RANDOM HOUSE SUNDAY *MEGA* OMNIBUS

VOLUME 1

EDITED BY

WILL WENG

Random House
Puzzles & Games

Published in the United States by Random House, Inc., New York, and simultaneously in Canada by Random House of Canada Limited, Toronto.

ISBN 0-8129-2708-7

Manufactured in the United States of America on acid-free paper.

8 9 7

1 Penny Ante By Elaine Schorr

Or some such coin to sweeten the pot.

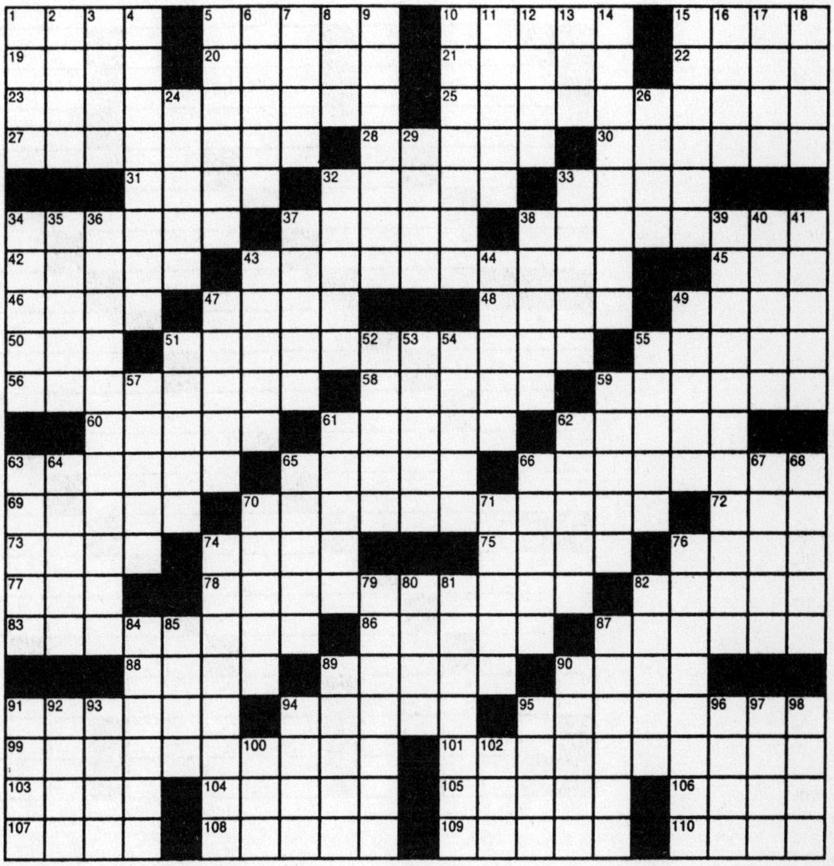

ACROSS

1 Guinness
5 Ballet wear
10 Kind of button
15 Name in neons
19 Short-tailed rodent
20 Make accustomed
21 Slur over
22 ___ stick
23 Fleeting
25 Having loose morals
27 Telephone operators of old
28 Adroit
30 Rich pastries
31 Top rating
32 Irma la ___
33 ___-gate (fugitive)
34 Incriminate
37 Egyptian corn
38 Study of regional properties
42 Here's partner
43 Commemorative event
45 French wheat
46 First name in fairy tales
47 Flat plinth
48 Otherwise, in Scotland
49 Biblical songs: Abbr.
50 Bone: Prefix
51 Kind of light
55 Character-actor Eric
56 Like some grapes
58 Sycophant
59 Formed a scab
60 "___ but you"
61 False fronts
62 Type, in Toulon
63 Red wine
65 He wrote about the burning-bright tiger
66 Workaday worries
69 Lemur of Asia
70 Clear as crystal
72 ___-Magnon
73 English actor Portman
74 Galway islands
75 Roy's mate
76 Fall fallout
77 Prefix for gram
78 Celsius reading
82 One of a seafarer's threesome
83 Searches for loot
86 Handles heavily
87 Seminary head
88 Passes time, in a way
89 Pinch-hit for
90 Pond
91 Actress Diane
94 Singer Haggard
95 Moral depravity
99 Underscore
101 Like mother-of-pearl
103 Vapid
104 Cuts and combines film
105 Range of the Rockies
106 Assam silkworm
107 State of bliss
108 Extinct birds
109 Deal with
110 Lethargic

DOWN

1 ___ plaisir
2 It makes the world go round
3 Zest
4 Monsters of myth
5 Herbal beverage
6 TV's "The Man From ___"
7 One of seven: Abbr.
8 Decorative piece
9 Gets on the way
10 Louisiana's bird
11 Carroll's girl
12 Hammett's Charles
13 Chemical ending
14 Hundredfold
15 Kind of notebook binding
16 Traffic tune
17 Fever
18 American seamstress
24 Jagged
26 ___ avail (fruitless)
29 Beguile
32 Gift giver
33 Dean Martin offering
34 One of a fictional threesome
35 Chief Justice: 1864–73
36 Venerable one
37 One of the Cyclades
38 Shoddy and shiny
39 Like a car once one buys one
40 Fixed frown
41 Gave the go-ahead
43 Salad-oil pot
44 Food, clothing, etc.
47 Scented
49 Land maps
51 Arctic sights
52 Wharton's Frome
53 Overcharges
54 Bedouin beast
55 Basque wear
57 Architectural order
59 Met's Marilyn
61 Point of view
62 Stone slab
63 In the ___ (free)
64 Blackmore heroine
65 Cereal byproducts
66 Oodles
67 Daughter of Zeus
68 Until now
70 Travels by ox wagon
71 Author of "Ralph Roister Doister"
74 Called attention to
76 Authorized, British style
79 Have an effect on
80 Scottish Highlander
81 Exclude
82 Paris parents
84 Fabric
85 Greek contest
87 Put in another chair
89 Flare-up
90 Valletta's island
91 Petruchio's love
92 Acquired character
93 Tip-top spot
94 Meter or bar
95 Poison
96 First name in architecture
97 Cut
98 Postpone
100 Japanese herb
102 Spiritual guide in India

2 Cooped Up By H.H. Reddall

What one might expect from a farm area.

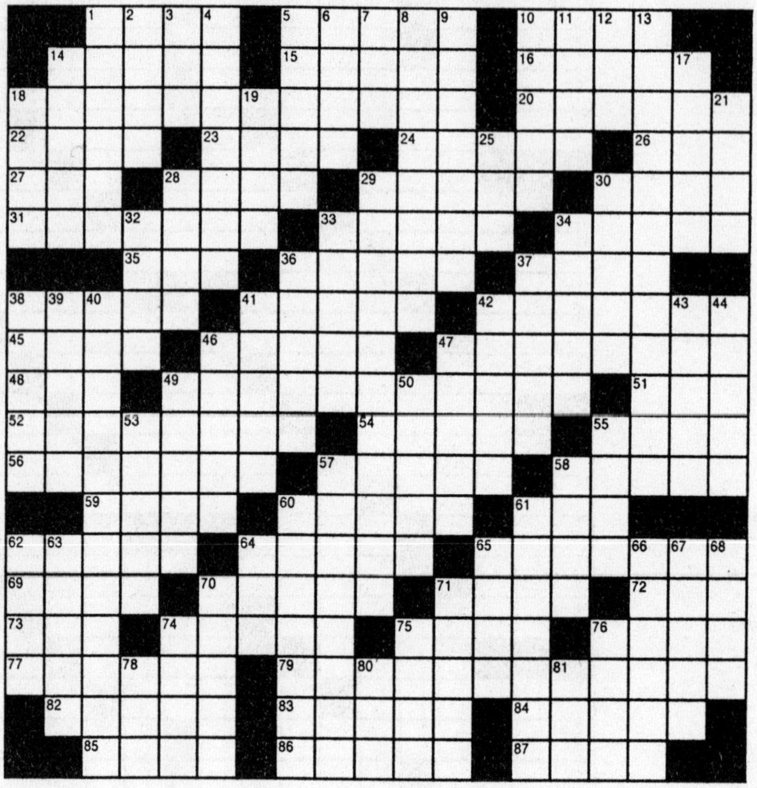

ACROSS

1 Family-business abbr.
5 Barbara or Clara
10 Revives a lawn
14 Frog sound
15 Love, in Rome
16 Mine entrances
18 Pâté ingredient
20 Pea or bean
22 Boat-hull features
23 Sheltered sides
24 King of Phrygia
26 Marsh
27 Chemical suffix
28 Halt
29 Dye plants
30 ". . . to buy ___ pig"
31 Defense bulwark
33 Medications
34 "Over ___"
35 Tabard, for one
36 Storage structures
37 Did gardening
38 Men of high rank
41 Fairy godmothers' gear
42 One kind of reaction
45 God of love
46 No ___ roses
47 Buck
48 ___ volente
49 Diner order
51 Dozen dozen: Abbr.
52 Cherish as sacred
54 Dilate
55 Sponsorship
56 Hires a lawyer
57 "Deutschland uber ___"
58 Liquor-bottle containers
59 Mild oath
60 Old weapons
61 Rod or dog
62 Friend of Solomon
64 Scorches
65 Yearly foursome
69 Sky science: Abbr.
70 Armadillos
71 Public-opinion ___
72 Letter
73 Depot: Abbr.
74 French mont
75 African nation
76 Constellation ingredient
77 Having folds
79 Machos of the roost
82 Type size
83 Sacred image: Var.
84 States
85 German family member
86 ___ Flow
87 Pot covers

DOWN

1 Corrupt gifts
2 Fabulous birds
3 Certain bucket material
4 English poet John ___
5 Dried tubers
6 Writer Kingsley
7 Mo. for balloting
8 Repetitive tones
9 TV lead-ins
10 Casa rooms
11 Poetic works
12 Work among ruins
13 Overfed burglars?
14 Crockery
17 Besmirch
18 Place for corn
19 Inert gas
21 Heraldry word
25 Counterpart of an M.D.
28 Goes wrong
29 Hunters of partridge, etc.
30 Showing the way
32 Rail holders
33 Western conifer
34 Realty sign
36 "Rain" girl
37 Troy girl
38 Jewish feast
39 Miss Bordoni
40 Sprays cast by speedboats
41 Breaks a habit
42 Small valleys
43 Strange
44 Refuse
46 Duck hunter's hideaway
47 Ancient Asians
49 King of Troy
50 Mr. Standish
53 Ishmael's mother
55 Consumes
57 Lawless
58 Anthracite or bituminous
60 Table-rapping sessions
61 Spiral
62 Door fastening
63 Basket fiber
64 Watering place
65 Recital pieces
66 Water animals
67 Approaches
68 Weights of India
70 Ethan or Fred
71 City on the Ganges
74 Old Saturday event
75 Between L and Q
76 Kind of cake or pearl
78 Labor initials
80 Abbr. on a most-wanted poster
81 Roman 56

3 Atonal By Bert Kruse

But having some music here and there.

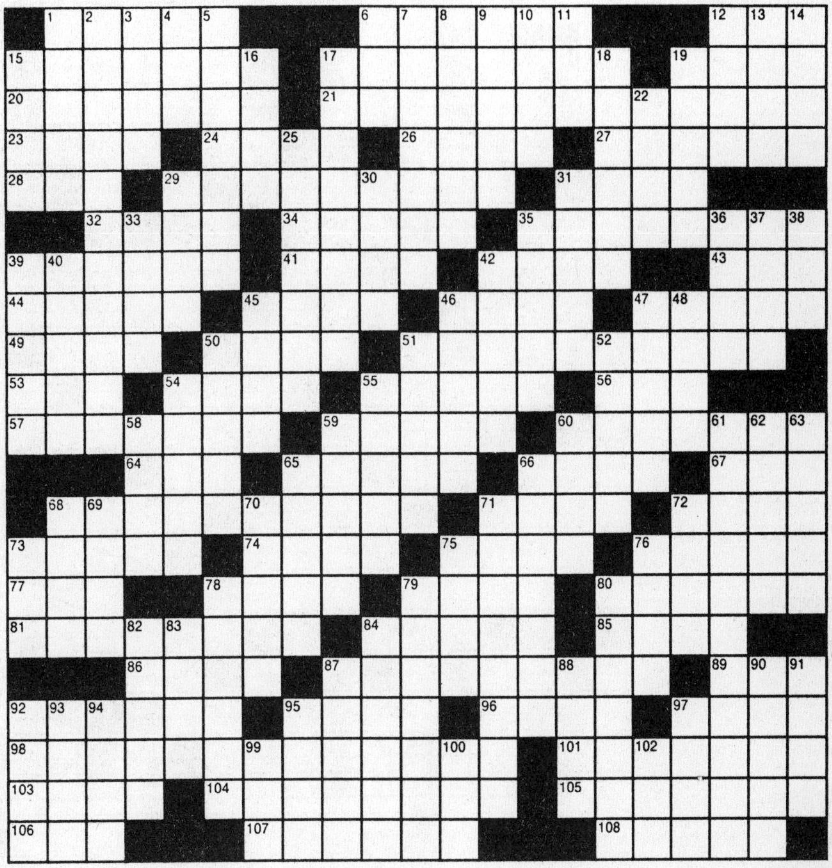

ACROSS

1 Sweet river
6 Chimps' relatives
12 Bill's partner
15 Philippine waters
17 Region of Turkey
19 Judge's seat
20 What meat is rich in
21 Nolan Ryan specialty
23 Sense organs
24 Insect
26 Maintained
27 Dull finishes
28 Whitney
29 Beach
31 Fictional tec
32 Info
34 Style
35 Love memo
39 Wheedled
41 Kind of nail
42 Type assortment
43 Tub
44 Crooked
45 Grassy dance
46 Cat, in San Juan
47 Discourse topic
49 Zilch, in Paris
50 Blackbird
51 Keen
53 Josephine of whodunits
54 Corn holders
55 Kind of man or maid
56 How some like it
57 Author Caldwell
59 Clair and Lacoste
60 Inge play
64 Part of i.e.
65 Blackfin snappers
66 Attractive
67 Exclamation
68 Furniture piece
71 Illustrator Gustave
72 Gem
73 Smut
74 Evergreen
75 Kind of glass
76 Cubic meter
77 Addition
78 Diana or Lanny
79 Truckle
80 ___ in (spoke up)
81 Certain rock
84 Pantagruel, e.g.
85 Elevation
86 Beliefs
87 Soft drink
89 Likely
92 Loose fold of neck skin
95 Seine tributary
96 Certain votes
97 Lyre's cousin
98 Urban dwellings
101 Normally
103 Reptiles
104 "___ Noel," holiday song
105 Gold-watch receiver
106 Piglet's word
107 Map features
108 Erased

DOWN

1 Of hearing
2 U.S. islands
3 Rebuking words
4 Simple sugar
5 Mimicked a mare
6 "___ Clear Day"
7 Coal-mine impurity
8 Go to
9 Earl, e.g.
10 Kind of rags
11 R.S.V.P. part
12 U.S. suffragist
13 Enough, often
14 U.S. publisher
15 Graf ___
16 ___ Domini
17 Nevertheless
18 Nearly
19 Was taken in
22 Primrose item
25 Bea and King
29 Gush
30 Leaping ___
31 Estate
33 Wagon power of old
35 Drive
36 Completed
37 Briar tool
38 Greek letter
39 A la ___
40 Willow
42 Daunts
45 Goddess of youth
46 "Bet-a-Million" promoter
47 Just one of ___ things
48 Items in the ring
50 January, e.g.
51 Err at bridge
52 "On the Beach" author
54 Whitefish
55 Middle, in law
58 "Show Boat" composer
59 Controls
60 TV's Ironside
61 Tailor's need
62 Airport
63 Faded
65 Silk sound
66 City's counterpart
68 Gallup product
69 Concorde site
70 Gives an edge
71 Words for Maine
72 Skinner of the stage
73 Zing
75 British royalty painter
76 Junk, e.g.
78 Boozer
79 Poetry, for one
80 Tripped up
82 Brothers of song
83 Glacial ridges
84 Kind of show
87 Brash utterances
88 Bosc
90 Punted
91 Palm or elm
92 Sketch
93 Alleviate
94 Help with the dishes
95 Garden
97 Seed jacket
99 Vedic sky serpent
100 Type of vessel: Abbr.
102 Rusted

4 Gambling By Ronnie Allen

Some things that can be found in the cards.

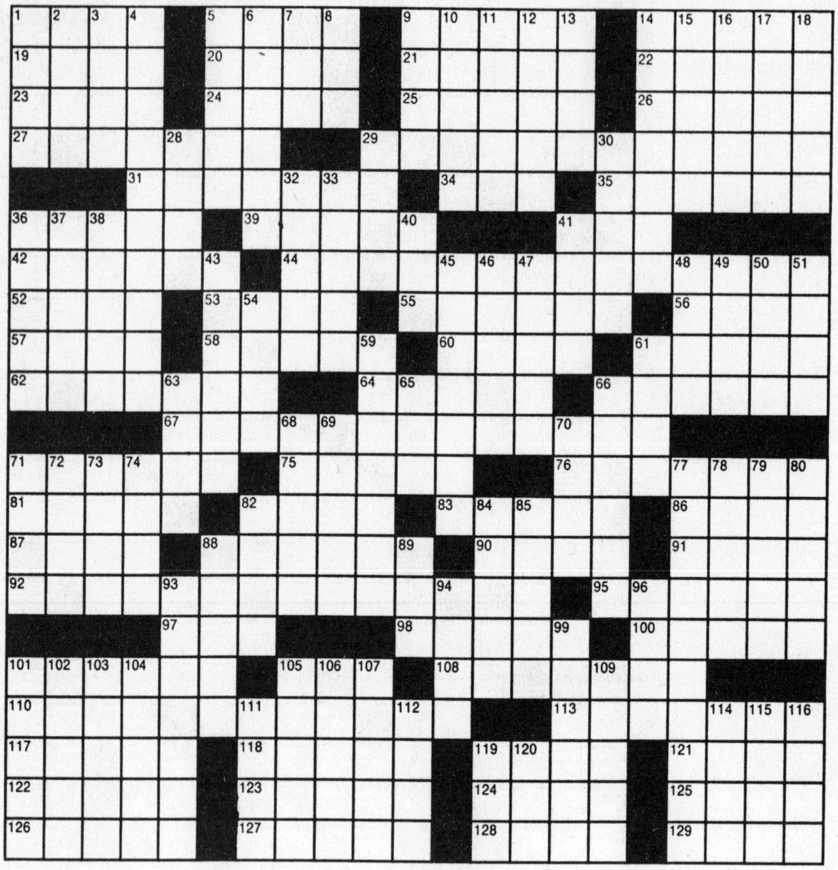

ACROSS

1 Charles's canine
5 Droops
9 Meal course
14 It's unlucky for three
19 Amaze
20 Type of sch.
21 Excuse
22 Author St. Johns
23 Seine sight
24 Paris airport
25 Yields
26 Ford's predecessor
27 Word of endearment
29 Prepare to testify
31 Prop up
34 Hesitant sounds
35 Not solids or liquids
36 Traditional robbery victim
39 Tribal symbol
41 Sculler's gear
42 Anoints, old style
44 Does business daringly
52 Reiner or Sagan
53 Esau, e.g.
55 Gets new service from
56 Crazed
57 Light color
58 Surface a road again
60 Exclamations in Bonn
61 Khomeini, for one
62 Ready for mailing
64 Light in the ciel
66 Tweed et al.
67 Like a gunslinger
71 Physicist Max
75 ____ nous
76 Disconcerts
81 Earring locations
82 Interlock
83 Straight: Prefix
86 Exam
87 German-Polish river
88 Hindu royalty
90 Victory margin, often
91 Pro ____
92 Certain walkouts
95 More expensive
97 Miss Gardner
98 Hairlines
100 Evenings, to Variety
101 Scan
105 Extinct bird
108 Raiding a Yiddish icebox
110 Cry of despair
113 Bacon quantities
117 Skip over
118 Intensity
119 Decorous
121 Do a tec's work
122 London leveler
123 Shoot from cover
124 Branch
125 Villa d'____
126 Doers: Suffix
127 Etta and family
128 Klutz's cry
129 Requisite

DOWN

1 Nile creatures
2 Pack
3 Tommy of musicals
4 Like the South in the 1850's
5 Spare the rod
6 Make a collar
7 Harden
8 Agent
9 Long yarn
10 Word for two peas
11 Basis for pâté
12 Helps a crook
13 Serve, with "out"
14 Sloping roof
15 Mine entries
16 Rangers' home
17 Duplicate
18 Crew
28 Raced
29 Place for a child's house
30 Old oaths
32 Namely
33 Of a people: Prefix
36 Sets the tempo
37 Legislate
38 Firma or cotta
40 Matelot's milieu
41 Change for a five
43 Revive a 60's fad
45 ____-lunged (raucous)
46 Bolivian capital
47 Burned completely
48 "I'm all ____"
49 Word after amo
50 Kind of wolf
51 Hits the slopes
54 Ties the knot
59 Jungle cat
61 "Music Man" locale
63 Charges of cpls.
65 Ship: Abbr.
66 Pampered
68 Adolescents
69 Beginning
70 "Peanuts" oath
71 Tool dating to the Bronze Age
72 City near Milan
73 Biblical fratricide victim
74 Insignificant guy
77 Align
78 Kind of felt
79 Cosmetician Lauder
80 Headliners
82 Heinous Hari
84 Beginning of an año
85 Overhead
88 Enthusiastic reviews
89 Drink
93 Furniture wheels
94 German philosopher
96 River to the Danube
99 Creole-dish ingredient
101 Port tie-ups
102 Success
103 Employee's gain
104 Word before cover or wear
105 French battle river
106 Rumor
107 Take over
109 Poetic measures
111 Chore
112 Annoys
114 Soothe
115 Baptism, for one
116 Coaster
119 Arafat's org.
120 ____ Grande

5 For Pollyanna By John Hales

Things don't always have to be grim.

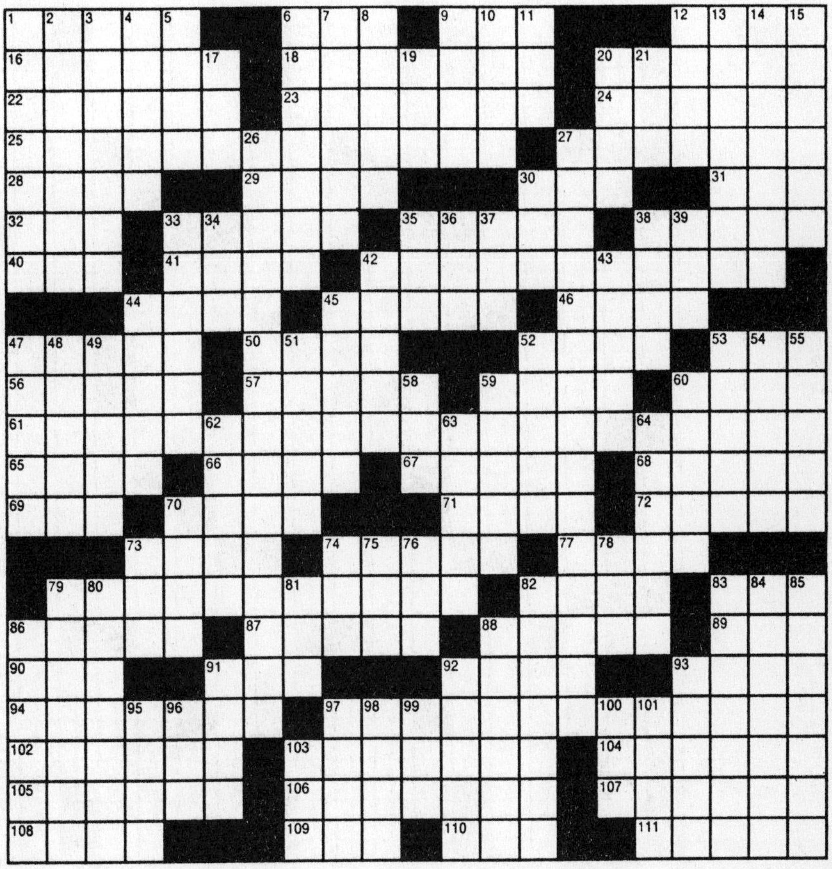

ACROSS

1 Scenic view
6 Massenet's "Le ___"
9 Two ___ kind
12 Small wedge
16 Bazaars in the Far East
18 Turkish president: 1923–38
20 Galahad's mother
22 One at an easel
23 All-purpose medicine
24 Miss Prentiss and namesakes
25 Agreeably
27 Hungary's gift to cookery
28 Bulrush
29 Medley
30 Legal matter
31 Native: Suffix
32 That, in Toledo
33 Stringed instrument
35 Brown weasel
38 Farm units
40 Dampen hemp
41 View from Taormina
42 Buffoon
44 Handle, in France
45 Implied
46 Moslem judge
47 Comic pianist
50 Goddess of hope
52 "Gotcha!"
53 Jet ___
56 ___ a time
57 City east of Frankfurt
59 Ethiopian people
60 Señor's residence
61 Sentiment for Charlie Brown
65 French women's magazine
66 Facility
67 Exactly
68 Prospero's servant
69 Like a malt drink
70 Hungary's Nagy
71 Dies ___
72 Like a honky-tonk piano
73 City map
74 In ___ (troubled)
77 Bone: Prefix
79 Deceive
82 Seethe
83 Master card
86 Resort lake
87 Earthenware vessels
88 Sacrament site
89 Lawyers' milieu
90 Scottish uncle
91 Fireplace warmer
92 Exchange fee
93 Spillage from Vesuvius
94 Pub worker
97 Marine Corps motto
102 Royal pelt
103 Enid's husband
104 Lombard or King
105 Showy headdresses
106 Guessing game
107 Laundry equipment
108 Main Street event
109 ___ longa . . .
110 Medical abbr.
111 Ranks

DOWN

1 Sprinkle
2 Go on a spree
3 Lily maid's home
4 "Common Sense" author
5 Gaelic
6 Star in Auriga
7 Benito's land
8 Aquarium fish
9 Cry of pain
10 Banjo feature
11 Rel. of alias
12 Author Bellow
13 Author Belloc
14 Fretful
15 Harmonizes
17 City ways: Abbr.
19 Word with dog or price
20 Major poem
21 Tepid, in Würzburg
26 Gratify
27 Enjoy
30 X or gamma
33 Ancient people of Gaul
34 "___ a deal!"
35 Fraction of a min.
36 Prefix with pod or cycle
37 Scrap
38 Skink
39 Shout, on the Champs
42 People of Kenya
43 Biblical prophet
44 Staring
45 Edgy
47 Black tea
48 ___ sides (surrounding)
49 Rejoinder
51 Obsolete
52 Guam's capital
53 Rabbit
54 Quaking, poetically
55 In a joyous way: Var.
58 Naval initials
59 Oscar or Emmy
60 Radium pioneer
62 River of Byelorussia
63 Imitating
64 Glib talk
70 Nastase of tennis
73 Prefix for found or pound
74 In toto
75 Feathery item
76 Officeholders
78 Wee, to a Highlander
79 Ancient Hebrew kingdom
80 Glider's updraft
81 Robe for a priest
82 Toyed
83 California seafood
84 One who quibbles
85 Rub-out agents
86 Hebrew months
88 Plan of procedure
91 Rushes
92 Beelike
93 "Vive ___!"
95 Involve, in a way
96 Memorabilia
97 ___ gut (very good, in Bonn)
98 Distinctive periods
99 Viña del ___
100 Here, in Soissons
101 Pub missile
103 Plane-landing syst.

Mix and Match

By Sara Helleny

Getting things together to make some points.

ACROSS

1 Obligation
5 "___ thief to catch . . ."
9 ___ impasse (stalled)
13 Similar things: Suffix
17 Hebrew month
18 One of the Ages
19 "Arrivederci ___"
20 Minot is here
21 Burroughs meets Brontë?
25 Neap and ebb
26 Monastery official
27 Italian physicist and family
29 Malayan knives
32 Jolson's boy
33 Start to fall, as an empire
34 Gland: Prefix
35 Prefix for bat
36 Actress Rowlands
37 Transportation gp.
38 Flavor for Mozart?
44 ". . . ___ I saw Elba"
45 To ___ (in addition)
46 Fate
47 De Staël and Bovary, for short
51 One at a will-reading
54 Days, in Dijon
56 Convent superior
58 Mother of Dionysus
59 Roman god of the dead
60 William Sydney or Katherine Anne
61 Merman stars in Genesis?
65 Understands
67 Stalin followed him
68 Betel palms
70 U.N. group
71 Lodged overnight
72 Dig in
74 Has it ___
75 Pelion's partner
76 Antony's love, for short
77 Interjection
78 Wagner-Fleming collaboration?
85 Season of the yr.
88 Between Phi and Kappa
89 Scintilla
90 Appears
91 Natives of Canea
93 Large pill
95 ___ of knowledge (Eden feature)
97 Makes a payment
98 Illinois city
99 Korean capital
100 Lanza sings with Hamlet?
105 Roman way
106 Wordsworth was this kind of poet
107 South or River
108 Ivan or Peter
109 Rents
110 Young or gang follower
111 Like Death Valley
112 Fast planes

DOWN

1 Beavers' creation
2 Dutch town
3 Arabian astronomer al-___
4 ___ thought (reasoning)
5 Dimensions
6 Christian and Mohammedan
7 Like a ___ of bricks
8 "___ in a storm"
9 ". . . a fascination frantic in ___ that's romantic"
10 Schiller's "Ode ___"
11 To love, in Spain
12 Miss Merriman
13 Street ball game
14 Pastoral poem
15 Enter quickly
16 Short swords of Ireland
22 One of the three R's: Abbr.
23 Whether ___ ___
24 Happening
28 Black or Red
29 Meadowlands entry
30 Dotes on
31 Made a new choice
32 Rabbit's tail
33 Te ___ (hymn of praise)
35 Stub ___
36 Italian poet Tommaso ___
39 Sent ___ (dunned)
40 Nine, in old Rome
41 Student
42 Where Cicero held forth
43 Hug: Var.
48 Rudolf Bing's position, once
49 Suffix for Japan
50 Ukr. or Lith.
52 Gathered
53 Purposive
54 First of two queens of Naples
55 Do ___ (last-ditch words)
56 Be ___ (join in)
57 One who portends
62 Hebrew prophet
63 Tidy up, in Dundee
64 Like a lion
65 Wrigley's output
66 Alfonso's queen
69 It's often nefarious
72 Fitzgerald
73 Omaha or Noor
75 Scraps
76 Tent installations
79 Moderating factors
80 Feeling, in Naples
81 Certain Egyptian
82 "Faust" composer and family
83 Tristram's wife and his beloved
84 Red-ink bottom line
85 Movie text: Abbr.
86 Adobe wall
87 Kind of control
92 High Asian country
93 Chap, in Charing Cross
94 Cousin of a weasel
95 Apollo's vale
96 Harbor barge
98 Med. course
99 Second-sight person
101 Literary monogram
102 Buzzer
103 Brewery item
104 Speech fillers

7 Intimacy By A. J. Santora

No need to be aloof all the time.

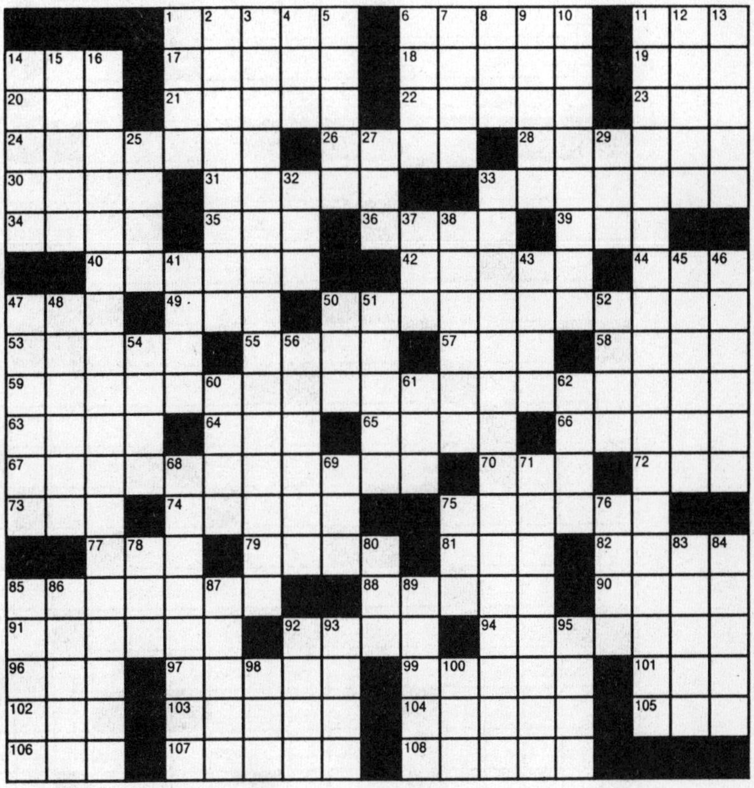

ACROSS

1 ___ off the old block
6 Like gardeners' hands
11 Kind of dance
14 Elec. unit
17 Escape
18 Comedienne Taylor
19 Owns
20 ___ around with (go together)
21 Hardship
22 Tinker-Chance link
23 Ending for hatch or station
24 Soon
26 Big Ten team
28 Revived
30 Word with jai
31 Orchestra instrument
33 Central American bird
34 Wine variety
35 Otho's govt.
36 A Bowl or skirt
39 Smattering
40 Zimbalist Sr. and Jr.
42 Silk fabric
44 Brit. fliers
47 Kind of fly in Calif.
49 Sun Devils' campus
50 "There's ___ things": Shakespeare
53 Float ___ (borrow)
55 Dorothy or Lillian
57 W.W. II agency
58 Bruins of college sports
59 Facing the music?
63 Uprising
64 Goddess, to the Romans
65 Shine
66 Storm, in France
67 ___ Morpheus (asleep)
70 Buckeyes' campus
72 Board's partner
73 ___ Moines
74 "Blue ___," Berlin song
75 Fatty solid
77 Arabian tea
79 Actress Talbot
81 Odd or job
82 Shown
85 Letting out froth
88 "Patton" actor
90 Meshed fabric
91 Like dessert toppings
92 Be told
94 "No pets ___"
96 Lament
97 Assign
99 "Tomorrow" girl
101 Historic time
102 Trimming tool
103 Sheer linen fabric
104 Inks
105 The sun
106 Thousand bucks
107 Miss Bagnold and namesakes
108 Works laboriously

DOWN

1 Flying word
2 Lovers' knots?
3 Keeping a secret
4 Two little words
5 Danger
6 Expanded
7 ___ motor (increase speed)
8 Ending for Clement
9 Thanks, to Gaston
10 Maybe?
11 Los Angeles Rams cheerleaders
12 With an ___ the ground
13 "___ Like It"
14 ". . . in ___ tree"
15 Actress Thomas
16 Fruit-store sign
25 Willing, to Shakespeare
27 Sound of surprise
29 Meadow sound
32 Mary Ford's partner
33 What it does, on the dance floor
37 A.P. rival
38 Pepe ___ (Boyer role)
41 Hindu queen
43 In that eventuality
45 Assert
46 Chipped off
47 Prado's home
48 Entertainer May
50 Kind of blonde
51 On ___ (busy)
52 German area
54 Pituitary hormone
56 "___ saw . . ." (Caesar's boast)
60 Neighbor of Minn.
61 Folklore creature
62 French yard
68 Calculate
69 Concorde
71 ___ up (paying)
75 ___-mo (TV term for retarded action)
76 European capital
78 Org. for M.D.'s
80 Sly ___ fox
83 January, to Pedro
84 Of a plant joint
85 Scrawny animal
86 Anthony Comstock, for one
87 Synthetic fabric
89 Rude
92 Clutch
93 Vous ___ (you are)
95 Minus
98 The year 52
100 Nothing

8 Selectivity

By Louis Baron

Choices that might be made by certain people.

ACROSS

1 Gangster's gun
7 Owner's paper
11 Kin of ands or buts
14 Freshwater tortoises
19 Kind of tax
20 Gudrun's mate
21 Poet's field
22 Flood controller
23 Mort's favorite program?
26 Autograph givers
27 Musical group
28 Bridges of screen
29 Math ratios
30 Links alert
33 Mme. Gluck's favorite ballad?
39 Fuji topper
42 Bertrand Russell was one
43 Produce
44 Greek letter
45 Miss Carroll's favorite Israeli?
49 "Can ___ true?"
52 Real
54 "When we are born, ___ that . . .": "King Lear"
55 Armstrong role in "King Kong"
57 Where Aaron died
58 Sacred figure
60 London timeout
62 Flour bleacher
63 Surrounded by
65 Babylonian god
66 Performs
69 Patch a roof
70 Good, to Gaston
71 Bonheur's favorite air?
74 Chang's inseparable
75 Assn.
76 Nonresident doctors
77 Faroe winds
78 Burnsian hillside
79 Godfathers' clan
81 Sandy's so
82 Rookie devils
84 Bireme mover
85 Loos favorite
87 In a cork-blowing mood
89 Admonish
93 Spanish muralist
94 Vivian Leigh's favorite comic?
98 Sis's rel.
99 ___ than a doornail
101 Old English moneys
102 Companion of lost or strayed
104 Stanwyck's favorite opera?
108 Dotted, as porcelain
109 Florida cigar center
110 Oversatisfy
111 Ply the scythe
114 Olfactory stimuli
115 Vanessa's favorite Indian?
122 Dancer Jeanmaire
123 Logo abbr.
124 Ben or Sue of films
125 Weber opera
126 Dill herbs
127 Long follower
128 Leapin' ___ (Model T)
129 Yucatán people

DOWN

1 Part of H.M.S.
2 Alfonso's queen
3 Exclamation in Aachen
4 Pre-Aztec native
5 Pasha's colleague
6 Italian painter Guido
7 Dit's partner
8 Beach time for Henri
9 Eleven, in Germany
10 Like Old Nick
11 Classical epic
12 Lateen-rigged ship
13 "___ uncle"
14 Actor ___ Cook, Jr.
15 Umpiring a strike
16 De Carlo's favorite despot?
17 Edited out
18 Meeting: Abbr.
24 One customer
25 Ferrer or Ott
30 Esne's turf
31 Septi plus one
32 Vic's favorite song?
34 Kashmir town
35 New Hebrides island
36 Shakespearean forest
37 Xmas-tree hanging: Abbr.
38 ___ one's way
40 Asian border river
41 Bluegrass
46 Most crafty
47 Russian co-op
48 Veldt scavenger
50 Oil or split
51 Become visible
53 Bushy clump
56 This does it
59 Pop artist Oldenburg
61 ___ in the bucket
63 Doomsday stockpile
64 Esprit
65 Batter's place
66 Monogram at Vailima
67 Menuhin's teacher
68 ___ judicata
71 Be a bibliophile
72 Cobra's relative
73 Nonfunctional
78 Dracula, at times
80 Construe
82 River in Zaire
83 Robot's flesh
84 Give the heave-ho
86 Wagnerian role
88 Most importantly
90 Part of Q. & A.
91 Utah city near Provo
92 Zilch
95 "Leave ___ to heaven . . ."
96 Blotting out
97 ___ Aviv
100 Humbles
103 Fish hawk
104 German spa
105 Vanzetti's codefendant
106 Letter of yore
107 ". . . ___ I saw Elba"
109 African antelope
112 Esau
113 Eban
115 Miss Farrow
116 Private or evil
117 Chaney
118 Genetic acid initials
119 Macaw
120 Stroheim or Sternberg
121 Nine has two

9 Atlas Doings By Arnold Moss

Fuller explanations from here and there.

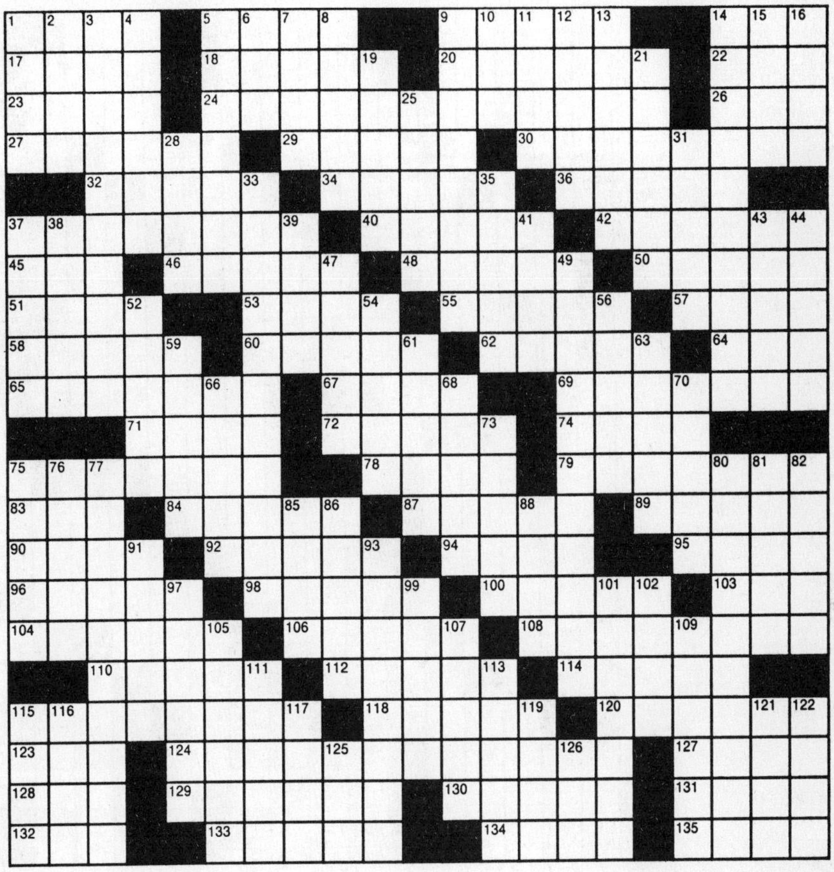

ACROSS

1 Pizarro's foe
5 Kind of bag
9 Indicative and subjunctive
14 Unruly hair
17 Thank-you-___ (road dip)
18 Atmospheres
20 One who hears in his mind
22 Mad. or Lex.
23 Cartoonist Peter
24 Finistère swimmers' fortes
26 Fisherman's need
27 Art of horsemanship
29 Cesare of opera
30 Give confidence to
32 "Christ Stopped at ___"
34 Part of an opera
36 Three Danish kings
37 Onslaughts
40 Obeys
42 Does legislative work
45 Thus
46 Rams and Colts
48 "The ___ and Daniel Webster"
50 Flynn of films
51 Scorch
53 Neapolitan wolf
55 Mubarak's predecessor
57 Director Wertmuller
58 Meara and Boleyn
60 Body passages
62 ___ stand (stet)
64 Kind of poker hand
65 Eyelash application
67 Rover's bark
69 In an awkward way
71 Below a jack
72 Swig
74 Patricia of films
75 Somewhat humid
78 ___ day (dosage)
79 Tied a shoe
83 Rio de ___
84 Elizabeth II to Edward VIII
87 She played Christie and Christina
89 Kind of cuisine
90 Miss Myerson
92 Ancient region in Asia Minor
94 Dnepr River port
95 Pokey
96 "Novum Organum" author
98 Senior
100 "___ cold, starve . . ."
103 Roman 151
104 Inclined
106 Threw cubes
108 W.W. I emplacements
110 Taoism term
112 Tony winner for "Cats"
114 "Dum ___ Spero" (motto of S.C.)
115 Colleagues
118 "The Rivals" role
120 Biblical Mount of ___
123 ___-Bakr, first caliph
124 Pasos
127 "One man's ___ . . ."
128 Mae West character
129 Carpenters' joints
130 Papal cape
131 Ending for pot or cog
132 Lawyer's payment
133 Oak ___, Tenn.
134 Radio's Freeman Gosden
135 Wimbledon winner

DOWN

1 Moslem priest
2 Honshu city
3 Boîtes on the Riviera
4 Simplest life form
5 Salt tax
6 Capek title
7 Greek Mars
8 Foundation
9 Afternoons on Broadway
10 ". . . ___ daily bread"
11 Fragrance
12 Walls for Holland
13 ". . . ravell'd ___ of care"
14 Pacific island writing
15 Ended
16 Sneaky name
19 Gormandize, in Glasgow
21 Ancient Jewish sect member
25 SST characteristic
28 Toe trouble
31 Gridlock
33 Eròe
35 In proportion to worth: Abbr.
37 Indian state
38 Palio festival city
39 Pornography
41 Kind of arms or dish
43 Like a fugue
44 Of a grayish cast
47 Erupts
49 Amatores
52 Reconditioned tire
54 Site of U. of Maine
56 Ringworm
59 Glossy fabric
61 Famous Chinese family
63 Emulate Mr. Chips
66 Convene once more
68 Sideshow star
70 Entreaties
73 Price list, in Pau
75 ___ Ferry, N.Y.
76 Of a space
77 Russian drink with a kick
80 Rotterdam and Ede in midsummer
81 Functional
82 Fairylike beings
85 Kind of chisel or cream
86 She was a lady, in song
88 Symbol of redness
91 Use a blotter
93 Lowered in social status
97 Most avant-garde
99 Shirer's "The Third ___"
101 Ousts, as a king
102 Indigo
105 More profound
107 Back: Prefix
109 Nightingale territory
111 Native of Shiraz
113 Four: Prefix
115 Fatted biblical animal
116 Theater award
117 Smooth, in Scotland
119 Coal bed
121 "To ___ his own"
122 Eye ailment
125 Participial part
126 Arafat's org.

10 Body Shop

By Sidney Robbins

Parts not to be found in a garage.

ACROSS

1 Shoot of a plant
6 More's partner
10 Excessively
13 Kind of com or lude
18 Prostrate
19 Aleutian isle
20 Theater org.
22 Mother of Aphrodite
23 Principal
26 Serfs
27 Actual being
28 Negative of sorts
29 Dearie's pal
30 Claiborne of cooking
32 Soak
33 River of Italy
34 Slapstick weapon
35 Oil or gas
36 Neighbor of Can.
39 Violinist Georges
41 Enemy
42 Overlay a wall
43 Soak through
44 Gait
45 Vegetable unit
48 Kind of fence
49 Southerly
51 Fall mo.
52 Biblical well
53 In a basic way
55 Sidestep
57 Remus or Sam
60 Circus dog
61 Interstice
62 Hawaiian flower
63 Wayside, for one
64 Reporter's asset
69 Outer: Prefix
70 Famed statue
73 Yen
74 Ones showing anger
77 Contempt
78 Hobgoblin
79 Handwriting move
82 Half a sawbuck
83 Narcotic drug: Abbr.
84 Flowing
85 Cash receiver
87 Idaho planting
89 Hula hoops, frisbees and such
92 Cupid
93 Additional
94 Dawn goddess
95 Railroad flares
97 Prefix for puncture
98 Essential part
99 Explosive
100 False god
102 It vanishes on rising
103 Haley book
105 Decay
106 Neighbor of Hung.
107 Scrawny animal
108 Phone opener
110 Delta
114 Zodiac sign
115 Helper
116 Cloy
117 Opera extra's weapon
118 Backslide
119 Moon vehicle
120 Greek god
121 Cloth for beach robes

DOWN

1 Orb
2 Roll-call reply
3 Oven bird
4 Shade of blue
5 Earth: Prefix
6 Amo, sum, puer, etc.
7 Race: Prefix
8 Let stand
9 Genus of swine
10 Western resort
11 "___ you noblest English!"
12 U.S. Indian
13 Goal
14 Unless, to Caesar
15 Insincerely
16 Opposite of WSW
17 ___ adjudicata
21 Charlemagne adviser: 735-804
24 Casino game
25 Heap-big guy
31 Aunt or uncle: Abbr.
33 Real
34 Relative of snooker
35 Productive
37 Grouping
38 Zoo animal
40 ___-so (somebody)
41 Deteriorate, as a collar
42 Butterfly's birthplace
43 Backbone
45 French season
46 Flight-study place: Abbr.
47 Hidden
48 Biblical king
50 British gun
53 Companion of Doric
54 "Cut the comedy!"
55 Came up
56 Margery of the seesaw
58 Filthy money
59 Truck-stop sign
60 Markings on cards
61 Home of a popular violet
65 Betting org.
66 Emerged suddenly
67 Shell crews
68 Spanish miss: Abbr.
71 Attempts
72 Field-lace queen
75 Goodly amount to carry
76 Certain Prado displays
79 Indians
80 Snoop
81 Observe
84 Chimney deposit
85 Kind of soup
86 Part of a circle
87 Blood component
88 Fifth halved
90 What de butcher chops
91 Arctic fur animal
93 Kind of rock
95 Destiny
96 Inventor Elmer
98 Oversized deer
99 Kind of pole
100 Montana city
101 Cigar products
104 Bullring cries
105 Obnoxious
106 Way off
107 Pickable
108 Henry V
109 Age
111 Black gold
112 She-bear in Spain
113 Between Q and U

11 This and That By Ruth W. Smith

And things that aren't like each other.

ACROSS

1 They're usually noires
6 Eye part
10 Baseball V.I.P.'s
14 Old hat
19 Simpson of fashion
20 Palo's follower
21 Jack-in-the-pulpit
22 Western skiing center
23 Tire parts
25 Astronauts' milieu
27 Scarlet bird
28 Kind of parts
30 Revive the lawn
31 Whitney and others
33 Pacific tree
34 Town on Lake Maggiore
37 Foot soldiers: Abbr.
40 One of the Five Nations
42 Untidy place
45 Slackened
46 Kind of stroke or bone
48 Cold time in Spain
50 India's ___ of Kutch
52 Young one
53 Know-it-all
55 Pale animals
57 Petty-cash item
58 Football get-together
60 Interlocks
65 Deli sandwich
66 Not ___ in the world
68 American vessel: Abbr.
70 Crew members
71 Large birds
73 Twain's Huck
74 One of the Little Women
75 Arabian demon
76 Pierre's nothing
77 Part of CBS
78 Major no-no
79 Rockefeller's oil co.
80 Use mouthwash
82 Cylindrical
84 Sorted into groups
88 Consents
90 Wordsworth, Coleridge, etc.
92 Coat part
95 Ruckus
96 Medium for David
98 Jewish greeting
99 Seldom-used towel
101 Genetic initials
103 Follows
105 Place for Spain's rain: Abbr.
106 More ___ (approximately)
108 Honshu city
110 Pickens of movies
112 English plotter Titus
114 Ring stones
116 Eastern Church cloak
121 Titian, Reubens et al.
124 Applecart upsetters
126 Flu variety
127 Wings
128 Makings of a dune
129 British racecourse
130 Tolerate
131 Tibetan beasts
132 Founder of Priam's land
133 Facing a glacier

DOWN

1 Hook addition
2 Actress Purviance
3 Neighbor of Ken.
4 Seat of an old Greek school
5 Suit material
6 Annie of song
7 Priestly robe
8 Fr. holy women
9 Traveler's stop
10 New Zealand native
11 Thin broths
12 Same old grind
13 Small duck
14 Like words ending in -ed
15 "Ad astra per ___"
16 Most meager
17 Relative of a mo
18 Nautical dir.
24 Communi-cations satellite
26 Cape
29 "I Love ___"
32 Old sword
35 Ross or Bering
36 Tack on
37 ___ la Douce
38 Prohibition drink
39 Extensive
41 Like a "South Pacific" evening
43 Attempts
44 Penn ___, New York town
46 Commercial degree
47 Scoreboard listings, for short
49 Like Nick or Vic
51 French appellations
54 Like trees in summer
56 Colorful plants
59 Container
61 Flatter
62 Pitchman's forte
63 Silkworm
64 Kennedy visitor
67 Water-storing tank
69 Toffler's is future
71 Work unit
72 Miss Farrow
74 Night flier
75 Biblical musician
77 Offshoot group
78 Mosaic piece
81 Custer's claim to fame
83 Good name, for short
85 German dramatist
86 Collar type
87 Army award
89 Spanish hero El ___
91 Nuclear groupings: Abbr.
92 Make ___ of it
93 Robot play
94 Organ stop
97 Expert with a couch
100 Crew member
102 Arctic jacket
104 African antelopes
107 His, in France
109 Naves' neighbors
111 Miss Hari et al.
113 Supporting rope
115 Go aloft
117 Certain sculpture
118 With the bow, in music
119 Boxing outcomes
120 Doers: Suffix
121 New World org.
122 W.W. II craft
123 High note
125 Número ___

12 Color Chart By Mary Murdoch

Concentrating mostly on one grouping.

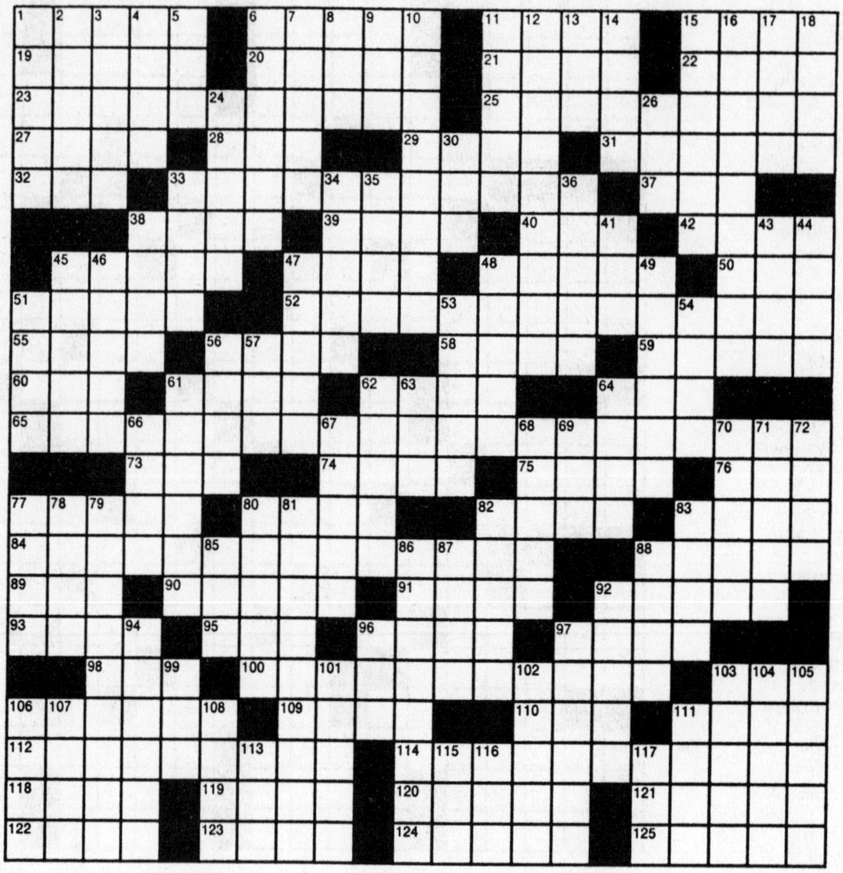

ACROSS

1 Etonian's dad
6 Wealthy one
11 Hormone initials
15 "It's ___ or us"
19 Small egg
20 Get rid of
21 Arabian craft
22 Roof part
23 Companion of Robin Hood
25 Dixon-Wrubel song, with "The"
27 Essay name
28 Sky Altar
29 Harvest
31 Burden, in a way
32 Beat the ___
33 English toy dog
37 "___ Girls"
38 Like a busybody
39 Piano and house
40 Nuclear-energy unit
42 It's Zimbabwe now: Abbr.
45 Clan
47 English river
48 Followed doctor's orders
50 Self
51 Sierra ___
52 Sherlock Holmes's debut, with "A"
55 Detective-film dog
56 Sandwich orders
58 Too
59 Hercules' captive et al.
60 Labor gp.
61 Row
62 Bellow
64 ___ rule
65 Sargent painting
73 Gives the nod
74 Long times
75 Tolkien creatures
76 Use O.T.B.
77 Framework
80 Vapor: Prefix
82 ___ War
83 Intend
84 Climbing rose
88 Port of Iraq
89 Greek letters
90 Like ___ (probably)
91 Inning enders
92 Southern breads
93 Russian hut
95 Have a bite
96 Burns word
97 Merit
98 Words before carte
100 Home of the cancan
103 Acct.
106 Typos
109 Leo of the zodiac
110 Time
111 Prison-window décor
112 River to the Wabash
114 It comes bob, bob, bobbin'
118 Jewish holiday eve
119 German zoologist Karl
120 West German port
121 ___ mer
122 Clears
123 Writer Seton
124 From, in Spain
125 Range animal

DOWN

1 Word with house or failure
2 Spanish city
3 Spring flower
4 Fitzgerald
5 Home: Abbr.
6 At hand
7 Imposing group
8 French party
9 Chemical suffix
10 Ratted on
11 Part of A.E.S.
12 Guardians of sorts
13 Bushy mass
14 Rtes.
15 Like Fitzgerald's night
16 Type of crab
17 Knievel
18 Ancient Asian
24 Effect's partner
26 Adjective suffix
30 Abstract being
33 Regal wear
34 Revue parts
35 High country
36 Cowboy gear
38 Actress Foch
41 Winter mo.
43 S-shaped curve
44 Dashes' partners
45 Inventor Nikola
46 Stator's opposite
47 Prefix for nomical
48 Lulu
49 Tandem-bike girl et al.
51 Not of the cloth
53 Small sailboats
54 Big noise
56 Bridle parts
57 Garland
61 "Death ___ Holiday"
62 Flourish
63 Before twa
64 Kind of sax
66 A Crosby
67 Thread: Prefix
68 King and Norman
69 Wayside place
70 Plump plus
71 Scorches
72 Lab burner
77 Roman 211
78 Molding edge: Var.
79 Ousted, as a lawyer
80 Per ___
81 Figurative interpretation
82 Kind of maid
83 Novelist Thomas
85 W.W. II org.
86 Subject of a Goya painting
87 Sally ___ (tea cake)
88 Tire
92 Called on the intercom
94 In two shakes of ___ tail
96 Traffic sign
97 Oregon city
99 Panay native
101 Rockies range
102 Sculled
103 Wire
104 Self-esteem
105 Actor Ed
106 Eternally
107 Soprano Grist
108 Edison's middle name
111 Tug or gun
113 Apollo's son
115 Scot's uncle
116 Dental degree
117 Boarding-house offerings: Abbr.

13 Celsius Readings By Mary Whitten

Ups and downs on the mercury scale.

ACROSS

1 Pilgrimage to Mecca
5 Door fastener
9 Hindu god of love
13 Pequod's captain
17 Toast addition
18 Mountain nymph
20 Leek's kin
21 Ditto
22 "___ you were here"
23 Book-cover item
24 One of a noted threesome
25 Aunts, to Juan
26 Poitier-Steiger film
30 Early riser's goddess
31 Venerate
32 Flightless bird
33 Land conquered by Pizarro
35 Resort near the Black Hills
41 Behavioral throwback
44 Presidential privilege
45 Guido's high one
46 Indian otter
47 "Olympian bards who sung ___ below"
49 Horoscope sign
50 Magna ___
51 Newspaper notices
52 Kind
53 Way to quit smoking
55 Silver residue
56 This, to a Spaniard
57 Reynard, e.g.
58 Hesitant sounds
59 Adds later
61 "No soap!"
62 They have a trill a minute
67 "___ pleasures and palaces . . ."
69 Cubs' box-office rivals
70 Hamlet's larger kin
73 Printing instruction
74 TV's terpsichorean contest
79 Bern's river
80 Choice seat location
81 ". . . but ___ forever"
82 Worshiper's place
83 Capote classic
85 Farm structure
86 Bog
87 Priest's calendar
88 Abandons
89 Paul Newman film
92 Neighbor of Ger.
93 Southern Calif. campus
94 Chariot routes
96 Naval off.
97 Ignore
105 Army grouping
106 Silly
107 Small antelope
108 Foolish
111 Walesa of Poland
112 Duo quadrupled
113 Jewish month
114 Almost shut
115 Professional stipends
116 Patricia of "Hud"
117 Almost: Prefix
118 Political cartoonist

DOWN

1 Frequent question
2 Three-time ring champ
3 Arnaz
4 ___ Q. Public
5 Sauna for flowers
6 Ram in the sky
7 A son of Adam
8 Plant bract
9 Betrays backhandedly
10 "___ Misbehavin'"
11 Mine's main vein
12 Lack of vigor
13 Wine town
14 Former Secretary Alexander
15 Oriental nanny
16 Actress Edna
19 Racing tie
20 Portugal's second city
27 European finches: Var.
28 Restaurateur Shor
29 Religious woman
33 Smoothing the way
34 Perón and others
36 British bobby's name-giver
37 Growl
38 Cutty ___
39 Location
40 Strong cart
41 Take as one's own
42 Leg bone with connections
43 Ole or near
44 Miles or Caspary
48 Part of a certain vowel
49 Bagel topper
50 Moon point
53 Wally of "Mr. Peepers"
54 Suffix for cyclo
56 Star in Pegasus
57 Repair
60 Portent
61 Connective
63 Roman magistrates
64 Vacation place
65 Mete
66 Sows
68 Reliance
69 How to save nine
70 Southwestern lunch item
71 Spanish gold
72 Tuesday of films
74 LP, for one
75 Exchange premium
76 ___ contendere
77 Indifferent
78 Sell
79 Playwright Maxwell
80 Ridiculous
83 Ticked off
84 Reporter's zero hour
86 Mode
87 Place for a plug
90 Crude shelter
91 Hampton or Barrymore
95 Trim, old style
96 Castro or Batista
97 Florida coast choice
98 Arrow poison
99 Versa's partner
100 Numerical endings
101 Prefix for comb or logue
102 Seine feeder
103 Actor Eddie
104 Eastern nabob
109 Cooking fuel
110 Linkletter

14 Nomenclature By Louis Sabin

In somewhat less than a literary sense.

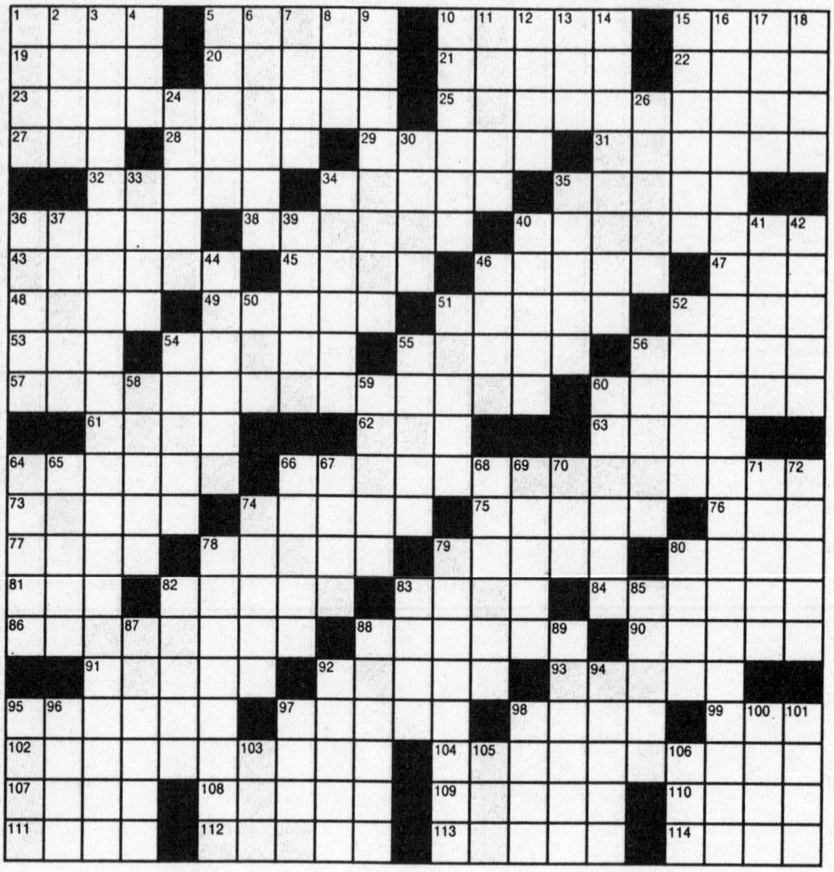

ACROSS

1 Ameche role
5 Kind of dance
10 Takes on cargo
15 War supplies
19 To the calm side
20 Dinner guest
21 "This ___ way to do it"
22 Cronus's wife
23 Boy barely making it to the "Kramer vs. Kramer" set?
25 They can ride, but can they sing like Maurice?
27 "___ aboard!"
28 King Cole and others
29 Dumas character
31 Powder maker
32 One of nine
34 Nail with a twist
35 One of a Christmas team
36 Central American
38 Annie was one
40 Annoyed
43 Rouses
45 Kind of sch.
46 Ali Baba's thieves
47 Time period
48 Welles role
49 Havelock or Dock
51 Othello et al.
52 Threatening
53 Sea bird
54 Cousteau's milieu
55 Herman or Allen
56 Troubled
57 Comic dance routines?
60 Mariners' calls
61 Algerian port
62 Crumb
63 Bolivian river
64 Do an editing job
66 Celeste-ial equestrienne?
73 Lubitsch of Hollywood
74 Pile-driving hammers
75 Some exams
76 Little one
77 Tree-trunk growth
78 Scout's master
79 Of value
80 "Hold it!"
81 Mrs. Cantor
82 Wastelands
83 Quarrel
84 Most reluctant
86 Rosemary Clooney song
88 Grass for lawns
90 Curves
91 Heraldic bearings
92 "___ they all, all honorable men": Shak.
93 Root or Yale
95 Storage areas
97 "Butterfield 8" author
98 "___ Indigo"
99 Dundee denial
102 Arlene's living quarters?
104 Comic turn?
107 Skating jump
108 Long-shot victory
109 Sir or madam, e.g.
110 Wine: Prefix
111 Russian communities
112 Cossacks protected them
113 Take the helm
114 Shoshoneans

DOWN

1 ___ California
2 Hebrew month
3 British beauty plays Lillian Roth?
4 Court call
5 French legislative unit
6 Sailor's artwork
7 Elevator man
8 ___-sahib
9 Sermonizes
10 Growths on rocks
11 Vote by ___ of hands
12 Forest creatures
13 Office desk item: Abbr.
14 Odessa and Boston
15 Greets the dawn
16 Butler takes the packet?
17 European blackbird
18 Return-mail enclosure: Abbr.
24 Pointless
26 Air-general Curtis
30 Coal-mine wagon
33 Autumn tool
34 Item for a benched skier
35 Cash's other half
36 Originator
37 In the know
39 Take it easy
40 Gat toters
41 Wading bird
42 Cooper's "Mr." role
44 Fiddle or rate
46 ___ the bill (be the host)
50 Actor Barker
51 "Veritas vincit" is one
52 Charles's lady
54 Tennyson's "The Palace ___"
55 1521 diet
56 Insists
58 Metal waste
59 Viking leader
60 Poplars
64 Offer payment
65 Wear down
66 Blues composer
67 Diamond trios
68 Make marginal jottings
69 Banal, to an Italian
70 Holbrook or Linden
71 Brant or graylag
72 ___-Unis
74 Gang gals
78 Exhausts
79 Wind currents
80 Longing
82 Actress Raquel
83 Scorch
85 Cab Calloway starts to sing about a girl?
87 Basic-training routines
88 Menu items
89 Streisand hit tune
92 Unqualified
94 Inferior
95 Rib donor
96 Kind of dancer
97 Pelion's base
98 Jot
100 Top-drawer
101 Grandson of 95 Down
103 Good times
105 Fired
106 Gehrig

15 Placement Bureau

By Olga Kowals

Getting things in their proper spots.

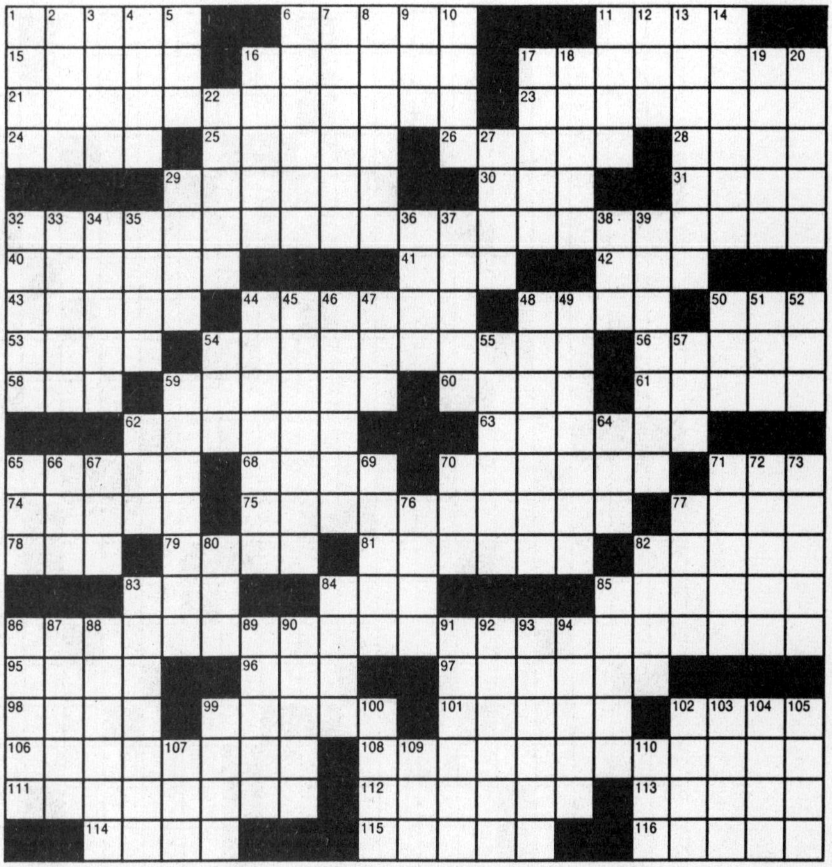

ACROSS

1 Westminster, for one
6 200-milligram unit
11 Parisian area
15 Schedule
16 Color
17 Algonquian people
21 Charge
23 Set aside
24 What children should be
25 Nicaraguan people
26 Junk
28 Hilarity
29 Go on a pension
30 C.I.A. forerunner
31 Waves on the Ebro
32 Look for trouble and get it
40 Spiral-horned antelopes
41 Roman 70
42 Son of Apollo
43 Bake-sale offerings
44 Town of Zaire
48 Kilns
50 Phiz
53 City near Des Moines
54 Pretend
56 Smidgen
58 Thailand river
59 Fancy
60 ___ homo
61 Penny-a-___ (hack writer)
62 Wall Street bulls
63 Equipped like a cat
65 Reach
68 Western Indians
70 Rained cats and dogs
71 Laughing or crying ___
74 In association with
75 Join a conversation
77 Forsyte or Arthurian
78 Kind of shoe or drop
79 Scrape
81 Blush
82 River-delta area
83 Nob's partner
84 Chamber in a harem
85 Wraparound for Lamour
86 Tidy the nursery, maybe
95 News story
96 "___, M'sieur"
97 Resolves
98 Room dividers: Abbr.
99 Large kangaroos
101 Fleeced
102 Pledge
106 Maybe, in France
108 Hoodwink
111 Checked
112 Summits
113 Bring on oneself
114 Gaelic
115 Kitchen equipment
116 Piquant

DOWN

1 Snakes
2 Kind of chip or book
3 Moderate
4 Collar
5 Urge
6 ___ de fer
7 Jockey Eddie
8 Stimulates
9 Postal abbr.
10 President after Roosevelt
11 Hiker's way
12 Prefix for gee
13 Burmese capital
14 ___ con carne: Var.
16 Cozy talks
17 Woman with ___
18 ___-Japanese War
19 Milieu for the QE2
20 Biblical verb
22 Shoe holders
27 Soup thickener
29 Boxing sessions: Abbr.
32 Praline ingredient
33 Moslem scholars' group
34 Claimed
35 Mind ___ manners
36 Fitzgerald
37 Colorless gas
38 In good shape
39 Pushed and shoved
44 Periodic car care
45 Rev
46 TV offering from a fence
47 Compass pt.
48 Obstruct
49 Solid part of a fat
50 Word after ape or yes
51 Hole-in-one
52 Prefix for mission or form
54 Nose around
55 Entente
57 Make free
59 What children do to clothes
62 Prohibit
64 Cyst
65 Quip
66 Ostrich's relative
67 Thumb or Sawyer
69 Broadway restaurateur
70 Pea or bean feature
71 Golden Fleece seeker
72 Ripening, as cheese
73 Lawless groups
76 Prosperous state, to Chaucer
77 Hindu lady's cover-up
80 Legal org.
82 Scrooge expletives
83 Pet rodent
84 Allegheny-Monongahela confluence
85 Pool member
86 Browning lass
87 Total
88 Hold
89 "___ the Top"
90 Treated tobacco
91 Hoffman of the films
92 Pawned
93 Rolling ones
94 Takes on
99 Suffix for kitchen or farmer
100 Saratoga, Hot Springs, etc.
102 Golfer Sarazen
103 Trajectories
104 Toe ailment
105 Shaw's 'iggins
107 Curve
109 News agcy.
110 Namely: Abbr.

16 Partners By Tap Osborn

People whose names turn out to be cooperative.

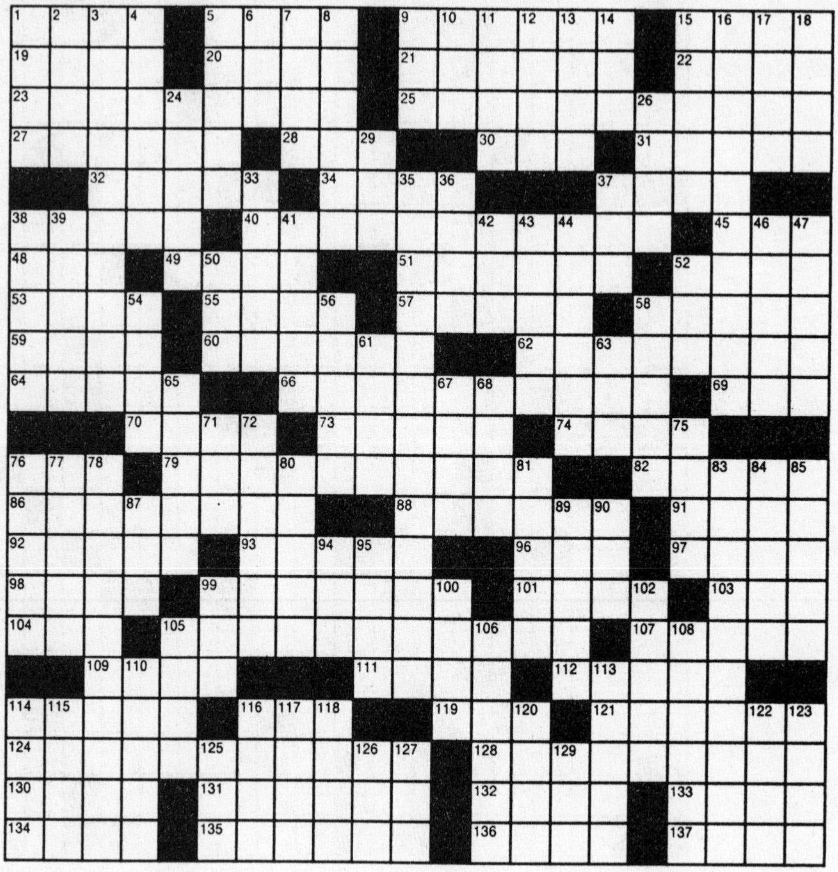

ACROSS

1 Haystack
5 Party loner
9 Ignoble
15 Air pollution
19 Geisha's box
20 Lima's place
21 Actor Peter
22 "Qué ____?"
23 Max and Melvin's paunch
25 Hot time for Elke and inventor George
27 Forward
28 Polo Grounds hero
30 Term of affection
31 Year, in Metz
32 ____ Devi, Himalayan mountain
34 Code word for A
37 Punjab sect member
38 Halt
40 State for Robert and Jenny
45 Nile creature
48 Counterpart of the Pac.
49 Entrance
51 Sovereignty
52 Theater org.
53 Martha of comedy
55 "Honi ____ qui . . ."
57 Villa ____
58 Waits
59 Color of an unwelcome slip
60 Straighten, as hair
62 Cipher experts
64 Kind of man or circle
66 Factory for Richard and John Stuart
69 Meriwether
70 A European
73 Weary
74 Does film editing
76 Part of a semi
79 Phyllis and Jane's plaudit
82 Old Indian term of respect
86 Beset with rage
88 On the upgrade
91 Ibsen heroine
92 More urgent
93 Tanoan people
96 Smooth: Prefix
97 Kind of iron
98 Major ending
99 Marine stations
101 Arab head cord
103 Course dir.
104 Stadium sound
105 Gregor and composer Ernest's hangup
107 Great quantity
109 Kind of bird or road
111 ____ over backward
112 Pulsate
114 Goes sky-high
116 Prior
119 Aquamarine or opal
121 Least
124 Gladys and Louis B.'s terror
128 Conrad and Johann's infirmity
130 One of the Near Islands
131 Obstruct
132 Spanish linen
133 Mine, in Paris
134 Lug
135 ____ saint (guardian)
136 Rams or Lions, e.g.
137 Butterfly catchers

DOWN

1 Spare or short orders
2 Subspecies: Suffix
3 Stiff cloth for performers Richard and Loretta
4 Film director Alexander and family
5 Please a store owner
6 Part of I.T.T.
7 Guthrie
8 Campfire instrument
9 Sea signal
10 Ear: Prefix
11 Easy victory
12 Cupola
13 "____ a Song Go Out . . ."
14 Bonn article
15 Courage
16 Rough up Thomas or George
17 Bone: Prefix
18 Stare
24 Filleted
26 Comics' Hazel, for one
29 Suit maker: Abbr.
33 "____ for the Misbegotten"
35 Arthur and Buster's shellfish catch
36 Egyptian dancer
37 Ship's plank curve
38 Wrists
39 French pewter
41 Sevareid and Blore
42 Certain recs
43 "____ Eat Cake": 1933 musical
44 Peaceful
46 Metric measure
47 Old hat
50 Columbus campus
52 Partner of abet
54 ____ out (manages)
56 Before frutti
58 Nuts' partners
61 Restraint
63 Actor Gulager
65 Happen again
67 Pope from 440 to 461
68 Murrow and Albee: Abbr.
71 Capek play
72 Fractured
75 Told all
76 Autumn quaff
77 Ekberg
78 Vital statistic of two Johns
80 Threesome
81 Spring bloom
83 Lena and Abe's birch tree
84 One of Chekhov's sisters
85 Black Forest locale
87 Charge
89 Owl's time
90 Tibetan antelope
94 ____ Miss
95 Street of finance
99 Seasoning in Metz
100 Scoria
102 Navigation aid
105 Word before mash
106 Kind of play
108 Biblical offering
110 Dispute
113 Wide-flanged support
114 Card game
115 Aware of
116 Poet Lazarus
117 Spellbound
118 Spotter
120 Slough
122 Highlander
123 "____ is a recording"
125 Gratuity
126 Tokyo of old
127 European period: Abbr.
129 Parrot of N.Z.

17 All the Keys By Dorothy Smitonick

At least those that constitute the alphabet.

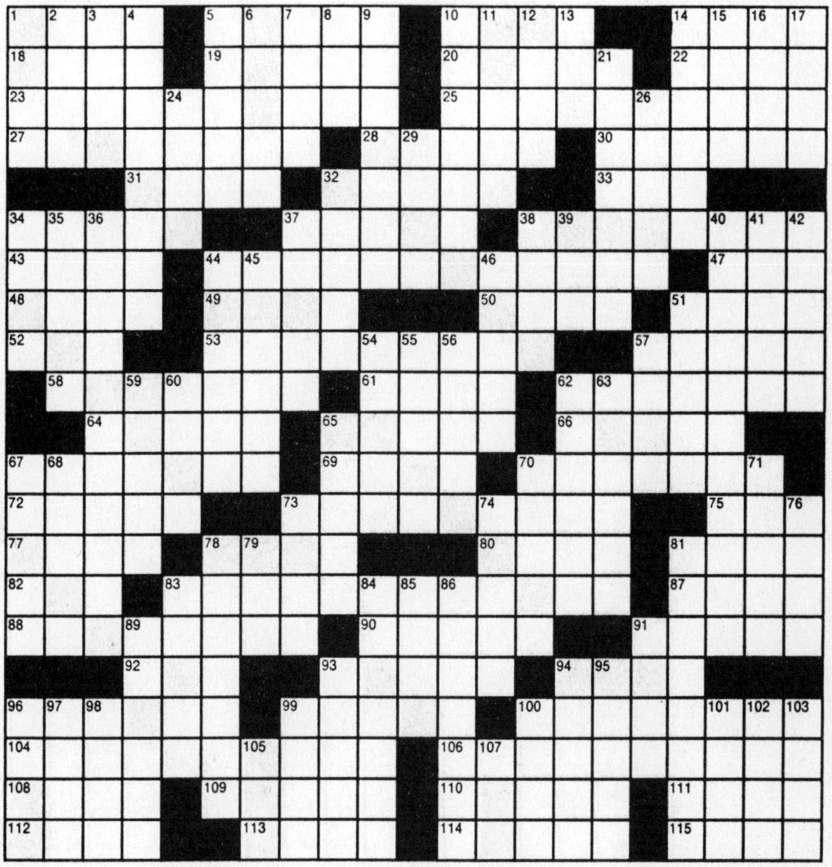

ACROSS

1 Essayist Charles
5 Arrange
10 Revise
14 Nods
18 City in Russia
19 In reserve
20 "Stille ___"
22 Pierre's date
23 Cosmetic counter?
25 Edenic greenery
27 Hash houses
28 Tear
30 Type of overcoat
31 Tantrums
32 Leading
33 Inlet
34 Outfit
37 Typing exercise: 3
38 All by my ___ (with no help)
43 Asks to be paid
44 Hobo's way to go?
47 Typing exercise: 4
48 Plate
49 Part
50 Beseech
51 Malayan boat
52 Law
53 Specialized schools
57 Unit of heat
58 Muscovites' change
61 Insect pests
62 Bottles
64 Check endorser
65 Casey or Davy
66 Win by ___
67 Not the smartest
69 Atop
70 Sneaky gunmen
72 Tests
73 United States citizens
75 Photography abbr.
77 Machine parts
78 Celsius reading: Abbr.
80 Molding
81 ___-Penh
82 Brooks or Ferrer
83 Rides through the gap
87 Figure
88 Pub dealings
90 Amusement-park features
91 Only ___ a customer
92 Typing exercise: 7
93 Humdingers
94 "I ___ You Truly"
96 Choice
99 French wine region
100 Ores
104 Finger ornament
106 What nobody was in Eden
108 Comedy act
109 ___ Hawkins Day
110 Roman robes
111 Snug
112 Louts
113 Tend
114 Excrete
115 Rds.

DOWN

1 Ear part
2 Space
3 Gist
4 Seafood item
5 "___ with Music"
6 Letters
7 Touts' offerings
8 Japanese salad plant
9 Favorite boutique?
10 Contest participant
11 Challenged
12 Chilled
13 Start of a typing exercise
14 Tropical trees
15 Leave out
16 Lot's ___
17 Prophet
21 Joust
24 Stumble
26 Handbill
29 Chops
32 Like some forces
34 Icelandic literature
35 Typing exercise: 2
36 Like a juggernaut
37 Semiprecious stone
38 ___ Porsena
39 Medical suffix
40 Letter ___ (testimonial)
41 Poet Marianne
42 Finals
44 Kick over the ___
45 July Fourth sight
46 Fencing swords
51 Stage of development
54 Escape, in a way
55 Unimportant
56 Ancient English tribe
57 Too much, in France
59 Buckets
60 Some are private
62 Film-festival site
63 Plants of the parsley family
65 Typing exercise: 5
67 Belief
68 Bay window
70 Epics
71 High-hat
73 Singer Ed
74 Manages
76 Between K and P
78 Abilities
79 Use sparingly
81 Like Maine's forests
83 Resort lake
84 Plodded
85 Hawaiian port
86 Teach
89 Is miserly
91 Typing exercise: 6
93 Russian leader
94 Beans
95 Start
96 ___ buco (veal dish)
97 Rabbitlike animal
98 Initials heard at work week's end
99 Skirt length
100 Wizard, old form
101 Acknowledge
102 Typing exercise: 8
103 Nicknames for Stallone and others
105 Astrological sign
107 Typing exercise: 9

18 Posted By Bernice Gordon

Some endangered species needing no-hunting signs.

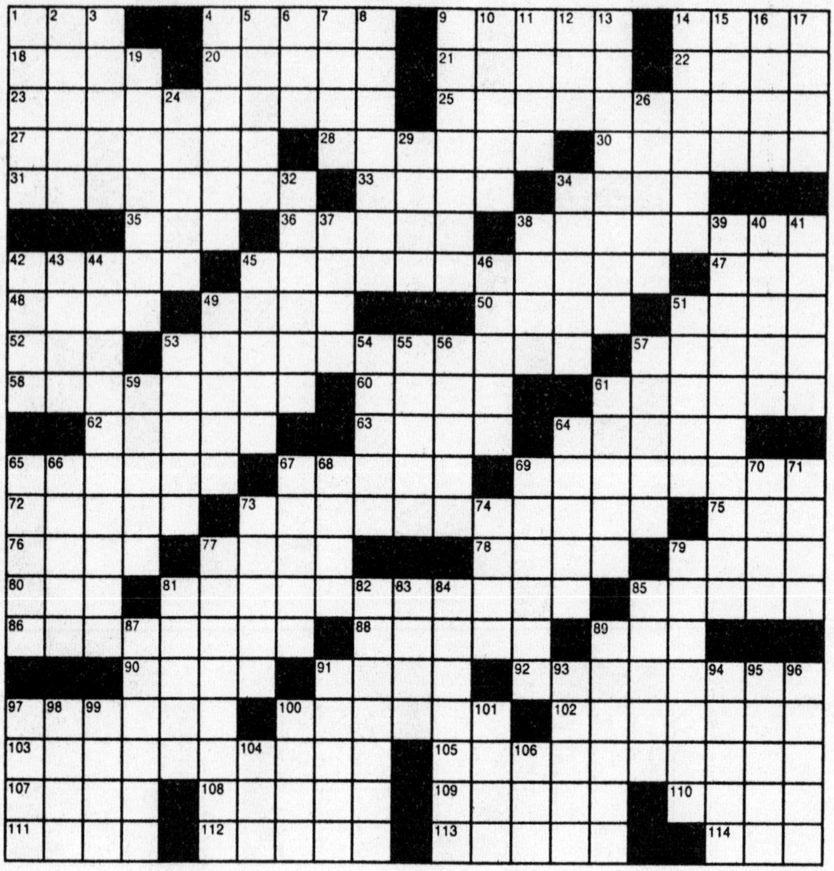

ACROSS

1 ___ Man of video games
4 Man on the lookout
9 Dean Martin specialty
14 Ebb's partner
18 Man, e.g.
20 Ruth of early aviation
21 Become a part
22 Large room, in Germany
23 African shortage
25 American shortages
27 Paint used for posters
28 Capable of change
30 In a tolerable degree
31 Tennis wear
33 Earthy deposit
34 Printing direction
35 Conducted
36 Walker or Eastwood
38 Weary
42 Hillsides, to Burns
45 Andes shortages
47 Gun a motor
48 Art media
49 Music critic Downes
50 Like a doornail
51 Cantrell
52 Costa del ___
53 American shortage
57 Simple organism
58 Backstabber's implement
60 Of the dawn
61 Electrical-switch joint
62 Aladdin's friend
63 Alfred of stage note
64 Hiding place for Laffite
65 Mexican president in the 1800's
67 "___ Got Nobody"
69 Ran in
72 Choir voices
73 Shortage in India
75 A vote
76 Bluebonnet
77 Kind of pipe cinch
78 Book of the Bible
79 Concerning
80 By means of
81 Australian shortage
85 Dispur's land
86 Writer Caldwell and namesakes
88 Map addition
89 Temple player
90 Adjective-forming suffixes
91 Insult
92 Larva of a marine worm
97 Large African river
100 Sewed roughly
102 Wagnerian tenor: 1831–1917
103 Shortage in Nepal and India
105 Shortages in Central and South America
107 Kind of warden
108 Extensive plain
109 "And ___ a goodnight!"
110 Onion
111 Originally, at one time
112 City of West Germany
113 Frolic
114 ___ Anne de Beaupré

DOWN

1 Early people of Britain
2 Gray
3 Poetic region
4 Adjusted
5 Of an arm bone
6 Tool for a carpenter
7 Lively dance
8 "Life is a ___ the night": Symons
9 Renaissance
10 ___ sides (surrounded)
11 Salt tree
12 But, to Livy
13 Climbing amphibian
14 Bundles for burning
15 Zinger
16 Cassini
17 Launder
19 Pierces
24 Lap dogs
26 Dills
29 Judge's seat
32 Prefix for phrenia
34 Kind of energy
37 Danube city west of Vienna
38 Kind of second-hand market
39 Indonesian shortages
40 Of the kidneys
41 Slip away from
42 Tweed, for one
43 An act to read
44 U.S. shortages
45 Goose grass
46 G.I.'s dog tag
49 President of Argentina: 1938–42
51 Trademarks
53 Heredity elements
54 Novel by George Sand
55 California pioneer
56 Guido ___, Italian physician
57 ___ âge (medieval days)
59 Dormouse
61 Pacific rootstocks
64 Word form for the English
65 Blended in colors
66 Worrier's ailment
67 Writer Dinesen et al.
68 Lover of Radamès
69 Creator of the Marches
70 Reddish wildcat
71 Have an opinion
73 Mosquito genus
74 Part of T.L.C.
77 Pendulum window
79 Of the Moslem faith
81 Beatle name
82 Swedish soprano Christine
83 Insect
84 Phases
85 Bearded
87 Thames feeder
89 Pro from Baltimore
91 River in France
93 Husband of ma tante
94 Respiratory sounds
95 Clumsy
96 Parts of Saturn's rings
97 Drive
98 Indian laboring caste
99 Objects
100 Bikini parts
101 Discontinue
104 City railways
106 Bireme necessity

19 Oxymorons By George Rose Smith

That is, paradoxes in the family of "sweet sorrow" and "cruel kindness."

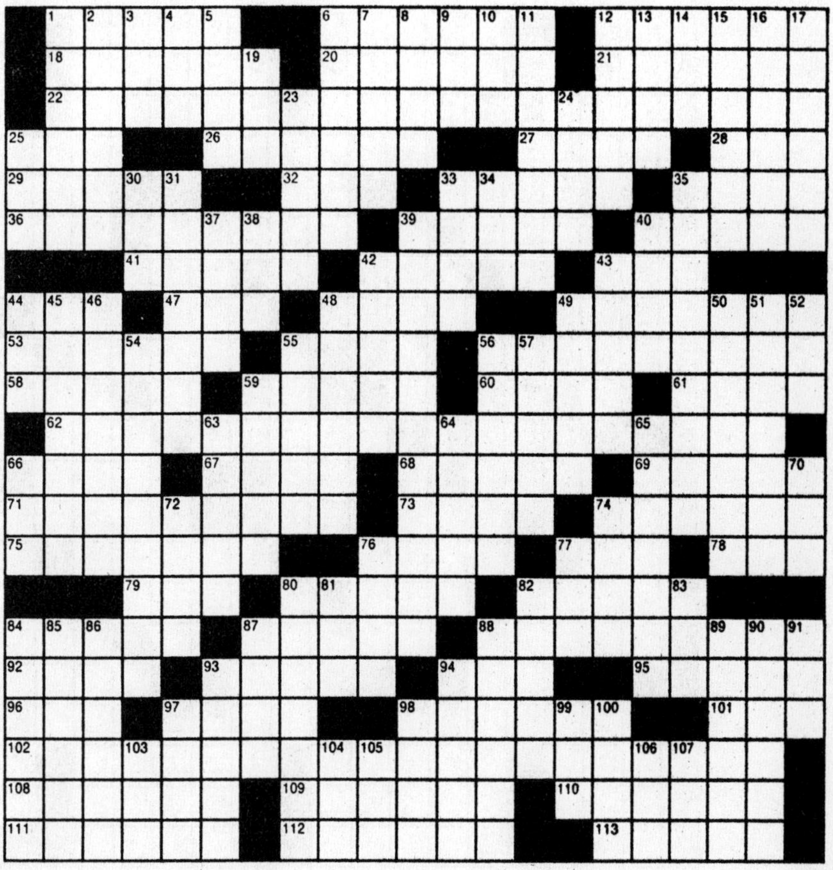

ACROSS

1 Kind of boom
6 Ostracized one
12 Squeezed oranges
18 Like the "Odyssey"
20 "Be it ___ humble"
21 Mysterious
22 Oxymoron in the armed services?
25 Racket
26 Repetitious fly
27 Kind of log
28 Be careless
29 Man the helm
32 Bill's partner
33 Jan. 1 china
35 Had on
36 Discontinuance
39 Wreck a car
40 Dwindled
41 Do a maidenly blackout
42 Abbey official
43 Back stroke of a sort
44 ___ Lippo Lippi
47 Oxonian fellow
48 "___ M for Murder"
49 Manifold
53 Bay tree
55 "Song ___ Blue"
56 Event at Belmont
58 Lost
59 Early arms discussion
60 Clock
61 Explorer Hedin
62 Oxymoron at college?
66 Fit to ___
67 Hawaiian bird
68 Like Woodworth's bucket
69 Last Commandment
71 Long-tailed cage birds
73 Van der Rohe
74 Unpawn
75 Like Rome
76 German title
77 Area of India
78 Graduating class: Abbr.
79 Mayday's relative
80 Rundown
82 ___ Ste. Marie
84 Attachment to a sports shoe
87 Floor
88 When "They're off!"
92 Lounge
93 Pointed
94 It's Big in Calif.
95 Weed eradicators
96 Wood sorrel
97 N.L. ball park
98 Wide river valley
101 Day: Abbr.
102 Oxymoron in the cities?
108 Colts or Dolphins
109 French star
110 Tenant
111 Put in more readable form
112 Thin-ice sign
113 Plays the lead

DOWN

1 Canaanite, for one
2 Expresses a belief
3 Nothing
4 Here, in Paris
5 Famed suffragist
6 Place on TV
7 Dispatch vessel
8 Descartes
9 N.Y. subway
10 Ibsen character
11 Embattled oxymoron?
12 Incarcerates
13 Press
14 Highball component
15 "___ to right of them"
16 Curtain re-raiser
17 Conveyed
19 Spanish article
23 W.W. II survey vehicle, for short
24 Respite
25 Mil. decoration
30 Sigmoid line
31 Unfair treatment
33 Seethe
34 Siouan
35 Point of division
37 Saw or hammer
38 Charged atom
39 Classic oxymoron
40 Breaker
42 Pub orders
43 Cheapskate
44 Sunshine st.
45 Knock-knock
46 Uncompromising
48 Sweet wines
49 Biblical cony
50 Gorges
51 Symbol of authority
52 Poet's time of day
54 Chore for a cast
55 Simon Templar
56 Dracula's creator
57 Floor pieces
59 Bethlehem output
63 Virgil's traveler: Var.
64 Like O'Neill's 66 Down
65 Stalker's asset
66 Primate
70 "___ Pinafore"
72 Cluster
74 Put to flight
76 With us
77 Steam, for one
80 Sinned
81 Aurora's counterpart
82 Marsh birds
83 Spanish relative
84 More stingy
85 Setting
86 Small kite
87 Prescient one
88 Happy cat
89 Pioneer in hypnotism
90 Wipes away
91 Fast flier
93 Macbeth, for one
94 Stone pillar
97 Small distance
98 Gulp
99 Norse god of victory
100 Parts of legislatures: Abbr.
103 English or ground
104 RR stop
105 Geological division
106 Explosive
107 Airboard abbr.

20 Banzai! By Ed Rehmus

Visiting the land of paper-folding and tree-dwarfing.

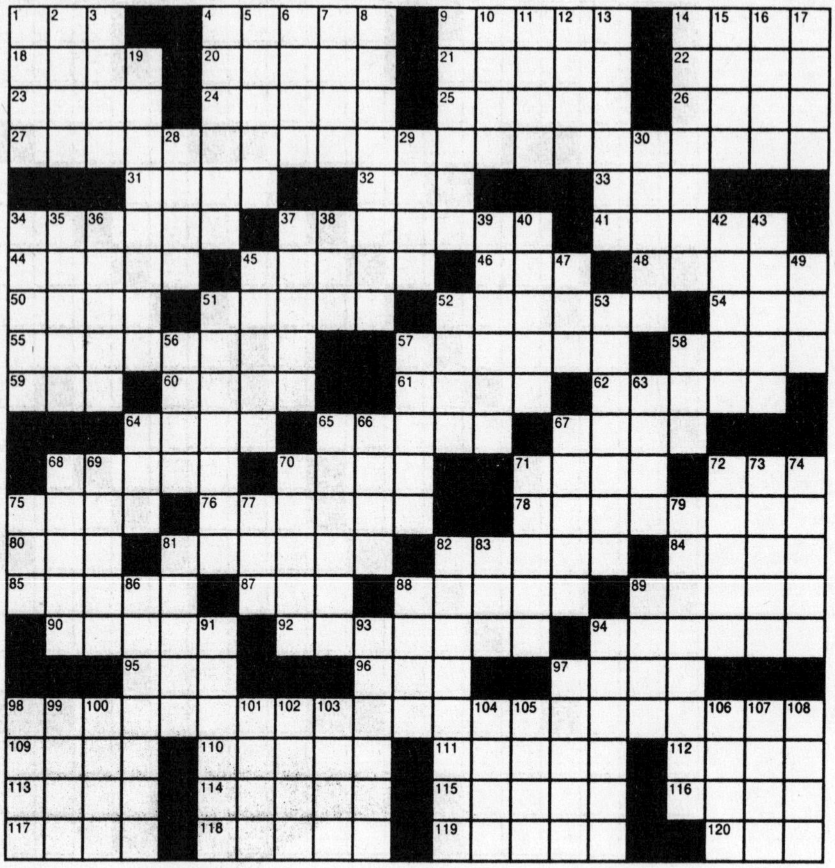

ACROSS

1 Put in voices
4 Gin bases
9 Greek letter
14 Religious picture
18 Columnist's tidbit
20 Deciduous pine
21 Perfect model
22 Blue river
23 Elephant Boy of films
24 Beloved, in Italy
25 Mediterranean island
26 That, in Paris
27 Spring fete in Japan
31 "The ___ have it!"
32 Mad-when-wet creature
33 Carson of the Old West
34 Mary Hartman portrayer
37 Pop the question
41 Revoke a legacy
44 Movie dog and namesakes
45 Intimidate
46 Cut
48 Very, in music
50 Writer Dinesen
51 Flat-bottomed boat
52 Northern
54 Blasting material
55 Lethal plane of W.W. II
57 Less naïve
58 Lunch-counter order
59 Elec. unit
60 Certain bills
61 Malarial illness
62 Vino ___ (red wine)
64 Lawyers: Abbr.
65 Glossy lacquer
67 Frustrate
68 "Coming of Age in ___"
70 Modest poker holding
71 English composer
72 Authors' submissions: Abbr.
75 Duchess of ___ (Goya subject)
76 Honshu city
78 Second victim of the atomic era
80 Form of Buddhism
81 Quaky poplars
82 Bandleader Shaw
84 Triplet
85 Golf meets
87 ___ of order
88 Inexperienced
89 Pickle juice
90 Path through the wilds
92 Sources of energy
94 Verges
95 Chemical suffix
96 Mideast nation: Abbr.
97 Alda or Bates
98 Far Eastern nickname
109 Things put on
110 Rome's river
111 Fine fabric
112 "___-daisy!"
113 Open-weave fabric
114 Zola
115 Step
116 Noble
117 "East of ___"
118 Homes of lovers
119 Connery and O'Casey
120 Edwardian ___

DOWN

1 Record
2 Provo's state
3 Silent film star Daniels
4 Killer
5 Dears
6 One type of surgeon
7 Prefix for plasm
8 Western Indian
9 Geisha wear
10 "___ Bede"
11 Ill-gotten gains
12 Head
13 Japan's nearest U.S. neighbor
14 Eggs on
15 Ukrainian capital
16 ___ podrida
17 Actress Patricia
19 Japanese authoress
28 Bread types
29 Fall mo.
30 Kind of wave
34 Soviet space dog
35 Indian state
36 Philatelic concern
37 Reduces
38 Mideast export
39 Clavell best-seller
40 Weird
42 These, in Spain
43 Tropical fruit
45 Stuns
47 Small
49 Japanese statesman
51 Certain roosters
52 Turnip variety, for short
53 Work with cut flowers
56 Japanese zither
57 Film director Frank
58 Sound of disapproval
63 The true olive
64 Physicians' org.
65 Pert
66 Gives succor
67 Egghead
68 Dozed
69 Li'l one
70 False: Prefix
71 Puts in the pot
72 County north of S.F.
73 Smooth-scaled lizard
74 Trig ratios
75 Nitrogen: Prefix
77 Mil. address
79 Do in a rustler
81 ___ dream (unworldly)
82 Seat dividers
83 Old car
86 Attaches in a way
88 Wound
89 Fiber food
91 Of the season after Mardi Gras
93 Saltpeters
94 Window shades
97 Oriental
98 19 Down's "The ___ of Genji"
99 Hurried
100 Sea bird
101 Stop on a ___
102 Geisha sashes
103 Hat material
104 Not well done
105 Willow
106 Graf ___
107 Addict
108 Honshu city

21 Bard Stoppers By Bert Rosenfield

Remarks that could have aborted Shakespearean classics.

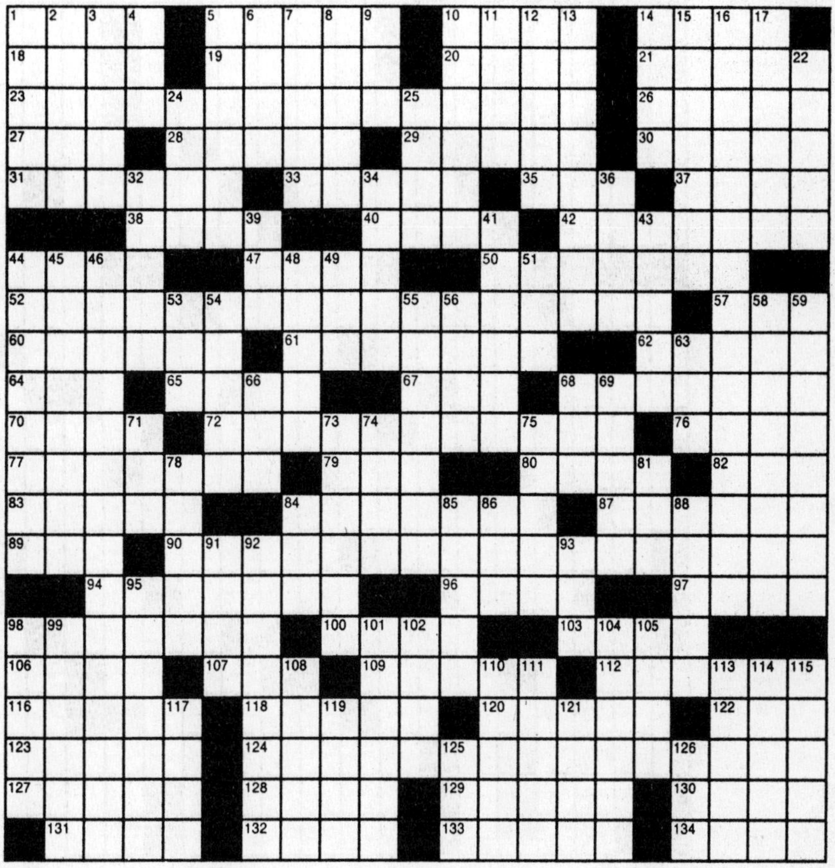

ACROSS

1 Pedestal part
5 Shade givers
10 Monte Carlo diversion
14 Streamlet
18 Fulda tributary
19 Attacked
20 To ___ (utterly)
21 Caribbean ritual
23 "King Lear"
26 Paris people mover
27 Prove to be human
28 Its capital is Grenoble
29 Aspirant to rank of capt.
30 A felony
31 "Macbeth," with 90 Across
33 Bean or Welles
35 ___ Na Na
37 Berlin's "___ Lovely Day Today"
38 Silas Lapham's movement
40 Cribbage-board units
42 Persian rug
44 Indian water buffalo
47 U.N. member
50 Trattoria dessert
52 "The Merchant of Venice," with 112 Across
57 Org. for Eagles, Bears et al.
60 Steele's journal
61 Bickering ones
62 Film director George
64 Away from: Prefix
65 ___ of the earth
67 Summer hrs. in Illinois
68 Breathe
70 "What ___ now?" (mom to junior)
72 "Julius Caesar"
76 Dele's antonym
77 14-line poems
79 Bar or rad ending
80 Pelion's perch
82 Bilbao bear
83 Sidles
84 Crowd ___ (popular one)
87 Eagles, Bears or Rams
89 Oona's brother-in-law
90 See 31 Across
94 Dreamlike
96 Count-out starter
97 Enniskillen's river
98 Adriatic port
100 Out of the gale
103 Entry point for a burglar
106 Relegated
107 Resp. to 74 Down
109 Sea access
112 See 52 Across
116 Word form with Saxon
118 Flier Balbo
120 He had 50 children
122 Sweet girl of song
123 ___ Robert (pitcher Feller)
124 "The Tempest"
127 Feed the boiler
128 Ange appendage
129 Tonic's companion
130 Golf-club part
131 Lars and siamangs
132 Striplings
133 Shed ___ (weep)
134 Fir pole

DOWN

1 Star in Cygnus
2 Idolize
3 Miss Paget of the cinema
4 Montana's motto metal
5 Rendezvous
6 The Charleston in the 20's, e.g.
7 Invierno month
8 Chow hound
9 Ave. crossers
10 Over the hill
11 François's friend
12 French philosopher-mathematician
13 "___ of a nation": F.D.R.
14 City NW of Napoli
15 Southern European
16 "Romeo and Juliet"
17 Singer Julius
22 Chinese province
24 Roman 503
25 ___ hemp (agave plant)
32 Fish professionally
34 Bouquet addition
36 Regarding
39 It's north of Afr.
41 ___ riot (make trouble)
43 Pigs, in Amiens
44 Fred and 114 Down
45 Liszt work
46 "Hamlet"
48 Defunct defense org.
49 Tel. operator
51 Connectives
53 V.P. under Cleveland
54 Weissmuller specialty
55 Argentine independence city
56 Hand over
58 Anticipated
59 Chintzy fabric
63 Bullish times
66 They take handoffs from qb's
68 Cogitans or judicata
69 One of the Fords
71 Bug killer also called DDD
73 Glass ingredient
74 Interrogative: Abbr.
75 Navigator's aid
78 Billy Sol ___
81 It goes around a 'ead
84 Greek letter
85 Skyscraper material
86 Before, in Baden
88 Confederate general
91 ___ single (get on base)
92 Peaceful
93 Scheldt joiner
95 Reticulate
98 Despots
99 Tebaldi or Scotti
101 Valley flowers
102 Slaughter of baseball
104 Where to find a glove compartment
105 Togo's capital
108 Narrow band
110 Disney mecca in Florida
111 Wind or last
113 ___ vitriol (sulfuric acid)
114 See 44 Down
115 Consumer's crusader
117 Pindaric and others
119 ___ lang syne
121 Song opener for Durante
125 Zsa Zsa's sister
126 Fighting Tigers' insignia

22 Places By Dorothea Shipp

Here and there on the school geography scene.

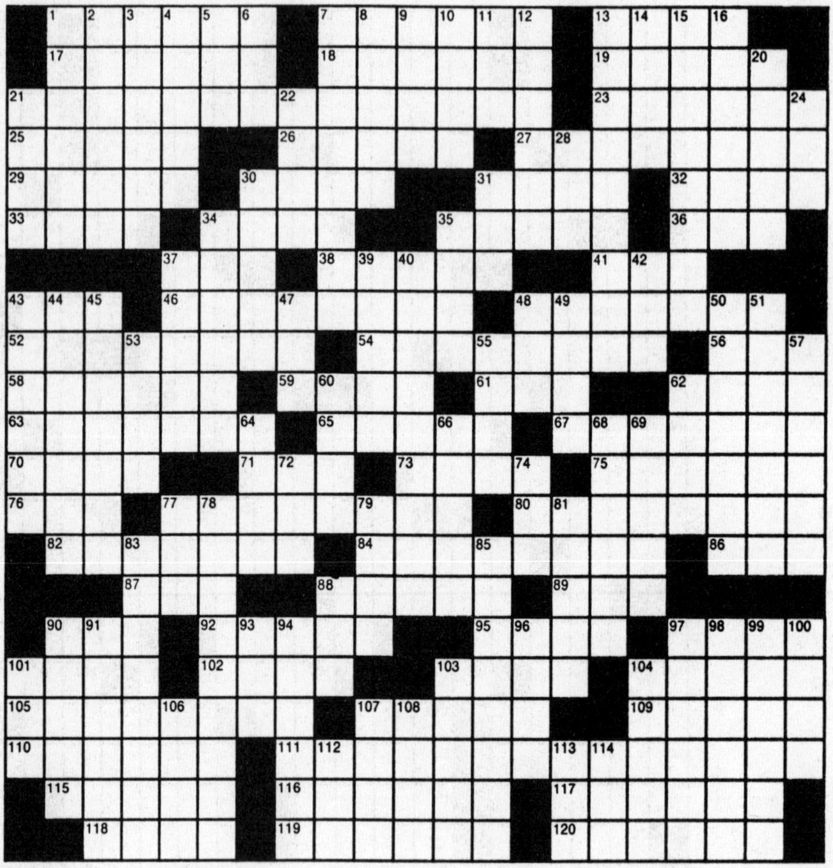

ACROSS

1 Mollusks
7 Dark blue
13 Eban of Israel
17 Hot Mexican fare
18 Mark Antony, for one
19 ____ Sainte Marie
21 Place for Western cenotaphs?
23 Was a good Samaritan
25 Equal, in Rouen
26 Actress Taylor
27 Fine silver
29 One-____ (partial)
30 Coin
31 Pier boss: Abbr.
32 Name in Genesis
33 Theater purchase
34 Worry
35 Robeson and Pinza
36 Thrice: Prefix
37 Parseghian
38 Brief summary
41 Welcome item for Don Ho
43 Alphabet starter
46 Sailor's gear
48 Gymnast's asset
52 Negligent
54 One who subjugates
56 Times of day: Abbr.
58 Like a goat's hoof
59 Work for
61 Call ____ day
62 Places: Suffix
63 Calif. Air Force base
65 Novelist Jameson
67 Cat's comfortable country?
70 Rackets
71 Cummerbund's relative
73 Dwarf: Prefix
75 War scene of 1854–56
76 Vane letters
77 One committing a crime
80 Icy-road occurrence
82 Arrange color shadings
84 Assert more strongly
86 Would-be capts.
87 Indonesia's old name: Abbr.
88 Writer Capek
89 Vista, in Paris
90 High ____ kite
92 Pose for another photo
95 Character in "The Grapes of Wrath"
97 "Dear me"
101 Work on copy
102 Thin covering
103 Red explorer
104 Go-ahead
105 Miss Burnett's state?
107 Martinique volcano
109 Rye disease
110 Charlotte ____
111 Washington's Mount ____
115 Handle, in Germany
116 Sarcastic
117 Plundered, old style
118 Do a floor job
119 Petroleum ingredient
120 Rate

DOWN

1 Cheap cigar
2 Certain goose's home base
3 Charm
4 Hobbled
5 Bar drink
6 Member of Cong.
7 Sent to ____ (ostracized)
8 Praying figure
9 Unit of hay
10 Salt tree
11 Affection, in Glasgow
12 Meetings
13 N.C. repository for fire leavings?
14 Heavyweight Max
15 Something to put on a board
16 Mountainous
20 Caruso, for one
21 Untidiness
22 Sir Herbert Beerbohm
24 Small metric wts.
28 Thy, in France
30 Endings for pluto and demo
31 Weaken
34 Quaker
35 They're under some eyes
37 Renata or Alfred
39 First German president
40 Artillery gunner
42 Thing to lend
43 Give in
44 Approaching alopecia
45 Officiator at a beauty show
47 Half a fly
48 Symbol of blindness
49 Grandparental
50 Chewy candy
51 Famous
53 LeGallienne and Braun
55 Describe
57 Anwar and family
60 S____ Samuel
62 Foul smelling
64 Kind of shoe or soap
66 ____ aves (unusual people)
68 Collect
69 Deal with a water pump
72 Spelling or sewing
74 Stupid person
77 Grecian urn inscribing
78 Conn. county-fete place?
79 Mild expletive
81 Kind of pride or minded
83 Part of Turkey
85 Girl for Italy?
88 Miss Novak
90 Kind of apple
91 Moslem bridges to paradise
93 German article
94 Czech or Serbian
96 Ukrainian capital
97 Turn up
98 French rail routes
99 Dodges
100 Bristle
101 Post-W.W. II agcy.
103 Remove, in law
104 Painter of "Foyer of the Dance"
106 Property right
107 A religion: Abbr.
108 Sicilian city
112 Before
113 Lyricist Gershwin
114 ____ publica

23 Whistling Dixie

By Wilson McBeath

A humorist's observation on some accents.

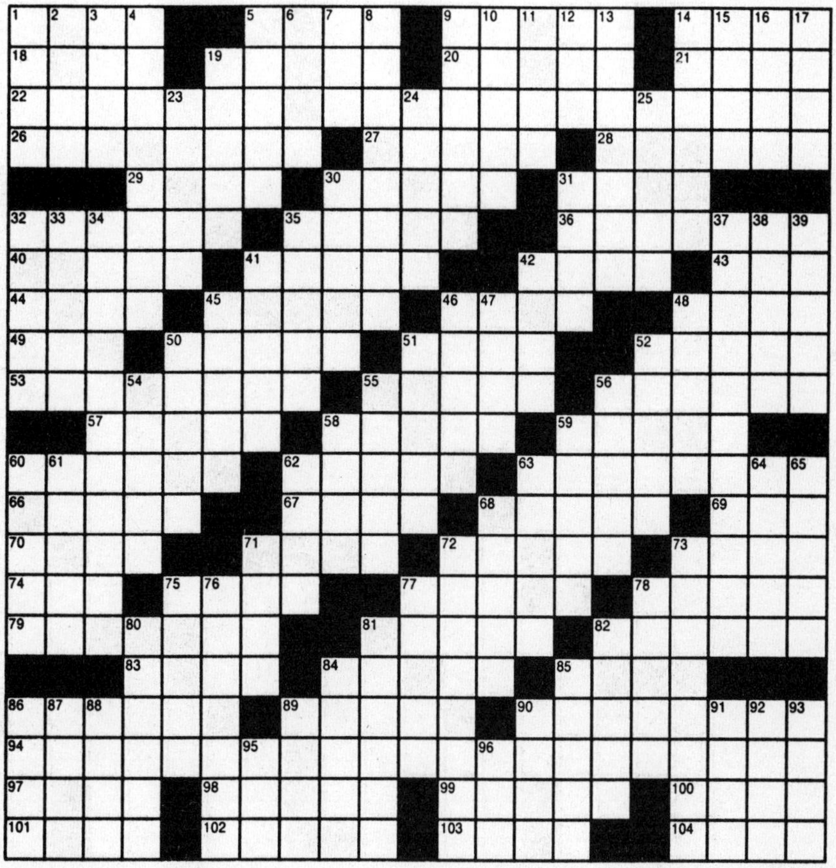

ACROSS

1 Pass over
5 Easy stride
9 Thistle appendages
14 Kind of sticks
18 Datsun or Chevrolet
19 Whistler's accessory
20 Rigel's constellation
21 Large kangaroo
22 Start of a Yankee quotation
26 Fingernail painter
27 Kind of conference or gallery
28 Prolific U.S. inventor
29 Prune, in Scotland
30 Part of a plow
31 Galena and pyrite
32 Event
35 Large quantities
36 Quartz or feldspar
40 Retreats
41 McKinley political adviser
42 Sets of tools
43 Ivy Leaguer
44 Light-giver for Debussy
45 Floor support
46 Comic sketch
48 Café au ___
49 Hydrocarbon: Suffix
50 Wino
51 Facial feature
52 Wimbledon champ Donald
53 Second part of the quote
55 Flaxen
56 Third part of the quote
57 Harass
58 Main rail line
59 Go down the ___
60 Fourth part of the quote
62 Rouen's river
63 Descends
66 Conducts
67 Kind of chair and street
68 Cereal-attacking fungus
69 Article
70 Autographs
71 Author of the quote, with 72 Across
72 See 71 Across
73 Sensitive leg part
74 Get even
75 Highlander
77 Kitchen utensil
78 Simpletons
79 Section of London
81 British cavalry sword
82 Store workers
83 Goals
84 Sprites
85 Son of Hera
86 Fillet for binding the hair
89 Robin of old song
90 Resident of Anniston
94 End of the quote
97 Item of interest
98 Upright
99 Astern
100 Miss Kett
101 Early church desk
102 Endures
103 Condiment
104 Secretary

DOWN

1 Glut
2 Nobelist in Chemistry: 1938
3 Virginia willow
4 "___ made by fools . . ."
5 Added liquor
6 Glacial ridges
7 Peevish state
8 Circus parader
9 Puzzles
10 Emerged
11 Papal name
12 Kind of shot or hole
13 What the meek shall do
14 Red
15 Attila's people
16 Mountain: Prefix
17 X-rated material
19 Swiss mathematician
23 Patron saint of France
24 Broadway offering
25 Paradises
30 Feeling
31 Leave out
32 Supreme Being, to an Arab
33 Flora's partner
34 Master bakers' achievements
35 Worker's goal
37 ___ chapter (keep on with one's book)
38 Straighten
39 Liquid measure
41 Colonel ___, Wilson adviser
42 Benevolent
45 Knightly combat
46 Sparkled
47 Twist in a rope
48 Sensational
50 Afternoon TV fare
51 Kind of lace
52 Speak with pride
54 Exigencies
55 Stimulating
56 Refrigerant gas
58 ___ down (raze)
59 Stray calf
60 Choice
61 City in Ohio
62 Decorative stamp
63 Cradle's counterpart
64 Kind of broom
65 Hawaiian geese
68 Pitchers
71 First-aid people, for short
72 Sea of Galilee
73 Teetered
75 Spirit in a lamp
76 Cain ___
77 Red cedar
78 Puffball core
80 Skill: Prefix
81 Inclines
82 Slyness
84 Decree
85 High up
86 Pet for F.D.R.
87 Part of a molecule
88 Use a stiletto
89 Cures, as meat
90 Arab head cord
91 Speck
92 University major
93 Neighbor of Manitoba: Abbr.
95 Time period
96 Org. for the Celtics

24 Arrival Board By Marjorie Pedersen

Results of going from place to place.

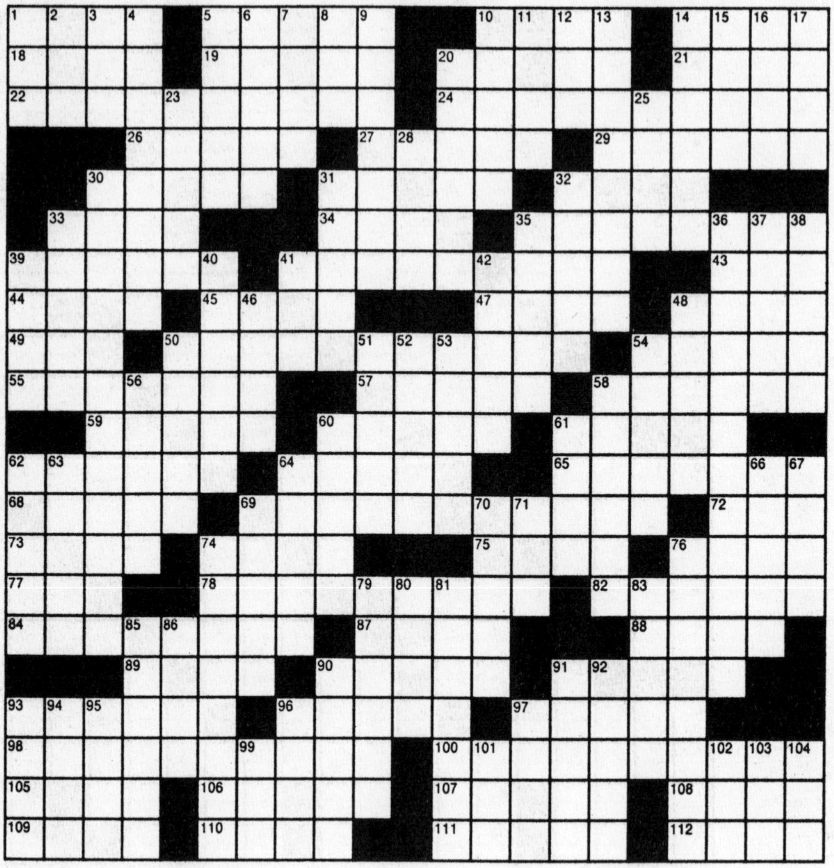

ACROSS

1 Diet staple
5 Snug
10 A leaper
14 Political adm.
18 King or Alda
19 Manifest
20 Alone, in Paris
21 Robt. ____
22 Doorstep installation
24 Pests at theaters
26 Property claims
27 Brings up
29 "____ Delight"
30 Paddock occupants
31 Short daggers
32 Take ____ bath (bask)
33 Garden rambler
34 Trick
35 Hostile
39 Ones showing promise
41 Inherits
43 Cheer word
44 Filled with wonderment
45 "Do ____ others . . ."
47 Chief
48 Give forth
49 French possessive
50 Enterprising
54 River of England
55 ____ leg (pants part)
57 Redeem
58 Classifies, as sentences
59 Shylock's forte
60 Kind of goat
61 Medit. tree
62 Sicilian nymphs
64 First Indian prime minister
65 Early stable workers
68 Dish or bath
69 Retribution
72 Pacific fish
73 Continent
74 Prefix for fact or fice
75 Writer Seton
76 Identical or fraternal
77 Cambridge campus
78 Intruders of a sort
82 Rio Grande city
84 Owing, in a way
87 Precious
88 Haberdashery items
89 Singer Alice
90 Clockmaker Thomas et al.
91 Old Nick
93 Angry
96 Violinmaker
97 Before
98 Criticize severely
100 Find by chance
105 Potentate
106 Fails
107 Slippery as ____
108 Fixed amount
109 My Gal and Mineo
110 Mass. state motto word
111 Hire
112 "____ But the Lonely Heart"

DOWN

1 Like a certain whip's hide
2 ____ de France
3 Neighbor of Nev.
4 Business-correspondence word
5 Halley's, for one
6 Places for roasts
7 Hebrew letters
8 Lippo Lippi
9 Metallic element
10 Sprees
11 Baseball-inning trios
12 Stout's relative
13 Judgment
14 Horoscope sector
15 Bread spread
16 Green, in heraldry
17 Hardy girl
20 Assuages
23 Kuwait visitor
25 Town of eastern Georgia
28 Gaelic
30 Reveals
31 Dickens's Edwin ____
32 ____ suit (astronaut's protective wear)
33 Oarsman
35 Trite
36 Divides
37 Kind of skirt
38 Baltic people
39 ____ of characters
40 Apartment-house V.I.P.'s
41 Shipping box: Abbr.
42 Ammonia compound
46 ____ a one (zilch)
48 Flynn
50 Customary
51 Hiding place
52 Hokkaido port
53 Complete a project
54 French pastry
56 Lichen
58 Celery variety
60 Having units of time: Suffix
61 Rabbit
62 Honshu resort
63 Red dye
64 ____ alike (words for snowflakes)
66 Forays
67 Word form for Chinese
69 Labyrinth's home
70 Peels
71 Reply, for short
74 Consolidate a joint
76 Test of a kind
79 Scads
80 Jeff's pal
81 Moral
83 House area
85 Tenders
86 Tail: Prefix
90 Kind of screen
91 Old knives
92 "____ of Two Cities"
93 Summer desserts
94 "Arrivederci ____"
95 Jannings of the films
96 Harding and Blyth
97 Swedish port
99 Triumph
101 ____-upmanship
102 Yoko ____
103 Transgression
104 Fr. holy woman

25 Seconds By Joan Whitman

Some who got to first, others who didn't.

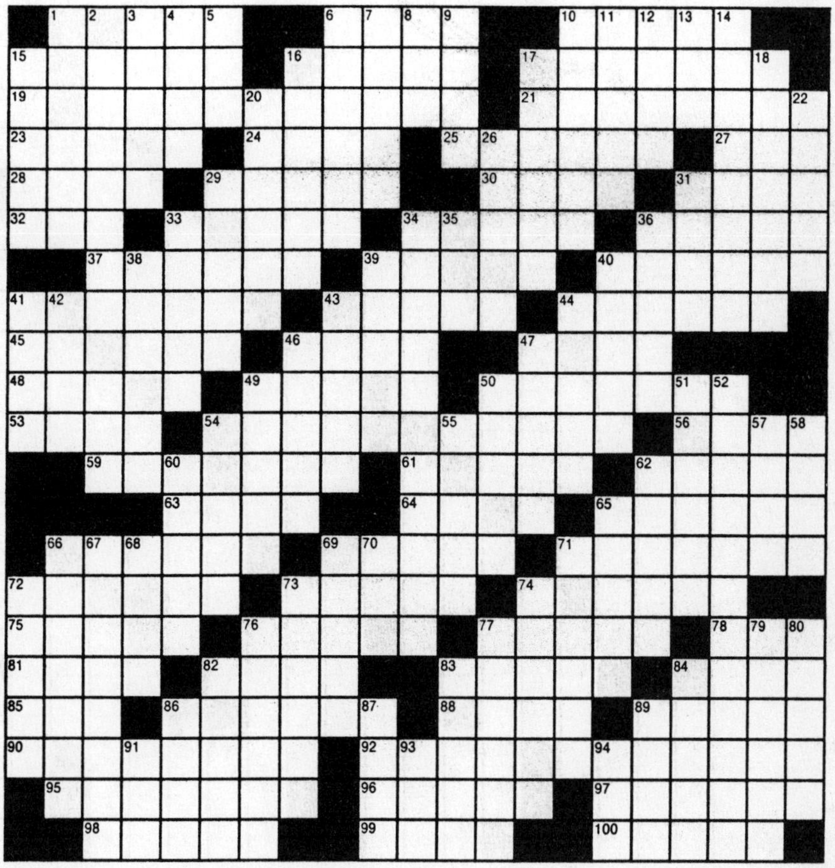

ACROSS

1 Natty
6 Bullfighter's cloak
10 Tied
15 Geronimo was one
16 Mountain ash
17 Resilient
19 McKinley V.P.
21 Wilson V.P.
23 Up ___ (stumped)
24 To love, in Spain
25 Été in the U.S.
27 Uncle, in Spain
28 French marshal and family
29 Sufficient
30 Pay attention
31 "Rule, Britannia" composer
32 Onager
33 Narrow passage
34 Sheds, as a lover
36 Darts
37 Colored
39 Relatives of mesas
40 Low-class guys
41 Low man on the peerage pole
43 U.S. naval historian
44 Danish Nobel poet: 1944
45 Chopin specialties
46 N. Eng. state
47 Silk, in Lyon
48 Philippine island
49 N.H. flower
50 Elaborate bash
53 Bit of info
54 Pierce V.P.
56 "___ Kampf"
59 Relentless rival
61 Hideaways
62 Home
63 ___ breve
64 Inkling
65 Cloister passages
66 Discordant sound
69 Blum and Edel
71 Asserts
72 Punctuation marks
73 Knave
74 Place side by side
75 "Pal Joey" author
76 Bittern
77 "The Green Hat" author
78 Mil. honor
81 Coptic Church title
82 Stupor
83 Chamber-music groups
84 Warsaw Pact opponents
85 Federal pension org.
86 Alamo or Hall of Fame
88 Furniture style
89 Felt pain
90 Monroe V.P.
92 Truman Veep
95 Homebodies of a sort
96 River to the Rhone
97 Filches
98 D.C. raider
99 Slow jog
100 "Steppenwolf" author

DOWN

1 Outpourings
2 Roosevelt V.P.
3 Large quantity
4 Former Korean leader
5 Fido, e.g.
6 Deep blue
7 Mindful
8 Level of equality
9 Social creatures
10 Censures
11 Rowed
12 Neighbor of Pol.
13 Utmost degree
14 Castro speech, often
15 Capital of Guam
16 Frolicked
17 Irish patriot Robert and family
18 Jefferson and Madison V.P.
20 Small town
22 Loamy deposit
26 European lancer
29 Chips in
31 Charity
33 Tube or circle
34 Adams and Jackson V.P.
35 Miss Hogg
36 Penalized
38 Chemical salt
39 Hawaiian island
40 Existence
41 Wife of 2 Down
42 Syllables after rat
43 Gangsters' gals
44 Links
46 Eyelashes
47 Symbol of generosity
49 Cotton thread
50 Washington's are Red
51 Permeates
52 Polk V.P.
54 Rose Trelawny's theater
55 Election bellwether, once
57 Thought, in Tours
58 Promontory
60 ___ cum laude
62 ". . . made some tarts, ___ a summer's day"
65 Mont Blanc et al.
66 Van Buren, Lincoln or Kennedy V.P.
67 George Wallace, for one
68 Nick's spouse
69 Navigation aid
70 Self
71 Poise
72 "The ___ is clear"
73 Negligent
74 Bluebeard's sixth wife
76 Jack of plum fame
77 Eager
79 Tatler founder
80 Buffalo Bill's family
82 Onion's kin
83 Banned
84 Antiaircraft missiles
86 Auto mishap on ice
87 Far or Mid
89 Comedian Johnson
91 School org.
93 Roman spirit
94 Timber tree

26 Question Time By Alfio Micci

With impertinent answers generally called for.

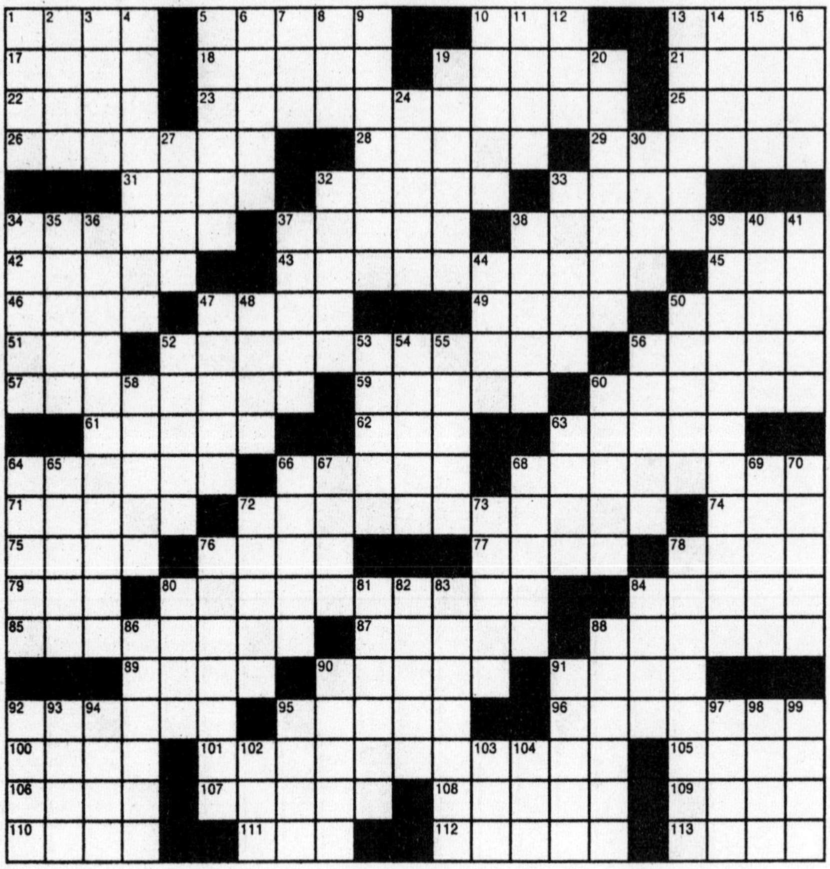

ACROSS

1 Veal source
5 Formal introduction
10 Swiss stream
13 Do a deck job
17 Monetary unit of Cambodia
18 Mortify
19 Mail
21 Elias or Julia
22 Greek theaters
23 Trap Lewis?
25 Presently
26 Like Beirut or Belfast
28 Confronts
29 Spanish dream home
31 Helen's foster home
32 Jury group
33 Budget item
34 Suva native
37 Straighten
38 Worthy
42 Habituate
43 Cancel a singing family's concert?
45 Former Mideast initials
46 Pinnacle
47 French sweetie
49 "___ a man with . . ."
50 Albanian river
51 Dine
52 Forsake Bob?
56 Matisse
57 Covering N.Y., N.J. and Conn., e.g.
59 Lures
60 ___ and conquer
61 Scandinavian
62 N.Y. subway
63 Dancer José
64 Stowe character
66 Another dancer José
68 Upset
71 "Tiny Alice" author
72 Thwart Cecil?
74 Arthur or Lillie
75 Seine sky
76 Guy Fawkes's forte
77 Time span
78 Laconic
79 Nepalese native
80 Throw Mike off balance?
84 Count of music
85 Simon's "The ___ Boys"
87 Acropolis sights
88 Vex
89 Appeared
90 On this side: Prefix
91 Miss Albright
92 Hidden
95 Bible book
96 Declaim
100 Preside at tea
101 Brought up Michael
105 Ajar
106 ". . . ere I saw ___"
107 Circe was one
108 Full of fluff
109 Roman 1551
110 Thick slice
111 Gumshoe
112 Singer John
113 Fearless

DOWN

1 Cornfield visitor
2 Radamès's beloved
3 Rake's expression
4 Motorist's woe
5 Synthetic fabric
6 Heavy wood
7 Taproom
8 Naval initials
9 What the brave deserves
10 Russian co-op
11 Andy's sidekick
12 White House nickname
13 Daisy variety
14 Custom
15 G.I. offense
16 Part of N.B.
19 Advancement
20 Purchase proof
24 Mountain chain
27 Old English money
30 Aardvark's diet
32 Worked at
33 Indian coin
34 Famine's counterpart
35 Bring on
36 Taking Orson by surprise?
37 "This is ___ romance . . ."
38 Coarse cornmeals
39 Annoying George?
40 Scottish squire
41 Pyle or Ford
44 Melee
47 Humble
48 Chess finale
50 Breed of cattle
52 Up ___
53 Off-Broadway awards
54 Undercover agts.
55 ___ miss
56 Ugandans
58 Deer in the third year
60 More serious
63 Mother of Pollux
64 Needs
65 Yale
66 Feel one's way
67 Philip or Lillian
68 Active ones
69 Eldritch
70 Librarian's need
72 Gradual change in a species
73 Laughing or spotted
76 Textbooks
78 Subterranean passageway
80 Comparison word
81 Up
82 Soft
83 Lourdes event
84 Large knife
86 Sacred beetle
88 Henry VIII's second
90 Trig ratio, for short
91 Slow, musically
92 Tarzan's friends
93 Bakery item
94 Land of the libre
95 Take on
97 Coiffeur feature
98 Uri's archer
99 Geraint's wife
102 Islet
103 Trouble
104 Bankbook abbr.

27 Alphabetics By Herb Risteen

Mostly from the back end of the list.

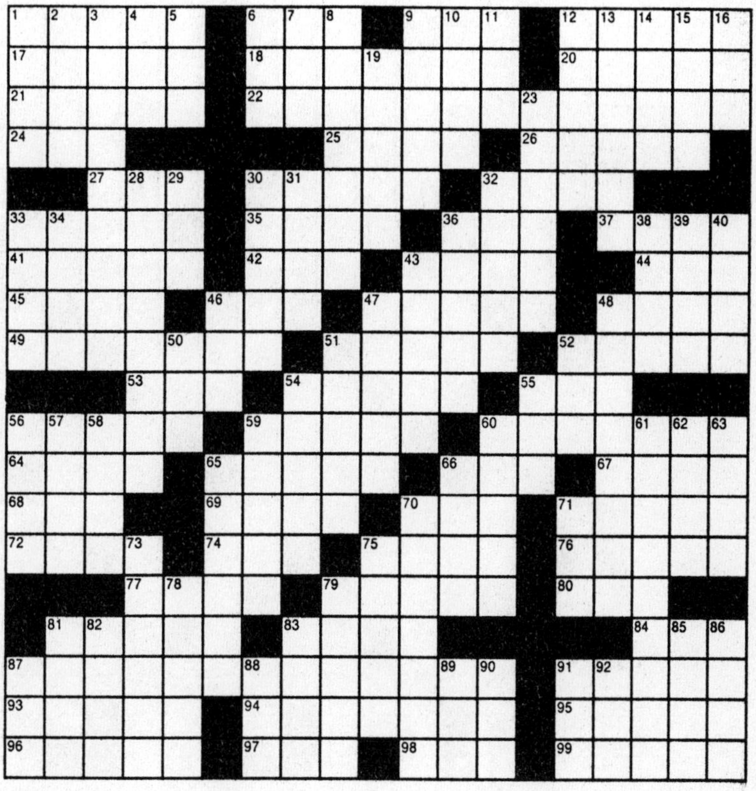

ACROSS

1 Hebrew letter
6 Add to a soundtrack
9 Hot Springs, for one
12 Keystone Kop event
17 Way down South
18 Farming problem
20 Of a cereal
21 Rocky Mountain resort
22 Musical semiquaver
24 ___ de mer
25 Superman, as a reporter
26 Carpentry files
27 Conceit
30 Facie or donna
32 Rational
33 Port of Brazil
35 Real-estate units
36 Liston's successor
37 Highschooler
41 Banish
42 "Cakes and ___"
43 Beasts of burden
44 Dupin's creator
45 Greeting for Zapata
46 Tournament draw
47 On the ___ (declining)
48 Zane Grey backdrop
49 Byzantine emperor
51 F.D.R.'s mother and others
52 Early Englishman
53 Tourist stop
54 ___ wave
55 Remiss
56 Human divisions
59 Part of 17 Across
60 Panthers, lions, etc.
64 W.W. II alliance
65 French painter
66 Follow
67 Having parts: Suffix
68 Roman 102
69 Fires from a job
70 Bewitch
71 Be sociable
72 Cooking direction
74 Fishing aid
75 Japanese city
76 Early Mexican
77 Stable fare
79 Puts in office
80 Car of yore
81 Yoga position
83 Bend
84 Religious title
87 Rouault was one
91 Variety of duck
93 Weather variety
94 Kind of account
95 Live
96 Does farm work
97 Tiny
98 Fetch
99 Hereditary factors

DOWN

1 Bede
2 Mona's follower
3 Drat or egad, e.g.
4 Symbol of easiness
5 Barnyard creature
6 ___ Moines
7 Tell's canton
8 Highflying toy
9 Italian city
10 Blake or Keats
11 ___ Arbor
12 He gave his regards to Broadway
13 Gretel's pal
14 At the summit
15 Bridge disasters
16 Chemical suffix
19 Checks
23 Brings a pet into line
28 Star systems
29 Cádiz cheer
30 ___ for time (stalls)
31 Function
32 Vehicles
33 Russian river
34 Leaf angle
36 Of a central line
38 Climax
39 Tolerable
40 O'Casey
43 Poddy plants
46 Bakery item
47 Eminent Egyptian
48 Intensify
50 Officeholders
51 Hockey teams
52 ___ soda
54 Belief
55 Triangle side
56 Pouches
57 Theater sign
58 Unlucky Roman number
59 Strains
60 Biblical vine spoilers
61 Close relatives
62 Great Lakes port
63 Good adjustment, for short
65 Southwestern cloaks
66 National burden
70 Deceiving
71 Deface
73 Showed anger
75 New Hampshire city
78 French writer Claude and family
79 Ski locale
81 Auto part
82 German admiral
83 Idée ___
85 Go up
86 Termites' relatives
87 Curve
88 Do handwork
89 Compass point
90 Hanoi holiday
91 Tent holder
92 English river

28 Bartender's Guide

By James and Phyllis Barrick

Partial manual for the professional mixer.

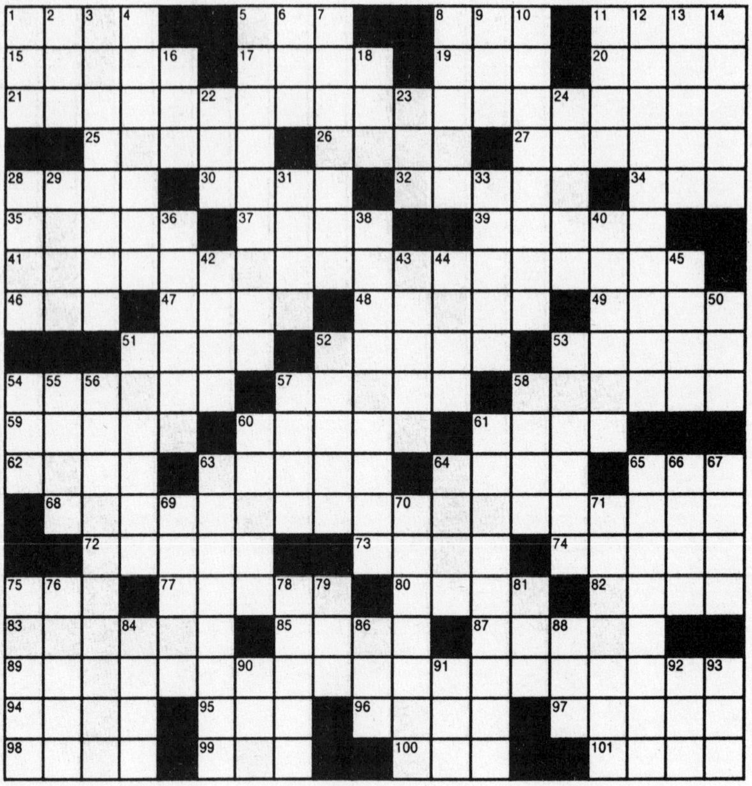

ACROSS

1 Game of Scottish origin
5 Kind of blonde
8 ___-disant
11 This, in Havana
15 Spa on Lake Geneva
17 "Believe ___ not!"
19 Fish eater
20 Agent: Suffix
21 Three with scotch
25 Like a soldier
26 Drinks
27 ___ del Fuego
28 Bhagavad-___ (Indian scripture)
30 Inland sea in Asia
32 McLuhan's concern
34 Curve
35 River in Italy
37 Name in fashion
39 Home to billions
41 Two with vodka
46 Counterpart of a Rep.
47 West and others
48 Revolts
49 Repented
51 Scoundrels
52 Openings
53 Something baffling
54 Dumas character
57 Playbill listings
58 Table articles
59 A Secretary of Defense under Nixon
60 What a jilted lover carries
61 Wind
62 Badminton item
63 Third: Prefix
64 Seed covering
65 Place for hay
68 Two with rum
72 What to do to noses
73 City in the Sooner State
74 Tricks
75 Hurok
77 "___ Kick Out of You"
80 Blind part
82 He wrote that the world of mules has no rules
83 Skilled ones
85 Order of a kind
87 Potato or artichoke
89 Three with gin
94 Jai ___
95 Long time
96 Food staple
97 Resulting from
98 Hawaiian goose
99 Pester
100 Chaney
101 Nautical ropes

DOWN

1 Part of Eur.
2 Ab ___
3 Hearty drink
4 Jumble
5 Relatives of heliports
6 Actor Erwin
7 Stableman
8 Feel
9 ___ pro nobis
10 Signs the short way
11 Naturalness
12 Granary
13 Travel-agency setups
14 Flemish tapestry
16 ___ de guerre
18 Abbr. on a map
22 Certain vote
23 Southern potato
24 Experts in fibbing
28 Chatters
29 Lacking basis
31 Wellaway!
33 Removes
36 Lowe of films
38 Stabilizer on a ship
40 Seat of power
42 Scotland ___
43 Beginning
44 Applications
45 Youthful ending
50 G.P.'s
51 Heart: Prefix
52 ___-colored
53 Kind of talk or fight
54 Priestly vestment
55 Attack of a kind
56 Master of the impossible
57 Coconut fiber
58 Secular
60 Corny
61 Even progression
63 Metal used in lamp filaments
64 Indigo
65 Bunk
66 Pindarics
67 Neighbor of Ore.
69 Fully
70 Impart slowly
71 Simple piece of engraving
75 "Bonjour Tristesse" author
76 Role in "Swan Lake"
78 Nasal quality
79 Timetable abbr.
81 Caucasian goat
84 Knee bend, in ballet
86 Hirobumi ___ of Japan
88 Auction move
90 Extinct bird
91 ___-Impressionism
92 French season
93 Sailors' cries

29 Here and There By Emory Cain

Some suggestions for the travel buffs.

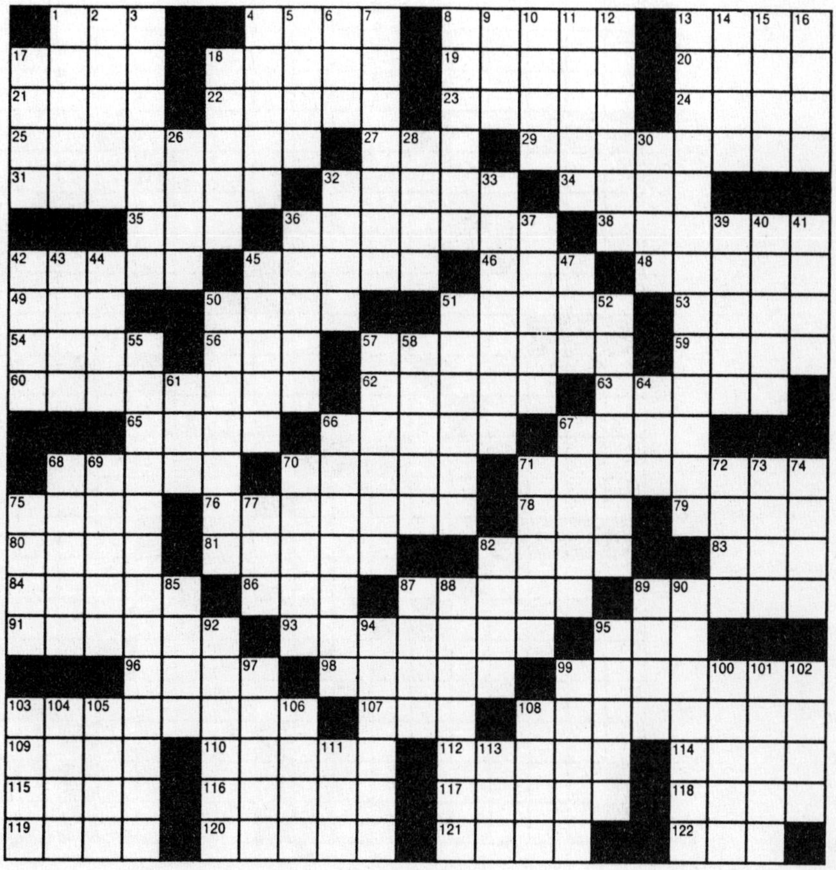

ACROSS

1 Prohibit
4 Fruit pie
8 Nasty-tempered one
13 Cogwheel
17 New Year's word
18 Kind of eclipse
19 A Lauder
20 Hard to find
21 What there ought to be
22 Words in a Stein line
23 Unyielding
24 Miss Moran of "Happy Days"
25 Its capital is Phnom Penh
27 "___ a creature was stirring . . ."
29 Philippine island
31 Add to the poker pot
32 Valuable violin, for short
34 5,280 make a mile
35 Rum, to Carlos
36 Like a bruised thumb
38 Garment part
42 Stand out
45 Orono's state
46 Turkish hat
48 Sample TV film
49 Word with tamale or dog
50 American suffragist
51 Chandler's "The Big ___"
53 Something for Moto
54 City on the Oka
56 Husband of Fatima
57 She gave Theseus some thread
59 Midterm event
60 City of Light resident
62 Tilts
63 14 pounds in Soho
65 Kind of street
66 Thanks, in Bonn
67 Animal for the Kremlin
68 Rio Grande feeder
70 Word with hog or hop
71 Paine and Revere, e.g.
75 Hebrew letter
76 Star of "Henry V"
78 Greek letter
79 Cruising
80 Formerly, formerly
81 Water wheel
82 Son of Aphrodite
83 Room at M.I.T.
84 Driving hazard
86 Joey was one
87 Baronial estate
89 René's school
91 Lendl's forte
93 Unit of explosive force
95 Suffix for ordinal numbers
96 Greek portico
98 Blunts
99 Muscular incoordination
103 Cultural center of Chile
107 Social event
108 Swedish port
109 African plant
110 Fasten firmly
112 Cohan's "Over ___"
114 Como or Mead
115 Tibetan Bigfoot
116 Happify
117 Lively airs
118 Singer Burl
119 Detected
120 Took out
121 ___ good example
122 But, to Caesar

DOWN

1 Society rulebook item
2 "What's in ___?"
3 North Carolina port city
4 City on the Po
5 Celebes ox
6 Ethiopian prince
7 City on the Delaware
8 Of a holiday
9 Suffix for near or dear
10 Particular
11 Fine line of a letter
12 Sawbuck
13 Desert area Down Under
14 ___ one's keep
15 Song
16 River of Italy
17 Algonquian Indians
18 Burdened
26 Siouan Indian
28 Heraldic border
30 Like one end of a pool
32 Actress Loretta
33 Bring down a peg
36 Silk's partner
37 Lacks
39 Writer Glasgow
40 Excite
41 Let it be
42 Word with worn or keeper
43 Israeli dance
44 Road for Caesar
45 Pacific peninsula
47 Buddhist sect
50 Underwater structure
51 Donut
52 Spanish money
55 Its capital is Vaduz
57 Evangeline's region
58 Grazing land
61 ___ Paulo
64 Gob
66 Like some eggs
67 Ulan ___
68 Mesta
69 Krupp's city
70 King of Tyre
71 Evita or Juan
72 Formerly Christiania
73 River duck
74 Quién ___?
75 Musical direction
77 Word before eared or sided
82 Son of Seth
85 Small monkey
87 Gender
88 Old Mexican spear throwers
89 Feminine suffix
90 French wine town
92 Hang-glided
94 Destroyed, as by fire
95 ___ Park, Colo.
97 Quick on one's feet
99 Blood carrier
100 Italian white wine
101 Annoyed
102 Matures
103 "Simon ___"
104 Safe, for a sailor
105 A-flat, e.g.
106 Elliptic
108 Moola
111 Season in Nice
113 Speed

30 Digital Computing By Calista Luminati

Things that need to be figured out.

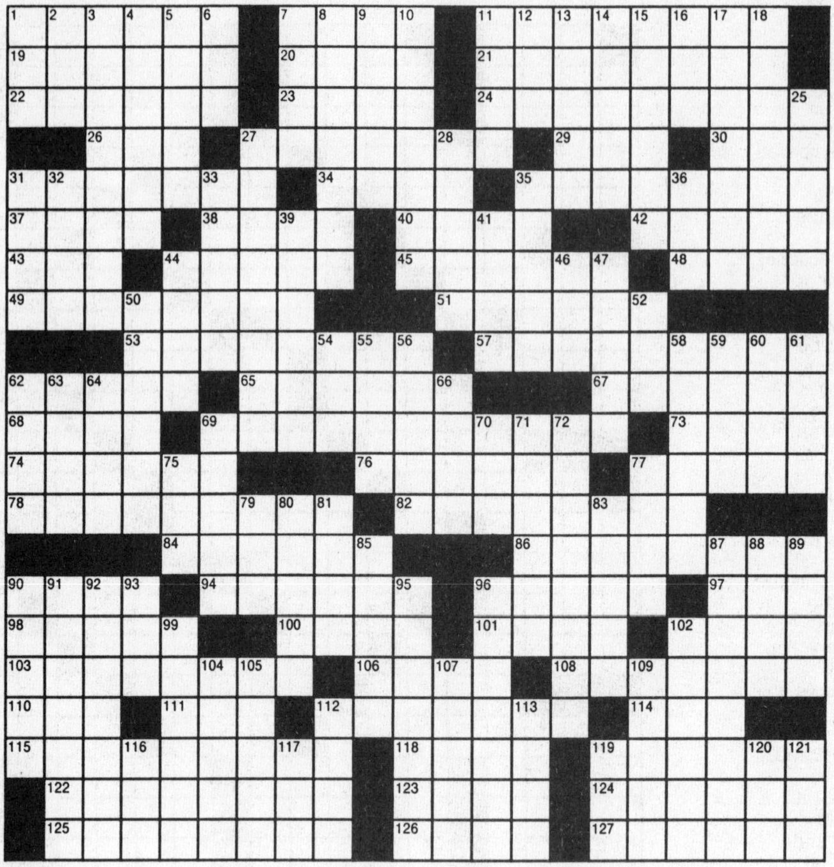

ACROSS

1 Resident of Mohammed's birthplace
7 Part of a play
11 Truck driver
19 Disinclined
20 Elaborate headdress
21 Framework used by sculptors
22 Vilify
23 One of a quartet
24 Words from John Silver's parrot
26 As, for Caesar
27 Entices
29 Stumble
30 Cotillion girl
31 Natural gifts
34 Munich's river
35 Border, in Spain
37 Note
38 Existence
40 Tale teller
42 Georges ___, French philosopher
43 Good Feeling was one
44 Helps with the dishes
45 One learned in law
48 German donkey
49 Ball-game length
51 Begin a journey
53 Welcome with ___
57 Apocalypse riders
62 Nigerian capital
65 Bert Parks and Dick Clark
67 Veto
68 Whitney and others
69 Pride, lust, envy, etc.
73 Archie Bunker's trait
74 Father of Agamemnon
76 Mexican town
77 Trappers' gatherings
78 King Cole's musicians
82 Part-time news correspondent
84 Butterfly or Bovary
86 Start of a book
90 Record
94 Most peeved
96 Twisted fibers
97 Musical notes
98 Film actor Lew
100 Feed the kitty
101 Brief for the boss
102 "Take ___ your leader"
103 Insight
106 Leisure
108 Not severed
110 "___ your heart out!"
111 Chemical prefix
112 ___ a pig
114 Gershwin brother
115 Popular Soviet Union agenda
118 Pearl Buck character
119 Christie of mystery
122 Highly regarded
123 Gambling city
124 Misuse a book page
125 Hollywood hopefuls
126 Kind of racing sled
127 Earth-moving machine

DOWN

1 Fairy queen
2 Adam's rib
3 Sky blue
4 Boxed
5 Patty Duke ___
6 Born
7 "Oh, What ___ Was Mary"
8 Sheep dogs
9 Dancers' wear
10 Part of a Musketeer slogan
11 Reveille's opposite
12 Silkworm
13 Moslem ruler
14 Large: Prefix
15 Violinist Isaac and family
16 Labor groups: Abbr.
17 Wind and rain, e.g.
18 Whistle blower
25 Something to be behind
27 Gave out homework
28 Lake and canal
31 Muses, as a group
32 Atmosphere: Prefix
33 Coated steel
35 English wooded area
36 ___ the line
39 TV street
41 About ready for school
44 Cocktail accompaniments
46 ___ Canals
47 Goes sour, as milk
50 Lassoed
52 Half a fly
54 NBC's parent
55 Ancient Asian
56 Markets
58 Saxon king
59 Armor
60 French political unit
61 Gangbuster Eliot
62 Caterpillar's tidbit
63 Prefix for tude or meter
64 Surround
66 Part of CBS
69 Global waters
70 Sun. message
71 Winter formation
72 Like infertile soil
75 Einstein's birthplace
77 ___ up (enlivens)
79 TV relative: Abbr.
80 Teasdale and namesakes
81 Contents of a tub
83 African country
85 Kefauver
87 Kind of railroad
88 Have status
89 Charlie Chan's No. ___
90 Rest
91 Nocturnal lemurs
92 Preliminary exam
93 Yet, to poets
95 Vincent Youmans song
96 "Bartered Bride" composer
99 Snorting snoozer
102 Unreality
104 Oust
105 U.S.S.R. town
107 Western capital
109 Hardship
112 Connectives
113 In a while
116 ___ glance
117 Aged: Abbr.
119 Do sums
120 Crone
121 Exist

31 Steeliness By Evelyn Benshoof

Some aspects of the solid sides of life.

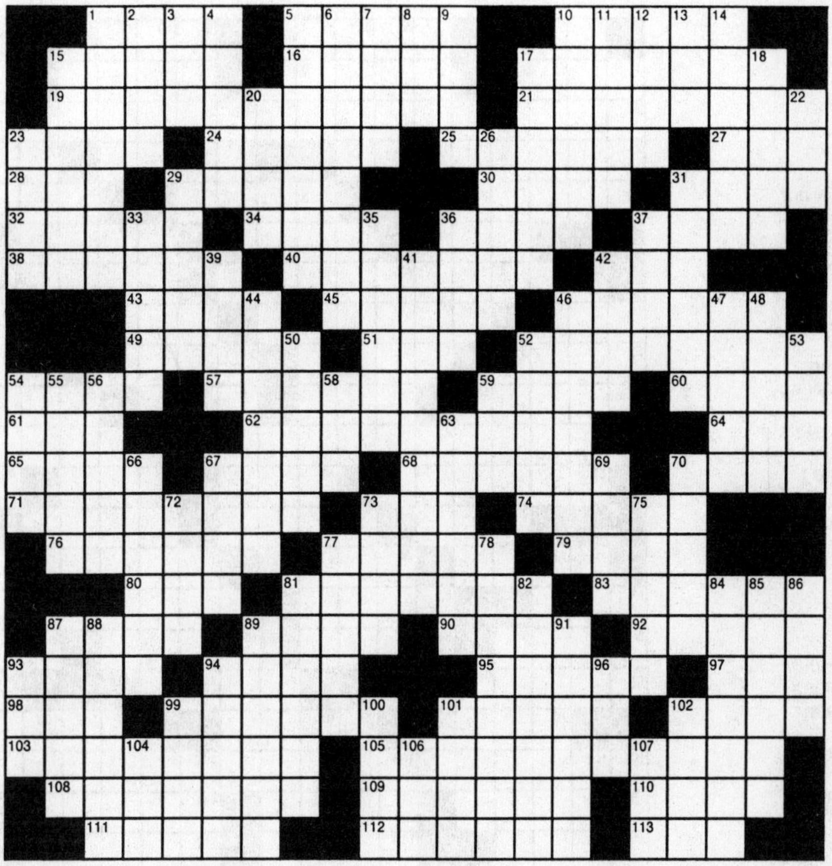

ACROSS

1 Stylish
5 Darken
10 Compressing device
15 Accra's land
16 Positive pole
17 Options
19 In a fix
21 Pushy advertising
23 Hereditary factor
24 Chemical compound
25 Ballet movement
27 U.N. pioneer
28 List-ending abbr.
29 Beer-hall item
30 Killer whale
31 Indiana's is South
32 Shovel or table
34 French Medit. port
36 Tremendous
37 Unlit
38 Sounded a knell
40 Put into a new form
42 Interdict
43 In good order
45 Extra
46 Civil War fort
49 One of the Fords
51 Tire
52 Hidden
54 Black or sea ___
57 Begrudged
59 Hyalite
60 Talk wildly
61 Preceders of king
62 No-longer-soft drink
64 Ott
65 Andes drug-yielding shrub
67 Fashion
68 Noble Moslems
70 Window part
71 Computer equipment
73 Nat. output
74 Art transfer
76 Operate on a steer
77 Movie director King
79 Dumb girl
80 Period preceding an event
81 Watched a moppet
83 Conjecture
87 Kind of bones or back
89 Sheriff's assts.
90 Coup d' ___
92 McQueen
93 Nucleus
94 Western lily
95 Figure of speech
97 Sty
98 Curve
99 Caruso et al.
101 Sicilian mount
102 Cherishing
103 Act sternly
105 Unyielding
108 Swerve
109 Vocalize
110 Parfaits' relatives
111 Consort of Zeus
112 Patriot Thomas and family
113 Flowers' home

DOWN

1 Church part
2 Lop-eared animal
3 Neighbor of Ky.
4 French king Hugh
5 Not as sensible
6 Agreements between nations
7 Kind of prize or key
8 Amin
9 Deal out
10 Fortune
11 Spanish city
12 Girl Friday
13 TV hosts
14 Kitchen gadget
15 Crowded city area
17 Indict
18 Move like Theda Bara
20 Puts into service
22 Persuaded
23 Story of derring-do
26 Jeweler's glass
29 Vilify
31 Joking exchange
33 "Iliad" king
35 Discerned
36 Listen!
37 May Whitty or Myra Hess
39 Cape Cod sight
41 Jawbreaker
42 Tree-trunk growth
44 Small-time
46 Disfigured
47 As a friend, in France
48 Make merry
50 Dodge
52 Exceed 55
53 Valley
54 Chorale composer
55 "Get ___ of this!"
56 ___-Coeur
58 Fury
59 Piece of writing
63 Obtrude upon others
66 Stick
67 ___ nostrum
69 Harbor vessel
70 Inclination
72 Contrived
73 Heavy fastenings
75 Appeared
77 Mist or fog
78 Squealed
81 "Scram!," to Shakespeare
82 Medit. vessel
84 Removed from office
85 Happenings
86 Sever
87 Suffering ennui
88 Bowed
89 Indicate
91 Metric weights
93 Truck part
94 City on the Meuse
96 Desk item
99 Singing group
100 Cause for an "Ahoy!"
101 Prefix for fact
102 Look forward
104 Bird: Prefix
106 Bits of information
107 Junior lie

32 Salad Days By Nancy Ross

Taking a look at the pre-adult world.

ACROSS

1 ___ Miguel
4 Prospector's turf
9 Parisian parent
13 Spain's longest river
17 File sound
18 Miss Loy
19 Chemical suffix
20 Scythe handle
21 Stevenson compendium
25 Film director's bible
26 Canadian pilots' org.
27 Mine, in the Midi
28 Red dye
29 Help for Sherlock
31 Warbled
34 Feed seed
36 Ishmael's captain
37 Biblical brother
39 River of China
40 Sally Benson novel
43 Wahine's dance
44 Edit film
45 Bubble material
46 Barflies' perches
47 Kind of straits
48 Tunisian port
50 "That's ___ need" (enough!)
52 Kind of farm
53 Reception hall
54 Japanese name
55 Serkin's instrument
57 Number for solitaire
58 Certain voter: Abbr.
59 Husky
62 "South Pacific" song
67 London theater section
68 "___ Maria"
69 Diamond score
70 Oozes
71 Mystery writer Josephine
72 Corn fancier
73 Aware of
75 Cruising
76 Finished
78 Pacific tree
79 Vipers
81 Board member: Abbr.
82 Hurricane center
83 China-shop visitor
84 Simplicity itself
86 Roman family clan
88 Author Bagnold
89 Elephantine adjective
90 "Jungle Books" python
91 Exceedingly
93 Slicker's place
94 Jazz singer Della
98 Prefix for dollar
99 Mare's nest?
101 Bold speaker
104 Goethe opus, with "The"
109 Liquid part of fat
110 Kind of happy or dash
111 Old British coin
112 Means' justifiers
113 Swan's queen
114 Queen's pie
115 Suspends
116 Chop suey sauce

DOWN

1 1927 radical martyr
2 Phoenix source
3 Belief
4 Superior of a Navy lieut.
5 Loosening: Prefix
6 Jason's ship
7 Actress Claire
8 Blemish
9 Magazine article
10 Sicilian smoker
11 Airstrip for Santa
12 Sprite
13 Register for class
14 St. Peter's, e.g.
15 Map abbr.
16 Exclamations
17 Tear down: Var.
20 Prefix for pro or circle
22 Oahu verandas
23 Trounces
24 Bulgarian port
29 Byron's pilgrim
30 Maiden
31 Floor piece
32 ___ de vie
33 Dash's companion
35 Wee ones
36 Sum
37 Yehudi Menuhin, once
38 Emanation
40 Italian silver coins
41 Sidewise colon
42 Stators' partners
45 Yawning, as a bird
47 Dapper ones
48 Men without women
49 ". . . and two ___"
51 Congenital
53 Muscular power
54 Charged atom
56 Lecherous looker
59 Intimated
60 Warm-country custom
61 Sovereignty
63 Isle of ___, former English county
64 Bard's river
65 Ladder step
66 Jacob's brother
72 Intestine: Prefix
74 City on the Ural
76 ___ and terminer
77 Glossed over
78 Like a runt
79 "I only wish ___ of stone . . .": Holmes
80 More meager
82 Queen-bee product
83 Opposite of topside
84 Pants material
85 Ophelia's brother
87 Reptile group
92 1982 computer movie
93 Chamber beneath a church
95 Race: Prefix
96 Down-at-heel
97 Leaves the straight and narrow
99 Lasso's cousin
100 A long way away
101 Stravinsky ballet
102 Boodle
103 Stage designs
104 Impresario Hurok
105 Hooray, in Seville
106 J.F.K. sight
107 Word of revulsion
108 Blue Eagle org.

33 Undercover By Norma Steinberg

Men who prefer to stay in hiding.

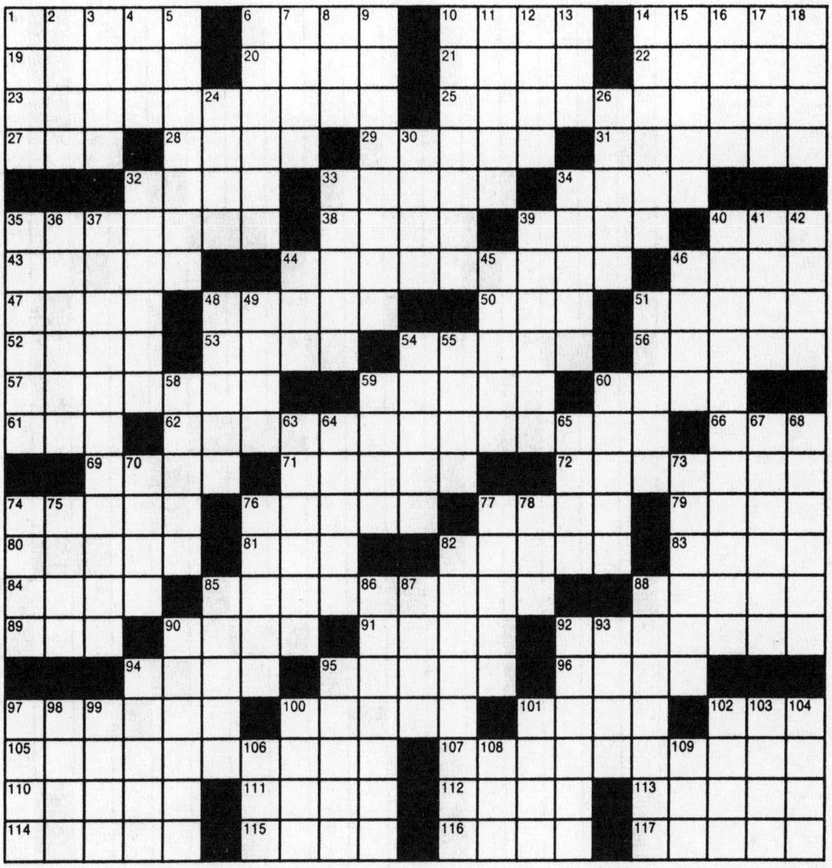

ACROSS

1 Caravan stop
6 Equally
10 Word in an ultimatum
14 Tiff
19 Embryonic tree
20 North American Indian
21 Dole out
22 Miss Jong
23 Cowboy's mess
25 Socrates's field
27 Early Siberian
28 Porgy's woman
29 All ___
31 Forward and lateral
32 Apartment
33 Make a buzzing sound
34 Spade and Goldwyn
35 Strands
38 Rifleman's need
39 Golden, for one
40 Mil. medal
43 Scratch, as a mission
44 Drab
46 Equine offspring
47 Winter Olympics gear
48 Ohio city
50 ___ fast clip
51 Actress Reed
52 Natives of: Suffix
53 ". . . a lamp ___ my feet"
54 Dress material
56 Boisterous
57 Procession
59 Estate house
60 Kind of car or arm
61 Spanish queen
62 Eleventh hour
66 Cribbage card
69 Marine: Abbr.
71 Moose genus
72 Cause to deteriorate
74 Circle measurements
76 "Beowulf" and others
77 Unassuming
79 Lambs' dams
80 Nicklaus equipment
81 Kind of bag or spoon
82 Mount
83 Seine crossing
84 Porn
85 "___ Trilogy"
88 ___ of Commons
89 N.Y. time
90 Broadway award
91 Sty sound
92 Had the lead
94 Progeny
95 "Put up your ___"
96 Nothing ___ (easy going)
97 Deli order
100 Like an easy job
101 Sixth for Henry VIII
102 Priestly garb
105 Personal pension savings
107 Neck
110 Stringed instrument
111 Florence's river
112 Abbr. after a list
113 Kangaroos
114 Something of value
115 Sharp
116 Snacks
117 Adolescents

DOWN

1 Santa's load
2 She loved Narcissus
3 Big defeat
4 Curve
5 Rorschach pattern
6 Animals
7 Assns.
8 Madre's brother
9 Go-fers
10 Caesar, for one
11 Hungarian composer
12 The clink
13 Long fish
14 Seed for a roll
15 Surly
16 Tears
17 Twinge
18 Makes slack, with "out"
24 Taper off from
26 Moonstones' relatives
30 Tart fruit
32 Sherwood or Black
33 American shrub
34 Anthony or Glaspell
35 It's often aforethought
36 Touch
37 Pilot's sign-off
39 Comeback
40 "___ gay apparel" (carol words)
41 Grit
42 Ali's name, once
44 Computer part: Abbr.
45 ___ the land
46 Sustenance
48 Zero
49 Leg joint
51 Not as damp
54 Does garden work
55 Spanish years
58 Small boxes
59 Roman 1300
60 Enjoy a pipe
63 Table linens
64 Of the pelvis
65 Sherbets
67 Danish port
68 Got the upper hand
70 "___ Misbehavin' "
73 Give the news
74 Shine's partner
75 Parts of some chairs
76 Wide collars
77 Religious men
78 Work unit
82 Hive dweller
85 Gin's partner
86 Astrodome's home
87 Hindu sect member
88 Snood
90 Alley dweller
92 Hedges
93 African antelope
94 German river
95 Actress Irene
97 Hindu god
98 Onassis and others
99 Neighbor of Vietnam
100 Spa visitor's goal
101 Braid
102 Land measure
103 Crazy bird
104 Overseer
106 19 Across, later
108 Call ___ day
109 Expected

34 Wassail By Ralph Beaman

Saluting a high time of the year.

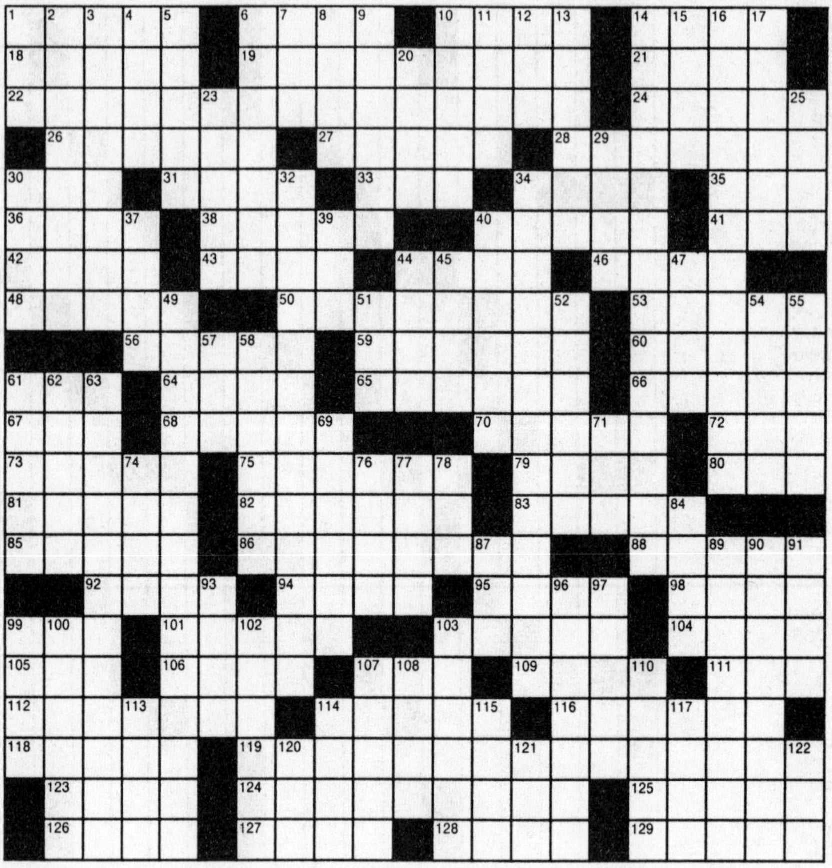

ACROSS

1 Prohibit
6 Sale condition
10 Type of code
14 Bank papers: Abbr.
18 Look intently
19 Surfeited state
21 Israeli dance
22 Largest Pacific atoll
24 Curbs
26 Win over
27 Based on eight
28 Put out a new edition
30 Spanish treasure
31 Uno, dos, ___
33 Querying sounds
34 Irish luck
35 J.F.K. visitor
36 A.P.'s stock in trade
38 Mind one's ___ q's
40 Verbal contraction
41 Caboodle's partner
42 Beer ingredient
43 Sandpiper
44 Scorch
46 Eastern ruler
48 Hostess Maxwell et al.
50 Emotionally unstable
53 Without end: Abbr.
56 Contaminate
59 Not at all
60 Mister, in Spain
61 Gas-flow rate: Abbr.
64 "High ___"
65 Bloodhounds' clues
66 Repeat sign, in music
67 Put this before the carte
68 Pith helmets
70 Strike
72 "___ Misérables"
73 Coconut meat
75 Repeats
79 Ambiance
80 Part of i.e.
81 Subject
82 Polite word
83 Show approval
85 Pastoral work
86 Paul Dukas's had an apprentice
88 Ragout of game
92 Precise
94 Armful
95 Rent
98 Kind of hog
99 ___ damnée
101 Prussian cavalryman
103 Atelier piece
104 Parasites
105 Present time
106 Old French coins
107 Franklin, the aphorist
109 Charles Lamb
111 O'Shanter
112 Sweet ___ (fragrant flower)
114 Pioneer in radium
116 Egg or lily
118 What an effective law needs
119 Seasonal story
123 Palm starch
124 Quiet
125 Sports place
126 Allowance for waste
127 Word of admonition
128 Italian noble family
129 Plaster city

DOWN

1 Army medal
2 Heavenly
3 Farm rodent catchers
4 Dry
5 Adjust
6 Car-seat ledge
7 Type of horse or scout
8 ___ facto
9 Hit a golf ball awry
10 Muscular man
11 Iranian coin
12 Billion years or so
13 Doria or del Sarto
14 Seasonal charity purchases
15 Does gardening
16 Name stemming from the Christ child
17 North African Moslem
20 Lett's neighbor
23 Canvas covers
25 Tartan pattern
29 Worker of yore
30 "This one's ___"
32 Ascribed source for pawnbroker's three gold balls
34 Buttercup's relative
37 Copy, for short
39 Surveyor's dir.
40 Lustrous fabrics
44 Gator's relative
45 See 97 Down
47 ___ fixe
49 Unthinkable seasonal headline
51 "Them guys is bad ___"
52 Soft white metal
54 Roman date
55 Jack, the fall guy
57 Deanna Durbin's "___ Men and a Girl"
58 Lease restriction
61 Desert growths
62 Inundation
63 Certain starting words
69 Rose of ___
71 Numerical prefix
74 Upset
76 Brazilian weight
77 Squeezed by, with "out"
78 Georgia or Ukraine: Abbr.
84 Rank above viscount
87 Greek letter
89 Dawdler
90 Feather, to Yankee Doodle
91 Footnote word
93 Friend's word
96 Set free
97 American inventor, with 45 Down
99 Med. subject
100 Annoy strongly
102 Radio's "___ Abner"
103 Isolate
107 Explode
108 Welland Canal terminus
110 Musicians' org.
113 Safekeeping of goods: Abbr.
114 Take it on the ___
115 French seasons
117 O'Hara estate
120 Bill's partner
121 Denver's time
122 ___ Cruces

35 No Problem By Marie West

Just follow the directions and have no trouble.

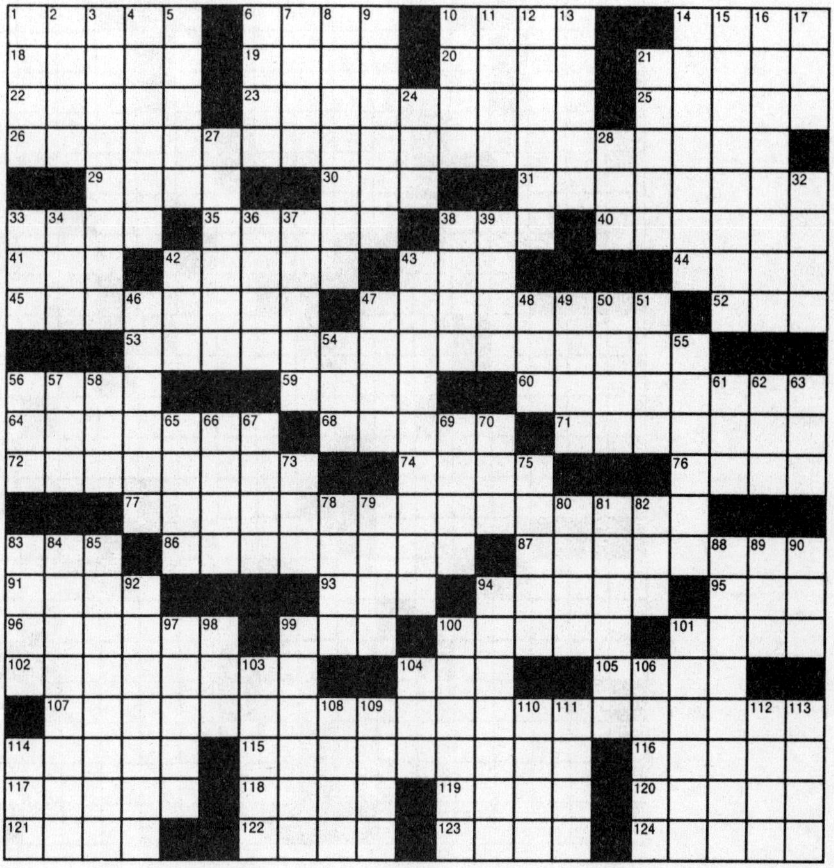

ACROSS

1 Seven: Prefix
6 Hannibal's crossing
10 Oxford's rival: Abbr.
14 Christie's title
18 Pungent
19 French station
20 Hwy. from Maine to Florida
21 State of Malaysia
22 Nonworker
23 Revised a text
25 Cat-____-tails
26 Label instruction
29 Seeger or Rose
30 Suffix with bombard
31 Short tunes
33 Quay
35 Ball-club deal
38 Alder, in Aberdeen
40 Part of NATO
41 Parabola
42 Investigate
43 Spanish year
44 Sandhurst weapon
45 Soak
47 Never
52 Before
53 Label instruction
56 Direction for Lynne
59 Progenitor
60 Stranded
64 Movie preview
68 "____ Solemnis"
71 Pod vegetables
72 Formal defense of an idea
74 Rainy-day rarity
76 Pollster Roper
77 Label instruction
83 Nile serpent
86 Roosevelt and Powell
87 Signed up
91 Office staff: Abbr.
93 Bullish times
94 Apprehension
95 Genetic initials
96 Corny actor
99 Altitudes: Abbr.
100 Eucharistic plate
101 Appear
102 Dated chit
104 Palindromic name
105 Major follower
107 Label instruction
114 ____ del Tronto, Italian town
115 Repairman
116 Heath plant
117 French seraphs
118 Foremost
119 Part of a bird's bill
120 Circle or tube
121 Borscht vegetable
122 Criteria: Abbr.
123 Those, in Spain
124 Pee Wee of baseball

DOWN

1 Pilgrimage to Mecca
2 Light color
3 Broad view
4 Colorist
5 Proficient
6 Author James
7 Beats it
8 Serve as chairman
9 Recipient of a letter
10 Bird's crop
11 Memo abbr.
12 ____ old friend (run into)
13 ____ pass (bridge player's option)
14 Signifies
15 Awned
16 Certain shark or tiger
17 Stretch out
21 Gondolier
24 June bug
27 Toward the back
28 Voter: Abbr.
32 Since, to Burns
33 Ballet step
34 A Gershwin
36 Moslem weight
37 Aids an arsonist
38 Part of A.D.
39 Cross
42 Girl's nickname
43 Ones bearing witness
46 Feature of a peaked hat
47 Hillside shelter
48 Pro ____
49 Type of type: Abbr.
50 Stable occupant
51 Social science: Abbr.
54 Draw a bead on
55 Travel-bureau listings
56 Airport abbr.
57 A founder of Dadaism
58 Saint, in Rio
61 Zilch
62 Shade tree
63 Honor medal
65 Napoleon's British custodian
66 Hero in Norse myth
67 Levitate
69 Enervates
70 Hewing tool
73 ____ glance
75 Sluggish
78 Bolt tightener
79 Word before sorry
80 Dirk of old
81 Old World kite
82 Subsidy
83 In ____ (sulking)
84 Half step, in music
85 Make public: Var.
88 Milestone for a mountain climber
89 Compass point
90 Aswan or Hoover
92 Source of caviar
94 Hebrew tribe members
97 Capital of County Clare
98 Uncooked, in Bonn
99 For this reason
100 Old vaudeville mecca
101 Creator of "Tristram Shandy"
103 Conditions
104 Calendar abbr.
106 "____ Finest Hour": Churchill
108 Playwright Bagnold
109 Cargo units
110 ____ song (cheaply)
111 Very, in Versailles
112 Commits a hockey infraction
113 Risk it
114 Taxi

36 Short Forms By Jim Page

Instances of cutting corners in some words.

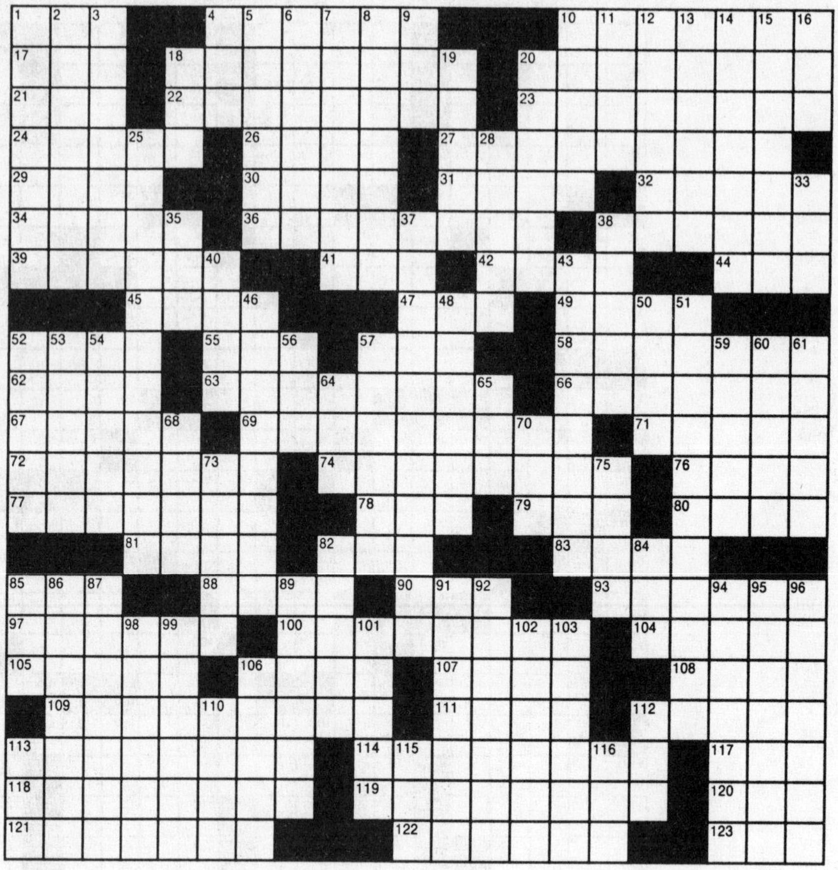

ACROSS

1 Big D univ.
4 Mine excavations
10 Easily split rocks
17 Follower of Attila
18 Threw like Sammy Baugh
20 Intensely illuminated
21 Plane formation: Abbr.
22 Native of an exotic isle
23 Former Senator from Miss.
24 Capital of Tibet
26 Dravidian language
27 Holding an Indian-chief summit
29 Actress Turner
30 North Carolina college
31 Folding money
32 Those opposed
34 Confuse
36 Sets up a detour
38 Pressing
39 Certain stage equal
41 Scottish alder
42 Bontok village units
44 Metric wts.
45 Pack away
47 Service-station purchase
49 Receipt-stamp word
52 Cummerbund
55 Feed-bag leftover
57 No ___ ands or buts
58 Swellheads
62 That, in Toulon
63 Has a go at
66 Reporter or editor
67 "He was ___ among scholars . . ."
69 Sheepskin, to a worried deg. seeker?
71 Light brown color
72 Word-for-word
74 Resin-yielding tree
76 Cassini
77 Dukes, earls, etc.
78 Opposite of WNW
79 NBC parent
80 Cores: Abbr.
81 Suffix for old or pun
82 He had many rounds of applause
83 Exile site
85 Mimic
88 Invitation letters
90 U.S.S.R. town
93 Cambridge inst. lacrosse team?
97 Bing Crosby's middle name
100 Polonius's daughter et al.
104 Actress Keaton
105 Witchcraft-trial city
106 Earthenware pot
107 Infield cover
108 Chances
109 Selector for a basketball tourney?
111 ___ homo
112 Computer fodder
113 Potato chip
114 Having shared, as a meal
117 Digger's quest
118 Like some horror flicks
119 Women's lib Gloria and family
120 Celtic sea god
121 Most reactive to sunbathing
122 "Gunsmoke" star
123 Asner and Ames

DOWN

1 Whip soundly
2 "___ About Nothing"
3 Lets go of
4 Baden-Baden, for one
5 Cheater at pinball
6 Athletic bird
7 Girl with a box
8 Soprano Steber
9 French possessive
10 Cabbage salads
11 Range in Calif.
12 Major shooting affair
13 Running in neutral
14 Like italic type
15 Making a bell-like sound
16 Regular: Abbr.
18 Shopkeeper's loan source: Abbr.
19 Where to meet buses
20 Smallest in number
25 U.S. and U.S.S.R. heads agreeing to an arms-cut pact?
28 Ryan or Tatum
33 City ways: Abbr.
35 "___, drink, and . . ."
37 Inchon landing in 1950?
38 Custom
40 Kind of beer
43 Kind of sandwich
46 Songbirds
48 Tristan's friend
50 Hawkeye State
51 Parris Island?
52 Theater-ticket scam
53 Eaglet's home
54 List of candidates
56 Spanish aunt
57 Six-Day War participant
59 Young salmon
60 Lion trainer
61 Pitfalls
64 Letter before tee
65 Narrow inlet
68 Part of Q.E.D.
70 Go amiss
73 Teen-___
75 Unruffled
82 New York's is big
84 One no-trump, e.g.
85 Jolson and Pacino
86 Easy bridge hand
87 Film actor James
89 Of people: Ger.
91 Tailor, at times
92 Sponge spicule
94 Frog-to-be
95 Was stick-toitive
96 Rookery birds
98 Pretends
99 Block progress
101 These come with strings attached
102 Mysterious
103 English Nile explorer et al.
106 Musical group
110 Suffix with laryng and bronch
112 Those elected to office
113 Kitchen fixture: Abbr.
115 ___ standstill
116 Printers' spaces

37 Ownership By Mary Whitten

Possessions of a variety of people.

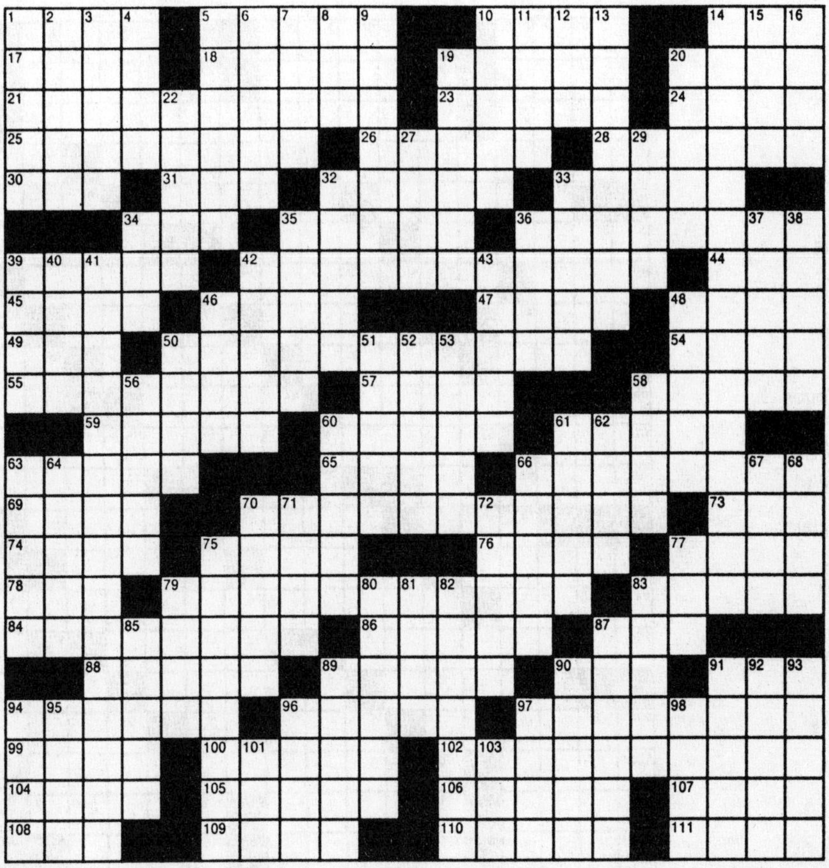

ACROSS

1 Old West schoolteacher
5 Biblical patriarch
10 Fibs
14 Morse signal
17 Exchange premium
18 Iranian cult believer
19 Miss Sawyer of TV news
20 Assistant
21 Where Jesus asked for a drink
23 Urged, with "on"
24 Olympic medal ingredient
25 Vetoed a veto
26 Grassy plain
28 Campaign managers' creations
30 Parted sea
31 Place for: Suffix
32 New Zealand tribesman
33 Public storehouse
34 Poke
35 ____ de León
36 Person of high rank
39 Titled
42 Original can of worms?
44 Work unit
45 Pequod's captain
46 Formerly, long ago
47 Like ____ of bricks
48 Continent
49 Golfer's goal
50 Bad money-good money theory
54 Eskimo's need
55 Alienate
57 "The ____ Love"
58 Rulers
59 Actress Signe
60 U.S.-born Japanese
61 U.S. artist John
63 Vise's relative
65 Latin being
66 Peppy
69 Actress Virna
70 She must be above suspicion
73 Prior to
74 Overhang
75 Red Skelton's "I ____ it!"
76 Tops
77 Briton's buggy
78 Black bird
79 His name was Hennery
83 Aunt, to André
84 Plunders
86 Concert hall
87 Comics' Garfield, e.g.
88 Biblical prophet
89 Oklahoma national park
90 Parseghian
91 Guido's high note
94 "____ the blue horizon . . ."
96 One of the Sierras
97 Woman, according to a chauvinist?
99 Relative of P.D.Q.
100 Wash out
102 Marching band of the 1890's
104 Steak order
105 Inexpensive veil material
106 Expensive veil material
107 Palms off
108 Failure
109 One of the ages
110 Mount
111 God of love

DOWN

1 Shaw's Barbara
2 Fiber plant
3 Prepared potatoes
4 Bleak English landscape
5 Soak up
6 Salacious
7 Korea's Syngman
8 Indian mulberry
9 Film actor Ray
10 Wood: Prefix
11 Othello's thorn
12 Compass pt.
13 Shays's crime
14 Cynic's illumination?
15 Unoccupied
16 Scatters hay
19 More costly
20 Wide open
22 Like some ways
27 More than daft
29 Tailless cat
32 May, e.g.
33 Form an arch, old style
34 Reb general Stuart
35 Old hat
36 Spanish pronoun
37 "All's well!" specialist
38 Old exclamations
39 Barber's clip area
40 Cries of discovery
41 Where George picked grapes?
42 Luigi's please
43 Hawaiian tree
46 Coastal fliers
48 Very, in music
50 Pant
51 Out of order
52 Southern slave's word for an owner
53 Villain's expression
56 Fiber plant
58 Sped
60 Has to have
61 Like cactuses
62 It's often insured
63 Easily understood
64 Climbing plant
66 Faint
67 Q.E.D. part
68 Greek commune
70 Consorts for hens
71 Astronauts' affirmatives
72 Clumsy shoe
75 Like the Jazz Age society
77 Way to stand
79 ____ in the neck
80 Give courage, old style
81 Hebrew month
82 Emulates Chan
83 Competitive groups
85 Skier's milieu
87 Petitioned
89 "Cry, the Beloved Country" author
90 Fred's sister
91 Fielding flaw
92 Forgotten-one's place
93 Bottomless pit
94 Shakespeare, for one
95 Birthright salesman
96 Stubborn one
97 Wheel shaft
98 Ump's call
101 Caustic item
103 Ump's call

38 Pairing Up By Stanley Newman

Odd couples that often come out even.

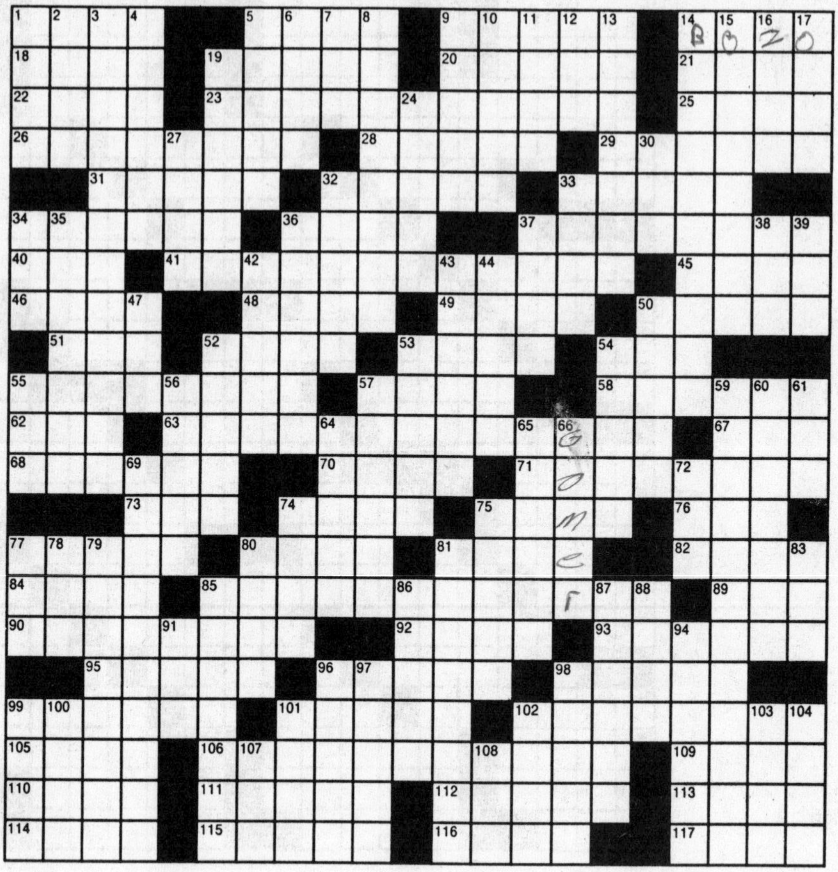

ACROSS

1 Ottoman ruler
5 Brothers
9 Cremonan artisan
14 TV clown
18 Ellington's was indigo
19 Soup-eating sound
20 ___ the manger
21 One of the Romanovs
22 Blame
23 Marsha-Gregory
25 ___ majesty
26 What echoes do
28 Tippecanoe's partner
29 Eskimo's quarry
31 Uneven
32 Whimpered
33 Daughter of Lear
34 ___ Mater
36 Harvest need
37 Alden or Standish
40 Coffee maker
41 Bret-David
45 Roman 604
46 Vallee
48 Something to feel
49 Bulwer-Lytton heroine
50 Listings, for short
51 ___ Na Na
52 Relative of a dodo
53 Wordman Willard
54 Part of Madame Butterfly's name
55 Kind of poisoning
57 Novel of the South Seas
58 "Now cracks ___ heart": Shak.
62 Ending for Dan or span
63 Walter-Wilbur
67 Suffer
68 Constituent
70 Has-___
71 Opposite of polygyny
73 One or more
74 Lola's Yankees
75 Thuds
76 Sounds of satiety
77 Singer John
80 Little, in Las Palmas
81 Innisfail
82 Humorist Bugs
84 Korbut
85 Clara-Clarence
89 Modernist
90 Boarded one's dog out
92 Like a night bird
93 Fifth-rate
95 Theater
96 Iloilo's island
98 Arabian leaders
99 Take chances
101 ___ by verdict (court phrase)
102 Microscopic animals
105 Corn lily
106 Howard-Anita
109 Ego
110 Top army off.
111 Of a skull bone
112 ___ cavae (heart feeders)
113 Lawrence Durrell novel
114 Pastorale
115 Vikings
116 Via Appia was one
117 Swan genus

DOWN

1 Pliny's passion
2 Part of "G.W.T.W."
3 Colonel-Celeste
4 Collect on a surface
5 Mozart's was magic
6 Mystic poem
7 Linkletter
8 Kitchen spreaders
9 Confuse
10 Scooter, updated
11 "Ain't She Sweet?" composer
12 Obsession
13 Classroom antique
14 Bailey-Stark
15 Too fastidious
16 Miss Pitts of films
17 Counterfeiters' "small potatoes"
19 California peak
24 Dress material
27 Biblical boatwright
30 Give it ___
32 Devoutness
33 Bounder
34 Upon, to Pierre
35 Board V.I.P.
36 Put on
37 Rabbit
38 Caesar
39 Rec-room sets
42 Network honcho Arledge
43 Renounce
44 Deep sleep
47 Thanksgiving fare
50 "It's a ___ Tell a Lie"
52 Spirited
53 West German port
54 Lyricist Sammy and family
55 Milne's Mr.
56 "___ we all?"
57 Kind of band or show
59 Birch-George
60 Oil source
61 English isle
64 Hemp fiber
65 "The Girl That ___"
66 Private Pyle
69 Masterson-George
72 Chat
74 "Harvey" hero
75 Bagel's relative
77 Korean G.I.
78 Pub pint
79 Disgrace
80 Kilmer creation
81 Model for "The Prince and the Pauper"
83 Rogers or Clark
85 Large tuna
86 "Movie Movie" director Stanley
87 Diffuse gradually
88 Least bit
91 Elusive one
94 Pitcher Jesse
96 Trendy breads
97 Allan-___
98 Clamorous
99 Oscar picture of 1958
100 Canned
101 Arabian region
102 Cornbread
103 Bread spread
104 At a distance
107 Twelve months, in Mexico
108 Permit

39 Plus Values By Reginald Johnson

A matter of fitting things together.

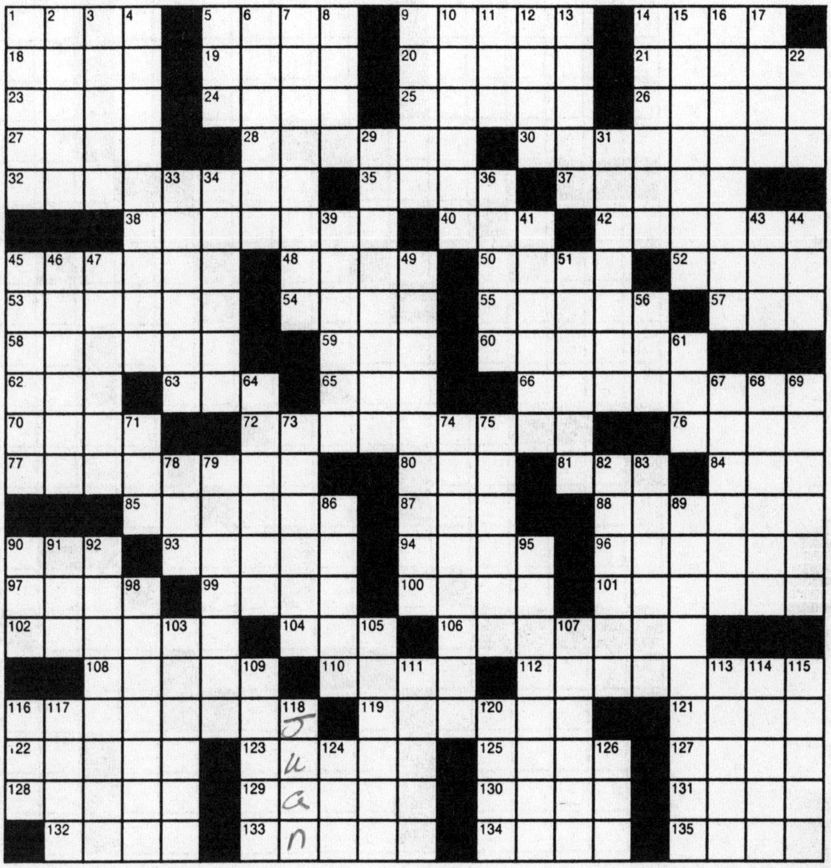

ACROSS

1 River spawner
5 Haze
9 Writer St. Johns
14 Native Egyptian
18 Lug
19 Entry fee of a sort
20 Mislays
21 "For want of ___ . . ."
23 Subtle emanation
24 Patriot James
25 Imaginations
26 Theater showings: Abbr.
27 Rainbow: Prefix
28 Filling in temporarily
30 Longitudinal
32 Like a close game
35 Underwater hazard
37 Molucca island
38 Less harsh
40 Kind of sister
42 On a slant
45 Handy kind of guess
48 Issue
50 Highway
52 Guitar's ancestor
53 Quickly
54 Paris menu word
55 Enameled metalwares
57 Hurried
58 Invisible
59 Highland wear
60 Sometimes they're false
62 N.Y. player
63 Moines or Plaines
65 Vacation time in Nice
66 Act of giving out
70 Wiesbaden donkey
72 Child's game
76 Sci. of rocks
77 Unclad
80 Bridge honor
81 Ozone
84 They called her frivolous
85 Inventor Pliny and family
87 Actress Claire
88 Prickly plant
90 Word with rock or stead
93 Place to relax
94 British title
96 Pilfered
97 Door or one
99 Prefix for tarsus
100 Short jacket
101 London and Pisa features
102 Device for Matthew Brady
104 Squeeze out
106 Speech, plus
108 Military subdivisions
110 Elbe tributary
112 Be romantic
116 Widespread
119 ___ value (car buyer's concern)
121 Kind of way
122 Doric-column edge
123 Shunned person
125 Laugh, on the Left Bank
127 ___ a barrel
128 Chemical compound
129 Violin name
130 Noun ending
131 Telegram
132 Havens
133 Extinguish
134 Stone and Bronze
135 Monster's home

DOWN

1 Blotch
2 Moslem nymph
3 Raised, as an anchor
4 Finished
5 Former Chinese V.I.P.
6 Uninjured
7 Nit-picker
8 Midterm event
9 Adjust
10 Avoids
11 Ending for Japan
12 Dining-room table part
13 Org.
14 Antics
15 Everybody
16 Lover
17 Quarrel
22 Invasion craft of W.W. II
29 Annoy
31 McGuffey's printings
33 Camped
34 Ruined
36 Wayne and Worth
39 Murdered Shakespeare
41 Infants' wear
43 School org.
44 Sunset, to poets
45 Froths
46 Seton or Bevin
47 Covent Garden vendor
49 Nonwaiters
51 Forget-me-not State
56 Symington, to friends
61 Droop
64 Postpone
67 Snuggle up
68 Refueling vessel
69 Terry and Drew
71 Recline
73 Conceive
74 Two or so of 100
75 Captivate
78 Tablet
79 High-ranking prelate
82 Implant
83 Prepare for a model change
86 Columbia River feeder
89 Poles-apart campus duo
90 College degree
91 Zeta follower
92 Legal objection
95 Empowering
98 Writing materials
103 Washes lightly
105 Long plumes
107 Large cask
109 Kind of dressing or days
111 Uncanny
113 Scot's henhouse
114 Extraordinary things
115 Evil ones
116 Craze
117 Melody
118 San ___
120 Region
124 City of France
126 Shoe widths

40 Groupies By Lois Hillis

Words that are compatible with each other.

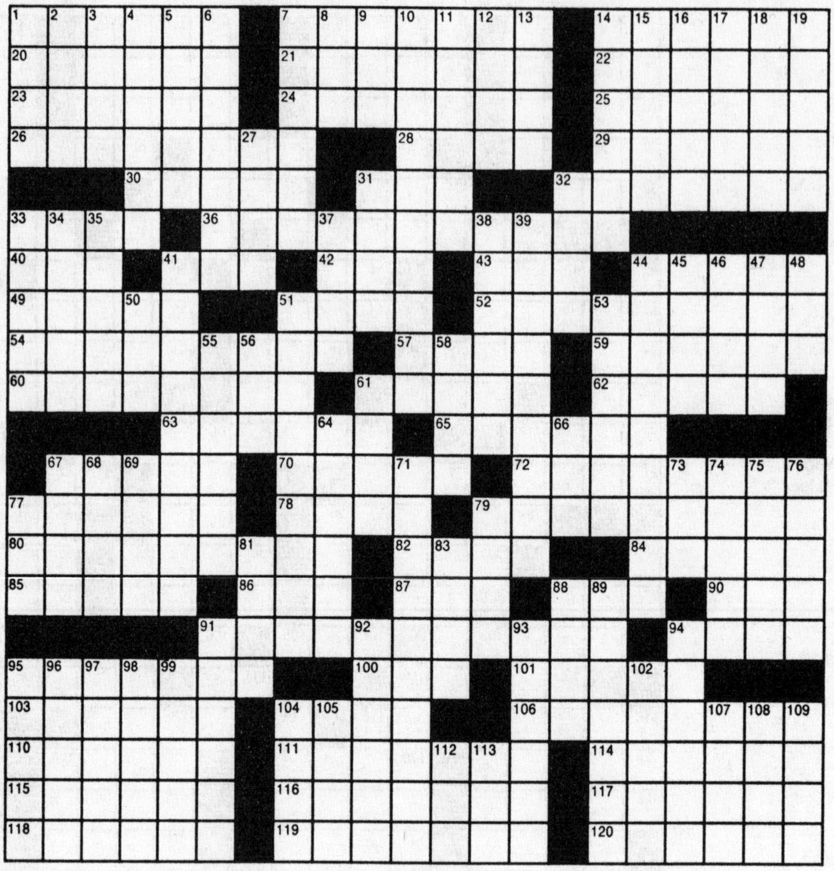

ACROSS

1 Hood's gun
7 Walks showily
14 Of the wrist
20 Mountainous
21 Charlatan of old
22 Unwilling
23 Criticize loudly
24 Character in a play
25 Inaccessible
26 Method for selecting servicemen
28 Neth. capital
29 Sneaky payer
30 Unworldly
31 Literary bits
32 Road to riches, for some
33 Greek letters
36 Make ___ (expect favors)
40 Young one
41 Beast of burden
42 Morse-code unit
43 Depression agcy.
44 Barmecide offering
49 Wish upon ___
51 Liver spread
52 Circulate
54 Johnny's waiting place
57 Kind of act that's read
59 Delicacy of taste
60 Italian violinist
61 Active
62 Kind of circle or parade
63 Fine, in France
65 Like a sot's eyes
67 Venetian traveler
70 Piece of bric-a-brac
72 Warns
77 Environment
78 "___ the mood for . . ."
79 Like city driving
80 Just missed
82 Drenches
84 Town in Aden
85 Teacher's charge
86 Chief Babylonian god
87 Deep wonder
88 Vigoda of TV
90 Goddess of healing
91 Yucca
94 Schliemann's digs
95 Travesty
100 Prove a subtraction answer
101 "Only God can make ___"
103 Crease again
104 20,000-league traveler
106 Moving in opposite ways
110 Involve
111 Kind of supermarket buying
114 Ennui
115 Candle holder
116 More substantial
117 Come forth
118 Had a feeling
119 Lab burners
120 Resident of Aleppo

DOWN

1 Writer Moss
2 Tribal leader of Edom
3 ". . . baked in ___"
4 Marks over letters
5 Finnish lake, to Swedes
6 Slows
7 This square's number, to Ovid
8 French soul
9 May's season: Abbr.
10 Towel inscriptions
11 Pleasing odors
12 Scottish ones
13 "Go away!"
14 Clone for a steno
15 Prevent
16 Respond to "Please pay"
17 Investigate
18 Fall bloomer
19 Suspicious
27 Accusing cries
31 Skeleton: Abbr.
32 Rich soil
33 Necklace part
34 "___ la vista"
35 Wear for a G.I.
37 Hebrew month
38 Straighten a rope
39 Lengthens
41 Sandy: Lat.
44 Once-upon-a-timer
45 Noun ending
46 Drinks
47 Some NCO's
48 Trifle
50 Moslem commander
51 Bright tropical plant
53 Finishes
55 Partial light reduction
56 "___ for the money"
58 Let ___ (give up)
61 Atmosphere: Prefix
64 Expanding bullet
66 ___ Paulo
67 Tenth of a cent
68 ___ breve
69 Spare barbecue items
71 Intricacies
73 Daughter of Cadmus
74 More baffling
75 Marsh of mysteries
76 Word before "wrong number"
77 Son of, to a Scot
79 German admiral
81 Angle of an ore vein
83 Fell behind in payments
88 Harmony part
89 Scolds
91 Confused
92 Chinese skiff
93 Library stamps
94 Hay spreader
95 Salad plant
96 Therefore
97 Sweet river of song
98 Certain horses
99 Blue girl
102 Hostile one
104 Ring of light
105 Large bird
107 Fishing industry org.
108 Wrinkle
109 Sign
112 Tell fibs
113 Old Japanese coin

41 Spring Stirrings By Dan Girardi

To help make the world go round again.

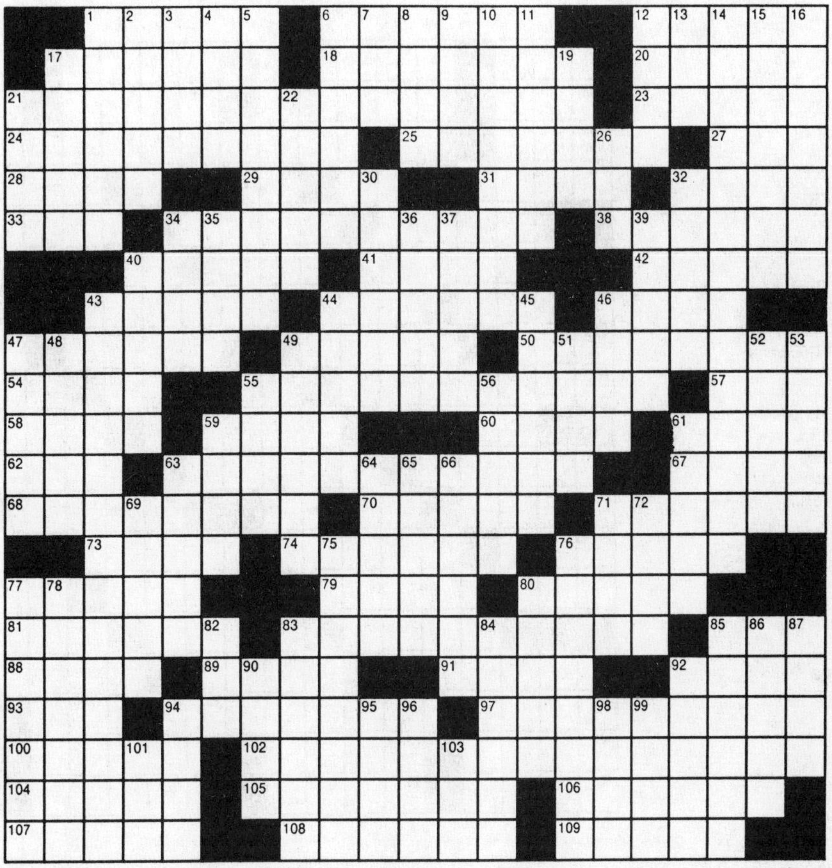

ACROSS

1 Polish city
6 Weather forecast
12 Garden pest
17 Pablo's money
18 Made good
20 Dancing Castle
21 Swain's ultimatum
23 Prepare chestnuts
24 Passionate
25 Unsettle
27 Way: Abbr.
28 Prefix for drama
29 Egg cell
31 It's mighty, at times
32 The Man of baseball
33 "___ was saying"
34 Elixir
38 ___ Cranston (the Shadow)
40 I is one
41 Wild oinker
42 Talents
43 Four-time Wimbledon champion
44 Circled the golf cup
46 Settle down
47 White poplars
49 Famous person
50 "P.S. ___"
54 Queens nine
55 Glenda Jackson film
57 Time periods: Abbr.
58 Little Elisabeth, in Essen
59 Sonora Indian
60 River to the Seine
61 Miss Daniels of the silents
62 Thor's wife
63 Friends plus
67 Simba's pad
68 With gusto
70 Yesteryear's song
71 What a sharp thwack does
73 Good earth
74 Franklins, e.g.
76 What Santa was making
77 Athenian lawmaker
79 New Zealand trees
80 Be smitten on
81 Miss Landi
83 Sorrows
85 Give the ax
88 Overhead item
89 Gun for Tommy Atkins
91 Feminine suffix
92 Run easily
93 Tennessean
94 Rickshaw pullers
97 Headdress streamers
100 ___ 1 (long shot)
102 Was unfeeling
104 Kind of servant
105 Evening affairs
106 In a prim way
107 Choose
108 ___ again (repeats)
109 Platinum wire loops

DOWN

1 Paris's Rue de ___
2 Pico de ___, Pyrenees mount
3 Word with tasse
4 Mountain: Prefix
5 Be mopey
6 Muster, as troops
7 Vein output
8 Toward the mouth
9 In the flesh
10 Always
11 Tarry
12 Yorkshire river
13 For
14 Sing-along song
15 Kind of coffee
16 Ratchet-wheel devices
17 Capitol features
19 Impression
21 Memorable golfer Tony
22 "Miroirs" composer
26 Solidify
30 Calder work
32 Umbrella, at times?
34 Tennis nonscore
35 Signs chits
36 ". . . peace ___ of good will"
37 Metrical feet
39 Century plant
40 Graceful dance in Nice
43 Suggestion by Romeo
44 Word on a bill
45 Rarefy
46 Pirate's hideout
47 Jacob Ammann's sect
48 Misrepresent
49 Jeff and Wendell
51 Tennis shots
52 Round trip for Glenn
53 Employers
55 Basket for fish
56 Part of the nose
59 Take a dip
61 Bored
63 Nixon Cabinet member
64 Oriental pipe
65 Young eel
66 "___ Fideles"
69 What chanticleer rules
71 Wild plum
72 Russian villages
75 Insect's tracheal fibers
76 Cling firmly
77 Tableware
78 Margarine base
80 Play part
82 Turku, to Swedes
83 Greek sun god
84 Finally
85 Varnish resins
86 Imitative doings
87 Egg holder
90 Mob's gats
92 City of Belgium
94 Stable youngster
95 Mr. 'iggins
96 Fr. holy women
98 "When you and ___ wed"
99 Greek letters
101 Spasm
103 Hawaiian game

42 Getting the Count By Ronnie Allen

In any number of ways.

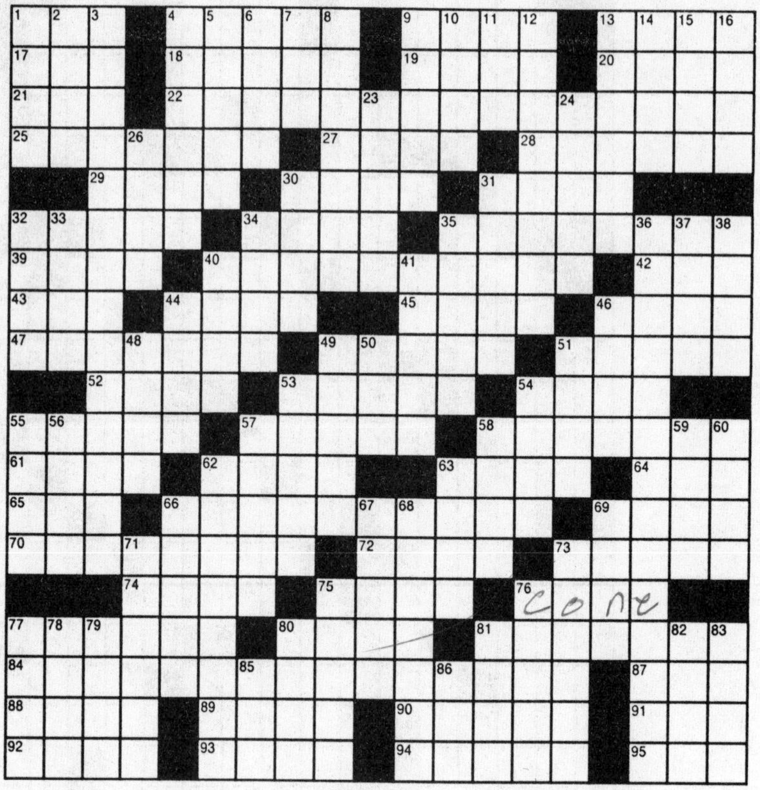

ACROSS

1 Opposite of syn.
4 Dexterous
9 Alternative to suspenders
13 Nuremberg negative
17 First word of a popular round
18 Trial's partner
19 Ogden's state
20 Escutcheon border
21 Forum greeting
22 Flapper era
25 Ship stabilizer
27 Roy's spouse
28 Like a Churchill hour
29 Casks
30 ___ majesty
31 Texas city
32 Grenoble's river
34 Gasp
35 Entrances
39 Hand or rags
40 Clementine's dad
42 Raven-ous author
43 Cold air's bite
44 Armstrong's was historic
45 ". . . going to St. ___"
46 Quiz choice
47 Adore
49 Cro-Magnon abodes
51 Wee one
52 Gratify
53 Extra restaurant charge
54 Roll up
55 Dayan's eyepiece
57 Homo sapiens
58 ___ joy
61 Wight or Man
62 Filly, eventually
63 Part of an Elgar march
64 "___ stranger in paradise"
65 Soissons season
66 Movie turned sit-com
69 ___ cry
70 Enlarges
72 Weathercock
73 Buddhist dialogue
74 Musical work
75 Parisian parent
76 Ice-cream holder
77 Town in southwest France
80 Tootsie, to Hoffman
81 Dawdles
84 Last minute
87 Nothing
88 Car designation
89 Fabrications
90 Better than a birdie
91 F.D.R. power project
92 Philippine knife
93 Easily managed, as a ship
94 ___ Janeiro
95 Garment part

DOWN

1 Arafat, for one
2 Variable star
3 Guests at the Last Supper
4 Add oxygen
5 Refuse
6 Part of Q.E.D.
7 "___ favor, señor
8 Neptune's symbol
9 Reveille sounder
10 Diminutive suffix
11 Order's counterpart
12 Atropos, Clotho and Lachesis
13 Later
14 Clinton's canal
15 Martinique and Corse
16 Avian nursery
23 Epithet for Ilie of tennis
24 More kind
26 Pastry ingredient
30 Frolic
31 Abates
32 Fiery prefix
33 Took a base dramatically
34 Vaulter's need
35 Donor
36 Doomsday for taxpayers
37 Possessive
38 What children should be
40 Disconcert
41 Actor David
44 "___ this ring I . . ."
46 Waterproof cover
48 Alençon product
49 Kohoutek, e.g.
50 Miss Gardner
51 Ecdysiast's maneuver
53 Heals
54 Reek
55 Variegated
56 Italian wine center
57 Horse-height units
58 Jupiter
59 Charles Goren's partner
60 ___ avis
62 Exactly
63 Yearn for
66 Land between India and Tibet
67 Observable
68 More distant
69 Mame, to Patrick
71 Klinger's home-town
73 Evening party
75 Parsonage
76 Was able
77 Ticket portion
78 Charlie Chan's interjection
79 Cassette's big brother
80 Equal
81 Corporate symbol
82 ___ Gauche
83 Bridge coup
85 By way of
86 "Bali ___"

43 Getting the Picture By Manny Miller

Usually one that got some kind of award.

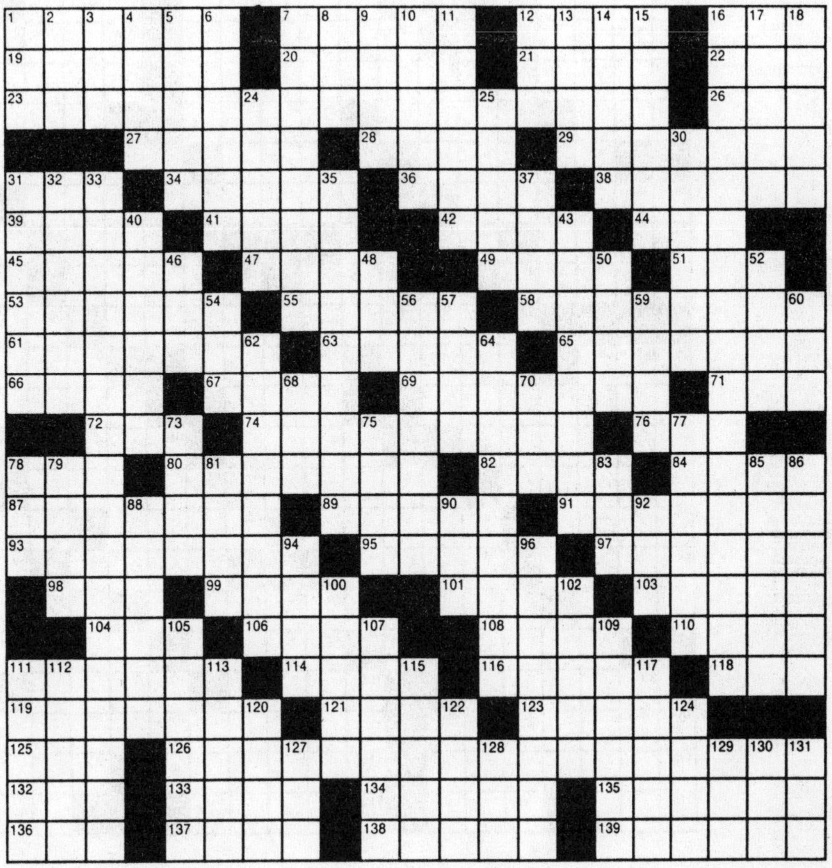

ACROSS

1 Hawkers
7 A ___ of Sundays
12 Follower of Shebat
16 Edible root
19 Oscar film for Olivier
20 Toughen
21 Challenge
22 Miss Gardner
23 Oscar film with Gene Kelly
26 Word in the mailmen's motto
27 Underfooting for a galosh
28 Garment for Indira
29 ___ off (cut short)
31 Wave, in Spain
34 Word with way or well
36 "Coal Miner's Daughter"
38 Selfish
39 Beats it
41 "Riders of the Purple ___"
42 "The Bad ___"
44 Mao ___-tung
45 Potato country
47 It was fatted in the Bible
49 Roman 507
51 Commercials
53 Area for grapes
55 Nostril
58 Minor-league planet
61 Excite: Var.
63 Cigar center
65 Minced-meat ball
66 Unearth, with "out"
67 Opposite of pro
69 Hanging ornament
71 Russia's quiet-flowing river
72 Whisky
74 Oscar film of a Coward play
76 ___ soda
78 College deg.
80 Sub's calling card
82 Cause to be accepted
84 Peter the pianist
87 Suribachi or Mauna Loa
89 Mubarak's predecessor
91 Obstructing agent
93 Guiding principle
95 Decoration
97 Kind of land at the front
98 Time in Wyo.
99 Wood sorrels
101 Where Nepal is
103 Spotted horse
104 Elephant feature
106 Box-office smashes
108 Gilbert and Solomon: Abbr.
110 Arabian gulf
111 Climbing plants
114 Downy surfaces
116 "___ of Two Cities"
118 Grid distances
119 Concurs
121 Billiard-ball holder
123 ___ ear and . . .
125 Arab gp.
126 Oscar films for Irene Dunne and George C. Scott
132 Remo or Mateo
133 Literary work
134 "The ___," Oscar scam film
135 Reproduction
136 Print measures
137 Network
138 Kefauver
139 Gaped

DOWN

1 Tea
2 Decamped
3 Miss Dodo
4 "Desire Under the ___"
5 Totters
6 Imitates mummers
7 Separator of some Great Lakes
8 "Cat ___ Hot Tin Roof"
9 Hebrew letters
10 Kind of lawyer
11 James and Morgan
12 Turkish title
13 "___ Victory"
14 Becoming mellow
15 It's sometimes last
16 Film for a Cagney Oscar
17 Refrain from
18 Oscar film for Borgnine
24 Father of Jacob
25 Had a yen
30 Rornero and others
31 Oscar film with a Twist
32 Mestizo
33 Oscar film for Paul Scofield
35 In-laws
37 Leningrad's river
40 Scottish pony, for short
43 Film for an Arliss Oscar
46 Mouths
48 Monk's title
50 Put ___ writing
52 Part of the farm scene
54 Singer Sumac
56 Burst inward
57 Not gen.
59 Superlative endings
60 Private spot
62 Make gradual inroads
64 Film for an Ingrid Bergman Oscar
68 Do a sneaky wire job
70 Successor to H.S.T.
73 Greek letters
75 Smith or Bede
77 Lack of vigor
78 Outstanding athlete: Abbr.
79 Lower the ___
81 Aware of
83 Alphabetic sequence
85 Leased
86 Bean and Welles
88 Liquid hydrocarbon
90 Miss Rehan
92 Explode in a small way
94 Joan Crawford flop film
96 Realtors' offers
100 Kay or Ringo
102 Finnish island
105 Malice
107 Thinly scattered
109 Inclines
111 Small error
112 Moslem religion
113 Mushroom stalk
115 Highlanders and bairns
117 Make into law
120 Soot
122 Make sweaters
124 Miss Kett
127 Chemical suffix
128 Scottish pronoun
129 Norse war god
130 Poet's start
131 Sparks or Rorem

44 Sitting Pretty By Richard Silvestri

On just about anything that might be around.

ACROSS

1 Misstepped
6 Lariat
11 Stupid one
14 Future status of a bill
17 Feudal sovereigns
19 Tom of "Happy Days"
20 Protein derivative
22 Loony
24 Send on a detour
25 Wedding-notice word
26 Miscellany
27 Animosity
28 Grew light
29 Assigned a PG or X
31 Velvety surface
32 Hay farmer's chore
34 Eden was one
36 Certain gavel pounders
38 Old English letter
41 Jai ____
42 Mine, in Metz
44 Wheel centers
45 Role for Liz
46 1945 conference site
48 Spoken
50 Flies like Lindy
51 Boston's is Beacon
52 Two-toned footwear
55 ____ up (appraised quickly)
56 Billboard displays
59 Dos follower
60 Atlantic fish
61 Legislative body
62 Not figurative
64 Toper
65 One snagging an olive
66 Footless
67 Apple leaving
68 Popular nonfiction subject
69 Dental deg.
70 Sullen
71 Longtime Cincinnati star
74 Earthenware jar
75 Tears down
76 Leif's father
77 Hot coal
82 Drops bait lightly
83 Yoko et al.
84 Dresden donkey
86 Drug plant
87 Silkworm
88 Center of local government
92 Rising
94 ____ Pointe, Mich.
96 Porker's sound
97 Kilmer opus
98 Stage direction
100 ____ Dimittis
101 Gargantuan
102 Spotted
105 Having tines
107 Former Turkish dominion
110 Closet items
111 "Sufficient unto ____ is . . ."
112 Checked
113 Voice votes
114 Q-U connection
115 ____ as a beet
116 French Impressionist

DOWN

1 N.C. college
2 Plentiful
3 Job-agency action
4 Part of the psyche
5 Indicate
6 Aussie animal
7 Island near Naples
8 It turns litmus paper blue
9 Waver
10 Point on the Isle of Man
11 Calendar abbr.
12 Like some grapes
13 Ankle injury
14 Society hanger-on
15 Feed the pot
16 Dandelion, for one
18 Moon goddess
19 Sib of sis
21 ____ crier
23 Caesar
30 Mine entrance
31 Small bottle
32 Relative of roulette
33 Early pulpits
34 Enola ____
35 Winglike part
36 Firewood measures
37 War yell
39 Took out
40 Items for pots and cigarettes
43 Poser
45 Crockery
47 Off the mark
49 School work
50 Sleep
53 Inland sea
54 Disdain
55 Boil
56 Pie order
57 Having opposite electrical charges
58 Finks
61 Risky venture, for short
63 Sagas' kin
65 Inasmuch as
67 Place for medals
68 Certain believer
71 Two-faced god
72 Fresh air
73 Pool-game beginning
75 Farm alarms
78 Medieval war club
79 Benediction
80 Eternity
81 Soak
85 More capacious
88 Marine eel
89 Lads
90 Geyser deposit
91 Put into cipher
93 Looked to be
95 Ladder part
97 Brewer's vat
98 Hebrew bushel
99 Roentgen discovery
100 Part of N.B.
101 Kind of ride or fever
103 Expanse
104 Ties the knot
106 Summertime initials
108 Sore
109 Pizza

45 Out of Control By William Canine

A look at the zanier side of things.

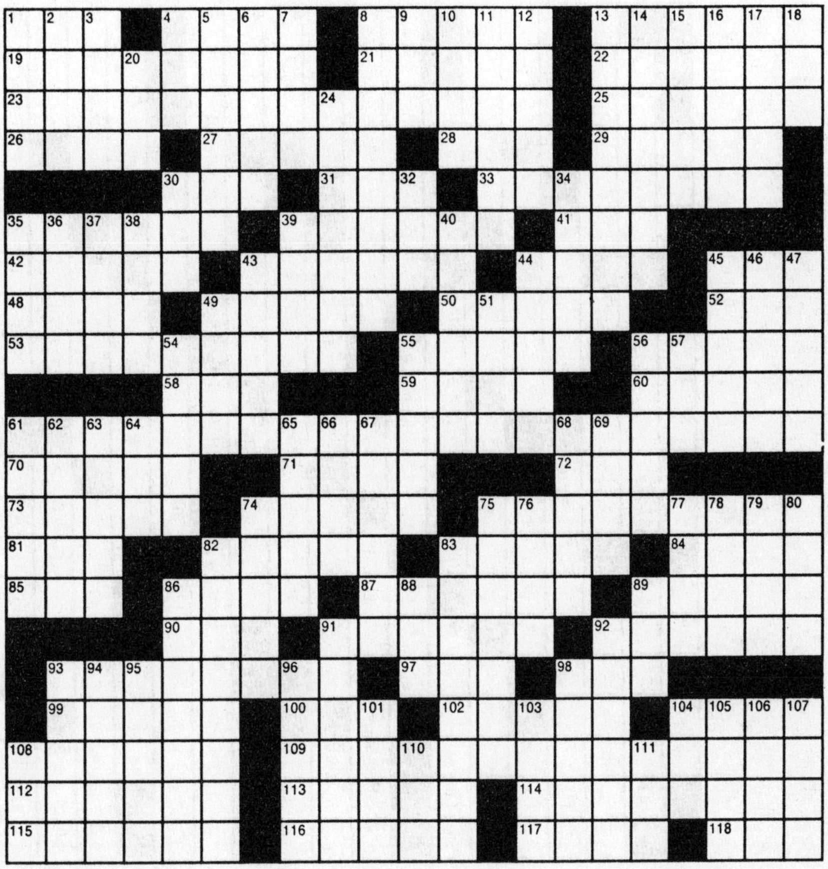

ACROSS

1 Dit's partner
4 Large part of Eur.
8 Neat piles of ropes
13 ___ hand (close by)
19 Be equivalent
21 Caucasian
22 Home of the Illini
23 Futile effort
25 Inquiry
26 No one, in old Rome
27 Boat for an Eskimo
28 How, in Bonn
29 Drudges
30 Court call
31 Golly!
33 One at a church console
35 Harangue
39 Rembrandt's birthplace
41 Hall of Famer
42 Onion relative
43 Songbirds
44 Common nicknames
45 Cook's abbr.
48 The tops
49 Give up
50 Poet Sylvia
52 ___ Jima
53 "What's up, Doc?" asker
55 Praises
56 Dravidian language
58 French soul
59 O'Neill's Christie
60 Care for abundantly
61 Zany film of 1963
70 Fragment
71 Notion
72 Title for Cupid
73 Western Hispaniola
74 Musical symbols
75 "He slud into third" broadcaster
81 Select
82 Its wall is famous
83 Reception
84 Scary figure
85 Meas. of speed
86 Solo
87 Terminates
89 Aristocles
90 Kind of lace
91 Responds
92 Like a certain goose's eggs
93 Case for a detective
97 Beetle
98 Poetic word
99 Vertical, at sea
100 Orangutan
102 Director for Mia, Diane and others
104 Brother of Jacob
108 Ester of an acid
109 Nonsense
112 Hand over
113 Tennessee ___
114 Spotted
115 Measure
116 Word after news or band
117 To be, in France
118 Cause damage to

DOWN

1 Awakening
2 Parisian girlfriend
3 Small island
4 Ointment: Abbr.
5 Fed the fire
6 Ermine
7 Blushful
8 Absurd
9 Kirghizian city
10 What vidi means
11 Injury
12 Bullock
13 Small bird
14 Knightly wanderers
15 Calculators
16 Frames
17 "___ of robins . . ."
18 Limey
20 Japanese salad herb
24 With panting breath
30 Light-horse Harry
32 Tokyo, once
34 Blame bearers
35 Strikebreaker
36 ___ En-lai
37 Surround
38 Periods prior to
39 Legal claim
40 His country, to Picasso
43 Decorated with tendrils
44 Polite title
45 Indonesian island
46 Eddy
47 Moved a gondola
49 Arizona city
51 Singer Art
54 Salten's fawn
55 Actor Fernando
56 Colored like 54 Down
57 Pother
61 For the gods, blood
62 "Sound of Music" family
63 Clubs and spades
64 Quant.
65 Skin nodules
66 Mideast gulf
67 Mutilate
68 Tools
69 Confuse
74 Lunchstand order
75 Subvert
76 Burl or Charles
77 Raggedy Ann or Barbie
78 "My word!"
79 "Vissi d' ___"
80 Kind of gas
82 Soup-order extras
83 Poisonous prairie plant
86 Flies
88 Stripling
89 By, in Madrid
91 Sound of a shot
92 Old Faithful, for one
93 Forces to court
94 Uncorks
95 Union general
96 Matrons
98 Inference
101 City in Sicily
103 Woodwind
104 Darkroom abbr.
105 Wrinkle
106 Nick and Nora's dog
107 Utility customer
108 ___ pro nobis
110 Relatives
111 ___ du Diable

46 Hard Knocks By John Hales

Aspects of the earthier side of life.

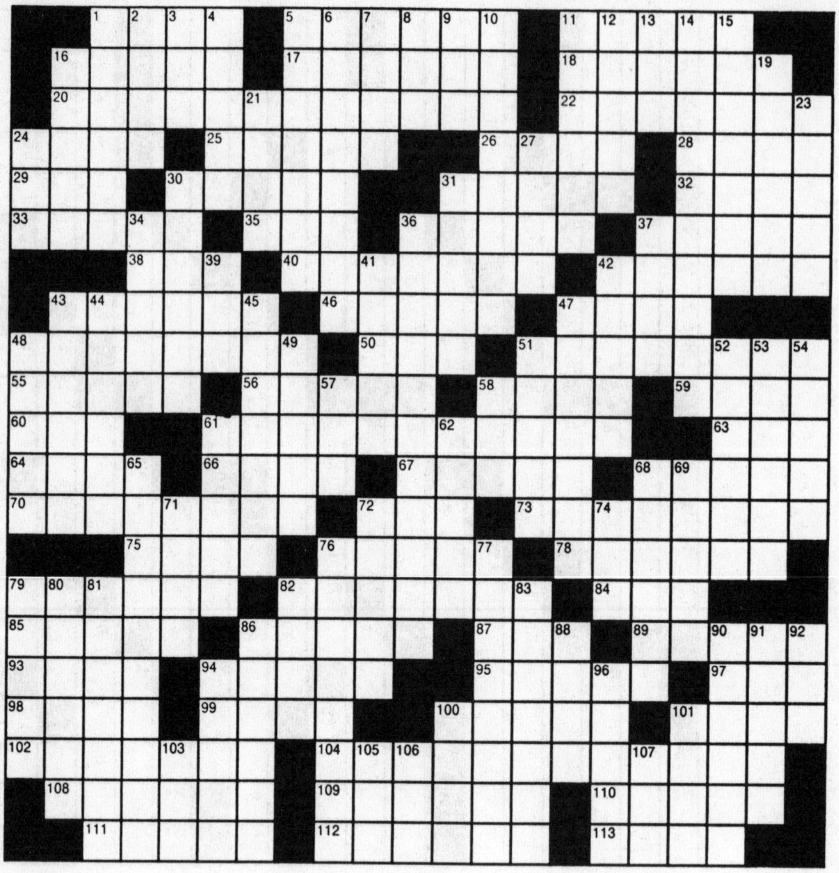

ACROSS

1 Use a stiletto
5 Bully
11 Skilled occupation
16 Lycée's relative
17 Of great size, to a Parisian
18 Letterpress proofs
20 Start trouble
22 Wise man of Troy
24 Volition
25 Neck cramp
26 Bivouac sight
28 Needle case
29 Italian goose
30 Small container
31 Enchantress
32 Come across
33 Hindu religious doctrine
35 October drink
36 Lustrous fabric
37 Weather-observing device
38 Ear: Prefix
40 Rainy-day funds
42 Fond stroke
43 Clandestine
46 Solemn acts
47 Lhasa figure
48 In loco ___
50 Big Board listing
51 Opposed authority
55 Director Lubitsch
56 Psalm pause
58 Loco
59 Swan lady
60 Slugger's stat
61 Grand-scale fight
63 "Vamoose!"
64 Taketh action
66 Writer Bagnold
67 Clumsy footgear
68 Piercing
70 In view
72 Writer Yutang
73 Late joiner
75 Baseball's Speaker
76 Antisub equipment
78 Intoxicated
79 Organized procedure
82 Like a Dalmatian
84 Never, to Hans
85 ___ Melba
86 Sturdy fabric
87 Stylist's concern
89 "Odd Couple" name
93 Nagy of Hungary
94 Gabs
95 Certain Easterner
97 Camel's-hair wrap
98 Sine qua non
99 Echoed
100 Quivering
101 Imperfection
102 Hay-fever patient, at times
104 Cole Porter song
108 Undertake, old style
109 Changes the décor
110 Kind of contract
111 Aspen gear: Var.
112 Take ___ (be neutral)
113 Earthenware jar

DOWN

1 Graduated, as a ladder
2 Drudgery
3 Martino and Pacino
4 Tree with gray bark
5 Soap operas, e.g.
6 Wage ___ war (use A-bombs)
7 Deduct from wages
8 Bother
9 Dallas sch.
10 Lab exercises
11 Bowsprit iron
12 Frenchman's income
13 Apropos
14 Brawl
15 Group annuity
16 Author Jong
19 Puget and Long Island
21 Offering by Miss Scotto
23 Nags
24 Stir-fry vessel
27 White-tailed birds
30 Kind of medicine
31 Crete's capital
34 Chess plays
36 Assaults
37 Likewise
39 Portion for Rover
41 Like some infections
42 Junta
43 Facsimile need
44 Bird: Prefix
45 Medicinal teas
47 Envoys
48 Hidden
49 Begin to happen
51 Synthetic material
52 Pea or bean
53 Checked copy
54 Receiving-clerk's equipment
57 Canadian version of inc.
58 Sailor
61 Obscure
62 Charged
65 1927 musical
68 Movement
69 Sheep sheds
71 Suffer, in the Highlands
72 Night criers
74 Prevailed
76 U.S. literary critic of early 1900's
77 Went over again
79 Tells a yarn
80 Sana native
81 Culls
82 Word before dig or plaster
83 Feel antipathy toward
86 Briefing graphics
88 Posture
90 Two-wheeled Philippine carriage
91 Degrade
92 Cold and windy
94 Suzette or de chine
96 ___-Saxon
100 Thine, to René
101 Paddock youngster
103 Tappan ___
105 Mod
106 Drapers' measures: Abbr.
107 Colloid

47 Triple Plays By Tap Osborn

None of them unassisted.

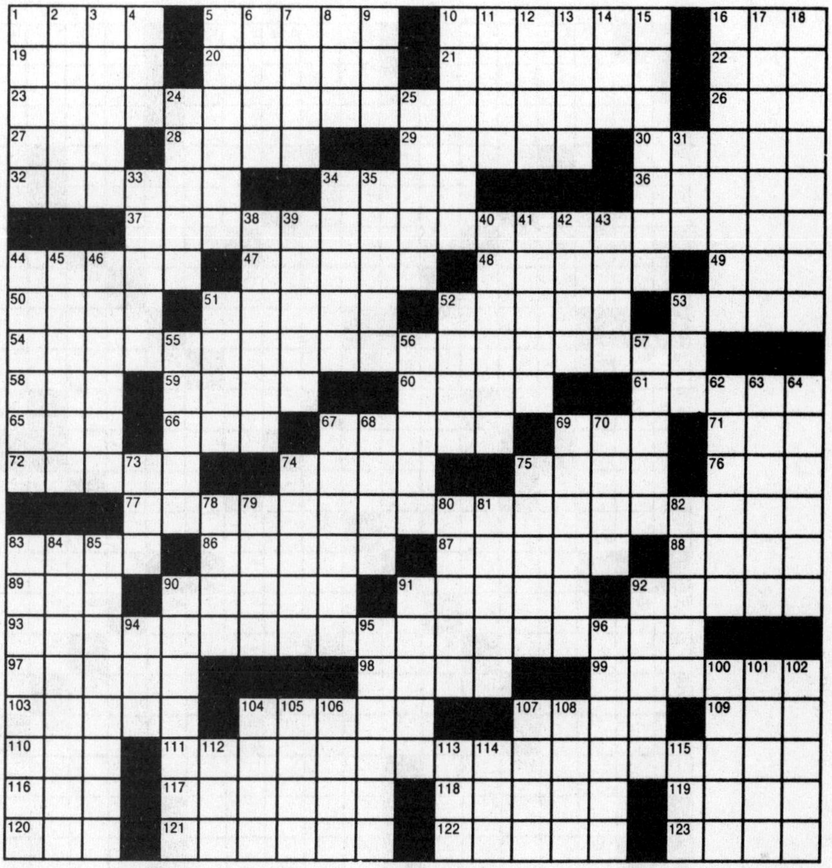

ACROSS

1 Snare
5 Did a lawn job
10 California resort city
16 J.F.K. visitor
19 O'Neill
20 Mideasterner
21 Ibsen dancer
22 Book-title word
23 Betting trio Ed, Pascal and Irwin?
26 Wine: Prefix
27 Old shield
28 "___ Misbehavin' "
29 Weedy plants of the Bible
30 Dried up: Var.
32 Tie in
34 Karate move
36 Arrow poison
37 Anglers Ralph, Frankie and Isaac Bashevis?
44 Italy's second city
47 Like a hay-fever sufferer's nose
48 Respond to
49 Ethnic suffix
50 Scent
51 Dinner course
52 Hopper or Gabler
53 Star: Prefix
54 Volunteers Helen, George and Walter?
58 Kind of time or doll
59 River islands
60 Approve
61 Of a bristle
65 Devotee: Suffix
66 Elevations: Abbr.
67 Head areas
69 Barfly
71 Before amas
72 ___comic
74 Word to a child
75 Uris's "___ 18"
76 Sand or chocolate
77 Marksmen John, Robert and Milton?
83 Singer Natalie
86 Lolling place in Waikiki
87 Door holder
88 Estonian measure
89 Mouths
90 Foul
91 V.M.I. student
92 Moves like lava
93 Hedonists John, Jane and T.V.?
97 Rooney's film father
98 Eye: Prefix
99 Writer Ambrose
103 Delighted in
104 In unison
107 Regarding
109 Slippery one
110 Ill humor
111 Theatergoers Lucille, Edward and William Sergeant?
116 Moslem spirit
117 Reach
118 Hess and Himmler, e.g.
119 Dormant
120 Titanic's call
121 Urban blight
122 Representative
123 Element

DOWN

1 Campanile
2 Rolls's partner
3 Void
4 Flash in the ___
5 Setting
6 North African port
7 Cool one's heels
8 Type measures
9 Machine tool
10 Party snack
11 Man: Prefix
12 Ascent
13 Time periods: Abbr.
14 Group of years
15 Noncourtly action
16 Warehousings
17 Most precipitous
18 More delicate
24 Twirler's need
25 Flabbiness
31 Ocean bird
33 "___ Day's Night," Beatles film
34 Grand or Kiel
35 India's main language
38 Killer snakes of Asia
39 Quiets
40 Action spots
41 Donkey, in England
42 Art cult
43 Strikebreaker
44 Kind of chair
45 Do brainstorming
46 Tenant
51 Loretta of TV
52 Food fish
53 Drink in a Maugham title
55 Uncouth person
56 "I ___ Right to Sing the Blues"
57 Founded: Abbr.
62 Iranian city
63 Charlotte——
64 Sophia and family
67 Spanish inn
68 One in opposition
69 Do a serenade
70 Kind of shoppe
73 Elba, to Napoleon
74 Heavy-duty cloth
75 Hair mops
78 Ball of yarn
79 Man's straw hat
80 Singsong
81 Relative of Bub or Mac
82 Funeral talk
83 Primroses
84 "Messiah" is one
85 Unwelcome travel delays
90 Serving tray, to a horse
91 Writer Karel
92 Thin paper, with 108 Down
94 Nautical dir.
95 Emphatic refusal words
96 Supplicate
100 "Hard Cash" author
101 Violin's cousin
102 Actress Terry
104 Old man, in Germany
105 Blind item
106 News notice
107 Bladed tool
108 See 92 Down
112 Part of N.C.A.A.
113 Literary collection item
114 Pester
115 Uproar

48 Incompletions By Bert Kruse

Singular ways of presenting expressions.

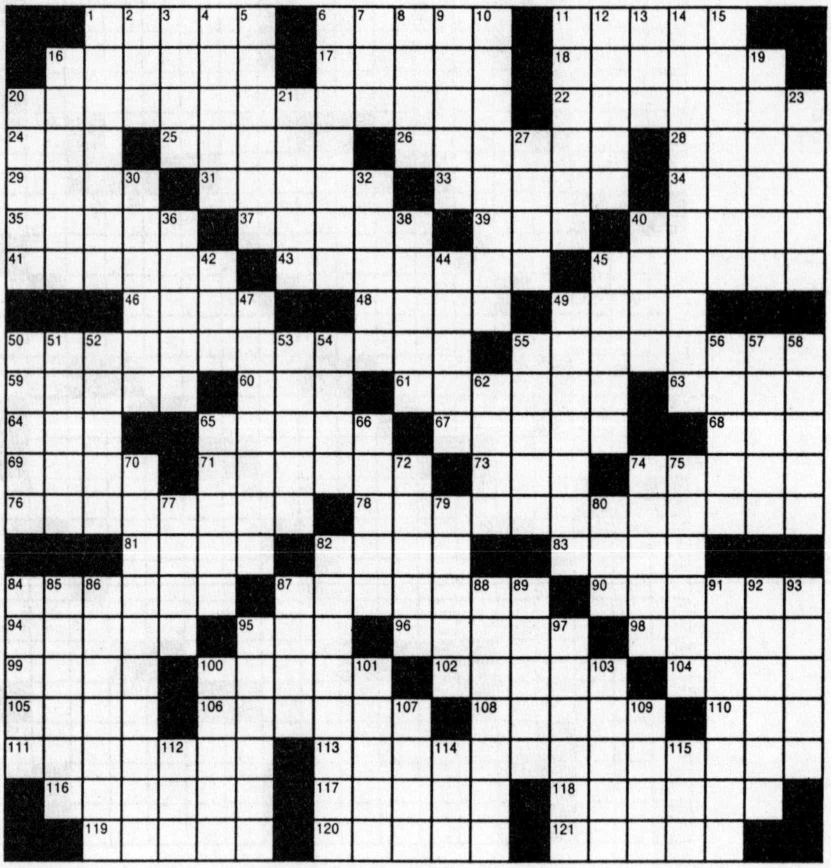

ACROSS

1 Bel ___ cheese
6 Digging tool
11 Chide
16 Hoi ___
17 Red dye
18 Begrudged
20 Half embarrassment?
22 Witty person
24 Tatum or Carney
25 Fortune people
26 Extreme
28 Asian water cock
29 Incursion
31 Palace, in old Roma
33 Breathing sounds
34 "___ True What They Say . . . ?"
35 Composers' org.
37 City lights
39 Lace
40 Stage line
41 Join forces
43 Yeti and Frosty
45 Was improvident
46 Egyptian goddess
48 Baron Munchausen, e.g.
49 Italian port
50 Hopeless mastication?
55 Cornmeal dishes
59 Finery
60 Dutch commune
61 ___ show (burlesque)
63 Moola
64 Moppet
65 "A Certain Smile" author
67 Spirals
68 Roman 1002
69 Hebrew letter
71 Action spots
73 Prefix for verse or form
74 Colorado resort
76 Sent a different way
78 Sign of being only half afraid?
81 Individualist
82 Island of ___ (brain lobe)
83 Chemin-de-fer stop
84 Lessened
87 Has a paper route
90 ___ oneself (be a loner)
94 Exit ways
95 ___ Rio or Mar
96 Gave birth to a lamb
98 Scatter
99 Mater or Gluck
100 Familiar boom
102 Flower footstalk
104 Bristle: Prefix
105 Pressure group
106 Virgil's nomad
108 Uncle of fiction
110 Wernher ___ Braun
111 Class members
113 Yellow Pages activity?
116 Famed alley
117 Harden
118 Buries, sort of
119 Writer's aide
120 Philbin of TV
121 Roman wash items

DOWN

1 Horace's "Ars ___"
2 Thirst quencher
3 Big U.S. game
4 Serious
5 "My Sister ___"
6 Rap or bull follower
7 "Phooey!"
8 That
9 Iranian money
10 Skilled metal worker
11 Many a book or story
12 Six Danish kings
13 Egg: Prefix
14 Unenthusiastic buss?
15 Down payment
16 Sentence part
19 Make fun of
20 Weight
21 Prods
23 Made an appraisal
27 Buck character
30 Actress Lily
32 Lizard
36 Possessed of gall
38 Dance
40 Rhine tributary
42 Movie
44 Merlin's bag
45 Richard Burton's birthplace
47 Actress Norma
49 Hot under the collar
50 Siberian
51 Papal cape
52 Garçon's concern
53 Nosed out
54 Cut apron strings
55 Make a bell sound
56 Musicians' beats
57 E.T., e.g.
58 Newman-Redford's "The ___"
62 Casanova was one
65 Had it up to here
66 In the buff
70 Echo from a nervous dad-to-be?
72 Kind of remark
74 Sheridan character
75 Shotgun contests
77 Individuals, in Paris
79 Fitzgerald and Cinders
80 Hard wood
82 Late-inning pitcher
84 Mideasterners
85 "Rodeo," for one
86 Floor-cleaning ingredient
87 Noted Quaker
88 Menu listings
89 More dry
91 Conductor Andre and family
92 Wyoming range
93 Due
95 Fails to
97 Stupe
100 Food wrap
101 Mutiny vessel
103 Fertilizer from Peru
107 Cozy
109 Snort of liquor
112 Start, poetically
114 Gypsy horse
115 Malayan monkey

49 Scale Models By Frances Hansen

Mostly a matter of keeping in shape.

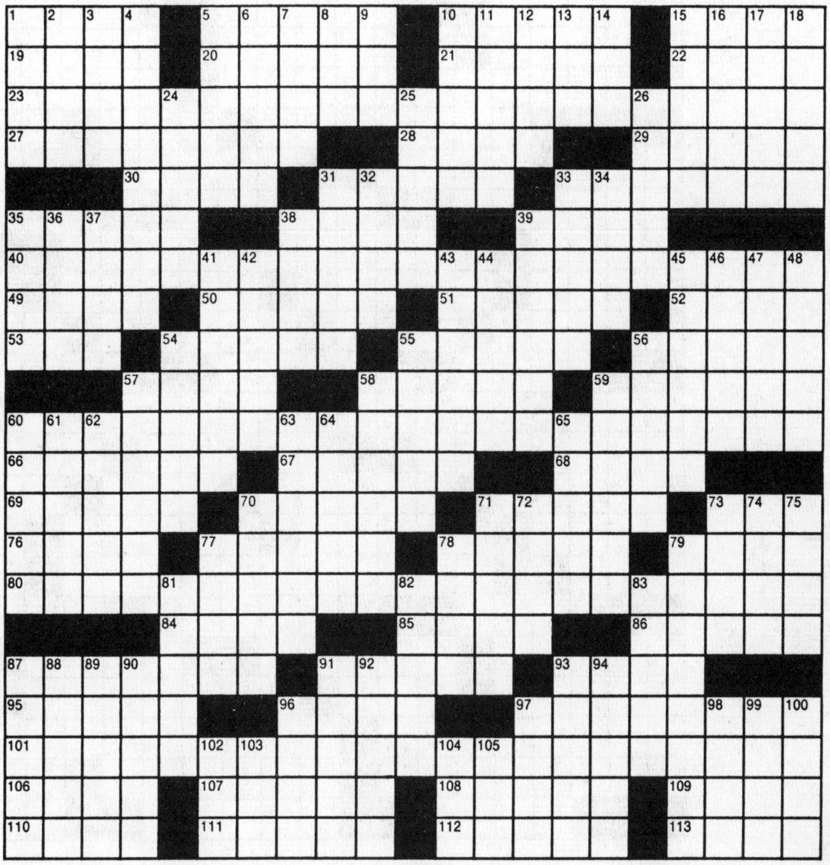

ACROSS

1 Egyptian Christian
5 Circuit
10 Plant pest
15 Raisa or Ponselle
19 U.N. air agency
20 He made his mark in films
21 Upright or grand
22 Kind of rain
23 How to join a dieters' club
27 In convoy
28 Music for 74 Down
29 Large halls
30 Thai coin
31 Crooner Ross of yesteryear
33 Yellow rag
35 Trim appearance, for one
38 Certain codes
39 Body, in biology
40 Encouraging words from St. John
49 Function
50 Artery
51 Candid camera shots
52 Financier's subj.
53 Pussycat's admirer
54 Orbit point
55 Afternoon TV fare
56 Where the action is
57 "This ___ it should be"
58 Thompson or Hawkins
59 Parts of the dock scene
60 Dieter's adage for fat cats
66 "___ Restaurant"
67 Heavy farm carts
68 "The Art of Love" poet
69 Conservative wing
70 Fencer's position, with "en"
71 Disclosed all
73 Assn.
76 German king
77 French toast word
78 Of the soft palate
79 Equal, in Evry
80 Admonition from Charles II
84 Ship hazard
85 Sole
86 Dined at home
87 Door opener, by request
91 One meatball
93 Condemn
95 Negatively charged particle
96 "The Jolly Toper" painter
97 Nimbi
101 How to quit a dieters' club
106 TV's Johnson
107 Latin American dance music
108 Squander
109 "Stride la vampa" is one
110 Mend
111 Make a hash of
112 Slaver
113 Heaviest U.S. President

DOWN

1 Quote
2 Big name in publishing
3 Where René goes barefoot
4 Overly corpulent
5 Quicksilver
6 "Haystacks" painter
7 Inculcated
8 Employer of C.P.A.'s
9 Drag
10 Of bees
11 Plump Muppet miss
12 Sounds of laughter
13 Bank abbr.
14 ___ job on (swindle)
15 Painter Dufy
16 Eye: Prefix
17 Biblical mount
18 Did some calculation
24 High dudgeon
25 Surrealist Max
26 Capital near Casablanca
31 London elevators
32 Upolu port
33 Theater awards
34 Freeman Gosden's radio role
35 Hairdo
36 Snaillike
37 Hawk
38 Thonged sandal
39 Molded
41 Yellowish fruits
42 Lou Grant's hotshot reporter
43 Uris book
44 Work out at the gym
45 Harbinger
46 Boadicea's tribe
47 Canonical hour
48 Grind the molars
54 Until now
55 River to the Rhone
56 Skunk cabbage or taro, e.g.
57 Key Korean War port
58 Miss Muffet's undoer
59 Meets a bet
60 By word of mouth
61 Mrs. Astor's crowd
62 After the gloaming
63 "Sweet ___ Avon!": Jonson
64 Have an ___ the ground
65 Quick raid
70 Stared
71 Feature of Santa
72 Confederate
73 Bugbear
74 Shankar
75 Small valley
77 Suffix for young or old
78 Duct
79 Dictum for Sprat
81 Chimp's cousin
82 Untrue
83 Less exciting
87 Hindu prince
88 Toughen
89 Ancient Roman receptacle
90 Room service is offered here
91 Hiatus
92 Bridal-path destination
93 Because of
94 "Tempest" sprite
96 Doughnut feature
97 Charlie Chan's phrase
98 Zhivago's girl
99 John Ciardi book
100 Coup d'___
102 Marquand's H.M. Pulham
103 St. Anthony's cross
104 Send on, at the P.O.
105 Feather's companion

50 Theater of the Absurd By Alfio Micci

Some shows that didn't get off the ground.

ACROSS

1 Nautical position
6 Sri ___
11 Ring
15 Authority
16 Abase
17 Court figures
21 Musical flop of 1951?
23 Hamlet's abode
24 Removed
25 Compass point
26 Town near Verona
27 Common abbr.
30 Bridge part
31 Ethereal fluid
33 ___ alia
34 Quickly, musically
36 Turkish title
38 Unconstrained
39 Alone, on stage
40 Musical flop of 1966?
45 Dieter's no-no
48 "My One and ___"
49 Songwriter Blake
50 Book by D.S. Freeman
51 Hindu deity
52 Ship to remember
54 Mix or Thumb
55 "Call Me ___"
56 Make-do money
57 Classify
59 Garden pest
61 Long coat
63 NCO
65 Musical flop of 1957?
69 Strauss's "___ und Verklärung"
70 Engraver's creation
72 Quebec peninsula
73 Rorem and Sparks
75 German writer Paul
76 Balts
79 Cricket positions
81 Prefix for rocket or grade
84 Concerning
85 Provide funds
86 Flower: Prefix
88 One of the Ages
89 Mixture of sodium salts
90 Musical flop of 1934?
92 Do ushering
93 E.P.A.'s concern
96 Take the stump
97 "I Am a ___"
99 Nonmetallic element
101 Pianist Jorge
103 Debussy's "Afternoon of a ___"
105 Cook's abbr.
106 Marketplace for Xanthippe
107 Common connective
108 In the best way
111 Stretch out
113 Musical flop of 1964?
118 Filled the tank
119 Miss Lansbury
120 Hogan material
121 Saharan
122 Grenoble's river
123 What matzohs don't have

DOWN

1 Pertinent
2 Bah!
3 Be indebted to
4 Petition: Abbr.
5 Most loyal
6 Vladimir Ilyich Ulyanov
7 Latin I word
8 Hawaiian bird
9 Part of a synagogue service
10 Cuckoo
11 More washed-out
12 Bar need, in Bonn
13 Dancer Markova
14 Trousseau items
16 Prefix meaning ten
17 Barcelona buss
18 Musical flop of 1980?
19 Unimpeded
20 Char
22 Bare
25 Was generous
27 Downs or salts
28 White mineral
29 Musical flop of 1964?
32 Parlor game
35 Ado Annie's "I Cain't ___"
36 Dresses up
37 King topper
38 Hurricane center
41 Ump's cry
42 Wolf-pack member
43 Dockers' org.
44 Musical speed
46 Dispatch boat
47 Not live
51 Bot. or phys.
53 Upright
55 He had a golden touch
56 More conniving
58 Sigma's follower
60 Wallendas' perch
62 Sea eagle
63 Take an oath
64 Furze
66 Member of a pool
67 Freeload
68 ___ two (1:50)
71 U.K. honor
74 Natural religion
77 Bit of ammo: Abbr.
78 "To have and ___ . . ."
80 Haggard title
82 Zoo sounds
83 Ready for use
85 Photographer's abbr.
86 Ten-percenter: Abbr.
87 Sponge orifice
91 Part of UNESCO
94 Horn-shaped figures
95 Wild ass
98 Whenever
99 Max or Buddy
100 Leer
101 Diminished
102 United
103 Aesop specialty
104 Serpent-constellation star
109 Venetian ruler
110 Fulda tributary
112 Baba or MacGraw
113 Merry, in Marseille
114 Keats creation
115 Mauna ___
116 Wts.
117 Still

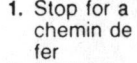

51 Ratings By Ronnie Allen

Some for leaders, others for also-rans.

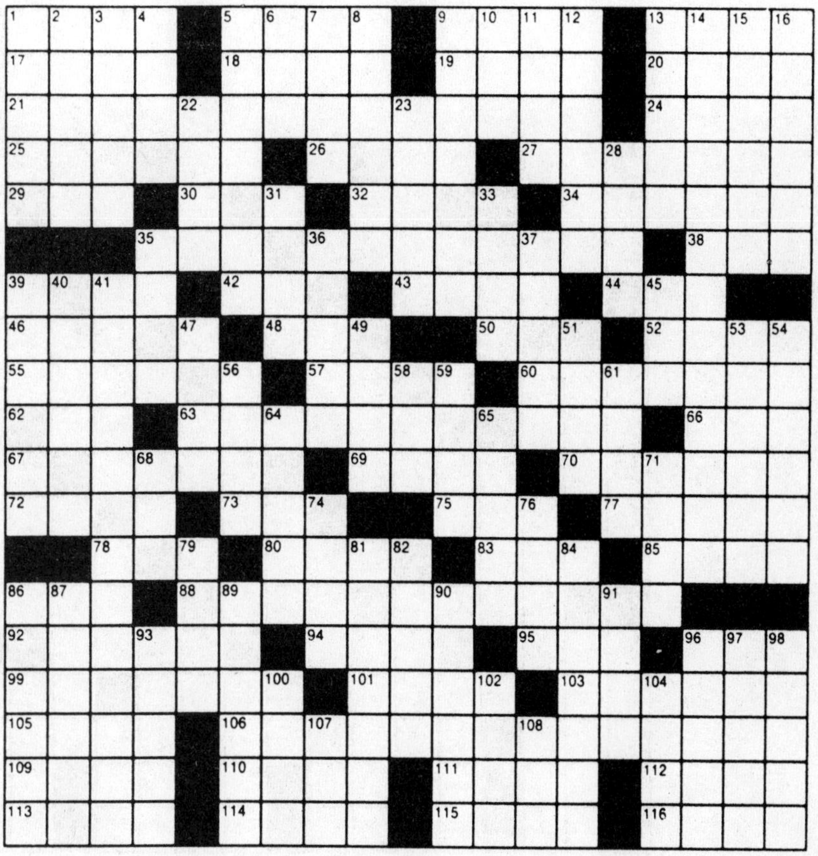

ACROSS

1. Stop for a chemin de fer
5. Took a base theatrically
9. Sitar player Shankar
13. "___ boy!"
17. Overlook
18. "See ya"
19. Tied
20. Restaurateur Toots
21. What some witnesses take
24. Greek Juno
25. Having the first bridge play
26. Artist Joan
27. "___ Hoffmann"
29. Caviar
30. Durocher's sobriquet
32. Royal word of address
34. Films
35. Press
38. Old-timer
39. Teen trauma
42. Damage
43. Great amount
44. Jeanne d'Arc, e.g.
46. Uses leverage
48. Miss Farrow
50. It has a long arm
52. Handle, in France
55. Ornamental plants
57. Naval stockade
60. Fodder grass
62. Emulate the Sprats
63. Adam, Eve, Cain, etc.
66. Make tracks
67. Olympic contender
69. Grain elevator
70. Cleans a cassette
72. ___ majesty
73. Western Indian
75. Mil. address
77. "It's ___ unusual day"
78. Word of assent
80. Org.
83. Mom's brother
85. Division word
86. V.I.P. of a fleet
88. Something Washington was
92. Mend
94. Roof part
95. Hot tub
96. Cleopatra's nemesis
99. Deter
101. Greens gadgets
103. Prophet of Israel
105. Stringed instrument
106. It started in Poland
109. Sea eagle
110. Fulda feeder
111. Stow cargo
112. Fun bird
113. Rogers and Clark
114. Concordes
115. Supplemented, with "out"
116. Odds' companions

DOWN

1. Attack
2. Kind of acid
3. Ransack
4. Ending for room or kitchen
5. Gridiron location
6. Con's escape
7. Bit of news
8. Breakfast roll
9. Guilty feeling
10. Partner of vale
11. Air hole
12. Whole
13. Pale
14. Psychic one
15. Where all roads lead
16. Mideast leader
22. Heavenly headgear
23. Laundromat appliance
28. Reclines
31. Nanny's carriage
33. Relative of etc.
35. Iambic measures
36. Lou Grant's paper and others
37. Valued violin
39. Judicial step
40. Invent
41. Beethoven's last
45. Chinese way
47. Umpire's decision
49. University department
51. Artifice
53. Most timid
54. Shut one's ___ (ignore)
56. In ___ (in position)
58. "___ Loved You"
59. Extravaganza
61. Dame Hess
64. Pave anew
65. Finish a battle operation
68. Southern general
71. Pierre's girlfriend
74. Actual existence
76. Change for a five
79. Tell ___ (lie a bit)
81. Dynamo parts
82. Author-actor David
84. Frolicked
86. "Cry Me ___"
87. Actor Robert
89. Eye parts
90. Tease
91. Telephone
93. French wings
96. Dam of the Nile
97. Pottery fragment
98. Former Miss America emcee
100. Spreads grass for drying
102. P.S. to a love letter
104. Unemployed
107. This, in France
108. Pindar product

52 Two-sided By Sidney Robbins

Many things have to have counterparts.

ACROSS

1. Restaurateur Toots
5. Russian river
9. Rodent of S.A.
13. Is, later
16. "___ of Two Cities"
17. Switch town
18. Ratite birds
19. Halloween mo.
20. Mismatch that backfired
23. Greek letter
24. State of Salem
25. Record for a deejay
26. French centuries
28. School org.
29. Soothsayer
31. Lawsuit
33. Chances
34. It takes a lot of pull
37. Paddle
38. Without
40. More snaillike
41. Like some peas
43. River of France
46. Neighbor of Syr.
47. Gawk
48. Lasted
50. Sky sight
53. Hence
54. Filching
55. Here, in Paris
56. Both sides
58. Paris season
59. Walking tall
62. Verve
63. Lawgiver
65. Insect
66. Pet
67. Auto
68. Excavation
69. Seven: Prefix
71. Taste sense
74. Pro ___
76. Fleur-de-___
77. Blue vs. Gray
79. Jannings
81. Condemn
83. ___ to a turn
84. Chemical suffix
85. Emerge
87. Handle copy
89. Took ten
92. Mrs. Johnson
93. Switches
96. Limb
97. Betel pepper
98. Scent
99. Desert sights
100. Hurricane part
101. Org.
102. Took off
103. Copied

DOWN

1. Begin
2. Take a fling, with "at"
3. Few: Prefix
4. Fix over
5. Container
6. More embarrassed
7. Ire
8. Weaving frame
9. Can. province
10. Accumulate
11. Lovelies
12. Tennis name
13. Certain sports final
14. Pained
15. Facing a hill slope
16. Take on
21. Satisfy
22. Site
27. Diplomat
30. Corn unit
32. Onassis
35. Dust-bowl victim
36. Clenched hand
37. Competitors
39. Popular opera
41. Norse tale
42. Rockies range
44. French income
45. Noses out
47. Seagoing drink
49. River of England
50. Sacred receptacles
51. Musical group
52. Reflection
53. Sea birds
54. Shoo!
56. Pendulum's partner
57. Roman 552
60. Skewer
61. Perennial best-seller topic
63. African country
64. Exam
66. Backbones
67. Howe or Luray feature
70. Tree
71. Bowler's target
72. Color scheme for an auto
73. Mounted, as an artist's canvas
75. X-rated-film watchers
77. Mather
78. Foxx and namesakes
79. Paris school
80. Shuffle along
82. Electrons' containers
83. Vacuum tube
86. West Indian fetish: Var.
88. Arabian vessel
90. Icelandic epic
91. Atlantic fish
94. Conquered
95. Buchwald

53 Misplaced Kin By Gayle Dean

Relatives who find themselves in unlikely spots.

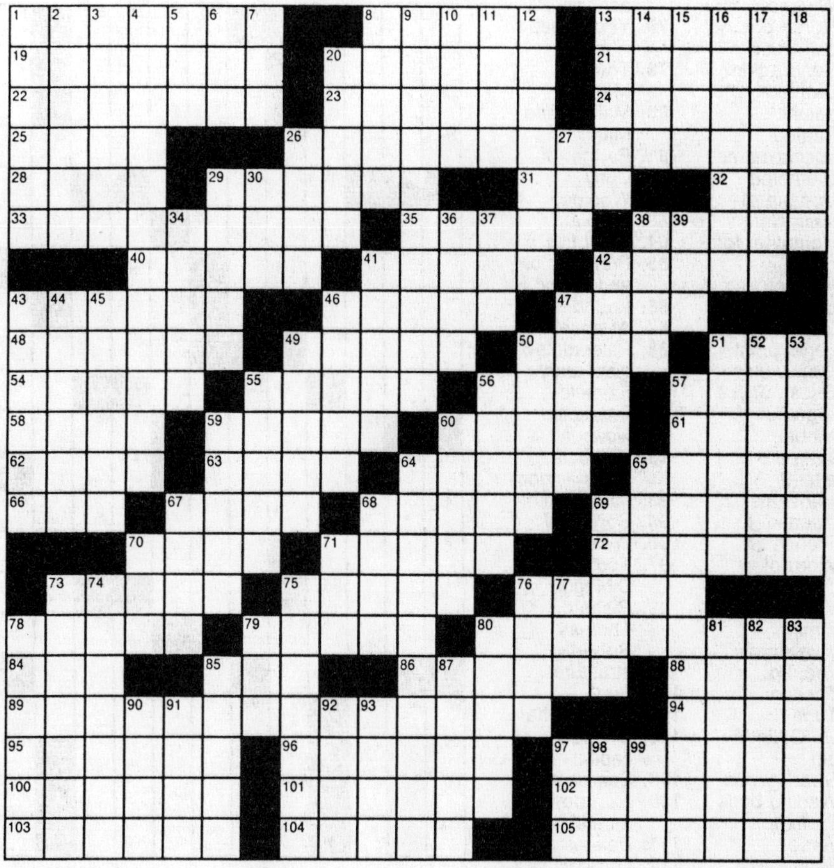

ACROSS

1. Shopper's quest
8. Reek
13. Summer wear
19. Weakness for Midas
20. Illinois city
21. Like some C.I.A. work
22. Added
23. Games honoring Apollo
24. Lack of vigor
25. Castor, for one
26. Convent intruder?
28. Touch down
29. Sandpaper grade
31. Native: Suffix
32. Diminutive ending
33. Sabu's charges
35. Wine river
38. Dished out
40. Mosquito genus
41. Hit by a hive guardian
42. Clothes hanger of sorts
43. Dell dweller
46. Straighten
47. Heap
48. Peter of films
49. Certain TV time
50. Gaiety
51. Tailless cat's home
54. Glacial word
55. Rice thrower's target
56. Earp's greeting to a foe
57. "___ the mornin' to you"
58. Location
59. Toper
60. Thor's chariot pullers
61. Annie or Carnegie
62. Raises one's dander
63. Pine-tree yield
64. Positive pole
65. Skater Sonja
66. Played first in bridge
67. Walking aid
68. Worship
69. Thesaurus man and family
70. ___ nostrum
71. Noise-makers
72. Wears away
73. Rulers
75. Wed
76. Make bread
78. Fidgeted, to a Scot
79. Asimov
80. Broadway musical remake?
84. Epoch
85. Mustangs' campus
86. Sun god
88. Spoken
89. TV spy-show remake?
94. Barber's offering
95. No. 1 Hun
96. Lung covering
97. Daley's political apparatus
100. Salacious looker
101. Poet Wylie
102. Lady in black
103. Infuriate
104. Carries on
105. Game-stat keepers

DOWN

1. Kind of ax or wagon
2. Open declaration
3. Coarse fabric
4. Anna Mary Robertson's husband?
5. Be indisposed
6. Surface for 65 Across
7. Sparks or Rorem
8. Factions
9. Scythe carrier?
10. Lake or Indian
11. Tale teller
12. Wolverine State capital
13. Artist's vista
14. Sharpen
15. Ham operator's word
16. Small feather
17. Eight-line poem
18. Gazed
20. Show host Jack and family
26. Cue expert Minnesota ___
27. American Indian
29. Basic group
30. "All for ___ . . ."
34. Bread extremities
36. Outsized
37. Hostelry
38. Chip's cartoon partner
39. What a torero hears
41. Park feature
42. Opinions
43. Ageless relic
44. Get-up
45. Joined the cheerers
46. Start the day
47. Food holder
49. Raisin's big brother
50. Road slope
51. Lamented
52. Granitic rock
53. Exactly as listed
55. Pat or Daniel
56. Open-and-shut items
57. Brando film remake?
59. Cicatrices
60. Dwarf of folklore
64. Wife of a stern scolder?
65. Goddesses of the seasons
67. Birthday greeting
68. Diva's offering
69. Film units
70. West or Murray
71. Genetic initials
73. Use a cinch
74. Biting pest, to a yokel
75. Power seizer
76. Do needlecraft
77. Sgt., for one
78. Femme ___
79. Org. started at Bretton Woods
80. Of the funny-bone nerve
81. Show up
82. Down Easter
83. Gantry and Fudd
85. Trap
87. Large kangaroos
90. Star in Cetus
91. Shake ___
92. Earthen jar
93. Half a Hitler book title
97. Metric units: Abbr.
98. Curve
99. Labor initials

54 Writers' Cramps By Robert Wolfe

Authors give new meaning in close quarters.

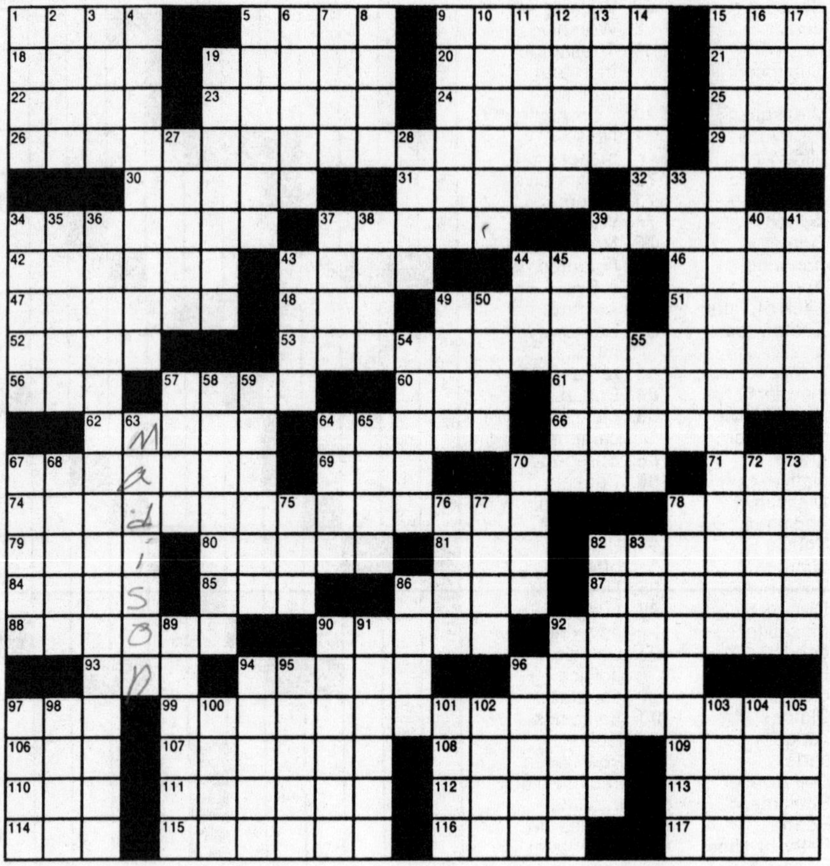

ACROSS

1. Winged
5. Norse poetry collection
9. Send again
15. Bathtub adjunct
18. Famed soccer name
19. Stumbled
20. Domain of Juan Carlos
21. Hematite, for one
22. Knievel
23. Lariat part
24. Cubic meters
25. Legal point
26. Elmer, plus Oscar, Joyce =grains
29. Nibble
30. Inexperienced
31. Hansen's disease, to French
32. Word of disgust
34. Vasco and family
37. Invalidates
39. Leaped
42. Thrilled
43. Tune
44. Uri Geller's gift
46. Swan genus
47. Wading birds
48. Prefix for verse
49. Simple fruit
51. "The Way We ___"
52. X-ray units
53. Alistair, Robert, Charles= mishap
56. Old Tokyo money
57. Graf ___
60. Electric ___
61. Vehement
62. Enamel, in Nice
64. Sound out noisily
66. Father Time attribute
67. Unsettle
69. N.R.C. predecessor
70. Sassy
71. Angelico or Diavolo
74. Charles, C.P., E.B.= assignment
78. You or he: Abbr.
79. Town in Madras
80. Malden and Marx
81. Partner of Curly
82. Woolen blanket
84. Food fish
85. Prefix for bar and metric
86. Pound down
87. At once
88. Paleontologist Henry Fairfield ___
90. Fearsome weapon
92. Highball-glass adjunct
93. Miss Merkel
94. Contempt
96. Welsh dog
97. Tool for DiMaggio
99. Richard, Thomas, Robert= structures
106. End-___
107. Canal or hat
108. Ghana's capital
109. Sea eagle
110. ___ down (abate)
111. Deletes
112. La Scala's city
113. Hair holders
114. Kind of ache
115. Loathe
116. 13th of April
117. Pairs

DOWN

1. Mimic
2. Son of Jacob
3. Author Waugh
4. Banishes
5. Wears
6. Overwhelm
7. Lucie's father
8. Nobility, in Nuremberg
9. Plant again
10. Bars legally
11. Javelin
12. Part of Bret's anatomy?
13. Arrow poison
14. Forgo
15. Thomas, Edward plus Robert= forecast
16. Province
17. Midterm or final
19. Groups of nine
27. Medieval helmet
28. Grad. degree
33. Guard dog, at times
34. Does
35. Pond scums
36. Erle plus Samuel= servants
37. Beverage in Asti
38. Stew
39. Pipe wrench
40. Standards
41. Diving bird
43. Playwright Clare
44. Old French coin
45. Penman
49. Bar drink
50. Comfort follower
54. Actor Stacy
55. RBI, e.g.
57. Sensible
58. Burden for O. J. Simpson
59. Verdugo et al.
63. Home of the Badgers
64. ___ out (scold)
65. Ayres and Wallace
67. Sky Dragon
68. Saarinen and namesakes
70. Bo-___ of shepherding
72. 1 or 66
73. Words of choice
75. Coronado's quest
76. Moslem leader
77. Catacomb sight
78. Corporate top banana
82. Highlander's purse
83. Ear protrusions
86. Secret society
89. Irritated
90. Oliver W. or Sherlock
91. Kind of plate
92. Charmers' pets
94. French upper house
95. "Avast!"
96. Bike
97. Ordered
98. Inter ___
100. Vetch
101. Branches
102. Kind of rain
103. Waxed
104. Within: Prefix
105. Meeting: Abbr.

55 Footloose By H. H. Reddall

Getting out of this world in a hurry.

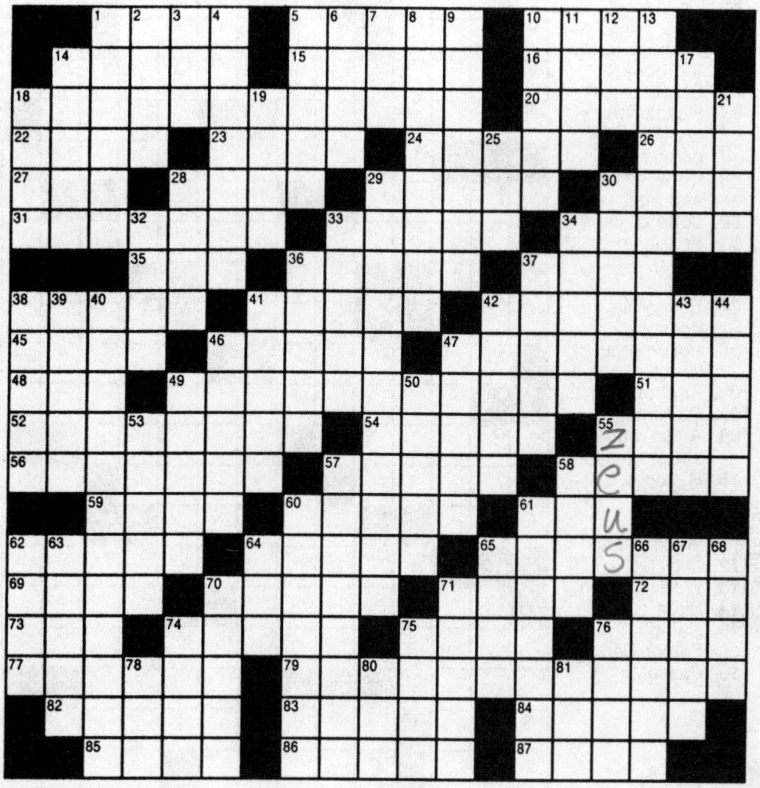

ACROSS

1. Glenn or Doe
5. Made a bird sound
10. Modish
14. Colonel ___, Wilson adviser
15. Having wings
16. Polynesian dances
18. Space-age city
20. Catkins
22. Down ___ in Maine
23. Trimming
24. Coin makers
26. Astronaut's response
27. Linkletter
28. ___ it (hep)
29. Some are barbed
30. Roman 107
31. Notwithstanding
33. Beat with a stick
34. A chosen few
35. Show to a seat, for short
36. Major blows
37. Food thickener
38. Rub out
41. Panama Canal features
42. Thankless person
45. Poison-ivy reaction
46. Tree-dwelling animal
47. Tempered
48. Summer time in N.Y.
49. Plane's underpinnings
51. Become weary
52. Massive slaughters
54. Wise men
55. Egyptian dancing girl
56. Mountie
57. Exhausted
58. Pentagon alloy
59. "A friend in ___ . . ."
60. ___ of burden
61. Charge
62. "They ___ not pass"
64. Comedy's relative
65. Got a space ship off
69. Debt chits
70. Prove false
71. Get wind of
72. French soul
73. Kettle's accuser
74. MacArthur's last campaign
75. Hops kiln
76. Neighborhood
77. Showed ill will
79. Installation at 18 Across
82. Alarm
83. Prefix for violet
84. Garden flower
85. Basks
86. Gradual disease declines
87. Kind of admiral or guard

DOWN

1. Contests on horseback
2. Give the gate
3. Successor of F.D.R.
4. Stone Age implement
5. Joseph Heller's was 22
6. Sheltered
7. Beehive constituent
8. Cotton fabrics
9. Wishes
10. Converses
11. Droning sounds
12. ___ de France
13. Blastoff locale
14. Sir Samuel ___ of England
17. Job was one
18. ___ over heels
19. Ex-cager Archibald
21. Revue unit
25. Writer Buntline
28. A word to the ___
29. Astronaut's stroll
30. Santa ___, Calif.
32. Kind of cart
33. Desert plants
34. Moth
36. Incites
37. Sten and Held
38. Standing
39. Detecting device
40. Science for space capsules
41. Single operator
42. Lifeless
43. Organized groups
44. Outside rims
46. Like some canaries
47. Real-estate worker
49. Part of a coat
50. Silly fowl
53. Christmas renderings
55. Greek god
57. In sequence
58. Sky animal
60. Ominous
61. Freight-train unit
62. Tastes
63. Barrel bands
64. ___-de-lance
65. Tops
66. More astringent
67. Middle East chief
68. "How ___ to my heart"
70. Presages
71. Sounds of merriment
74. Songwriter Jerome
75. Monster
76. Architectural pier
78. Greek letter
80. Possessive
81. Compass dir.

56 Cap-a-Pie By Louis Sabin

And several places in between.

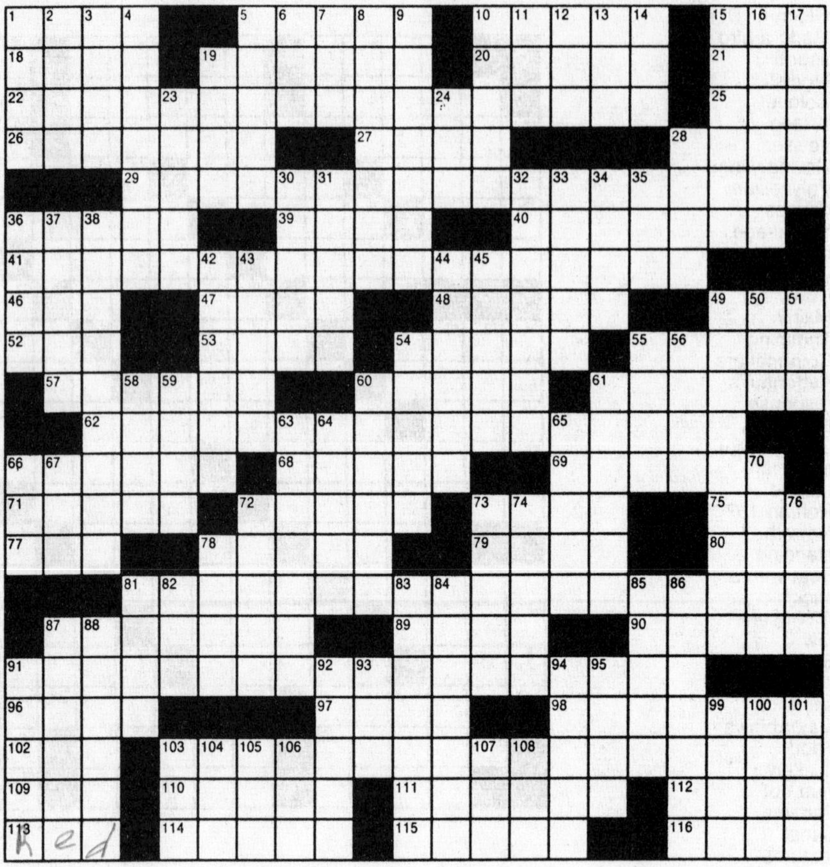

ACROSS

1. Relative of egad
5. Ending for ecto or endo
10. Kind of power
15. R. E. Lee's side
18. Apiece
19. Pamplona hero
20. Of value
21. Electrical unit
22. Rodgers-Hart standard: 1927
25. Pen point
26. Basketball two-pointer, at times
27. Memphis deity
28. Like the rich, traditionally
29. Gets to first base, saleswise
36. Galley goofs
39. Bridge seats, reading clockwise
40. "Baloney!"
41. Lefty Grove's blazers, e.g.
46. Madison Ave. lifeblood
47. Gregory Peck role
48. Consumers' defender
49. Author LeShan
52. In medias ___
53. ___ a one (none)
54. "___ lost save honor"
55. April 15 individual
57. Schools for French preppies
60. Irregular
61. A Benchley
62. Do a Romeo
66. Lady-killer
68. Acute or obtuse item
69. Ants
71. Regional life
72. Bandsman Shaw
73. Try a come-on
75. Bitter herb
77. Suited
78. Talk endlessly
79. Bills' partners
80. Connector
81. "___ what exercise is to the body": Steele
87. Revolutionary War general
89. Between hic and hoc
90. Lotte of films
91. Preparing to speak
96. Pile
97. Seven big ones
98. Pollen grain layers
102. Kind of muff
103. Be honest
109. A film was all about her
110. Raccoon's cousin
111. Oscar Wilde's Gray
112. Miff
113. W.W. I Baron
114. Birch
115. Hall-of-Famer Cap
116. Passel

DOWN

1. D.C. politicos
2. Comedienne Martha
3. Otto's eight
4. X marks it
5. Abolitionists James and Lucretia
6. Words of choice
7. Soak flax or timber
8. Suggest
9. Night caller
10. Osaka fish dish
11. Master Melvin
12. Weeks in an annum
13. Utterly
14. Electrical unit
15. High-rise offerings
16. Civil War battle
17. Red-green divider
19. Pony
23. "And ___ with the setting moon": Tennyson
24. Gram. case
28. Lupino and Kaminska
30. Gamal's successor
31. Getting supplies from
32. More deprived
33. Occasional London flats
34. Legal successor
35. Field animal
36. Peter the Great, for one
37. Do an Alpine routine
38. Tread warily
42. Skirt strips
43. Make ___ of (bollix up)
44. Smitten
45. "___ Triste"
49. Bibliophile's hazard
50. "___ Rosenkavalier"
51. Cunning
54. Play ___ (be in the cast)
55. A tree, to Kilmer
56. Up to it
58. Bias
59. A.k.a. Lamb
60. Border
61. Engage gears again
63. At work
64. Bruckner
65. Spartan serf
66. Desert wear
67. Fox-trot flourish
70. Cheerful
72. "The Age of Anxiety" author
73. Chamber group
74. Type of chemical filter
76. Icelandic epic
78. Nobel physicist I. I.
81. Do a fall farm job
82. Ger., G.B., etc.
83. "___ bird at break of day": Percy
84. English writer Siegfried
85. Israeli port
86. Lines of work
87. ". . . ravell'd ___ of care"
88. Wept
91. Encourage
92. Werner of films
93. Kind of clock
94. Actress Ada
95. Draft animals
99. Kind of file or polish
100. First name in mysteries
101. Fret
103. Saratoga or Hot Springs
104. Stan, to Ollie
105. Bottom line
106. July juice
107. Counterpart of Mme.
108. Spanish uncle

57 Doing Things By Judson Trent

Having no part of the sedentary life.

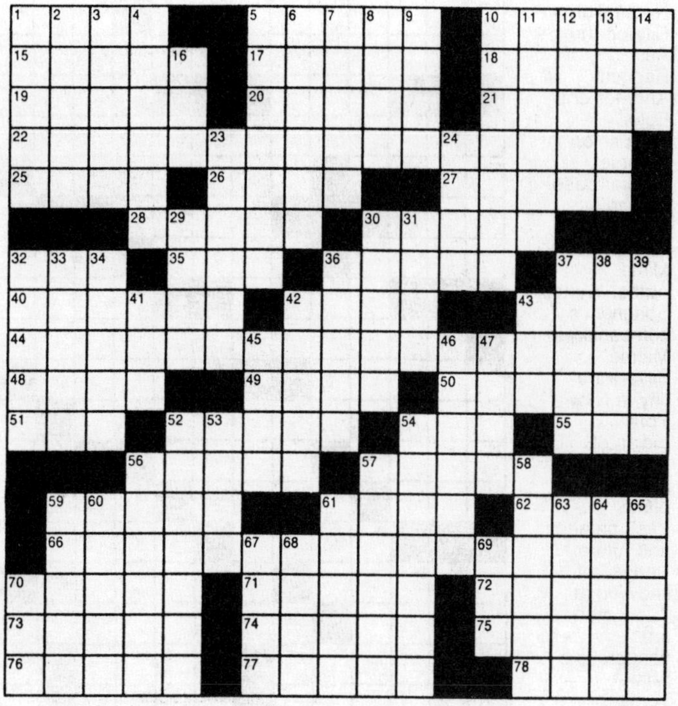

ACROSS

1. Sheik, usually
5. Polio pioneer
10. Spanish homes
15. Olympic gold
17. Track winner's share
18. Eye: Prefix
19. "Fidelio," for one
20. Blacks, for Byron
21. Simon and Diamond
22. Call on the carpet
25. "I got ___ asked for"
26. Henry James biographer
27. Man's counterpart
28. Shrewd
30. Junta
32. G.I. address
35. Skimmer
36. Place of confusion
37. Uzbekistan or Kirgizia: Abbr.
40. Having more dampness
42. Caen's river
43. Comics' Kett
44. Cater to
48. Robt. ___
49. Lab burner
50. Segal or Abbott
51. ___ Führer
52. Light helmet
54. Female ruff
55. Humorist Bill
56. Campaign tactic
57. Extends credit
59. Awry, in Scotland
61. Kind of paper
62. She, in Salerno
66. Toast
70. Dolphins' home
71. Asian antelope
72. Lagoon feature
73. Irish patriot
74. Nose part
75. Mysterious
76. Untidy
77. Fixed potatoes
78. "Never ___ sentence with . . ."

DOWN

1. Early Jewish scholar
2. Turn away
3. "It's ___!" (Shake!)
4. Poetic
5. Drove like a jehu
6. Actor C. ___ Smith
7. Cook chops
8. "Money ___ object"
9. Set of tables
10. Cache
11. Sedative compound
12. Spades, clubs, etc.
13. Mete
14. Mayday
16. Lang. for Brutus
23. Mass exodus
24. Cleric's title
29. Sheltered
30. Large garden plant
31. Retired
32. Made a postscript
33. Colonial artist
34. Proprietor
36. Borough of London
37. Austere
38. Cigar for a cowpoke
39. Indian princess
41. Bar rocks
42. "Ring of Bright Waters" pet
43. Environmental prefix
45. Melodic subject
46. Schedule
47. Lack
52. Convenience
53. Fume
54. Replenished
56. Mucks
57. Punjab city
58. High-backed bench
59. Stop on ___
60. Metric weights
61. Glacial pinnacle
63. Clipped
64. Kind of geometry
65. Have ___ in one's ear
67. Romanov title
68. Prefix for copter or port
69. New Guinea port
70. Hebrew letter

58 Dining Out By Mary Whitten

Samples that are available here and there.

ACROSS

1. Initials on the borscht front
5. ___ de plume
8. Vacation wheels, briefly
11. Animal
16. Comic actor Jacques
17. Jannings or Ludwig
19. "___ ever so humble . . ."
20. Fifth or Madison
22. Plenitude
24. Western Indian
25. He pays dollars for quarters
26. Course in Budapest
29. "___ go bragh"
30. Seine sight
31. Wear away by friction
32. Wood for rafts
33. Fixings in Barcelona
39. Sturgeon products
41. Sled
42. Prefixes for monsters
43. Enthralled
44. Bed for a visitor
47. Caravansary
48. Lad's love
49. Cousins of Mickey
50. Smear
51. Russian denial
53. Posted
54. Filling in Geneva
57. First place
59. Pat or Debbie
60. Gladden
61. Sonora nonedibles
67. Ambiances
68. Dr. Salk
69. Confederate
70. Day starter in Arles
73. Tomlin or Pons
75. Kind of porridge
79. Leaping lights
80. Get one's just due
81. Sensible
82. Golfer's concern
83. Slum denizen
84. Like Telly Savalas
85. Certain NASA flights
88. City on the Aar
89. Raggedy Ann, for one
90. Eggs' companion in Toronto
92. Rubber base
95. African ruminants
97. Fair and Milne
98. Author Wister
99. Spaghetti's companion in Malmö
106. Silverware city in New York
108. Indian of Canada
109. Material for plates
110. Past, present and future
111. Ranges of knowledge
112. "___ men are dangerous": Shak.
113. Turner or Louise
114. Hairdressers, at times
115. J.F.K. sight
116. Bashful
117. It's found between risers

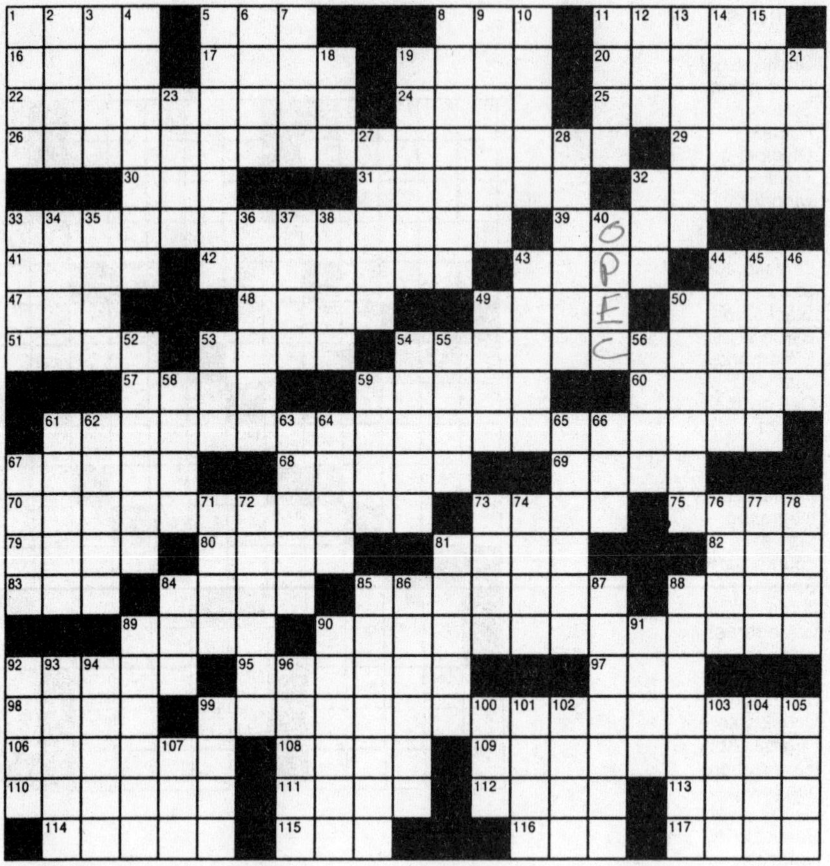

DOWN

1. Deseret, today
2. Elephant Boy of old films
3. Daze
4. Unanswered-phone activity
5. Closest
6. Atlanta arena
7. Isinglass
8. Emulates a boomerang
9. Stringed instruments
10. Lieu
11. Steam or sitz
12. Second person
13. Trojan hero
14. Wolf's warning
15. African city
18. Author Deighton
19. Error
21. Lab burner
23. Surrealist painter
27. Paces
28. Ice pinnacles
32. Put a fin on a nose
33. Rotate
34. Piddling
35. Boleyn or Bancroft
36. Rubinstein of cosmetics
37. Mediterranean port
38. Boss Tweed's twitter
40. Oil cartel
43. Up
44. Scrub
45. Evicts
46. Brooklyn novel subject
49. Skirt type
50. Fastens a sail rope
52. Natives of Lubbock
53. Dry, as wine
54. Body: Prefix
55. Thrashes
56. Command for Fido
58. Kind of jockey
59. Hot cross ___
61. Wine cup substance of old Rome
62. Upright
63. One of the Vanir
64. Collins or Crawford
65. Source of lead
66. Travelling Nellie
67. From a distance
71. Make sound
72. Candle ingredient
73. Praise
74. Cross inscription
76. Guinness or Waugh
77. Painter Joan
78. Quaker State name
81. Hide away
84. Emulate Ali
85. Wise
86. Drink flavorings
87. Spasmodic
88. Volcanic rocks
89. Lor or Levertov
90. Trained groups
91. Athlete Didrikson Zaharias
92. Booty
93. Bearded, as wheat
94. Partner of weeny
96. Coarse herbs, in England
99. Talk back
100. They seek AWOL's
101. Ending for gas or beaut
102. Like some enemies
103. Café au ___
104. Kind of drive
105. Imperative finger action
107. ___ Bingle (Crosby)

59 This and That By John Hales

With some tonsorial doings in the fare.

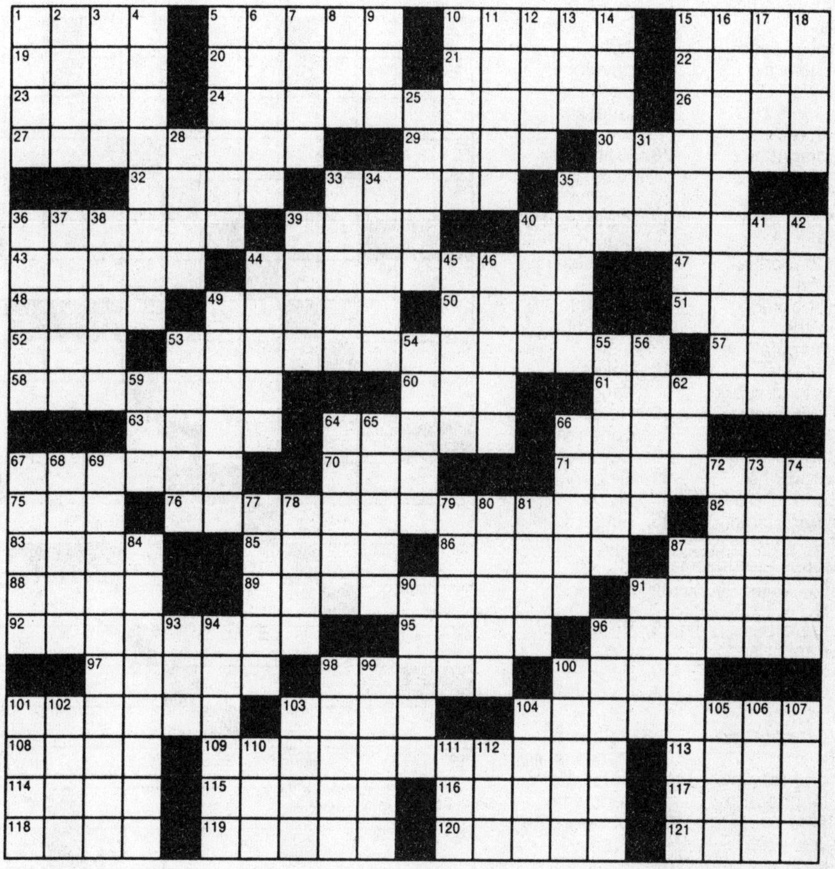

ACROSS

1. Involuntary inhalation
5. Tapioca base
10. Less corrupt
15. Apothecary: Abbr.
19. Kett of the comics
20. Soap substitute
21. "Manon," for one
22. Bacteriologist's wire
23. Catchall abbr.
24. Gardener's activity
26. Overstuff
27. Birthday-party cry
29. ___ off (angry)
30. Surpassed
32. "___ we got fun?"
33. Explosion
35. Latin gold
36. Speculate
39. Galway Bay islands
40. Something causing change
43. ___ sides (surrounded)
44. Somewhat superior to
47. Son of Rebekah
48. Enjoy the cuisine
49. Type of acid
50. "And ___ man hath power . . ."
51. Sandpiper
52. W.W. II theater
53. Engage in a brawl
57. Miss Arden
58. Sauce ___ (fish dressing)
60. Word with plane or borne
61. Tidal bores
63. Getting ___ years
64. Andrea del ___
66. Northern capital
67. Mires
70. Explosive stuff
71. ___-faire
75. "High ___"
76. Maugham novel
82. Peer Gynt's mother
83. Kind of glass or hand
85. Earth goddess
86. Grotesque
87. Qualifying words
88. Common Latin verb
89. Mad Hatter's tea partner
91. Allegorical card
92. Discussed anew
95. Poetic prepositions
96. Kind of bed covering
97. Person with lines
98. Lab microscope subjects
100. Bamako's country
101. Mixed-nuts ingredient
103. Medieval ballads
104. Certain Frenchman
108. "___ I didn't know"
109. American jurist: 1872–1961
113. Part of Sulla's wardrobe
114. Island near Venice
115. Verse form for Horace
116. "It tolls for thee" poet
117. Camelot lady
118. River in Bohemia
119. Early ___
120. Ravi's guitar
121. "It ___ a hundred years . . ." (Holmes's shay)

DOWN

1. Relatives of goshes
2. Westernmost bit of the U.S.A.
3. Marshal's symbol
4. Tangible
5. Brazilian timber tree
6. "It's ___ unusual day"
7. Something less than a gallop
8. Antiquity
9. Prefix with diem or capita
10. Attitudes
11. Win against the odds
12. Wallace of the silents
13. Raptorial sea bird
14. Meat dish
15. Attitudes
16. Private-school principal
17. Italian wine center
18. Papyrus, for one
25. Babylonian hero
28. Rivulet
31. Yorkshire river
33. Spread a rumor
34. Door fastening
35. Shake like ___
36. Skirt insert
37. Miss Gillette
38. Stately home
39. Teen-ager's woe
40. Declare
41. Ingenuous
42. London underground lines
44. Pulitzer poet Conrad
45. Suit
46. City of Bolivia
49. Church community
53. Labor's counterpart: Abbr.
54. Give an ___ (listen)
55. Gil Blas creator
56. Collegian from New Haven
59. Overly
62. Hawk variety, for short
64. Single step
65. Aussie soldier
66. Song of yesteryear
67. Heavens
68. Big-racked animal
69. Dismiss curtly
72. Lizard: Prefix
73. Prohibit, by law
74. Piquant
77. Kind of wheat
78. Electric catfish
79. Stitch anew
80. Roebuck's partner
81. Sins
84. Try to touch
87. Handrail
90. Word with hair or feathers
91. Anklebones
93. Fr. holy woman
94. Ridiculous blunder
96. Textile worker
98. Avant-___
99. Indefinite one: Ger.
100. Heavenly fare
101. Colombian city
102. Sale provision
103. Land on the Mekong
104. React to push-ups
105. One of the Inner Hebrides
106. Opposed to, in Dogpatch
107. Nothing, to a Spaniard
110. Roof ornament
111. Periodontist's deg.
112. ___ polloi

60 Mergers By Louis Baron

Appropriate pairings for certain people.

ACROSS

1. Noncommittal
5. Hackneyed
10. Whom a Lowell speaks to
15. Retired
19. Emanation
20. "Maria ___": 1933 song
21. Wide open
22. Bach's "Chaconne" is one
23. Hot combo on the "Dracula" set
26. Rail rider
27. Historic years
28. Thun's river
29. Circle or tube
30. Bad-tempered one
32. Sung or Ming
34. Where oinks are heard
35. Moses' camp after crossing the Red Sea
36. ___ off
37. Shankar's instrument
38. Oilable servants
41. Vestment for Eli
44. Song for Blanche and David
46. Tuck's pal
47. Skyrocket
48. Sir, in Penang
49. Alternative in Bonn
50. Part farthest from the center
51. Ad ___ (to the point)
52. "Spartacus" prefers blondes
56. Heat, to Ovid
57. Avenue of the ___, in N.Y.C.
59. Cuprites
60. Like a glossy fabric
61. Batman's sidekick
62. Talk foolishly
63. Kierkegaard
64. Cottage
66. Air: Prefix
67. Social and Christian
70. Cruise queen
71. The Johnny & Grant Co. sales policy
74. Orel's river
75. Auto developer
76. Cork port
77. Guesses awry
78. Treble or bass
79. Have a bite
80. Zane-y duo, starring Ben
84. Schnitzler's "La ___"
85. Resettler
87. Assembly halls
88. Loki's daughter
89. Heathen's opposite
90. Complete
91. Diogenes prop
95. Singer Leslie
97. Halloween choice
98. Havoc or Allyson
99. Be an alibi pro
100. Bank
101. Pair of arty girl-watchers
105. Medicinal lily
106. Defalcator's doomsday
107. Elbow in the ribs
108. Retained
109. Black or back
110. Cloister-hearth chronicler
111. Kind of wool or guitar
112. Zero toppers

DOWN

1. Did a pre-heist job
2. Singing Texan
3. Complain
4. Sherpa's ox
5. Call down
6. Winged
7. Rare goose
8. Plus
9. Corsair Jean
10. Heavyweight Primo
11. Saint martyred at 13
12. Boxer Max
13. Goddess of plenty
14. Will-ful one
15. Hindu hermitage
16. Shirley plays Mary Todd
17. Isle in a palindrome
18. Room shutter
24. Let up
25. Eastern Christian
31. Lined up
33. Power yielder
34. Palio festival city
35. Hinnies' cousins
37. Smacks
38. ___ Elephant Park of Africa
39. Tiger-lion hybrid
40. Mime's art
41. Poet Pound
42. "Trees," for one
43. Two birds that deliver
44. Lazy or black-eyed
45. Snare
48. Understood
50. Corroded
52. Moral ___
53. Part of NNW
54. Aeschylus's forte
55. Spill some beans
56. Actor Harry
58. Parts
60. Before nuits
62. Old Turkish title
63. Causing goose pimples
64. Getting warmer
65. Seed scar
67. Landslide stones
68. Scraped by
69. Sound's partner
71. Have weight
72. Co-perpetrate
73. Succeed as a Pied Piper
76. Marxian premise
78. Early revolver
80. Fill to the
81. Double-negative girl
82. Of a noble rank
83. Wheat proteins
84. Revivify
86. Adapted for
88. "Water Music" composer
90. Grizzly bear, for one
91. Duelist's ploy
92. "Lady of the Lake" heroine
93. Updated musket
94. Has to have
95. State with a salty lake
96. Desert lizard
97. River in Sweden
98. Green necklace material
102. Cry's partner
103. Stale routine
104. Cry of surprise

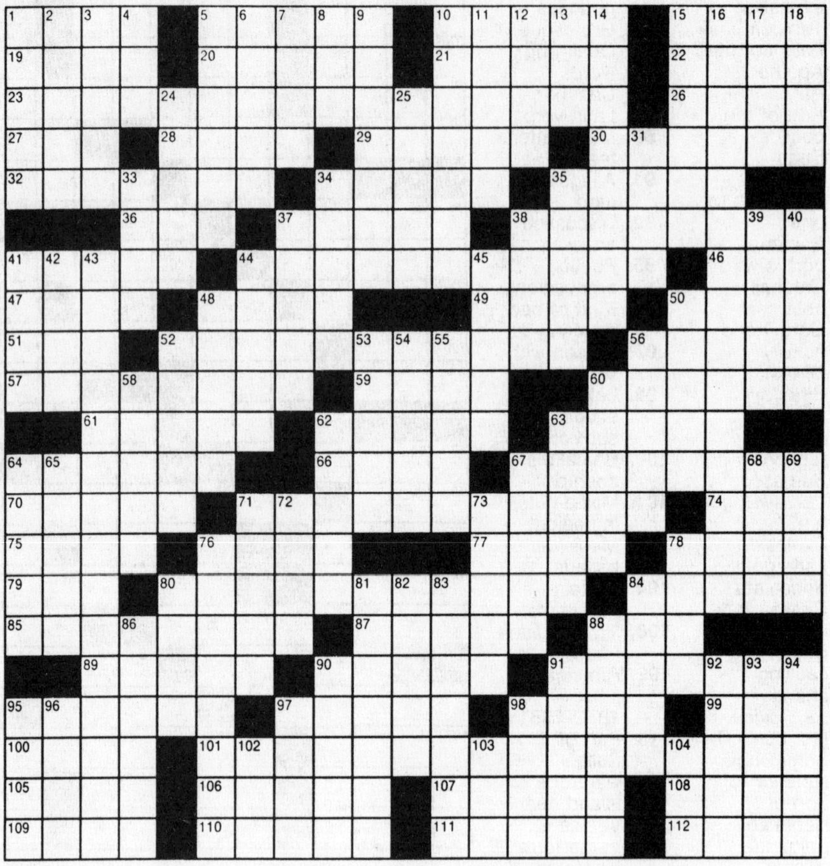

61 Echoes By Barry Tunick

Getting into the sound of things.

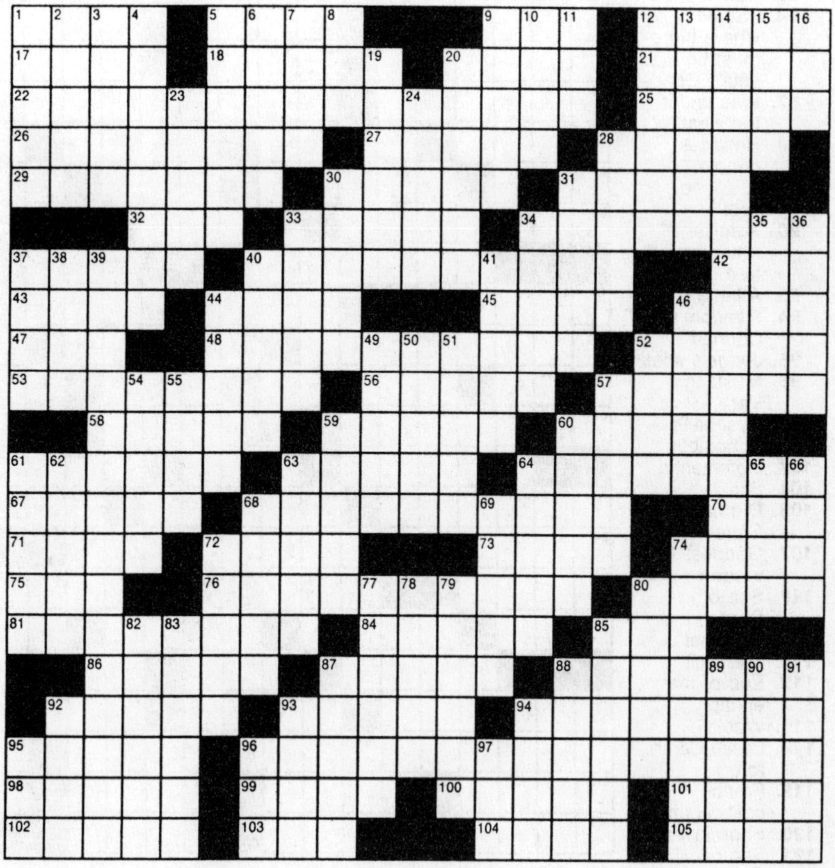

ACROSS

1. European coal region
5. Tiff
9. Board companion
12. Pasadena float components
17. "It was him ___!"
18. Books of Moses
20. Choir member
21. Conceder's cry
22. Appraise gold?
25. Micah's follower
26. Billet-doux
27. U. S. Grant's rival
28. "The Overcoat" writer
29. Attacks
30. Money, to Manuel
31. Heartless
32. City-hall pro
33. Writer Anya
34. Draw out
37. Steps
40. C.I.A. or K.G.B.?
42. Louis XIV was one
43. Misplays
44. Observed
45. Seine tributary
46. Invitation initials
47. ___ doggo (hide)
48. Runt?
52. Fashions
53. Kind of laundry
56. Get up
57. Computer feature
58. Takes a stab at
59. Gush out
60. Castro
61. Salad-oil holders
63. Act part
64. Comforted
67. Long-eared animals
68. Little tipple?
70. Exist
71. Persons
72. Substance
73. Classified abbrs.
74. Stable stall
75. Place
76. Equator?
80. Joins the also-rans
81. Watch an event
84. Sea birds
85. Card player's cry
86. Alda and namesakes
87. Special-interest groups
88. Eyelash darkener
92. Bouquet
93. Latin dance
94. O'Hare tenants
95. Couturier Marc
96. Teases hair?
98. Ecole attender
99. Meager
100. Cosmetician Lauder
101. Facility
102. Done in by a bull
103. Grass bristle
104. Separate
105. Western Indians

DOWN

1. Volcanic crater rim
2. Regions
3. Gather
4. Molds anew
5. Ramble
6. Masters and Jonson, e.g.
7. Commedia dell'___
8. Swabbie
9. Wabash or St. Louis moods
10. French I verb
11. John or Jane
12. Lapse
13. Old catapult
14. College tuitions?
15. Jewish month
16. Relig. school
19. To this document
20. "___ as you're up . . ."
23. Freshwater mussels
24. Fabulous writer
28. Fumble about
30. Menials
31. Audacity
33. Skulk
34. Balance
35. Spy's necessity
36. Fuddled
37. Riches
38. Seed appendage
39. Lion tamer?
40. Prognosticators
41. Use the oven
44. Blackthorns
46. Young Montague
49. Slender candle
50. Impact
51. Of De Valera's land
52. T-shirt sizes
54. Tamarack and tamarind
55. Sanity
57. Coins coins
59. Ivanhoe's creator
60. One of the firths
61. Karate moves
62. Accumulated, as a bill
63. Portion
64. Egyptian Christians
65. Buffalo's county
66. Socialist leader
68. Does ushering
69. Nostrils
72. Intended
74. More succinct
77. "Catch-22" writer
78. Dozen dozen
79. "___ you should ask"
80. Cotton thread
82. Split
83. Made leather
85. Poet's traditional room
87. Nobleman
88. Bishop's headdress
89. Handles
90. Noted shortstop
91. Fools
92. Aria, e.g.
93. Put away
94. "Thin Man" pet
95. Implore
96. Mineral spring
97. Sixth sense

62 Observation By Wilson McBeath

Reflection on the alternatives of ownership.

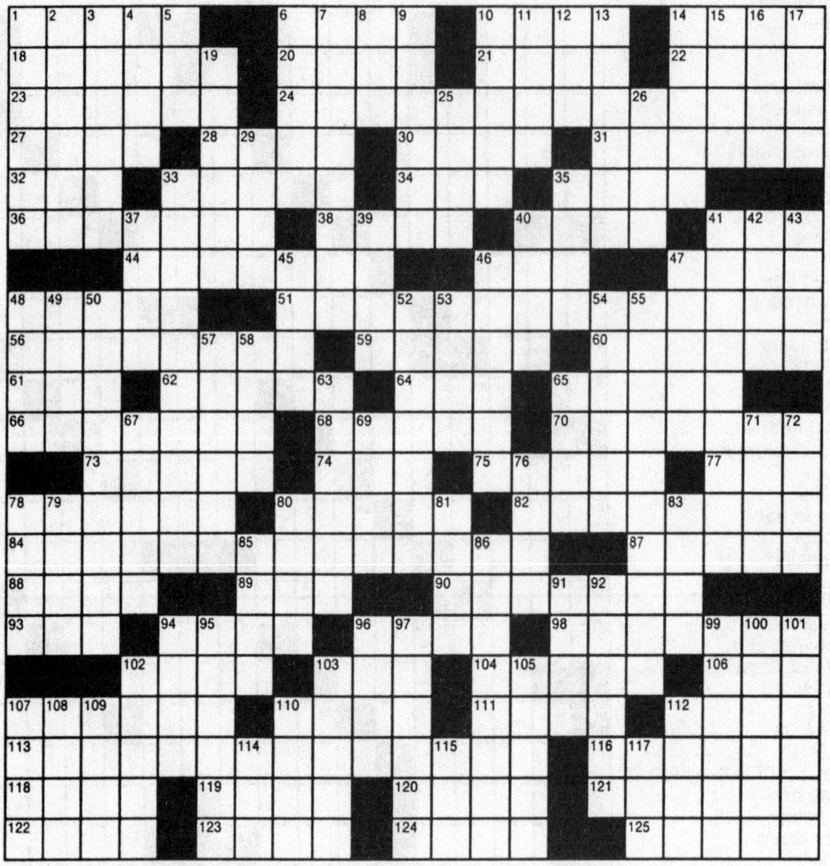

ACROSS

1. Cavalry sword
6. Israel's Eban
10. It may be in one, in golf
14. Curve
18. Of a one-celled animal
20. Unmixed
21. Seed covering
22. Culture medium
23. Wisconsin city
24. Start of an old epitaph
27. ___ for one's money
28. Scottish hillside
30. And others: Lat.
31. Nullified
32. L.A. player
33. Warning
34. Knight's title
35. Kind of ray
36. Egg white
38. Mel's family
40. Rainstorm in Hawaii
41. Pronoun
44. Having left a will
46. Poetic word
47. Hurried
48. Autumn perennial
51. Second part of the epitaph
56. Napoleon was one
59. Thanks, to Pierre
60. Main thorough-fare
61. Be sorry
62. "Thou ___ not then be false to . . ."
64. Aviation org.
65. "Robin ___"
66. Smudge on a typesheet
68. Goose genus
70. Fight to the ___ (Helsinki version)
73. Examina-tions
74. Formerly named
75. Great effort
77. French business org.
78. Reverence
80. Discharge
82. Star-shaped
84. "Some-where there must be ___ soul": Cory
87. Was under the weather
88. Religious people
89. "___ no use!"
90. Tropical American tree
93. Atlanta's time
94. Filmdom's Conried
96. Judge's seat
98. Mustang: Var.
102. Baseball's Schoolboy
103. Detrimental
104. Slip
106. Drama by Capek
107. Goddess of wisdom
110. Sea off Borneo
111. Fastener
112. Transmit
113. End of the epitaph
116. Woolly
118. Leslie Caron role
119. French political unit
120. Shoe insert
121. Sea duck
122. Snick's partner
123. What Hubbard's dog had
124. Approved models: Abbr.
125. Pitchers

DOWN

1. Winged fruit of the elm
2. Having no principles
3. Stupefy
4. Black
5. It precedes a pair of Tins
6. Sadat
7. Monstrous creature
8. Cote sound
9. Certify
10. Horrible cartoon Viking
11. Viva voce
12. Miss Ullmann
13. XI
14. Coastal state of Brazil
15. Mild oath
16. Church area
17. ___ Scott
19. Heavy ropes
25. Suffix for tonsil
26. Whit
29. Bombast
33. City near Plains
35. Femur, for one
37. Shoshonean Indians
39. Harnessed animals
40. Poilu's cap
41. Globular
42. Listen
43. Singer Nelson
45. Barley beards
46. Steep slope
47. Union job action
48. Israeli port
49. Tart
50. Osteopath's offering
52. Most taut
53. Dies ___
54. Singer Conner
55. International conference worker
57. Drayed
58. French donkeys
63. Sinuous dances
65. Throw ___ (become angry)
67. Layers of ore
69. Poetic contraction
71. Place
72. Pay attention
76. Part of Y.M.C.A.
78. Sharpen
79. Burden
80. Newts
81. Holier-___-thou
83. Member of a service club
85. German article
86. Enraged
91. Dugout shelter
92. Folklore dwarfs
94. "___ soit qui . . ."
95. Arouse
96. Indonesian island
97. Grown-ups
99. Originate
100. Orion was one
101. Directs
102. Bind again
103. Isolated hill
105. Values
107. Cobblers' tools
108. Lank
109. Robust
110. Airplane wing length
112. Kind of job
114. Ike's command
115. Scrap
117. Expert

63 Broadway By Norma Steinberg

Shows that might have had other names.

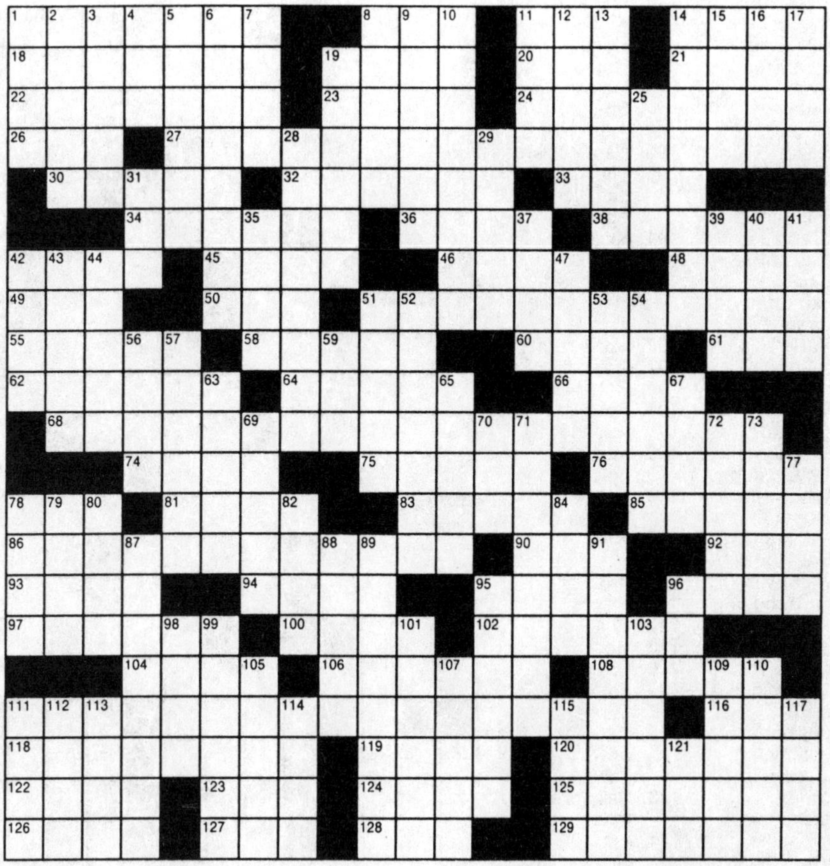

ACROSS

1. Take back
8. Churchill's "few"
11. Wee, to a Glaswegian
14. Secure
18. Put in order
19. London gallery
20. Carson
21. Stravinsky
22. Avert
23. Lulu
24. Kind of calculus
26. Asian holiday
27. "Amadeus"
30. Strong cotton
32. Pay attention
33. Puppy sound
34. Eaves dropping?
36. Lop off, in Scotland
38. Conveying nervous impulses
42. Univ. course
45. Entre ___
46. Japanese base of W.W. II
48. Cain's kin
49. A Reiner
50. Hebrew letter
51. "Oklahoma!"
55. Lends an underhand
58. Seas' number
60. Café additive
61. Moo
62. Nabokov girl
64. Crown
66. Carter's predecessor
68. "Of Mice and Men"
74. Festive
75. Roman dictator
76. Star, in Arles
78. Kind of cap
81. ___-winded
83. Purposeful
85. Word before head or mint
86. "Oliver"
90. Our, for Pierre
92. Navy rank
93. Walt Kelly creature
94. Section of London or N.Y.C.
95. Native of Aberdeen
96. Eleanor's successor
97. Big name in boxing in 1978
100. Gee's relative
102. Spanish sword city
104. Within: Prefix
106. Teaching devices
108. Pub orders
111. "Cats"
116. Part of a jug
118. Native Alaskan
119. Counterfeit: Abbr.
120. Part of the Capitol
122. Actor Guinness
123. ___-picking (carping)
124. Old-timers
125. Estimate
126. Unconsidered
127. Juan's wife
128. Noun ending
129. Municipal arteries

DOWN

1. Carried away
2. Goofed
3. Minotaur's homeland
4. Washroom, for short
5. Thin-blooded
6. Shame
7. City on the Moselle
8. Carries on
9. Alamogordo events
10. Becomes wine
11. Ice hazard
12. Mork's friend
13. English P.M.: 1945–51
14. Obvious clue
15. Indian tourist spot
16. Suds
17. Mystery writer Gardner
19. Certain American colonists
25. Snaky creatures
28. Suggest indirectly
29. Like some gases
31. Famous diarist
35. Sounds from a cote
37. Burr-Hamilton event
39. New or raw
40. "Tell ___ the Marines"
41. ___ the scenery
42. Of a time period
43. Computer talk
44. Notations in manuscripts
47. Brown wrapping paper
51. Frays
52. Coming
53. Daughter of Tantalus
54. Moves like a majorette
56. Ringing sound
57. ___ the spotlight
59. Energy
63. Either a success or ___
65. Less inept
67. Kind of cloth or kick
69. Indian nobles
70. Old measure of cloth
71. Garb for Columbo
72. Your brother's daughter
73. Strikes
77. Cupid
78. Cookbook abbr.
79. On
80. Word in an O. Henry title
82. Booze on board
84. Aloof
87. Paragon
88. Rose's drawback
89. Precipitate decline
91. Lives it up
95. Clown props
96. Before appétit or voyage
98. Make a sweater
99. Dry-cleaning problems
101. Spillane hero
103. Calorie counter
105. Walking ___
107. Nonclergy
109. High-strung
110. Egyptian statesman
111. TV talk-show host
112. Miss Fitzgerald
113. Female ruffs
114. Pillar
115. Work units
117. Charlie Brown's expletive
121. Function

64 Uptight By Bernard Meren

Sometimes one has to give vent to exasperation.

ACROSS

1. An ogee is one
5. Fabric named for a French town
11. Part of a semi
14. Ski lift
18. Host to Goldilocks
19. Self-contradiction
20. Thai native
21. Medley
22. Like an iron horse
24. Water
26. Cul-de-____
27. It gives a hoot
28. Beverage
29. Bacchante
30. René's floor
32. Abbr. on a bargain-clothing label
35. Like Rome when Nero got through
39. Dry
40. Daub
42. Tennis unit
43. Cenozoic is one
44. Afternoon break in London
46. One of Hitchcock's thirty-nine
48. Artie
51. Campus org.
52. Fortes, with 58 Across
55. "____ Didn't Care"
56. Antitoxins
57. Man or Wight
58. See 52 Across
59. Meat cuts
61. What Murphy's law expects
63. Word with tube or circle
64. Poetry form
65. Cut off
69. Café server
70. Essential being
71. Raines or Logan
73. Pacifists
74. Luxe
76. Spur parts
78. First president of Germany
79. Nebraska Indians
80. Catches flies
81. Endless, to poets
82. Kind of ray
85. Repute
87. Noted iceman of Boston
88. Alef or zed
89. Came down
90. This goose can "lei" eggs
91. Kind of pupil
93. Cuckoo
94. Molasses juice with a zing
95. Curvy turn
97. Tizzies
99. Otherwise
103. Aped a volcano
109. Musical notes
110. Greek theater of yore
111. Place for Aries and Pisces
112. Bad
114. Goof
116. Upward: Prefix
117. Cupid
119. Like an overblown balloon
123. Sally of the fans
124. Auto pioneer's monogram
125. Least taxing
126. Ko-Ko's weapon
127. Minor card
128. Join the service: Abbr.
129. Ancient ascetic
130. Fast jets

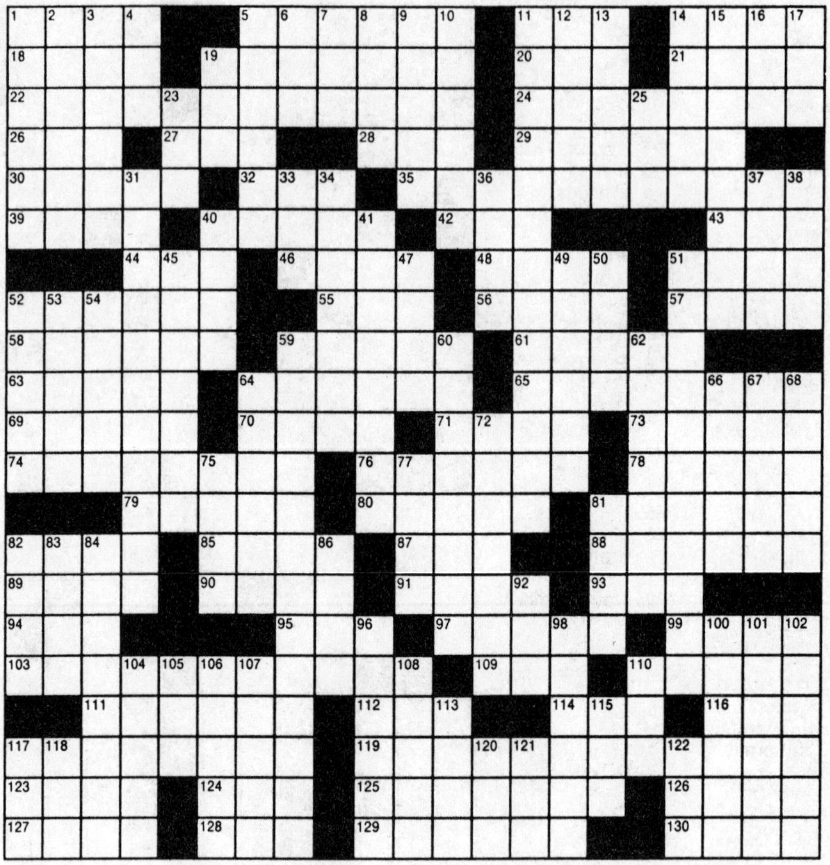

DOWN

1. Demeans
2. Tell
3. Clawlike spur
4. Many mins.
5. Semitic gods
6. The law's is long
7. "Norma ____"
8. Norse saga
9. Cheese from Holland
10. Ousts
11. What Spiderman can do best
12. City west of Zurich
13. Corn pest
14. Forum wear
15. Vesicles
16. Small island
17. Baseball's Preacher ____
19. Worshiper's spot
23. Word with hold or nail
25. Lodging place
31. Latch on to somebody's capra
33. Matter, in law
34. G.I. "C" meals
36. Minus
37. Caspian feeder
38. Cocktail-cracker spread
40. Droops
41. OPEC middlemen
45. Petition
47. Lonesome tree
49. Bouquets
50. Deform
51. Passed the prenuptial health test
52. Malice
53. Of musical quality
54. Before tumble dry
59. Misplaces the air conditioner
60. James and Donald Ogden
62. Czech range
64. Quit the Union
66. Ward off
67. Coat with tin and lead
68. Acid compound
72. French composer Michel
75. "Darkness at ____"
77. Cries of discovery
81. High notes
82. Fishhook feature
83. Jewish month
84. One of four between N.Y. and L.A.
86. Remainder
92. Dolores Del ____
96. Evening party
98. Deadly fly
100. Becomes educated
101. Gloria Swanson's boulevard
102. Does the ham
104. Loquacious
105. Pindar's thing
106. Saltpetre
107. Ingested
108. Bargains in the courtroom
110. Sphere
113. Bonnie one
115. Balderdash
117. Canvas product
118. Spoil
120. One of a pair at Atlantic City
121. Longing
122. Naval initials

65 Duality By Don Nardizzi

Getting two definitions for the price of one.

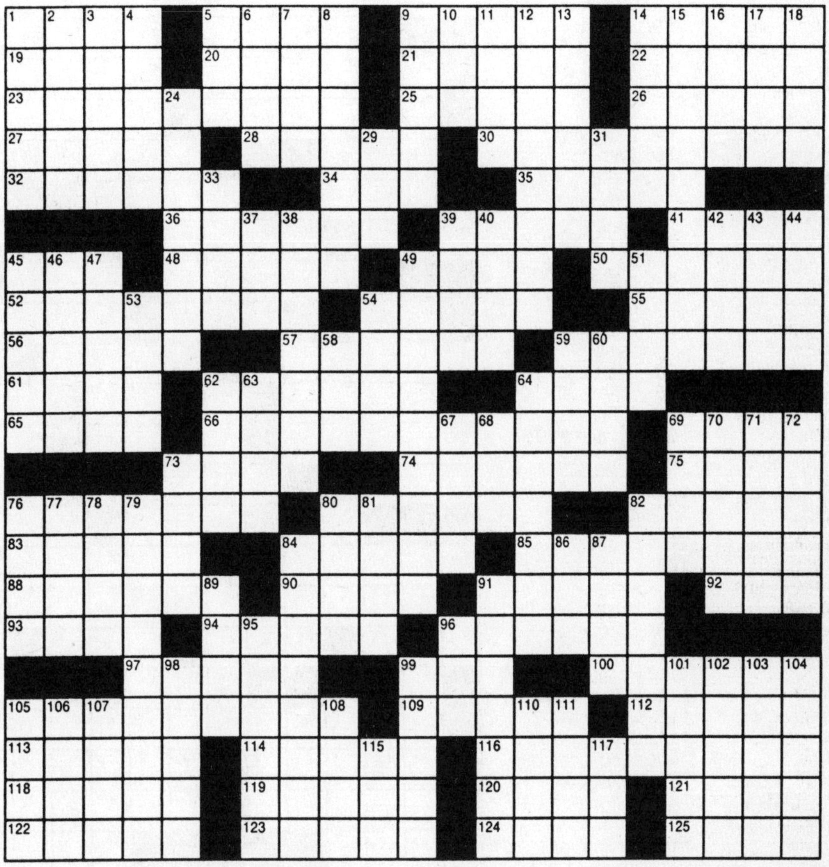

ACROSS

1. Tibetan monk
5. Relative of a gulp
9. Subject for Asimov
14. Microscopic animal
19. Three-banded armadillo
20. Pilaster
21. Site of La Scala
22. Consumer advocate
23. Movie star or Eastern city
25. Concerning
26. Star of "Ninotchka"
27. Did stage work
28. Stone chip
30. Princesses or Pacific islands
32. Veteran sailor
34. Sal of song
35. One of a friendly pair
36. Musical movements
39. Pilfer
41. First garden man
45. Ship's dir.
48. Keep an ___ things (look after)
49. Old Roman markets
50. Small lump
52. Spanish red or state
54. Half a German spa
55. Of the kidneys
56. A.k.a.
57. Gray of the dissolute portrait
59. Drinks after drinks
61. King Cole and Turner
62. Kind of diplomacy
64. Racegoer's vantage point
65. Waste allowance
66. Vietnam War figures
69. Room in a hacienda
73. Deneb, e.g.
74. Poplars
75. Elbe tributary
76. Stray from the subject
80. Mackerel's relative
82. Violinmaker
83. Noun suffix
84. Eskimo garb
85. Early American Dare or state
88. Spanish snowfall or state
90. Barbecue items
91. Jason's lover
92. Town near Liège
93. "O, my Luve is like ___ . . ."
94. Highlanders
96. Type of hound
97. Steep slope
99. Luau staple
100. Some October people
105. Comedian or Dutch city
109. Proportion
112. Artless
113. City on the Seine
114. Wear away
116. Comic's valet or N.Y. city
118. On one's toes
119. Emperor and fiction detective
120. Inner: Prefix
121. Chinese dynasty
122. Cowboy's need
123. Nicholas and Peter
124. Coal basin of Europe
125. In ___ (actual)

DOWN

1. Singing syllables
2. Speedily
3. Kind of ray
4. Moved in a curved course
5. Tear or laughing
6. Social insects
7. "That's one small ___ for a man . . ."
8. Model of excellence
9. Fry or talk
10. Bowling-alley fixture
11. Guinness
12. Club or bacon
13. Decoy
14. Kind of Saxon
15. Pickling mixtures
16. Where 41 Across lived
17. ___ noire
18. Textile screw pines
24. Admiring lovers
29. ___ Palmas
31. Augury
33. "Maja" painter
37. Actor Sparks
38. Phone-booth scribbler
39. Kind of cracker
40. Small songbird
42. Sahara sight
43. Having wings
44. Blanc and Brooks
45. Meager
46. Energy or system
47. Typewriter type
49. Actor or Alaskan city
51. Using speech
53. Kiln
54. Fiber food
58. "Bravo!"
59. Roman statesman
60. Snaky sound
62. Female offspring: Abbr.
63. Old moneys of account, in England
64. Ousts
67. Famous pen name
68. Stool pigeon
69. Kind of trailer rig
70. Guam's capital
71. Admit
72. Melodies
73. Transmit
76. Actor Andrews
77. Road to Rome
78. Grant
79. Snazzy autos of yore
80. Dip out a boat
81. Poetic eyes
82. Like chalcedony
84. Gets ready
86. Ego sources
87. Unit of film
89. Seaweed
91. Restaurant V.I.P.'s
95. Fervent
96. Fur scarf
98. Literary patchwork
99. One of the estates
101. Moisten the roast
102. Hayworth and Moreno
103. European herb
104. Suit cloth
105. Russian sea
106. Ocean sunfish
107. Petitions
108. Italian finger game
110. New Rochelle college
111. Eight: Prefix
115. Flying insect
117. Opposite of vert.

66 Dark Shades By Ralph Beaman

Converting some white squares into the opposite should help.

ACROSS

1. Judo honor
6. Left: Prefix
10. Small type
14. River for Stephen Foster
15. Take in food
18. Part of a parapet
20. Gauzy paper
21. One using a trap
22. Handsome man
23. Kind of fountain
24. Thermal nuclear emission
26. Philadelphia suburb
28. Australian plant
29. G.I. address
30. Switch positions
31. Evergreen
32. Great Plains roamer
34. Hawaiian food
36. One ___ kind
39. Explorer Johnson
41. Bridal-wreath flower
43. ___ Lanka
44. Cocktail
46. Imitate
47. Rowboat fixture
48. Rice dish
50. Crummy
51. Prolific inventor
53. Remnant
55. Turn up one's ___
57. Nutty acts
58. What a door is when it isn't
59. Paving surfaces
60. Defame
63. Simpletons
64. Famed naturalist
65. In ___ (positioned)
66. Stupid one
68. Cont.
69. Marlo's father
70. Barber's target
71. Bears, mice and pigs of note
72. Pang of pain
74. House plant
75. Abundance
76. Edward Teach
79. French school
81. Morse dash
83. ___ de France
84. Munitions
86. With it
87. Cake coverings
89. Regret
90. Go to next page: Abbr.
91. Off one's rocker
92. Scottish terrier
93. Draft agcy.
96. Chemical suffix
98. Roman 2001
100. ___ blue (livid)
101. Kind of handed or headed
103. Crude type of syrup
108. Desertlike
109. Coronets
110. Souls
111. Pestilence
114. Matriculates
115. Caviar fish
116. Science of acoustics
117. Like good cheese or wine
118. Ending for young or old
119. "___-Told Tales"

DOWN

1. Treacherous female
2. ___ metabolism
3. Nav. officer
4. Rumanian coin
5. Palmer's peg
6. Port on the Tagus
7. Pester
8. Proper British oath
9. Part of VHF
10. Prefix for type or zoan
11. Big Ten school
12. Circus-poster word
13. Soon
14. Greek promenades
16. Turkish inn
17. Part, backward
18. Spring month in Paris
19. Watchdog agcy.
23. Sneaky Northern apple
24. Ghetto school, sometimes
25. What to show a rude guest
27. There, to Caesar
28. Turkey's northern border
33. What some athletes pump
34. Prissy person
35. Black gold
37. Exhalations
38. Cruising
40. "Have you ___ wool?"
42. Cuban coins
43. Gyroscope pioneer
44. Algonquians
45. Had a portrait painted
46. French leave
49. Upas arrow poison
51. Where this word is
52. Ending for verb or nod
54. U.S. explorer Paul
56. Goad
58. To ___ (all)
59. Family's disgrace
60. Ornamental tree
61. Act in excess
62. Cheat on a diet
66. Jeanne d'Arc, e.g.
67. Gourmet Claiborne
69. Common contraction
72. Light color
73. ___ up (conclude)
74. Put coins in a juke box
75. Revolve noisily
76. ___ white (all out, either way)
77. Causing injuries
78. Having no teeth
80. Half a dance
82. Sulfuric or amino
85. Pennsylvania is one: Abbr.
88. Compass dir.
91. Pooh's creator
92. Kind of salad
94. Piggeries
95. A Chaplin
97. Made a gaffe
99. Ancient part of Jordan
100. Flammable Western weed
102. Black ___ (sorcery)
103. Beverage
104. Swiss river
105. Letter addenda: Abbr.
106. Bothers
107. Obscenity
111. Coast time initials
112. Relative of a moo
113. Black cuckoo

67 Table-Hopping By Calista Luminati

And coming up with some suitable fare.

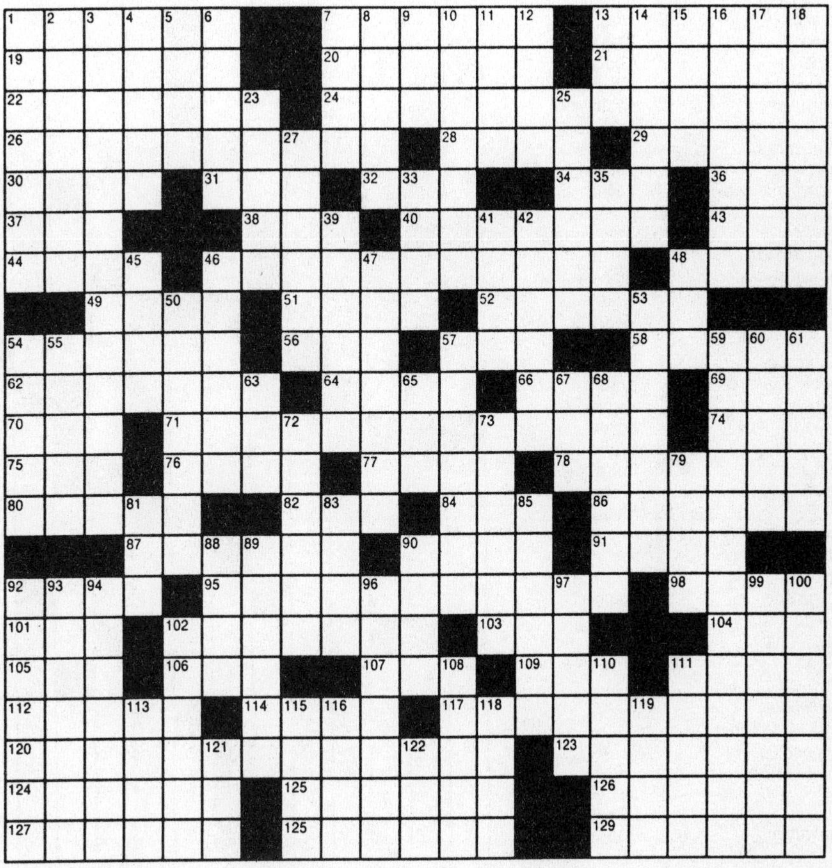

ACROSS

1. Truman and Myerson
7. Cowboys' home
13. Sunday meal, often
19. Charm
20. Plaza Hotel girl
21. Do shoe repairing
22. Wined and dined
24. Consummate consumer of TV
26. Carrier of easy money
28. Latin-class word
29. Kind of boat or land
30. Yorkshire river
31. Vesicle
32. D.D.E. was one
34. Asian deer
36. Tickbird
37. Call ___ day
38. Parts of dols.
40. Lining for a beverage chest
43. Concorde
44. Nursemaid
46. Formal wear
48. Looks at
49. Spanish coin
51. Ancient chest
52. Chinese port on the Yalu
54. Hot as a ___
56. Resinous substance
57. Samovar
58. Staring bug-eyed
62. Debunked
64. Rebecca or Mae
66. U.S. bridge engineer
69. "___ my word!"
70. Roman 52
71. Insignificant
74. Greek letter
75. Opp. of an express
76. Sumerian water god
77. Nautical ropes
78. Tolled
80. Villain's grimace
82. Graduate degrees
84. Kind of bread or whisky
86. Blotters, e.g.
87. Light into
90. French salts
91. Ans. requested
92. Mast
95. All-purpose flavor
98. Dog utterances
101. Table scrap
102. Busy, to Anatole
103. Unit of conductance
104. "___ your heart out!"
105. Suffix for ring or book
106. ___ nouveau
107. Big ___ house
109. Business-letter abbr.
111. Short-billed rail
112. Word with sacro
114. Limitless times
117. Ragtime dance
120. Alger Hiss's undoing
123. Find ___ in a . . .
124. Urfa, formerly
125. Epic poem
126. One's livelihood
127. Remove surface defects
128. "The Song of the Lark" author
129. French department and river

DOWN

1. Shopper's quest
2. Title for a retired woman
3. Ingredients of little girls
4. Dred Scott, for one
5. Squirming
6. Marks on proofs
7. Tenth: Prefix
8. Get ___ with (be compatible)
9. Old card game
10. Compared
11. Sale condition
12. Bishoprics
13. Rel.
14. Tore apart
15. U.S.A. antagonist
16. Difficult
17. Purge
18. Loners
23. Harsh lawgiver of Athens
25. Slightest
27. Authentic
33. Sicilian volcano
35. Honolulu's location
39. Spread
41. Remotely
42. Finch
45. Reo or Edsel
46. Grave
47. Takes
48. "Which-came-first?" item
50. Loggers
53. Family of Gamal
54. Old parchments
55. King punished for his love of Hera
57. One who pronounces
59. Neatness exemplified
60. Tough problem
61. Bagnold and Markey
63. N. or S.
65. Oriental sauce
67. Perfect, to an astronaut
68. Tree: Prefix
72. Allowable maximums
73. Refuge
79. Roman historian
81. Corn unit
83. Can. province
85. Biblical heroine
88. Magi's guide
89. Novelist Jane
90. Mine passages: Abbr.
92. Single-hoofed
93. A Chopin specialty
94. Occasionally
96. Having trouble
97. Perfumery bean
99. Certain con on the loose
100. Old Greek coins
102. ___ wallop (hits hard)
108. ". . . poem lovely as ___"
110. Beatrice ___, subject of Shelley tragedy
111. Cubic measure
113. Church area
115. Petroleum cartel
116. California wine valley
118. Employer
119. Senate votes
121. "___ Woman"
122. Book of the N.T.

68 Plus Qualities By Lois Hillis

Some things on the black side of the ledger.

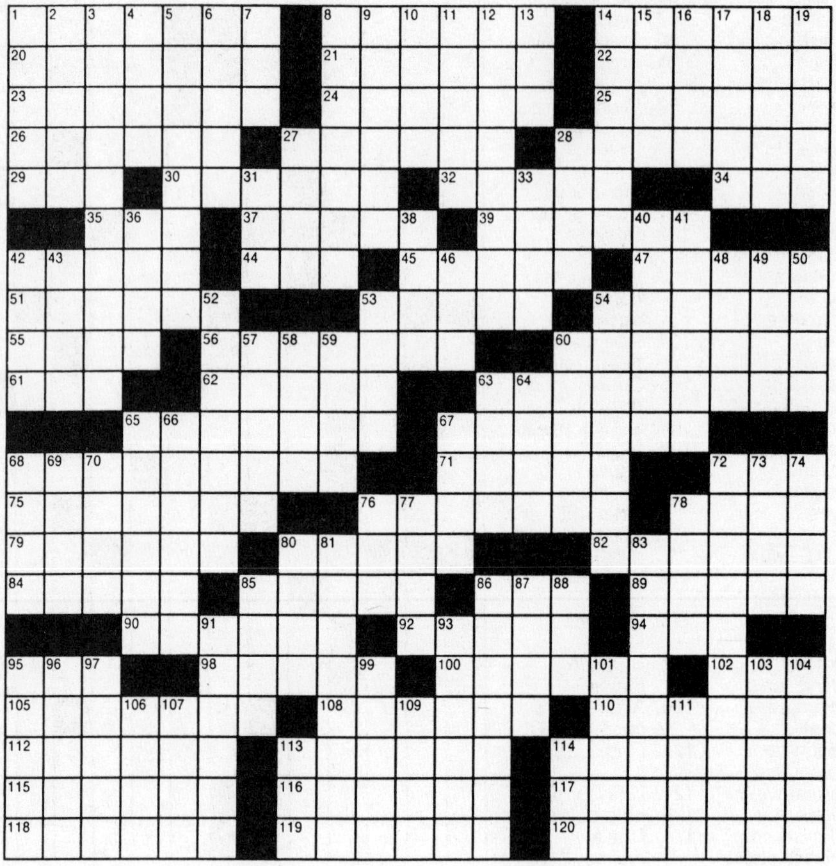

ACROSS

1. One of two words of pardon
8. Boxing periods
14. Companion of 1 Across
20. Chemical esters
21. Send abroad
22. Sherbet flavor
23. Degree of excellence
24. Slaggy lava
25. Admire
26. Joins
27. Railroad-track feature
28. Erased
29. Noises: Abbr.
30. "The only thing we have ___ is . . ."
32. Moves slowly
34. Chicken coop's neighbor
35. Warm plus
37. Like rural roads
39. Ejected
42. Permission
44. Writing on an urn
45. True grit
47. Get ___ review (win plaudits)
51. Set sail
53. Karate awards
54. Sluggards
55. Window ledge
56. Covered with suds
60. Signifies
61. Summer on the Loire
62. Skull bulge
63. Smoke for an Indian
65. Managed
67. Gun-loading implements
68. Rainbow's largess
71. Supplied weapons
72. Thing to do in Aspen
75. Fishing craft
76. Let go
78. Food fish
79. Eyelike
80. Motto
82. Take turns
84. Gratifies
85. Oat genus
86. Who "stoops to conquer"?
89. Peak of Colorado
90. Oxford scholarship
92. Mother of Perseus
94. Before
95. Like Alice's hatter
98. Nostrils
100. This many cents
102. Evil woman
105. Oscar Wilde's forte
108. Go back
110. Paste of boiled flour
112. Variety of computer
113. Without profit
114. Imitation silky fabric
115. Mislead
116. Perform for the class
117. Scam
118. Spring holiday
119. Eaten away
120. Puts in a box

DOWN

1. Center of attention
2. Charlie Chan actor
3. Pleasant to the appetite
4. Trot or gallop, e.g.
5. "___ be a good one"
6. Opposite of recto
7. Native of: Suffix
8. Change the time of
9. Farm wagon of yore
10. Atop
11. Oslo's land, in Oslo
12. Recovered from a lost weekend
13. Depot: Abbr.
14. Germany has a black one
15. Russian city
16. Hot fashion
17. Small insects
18. Heron
19. Bear or Roosevelt
27. Hatfield specialty
28. Secretary, for one
31. Opposite of to
33. Water and cap
36. White House room
38. River to the North Sea
40. Merited
41. Sags
42. ___ majesty
43. Give off
46. Work steadily
48. Counter: Prefix
49. Alben Barkley
50. Actual being
52. Jamie Farr role
53. Yield
54. One who deciphers
57. Words on each side of /
58. Money drawer
59. Worked the soil
60. Has the nerve
63. Shave off
64. Jane Austen novel
65. Ridiculous blunder
66. "Mirth is like ___ of lightning"
67. Chest sound
68. Instructions at page bottoms: Abbr.
69. Killer whale
70. Not slack
72. "___ and come out fighting"
73. "God Bless America" singer
74. 13th or 15th of some months
76. Fled
77. Mild oath
78. Move slightly
80. Declare
81. Rat on a sinking ship
83. Like Met performances
85. Garden inhabitant
86. Made a horsy sound
87. Stop
88. Slippery fish
91. Old catapult
93. "___ Fidelis"
95. Union general
96. Suspension of breath
97. Clock features
99. Painting on dry plaster
101. Act as ___ (be servile)
103. An Astaire
104. Water-controlling devices
106. Gorge
107. Performed dressage
109. Null's partner
111. Companion of the Pinta
113. Common verb
114. Direction: Abbr.

69 Music Lesson By Herman Surasky

A matter of matching composers with their specialties.

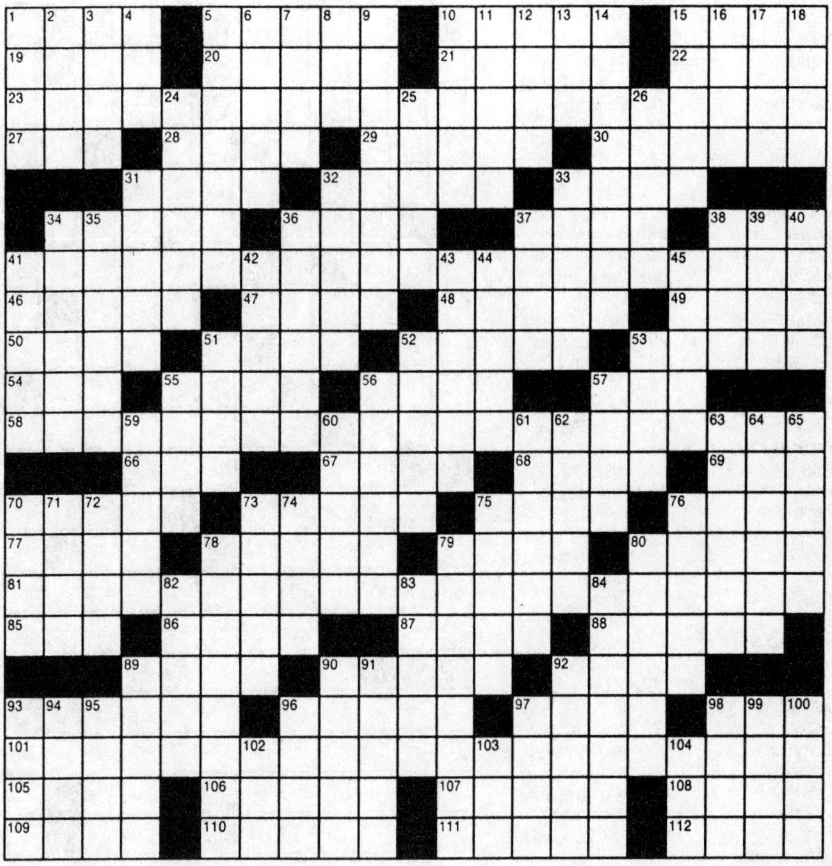

ACROSS

1. Cupbearer to the gods
5. Lower
10. Feel
15. Glazing compound
19. Arabian Sea land
20. Production at the Met
21. Debussy's "___ de lune"
22. French composer
23. LA BOHEME-IANS
27. Sort of: Suffix
28. Heaven, to Monet
29. Ancient Greek region
30. Abhor
31. German song
32. Mohammedan scripture
33. Pieces
34. Smiley's people
36. Crimson Tide, for short
37. Bric-a-___
38. Urban lines
41. MASS PRODUCERS
46. Scented
47. Word after red or onion
48. Weird
49. California rockfish
50. House members: Abbr.
51. Related
52. Meager
53. Shaving aid
54. Memorabilia
55. Portent
56. Tiff
57. Thee, in France
58. MUSICAL CHILD-LOVERS
66. French assent
67. Carry on
68. Land of hostage infamy
69. Old car
70. Watchful guardian
73. Bil or Cora
75. Moslem call to prayer
76. Pant
77. Word after slam
78. Arm bones
79. Rip-off
80. Royal, in Italy
81. PAGAN-INIANS
85. Nevertheless
86. It's often pura
87. Murray and West
88. Concerning
89. Emile ___, optimist of the 1920's
90. Hiawatha's months
92. Newton fillers
93. Mountain range
96. Facial décor
97. Haste, in Berlin
98. Burrows or Beame
101. SHAKE-SPEARE ADMIRERS
105. Throat-clearing sound
106. Cantor or Albert
107. Hermit
108. Repute
109. Entre ___
110. Eastern church cloak
111. Headliners
112. Ali ___

DOWN

1. Arizona Indian
2. Birds of Australia
3. Another for 41 Across
4. Envelope filler: Abbr.
5. Most scrawny
6. On foot, in Paris
7. Ball-balancing animal
8. Sea eagle
9. Sparks, nautically
10. Part of 20 Across
11. Remove, in law
12. Zola heroine
13. Thus
14. Shoot forth
15. Musical symbols
16. Chest sound
17. Misfortunes
18. Binge
24. Most aloof
25. Navigation aid
26. Fodder plant
31. Waterfalls, in Scotland
32. Garson of the theater
33. Wide, in Germany
34. Moon goddess
35. Compensate in advance
36. Swimsuit
37. Swiss city
38. Always
39. Soft fabric
40. Break off
41. Famous Idaho senator
42. Glacial ridge
43. Pour off gently
44. ___ retreat
45. Spanish composer
51. Prefix for dextrous
52. Disburse
53. Anon
55. Burden
56. Ogler
57. Govt. agent
59. Moola
60. Common chord
61. Hyderabad V.I.P.'s of yore
62. Broadway production
63. Spanish region
64. Put through the sieve again
65. "On ___ Old Smokey"
70. Ann Landers' twin
71. Underdone
72. Insect
73. Blue, in Bonn
74. "___ Karenina"
75. Pains
76. Autry and Rayburn
78. William Penn was one
79. Fodder for Sheridan's school
80. Horseshoes bull's-eye
82. New Zealander
83. Writer Cleveland
84. Carpenters, at times
89. Packs tightly
90. In the middle: Prefix
91. "The Old ___ Bucket"
92. Nutritional food
93. Musial
94. Ginkgo tree
95. Alas, to Cicero
96. Underwear initials
97. Ferber
98. Example of 20 Across
99. Simpleton
100. Poet Pound
102. Harem room
103. Negative
104. Tennis stroke

70 Sleuthing By Dorothy Smitonick

A glance at the world of undercover doings.

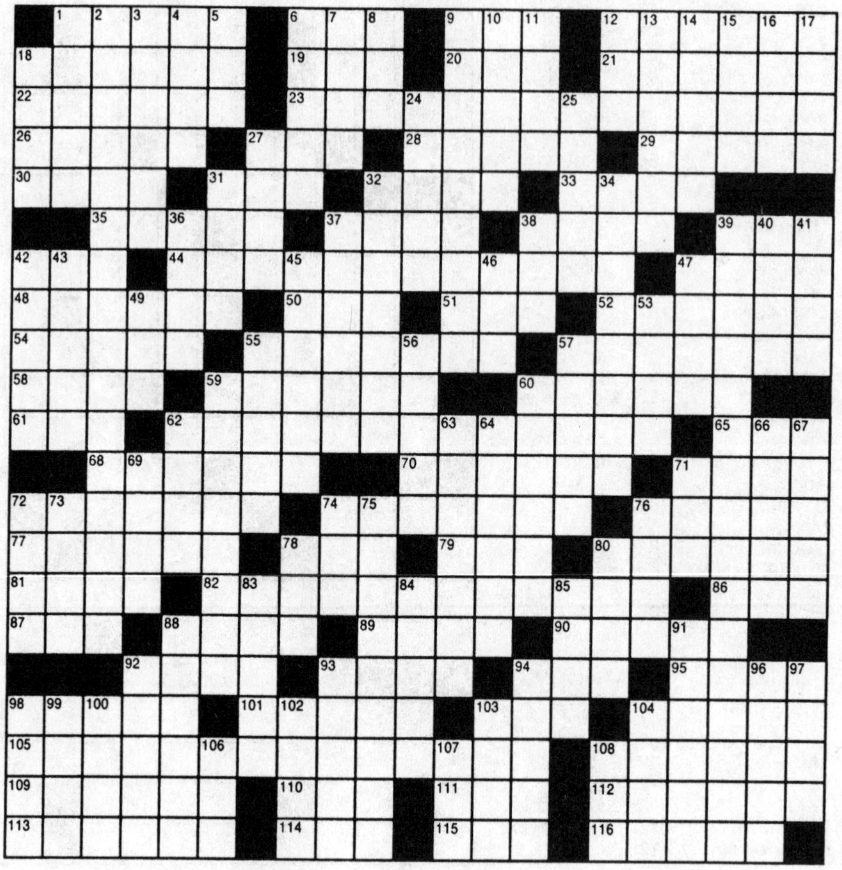

ACROSS

1. Hit
6. Psychedelic-drug initials
9. Equip
12. Trade
18. Flew high
19. Debtor's initials
20. Mauna ___
21. Not away
22. Musical instruments
23. Baker Street address?
26. Quaker William and family
27. G.I. address
28. Tripod
29. Perfect
30. Cozy
31. Partners of outs
32. Spar
33. Radius's bony partner
35. Intended
37. Impressionist Little
38. Hart
39. England's Bonar
42. Afterthoughts: Abbr.
44. Ellery Queen offerings
47. Somewhat, to Solti
48. Find
50. W.W. II spy org.
51. Word after tommy
52. Heat: Prefix
54. Ruins
55. Worried
57. Gave an Oscar to
58. Ruler of yore
59. Two-___ (roadster)
60. Enlarge, as a photo
61. Border
62. Sleuth's basic training?
65. Conservation dept.
68. Book of the Bible
70. ___ gown (commencement wear)
71. Astound
72. Cornered
74. "Some Enchanted ___"
76. Some South Africans
77. Goddess of health
78. Resort
79. Appellate bench: Abbr.
80. Entree, e.g.
81. Vases
82. Posers
86. Concert piece: Abbr.
87. Do weeding
88. Shorten
89. Singer Ives
90. Take up again
92. Mets' home
93. Threads
94. Smash hit
95. Ceremony
98. Bewildered
101. Bull: Prefix
103. Dutch cupboard
104. Pythias's friend
105. It hits the nail on the head?
108. Tenant
109. More commonplace
110. Criticize
111. Anonymous Richard
112. Moslem titles
113. Relatives of misters
114. Draft initials
115. Ship: Abbr.
116. Nineveh was its cap.

DOWN

1. Writer Kierkegaard
2. Sleuth's bubbly?
3. Controversial Agent
4. Some bills
5. Asner and Koch
6. Speaks imperfectly
7. Arty center of New York
8. Payable
9. Final call to ship visitors
10. Perch
11. A spice
12. Coll. degrees
13. "I haven't ___ to wear!"
14. Mary Richards's friend on TV
15. Kind of enamelware
16. ___ Bovary
17. Virginia ___
18. Bribes
24. Take the bait
25. Jane Fonda thriller
27. Against
31. Concerning
32. Trip
34. The rage
36. Performs
37. Puts in a new place
38. Be in session
39. Sleuth's quaint notion?
40. Peak
41. Grant ___, American painter
42. Poet Sylvia ___
43. Rustlers' downfall
45. Bog
46. Taylor or Steiger
47. Andean land
49. Gas: Prefix
53. Peddle
55. ___ fatale
56. Small amount
57. All ___ (from the beginning)
59. Suitable for marketing
60. Masters, in Africa
62. Indian wraparound
63. Fred and Ginger, e.g.
64. On a grand scale
66. Race horse's winning
67. Photographer Adams
69. French holy women
71. Trivial bit
72. Negative response
73. Prefix for maniac
74. Roof ornament
75. Martin and Dear Abby
76. Deck officer
78. Weaken
80. Type of haircut
83. Cowboy's rope
84. Once ruling family of England
85. God of love
88. Water or beer, at times
91. Wipes out
92. Take care of
93. Novelist Alexandre
94. Bet
96. "___ is human . . ."
97. Chemical suffixes
98. Quantities: Abbr.
99. Weary
100. Kind of flint
102. Elec. measures
103. Nautical speed unit
104. Party members: Abbr.
106. Daily 24: Abbr.
107. Tax initials
108. Meadow

71 World Records By Stanley Newman

According to Mr. Guinness and his book of unusual distinctions.

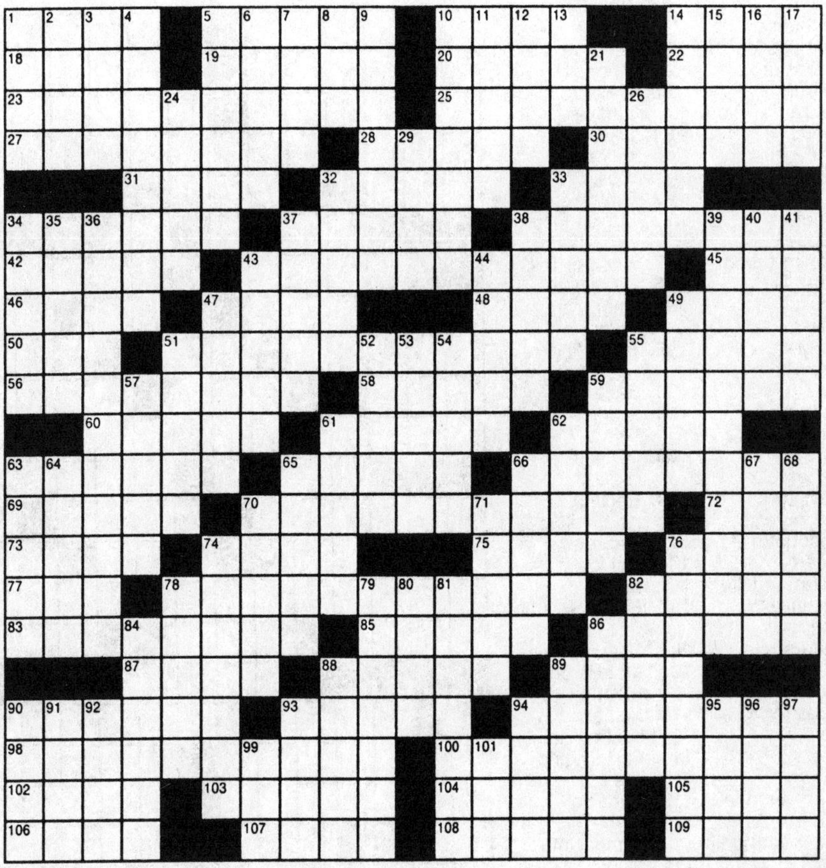

ACROSS

1. Showman Mike
5. Gripping device
10. Western city
14. Beginning
18. South Seas story
19. ___ by verdict (legal term)
20. Port of Israel
22. Suffix for switch
23. Etosha Reserve, Namibia
25. Walt Disney
27. He's run in
28. Power-outage cause
30. Sterne man
31. Comment ending
32. Word form for lizard
33. Male red deer
34. Sports-event official
37. Leg parts
38. Careless
42. City on the Rhone
43. 2.97 miles, in Antarctica
45. Adjective suffix
46. One-time Angel Cheryl
47. Tragedian Edmund ___
48. Fencing piece
49. Gets better in the bottle
50. French donkey
51. Sun, technically, or Proxima Centauri
55. Not ___ (pretty bad)
56. Asset off the tee
58. TV test show
59. Barbers, at times
60. Tyler's position as President
61. Chambermaid's charge
62. Put-ons
63. Neutral vowel sounds
65. The funny pianist
66. Place of reclusion
69. Tonic plants
70. Atacama Desert of Chile
72. Gun-guardian org.
73. Porsena
74. Openers, sometimes
75. Squiffed
76. Soprano Lucrezia
77. Bar rocks, in Bonn
78. Femur
82. Discover
83. Sixth graders
85. Little Nell ___
86. Company lover
87. Part of D.A.
88. Pal
89. Peacenik
90. Stew within
93. Having wings
94. Cycle attachments
98. Robert Wadlow, 272 cm, 8′11″
100. Himmy, 45 lbs.-plus
102. One of HOMES
103. Goodman's kingdom
104. Fakes: Abbr.
105. First name in mysteries
106. Nieuwpoort's river
107. "A Loss of Roses" author
108. One of a deck of 22
109. Like a river of song

DOWN

1. Indian weight
2. Actor Sharif
3. Rhode Island rebel
4. Like a well-read book
5. Olive Oyl's brother
6. Metric gasoline unit
7. Wood trimmer
8. Agricultural caste of India
9. Humdrum
10. Atoner's emotion
11. Ecuadorean province
12. Publisher Condé
13. Man of 511 homers
14. Goes bad
15. Galway islands
16. Tidings
17. Like Paul Pry
21. Traveler's stop
24. Adlai's '56 partner
26. Form
29. He-man
32. Shoe job
33. More tricky
34. Youthful days
35. Skull: Prefix
36. Billy, 62, of England
37. Partake of
38. Mar. honoree
39. 12,544 cycles/sec, on the organ
40. ___ the other
41. Airline-board abbrs.
43. Blackbeard, by birth
44. Attack
47. Clark and family
49. Insurance ratings
51. Pram pushers
52. Part of a town skyline
53. Knife-to-goblet sounds
54. It comes down frozen
55. Identical twin
57. Lauren of "Love Boat"
59. Booze
61. French river
62. Resort beach
63. Tapioca ingredient
64. French director René
65. Seagoing lockups
66. Eastwood
67. Diamond stat
68. Like a monsoon season
70. Marlo's father
71. Spurious
74. Dickinson or Moore
76. Divided equally
78. Forgetfulness
79. Peculiar
80. Dog or turkey
81. Charity performance
82. Apiarists' charges
84. Steele's mag
86. Unassuming
88. "Trolley Song" sound
89. "Me too!"
90. Steep, in Scotland
91. Walls' features, sometimes
92. Writer Wiesel
93. Ugandan exile
94. To-do
95. Suburban plot
96. Raspy sound
97. Something to watch
99. Start for night or light
101. "Today I ___ man"

72 Typecasting By Alfio Micci

People who fail to live up to their names.

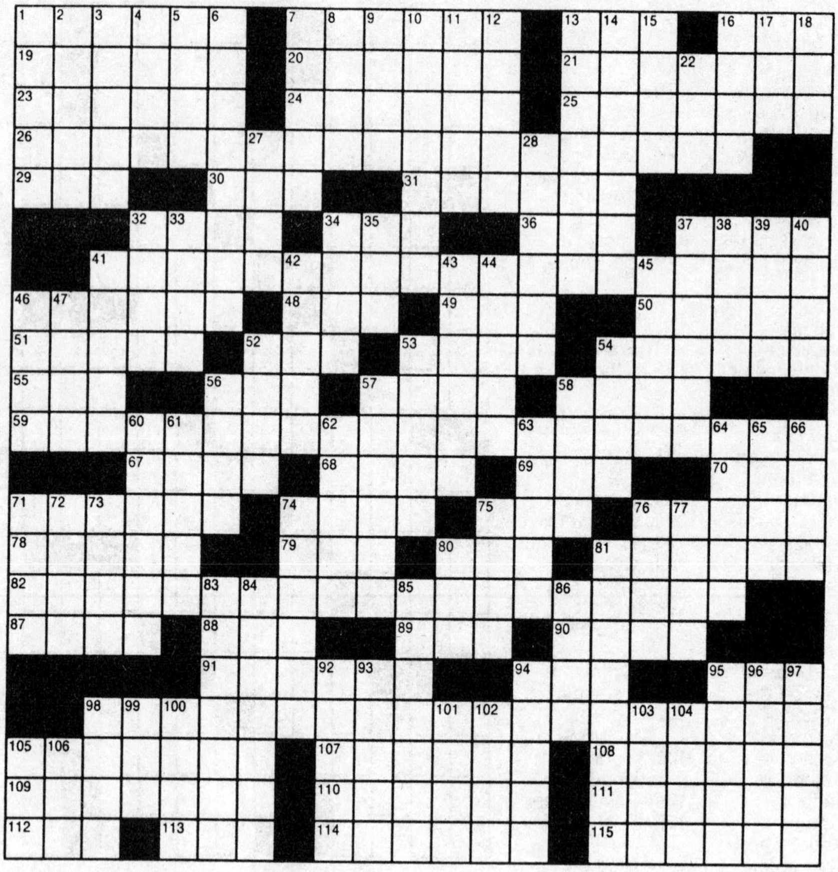

ACROSS

1. Tribal emblems
7. Get started
13. Labor org.
16. Expert
19. Tarzan's little friend
20. Shea hit
21. More spacious
23. Plantain
24. Loosely woven fabric
25. Sang like Crosby
26. Millers, but no grain experts
29. Pts. of dollars
30. King Arthur's brother
31. Debatable matters
32. Fibbed
34. Conductor de Waart
36. Liking, in Lille
37. Primitive weapon
41. Bakers, but no cake experts
46. Place for a tempest
48. Cleo's undoing
49. Writer Santha Rama ___
50. ___ hand (help)
51. Gibson garnish
52. Supped
53. Liner's V.I.P.
54. Push a light switch
55. Servicemen, for short
56. Presidential nickname
57. Saint of sailors
58. Puccini heroine
59. Smiths, but not forge experts
67. Heaps
68. Navy men: Abbr.
69. Actor Scheider
70. Caviar
71. Do a cobbler's job
74. Geological period
75. Kind of talk
76. Participate in a bee
78. Port for Caesar
79. River to the Rhone
80. Cyclotron particle
81. Like much modern music
82. Chandlers, but no tallow experts
87. Knox or Dix
88. Expected
89. Feed-bag item
90. Butterfingers' exclamation
91. Save
94. I, in old Rome
95. "O sole ___"
98. Carters, but no trucking experts
105. California seafood
107. Fabric weight unit
108. More comely
109. Motors or Electric
110. Spiritual indifference
111. Part-singing lines
112. Canticle
113. In the manner of
114. Mugs
115. "The ___ silence"

DOWN

1. A smoke for Pierre
2. MOMA offering
3. Camping quarters
4. Biblical king
5. Waiter's presentation
6. Least ornate
7. Wander
8. Historic times
9. Josip Broz
10. Point of view
11. Arm bones
12. Adolescent years
13. Tell and others
14. Divine
15. Diving bird
16. Like a cedar tree
17. Sandpiper
18. Calif. fort
22. Forest humus
27. Fatigue
28. Canoe
32. Wolf, in Milano
33. "When the frost ___ the punkin . . ."
34. If not
35. Drop bait lightly
37. Darling, in Dieppe
38. Scottish waterfall
39. Ruin
40. Castor or snap
41. Soprano Rosa
42. Rubber-tree secretion
43. Broadway offerings
44. Tokyo's land, to the French
45. Probe
46. Forum garb
47. Author Bagnold
52. Encourage a felon
53. TV-ad awards
54. Neat
56. Medicinal plant
57. Madrileño's land
58. L-Q connection
60. Follower of a former Chairman
61. Islamic god
62. Without warmth
63. Bout site
64. Movement
65. Altman's "Welcome ___"
66. Cry
71. Santa's landing strip
72. "___ Perpetua," motto of Idaho
73. Fuss
74. City on the Rio Grande
75. After-dinner wine
76. Prevent
77. Coloratura Lily
80. Mrs. Cantor
81. "___ the Misbegotten"
83. Steroid gland
84. Paris's ___ Paix
85. Person on a slate
86. Mental discipline
92. Calder Willingham's "___ a Man"
93. Oust
94. Wildcats
95. Corday's victim
96. Ancient British people
97. Gumbo ingredients
98. A Fonda
99. Rubber tree
100. Mrs. Helmer
101. French region
102. "___ Kampf"
103. Challenge
104. Lively dances
105. Past
106. Garden unit

73 Down Under By Reginald Johnson

Into a classic world that never was.

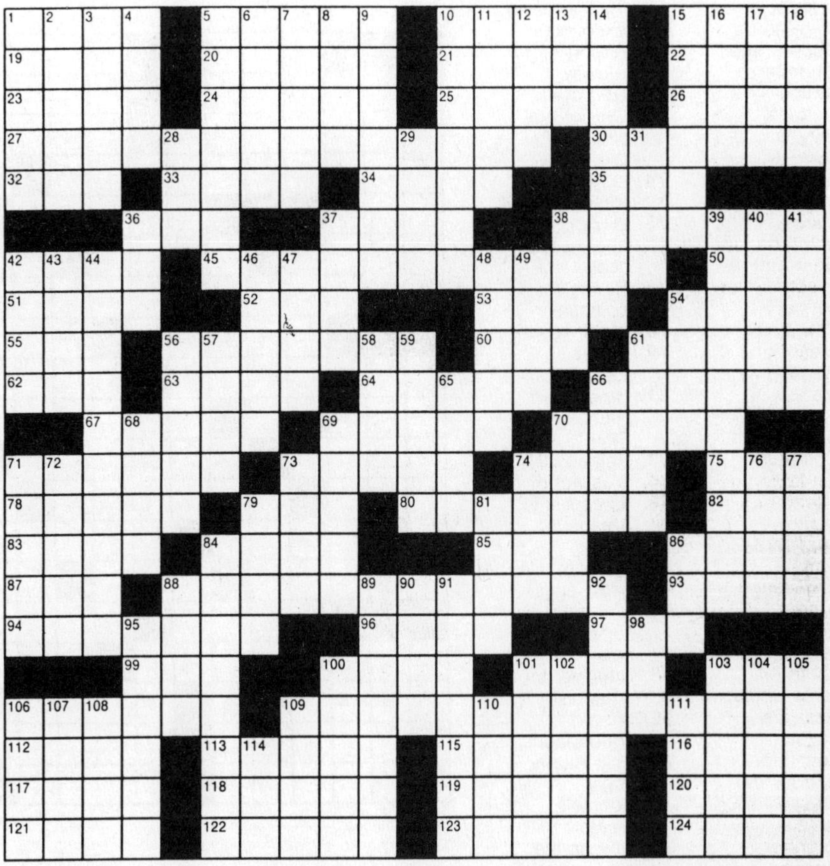

ACROSS

1. Rider of the slopes
5. Deserves
10. April happenings
15. Kind of cracker
19. Last of Henry's spouses
20. Leave out
21. Certain bones
22. Having a part of
23. Pierre's being
24. Like an arrow
25. Swiss city
26. Harrow's rival
27. Carroll character
30. Store fodder
32. Virgil's but
33. Employ-ments
34. Lamb cut
35. That, in Quebec
36. Friend, in Lyon
37. Bothers
38. Kind of clam
42. Kind of mower or tennis
45. Carroll character
50. Chemical prefix
51. English river
52. Poetic eye
53. "The ___ to Morocco"
54. Roman 301
55. ___ ordinaire
56. Carroll character
60. Neighbor of Ky.
61. Gathers leaves
62. Do figure work
63. Madrid time period
64. Clean the board
66. To-do
67. Jannings and Ludwig
69. Spartacus was one
70. African language
71. Short job
73. Diplomat Silas
74. Prefix for drome or naut
75. Commit a crime
78. Acts lazily
79. ___ Aviv
80. Carroll character
82. Guido's three
83. Form of a Latin verb
84. Prison stretch
85. Italian possessive
86. Corse and de la Cité
87. Work on hides
88. Carroll character
93. Robin's construction job
94. Provided funds
96. Essay name
97. Compass reading
99. Inlet
100. Lath
101. ___-de-camp
103. Reply: Abbr.
106. Easily remem-bered
109. Carroll
112. Plod through mire
113. Acclaim
115. Chemical compound
116. Italian erupter
117. Security Council move
118. English novelist
119. Porticoes
120. Narrow strip of land
121. Hammer part
122. Used a needle
123. Horse or common
124. Corner

DOWN

1. Small barracudas
2. Shaping tool
3. Took the wrong road
4. Sketched
5. Come again
6. Having wings
7. Prongs
8. German river
9. City in Missouri
10. Worthless stuff
11. Actor Delon
12. Part of M.I.T.
13. Highland negative
14. Chosen
15. Afternoon break
16. Pro's opposite
17. April 1 V.I.P.
18. Nine: prefix
28. Prefix for drum or bug
29. Brazen
31. Kind of do-well
36. Massachu-setts cape
37. Early pulpit
38. South African village
39. Carroll character
40. Surpass
41. Poker move
42. Crater's issuance
43. Greedy
44. Carroll creation
46. Gardeners, at times
47. Brünne-hilde's mother
48. Hit the deck
49. Pitch
54. Go for a trout
56. Dilutes
57. Stop the action
58. Of the, in Paris
59. Chimp's relative
61. Talk and talk
65. Declare
66. Pressure: Prefix
68. Brewer's need
69. City in Alabama
70. State in India
71. Buck up
72. Cicero or Virgil
73. Skin: Prefix
74. Samoan capital
76. Metal carriers
77. Overcome
79. Ready to drive, with "up"
81. Org. for youth
84. Broadway attractions
86. Chemical ending
88. One of two of a kind
89. Like John and John Quincy
90. Woodwind inst.
91. Like a batter, on some days
92. Approve
95. Pac Ten team
98. Raise ___ (act up)
100. Relative obscurity
101. British scientist
102. Thoughts
103. Late bloomer
104. Present time
105. ___ in the grass
106. "Are you coming or not?": Abbr.
107. Robt. ___
108. ___ d'Azur
109. Crab's weapon
110. This, to Juan
111. Dude
114. Letter

74 Soreheads By Bert Rosenfield

A recurring first syllable that might give that impression.

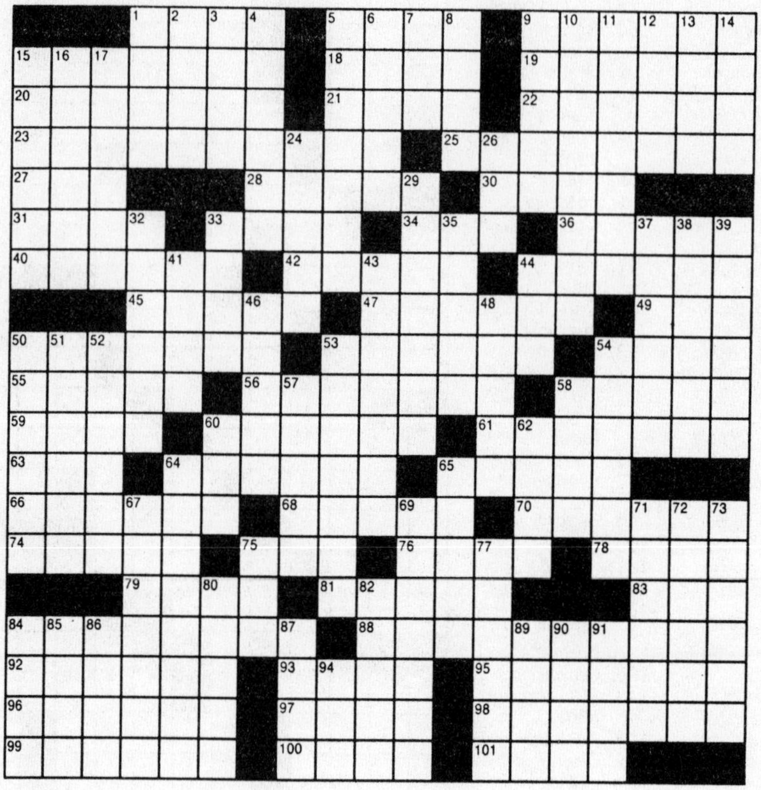

ACROSS

1. Ivan or Peter
5. Beechnuts, acorns, etc.
9. Thunder-struck
15. Lettuce variety
18. 1966 N.L. batting champ
19. Dark-colored cigar
20. East and West, in New Jersey
21. Whipped-cream unit
22. Handsome man
23. Wayne of Stony Point
25. Commun-ion-table attendant
27. Southwest-ern lizard
28. Upright
30. Chevalier song
31. Red-ink entry
33. Loretta of Tv
34. South or north windup
36. Pizarro's victims
40. Revelator
42. Title for de Grasse
44. Zaire's neighbor
45. Paris's ___ Rivoli
47. Grain beard
49. Branch of biol.
50. Strong white wine
53. Barber wrote one for strings
54. Useful part of a fork
55. Zodiac sign
56. Like Thomas Hardy's crowd
58. Demagne-tize a tape
59. N's, to code men
60. On this document
61. Between Fifth and Park, in Manhattan
63. "___ now!" (Soho protest)
64. Kimberley activity
65. TV's stellar expounder
66. Airport runway
68. Red dye
70. One of the singing brothers
74. ___ firm (resisted)
75. Lilly of pharmaceu-ticals
76. Rouge's companion
78. Woolly prefix
79. Where Esfahân is
81. He created Nathan and Sky
83. Roman 601
84. Trustworthy
88. Its capital is Antanana-rivo
92. Study of birds' eggs
93. ___ price, in supermar-kets
95. Haulover for a canoist
96. Woven cotton fabric
97. ___ Ahern, Major Hoople's creator
98. One on the run
99. Collectors' items from Detroit
100. Potato parts
101. Heavenly hammer heaver

DOWN

1. Kenya's longest river
2. Omen
3. Cast ___ (start trawling)
4. Run the film again
5. Current generator
6. ___ McLerie of stage and TV
7. U.S.–Canada canals
8. Big brass
9. Famous Cremonese name
10. Leporello aria in "Don Giovanni"
11. Showing affection
12. Pueblo dweller
13. Trouble-making deity
14. "___ thou hear me, Hal?": "Falstaff"
15. Carlos ___, early U.N. leader
16. Dirksen was one
17. ___ hatter
24. In the bag
26. K-O filler
29. Quit the Metroliner
32. Rock heaps
33. Prescient one
35. Sway
37. Warm-seas game fish
38. Ferdinand's father in "The Tempest"
39. Lining material
41. ___ Angel Firpo
43. English-men's midday companions
44. From ___ Z
46. They accompany herren
48. Greek letter
50. Expensive French paintings
51. Mountain also called Agri Dagi
52. Moola
53. Nasal-pas-sage blocker
54. Threefold
57. Caliban's antithesis
58. Age, in Seville
60. Sot's sound, in cartoons
62. Radio-tube worker
64. Part song
65. Tress hammock
67. Old Portuguese coin
69. Cell dwellers
71. Devil-may-care
72. Confine
73. Evening do
75. Photo-lab abbr.
77. Piqued
80. Yawning depth
82. Chemical compound
84. Arrive
85. Kind of hog
86. Antiquities
87. Bravo
89. Cousin of gee whiz
90. With the bow, in music
91. Pollux or Spica
94. The Duke of Elchingen

75 Livestock By Bert Kruse

And its contributions to the human scene.

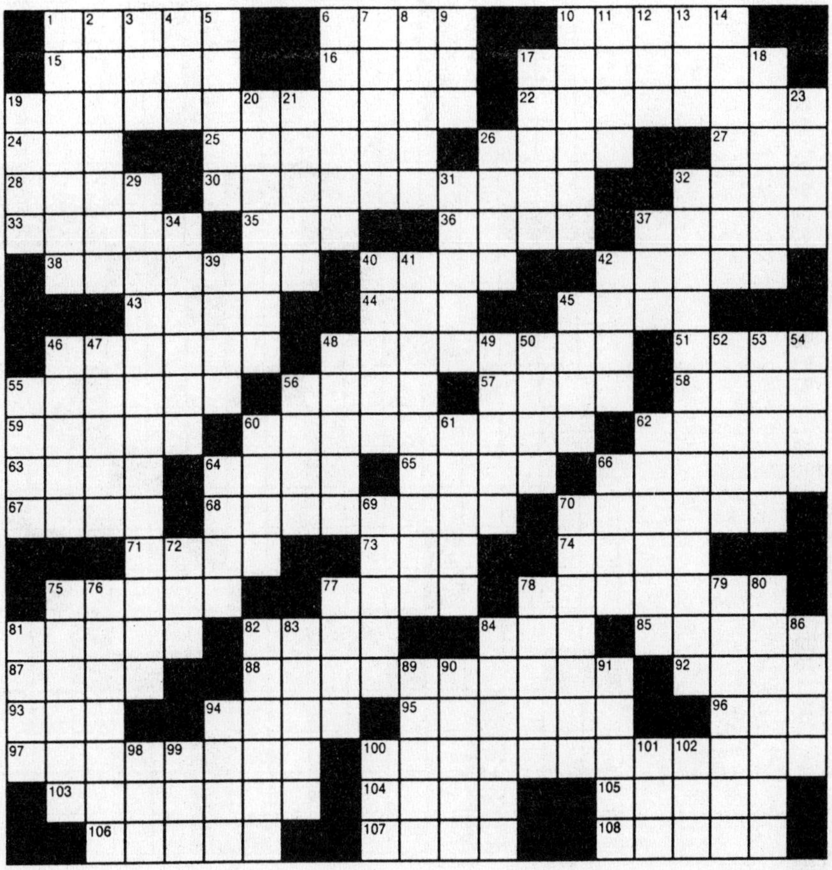

ACROSS

1. Pola of the silents
6. A Lane
10. Waste
15. Hero in David's army
16. Factual
17. Watery
19. Spanish athletes
22. Successful hit
24. Onassis
25. Flowering plants
26. Marina unit
27. English doctors' org.
28. Native Egyptian: Var.
30. Locomotive front
32. High cards in gleek
33. Not retiring
35. Kind of picker
36. Heckled
37. Daphnis's love
38. Mexican garments
40. State
42. Shore find
43. Swan genus
44. Castilian hero
45. Page
46. Lapwings
48. Calf's parent
51. Pine
55. Knots up
56. Playwright Simon
57. Horse color
58. Thunder god
59. ___-Unis
60. Cartoon flower-lover
62. Flimflam
63. Clock name
64. Partner
65. Zilch
66. Public to-dos
67. Hat holder
68. Corrida center
70. Salary or allowance base
71. French cheese
73. Native of: Suffix
74. Auricular
75. "On the Beach" author
77. Dillon of "Gunsmoke"
78. Plains Indian
81. Oil source
82. Waugh
84. Articles
85. Toil
87. Wet blanket
88. Pusillanimous
92. Worry
93. Kind of will
94. Sherbets
95. Eye part
96. Old English money
97. Leather sources
100. Papal papers, in a way
103. Equine rig
104. Harem apartments
105. Restaurateur of N.Y.
106. Agreements
107. Rebecca or Benjamin
108. Clear

DOWN

1. Nerve cells
2. Compressed circle
3. Hodges of baseball
4. Dict. or encyc., e.g.
5. Large artery
6. Greek province
7. Dutch city
8. Explosion
9. Honor and enlist followers
10. Country gentleman
11. Fruit-juice leftover
12. Sea scavanger
13. Certain votes
14. Debt acknowledgment
17. Made possible, old style
18. Sign or figure
19. Metropolis on the Caspian
20. Uncertain ones
21. Julia Ward and Elias
23. Facilitate
26. Restaurateur Toots
29. Talks nonsense
31. Faith confession
32. Prodigal son's fare
34. Elis
37. Half a dance
39. Plant holders
40. Sharp
41. Bull of Norway, e.g.
42. Basted
45. "Get a ___ of this!"
46. Leningrad builder
47. Growing out
48. Gemstone
49. Sturm und ___
50. Double-dip treat
52. It's 'crost the Bay, to Kipling
53. Kind of bear
54. Work units
55. Try
56. Dickens girl
60. Chimney part
61. Choral piece
62. Shinplasters
64. Nichols creation
66. Bristle
69. Boarding-house ___ (diner's asset)
70. Lars ___
72. Hwy.
75. Tennessee military park
76. Foyer
77. Cat sounds
78. Dido
79. "Childe ___ Pilgrimage"
80. Rest upon
81. ___-and-span
82. Availability
83. Fine-grained soil
84. Wyeth was one
86. Greek letters
89. Scrape off, old style
90. Philippine natives
91. "___ Macabre"
94. French notion
98. Charlemagne's org.
99. The Government
100. Swear
101. It's sometimes sinister
102. Hogg sister

76 Planetarium By Robert Wolfe

Offering mostly obscured views of the sun's orbiters.

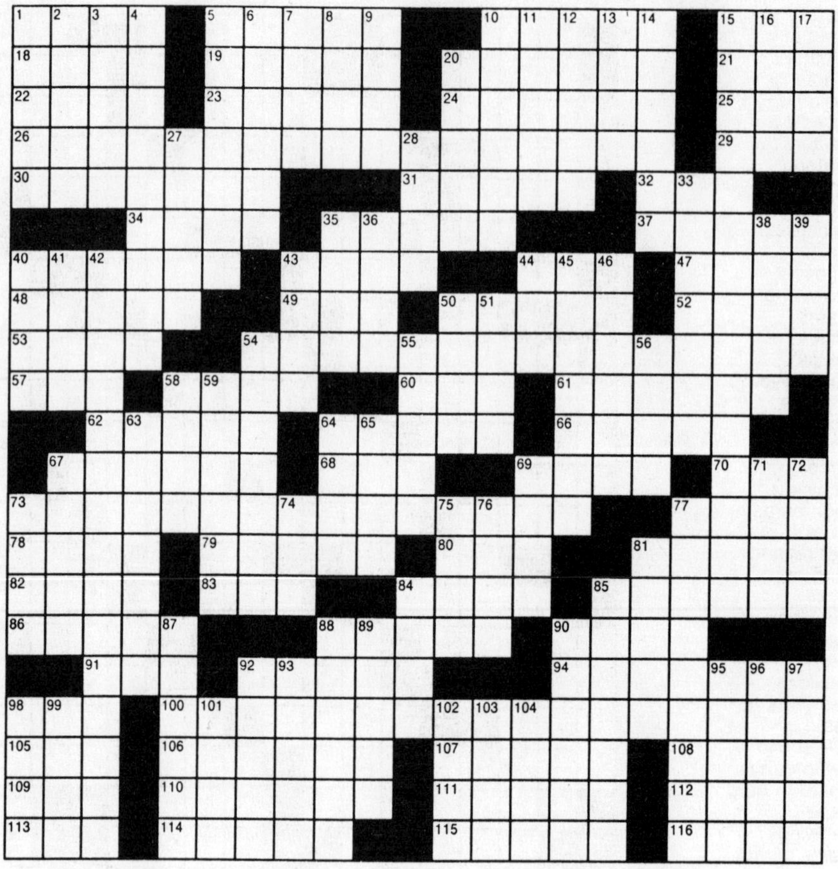

ACROSS

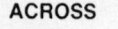

1. Auto or demo follower
5. Musical group
10. Spurt of activity
15. Child's pie material
18. Suborder of gulls
19. Pulitzer novelist Ernest
20. Mouthwash
21. Metric area measure
22. Aid in hanky-panky
23. ___ Gay
24. Father of the Titans
25. Scurried
26. ___ for the better (hospital-chart entry)
29. Furtive
30. Outstanding
31. Lenten applications
32. Nautical direction
34. Miss Horne
35. Livingstone and Pickford
37. Earthquake
40. ___ tuck (very close)
43. Foldaway items
44. Cretan mount
47. Nile queen
48. Conference site of 1945
49. Turmoil
50. Room style
52. Racist group
53. Swing around
54. Bungling orbital songsters?
57. Superlative ending
58. Frequent fourth-down play
60. What Liz did many times
61. Printing lines
62. Due
64. Makes corrections
66. Glacial ridge
67. Denounce fiercely
68. Junior, for one
69. Leftovers
70. Beame or Fortas
73. Ollas
77. Growl
78. Smell
79. Hawaiian feasts
80. Sash
81. Bobby Unser, e.g.
82. Actress Shaw
83. Mal de ___
84. Farm sounds
85. Stairway parts
86. Janet or Vivien
88. Irritate
90. Mock
91. Bee follower
92. Spread apart
94. Apply excessively
98. Wing
100. Modern housewife, at times
105. Hurok
106. Extol
107. In motion
108. Follower of black or iron
109. Sesame
110. Deserved
111. Ermine
112. Italian river
113. Before how or where
114. Chinese soup bases
115. Acne sufferers
116. Young oyster

DOWN

1. Applauds
2. Morocco's capital
3. Mountain crest
4. Excite pleasurably
5. An ___-shut case
6. Prefix for band or dict
7. Blow the horn
8. Fitzgerald
9. Hard wood
10. Vaughan and Miles
11. Chatter
12. ___ Dei (prayer)
13. Cast aspersions on
14. Feudal lords
15. Gulf of Lions address
16. Russian range
17. Gainsay
20. ___ up (dress fancily)
27. Miss Verdugo
28. Rabbit features
33. Gift for father
35. Fashion
36. On the summit
38. Scorches
39. Days of the wk.
40. Wall St. initials
41. Adjective suffixes
42. In the manner of a nabob
43. Whining speech
44. Polar abundance
45. Divining rods
46. Stop
50. Twosome
51. ___ of the earth
54. Aspirant to a heroine role
55. Interlace
56. Bothers
58. Substance
59. Remove a headpiece, old style
63. Amount of electrical power
64. Birthright seller
65. Beetles
67. Hindu garment
69. Actor Skinner
71. Loser to Braddock in 1935
72. Misplays
73. Biggers or Warren
74. Start of a Tolstoy title
75. Cry of disdain
76. Hautboy
77. Embryonic stages
81. Gone up
84. Yucatan Indian
85. Goes back
87. Made of cordage fiber
88. Terminates
89. Partner of hemmed
90. Of a mighty god
92. Leavings of wounds
93. Publish
95. Arrogate
96. Medicinal herb
97. Plant disease
98. Nora's dog
99. Kind of cloth
101. Dies ___
102. Like an ocean
103. East, in Palma
104. American Indian

77 Matched Pairs By Manny Miller

Combos that generally get along well together.

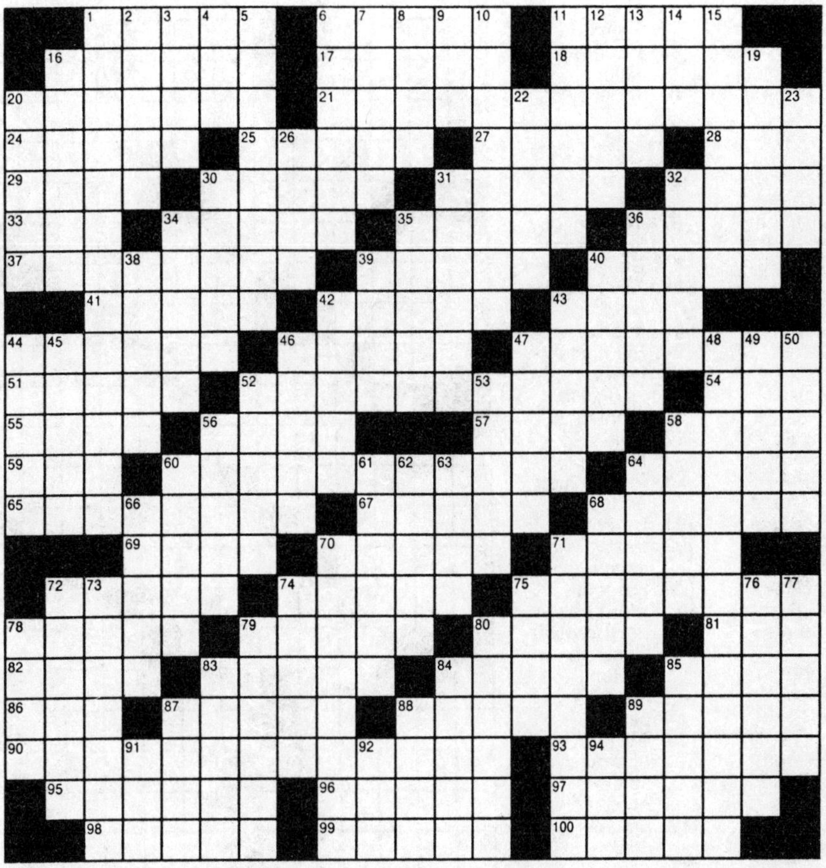

ACROSS

1. Stage items
6. Furthermore
11. Wild talker
16. Grimm Brothers character
17. Dance for two
18. Patron saint of Norway
20. Italian satirist: 1492–1556
21. Teachers' wooers
24. Apples and pears
25. Writer Zola
27. Delaying tactic
28. Make edging
29. Do the butterfly
30. Changes direction
31. State of Brazil
32. Narcotic, for short
33. Parisian season
34. Crystal, the singer
35. Pamby's partner
36. Kind of salad
37. Cried in a high pitch
39. Telegraph systems
40. Suppose
41. High-spirited horse
42. Troy name
43. Grant
44. Island off Brittany
46. Full dress
47. Collector of a sort
51. Coins in Qum
52. Helter-skelter
54. Roman 102
55. "___ Valentine"
56. Tiny creature
57. Lily
58. Noggin
59. Black bird
60. Disorganized
64. Open
65. Gives an account
67. Board plays
68. Fastidious
69. Newspaper page
70. Orphant Annie's creator
71. Common ailments
72. Tunes in
74. Shoe parts
75. Butler, for one
78. Glittering
79. Lugs
80. Hope, the actress
81. Alphabetic predecessor of Pa.
82. Strikes smartly
83. Pungent seasoning
84. Become dry
85. Sicilian mount
86. Words before king
87. Code man
88. Coat-collar continuation
89. Persistent worker
90. Minor accidents
93. Perplexed
95. Mideast body of water
96. Discontinue
97. Nolens ___ (unwilling)
98. Memorize
99. Beginning of a toast
100. Pleasant places

DOWN

1. Israeli leader in 1984
2. Desert shrub
3. Elevator inventor
4. Word after ball or bull
5. Having exotic optics
6. Dress
7. Frenchmen
8. Enter the pot
9. "Where did ___ wrong?"
10. Scandinavians
11. Series of prayers
12. Part of a bird's wing
13. Colorado resort
14. Newt
15. Turbulent
16. Expansion
19. Basra citizens: Var.
20. Building recesses
22. Wounds
23. Printer's term
26. Pinochle combination
30. Gielgud's "Arthur" role
31. Affectionate gesture
32. Fish basket
34. Singer Campbell et al.
35. Willy's accompaniment
36. Start for duddy
38. Boot-shaped country
39. Small dam
40. Everyday-life painting
42. Odalisque's home
43. Billiard shot
44. Citified
45. City near Florence
46. ID's for Pavlova
47. Beauts
48. Sea swells
49. Mirthful
50. "Hinky ___ Parlay Voo"
52. Chartered
53. Silent star Harry
56. Counterparts
58. Wedding-party member
60. By chance
61. Le Carré character
62. Frisky animals
63. Salutations
64. Kind of arrest or teeth
66. What a buffalo does
68. Moola
70. Economize
71. Private meeting
72. Wheeler's follower
73. Choose for jury duty
74. Inferior
75. Hounds' quarry, in a game
76. James of TV
77. Comes close
78. German title
79. Headwear in the Mideast
80. Minor errors
83. Kitchen device
84. Describe grammatically
85. Actress Burstyn
87. Arizona city
88. TV producer Norman
89. Ashen
91. J.F.K.'s predecessor
92. Sandra or Ruby
94. Wool weight

78 Nothing To It By Wilson McBeath

Some things require little or no effort.

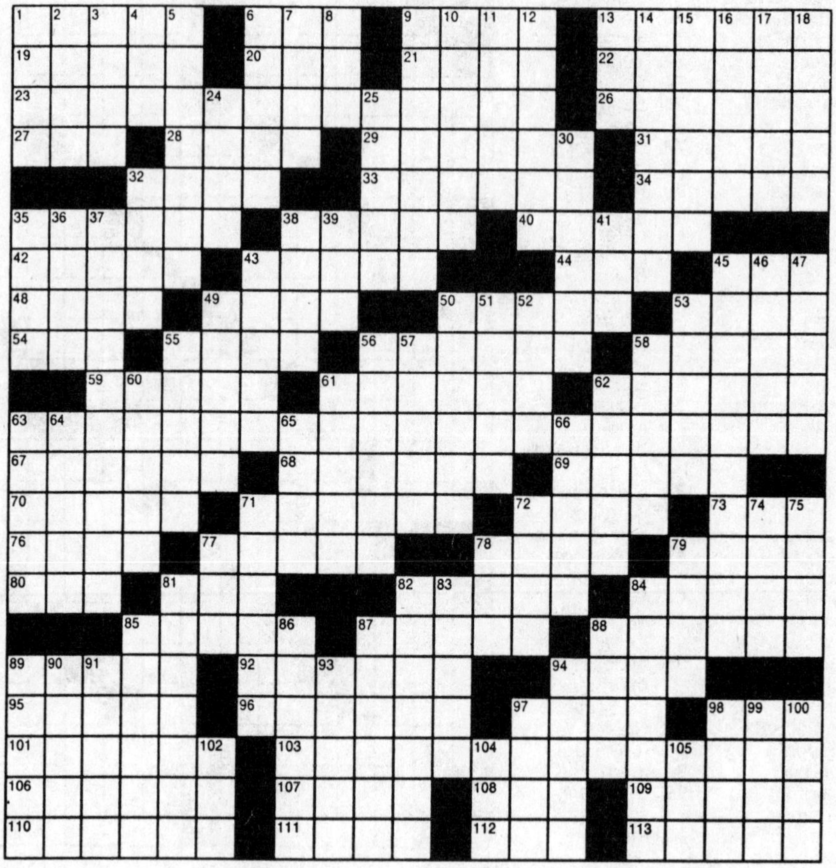

ACROSS

1. Wounds
6. Confederate-flag unit
9. Arab prince
13. Moderating agent
19. Express a view
20. Greek vowel
21. Weight adjustment
22. Land of the Mounties
23. Easy job
26. Cure-all
27. Companion of cakes
28. Layer of ore
29. Chemical compounds
31. Clerical vestment
32. So be it
33. ___ Creed
34. Discernment
35. Like some prose
38. Frontiersman of note
40. Corporate off.
42. Imperturbable one
43. Vine
44. Approves
45. Baby food
48. Cub Scout groups
49. ___ soup (easy job)
50. La ___, naval-battle site of 1692
53. Old Greek platform
54. Hit sign
55. Gentle
56. Auction decoys
58. Certain Louisianian
59. Verify
61. Orbital point
62. Melodic
63. Easy job
67. Head protection
68. Ruth McKenney's sister
69. Miraculous food
70. Iroquoian Indians
71. Police action
72. Ascend
73. Summit
76. Fellow
77. Blockheads
78. Something easy, with 74 Down
79. Prima donna
80. Chemical suffix
81. As easy as ___
82. Checks
84. Donated
85. Champ or Mark
87. Women, in legal terms
88. Chair workers
89. City on the Rhine
92. Intertwine
94. Big name in Hawaii
95. Habituate
96. Frankfurter
97. Twirl a floating log
98. Before Juan or José
101. Be present
103. Easy acquisition
106. Harangue
107. Word before deep or high
108. Comedian Buttons
109. Count or baron
110. Tip the ___
111. Approved models: Abbr.
112. Summer drink
113. Chirp

DOWN

1. Couch
2. Iridescent gem
3. Irritate
4. Photographer's abbr.
5. Of an earthquake
6. Initiated
7. Part of a molecule
8. British military org.
9. Light fabric
10. Lincoln wanted this toward none
11. Liquid from orris roots
12. University officer
13. Expert
14. Golf-ball cover materials
15. Souls
16. Cabs
17. Decree
18. Peep show
24. Urgency
25. Vestment
30. Of body fluid
32. Sacred bull of Egypt
35. Vessels of W.W. II
36. Roman road
37. Take over in toto
38. Shade of blue or green
39. Grown-up acorn
41. Supplement, with "out"
43. Measure of light
45. Deprecatory
46. Divert
47. Type of truck
49. Ship's crane
50. Author Helen MacInnes ___
51. Acid in vegetable oils
52. Secluded valley
53. Scottish child
55. Carries
56. Barrel spigots
57. Waters the garden
58. Maneuver one's neck
60. Lover
61. Blazing
62. Disconcert
63. Solomon's queenly visitor
64. Bittern
65. River to the Garonne
66. Astray
71. Have ___ loose
72. Baseball bottom lines
74. See 78 Across
75. Rotates a camera
77. Arabian garment
78. As easy as ___
79. Eat
81. President of Chile: 1970–73
82. Withdraws
83. Abrasive substance
84. Chivalrous
85. Breakfast food
86. New York's N.B.A. players
87. Struck out
88. Crocus bulb
89. Tempos
90. Caper
91. Buddhist sermon
93. Slanted
94. Electronic device
97. Nurtured
98. "Quién ___?"
99. Competent
100. U.N. vote
102. Before Moines or Plaines
104. Monk's title
105. Forward end of a vessel

79 Caretaking By Connie Cowan

Phrases that reflect a watchful nature.

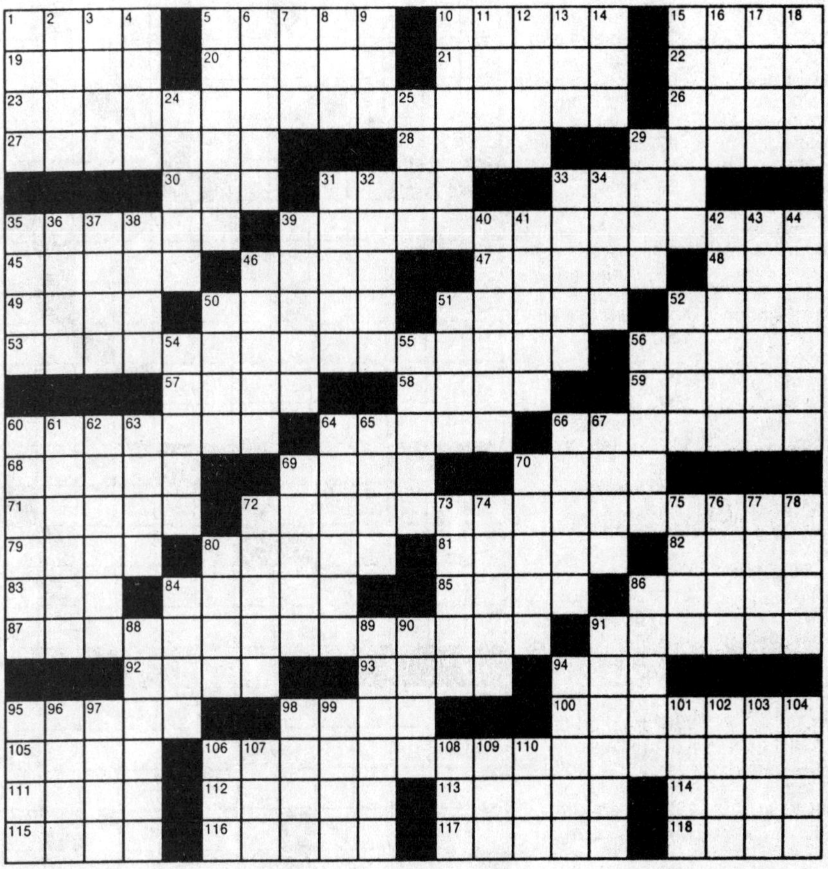

ACROSS

1. ". . . no in Gilead?"
5. African fox
10. Becomes full
15. Moslem official
19. Away from the windward side
20. ___ of the world
21. Make a payment
22. ". . . with the blue ribbons ___"
23. What Washington wanted for a special guard
26. Southern U.S. staple
27. Notorious Nazi police
28. Direction
29. Of superior quality
30. Word with ton or voyage
31. O'Casey
33. Anew, to a hillbilly
35. "Nine, ten, a big ___"
39. Caretakers of a sort
45. Remains
46. John Dickson of mystery
47. Orient Express, for one
48. Eggs
49. Like a sourpuss
50. Syrup base
51. Silk's partner
52. Fine, to Harry Lauder
53. "Angels and ministers ___!": "Hamlet"
56. Abyssinian weight
57. Taken for a ___
58. Prejudice
59. Etonian's parent
60. Decorative appendages
64. Like a fountain drink
66. Standpatter
68. Kyushu city
69. Hawaiian precipice
70. "They have ___ the wind . . ."
71. Movie vamp and family
72. "Then felt I ___ of the skies": Keats
79. Summers in Rouen
80. As ___ a pig
81. Soft leathers
82. Hercules's captive
83. Perform
84. Tree, in Spain
85. Becomes unclear
86. Apportion
87. "Get ___" said Hamlet
91. Cathedral city of France
92. Egyptian god
93. Epoch: Var.
94. One of a Latin trio
95. Communist secret police
98. African antelope
100. "___ dare!" (Lay off!)
105. Arizona Indian
106. G. & S. protectors
111. Participating
112. Conger catcher
113. Mediterranean evergreen
114. Campus soc.
115. Promontory
116. Very insignificant
117. Betel palm
118. Augments

DOWN

1. "Chitty Chitty ___ . . ."
2. African plant
3. Item used by Steichen
4. Encounter
5. Clipping for a bargain hunter
6. Bruckner
7. ___ discount (cheap)
8. Caring caretaker
9. Rue Morgue killer
10. He and Kellogg created a pact
11. Family rooms, for short
12. "___ my wits' end"
13. Counterpart of max.
14. City rtes.
15. Managing
16. At another time
17. Have a repast
18. Caesar's highway
24. Toyland residents
25. Kind of guard
29. Helsinki native
31. Sudden rise
32. ___ corn
33. Writer Nin
34. Achieve
35. Portuguese folk song
36. ___ now (currently)
37. Gangster
38. Gentleman, in Germany
39. French caretaker
40. Call ___ (retire)
41. Narrow, to Cicero
42. Printing mistakes
43. One who puts cargo aboard
44. Alaskan peninsula
46. Campus people
50. To wit: Abbr.
51. Pique
52. Insipid
54. Regions
55. Arabian Satan
56. Catkin
60. Hard ___ (unstoppable)
61. Three on
62. French security arm
63. Train stops: Abbr.
64. Peak in Nepal
65. Drinks
66. They're often first, in football
67. "As ___ saying"
69. Climber's wedge
70. ___ side of life
72. Father of Rachel
73. Class
74. Dancer Shearer
75. Eyelash: Prefix
76. Calcutta's was black
77. College in N.C.
78. Steeps flax
80. Cleaving tool
84. Tropical ant genus
86. Surrounded by
88. American painter Thomas
89. Table accessories
90. Refusal in Bonn
91. Unicellular animal
94. For this purpose, to Caesar
95. Facial feature
96. Sharpen
97. Classic poetry
98. Painted tinware
99. Augury
101. Porous rock
102. London's Scotland
103. Toward the mouth
104. Offshore assault units: Abbr.
106. In addition
107. Shoe width
108. Wood sorrel
109. Distant
110. Italian numeral

80 Foursomes By Tap Osborn

Not the kind found on a golf course.

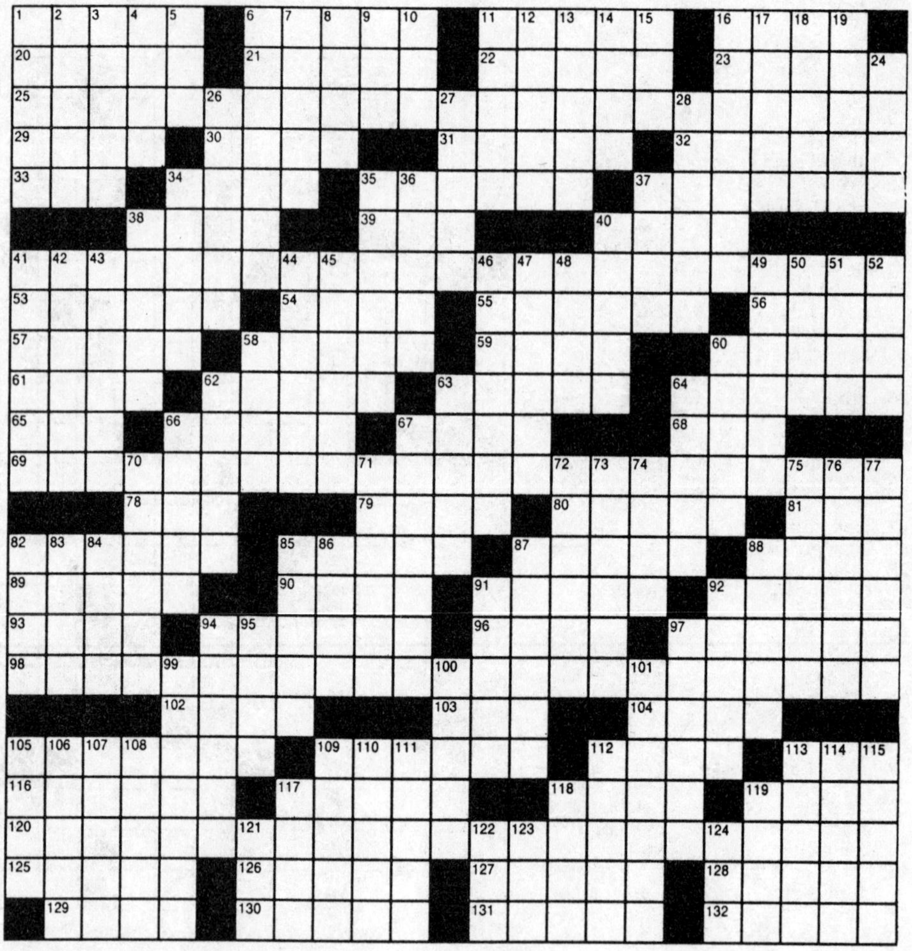

ACROSS

1. Imitated Marceau
6. Aspic shapers
11. Nevil Shute locale
16. Beautiful: Prefix
20. "A miss is as good as ___"
21. Embellish
22. Knightly wear
23. Papal cape
25. Actor, poet, golfer, singer
29. Fierce one
30. Choler
31. Stein-song state
32. One who climbs
33. Olds's car
34. Lawyer: Abbr.
35. Rang
37. What hams chew
38. ___ Caliente
39. Blyth or Miller
40. Poker holding
41. Comics character, royalty, actress, actress
53. Transmit again
54. Old fogy
55. Light tunic
56. Mine access
57. Marquand's George
58. Poet Guest
59. Scottish swift
60. Talk endlessly
61. Courts
62. Word in a letter closing
63. Abounding in greenery
64. Sty occupant
65. Service initials
66. Before nez
67. "In ___ veritas"
68. Bar order
69. Chanteuse, actress, artist, comedy great
78. "You ___ Woman"
79. Part of B.P.O.E.
80. Siren, e.g.
81. Opposite of WNW
82. Infatuated one
85. Lewiston college
87. Bristles
88. Half a spy
89. Wood units
90. Portent
91. Cruel one
92. Singing group
93. Dial ___
94. Volcanic rock
96. Old man, in Bonn
97. Longfellow subject
98. Actress, impressionist, novel character, Argentinian
102. Failures
103. Like Nairobi
104. "___ corny as . . ."
105. Dulls
109. Unpigmented animal
112. Relative of etc.
113. Iron or coon's
116. Father of electrodynamics
117. Sound of disappointment
118. Dressed
119. Severn tributary
120. Painted lady, actress, actor, golfer
125. Gravestone
126. Taking off
127. "___ in Paris"
128. End a curtsy
129. Beanery sign
130. On edge
131. Minuscule
132. Put into cipher

DOWN

1. Shaw's Barbara
2. Candidate's concern
3. Small: Prefix
4. Miss Sommer
5. Andrea ___ Sarto
6. Kind of bliss
7. In an offbeat way
8. Earring holder
9. High's partner
10. Last year's jr.
11. Twice-told
12. Banks or Pyle
13. Modify
14. Singer Natalie
15. Time periods: Abbr.
16. Anxiety
17. Of the planet Mars
18. Server
19. More advanced in years
24. High nest: Var.
26. Blunt
27. Arabian native
28. Class of perching birds
34. "The ___ and the Ecstasy"
35. Wage earner's big moment
36. Home of a witch
37. Asserts
38. Writer James and family
40. Elder or Younger writer
41. Write, as a document
42. Tranquillity
43. "___ as you're up, get me . . ."
44. Cite as proof
45. Tough golf hole
46. Stress marks
47. Cramped
48. "___ for All Seasons"
49. Illegal Niagara Falls transit
50. Aleutian isle
51. Confirmation, e.g.
52. Road to Roma
58. Coastal flier
60. Of Santa's home
62. Construction specialist
63. Squealers
64. Bet winner
66. Bonfire stacks
67. Film industry's Jack
70. Rock or Madison Square
71. Repeat
72. Ester of an acid
73. Surpass in insight
74. Mild oath
75. Horseshoes shot
76. Marshy inlet
77. Tidy up
82. Play opener
83. Room access
84. French river
85. Pears
86. Asian nurse
87. Dispose of for cash
88. Chess plays
91. Bernstein prop
92. Katmandu's locale
94. Borneo sultanate
95. Helps
97. Open porch
99. Swimmer Gertrude and family
100. Believe
101. In a key manner
105. Hoover and Grand Coulee
106. Wax dramatic
107. Respiration hiatus
108. Served up
109. Actor Alan
110. Meat cuts
111. Harbor boat
112. Famous marbles
113. Shun
114. Furze
115. Over
117. Look of astonishment
118. Restorative
119. Coiffure
121. Day of the wk.
122. Black bird
123. Expose, poetically
124. Air defense sys.

81 Dew Point By Sidney Robbins

Where moisture starts to set in.

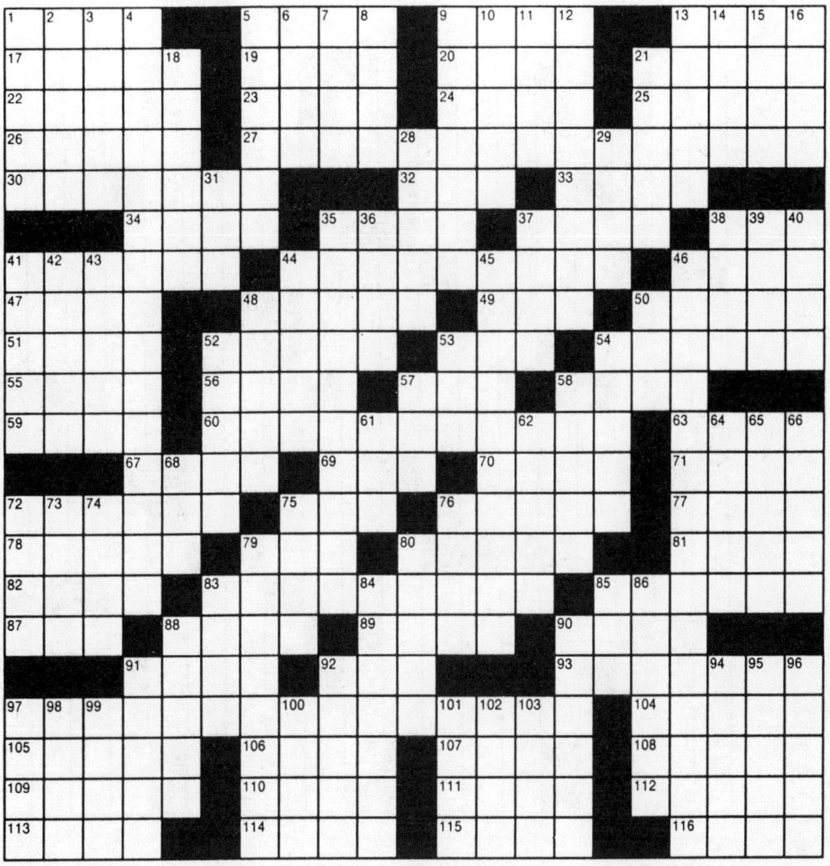

ACROSS

1. Watering holes
5. Noble
9. Stadium in N.Y.
13. Word after slap
17. Complete: Prefix
19. Tardy
20. Kind of jerker
21. Belief
22. Arden
23. Israeli port
24. Bridge seat
25. God of the east wind
26. Have ____ (watch out)
27. Shower curtains, so to speak
30. Protection
32. Mornings: Abbr.
33. Gait
34. Stepped
35. Made baskets
37. Silent
38. Article
41. Stalls
44. Pads
46. Acne age
47. Tentmaker
48. Louisiana's is Rouge
49. Suffix for station
50. In front
51. ____ Barrani of W.W. II note
52. Diamond stops
53. Follower: Suffix
54. Takes by force
55. Miss Cinders
56. Heavenly science: Abbr.
57. Residue
58. Flotilla unit
59. Film unit
60. Warm up
63. Copied
67. Entreaty
69. Slum menace
70. Triumphal moment
71. Miracle spot
72. Fish group
75. Steadying rope
76. Boxers Max and Buddy
77. He was Terrible
78. Poet T. S.
79. Half a gun
80. At this time
81. Gala party
82. Word on a door
83. Reacts to heat
85. Comes up
87. Offensive of 1968
88. Appropriately
89. Inheritor
90. Smart one
91. Low-caste Hindu
92. Connective
93. Translates, in a way
97. Sweaty joint
104. French school
105. Name for a cow
106. Atmosphere: Prefix
107. Type of judgment
108. Mongol of Nepal
109. Metric measure
110. Astronauts' boss
111. Clue
112. Savor
113. Play the first card
114. Goddess of hope
115. Greek letters
116. ____-do-well

DOWN

1. Advantage
2. Money in England
3. "Half ____ is better . . ."
4. Typist tank
5. Like some silverware
6. "Into ____ life . . ."
7. To be, in Paris
8. Woodwind
9. Certain clam
10. Scads
11. Life of Riley
12. Museum course
13. Question
14. Taj Mahal site
15. Porn
16. Hodgepodge
18. Author Porter
21. Author Daniel
28. Nevermore bird
29. Bits
31. Mayday
35. Herbs found in bogs
36. Nebraska Indians
37. Only
38. English river
39. Pressure
40. ____ of the earth
41. Pill giver
42. Zola
43. Soup-pot aide
44. Kind of basket
45. Child, often
46. Big piece of the world
48. Port of Iraq
50. Onassis
52. Communications breakdown site
53. Kabibble
54. Curds' partners
57. Lawyer: Abbr.
58. Goosebumpy
61. Round Table knight
62. Plans
64. Macadamizes
65. Related maternally
66. Hamlet's folks
68. He had a salty wife
72. Before Oct.
73. Suggestion
74. Dagger top
75. Like some whodunits
76. Soprano Lucrezia
79. Fish eaters
80. Rows
83. Word on a door
84. Unfounded fears
85. Pub drink
86. Just a bit ago
88. Librarian's aid
90. Conforms
91. Worked at
92. Edith Cavell, for one
94. Divine for water
95. Buoy up
96. More withered
97. Hot spot
98. Wiesel or Siegmeister
99. Movie dog
100. Type of year
101. Tennis name
102. Section
103. Zola novel

82 Forced Entry By Mary Murdoch

Some ways of gaining admittance.

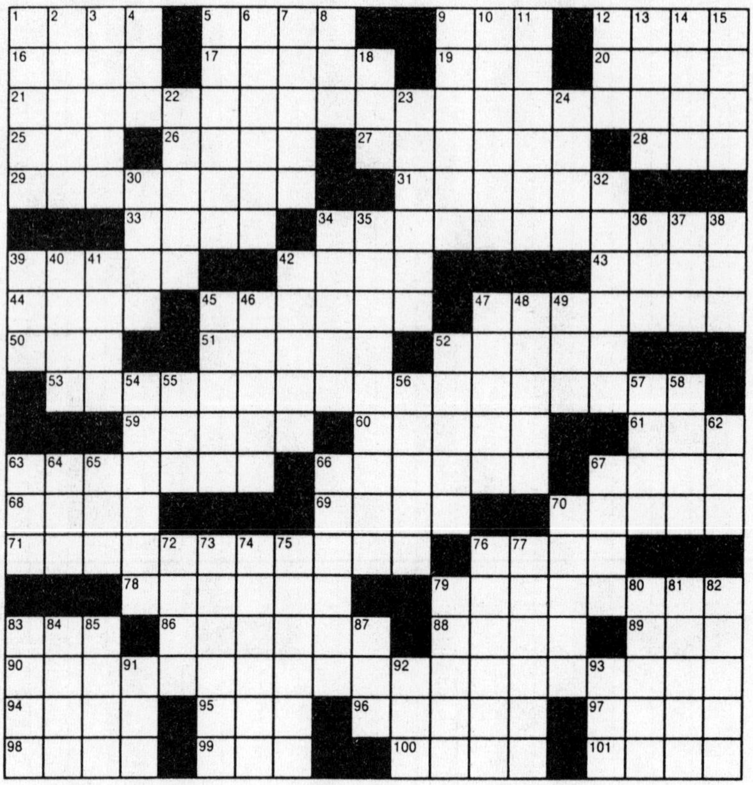

ACROSS

1. Previously owned
5. To be, in France
9. Something to pay
12. Portly President
16. Shade of green
17. ___ khan (Kipling tiger)
19. Japanese admiral
20. Gen. Bradley
21. Earl Derr Biggers novel
25. Miss Arden
26. Platinum loop
27. Awn
28. Eastern holiday
29. Breathes
31. Teen-age activity
33. Bear of the sky
34. She portrayed a sister of Scarlett O'Hara
39. Jacques, for one
42. Winglike
43. Literary villain
44. Cotton unit
45. ". . . now that ___ here"
47. Yukon sergeant of radio-TV
50. Daughter of Cadmus
51. Oriental inn
52. Angry
53. Observation of a smug sleuth
59. Clarinets, e.g.
60. Mussolini's son-in-law
61. Ancient times
63. Firecrackers
66. Damrosch
67. Count portrayer
68. Solar disc
69. Nora's pup
70. Composer Ned
71. Alan Ladd movie of 1942
76. Ambitious bridge bid
78. France's police arm
79. Erred
83. Autumn mo.
86. Have application to
88. In ___
89. Silkworm
90. A. J. Cronin novel
94. Membrane
95. Alley ___
96. March animals
97. Abie's spouse
98. Suburb of Paris
99. French articles
100. For fear that
101. Adjective suffixes

DOWN

1. Racing's Bobby
2. Puree
3. Sprites
4. River of Scotland
5. Sandy ridges
6. "___ Around Us"
7. Spanish royalty
8. Hesitating sounds
9. Of the shinbone
10. Have ___ meal (dine well)
11. Bundle of straw, in England
12. Kind of dollar
13. Latin I word
14. Kismet
15. Waste allowance
18. Greek letter
22. Bête ___
23. Waiters' concerns
24. Like a wet cellar
30. Simple's partner
32. Teahouse hostess
34. Of a Greek city
35. Well-grounded argument
36. Between Sun and sen
37. Self
38. Offspring
39. U.S. parallel of 78 Across
40. Frog genus
41. N.C. college
42. Tapestry
45. ". . . things require ___ to start from": Lucretius
46. Hangs
47. Wrinkled fruit
48. Machine part
49. Catchall abbr.
52. "Oh, ___ Beautiful Mornin' "
54. Apes, for short
55. ___ diem
56. Like a river delta
57. Oracle
58. French magazine
62. Hoover, e.g.
63. Way to stand
64. Old English letter
65. Part of Italy
66. "___ the Red Witch": Wayne film
67. Turkey
70. Actor Novarro
72. Grease monkey's job
73. "How ___?" (greeting)
74. Summer, e.g.
75. Razor sharpeners
76. Feeds the furnace
77. Certain musician
79. Cordwood measure
80. Lured
81. Uneven
82. Charity-march offerings
83. H.R.E. name
84. Sonny's ex
85. A William
87. Degree
91. Letter
92. Holbrook
93. Gypsy horse

83 Turnabout By Ronnie Allen

It's fair play for some of the people.

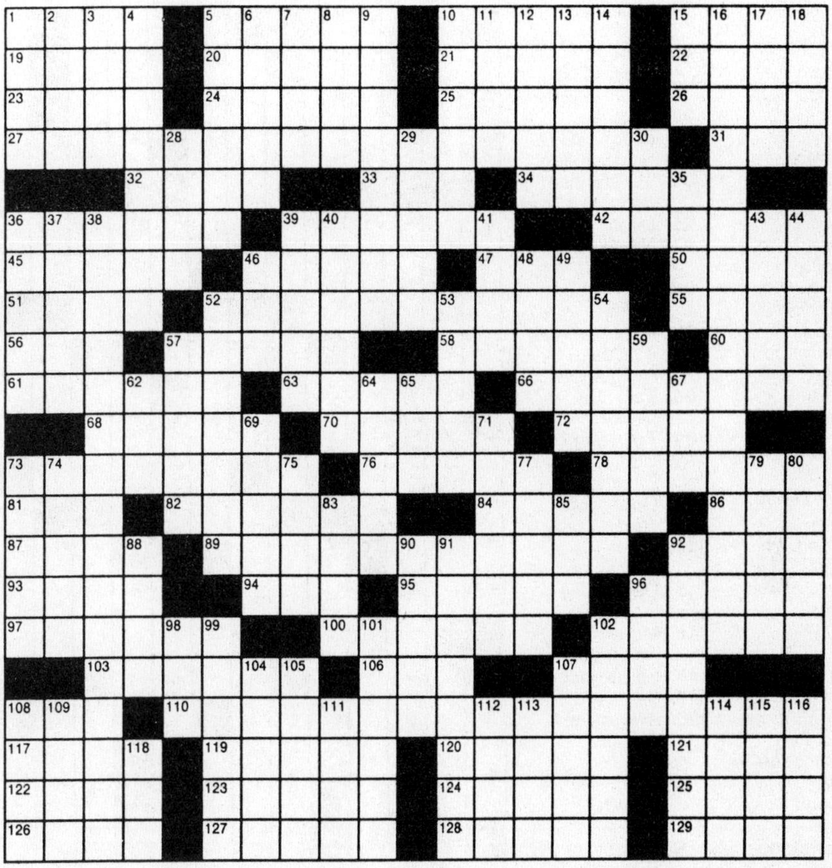

ACROSS

1. Heroic tale
5. Podium adjuncts
10. Price anew
15. Make eyes at
19. Feline sound
20. ___ as two peas
21. Señora Peron
22. Landed
23. Columnist's tidbit
24. Intimidated
25. Instruments for Casals
26. Game of chance
27. Donne's feminist philosophy
31. D.C. title
32. Home for a Hawkeye
33. Play an ace on a king
34. Chimney cleaners
36. Rejects a lover
39. Dawdle
42. Bureau compartment
45. British composer and family
46. Birchbark boat
47. Doer: Suffix
50. Cell body
51. Curtain-call actions
52. Female beggar
55. L.A. skyline sight
56. Ab ___ (from the start)
57. Wahine's porch
58. Painful struggles
60. Season in Nice
61. Small bird
63. Vegas depositories
66. Plane trees
68. Roof overhangs
70. Blue Ridge caverns
72. Scent
73. Paced a horse
76. A classic macho
78. Asian wild ass
81. G-man
82. Meal
84. Poker ploy
86. Yalie
87. ___ out (hit the silk)
89. Take a lady apart
92. Chief exec.
93. Stub ___
94. Sound of discovery
95. "Golden Boy" playwright
96. Relinquish
97. Pointed arch
100. Table linen
102. Life's work
103. Swap for Richard III's kingdom
106. Demand payment
107. Traditionally blind emotion
108. Reporter or Scout
110. Out of her mind
117. Exclusively
119. Mother: Prefix
120. Foolish
121. Fictional plantation
122. ___ fixe
123. Small goose
124. Cut up small
125. Soprano Gluck
126. Cowley's or Stein's generation
127. Everybody, to Hans
128. Building-height unit
129. Jet designer

DOWN

1. Quick tour
2. Prefix for graph or biography
3. Emulated Topsy
4. Cabinets
5. Big-beaked birds
6. Actress Massey
7. Fruit from New Zealand
8. ___ out (supplements)
9. Tranquilized state
10. Julia Child offering
11. Christmas and New Year's ___
12. Cultivates
13. Attorney-___
14. Put on pounds
15. Klutz
16. Laura and Amanda's zoo
17. Italian bread?
18. School jacket
28. Belgian city
29. Famous
30. Aachen article
35. Weak-hand holder's call
36. Shoe for Hans Brinker
37. Utah city
38. Slips and brassieres, possibly
39. Actor Fernando
40. Chaplin's father-in-law
41. Affluent
43. Chew the scenery
44. Storms
46. Direct the ship
48. Canvas cover
49. ___ Gay
52. Irrigated the garden
53. Where ___ (scene of action)
54. Yellow-pink bloom
57. Meat order
59. ___ of Scone
62. Do lacework
64. ___ lunch (door sign)
65. Prefix for dent or pod
67. Doctors' org.
69. Old photo color
71. Teller of stories
73. Secret organization
74. American glassware
75. Sprint
77. Cooper's natural man
79. Ecole attendee
80. Stair part
83. Ugly duckling, eventually
85. Parisian pronoun
88. Poland's Walesa
90. Swab clean
91. They're often removed with tonsils
92. The P in P.G.
96. Surfer's transportation
98. Ages and ages
99. Trumpet stop on an organ
101. Owns up to
102. Dante's was Divine
104. Growl
105. Outer
107. Antisocial one
108. Innerspring section
109. Loosen
111. Caen's river
112. Temperamental state
113. Texas city
114. One of Chaucer's offerings
115. La Douce
116. European coal region
118. So far

84 Romance By William Canine

It comes in many ways to the young at heart.

ACROSS

1. Love, Cádiz style
5. Puts the muzzle on
9. Bambi, e.g.
13. Dazzle
16. Where Minos reigned
17. Locale for Margaret Mead
18. "Born Free" heroine
19. ___ Gwyn, flame of Charles II
21. Vital tendon?
23. Treat clumsily
25. "And what ___ as a day in June?"
26. "The Mating ___"
28. Bullring, in Spain
29. Came down
30. "Pure ___ angel"
32. Deficient
33. Romantic girl's quest
40. Tarkenton or Allison
41. Most risqué
42. Kelly-Garland movie
46. Great stories
47. Collars
48. "___ Poetica"
49. Payable
50. Former Iranian V.I.P.
51. Den
53. Raindrop catcher
56. Paraseghian
57. Dueña's concern
59. "Ad ___ per aspera"
61. Hungarian
64. Virgilian aphorism
67. Egyptian king
70. Native of Basra
71. Generosity
75. Kind of port in a storm
76. Military group
77. Cincture
78. Mauritanian town
79. Boo's follower
80. Mischief-maker
82. Gentle expletive
84. "Chanson d' ___"
85. Time for expressing tenderness
90. Football coach Joe
92. Singer's deg.
93. Substandard contract
95. Direct
97. Novelist Wister
98. A sin, in a saying
99. Malaise
101. Political cartoonist
104. Taking a peek
109. Traveling bag
111. Don Juan or Casanova
113. Dotted with stars
114. Actor Guinness
115. Dangerous mosquito
116. Muse
117. Actor Beatty
118. Parrot feature
119. Spruce
120. Aykroyd and Rather

DOWN

1. Consort of Aphrodite
2. Tsp. or tbsp., e.g.
3. Other, in Spain
4. Goes back over
5. Nephew of King Arthur
6. "Mon cher ___"
7. Signal from Major Bowes
8. Story of great deeds
9. Estate land
10. New Haven denizen
11. Site of the Krupp works
12. Cheers
13. Actress Wong
14. Time of great expectations
15. Author Havelock
16. "The Sweetheart of Sigma ___"
17. Puritanical
20. Thirteen popes
22. Willy Loman's line
24. Sergeant ___
27. Injure severely
31. ___ Khan
33. One of the estates
34. Anatomical seam
35. Specializing in: Suffix
36. Director Mike
37. ___ cry
38. Roy or Reiner
39. "___ Miniver"
40. E.R. was his First Lady
43. Glaswegian's denial
44. Emanation
45. TV's Norman
47. Nicotinic acid
51. Ullmann and others
52. Supped
53. Needle case
54. Surface measure
55. Scoundrel
58. Caviar
59. Med-school course
60. The following ones: Abbr.
61. Trading center
62. High-school subj.
63. Shone
65. Mouth: Prefix
66. "My gal"
67. Critic Philip
68. Indonesian ox
69. "Belle of the Nineties" hit song
72. Boutique
73. Finns' gift to fitness
74. Flynn of films
76. News agcy.
77. Indianian Birch
80. Habituates
81. Rockies or Alps: Abbr.
82. M.D. was his First Lady
83. V.M.I. freshman
84. Was a guest at
86. Made improvements
87. Aust. state
88. Malformation on a horse
89. Town on the Zambezi
90. One of Athena's names
91. Certain believer
94. Immature raptor
95. Carriages
96. Actress Terry
97. "___ mio"
100. Thrust
102. Stretch across
103. "How do I love ___ . . ."
105. Wax, to Livy
106. Land south of the Caspian
107. Clears
108. Twelve doz.
110. Teachers' org.
112. Apple-cider girl

85 Music Stand By Sara Helleny

Appropriate terms spotted here and there.

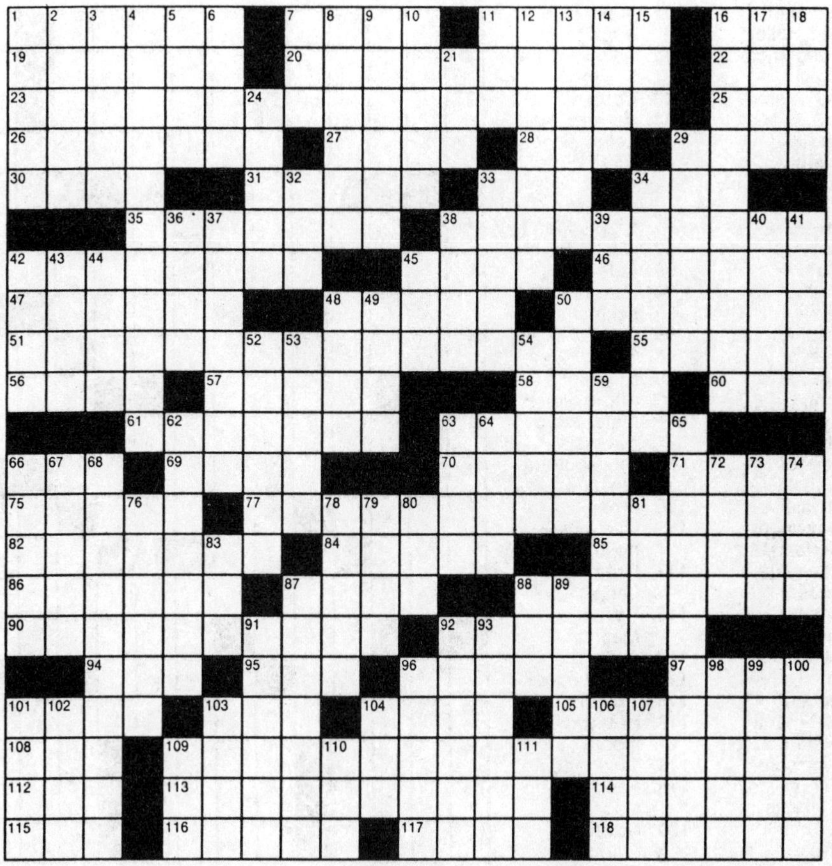

ACROSS

1. Scene of Hannibal's victory
7. Govt. info org.
11. Writer Seton and others
16. Before Beta Kappa
19. Interstice
20. Tabloids' offerings
22. Charged particle
23. Duck an issue
25. Give ___ to (heed)
26. Pismire's pad
27. Words of despair
28. Huon Gulf town
29. Rhine feeder
30. Caucasian Moslem
31. Fragrant compound
33. Prefix for enchanted
34. Ocean: Abbr.
35. Puts into writing
38. Thackeray schemer
42. New York slammer
45. Cloud or fog formation
46. Similar compound
47. P.L.O. leader
48. Actress Keaton
50. Windflower
51. Get ready to order redeye
55. Donkey, in England
56. She, in Italy
57. Comedian Bert's family
58. Mardi ___
60. Snake shape
61. Junkman, in Jerez
63. Arnold Schoenberg device
66. Skip a stone
69. Smell ___
70. Sea call
71. "___ you can't do it"
75. Ending for Unit or octogen
77. Didn't make a ripple
82. Rough sheds
84. Pseudonym
85. English composer and family
86. Oakley and Laurie
87. Word to Tabby
88. What the I.R.S. does
90. Song for Ethel Merman
92. Sauce to go easy on
94. Money officers: Abbr.
95. Altar constellation
96. Kind of eclipse or loss
97. Campus org.
101. Water, to Caesar
103. Initials for 84 Across
104. Turkish city
105. Attached directly, as a leaf
108. Accouterment for a marshal
109. Booze for one of the three B's
112. ___ one on
113. Spring or summer, e.g.
114. Renter
115. Ocean farer: Abbr.
116. Breathless
117. Burmese rice
118. Acute and obtuse

DOWN

1. Intrigue
2. Sports place
3. ___-foot oil
4. Words for lightning speed
5. U.S.S.R. range
6. Fatha Hines
7. As a rule: Abbr.
8. Stepping stone to the White House
9. East or West ___
10. Bright flower
11. Dined
12. Golf club
13. "Did ___ me a question?"
14. French handle
15. "Quiet!"
16. Dessert
17. Ancient
18. Regarding
21. Satisfied sounds
24. Upstate N.Y. city
29. Receiving guests
32. Silver abbr.
33. Star in Cygnus
34. Agreement, in Italy
36. "___ can you . . ."
37. In name only
38. ___ of one's existence
39. Yang's partner
40. Tears
41. Plunders
42. "Quién ___?"
43. Feelings of anger
44. Giant reeds of India
45. Humbug's companion
48. R.I. rebel in 1842
49. "Wishing will make ___"
50. Run in
52. Custard apples
53. Between eta and iota
54. Related on the father's side: Var.
59. Naïve
62. People who carry on
63. S.A. timber tree
64. Sheep, in old Rome
65. Mendelssohn's "On ___"
66. ___ Lama
67. Malayan palm
68. String expert of a sort
72. Aboma and anaconda
73. Basic French verb
74. Novel heroine
76. Grieg's dancing girl
78. Actor Guitry
79. Infinity
80. Like a fiddle, supposedly
81. Energy source: Abbr.
83. Kirghiz city
87. Fires from low-flying planes
88. Arab robe
89. Mud volcano
91. Washington city
92. Chewy candy for Diana
93. Moorish tabor
96. Donahue and others
98. Minor enemy
99. Coeur d'___
100. Sheiks' quarters
101. Ten-per-centers: Abbr.
102. Discontinue
103. Not care ___
104. TV reception letters
106. Miss Kett
107. Biblical locale near Bethel
109. ___ loss for words
110. The circus's is big
111. Historic time

86 Overlaps By Peter Swift

Yielding a lode of familiar personalities.

ACROSS

1. Ear parts
6. Storytellers
11. Turkish chief
15. Chichi
19. Be in store for
20. Nora's creator
21. Beat severely
22. Word to a chicken
23. Actress Anne
24. Ruth's mother-in-law
25. ___ en scène
26. Fragrant flower
27. Psychologist, lyricist, painter, author, physicist, playwright
31. Certain cats
32. Server
33. Angst
34. Smutty
38. Plaid
41. Bedazzle
42. Artist, dictator, actor, actor, Pilgrim, actor, songwriter
48. Horned deity
49. Topkicks et al.
50. "No ___ is an island"
51. Anatomical duct
52. Shipped
53. Links blemish
55. Toady's words
58. Retreats
59. Cream
61. More robust
62. Twilled fabric
63. Novelist, two composers, actor, civil libertarian, painter, journalist
69. Lublin natives
70. Cosmetic
71. Ridge of glacial ice
72. Rebuked, with "off"
73. Run out, as a subscription
74. Bind tightly
76. Charity
80. Sherbet, for one
81. Make lace edgings
82. Painter in the Prado
83. Carol
84. Actress, king, actor, singer, Biblical victim, violinist, Cleo's friend
92. Cue followers
93. Lets
94. Famed Dutch scholar
95. Joey or Don
98. Stinger
99. KO punch
100. Three film stars, three novelists
109. City south of Moscow
110. Frost
111. One of the media
112. Greeting in Lanai
113. Painter Magritte
114. Avouch
115. Derisive look
116. Ocean queen
117. Hebrew month
118. Govt. agents
119. Food stabilizers
120. Novelist Françoise

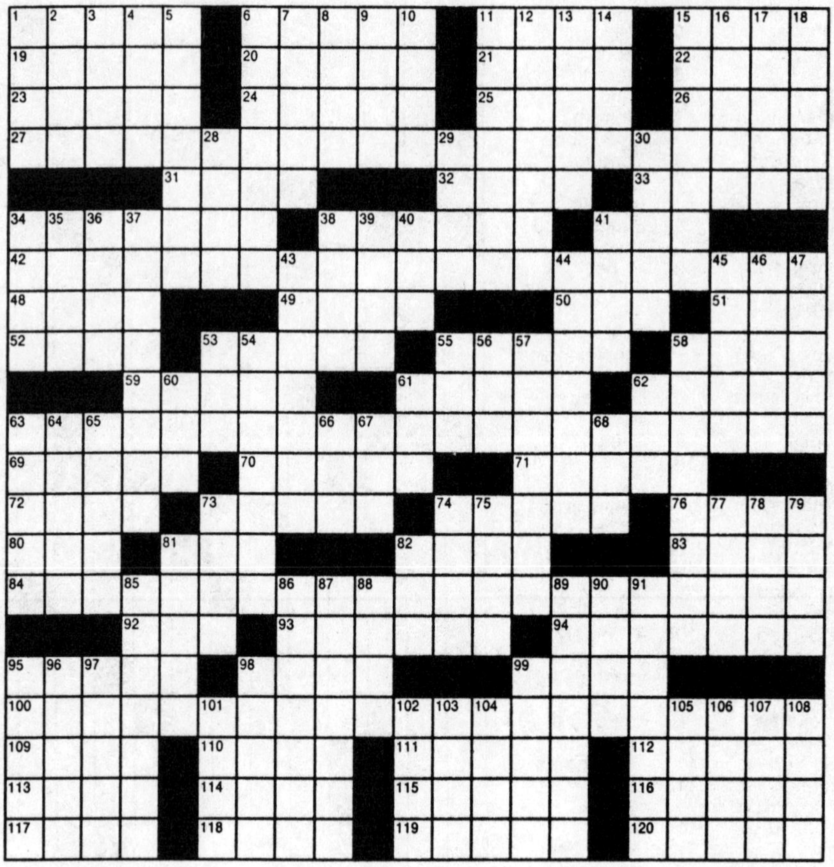

DOWN

1. Lhasa monk
2. Was a debtor
3. Idol
4. Where Dingle Bay is
5. Race official
6. What most footballers are
7. Steel construction pieces
8. ". . . unto us ___ is given"
9. Radiation dosages
10. Dither
11. Bright butterfly
12. ___ bear it
13. Minx
14. Incite
15. Ambitious one
16. Cologne's river
17. Islands east of Fiji
18. Joined together
28. Licking one's knife at the table is one
29. Comic-strip girl
30. Newsman Newman
34. Dolts
35. Highland hillside
36. Twirled
37. Concentrated
38. Mexican dish
39. Very much
40. Tpks.
41. Collections of writings
43. Surround
44. Crops up
45. Patent
46. Tropical fruit
47. Ruhr city
53. Roman 504
54. Repeat
55. Jabber
56. Clockmaker Terry
57. Voluptuous
58. Discusses at length
60. Palmas or Vegas
61. Historic Eur. dominion
62. Beaufort or Kara
63. Of the eye
64. Booze
65. Lyon lane
66. Songwriter Kahn
67. Golden ___
68. Amtrak and others: Abbr.
73. Striplings
74. Opener for Hamlet
75. Bar supplies
77. Appear imminent
78. Preprandial reading
79. Rock star Stone and namesakes
81. Sculptor's work
82. Xenon, for one
85. Climbing rose
86. Fearful
87. Western squatters
88. Hebrew letter
89. Counselors
90. Mars: Prefix
91. Tusked arctic mammals
95. Old Athenian hub
96. Had the courage
97. The Omni is one
98. Relinquish
99. Willow
101. German count
102. Major or Minor
103. Pealed
104. Plan
105. Essay name
106. Hanker
107. Camellia
108. Tall tale

87 Accounting By Peggy Devlin

Presenting things in a number of ways.

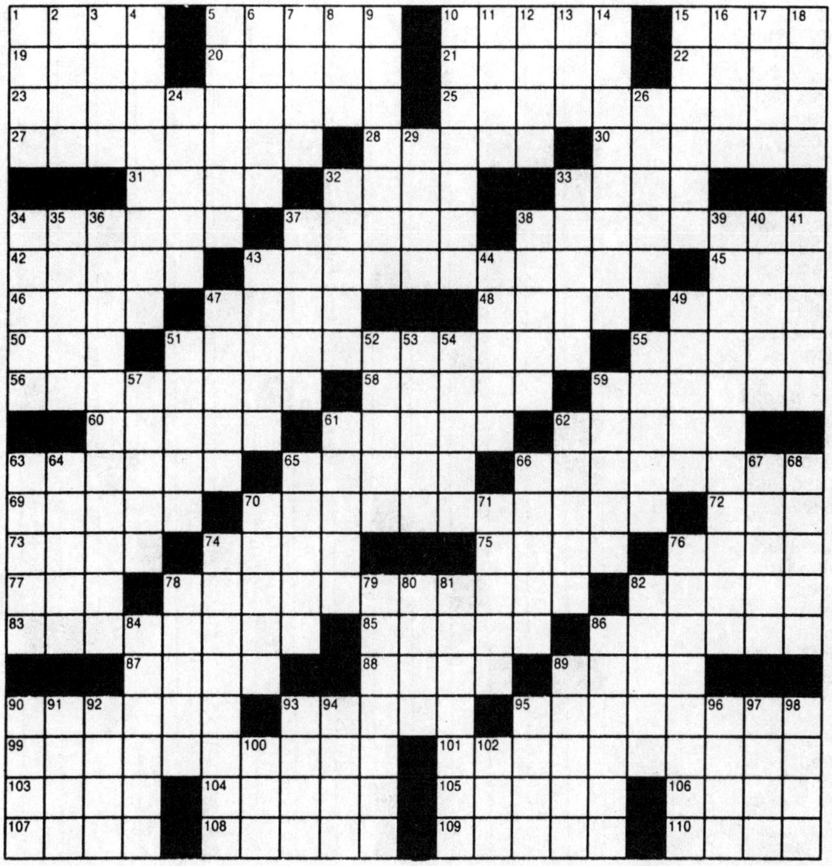

ACROSS

1. "Bye-bye"
5. Grinder
10. Lazy one
15. ___ on a dime
19. Gen. Bradley
20. Repay morally
21. Spread about
22. Westchester college
23. Necktie
25. Starfish
27. Like some leather
28. Wagnerian maidens' milieu
30. Bergen and Burroughs
31. North Sea feeder
32. Word before heat or beat
33. Acorn's issue
34. Charts again
37. Cotton thread
38. Policeman, sometimes
42. Ludwig and Jannings
43. Eleanor, Bess et al.
45. Rush
46. Elvers
47. Paean
48. Comedian Allen
49. Wait
50. Rate of speed: Abbr.
51. Ship with more than one captain?
55. Was loving
56. Asmara native
58. Argot
59. Divers
60. Rigel's constellation
61. Disdain
62. W.W. I city of song
63. Heat and cool, as steel
65. Vermont city
66. Stroked
69. Article of food
70. Quick ones on the watch?
72. Uncle Remus's ___ Baby
73. Tart
74. Biblical wall word
75. Work units
76. Goalie's milieu
77. Indian weight
78. Elba-Waterloo hiatus
82. Cocktail spreads
83. Musical vibratos
85. "Bon voyage" locales
86. Rattan workers
87. Actor Mischa
88. Doctrines
89. ___-Saint-Michel
90. Like shoptalk
93. Famous designer
95. Believer in "Ars gratia artis"
99. Perceptive bonus
101. Oater weapon
103. Exaction
104. Further
105. The haut-monde
106. Sometimes they're wild
107. Old-time dagger
108. Less favorable
109. Kind of year or day
110. Swiss artist

DOWN

1. Bean-curd food
2. Egyptian deity
3. Showing strain
4. Impressive displays
5. Author Marya
6. Different
7. Onus
8. ___ Arbor
9. Compensation
10. Unbeliever
11. Slay
12. Kind of wire
13. Dir.
14. Sent on
15. Does a hair job
16. Robe of office
17. Ace
18. Good golf scores
24. Police offs.
26. Pierre's thoughts
29. Crippled
32. Threnody
33. City on the Moselle
34. Run a rope through
35. Moslem title
36. Daddy Warbucks, e.g.
37. Napery
38. Legalese for "to the point"
39. Bourgeoisie's residence?
40. Duck
41. Piping
43. Actor Dick
44. River for Burns
47. Biblical underworld
49. Harmful things
51. Musical chord
52. Prefix for scope or cosm
53. Bedizen
54. Begat
55. Preserves
57. General course
59. Jewel stones
61. Holy, to Cicero
62. Spasms
63. "Halt!", at sea
64. More precise
65. Diver's bane
66. Actor Grant's namesakes
67. Ardent
68. Go formal
70. Mexican title
71. Learns
74. Cutting tool with clamps
76. Pole used in logging
78. U.S. writer Emerson ___
79. Common to both sexes
80. Kind of jockey
81. Transfers, as an estate
82. All: Prefix
84. Cloak
86. Be a sponger, in Ireland
89. Hostess Perle
90. High fliers
91. African king
92. Wheel holder
93. Growl
94. Govt. radio arm
95. Leaf-stem angle
96. Common abbr.
97. Half a head-on talk
98. Gaelic
100. Self
102. U.N. group

88 Low Finance By William Lutwiniak

On a level where money really matters.

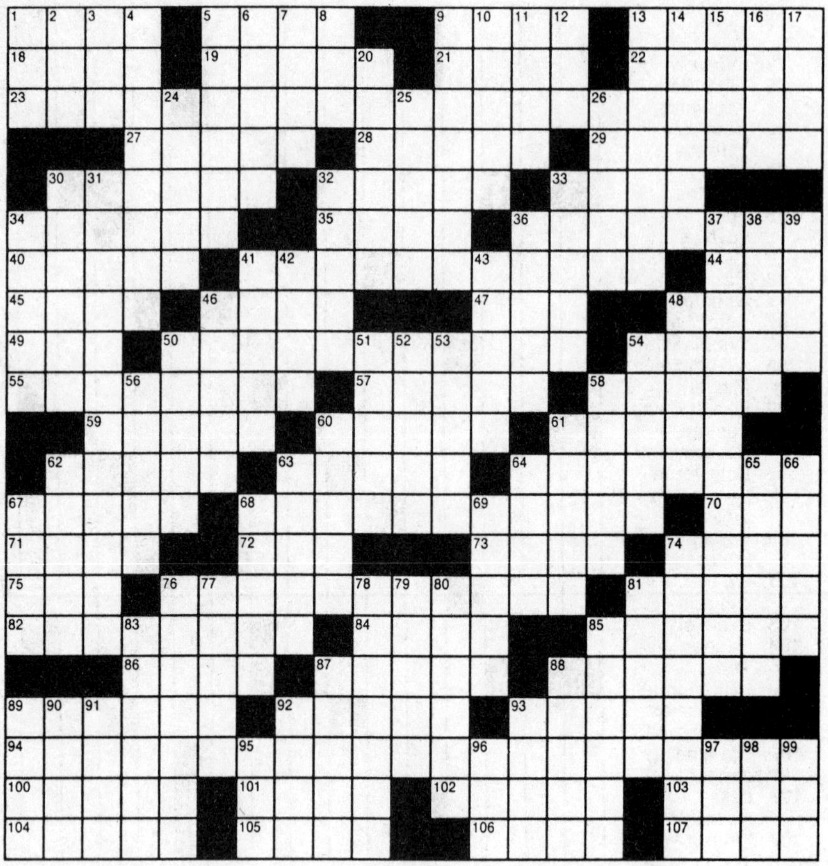

ACROSS

1. Shakes a leg
5. Actress Pitts
9. Marriage, e.g.
13. First-rate, in India
18. Rights org.
19. Airborne
21. Ivy Leaguers
22. Late Marquand hero
23. Budget, with 50, 68 and 76 Across
27. Snoops
28. Spring bloomer
29. Things to know
30. More painful
32. State of Brazil
33. Gas or coal
34. Jack-in-the-pulpits
35. "___ well!"
36. Sour cherries
40. Makes an impression
41. Capital punishment?
44. Freudian word
45. Zilch, in tennis
46. Sheepshank or granny
47. Westchester city
48. First place
49. ___ du Diable
50. See 23 Across
54. Challenges
55. Old Greek lyre
57. Has coming
58. Attitudinizes
59. Gypsy card
60. "___ there!" (let's shake)
61. Energetic one
62. Lionel Hampton's instrument
63. Penthouse
64. Forebear
67. Like oak leaves
68. See 23 Across
70. Coronado's gold
71. Bad things
72. Bambi's mother
73. Diamond group
74. Fukien port
75. Quebec season
76. See 23 Across
81. What to put on Mame
82. Banded with color
84. Large bird
85. Certain English socialist
86. Danube feeder
87. Karloff
88. Navigational systems
89. N.L. team
92. Spite
93. Of an Asian people
94. Sinking fund?
100. Cape of Brazil
101. Consumer
102. Provoke
103. Physics Nobelist in 1944
104. Deed holder
105. Makes book
106. Cave dwellers
107. Lambs' dams

DOWN

1. Tarboosh or fez
2. Most of Antarctica
3. Old 45-inch measure
4. Chemical compound
5. Jesters
6. Tattered Tom's creator
7. Oriental sauces
8. Sky sighting
9. Self-reproach
10. Miss Massey
11. Minuscule
12. Opposite of WNW
13. Plains Indians
14. Laborious
15. Role for Liz
16. "Roberta" composer
17. Votes for
20. Black gum tree
24. Flag and orris
25. Domain
26. "___ the Top"
30. Small hollow
31. Cars for bond sellers?
32. Saguaros
33. Outwitted
34. Off the cuff
36. Yucatán natives
37. C.P.A.'s turf?
38. Certain arches
39. Progeny
41. Bullion mold
42. Lunchtime
43. English river
46. Tokyo zithers
48. Let up
50. All in
51. Nerve: Prefix
52. Took part
53. Made a stab at
54. Current
56. Ruth and Herman
58. Airliner
60. Flycatcher
61. Patterned cloth
62. River in Ghana
63. Up front
64. Big smile
65. Fragrances
66. Senior member
67. Gladly
68. "Golden Boy" author
69. Virgil hero: Var.
74. Large tuna
76. Persuade
77. Medieval guild
78. Mangles
79. Heartbeat
80. Where Goethe lived
81. Of pressure
83. Waxy ointment
85. Armed strength
87. Sire
88. Part of l.c.d.
89. ___ time (never)
90. Put in an appearance
91. Sea swallow
92. Urn's relative
93. Arctic bird
95. Massage
96. Soho V.I.P.
97. Detroit-based union
98. Helmsman's course
99. ". . . ___ of thee"

89 Family Matters By Mary Russ

In one way or another.

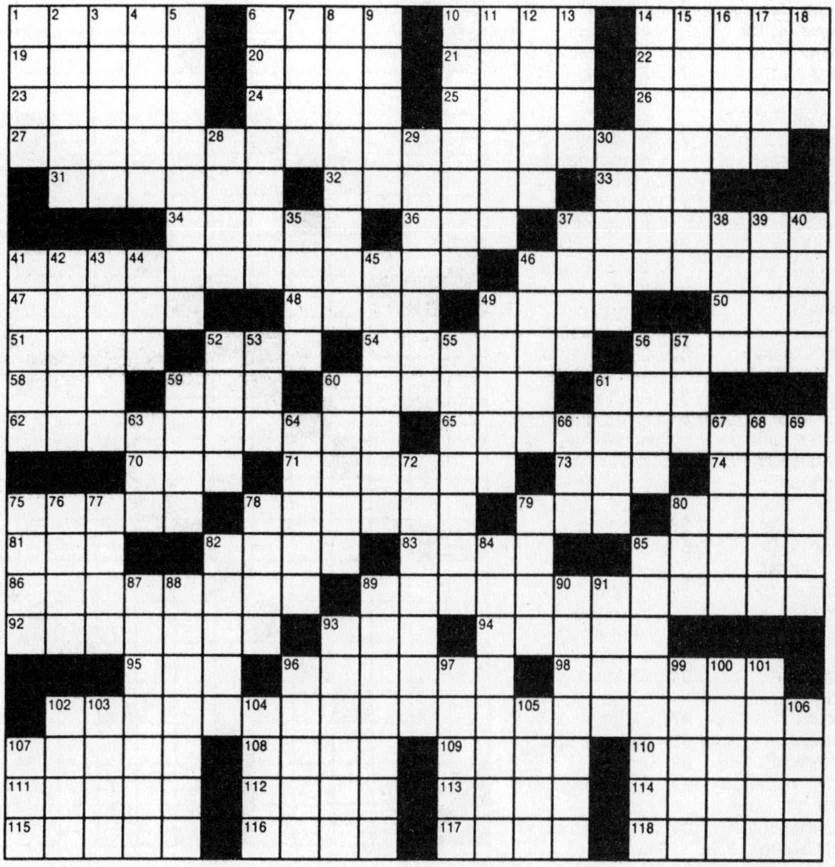

ACROSS

1. Wasps' inflictions
6. Panama and derby
10. Ancient chest
14. Do the fandango
19. Knock for ___
20. "___ a Man": Ciardi
21. Where to spend a krone
22. Standing straight
23. Terra ___
24. Señora's room
25. Essential point
26. Mexican sandalwood
27. Dostoyevsky clan
31. U.N. cultural org.
32. Complains
33. G.I. address
34. Baseball stat
36. Blas or Hodges
37. They sometimes buck
41. Amateur-theater standby
46. Burl Ives portrayal
47. Queen's fare, in rhyme
48. Elec. units
49. Allot
50. Poetic time of day
51. On the briny
52. Road surface
54. One of the Horae
56. Pierre's proposal
58. Swamp
59. Buddy
60. Ringlike marking
61. Upper-class water hole
62. Native country
65. Big time for florists
70. Cenozoic, for one
71. Novelist Zweig
73. Untidy dwelling
74. Violinist Bull
75. Actress Hasso
78. She took an ax
79. Miss Hagen
80. Solo
81. Darkroom abbr.
82. Quite normal
83. Journalist Jacob
85. Decree
86. Surrender
89. She painted rural scenes
92. Rear part of an old limo
93. Cote sound
94. French philosopher
95. Hole puncher
96. Homeland, to Bardot
98. Jewelry paste
102. Words to a certain hopeful swimmer
107. Hooded jacket
108. French menu word
109. Persian elf
110. Rhone feeder
111. Johnny of TV game shows
112. College in N.C.
113. ___ and Thummim
114. European magpie
115. Mr. who went to town
116. Feathery elevator
117. Cooking meas.
118. Dwarf

DOWN

1. Blow in the breeze
2. Statesman Root
3. Actress Sophia
4. Resting place for Napoleon
5. In a meager way
6. Trevelyan's field
7. Nanking nurse
8. Wire
9. Bart or Belle
10. Pilot's place
11. Knesset's land
12. Slanders
13. Sponge spicule
14. Lobster or squid
15. Petrified Forest's state
16. Pianist Peter
17. Cicero's 204
18. Ike's command
28. Renoir's paint pigment
29. Reports to work
30. ". . . on the ___ of Lake Lebarge"
35. Gravel ridges
37. Light snack
38. B–G connection
39. Polish border river
40. Ago, to Scotty
41. Banter
42. Hebrew prophet
43. As to
44. Caricaturist Gardner
45. Topsy-turvy
46. Stephen Vincent or William Rose
49. Cut a ___ (share profits)
52. O'Hara mansion
53. Winner take ___
55. Bulgarian neighbor
56. Nashville's grand old place
57. Scale notes
59. Pierre's relative
60. Poetic cave
61. Bristle
63. Coop dweller
64. All together
66. V.P. under F.D.R.
67. Miss Day
68. Mad-tea-party intruder
69. Irish poet
72. Composer Wolf-___
75. Denomination
76. Japanese box
77. Author of "Three Weeks"
78. Sumatran wildcat
79. Govt. meat stamp
80. Hubbub
82. Like fish
84. Entities
85. Coming into view
87. Not invited
88. Paul and Phyllis
89. Early machine gun
90. Goes wide of the mark
91. Rat-poison chemical
93. U.S. Red Cross founder
96. Philadelphia suburb
97. Opposite of outtake
99. "The heathen Chinee"
100. Office gal
101. Antitoxin
102. Bulldogs' home
103. Gaelic
104. Made a picture
105. Faucet problem
106. Network
107. Pea container

90 Stoneware By John Hales

But not exactly of the kitchen variety.

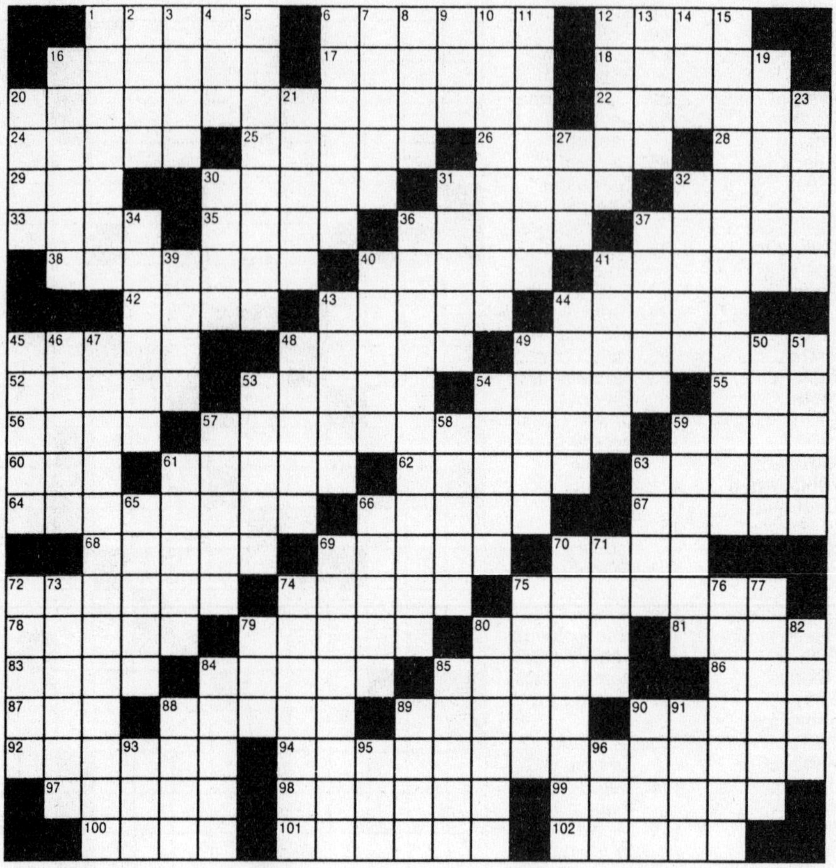

ACROSS

1. Companions
6. Timorous
12. Bowsprit, for one
16. River to the Yukon
17. Take turns
18. French landscapist
20. Small roasting fowl
22. Highest points
24. Certain Buddhist monk
25. Likes excessively
26. Moon valley
28. Krazy animal
29. U.S. architect
30. Pouter pens
31. Benumbed
32. Fungus: Prefix
33. Adjust the pitch
35. ___ about
36. Liturgies
37. Take exception
38. Be fitting
40. Name in bridge
41. Cocktail snack
42. Military off. pool
43. Parts of bushels
44. High trump
45. Bestial
48. Subsides
49. Courted
52. "When found, make ___ of": Dickens
53. Place for household discards
54. Does cataloguing
55. U.N. org.
56. Comedienne Imogene
57. Football coach of note
59. "___ in the U.S.A."
60. Wapiti
61. Controls
62. Mickey Rooney's family
63. Recluse
64. Most witless
66. Fall bloom
67. Offhand remark on the Champs
68. Scarflike vestment
69. Less gabby
70. Splitting tool
72. Kitchen wraps
74. Weather-detecting system
75. Acted in a fussy way
78. I.R.S. action
79. Switchboard face
80. In-group
81. Vetch seed
83. Landon and namesakes
84. Act the fink
85. Humble home
86. W.W. II fliers
87. Chou En-___
88. Lapwing
89. Be penny-wise
90. Bubbly measure
92. Heckart or Brennan
94. Western U.S. range
97. Clipped
98. Store fodder
99. Incites
100. Fujiyama topping
101. Gathered at the table
102. Home of Saul's witch

DOWN

1. Product of the Industrial Revolution
2. Singer Paul
3. Savoir-faire
4. Wine: Prefix
5. Scornful
6. More common-place
7. "___ have thorns . . ."
8. Old English letters
9. Expression of contempt
10. Recapitulates
11. Regular frequenter
12. Bring to a sub-boil
13. Vatican City figure
14. Greek nickname
15. Heavyweight champ of the 1950's
16. Shredded
19. Important afternoon item, in Britain
20. Absorbed
21. "___ your life!"
23. Hold for later
27. French article
30. Word with tail or rack
31. Daggers
32. "Three ___ a Horse"
34. List of corrigenda
36. Transparent quartz
37. Andrews and Wynter
39. Kind of metalware
40. Supernatural creature
41. French philosopher of the 1800's
43. Two English P.M.'s
44. ___ of a dilemma
45. Turned toward
46. ___ Gay
47. TV vehicle for James Garner, with "The"
48. Tour de force
49. One of the ray family
50. Church officer
51. Active ones
53. Flavoring for ouzo
54. Hard: Prefix
57. ___ over (swoons)
58. One of the Hebrides
59. Annoy
61. Mirthful
63. Vientiane's country
65. Expenses, in Cannes
66. Poet W. H.
69. Singsong delivery
70. Skiing disaster
71. Dick Button's old place
72. Halle's river
73. Café ___
74. Swiftian writings
75. Having a flat surface
76. On a previous occasion
77. Sewers
79. Hillbilly's parent
80. ___ in (interrupted)
82. Newts
84. Extend, as a contract
85. Bill Blass's concern
88. Money in Matamoros
89. Revue feature
90. Fancy button
91. ___ Robles, Calif.
93. Shore bird
95. General Pickett's insignia
96. ___ compos mentis

91 Title Revisions By Louis Sabin

For the zanier rather than for the better.

ACROSS

1. Eagle variety
5. Wences of the Ed Sullivan show
10. Carrie Chapman and family
15. Musical sign
19. Seaweed
20. Old-womanish
21. Brundage of Olympic note
22. Israeli dance
23. Florentine river
24. Overalls material
25. Neophytes: Var.
26. Tamiroff of film
27. Benny's theme, after an overdue library book?
31. Dupe
32. In that case
33. Be obliged
34. Tarzan friend
37. Mongol tribesman
39. Weevil's abode
41. Humdinger
44. About
45. Sharif of the bridge table
46. Highway rig
47. Greek Olympian
48. Masochist's melody?
53. Hebrew reading aid
54. Osiris's wife
55. Maugham weather
56. Maine college town
57. Atlantic route
60. Metric measure
62. False show
63. Cry uncle to a plow maker?
67. Gentle touch
70. Out of whack
71. Perpetual
75. Bottom line
76. Move
77. Washed-out
79. Basic unit
80. Sugar daddy's theme?
86. Rock metals
87. Flirting one
88. Archipelago unit
89. Uncanny
90. Electrical unit
91. Nero's route
92. Word on a door
93. Life work
94. Franklin's 1936 opponent
95. Plastic surgeon's target
96. Kind of head or point
97. "Brief Encounter" theme?
106. Kitty's feed
107. U. S. Grant's foe
108. Relating to form
109. Flag
111. Connery or O'Casey
112. Mythical dwarf
113. Top-drawer
114. Opera wear
115. Response to a joke
116. Equine measures
117. Quell, by fear
118. Merganser

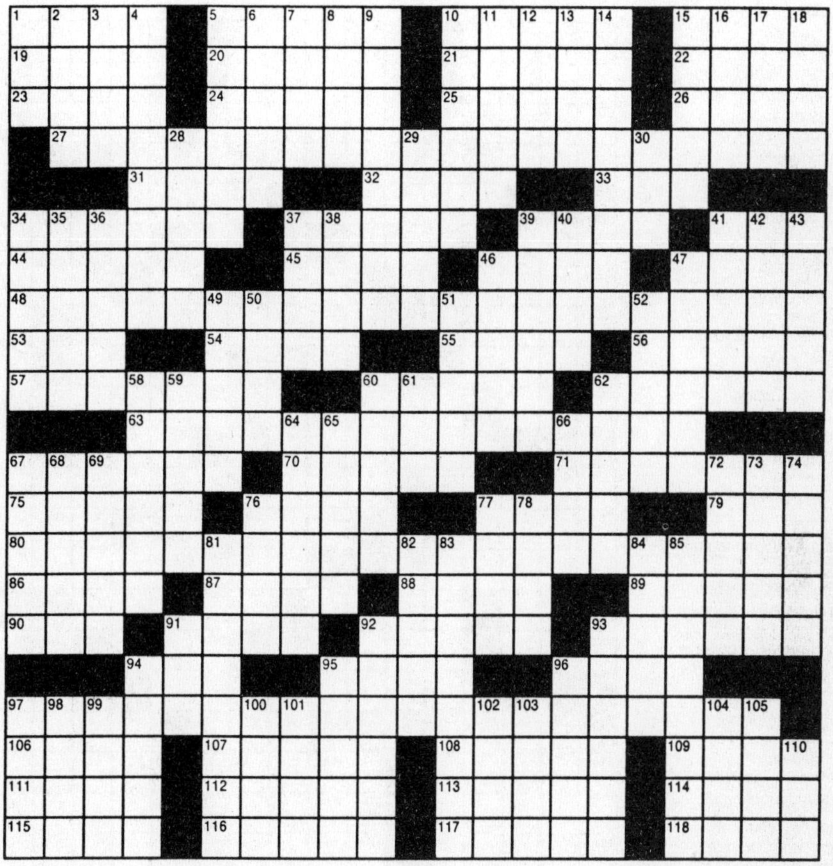

DOWN

1. Bleat
2. Shah Jahan's building site
3. Film director Fritz
4. Down in the dumps
5. Make blue
6. Challenger
7. Very early Atlantic crosser
8. Music critic Downes
9. Payment
10. "O Pioneers!" author
11. Of birds
12. Part of Canada's N.W.T.
13. Walked
14. Of one's heartbeat
15. Irritate
16. Mischief-maker of myth
17. Innisfail
18. Fortune's partner
28. Emulate Bryan
29. Miss Lewis of TV
30. Swivel-neck bird
34. Gives the boot
35. Build immunity
36. Radio, press, etc.
37. Pith helmet
38. Loving Latin word
39. Proved false
40. Augury
41. Monterrey money
42. Embodiment of peace
43. Word of mouth
46. Belle or Brenda
47. Plum-fancier Jack
49. "Peanuts" character
50. Junkie
51. Rowans and aspens
52. Bay of Biscay feeder
58. Feudal lords
59. Brazilian fruit drink
60. Emulates Atropos
61. Six-pointers: Abbr.
62. Gallic heads
64. "I'd ___ be right . . ."
65. Mideast bigwig
66. Hard to hold
67. Blush
68. Livorno love
69. Make merry
72. Bête ___
73. Laurie or Oakley
74. Painter Fernand
76. Eye problem
77. Soccer name
78. ___ of Hezekiah: Ezra 2:16
81. Start a journey
82. Hoisting machine
83. Valued
84. Niobe's production
85. Unorthodox believers
91. Off one's feed
92. Atelier staples
93. Lockup
94. Theater type
95. Eugene or Sally
96. D.C. department
97. Beanery listing
98. Classy
99. Deseret state
100. Vague or Miles
101. N.C. college
102. Certain kind of model
103. Correct
104. Ancient Syria
105. Pound sound
110. Baste

92 Bargain Day By Judson Trent

Wherein the solver gets an extra one free.

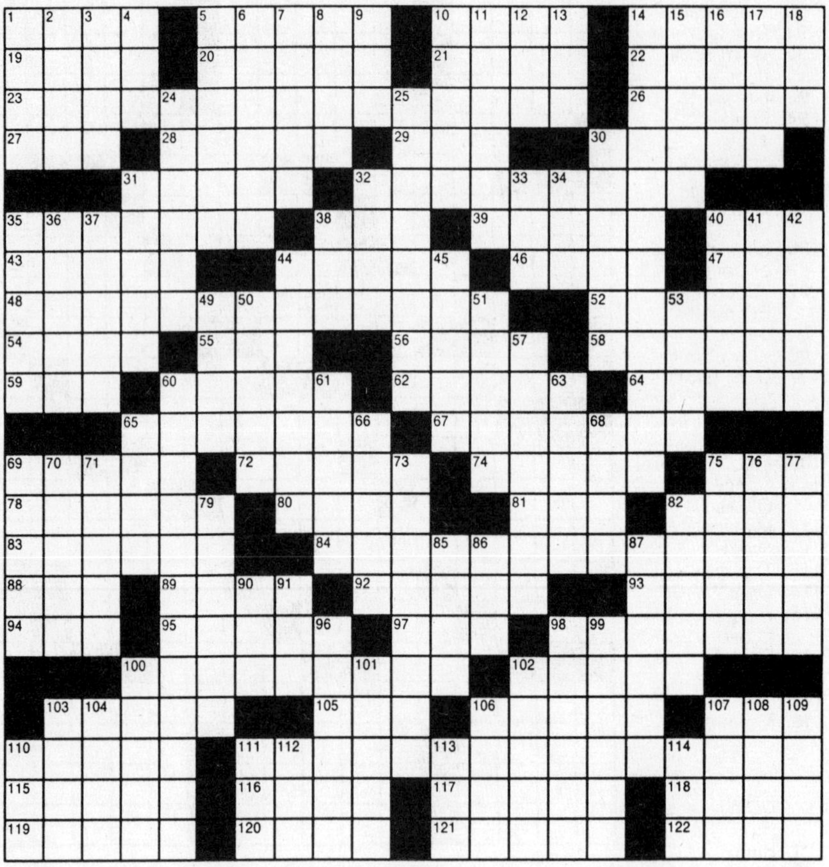

ACROSS

1. Bristle
5. "____ war": F.D.R.
10. Latin I word
14. Black buck
19. Not give ____
20. Kind of code
21. Wisdom
22. Horace specialty
23. Comedy about racing addicts
26. Man's man
27. Id ____
28. "Excavating for ____ . . .": "Clementine"
29. Salamander
30. Ancient capital of Ethiopia
31. Chimp's relative
32. Puma
35. Emulating Roper
38. Kind of pole in a pond
39. Part of l.c.d.
40. A fjord is one
43. Liquid in a fat
44. Ointments
46. Writer Sholem
47. A Murray
48. B.S.A. rank
52. Maintain
54. Rip or neap
55. Brit. lexicon
56. Bandy
58. Sawbuck
59. His, in France
60. White-tailed eagles
62. Am. Samoa and Virgin Is.
64. Explosive, for short
65. Ermine
67. Like the Pacific's Mariana Trench
69. Rawboned animal
72. Talking birds
74. Rural crossing
75. Berliner's word of distress
78. Considers
80. Reindeer herdsman
81. Marshall Plan org.
82. Lily plant
83. Stone Age tool
84. Variety store, familiarly
88. "Blessed ____ the meek"
89. Tom Watson's goal
92. Acclaim
93. Model
94. Samoan monogram
95. Hurl
97. Loch Ness headwear
98. Ancient ascetics
100. Hessian, in 1776
102. Constellation Ara
103. Greek walkways
105. ____-la-la
106. More loyal
107. Brenda or Peggy
110. Pope in 847
111. Insurance proviso
115. Love, for Luigi
116. Miss Vague
117. Snoopy one
118. Gen. Bradley
119. Famed opera's home
120. Emulated Little
121. Listens
122. Take out

DOWN

1. Item for Jimmy Valentine
2. Piccadilly statue
3. Strained
4. I.R.S. time
5. "The ____ Cometh"
6. Sharpening
7. Beside
8. Resiliency
9. Pitcher's stat
10. Up in the air
11. Human
12. ____ poetica
13. Before total
14. ESP
15. Dissociated
16. Aria
17. ____ fixe
18. Kind of proceeds
24. Gyrene
25. Leading
30. Oman's capital
31. Part of O.D.
32. Fine leather
33. ____ culpa
34. Hemispheric assn.
35. Frost and Eliot
36. Fran's friend
37. City on the Aire
38. Cigarette no-no
40. Catkin
41. Thinner
42. D.C. subway
44. Torment
45. Strewed
49. Urd, for one
50. Mod fabric
51. Weeds
53. In a ____ (piqued)
57. Excuse
60. Janet Gaynor film
61. French upper house
63. Star in Virgo
65. O. Henry's gift givers
66. Anatomical seam
68. Verve
69. Vow
70. Anglo-Saxon menial
71. Vexes
73. Ghostly
75. U.F.O. visitor
76. Plant clusters
77. Cads
79. Smiths, at times
82. Krait
85. Do in
86. ". . . the King of Siam, ____"
87. Render harmless
90. Resin
91. First lady
96. Whole
98. Dodged
99. Controls
100. Dancer Shearer
101. Old Hungarian hero
102. He had an army
103. Highway rig
104. Kind of chest
106. Flag
107. Gin-and-tonic additive
108. Common abbr.
109. Literary governess
110. Thrash
111. Power org.
112. Hill V.I.P.
113. N.T. epistle
114. Nap

93 Missing Links By Nancy Ross

In which something is always lacking.

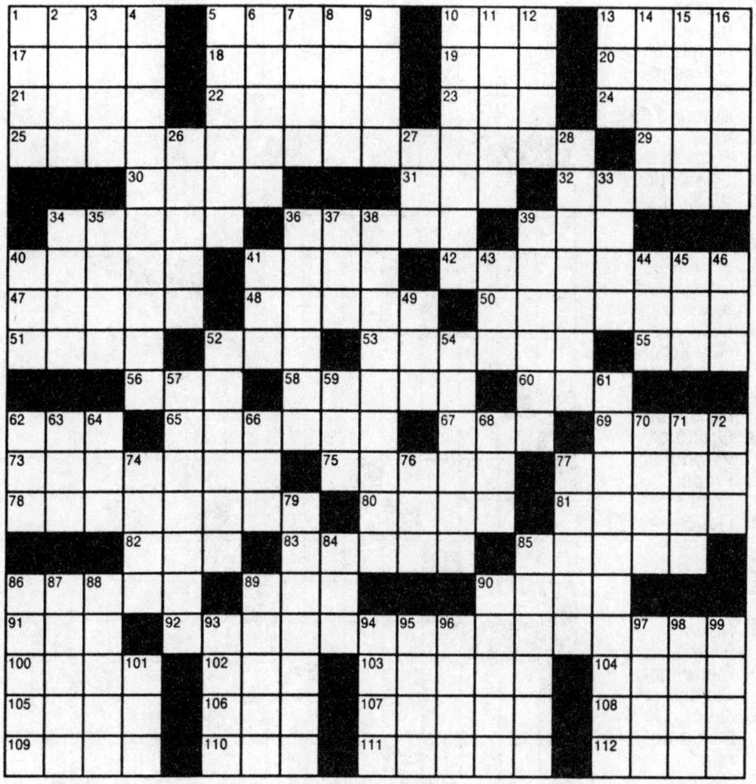

ACROSS

1. Heedless
5. Halloween creature
10. Sound from the fold
13. Makes logs
17. Best or Ferber
18. Old Greek temple part
19. College deg.
20. ___ du jour
21. Accompanying
22. Less green
23. Honest ___
24. Baseball's Berra
25. Minus 100
29. Coop dweller
30. Breakfasts
31. Lamb's dad
32. Bread ingredient
34. Intimations
36. Mephistopheles
39. Ministerial abbr.
40. River of forgetfulness
41. Coconut fiber
42. Minus 3
47. Bring up
48. Esteem
50. Droopy-eared dog
51. Gandhi garment
52. Long time: Abbr.
53. Actor Zero
55. Hog's habitat
56. Chorus syllable
58. Curve into an arch
60. Pub quaff
62. ___ de Cologne
65. Crater lake near Naples
67. Conger
69. Charles's pooch
73. One who slanders
75. Ryan or Tatum
77. Ordinary
78. Minus 3
80. Professor 'iggins
81. Waffle topper
82. Feed-bag grain
83. Nincompoops
85. Patsies
86. Scorn
89. One of a Latin trio
90. Spore clusters
91. Keats subject
92. Minus 6
100. Evening in Paris
102. Poet's before
103. Muddle
104. Ring up
105. Poker stake
106. Tune
107. "___ Ben Jonson!"
108. Poem
109. Want
110. Vertebrate's foot
111. Traditions
112. ___ precedent

DOWN

1. Damp
2. Ernie's widow
3. Theater org.
4. Minus 459
5. Hurries
6. Riches
7. Motor magnate
8. The cheaper spread
9. Actor Malden
10. Obtrusive
11. Snapshot spot
12. Not yet risen
13. Le Carré mole
14. Oahu word
15. Pay
16. Be sparing with
26. Glutted
27. George's brother
28. It's under a lid
33. Tied
34. Juno, in Greece
35. Road, in old Rome
36. Oklahoman
37. Rhone tributary
38. Minus 76
39. Rescind
40. Certain wts.
41. Fidel's one-time comrade
43. D.D.E. predecessor
44. Three-toed sloths
45. Put to pasture: Abbr.
46. Shakespearean tinker
49. Kanga's child
52. Warning
54. Shocks Grandmother
57. Widespread
59. P predecessors
61. Minus 5
62. Ames and Asner
63. Predecessor of the N.R.C.
64. Skywatcher's abbr.
66. Sea bird
68. Isle of ___
70. Steady
71. Greek letters
72. One of a range
74. Cupid
76. Opposite of WSW
77. Appropriate
79. Whines
84. ___ Canals
85. Eludes
86. Hayward or Anthony
87. Disposed to
88. Wed
89. Eagle's nest
90. Snoozer's sound
93. Rattletrap
94. Ancient Greek coin
95. Agrippina's son
96. At a distance
97. Neck part
98. Lump
99. Wagner heroine
101. Leftist hue

94 Video a.k.a.'s By Bette Sue Cohen

Roles that should be familiar to tube buffs.

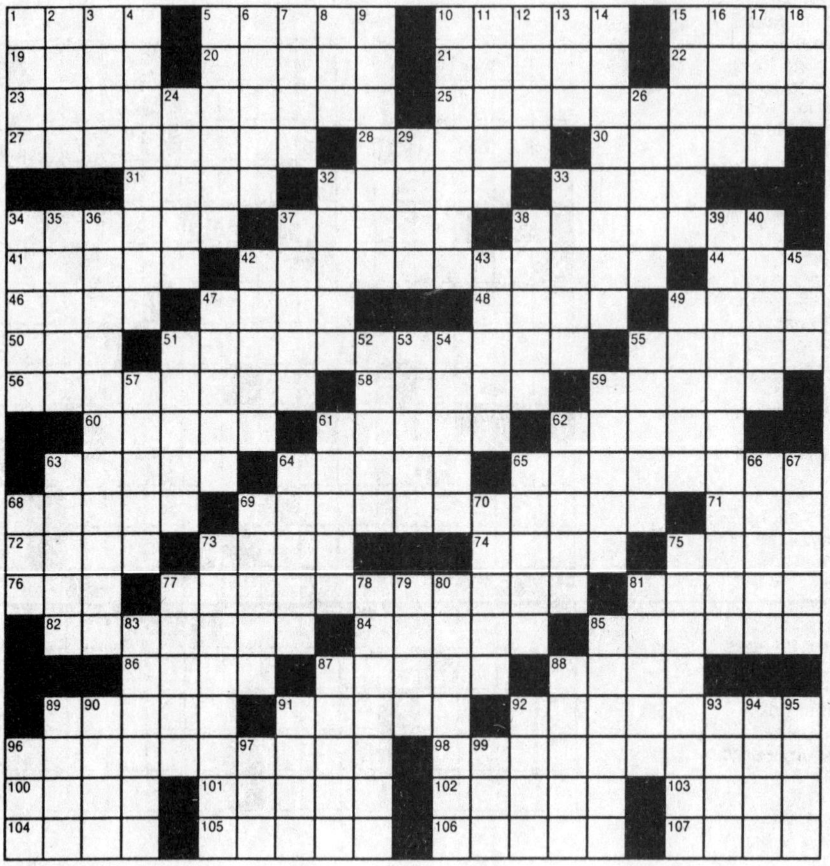

ACROSS

1. Soothing ointment
5. Bandleader Shaw
10. Leg of mutton
15. Partake in a marathon
19. Helm position
20. Barber's instrument
21. City south of Gainesville
22. Pearl Buck heroine
23. Krystle Carrington
25. Simon Templar
27. Edith Head, e.g.
28. Greek language
30. Winslow of the seascapes
31. "___ Hand Luke"
32. Nob and Bunker
33. Head, in Grenoble
34. Leave
37. Conclusive
38. Comforted
41. ___ barrel
42. B. J. Hunnicut
44. Kildare and Ben Casey, for short
46. Formality
47. ___ and hounds
48. Props for strokes
49. Work on a manuscript
50. Native: Suffix
51. Tony Baretta
55. Behaved nosily
56. Did a wall-to-wall job
58. Get ___ out of (provoke)
59. ___ eggs
60. Auctioneer's mallet
61. "I will come within ___ of wine"
62. Miss Verdugo
63. Porridge
64. Choctaw or Creek
65. Tugboat Annie
68. ". . . and ___ a goodnight!"
69. Julie McCoy
71. Sound from Mary's pet
72. Edison's middle name
73. Gangster's girl
74. Dismounted
75. House plant
76. President before J.F.K.
77. Irma Peterson
81. Strong point
82. Waldorf's partner
84. Owlish sounds
85. One ___ money
86. U.S. Revolutionary statesman
87. Clergyman's residence
88. Grotto or moon color
89. Prepare onions
91. Reached effectively
92. Frightful
96. Susie McNamara
98. Sister Bertrille
100. Playwright Simon
101. Jay Silverheels role
102. Roman magistrate
103. I have said, as Caesar said it
104. Proofreader's mark
105. "Sir, we are ___ of singing birds": S. Johnson
106. Did
107. Author Wiesel

DOWN

1. Like Daddy Warbucks
2. "I cannot tell ___"
3. Dawson and Deighton
4. Program for the older set
5. "We ___ amused"
6. French composer
7. Russian ruler: Var.
8. Charged particle
9. Author Caldwell
10. Mobster
11. Religious images
12. Token of defiance
13. Rah!, Spanish style
14. Natives of North Carolina
15. Customer for Mrs. Hoople
16. African plant
17. Singer Vikki
18. Chemical suffix
24. Marketplace
26. Where to stay the night
29. Norwegian king
32. Boy Scout, at times
33. "Being ___": 1979 film
34. Style of architecture
35. Patti LuPone role
36. James Phelps
37. Axed, as from a job
38. Wading bird
39. Frank McBride
40. Partner of cut
42. Miss Normand of the silents
43. Friars' event
45. Avg.
47. Vicki Baum's was grand
49. Miss Moran and namesakes
51. Wild party
52. Snouty animal
53. Money under the table, e.g.
54. Sheets, pillowcases, etc.
55. Kind of agent or conference
57. Actress Prentiss
59. Admiral's charge
61. As ___ (generally speaking)
62. Stu of "Trouble with Father"
63. Ingrid portrayed her
64. Actress Shire
65. Aegean island
66. Neighbor of Mars
67. Hindu queen
68. Youngster
69. Lemur
70. Savor
73. Ohio college city
75. Front
77. Homey wall hanging
78. Thingamajig
79. College in New Rochelle
80. ". . . and the ___ voices": T. S. Eliot
81. Draft flunker's class
83. Dishevel
85. Criticized harshly
87. Sahl et al.
88. Miss Starr the outlaw
89. Snick's partner
90. Indigo dye
91. Kelly or Sarazen
92. Emulate a butterfly
93. ___-de-boeuf
94. Roman 1061
95. Singer Adams
96. Plus
97. Brief word of endearment
99. Asst. at Camp David

95 Quiet, Please By Alfio Micci

An observation on the drawbacks of obtrusiveness.

ACROSS

1. Impose a tax
7. Miss or Bull
10. Recede
13. Actress Rigg
18. Purchased
19. Of a phonetic speech sound
21. Stuck out
22. Italian herb mixture
23. Gourmet
24. E.T. et al.
25. Start of an old saying
28. Bog
29. Legal beneficiary
30. Unified
31. Campus group
34. Prefix for appear or appoint
36. Hateful
38. Kind of wit
41. Yalies
42. Flub
43. "Rory ____" Samuel Lover novel
45. Not much, musically
46. More of the saying
52. Goddess of wisdom
53. Foolishness
54. Pierre's digs
55. Della of song
56. Fishermen
57. Nursery-rhyme boy
58. Work with an archeologist
59. Harbor craft
60. Overseas
64. Spanish-American War admiral
69. Scottish poet Macleod
74. Cyclades native
75. Brussels exports
76. Look to for support
77. More of the saying
80. Wrongful act
81. Bruckner
82. Roof adornment
83. City on the Aar
84. Mimic
85. Toot
87. Freshwater fish
88. "The ____ Report": 1976
89. Rat-____-tat
90. African nation
93. Modernist
95. End of the saying
103. Detective's quest
104. Kind of lamb
105. Where Livorno is
107. Up
108. Facing trouble
109. Wyoming range
110. Fowl
111. White House nickname
112. Compass reading
113. Ridges

DOWN

1. German composer Vogler
2. Child's mouthwash of old
3. Japanese wrestling
4. Equal, to Pierre
5. It's usually short
6. One of 50
7. Oil cartel
8. Mistake, in old Rome
9. Howe
10. Chopin work
11. Fermenting yeast
12. Cordon ____
13. Sweet-sounding
14. Homer classic
15. Teen or golden follower
16. Hawaiian bird
17. Classified items
20. Skin woe
21. French spas
26. Madagascar lemur
27. More miffed
31. Orchestra instrument
32. Nouveau ____
33. Leavings
35. Being a pest
36. Native Egyptians
37. Nobel physicist Harold
38. Use a divining rod
39. Fluid of the gods
40. Tide regulator
41. "Cielo ____!," Ponchielli aria
42. Guidonian note
43. Without, in Wittenberg
44. Golda
45. Nabokov novel
47. Donkey, in Dieppe
48. Chang's twin
49. Oriental cymbals
50. Pollutant
51. Scull
56. Foreign or first
57. Follower of Attila
58. Clammy
59. Fixed the salad
60. Fabler of note
61. Eric of old films
62. Chasm
63. Lout
64. Freshet
65. Guthrie
66. New ____ hay
67. ____ hemp (Asian shrub)
68. Piggery
69. Charge
70. Metrical feet
71. Beginning
72. ____ Dame
73. Presently
74. Philippine tree
75. Auld lang ____
76. Oahu garland
78. Kind of worm
79. Exhausted
85. Even-____ (tied)
86. Eucharistic plate
87. Principles
88. Owl
89. Dispatch boat
90. Sea off Australia
91. Librarian's admonition
92. Ta-ta, in Tijuana
94. Long-running musical
95. Israeli dance
96. Expectant
97. Grandiose
98. Miss Horne
99. Ko-Ko's weapon
100. "It must be something ____"
101. Coagulate
102. "____ kleine Nachtmusik"
103. Raincoat
106. Balaam's mount

96 Absent-Minded Prof By Bert Kruse

Activities that make up a day's work for him.

ACROSS

1. Do electioneering
6. European
10. Persona non ____
15. Mr. Magoo's problem
16. Balkan capital
17. Imperfect paper
19. Sport fish
20. Intended to lecture on treaties, instead ____
23. Blah
24. Peter and Ivan, e.g.
26. Minty quaff
27. Geisha garb
28. Kind of type
29. Gesture of respect
31. Midnight item
32. German industrial city
34. Word before Saxon
36. Agnus ____
37. West's grid rival
39. Lords' houses
40. Intended to lecture on Keats, instead ____
43. Exams
44. ____ alai
45. Cinch, with "up"
46. Approach quietly
49. Cactus
52. Social org.
54. Québec traffic alert
55. Here's companion
58. Small versions of tomes
60. Missouri military school
62. Hoard
64. Rim
65. Intended to take the bus, but ____
68. Last write, as it were
69. Word for a male chauvinist
71. Prayer
72. Musical flutterings
74. Sea flier
75. Wine pitchers
77. Letter abbr.
79. Greatly disturbed
80. Poet Bogan and namesakes
82. Exclamation
84. First name of 67 Down
85. High laced boot
87. Meant to confer with the dean, but ____
93. Praying insect
94. Suds
96. Wire measure
97. Cabbage or lettuce
98. That is, to Plautus
99. Period
100. Skewered foods
103. Jour's opposite
104. Neighbor of Ga.
105. Moor
107. Belief
108. Plucky
109. Strode to the dictionary, then ____
113. More like April
115. Oolong experts
116. Gas displays
117. Mighty gods
118. Kind of parade or circle
119. Cuxhaven's river
120. Become a parent

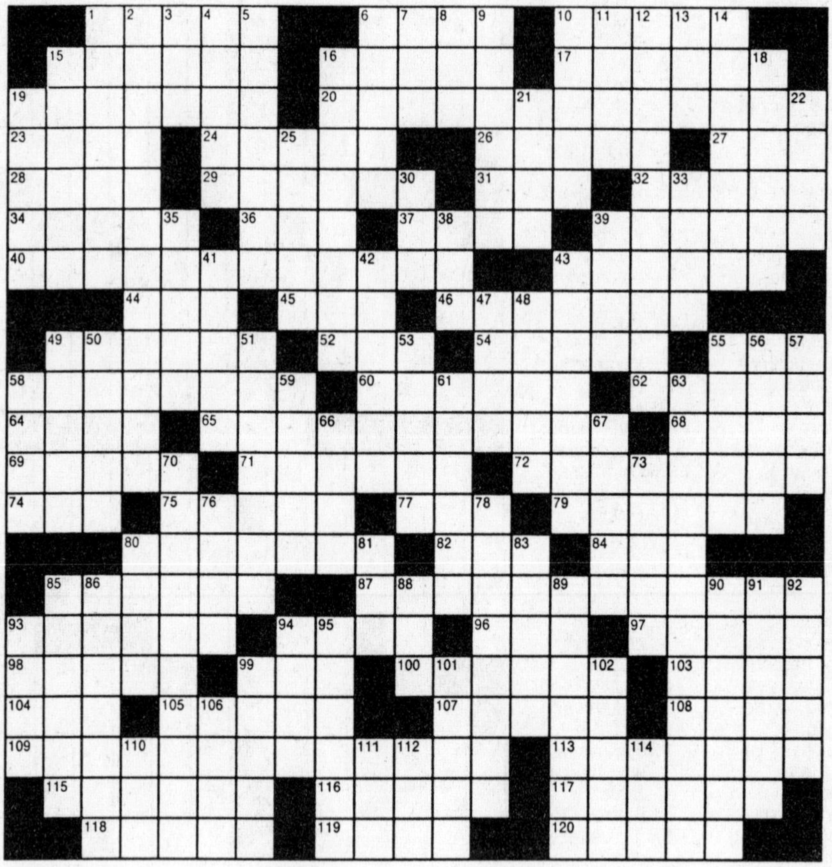

DOWN

1. Idaho's flower
2. Intended to demand discipline, but ____
3. A.P. news rival
4. Coins
5. Fencing thrust
6. He played in Offenbach's orchestra
7. Newt
8. S.A. city
9. Knee instruments
10. Bar's partner
11. Explain, old style
12. Intended to go out to lunch, but ____
13. Joyful syllable
14. Type of spray
15. Serviceman
16. Got an ankle injury
18. Warm memories
19. Of the cheek
21. Please
22. Confessional reports
25. Turkish flags
30. ____ amis
33. Fastener
35. "____ things!" (Mercy!)
38. Sighs of contentment
39. Kind of run or post
41. Steamed up
42. Stirs up
43. Geraldine and Margaret
47. Lights out
48. Build
49. Symbol expert
50. Golf immortal
51. Eye-dilating liquid
53. Go after weeds again
55. Charlie ____ (galley pipe)
56. Constellation
57. Volstead foes
58. Silent actress Daniels
59. Boils and blisters, e.g.
61. Bait fish
63. Intended to grade themes, but ____
66. Clamping tool
67. Comedy actress of the 1800's
70. Meant to return a library book, but ____
73. Lady
76. San ____ Rey of bridge note
78. Judges' places
80. Assault boats: Abbr.
81. Opposite of NNW
83. Russian-dome shape
85. Worthless person
86. Like many seals
88. Ship for couples
89. Edmonton's province
90. "____ seen nothin' yet"
91. Oozes
92. It grows in Virginny
93. Offend
94. The two
95. Gas component
99. Beginnings
101. Make up for
102. Without zing
106. Summers in Sens
110. Billfish
111. ____ Aviv
112. ____ off (swindle)
114. Japanese admiral

97 Malapropisms By Maura B. Jacobson

In which the medical field is manhandled.

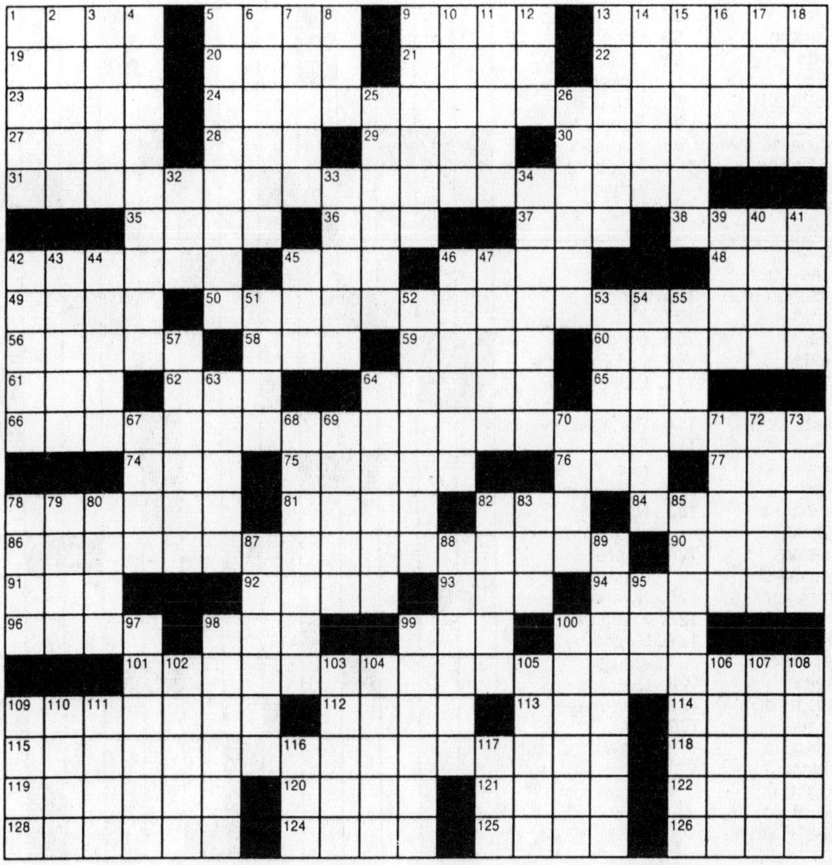

ACROSS

1. Banana-peel mishap
5. Bacchanalian yell
9. Winglike
13. "___ ancient Mariner"
19. Neighbor of Twelve Oaks
20. Merchandising place
21. Buffoon
22. Power of recall
23. Second caliph
24. Botanical scourge in the Middle Ages?
27. First name in spydom
28. Dawn goddess
29. Length times width
30. William Randolph and Patty
31. Killing by antedose?
35. Auto pioneer
36. Kind or bag or mask
37. Ballerina's prop
38. Saint Laurent
42. Read
45. Anecdotal collection
46. Egyptian deity
48. Pier gp.
49. Algerian port
50. Strutters' paranoia?
56. Jousting field
58. First gear
59. Frosh course
60. July birthstones
61. Opposite of nope
62. Sampled the menu
64. Neural networks
65. News agcy.
66. Crackpot ailments?
74. Writer Fleming
75. Thesaurus man
76. Peer Gynt's mother
77. U.S. border canals
78. Havana honcho
81. Qatar ruler
82. English botanic gardens
84. Energetic one
86. "Nor Hell a fury ___"
90. Passport entry
91. Uris hero
92. European fish
93. Impersonate
94. Inquiry into lost goods
96. Hankerings
98. Banned pesticide
99. Numbered rd.
100. Fetal membrane
101. First aid from Socrates?
109. Beatrix's predecessor
112. Delhi nursemaid
113. Fort near Monterey
114. Lloyd's rating
115. What I've come from Alabama with?
118. Fork feature
119. Amalgamation
120. River of Ireland
121. Suit to ___
122. Ivy League team
123. Tinhorn
124. Prevaricated
125. Sawbucks
126. Partner of dem and dose

DOWN

1. Jazz dance
2. Truman's birthplace
3. Seeing red
4. Of prime importance
5. Infixed
6. Royal house of France
7. Go to U.C.L.A. (college choice in L.A.)
8. French summer
9. Portuguese islands
10. Like most highways
11. Region of Vietnam
12. Meadow crop
13. Hinder
14. Weblike tissues
15. "The Girl That ___"
16. Soaks, in the Ozarks
17. In ___ (habituated)
18. Comedian Louis and kin
25. Pacific battle site
26. Seat of authority
32. City RR's
33. V.P. who resigned
34. Shangri-Las
39. End of Caesar's boast
40. Sommer of films
41. Back talk
42. Sex-life subject for Benchley
43. Senecas' foes
44. Hoarse
45. Lover's Latin verb
46. "___ the truth!"
47. Doug Henning's forte
51. Power provider: Abbr.
52. Certain steelworkers
53. Wake-robins
54. Like a ball catcher's hands
55. News notice
57. African sands
63. Up ___ (so far)
64. Blustering
67. Quote
68. Recluse
69. Kind of nose or candle
70. Display ennui
71. Of a metallic element
72. Largest deer
73. Sub detector
78. Ali, once
79. Leeds's river
80. Kind of deep or flint
82. Part of a ruble
83. Prior, in poems
85. Appraised
87. Crone
88. Intriguing, as a tune
89. S.R.O. people
95. One of Ophelia's herbs
97. Smarts
98. Tenfold
99. Was a vagabond
100. Lurch
102. Pluto's realm
103. New Zealand native
104. "East ___" of tear-jerking note
105. Three-card game
106. Sheer fabric
107. Baseballer Del
108. Singer Della
109. Doorway piece
110. "Deutschland ___ alles"
111. Zhivago's love
116. Slitherer
117. Krazy

98 Facing the Bar By Ruth W. Smith

Not the kind you drink at, though.

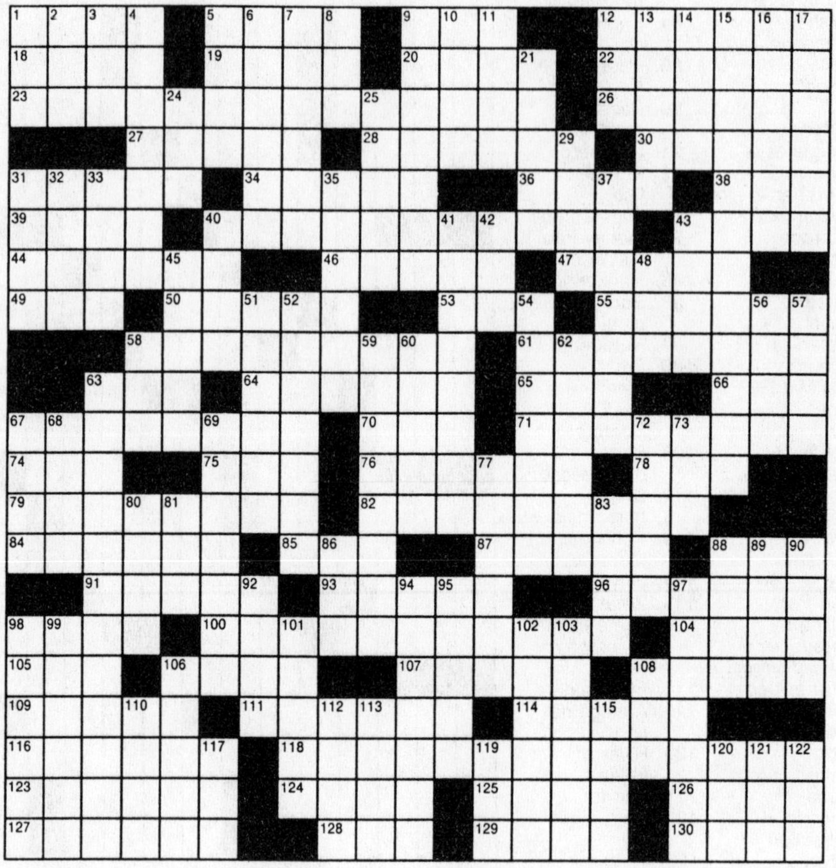

ACROSS

1. Tear
5. Show boredom
9. Cards for G.I.'s
12. Region of Spain
18. Old name for the Saône
19. Part of the eye
20. Lack
22. Decline
23. Come-on in subscription ads
26. Order of priests
27. Hindu guitar
28. Wing-footed
30. Realty sign
31. Lariat
34. Rapidly, in music
36. Venezuelan town
38. Sesame
39. English composer
40. Frustrated athlete
43. Teen-ager's problem
44. What to do to a fever
46. Seated, in heraldry
47. Gadget
49. Kind of cat
50. Hall-of-Famer Cap
53. Stock privileges: Abbr.
55. Canned fish staple
58. Suer
61. Slip forward
63. Game, in Nice
64. Havana cigar smoker
65. Charged particle
66. Order's partner
67. Persian Gulf shipment
70. Civil or cold
71. Cattle thieves
74. Possessed
75. Caesar's 151
76. Old, in Marseille
78. ____ -la-Chapelle
79. Wisconsin city
82. Scram
84. Open porch
85. One belonging to: Suffix
87. State in India
88. Droop
91. Collars or jackets
93. Pomace
96. Baby's toy
98. Soprano Lily
100. Place for service
104. Pearl Buck heroine
105. Can. province
106. African fox
107. Middle, in law
108. Irregular
109. Old Persians
111. California's ____ Sea
114. Eur. country
116. Scenic drive near Naples
118. Gets strict
123. Naturally illuminated
124. Spore clusters
125. Swerve
126. Pianist Peter
127. Sword-shaped
128. Distress call
129. Advantages
130. Do a TV show

DOWN

1. W.W. II heroes
2. Slip up
3. Denial in Aberdeen
4. Actor's helper
5. Siberian tent
6. Fly
7. Become tedious
8. Giant reed of India
9. Accretions of money, for example
10. Challenge
11. Ooze
12. Branch
13. Vaquero's rope
14. Kind of hairdo
15. Troubled conscience
16. Bone-tissue substance
17. Irritate
21. Life, to Montaigne
24. Uncle, in Cádiz
25. Pledges
29. Bit of sediment
31. Flog
32. Johnson of TV
33. Shot or dragon
35. Provides meagerly
37. Prayers
40. Bantu-speaking people
41. Branch of the military
42. Between Q and U
43. Village in Norway
45. Worth
48. Mineo
51. Word form for Palermo's land
52. Forming a row
54. Garden shrubs
56. Glacial ridges
57. "What ____ on the Rialto?"
58. Foot: Prefix
59. Expression of innocence
60. Candid
62. Outbursts of applause
63. Certain moments of truth
67. Dear, in Lyon
68. Ukrainian legislature
69. Angle-measuring instruments
72. Large cape of the 1800's
73. Prevaricate
77. Baking potatoes
80. Consumes
81. One of the media: Abbr.
83. Move suddenly
86. Info on a G.I.'s record
88. Market town of France
89. Word of sorrow
90. Wilder or Hackman
92. Meeting: Abbr.
94. Process of absorption
95. Pitch, as a ship
97. Raging flood
98. Hair ointment
99. Kind of show or band
101. Actress Patricia and family
102. Not impressed
103. Got together, as alumni
106. ____ as a fiddle
108. Ordinal suffix
110. Singer Fitzgerald
112. Neighbor of Thailand
113. Novice
115. Ships: Abbr.
117. Resident: Suffix
119. Ab ____ (from the start)
120. Grazing place
121. French surrealist
122. Misery

99 Anonymity By Frances Hansen

Sometimes it can be downright unfair.

ACROSS

1. Statue of Liberty feature
6. Echo oneself
13. "It lies not in our power to love, ____": Marlowe
19. Wealth
21. Arsonist's spoilsport
22. Dreaded
23. Start of a verse
26. High-hat
27. Assn.
28. Old washtub adjunct
29. Greek resistance org.
30. Peninsula of Asia
32. Vegas preceder
33. Horse-hock swelling
36. Bumpy beast
37. Julep embellishment
38. Angel's favorite letters
41. Slosh through surf
42. Egyptian cotton
43. Free-style dance
44. Not pro
45. More of verse
51. Slippery customer
52. Goal for 36 Across
53. Pub offerings
54. Mediterranean port
55. Musical intro
57. Bartók or Lugosi
58. Displease
60. German-Swiss theologian of the 1500's
64. Rodgers-Hammerstein musical
66. Come ____ (meet)
69. City founded by Harold III
71. Pope's "____ of the Lock"
75. Steer clear of
76. Rack's partner
77. One of the Golden Horde
79. Bar bill
80. More of verse
86. Ending for drunk or cow
87. Metal alloy
88. "Gentlemen Prefer Blondes" author
89. Feed the kitty
90. Originally named
91. M.I.T. grads
92. Silly
94. Koestler's "Darkness ____"
96. Panay people
97. Troll
98. Political coalition
99. Norma or Moira
103. Noncom rank
104. Part of S.W.A.K.
106. End of verse
112. Novelist de Beauvoir
113. Dr. ____ of TV series
114. Having teeth: Suffix
115. Like hip talk
116. Deeply felt
117. Mr. Toad's friend

DOWN

1. Dernier ____
2. Moroccan mountain range
3. Name in publishing
4. Unspecified time
5. Oil used in perfumery
6. Unresolved
7. Man's need at a posh cafe
8. "____ tu," Verdi aria
9. Do a shoemaker's job
10. Ethically neutral
11. Full of zest
12. Compass point
13. "The King ____ went up . . ."
14. Electric circuit device
15. Nobelist in chemistry: 1944
16. First of a Kipling trio
17. River to the Severn
18. River to the Fulda
20. Writer Wilson
24. "____ Magic," song of 1948
25. Like a wise old bird
30. "Does Gimbels tell ____?"
31. Running wild
33. Overwhelming victory
34. Road worker
35. Couturier Simpson
36. Moslem judge
37. Prayer book
38. Alarm
39. Brutus was the noblest one
40. Vertical
42. Babe in the bulrushes
43. ____ on (persist)
46. Brief letter sign-off
47. Not as ____ it looks (a bit better)
48. Collar
49. True olive
50. "Don't take ____ an answer": Churchill
56. Venezuelan president: 1964–69
58. Old Irish alphabet
59. Jacques of song, for one
61. Colonial Loyalists
62. Customary
63. Like a fashion model
65. Miss Kett and others
66. Nile dam
67. Task
68. ____ la Paix
70. Cricket sides
72. ". . . dollar, ____clock scholar"
73. Luigi's repast
74. Actor Buddy
77. Steak cut
78. Plant that sounds like a greeting
81. Tot's finger-painting activity
82. Pre-1847 California capital
83. Wrapped around
84. Hebrew infinity
85. Round Table macho
92. Compliment's opposite
93. ____ plume (literary aliases)
94. "Cradle of Texas Liberty"
95. Holy city of Spain?
97. Vault line in architecture
98. Lillie or Arthur
99. Sibilant sound
100. Accost
101. Pip or ack follower
102. Shakespeare's river
104. Snick's partner
105. Fender bender
107. "____ Gumo," Futabatei novel
108. Swedish district
109. Pts. of decades
110. Sault ____ Marie
111. Island in the Medit.

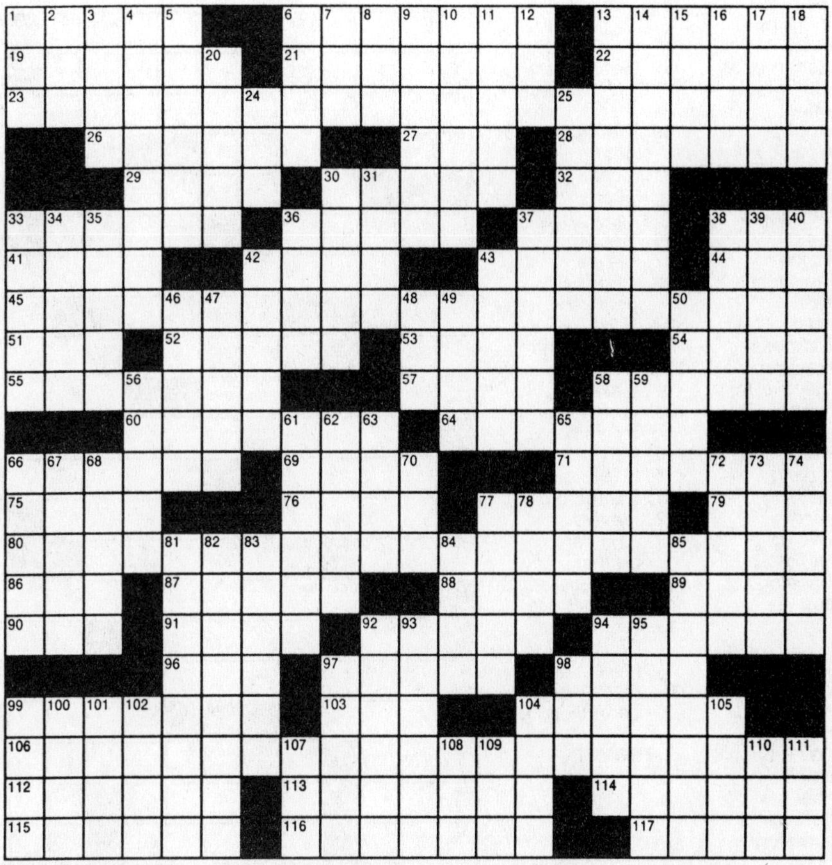

100 Apt Remarks By Louis Baron

There's always an off-key way to describe things.

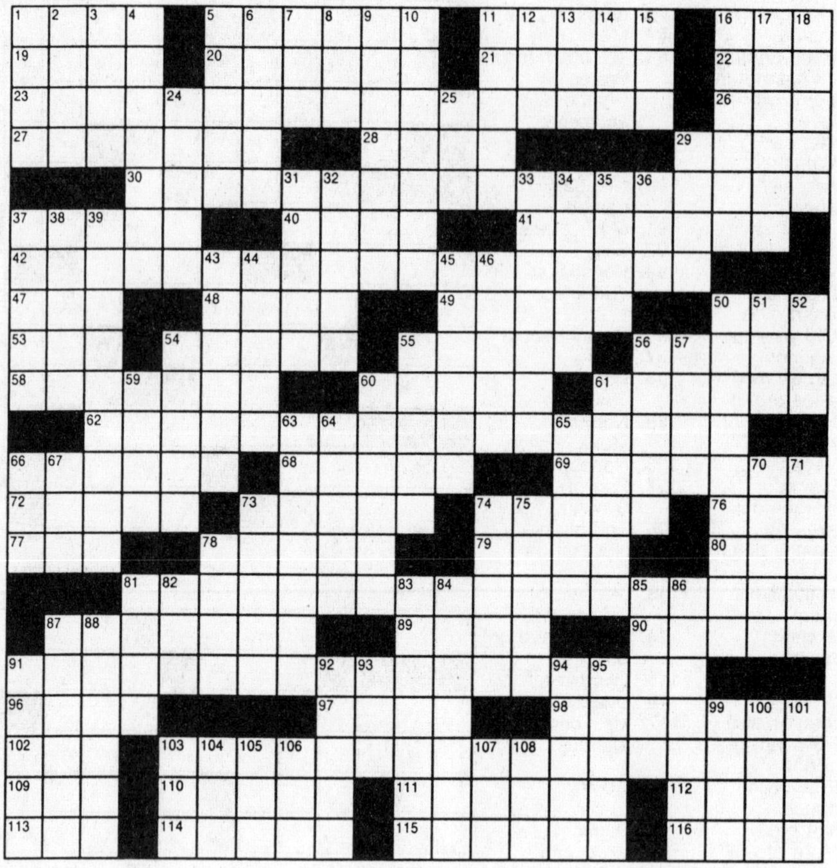

ACROSS

1. Sidekick
5. Opera by Gluck
11. Kitchen opus
16. Fiddler-crab genus
19. Kin of a Dagwood
20. Induce by sweet talk
21. Ill-wisher
22. Hammock quickie
23. Manicurist's line
26. Part of TNT
27. Thickness measurer
28. Adjective for shoppe
29. Bauxite and galena
30. Starving artist's lament
37. "Vive ___!"
40. Tuamotu atoll
41. Genealogical trees
42. Jogging dropout's bio
47. Wallaba tree
48. Pick over
49. Copperhead, for one
50. W.W. II agcy.
53. Cuisinier's pinch
54. Eisenstein's cinematographer
55. Skin redness
56. Not mine
58. Province of Ethiopia
60. Stacked
61. Samples
62. Belly dancer's review
66. Be the hungriest
68. Botches up
69. Smile-inducing
72. It's fine on contracts
73. Breakwaters
74. Small bit of land
76. Oxford tutor
77. "___ transit gloria . . ."
78. Powder and cream
79. TV's
80. Braun or LeGallienne
81. Soda jerk's advisory
87. Hansberry's "___ in the Sun"
89. Saroyan's "My Name Is ___"
90. Fire-truck gear
91. Cryptographer's sick-call
96. Hangouts
97. Plexus
98. Genesis patriarch
102. N.Y.C. subway line
103. Exorcist's plaint
109. Lunch hour for some
110. Part of H.R.E.
111. Parade order
112. Players
113. J.F.K.'s brother
114. Saratoga or steamer
115. Writer Cousins or Mailer
116. Place where Zeno thought

DOWN

1. "Blondie" creator Young
2. Blood: Prefix
3. Russian river
4. Large lizard
5. Tree-lined walk
6. Run through an oast twice
7. ___-jongg
8. G. & S. princess
9. O.S.S. chief
10. Book-cover backing
11. Mediterranean craft
12. Grasshopper's antithesis
13. Ladakh capital
14. Etienne's buddy
15. Bad: Prefix
16. Not so
17. Soft touch
18. Imitative
24. Of snakes
25. Navy V.I.P.
29. Bacchanalia
31. Celts
32. Old-womanish
33. Camera adjuncts
34. Prague cash
35. Arabian title
36. Belfry flier
37. Tenant's paper
38. Lab test: Abbr.
39. Lifelike
43. Least cordial
44. Actress Hayward
45. Tonsil's neighbors
46. Lhasa's land
50. Nonmembers
51. Opposite of post
52. Fool
54. Halloween choice
55. "Les petits ___," Mozart ballet
56. Turkic Siberian
57. Simple sugars
59. "___ there were none"
60. Man of the cloth
61. Least apt to bite
63. City of Idaho
64. Chasms
65. Stops
66. Roman goddess of plenty
67. William Tell's canton
70. Variable stars
71. Worries
73. Chamber ___
74. Moslems, collectively
75. The ___ side of life
78. Galileo's home
81. Hebrew letters
82. Speed
83. Duvalier, for one
84. Che Guevara's first name
85. Entertainer Lewis
86. "It is sweet ___ to violins": Wilde
87. Actor Brian
88. Spoke wildly
91. Dope
92. Between "eat" and "be merry"
93. Smorgasbord fish
94. Lake Chad people
95. Barnaby Jones portrayer
99. Make sound
100. African fox
101. River to Lake Ilmen
103. ___ Nouveau
104. "Le Coq ___"
105. Cassowary's kin
106. Big truck
107. Part of H.R.H.
108. Funnies explosion

101 Trigger Happy By Sidney Robbins

Back in the days when people knew how to shoot.

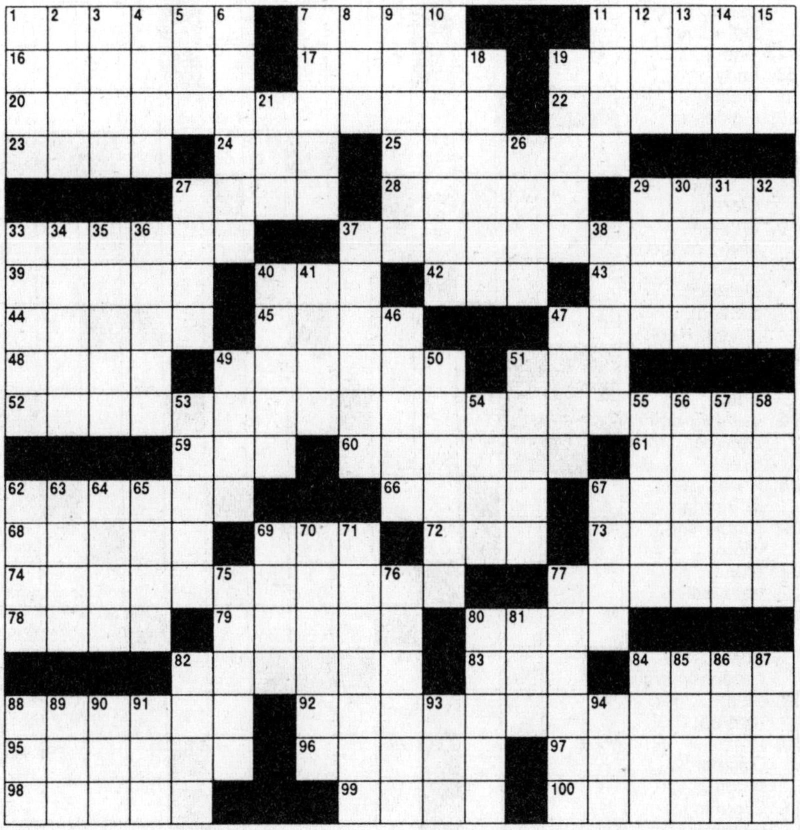

ACROSS

1. Camel riders, often
7. Grate
11. Roper's gear
16. Spain and Portugal
17. Notions
19. Jai alai
20. Wild and woolly frontierswoman
22. Morse-code sender
23. Football linemen
24. Poet's meadow
25. ___ out a claim
27. Gallup endeavor
28. Cargo ship
29. "For goodness ___!"
33. Dreiser's ___ *Carrie*
37. Wild and woolly frontierswoman
39. Add up
40. Twice as much, for short
42. Nat'l output
43. Africa's Sierra ___
44. Harden
45. Long fish
47. Wild and woolly exhibits
48. Name for a dog
49. Implant deeply
51. Scenic setter
52. Title claimed by a wild and woolly one
59. Pts. of dollars
60. More like Tim
61. Wine: Prefix
62. Certain Louisianian
66. Teen woe
67. Seoul-food land
68. Blood vessel
69. N.Y.S.E. listing
72. Nasser's org.
73. Singer Adams and others
74. Wild and woolly frontiersman
77. Most of North Africa
78. Speedy planes
79. Degrade
80. Bearing
82. Like hens' teeth
83. Cleo's bosom companion
84. Back talk
88. Cowboy with a reata
92. Wild and woolly frontiersman
95. Famed sister
96. Spinning
97. Evening party
98. Charlie Chan portrayer
99. Arthur of tennis
100. Engage in overseas trade

DOWN

1. French resort
2. Old Japanese coin
3. Pinochle play
4. Turkish river
5. Poorly lighted
6. Popeye or Sinbad
7. Saudi Arabian money
8. Kind of gen.
9. One of a year's four
10. Out of breath
11. Kind of pencil
12. Mountain
13. Drench
14. Anne or Marie: Abbr.
15. Paddle
18. Close tightly
19. Wing: Prefix
21. Far: Prefix
26. "___ off the grass"
27. Star with a kick
29. Timetable, for short
30. Tonic plant
31. Lotto's relative
32. Ogles
33. Formal
34. Old Greek region
35. Lonigan of fiction
36. Seer's card
37. Lifeguard's words on sighting a shark
38. Hermitlike
40. Fender bendings
41. North Atlantic menace
46. Princess in *The Merry Widow*
47. Coal valley
49. Italian city
50. Beggar's prop
51. Take the wheel
53. Renown
54. Miss Foch
55. Junior forests
56. Wildly strange
57. Do lip-curling
58. Skoal, for one
62. Cornfield sounds
63. Campanella and Rogers
64. He was, in Rome
65. Mel's family
67. Sharp
69. Russian log hut
70. "Don't ___ lion in his den"
71. Makeup item
75. Sir Francis
76. English overseers
77. Oust
80. Twin crystal
81. Neighbor of Syr.
82. Dispose of
84. Pass over
85. Prefix for space
86. Gang or mob follower
87. Let stand
88. Part of G.W.'s sig.
89. Bother
90. Gums
91. 100 yrs.
93. Relative of uh-huh
94. Crew coaxer

102 First Ladies By Sara Helleny

And what they were known for in the White House.

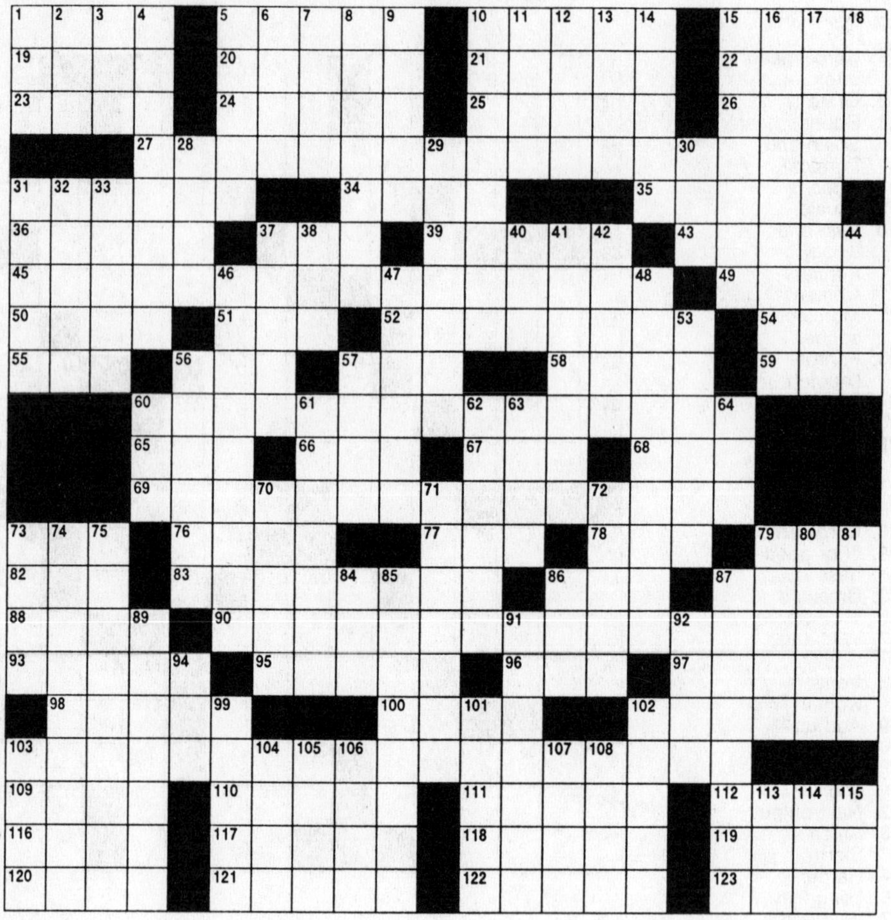

ACROSS

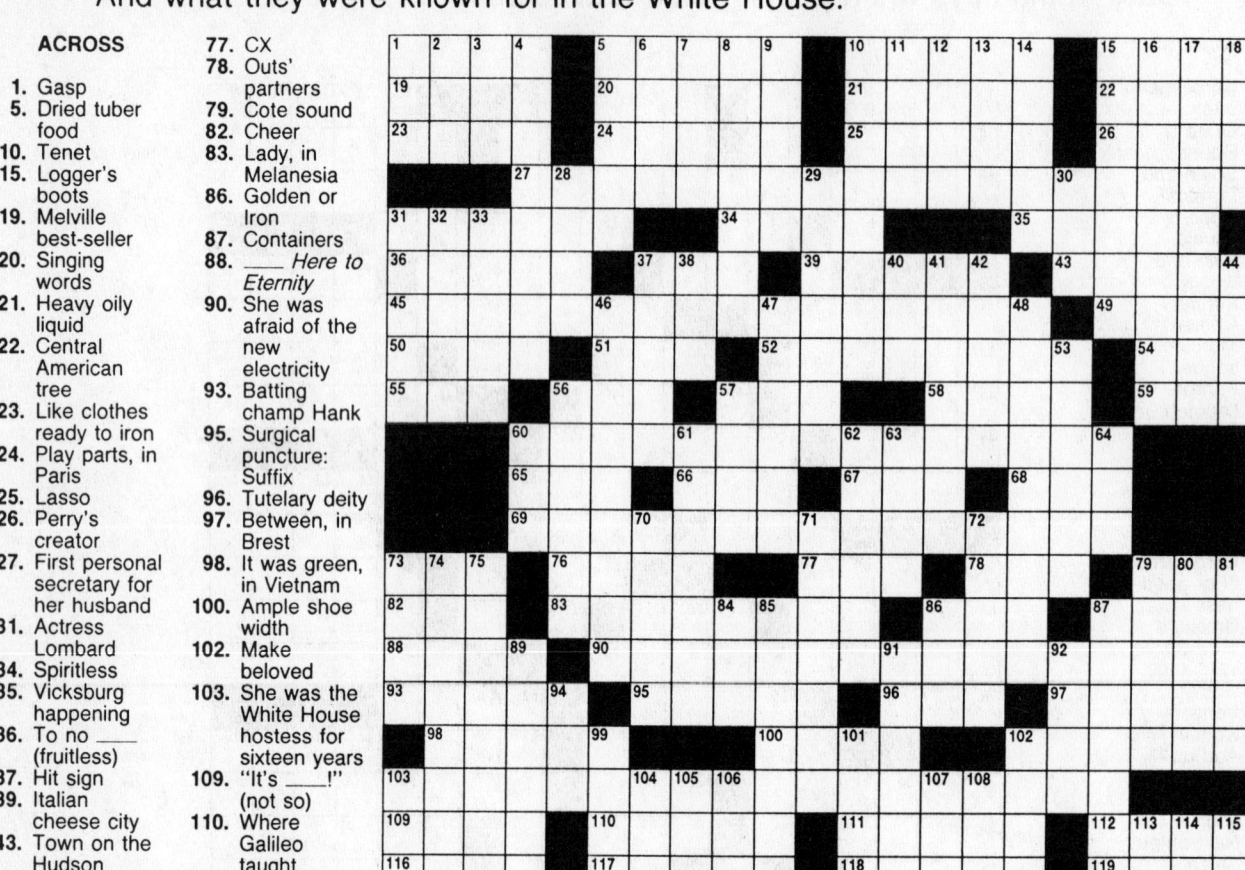

1. Gasp
5. Dried tuber food
10. Tenet
15. Logger's boots
19. Melville best-seller
20. Singing words
21. Heavy oily liquid
22. Central American tree
23. Like clothes ready to iron
24. Play parts, in Paris
25. Lasso
26. Perry's creator
27. First personal secretary for her husband
31. Actress Lombard
34. Spiritless
35. Vicksburg happening
36. To no ___ (fruitless)
37. Hit sign
39. Italian cheese city
43. Town on the Hudson
45. She was responsible for the cherry trees
49. Ending for vend
50. Maddens
51. Mike's friend
52. One who declares
54. Eternity
55. Louis and James: Abbr.
56. Spanish hero
57. French counterpart of Mrs.
58. Volcano top
59. Seminary degree
60. She was into environment
65. Brown drink
66. Nigerian people
67. Gums: Prefix
68. Relative in Nogales
69. She witnessed an assassination
73. Downs' counterparts
76. "___ a man . . ."
77. CX
78. Outs' partners
79. Cote sound
82. Cheer
83. Lady, in Melanesia
86. Golden or Iron
87. Containers
88. ___ *Here to Eternity*
90. She was afraid of the new electricity
93. Batting champ Hank
95. Surgical puncture: Suffix
96. Tutelary deity
97. Between, in Brest
98. It was green, in Vietnam
100. Ample shoe width
102. Make beloved
103. She was the White House hostess for sixteen years
109. "It's ___!" (not so)
110. Where Galileo taught
111. Organic compounds
112. Ardor
116. Word for Tim
117. How to stand
118. Sot
119. Withered
120. Serves impeccably
121. Mother of Perseus
122. Tapestry
123. N.Y.S.E. accommodation

DOWN

1. Jet enclosure
2. Org. for M.D.s
3. ___ de plume
4. Loams
5. Look rudely
6. Alms box
7. Wood strip
8. College member of a kind
9. Former Turkish title
10. Duc ___ (French royal title)
11. Fetid
12. Parapher-nalia
13. Trumpet attachment
14. Gather
15. Nursery game
16. Abolished
17. Coin or stamp fan
18. Partner of hide
28. "___ want for Christmas . . ."
29. Intruded
30. "It's a ___ to . . ."
31. Major or Minor
32. Prevent
33. Abnormal breath sounds
37. Kind of lady
38. Steep flax
40. Map abbr.
41. "Forward!"
42. Burns's sweet river
44. A Citizen
46. Relating to the outer skin
47. Strict disciplinarian
48. Englishman who weighs 140 pounds
53. Does another lube job
56. Port opposite Dover
57. Spanish painter Joan
60. On the ___ (fleeing)
61. Assault's partner
62. Kind of calendar
63. Medley
64. Negative prefix
70. Shensi town
71. "___ what I thought I saw?"
72. W. C. Fields prop
73. Turkish city
74. Bowl-shaped
75. Coastal area
79. Of top quality, in Berlin
80. Meeting place in Athens
81. Lou Grant portrayer
84. Kind of elder or car
85. What not to do with affections
86. Cry of triumph
87. A cupful for auld lang syne
89. Actor Robert and family
91. Between Lou and Bess
92. City on the Truckee
94. Wedding-announce-ment word
99. Identified a blood sample
101. Ancient Syrian city
102. Curves
103. Info
104. Meter or trooper preceder
105. Arabian port
106. Cassava
107. Sullen
108. *Casablanca* role
113. Majors or Radziwill
114. Altar constellation
115. Kind of ball or proceeds

103 Getting There By John Hales

Various ways in which it can be done.

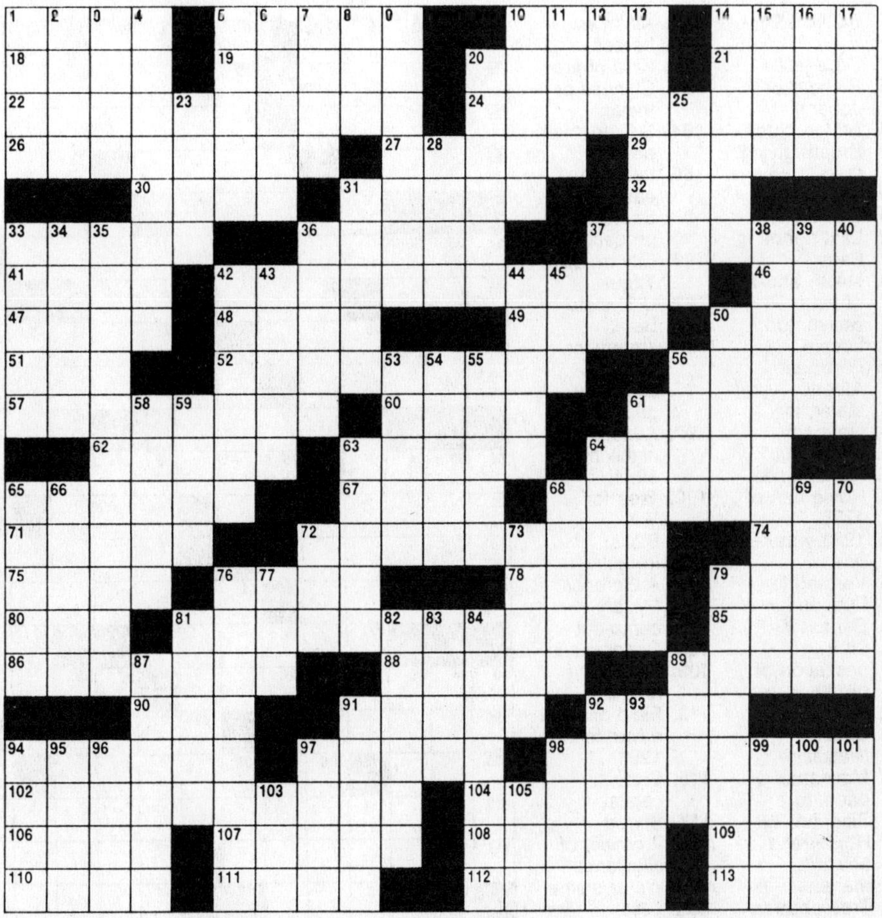

ACROSS

1. Mountain of Thessaly
5. Basilica areas
10. Vamp in old movies
14. Teheran money unit
18. Make turbid
19. Bull: Prefix
20. Abalone
21. Sicilian resort
22. Tennessee Williams play
24. *Porgy and Bess* locale
26. Took to a higher court
27. Loves excessively
29. Boyfriends
30. Asp's habitat
31. Takes on
32. ". . . ___ of thee"
33. Artistic theme
36. Alluvial matter
37. One-time laundry unit
41. Writer Leon
42. Route for a satyr
46. Put ___ show
47. Carry on
48. Vishnu incarnation
49. Venetian magistrate
50. ___ of all right
51. Sight from Gstaad
52. Spacious public walk
56. Do earbending
57. Like most trees in winter
60. He wrote about two years at sea
61. Affects daintiness
62. Not a soul
63. Small monkeys
64. One-liner expert
65. What Mennonite men have
67. Restore
68. Tenderly, in music
71. Loser to Dwight
72. Access to l'Etoile
74. Legal point
75. Bank on
76. "Where angels ___ to tread"
78. "Never ___ sentence with a preposition"
79. "Honi ___ . . ."
80. Family member in Dundee
81. Route to Fairbanks
85. Welles role
86. Kind of diary
88. Little one: Suffix
89. Golfing cup
90. Hockey name
91. Pilot
92. Skedaddled
94. Tropical rodent
97. ___ precedent (shows the way)
98. Millet's gleaners, e.g.
102. Corridor
104. Sinclair Lewis's way
106. Mechanical method
107. Escape hatches of sorts
108. Choose
109. Sup
110. Pub orders
111. 20,000-league man
112. Virginia family
113. Like some boats to China

DOWN

1. Killer whale
2. Soft or castile
3. Silly one, for short
4. One who judges mental competence
5. Bikini, for one
6. Gay ___
7. Involved legally
8. Pitching stat.
9. G.I.
10. Hillsides of Scotland
11. Aggregates: Abbr.
12. Grid official
13. Having an awn
14. Go over the same ground
15. Christian symbol
16. In a while
17. Legislative aims
20. Musical groups
23. Ingenuous
25. Sound of a taffeta skirt
28. Thereabouts
31. Relating to blood
33. Wall display
34. Scarflike vestment
35. Tunesmith's milieu
36. Upholstery trimmings
37. Fun lover
38. Jeeter Lester's address
39. Wed
40. Moderates
42. Primps
43. Civet of Asia
44. Old collections of verse
45. Author of macabre poetry
50. Ludwig von ___, German poet
53. Parting word, on the Champs
54. Brazilian port
55. Old-womanish
56. Strong cotton cloth
58. Sudden raid
59. Napoleonic victory site
61. ___-morning quarterback
63. Sticker for Androcles
64. Bohemian botanist
65. Revealed
66. Disease of plants
68. "___ do something for you?"
69. Versailles royalty
70. Glyceride
72. Fold sound
73. Lake in Bombay
76. Hormone that promotes blooming
77. Martin Luther's antagonist
79. Toward the heavens
81. Vital vessel
82. Eccentric financier Green and namesakes
83. Areas in the Seine
84. Shone
87. Pulls with a tackle
89. Respite
91. "From ___ shining . . ."
92. Seller of hot goods
93. Foot models
94. Port of Guam
95. Prison, in England
96. Bone: Prefix
97. Enter a butterfly race
98. Breakwater
99. Sedaka or Simon
100. ___' clock scholar
101. Savory mix
103. Cornwall river
105. Tuscaloosa's state: Abbr.

104 1984 in Retrospect By Calista Luminati

A year that wasn't quite what Orwell had imagined.

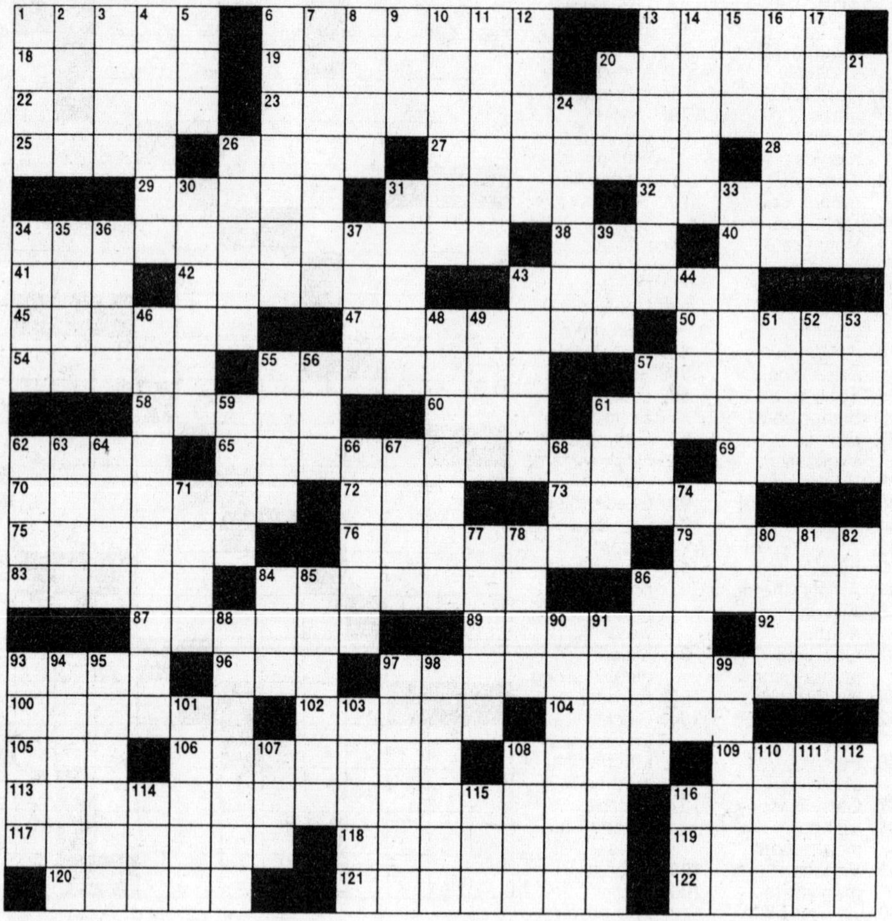

ACROSS

1. Do a jeté
6. Richard or Johann
13. Bridge bids
18. Breath-giving bulb
19. Awns
20. Silly tricks
22. Last dance in Paris
23. NASA abort of June 26
25. British gun
26. Locale
27. Port near Athens
28. Major, in Germany
29. Texas star?
31. Newsstand
32. Horseman of 1775
34. 1984 was one
38. Verb suffix
40. Furious
41. Set-to
42. Of a cessation of breath
43. "God ___," said Nietzsche
45. More than a pace, to a Siberian
47. Horse-race finish margins
50. Tree abodes
54. Alpine region
55. "___ is lessen'd by another's anguish": *Romeo and Juliet*
57. Parasite of W.W. I trenches
58. Venezuelan president
60. For
61. Touching, as a math line
62. River to the Caspian
65. United States and Russia, e.g.
69. *The Thin Man* dog
70. Fruits
72. Originally named
73. Point again
75. Living-room piece
76. Asian wild horses
79. Kind of fire
83. Chinese or Indian
84. S.C. football power
86. Lend an ear
87. Sadat's predecessor
89. City on the Tagus
92. U.S. state
93. Bank statement: Abbr.
96. Dawn goddess
97. Athletic highlight of 1984
100. Tree for Yule
102. Bicker
104. Irregular
105. A Gardner
106. Military camp-out
108. Connections
109. Method of learning
113. Field of great advance in 1984
116. Crete's capital
117. Stirred
118. Promiser of allegiance
119. Water animal
120. Tests
121. Platters and trays, e.g.
122. Laborers

DOWN

1. Sentence enders
2. Premed. subject
3. Baseball number
4. Brandy
5. Wine: Prefix
6. Presser for grandmother
7. Musical interval
8. Partner of shine
9. Mil. unit
10. Shangri-La
11. Deliverer
12. Fortune-tellers
13. Go on a spending spree
14. Charter
15. Indonesian island group
16. Baby-sitter, in England
17. Make fast
20. Friendly vote
21. Sliver
24. Dashing
26. Stalk
30. Rice, to the Asians
31. Stinging ant
33. Arcade favorites in 1984
34. One-time, of old
35. Novelist Pierre
36. Pitcher
37. Ivy League member
39. Fargo univ.
43. Murrow's "See ___"
44. In a while
46. Environ-mental villains
48. Dozers
49. Copter
51. Jeanne and Thérèse, for example
52. Shade
53. Bristle
55. Duty
56. Little drink
57. ___ Grande
59. Bone: Prefix
61. Very, in Nancy
62. Major or Minor
63. Female ruffs
64. ___ spumante
66. Take the stage
67. Clean a pipe
68. Sea eagle
71. Horne
74. Toppings
77. Simple animal form
78. Lively, in music: Abbr.
80. Iota
81. Very dry
82. Chemical suffixes
84. Head of a U.S. Army branch
85. Renter
86. Madmen
88. Descendants of Shem
90. One of Churchill's names
91. Audubon followers
93. Fiber plant
94. Frolic
95. Racket
97. Delphi resident
98. More netlike
99. Use a room freshener
101. Maltreat
103. Crescent-moon horns
107. Indian-American writer Mehta
108. French seraph
110. Aware of
111. Preadult
112. What hotel walls have
114. Last emperor of China
115. Heart doctor's abbr.
116. Beat walker

105 Flying the Coop By Gary Schmunk

Without any left or right wingers.

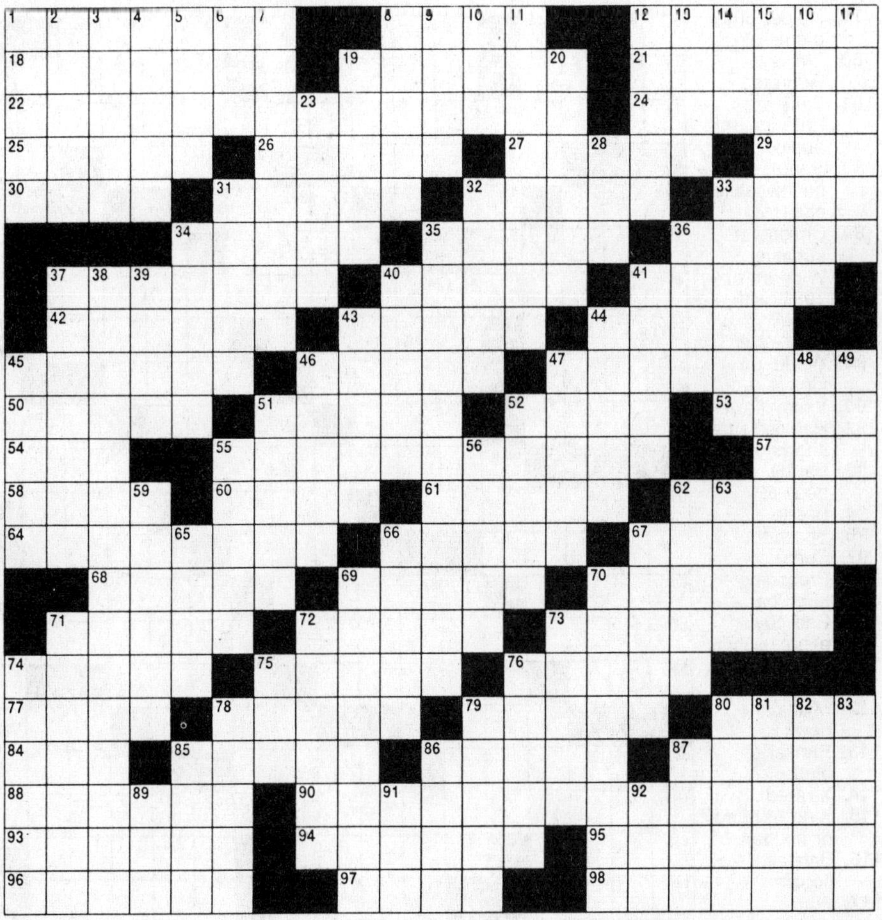

ACROSS

1. Launch a rowboat
8. Snide remark
12. Dogwood genus
18. City named for a fur trader
19. Open-mouthed ones
21. Quantity
22. Advantageous position
24. Ma, Pa or tea
25. Show again
26. Habit
27. Basketball player
29. Vine stock, in France
30. Angers
31. Omit
32. King of Judea
33. Golf-green protector
34. Sheepshank and cat's-paw
35. Bulgarian hub
36. Aspect
37. Portentous
40. Plains animal
41. Coniferous tree
42. Drives back
43. "The universal solvent"
44. Impresario Sol
45. Humiliates
46. North Pole denizen
47. "Dragnet" star
50. Takes a bus
51. Movie dog
52. Convex moldings
53. Guthrie
54. Sioux Indian
55. Assigned to File B
57. ___ Paulo
58. Bryn ___
60. Clamorous
61. Manners of movement
62. Grieve
64. Portion out
66. Revises
67. Crystalline amino acid
68. Iowa community
69. Letter-ending word
70. Contribute
71. Alla ___
72. Actor Vincent
73. Omar, the general
74. Black tea
75. Acutely perceptive
76. Failures
77. ". . . ___ well" (crier's words)
78. Spiritual guides
79. Swains
80. Vapor: Prefix
84. Never, in Nuremberg
85. Demand
86. Performing
87. White-faced
88. Venus ___
90. Dowagers are no longer these
93. Calls forth
94. Separate ___ from the boys
95. Adriatic gulf
96. Begins again
97. Went like lightning
98. Like Whittier's "It might have been!"

DOWN

1. Gloria ___
2. Aisle escort
3. Cubic meter
4. Deceive
5. Algerian port
6. Conniption
7. Like Ophir's wealth
8. Sheriff's star, e.g.
9. Church area
10. Caddoan Indian
11. ___ the shock (prepare)
12. Encrusted
13. Hebrew measure
14. "Bosh!"
15. Yuletide stage music
16. Free
17. Great plain, Russian style
19. Alumni, for short
20. Play the leading role
23. "Virtue ___ own reward"
28. Western Indian district
31. Organic compounds
32. Biblical book
33. ___ monkey wrench into
34. Patella locations
35. Easy target
36. Central or Hyde
37. Like a space shuttle's path
38. Harlem Globetrotter name
39. ___ dixit
40. Eddie Cantor's kind of eyes
41. Clear
43. Ebbed
44. Belgian hoppers
45. Redolence
46. Continue without a break, in music
47. Shocks
48. Earbender's stone
49. Daniel or Pat
51. Life of a region
52. Hoity's partner
55. Leveling tool
56. Selassie
59. Lovers
62. Repairs
63. Voiced
65. Spelunker's hangout
66. Sevareid et al.
67. TV serials
69. Victories
70. Prolonged shortages
71. Accept on faith
72. Strict adherent
73. Mont ___
74. Toady (to)
75. Sine ___ non
76. Pretend
78. Luster
79. Filleted
80. Fixed a price
81. "___ are the times . . ."
82. Endings for develop and depart
83. Beginning
85. Ball of yarn
86. Coin
87. Biting
89. Follower of Harry
91. Corded fabric
92. Retirement acct.

106 Saddle Up By Louis Sabin

And spend a little time in the old West.

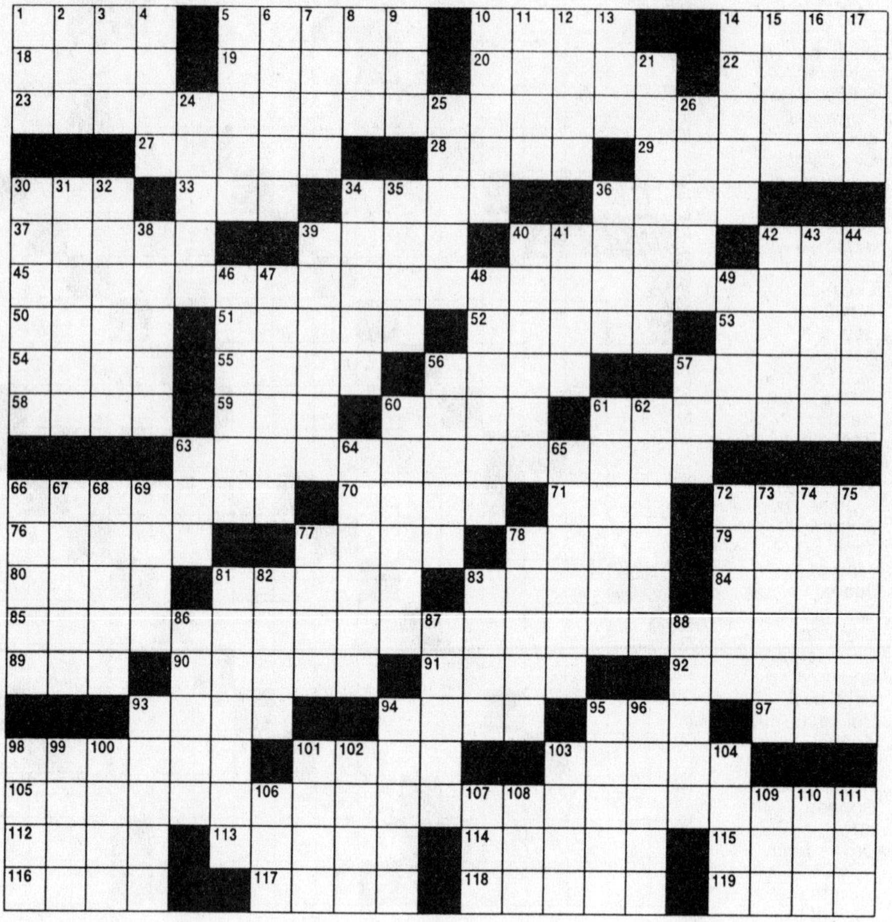

ACROSS

1. Parker who played Boone
5. Gangland Bugs or tennis Gussie
10. Miracle site
14. Finish line
18. Melville opus
19. Expiate
20. Horse ___
22. Mickey Rooney's real name
23. Western confrontation movie
27. Aconcagua site
28. Serve notice
29. W.W. II wolf pack
30. Indian title
33. G. & S. role
34. Related
36. Western Indians
37. Jacques's aunt
39. Mediter-ranean port
40. ". . . but ___ will never hurt me"
42. Held
45. Zane Grey people
50. Cow-horned deity
51. Fairylike
52. Like trigger fingers
53. Spoken
54. Certain tone
55. Miss Adams
56. Beliefs
57. Composer Erik
58. Sicilian resort
59. Kind of badge or horn
60. Poker fee
61. Income
63. Western of 1950
66. Geronimo's followers
70. December song
71. Gold holder
72. Evian and Ems
76. Asian peninsula
77. Deceiving one
78. Let loose
79. Holder of plenty
80. "Miss ___ Regrets"
81. Take ___ (join the audience)
83. Shoot, bushwhacker style
84. Christie or Lucasta
85. Western of 1981, with "The"
89. Shore flier
90. Works on film
91. Valley flower
92. Hall-of-Fame shortstop
93. Earthy deposit
94. Bristle
95. Sharp tool
97. Curve
98. Preceding
101. Mine car
103. Bad guy's expression
105. Clark Gable western
112. Mythical hawk
113. Brinker's blade
114. X-rated
115. Kind of horse or maiden
116. Balalaika's cousin
117. Was obligated
118. Certain income
119. Welsh emblem

DOWN

1. Confused state
2. Long-legged bird
3. Offspring of a gun
4. Fancy couch
5. A Gabor
6. Different
7. Goes bad
8. Sayings
9. Bottom line
10. George M.
11. Mimic
12. Strip light
13. "Two by Two" vehicle
14. First-timers
15. Atmosphere
16. Locality map
17. Slippery ones
21. In a shrewd way
24. Preceder of com or cept
25. Packer's cord
26. Like Sydney Greenstreet
30. Long pace
31. Rice-pudding additive
32. Brave
34. Bandman Shaw
35. Lyricist Gus
36. Cry of disgust
38. Electrical genius
39. Near future
40. Eggnog covering
41. Bows
42. He created Roaring Camp
43. Besides
44. Struck from the galley
46. Froth
47. Tom Mix films, e.g.
48. Flower part
49. Saddle ___
56. Deduce
57. Dear one
60. Take ___ (swear)
61. Hash mark
62. Sway
63. "___ wish is my . . ."
64. Eastern Christians
65. Grits
66. Plant for 49 down
67. Etonian dad
68. True up
69. Ellery Queen job
72. Western of 1953
73. Silk fabric
74. TV's Matt Dillon
75. Set of drums
77. Departed
78. ___ Gay
81. Gettysburg, for one
82. Farmland
83. Kind of trench
86. Approaches
87. Lacquer base
88. Van Gogh setting
93. Lodge member
94. Played a violin badly
95. Infirm
96. Mae and Rebecca
98. Semitic deity
99. Tan shade
100. Ridge on 116 across
101. Soften
102. Nerve network
103. Complacent
104. Vex
106. Ring finish
107. Grackle's cousin
108. Author LeShan
109. Actress Mary
110. Hind
111. Sign

107 Countrified By Louis Baron

Things that seem to fit in their natural slots.

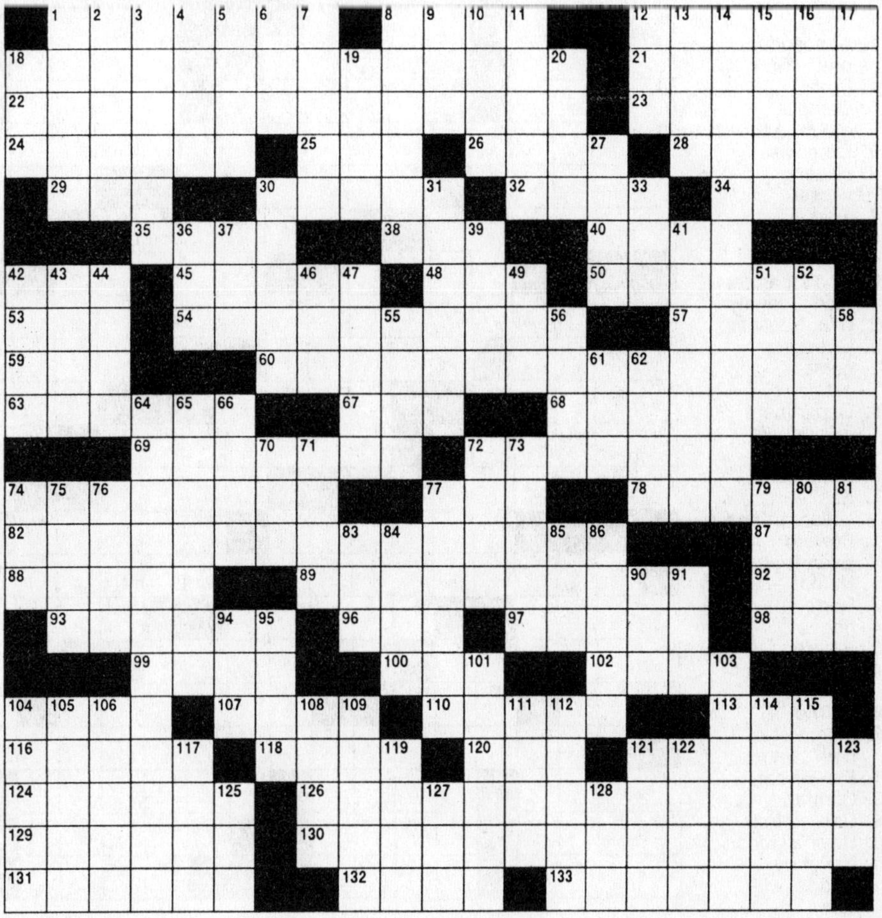

ACROSS

1. In an ethical way
8. Outrigger
12. Felt hat
18. Volkswagen, Tokyo version
21. Entertains
22. Couturier's concern?
23. Interfere
24. More gentle
25. Chiropter
26. TV's Jack
28. Setting
29. Kyushu volcano park
30. Token appearance
32. Nigerian natives
34. Frosty coating
35. Promenade
38. After pi
40. Old Mexican coin
42. Order's partner
45. Pacific swimmers
48. Work unit
50. Traveled like Hiawatha
53. Ending for pay or boff
54. Tom from Teheran?
57. Spanish silver dollars
59. Gallic chum
60. Outback snake dance?
63. Bluebeard's last wife
67. Ex-husband of Rita
68. Fawned over
69. Funny
72. Levee prop
74. Womanly
77. Architect I. M.
78. Deviate from a course
82. Marxman's machismo?
87. Isn't out of
88. Before dox or dontist
89. Headline for angry Ari?
92. Print measures
93. "___ to dullness": Franklin
96. So. state
97. Prefix for trope
98. Siamang
99. Tartu native
100. Common abbr.
102. Like a certain duckling
104. Young trout
107. Malt drier
110. Petemen's targets
113. Fuss
116. Burglar's bane
118. Large hartebeest
120. Dogpatch diminutive
121. Adulterated
124. Flight feather
126. Down Under demon?
129. Agree
130. Great knead in Uppsala?
131. Eyed unpleasantly
132. Miss
133. Plays out, as a fish line

DOWN

1. Ouspenskaya or Schell
2. Has a premiere
3. Lacking design
4. Allow or annoy ender
5. Glassmaker's oven
6. Narc's evidence
7. ___ Buena Island
8. Be a nuisance
9. ___ judicata
10. "Take ___ from me"
11. Bones above wrists
12. Manufactured: Abbr.
13. Flightless birds
14. Valor in the Cider Zee?
15. Bone: prefix
16. Rey's consort
17. Actor Ed
18. Where SST's land
19. Show pleasure
20. Hoople's cry
27. Mil. training group
30. Mrs. Schumann
31. William Sydney Porter
33. Moroccan port
36. Lethal serpent
37. Annabel of poetry
39. Seal-eating whale
41. "Nature, red in tooth ___": Tennyson
42. Goldbrick
43. Mrs. Mahler
44. Tend table
46. Baton Rouge campus
47. Agave fiber
49. Dame
51. Middle of Q.E.D.
52. "Where ___ Go From Here?"
55. Tamarisk tree
56. ___ Shan Range, U.S.S.R.
58. Left port: Abbr.
61. Say further
62. Cruxes
64. Eiredale?
65. Servile agents
66. ___ Minor
70. Stopover
71. Composer Alban
72. Track down
73. It is dropped in Soho
74. To's partner
75. Seine joiner near Rouen
76. River to Lake Ilmen
77. Garment folds
79. Large S.A. bird
80. Femme fatale
81. To be, to Ovid
83. ___ pro nobis
84. Ubangi feeder
85. Cousin of trois
86. God of the winds: Var.
90. Ruman of films
91. Tarzan producer Lesser
94. Palindromic Indian
95. "Take ___!"
101. Channel port
103. Resident of the Carolines
104. Kind of bull
105. Tea-party guest
106. Belgian marble
108. Lushes
109. Dragged net
111. Five-spots
112. Nobelist Root
114. Armand ___, Camille's lover
115. Not copies: Abbr.
117. Method
119. Far from harbor
121. Old Irish garment
122. Gds.
123. Wiggly fish, old style
125. Sparks or Rorem
127. A.M.A. people
128. Flier: Abbr.

108 Literary Moment By Wilson McBeath

Some fruits of library browsing.

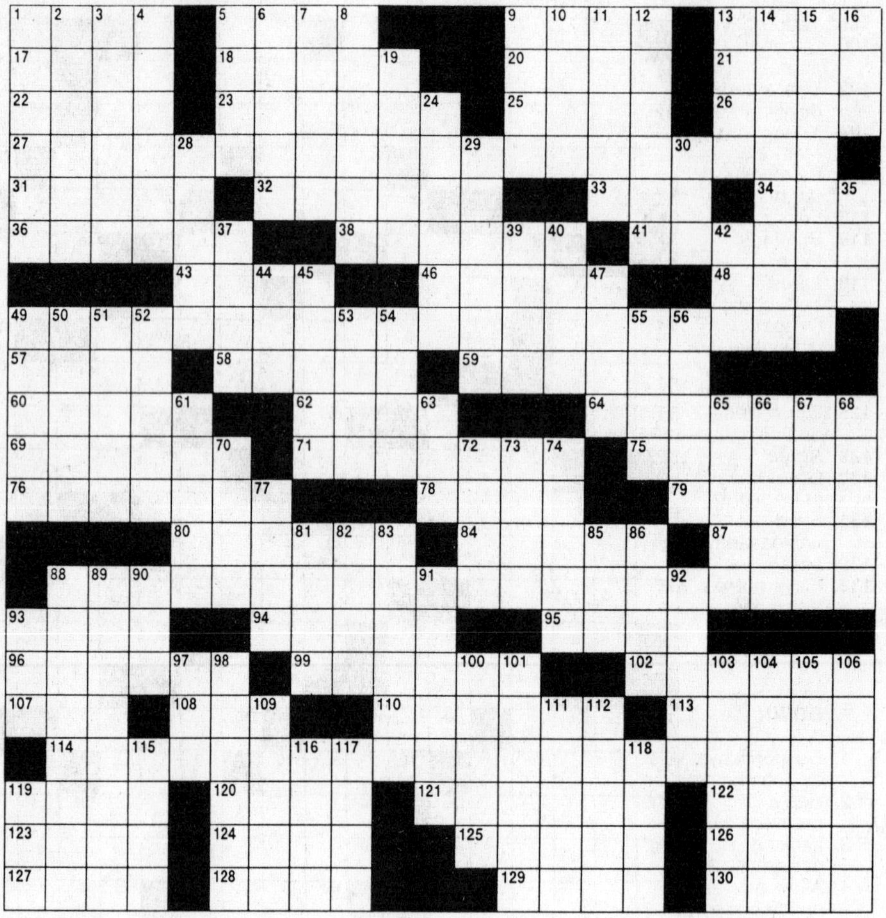

ACROSS

1. Atmospheric pressure: Prefix
5. Campus group: Abbr.
9. Otherwise
13. Heating vessel
17. Tied
18. Assessed amount
20. Rod's partner
21. Muffin variety
22. Diva Ponselle
23. Guessing-game category
25. Department in southern France
26. Demolish
27. Shakespearean pair
31. Edward Everett and Nathan
32. Narrow ridges
33. Before
34. Indian title of respect
36. Warns
38. Margaret of birth control
41. Flower part
43. Comfort
46. Cafe patron
48. River islands
49. Novel by Reade, with *The*
57. Listen
58. Musical work
59. Palestinian sect member
60. Grain disease
62. Parcel's companion
64. *Lusitania's* undoing
69. Belonging to Guam's capital
71. Mountie
75. One who blockades
76. Stretchable
78. Inside info
79. Merits
80. Boring tool
84. Percolate
87. Mother of the Gorgons
88. Barrie's resourceful butler
93. Will of the Waltons
94. Blazing
95. It needs air
96. Apprehensions
99. Isolate
102. Shield loop, in armor
107. Lincoln Center hub
108. Consumed
110. Tentacle
113. "Don't ___ on me"
114. Uncas's father
119. Queens arena
120. Noisy god
121. Heavy silk fabric
122. Pierre's friend
123. Ages and ages
124. Yesterday, in Milano
125. Irritates
126. Vale
127. Educational org.
128. Rugged rock
129. Mtg.
130. Distinctive times

DOWN

1. Krupp's big gun of W.W. I
2. Acknowledgment
3. Repair a shoe
4. Wild ass
5. Kukla's friend
6. Bombasts
7. Leaning
8. Circus performers
9. Therefore
10. Table part
11. Start a tennis game
12. Church officials
13. Saragossa's river
14. Convey
15. Biblical city
16. Donkey, in Rouen
19. Vampire
24. Inclined
28. Billie Sol
29. Nullify
30. Soak, as flax
35. Officeholders
37. Gorge
39. Old English letters
40. Females of the ruff
42. Swiss river
44. Bridge player's backslide
45. Burst forth
47. Showy prose: Abbr.
49. Do a scam on
50. Bulky
51. Musical instrument
52. Images: Var.
53. Jewish month
54. Black, to an Italian
55. Biblical patriarch
56. High habitat
61. Subarctic forest
63. Bushy mass
65. Melba base
66. White heron
67. Tooth: Prefix
68. Welles or Bean
70. Encountered icy footing
72. Canvass
73. Rapier
74. Respond
77. Jane Austen heroine
81. Animation
82. "___ go bragh"
83. Importer's burden
85. Dernier ___
86. Engage
88. Protracted TV show
89. Missionaries' targets
90. Go astray
91. Assails
92. Prefix for grade or meter
93. School of whales
97. Bad: Prefix
98. Kind of electricity
100. Hungarian composer
101. Resins
103. Shopping area
104. Enlarging tool
105. Strong paper
106. Vintage cars
109. London suburb
111. Zola
112. Fixed procedures
115. Far or Middle
116. Pentateuch
117. Not a copy: Abbr.
118. Dame Myra
119. Six, in Pisa

109 Growth Factor By Judith Perry

To be investigated with a fine-tooth comb.

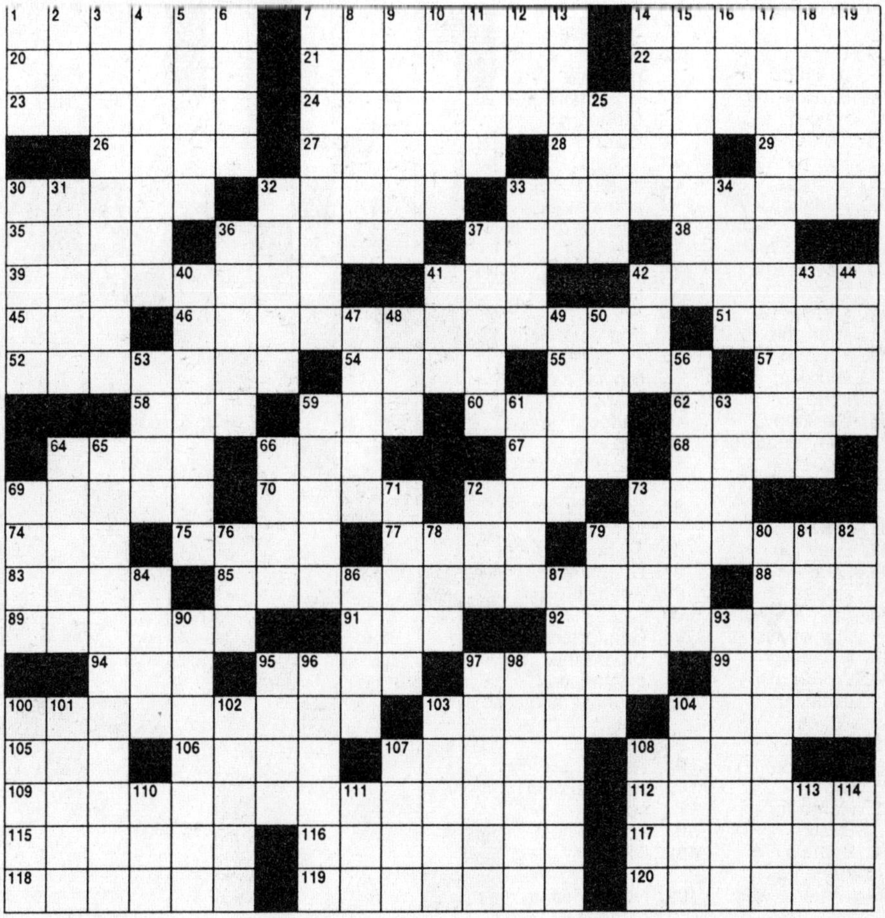

ACROSS

1. One-seeded fruit
7. Gobi and Arabian
14. English ornithologist
20. Oklahoma resident
21. Scrutinize
22. Geological epoch
23. Ride ___ (keep in check)
24. Drawing a fine line
26. Celestial bodies
27. French hen
28. Muses' number
29. Cartoonist Gardner
30. Jury components
32. Trumpeter Al et al.
33. Adds the icing
35. Tooth or heart
36. Ersatz-gem material
37. Physician's patient
38. Hockey great
39. Kind of stand for motorists
41. Word before havoc or wolf
42. Oakley and Laurie
45. Whitney
46. Macho
51. Leer
52. Eve's nemesis
54. News notice
55. Guinness
57. Hiatus
58. Pizarro's acquisition
59. Approves
60. British noble
62. Catkin
64. Kind of talk or steward
66. Luau instrument
67. New Deal org.
68. Balm
69. Stiller's sidekick
70. Enormous
72. Messy place
73. Alcoholic delusions
74. Cuckoo
75. Out of ___ (nonconforming)
77. Russian range
79. English conductor
83. Sharp
85. Road hazard
88. Onassis
89. Giant step
91. Joined in a child's game
92. Lunch hour
94. Nut-brown brew
95. German quaff
97. Coat fur
99. Architect Christopher
100. Glider
103. Quibble
104. ___ up (gets savvy)
105. Times of day: Abbr.
106. Santa's reference
107. Of a grain
108. Corned-beef dish
109. Plant with feathery fronds
112. Eventually
115. Rococo
116. Gentle touch, in France
117. Sound system
118. Drooped
119. Honored, in a way
120. Scottish plaid

DOWN

1. Hard wood
2. College in Cedar Rapids
3. Stiff cloth
4. Lasted
5. Lights
6. Sea birds
7. One who loathes
8. Send abroad
9. Greet
10. Actor Jannings and others
11. Ceremonial act
12. Explosive
13. Nets
14. Wood: Prefix
15. Mythological River of Woe
16. Hyson
17. Easily activated
18. Coincide
19. Flat-topped hills
25. Riviera city
30. Reduces
31. Paris pupils' place
32. "I've ___!" (Enough!)
33. Family in *Life with Father*
34. Italian river
36. Instrument for Horowitz
37. Site of Minoan culture
40. Hillary's helpers
41. Greek letter
42. Soft drink
43. African antelope
44. Calendar abbr.
47. Harnesses
48. Network with an eye
49. Loiter
50. Fitzgerald
53. Richard or box
56. Stage-door ___
59. Relative of the giraffe
61. Caper
63. A gender: Abbr.
64. French legislative body
65. Horrific
66. Part of the eye
69. Door and place
71. Snouty animal
72. ___ Clemente
73. English county
76. Article
78. Cover
79. Cook a steak
80. Penitent's garment
81. Napoleon's force
82. Manners
84. Cultivate
86. Korea's Syngman
87. Readied a new shirt
90. Exhaust
93. Tornado
95. Shindig
96. Unimpaired
97. Hot fashion
98. Feeling distaste
100. Aegean island
101. Genus of ground beetles
102. Winterized a light coat
103. Eating spots
104. "I ___ Girl . . ."
107. Odd, in Scotland
108. "Listen!"
110. Hammarskjöld
111. Hawaiian bait fish
113. ___ culpa
114. Age

110 Tennis Courtship By Norman Steinberg

Terms of affection for Wimbledon fans.

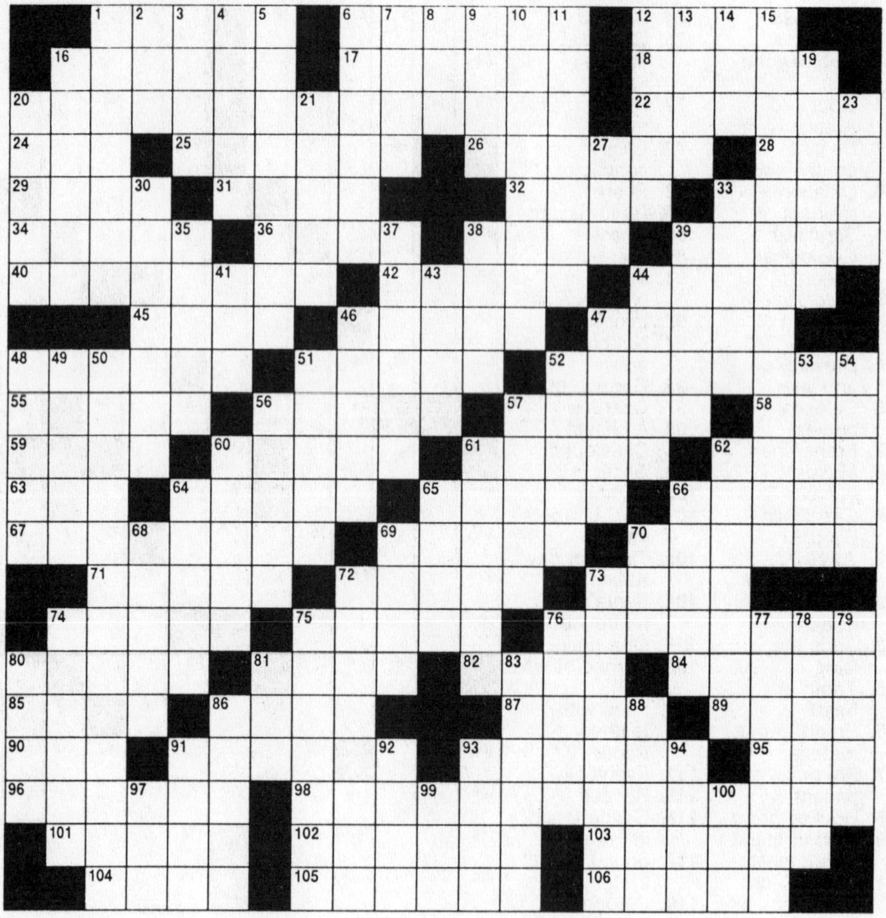

ACROSS

1. Units of laughter
6. Explicit
12. Hair style
16. Contemptuous term of address
17. Atlantic City spot
18. Kind of fund
20. Ray Bolger solo
22. Messages sent abroad
24. "____ on your life!"
25. Imps
26. Vacillate
28. Lumberjack's tool
29. Like the fox's grapes
31. Hawk
32. Easy job
33. Gear on the slopes
34. Poet Pound and others
36. Meadows
38. Words of disbelief
39. Pokes
40. Between twelve and twenty
42. Home for a Sioux
44. Santa's surname
45. "When I was ____ . . ."
46. Bare
47. Possessive
48. More snail-like
51. "This seat is ____"
52. Part of the Pacific
55. Relatives of 1 Across
56. Handled successfully
57. Actor Karloff
58. Bulgarian coin
59. Island off China
60. Partners of bounds
61. Salk of polio note
62. Center
63. Period of revival: Abbr.
64. Singer Newman
65. Neighbor of Nuremberg
66. Plebe's negative
67. Undertakings
69. Ciphered
70. Edict of ____
71. Yokels
72. Helen's abductor
73. ____ *of the Flies*
74. Two-faced god
75. An Impressionist
76. Piccadilly and others
80. French bridges
81. Thaw
82. Warmth
84. Perfume
85. Dept. for farmers
86. Tranquil
87. Guinness
89. Spanish cup
90. "____ nuff!"
91. Comforters
93. Big brother of monaural
95. Mideast land: Abbr.
96. Uproar
98. Romberg-Hammerstein song
101. Eagle's nest
102. "____ My God . . ."
103. New Orleans campus
104. Jabbers
105. Marsh plants
106. Moslem priests

DOWN

1. Equal of 1,000 words?
2. Before
3. Unfertile
4. Bowling alleys
5. Dug a hole
6. Lilylike flower
7. Does lacework
8. Kind of tray
9. Aunts in Tabasco
10. Caught
11. Senior woman in a group
12. Songwriters' group
13. Imperfection
14. Massage
15. Shakespearean play
16. Forty winks
19. Groups of six
20. Beginning
21. Enticed
23. Sun. speeches
27. ____ Paulo
30. Escaped
33. Chisholm, e.g.
35. Soupy of comedy
37. Major horse races
38. Unwrap
39. Entreaties
41. Civil War gp.
43. Made do, with "out"
44. Opponent for Martina
46. Diaper, in England
47. Hebrew body of law
48. Musical sign
49. Debussy opus
50. Outdated marriage vow
51. Amphibians
52. Abbr. at a page bottom
53. Strange
54. Swears
56. Coins
57. Tedious ones
60. Thongs
61. Actress Anderson
62. Lead
64. Pictograph puzzle
65. Golfer's cry
66. Drug cops
68. Political intrigue group
69. Argot
70. Neighbor of Swed.
72. Coconut producer
73. The intellectual elite
74. He fit at Jericho
75. Philanthropic family
76. Biblical spy
77. Temperate-zone quartet
78. Pepsin, for one
79. Ogle
80. Word on a door
81. After avril
83. Restaurant patrons
86. Freezer contents
88. Pouch in the body
91. Mot
92. Warm-sea fish
93. Pintail duck
94. Musical-show state: Abbr.
97. Bikini half
99. Assn.
100. Kind of cap

111 Meet the Press By Gayle Dean

Some familiar bylines in the media field.

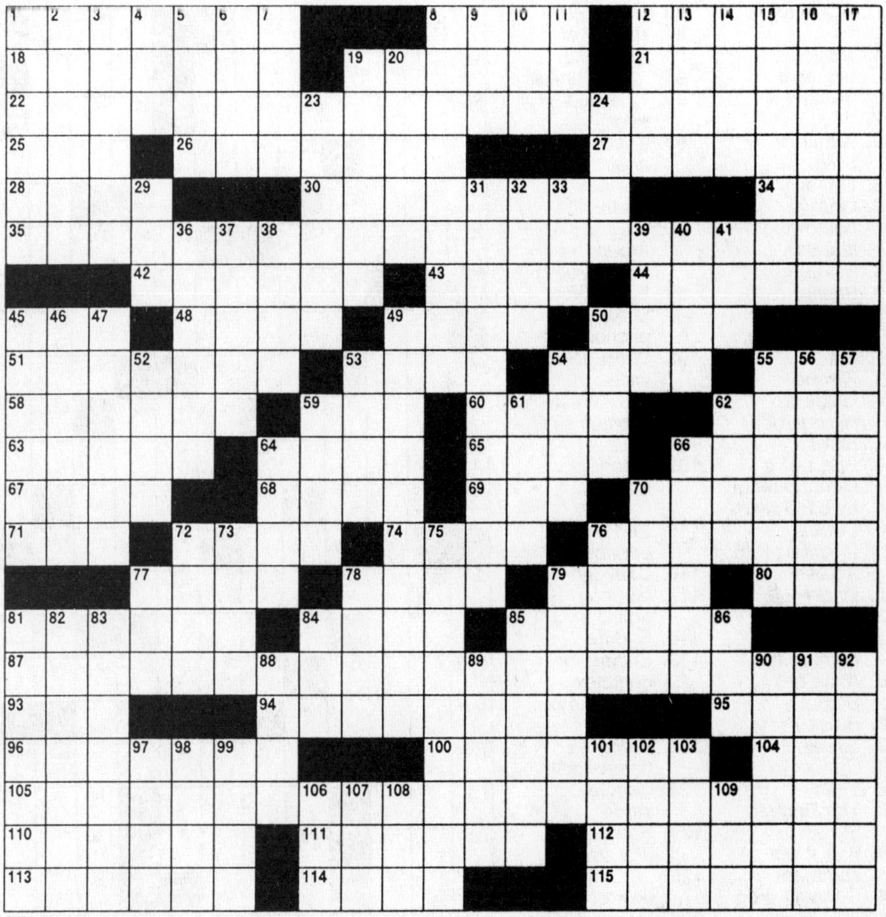

ACROSS

1. Nome native
8. Very, to Pierre
12. Put the ___ on (squelch)
18. Detour
19. Musical note
21. Punish with a fine
22. *South of Freedom* author and Livingstone's tracker
25. Summer drink
26. Viscera
27. London commercial district
28. Delicate, old style
30. Paroled one
34. One day ___ time
35. Humorous columnist and "Stand by for News" man
42. In ___ and out the other
43. Upolu port
44. Commands
45. Embassy head: Abbr.
48. Waiter's item
49. Agreeable votes
50. Thumb and Jones
51. More spicy
53. M.I.T., for one
54. In a comical mood
55. Hosp. employees
58. Drums
59. Not even
60. Discharge
62. Old English court
63. Over
64. Victim
65. Zero
66. Kind of city maid
67. Unpleasant smell
68. Shakespearean king
69. Archibald or Wally
70. The Rockies have a great one
71. Football six-pointers
72. Makes reverent
74. Poems
76. Lions, leopards, etc.
77. Pelvic bones
78. Does garden work
79. Singer Tennille
80. Commercials
81. Points of view
84. Barrett of Tinseltown
85. Specie sums
87. Hosts of a late TV show and of "Person to Person"
93. Brit. military center
94. Point between opposing currents
95. Painful
96. Affect deeply
100. Repeat
104. "___ the season to be . . ."
105. *Why the Right Has Failed* author and Tammany Tiger originator
110. French star
111. Flower nectars
112. Spot for an aerie
113. Large sandstone block
114. Puts with
115. Not bankrupt

DOWN

1. Secrets
2. Brigham Young, to the Mormons
3. Police-blotter entry
4. Impresario Hurok
5. Russian village
6. Like ___ of bricks
7. TV evening staple
8. "Some of ___": Sophie Tucker's song
9. Fled
10. Go amiss
11. Le Carré character
12. Judo exercise
13. "___ corny as Kansas . . ."
14. Inclination
15. Take it ___ it
16. Bloodhound, for one
17. Peaks of power
19. Make fond
20. Egg part
23. Plane route
24. Stitch a hawk's eyelids
29. Pay-TV channel
31. Strong cravings
32. Capuchin monkeys
33. U.S., to the French
36. Like some shoelaces
37. Demeter's counterpart
38. Part of a town crier's shout
39. *Peter Pan* villain
40. Salvation or Coxey's
41. Hwys.
45. Maintain
46. Having a work complement
47. Turbine parts
49. "Sixty Minutes" observer
50. Carry
52. Journey
53. Concept
54. Bring bad luck
55. Eye part
56. Required
57. Emphasize
59. Mine products
61. Sounds from Old MacDonald's place
62. ___ Morton, V.P. in the 1890s
64. Guilty or not guilty, e.g.
66. Environment
70. Durable material
72. Female voice
73. Will-o'-the-___
75. Reporters' banes
76. Having affection
77. Red or black material
78. "___ that tiger!"
79. Bullfighter
81. Stars' partners
82. Syllogism premises
83. Film writer, at times
84. Grange or Buttons
85. Ancient Hebrew weights
86. Grad. class
88. Pakistan city: Abbr.
89. Clever
90. Revolve
91. Prayer
92. Home of the U.S.M.A.
97. Sluggers' stats
98. Owl, in Berlin
99. Movie script: Abbr.
101. Quantities: Abbr.
102. Pacific food
103. German donkey
106. Cry of triumph
107. One of a Eugene Field trio
108. Common conjunction
109. Neighbor of Cal.

112 Broken Record By A. J. Santora

Typical put-down administered by a veteran put-downer.

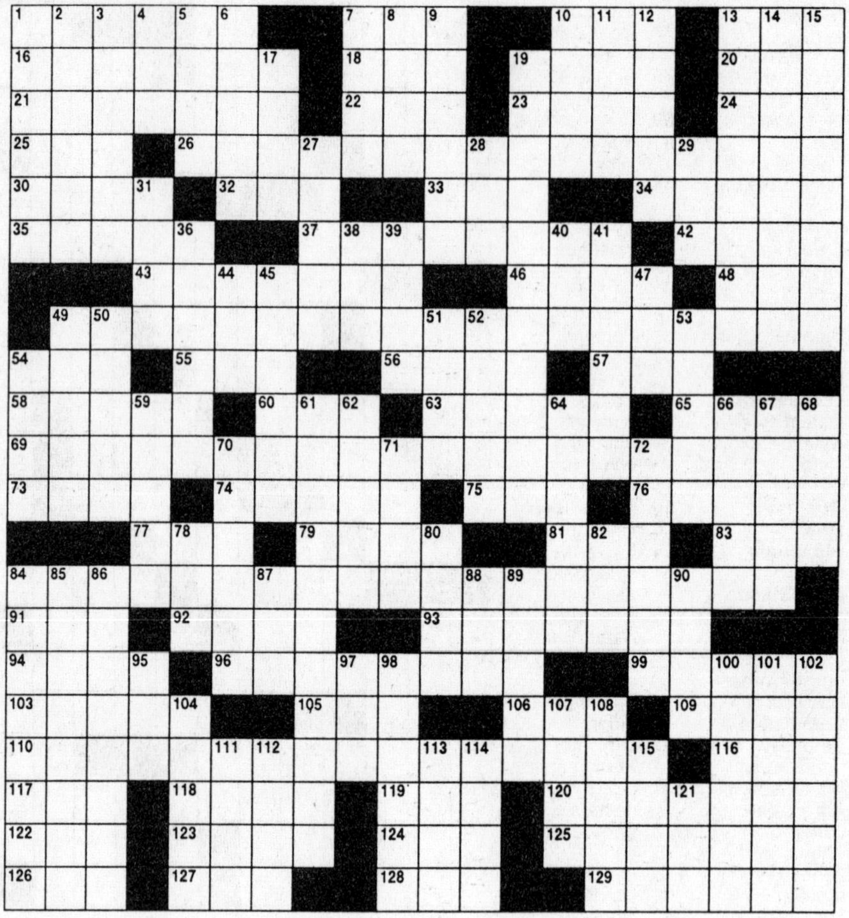

ACROSS

1. Nip in ___ (squelch quickly)
7. Peculiar
10. Arthur or Lillie
13. G-man
16. One bestowing laurels
18. Favoring
19. Prickly ___
20. Pinochle card
21. Prado artist
22. Stir
23. Risque
24. Guide a racing shell
25. Sickish
26. Part I of a film comment by 61 Down
30. *Duck* ___ (source of 26 Across)
32. Desire
33. Pouch
34. Smell of burning fat
35. Alma or Stabat
37. Brain: Prefix
42. Singer Perry
43. Queue
46. Scans
48. The Badger St.
49. Part II of comment
54. G.I. mail drop
55. ___ favor (señor's please)
56. A Truk island
57. Goldie, to cockneys
58. Kiel or Erie
60. Metric weights: Abbr.
63. ___ means (certainly)
65. Stepped on
69. Part III of comment
73. Crème ___ crème
74. Sneak away, in a way
75. Miss Lindstrom
76. A Hayes
77. Ending for cash
79. Wahwah Mountains' home
81. Neither's partner
83. Leverage
84. Part IV of comment
91. ___ Palmas
92. Xanadu's river
93. Tacks on again
94. Correct: Prefix
96. Playing around, pencilwise
99. Ex-Yankee junkball pitcher
103. Word before wise
105. Miss West
106. Women's ___
109. "Mens ___ in corpore . . ."
110. End of comment
116. Coolidge
117. German article
118. Endure
119. Ending for complex
120. Slim kind of chance
122. Peixe-___ (large smelt)
123. Cameo stone
124. Nanty ___ (Pa. town)
125. ___ hair down
126. Madrid Mrs.
127. Letter
128. Experiences
129. Biblical dancer

DOWN

1. Belief in God
2. Shout for attention
3. Gulp down
4. Brooklyn or Queens: Abbr.
5. 1934 Nobelist in chemistry
6. Lure
7. In the blink ___ eyelash
8. A bird no more
9. Be half asleep
10. Kind of geste or monde
11. Apiece
12. Indo-European
13. In the hole, as in poker
14. Of fiscal management
15. Corn sugar
17. Profligate one
19. Close friend, in law
27. Make dough
28. Mouth off
29. London's is Old
31. Melon or squash
36. Small wave
38. Kind of wit
39. Uncommunicative one
40. Writer Rand
41. Certain paid ads
44. Mail center: Abbr.
45. Hawk, in falconry
47. Opposite of NNE
49. Sally Ride's frontier
50. Of sound
51. Timber wolf
52. Cause nervous tension
53. ___ pink (healthy)
54. Kind of rain or test
59. With force
61. Speaker of the comment
62. Seven: Prefix
64. Capital of Angola
66. Houk or Rackstraw
67. ___ barrel
68. Turn down
70. Proclaim
71. Bring forth lambs
72. Sensation
78. Miss Le Gallienne
80. Mata ___
82. Information agcy. of W.W. II
84. Stupid boners
85. More unrefined
86. Tallinn's land: Var.
87. Navy noncom
88. "___ Little Indians"
89. American poet
90. Village divisions: Abbr.
95. Fowl
97. Bob a fishline
98. Bethlehem, Pa., campus
100. Actor Al
101. Head wreath
102. *Thy Neighbor's Wife* author
104. Mechanical man
107. Adored one
108. Sadness
111. Kelly or Sarazen
112. Martha of comedy
113. Lopez theme
114. Son of Seth
115. Comics' Kett
121. The sun

113 Around the House By Dorothea Shipp

Concentrating on a certain room.

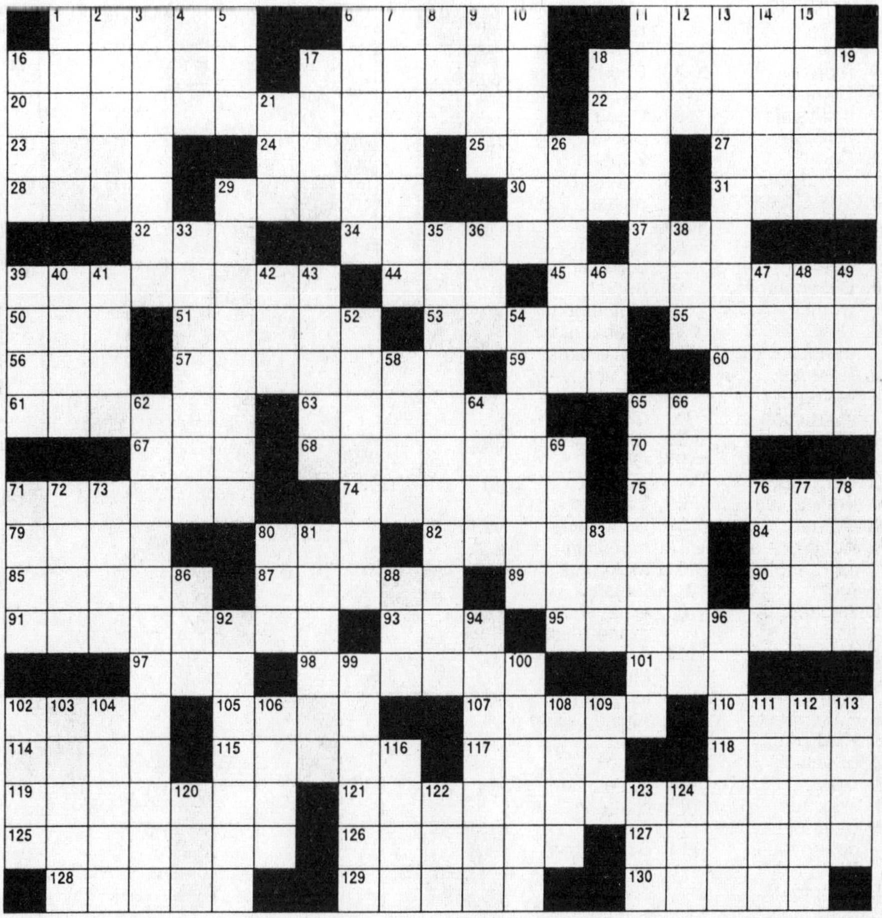

ACROSS

1. Did a potato job
6. "Ad ___ per aspera"
11. He's in "de cold, cold ground"
16. Carbonate
17. Reach
18. Horse's retirement place
20. Momentary sensation
22. Classifies
23. Network
24. Violinist Leopold
25. Lawmaking gp.
27. Some necklines
28. Baltic feeder
29. Native of Muscat
30. Irish exclamation
31. Della's creator
32. Feature of velvet
34. It turns litmus blue
37. Stop or Delaware Water
39. Board members
44. Article, in Bremen
45. Emulates an astrologer
50. Ben ___
51. Prefix for dox
53. ___ over (helped along)
55. Go bad
56. Actor Wallach
57. Of a fraternal order
59. Psyche parts
60. Sicilian resort
61. Vest
63. Swimmer Williams
65. Prepare leftovers
67. Village near Nice
68. Pittsburgh athlete
70. Alfonso's queen
71. Declared
74. Liniment
75. Connected series
79. Kentucky Derby entrant
80. S.A. country
82. Bird fancier
84. Russian village
85. Of age
87. "I am sure, if I had ___ ghost . . ."
89. Occurrence along a fault line
90. Here, in Paris
91. Maid
93. Swedish money
95. Left high and dry
97. "The voice that breath'd ___ Eden"
98. Early ascetic
101. Dutch commune
102. Beach pounder
105. Prefix for carp or derm
107. Hard work
110. ___ le Moko
114. Royal Scandinavian name
115. House of Lords people
117. Kind of bellum or room
118. Part of the eye
119. Hun leader and namesakes
121. Multihued stove?
125. Roll-call answer
126. Departure
127. Flower gatherer's need
128. Sackcloth's companions
129. Minimal
130. Indians of Ontario

DOWN

1. Expunged
2. Out of temper
3. Old military barracks
4. Old English letter
5. Gods, to Cicero
6. Goddess of wisdom
7. Like a surgical dressing
8. Kind of dance or room
9. Coin of Iran
10. Toughen
11. Kind of parlor
12. Jenny
13. Headgear of Lincoln's day
14. More definite
15. Russian collective
16. Hair style
17. Polynesian spirit
18. Unit of socks
19. "___ Quam Videri" (N.C. motto)
21. Business-men's org.
26. Complained
29. Did an appendix job
33. Spray
35. Apron?
36. Black bird
38. Newspaper insertions
39. Muscle
40. "___, Britannia"
41. Writer Leon
42. Diminutive endings
43. Mules or loafers
46. Thorough-fares: Abbr.
47. Volcano topper
48. Singer Turner
49. Blind part
52. Before an audience
54. Steers
58. Brain passage
62. Sorry state, often pretty
64. Lamb's other name
65. Took time off
66. Ready for war
69. Sped
71. Marine fish
72. Flurry
73. College grad
76. Give off
77. Resort in southern France
78. Like the Sahara
80. "___ was going to . . ."
81. What some hairlines do
83. Hurry
86. Mao ___ -tung
88. Our, in France
92. Cutting tools
94. Takes on
96. Drive back
99. Horse color
100. Hemingway or Bloch
102. Kind of opera
103. Ne plus ___
104. Has status
106. Fledgling's home
108. Japanese admiral et al.
109. Ship-shaped clock
111. Call forth
112. Goriot and others
113. One of London's Ends
116. Stuffing ingredient
120. Peggy or Pinky
122. Gun owners' org.
123. Network for Toronto
124. Trireme necessity

114 Nonprescription Drugs By Bert H. Kruse

Or, to be more accurate, nonexistent ones.

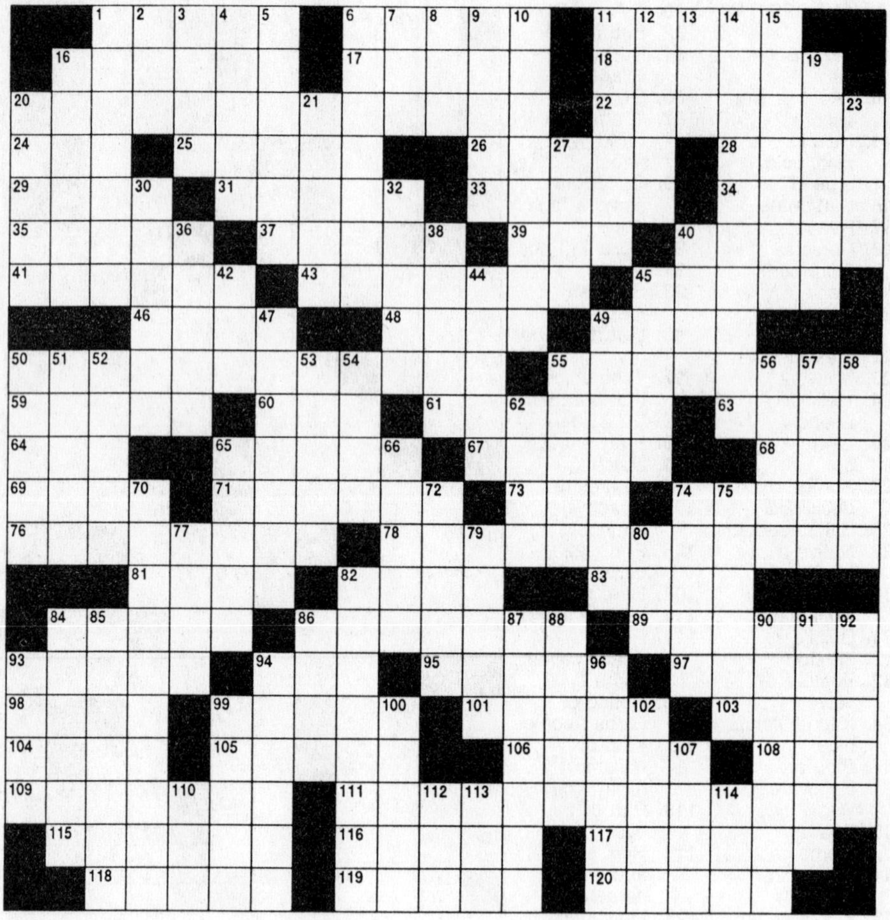

ACROSS

1. Give a ___ (boost)
6. Common children's disease
11. Corn porridges
16. The Green Wave
17. On the qui vive
18. Disreputable women
20. New tranquilizer?
22. Reverse faulty instruction
24. Slippery one
25. Permitted
26. Trifling sum
28. Corner
29. Keep one's ___ shut (be mum)
31. Aquarium fish
33. Careless speech sounds
34. Safecracker
35. Kind of day or vitae
37. Gawk
39. Prior to
40. Belgian city destroyed in W.W. I
41. Nonprofessionals
43. Blithe ___ (blues remedies?)
45. Wide of the mark
46. Dancer's bend
48. Sea raptors
49. Watch part
50. Medicine for the classroom?
55. Common lawn weed
59. Spoil
60. Highest note
61. Narrow valley
63. Luge
64. Neighbor of Que.
65. Understanding
67. Brooks
68. "___ Got My Eyes on You"
69. Loved figure
71. Toughen
73. Grassland
74. Lucky number
76. Flower parts
78. Ego-building dispensers?
81. Close
82. Son of Zophah
83. Spanish painter
84. Zones
86. ___ conscience (moral ointment?)
89. Grabbers for some birds
93. Be uppity
94. Counterpart of the Pac.
95. Smithy fixture
97. Gone ___ (ruined)
98. Liberal things
99. Conquer a mountain
101. Male and female
103. What you did at the office
104. Ancient Mideast kingdom
105. Alpine region
106. Start to attack
108. Writer Yutang
109. Name in film dance
111. Concoction for concerned voters?
115. Stock-market figure
116. Nary a soul
117. Fix a coat, e.g.
118. Mergansers
119. Arose
120. Lauder of cosmetics

DOWN

1. Broadway song
2. Tooth wearer
3. Quarters for Wilde
4. Not up to it
5. Periods between wars
6. Sinclair Lewis novel
7. Rubber tree
8. Mine, in France
9. Punctilious people
10. Hollywood hopefuls
11. Kind of root sometimes hard to find
12. Family members
13. New York athlete
14. Medicine hard for hosts to take?
15. Ones setting traps
16. ___ del Fuego
19. Wartime blockades
20. Iron or gold
21. Catchers' gear
23. Darkroom products: Abbr.
27. Possessive
30. Chrysanthemum
32. *Paradise Lost* angel
36. Apportion again
38. Slipped up
40. Singer Sumac and namesakes
42. Zilch
44. Bury
45. Buenos ___
47. Timeless
49. Slow-witted one
50. Zeno pupil
51. Motto of the Seabees
52. ___ -miss (haphazard)
53. Alda and King
54. Foundation
55. Heaped
56. Breathing
57. At no time
58. Paradisiacal sites
62. Office item
65. Celebrations
66. TV group
70. Soothing agent for also-rans?
72. Caterpillar
74. Chair part
75. Afterword
77. Meager
79. Deportments
80. Kind of cake or meal
82. Comic-strip areas
84. ". . . crucify mankind upon ___ of gold"
85. Spins
86. Sapphire variety
87. Like fatsos
88. Devise
90. Milk glass
91. Beginner
92. Office worker
93. River of Peru
94. Quaker grays
96. Poe's mourned blonde
99. Scatter
100. Author of *Middlemarch*
102. Kind of tax
107. Joust
110. St. Lawrence River sight
112. Old card game
113. Yoko ___
114. Lash

115 Numbers Game By Ronnie Allen

Concentrating on one phonetically anyway.

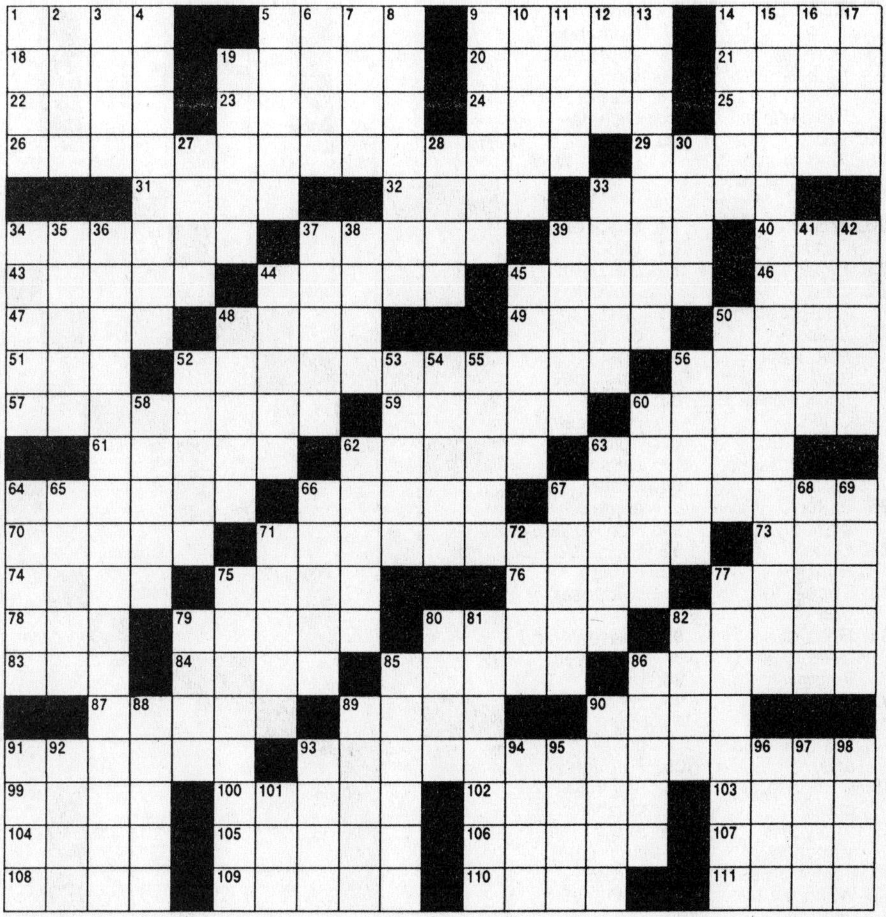

ACROSS

1. Like nails
5. Hip habitations
9. Must
14. Attempt
18. Pitcher
19. Greenstreet's sidekick
20. Poe's foster father
21. Sound from the little engine
22. Temptress in *Damn Yankees*
23. Organic compound
24. Strays
25. Split
26. See-through storefront
29. Rose's origin
31. Majestic term of address
32. Elephant's offspring
33. Monkey or man
34. Item lost in a nursery rhyme
37. Milking-machine milieu
39. Stagehand
40. Pinup's underpinning
43. Was painful
44. Interest for Shylock
45. Satisfy
46. Yalie
47. Active person
48. Dandelion's domicile
49. Volcano's top
50. Earth
51. The law, to Mr. Bumble
52. Audrey Hepburn thriller
56. Ulysses foiled her
57. Princess-pea separator
59. Piping
60. He was "Once in Love With Amy"
61. Increase
62. Clues
63. Seaweeds
64. Backer of centralized government
66. T. S. Eliot's land
67. Negotiate
70. U ___ of U.N. note
71. Ultimatum to a shirker
73. Arafat's org.
74. "___ that a shame!"
75. Baptismal basin
76. Arena exclamations
77. Talon
78. Neighbor of Ill.
79. Compassion
80. Moonshiner's need
82. ___ Khan, Kipling tiger
83. Scouting unit
84. Der ___
85. Once in a ___
86. Hung around
87. Endure
89. It's less lovely than a tree
90. Figure-skating combo
91. Destroys documents
93. San Fran span
99. African antelope
100. Classic kidnapper
102. Longest French river
103. Elected position
104. Andy's pal
105. Chemical compound
106. Passion
107. Brief message
108. Ingredient in a *Macbeth* recipe
109. Like a puny animal
110. Feds
111. The last word

DOWN

1. Assist
2. G.I. misconduct
3. Pertain to
4. Hot-rod driver
5. Sheriff's retinue
6. Part of M.A.
7. Sketched
8. Protein of silk fiber
9. Only just
10. Reserved
11. Cabbage dish
12. Highland hat
13. Picket-sign words
14. "Beat it!"
15. Marquand character
16. Top rank at Lloyd's
17. Portend
19. Profit from experience
27. German song
28. Balm
30. Mature
33. Bit of mischief
34. *Call Me* ___
35. Twenty: Prefix
36. Honest path
37. Epsom ___
38. Charley's theatrical relative
39. "Battle Hymn" refrain word
41. Mad Hatter's guest
42. Distance runner
44. Hesitate
45. Oodles
48. Up to the minute
50. Eliot's Marner
52. Arm joint
53. Their luck is traditional
54. Musically slow
55. Inhibit
56. Related by blood
58. Spoil
60. Spills the beans
62. Pudding variety at Harvard
63. Russian cooperative
64. Proper
65. ". . . with ___ eyes"
66. Shrink from
67. Veil material
68. County in Ireland
69. Used a trailer hitch
71. Strong point
72. Shape of a spring
75. Shiny mineral
77. Magnetic quality
79. Downstairs occupant
80. Molt
81. Cause-effect interval
82. Kind of crazy
85. Henry VIII's adviser
86. Dueling weapon
88. Beauty's beau
89. West ___
90. Alba, to Goya
91. A.k.a. The Man
92. Heart's proverbial location
93. ___ and bear it
94. Standard
95. Author of *The Immoralist*
96. Consider
97. Plucky
98. School jacket
101. ___ Darya, Asian river

116 Getting Literal By Robert Wolfe

Extra ways of looking at the obvious.

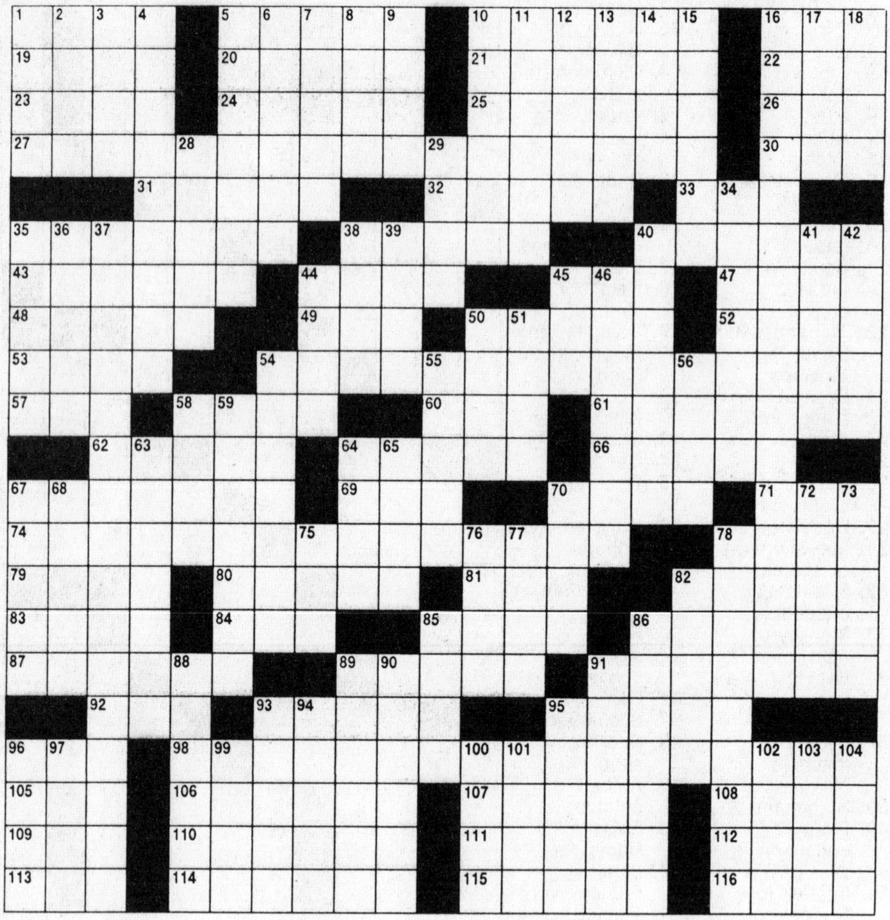

ACROSS

1. Hunk of bread
5. French Revolutionist
10. Sultry
16. Kind of suit
19. Holy man of Tibet
20. Emulate Cicero
21. Small space
22. ___-de-France
23. Miss MacGraw and namesakes
24. Lion's instructor
25. Quarterback, at times
26. Latten component
27. Christie Brinkley
30. Topee, for one
31. Units of syllabic length
32. Composer Harold
33. Conservation agcy.
35. Compose for print
38. Analyze a sentence
40. Full of dross
43. Withdrew by degrees
44. Surfeit
45. Impertinence
47. Dies ___
48. Radiates
49. Habitat: Prefix
50. Lizard
52. Seizes
53. Poetic nights
54. What Wilt might do in a Piper Cub
57. Blasting material
58. Gulf off Arabia
60. Eye part
61. Brings into agreement
62. Narrow groove
64. Certain jars
66. Ponti of films
67. Copy of a court record
69. Inlet
70. Sicily's sword of Damocles
71. Backward
74. What Comaneci and Korbut do
78. Ivan or Nicholas
79. El ___, Libyan W.W. II town
80. ___ Gay
81. Smidgen
82. Label
83. Genus of mollusks
84. East Lansing campus
85. Brief biography
86. Kerry's county seat
87. Young salmon
89. Mine approaches
91. Hunting dog
92. "___ is me"
93. French composer Erik
95. Teasdale and Roosevelt
96. Bristle
98. What Vulcan might have done
105. Through
106. Singing syllables
107. Stony landmark
108. Barbara or Anthony
109. Chemical suffix
110. McCarthy or Debs
111. Medieval helmet
112. Nevada city
113. Tack on
114. Early chariots
115. Authority
116. High-sch. tests

DOWN

1. Grand bridge bid
2. Composer Edouard
3. In the center of
4. Bargain-sale places
5. Went for a spin
6. P.L.O. head
7. Gradients
8. To ___ (exactly)
9. Pre-statehood: Abbr.
10. Candles
11. Apollo's voice at Delphi
12. Remainder, in Rouen
13. Aid for Seaver
14. Intestine: Prefix
15. Rye grass
16. How Lot's wife took the warning
17. Lamb
18. Big top
28. Forfeits
29. Diet
34. Sore
35. Bird sound
36. Where Sana is
37. What Gromyko does gaily in Moscow
38. New York university
39. Perched on
40. Stoical
41. Famous Butler
42. Sycophants' responses
44. Noted
45. Solon's specialty
46. Brunts
50. Inter ___
51. Olympus dwellers
54. Diane and Buster
55. Alms are given in his name
56. Another, in Avila
58. Region
59. Crowns
63. Quivery musical passage
64. City on the Oka
65. Modena money
67. Remarks by Major Hoople
68. Wicked biblical city
70. Exile isle
72. Indian royalty
73. In ___ (sequential)
75. Proof of payment: Abbr.
76. Do a newsroom job
77. Consumes
78. Decals
82. Actor Keith
85. Opinion
86. Lake Ontario port
88. Quiz taker
89. Near
90. Double daggers, in printing
91. San Diego club
93. Harts
94. Salt tree
95. Like a fish's skin
96. Samoan port
97. Go on one's way
99. Household head, to Brutus
100. Wood sorrels
101. ___ avis
102. Thought
103. Schism
104. Son of Seth

117 Locomotion By Evelyn Benshoof

Getting around in one way or another.

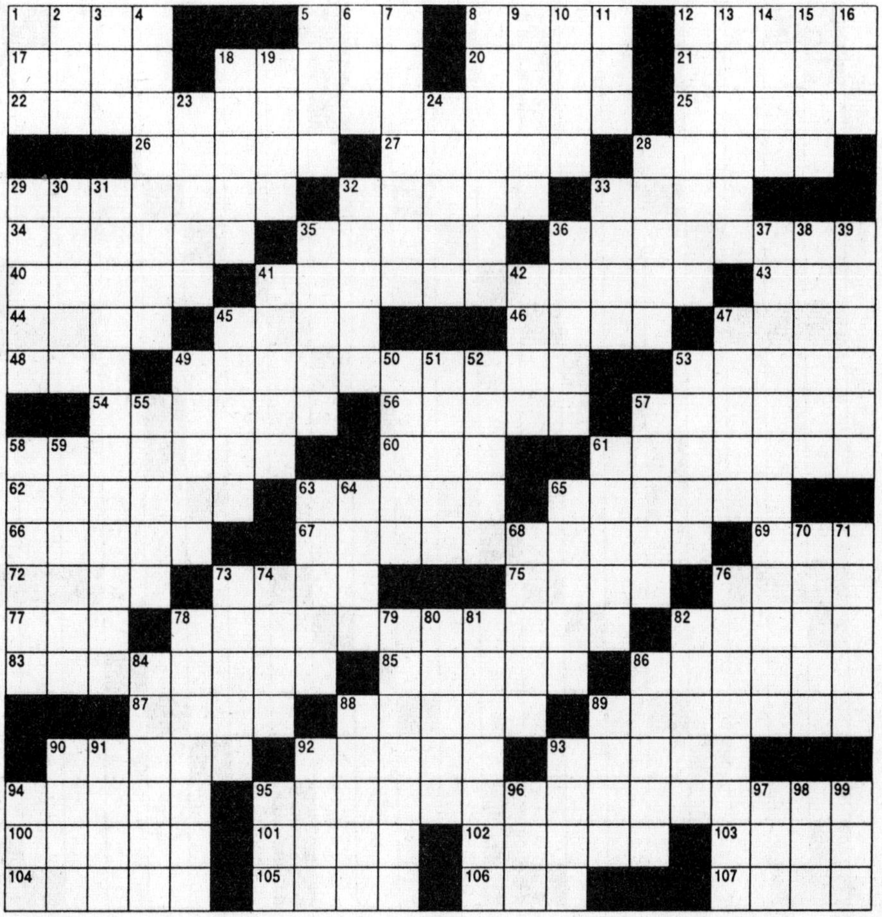

ACROSS

1. Teddy or Kodiak
5. Cobra of Egypt
8. Lively party
12. C.P.A.'s entry
17. French river
18. Machine part
20. Play part
21. Crème de la crème
22. Behaved cautiously
25. Distributed
26. Kept going
27. Paris quarter
28. One who actuates
29. Side-show barker
32. Rabbit fur
33. Recent
34. Lavish
35. Attack
36. "The ___ Sleepy Hollow"
40. Baseball gear
41. Make progress
43. Regret
44. Hurt
45. German river
46. Andean Indian
47. Makes trimming
48. Discern
49. Slow going
53. East Indian cereal grasses
54. City near San Diego
56. More novel
57. Chicago's Scarface
58. Yankees or Packers, for example
60. Philippine volcano
61. Shoe ties
62. Summer cottage, often
63. Terrible
65. Part of H.S.H.
66. Moth
67. Head for the second floor
69. Wee, in Scotland
72. John Dickson of mysteries
73. Reply from a cliffside
75. Entr' ___
76. Remotely
77. Eskimo knife
78. Gain advantage over, with "on"
82. On the qui vive
83. Sawbucks
85. Bit of sculpture
86. Actress Francis
87. Rustic way
88. Emporium
89. Arouses
90. Prophets
92. Pester
93. Dutch painter
94. Handyman
95. Be obsequious
100. Vibrant
101. Piece of china
102. Use the oven
103. Sparse
104. Famous
105. Robert ___
106. Indian weight
107. Impart

DOWN

1. Do a salaam
2. ___ of Good Feeling
3. Picnic denizen
4. Form a new image
5. Like ___ of bricks
6. Heir
7. Bishop or abbot
8. Stitching
9. Muscle protein
10. British gun
11. Sophisticated
12. Reduced in class
13. Football team
14. Snack
15. Anatomical passage
16. A Kennedy
18. Actress Taylor
19. Fragrance
23. Aborts
24. Flavor
28. ___ Carta
29. East Indian vines
30. Vincent or Leontyne
31. Eventually
32. Balanced
33. White: Prefix
35. Province of Spain
36. Recluse
37. Be reluctant
38. Pleasure trip
39. Actor Parker and namesakes
41. Gorge
42. Pilaf base
45. Actress Tatum
47. Basketball shot
49. Daub
50. Foul-up
51. Animate
52. Decamping G.I.s
53. Grand-prix events
55. Rose oil
57. Spy writer John le ___
58. Like some building lumber
59. Entertain
61. Scottish port
63. Turkish titles
64. Eye pull-over
65. Vanzetti's friend
68. Silken stuff of old
70. French river
71. Crafts, in Mexico
73. College and collar
74. Whale
76. Everything considered
78. Shadow-boxed
79. Kind of case
80. Big deer
81. In ___ (owing)
82. Moved in a curve
84. Garment part
86. Concerning
88. Acuity
89. Followers: Suffix
90. Farm structure
91. Stage direction
92. Coat or shirt follower
93. Nova
94. Devotee
95. Ike
96. Shoe part
97. Formerly named
98. Fire
99. ___ of the line

118 Plus Values By Barbara Weakley

Giving the high sign to some combinations.

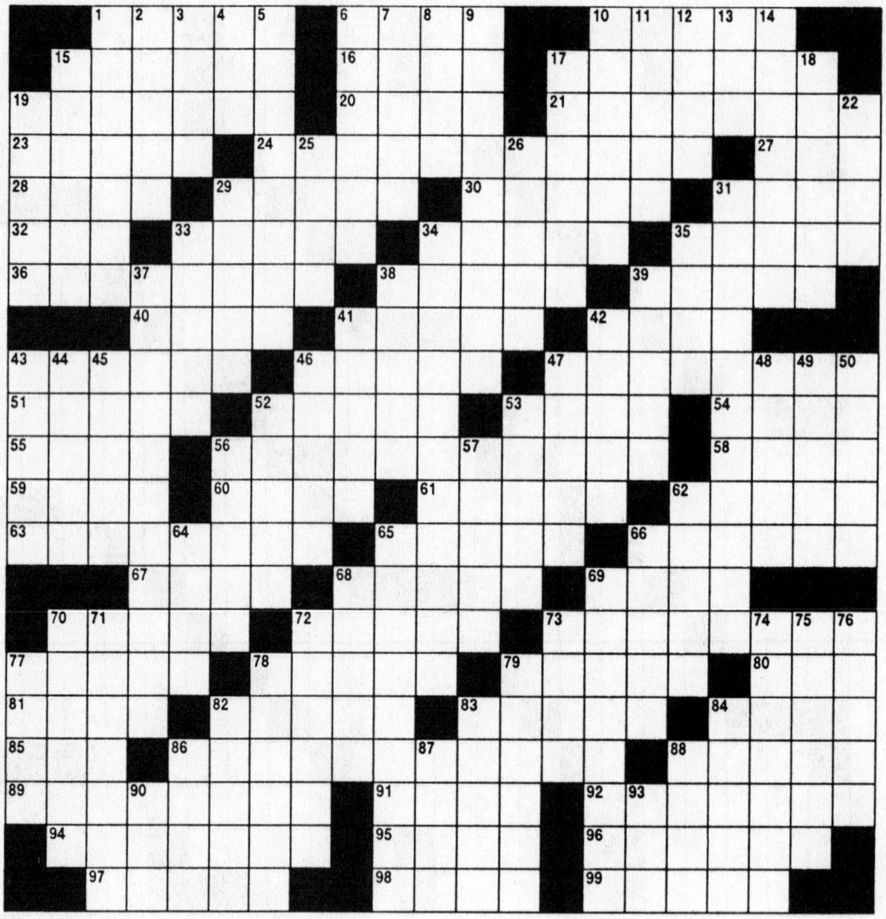

ACROSS

1. Singing family
6. Nomadic northerner
10. Philippine island
15. Menace after a disaster
16. "Deutschland ___ Alles"
17. Receiver of property
19. Full
20. Country road
21. Chiropody
23. Colorado resort
24. Hair color of the middle ages?
27. Doctors' gp.
28. ___ irae
29. Brawl
30. Austrian psychiatrist
31. Play truant
32. Follower of super or infer
33. Yearned
34. Produce
35. Unlocks
36. Example
38. Kadiddlehopper et al.
39. Marinating solution
40. "Vissi d'___"
41. Barton or Bow
42. Idyllist
43. Sergeant-___
46. Guinness and namesakes
47. Like Ali's opponents?
51. "To a ___ bone . . ."
52. Haunted-house sound
53. Atmosphere: Prefix
54. Pueblo Indian
55. Star in Pegasus
56. Ingredients of little girls
58. Gymnast Korbut
59. Waxy fabric finish
60. Love god
61. Baby-sit
62. Extort
63. Legendary continent
65. Santiago's country
66. Puppeteer Bil et al.
67. An age
68. Polished
69. Prepare a salad
70. Ruins
72. Indian caste members
73. Haberdashery item
77. Modify
78. Flower, in Italy
79. Convenes
80. ___ Paulo
81. Bring up
82. Marine animal
83. Flies high
84. Struck, old style
85. Farming: Abbr.
86. Be selective
88. Electron tube
89. One of five
91. Travel-agency offering
92. Light desserts
94. Secondhand tire
95. Early worker
96. Weaken
97. Badgerlike mammal
98. Radicals
99. Coward et al.

DOWN

1. Opera hats
2. Functions
3. Solar disk
4. Kind of peeve
5. A ghost, perhaps
6. Made tranquil
7. Moderate
8. ___ ink
9. They fill out tax returns
10. Canted
11. One giving help
12. Golda
13. Literary bits
14. Captured anew
15. Injury
17. Doctor repellents
18. Weasel with fine fur
19. Arm bones
22. Babbles
25. Toward shelter
26. Dropsy
29. After-dinner sweets
31. Soldier's appearance
33. Italian city
34. Something to get it down in
35. Masculine name
37. Prepare one for a trip out of town?
38. Exonerate
39. Knife named for a Texan
41. Kind of cut or sailing
42. Lanai
43. Betel palm
44. Carthaginian goddess
45. Announcement words, with "It's"
46. Ancient Greek city
47. Clear a plane wing
48. Houston athlete
49. Prodded
50. Hoppers
52. Flavoring herb
53. Fittingly
56. Overfills
57. Ex-pitcher Johnny and others
62. Supply centers
64. Poetic word
65. Weirdo
66. Wear for a puss
68. ___ save (supermarket words)
69. Electronic musical instrument
70. Sour liquid
71. More desolate
72. Cheated
73. Red and Black
74. Absorption
75. L.A. footballer
76. Observes
77. Russian sea
78. Beauty treatment
79. Mary Tyler and Garry
82. Emphatic suffix for yes or no
83. Partner of safe
84. Agave fiber
86. Flippant
87. Nylons
88. Fool
90. Greek vowel
93. Shoulder: Prefix

119 Escapism By William Canine

Some things involved in getting away from it all.

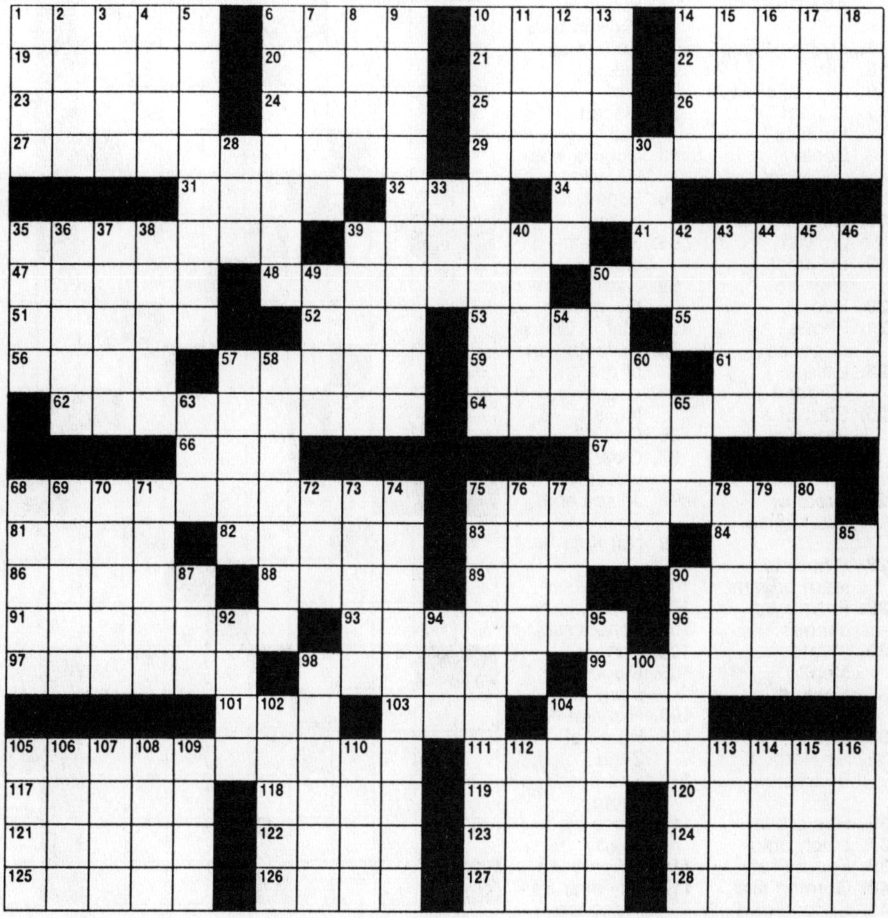

ACROSS

1. Early pulpits
6. Track event
10. Leaves "that old gang"
14. Uncover
19. Victim of Corday
20. Glee-club member
21. Other, in Iberia
22. Muse
23. Buoy up
24. "The ___ of the crowd"
25. Had regrets
26. Chairman's prop
27. Spots for the convivial
29. Romberg specialty
31. Port ___
32. The earth, old style
34. Word before whiz
35. Actor of many parts?
39. Relative of crunchy, in ads
41. Andean beasts
47. Shallot
48. Zoo skyscraper
50. Hold in contempt
51. Horace and Thomas
52. Ad ___
53. Chemist's abbr.
55. Shy
56. Not pro
57. Michener title
59. Burned up
61. Helpmate
62. Features of adventure films
64. Big-top performer
66. Nickname for a Nile king
67. Caesar
68. Where stars perform
75. Features of horse operas
81. Smirk
82. Deep sleep
83. Sea birds
84. Harpers Ferry event
86. Solos
88. Buddhist priest
89. Kind of pocket or port
90. Passageway
91. Comedian Phil
93. Bit of letter juggling
96. Annoying
97. Offenbach's *La Belle* ___
98. Befuddles
99. Utilizes
101. Vets' org.
103. Sibilant sound
104. Ice sheet
105. Garry Trudeau or Peter Arno
111. Specialty of 64 Across
117. D-day beach
118. Okinawa's capital
119. Exigency
120. Of the neighbor-hood
121. Team on the short end
122. Town on the Thames
123. Number after zwei
124. Irregular
125. Residue
126. Grain
127. Mixer
128. Supped

DOWN

1. ___ corner
2. Mauritania's neighbor
3. Vaunt
4. Word of honor
5. Western toppers
6. Word for Clementine
7. Audibly
8. Puncture
9. Meadowlands events
10. 1970 Osaka presentation
11. Needlecase
12. Full of sediment
13. Hebrew letter
14. Western lily
15. Kind of door or shooting
16. Rhapsodize
17. Roman road
18. Negri of the silents
28. Gondola
30. Prefix for graph
33. Moroccan hilly region
35. Capital of Italia
36. Fatuous
37. Half ___ (young squirts)
38. Stimulant
39. Philosopher Benedetto
40. Rock: Prefix
42. W.W. II vessel
43. Of bees
44. Parrot
45. Not in the center
46. Feast of the Exodus
49. "If ___ a Million"
50. Is mad about
54. Siesta
57. Exhorts
58. Lookouts
60. Arranges news items
63. Brunched
65. Hubbub
68. Jar
69. Uncanny
70. Eugene O' ___
71. Crossbeam
72. Argentine native
73. Wanderer
74. What some people play to
75. Set builders
76. Successors
77. Weirdo, in Glasgow
78. Milton archangel
79. Italian poet
80. Oozing smoothness
85. Ottoman rulers
87. Wash. lawmaker
90. Went to a higher court
92. Make a change
94. Pacino and others
95. Organ stop
98. Fly a plane
100. Multitude
102. Two of Henry's six
104. Let go
105. Tropical tree
106. Biblical book of prophesies
107. Headlong
108. "How do I love ___?"
109. Paddles
110. Brogan
112. Atlantic sport fish
113. Convex moldings
114. Image
115. Carryall
116. Coaster

120 Upper Regions By Helena Farmer

Where things are more orderly and pleasant.

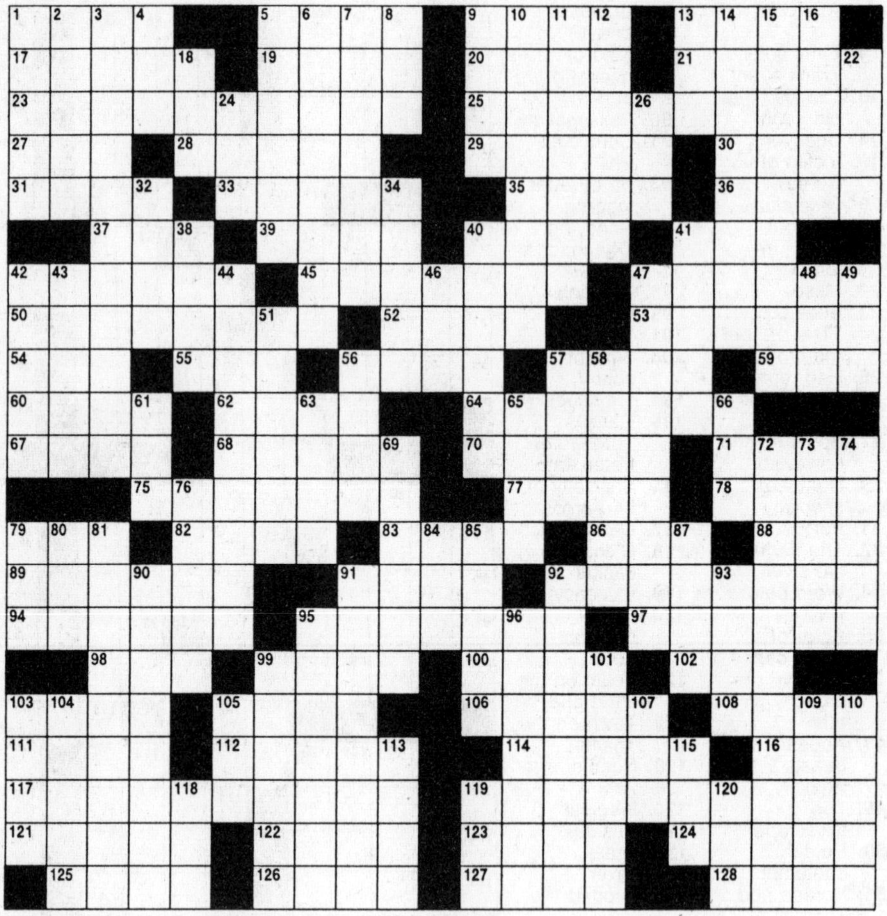

ACROSS

1. Fly-home bug
5. Tiff
9. ". . . against ___ of troubles"
13. Book addenda: Abbr.
17. German war prowler
19. Syllables after tra
20. Hue
21. Shows diligence
23. Little braggart
25. Start of a Browning observation on nature
27. Great or razor-billed ___
28. Where to learn origami
29. Polynesian canoes
30. "Watch ___ step"
31. Cooking direction
33. Doc
35. Sir Herbert Beerbohm ___
36. Has a bite
37. Latch onto
39. Food: Prefix
40. German title
41. Second part of the quote
42. Third part of the quote
45. Original
47. Atom constituent
50. Wiry-coated dog
52. Son of Seth
53. ___ day (have regrets)
54. Science place
55. Miss Arden
56. Smell ___
57. Between hic and hoc
59. Diplomat's res.
60. Minor error
62. Fourth part of the quote
64. Raised
67. Piedmont wine town
68. Classic keepsake
70. Fifth part of the quote
71. Small drinks
75. Buddhist state of bliss
77. Certain age
78. Indigo
79. Vim
82. Placed the ball
83. Octavia was his wife
86. Superlative ending
88. Sympathy drink
89. Sixth part of the quote
91. Star in Cetus
92. Seventh part of the quote
94. ___ only (titular)
95. Operated
97. *Oklahoma* vehicle
98. Jolson and Smith
99. Nat King ___
100. Deadly sin
102. Shoe width
103. School subj.
105. Portend
106. Diagonal mark
108. Nicholas I or II
111. Home of Zeno
112. End of the quote
114. Close by, to poets
116. Italian three
117. City near San Francisco
119. Charge of wrongdoing
121. City in Florida
122. "And all ___ is a merry yarn . . ."
123. Virginia ___
124. Hawthorne lived in an old one
125. Jacob's twin
126. Gaelic
127. Helper: Abbr.
128. Type of arch

DOWN

1. George ___, film bigwig
2. Concerning
3. Do a space maneuver
4. Tibetan ox
5. Skiing places
6. Jug of wine, etc., to Omar
7. Sulfate mineral
8. Scottish wear
9. Above
10. Ole Blue Eyes and family
11. Hold spellbound
12. "Set ___ to catch . . ."
13. Mimic
14. Leisure footwear
15. Do a ballet turn
16. Arrangement
18. ___ Mahal
22. Wall St. purchases
24. Getaway
26. Direction: Abbr.
32. He had a Progress
34. One with a future
38. The Venerable ___
40. "___ seauton" (know thyself)
41. War respite
42. Model-airplane wood
43. Coins of Iran
44. Of a Spanish region
46. ___ rut (mired)
47. Play actings
48. Electrical unit
49. Lincoln's state: Abbr.
51. The dream, in France
56. "It's ___ to tell . . ."
57. Sex-book author
58. What a wolf needs for clothing
61. Linch or rolling
63. Dressed
65. Aware of
66. Genetic initials
69. Eye tooth
72. What a bore is not
73. Recital number
74. Like some roofs
76. Parts of lists
79. Greek letter
80. Poetic word
81. Slim cigars
84. Edwardian, for one
85. Fads
87. Certain exam choice
90. HQ for the Valkyries
91. Machismo
92. What authors like on royalties
93. Ridge on a guitar
95. Like a space vehicle
96. Intertwines
99. Chinese laborer
101. Tristram's beloved: Var.
103. Office note
104. Shade of blue
105. Women's-lib discard
107. Owns
109. Ascended
110. Adorée of films
113. Henry van ___, U.S. educator
115. Animal in the sky
118. Early Greek letter
119. Parseghian
120. Chinese truth

121 Word Play By Judson Trent

Some combinations that might seem appropriate.

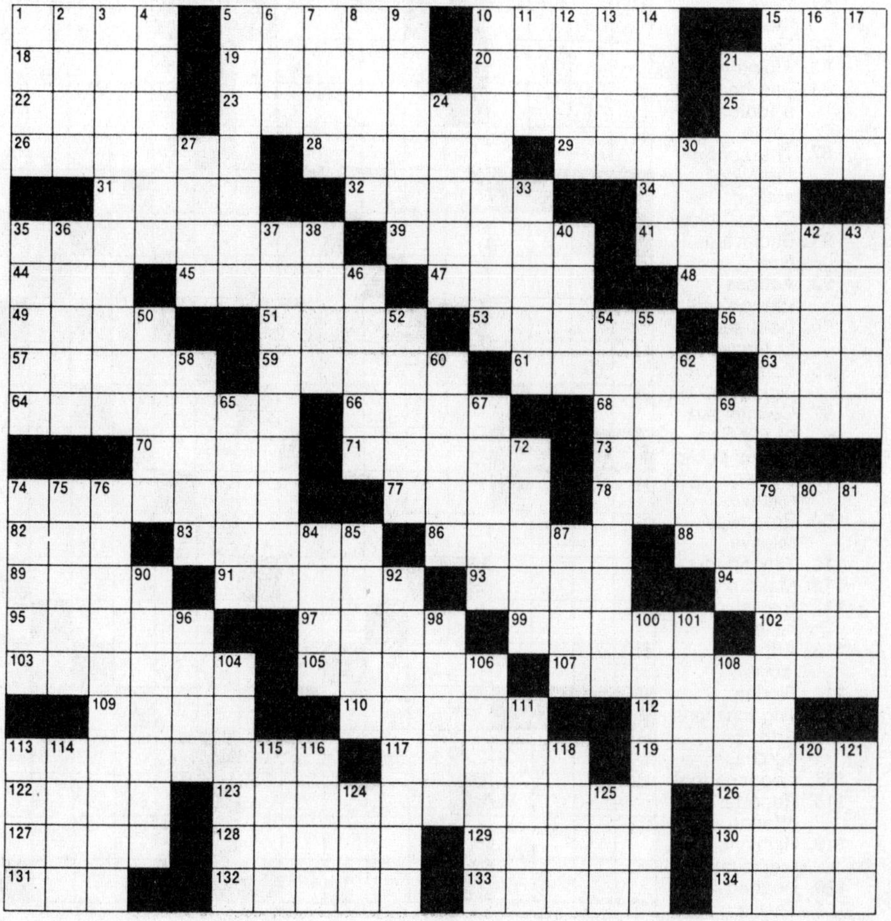

ACROSS

1. Egyptian cotton
5. Trattoria fare
10. ___ Flow
15. Deface
18. "Thanks ___"
19. Knock for ___ (wallop)
20. Stopwatch
21. Spanish conifer
22. Touch
23. Atonement?
25. Pisa's river
26. Atoms
28. A Longworth
29. Hauled away again
31. Minnesota player
32. Pink ones are dreaded
34. Oriental nurse
35. Dissertation
39. Kind of energy
41. Kind of centennial
44. Always, poetically
45. Spread outward
47. Maui goose
48. "Scotland's Burning," e.g.
49. Girl Fri.
51. Glacial ridges
53. Uses a dirk
56. Serve chowder
57. Turn away
59. Lapwing
61. Make suitable
63. N.Z. parrot
64. Plastic material
66. "Hark, hark" bird
68. Fans
70. Run a combine
71. Smarted
73. Bumpkin
74. Niagara's outlet
77. Hebrew lyre
78. Emulated Circe
82. French statute
83. "___ alive!"
86. Endured
88. Singer Lena
89. Part of O.E.D.
91. Souvenir sticker
93. Arias
94. Unit of loudness
95. Inquiring one
97. Caky deposit
99. Corday's victim
102. Joined
103. Started a garden
105. Trencherman
107. Piazzas
109. Edgar ___ Burroughs
110. Recoiled
112. Famed Chi paper
113. Flabbergasts
117. Kefauver
119. Tristan's love
122. Dandy
123. Apathy?
126. Shank
127. Indy segments
128. Abstract beings
129. Parts of cows' stomachs
130. This, in Spain
131. Midi season
132. Lac, for one
133. Moslem holy writ
134. Ending for young or ham

DOWN

1. Palindromic title
2. White: Prefix
3. Comparison shopper?
4. Northern capital
5. Root vegetable
6. Pub drink
7. Cell body
8. Saws and screwdrivers
9. Spring months
10. New England town sights
11. Presidential rank: Abbr.
12. Mythical archer
13. Suffix for centi
14. Betel palms
15. Belly laugh?
16. Diarist Frank
17. Cross
21. Lady's prop at Ascot
24. Heir
27. Relatives of dahs
30. New World native: Abbr.
33. December figure
35. Rips
36. Change the thermostat
37. Novice skier?
38. Riley's forte
40. Learn from McGuffey
42. Below
43. Notions
46. Jolly boats
50. ___ cotta
52. Cowboy's gear
54. Sarcasm?
55. Edgar Lee Masters's river
58. Ogles
60. Bind
62. Place for a crown
65. Water nymph
67. Grannies and half hitches
69. Combos
72. Get a horse ready for showing
74. As ___ Methuselah
75. Cacophony
76. Electro-cardiogram?
79. Melee?
80. Nine: Prefix
81. Boy Scout specialties
84. "___ homo!"
85. Teasdale and Roosevelt
87. Oslo regal name
90. Boring
92. Synodical church
96. Received, in Paris
98. System of belief
100. Ceramist, e.g.
101. Sea dogs
104. Highest U.S. capital
106. Seized anew
108. Relatives
111. Skin: Prefix
113. Competent
114. Catbird ___
115. Patronize a refectory
116. NCO's
118. Principal
120. Troubadour's instrument
121. Romanov, for one
124. Muttonbird
125. "Rose ___ rose . . ."

122 Siblings By Emory Cain

Coming from all or no sides of the family.

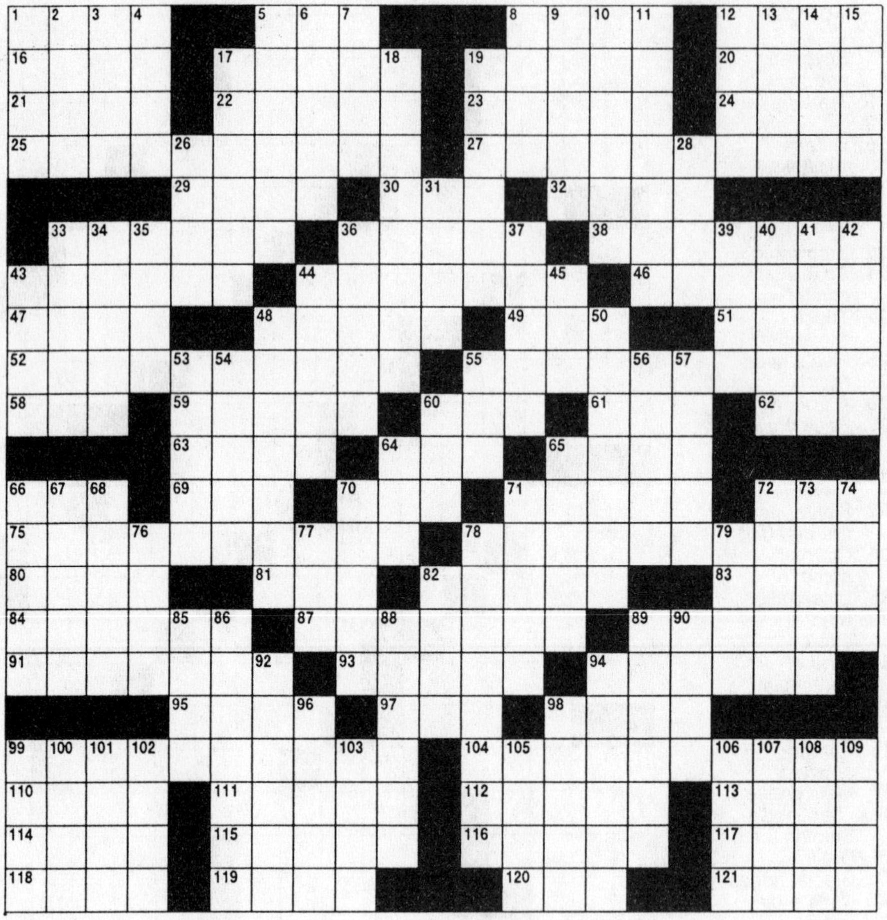

ACROSS

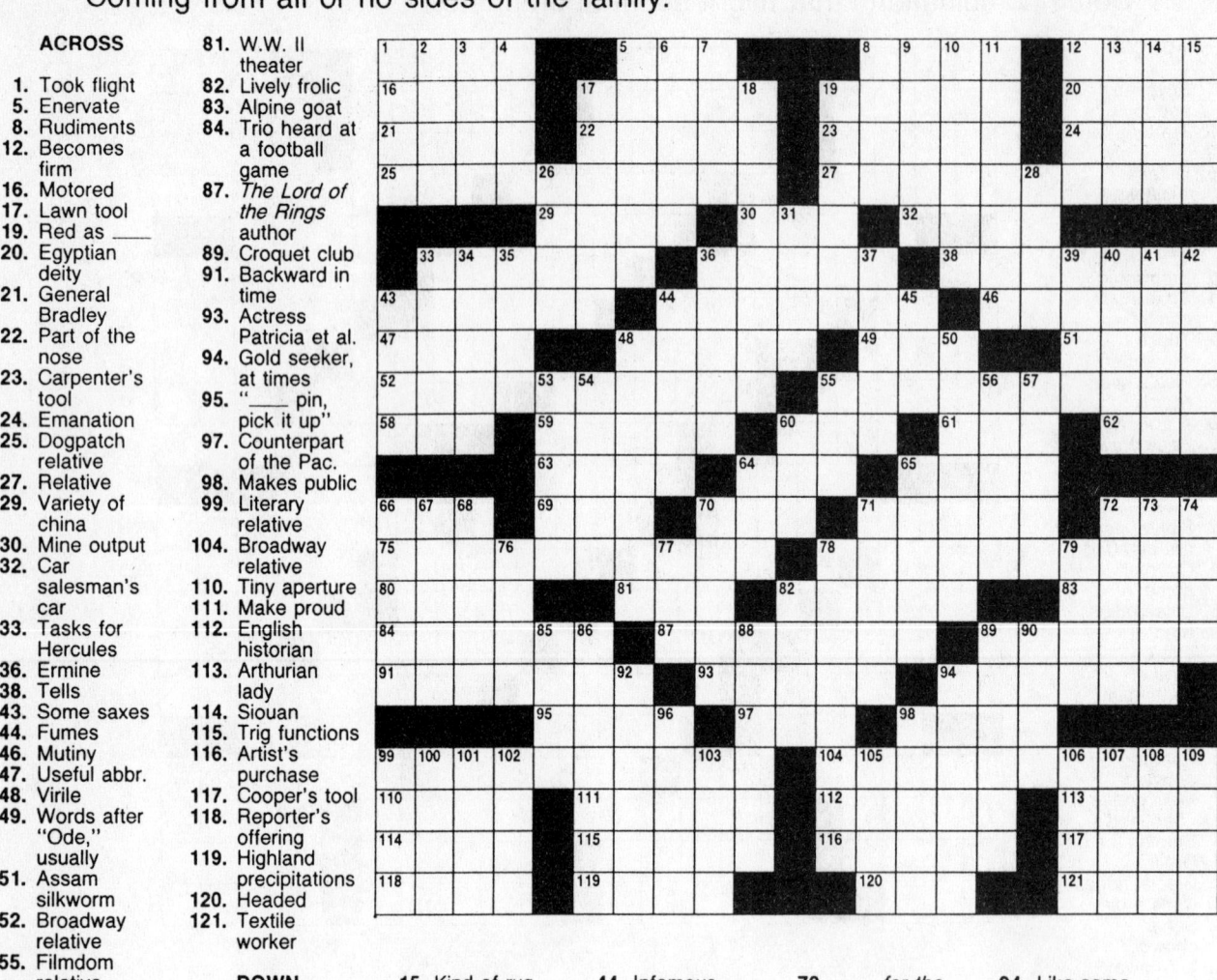

1. Took flight
5. Enervate
8. Rudiments
12. Becomes firm
16. Motored
17. Lawn tool
19. Red as ___
20. Egyptian deity
21. General Bradley
22. Part of the nose
23. Carpenter's tool
24. Emanation
25. Dogpatch relative
27. Relative
29. Variety of china
30. Mine output
32. Car salesman's car
33. Tasks for Hercules
36. Ermine
38. Tells
43. Some saxes
44. Fumes
46. Mutiny
47. Useful abbr.
48. Virile
49. Words after "Ode," usually
51. Assam silkworm
52. Broadway relative
55. Filmdom relative
58. Dir.
59. Coastal fliers
60. Grazing land
61. Son of Noah
62. Curve
63. Gives a leg up
64. Corrode
65. Nastase of tennis
66. G.I. address
69. Goddess, in Rome
70. Trajectory
71. White poplar
72. Kennedy lander
75. New Year relative
78. Shimmying relative of song
80. Davis Cup captain
81. W.W. II theater
82. Lively frolic
83. Alpine goat
84. Trio heard at a football game
87. *The Lord of the Rings* author
89. Croquet club
91. Backward in time
93. Actress Patricia et al.
94. Gold seeker, at times
95. "___ pin, pick it up"
97. Counterpart of the Pac.
98. Makes public
99. Literary relative
104. Broadway relative
110. Tiny aperture
111. Make proud
112. English historian
113. Arthurian lady
114. Siouan
115. Trig functions
116. Artist's purchase
117. Cooper's tool
118. Reporter's offering
119. Highland precipitations
120. Headed
121. Textile worker

DOWN

1. "___ the halls of . . ."
2. Glen Gray's Casa ___ Orchestra
3. Mild cheese
4. Skin
5. Lawmakers
6. Up and about
7. Andean country
8. Kind of bodied
9. Boy Scout organizer
10. Man between two guards
11. Stanley ___ (old car)
12. Pair of horses
13. Needle case
14. Mountain pool
15. Kind of rug
17. Civic brass
18. Opposite of closely
19. Seem
26. Tampa's ___ City
28. Captive of Hercules
31. Optimistic
33. "___ pray"
34. Of ___ (in a time period)
35. Gaucho's weapon
36. Transmits
37. Aquarium fish
39. State
40. Baseball manager Joe
41. Inventor Howe
42. R.B.I. and E.R.A.
43. Dick Tracy's wife
44. Infamous marquis and family
45. Gadgety kind of dad
48. Fiat
50. Gymnast, for one
53. English novelist
54. Paint additive
55. Aqueduct action
56. Selassie
57. Mideast ruler
60. Varnish ingredient
64. Before
65. Norwegian dramatist
66. ___ *in the Crowd*
67. Turkish title
68. Word before wise or worldly
70. ___ *for the Misbegotten*
71. Buenos ___
72. Fine fur
73. ___ clear of
74. Kind of book
76. Command to a dog
77. Big Board initials
78. Overflow
79. Furnace
82. Card game for three
85. Diva Stevens
86. Sibyl
88. Legal documents
89. Cuban boat-lift center
90. Handle, in France
92. Land one's catch
94. Like some prunes
96. Iowa society
98. Win by ___
99. Atop
100. Memo
101. Cornfield visitor
102. Dregs
103. Western Indians
105. Caspian feeder
106. U.S. anthropologist
107. Capp of cartoons
108. Baseball slugger Johnny
109. German river

123 Catalogue By Jo Lundy

List that seems to favor certain pets.

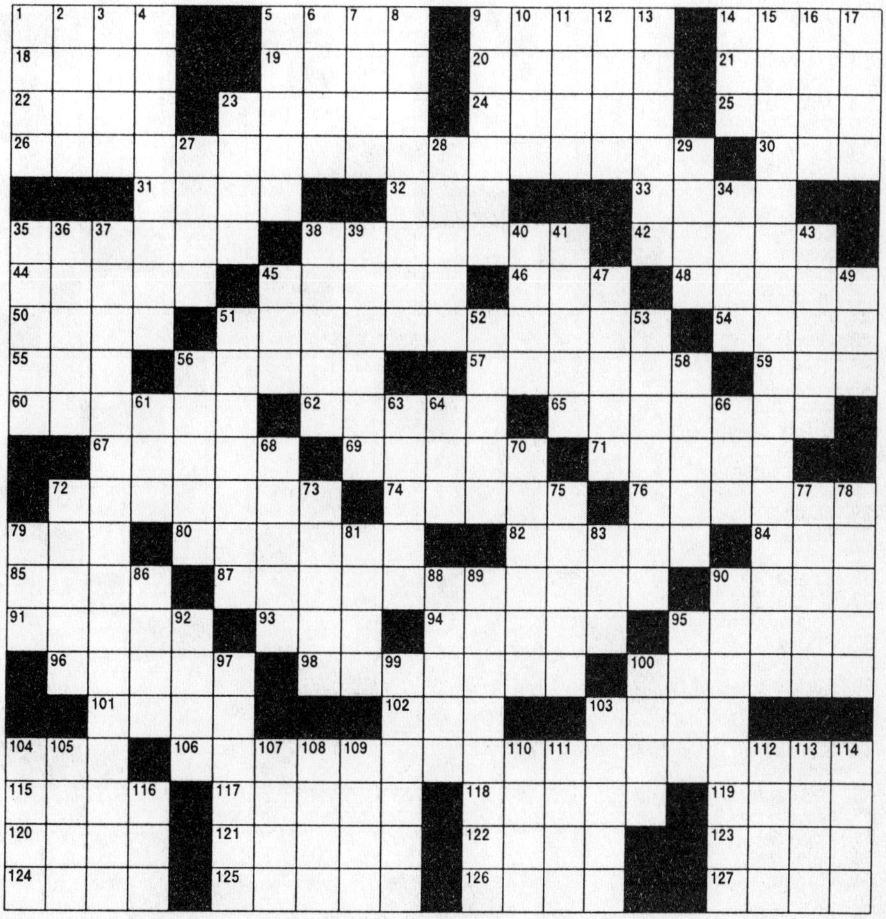

ACROSS

1. Erode
5. Central African lake
9. Contents of a hatch
14. Amounts
18. Opera singer Frances
19. Traditional knowledge
20. Gazelle of Arabia
21. Send out
22. Came down
23. Printing flourish
24. Set aside
25. In a competent way
26. Advice from John Donne
30. He wears a crown
31. This is often dropped
32. Cuckoo's kin
33. Do a steno's job
35. Admittance
38. It pulls out the chestnuts
42. English relatives of counts
44. Makes small talk
45. Baby food
46. "My country ___ of thee"
48. Early spring flower
50. Spoils
51. Disaster
54. Trumpeter perch
55. Choler
56. City on the Willamette
57. *Aïda* and *Rigoletto*
59. Beanie
60. Of the skin
62. Competitor
65. Garment worn over armor
67. Flight-path marker
69. Locales
71. Crow over
72. Smoke for a vamp
74. Bend over
76. Turkey's capital
79. ___ -de-sac
80. Partial power failure
82. Arrange in folds
84. Juan's "the"
85. Flat plinth
87. Stock-market junk
90. Mineral springs
91. Frog and year
93. Conical buoy
94. Goddess of peace
95. Novelist John
96. Theater offering
98. Serve as emcee
100. Impudent
101. Therefore
102. ___ Yat-sen
103. Hollywood status item
104. Craggy hill
106. Mountain in a Hudson River range
115. Pointed arch
117. County in Ireland
118. Showing no emotion
119. River to the Baltic
120. ___ Bator
121. Up and about
122. Recorder input
123. Fly catchers
124. Foxx of TV
125. Requires
126. Cheers
127. Glut

DOWN

1. Woman soldier of W.W. II
2. Miss Fitzgerald
3. Way in, to a miner
4. Pawls
5. Like the Rock of Ages
6. Israeli dance
7. Seed coat
8. Collapses
9. Tabby's favorite mint
10. As limp as ___
11. Veins in a leaf
12. Moola
13. Type of acid
14. Hamlet's ___ of troubles
15. Spreading trees
16. Distance for Sebastian Coe
17. Noted river with a ferry
23. ___ souci
27. Relative of a boo
28. Gore in a dress
29. Old English coin
34. ___ and proper
35. Caustic
36. Odd job
37. Device over a tank's wheels
38. More clever
39. One of a French three
40. Over
41. Dries the dishes
43. 1978 Nobel Peace Prize winner
45. Bosom friend
47. Motion of indifference
49. ___ a plea
51. Pertaining to heat
52. Loggers' contest
53. Parts of winter caps
56. Certain days
58. Tea cake
61. Metric weight: Abbr.
63. Pleasant view
64. Part of D.A.
66. Sturdy tree
68. Soviet river
70. Revived the lawn
72. Smoked, as ham
73. Add the figures
75. Disposed to
77. Noisy outbreaks
78. Appraise
79. Gap between mountains
81. Serv. branch
83. Iron or Stone
86. Colorful ocean fish
88. Inclination
89. Joins a toast
90. Inshore areas
92. Plant disease
95. Spanish golds
97. Depth charge, to a sailor
99. Chemical compounds
100. Pear
103. Thicknesses
104. Excursion
105. Eye
107. Additional to
108. Choice food, old style
109. Dehydrated
110. Slanted type: Abbr.
111. Run easily
112. Thought
113. Obligation
114. Gaelic
116. Finis

124 Single Track By Sidney Robbins

Getting down to a basic figure.

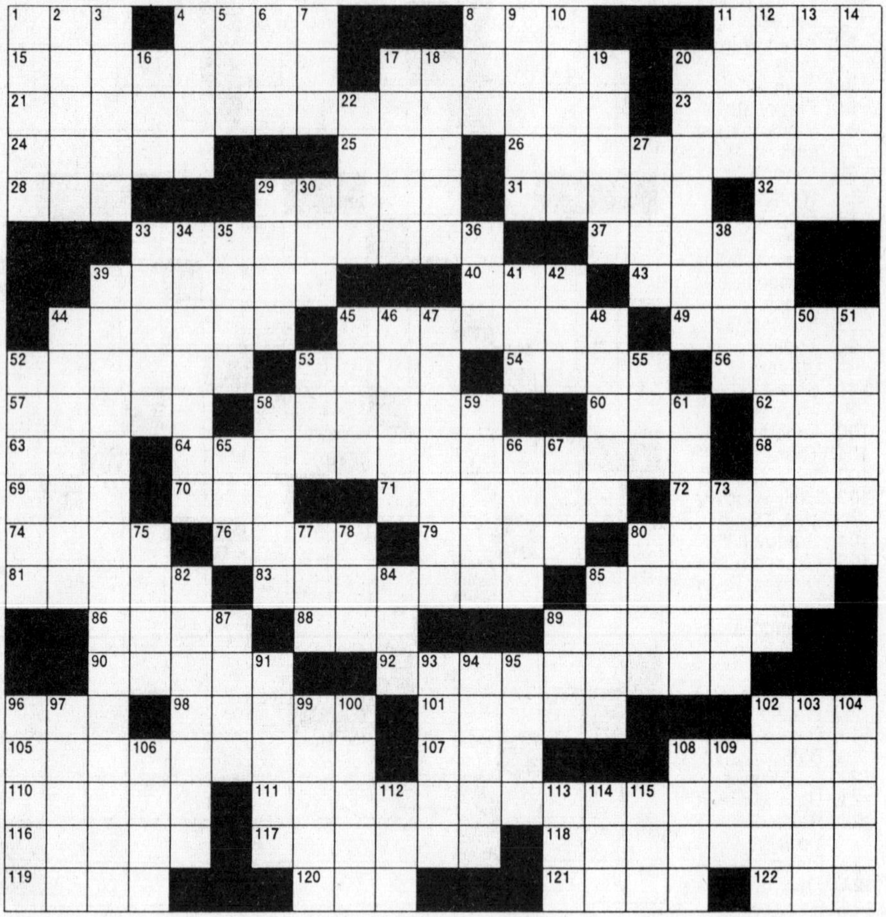

ACROSS

1. Harvest goddess
4. Mild oath
8. Vigor
11. Early Egyptian
15. Harassment
17. Old Greek colony
20. Kind of NASA landing
21. One
23. Sports site
24. Indian title
25. ___ tight (stay put)
26. "They asked me so ___"
28. Basic Latin word
29. Leather
31. Played a violin poorly
32. Snake
33. Nassau hockey team
37. Phony customer
39. Furtive ones
40. Harem unit
43. Coral ridge
44. Sits like an Indian
45. Ham actors
49. Cloys
52. Fountain
53. Solar disk
54. Wagers
56. Idée ___
57. Soft, musically
58. Furthest orbital point
60. Kind of well
62. Of a city: Abbr.
63. Hockey name
64. Victors' cry
68. Building addition
69. Born
70. Famed uncle
71. Performed a plane stunt
72. Italian specialty
74. One of Odin's wolves
76. Papal court
79. Foray
80. Strategy
81. Fable man and family: Var.
83. Has qualms
85. Fame
86. Condition: Suffix
88. Golf mound
89. South: Prefix
90. Sum
92. One
96. Chinese V.I.P.
98. Upstate N.Y. river
101. Nay or sooth follower
102. Paid in adv.
105. Eccentric
107. Shooting match, in France
108. Kukla's friend
110. "The days ___ years are three-score . . ."
111. One
116. Peelings
117. Golf-club swinger's concern
118. Asserted firmly
119. Divorcees
120. Spanish queen
121. Household members
122. Former campus org.

DOWN

1. *Aïda*, for one
2. King of Troy
3. Musical repeat notation
4. Italian city
5. Chewy item
6. Onassis
7. Lair
8. Edgar Allan
9. Presley
10. Famed statue
11. Brusque
12. One
13. Window parts
14. Chaplin character
16. Pronoun
17. Stage whisper
18. Chemical compound
19. Flaky fallings
20. Highland youths
22. Kind of car
27. Comic Lew
29. Egyptian cottons
30. Us, in Berlin
33. Encase
34. Manatees
35. Like midnight
36. Wino
38. Aspen quiverer
39. One
41. Lass entering society
42. Exist
44. Musical evenings
45. Collar
46. V.I.P.
47. Encore!
48. Got up
50. Get a thrill from
51. Hastings battle site
52. Be a cadger
53. Mimic
55. Sermon target
58. Knight's need
59. W.W. II vessel
61. Greek port, to Italians
65. Corn unit
66. Roof toppings
67. Moscow square
73. Squash variety
75. ___ facto
77. Offensive of the Vietnam War
78. Mature
80. Exam
82. Parents' helpers
84. ___ adjudicata
85. One who regrets
87. Spahn's pitching partner
89. Pub drink
91. Dreamer's fruit
93. Suffix for real or modern
94. Ingenuous
95. Cerebral ridges
96. Actor Dudley
97. Attach
99. People, in Spain
100. Of the planet Mars
102. Land divisions
103. Moped
104. Land contracts
106. Cows' chews
108. Sashes
109. River to the Schelde
112. Life-force initials
113. Quick swim
114. Opposite of WSW
115. Time initials

125 Phonetic Code By Marjorie Pedersen

How the armed forces and the police break up the alphabet.

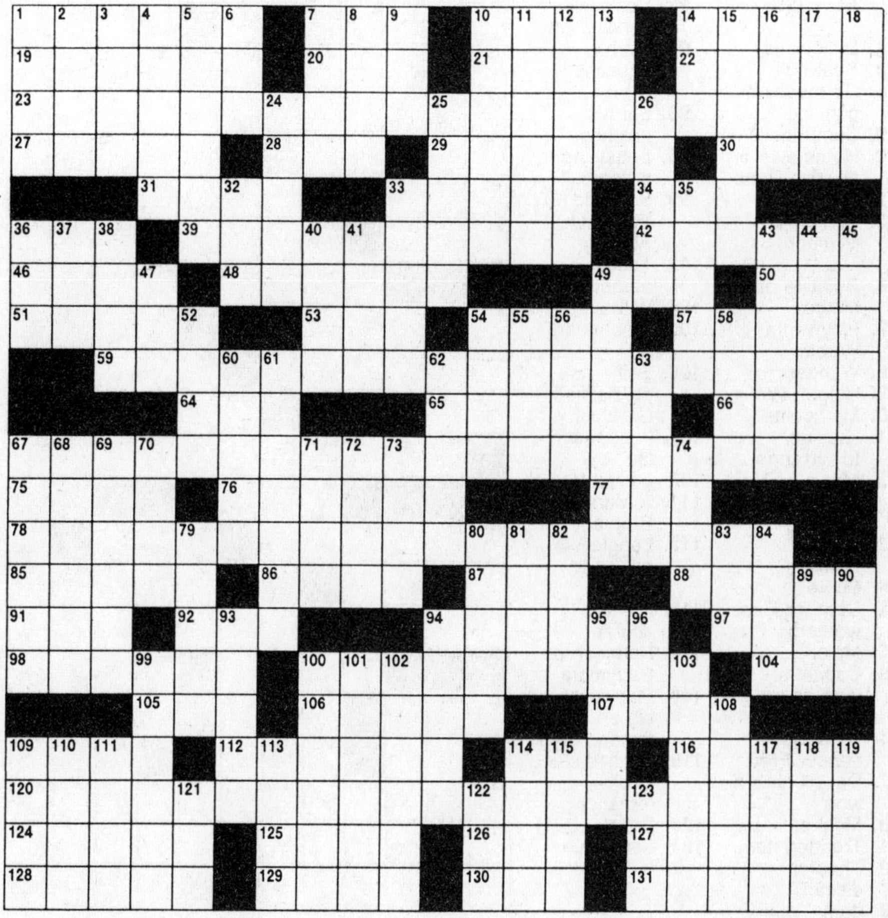

ACROSS

1. Ingredient of sand
7. Viper
10. Rio's famed beach
14. Make corrections
19. ". . . as rivers of water ___ place": Isaiah 32:2
20. Mauna ___
21. Irregular: Prefix
22. Home of Circe
23. M I N X
27. Mr. T's TV group
28. Chat
29. Smudge anew
30. Troubles
31. Vaccines
33. Ethan or Hervey
34. Incorrect: Prefix
36. Catchall abbr.
39. A D
42. "___ it" (questioning words)
46. Late-July people
48. Fishnets
49. Roman 401
50. Negative of sorts
51. Immortalizer of Beatrice
53. Genetic letters
54. Egyptian god
57. America's bird
59. J A Z Z
64. Certain word: Abbr.
65. Film actor Power
66. Son of Troy's founder
67. C H O P
75. Tops
76. Surgical instrument
77. Senate's counterpart: Abbr.
78. W E E K
85. French nobleman
86. Capital of Yemen
87. Twelve doz.
88. At no time
91. Cry of discovery
92. Lake Nyasa people
94. Centers of action
97. Procrastination's thievery
98. Greedy eater
100. Y E
104. One of the Tweedles
105. Strange
106. Coastal raider of W.W. II
107. Hit on the head
109. Loot
112. Buy ___ (trader's choice)
114. Go astray
116. Growing out
120. T R I S
124. Migratory workers
125. But, to Pierre
126. Asner and Sullivan
127. One of a seven-star group
128. Fuses metal pieces
129. Harding and Sheridan
130. Observe
131. Relieves

DOWN

1. Igneous rock
2. "What's ___ for me?"
3. Superior or Huron
4. Concepts
5. Where Yalta is
6. Author Rand
7. Inter ___
8. Lather
9. Peter or frying
10. W.W. I nurse-heroine
11. Single tennis division
12. City near L.A.
13. Prefix for dextrous
14. Otologist's concern
15. Land south of the border
16. Warren or Weaver
17. Actress Patricia
18. ___ *of Wine and Roses*
24. Arrange fabric
25. Escutcheon borders
26. Spanish hero
32. "Kidnapped" monogram
33. "Let's Make ___!"
35. Farewell
36. Antiquity, to poets
37. Oolong, for one
38. "And" or "but": Abbr.
40. Al of the trumpet
41. Moffo or Held
43. Hoof or claw
44. Make a botch of
45. Dos Passos trilogy topic
47. Actor Erwin
49. Jungle native of South America
52. Israeli airline
54. Tribe: Prefix
55. Poi plant
56. Certain dye types
58. Move with ___ (go fast)
60. Chemical alcohol
61. ___ often (occasionally)
62. Feather: Prefix
63. Saskatoon neighbor
67. Cornfield sounds
68. Santa's line
69. Kind of cracker
70. Siesta
71. ___ garden (do digging)
72. Happening: Abbr.
73. African weaverbird
74. Check
79. Attuned
80. Fine-feathered bird
81. Canadian Indian
82. Whet
83. Permit
84. Roman poet
89. Rhea
90. Ad ___ (to the point)
93. Zeal
94. Militant Sikh
95. Ghana's capital
96. "___ 'nuff!"
99. Steamed up
100. Sycophant
101. Have ___ one's bonnet
102. Incurred ___ (broke even)
103. Oona's maiden name
108. Genuflect
109. Put away
110. Pacific island of W.W. II
111. Indigo
113. City of Italia
114. Whirl
115. Opera's Stevens
117. Solo
118. Trunk compartment
119. American bridge engineer
121. C.I.A. predecessor
122. Born
123. Watering place

126 Helpful Celebrities By Olga Kowals

Some whose names come in handy for a twist.

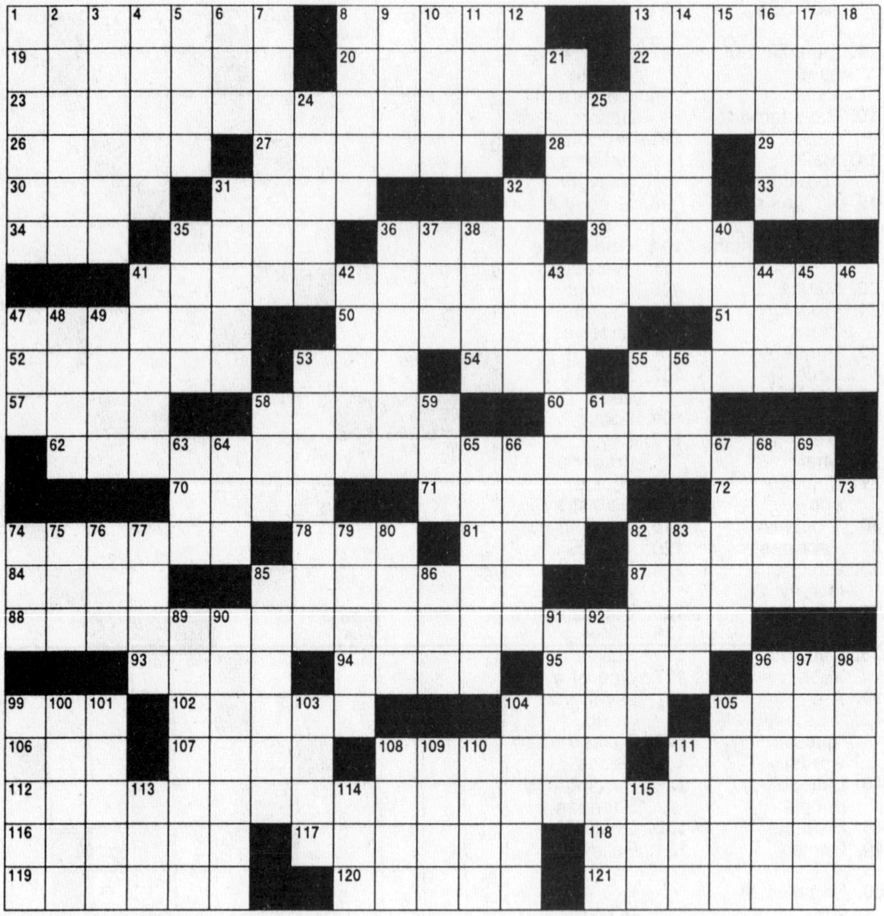

ACROSS

1. Difficulties
8. Seat belt
13. Do machine-gunning
19. Component
20. Hometown of an Irish Rose
22. Up
23. "To err is Ullmann, ___"
26. Relative of a bimbo
27. Playwright Harold
28. Wanders
29. Height: Prefix
30. Mr. 'iggins
31. ___ up (disarrange)
32. Made another bull's-eye
33. Modern: Prefix
34. Curve
35. Dem. or Rep. workers
36. Major-___
39. Capital of long days and nights
41. Movie for dancer Fred
47. Desert farer's woe
50. Meshes
51. Treaded item
52. Theater district
53. Item sometimes in the fire
54. Certain people
55. Kind of minded
57. Der ___ (Adenauer)
58. Bach's "The ___ the Fugue"
60. Baby's word
62. Song for Miss Fawcett
70. Soon
71. Sherwood Forest's Hood
72. Rubber trees
74. Bounty
78. Kind of dance
81. British alder fly
82. Termagant
84. One who does: Suffix
85. African ring money
87. Naval officer
88. Commandment for a TV interviewer
93. Comparative conjunction
94. Math equating words
95. Earth's neighbor
96. Substitute for a doorbell
99. Scotland Yard unit: Abbr.
102. Tourist attractions
104. Without
105. What gears do
106. Self-proclaimed Greatest
107. "___ each life . . ."
108. Locust tree
111. A Marx Brother
112. Longfellow's advice to Sophia
116. Dinner course
117. Hampton or Barrymore
118. Playwright big on rhinoceroses
119. Spirited steed of old romance
120. Ballet ___
121. Spruce up

DOWN

1. Small sofa
2. Zanies
3. Directs to
4. Writer Cleveland ___
5. Horizontal's opp.
6. Chang's twin
7. Leaflike appendage: Var.
8. British guns
9. Third: Prefix
10. Demolish: Var.
11. Winglike
12. Mighty implement
13. A bit on the morose side
14. Bridge support
15. *Six Rms ___ Vu*
16. Indian or Chinese
17. Easel for Tom Sawyer
18. Spanish month
21. Maugham's *The Razor's ___*
24. "___ d'arte" (*Tosca* aria)
25. Houyhnhnms' subjects
31. Homey maxim
32. Rolls's partner
35. Attention getter
36. City near Dallas
37. Pussycat's companion
38. Address for a princess
40. Breakfast food
41. *Green Hat* author Michael
42. Gaucho's gear
43. Threadlike plant part
44. Compete
45. Fish-eating bird
46. Trapeze performers' standby
47. Leader for la-la
48. Jack and Jill's Waterloo
49. Hiatus, in Italy
53. Kind of attack or lobe
55. City of Oklahoma
56. Word before humbug
58. Have ___ at (venture)
59. Predecessor of H.S.T.
61. Scottish alder
63. Needlefish
64. Connective
65. "I was a ___ love you"
66. Bric-___
67. Knack or brat follower
68. Kirghiz mountains
69. Safecracker
73. "Chacun à ___ goût"
74. Despicable person
75. Biblical verb ending
76. Court
77. In ___ (mired)
79. Naysayers
80. Needle-trade supplies
82. Turns
83. U.N. language people: Abbr.
85. Indian spirit
86. Chance
89. Lodge member
90. Kind of house
91. At full speed
92. A name of Freya
96. Meal
97. "___ viator" (Roman-tomb words)
98. Light quantum
99. Biblical spy
100. Miss Massey
101. Kind of dozen or trick
103. Little Oliver
104. Climb
105. Kitten, at times
108. Ben Adhem
109. Those not pros
110. Greek god
111. Writer Gale
113. Time period
114. Bearing
115. Piper's son

127 Capital Ideas By Manny Miller

Looking for assorted seats of government.

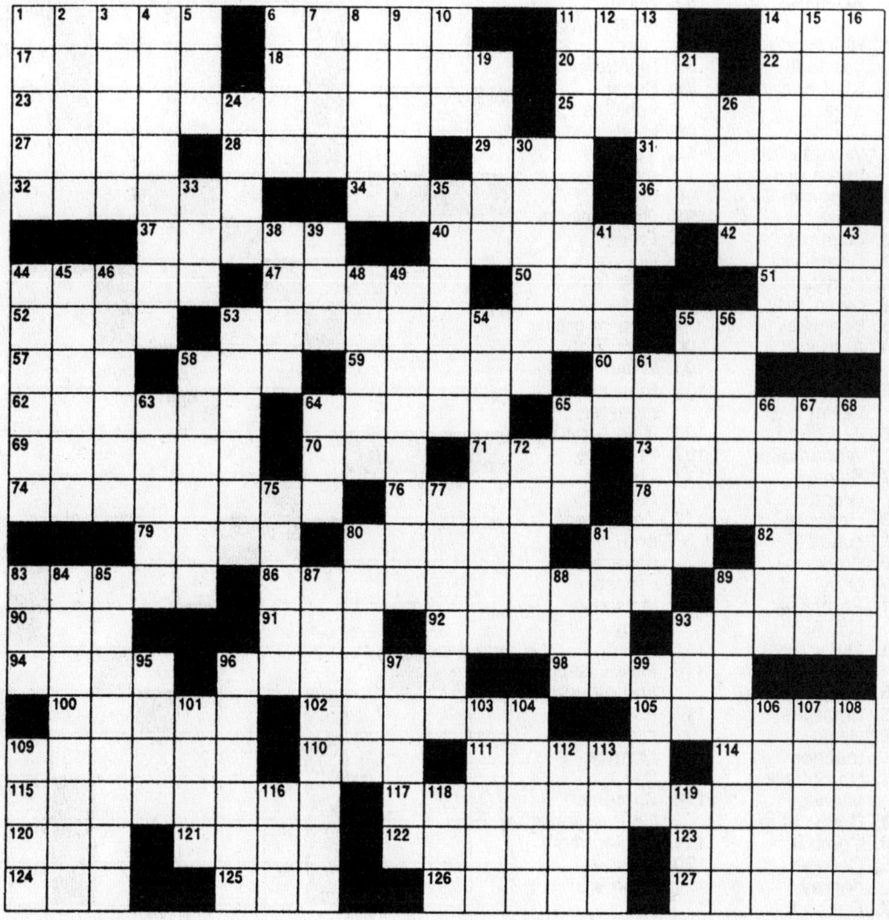

ACROSS

1. Fall flower
6. Condition
11. ___ es Salaam
14. Readdress a letter: Abbr.
17. Soft cake
18. Capital with 9 million or so people
20. Knievel
22. Capital of cruise note, for short
23. Caribbean capital
25. Banjolike instruments
27. Winglike
28. Task
29. Open a beer keg
31. Interfere with
32. Equatorial Guinea capital
34. Half mask
36. Speak, biblically
37. Mean
40. *The Old Man ___ Sea*
42. Recess
44. Red-ink items
47. Scads
50. Inlet
51. Diminutive
52. Son of Aphrodite
53. Nellie Forbush's capital
55. Vilma of the silents
57. Like Ben or Sur
58. Boggy land
59. Yugoslav money units
60. Nile bird
62. Long-legged bird
64. Hoard
65. Ironed out
69. Badgerlike animals
70. Soc.
71. Darling
73. A founder of *The Tatler*
74. Tangling, as hair
76. Hokkaido port
78. Excellent
79. Strengthen
80. Discover
81. Peruse
82. Massachusetts coll.
83. Edict
86. Capital on the Kanawha
89. Deep cut
90. Half a sawbuck
91. Boo's opposite
92. "___ Be," Beatles' song
93. People of Odense
94. Medical subj.
96. Comoro Islands capital
98. V.I.P.
100. Inclined surface
102. Spiritualistic state
105. Ethically neutral
109. Clavell novel about Japan
110. G-man
111. Mideast capital
114. Capital of Italia
115. American Samoan capital
117. Capital of the Colts
120. "___ was going . . ."
121. Gelling agent
122. Loose overcoat
123. Regarding
124. Pouch
125. Football player
126. Ted the bandleader
127. Assents

DOWN

1. Indian state
2. Milan's La ___
3. Of sounds
4. Contestants
5. Old car
6. What X marks
7. Half: Prefix
8. Of ___ (alike)
9. Piebald pony
10. A lang.
11. Like an autocrat
12. Former capital of Burma
13. Release claim to
14. Capital of Sierra Leone
15. Capital of Namibia
16. Give medicine to
19. Entered
21. Bean capital?
24. Service medals: Abbr.
26. Narrate, as a yarn
30. Bahamas island
33. ___-relief
35. Lesotho capital
38. ___ as a rail
39. But
41. Moslem doctor
43. Principal
44. Excludes
45. Armenian capital
46. Capital of Colombia
48. Stock-market phrase
49. Frequenter of shows
53. Admits
54. Vagabond
55. Egg-yolk component
56. ___ in the right direction
58. Circular rim
61. Another bean capital?
63. Documents: Abbr.
64. Record
65. Actor Erwin
66. Cossack chief
67. Plaza girl
68. Ocean bottoms
72. Director Lubitsch
75. Dead: Prefix
77. Estonian capital: Var.
80. Pakistani city
81. Shelter
83. Capital of the Bashkir Republic
84. Capital of Zaire
85. Similar
87. Nutmeg State capital
88. Twitching
89. Capital of Botswana
93. Partner of dese and dose
95. Its capital is Lomé
96. It's sometimes for trois
97. Zenith's opposite
99. Juan's wool
101. Insect stage
103. Be a sponge
104. *Nana* author's first name
106. Actors' quests
107. Chemical compound
108. Endures
109. Bad Ems and Ballston
112. Respectful term of address
113. Blyth and Harding
116. Started, to a poet
118. Pappy's negative
119. Kind of check

128 O-missions By Robert Roop

Getting along with only four vowels.

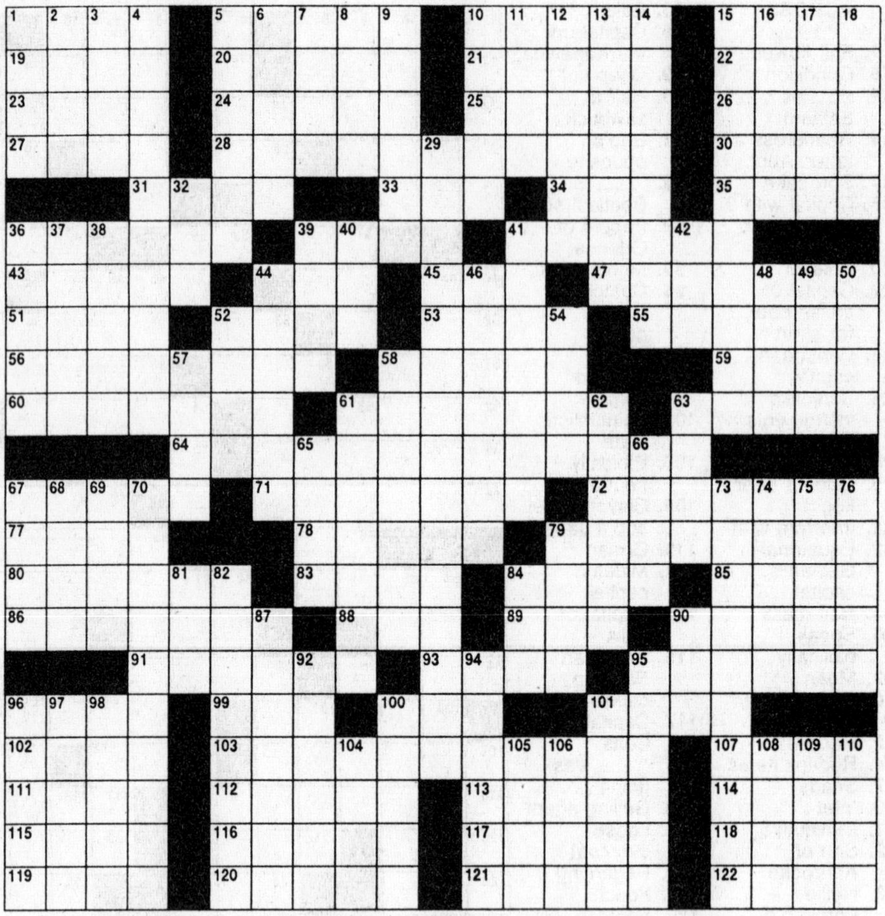

ACROSS

1. Help underhandedly
5. Kind of cart or jack
10. Criticizes
15. Word before broke or tire
19. Long-run TV show
20. Gymnast Comaneci
21. Humiliate
22. Swan lady
23. Winglike
24. Actress Stevens
25. Musical Count
26. Jaffe and Wanamaker
27. Savage Island
28. Unappreciated
30. Work on copy
31. Part of N.E.A.
33. Outer: Prefix
34. Illuminated
35. Have it made
36. Emerges
39. Hindu teacher
41. Unit of silk fineness
43. Comic strip
44. Combat
45. College degree
47. Daubed
51. Biblical king
52. Excavation
53. Poet Lazarus
55. Hemingway
56. Going back on a promise
58. Computer food
59. Sand hill, in Britain
60. Starchy products of a flower
61. Goddess of fertility
63. Inquired
64. Peddler
67. Ballet movement
71. Qualities
72. Golf club
77. "___ kleine Nachtmusik"
78. Relative of curds
79. Of third rank
80. Skin: Prefix
83. Shore noisemaker
84. Hurl
85. Plunderer
86. Snow vehicles
88. Hindu sage
89. Towel marking
90. Oxlike
91. Gem weights
93. Frees
95. Act parts
96. First father
99. Prefix for carp or gram
100. Sum: Abbr.
101. Wharf
102. Kind of monster
103. Rifle experts
107. Preserve
111. Trot or canter
112. Zeus's wife and namesakes
113. French legislative body
114. Victim
115. Miss Claire and others
116. As a friend, in France
117. Licorice flavor
118. Supreme Court number
119. Contentment
120. Scrapes
121. "The wild blue ___"
122. Port ___

DOWN

1. ___ *for All Seasons*
2. Isle of romance
3. Jacob's brother
4. Curly, Larry and Moe
5. Hatred
6. Wall Street event of 1929
7. Examples: Abbr.
8. Stead
9. One who brings home the bacon
10. French founder of Illinois Utopian community
11. "Neither is poverty ___": Thucydides
12. Do a grunt-and-groan routine
13. Situations
14. When to sow
15. Needless trips
16. ___ dog's life
17. Own up to
18. One of the senses
29. Public-TV offerings
32. Rumpus room
36. Mites
37. One who storms
38. Khomeini, for one
39. ___ busters
40. Actress Mary
41. Acts coyly, old style
42. Poetic word
44. Churchill
46. Pierces
48. Strong smell
49. Laborer
50. Bestowed fondness
52. Lesser
54. Lawyers: Abbr.
57. Author André
58. Publishers
61. Treacher and Godfrey
62. Coals
63. Med. course
65. Crows
66. Bow and ___
67. Greenhouse areas
68. Cambodian currency
69. Concerning
70. In a partial stupor
73. Contents of rich babies' mouths
74. Glossy fabric
75. "Goodnight" lady
76. Jane and Simon
79. "___ is it!"
81. ___ Khan
82. Farm machine
84. Definite article
87. Large leg vein
90. Tech.-school degree
92. Coronets
94. Predict
95. *My ___ Eileen*
96. Student of farming
97. Charles's mate
98. Nom de plume
100. Orbital point
101. Chalcedony
104. Slope
105. Vol's home
106. Actress Markey
108. Sutherland's offering
109. Word from Caesar
110. Ogled

129 Big Apple By Ron Aigen

Some of the people who helped give it polish.

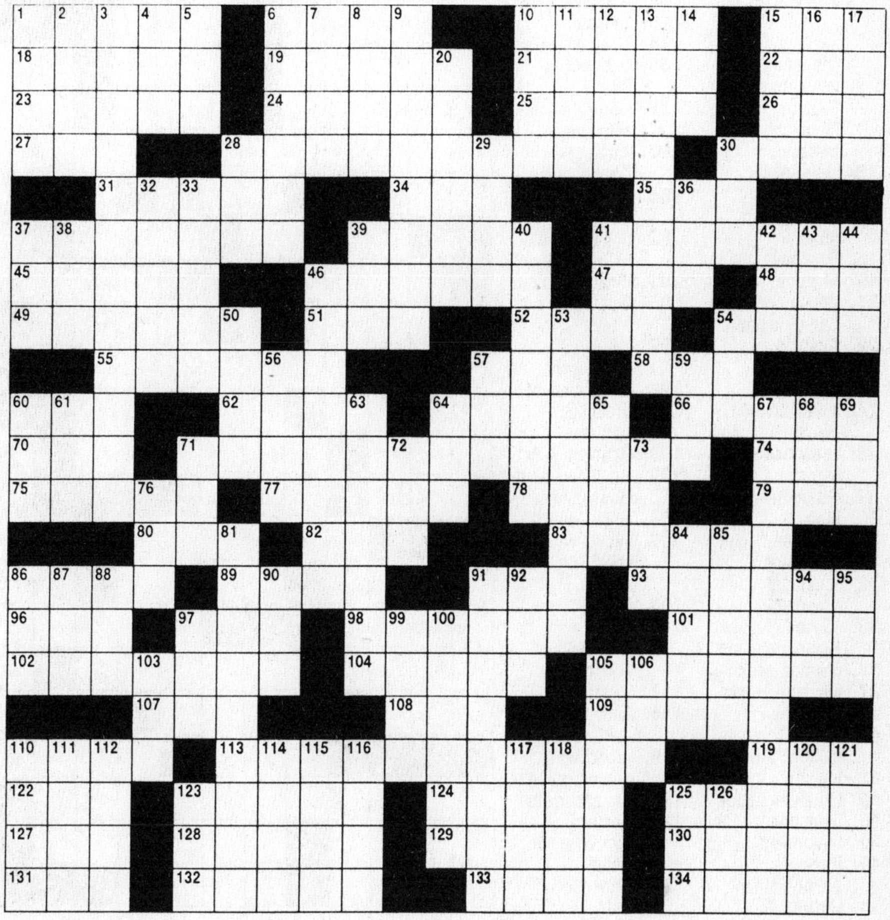

ACROSS

1. Union member
6. Clean a pipe
10. Small bit of land
15. Curse
18. Michigan's Ann
19. Millay and Ferber
21. Lorna of Devonshire
22. Pitcher part
23. Funnyman Victor
24. Down East state
25. Made waves
26. Jolson's given name
27. Screen's Merkel
28. N.Y. man about town
30. Deuce topper
31. Mideast dances
34. My, in Paris
35. Contend
37. Tax cheaters
39. Civil wrongs
41. Oriental
45. Small change
46. Clergyman
47. Polo Grounds' Mel
48. Tic-tac-toe winner
49. Scribe's surface
51. Shake a leg
52. Seine feeder
54. Cold sort of job
55. El matador's quarry
57. War detainees: Abbr.
58. A John for suing
60. Half a dance
62. Gasp for breath
64. West's legendary Bill
66. Hindu royalty
70. Resistance unit
71. N.Y. son of a New Deal pioneer
74. Northwestern st.
75. Bit of school writing
77. News bits
78. School head: Abbr.
79. Certain actor
80. Apple-cider girl
82. Plural endings
83. Reach
86. Yell
89. Ref. book
91. Family member
93. Wildcat of Africa
96. Stage Door Canteen org.
97. Medical-exam sounds
98. Reddish-brown pigments
101. An emperor of Rome
102. Demonstrable truth
104. Aristocles's assumed name
105. More prickly
107. Man, in old Rome
108. Airline abbr.
109. Red dye
110. ___ Scotia
113. N.Y. Chinese-food lover
119. Radio's Uncle ___
122. Possess, cockney style
123. Be snobbish
124. Place for an étudiant
125. Italian sauce
127. Angelo or Antonio
128. Head or false
129. Smoothed a garden
130. Muse of love poetry
131. Neighbor of Miss.
132. Ruhr city
133. ". . . ___ or draw"
134. Unnatural fiber

DOWN

1. Elephant Boy of films
2. Disney space film
3. N.Y. short man
4. ___ out (dress up)
5. Before
6. Lax
7. Cheese center
8. Spirited, in music: Abbr.
9. ". . . birthday and ___"
10. Film or fallen
11. Overcharge
12. Traditional belief
13. Sapped
14. E.M.K., informally
15. Get wind of
16. Contentment
17. Lab photo
20. City mains
28. Home for olives
29. About
30. Historic Vietnam attack
32. Digger of radio days
33. Alter a chronometer
36. Doer: Suffix
37. N.Y. summer time
38. Veneto is one
39. Southeast Asian
40. Everest topper
41. Dawn goddess
42. Long time
43. Aussie animal
44. "___ hear this!"
46. Of speech sounds
50. Venetian fishing vessel
53. Weather-map lines
54. Mer, to us
56. Moslem month
57. Sabbath seat
59. Skating great
60. Folding item
61. Former Minn. senator
63. Risky place for a cradle
64. Basketball stats
65. Irritated state
67. Fun City promoter
68. Southern constellation
69. Stitch selvage
71. Barber or Grange
72. Logos, often: Abbr.
73. Bldg. accesses
76. Wire measure
81. Followers
84. Sponsorship
85. Iraqi's foe
86. Not if or and
87. Mount St. Helens stuff
88. Surfeit for Wednesday's child
90. Doctrine
91. Of a measurement system
92. Gold, in Ronda
94. 3 Down, to friends
95. Roman deity
97. *Exodus* name
99. Woodwind inst.
100. More challenging
103. Eggs ___ lightly?
105. Quit an alliance
106. Cry of disgust
110. Shuttle org.
111. Derby course
112. Blood carrier
114. "___ you are told"
115. Had on
116. Business letter abbr.
117. ___ Nor, Chinese lake
118. Corrida approvals
120. Graham or Kruger
121. *High* ___
123. Compass dir.
125. Word before cent
126. Time span

130 Reverse Gear By Ernie Furtado

Wherein the last shall be first.

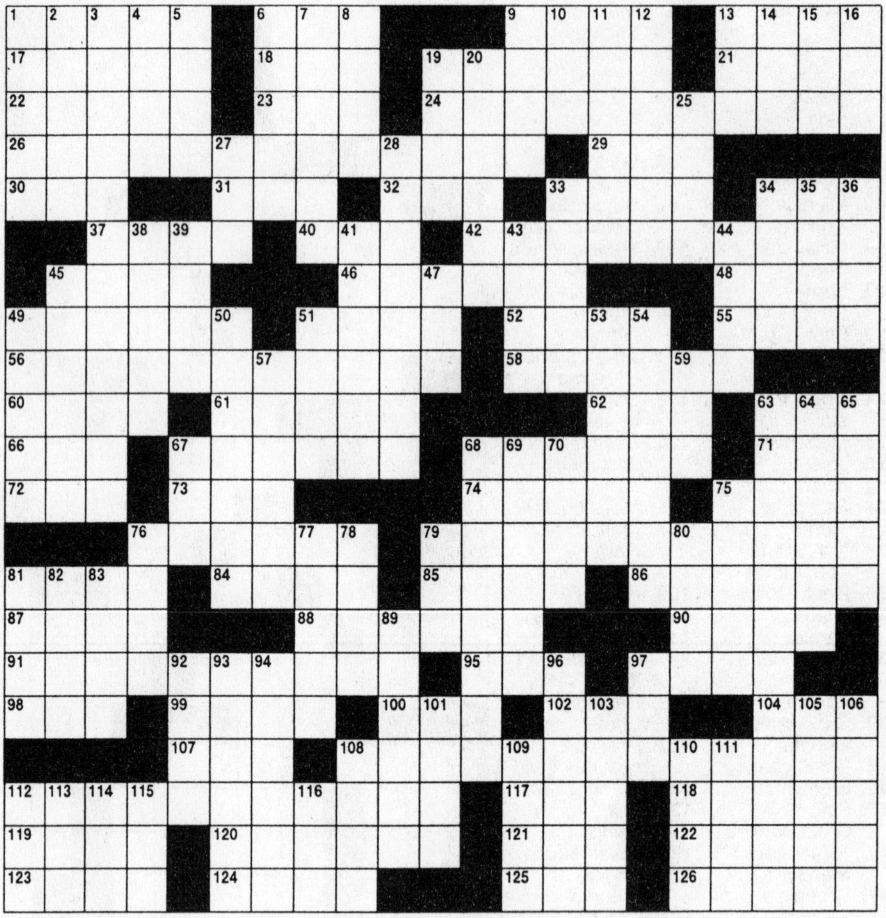

ACROSS

1. This, in Marseille
6. It's dernier, in France
9. Rival of Ole Miss
13. ___ and anon
17. Household spirits
18. *Brother* ___
19. More in want
21. Word with flat or spare
22. Actor's need
23. French donkey
24. Inseparable ones
26. Steinbeck topic
29. Sesame
30. Ready
31. ___ Ann de Beaupré
32. ___ de guerre
33. "The ___ of Spring"
34. Dance step
37. Horatian and Pindaric
40. East German police: Abbr.
42. Hymn
45. Cleaving tool
46. Bait fish
48. Opposed
49. Parents, sometimes
51. Blithe
52. Old English court
55. Like a golf ball, at times
56. Drinking companions
58. Loves
60. Novelist Kingsley
61. *The Dirty* ___
62. Companion of long.
63. Understand, at a rap session
66. Gumshoe
67. Goes onstage
68. "Thou shalt deny me ___"
71. Companion of only
72. Sign
73. Meadow
74. Singer John of musicals
75. World mover
76. Method
79. Something to beware
81. Nanny in the Orient
84. Utah flower
85. Lamech's wife
86. Leave active service
87. Actress Lange
88. Astaire and Jergens
90. It's high in Manhattan
91. First couple
95. Opposite of NNW
97. Young ___ (insurgent)
98. Neighbor of the U.S.
99. Curves
100. Roman 1051
102. Bourbon and Basin: Abbr.
104. Shoe width
107. Word with chick or sweet
108. Blab
112. Rain contents, sometimes
117. Digit
118. *Last* ___ *in Paris*
119. Word with rug or code
120. African cats
121. Certain records, for short
122. Poet Conrad
123. Spanish cat
124. Long-run Broadway musical
125. Ending for verb
126. Bugle's sound

DOWN

1. Cat's weapons
2. Tidal bore
3. Halloween challenge
4. Something to pitch
5. Balt
6. Découpage, e.g.
7. Stoves
8. What Caesar traveled on
9. Mires
10. Parseghian
11. Non compos ___
12. Bold, to Menotti
13. Poetic word ending
14. ___ Dolorosa
15. Ending for north or south
16. 40 ___ (suit-size label)
19. Gourd or melon
20. Kind of band or gang
25. Musical symbol
27. C.I.A. predecessor
28. Fireplace staples
33. Emulate Taylor and Burton
34. Player on the dealer's right
35. Deed, in Marseille
36. ___ Row
38. Achievers
39. Weird
41. One delivering a blow
43. Curved molding
44. Squeals
45. Enemies, old style
47. Follower of Falstaff
49. Teak tree of Malaysia
50. Dejection
51. Cutting tool
53. Stone Age tool
54. Farm vehicle
57. Make marginal jottings
59. After printemps
63. Jimmy Durante song
64. Turn upside down
65. Simpletons
67. Culbertson
68. Uses one's car for a new model
69. Pester
70. In the chips
75. Quart-plus
76. Home of the Mets
77. Hoople expressions
78. Fashion, in Rome
79. ___ de mer
80. Rope fiber
81. Attention getter
82. Excite
83. Summit
89. Famed clown Kelly
92. Calif. wine valley
93. Soak
94. National park in Maine
96. Legally hinders
97. Poetic monogram
101. Lad's friend
103. "We hold ___ truths . . ."
105. Hiss of the pumpkin papers
106. Like the Mariner at sea
108. Max or Bugs
109. Normandy town
110. Sometimes it's in the back
111. Dairymaid's need
112. Hammarskjöld
113. Openings
114. Obtain
115. ___ Paulo
116. Brutus's 106

131 Fourth Estate By Herman Surasky

Culled from the pages of *Editor & Publisher.*

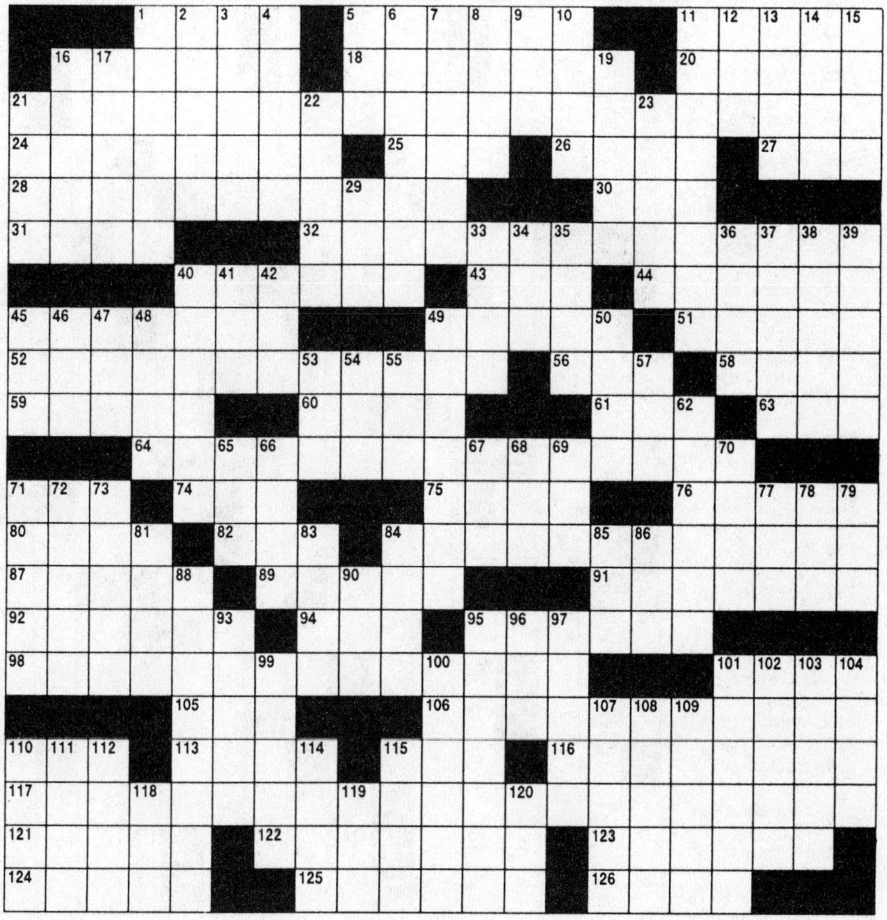

ACROSS

1. Silent movie star Wallace
5. Child's bakery product
11. Word before tease
16. "Do not ___" ("I'm harmless")
18. New York city
20. Wear away
21. *West Side Story*
24. Ward
25. Timetable abbr.
26. Condiment
27. Range of knowledge
28. Epee
30. Buzzer
31. Scorch
32. Channel watcher's staple
40. Impudent
43. Freshwater fish
44. Picturesque
45. Fragrant
49. Respond
51. Ethyl compound
52. E.S.T. and E.D.T.
56. Draw
58. Narrative
59. Prorate
60. First man
61. School subj.
63. Ike
64. Paul Revere
71. Edge
74. Stopping place: Abbr.
75. Bass ___
76. Caribbean island
80. Rival of Babylonia
82. ___ *My Sons*
84. Southern comfort
87. Canonical hour
89. Not express
91. Posh
92. Rumanian composer
94. Hockey great
95. Dreiser's Carrie
98. Sousa favorite
101. Rind: Prefix
105. Tune
106. Regaled
110. Bribe
113. Pigeon-___
115. Miss Rehan
116. One of a dorm pair
117. Queen City investigator
121. Brave, in Soho
122. Like the earth's path
123. Protective garment
124. Wagner heroine
125. Author of *Honor Thy Father*
126. Beholds

DOWN

1. Supporting beam
2. Bungled
3. Adult insect
4. Star in Cygnus
5. French pronoun
6. Not morosely, old style
7. Edict
8. Impoverished
9. Business abbr.
10. Numerical endings
11. Parser's target
12. Numerical prefix
13. Plymouth or Inchcape
14. Like some rumors
15. Hammer end
16. North Atlantic islands
17. ___ Gay
19. Egyptian leader of the 1800s
21. N.Y.C. and Bost.
22. Early Britons
23. Fats
29. Loser to 63 Across
33. Competes
34. G. & S. princess
35. Denomination
36. Snug abode
37. Inward
38. Handle
39. Debris
40. Shirley and John Wilkes
41. Capek play
42. Invite
45. "Go sit ___ tack"
46. Neighbor of Md.
47. Hooked-bill bird
48. Peasant of India
49. Dismissal
50. Row
53. Confucian code
54. License, passport et al.: Abbr.
55. Gym piece
57. Spanish queen
62. One looking daggers
65. Greek letter
66. Lucille or George
67. Nothing
68. Kind of dog or tamale
69. Whitney
70. Bit of sediment
71. Be a good subscriber
72. Miss Massey
73. Lion growths
77. Neighbor of Can.
78. Hairdo
79. Emmet
81. Netting
83. Swag
84. Drafty place
85. N.L. player
86. Violinist Bull
88. Lower-back pain
90. ___-Magnon
93. Hamburger addition
95. Musical pieces
96. Follower: Suffix
97. Cubic measure
99. Painter El ___
100. Having a foot
101. Restricts
102. Finnish lake, to Swedes
103. Pumpkin eater
104. ___-Neisse Line
107. French circles
108. Brimless hat
109. Provide pleasure
110. Fr. holy women
111. Czech river
112. Laborer
114. Kind of cheap
115. Blue dye
118. Townsman
119. Sports org.
120. Seine sight

132 For the Handyman By Peggy Devlin

Or anyone puttering in the basement.

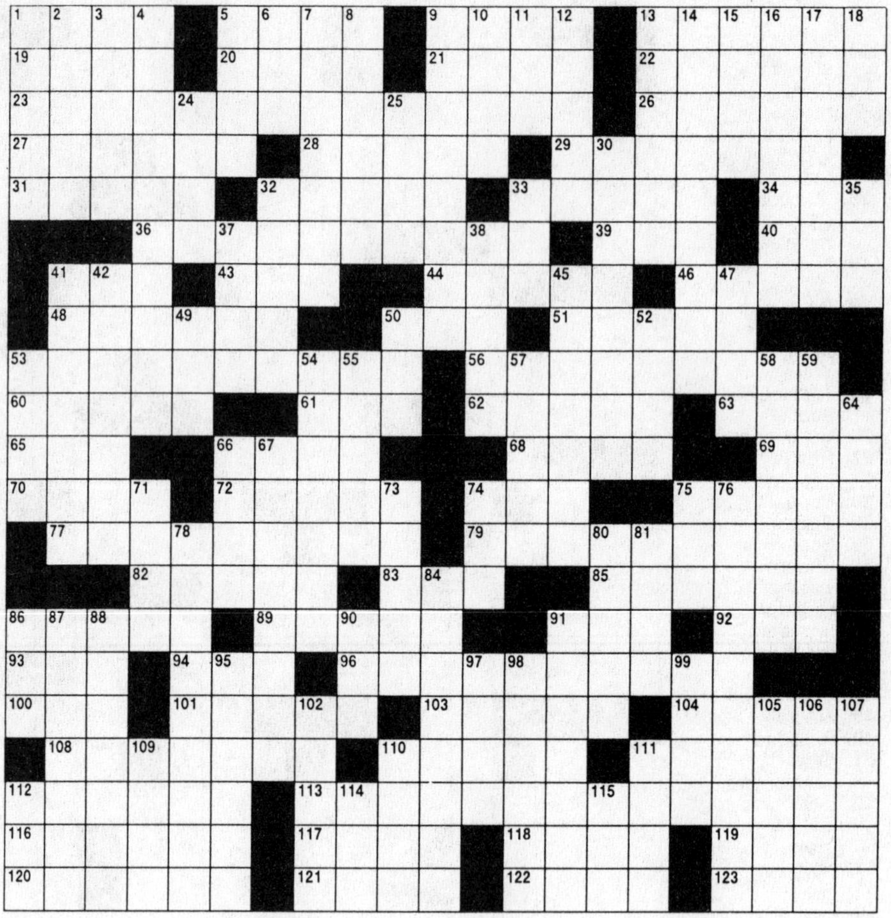

ACROSS

1. Hebrew letter
5. Dull sound
9. Lion's greeting
13. Biblical songs
19. Spicy dish
20. Whether ___
21. This, in Spain
22. Zoological sheaths
23. Feel utter despair
26. Dolls up
27. Atkins and Tune
28. Befuddle
29. Entered a conversation
31. Like Sue of song
32. Place of action
33. In ___ (perturbed)
34. Agent, for short
36. Hurdle for a space shuttle
39. College degree
40. Popular bank acct.
41. Beer container: Abbr.
43. Old English letter
44. Carrier
46. Pile up
48. Brigand
50. Ending for patriot
51. Philadelphia suburb
53. Blues numbers, sometimes
56. Most frangible
60. ___ *and Sing*
61. Pitching stat
62. Agog
63. Respectful title
65. French nobleman
66. Ionian gulf
68. Lake Chad native
69. Miss Ullmann
70. Barbecue adjunct
72. Sect, in Italy
74. Miss Farrow
75. Faye or Longworth
77. Made cutting remarks
79. Shirks
82. Memorize
83. Russian village
85. Adapt machinery
86. Kind of stock or horn
89. *Play It ___, Sam*
91. Wax: Prefix
92. Dir.
93. Shell-game piece
94. Murky
96. "Meanwhile, back ___"
100. Hebrew letter
101. Swelling disease
103. Goren's king or queen
104. Hire
108. Place with many keys
110. "___ beaucoup"
111. Took to the skies
112. Lexicographer of Elizabethan days
113. Was self-seeking
116. Eastern Mediterranean area
117. Flat spinner
118. Roman 1502
119. Ritzy
120. Film actor Arnold et al.
121. "___ a man with . . ."
122. Rind
123. Amtrak stops: Abbr.

DOWN

1. Some Egyptians
2. ___ for (leave room)
3. Ostrich feature
4. Wrestling hold
5. Adds up
6. Royal initials
7. Dig up
8. Walk unsteadily
9. Moves the shrubbery
10. Bone: Prefix
11. Part of N.C.A.A.
12. Carpentry tools
13. ___ the question
14. Wacko
15. Barren
16. Fabled continent of the Indian Ocean
17. Cartographers
18. French possessive
24. Computer word
25. ___ May Oliver
30. Repeated
32. Man: Prefix
33. Aged: Abbr.
35. "N'est-ce ___?"
37. Wide shoe sizes
38. Valley, in England
41. Photo enlargements
42. Kind of acid
45. Growing on the ground
47. ___ van der Rohe
49. Article
50. "There ___ tavern in . . ."
52. Other, to Pablo
53. Little ones
54. Mosquito barrier
55. Furnace part
57. Proportion
58. High-tech Valley
59. Faulty-faucet flow
64. Holiday times
66. ___ Minor
67. Changed a door or window
71. Yarn
73. Own up
74. Baseball-dugout V.I.P.
75. Wile
76. Brave people
78. Architect's drawing
80. Melancholy, to a poet
81. Swiss city
84. Caught ___ (nailed)
86. Suited
87. Folder
88. Famous ballerina
90. Motorists' org.
91. ___ guerre
95. Fools
97. This can be tooted
98. Set up a bivouac
99. Shoe
102. Moslem leader
105. Running wild
106. Medicinal plant
107. Singer Nelson and family
109. Algerian city
110. Retailers' gds.
111. Country
112. Stories: Abbr.
114. Use a gunsight
115. Four-in-hand

133 Impertinences By Don Nardizzi

Taking liberties with some familiar things.

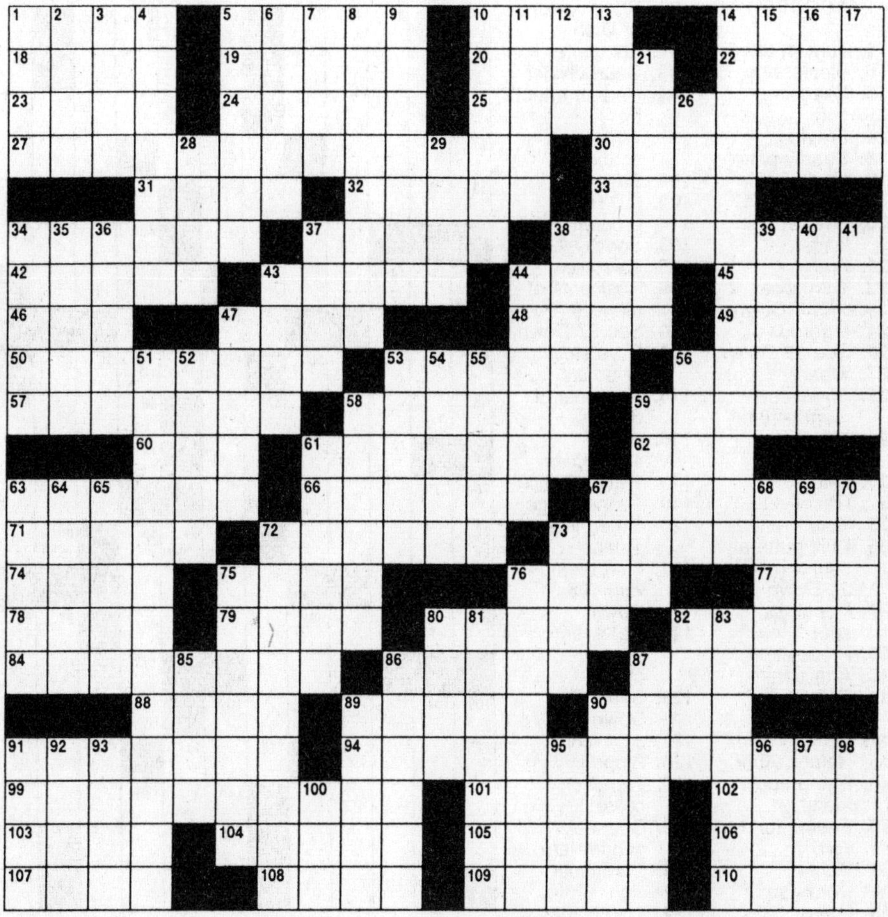

ACROSS

1. Gas light
5. Extent of perception
10. School org. units
14. Seat of Hawaii County
18. "It's ___!" (words of denial)
19. ___ in (duped)
20. Huck Finn vessels
22. Perfume
23. Return-mail initials
24. African antelope
25. Lineage
27. Ropesville, Texas, publication?
30. Unwelcome
31. Miss Turner
32. City on the Rhone
33. Impecunious
34. Blacksnakes
37. Attack
38. A motel, usually
42. Expunge
43. Mouthfuls
44. Sound on a paging device
45. Western lily
46. Word before brush or brake
47. Adjective suffixes
48. Retirement accts.
49. Roosevelt's mother
50. Earrings
53. Billiard shots
56. More skillful
57. Green items of a song
58. Place to buy redeye
59. Ices
60. Affirmative of sorts
61. Ship-ladder unit
62. Writer Fleming
63. Obliquely
66. Chemical compounds
67. Schweitzer and Finney
71. Escutcheon blemishes
72. Mechanic's tool
73. Lobbyist's stock in trade
74. Inferior diamond
75. Gaelic poem
76. Pig's ancestor
77. Actor's aid
78. Moonfish
79. Newts
80. Laurel and Musial
82. Jacob's son
84. Canary island
86. Bulls' counterparts
87. Members of the wedding
88. Biblical word of reproach
89. Signified
90. Prefix for aircraft or body
91. Generated
94. New England barber?
99. Getting rid of
101. Palmer
102. Prefix for mutuel
103. Container
104. Of an ecological stage
105. Foxx and namesakes
106. Camelot lady
107. D'Oléron and d'Yeu
108. High ground
109. Slag
110. Poor grades

DOWN

1. Satirical cartoonist
2. A king of Israel
3. Seine feeder
4. Goads
5. Tavern servers
6. Lily type
7. All right
8. Stadium-top flappers
9. Sanction
10. Establish beforehand
11. Puts a strain on
12. Astern
13. Afternoon events for an ecdysiast?
14. Eastertime Jolly Roger?
15. Personal: Prefix
16. Appear indistinctly
17. Caen's river
21. Sassafras drinks
26. Hoofbeat
28. River into Lake Biel
29. Sporting sounds in Madrid
34. Harvests
35. *The Tempest* spirit
36. Chile's companion
37. Does a lube job
38. Tranquil
39. Calves
40. Plumed heron
41. Sounds from a den
43. Vampires
44. Shaggy-maned animals
47. Inefficient
51. Ottoman ruler at Santa Anita?
52. Herb genus
53. Dull finish
54. To go, in Gascony
55. Evenings, in Paris
56. Longfellow's tent folders
58. Black bucks
59. Office worker
61. Narrate
63. Chief monk
64. Ski site
65. Navigational system
67. Macaws
68. Dress trimming
69. More loyal
70. Prescient ones
72. Viper with an abacus?
73. Lily of the opera
75. Plane-wing antifreeze devices
76. Trader
80. Connery or O'Casey
81. Drinking mug
82. Vino city
83. Transported
85. Pro ___
86. Snoopy, for one
87. Except that
89. Talking birds
90. Muriatic and formic
91. Roman 406
92. Coin of Iran
93. Being
95. Within: Prefix
96. Window division
97. Iroquoian
98. Disencumbers
100. Grandson of Benjamin

134 Pairs By Reginald Johnson

Ones that show an affinity of sound.

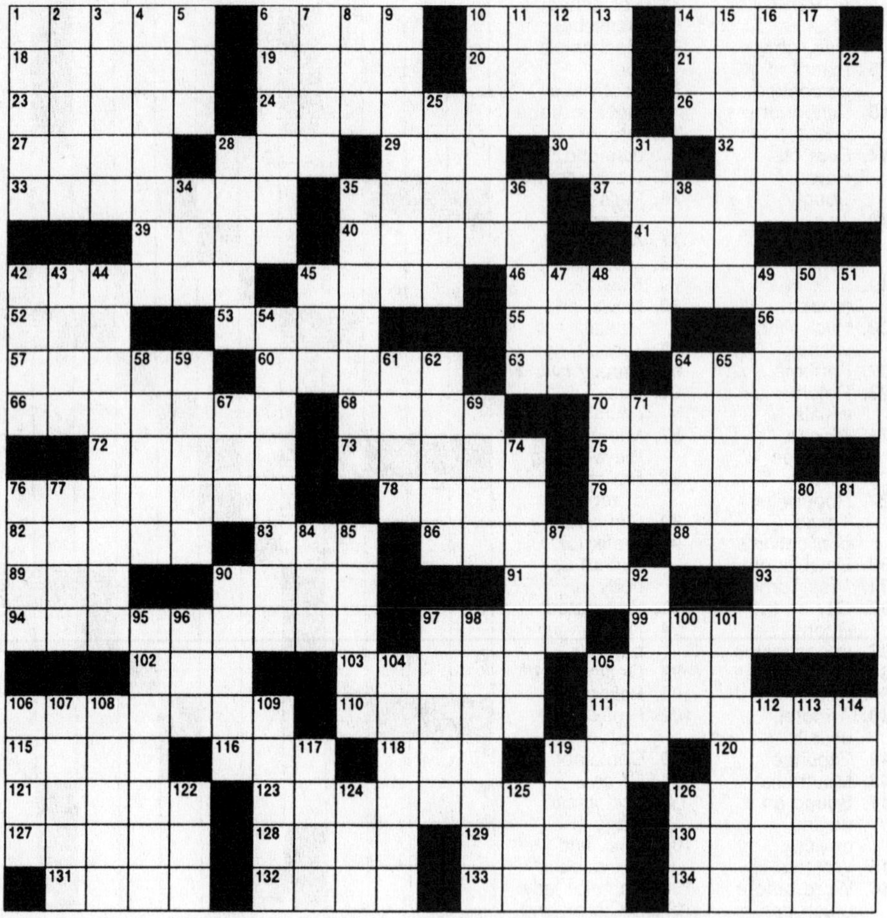

ACROSS

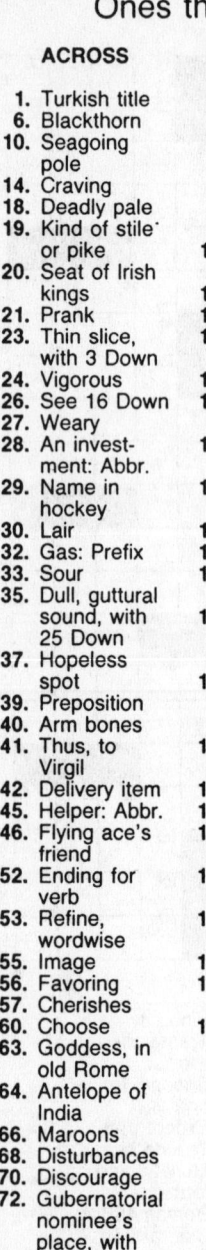

1. Turkish title
6. Blackthorn
10. Seagoing pole
14. Craving
18. Deadly pale
19. Kind of stile or pike
20. Seat of Irish kings
21. Prank
23. Thin slice, with 3 Down
24. Vigorous
26. See 16 Down
27. Weary
28. An investment: Abbr.
29. Name in hockey
30. Lair
32. Gas: Prefix
33. Sour
35. Dull, guttural sound, with 25 Down
37. Hopeless spot
39. Preposition
40. Arm bones
41. Thus, to Virgil
42. Delivery item
45. Helper: Abbr.
46. Flying ace's friend
52. Ending for verb
53. Refine, wordwise
55. Image
56. Favoring
57. Cherishes
60. Choose
63. Goddess, in old Rome
64. Antelope of India
66. Maroons
68. Disturbances
70. Discourage
72. Gubernatorial nominee's place, with 59 Down
73. Pretty bird song, with 62 Down
75. See 64 Down
76. The Red Baron, for one
78. Wanton look
79. Kindles
82. Your, in Paris
83. Bill
86. Made an effort
88. Linden trees
89. Nice season in Nice
90. State flower of Utah
91. Encounter
93. Court divider
94. Had an effect on
97. Whale schools
99. Sayings
102. F.D.R. program
103. Spooky
105. Taleteller
106. Residents of manses
110. See 97 Down
111. Buys stocks or bonds
115. Accounts of deeds
116. ___ *Misérables*
118. Within: Prefix
119. Tunnel digger
120. Other, in Toledo
121. Fast break, with 108 Down
123. Not even second-class
126. See 112 Down
127. ___-comic
128. Ripped
129. Turnover collar
130. Goose-gander fare
131. Octagonal sign
132. Thin blade
133. Endangered trees
134. Heads, in Caen

DOWN

1. Macaroni, for one
2. Cold dish
3. See 23 Across
4. Dissenter
5. Chemical ending
6. Sound system
7. Moon goddess
8. Bauxite, e.g.
9. Signs up
10. Breastbones
11. One way to stand
12. Like parts of Arizona
13. Bobby Unser, e.g.
14. Varnish ingredient
15. Open, as a door
16. Keep away, with 26 Across
17. Valuable headpiece
22. Season's yield
25. See 35 Across
28. Fiber plant
31. Twangy
34. Two's predecessor
35. Keaton and Brown
36. Lukewarm
38. Spasmodic contraction
42. Kind of vault
43. " . . . unto us ___ is given"
44. Called on again
45. Be under the weather
47. Citrus refresher
48. Kind of market
49. Disquieting
50. Hall of Fame's Speaker
51. Ages
54. Abandoned
58. To be, in Spain
59. See 72 Across
61. Hood
62. See 73 Across
64. Vapid perfume, with 75 Across
65. Palmer of golf
67. Ike's war area
69. Prophet
71. Device for heart tests: Abbr.
74. Added lace
76. Declare
77. Ballot
80. Robert ___
81. Fast planes
84. Iron or Bronze
85. Is an omen
87. Letters
90. Traffic tie-up
92. Relative of 'tis
95. New York neighbor
96. Tail: Prefix
97. Kind of stadium, with 110 Across
98. Grand National course
100. Org. for war injured
101. Interstices
104. Everlasting, of yore
105. Sheets, etc.
106. Stay out of the bidding
107. Summits
108. See 121 Across
109. Seven, in Siena
112. Heavy blow, with 126 Across
113. Cease-fire
114. Indulges to excess
117. Store
119. Mighty mite
122. Kind of banana
124. Anger
125. One of five: Abbr.
126. Chi. time

135 Getting Familiar By John Ohlsen

One can't always be formal with well-known people.

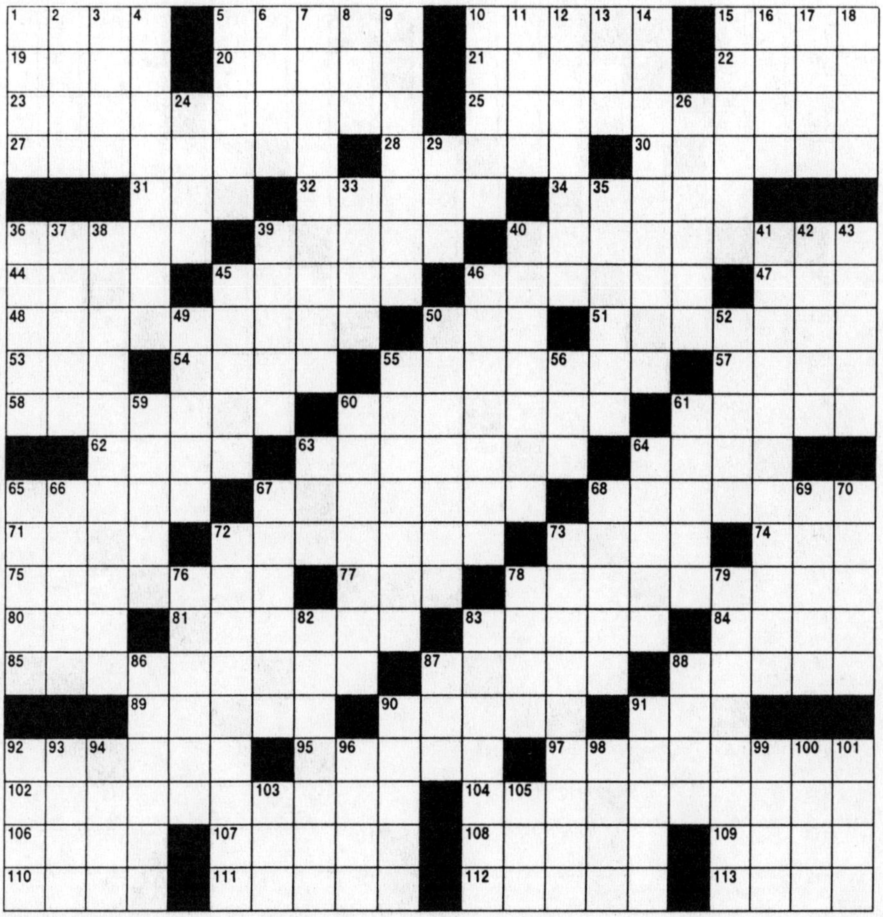

ACROSS

1. Uncle Remus's rabbit
5. Old Turkish coin
10. Rome divider
15. Mine entrance
19. Congo river
20. Wilkes-___
21. Soap plant
22. Pro ___
23. Mark Twain
25. O. Henry
27. Small seeds
28. Shades
30. Revokes, as a legacy
31. Dir.
32. Kind of tower
34. Takes a stab at
36. Indian ruler
39. Worship
40. Tavern article
44. Skip
45. Anoint, old style
46. Ropes, in France
47. Gene component
48. Cheese variety
50. Corn unit
51. Removable fence piece
53. Kipling character
54. "Too bad!"
55. Mexican men
57. Finnish poem
58. Sneaky laugh
60. Like worse gravy
61. French parents
62. Stage and TV actress
63. Jewish title of respect
64. German coal area
65. Source of Solomon's wealth
67. Club personnel
68. Gestures
71. Stagger
72. "Each must do ___"
73. Furnace input
74. Not in, to a Boer
75. Blessing
77. Certain carriers: Abbr.
78. U.S. emblem
80. "___ Got My Love . . ."
81. ___ oneself on (felt satisfied)
83. Craftily: Var.
84. "___ in the Course of . . ."
85. Yukon, for one
87. Goads
88. Low-pitched voice
89. Turkish city
90. Astringent
91. Norm
92. Shore bird
95. Lose one's head
97. ___ Angus
102. *Silicon Valley* author
104. *Arundel* author
106. Glacial leavings
107. Street show
108. Compare
109. Carry on
110. Mantas
111. Toys with strings
112. Attempt
113. African village

DOWN

1. Osculate
2. Harvest
3. Sailors' saint
4. Put fresh life into
5. Poplar
6. Identical
7. Chairmen
8. Sea bird
9. Work on an old painting
10. Lion-colored
11. Not orig.
12. Reinforce
13. Building wing
14. People who fix things
15. Stop
16. Fruitcake ingredient
17. Article
18. Gobs
24. Like a rain forest
26. Ukrainian port
29. Choler
33. Electrical unit
35. More rubious
36. Diamonds, to a heister
37. With full force
38. *Iberia* author
39. Close, poetically
40. Spools
41. Ape-man creator
42. Foolish
43. Nostrils
45. More capable
46. Conduct
49. Creator
50. Waves
52. Inflict
55. Elbert or Mother
56. Defendants, in law
59. Pepper pod
60. Eel
61. Twin crystal
63. Legal thing
64. Down at the heels
65. Space path
66. Irk
67. Servile follower
68. ___ one's way (gets pushy)
69. Ohio city
70. Office worker
72. Giving encouragement
73. Alcan Highway terminus
76. Expert spinner
78. Become hazy
79. Ones giving prizes
82. Window décor
83. Small splotch
86. Indy 500 people
87. School subj.
88. Catty remark
90. Handles, in France
91. Garden flower
92. God of love
93. Passport entry
94. Word of agreement
96. Mars: Prefix
98. La ___ tar pits (L.A. area)
99. Latin verb
100. Burner
101. Fitted together: Abbr.
103. Fed. fiscal body
105. German cooler

136 Recipe Directions By Virginia Yates

With no guarantee of edible results.

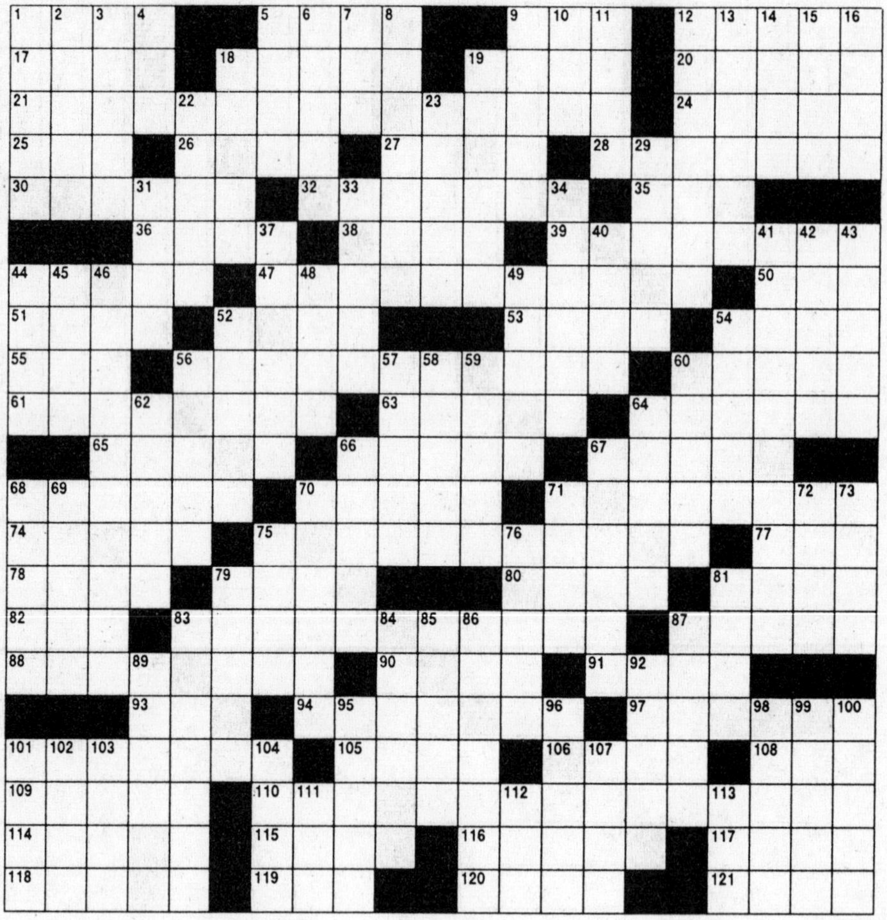

ACROSS

1. Gist
5. Animal protection agcy.
9. Gullet
12. Spanish steps
17. ___ domini
18. Fume
19. Blackjack, in Soho
20. As ___ (usually)
21. STIR
24. Gadabout
25. Mesabi output
26. Cousin's mother
27. Civil wrong
28. Mollify
30. Soften
32. ___ the crime
35. They, in Paris
36. Virginia willow
38. Gargantuan
39. ___ the switch
44. Adds one's John Henry
47. BROWN
50. Wallach
51. Exhausts, with "up"
52. Response to the Little Red Hen
53. River past Mt. Ararat
54. Ending for pony
55. Aegir's wife
56. MIX
60. English philosopher
61. New member of Congress
63. Notwith-standing
64. Places for mascara
65. American ostriches
66. Shows pleasure
67. Its quality isn't strained, said Portia
68. Tick or mite
70. Pith helmet
71. Afternoon snacks
74. Provide the food
75. BASTE
77. Paleozoic, for one
78. Arthurian lady
79. Bracken
80. "Bravo!"
81. Gripe
82. Auto pioneer's initials
83. SALT
87. Sesame Street character
88. Feasts
90. Coconut fiber
91. Calhoun of films
93. Jardiniere
94. Confronts
97. Bit of candy
101. Oz denizen et al.
105. Go to pot
106. Tints
108. Shoshonean Indian
109. City near Lisbon
110. BAKE
114. Piquant
115. Street sound
116. Part of R.N.
117. Put on the ___ bag
118. Volcanic rock
119. Chip off the old block
120. Bristle
121. Whig's opposite

DOWN

1. Shaw's Barbara
2. Accustom
3. Play backer
4. To boot
5. Overwhelm
6. Hides
7. Presidential nickname
8. Tyro
9. Very, in music
10. ___ -san, Kyushu volcano
11. Command to Dobbin.
12. Garnish item
13. Waken
14. Fiji capital
15. A Cassini
16. Dried up
18. *On the Beach* author
19. Profession
22. Declaims
23. Drum
29. Sediments
31. One, in Ulm
33. Preside
34. Atlantic islands
37. Large snakes
40. Common back wound
41. COOL
42. Same
43. Mah-jongg pieces
44. Breakers
45. River to the Danube
46. BEAT
48. Coat or collar
49. Combos
52. Bedouin
54. Puccini work
56. Possessive
57. A Marx
58. Source of wickerwork material
59. I.Q.-test originator
60. Tamarack
62. Smidgen
64. Contract of a sort
66. Frocks
67. Scanty
68. Sharp
69. Capital of Crete
70. Brewer of song
71. Japanese naval base of W.W. II
72. Palindrome words
73. Umpire's decision
75. Transmitted
76. Thing to have in the right place
79. Rabid enthusiast
81. ___ Mawr
83. Anne and Arthur
84. Mystic's field
85. Perch
86. Heeds
87. Notched, as a leaf
89. Milk units
92. Stout
95. Antigone's uncle
96. Kind of cut or coming
98. Hawk
99. Different
100. Eligible for welfare
101. ___ Point
102. Match-king Kreuger
103. Dreyfus's defender
104. Ocean crossers
107. Bear, to Brutus
111. Court
112. Wish undone
113. Newt

137 Stacked Decks By H. H. Reddall

A few glances at the world of cards.

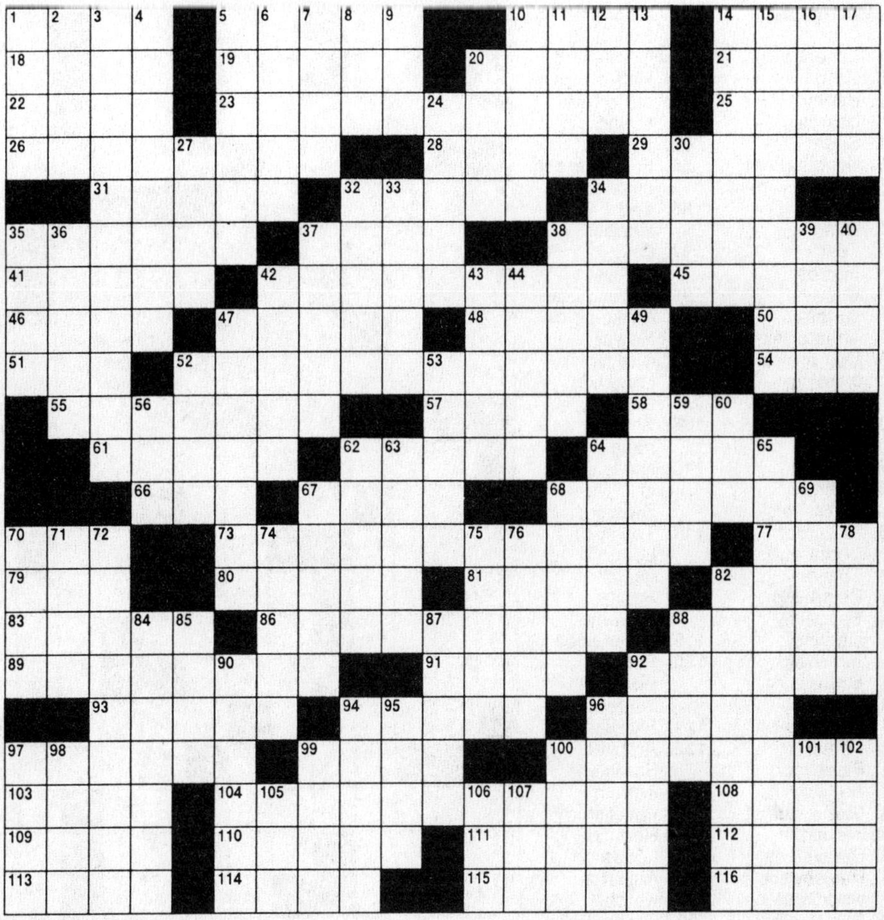

ACROSS

1. One ___ (bridge bid)
5. Northern nomads
10. Ring stone
14. Roman 1300
18. Nathan ___
19. Stevenson of politics
20. Suppose
21. Guthrie
22. Totals: Abbr.
23. Bridge events
25. Carol
26. North and South, at bridge
28. Golconda
29. Tics
31. Stand up
32. Longfellow and Frost, e.g.
34. Prepares eggs
35. Mourn
37. Horse or yacht event
38. Puzo's Godfather
41. Be ___ of (look up to)
42. Winner's words
45. Cut
46. Honorary titles
47. Composer of marches
48. Prefixes for farming
50. Pitcher's stat
51. Greek letter
52. Bridge bid
54. Go bad
55. Dinner courses
57. Lorelei and R. E.
58. Unit of hope
61. Indians
62. Member of Reagan's team
64. Annoys
66. Spring mo.
67. Arias
68. Relative of rummy
70. Horseplayers' convenience: Abbr.
73. Gun platforms
77. Free of
79. Triumphant cry
80. Showed a film again
81. Column molding
82. Like pastel colors
83. Piece of sculpture
86. Unwelcome member of a game
88. Badgerlike animal
89. Deduct
91. Form of lotto
92. Gentle touch
93. Amphitheater
94. Dens
96. ___ home the bacon
97. Old English coins
99. Word before A-Wee
100. Foot parts
103. Jack and Jill's burden
104. Devices for 86 Across
108. Relating to: Suffix
109. Spoken
110. Writer James and family
111. Red as ___
112. Theda the vamp
113. Wash. figures
114. What to do with a hand
115. Documents
116. Moonshine

DOWN

1. Fellow
2. Priest in Tibet
3. Brilliant blue
4. Scatters
5. Hot off the press
6. Revere
7. Kind of fours
8. Norm
9. Transgress
10. Starts the bidding
11. Evergreen
12. Emmet
13. One of two evils
14. Sea cow
15. Track linking two rail lines
16. Attlee, to friends
17. Mountain passes
20. Leave out
24. Arabian chieftain
27. Baseball team
30. Buddies
32. Dated
33. Indian or Arctic
34. Kind of friend
35. Speech impairment
36. Aromatic herb
37. Rakes
38. McCormick of reaper note
39. Pianist Peter
40. Latin-class word
42. Bodies of knowledge
43. Heads
44. Assent
47. More inclined
49. Short races
52. Ego experience
53. Containing a fatty acid
56. Predecessor of la
59. "Too bad"
60. "___, We Have No Bananas"
62. Back tooth
63. African antelope
64. What the mouse did to the clock
65. Of military planning
67. Small herring
68. Hill, in Spain
69. Wings, in France
70. Feed-bag items
71. Command-ment word
72. Uncivilized person
74. Ultimate goal
75. Clear sky
76. Eerie wind sounds
78. Convention people: Abbr.
82. River in Brazil
84. Walks leisurely
85. Russian city
87. Hit a high fly ball
88. Occurrence in Spain
90. Companion of vegetable and mineral
92. Tops of mountains
94. Favored
95. Drinks
96. Portended
97. Navy noncoms
98. Swiss river
99. British gun
100. One grew in Brooklyn
101. Songbird
102. Do in
105. Dog's or coon's ___
106. Heel
107. Theater's Burrows

138 Supermarket By Threba Johnson

Where to pick up some unlikely bargains.

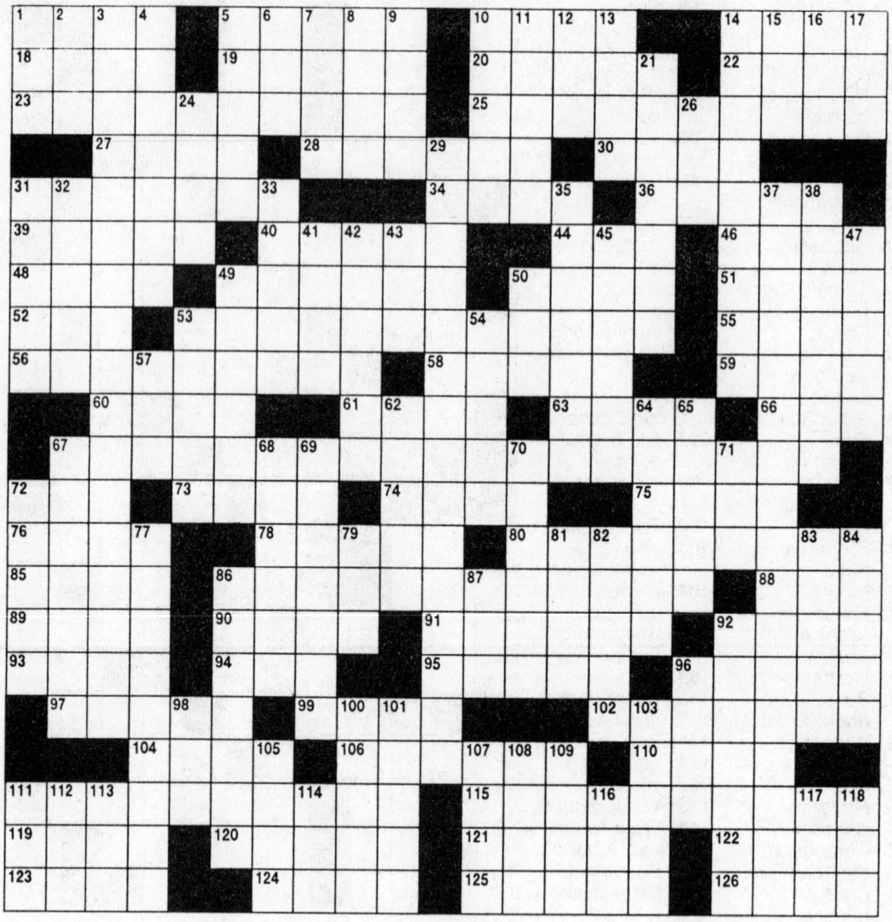

ACROSS

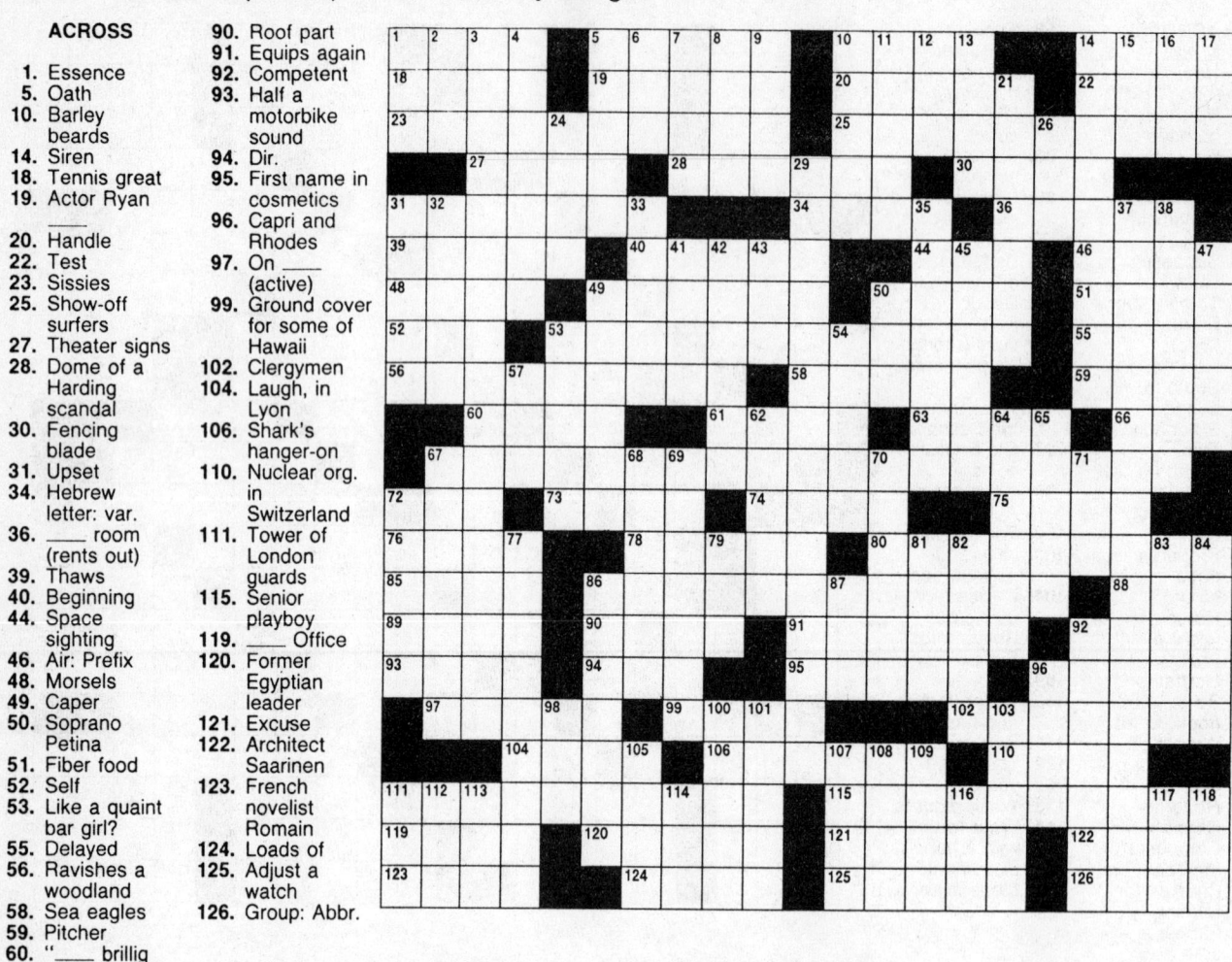

1. Essence
5. Oath
10. Barley beards
14. Siren
18. Tennis great
19. Actor Ryan ___
20. Handle
22. Test
23. Sissies
25. Show-off surfers
27. Theater signs
28. Dome of a Harding scandal
30. Fencing blade
31. Upset
34. Hebrew letter: var.
36. ___ room (rents out)
39. Thaws
40. Beginning
44. Space sighting
46. Air: Prefix
48. Morsels
49. Caper
50. Soprano Petina
51. Fiber food
52. Self
53. Like a quaint bar girl?
55. Delayed
56. Ravishes a woodland
58. Sea eagles
59. Pitcher
60. "___ brillig . . ."
61. Arizona city
63. Blade of yore
66. ___ *Stop*
67. Straus's candy man?
72. Guevara
73. Tree toad
74. Chemical endings
75. European wheat
76. Dear, in Düsseldorf
78. Dickens's Edwin ___
80. Shaped
85. Two-toed sloth
86. Clever brownies?
88. Ending for law or saw
89. Comedian Sahl
90. Roof part
91. Equips again
92. Competent
93. Half a motorbike sound
94. Dir.
95. First name in cosmetics
96. Capri and Rhodes
97. On ___ (active)
99. Ground cover for some of Hawaii
102. Clergymen
104. Laugh, in Lyon
106. Shark's hanger-on
110. Nuclear org. in Switzerland
111. Tower of London guards
115. Senior playboy
119. ___ Office
120. Former Egyptian leader
121. Excuse
122. Architect Saarinen
123. French novelist Romain
124. Loads of
125. Adjust a watch
126. Group: Abbr.

DOWN

1. Lumberman's boot
2. Neighbor of Syr.
3. Society's tops
4. Newspaper family
5. Thicket
6. Burmese leader
7. Torn
8. Secure
9. Miss Maxwell
10. Massachusetts town
11. Penned
12. Bottom line
13. Notorious marquis
14. Twenty Questions category
15. Chop
16. Deface
17. Times of day: Abbr.
21. Heap of lumberers' logs
24. Witty remarks
26. Relative of gosh
29. Skin tone
31. Plant
32. Snow on the Seine
33. Sections of a hospital
35. TV watchdog Betty ___
37. Fair-haired ladies
38. College athlete
41. SoHo studio
42. Lymph: Prefix
43. Towel monogram
45. City in California
47. Unique people
49. Plump
50. Charged particle
53. Spinachlike plant
54. Angry
57. Be obligated
62. George or T. S.
64. Gladdens
65. Taro roots
67. Do pruning
68. Hemingway character
69. Lateen-rigged ship
70. Convoy
71. Chit
72. Tuft
77. Frivolous socialite
79. Metal
81. Migrant farm worker
82. River in west Africa
83. Fisherman of a sort
84. Clothe
86. Ladies of Spain
87. Faroe whirlwinds
92. Goddess of justice
96. Chilled
98. ". . . the giftie ___ us . . ."
100. Island in the Firth of Clyde
101. Endows
103. Writing: Fr.
105. "L'___ c'est . . ."
107. Eskers
108. ___ of thumb
109. Spartan king
111. Marsh
112. Stowe girl
113. Corn unit
114. Tokyo, once
116. Presidential nickname
117. Med. men
118. Over there

139 True Love By Bert Rosenfield

Tracing its nonstraight path through the medium of song.

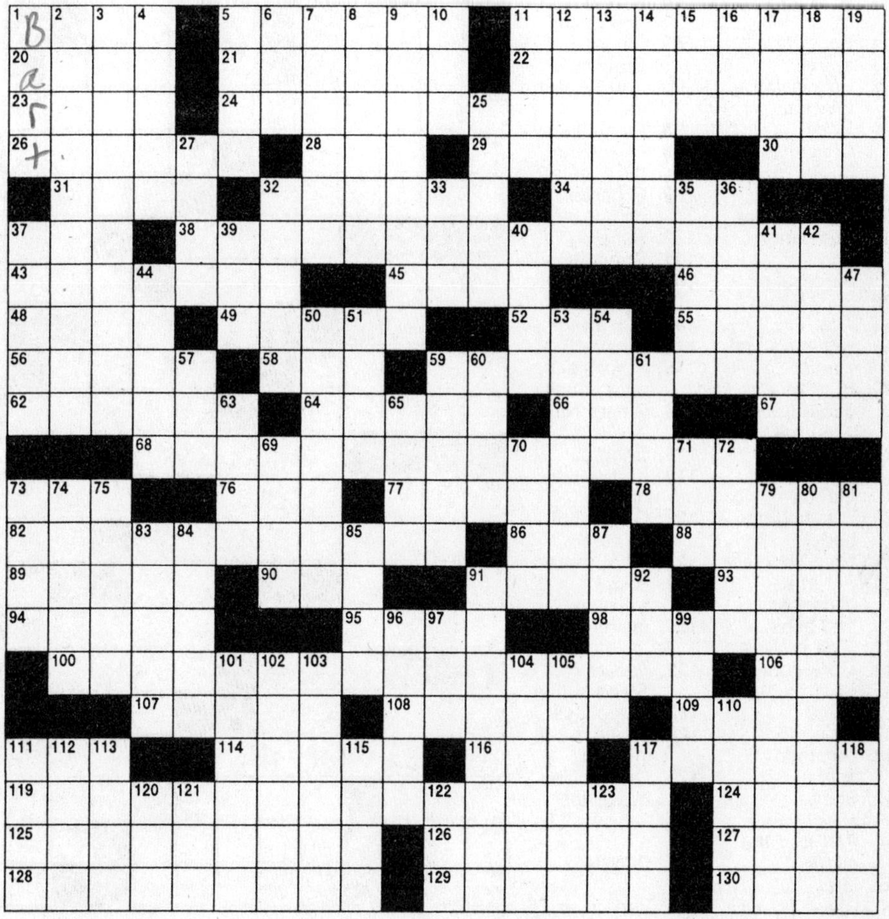

ACROSS

1. Woods waif
5. Constituent
11. Like lady wrestlers
20. Author Seton
21. Glowing
22. Bows to urban renewal
23. 90 and 95, e.g.
24. *The Sighting*
26. Fabrics from Asia
28. "Who ___ that lady . . .?"
29. Los ___, near San Jose
30. Narcotic initials
31. Ernie of W.W. II
32. Florentine family of note
34. Willow
37. It follows a do
38. *The Approach*
43. Paul who starred in *The Emperor Jones*
45. One who ogles
46. Revoke a legacy
48. ___ impasse
49. ___ over (carried through)
52. Org. of the Knicks and Lakers
55. Porridge of uncertain temperature
56. Often-charmed snake
58. It's found on la table
59. *The Chemistry*
62. "Tennis, ___?"
64. Prima ___ (apparent)
66. Porter's relative
67. "The Cruel ___"
68. *The Offer*
73. Wee, in Dundee
76. Boston Garden great
77. Field mice
78. Congressional hang-up
82. *The Response*
86. Appia or del Corso
88. ___ Lane Theatre
89. Pineapple
90. Quite a few: Abbr.
91. Finnish coin
93. Salinger girl
94. Partook of the sauce
95. "___ Arms": Loesser song
98. Kind of speech stop
100. *The Suspicion*
106. Half a Broadway play title
107. Go for a new tenant
108. Standard
109. Singer Tennille
111. Dutch airline
114. Swiss city on the Aare
116. Russian money: Abbr.
117. Expensive
119. *The Accusation*
124. Eight furlongs
125. Ethiopia
126. Walled city
127. Texas publisher Carter
128. One of the Bible's two
129. Sudra and Vaisyà
130. Good or Loch ending

DOWN

1. Starr of football
2. Negatively charged particle
3. *The Dismissal*
4. Atelier accessory
5. Domino or Waller
6. Hard wood
7. One working on a tough steak
8. Harangue
9. Partial
10. Jacket size: Abbr.
11. Kind of code
12. Pensive musical pieces
13. Well nigh
14. Manila grass
15. Alas, Gaelic style
16. Denial in Nairn
17. Kind of type: Abbr.
18. Chalice veils
19. Fitted, as tables: Abbr.
25. Pointed arch
27. Writer Josephine and family
32. *Scarface* star and family
33. Ron of baseball
35. Warehouse for goods
36. "___ cock-horse. . ."
37. Brazilian timber tree
39. Scottish umpire's call
40. "Rule, Britannia" composer
41. Inches up on
42. Deed of derring-do
44. Join the class
47. City near Phoenix
50. Madame ___ of knitting note
51. Joie de vivre
53. ___ mind (remembers)
54. Hunnish king of myth
57. Upward: Prefix
59. What he says, you do
60. Prosperity
61. Restore
63. Boozy cry of old
65. Roman 406
69. Mesozoic and Cenozoic
70. Dream, in Paris
71. Allah or Set
72. Everglades bird
73. Game with 32 cards
74. He called TV a wasteland
75. Biblical psalmist
79. *The Conclusion*
80. Thick-plated animals
81. Spinal cord: Prefix
83. Von Stroheim expression
84. Tia's relative
85. Tel ___
87. Gabriel, for one
91. Gum infection
92. ___ de France
96. Italian Socialist leader
97. Prefix for cardial or neural
99. Aware of
101. God, in Hebrew scripture
102. Offenbach's *La Belle ___*
103. Achieve
104. Raw and burnt
105. Volcanic rock
110. Ottoman Empire founder
111. Burmese coin
112. Pierced item
113. Spanish adverbs
115. Pennsylvanie or Californie
117. Containers for pkgs.
118. Hankerings
120. Q-U filler
121. Entity headed by J. Davis
122. Initials for a peacock network
123. ___ grass (meadow barley)

140 Non-Profession By Peter Swift

There's at least one impossible source of income.

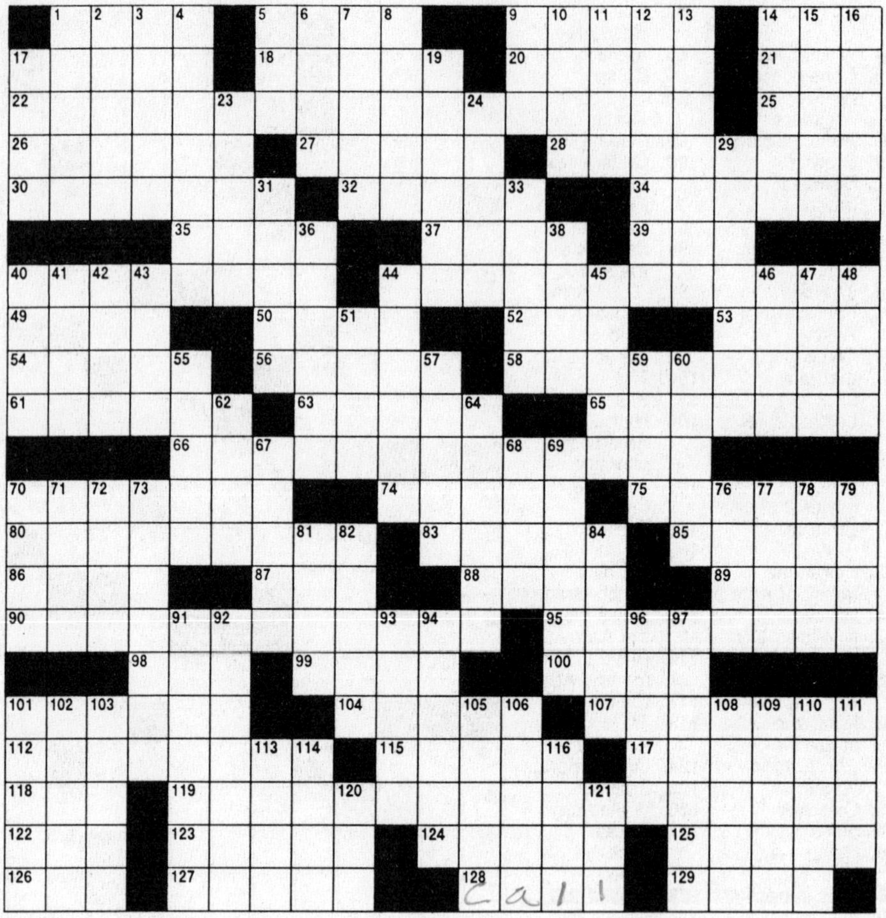

ACROSS

1. Food for swine
5. Polynesian loincloth
9. Does Christmas buying
14. Spree
17. Water wheel
18. Templeton and namesakes
20. ___ Haute
21. Trial witness's first words
22. Start of a quote from Jean Kerr
25. Actress Fabray, to friends
26. Washington body
27. Miss Thomas
28. Put at a distance
30. Fell behind
32. Riga natives
34. More goofy
35. Notable pen name
37. Inning trios
39. Common abbr.
40. Shows affection for
44. Part II of the quote
49. Inter ___
50. Ukase issuer
52. Arafat's gp.
53. Designer Cassini
54. Word before iliac
56. Sudden onrush
58. Calling for Popeye
61. Paint pigment
63. Iranian coins
65. Victorian under-garments
66. Part III of the quote
70. Beguile
74. Spring time
75. Western desert
80. Meandering
83. Used a sniggle
85. Meddlesome
86. Race track
87. "___ Love Is Here to Stay"
88. Son of Jacob and Leah
89. Singer Stevens
90. Part IV of the quote
95. Plants firmly
98. Chaney of the silents
99. Organic compound
100. Saharan
101. Strengthens
104. City on the Missouri
107. Scalawags
112. Trusted
115. Actor's line, occasionally
117. Where Napoli is
118. Bring out
119. End of the quote
122. Garland of flowers
123. Plant disease
124. Bridal walkway
125. Instrument for a combo
126. *Fables in Slang* author
127. Percolates
128. Meets a bet, in cards
129. Certain New Havenites

DOWN

1. Van driver, often
2. Sports palace
3. Mideast peninsula
4. Snitches
5. ___ Tse-tung
6. Grad
7. Majestic
8. Earthy pigment
9. Erwin of films
10. Red pigment
11. Heavenly bodies
12. Bar tidbit
13. Having notched edges
14. Supernatural spirit
15. Saying
16. Dead duck
17. Airport of a sort
19. ___ the earth
23. Tilts, as a ship
24. ___ to par (below normal)
29. They're often aweigh
31. Eats care-fully
33. Rome's Spanish ___
36. Guarantee
38. Shoe part
40. Comedienne Peggy
41. Russian range
42. Wedding debris
43. Deserve
44. Types of vocal music
45. Trespass
46. "I cannot tell ___"
47. Opening
48. Grocery purchase
51. Parched
55. Available for use
57. Go on the lam, romantically
59. Kind of rubber
60. Incendiary act
62. Curves
64. Grievously
67. Ending for rend or part
68. Shade of blue
69. Henri's classmates
70. A.B.A. member
71. Faithful
72. Pungent
73. Shuffled cards
76. Rumanian dance
77. "___ anybody cared"
78. Three-piece suit unit
79. Peepers
81. Stripped
82. Cum ___ salis
84. Waiter tipper
91. Grainy rocks
92. Remove from the stockroom
93. ___ *of the Year,* Broadway show
94. Seward's purchase
96. Galahad's find
97. Fidgety
101. Milan's La ___
102. Sampled
103. Spooky
105. Radio-shop merchandise
106. ___ of one's own medicine
108. Quibble
109. Excuse
110. Wrinkles
111. Droops
113. Advantage
114. Globule
116. Author Gardner
120. "___ De-Lovely"
121. He lost to D.D.E.

141 Shady Films By Bernice Gordon

But they aren't necessarily X-rated.

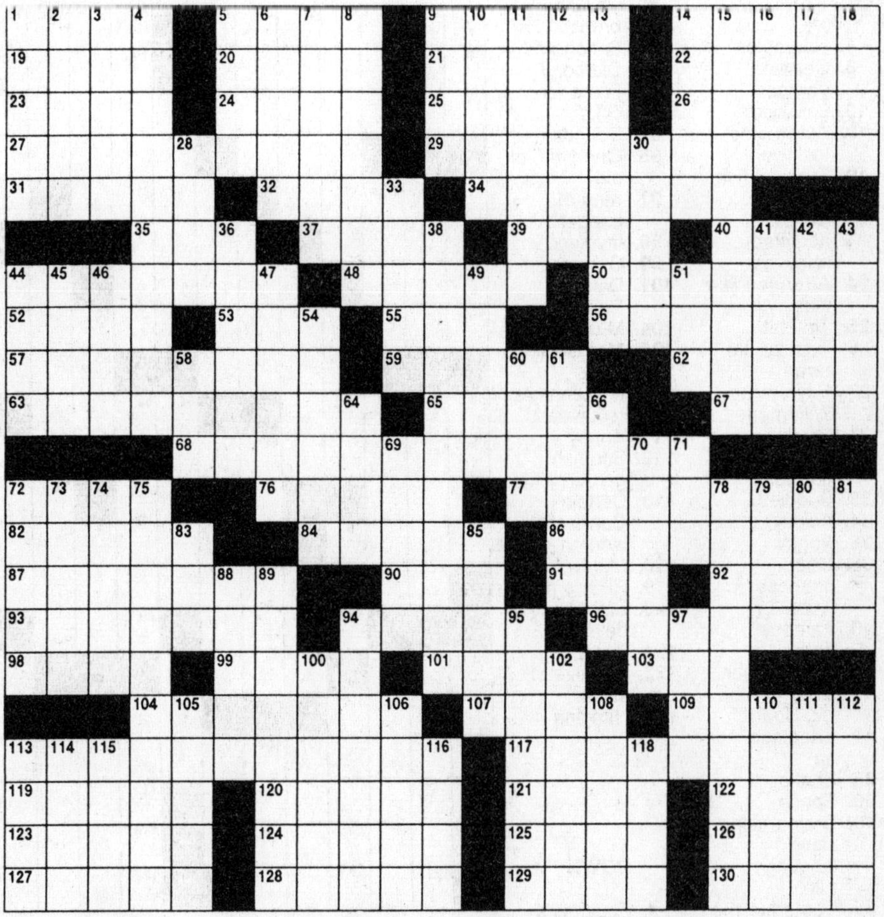

ACROSS

1. Effort
5. Elec. units
9. Bird known as the honey guide
14. Mexican measure
19. "___, dark and handsome"
20. Gila River feeder
21. Old Venetian medal
22. Take part in a drama
23. Adhem of poetic note
24. "___ she blows!"
25. Discolor
26. "Barnaby Jones" actor
27. Film with Eddy as a Mountie
29. Valuable animals for a Michael Caine film?
31. Neat, in Scotland
32. Greek letters
34. Work area for Miro
35. Cuckoo
37. Gambol
39. Part of a heraldic shield
40. Querying word
44. Toward the center, old style
48. More underhanded
50. Daddy Long Legs in the movies
52. Old mining town in Venezuela
53. ___ *Town*
55. Colonizer
56. Trays
57. City near Tallahassee
59. Straw beehives
62. Pertaining to wax
63. Hoped for
65. Shrimp
67. Protein-rich bean
68. Film with Audrey Hepburn as the bird girl
72. Draw nautical ropes
76. Marbles now housed in England
77. Places in jeopardy
82. Prepared the way, with "to"
84. Something one is often out of
86. Small craft used in Venice
87. Ham it up
90. In spite of: Var.
91. South, in France
92. Fabulist
93. Molasses' partner
94. Kitchen V.I.P.s
96. Unites, as metals
98. Circus performer
99. Former emcee on "Tonight"
101. Sounds at the Omni
103. This is sometimes me
104. Shows
107. Legendary birds
109. Biting insects
113. Film with Moira Shearer as a ballerina
117. Film in which Cagney plays a hood
119. Where Kaifeng is
120. Intervening, in law
121. O'Neill's daughter
122. The Ponte Vecchio spans it
123. Job for a C.P.A.
124. Hole-___
125. Kind of rubber
126. Something slight
127. Actor Jeremy
128. Of tissue
129. A Wilson
130. Largo and West

DOWN

1. Set out
2. No-no
3. At ___ for words
4. Film with Presley as a tour guide
5. Movie pet
6. American skiing champ
7. Hair braids
8. Brief runs of luck
9. Thespian Arnold
10. Old Tiber port
11. Agent for a house hunter
12. Hardy or Twist
13. White cinnamon trees
14. User of the bathysphere
15. Film set in the wheat belt
16. Painter Bonheur
17. Road to Rome
18. Camera part
28. Talking bird
30. Harbor on the Elbe
33. Miser Marner
36. Mangle
38. Beast for Peter Sellers?
41. Sacred: Prefix
42. Finery
43. Inventor Nikola
44. Peggy Wood role
45. Cleopatra's attendant
46. Village, in Africa
47. Port in Scotland
49. Infinite time, poetically
51. Thoughtful treatment, for short
54. Badgerlike animals
58. Land of the Pampa: Abbr.
60. Matador's maneuver
61. Playground fixtures
64. Proceed, old style
66. Knotty
69. Glee
70. Rhea
71. Puget or L.I.: Abbr.
72. Dental aid
73. *Ziegfeld Follies,* e.g.
74. Writer St. Johns
75. Rare film phenomenon for Prince?
78. Film bird for Sterling Hayden?
79. Author Wiesel
80. Like Hitchcock's window
81. Ocean liners: Abbr.
83. Cry of disgust
85. Preceder of "so good"
88. One with a romantic arrow
89. Forward
94. Antiseptic liquid
95. Play by George Kelly, with "The"
97. Theater section
100. One-seeded fruit
102. Sheridan had one for scandal
105. Parts of some jackets
106. Medicinal shrub
108. Where Moses received the Commandments
110. Home on high
111. Aromatic herb
112. Pipe-organ parts
113. Native of Bangkok
114. *The Children's ___*
115. Prefix for carp or crine
116. Prescient one
118. Drive in

142 Kinfolk By Rhoda Kraus

People who might be near but not necessarily dear.

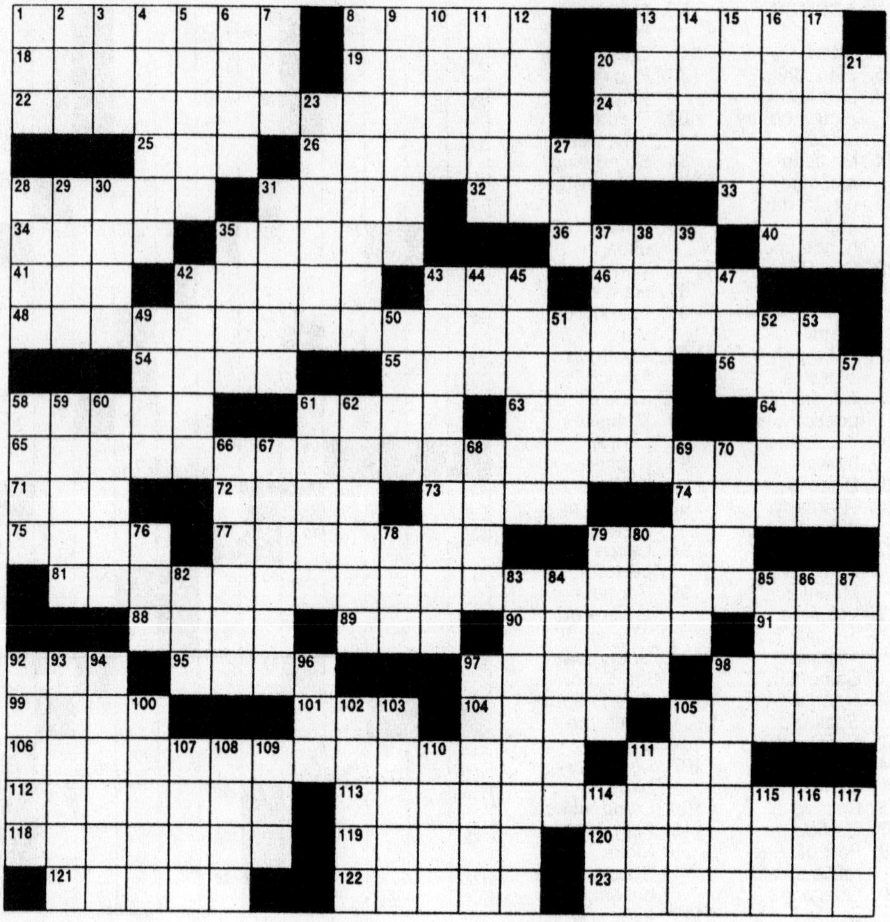

ACROSS

1. Harvester
8. Certain parties
13. Lassoed
18. Alarm clock, for one
19. Tropical fish
20. Betrayal
22. Certain acquired relatives
24. Arranged like tiles
25. Tiny bit
26. Popular TV rerun
28. City on the Willamette
31. Gratis
32. African garment
33. Buddies
34. Acidity
35. Foggy
36. Good chances: Abbr.
40. Famous news-paper: Abbr.
41. Corp. on the Big Board
42. Shoelace tip
43. Shake
46. Space
48. Drama using sign language
54. Kiln
55. Catherine the Great was one
56. Yeses, to Pierre
58. Bret Harte character
61. Bedouin
63. "What's ___ for me?"
64. Excessive
65. Mary Martin's pronounce-ment
71. Spring month in Nice
72. Khachaturian
73. Pete or Broadway Danny
74. Medicinal plants
75. "___ long way to. . ."
77. Soldier, frequently
79. Pinnacle
81. Mexican relatives
88. Parts of yards
89. Roman bronze
90. Simon and Diamond
91. Place for G.I.s
92. Bounder
95. One-time, of old
97. Kind of hanger
98. Involved with
99. Over again
101. Dancer Reinking
104. Meager
105. Map section
106. Ruth McKenney's relative
111. Annoy
112. Scottish genre painter
113. Certain Connecticut women
118. Mutes
119. Hiker's milieu
120. Sighting devices
121. Teary
122. Relative of Junior
123. Hanging

DOWN

1. Engineer's domain
2. Hockey star Bobby
3. Lowing sound
4. Churn's product
5. Bandleader Jones
6. Lack
7. Sin
8. Sneaky weapon
9. Olympic skater Albright
10. Gudrun's husband
11. Ulysses S. or Cary
12. Took care of
13. Navigational menace
14. Gymnast Korbut
15. Not quite obese
16. Wind-produced
17. Doubly
20. Jeanne d'Arc: Abbr.
21. Tête-à-tête, perhaps
23. Loose mass of stone
27. Pay-TV movie channel
28. Eastern ketch
29. Arthritis drug
30. French writer Pierre
31. ___ mignon
35. Overseers: Abbr.
37. ___ along (spread the news)
38. Magician's shout
39. Indian weight
42. Turkish city
43. Scout get-togethers
44. High mountain
45. Makes equipment changes
47. In the past
49. Dancer Fuller
50. Loyal, in olden days
51. "Common ___"
52. Exceed
53. Electron tube
57. Beans
58. Bishop's weed
59. Hotel-chain name
60. ___ kebab
61. Having ___ (carousing)
62. Herd of horses on a ranch
66. Bacon slice
67. Character-istics
68. Norse goddess of fate
69. Condemns
70. Guinness
76. Pershing's command: Abbr.
78. Uno, due, ___
79. Far Eastern
80. Irish limestone
82. Average grade
83. Very busy
84. Fierce, in Spain
85. Vandals
86. Noble Italian family
87. Baggy suit of earlier years
92. Outdoor shelters
93. Haphazardly
94. Streetcar name
96. Roofing material
97. Enter
98. Similarly
100. Playwright Oscar
102. Aeries
103. Part of an explosive combination
105. Novelist Shaw
107. Kind of cover or knot
108. Wee
109. Roof adornment
110. Film director David
111. Unemployed
114. Gab
115. Type of neckline
116. Sea bird
117. Rapid transit

143 Paging George Orwell By Connie Cowan

And offering a few additions to his newspeak file.

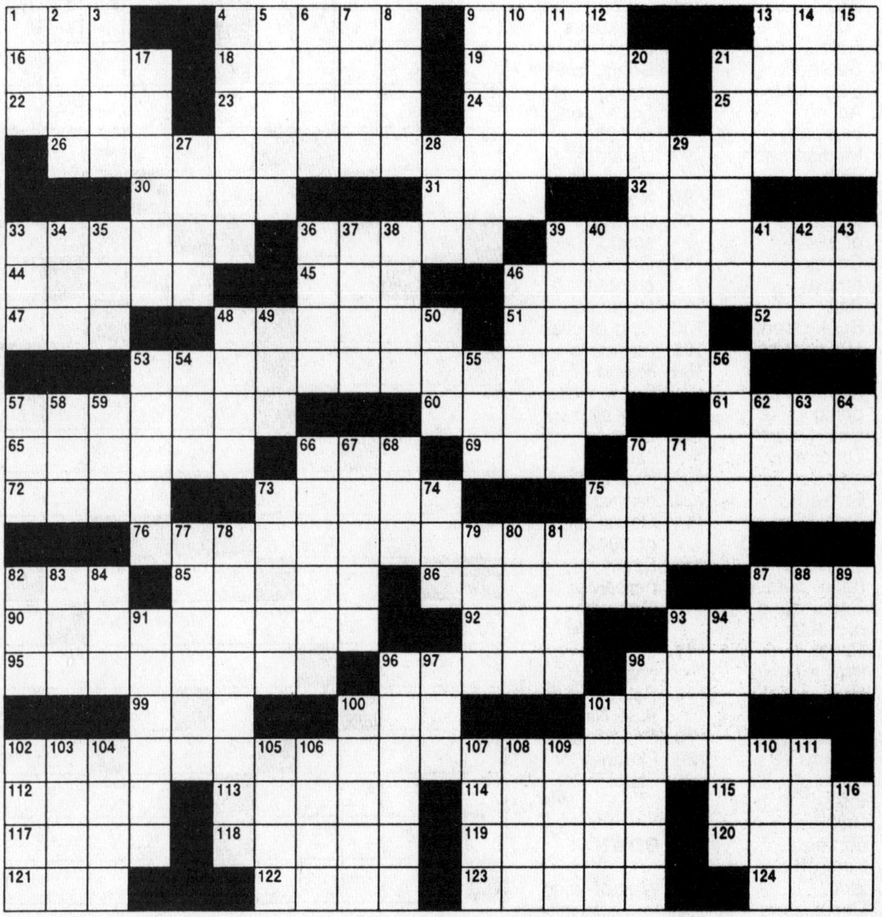

ACROSS

1. Part of Canada: Abbr.
4. Loses color
9. Support
13. Bed for Junior
16. Olympic skater Heiden
18. Gertrude Stein words
19. ___ *of One's Own*
21. Island near St. Kitts
22. Max or Bugs
23. Believe
24. Ruth's mother-in-law
25. Customer
26. Undertaking parlor, in officialese
30. Opposite of a lump
31. Some
32. Amount
33. Hooker, in newspeak talk
36. Bewildered
39. Forms of mica
44. Sculpture piece
45. Medieval French tale
46. Doing a debate routine
47. Cuckoo
48. Items in bierstuben
51. River of France
52. ___ peeve
53. Garage repairs, in newspeak
57. Suitable for drinking
60. Md. city
61. It, in Naples
65. Sound system
66. Burro
69. Curve
70. ". . . what can the ___ be?"
72. Go it alone
73. Maples and oaks
75. Courageous
76. Obfuscating words for a company's profit
82. NBC's parent
85. Geometrical line
86. Contrivance
87. Swarmer
90. What 26, 53, 76 or 102 Across is
92. Vegas or Cruces
93. Fish receptacle
95. Swiftest
96. Kind of nonwinning heart
98. "___ but to do and die"
99. Tennis call
100. Greek name
101. Enroll in
102. Secondhand vehicles
112. Galway islands
113. Lobster state
114. Alaskan native
115. Join the cheerleader
117. Poet Teasdale
118. Ocean eagles
119. Pester
120. Lady, in Spain
121. Center
122. Breeding place
123. Civil wrongs
124. Place for a TV

DOWN

1. Bird's bill
2. Prepare a gift
3. Row
4. Inventor's need
5. Stop sign in Quebec
6. Flashy
7. To be, in old Rome
8. Puts into type
9. Fruit for a split
10. Sheik's home
11. Calm
12. Soviet republic
13. Oddball
14. At the top, in Bonn
15. Sharp
17. Beliefs
20. 1985 Series state
21. Meeting of a sort
27. Roman dictator
28. U.S. inventor's monogram
29. Associate of Martin Luther
33. Greek letter
34. Gun's offspring
35. Dernier ___
36. Toward shelter
37. Tin plate
38. "___ for your supper"
39. Harasses
40. Word form for Spain's peninsula
41. Ex post facto bribe
42. Compass reading
43. NCO
46. Cambodian money units
48. Battle site in France
49. ___ the line
50. Relative
53. Burr
54. Honshu city
55. Scottish denial
56. ___ right (be accurate)
57. Letter addenda: Abbr.
58. Of the ear: Prefix
59. ___ Aviv
62. Depot: Abbr.
63. Old coin of Japan
64. Table scrap
66. Skilled performer
67. Earth shaking
68. Quite a few: Abbr.
70. Medieval club
71. Pasha or Baba
73. Metered conveyances
74. But, to Cicero
75. London's Old ___
77. City near Fresno
78. Kickoff moment
79. Food store
80. Author Hunter
81. Kind of fight
82. Game official: Abbr.
83. ___-de-sac
84. Man's ancestor, to Darwin
87. "___ Mir Bist. . ."
88. Always, to Shelley
89. Loop trains
91. Western capital
93. Stylish
94. Fox, in a bois
96. Least restrained
97. First ___
98. Sweet cakes
100. Teen-age problems
101. Knightly combat
102. Take one's
103. Photo of a kind
104. Diminish
105. Deserve
106. Number for a cat's life
107. Dillon
108. Spread
109. Kind of sheet
110. Tryout place for a show
111. Indefinite number
116. Color

144 Winners By Alfio Micci

Top-notchers of Academy Award nights.

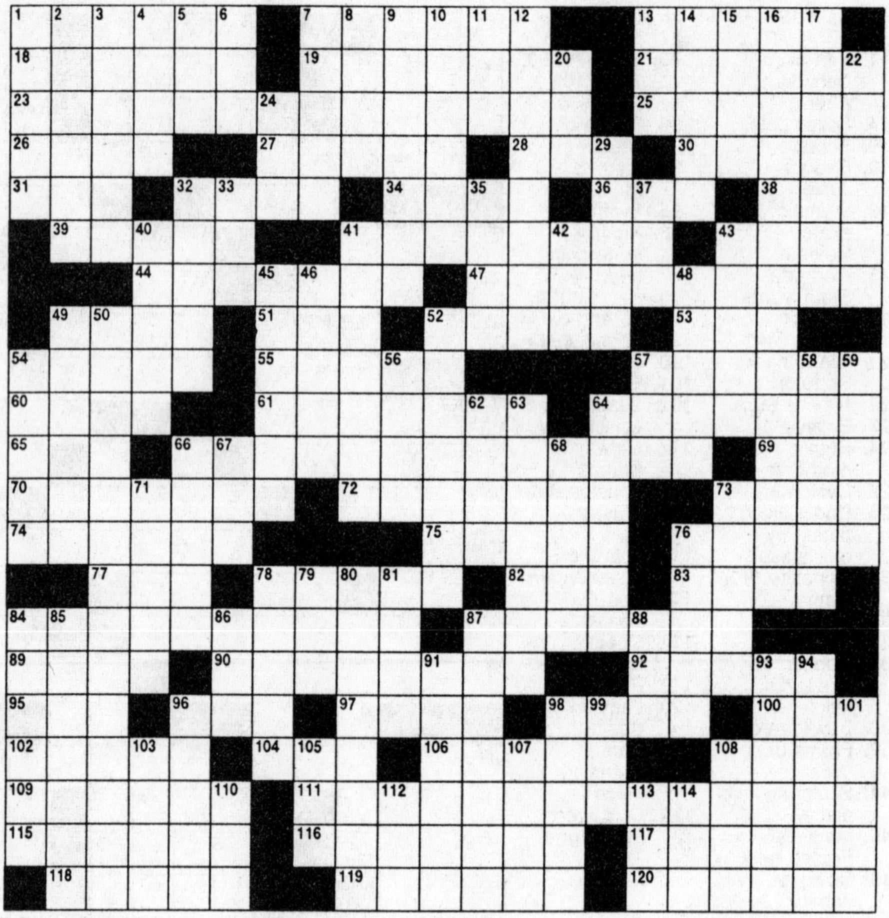

ACROSS

1. Holy
7. Soothe
13. ___ lamb
18. Acting company
19. Madison and Fifth
21. Oil yielders
23. Oscar song of 1943
25. Campus official
26. Bait
27. Book opener
28. Molar: Prefix
30. About
31. Abstract being
32. Heavy cart
34. Ox of the Celebes
36. Scrap for Fido
38. Young sheep
39. ___ tort (legal phrase)
41. Oscar song of 1952
43. Czech river
44. Had a fitting
47. Err
49. Retired
51. Force, in the Forum
52. Racer A. J.'s folks
53. Balloon contents
54. Kind of lace
55. Zinc ___
57. Oscar song of 1975
60. Singing voice
61. Gothic vaulting ribs
64. Sweet girl of song
65. Place
66. Oscar song of 1960
69. Singer Merriman
70. Court handling estates
72. "The Faerie Queene" poet
73. News notice
74. Classic hero
75. Forsake
76. Robe
77. Pouch
78. Quits eating
82. Author Anais
83. Captured personnel, for short
84. Gym apparatus
87. Exalt
89. Brings forth young
90. Oscar song of 1950
92. Usher's milieu
95. Norm: Abbr.
96. Barnyard sound
97. Omar creation
98. Misplaced
100. Kind of chair
102. Put aside
104. Friend of Snow White
106. Use clippers
108. Fictional Jane
109. Principal dancer
111. Oscar song of 1942
115. Begin to perceive
116. One who bequeaths
117. Undergoing change
118. Source of the Blue Nile
119. Razor clams
120. Plummer or Blake

DOWN

1. Way of living
2. In the vicinity
3. Soup or dessert
4. Hold sway
5. Spring mo.
6. Cariou of the stage
7. Old court dance
8. Declare
9. Sure
10. Affixing one's signature
11. Partner of games
12. Small land owners, in England
13. Moon-probe abbr.
14. Do a November job
15. Oscar song of 1958
16. Oscar song of 1939
17. Users of epees
20. Australian game of two-up
22. Where boards are trod
24. Roof adornment
29. Diving birds
32. Verbose
33. Black bird
35. "___ be in England. . .": Browning
37. Hosp. workers
40. Office worker
41. Socks experts
42. Feed-bag tidbit
43. Bay window
45. Develop
46. Land of cotton
48. Like overripe meat
49. Fascinate
50. Oscar song of 1948
52. Flavoring herbs
54. Ecclesiastical robe
56. Mail or lemon
57. Mrs. Cantor
58. Escargots
59. Gossipy woman
62. Menial of yore
63. Girl in a Foster song
64. Of a gland: Prefix
66. Rights gp.
67. French connections
68. Composer Ethelbert
71. Shows pleasure
73. Sioux Indians
76. Banana concoction
78. Johnstown event
79. River of France
80. Takes forcibly
81. Type or vision prefix
84. Used the lab
85. Door knock
86. River of Ethiopia
87. Artistic type
88. Kind of relief
91. Put in a fixture
93. Nonprofessional person
94. Low-level mission
96. Casaba
98. Comic Bert's folks
99. Bobby of hockey fame
101. Celebrated hostess
103. Director Wertmuller
105. Keen-eyed bird
107. Social-science subj.
108. Ending for vend or Henri
110. Bambi's aunt
112. ". . . but ___ on forever"
113. A Hogg
114. Total

145 Personal Menu By Bert Kruse

Stretching an occasional point on how to serve some people.

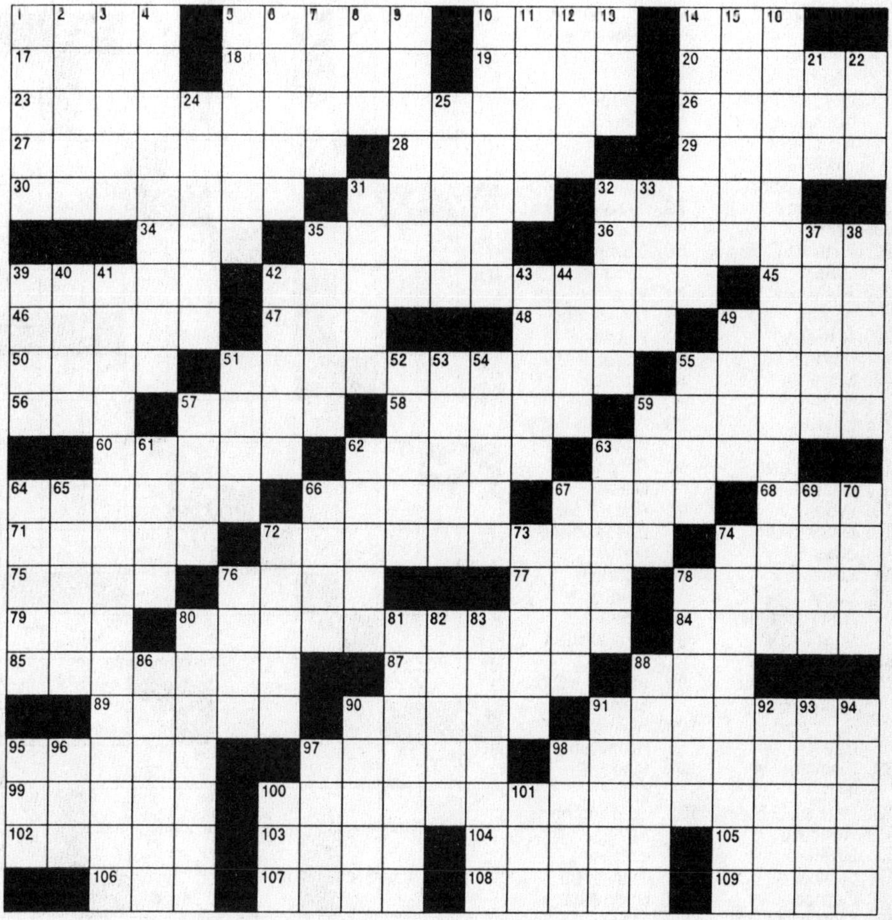

ACROSS

1. Teapot ___
5. Furnish with a hairpiece
10. Swindle
14. Beer source
17. Biblical mountain
18. Former batting champ Tony
19. First miracle site
20. Arab bigwig
23. Dean Martin affairs
26. Coward and Harrison
27. Shaded malls
28. Wows
29. Luca ___ Robbia
30. Dalmatian owners, often
31. Labyrinths
32. West Pointer
34. Religious woman
35. Kind of shower
36. Moslem relative of Lent
39. Not-to-be-missed things
42. Brats, usually
45. ___ *Stoops to Conquer*
46. Pilasters
47. Work unit
48. Grandson of Eve
49. Prepare prunes
50. Heavy hammer
51. One with a big load on
55. French Revolution bather
56. North Pole denizen
57. Bullring cries
58. Mailman's concern
59. Stays in the bridge auction
60. Impostors
62. Pocket accumulations
63. Reacted
64. College course
66. Ankle-length robe
67. Sacred Egyptian bull
68. Turn critical thumbs down
71. Singer Helen
72. Third-degreed prisoner
74. Saarinen
75. Classical villain
76. See the sights
77. Wife of Athamas
78. Suburb of Tucson
79. Place for undeliverable mail: Abbr.
80. Injurious-habit kicker
84. Lazy girl
85. Strive to equal
87. Records
88. Air-wave org.
89. Fictional uncle
90. Presaged
91. Stritch et al.
95. Plan again
97. Violinist Mischa
98. Exaggerated
99. Bordoni or Papas
100. Irate April 15 person
102. Dad, to some Britons
103. Farm vehicle: Abbr.
104. "___ in his right mind . . . !"
105. Actress Garr
106. Grads-to-be
107. Abel's brother
108. Kind of code
109. Ending for stink or switch

DOWN

1. Certain coffee, for short
2. Printing marks
3. Of the cheek
4. Rudimentary
5. Ax lady
6. Like a Lamb
7. Old Algonquin crowd, e.g.
8. Venerable league
9. Hamlin or Judy
10. Kind of triangle
11. ___ belli (war cause)
12. House pests
13. Mates of pas
14. Certain bicycles
15. Protozoan
16. Undressed performers
21. Building part
22. Scottish inst.
24. Muddle
25. Thrush
31. Gnat's relative
32. Earlier
33. Boys
35. Lemur
37. Winning
38. Efts
39. Famed aunt
40. Single
41. Pigged-out diners
42. Harvest goddess
43. Govt. units
44. Kind of bend
49. Elephant boy of films
51. Took a jet
52. Train
53. Of a sound
54. Bizarre
55. N.Y. players
57. "Right on!"
59. Flood beginning
61. Actor Ray
62. Scottish landowner
63. Animal trail
64. Partner of prejudice
65. Domain
66. Exam-question choice
67. Teen problems
69. Solo
70. Twelve
72. Dressmakers' inserts
73. Like the Netherlands
74. Explain
76. Ballet wear
78. Steep declivity
80. Tourists' vehicles
81. Tolerate
82. Sir's counterpart
83. Like some investment funds
86. Horseshoe throw
88. Bends
90. Cote cry
91. Madge or Maurice
92. Drown, in Dijon
93. Cold Spanish month
94. Kind of comedy
95. Celebrated sleeper
96. Age
97. Raison d' ___
98. Western Indian
100. Urban rtes.
101. Buzzing insect

146 Familiar People By Virginia Yates

Or, more likely, getting familiar with them.

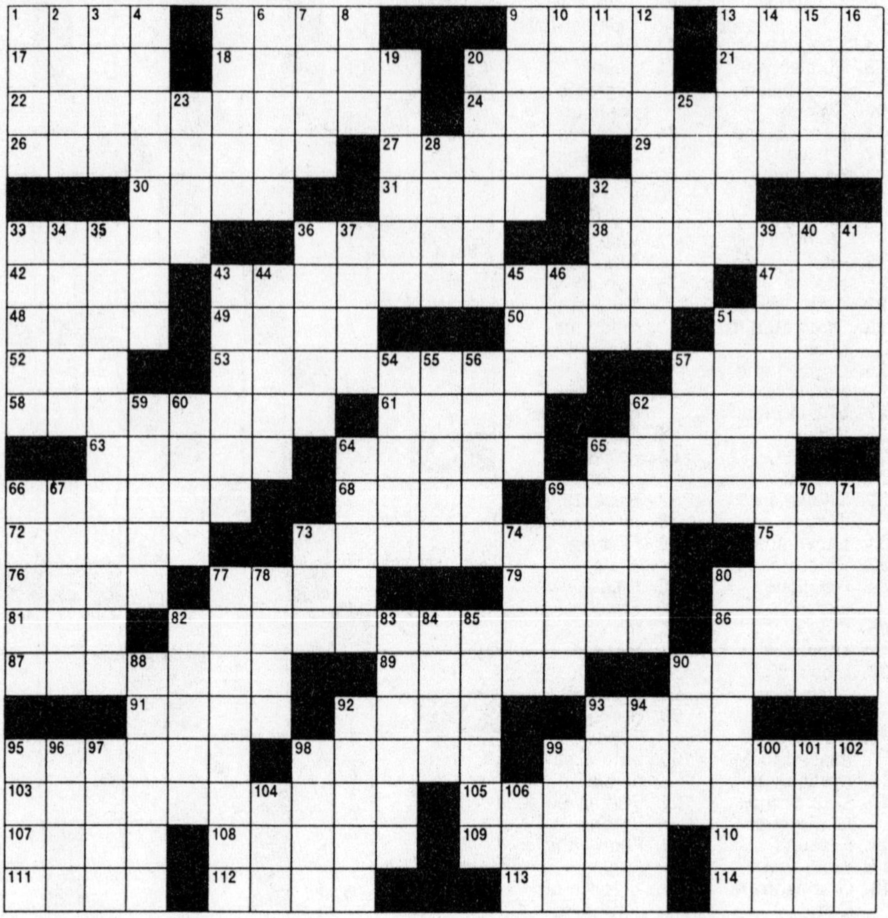

ACROSS

1. Lettuce variety
5. Degree for a boss-to-be
9. Do street work
13. Sail support
17. Bailiwick
18. Tart
20. Firth of Clyde island
21. Prefix for globin
22. A merry Mudd?
24. Martin's memos?
26. Literary excerpts
27. Well-known chorus
29. Woolly
30. Disdainful cries
31. Letters
32. Lady Baltimore or angel food
33. Western lily
36. "They sailed away, for ___ and a day"
38. Coincide in part
42. Part of U.S.A.
43. Reticent Rhett?
47. Lupino or Cantor
48. Kind of barrel
49. N.W. state
50. Tops
51. Ski lift
52. Do wrong
53. Denver and Gielgud standing tall?
57. "Fine!", to Pedro
58. Kops of the silents
61. Samoan capital
62. Spacecraft rockets
63. Expiate
64. Pita fiber
65. Where Valletta is
66. Wicker-work
68. Snaky shape
69. Señora's scarf
72. In a strange way
73. Dailey and Rowen gussied up?
75. ". . . Good News from Ghent to ___"
76. Second-helping seeker's word
77. Kind of deep
79. "Answer yes ___!"
80. Composer Jacques
81. Wrath
82. Mellifluous Bard?
86. Major suffix
87. Marsh marigold
89. "And thereby hangs ___"
90. Steps, in Madrid
91. *Pure Reason* philosopher
92. Harte
93. Spanish painter
95. Robust
98. She's often fatale
99. Flower-shop standbys
103. Skater Hamilton takes the gold?
105. Joel acting up?
107. Cultivate
108. Thin soup
109. Bridge-hand asset
110. Ku Klux ___
111. Sauces for chop suey
112. Kind of log
113. Place in Parliament
114. Parched

DOWN

1. ___ California
2. Tool for Trevino
3. Bartók
4. ___ figure (estimation)
5. Hare's month
6. Burns et al.
7. Wheedles
8. Metric measure
9. Cost, in Thuringia
10. Asian sea
11. Foremost position
12. Subjugates
13. Mouse
14. Money in Mexico
15. Quantities: Abbr.
16. Pete or Billy
19. Cheeky
20. Word modifier
23. Affirmatives
25. L.A. cager
28. Way to have one's Scotch
32. Feet, at times
33. *R.U.R.* dramatist
34. Love, in Italy
35. Lighthearted prince?
36. Coeur d'___
37. Thug
39. Buchwald and Garfunkel acting generously?
40. Bell city
41. One of the Cyclades
43. "___ Oo Long"
44. Perfume additive
45. Radii's neighbors
46. "Whether ___ nobler in the mind . . ."
51. Everybody, in music
54. Actor Robards
55. Of the eye
56. Like Rome or S.F.
57. Sun or Bible
59. Steps on the farm
60. Randall of films
62. Kidnapper's demand
64. "___ give you anything but. . ."
65. Divine aid
66. Mostel or Silvers, e.g.
67. To worship: Lat.
69. One of the Osmonds
70. Be stationary, asea
71. Wheel parts
73. "For shame!"
74. Pretty child
77. Makes a side trip
78. Retained
80. Social rebels of the 50s
82. Bias
83. Cordiality
84. Agenda unit
85. Most up-to-date
88. Toasts
90. Math chore: Abbr.
92. Midler
93. Writer Lagerlöf
94. Land of Ra
95. Some milit. men
96. Threesome
97. Depend
98. April 1 V.I.P.
99. Downcast
100. *Winnie ___ Pu*
101. Winglike
102. Auld lang ___
104. French vineyard
106. Tax agcy.

147 Substitutions By Dan Girardi

Just to give a slightly different slant on things.

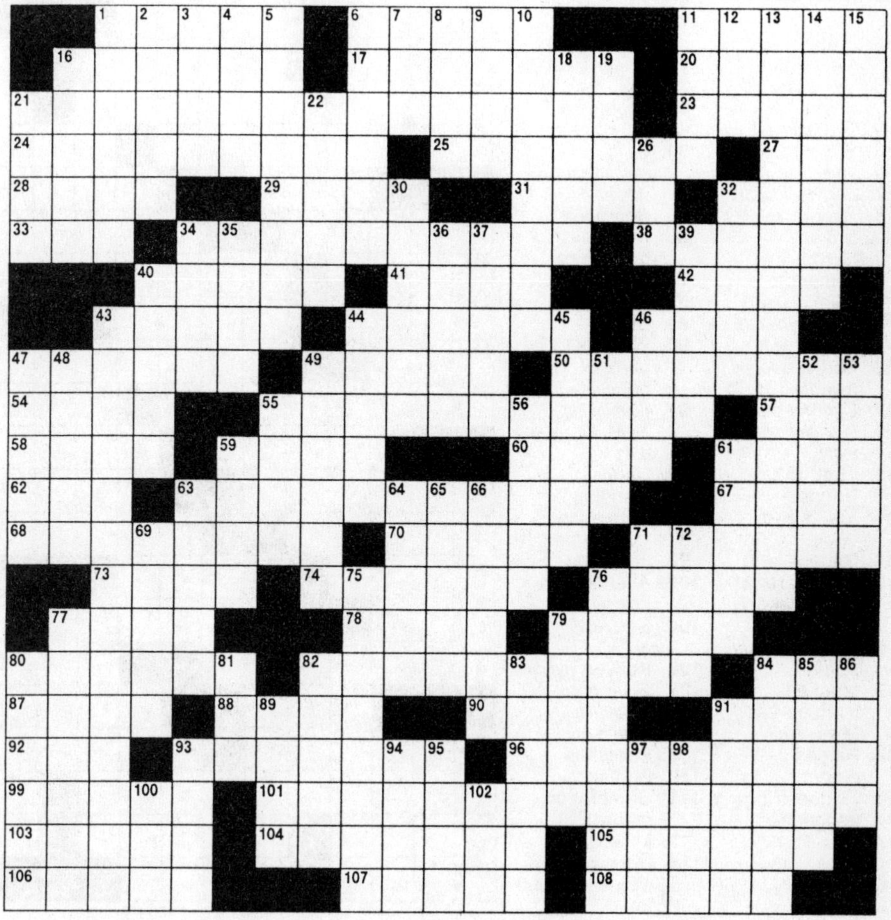

ACROSS

1. Amati's relative
6. French Impressionist
11. Anguished feelings
16. Skirt's topper
17. Neighbor of San Francisco
20. White poplar
21. Alternate for a Miller drama
23. Evildoer
24. Butt in
25. Mechanical levers
27. Grid scores
28. Memorable Will of TV
29. Put to flight
31. Of the dawn
32. Relinquish
33. City ways: Abbr.
34. Alternate for a drug
38. Like some roads
40. ___ system
41. Mae or Wild
42. Enter
43. Stone chip
44. Philippine carriage
46. Mideast nation
47. Writer's device
49. Hearth gods
50. ___ apple cart
54. Assert
55. Alternate for a Maugham novel
57. Barnyard denizen
58. Erudition
59. River to the Aisne
60. DeValera's land
61. Cozy place
62. "Ich bin ___ Berliner": J.F.K.
63. Alternate for a Philadelphia landmark
67. Old tongue
68. Deep
70. Curtain material
71. Twain boy
73. Standard
74. Liquid part of fat
76. Short story
77. E.R.A., e.g.
78. Once, formerly
79. Puts on an unhappy face
80. Composer Gustav
82. Alternate for a paschal symbol
84. Three, in Turin
87. Summer quaffs
88. Not give ___
90. Where the bigwigs sit
91. Boast
92. Leader: Abbr.
93. Social rank
96. Churchill's *The ___ Storm*
99. Came up
101. Alternate for a children's rhyme
103. Archie of ring fame
104. Cather's *My ___*
105. Gun, to a hood
106. Finally, to Renée
107. Zoo animal
108. Dutch painter

DOWN

1. Schedules
2. Safari member
3. German valley
4. ___ now (from here on)
5. Postponement
6. Concocted
7. Pre-marriage monogram for a 1906 White House bride
8. Suffix for astro
9. Jane Austen novel
10. Teapot tumults
11. Stay out of the bidding
12. Org. for attorneys
13. Alternate for a Salinger novel
14. Elate
15. Had a feeling
16. *The Devil and Daniel Webster* poet
18. Amtrak stop
19. Zone
21. Pad for a hippie
22. Bellowing
26. Dynamite initials
30. Frustrate
32. Central European
34. Climb
35. She, in France
36. Strikes out
37. ___ hammer (does carpentry)
39. Jibe
40. Steeple
43. Alternate for a Mostel musical
44. Minded
45. Of hearing
46. Man or Wight
47. Orchid meal
48. Have, in Le Havre
49. City on the Rio Grande
51. Brit. legislative body
52. *Steppenwolf* author
53. Join
55. Chinese heaven
56. Pro-football coach Greasy
59. Cuckoopint
61. Salamanders
63. Strong point
64. Calls on the rifle range
65. Like a good cake
66. Intimated
69. Dams' offspring
71. Tart
72. Part of A.M.
75. Enter enthusiastically
76. Scotch-and-soda supporters
77. Grandma's presser
79. Small bottle
80. Lady of the house
81. Kind of race
82. Ingested
83. Like Coxey's Army
84. Zodiac division
85. Indian queen
86. Cake ingredients
89. Pro ___
91. Support
93. Spotted
94. Swan genus
95. Historic vessel
97. Razz
98. Actual being
100. ___ Lanka
102. Kind of horn

148 Singsong By Jack Steinhardt

A matter of putting appropriate words together.

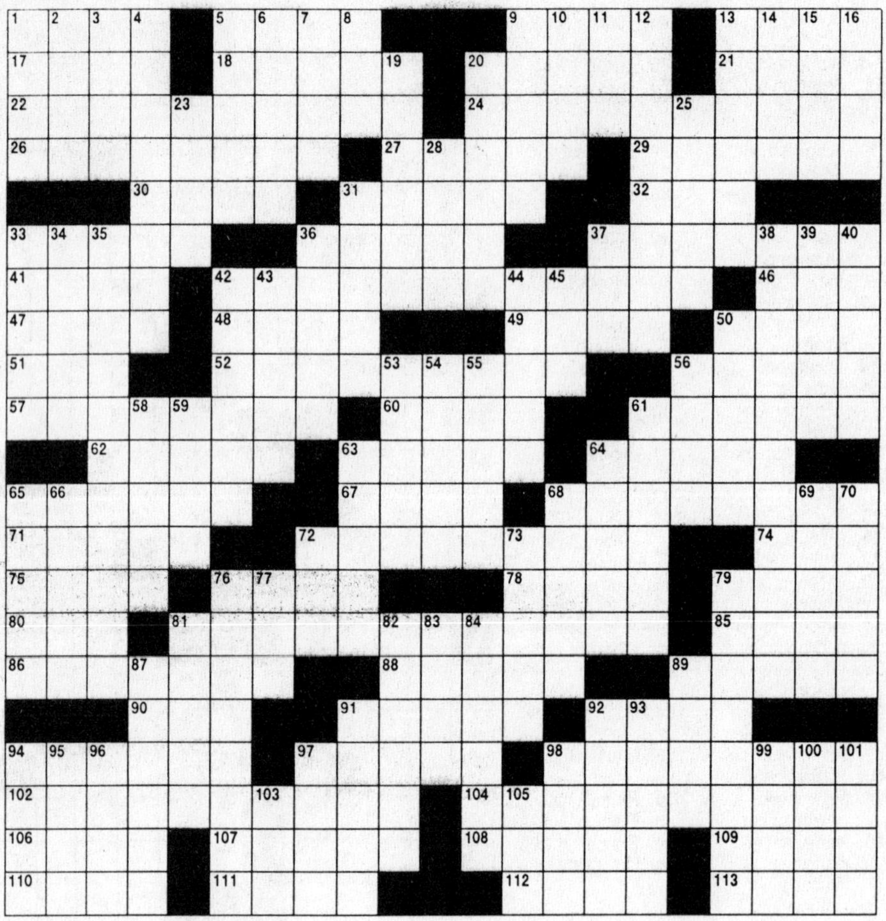

ACROSS

1. French clergyman
5. Early church desk
9. Dispatched
13. Provençal love song
17. Lady's escort
18. Hirsute
20. Snap
21. Luzon volcano
22. Queue dish
24. Top-level recruitment
26. Perceptively aware
27. Circumspect
29. Narrow sea arms
30. That, to Brutus
31. King-sized deer
32. Danube port
33. Discoverer of the American mainland
36. Revolutionary patriot
37. Mocked
41. Heroine for Miss Buck
42. Ridged planet
46. Goddess of vengeance
47. ___ libre (free verse)
48. Spikes of grain
49. Out
50. Terrible-sounding container
51. Fail to touch base
52. Eyeball
56. Actress Hope
57. Without faltering
60. Part of R & R
61. Up-tight
62. Gaudy lamps
63. Concoctions
64. Thrifty person
65. Danish city
67. Dashiell's dog
68. West
71. Midwest church sect
72. Insect power
74. Ending for cash or bombard
75. Pitches
76. Revenue agt.
78. Pointer Sisters, e.g.
79. Shah Jahan's city
80. Japanese board game
81. Hold on architectural décor
85. Begrudge
86. Kind of heating or intelligence
88. Smirks
89. Burros
90. Word before peck or house
91. Site of a 1521 German diet
92. Under-standing
94. Cuts short
97. Horned beast
98. Leverage
102. Abandons chigoes
104. Converts gulls
106. Kenyan river
107. Tidal bore
108. Sister to Thalia
109. Stretched
110. Booted
111. Gambrel or mansard
112. Miss Cannon
113. Relatives of dynes

DOWN

1. Ligurian and Bernese
2. Pigment clay
3. Fiber food
4. Book printings
5. Fencing stroke
6. Author A. A.
7. Cry of a calf
8. Type of grass or cake
9. Talia of the cinema
10. Sluggish
11. Old English letter
12. In a pitiful way
13. In
14. Haunt
15. Avon denizen
16. Porters' relatives
19. Backlash
20. Synchronized
23. Joust
25. Offended
28. Sharpen
31. Mallow or marigold
33. Shoreline recesses
34. Attentive
35. Childless peer
36. Bess's love
37. Angelico or Diavolo
38. Claude prevails
39. Floor, in Menton
40. Excised
42. ". . . how shall ___ to her . . . ?": Swinburne
43. Accosts
44. English hymnist: 1674–1748
45. Be obliged
50. Feathered, as an arrow
53. Assignation
54. Lucky number in Lucca
55. Bandleader Jones
56. Son of Leah
58. Endless times
59. Copperfield miss
61. Tic-___
63. West German port
64. Split: Prefix
65. Prophetlike
66. Candidate's concern
68. Mean creatures
69. Temerity
70. Servers
72. Marsh or Busch
73. Anatomical passages
76. Hand over
77. Wire measure
79. Dilettante
81. Border designs
82. Plaza girl
83. House plant
84. Outside broadcast
87. Filament
89. Aud.
91. Pier
92. ___ Gorda or Arenas
93. Flaming felony
94. P.M.s
95. Nonsense
96. She could turn anything into wine
97. ___ Park in Queens, N.Y.C.
98. Implore
99. Sandarac tree
100. Fitting closely
101. Approxi-mations: Abbr.
103. Thai language
105. Scandinavian giantess

149 Another Language By Frances Hansen

How grandmother, or great-great grandmother, would be groovy.

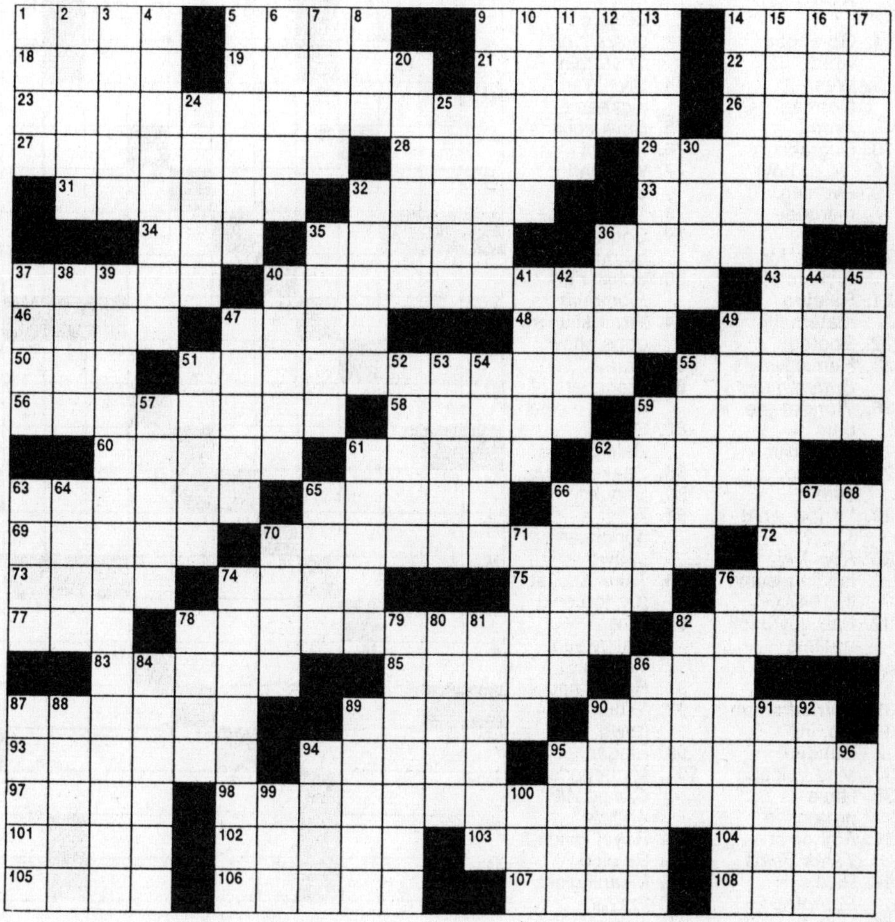

ACROSS

1. Wet blanket
5. Dumb girl
9. Circa
14. Mining nail
18. Cleveland's lake
19. "___ My Souvenirs"
21. Greet, in a way
22. Wild water buffalo
23. Bewildered first man, in old lingo
26. Chain unit
27. Even-steven pairing
28. Pile up
29. Ballerina Markova
31. Surly-sounding fish
32. Odorous-sounding fish
33. Canada goose or traffic hog
34. Cartoonist Gardner
35. Marianne or Mary Tyler
36. This has a fragrant oda
37. Westminster, for one
40. Old words for strong ale
43. Bad ___, German spa
46. Scout's good thing
47. Withered
48. Plug for an Irish county
49. Neighbor of Minn.
50. Ailing
51. Licentious men of yore
55. Title for Macbeth
56. One of Rome's hills
58. Actor Jack of gangster roles
59. Prompter's activity
60. Europe's Boot
61. Coin that sounds like a cafe-car
62. Wise-sounding gannet
63. Argue
65. ___ noster (Lord's Prayer words)
66. Sliver of wood
69. Soap plant
70. Cuff on the ear, old style
72. Seine sight
73. Fork part
74. Spring from the slammer, with "out"
75. Off ___ (light-switch choice)
76. Trotsky or Uris
77. Consumed
78. Food, in days of old
82. W.W. II riveter of song
83. Summer ermine
85. Trite
86. Presidential nickname
87. Martin ___
89. Twin crystal
90. Left the dock
93. "Do unto ___ . . ."
94. Abram's wife
95. Italo-Swiss alps
97. Architect ___ van der Rohe
98. Cackling blockhead of the past
101. Medicinal herb
102. Kills time
103. Twangy
104. Trieste wine measure
105. "Man bites dog," e.g.
106. ___ home (out)
107. Unit of force
108. Chaucer or Frost

DOWN

1. Gourd or melon
2. Annoying
3. One cubic decimeter
4. Spoke
5. Western Indian
6. Shadows of coming events
7. Mechanical repetition
8. Industrious insect
9. Cost an arm ___ (come high)
10. Brag
11. O.T.B. concern
12. Actress Hagen
13. Crazy Horse wielded one
14. Salty
15. Finicky dressers, once
16. The "Tomorrow" girl
17. Senegalese port
20. Show-biz allure: Var.
24. Bee product
25. Manicurist's kind of board
30. "I am a lone ___ creetur . . .": Dickens
32. *The Red and the Black* hero
35. Hollywood's Oberon
36. ___ d'oeuvre
37. Take ___ (swim)
38. Lugosi
39. Beautiful girl's servant, formerly
40. "Eeny, ___, miney . . ."
41. Happen
42. Okey-___ (uh-huh)
44. *The Magic Mountain* author
45. Keel extension
47. It's your umbrella, in song
49. Gallagher's vaudeville partner
51. Aver
52. Narrow apertures
53. Impressionist Edouard
54. "___ Ben Jonson"
55. What you wore, in song
57. ___ *of Two Cities*
59. Punctuation mark
61. Every morning
62. Animal's track
63. Computer input
64. Give forth
65. Mr. Silvers
66. Binge
67. Patron saint of artists
68. Coty or Descartes
70. Disney or Whitman
71. California white oak
74. Tall fur hat for parade uniform
76. Shirley's "good ship"
78. Afrikaner
79. Adherent of Russian royalty
80. "Talent does what ___": Meredith
81. Disparage
82. Day to save for
84. Last-term papers
86. Taper
87. Miller's salesman Willie
88. Practical
89. ". . . only God can ___ tree"
90. Car style
91. January in Júarez
92. Diplomat Silas of Colonial days
94. Attic wit
95. Small bouquet
96. Three-handed card game
99. Tokyo, formerly
100. Owned

150 Second Choices By Louis Baron

Subtitles of sorts for literary entries.

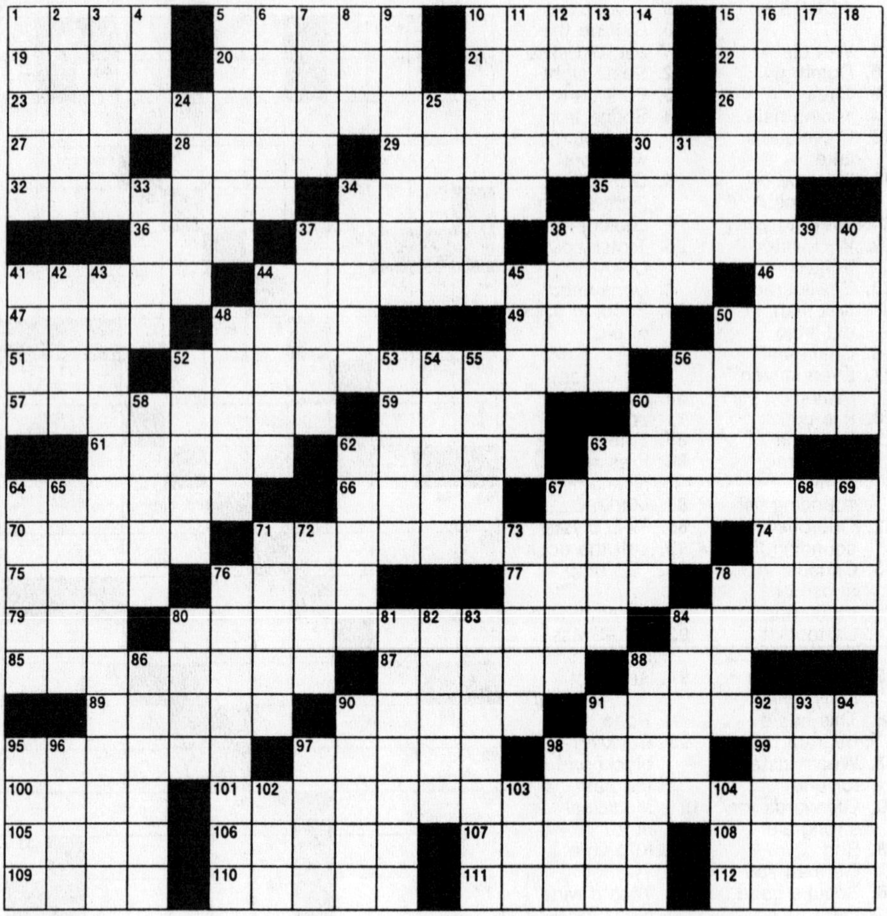

ACROSS

1. Go-ahead word
5. West German river
10. Degrade
15. "___ boy!"
19. Evening, marquee style
20. Swift's Mr. Bickerstaff
21. Related maternally
22. Booted
23. Hemingway's *Butterfingers*
26. Work at the bar
27. Have bills
28. "Cogito, ___ sum"
29. "Know what ___?"
30. *Kon-Tiki* landing island in 1947
32. Bad guy Jack of films
34. Say rashly, with "out"
35. Berried shrub
36. Go, in Dundee
37. Mud volcano
38. Gave protection
41. Author of *Taras Bulba*
44. Rice's *Potholes*
46. Hell, to Sherman
47. "___ my word!"
48. Adriatic port
49. Covers
50. Bit
51. Jose or Antonio
52. Caldwell's *First Puff*
56. U.S.N. women
57. "One for ___"
59. Working group
60. Cooks' tools
61. Dilute
62. Climbers' problems
63. For the ___ (useless)
64. Made parallel
66. Gland parts
67. Bach works
70. Biblical juniper
71. Meyer Levin's *Grapes of Yesterday*
74. Civil War nickname
75. Bowl sounds
76. Litigant
77. Word after dies
78. Surplus
79. Corot's output
80. Schiller's *Bigmouth*
84. What snarling dogs show
85. Safe
87. Preceders of nuits
88. Solti or Raleigh title
89. Snake genus
90. Shocks
91. What a nondieter shows
95. Take ___ at (try to conk)
97. Like Halloween visitors
98. Rough nap
99. "Thumbs down"
100. Elegant
101. Michener's *Calling All Angels*
105. Royal Hindu
106. Rejoice
107. Meaningless
108. Prayer sign-off
109. Norse poetry
110. Twofold, to a Spaniard
111. Grades
112. Yucatán native

DOWN

1. Champ's status
2. Plains Indian
3. Tamarisk tree
4. "Thumbs up"
5. Savage
6. Application
7. Wool: Prefix
8. Famed bill-payer
9. ___ *Lauro*, hijacked Italian liner
10. Young hare
11. ___ a time
12. When, to Heine
13. Ike's front
14. Rehabilitates
15. Starry
16. Arnold Bennett's *Stay Single!*
17. Singer Tennille
18. Egyptian lizard
24. Bribable
25. Keep cheerful
31. Sheltered, at sea
33. Dramatic conflict
34. Of atmospheric pressure
35. Chicago aquarium
37. Dogie, for one
38. Shadow: Prefix
39. Lotus ___ (dreamy one)
40. Kind of circle
41. Outburst
42. Large ocean fish
43. Mitchell's *Dandelion*
44. Fencing weapon
45. Vegas openings
48. Filleted
50. Word before Gras
52. Tribal symbol
53. Objet d'art
54. ___ fours
55. Uncompromising
56. Fort near Dallas
58. Lions' features
60. Famed pig-maker
62. Darling, Paris style
63. Common-place
64. Pianist Claudio
65. Absorb, in one way
67. Knitting stitches
68. Be contiguous
69. Abel's younger brother
71. Bulrushes
72. Controlled
73. Catafalques
76. Showed an affected smile
78. Nucleus
80. Shawl
81. Fertility goddess
82. Be sorrowful
83. Appealing Dickensian
84. Upstate New York county
86. Pianist de Larrocha
88. Goggles
90. Racing boat
91. ___ of the evening
92. Soul
93. Jones or Stengel
94. Scavenger with a bad press
95. Land section
96. Roe yielder
97. Suffer a toe mishap
98. Work out in the ring
102. Outer: Prefix
103. Stop ___ dime
104. Equine mother

151 On High By Mary Murdoch

Scanning the ether via various vehicles.

ACROSS

1. Carry's partner
5. Jeweler's weight
10. Ruin's partner
14. Herr's partner
18. Italian instrument
19. Declares
20. Concerning
21. Botches
22. ___ of Avon
23. ___ ray
24. Pintado fish
25. Grow dark
26. Broadway musical of 1942
28. Theodore Morse–Edward Madden song
30. Propels a gondola
31. Loose soil
32. School subj.
33. Sought diamonds
37. Bother
38. Word before haste
40. Cowbell accompaniment
43. Broadway musical of 1943
49. Long
51. Other, in Spain
52. Necktie for a rustler
53. Rear
54. *Pinta*'s fellow traveler
55. Old autos
56. Siren, e.g.
57. Drums' accompanists
59. Charlotte and Norma
60. Photog's abbr.
61. Raincoats
62. Grassland
63. Bill's partner
65. Jerome Kern hit song
73. Marriage or driver's cert.
74. ___ Claire
75. Table d'___
76. ___ and Abner
78. Israel's Eban
81. Pursue
84. Parade unit
86. Be up to
87. Author Stoker
88. Seagoing inits.
89. Counting devices
90. Kind of kiln
91. Capital of Morocco
93. Phrase that inspired a 1943 film
97. Freshwater fish
98. Certain climber
100. Actress Mary
101. Bewildered
102. Part of A.B.A.
103. Frog genus
105. Draw ___ on (aim)
109. Halley's, Kohoutek, and all
112. Victor Herbert song
116. Shade for hosiery
117. Over
118. Decorate
119. *Stardust* ___ (Hoagy Carmichael autobiography)
121. Kind of days
122. ___ time (never)
123. Newspaper pieces
124. ___ Hari
125. *East of Eden* son
126. Sit
127. Ex-Yankee Roger
128. Part of 98 Across

DOWN

1. Engineer's place
2. Certain steed
3. Agile
4. Meccan pilgrimage
5. South American plain
6. Be of service
7. French income
8. Comedian Johnson et al.
9. Autocrat
10. Small filled pastry
11. One of the Santas
12. Namby-pamby person
13. Deborah or Jean
14. Painter James Montgomery
15. Actress Gordon
16. Aid, in a way
17. Service initials
21. Obdurate
27. Hair style
29. Bandman Brown
31. Miss Ullmann
33. Roger or Dudley
34. Purpose
35. Perfume ingredient
36. Greek letters
37. Southwest wind
39. Italian innkeeper
40. Mother of Hermes
41. Caen's river
42. Miss Munson and others
44. Open
45. Place to lounge
46. One of the latitudes
47. Full of: Suffix
48. Water nymph
50. Sign up
57. Pot-au-___
58. Highlands pet
61. Roman 1051
62. "Skip to my ___"
64. Olsen or Bull
66. Andes denizen
67. Spread perfume
68. *A Shropshire* ___
69. Young hog
70. Producer Hal
71. Flourishes
72. Up-and-coming one of the 80s
77. Hostess Perle
78. Dugout
79. Nail
80. Nickname for a Sultan
82. On the ___ (feuding)
83. Certain seater
84. Songstress Alice
85. Wts.
86. Tab
92. Delineated
94. Solar sight
95. Asian monkey
96. Do a longshore job
99. Rio de ___
102. Started the beguine
104. Make up for
105. Body trunk
106. Corn pest
107. As a friend: Fr.
108. Immeasurable space
109. Speed
110. Place to play a uke
111. Term of address
112. Impair
113. Subject for Virgil
114. Castle feature
115. Surfeit
116. Youth grp.
120. Aswan sight

152 Communicating By Olga Kowals

Getting things across in one way or another.

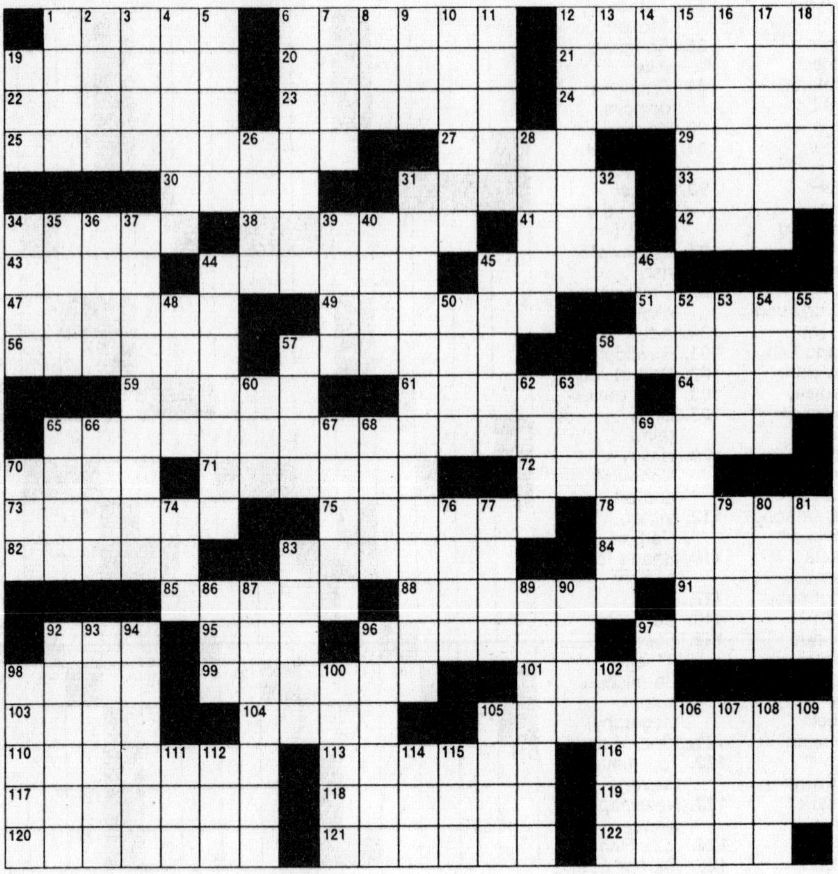

ACROSS

1. Fauna's predecessor
6. Presides
12. Garrulous one
19. Pencil-box item
20. Become callous
21. Cross-country runner
22. Cuddle up
23. Fleet
24. Enrage
25. Cozy confab
27. Trajectories
29. Excited
30. Day before: Abbr.
31. Brews
33. Leaves: Abbr.
34. Mine passages
38. Poncho's relative
41. "I'd lay me doun and ____"
42. Draft initials
43. Soprano Petina
44. Convict's quest
45. Opening segment
47. "Indeed!"
49. Infant attire
51. Like the rock of ages
56. ____ swim (desperate choice)
57. Lab vessel
58. Cindery lava
59. Nest on a tor
61. City on the Douro
64. El ____, Egyptian oasis village
65. Manipulate a puppet
70. Coordinate
71. Argentine measure
72. Met offering
73. Having branches
75. Passageways
78. Time period
82. Point of view
83. Fate
84. Stage speeches, O'Neill style
85. Stumper
88. "Rome wasn't built ____"
91. Bath powder
92. W.W. II command
95. Spring mo.
96. Becomes one
97. Aleppo's country
98. At a specific time
99. Heraldic strip
101. Tilt
103. "Is ____ so?"
104. Psychic gifts: Abbr.
105. Blarney Stone's offering
110. Kind of football pass
113. Salivating-dog physiologist
116. Narcotic
117. "____ all?" (no exceptions)
118. Relative by marriage
119. Yearned
120. Fisherman, at times
121. More wanton
122. ____ *a Man*

DOWN

1. ____-for-all
2. Like a Paris tango
3. Bone: Prefix
4. Team races
5. Mountain ridge
6. Chipmunk language
7. Tortoise competitor
8. Chair part
9. Mount of Crete
10. Set a new time
11. Kind of drum
12. Talk secretively
13. Fleming
14. Successor to the A.E.C.
15. Apprehensions
16. Toots
17. ____ *Fables*
18. Peck and Ratoff, for short
19. Inner: Prefix
26. She, in Italy
28. Closet wood
31. Be forthright
32. Inflict a bridge loss
34. They're sometimes put on
35. German three
36. Ayatollah's land
37. Filibuster
39. Enjoyed Rotten Row
40. Inter ____
44. Coal-tar product
45. Prominent Argentine
46. RR watchdog
48. Early film-chain name
50. Gourd-family member
52. Glibness
53. Common Latin verb
54. What to do in troubled waters
55. Feathers' partner
57. Flower and hot
58. "____ My Prince Will Come"
60. Retirement acct.
62. Vintage cars
63. Recipe amt.
65. Bell or laughter sound
66. West Point, for short
67. Case, way or well
68. Spring bloom
69. Mines' contents
70. Relative of Sra.
74. Halt: Abbr.
76. ____-Lenape (Delaware Indian)
77. French state
79. Jewish month
80. Pastrami emporium
81. Bait, to an Italian
83. Sidewalk edges, in London
86. Row
87. Pitchman
89. What to do to the goods
90. "____ I cared" (not interested)
92. Musical key
93. Precisely
94. "____ bridesmaid but . . ."
96. Open to danger
97. ____ a dime
98. Geographic volume
100. Dismay
102. Did shoplifting
105. "____ but not forgotten"
106. Unearth
107. Batty
108. Sweetsop
109. Water or river
111. British mil. unit
112. Reverence
114. Org. for ex-soldiers
115. Skimmer

153 Wild Life By Gary Schmunk

Most of it on the not-too-feral side.

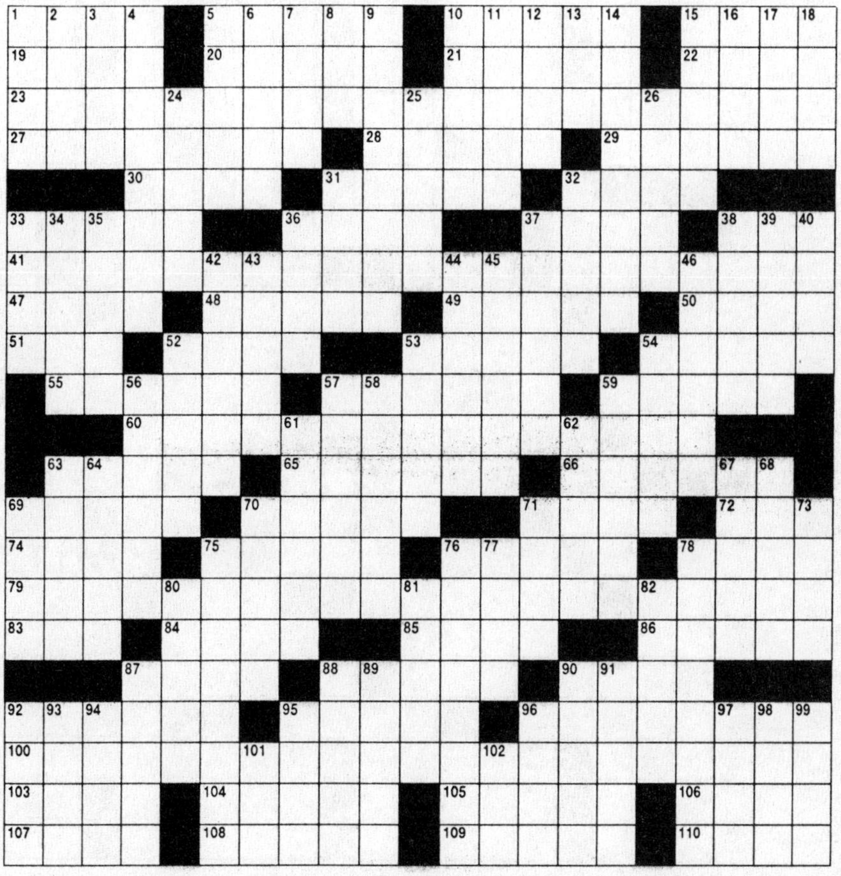

ACROSS

1. Wingspread
5. Join Mr. Chips
10. Cake ingredient
15. Big Ben sound
19. Church calendar
20. Follow
21. Liquid measure, in Britain
22. Medicinal plant
23. Asks for trouble
27. Balanced proportions
28. Stirs
29. Isolate
30. Wings
31. Corundum
32. First king of Israel
33. Recommended daily fare
36. Actor James
37. O–T connection
38. Critic Huxtable
41. Outdo
47. Carousal
48. Religious-cloth container
49. Strange
50. Wading bird
51. Peruke
52. Columbus' ships, e.g.
53. Speak off-the-cuff
54. Fern seed
55. "Why, bless ___!"
57. Eyesight
59. Vestibule
60. One-time children's TV show
63. Hallowed
65. Balancing devices
66. Glass bottles
69. Item
70. "What else ___?"
71. Rat-___
72. Chafe
74. Wheel shaft
75. Scrutinizes
76. Home of some mustard
78. Astronaut Sally
79. Blabs
83. Wiggs or Miniver
84. River through Leeds
85. Fasten, in Glasgow
86. Oasts
87. Mont Blanc et al.
88. Catches fly balls
90. Quote
92. Circus
95. Overcharge
96. Songstress Flack et al.
100. Way to travel, from a seasonal song
103. Beat or stick beginning
104. Garments
105. Push gently
106. Pianist Peter
107. Moray and conger
108. Like a porcupine
109. Lear's runcible utensil
110. Attract

DOWN

1. Weeps
2. Rabbit, to a fox
3. Cain's father
4. As a rule
5. Seed coat
6. ___ nous
7. Colorless
8. Prompt
9. Eve was one
10. Flabbergast
11. Jitterbug relative
12. American patriot
13. Vase
14. Go through one's lines
15. Minty herb
16. Automobile name
17. Carol
18. Mr. Autry
24. Removed
25. A Castle
26. Occupied
31. Diner sign
32. Short news piece
33. Take ___ (react to applause)
34. Jewish holiday
35. Kind of bank
36. Mackerel's relative
37. Reading studiously
38. Garden spot
39. Kind of farm
40. Vaulted alcove
42. Brusque
43. Constructed
44. Phone again
45. Cantaloupes
46. Go through the tulips
52. Drink to
53. Crooked
54. Schnozzle
56. Public spats
57. Schnitzel's home
58. Put money in
59. Wandering
61. Region of France
62. ___ God (natural occurrence)
63. Dog breed
64. Spirited tunes
67. Mohawks' group
68. Khartoum is its capital
69. One of the Sundays
70. Wine coolers
71. Do ___ on (swindle)
73. Panhandles
75. Cargo dealers
76. Castle keeps
77. "___ an ancient mariner . . ."
78. Clergyman's title
80. Eagle claw
81. Missouri River feeder
82. Ritz or Waldorf-Astoria
87. Minute particles
88. Writer Kierkegaard
89. Brazen girl
90. Major African river
91. Creator of Nora and Hedda
92. ___ one's time
93. Concerning
94. Caesar's conquest
95. Mongolian desert
96. Decorate again
97. Stadium unit
98. Indian city
99. Display
101. ___, skip and jump
102. Young dog

154 Sound-Alikes By Reginald Johnson

Making two words merge phonetically into one.

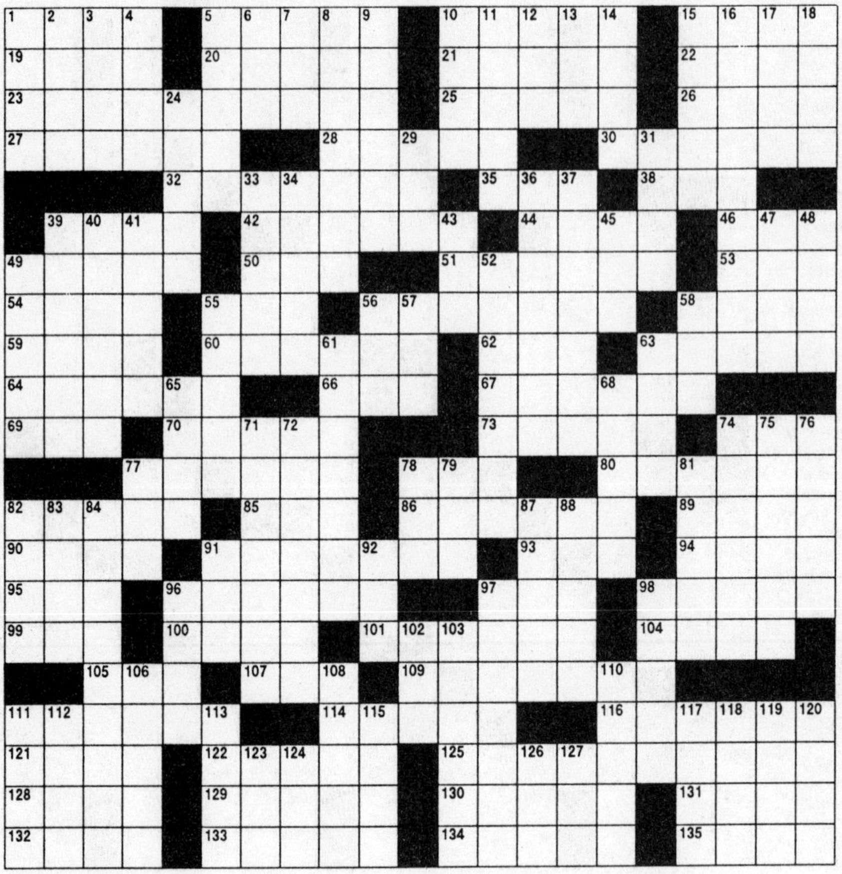

ACROSS

1. One of the tenses
5. Fireplace leaving
10. Zeno follower
15. Semiprecious stone
19. "A foolish thing was but ___": Shak.
20. ___ de Poitiers, French duchess
21. Bingo's relative
22. Highway part
23. Brings together?
25. Come out ___ (win)
26. This, in Cuba
27. Bad temper
28. Rent again
30. Blackboard need
32. Decree?
35. Food morsel
38. French article
39. Look at quickly
42. Eye inflammation
44. Periods
46. Wedding-notice word
49. Humdingers
50. One of a hundred: Abbr.
51. Rent payer
53. "You may talk o' ___ an' beer"
54. "I met ___ with . . ."
55. Red or Black
56. Kind to animals?
58. Relating to aircraft
59. Tease
60. Erie, e.g.
62. Mischievous child
63. Lots of land
64. Fooled around
66. Unit of conductance
67. Vacation place
69. Compass point
70. Necklace part
73. Skillful
74. Farmyard sound
77. Loyal obligation?
78. Tennis or bridge word
80. Chemical substances
82. Symbols of office
85. Ethiopian title
86. More humble
89. Acclaimed one
90. Where they learn cricket
91. Thing often seconded?
93. Neighbor of Ga.
94. Where it all began
95. Sawyer or Thumb
96. Coins in Bombay
97. Troy coll.
98. Travel way
99. Elec. unit
100. Wimbledon winner
101. No-nos
104. Robert ___
105. Assn.
107. Football meas.
109. Large lab vessels
111. Bride's wardrobe?
114. Early Mexican
116. Loads
121. Tops
122. Make cloth
125. Toll road?
128. Caps
129. Puts on cargo
130. Legal document
131. Advantage
132. Otherwise
133. Head follower
134. Kefauver
135. Painter Bonheur

DOWN

1. Meets an obligation
2. Above
3. Kind of searching
4. Small child
5. Town near Minneapolis
6. Soviet fighter plane
7. Scrooge word
8. Board the Amtrak
9. Express annoyance
10. Blackthorn
11. Lone Ranger's pal
12. Polo Grounds star
13. Japanese statesman
14. Be a match for
15. Upstate N.Y. city
16. Backseat occupant
17. Price of admission
18. Shake-spearean king
24. Signs
29. Neckwear in Oahu
31. Reddish brown
33. In the air
34. Fear
36. Changed the title
37. Walk about idly
39. Unspecified person?
40. Actress Ina
41. ". . . and his cousins and his ___"
43. French holy woman: Abbr.
45. Mass. cape
47. Leprechaun land
48. Baseball's Slaughter
49. Shaping tool
52. Arabian jurisdiction
55. Move stealthily
56. Cry of satisfaction
57. One, to Juan
58. Moss Hart's One
61. Deadlock
63. Beaux-___
65. Old French coins
68. Kind of hat or house
71. Wasting-away process
72. Kelp
74. Form morning dampness?
75. Stopped, in France
76. In unison
77. Lair
78. Dallas coll.
79. After sundown, to poets
81. Relig. study
82. Kind of physician
83. Mighty mite
84. Mixtures
87. Padding material
88. Beethoven's "Für ___"
91. Greek letters
92. Winner over T.E.D.
96. Alger hero's early wear
97. Kitchen pests
98. Seed again
102. Approx-imately: Abbr.
103. Kind of brow
106. Dodger Pee Wee
108. Frugal person
110. Poet laureate (1715) and family
111. Story
112. Make muddy
113. Wise ones
115. Spice
117. Stag
118. Venetian resort
119. Cake ingredients
120. Mets' stadium
123. Gobble
124. Ohio college town
126. Inform on pals
127. Sailing course

155 On the Offensive By Robert Wolfe

And wielding appropriate weapons on the way.

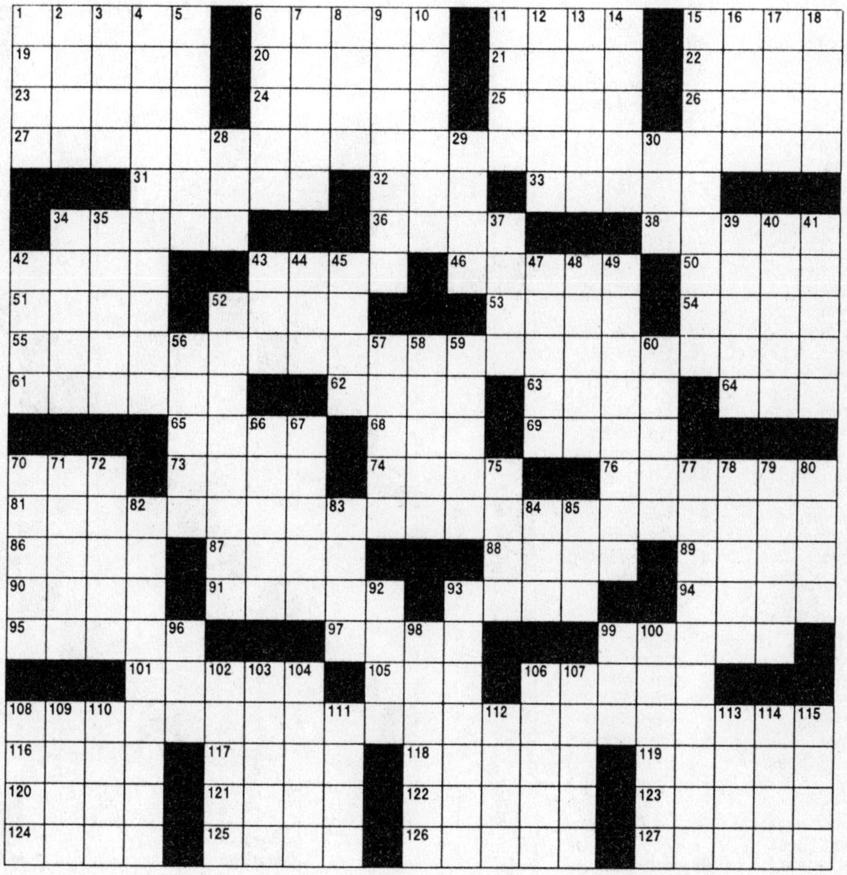

ACROSS

1. Mops
6. Gather
11. Nile bird
15. Actor Cronyn
19. Paia porch
20. Thread: Prefix
21. Shore sight
22. Plenty, once
23. Perfumery liquid
24. In-law of Ruth
25. Dash
26. Adjutant
27. Tennis aces by Cary Grant's ex?
31. Where the Reno runs
32. Lifetime
33. Winter hazard
34. Kind of metabolism
36. No, in Novgorod
38. Oscillates
42. Wear for Orion
43. Units of work
46. Rich man
50. Arch type
51. "I cannot tell ___"
52. Image
53. Wear for Gabriel
54. Partner of rave
55. Silent actress with idealistic doctor?
61. Squabble
62. Adz or hammer, e.g.
63. Dill of biblical days
64. Pensacola mil. installation
65. Militant god
68. Naval spy org.
69. Actress Thompson
70. Linger
73. Laugh, in Loos
74. Snicker-___
76. Ejection
81. Deli order?
86. Bosox or Cubs
87. Zilch
88. Came down
89. Ryas and runners
90. Site of Christ's first miracle
91. What Macbeth "does murder"
93. Sooty matter
94. Greek letters
95. Follow
97. Monte ___, Pennine Alp
99. Asparagus weapon?
101. Poodles' pests
105. Equal status
106. No ___ (easy)
108. Actress defends her blade?
116. Haunt
117. Coin in Qum
118. Short bios
119. Mount for Moses
120. Formerly, of old
121. Kind of rumor or threat
122. Walk ___ (feel great)
123. Addicts
124. Drivers' needs
125. Some are electric
126. Fencing piece
127. Malaysian state

DOWN

1. Coasted
2. Cautious
3. Celebes animal
4. Miler Roger and family
5. Midday break for a señor
6. Record of a year
7. George of A.F.L.-C.I.O. note
8. Theban deity
9. Subjects for Margaret Mead
10. Miserly
11. Concept
12. Wall St. buyers
13. Completely
14. Touch, for one
15. Dog parasite
16. Part of U.C.L.A.
17. Style
18. Sheep
28. ___ Tech
29. Has-___ (one of past fame)
30. Technical-school grads
34. Abzug of politics
35. Wanted-poster word
37. Wild goat of Asia
39. Encore
40. Gossip
41. Clockmaker Thomas et al.
42. One of the three B's
43. Kind of sphere or system
44. Brawl
45. Midge
47. Vamp Theda and family
48. Hawaiian shrub
49. Retired gracefully
52. Spaniards' predecessors
56. Clock variety
57. Item of Western justice
58. Miss Reed
59. Nonvoter, often
60. Ex-Met Rusty ___
66. Actor Flynn
67. Net
70. Weapon for Guinevere's lover?
71. Kind of flu
72. Weapons for Ben and Moses?
75. Dutch export
77. Like some slum youths
78. ___ fait (quite, in Paris)
79. Actress Samantha
80. Diana of song
82. Wind-scale deviser and family
83. At no time, to Tennyson
84. Actor Gulager
85. Illuminated
92. John, Paul or John Paul
93. Tightly packed fish in Firenze
96. Wapiti
98. Broadside discharges
99. Espy
100. Forgo
102. Mysterious
103. Stage whisper
104. "I ___ return"
106. Flight part
107. ___ *the Boys Are*
108. Fruit decay
109. Infrequent
110. French river
111. Corse and d'Yeu
112. Wound for Caesar
113. Top banana
114. ___ avis
115. Vertebral cushion

156 Playpen By Dorothy Smitonick

A brief visit with the younger generation.

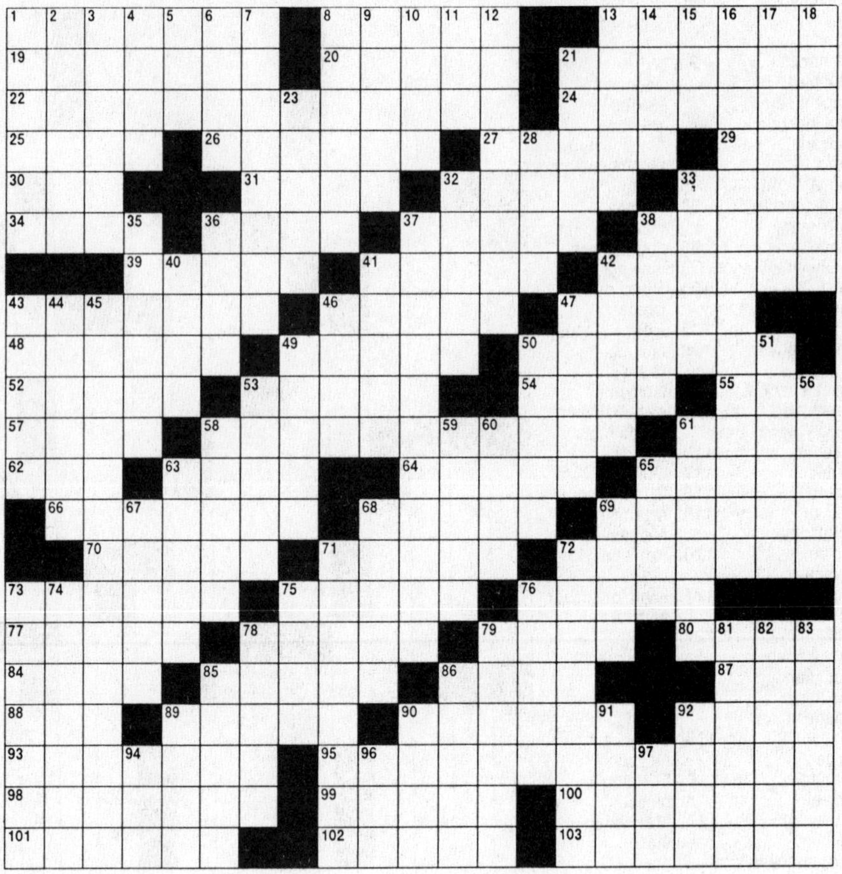

ACROSS

1. Coastal area of India
8. Unspoken
13. In fine ___
19. "I Love ___"
20. Seaman Arden of poem
21. Like the proverbial cat
22. ___ *Mohawk,* Edmonds novel
24. Elia and Twain, for example
25. Evergreens
26. Mend a shoe
27. ___ off (resists)
29. Opposite of NbW
30. Urn writing
31. ___ time (never)
32. Oop of the comics
33. Trumpet call
34. Get a tux for a while
36. Bargain term
37. At ___ (puzzled)
38. Trace
39. "___ nice day!"
41. Give ___ to (medicate)
42. "God Bless Our Home," etc.
43. Strained
46. Ages
47. Fraction
48. Type style
49. Set of steps
50. Sweetened
52. Prize name
53. Kind of pigeon
54. Sponsorship
55. Prefix for flying
57. Certain bills
58. "Professor" Harold Hill
61. Island of an Alaskan chain
62. French possessive
63. Part of Cassius' look
64. Relatives of zithers
65. ___ Park, Colo.
66. Actor Montalban
68. Specks
69. Tax on commodities
70. Scandinavian
71. Does sightseeing
72. Awaits
73. "To thine own self ___"
75. Unpoetical
76. The brain and spinal cord
77. Battery part
78. Reagan's friend Edwin ___
79. Mongrel
80. Reveille's counterpart
84. Charles and Noble
85. Prickly shrub
86. Ordered
87. Put the lid on
88. Wooden container: Abbr.
89. Agricultural region in Europe
90. Prone's opposite
92. Chapter of the Koran
93. Crimson Tide's home
95. Le Carré's *The ___ Girl*
98. Broke a promise
99. Cheer
100. Brennan and Farrell
101. Snakes
102. Gratifies
103. Easing of hostility

DOWN

1. Crazy about
2. ___ of lions
3. Hutton or Bacall
4. Weapons
5. Coll. degrees
6. Jewish month
7. Let go of
8. Mortises' partners
9. ___-Saxon
10. ___ d'Azur
11. "___ *bin ein Berliner*"
12. Site of George Eliot's mill
13. Bay known for its tides
14. God of love
15. Cheap kind of horn
16. Lillian Hellman play
17. Back pain
18. Jewish ascetics
21. Walking sticks
23. Ancient Roman port
28. Otherwise
32. Without equal
33. Sailor's bag
35. Oar pins
36. "*___ plaisir*"
37. Nora's domicile
38. ___ down (moderates)
40. Seed covering
41. The vowels
42. Kingsley's *___ White*
43. Typesetters, for short
44. One doing penance
45. Victor Herbert operetta
46. Jot
47. What Romans wore
49. Office gal
50. Rope materials
51. Abhor
53. Awning
56. Tricks
58. Succinct
59. Healing: Suffix
60. Louder, in music: Abbr.
61. Advancement
63. Movie villain Jack ___
65. Montreal fair
67. Strings
68. Large deer
69. Way out
71. Frameworks
72. Drawn out
73. Bel Geddes or Eden
74. Made possible
75. Section of Istanbul
76. W.W. II hero Murphy
78. Unit
79. Trees with sap
81. Shrewdness
82. Sire
83. Meager
85. Fun's partner
86. City in Montana
89. Deg. for a granger
90. Bit of info
91. Border lake
92. *Peter Pan* pirate
94. Quilters' event
96. Pier org.
97. Utmost: Abbr.

157 Tuning In By Wilson McBeath

Presenting selections on the musical front.

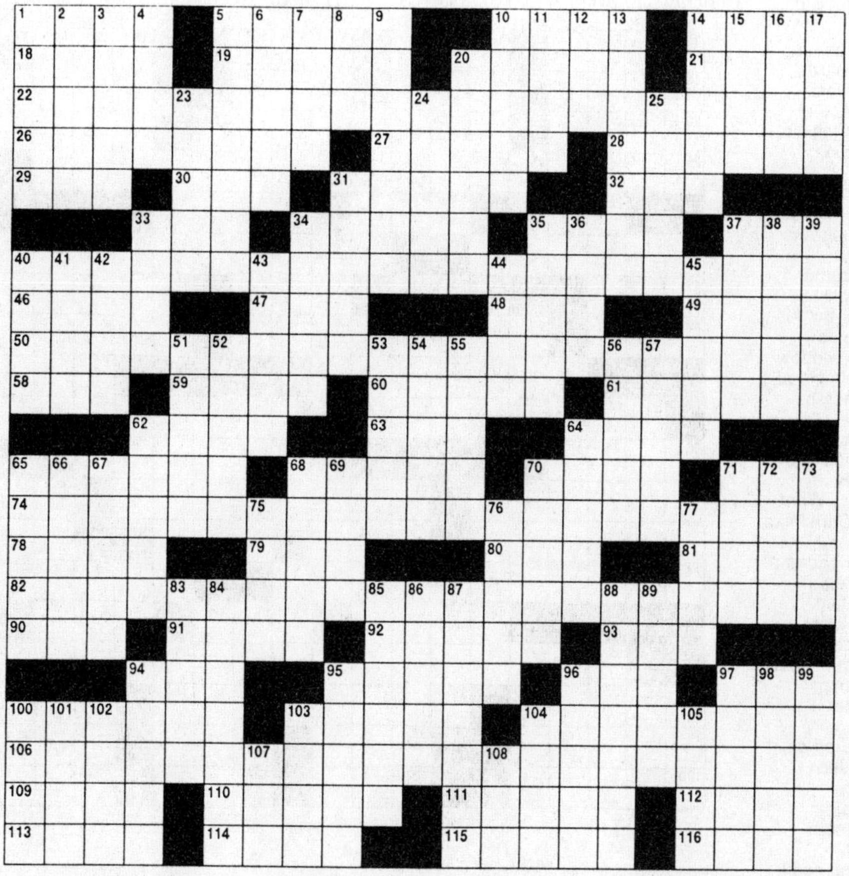

ACROSS

1. Shoulder of a road
5. Milan's La ___
10. U.M.W. output
14. Formerly, in earlier days
18. Zoological suffix
19. To go, in Paris
20. Flora's partner
21. Travel
22. Dvořák's childhood memories
26. Everest's is high
27. Diviners' sticks
28. Type of photo print
29. Golfer Elder
30. 100 square meters
31. Spools
32. Possesses
33. Spanish lady: Abbr.
34. Seven, in Ravenna
35. Desserts
37. *Norma* ___
40. "___ By" (anticipate sunshine)
46. Mountain in Thessaly
47. Scottish river
48. No good wind
49. German donkey
50. Lament for a forty-niner's daughter
58. Brown of renown
59. Black
60. Tapestry
61. Spoilsport
62. Old horses
63. Bee's follower
64. Family member
65. Mysterious
68. Rich pastry
70. Dilatory
71. Fall mo.
74. Symptom of aging, with 113 Across
78. Blackthorn
79. Author Levin
80. Dernier ___
81. Type style: Abbr.
82. "I've ___" (new experience)
90. Nautical dir.
91. Ye ___ Tea Shöppe
92. Personification of fate
93. Garfunkel
94. River of Malawi
95. Maple-sap spout
96. Cuckoo
97. Doer: Suffix
100. Allotments
103. Dais ritual
104. Complete deafness
106. Well-known airman
109. Miscellany
110. Weird
111. Water wheel
112. City on the Oka
113. See 74 Across
114. Prefix for mite
115. Kind of widow
116. Monster loch

DOWN

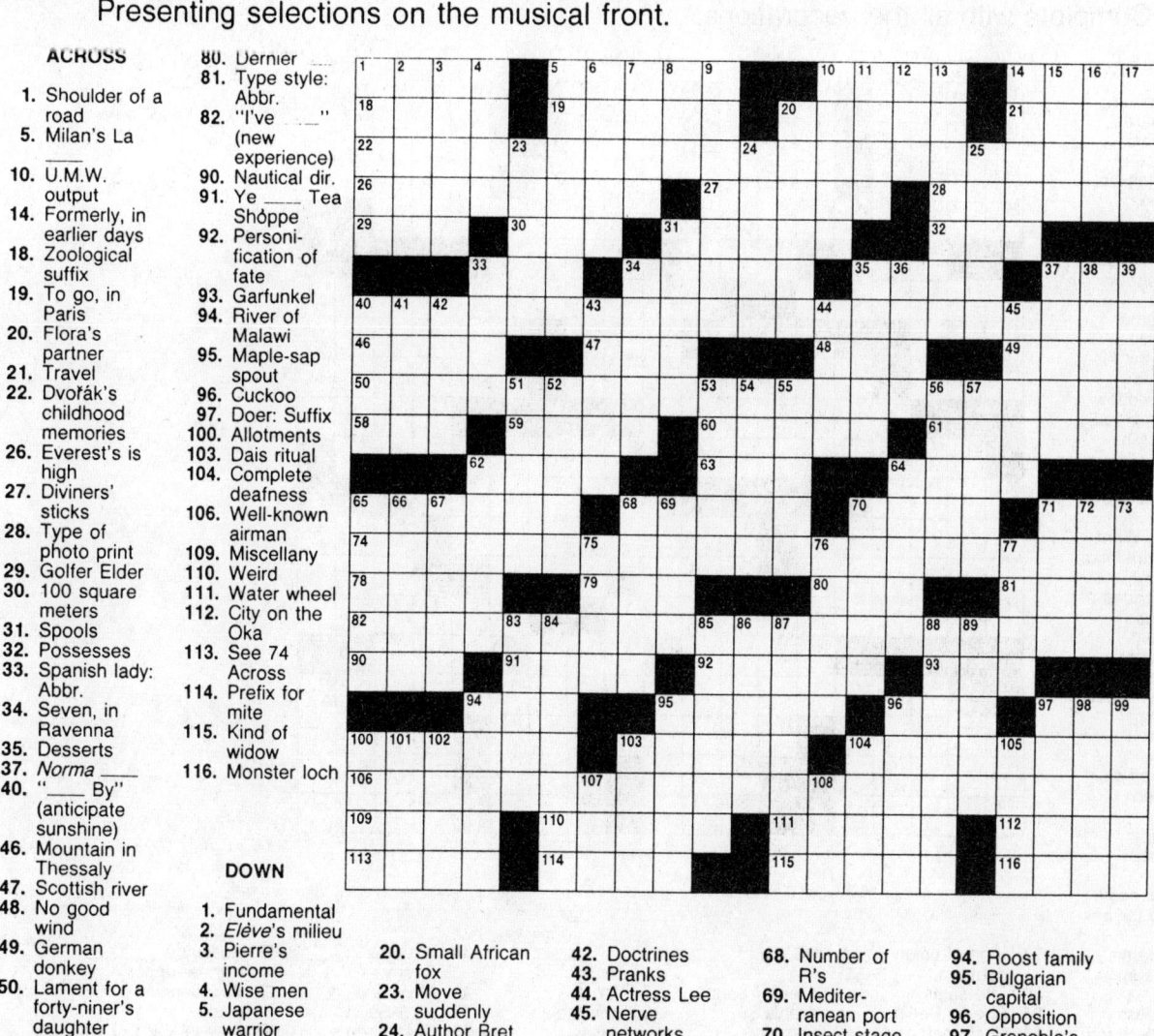

1. Fundamental
2. *Elève*'s milieu
3. Pierre's income
4. Wise men
5. Japanese warrior
6. Scottish firth
7. Egyptian dancing girl
8. Papal name
9. ". . . for thou ___ me": Psalm 23
10. Amusing persons
11. Six in an inning
12. Anecdotal item
13. Giggled
14. Community character
15. Goes bad
16. Aggregates
17. Deuce beater
20. Small African fox
23. Move suddenly
24. Author Bret
25. Tumbler
31. Kind of dish for cultures
33. Brace
34. In a cunning way
35. Hercules' captive and namesakes
36. Coal refuse
37. Violinist's necessity
38. Coeur d'___
39. Aunt in *Oklahoma!*
40. Shearer's gathering
41. Name in tennis
42. Doctrines
43. Pranks
44. Actress Lee
45. Nerve networks
51. Actress Keaton
52. Choler
53. Mother-of-pearl
54. Garbo
55. Nicene ___
56. Muse of poetry
57. Divine power
62. ". . . the Ruler of the Queen's ___!"
64. Ike's spouse
65. Orgs.
66. Irritates
67. Kind of hitch
68. Number of R's
69. Mediterranean port
70. Insect stage
71. Preminger
72. Scorch
73. Prefix for graph or scope
75. Bound
76. Tally
77. Talent
83. City on the Seine
84. Worked with explosives
85. Pierce
86. Tumultuous
87. Singing rhythmically
88. Uttar Pradesh area
89. Heath
94. Roost family
95. Bulgarian capital
96. Opposition
97. Grenoble's river
98. Magnitudes
99. Far East weights
100. Urban problem
101. Nimbus
102. Indigo
103. Aquatic bird
104. Site of the Taj Mahal
105. Above
107. Cry of surprise
108. Conjunction

158 Valentine Card By Nancy Ross

Complete with all the decorations.

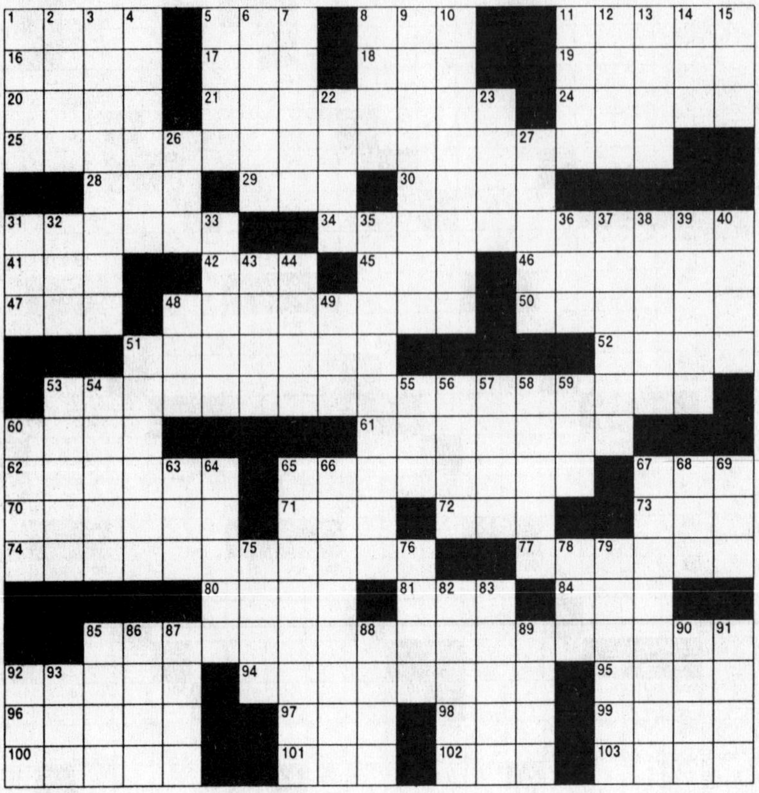

ACROSS

1. Astronaut Shepard
5. 100 lbs.
8. Computer-land initials
11. Earnest
16. Dover specialty
17. Old Mideast monogram
18. Oahu welcome
19. Touch
20. ____ the kill
21. Shields
24. Bay window
25. Robin Hood's monarch
28. Dem. opponent
29. Opposite of NNW
30. "____ Want for Christmas . . ."
31. Like shoes or gloves
34. Captain Shotover's home
41. Height: Abbr.
42. German cooler
45. ____ *Misérables*
46. Merited
47. Voice
48. Heraldic crosses
50. Lost spontaneity
51. Place for a ring
52. Substantial, as a sum
53. Alec Guinness tour de force
60. Like Sullivan's chord
61. Antiseptics
62. Play it for ____ worth
65. Speculated
67. Govt. emissary
70. ____ bet (wager)
71. Gerund former
72. Pulpit speech: Abbr.
73. Certain vote
74. "The band is playing . . . , and ____ are light"
77. Kind of union contract
80. The same
81. She, in Berlin
84. Circle part
85. Mary Martin number
92. Organic compound
94. Stubbornly opposed
95. Tender
96. Confiscated
97. Item on an env.
98. Pied Piper's follower
99. State for Louis
100. Cruel
101. Wild Asian sheep
102. That, to Juan
103. Prefix for god or john

DOWN

1. Area of Saudi Arabia
2. Actress Anderson
3. Dispatch
4. One of the worlds
5. Copper: Prefix
6. Hospital areas
7. Yonkers events
8. Robert ____
9. Bridge player, at times
10. Without mercy
11. Kind of talk
12. Discharge
13. Writer Bagnold
14. Opp. of small
15. Communi-cations abbr.
22. ____ *Is a Lonely Hunter*
23. East Indian herb
26. Simian
27. Winged Victory statues
31. Ballet step
32. King lead-in
33. Love-letter salutation
35. Oversenti-mental one
36. Bowler
37. Does earbending
38. Like lamps, sometimes
39. Tournament choices
40. MacDonald's partner in song
43. Woes
44. Walk for Socrates
48. Morose
49. ____-Saud
51. Do a siren's job
53. Wagnerian tenor René
54. Moslem's world
55. Boston fish
56. Sonnets' kin
57. To laugh, in Lyon
58. Unique things
59. Raise ____
60. Race segments
63. Fuss, old style
64. Master, in India
65. Radio, to a Londoner
66. Fraction of a year
67. Audience warmer-upper
68. Wrestlers' place
69. Way to learn
75. German river
76. Army NCO
78. Roll of bills
79. Took out
82. Rhone feeder
83. Lab heaters
85. Pat's partner
86. Chemical suffixes
87. Encourages
88. Asian palm
89. German king
90. Wee drop
91. Himalayan haunter
92. Funda-mentally
93. ____ de mer

159 Solving Tips By Sidney Robbins

Not quite the kind given at the racetrack.

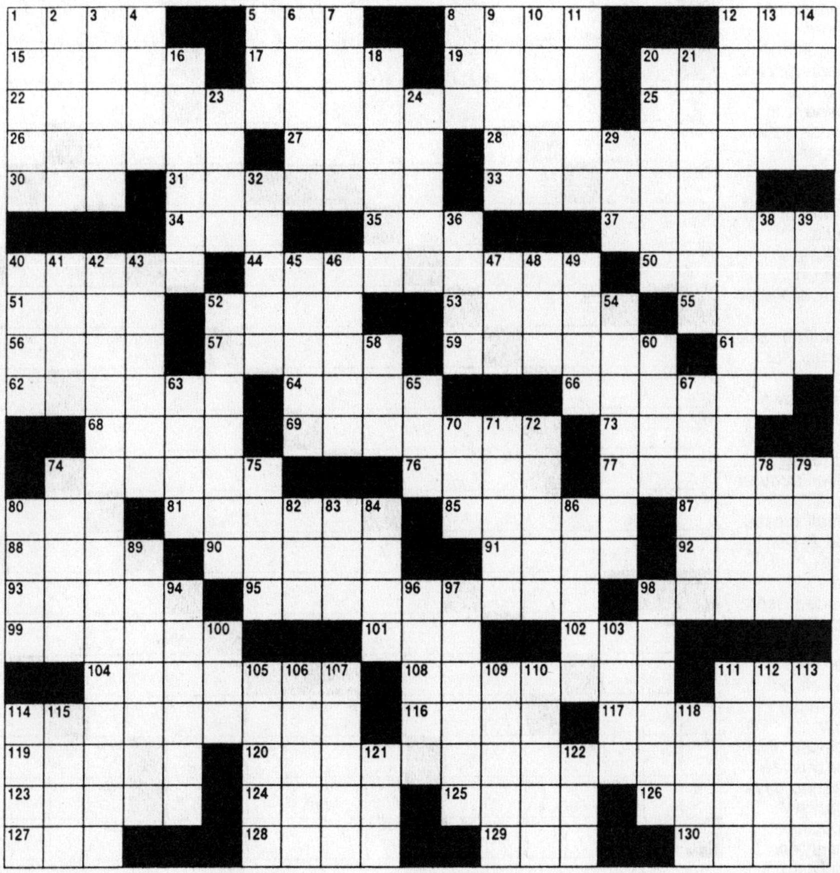

ACROSS

1. Amontillado container
5. Siesta
8. Oily org.
12. Burmese governor
15. Arm bones
17. Crackle
19. Judicial robe
20. Lucia had a mad one
22. Critical time
25. Elmer's mate
26. Notify
27. Relative of Alicia
28. Fell back
30. Dict. entry
31. ___ quarters (confined)
33. Clogs completely
34. Miss Lindstrom
35. Globe
37. Wall sections
40. Actor Alan's family
44. Directs attention to
50. Use scales
51. "It's a sin to tell ___"
52. Atmosphere
53. Money substitute
55. Dirk of old
56. Pear
57. Knights of ___
59. Is unable
61. Recipe meas.
62. Sprinkle
64. Heraldic band
66. Like a crow-flight line
68. Heraldic fur
69. Setter's kennel pal
73. Ship for Columbus
74. Mr. Gonzalez
76. French author
77. Baby's gait
80. Before dunit
81. Ancient Asia Minor colony
85. Shaping tool
87. Check
88. Angora's pride
90. Vat workers
91. Chilled
92. Indians of the West
93. Sea birds
95. Scores more
98. Follow
99. Group of four
101. Opposite of nord, to René
102. One-time jrs.
104. Song thrushes
108. Vamooses
111. Hezekiah's mother
114. 8:59
116. Sunken fence
117. Eden
119. Reclusive one
120. Inanity
123. Easy mark
124. Otherwise
125. Struck, old style
126. "Remember the ___!"
127. Querying words
128. No different
129. "Have you ___ wool?"
130. Vehicle

DOWN

1. Eros
2. Unattended
3. Do a nose job
4. Nigerian city
5. Initials on a bounced check
6. Record of a single year
7. Lover of Francesca da Rimini
8. Baseball great
9. Teems
10. Feather yielder
11. Poem division
12. Future officers
13. Unicorn fish
14. Necessity
16. Apes Gypsy Rose Lee
18. Warden's place
20. Item for Margery Daw
21. Monet and Rains
23. Prefix for bus
24. Make an effort
29. Harbor official: Abbr.
32. Town where Spartacus fought
36. Degree in sci.
38. Cast out
39. Name for a collie
40. Research spots
41. Awry
42. Letdowns
43. Fiat
45. Lowest deck
46. Medicine: Prefix
47. Wood sorrel
48. Container
49. Kindle, in England
52. Altered
54. Used one's finger
58. Clay's new name
60. Combo
63. Earth goddess
65. Siamese twin
67. Route for a halfback
70. "My country, ___ of . . ."
71. Booth of the stage
72. Respond
74. Portion
75. Toy on a string
78. Kind of tenant
79. First word of the Mass. motto
80. Hone
82. Rumanian coin
83. N.Y. subway line
84. Cleo's snakes
86. Bas-relief material
89. Puts a new value on
94. Tasty
96. Should
97. Goals
98. Regard highly
100. Clatter
103. Coal valley
105. Tire-tread grooves
106. ___ Gay
107. Earthquake
109. Musical subject
110. Black buck
111. Advantage
112. Swiss city
113. Signed
114. Old Greek flask
115. Biblical sailor
118. Latin love word
121. Born, in France
122. Pig pad

160 Country Life By John Hales

Not exactly designed for roughing it, though.

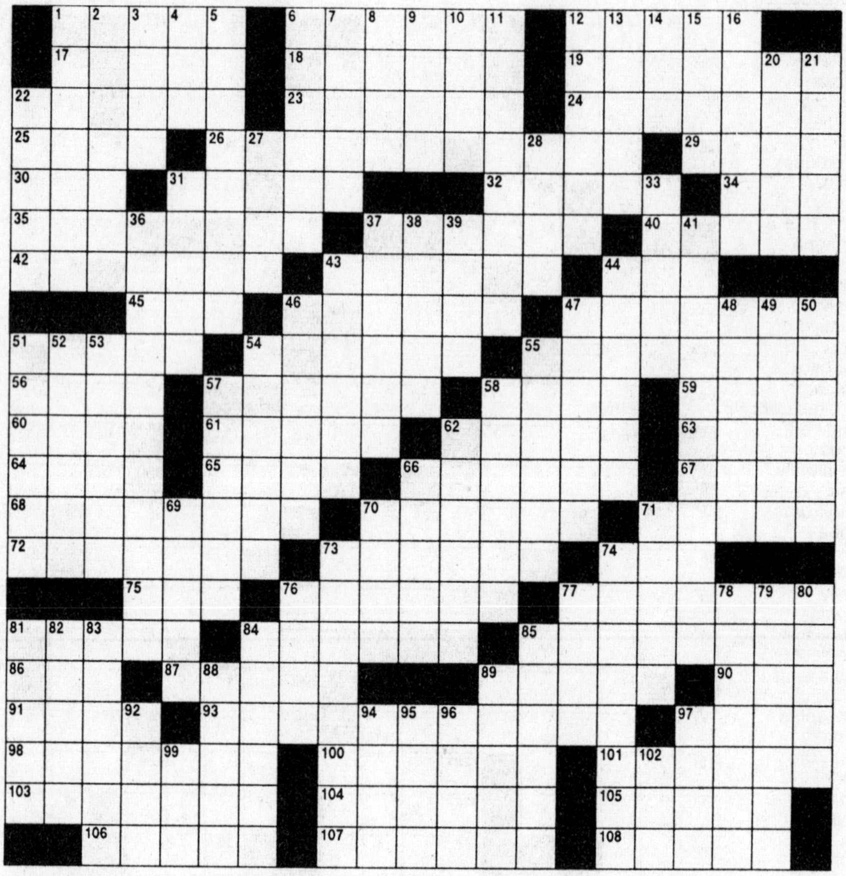

ACROSS

1. Egg white
6. Piña ___ (rum drink)
12. "Hands Across the Sea" composer
17. Money in Smolensk
18. Arthurian place
19. Musical intervals
22. Shout
23. Mussolini
24. American Revolutionary poet
25. Exclusively
26. Asian jujube
29. Italian wine area
30. Food regimen: Abbr.
31. Mongoloid people
32. Faultless
34. Gala in the Far East
35. Involves in difficulties
37. Role for Weissmuller
40. "___ and sacred death": Whitman
42. French port on the Adour
43. More lacking in plumpness
44. Wightman or Davis
45. Publication, for short
46. Vilified
47. Woolly creatures of the Andes
51. Perfume
54. Prepare cattle for the market
55. Sever friendly ties
56. Financial arrangement
57. Badinage
58. Jack Horner's extraction
59. Adherers
60. Wooded area, in Soissons
61. Del of baseball note
62. ". . . punishment fit the ___"
63. Patio facility
64. Kett of the comics
65. Hired hoodlum
66. Jidda citizens
67. Nimbus
68. Renew, in consecration
70. Sugar-yielding substance
71. Trees of India
72. Offers
73. Put on
74. Harper Valley org.
75. Wartime tank carrier, for short
76. Like drawn butter
77. Long-suffering
81. River through Berlin
84. Small mesas
85. Old British ship
86. Haw's predecessor
87. Tippler
89. Of the pelvis
90. Carter or Lowell
91. Financier Kahn
93. Posture of the bustle-wearing days
97. Spanish huzzahs
98. Enlightens
100. Knobbed
101. Maintain firmly
103. Area of Ethiopia
104. Spoke at length
105. Actor Nick
106. Wind-borne soil
107. Actor Novarro and namesakes
108. Blackthorn fruits

DOWN

1. Family member
2. Nursery tune
3. In a competent way
4. U.N. workers' org.
5. Seeking something on the top shelf
6. Aircraft compartments
7. Oasts
8. Byway
9. Muhammad et al.
10. Love excessively
11. Put a coating on metal
12. Use an emollient
13. Plant sheath
14. Multi-purpose truck
15. Capital of Yemen
16. Zoroastrian writings
20. Used up
21. *Tout de ___* (immediately)
22. Biblical mount
27. Hearty's partner
28. Hebrew month
31. Submarine spotter
33. Jeweler's glass
36. July 4 display
37. Viennese desserts
38. Goose genus
39. Zilch, in Le Havre
41. Scene of Caribbean piracy
43. Meddle
44. Poetic regions
46. "He who ___, teaches": Shaw
47. Prefix for a light metal
48. Weinberger or Milquetoast
49. King of the Huns
50. Scene of the Hero and Leander legend
51. Musician Herb
52. Precisely
53. Plaid
54. Liturgical vestments
55. Part of an astrolabe
57. Encompassed
58. Cut tree branches
62. Film-festival city
66. *"A votre ___!"*
69. Bacteriologists' instruments
70. Shed
71. Place for home castoffs
73. Device sensitive to smoke or metal
74. Heroic champions
76. Clio or Melpomene
77. Bread, in Brest
78. *"Liberté, ___, fraternité"*
79. Avengers
80. Assignation
81. Young hog: Var.
82. Finch or Fonda
83. Sell to the consumer
84. Body sacs
85. Extorts
88. Certain moldings
89. *Hedda Gabler* author
92. Prefix for pus
94. Asian songbird
95. Khachaturian
96. Say ___ (refuse)
97. Capital on a fjord
99. Otto's realm: Abbr.
102. ___-pros (discontinue legally)

161 Pairings By Robert Wolfe

A matter of getting unlikely couples together.

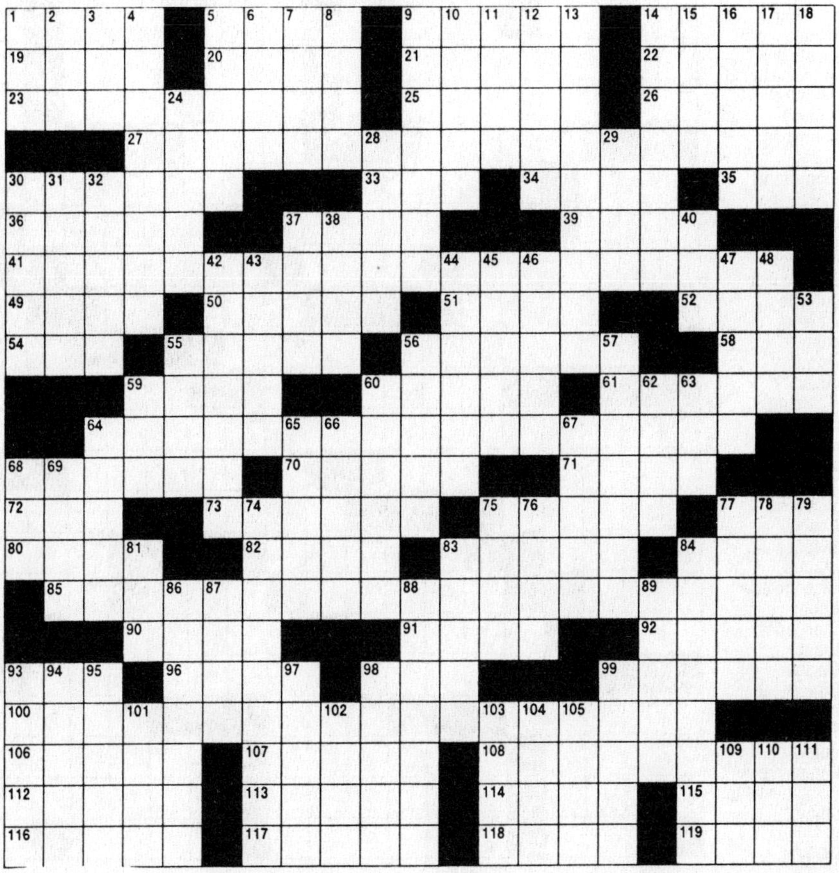

ACROSS

1. Piedmont center
5. African country
9. Prank
14. Flat roll: Var.
19. Paper measure
20. Copied
21. Coliseum part
22. Fame
23. Truce
25. Number for a ménage
26. Over
27. Haunting TV duo
30. Prayer beads
33. Three-toed sloths
34. Bird feed
35. ___ Plaines
36. Sharp
37. Lairs
39. French town
41. Seagoing duo
49. German title
50. Psi follower
51. A sainted Thomas
52. Kind of toad
54. Speakers' pauses
55. Elliptical
56. Lac and elemi
58. Ship channel
59. Dill
60. Craze
61. Cat or rabbit
64. Bora with Leo?
68. *Potemkin* locale
70. Atmospheres
71. Engrossed
72. Scarf
73. Summer wear
75. Goshen and Nod, e.g.
77. Hiatus
80. Kind of worm
82. Oriental nurse
83. Miss McPherson
84. Fairway call
85. Department-store duo of films
90. Louvre goddess
91. Fulda feeder
92. Pico de ___
93. Cinder
96. Diamond shape
98. Grown-up lamb
99. Caves, to poets
100. Father Time with Neptune?
106. Dialect
107. In a stew
108. What Waugh's Brideshead was
112. Stranger
113. Spanish infants
114. Waterless
115. Fleeting star
116. Winter hazard
117. School officials
118. Barbershop ID
119. Cheese

DOWN

1. Altar constellation
2. Indian weight
3. Cap
4. Rich Little, e.g.
5. British chum
6. Buy ___ in a poke
7. Walesa of Poland
8. Prefix for gram or logical
9. Spiteful
10. Tapestry
11. Laborer
12. Actresses Bennett and Markey
13. Danish explorer Knud ___
14. Like bad English weather
15. U.S. missile
16. Audible
17. *"C'est ___"*
18. Anatomical passages
24. Nag
28. He clears the chimney
29. Soaks flax
30. Early, to Tennyson
31. Dark yellow
32. Litigants
37. Letter-shaped seine
38. Lip
40. Cal. part
42. "And ___ not a little thing": Chesterton
43. Stradivari's teacher
44. Improves
45. Set in place
46. Bathsheba's spouse
47. Inert gas
48. Use the dotted line
53. Air-board abbr.
55. Individuals
56. Indian princes
57. Calais dinner courses
59. Cries of delight
60. George's spouse
62. Small drinks
63. Received
64. Pirate Blackbeard
65. Ruth's in-law
66. Of a brain membrane
67. Eagles
68. Sash
69. ___ *Go Near the Water*
74. ___ to (intend)
75. Kind of light
76. Moslem prince
77. One beyond help
78. Sharp ridge
79. Merida money
81. Word before pecked or party
83. Tacked on
84. Actress Joan
86. Plant with twofold cells
87. Made out, barely
88. Quality of originality
89. Seymour and Eyre
93. Reference book
94. Pitchman's plant
95. Skater Sonja
97. Street show
98. Dined
99. Certain whisper
101. Molding
102. Wendy's dog
103. Snare
104. Medal of Honor winner
105. Wickedness
109. Clump
110. ___ Marie Saint
111. Hoover, e.g.

162 Space Saving By Ernie Furtado

It is especially valuable for closing some eyes.

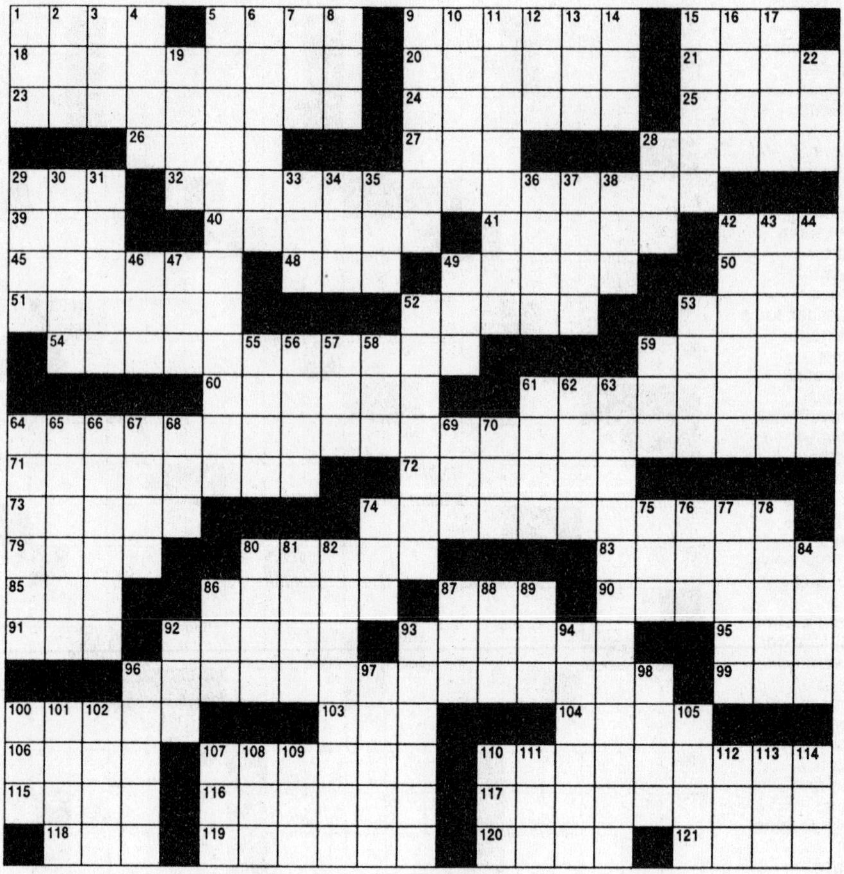

ACROSS

1. French composer
5. Cote birds: Abbr.
9. Grieg dancer
15. Dog tags, e.g.
18. Revenge
20. "Scat!"
21. Aladdin's loss
23. Wabash River trees
24. Lacking reverence: Var.
25. One way to see
26. Leningrad's river
27. "___ for Two"
28. Proverb
29. MacGraw or Baba
32. Pleasant surprise
39. Coagulate
40. Closer
41. Word for Aleck
42. Shade tree
45. Related on the mother's side
48. Pole month
49. Hosiery color
50. ___-disant
51. Tennessee's streetcar
52. *Beau* ___
53. Strong ___ ox
54. Like some cats
59. Topple
60. Distanced
61. ___ respects (made a formal call)
64. "As all looks ___": Pope
71. ". . . such beauty as ___": Shak.
72. Find a buyer
73. Scottish pools
74. Clams
79. Of a subcontinent: Abbr.
80. Elias and Julia Ward
83. Pitcher Luis and kin
85. Id's companion
86. Occupant of 21 Across
87. Diamond arbiter
90. Resident of a divided country
91. Draft org.
92. Administered
93. Minstrel troupe member
95. Ike's command
96. "___ You," 1934 song
99. Author Wallace
100. Feathered friends
103. Charlemagne's domain: Abbr.
104. "___ the night . . ."
106. Jesuit scholar: 1656–1727
107. Word for Christ
110. Display places
115. Change the décor
116. Biergarten toast
117. Cadge
118. Dinner-tab extra
119. Three-D objects
120. Legis. group
121. "I ___ at the office"

DOWN

1. Word before Vegas
2. Some
3. Auto plate: Abbr.
4. "With the jawbone ___ ass . . ."
5. Cape Cod resort
6. Shelter for a Rolls
7. Compass dir.
8. Sibling, for short
9. Writ voider, in law
10. More recent
11. Spectacles
12. Mark or line toucher
13. T.L.C. dispensers
14. D.D.E. opponent
15. Head-part coverings
16. Information
17. Haze
19. Cockney abodes
22. Word with humble or pecan
28. Islet
29. Like good wine
30. Smooth consonants
31. Place for mascara
33. Son of Noah
34. Refrain bit
35. Puckish
36. Leave out
37. "In" thing
38. Word before long or now
42. Ancient ascetic
43. Did a banking routine
44. Imagination
46. Chico's uncle
47. Sales-tag marking
49. Companion of board
52. Origin
53. Ult. revelation
55. Shanties
56. Thine, in Tours
57. N.Y.C. subway
58. Olé's counterpart
59. Caucasic language
61. Influence
62. Poker start
63. "___ I Love You Like I Do"
64. Elis
65. Patrick and J. R.
66. One-time matman Jim
67. K–P connection
68. Western org.
69. Namath, once
70. Height: Abbr.
74. Pinky or Peggy
75. Refrain ending for Old MacDonald
76. Word after box or side
77. Genuflect
78. One of 50
80. Restore
81. Lone
82. "And cursed me ___": Coleridge
84. Kind of job or tire
86. Patton, e.g.
87. French article
88. Roman 1501
89. Mrs. Thatcher et al.
92. ___ Passos
93. Turns outward
94. Towns in N.Y. and Okla.
96. Tear that's shed
97. Wake-robin
98. ___ avis
100. Pub
101. Shoelace hole
102. Cheap whisky
105. "The ___ Is You": Kern
107. Cousins of M.P.s
108. Nigerian people
109. Tenn. athlete
110. Relaxing spot
111. Owns
112. Harem room
113. 1055, to a Latin scholar
114. Bishop's bailiwick

163 Globe-Trotting By Don Nardizzi

Providing stopovers here and there.

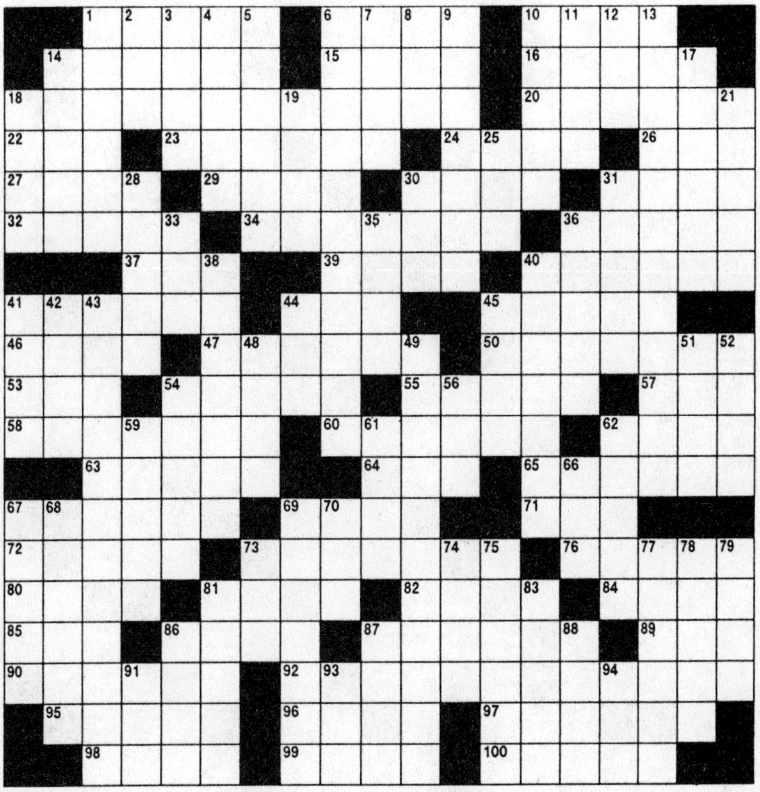

ACROSS

1. Bewildered
6. Capitol feature
10. Tree genus
14. Actress Louise et al.
15. "Once ___ a midnight dreary . . ."
16. Tribunal
18. Roman landmark
20. Menlo Park's wizard
22. Be indisposed
23. Mementos
24. Weary
26. Mrs., in Mazatlán
27. Supercilious one
29. Plaster base
30. Le ___, auto-race city
31. Where Anna taught
32. Urged
34. Warms over
36. Like yesterday's beer
37. High custom in England
39. Away from the wind
40. "Well, I'll be ___!"
41. Puts off
44. Numerical prefix
45. Word before band or box
46. Carter's middle name
47. A bird carried him
50. Harvesting
53. Hail or farewell
54. Dividing wall: Prefix
55. Single things
57. Seven, to Seneca
58. Performs
60. Get the piano back in shape
62. Knock down
63. Ten times ten, to Tintoretto
64. Dramatic division
65. Brought up
67. Place for Timon
69. Sumptuous
71. Scholastic test, for short
72. Between iota and lambda
73. Conditioning exercises
76. Succinct
80. Inlets
81. Batting strategy
82. King Charles's Gwyn
84. Small religious group
85. Saturn's wife
86. Beethoven's birthplace
87. Sound at a horror movie
89. Tabu
90. Realized after deductions
92. *Rigoletto* or *Pagliacci*
95. Like Donald Duck, often
96. The ___, Thames area
97. Othello's home
98. Affirmatives
99. Fat, in Fontainebleau
100. Kefauver

DOWN

1. Parallel
2. Kind of ear
3. Slammer
4. Atelier fixture
5. Building stone
6. W.W. II Aleutian air base
7. Unlocks, to poets
8. Thick head of hair
9. Put in office: Var.
10. Southwest winds
11. Area or ZIP
12. Silkworm
13. California stream
14. Copying
17. Courageous attitude
18. Return-mail initials
19. Locale
21. Called
25. Officeholders
28. Asian palm
30. Fannie ___, mortgage org.
31. Kind of hanger
33. German article
35. Noted nom de plume
36. Long narratives
38. Maintains
40. Weight watchers
41. Costly
42. Overhang
43. Menu item at Maxim's
44. Explosive letters
45. Coarse cloth, for short
48. ___ facto
49. Certain scolds
51. The White or the Blue
52. Gold-plate
54. Medicinal herb
56. Kooky person
59. Ocean trenches
61. Apiece
62. Destinies
66. ___ humble pie
67. Ill-fated dirigible of 1933
68. Pacific capital
69. Continuous
70. Doer: Suffix
73. Lowly form of wit
74. Persian elf
75. ". . . the ravel'd ___ of care"
77. Stringed instruments of old
78. Panic
79. Laboratory item
81. Augurs
83. Highway divisions
86. Kind of electron ray
87. Roosevelt's mother
88. Blanc or St.-Michel
91. Toe, on the Tweed
93. Pinnacle
94. Mince, e.g.

164 Recommended Reading By Norma Steinberg

Assuming, of course, that one knows the authors.

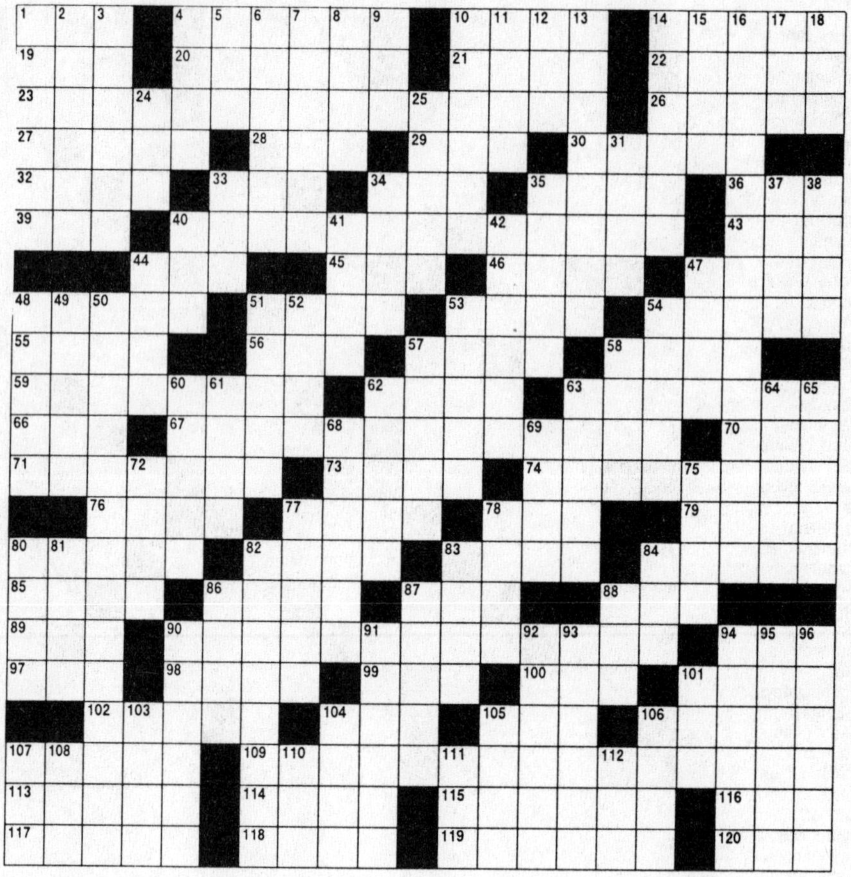

ACROSS

1. Snake
4. Library catalogue listings
10. Title for a rabbit
14. An S.S.R.
19. Feather ___
20. Madden
21. Meander
22. "What's in ___?"
23. *Bellefleur*
26. Kind of flush
27. Labor group
28. Pluto's counterpart
29. Greek letters
30. Wreck a car
32. Torn
33. Oolong, for one
34. Word on a towel
35. Goya's duchess
36. Twice-told
39. Work unit
40. *The Autobiography of Alice B. Toklas*
43. Dale's husband
44. ___ of a gun
45. Rush
46. Hardy heroine
47. Read quickly
48. Kind of new
51. Moue
53. Without: Suffix
54. Ladd part
55. Como, e.g.
56. On the ___
57. Pub missile
58. Assume a snaky shape
59. Without foreknowledge
62. "___ for a change"
63. Lie about
66. Soak flax
67. *The Tale of Peter Rabbit*
70. Initials on a job record
71. Sees
73. Egyptian sacred bird
74. Zero
76. Imitated
77. Pintail duck
78. ___ *ordinaire*
79. Paris magazine
80. Tinsel Town award
82. Ado
83. Spouse
84. *"Deutschland über ___"*
85. Cosmetic for Cleopatra
86. Musial or Laurel
87. Article
88. Roman money
89. Capek play
90. *To the Lighthouse*
94. Bomb of a bomb
97. Mr. Baba
98. Medicinal lily
99. Can. province
100. NBC rival
101. Descartes
102. Mountain-dew equipment
104. Sault ___ Marie
105. Gallic summer
106. Red dye
107. Morning on the Loire
109. *Jo's Boys*
113. One of the Durants
114. Ambler
115. Various
116. Gadget for Snead
117. ___ board
118. Learn by ___
119. Kind of hammer
120. Out of the ordinary

DOWN

1. Renounce
2. Oklahoman
3. Remitting
4. Adolescent
5. Business abbr.
6. ___ *Horn,* Harry Carey movie
7. Cowboy gear
8. Shrinks' concerns
9. Choice: Abbr.
10. Cook meat, in a way
11. Goes bad
12. Miss Arden
13. Antsy
14. Clansman's wear
15. Small ox
16. *Dear and Glorious Physician*
17. M.D.'s group
18. Bro. or sis
24. Camp accommodation
25. Zinc ___
31. Geishas' accessories
33. Count to ___
34. Eight, for Pierre
35. Bikini atoll event
37. Bank transaction
38. Force unit
40. Zeus or Triton
41. Baba au ___
42. Home music maker
44. Skier's delight
47. Leg part
48. Book-jacket comment
49. Rajah's mate
50. *Death on the Nile*
51. Entreaties
52. Hops oven
53. Hurricane and Tiffany
54. Flies
57. Land of cotton
58. Tony's friend on the Nile
60. More capable
61. Mr. Foxx
62. "Let Rome in ___ melt": Shak.
63. Jackson's kind of wall
64. Aerie resident
65. Roman kings
68. Francesca da ___
69. Week's end initials
72. Milky gem
75. Cockney cads
77. "All the world's a ___"
78. Vista
80. Gumbo ingredient
81. Essence
82. Baby carriage
83. "Eh?"
84. W.W. I army
86. Window part
87. Fork parts
88. Smith and Capone
90. Without success
91. Two weeks' ___
92. Eight notes
93. Heeded
94. Explorer in Florida
95. Part of U.K.
96. Dimpled
101. Bird of fable
103. Stratum
104. Befit
105. Actor Jannings
106. Otherwise
107. A West
108. Long ___ of the law
110. Gold for José
111. Madison Ave. output
112. Perón's country: Abbr.

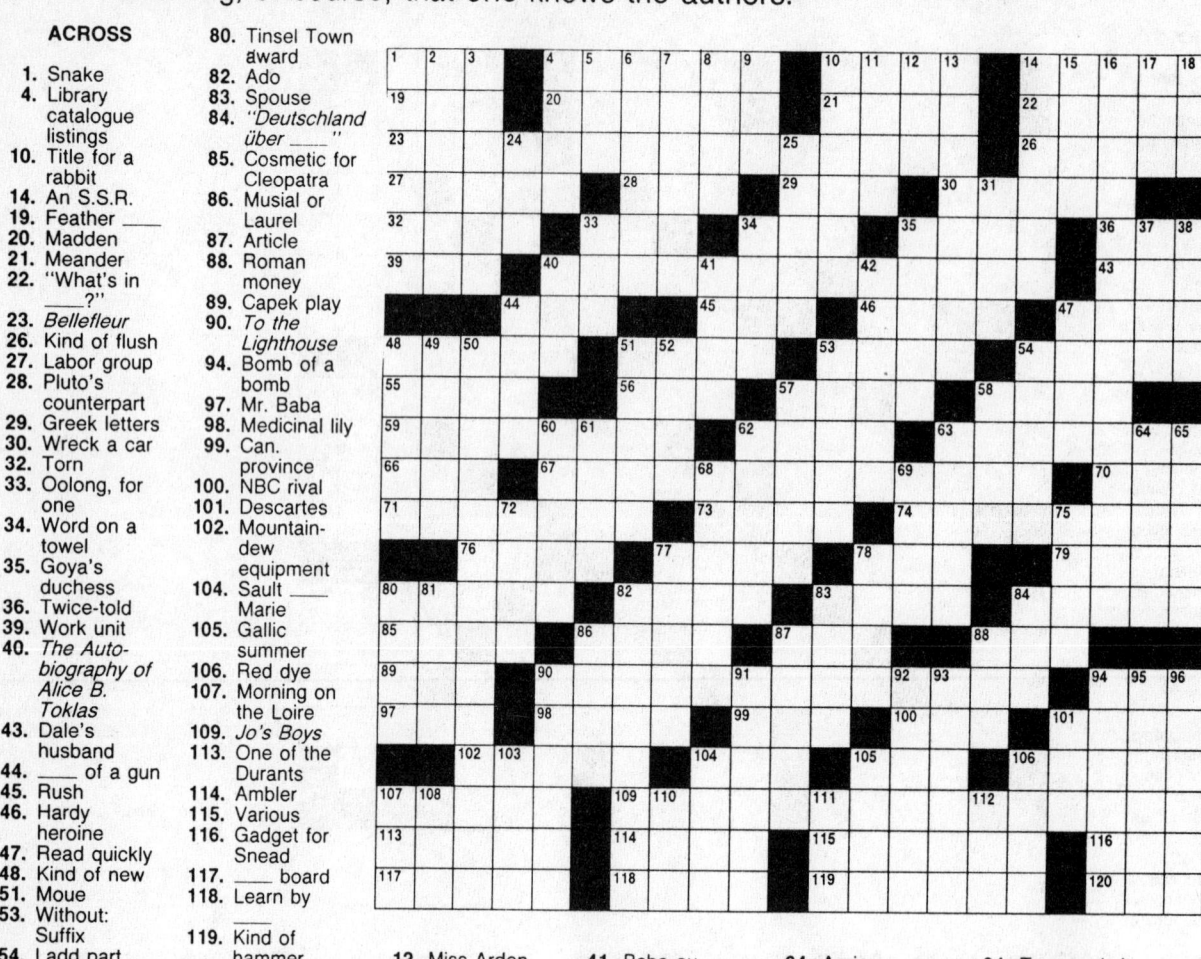

165 Exercise in Futility By Ruth W. Smith

Not everybody can be a winner.

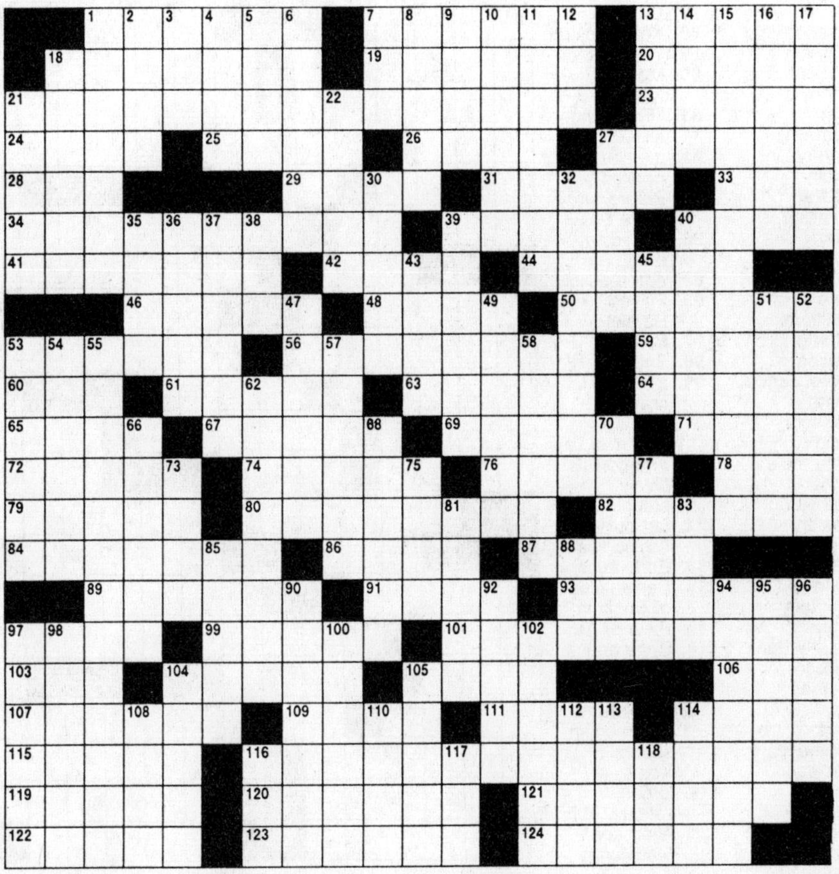

ACROSS

1. Tedious writer
7. Van Gogh, for one
13. Like a he-man
18. Apportion
19. Home of a certain wild man
20. French actor Delon
21. Words to an also-ran
23. Toulouse-Lautrec's Moulin
24. Have no use for
25. Genus of mussels
26. Wood burr
27. Looked for
28. Unit
29. Degrees
31. ____, *With Love,* Poitier film
33. Cut down
34. Like an also-ran
39. Form
40. Black: Prefix
41. True copy, in law
42. Miss Sommer
44. Once more, to Caesar
46. Street show
48. Animal skin
50. Containers for wine
53. Remove by melting
56. Created an also-ran, just barely
59. Of an alcohol product
60. Queen or honey
61. Certain data, for short
63. Miss Doone
64. Peer
65. Port, in yachting
67. News items
69. Fountain drinks
71. Estonian weight
72. Ready
74. March–April sign
76. Uriah and namesakes
78. Concert piece: Abbr.
79. Mexican basket grass
80. Target shot for an also-ran
82. Napery
84. Having a maxim
86. Hepburn's winter animal
87. Hard-heart material
89. Stretching muscle
91. Exchange fee
93. Houdini feats
97. Very, in Germany
99. Entangle
101. Nearing an also-ran status
103. Half a fly
104. Hostess Perle
105. ____ B'rith
106. Writer Serling
107. Fruit-bowl items
109. Yesterday, in Paris
111. Between Q and V
114. Weak
115. Devout
116. Game for also-rans
119. Lariat
120. No. 49 of 50
121. Ill-wishers
122. Singer John
123. Starts again, at golf
124. Pill pushers

DOWN

1. Guard
2. Ascended
3. Iron or lead source
4. Elephant Boy
5. Vingt-____
6. Part of the eye
7. Australian native
8. On the ____ (bankrupt)
9. Triplet
10. "Tell it not ____"
11. Path for an ocean liner
12. Rocky peak
13. Herb eaten at Passover
14. Matty or Felipe
15. Reduced to also-ran status
16. Superior
17. Prelude to "Buckle my shoe"
18. SST's
21. Opted
22. Night, in Naples
27. City near Florence
30. Assists
32. Watch, as a sports event
35. Odd, to Sandy
36. ____-foot oil
37. Have the nerve
38. Road-map abbr.
39. Rarely
40. Island for King Arthur
43. On an even ____
45. Algerian port
47. Complete
49. Pentateuch scrolls
51. Famous sister
52. Fishhook attachments
53. Flowering
54. "I've ____ London to . . ."
55. Converted quickly to an also-ran
57. Of a heart part
58. Except
62. Deserts
66. Torn piece
68. Pearl White vehicle
70. Spatter: Var.
73. Mexican laborer
75. Los Angeles plague
77. Because
81. Part of the skull
83. A tide
85. Letters
88. Hebrew letter
90. Bottomless pit of a sort
92. Works ____ (painting, e.g.)
94. July 4 events
95. Schools, in France
96. Ceremonial dinner
97. Basic food item
98. Observation
100. Revile
102. Went for a bass
104. Unstable nuclear particle
105. Bankrupt
108. Word form for Portuguese
110. Besides
112. ____ 'clock scholar
113. Rubber trees
114. Duo or brace
116. Kind of cry
117. Existed
118. Uncle, in Aberdeen

166 Pet Project By Calista Luminati

Not limited to those around the house.

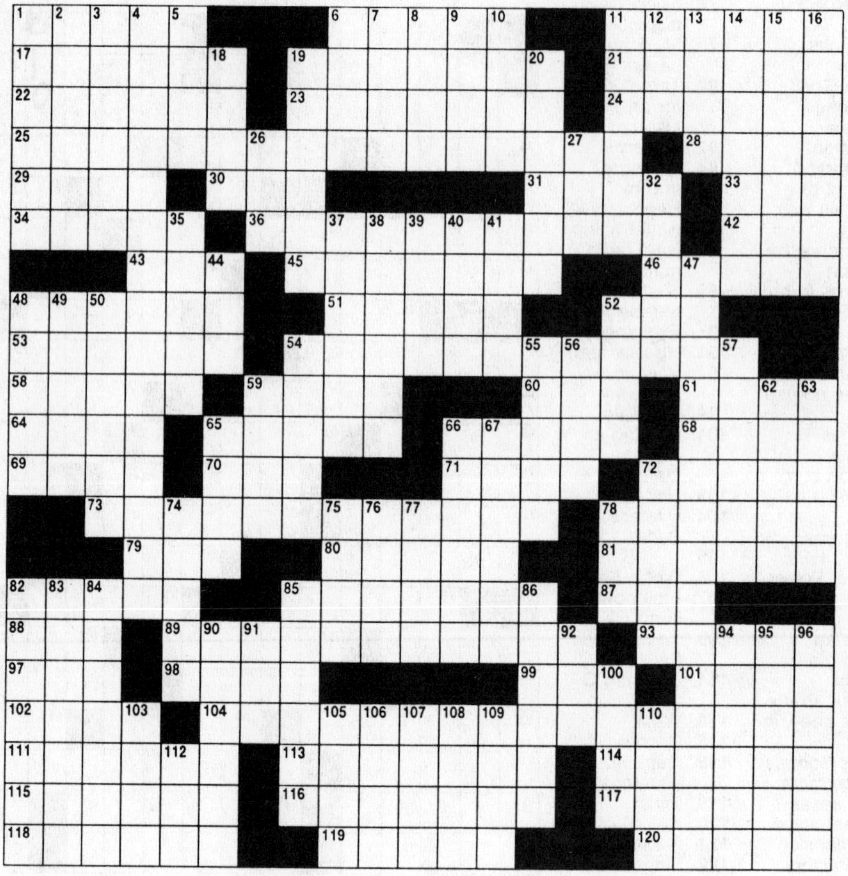

ACROSS

1. Tobacco and gum, e.g.
6. Caesar's and Antony's wear
11. Term of address, in Britain
17. Did frat recruiting
19. Feted
21. Twist or Goldsmith
22. Have ambitions
23. Put into position
24. Inflorescence
25. Wheezy question
28. Cupid
29. Fontanne's partner
30. Ship: Abbr.
31. Russian range
33. Hesitant sounds
34. Quixote's milieu
36. Stealthy ones
42. Suffix for enzymes
43. Fuzz
45. Doers of grammatical exercises
46. Chose
48. Athletic dance duet
51. Botch
52. Babylonian sky god
53. Some snakes do it
54. "___, if you please" (Disney movie line)
58. Fundamental spirit
59. Wife of Henry VIII
60. Compass pt.
61. Easy job
64. Youthful one
65. Bridge support
66. Jewish month
68. ___ of Man
69. Sea eagles
70. Place for a contented bug
71. "___ a man who wasn't there"
72. Nasty
73. Grin like ___
78. Knife repairer
79. W.W. I force
80. More withered
81. "Forsaking all ___ . . ."
82. ___ Brava
85. Spoiled
87. Before tense or fix
88. Canadian prov.
89. Acted timidly
93. Played Hamlet
97. Born
98. Snicker___
99. It is cast or drawn
101. You ___ (either of us)
102. Antagonists
104. Lively stepper?
111. Let out fishing line
113. Endurance
114. Danish king of England
115. Plain of Asia
116. Debs and McCarthy
117. Sifter
118. ". . . round ___ human shores": Keats
119. Organizations: Abbr.
120. Allen and MacMurray

DOWN

1. Inches along
2. "Be quiet!"
3. Spanish name for 34 Across
4. Famous British mouser
5. Indian weights
6. Weather abbr.
7. Former Russ. secret police
8. Guys' friends
9. "___! poor Yorick"
10. Off. worker
11. Pestle's need
12. Dockworkers' org.
13. Pests
14. Gorge
15. Contrition
16. Clothed
18. Thieves' places
19. Try again on a Christmas package
20. Transfers
26. Common abbr.
27. ___ mode
32. "What ___ to do?"
35. Brads
37. Domesticators
38. Pipes
39. Largest country: Abbr.
40. Counsel, old style
41. ___ point (canvas stitching)
44. He featured a raven
47. Children's game
48. Mountain ridge
49. Post-office equipment
50. Goddess of wisdom
52. Final word
54. Alec or Evelyn
55. Gusset
56. Medical subj.
57. Store fodder
59. Former German state: Abbr.
62. Birch-family tree
63. Equals
65. Nonkosher
66. "Oh, it's ___ get up in the morning'"
67. Turkish hospice
72. Hindu precept
74. Oodles
75. "Do as ___, not . . ."
76. Plunder, in Scotland
77. Conductor Rapee
78. ___ a plea
82. Muddle
83. Upstate New York city
84. Pilot
85. Fly of Africa
86. Greek letters
90. Sam and Remus
91. Red or Black
92. Period
94. Found, to Pierre
95. Expressed feelings
96. Postpones
100. Facial movements
103. Fall mo.
105. Giant of Greek myth
106. Hungarian premier
107. Ed and his brothers
108. Cue
109. Bills
110. Artless
112. N.T. book

167 Screen Test By Louis Sabin

Designed to find out who appeared in what films.

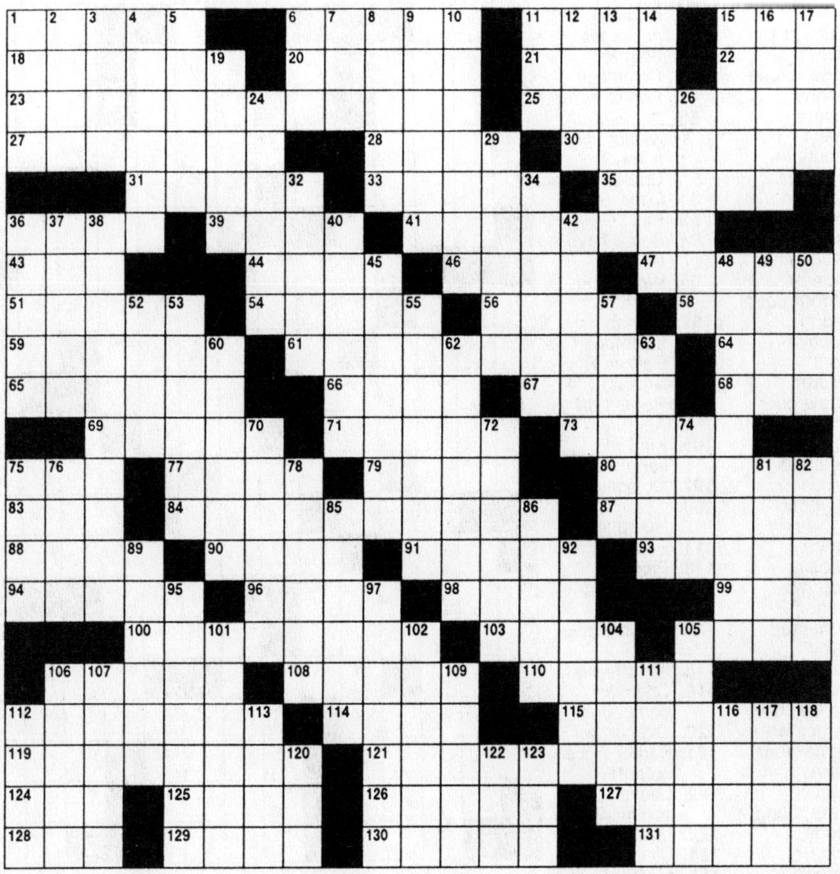

ACROSS

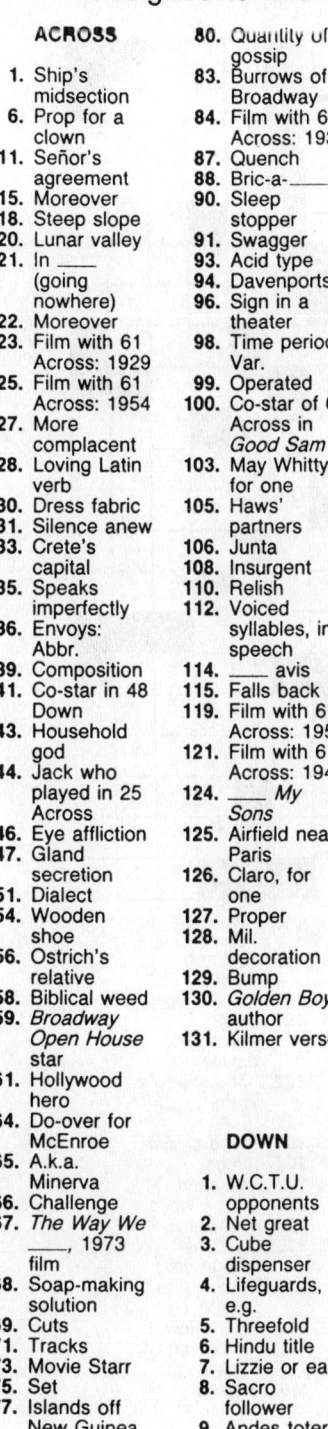

1. Ship's midsection
6. Prop for a clown
11. Señor's agreement
15. Moreover
18. Steep slope
20. Lunar valley
21. In ___ (going nowhere)
22. Moreover
23. Film with 61 Across: 1929
25. Film with 61 Across: 1954
27. More complacent
28. Loving Latin verb
30. Dress fabric
31. Silence anew
33. Crete's capital
35. Speaks imperfectly
36. Envoys: Abbr.
39. Composition
41. Co-star in 48 Down
43. Household god
44. Jack who played in 25 Across
46. Eye affliction
47. Gland secretion
51. Dialect
54. Wooden shoe
56. Ostrich's relative
58. Biblical weed
59. *Broadway Open House* star
61. Hollywood hero
64. Do-over for McEnroe
65. A.k.a. Minerva
66. Challenge
67. *The Way We* ___, 1973 film
68. Soap-making solution
69. Cuts
71. Tracks
73. Movie Starr
75. Set
77. Islands off New Guinea
79. Curare's kin
80. Quantity of gossip
83. Burrows of Broadway
84. Film with 61 Across: 1937
87. Quench
88. Bric-a-___
90. Sleep stopper
91. Swagger
93. Acid type
94. Davenports
96. Sign in a theater
98. Time period: Var.
99. Operated
100. Co-star of 61 Across in *Good Sam*
103. May Whitty, for one
105. Haws' partners
106. Junta
108. Insurgent
110. Relish
112. Voiced syllables, in speech
114. ___ avis
115. Falls back
119. Film with 61 Across: 1952
121. Film with 61 Across: 1941
124. *___ My Sons*
125. Airfield near Paris
126. Claro, for one
127. Proper
128. Mil. decoration
129. Bump
130. *Golden Boy* author
131. Kilmer verse

DOWN

1. W.C.T.U. opponents
2. Net great
3. Cube dispenser
4. Lifeguards, e.g.
5. Threefold
6. Hindu title
7. Lizzie or ear
8. Sacro follower
9. Andes toters
10. Rent-bill recipients
11. Kind of bank acct.
12. Peeved
13. Indeed!
14. Type styles
15. Suspended, as an anchor
16. Some words
17. Nod off
19. Please, in a trattoria
24. Wine producers
26. Box for valuables
29. Place for a Spanish drama
32. *The ___ Archipelago*
34. One way or another
36. Actress Valli
37. Furious with
38. Film with 61 Across: 1950
40. Matinee day, in Madrid
42. Loser, at times
45. Czech region
48. Film with 61 Across: 1942
49. Nobel chemist
50. Apportion
52. Hebrew measure
53. Obsessions
55. Dictators
57. Ivory towers
60. Cannoneer's tool
62. Piano's old cousin
63. Tebaldi or Adler
70. More tart
72. Grow furious
74. Stern
75. Chats
76. Spanish river
78. Cure-all
81. Arm bones
82. Errol and Uris
85. Fly's hopeful host
86. Aromas
89. Haunt for Charles Boyer
92. Actress Geva
95. Irish airport
97. Mexican state
101. Foe for the matador
102. Sea nymph
104. Levels
105. More ashen, in England
106. Rings
107. Saxon's other half
109. Coat size
111. Chamber group
112. Roe producer
113. Sign on a mover's lawn
116. Cupola
117. First name in detective stories
118. *The ___ the Limit,* 1943 Astaire film
120. Louis or Carrie
122. Capone's rod
123. Hesitaters' sounds

168 Determination By Jo Lundy

Exploring various ways to express it.

ACROSS

1. Youth org.
4. Taxi
7. Metal refuse
11. Johnny ___
14. Actress Cheryl
16. County in England
18. Young salmon
19. Ancient Syria
21. Holy Roman emperor
22. Without equal
23. Chip in
24. Infective agent
26. Children's curfew crier
29. Tarsus
30. Tranquil
31. Sketched
32. Certain partygoer
34. ___ de France
35. Curiosity Shop girl
36. Meager
39. Tormented
41. Put by
44. *The ___ Around Us*
45. Strange thing
46. Thames area with gardens
49. Elusive object
55. Part of Cong.
56. Melody
58. God, in Hebrew writings
59. Corp., for one
60. Fresh
61. Sergeant's order
63. Irrational number
64. Little Sir ___
66. Anger
69. Treasure or Ellis
70. Recipe abbr.
71. Possesses
73. Charm
75. Car of earlier days
76. ___ buco, veal dish
78. Angle
79. Arthur's teacher
80. Sports-ticket buyer
82. Small shelter
84. Lilting musical passages
86. Ship for Columbus
87. Porker home
88. "___, and wisdom finds a way": Crabbe
91. Cape
92. Plot
94. Some have a tin one
95. Woodwind: Abbr.
97. French sweetheart
98. Bottom lines
101. Arizona city
104. Rogers or Acuff
105. Kind of sapphire
107. Objective
109. ___ Humphrey
111. Escape
113. Piece of decorated china
117. Alarm clock, e.g.
118. It's often rara
119. Chemical compound
120. Old garden
121. Parker House output
122. Loose sediment
123. Lively dances
124. Classify
125. Marshal under Napoleon
126. Early movie censorship czar
127. Attempt
128. Western state: Abbr.

DOWN

1. "Thar she ___!"
2. Glossy fabric
3. Hold fast
4. Con's quarters
5. Steer clear
6. Boo-boos
7. Stretch over
8. Long and skinny
9. Creative worker
10. Say "Howdy"
11. Devastated
12. St. Patrick's country
13. Message for Dickens' Piggotty
15. Wooden plugs
16. Valley
17. Stair post
20. Food fish
25. Rundown
27. Wife's brother
28. "___ said that": Wilde
33. Above
37. Word before whiz
38. Actress Goldie
40. Together, in music
42. Foods
43. Days of yore
46. Afghan people
47. Wipe out
48. "This is the ___": Service
50. Missed the victory
51. Burden
52. Canvas cover
53. Showcase for 65 Down
54. Relative of an org.
57. Words before mode
60. Alaskan city
62. Get ___ the ground floor
65. Skater Dorothy
67. Marie Antoinette was one
68. Laboratory vessels
71. Give a job
72. Eastern hemisphere unit
74. Samovar
77. Haggard novel
78. Hodgepodge
81. Town in Massachusetts
83. Kojak or a Van Gogh
85. "___ transit . . ."
87. Student
88. Borscht ingredient
89. Corrode
90. Basketball shot
92. It needs a driver
93. Penny-pinching
96. Russian money
98. Bits and pieces
99. Farther down
100. Tool-sharpening device
102. "The sheep's in the ___ . . ."
103. Blood carrier
106. Almost swamped
108. After a while
109. Possessive
110. ___ one (good odds)
112. Take out, in printing
114. Easter flower
115. Naval craft of W.W. II
116. Depend

169 All in a Year By William Canine

And not too long ago to blot out memory.

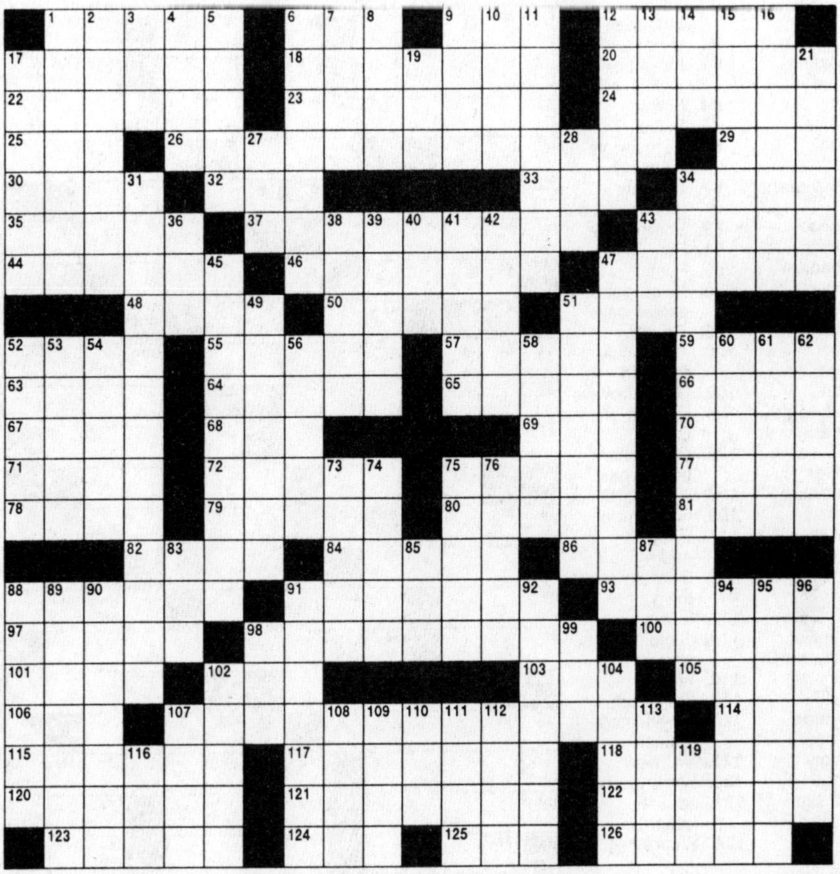

ACROSS

1. Freighter's load
6. Call from police HQ
9. Peak
12. Handicap, as one's style
17. Of a Frankish tribe
18. Brno's region
20. Shark's hitchhiker
22. Pass
23. Most valiant
24. Holds dear
25. Sailor
26. 1977 award to *The Shadow Box*
29. Dolt
30. Syria, once
32. Dupin's creator
33. Cheer for Escamillo
34. Revolt
35. Demarcate
37. 1977 Academy Award film
43. Playwright Jean
44. "'Tis the ___ to be jolly"
46. Tone-deaf ones' features
47. Boring tools
48. Kind of goose or shoe
50. Burst of applause
51. Caroled
52. Border
55. White hydrocarbon
57. Harbingers
59. Doubtful
63. Anderson of WKRP
64. Woman in a *palais*
65. Citadel student
66. Clinton's canal
67. Valhalla host
68. Stowe heroine
69. Long-nosed fish
70. German city on the Saale
71. Gas for signs
72. Yugoslav coin
75. Yugoslav port
77. Approving votes
78. Ready to eat
79. It's acute or obtuse
80. Forgettable Detroit export
81. Trout-fishing move
82. Dotted, in heraldry
84. "What's in ___?"
86. Haystack
88. Strauss opera
91. Foremost
93. Maintain
97. Jogs
98. 1977 Masters champion
100. *Pagliacci* role
101. ___ avis
102. Strudel's relative
103. Buck's mate
105. Fleet
106. Broadway's Burrows
107. Seattle Slew victory in 1977
114. Angolan province
115. Coal miners
117. *Invisible Man* author
118. Mystery-story mainstay?
120. God of agriculture
121. Most insinuating
122. Offspring of 40 Down
123. Nursemaid
124. Vital juice
125. In medias ___
126. Mary of wreck note

DOWN

1. Dieter's concern
2. Home for Tallulah
3. Sleeper of note
4. Make a wheezy sound
5. In golf, a bare lead
6. Encompassing
7. Any one will do, in a storm
8. Land north of Uru.
9. Declare
10. Speech flaw
11. Reconnaissance groups
12. Hottest fad
13. Counsel, old style
14. "I love," to Calpurnia
15. Glacial deposit
16. Laundry worker
17. Vivienne and George
19. Hail!
21. Goods and chattels
27. Mauna ___
28. Indisposed
31. Dorothy Benham, 1977 Atlantic City winner
34. 1977 World Series MVP
36. Vogue
38. Jewish month
39. Sappy
40. Conger
41. Devastation
42. Scent
43. Squirt or BB
45. College football's 1977 champion
47. Davis Cup winner in 1977
49. Dodder laurel
51. Tennis footwear
52. Pale
53. Cowboy show
54. Skull part
56. Old Chinese weight
58. Selvages
60. Valkyries' leader
61. Penalties
62. Fungus for a baker
73. Tocsin
74. Begin again
75. Forgive
76. Parisians' notions
83. Dorothy's aunt and others
85. *I ___ Camera*
87. Winter time in K.C.
88. Wristlets
89. San'a resident
90. Young or Lynn
91. Marianne Moore, for one
92. Beavers and others
94. Person giving power
95. Diamond necklace
96. Persons who dally
98. Kind of pan or soldier
99. ". . . ___ any drop to drink"
102. Actress Singleton
104. Went into decline
107. *Show Boat* composer
108. Forelimb bone
109. Mow
110. Josh
111. North Sea feeder
112. Administer aspirin
113. Christmastide
116. Town: Abbr.
119. Dam-building org.

170 Reunion By Richard Silvestri

Wherein members of the clan get together.

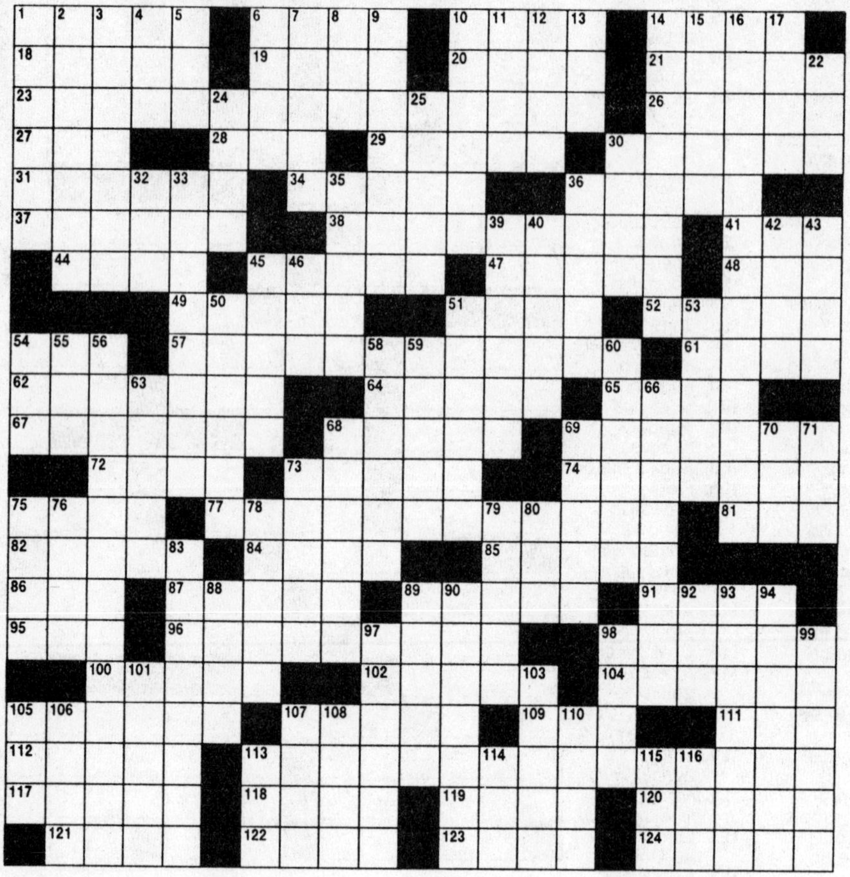

ACROSS

1. Aids evildoing
6. Mideast cartel
10. Part of a fishhook
14. Pealed
18. Variable stars
19. ___ morgana
20. Shawm's descendant
21. Audibly
23. Robert Vaughn TV series
26. Actress Oberon
27. L.B.J. beagle
28. Superlative suffix
29. Slur over
30. In a morose manner
31. Improves a text
34. Dieter of note
36. Singer O'Day
37. Admirers of Silas Marner
38. "I'll be darned!"
41. Bird's beak
44. "___ boy!"
45. Adult ugly ducklings
47. Clear a tape
48. Austin or Essex
49. Muckraker Sinclair
51. Scads
52. Germ cell
54. Promoted capt.
57. American painter
61. Peck's partner
62. ___ and cold (be inconsistent)
64. Simultaneously
65. Egyptian goddess
67. Newborn's outfit
68. ___ *Andronicus*
69. Workshop
72. Container for six-packs
73. Art gallery
74. One of the languages
75. Asseverate
77. Native language
81. U-boat
82. Neighbor of Chad
84. Foray
85. Sulks
86. ___ Bingle (Crosby)
87. Ultimate gambling loss
89. Sharp ridge
91. Flip
95. Fuss
96. News gal of earlier days
98. Tin alloy
100. Three-coin fountain
102. Greek vowels
104. Francis or Dahl
105. Component of fuel gas
107. ___ Carta
109. Gas: Prefix
111. Enzyme ending
112. Belgian treaty town
113. Santa ___
117. Junior canyon
118. Wings
119. Bump off
120. King Minos' realm
121. Not new
122. Work the bar
123. ___ it (amen)
124. Wears out

DOWN

1. The "Marseillaise" is one
2. Place for arty people
3. Hillary's conquest
4. Aberdeen cap
5. Red, Yellow or Black
6. Switch positions
7. Constituents
8. W.W. II area
9. Actor Rod
10. Skipjack
11. Start of the alphabet
12. Lead or cameo
13. Bonnet inhabitant
14. Mast markings
15. Adak native
16. Noted *Saturday Review* editor
17. Trick
22. Old Algerian governor
24. Mysterious loch
25. European lancers: Var.
30. Wildebeests
32. Seine
33. Drinks
35. Mind one's ___ Q's
36. Playing marble
39. Criminals
40. Cropped up
42. Make money
43. Author Harte
45. One of 50
46. Came in first
50. For the time being
51. Total
53. Pa. city
54. Easily changed: Abbr.
55. In the style of
56. Popular psychologist
58. Posted
59. Dictator of the 400
60. Take no part in
63. Spent
66. Half a school year
68. South Pacific island
69. Dispute
70. Medieval shield
71. Johnny of the Confederacy
73. Marquee names
75. Hawkeye portrayer
76. Competed
78. Pygmy antelope
79. Horse or soap follower
80. "___ on a bet!"
83. Answered affirmatively
88. ___ to (positioned a ship)
89. Make amends
90. Holds back
92. Hooter
93. Paddle wheeler
94. Capable of feeling
97. Breathed an "alas"
98. Prefix for mutuel
99. Della and Pee Wee
101. Scope
103. Hindu term of respect
105. Bird-to-be
106. G
107. Smoker attendee
108. ___ impasse
110. Sea eagle
113. Portly
114. Dove call
115. Cub or Eagle: Abbr.
116. Prefix for color or corn

171 Couplets By Alfio Micci

On a minimal scale, as far as poets are concerned.

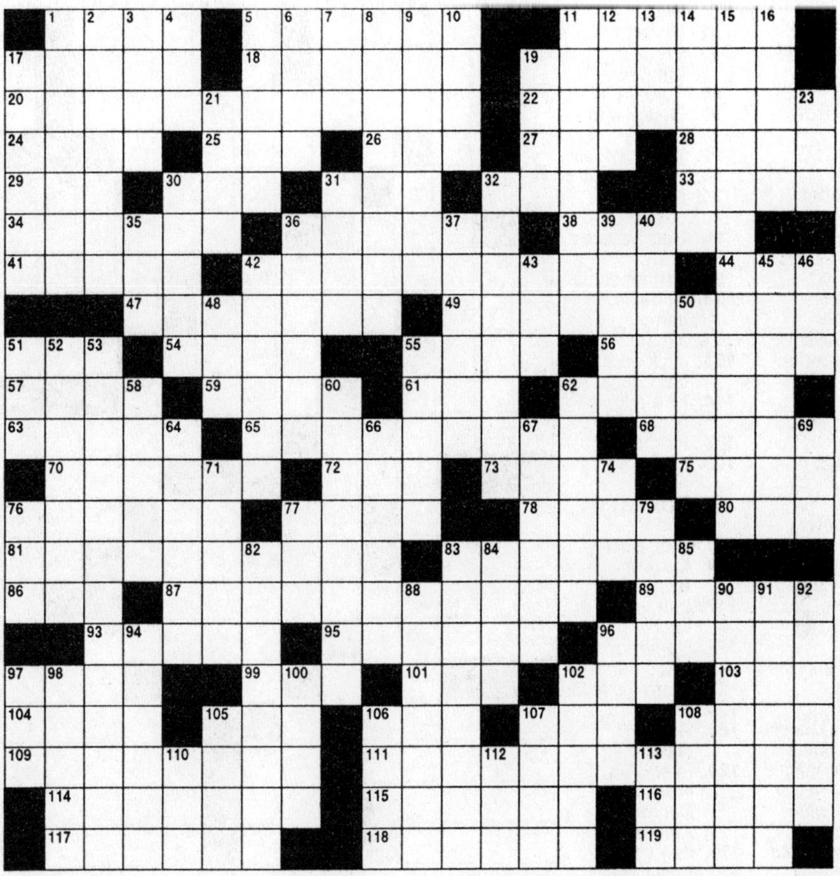

ACROSS

1. Mind
5. Sells hot tickets
11. Forth and Clyde
17. ". . . and behold ___ horse": Revelation
18. "Do ___ Waltz?"
19. Loser
20. Leipzig lecture?
22. Gave
24. Mine finds
25. East, in Essen
26. Ltr. afterthoughts
27. Mil. officer
28. Egyptian heaven
29. Word before a-tat
30. Bean variety
31. ___ tee
32. Morse-code word
33. Pottery drier
34. Criticize
36. Option
38. Very, to Verdi
41. Bobby ___ of *A Lonely Rage*
42. Soissons seat?
44. Critic Huxtable
47. Raipur natives
49. Wile E. Coyote's cartoon prey
51. Scott's *The ___ Quartet*
54. Dusting powder
55. Cement
56. Subterranean events
57. Blind as ___
59. Word before work or pile
61. That, to a Spaniard
62. Punish with a fine
63. Mead's milieu
65. Chalet cutie?
68. ___-Exupéry
70. Eric Knight's collie
72. Pal to Larry and Curly
73. Writer Philip
75. Hindu water vessel
76. Cry to the hounds
77. Disturbance
78. Small amount
80. Not pos.
81. Covering
83. Child's drink
86. Soup variety
87. Samawa sport?
89. Aspect
93. Relatives of the ides
95. Hudson Bay feeder
96. Stage whispers
97. Ali ___
99. Acad.
101. Bambi's aunt
102. "Have you ___ wool?"
103. French connectives
104. Winglike
105. Author Santha Rama
106. Monk's title
107. Degree for an atty.
108. Utah resort
109. Adhesive
111. Nazareth newspaper?
114. Winter underwear
115. Kyoto entertainer
116. Sea birds
117. Producers' saviors
118. Visit
119. Tear's companion

DOWN

1. Run
2. Robert Blake TV role
3. O'Neill trees
4. Voice vote
5. Miss Spacek
6. Huntley
7. Flying prefix
8. National and Harvard
9. Dull
10. ___ souci
11. ___ *the Devil,* Garbo film
12. "This ___ sudden!"
13. "Balderdash!"
14. Russian vehicle
15. Hilo heir?
16. Fish-line leader
17. Athenian squares
19. Girl in *East of Eden*
21. Cranny's partner
23. Press for payment
30. Aroma
31. "And ___ there were none"
32. Jaunty
35. Miss MacGraw
36. City on the Vistula
37. Baptismal oil
39. "Get lost!"
40. Author Nevil and others
42. Threadlike
43. The same: Latin abbr.
45. Easing of discord
46. Preceders of esses
48. Crow's relative
50. Form of citral
51. Cape
52. Shellfish
53. Port Royal pork?
55. Harass
58. Operatic heroine
60. Reduce
62. Wandering
64. Invites
66. Calm
67. Like underbaked bread
69. Convention lapel wear
71. River to the Rhone
74. Gen. Arnold
76. On to
77. Necessary: Abbr.
79. Peter Rabbit sib
82. Health-club offerings
83. Script
84. Gumbo
85. Key letter
88. Excess newspaper type
90. Soprano Patti
91. Colonist
92. Elian works
94. Propelling a dinghy
96. *The King ___*
97. Dull noise
98. False wing of a bird
100. Hints
102. Poe's middle name
105. Shore bird
106. Pear-shaped fruits
107. City near Utah Lake
108. Bern's river
110. Sweater size: Abbr.
112. Cleo's killer
113. Morning mist

172 Torrid Zone By Tap Osborn

Getting to the warmer side of things.

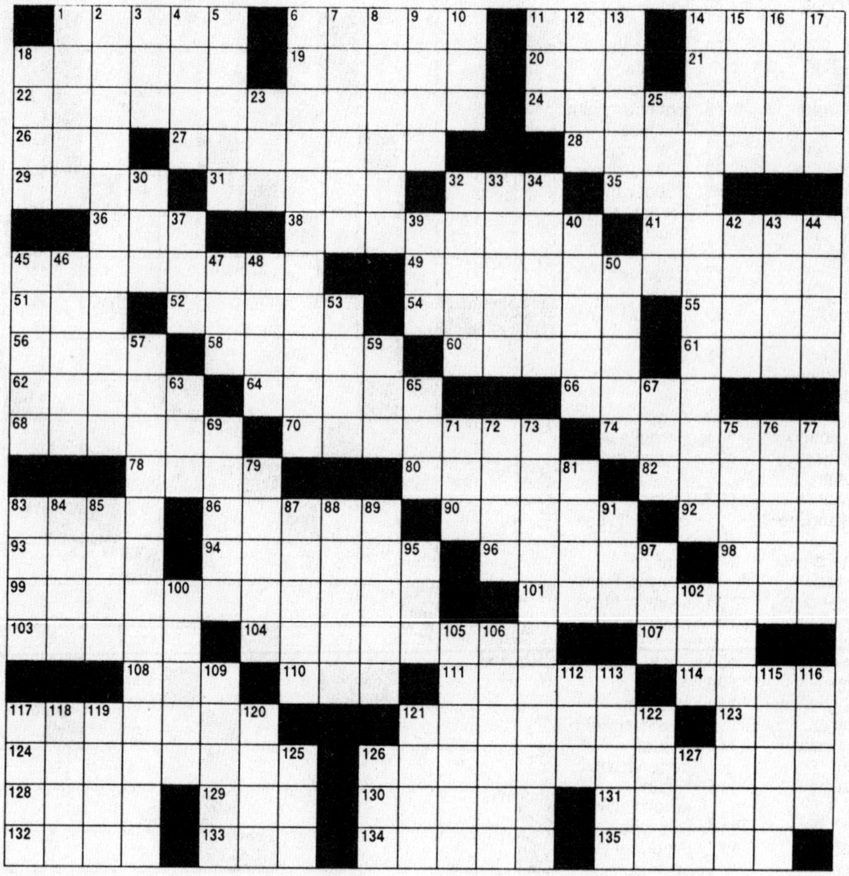

ACROSS

1. Melville's captain and family
6. Orale
11. Hunter of films
14. Gambler's game
18. Michener opus
19. Repeat, to Cato
20. Prior to
21. Solzhenitzyn's Denisovich
22. Hot weapon
24. Foundation material
26. Like a mad hen
27. Extends the lease
28. Sticks
29. Film-actor Blore
31. A fresco technique
32. "When ___ a door not . . . ?"
35. It flows in the spring
36. Rapa ___, Easter Island
38. Subscribers' acts of faith
41. Like Mercury
45. Sweet wine
49. Olympic-games herald
51. Saturate
52. ___ on wood
54. Involve
55. Persian gazelle
56. One-time Asian monarchy
58. Another sweet wine
60. Heavy French weight
61. Fabulist: Var.
62. Sonar's relative
64. It enhances fish
66. Star in Pegasus
68. Mexican liquor
70. Went berserk
74. Club for Snead
78. Old English coin
80. Hostess Mesta
82. Undermine
83. Prefix for gravure
86. Took heed of
90. Glasgow land baron
92. Writer Wiesel
93. Under, at sea
94. Rickshaw puller
96. Red Square draw
98. Lab amounts
99. Certain cork items
101. Initiate
103. Jack, in a card deck
104. Like migrant field hands
107. Pale color
108. Kind of phone
110. Between L and P
111. Prot. sect
114. Current fashion
117. Left in the lurch
121. Name for Napoleon II
123. Darrow's field
124. Met
126. Warmer-upper
128. First president of Central America
129. Salt Lake pro
130. Baseball-shoe item
131. 1968 Oscar film
132. Youthful one
133. Bench with a back
134. Flax fibers
135. Rites setting

DOWN

1. More adept
2. Ache soothers
3. Fortify
4. German drink
5. Fills
6. Noisemaker
7. Pronto
8. Isaac of apple note
9. Cassiterite and galena
10. Conjunction
11. Shamus
12. Venezuelan mine center
13. Diver's malady
14. Cozy parlor heat source
15. Affirm
16. Have status
17. Do ___ thing
18. "Victory is ours ___ try"
23. Medieval reign: Abbr.
25. Rub raw
30. Kind of bid or ball
32. "___ Dance"
33. Andrea del ___
34. Continental highway
37. Sort
39. Paris season
40. Do a shoe job
42. Cupid, to Homer
43. Saarinen
44. Ensnare
45. Indian state
46. Ear pollutant
47. Usurer's take: Abbr.
48. Unshaken
50. Coffee expert's creation
53. River to the Volga
57. Cookstove's progeny
59. Over there
63. Islet
65. Siesta
67. Spleen
69. Armor piercer
71. Blanc or Allen
72. Not written
73. Illumination producers
75. Heat-producing stuff
76. Decree
77. Famed shortstop
79. Riot hauls
81. Fish-eating flier
83. Off the ___ (not tailored)
84. 1932 P.G.A. champ Dutra
85. Garb for Gaius
87. Tribal emblem
88. Lamb-like
89. Prospect for the d.t.'s
91. Hullabaloo
95. Inner: Prefix
97. Court divider
100. English author Charles
102. Wool producer
105. More orderly
106. At the top
109. Sew hastily
112. Road warning
113. Milk drink
115. Office gadget
116. Water holder
117. Ella's forte
118. Flew
119. It's usually enough
120. Fountain of music
121. Getter of *Damn Yankees*
122. Football coach Chuck
125. Mountain ___
126. F.D.R.'s predecessor
127. ___ into (assailed)

173 20/20 By Evelyn Benshoof

Checking up on one's sense of sight.

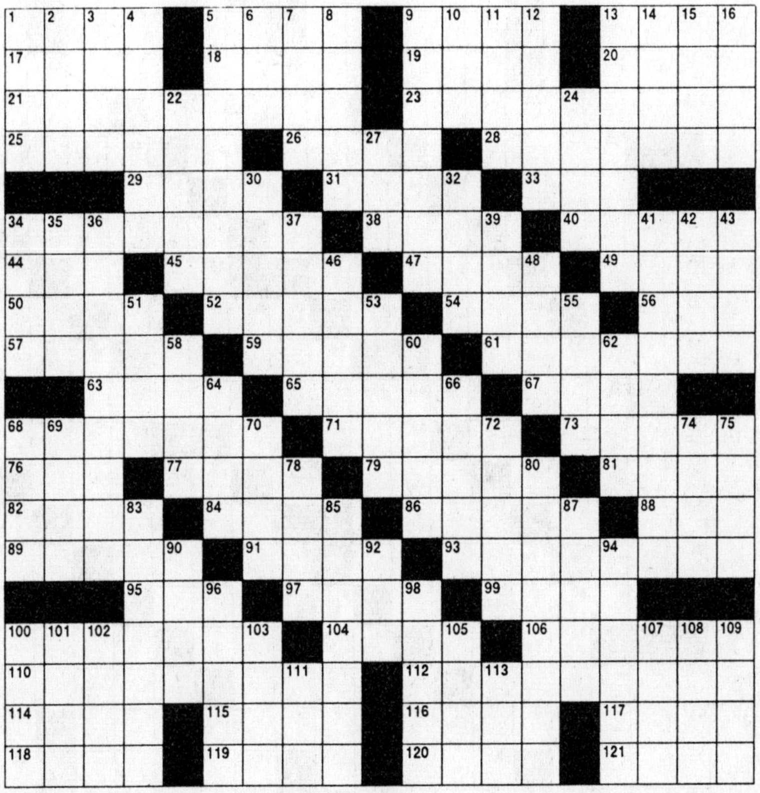

ACROSS

1. Kind of hat or heart
5. Florida neighbor
9. Local map
13. Islamic judge
17. Indonesian islands
18. Danube feeder
19. Indian princess
20. Focal line
21. Casual glance
23. Beauty
25. Burning
26. It's dangerous if split
28. Foot lever
29. Do a doctor's job
31. Impressively great
33. Low-grade wool
34. Immigrants' accommodation
38. Part of a school year
40. Hebrew letter
44. Scottish river
45. Bluish green
47. Cross
49. Australian lake
50. Mimicked
52. Make sense
54. Puffy headdress
56. Always, to poets
57. Confusion
59. Column type
61. Slip back
63. Off center
65. Early Germanic law
67. Identifying tag
68. Complete a questionnaire
71. Splendid
73. Famous diarist
76. Kind of wind or bred
77. "Shoo!"
79. Roosevelt and Teasdale
81. Tiff
82. Falsified
84. Depart
86. Bridge-game response
88. Wallach
89. Exemplary
91. Sacred painting
93. Objection
95. Trivial bribe
97. Mop
99. Erudition
100. Japanese fish dish
104. Cross- or bug-___
106. Site
110. Morning nip
112. See
114. Island off Ireland
115. Type of terrier
116. Mountain: Prefix
117. Dispatch
118. Alight
119. Effuse
120. Estrange
121. Pudding starch

DOWN

1. Merry sound
2. Mecca visitor
3. Undulate
4. Spoil
5. Wide-angle movie of yore
6. Avail
7. East Indian weaverbird
8. Mountain ridge
9. Canadian V.I.P.
10. ___ of the land
11. Dill
12. Headdress
13. Skilled
14. Fired
15. Radio part
16. ___ of Man
22. Blue
24. Small armadillo
27. Elect
30. Islands off Sicily
32. Cut closely
34. Pierce
35. Polynesian cloth
36. Took a gander
37. Logical structure
39. Tie up at a pier
41. Lollapalooza
42. Company off.
43. Now's partner
46. Type of eclipse
48. Contest
51. Farmer's place
53. Wharf timbers
55. Lay an egg
58. Writer about blondes
60. Cheroot
62. Periods
64. Brownish purple
66. Minded
68. Make a movie
69. Pelvic bone: Prefix
70. Rental car of a sort
72. Tag for a buyer
74. Lockmaker
75. Pother
78. Spasms
80. Buck
83. Feel blue
85. Reached great heights
87. Old English woolen cloth
90. Cloth mask
92. A vote
94. Coffee break
96. One of the estates
98. ___ the salt
100. Greenish blue
101. South American wildcat
102. Shabby
103. Cross of old Egypt
105. Hazard
107. Cruising
108. Kind of shoreman
109. Within: Prefix
111. Part of a needle
113. Affirmation

174 Alfresco By John Hales

Letting nature have its day.

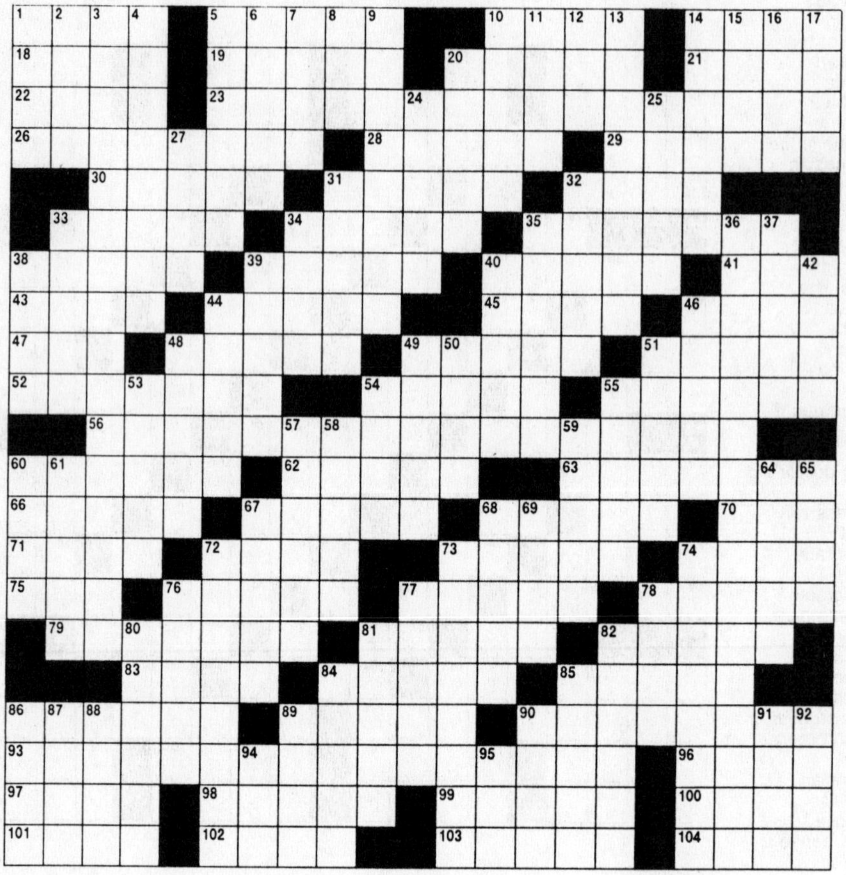

ACROSS

1. Wall pier
5. Manila hemp
10. Boxers' moves
14. Plethora
18. Auto route, in Berlin
19. Meeting place for academia
20. Borne by the wind
21. Innkeeper, in Italy
22. Unvarying
23. "Song of the Chattahoochee" locale
26. Nimbleness
28. Maurice of drama
29. Fonda and Piper
30. Scheduled costs
31. Nasty kids
32. Feather: Prefix
33. Conger catcher
34. Night spot
35. Like Noel Coward's lives
38. Grove features
39. Meet with old grads
40. Electricity, to a wirer
41. ___ *Pinafore*
43. It's often glad
44. Florence's ___ Vecchio
45. Sea extensions
46. Vantage point for Moses
47. Egyptian cobra
48. Wild buffaloes
49. Mea ___
51. Witchcraft city
52. Sapped of energy
54. Kind of wave
55. Actor Michael
56. Whitman poem
60. Source of a certain chip
62. Stirs up
63. Church assistant
66. Hebrew months
67. Satyrs
68. Cipher
70. Sweep
71. Badminton piece
72. Put up a painting
73. Allen's or Gasoline
74. Newts
75. "Hello!" from Caesar
76. European food fish
77. Jury affair
78. Smelting byproduct
79. *CHiPs* star
81. Creator
82. Full of meaning
83. Pete Rose's old buddies
84. Disputed Israel–Syria heights
85. "___ Macabre"
86. Montana Indian
89. ___ a limb
90. Extraordinary events
93. Ferde Grofé composition
96. Not common-place
97. Seine feeder
98. Painter Winslow
99. Jack Jones' father
100. Gumbo ingredient
101. Dregs
102. Supplemented a bit at a time
103. Refine ore
104. "Out where the ___ begins"

DOWN

1. Biblical shepherd
2. Church area
3. Connelly play
4. Toughened, as steel
5. Less colorful
6. Torments
7. Confederate
8. Mountain pass
9. Gooselike
10. Updike and Steinbeck
11. "How sad!"
12. Apron part
13. Doubters: Var.
14. Places for orators
15. Tennis star
16. Luminary
17. Partner of haws
20. Pacific island
24. Egg-shaped
25. Female of the ruff
27. Atlas entries: Abbr.
31. Ring-card listings
32. Kind of donna
33. Nullify
34. Lake Nyasa people
35. Like Burgess' cow
36. Scott poem
37. Glowing coal
38. Ease tension
39. Musical form
40. Drug-yielding plant
42. Body of an animal
44. Courteous word, in Firenze
46. Twangy
48. Words that offend purists
49. Sky-blue colors
50. Japanese herbs
51. Be uppity toward
53. Amundsen
54. ___ as a rail
55. Mehitabel's friend
57. Lingua ___
58. Durable
59. Conrad of old films
60. Small armadillo
61. Drab color
64. Cheap
65. Gaelic
67. Trust and sinking items
68. Outlander
69. Suffix with jug or mod
72. Migraine
73. Land of Opportunity state
74. Acknowledges an error
76. Drift
77. Claw
78. Ancient weight
80. Groups of three
81. Prime mover
82. Report-card inspector
84. Reinforced
85. Harp-guitar key
86. Band for an Arab's kerchief
87. Irrefutable
88. *"Quién ___?"*
89. "That's one ___!"
90. Word before stone or post
91. Slips
92. Stock-exchange purchase
94. Perfect, to an astronaut
95. City on the Danube

175 Possessions By Dorothy Smitonick

Possible alternatives to the Oscar awards.

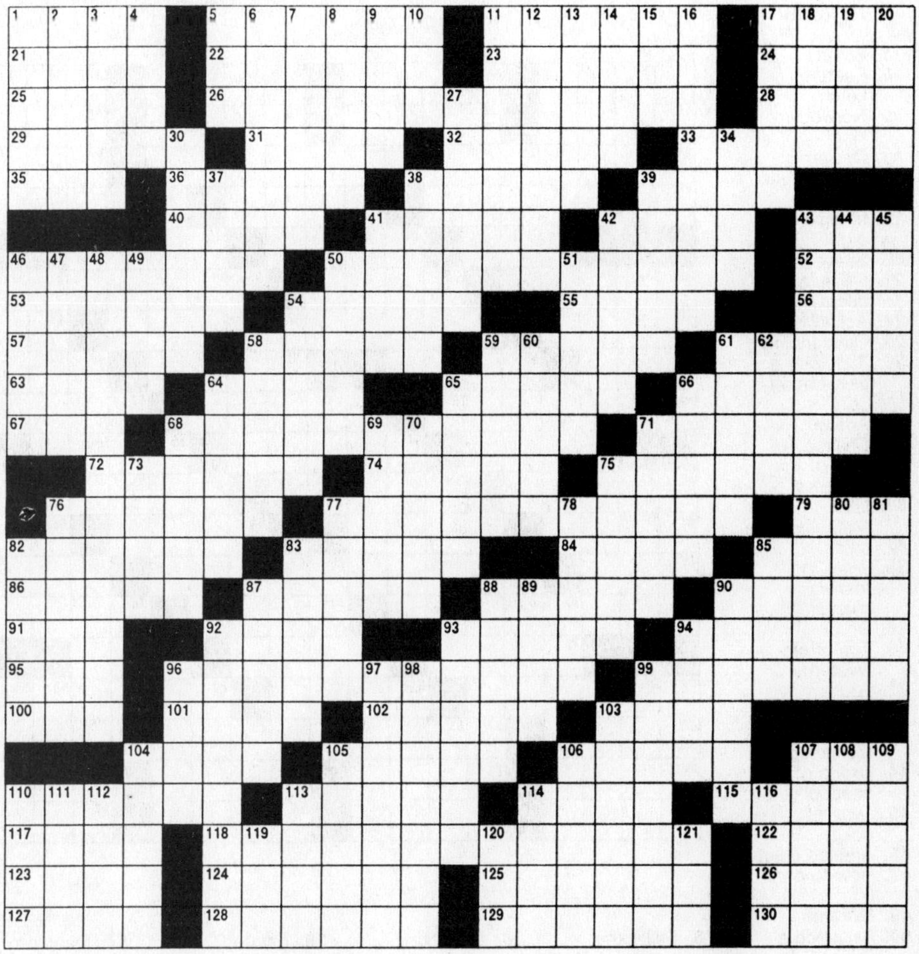

ACROSS

1. Gem stone
5. Skilled people
11. Cause a blockage
17. Roof ornaments
21. Kind of eye
22. Win back
23. List of corrections
24. Like Ben Jonson
25. Sinking-ship deserters
26. Art's sideshow?
28. Actor Richard
29. Tampered with a check
31. Tennis play-overs
32. South American monkeys
33. New
35. Stallone, for short
36. Issues
38. Bandleader Shaw
39. ___ out (arrange)
40. Bogs
41. Farewell
42. Escapees from Pandora's box
43. Instance, in France
46. Repeating
50. Harrison's old vehicle?
52. The law's is long
53. Furrowed
54. Rajah's wife
55. Zuider and Tappan
56. Pier workers' org.
57. Four-star janitor?
58. No man's land of a sort
59. Meager
61. Li'l Dogpatch resident
63. Augur
64. Hawaiian wreaths
65. Separate
66. Glib
67. Brit. officials
68. Audrey's songbird?
71. Melodic
72. Woodnymphs
74. Sluggish
75. Nameless person
76. Choice dishes
77. Robert's deal?
79. Swiss canton
82. Lassos
83. ___ at (eats like a bird)
84. Russian city
85. Doer: Suffix
86. Singer Gluck and others
87. Use a spa's facilities
88. Earn
90. Feel for concealed weapons
91. Half a Philippine city
92. Indian weight
93. Most dire
94. Mickey's partner
95. *Dombey and* ___
96. Orson's express?
99. Affluent
100. Finish
101. Actress Charlotte and family
102. Goddess of agriculture
103. Gala
104. Draws a bead on
105. Metric weights
106. Extinct birds
107. Taboo
110. Church vaults
113. Shy of
114. Atmosphere: Prefix
115. Succinct
117. Irritate
118. Dustin's yarn?
122. "___ horse!"
123. Actor Walter
124. "___ bragh"
125. ___ leave (at liberty)
126. ___ a barrel
127. Swampy place
128. Actress Thelma
129. Strait off the Coral Sea
130. Sun. talks

DOWN

1. Dopey people
2. Advantage
3. Simple song
4. Or ___
5. Bow
6. Wheeling's partner
7. Wading birds
8. Sam made them too long
9. Standoffs
10. Curve in a ship's plank
11. Descendants of Shem
12. Radioactive isotope
13. ". . . a case of do ___"
14. Handles roughly
15. American lizard
16. Armored trucks' load, often
17. Build
18. Summon by intercom
19. Oil country
20. Mailed
27. Step
30. Nonconformist
34. Formerly, old style
37. Darn
38. Relevant to a matter
39. Winter fall
41. First-rate
42. Part of I.D.: Abbr.
43. Michael's rebellion?
44. Miss Dahl
45. Clever
46. ___ Downs
47. Tuft
48. Bob's bauble?
49. Author Wister
50. "So ___ good"
51. Arkansas range
54. Attacks
58. "___ up!" (look out!)
59. Ignite
60. Menu
61. ___ with the past (keepsake, i.e.)
62. Float
64. Is in front
65. Templeton and Guinness
66. Dress
68. Tropical birds
69. Kind of doctor
70. Kind of charmer
71. "___ of robins in her hair"
73. Pro ___
75. Confess
76. Poet François
77. Bristles
78. Back: Prefix
80. Miss O'Grady of song
81. Annoyed
82. Lift
83. Bores
85. English composer
87. Tree trunks
88. Customs
89. Work units
90. "This was their ___ hour": Churchill
92. Truck driver
93. Cordiality
94. Marquand's sleuth
96. Legal document
97. Cratchit's employer
98. ___ one's life (be in danger)
99. Go between
103. Preceding
104. Daily anti-doctor fare
105. Treaty city
106. Postpone
107. Mark over a vowel
108. Fall flower
109. Approaches
110. Bone up for an exam
111. Nobel physicist
112. French-Belgian river
113. Cut
114. Hair style
116. Some are inflated
119. Onassis
120. Many times, to poets
121. Figs.

176 Split-Ups By Arthur Palmer

A matter of taking some liberties with words.

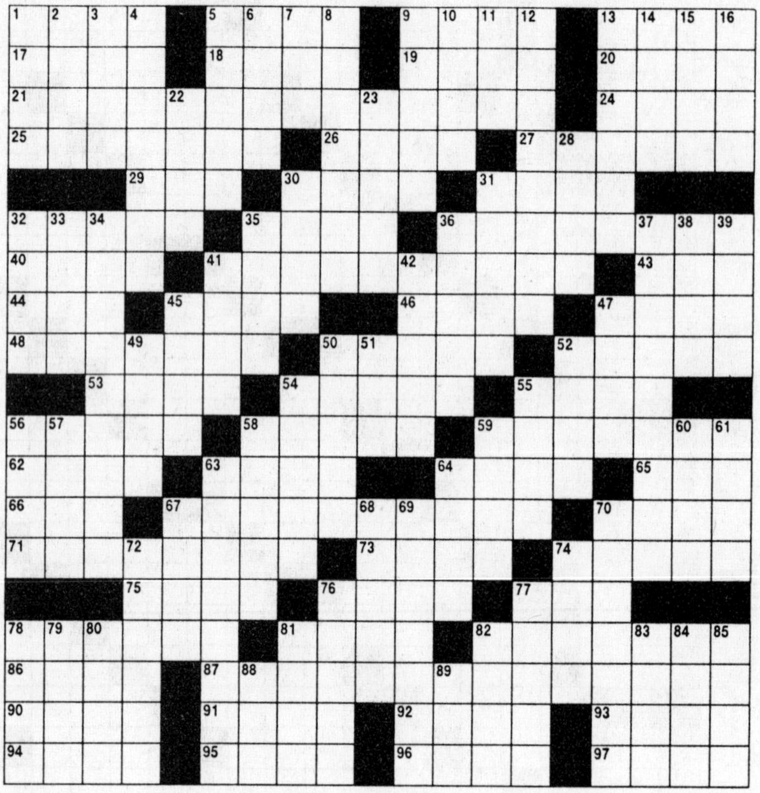

ACROSS

1. Smart ___
5. Eastern ketch
9. Norwegian king
13. Design
17. Wool: Prefix
18. Bones
19. Maggiore, e.g.
20. Stray
21. C.P.A.'s talent?
24. Acknowledge
25. Outstanding
26. ". . . with a blue ribbon ___"
27. Arrival
29. Chalice veil
30. One of the Rangers
31. Like Methuselah
32. Inks
35. Word in many mystery titles
36. Docile
40. Tim of old westerns
41. Grumpy German?
43. Former Mideast org.
44. Group of anecdotes
45. Type of poker
46. Arabian chief
47. How to bear it
48. Extreme
50. Assigned a PG or R to
52. *La ___ Vita*
53. Advice to a cat
54. Referred to
55. Top-notch
56. Drive
58. Slackens
59. Pardon
62. One of the Ages
63. Swiss river
64. Medicinal plant
65. Part of S.P.Q.R.
66. Marsh
67. Add refrigerants?
70. ___ libre
71. Place catering to luxurious tastes
73. Concerning
74. Diaphanous
75. Biblical weed
76. Spike the punch
77. Air-board abbr.
78. Summer-house
81. Supermarket counter
82. Some anesthetics
86. Cupid
87. Vessel for an envoy
90. Woodwind
91. Winter affliction
92. Toward the mouth
93. Chaplin's widow
94. Vehicle to the airport
95. Pianist Myra
96. Libertine
97. Moscow negative

DOWN

1. "Woe is me!"
2. Milk: Prefix
3. Differ or refer follower
4. Suave insect
5. Marine detector
6. Star: Prefix
7. "It ___ far, far better thing . . ."
8. Freight-train unit
9. Stan's friend
10. Café au ___
11. Rep.
12. Canadian woodsman
13. Soviet paper
14. Tennis word
15. Stratford's river
16. Salamander
22. Caucho sources
23. ___ sanctum
28. Fender blemish
30. Acclaim
31. "And the way of a man with ___"
32. Body of Islamic law
33. Scottish island
34. Happy Irving, the author?
35. Heated sheet of metal
36. With sword in hand
37. Like Ives?
38. Secular
39. Sea bird
41. R.B.I., e.g.
42. Singer Smith and others
45. Disfigure
47. Lost
49. Image
50. Up and about
51. Lunched
52. Not rare
54. Insertion mark
55. Andy's radio pal
56. Offend
57. U.S.S.R. city
58. Author of "The Raven"
59. Sheltered
60. Toothpaste unit
61. Once around the sun
63. Get near
64. Farmer's asset
67. Moby Dick's pursuer
68. Clock faces
69. Canine's neighbor
70. Detective Charlie's heir?
72. Equipment in many dens
74. Ado
76. Aids for detectives
77. Horace's forte
78. "The Ballad of Reading ___"
79. Prefix for dextrous
80. Camera-lens type
81. Bridge bids: Abbr.
82. Neighbor of Minn.
83. Tar's cry
84. Seven on a football team
85. Tiff
88. One of the Stooges
89. Parseghian

177 Card Shuffling By Norman Wizer

And coming up with names by which some were once known.

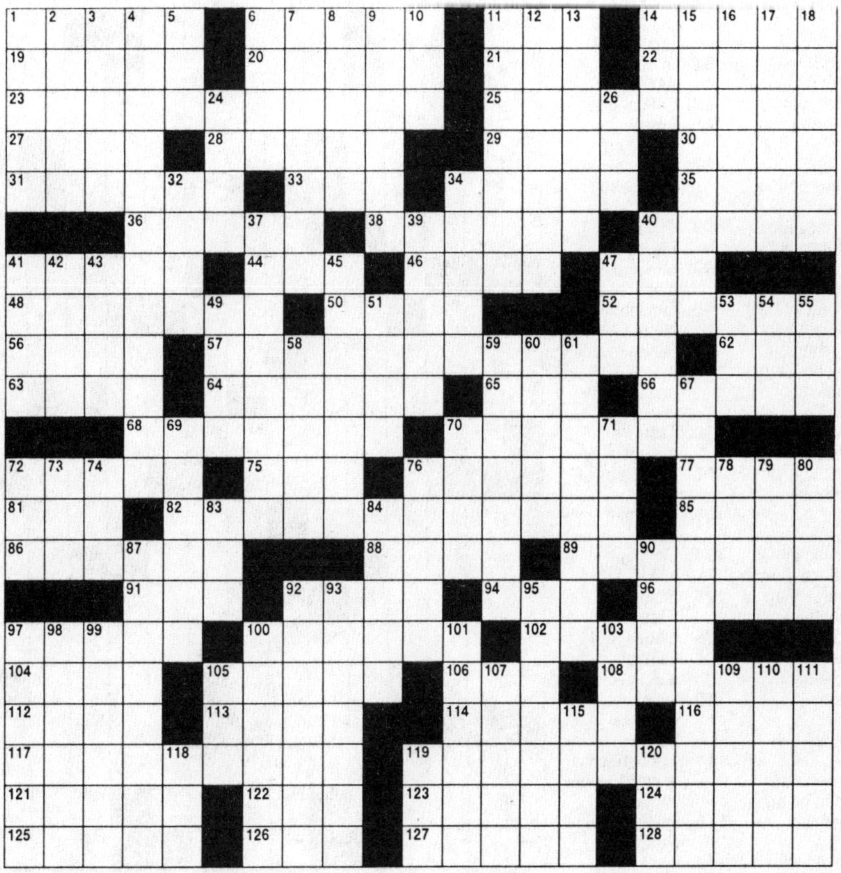

ACROSS

1. ____ Eyes (Eddie Cantor)
6. King of spades, named for a biblical ruler
11. Letter addenda: Abbr.
14. Sneer
19. Not sotto voce
20. Irregular
21. Balderdash
22. Actress Thomas
23. Jack of clubs
25. King of clubs
27. Highway vehicle
28. Kind of work or worm
29. Unemployed
30. Consider
31. Underwrite
33. Honshu bay
34. Aft
35. Add booze
36. Embellishment on a letter
38. Jack of hearts, named for a French soldier
40. Heaped up
41. Rope fiber
44. Defendants, in law
46. Turns to the right
47. Cupid
48. Prohibition
50. Zola heroine
52. Queen of clubs, a French anagram of Regina
56. Garment
57. Two cards in a modern deck
62. Camper's item
63. High cards
64. Admonishes, old style
65. Spanish wave
66. Swelling disease
68. Lends a hand
70. Wine cup
72. British measure
75. Garland
76. Hibernate
77. Way off
81. Japanese pearl diver
82. Queen of spades
85. Over
86. Queen of hearts, named for a biblical heroine
88. Name for 82 Across
89. Pop singer Johnny
91. Teachers' org.
92. Treadless, as old tires
94. Affirmative vote
96. Twice-told items
97. Philippine marsh grass
100. Jack of diamonds
102. Unruffle one's feathers
104. Economist Smith
105. One over par
106. Character in *Exodus*
108. Map features
112. Kind of bus
113. "____ Plenty o' Nuthin'"
114. Panatella
116. Acclaim
117. Ten of diamonds, in a modern game
119. King of hearts
121. Spaces
122. An, in Ems
123. Posy part
124. "The Lady ____"
125. Uncle Miltie
126. *Norma* ____
127. Site to remember
128. Think-tank products

DOWN

1. Male singers
2. E.T., e.g.
3. Standards
4. King of diamonds
5. Harem room
6. Numerical prefix
7. ". . . and prejudices ____": F. L. Mott
8. Electrical units
9. Connecting line on a map
10. Mil. unit
11. Buffaloes' home
12. Lands reclaimed from water
13. Carved pillars
14. Wee, to Ian
15. Egg inspector's job
16. Painful experience
17. Jason's quest
18. Created
24. At no time, to Burns
26. Dry: Prefix
32. Rise up
34. In store
37. Determination
39. ____ *of God*
40. Interstellar space measure
41. Time period: Var.
42. Important student: Abbr.
43. Singer Lane
45. Tendency to stay put
47. East Indian tree
49. Tibetan gazelles
51. Author Rand and namesakes
53. Kind of house or boat
54. Etienne or Pierre, e.g.
55. Greek letter
58. Artist's stand
59. American diplomat and writer
60. Winged
61. Perpetual or Gregorian
67. Aces and eights, as held by Wild Bill Hickok
69. Musical group
70. Quote
71. Dies ____
72. Mil. rank
73. Down Under bird
74. Wee bit
76. One of Emerson's names
78. April 1 figure
79. Miss Frank of the diary
80. Beatty film
83. Eureka
84. Piquant
87. Hostile
90. British gun
92. Ornamental plant
93. Solvent
95. Witty saying
97. Tropical tree
98. Hold in high regard
99. Forest warden
100. Jack of spades, named for a battling Dane
101. Queen of diamonds
103. Hibernia
105. One more time
107. Roper's gear
109. Tidal bore
110. Skin disorder
111. Luges
115. Different: Prefix
118. Peer Gynt's mother
119. Auditor: Abbr.
120. Roman 1002

178 Writer's Cramp By Sara Helleny

Catching some authors out of character.

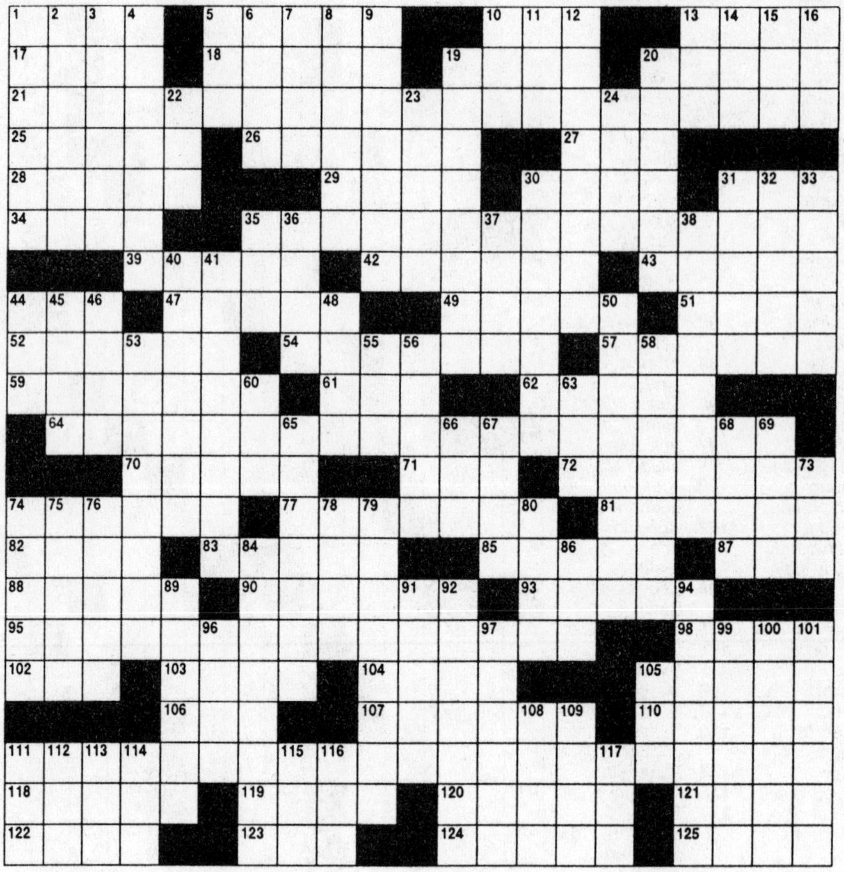

ACROSS

1. *"Qui ___?"* (French sentry's challenge)
5. Soft drink, for short
10. Five-spot
13. Footless animal
17. Med. subject
18. Madame de ___
19. Prefix for an element
20. Stick out like ___ thumb
21. "Do you own a book by Bret?"
25. Pulitzer writer Ernest
26. As ___ a pin
27. Carpentry abbr.
28. Enter
29. Actress Virna
30. Make sewing gathers: Var.
31. Fleur-de-___
34. Sandra and Ruby
35. Abode for Oliver Wendell
39. Holy, to Cicero
42. Cosmetician Lauder et al.
43. Robert or Andrew
44. Cambridge campus
47. Dry up
49. Over
51. Between "once" and "a time"
52. A turn around the track
54. Danish cheese
57. ___ the occasion (coped)
59. Uneasy feeling
61. ___-disant
62. Book part
64. What essayist Francis forgot
70. Something that seeps
71. "___ tu," Verdi aria
72. Smoothed off
74. Pier, to the early English
77. Certain numbers
81. "I've got ___ time" (no hurry)
82. *If I ___ Million*
83. Office gadget
85. Local hayseed
87. Abbr. on a business letter
88. Then, to Pierre
90. Mineral silicate
93. Inventor Nikola
95. Policeman's words to poet Henry W.
98. Tatter's output
102. Opposite of NNW
103. Go for the lure
104. Egyptian town
105. Actor Fernando
106. Cheer
107. Part of A.S.A.P.
110. "It's ___ Unusual Day"
111. Publisher's query to poet William
118. Poilus' weapons
119. Pant
120. To be, in Toledo
121. Withered
122. Part of a decade
123. Mrs., in Montmartre
124. Schoolroom necessities
125. Hebrew lyre

DOWN

1. Improvised an accompaniment
2. "___ for tennis?"
3. City of Pakistan
4. ___ for words
5. Atlantic crosser
6. Two fives for ___
7. Playwright David
8. What Santa can do
9. Kind of sports record
10. Driving hazard
11. Tags for G.I.'s
12. Those
13. As cute ___ button
14. Jet housing
15. California fort
16. Former Turkish official
19. Pushy person
20. "It's ___ shame!"
22. Sis, for one
23. Green spots
24. English painter John
30. Kind of meatball
31. Jeweler's lens
32. Answer to "You are!"
33. Music notation
35. Part of H.R.H.
36. Symphony org.
37. Mailed
38. Family pet
40. "___ star-cross'd lovers . . ."
41. Turned turtle
44. Apple-pie baker
45. ___ the finish
46. Distant: Prefix
48. Leftover concoction
50. Bounces a basketball
53. *"___ est orare"* ("To work is to pray")
55. Doo preceder
56. Evangelist McPherson
58. Having a winning streak
60. Vane reading
63. Shooter ammo
65. Having a cheese crust
66. Sea eagle
67. Neat
68. Bone: Prefix
69. Gas for lights
73. Air medal
74. Strikes hard
75. Wear for harp players
76. "Oh that I had wings like ___!"
78. China's ___ Xiaoping
79. Floats, as a feather
80. "And ___ bed"
84. Maxim
86. London suburb
89. Prickly pears
91. "Coffee, ___ me"
92. Pushed through a crowd
94. Colorado city
96. Taleteller
97. Woolly
99. Love elegies by Ovid
100. Fidel or Raul
101. Rolle of TV
105. Letter of the ___
108. Crafts' partner
109. Its cap. is Pierre
111. Appian or Swann's
112. Charlemagne's realm
113. Org. for doctors
114. Part of N.W.T.
115. Sweet potato
116. Simple sugar
117. Grads-to-be

179 Groupies By William A. Smith

Some less-than-scientific labels for species.

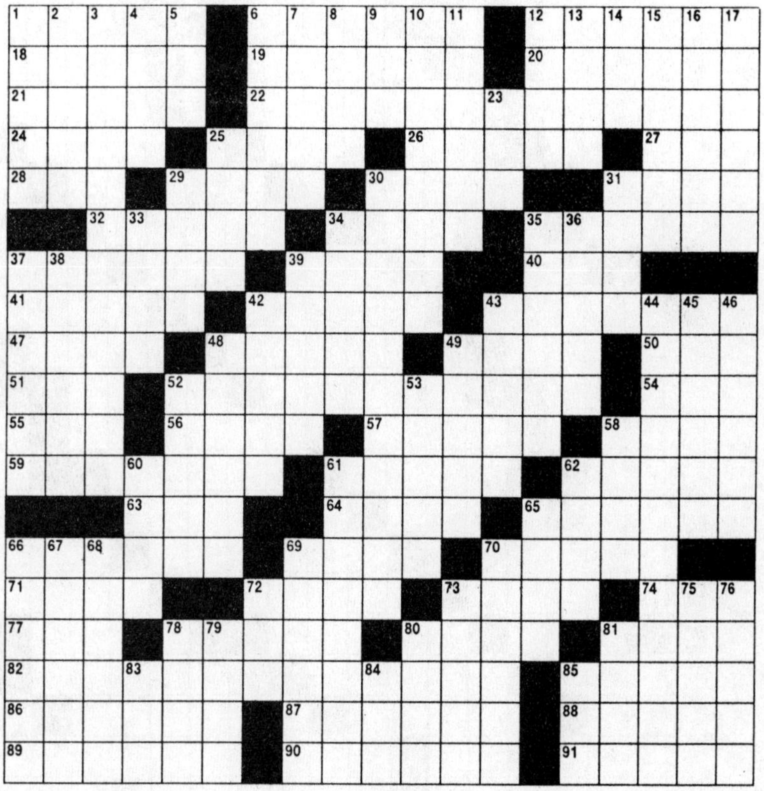

ACROSS

1. Daub
6. Coddle
12. At the top
18. Mexican resort
19. Small space
20. A ___ of ants
21. Portrayer of Chan
22. A ___ of snobs
24. Fury
25. Emeralds, diamonds, etc.
26. Aspect
27. "No soap!"
28. Work unit
29. O'Hara place in Georgia
30. ___ and there (immediately)
31. France's Coty
32. Lets out
34. Scorch
35. Plays at love
37. Sea painting
39. Caution
40. Rub-on for aches: Abbr.
41. Egg-shaped
42. Land of lamas
43. Tropical fruits
47. Rose or Fountain
48. City near Grand Rapids
49. Kind of brush
50. Bikini part
51. Greek letter
52. An ___ of peacocks
54. Mr. Spade
55. W.W. II theater
56. Pastoral pipe
57. Of a Great Lake
58. Place for an R.N.
59. A ___ of decorators
61. ___-trump (bridge bid)
62. Helmet-shaped flower part
63. Bother
64. Ale serving
65. Drinking place
66. Annoy
69. Forwarded
70. Wayside Inn accounts
71. Seed covering
72. Phyllis Diller's spouse
73. Father, to Pierre
74. Chinese tea
77. Army Joes
78. ___-needle (yucca)
80. First-class
81. Place for a cold
82. A ___ of tadpoles
85. Large African river
86. Lacking vitality
87. Small lump
88. Writer Wilde
89. Move, as lightning
90. Ancient Greek land
91. Cubic measure

DOWN

1. A ___ of tradesmen
2. Of the cheek
3. An ___ of fishermen
4. An ___ of adolescents
5. Diviner's gadget
6. Some race horses
7. An ___ of bakers
8. *"___ sana in corpore . . ."*
9. Group of seals
10. G.O.P. mascot
11. Bacon slice
12. Experts
13. Corn bread
14. They, to Pierre
15. Inventor of words
16. Consecrate
17. Wildcats
23. Give the ax
25. Golden or Hell
29. Fork part
30. A ___ of muggers
31. A ___ of jewelers
33. Widow's offering
34. Uncle Tom had one
35. Large liquor bottle
36. Table décor
37. Child
38. Sacred Zoroastrian writings
39. Partner of dined
42. Kind of pole
43. A Society island
44. An ___ of appliances
45. Mistake maker's aid
46. Boat on the Yangtze
48. Beloved of Tristram
49. Restrict
52. Species of iris
53. Common contraction
58. Possess
60. Chinese weight
61. Union card not needed to work here
62. Strong wind
65. Weight allowance
66. Molten rock materials
67. Adjust
68. Antiseptic pioneer
69. A ___ of salesmen
70. Pluperfect and present, e.g.
72. Remote
73. French soldier of W.W. I
75. Horrible one of the comics
76. Regard with high esteem
78. Bowfin
79. Deduct from wages
80. Assyrian war god
81. A ___ of angels
83. Henri's soul
84. Tokyo sash
85. Romaine lettuce

180 Accounting By Gary Schmunk

Getting ahead in the numbers game.

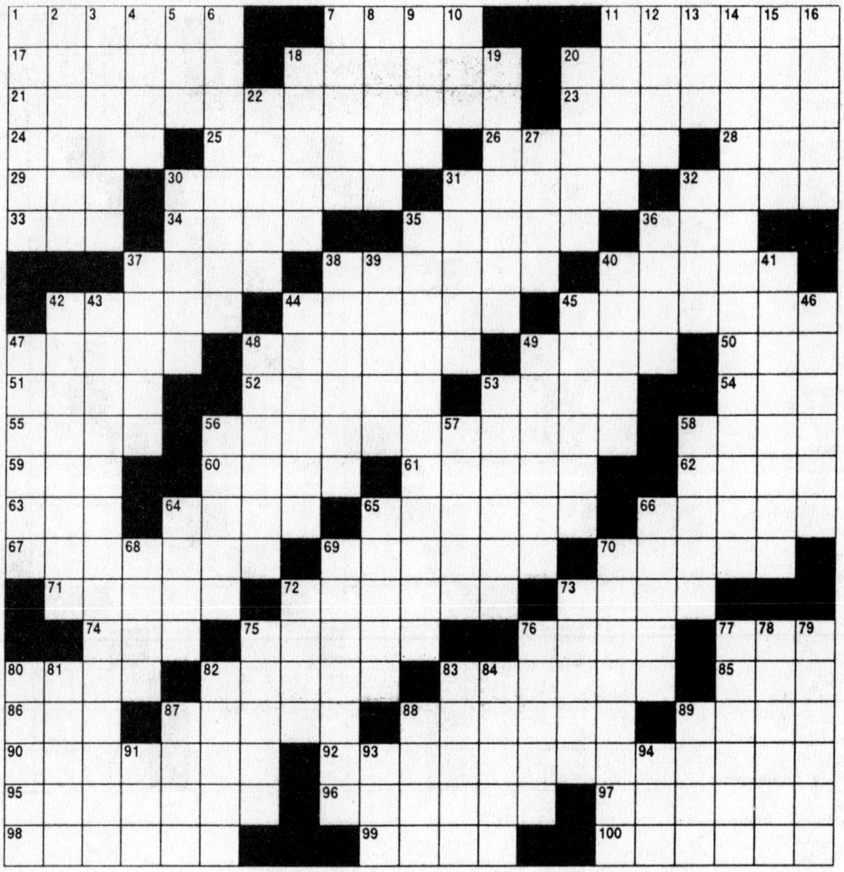

ACROSS

1. Landed estates
7. Nobel physicist: 1922
11. Ned or Warren
17. Garden flower
18. Make dirty
20. Irish wailer
21. Disney cartoon movie
23. French resort region
24. Refrain syllables
25. Whirlpool
26. Like some winter weather
28. Elementary curriculum
29. ___ Cross
30. Finishing tool
31. Film actress Lee and others
32. "___ a man with . . ."
33. Snaky letter
34. Ten-percenters: Abbr.
35. Golfer's item
36. Heat unit, for short
37. Mirth
38. Ester of an apple acid
40. Batch of grain
42. Canyon mouths
44. Baffling questions
45. Fairbanks resident
47. False: Prefix
48. Venomous snakes
49. Comply
50. Devon river
51. Tennis star
52. "___ by land . . ."
53. Nerve-cell process
54. Gratuity
55. Hoosegow
56. State of confusion
58. Ten: Prefix
59. Writer Rand
60. Treaty
61. Navigation help
62. Genuine
63. Kind of way or town
64. Howls
65. Taft's middle name
66. Actress Benton
67. Stag's pride
69. Person of learning
70. Type of cheese or steak
71. Haunted-house dweller
72. Rhythmical
73. Chinese Zen
74. Psyche part
75. Pencil-box item
76. Irish islands
77. Like some verbs: Abbr.
80. *Around the World ___ Days*
82. Whale constellation
83. Movie house
85. Yellow River feeder
86. Johnny ___
87. Canteen
88. Pulverize
89. Moreno
90. Profited
92. Periodic pests
95. Invalidate
96. Gospel writer
97. Dark blue shade
98. Holms
99. In the ___ and now
100. British economist

DOWN

1. ___ d'hôtel
2. Portuguese islands
3. Water nymphs
4. Auto name
5. Cartoonist Gardner
6. Rescues
7. Midler of *The Rose*
8. Willow
9. Deception
10. Reagan, to friends
11. ___ out (takes off the hook)
12. Covet-ousness
13. "___ was saying . . ."
14. Famous friends
15. ___ Haute
16. Leavening agent
18. Poets
19. Articles of clothing
20. Actor Keith
22. ___ Carlo
27. Medicinal plant
30. Chef's or Caesar
31. Storytellers
32. Suffix for tonsil
35. Good-luck charm
36. Mulish sound
37. Thin porridge
38. Trice
39. ___ as life
40. Secluded valleys
41. City sights
42. Analyzing
43. In a fix
44. Wall Street frights
45. Teem
46. Katmandu native
47. *The ___ Game*, 1957 film
48. Eels
49. Primitive conveyance
53. Outright
56. Like some harmony
57. Des Moines resident
58. Down the ___ (lost)
64. "Don't ___ sure!"
65. Nether world
66. African master
68. Company symbol
69. Greyhound-like dogs
70. March 17 lapel wear
72. Mows
73. Angler's item
75. Prepared
76. Conductor Previn
77. "___ ancient Mariner"
78. Baby's toy
79. Dean Martin specialties
80. Tabriz resident
81. Birthmark
82. Treble and bass
83. ___ d'Alene
84. ". . . before ___, I pray the Lord . . ."
87. Dart about
88. Gomer or Ernie
89. Precious gem
91. ___ de France
93. ___ heaven (bliss)
94. Cedar Rapids college

181 Gambit By Kenneth Haxton

With the right moves, everything falls in place.

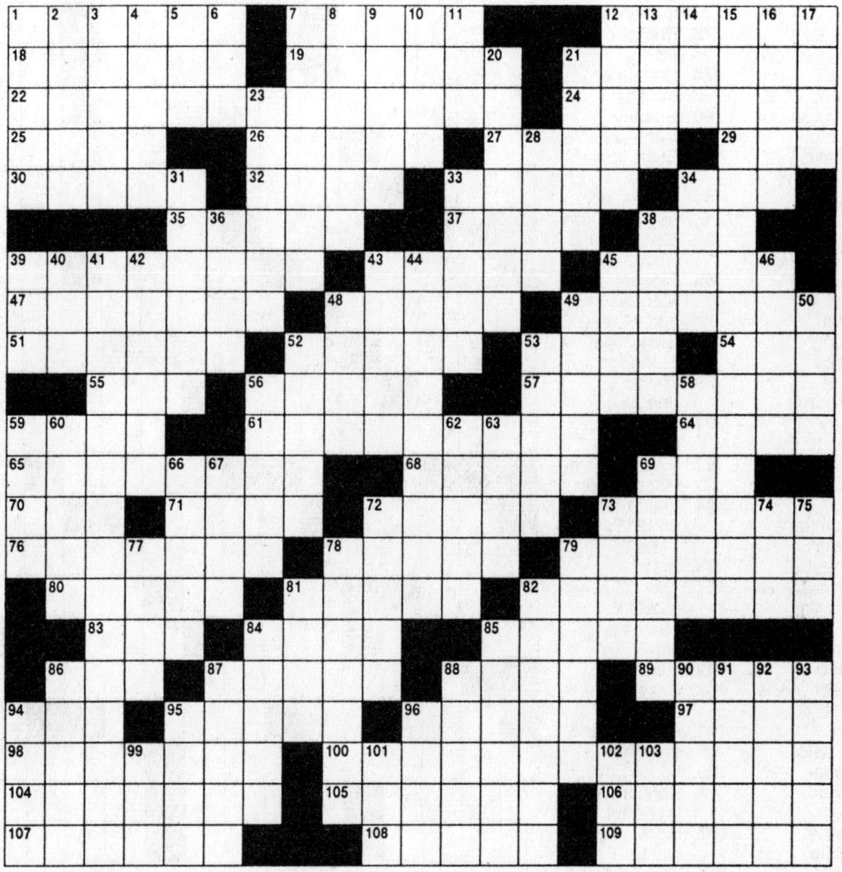

ACROSS

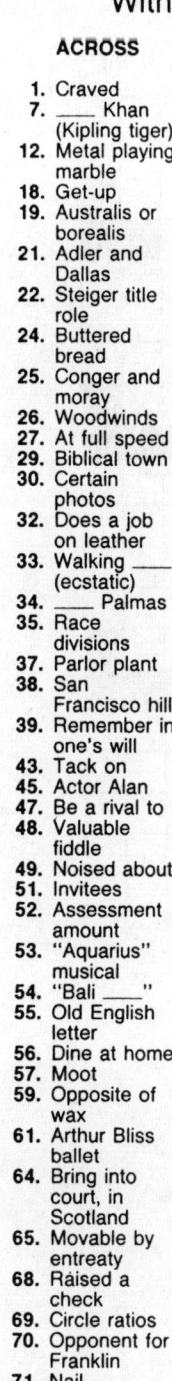

1. Craved
7. ___ Khan (Kipling tiger)
12. Metal playing marble
18. Get-up
19. Australis or borealis
21. Adler and Dallas
22. Steiger title role
24. Buttered bread
25. Conger and moray
26. Woodwinds
27. At full speed
29. Biblical town
30. Certain photos
32. Does a job on leather
33. Walking ___ (ecstatic)
34. ___ Palmas
35. Race divisions
37. Parlor plant
38. San Francisco hill
39. Remember in one's will
43. Tack on
45. Actor Alan
47. Be a rival to
48. Valuable fiddle
49. Noised about
51. Invitees
52. Assessment amount
53. "Aquarius" musical
54. "Bali ___"
55. Old English letter
56. Dine at home
57. Moot
59. Opposite of wax
61. Arthur Bliss ballet
64. Bring into court, in Scotland
65. Movable by entreaty
68. Raised a check
69. Circle ratios
70. Opponent for Franklin
71. Nail
72. Forty-niner
73. Kind of cracker
76. Den
78. Forces
79. Beethoven heroine
80. Basketball throws
81. "And thereby ___ a tale"
82. Premolar tooth
83. Dawn goddess
84. Japanese wrestling
85. "And as the sun ___ slowly in the west"
86. Insect
87. Sired
88. Sink in the mud
89. Kazan native
94. Dernier ___
95. Cord and Edsel
96. Bet
97. Weight of India
98. Henley event
100. Faulkner opus
104. One with physical talents
105. Petrarch form
106. Interstice
107. Davis and Balzac's Cousine
108. Stiller's partner
109. African dormice

DOWN

1. Rubber-tree juice
2. ___ Pendragon, King Arthur's father
3. Stone slab
4. Sloshed
5. Roman or Christian
6. Type of berry
7. Time of rest
8. North American Indians
9. Cockney idols
10. Korean soldiers
11. Prior to, to Poe
12. Flight
13. Sea bird
14. Knead, old style
15. Pulitzer poet of 1956
16. Bowling areas
17. Belgian river
20. Spider
21. Blotch
23. Write down jottings
28. Chico or Harpo
31. Sword case
33. Garbage
34. Viaud's pen name
36. Highway sign
38. Pacific island
39. Implore
40. Nonflying bird
41. *Magic Flute* character
42. Irish trouble area
43. Home catchall
44. Singer known as Pee Wee
45. Naval lockup
46. Flippered performers
48. Glut
49. Showed, as fangs
50. ___ of Worms
52. Engaged in cheering
53. Misanthrope
56. Acclaim
58. Nepalese and Thais
59. Companion of wash
60. Wheel rods
62. Coins
63. Stuttering Roscoe of films
66. Backs
67. Arm, in France
69. Swann's creator
72. North Dakota city
73. Show scorn, in Scotland
74. Onassis
75. Field for an M.D.
77. Statesman Elihu
78. Linens
79. Eye accenters
81. Author Victor
82. Cardinal's cap
84. Bristles
85. One who says "alas"
86. Crest of an alp
87. Ashtray contents
88. ___ Carta
90. Military equipment supplier
91. No-no
92. Like Pisa's tower
93. Ceremonies
94. Kind of apple or grass
95. Suit to ___
96. Port or Bordeaux
99. Height: Abbr.
101. ___ de plume
102. Sal, for one
103. Exist

182 Singing Along By Mary Murdoch

And making progress up the scale.

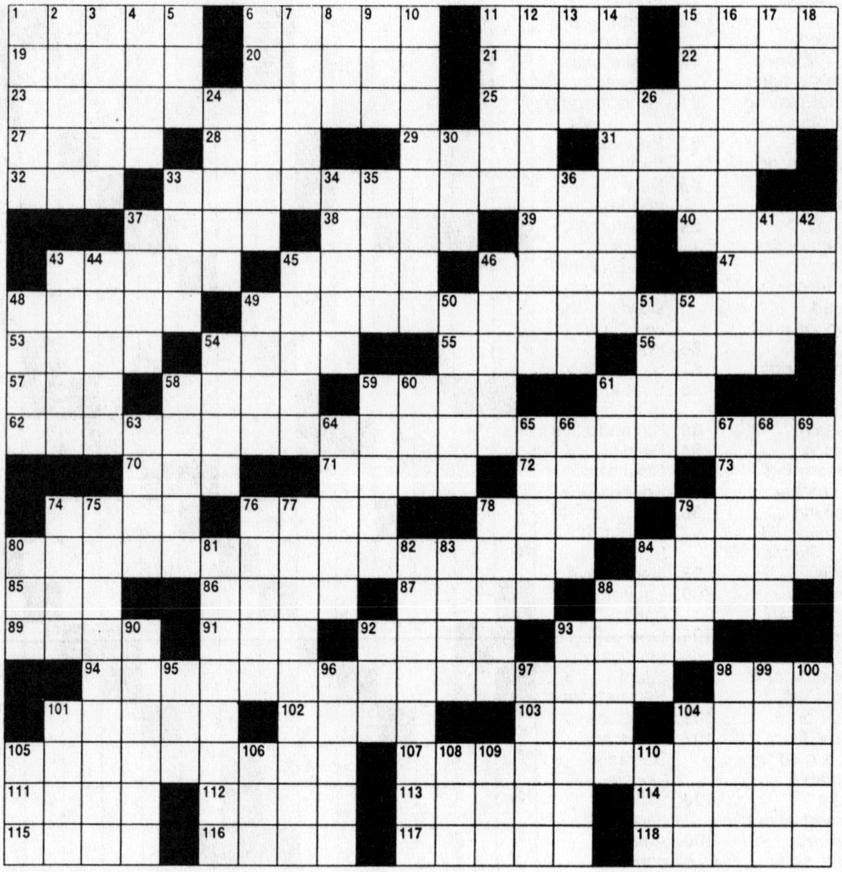

ACROSS

1. Plow part
6. Like ___ on a log
11. Johnny et al.
15. Converse
19. Hawk's defense
20. Photo tone
21. Door sign
22. Western Indian
23. Hy Zaret–Lou Singer hit about a dinner serving
25. Musical works
27. Additional
28. Overly
29. River to the Elbe
31. Clyde Beatty, e.g.
32. Pendulum's partner
33. Orchestral work by Duke Ellington
37. Jeté for Pavlova
38. Tempo
39. Perfect grade
40. Deneb or Mira
43. One who snoops
45. Deliver
46. Part of Y.M.C.A.
47. "O Sole ___"
48. Menial workers
49. Lionel Richie song: 1978
53. "In thunder, lightning, ___ rain?": Shak.
54. Orderly
55. Literary lioness
56. Actress Rowlands
57. Art medium
58. Oracle
59. Window part
61. Where to do a stretch
62. Hal David–Don Rodney song, with "The"
70. Chinese dynasty
71. Some golfers
72. Naldi of the silents
73. Actress Joanne
74. South African settler
76. Early Olympics site
78. Publisher Henry
79. Statute or nautical
80. Sammy Cahn–Jule Styne tune: 1946
84. Like some hay or cotton
85. Song from *A Chorus Line*
86. Singer Merriman and others
87. Swiss river
88. Thin fogs
89. Titanic's nemesis
91. Depression org.
92. Heraldic term
93. Honshu port
94. Fiddle tune of 1815, with "The"
98. Brat
101. *The ___ Incident,* 1943 Fonda film
102. Hence
103. F.D.R. agency
104. Punchy word ending
105. "___ Love," Bacharach–David hit
107. Merle Travis hit: 1947
111. Yorkshire river
112. Ancient letter
113. Green-blue shade
114. Queen ___ lace
115. N.Y.C. Chinatown street
116. Otis or America
117. Fills to excess
118. Sample

DOWN

1. Heavy-footed dance
2. Vietnamese capital
3. Warn
4. It's an eternal city
5. Chemical suffix
6. Tilted
7. Jazz style
8. ___ tree
9. Wire measure
10. Hudson River sight
11. Meet again
12. Anti-Satan rituals
13. Coal container
14. WKRP and WJM-TV, for two
15. Wind or door items
16. Diogenes' quest
17. Armadillo
18. Poetic contraction
24. Feuding
26. Hebrew letter
30. N.Y.C. or Balto.
33. English river
34. German president
35. Descartes
36. Where Bobby Shaftoe went
37. Scottish waterfall
41. Musical opus that opened in Cairo
42. Rogers or Bean
43. ___-comic
44. French doughboy
45. Fragment
46. *Ange* appendages
48. Cry of contempt
49. Certain age
50. Does bar work
51. Rocket stage
52. Camera part
54. Hitler's denial
58. Bee gathering
59. Describe a sentence
60. Spanish year
61. Rose of the diamond
63. Syngman ___
64. Barbecue needs
65. Toughen
66. Kind of squad
67. Roman magistrate
68. Van Gogh setting
69. Went to court
74. Twining stem
75. Strain one's muscles
76. Put into law
77. Three-martini events
78. Sophia of films
79. Minotaur's home
80. Watch pocket
81. It measures its way along
82. Cities in California and Costa Rica
83. Hari of W.W. I
84. Coddle
88. Goddesses of the seasons
90. Gravy type
92. Between D and H
93. Capek et al.
95. Sound from the nursery
96. Golden ides
97. Separate
98. Actor Jeremy
99. Water-lily artist
100. Sheriff's group
101. "Beautiful ___," old waltz
104. Lab device
105. Topper in Dundee
106. Thai people
108. Miss Hogg
109. Totem pole
110. Cole of songdom

183 Simple Arithmetic By Louis Sabin

Various ways of arriving at the number 40.

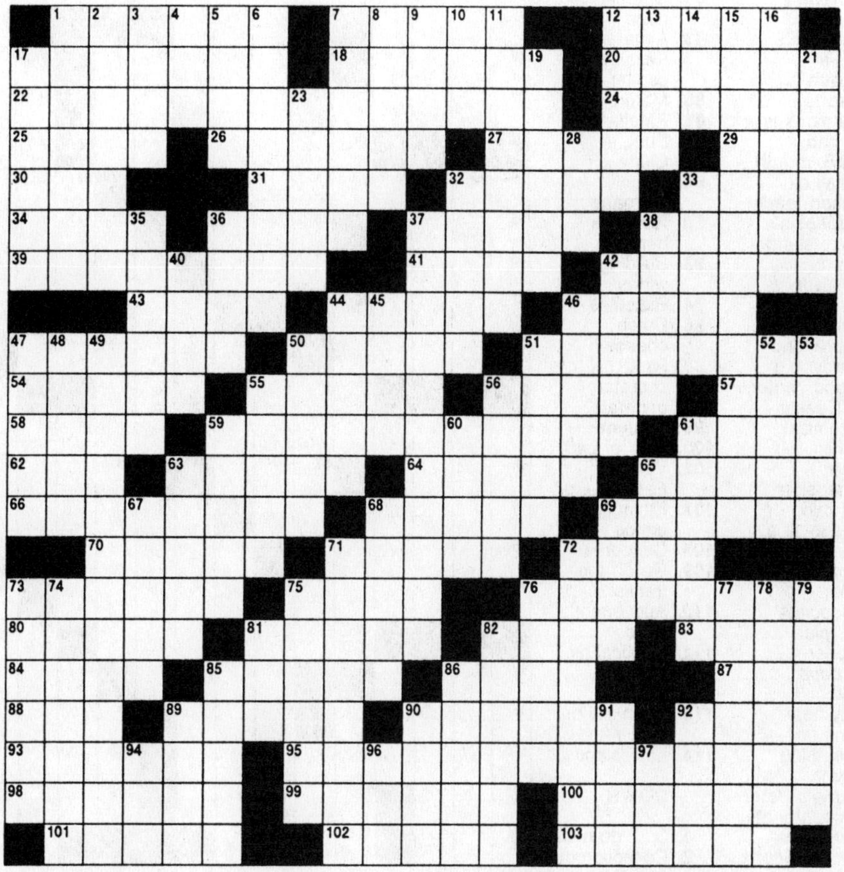

ACROSS

1. Dozes
7. Violin collector's item
12. Bring joy
17. Atlantic cruise
18. Grumble
20. Bewitchers
22. Forty
24. Where the medium gets the message
25. Competition
26. Formal malls
27. Well ___ (rich, to a cockney)
29. Stuff
30. Nigerian people
31. Flab
32. "Over the Rainbow" composer
33. Martinelli of the films
34. Earth turner
36. Tax
37. Shouted
38. Table-oil dispenser
39. One-time A.L. nine
41. Dimwit
42. News medium, in France
43. "In" things
44. Bulldog's relative
46. Special people
47. Conceal, as a noise
50. Embers
51. Dinner fowl choice
54. Grand-motherly
55. Blood fluid
56. Hands in gloves
57. Author Levin
58. Bio
59. Forty
61. German theologian
62. Little one
63. Between twins and quads
64. Film portrayer of Phileas Fogg
65. An ex of Ava
66. Porter's "___ Goes"
68. Ages tobacco
69. Stalking animal
70. French revolutionary
71. Tough question
72. Japanese diplomat
73. Black eye
75. Bath powder
76. Inept knitters, at times
80. Slight flavor
81. Column style
82. Cotton-field cube
83. Help pull a job
84. Composition
85. Face the ___
86. Cigar source, once
87. Eggs
88. Harvest goddess
89. Stab
90. Area of Algiers
92. Indigo
93. Showed compassion
95. Forty
98. Ranked, in sports ratings
99. Lion's-den visitor
100. Applied strength
101. Twisting
102. Edith Cavell, for one
103. Pedestal parts

DOWN

1. Capable of a needle job
2. Trojan destroyed by serpents
3. Ending for major
4. Silkworm
5. Denim's kin
6. Grade-school texts
7. Major road
8. Made cat sounds
9. Imitates
10. Kind of ear or badge
11. Kind of decorator
12. Ruhr city
13. German song
14. Southern constellation
15. Forty
16. Puts in a package
17. Gaza and Sunset
19. Grommet
21. Give opiates to
23. Czechs or Croats
28. Showed the way
32. Indonesian islands
33. Standing
35. Show uncertainty
36. Mine deposit
37. Forty, to Flavius
38. Salad addition
40. Account
42. *Republic* author
44. Tuskers
45. Kiln
46. Rose-colored dye
47. Neighbor of Sicily
48. It has locals
49. Forty
50. Held on
51. What Hemingway's sun also does
52. Reporter Pyle
53. Detroit gadfly
55. Game-score unit
56. Scarlet or Saturday Night
59. Robin Hood's Tuck
60. Sticky stuff
61. Interstice
63. Non-number for a match
65. Commedia dell'___
67. Sharp scents
68. Child's ailment
69. Do street work
71. Montmartre homme
72. Bowed
73. Brownstone hangouts
74. Cool cats, once
75. Kind of salad
76. Synagogue V.I.P.
77. Hard rubber
78. Brings back
79. Became trite
81. Payable
82. Lillian Russell purchase
85. Unclear
86. Choice viands
89. Carnival wild man
90. East Indian pine
91. Six: Prefix
92. Hair style
94. Actress Kaminska
96. Short-maned antelope
97. But, to Nero

184 Toujours Gai By Joy L. Wouk

In which the puzzle's author capitalizes on her own first name.

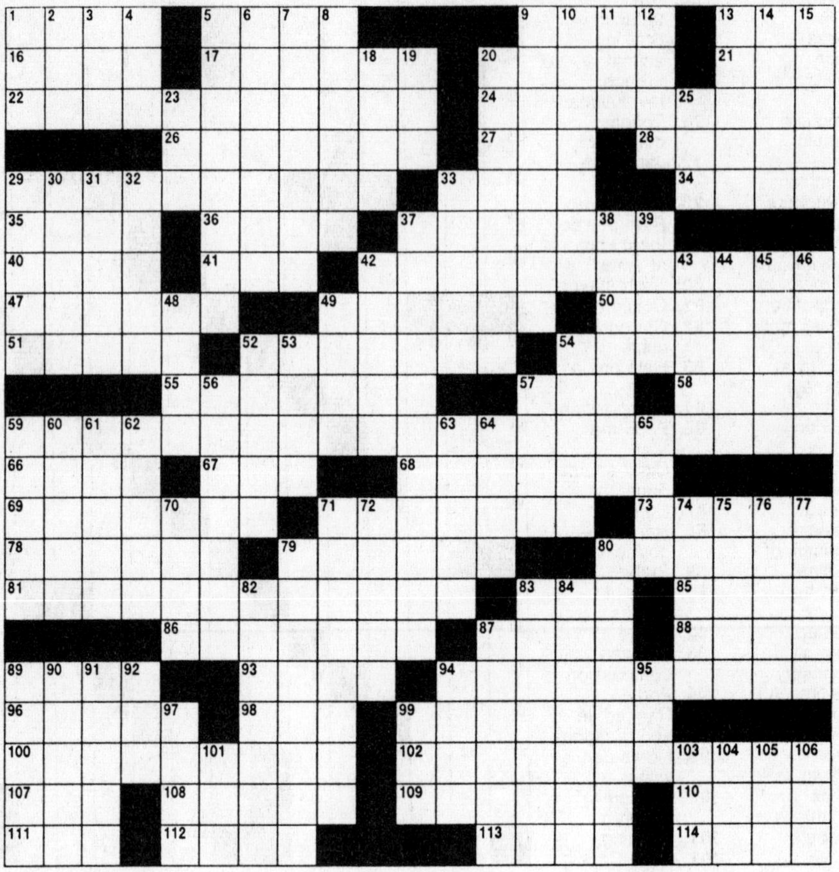

ACROSS

1. Baseball's Willie
5. Health resorts
9. Bismarck is its cap.
13. I.R.S. month
16. Small ox
17. Yukon feeder
20. Indonesia's ___ Islands
21. Sigma follower
22. La Farge Pulitzer novel
24. Laurel and Hardy, e.g.
26. Blood carrier, to Caesar
27. Chemical suffix
28. Sea extension
29. "A thing of beauty is a ___"
33. Mixtures: Abbr.
34. Associate
35. Caspian feeder
36. *Exodus* author
37. City near Etna
40. Breathing sound
41. Barrie's Peter
42. A country at Christmas-tide, to Scott
47. Aquatic mammals
49. French bullets
50. Taiwan's chief city
51. Gaucho's rope
52. Belgian festival
54. Madden
55. Electric-charge unit
57. Tear raggedly
58. A Wolfe
59. F.D.R. campaign song
66. An Adams
67. Overhead subways
68. Expiators
69. Wide pasta
71. Anchor beam
73. Florida city
78. Pluto or Uranus
79. Mrs. Thatcher's supporters
80. Drive forward
81. Gagman's need
83. Alma-___, Kazakh capital
85. Mature
86. Patella
87. Shut, in Cluny
88. ___ Morgana
89. Reindeer herder
93. Building wings
94. Ridicules
96. Dutch cheeses
98. First U.N. secretary-general
99. Diadem
100. Kind of park
102. Verdi's *Falstaff,* e.g.
107. Ethiopian prince
108. Concerns
109. Go off the tracks
110. Auctioneer's word
111. Nautical dir.
112. Soviet agency
113. "Drink to me ___ with . . ."
114. Low islands

DOWN

1. ___ de mer
2. Collection of anecdotes
3. "How do ___ do?"
4. Droop
5. Saddle adjuncts
6. Cougar, south of the border
7. Of the Plantagenet line
8. Light Brigade weapons
9. High sun times
10. Land of an estate
11. Pub order
12. Moslem judge
13. In the least
14. Cartoon-strip unit
15. Out of practice
18. Roulette color
19. Babylonian consort
20. Staffs for Victoria and Elizabeth
23. Chinese weight
25. ___ rut
29. Courtroom figure
30. Emulate W. J. Bryan
31. Black Sea port
32. Rapid
33. Sandburg and Sagan
37. Convivial good time
38. Whole number
39. Culture medium
42. Baby's word
43. Old Chinese weight
44. Temporary breath stoppage
45. Pola of the silents
46. ___ base (be stranded at Shea)
48. Pungent
49. Rels. of sis
52. ___ Lumpur, Malaysia
53. Culbertson et al.
54. Was presumptuous
56. Village near Annapolis
57. Where Napoleon won in 1806
59. Lends a hand
60. Robin Hood's Allan
61. Galileo was one
62. Heraldic furs
63. Clear sky
64. Does a gardening job
65. Hebrew lyre
70. Carnival performer
71. Successive lines of poetry
72. Juan's weapons
74. Island off Greece
75. Pertaining to bees
76. Slender: Prefix
77. Take ___ from someone's book
79. Read between ___
80. Well enough
82. Insect antennae
83. Moslem sacred book
84. Target of some clippers
87. Profit-hungry, in Mexico
89. Memorize
90. Madison Avenue denizen
91. Delay
92. Matinee times: Abbr.
94. Be dispirited
95. Ziegfeld
97. Zen Buddhism, e.g.
99. Food fish
101. Pasture sound
103. Welsh river
104. Goliath, to David
105. Aviate
106. Asner and Begley

185 People By H. Hastings Reddall

Some women who have made it to the top.

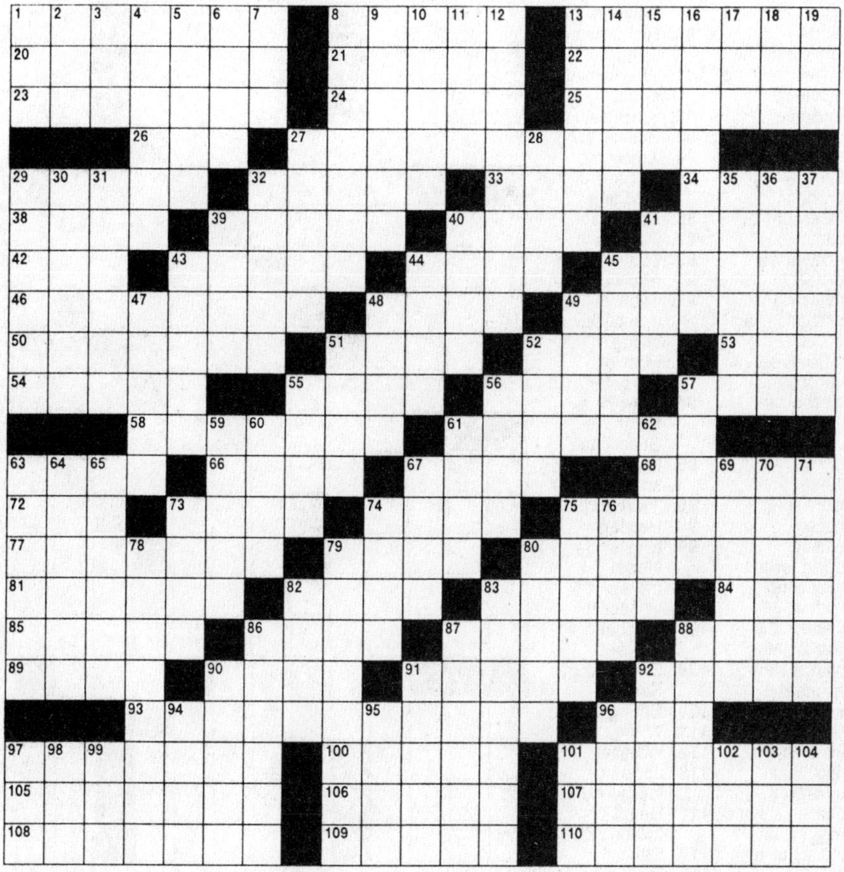

ACROSS

1. She used to be Snow White but she drifted
8. Level with the waves
13. Not naturally formed
20. Rising above the water
21. Paper, in Milan
22. Eastern Christians
23. Despots
24. ". . . sweet as apple ___"
25. Units over door tops
26. Boston party jetsam
27. She overcame many handicaps
29. Spa treatments
32. German place for 29 Across
33. Dueling sword
34. Within an ___ of (very close)
38. Collections of sayings
39. Did shoe repairs
40. One nautical mile per hour
41. Music-lesson hurdle
42. Companion of outs
43. Less cordial
44. Fixed charges
45. Weight watcher
46. Football passes
48. Scout's daily thing
49. Causing nervous strain
50. Football teams
51. Observed
52. Cronies
53. Former G.I.
54. City on the Ruhr
55. ___ over heels
56. Lean over
57. Whey: Prefix
58. Village in Connecticut
61. Church dignitary
63. NNE and SSW, e.g.
66. Ventilates
67. Wild hog
68. Accented parts of a verse
72. Piece of poetry
73. Wins a certain card game
74. Refute
75. Religious vestment
77. In the van
79. Yearn for
80. America's Sweetheart Mary
81. Strong beams
82. Thirteen cards, in bridge
83. Arias
84. New Zealand parrot
85. Coral island
86. Not his
87. Observes Ramadan
88. Fellow
89. Painter Guido
90. Wading bird
91. Wind instruments
92. Craft for Pocahontas
93. Founder of the American Red Cross
96. Word after bon
97. Reaches a goal
100. Aroma, in London
101. Charlotte and Emily
105. Assert anew
106. French river
107. Rescinds
108. Expressed scorn
109. Resource
110. Solar and Columbia Broadcasting

DOWN

1. N.Y. opera house
2. Poet Lowell
3. Suffix for ballad or command
4. Fits of anger
5. Domestic slaves
6. Bristle
7. Football six-pointers
8. One who concurs
9. Lamented loudly
10. Elizabeth of cosmetics
11. British carbine
12. Listened
13. Edible fish
14. Like an old woman
15. Baseball team
16. Type molds
17. Consumed
18. Neighbor of Md.
19. Feminine suffix
27. Forces to court
28. Early unwritten poetry
29. One receiving goods in trust
30. Records of events
31. Samples
32. Prepares salad eggs
35. Indigenous
36. Smart
37. *From ___ Eternity*
39. Look over
40. Sharp
41. Goes astray
43. Vernon's dancing partner
44. Kind of bag
45. Mississippi River feature
47. Smooths over
48. Pitcher Dizzy
49. Kind of tale or drink
51. Fixes a hem
52. Ship's dock
55. ___ de combat
56. Serving implement
57. Stroke on a letter
59. Farm wagons
60. Light metallic sound
61. Corn ___
62. Combat vehicles
63. Kind of diplomacy
64. Conceive a thought
65. Sanity
67. Turn in a river
69. Oral
70. City in Oklahoma
71. Prim
73. "___ of My Dreams"
74. Cacophonies
75. After-dinner items
76. Tops in cards
78. Like lace
79. Plane curve
80. South Korean city
82. Wife of Zeus
83. Low stool
86. ___ around (romped)
87. Fortune-teller's field
88. Sea bird
90. *"A votre ___!"*
91. Number for les Mousquetaires
92. Chickens' residences
94. Prevaricator
95. Bothers
96. Low card
97. "___ longa, vita . . ."
98. Top-rating number
99. Half a fly
101. Abbr. in an apartment ad
102. ___ Han Min'guk (South Korea)
103. Shade tree
104. Draftee's org.

186 Floral Offering By Judith Perry

For people with a knack for drawing.

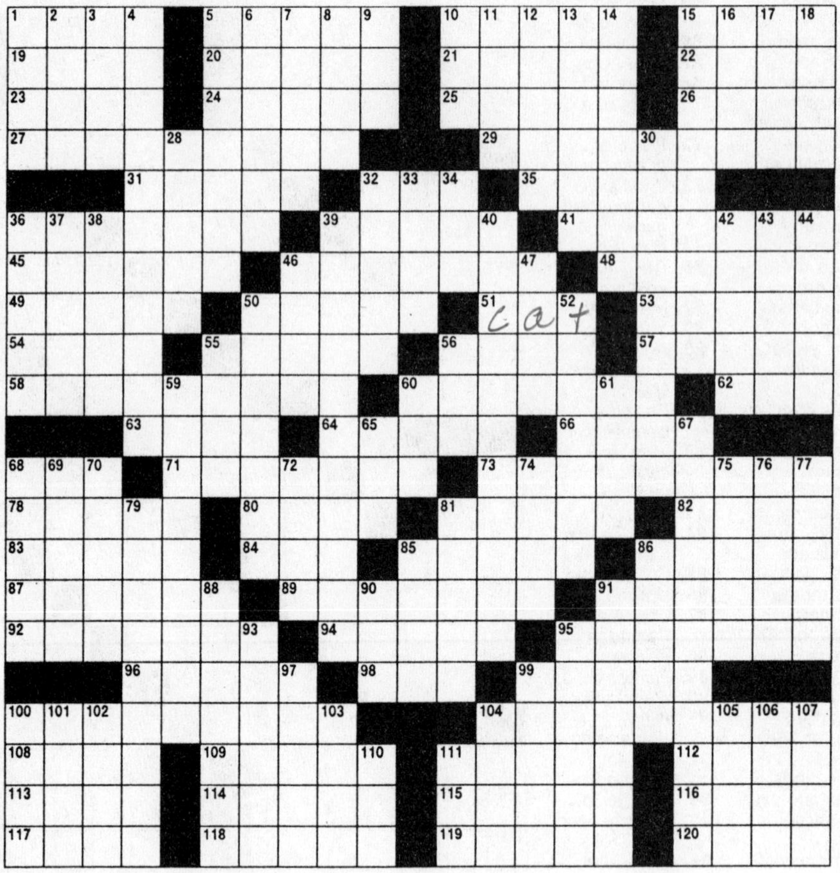

ACROSS

1. Deeds
5. Fine violin
10. Flower fragrance
15. Pleated ribbon ornament
19. Slovenly person
20. Statement of belief
21. Annoyance
22. Verbal
23. Trailer rig
24. Addition to a bill
25. Hackneyed
26. Evergreens
27. Not the life of Riley
29. Egyptian discovery of 1799
31. Opera director Beverly
32. Boring writer
35. Word after sooth
36. A, an or the
39. Killer whales
41. Make a new appraisal
45. Heraldic patterns
46. Like a tapir
48. Arctic explorer
49. Robin ___ of song
50. Belgian treaty city
51. Felix or Garfield
53. Income, in France
54. Violates a Commandment
55. Figure of speech
56. La Scala numbers
57. Shield of Zeus
58. Precarious situation
60. Blessing
62. Movie stage
63. Fruit of a thorny shrub
64. Like King Arthur's table
66. Plant sugar
68. Units of energy: Abbr.
71. Inspires
73. Congressional winner's prize
78. Bring into position
80. Hot times in Paris
81. West Point figure
82. Korbut
83. Biblical king
84. Xmas mo.
85. Rubber and wedding
86. Append
87. Poplars
89. Leaves high and dry
91. Type of competitive skiing
92. Men of Barcelona
94. Start of a Gertrude Stein line
95. Metallic shavings
96. Twining plant
98. Harden
99. English Nobel physicist
100. In secret
104. Biblical flower
108. Diamond or Simon
109. Spring bloom
111. Weird
112. Wander
113. Jones of locker note
114. React theatrically
115. Stain
116. Of two parts
117. Industrious
118. Gluts
119. Rugged cliffs
120. Shout

DOWN

1. Org.
2. Egypt's femme fatale
3. Grant's ___
4. Long-running Broadway show
5. Dead Sea yields
6. Dally
7. "___ for a Blue Lady"
8. Fruit coolers
9. Beetle
10. Police-radio msg.
11. Fragrant bloom for a P.M. ritual?
12. Omar's wares
13. Hindu incarnation
14. Passed along
15. Song for Irish tenors
16. Blind-mice grouping
17. Mountain lake
18. Otherwise
28. Kitchen gadget
30. Kind of pay
32. Recumbent
33. Shaped in a way, as a diamond
34. Stoolie
36. Nautical call
37. Spokes
38. African antelope
39. Dorothy Parker's lament
40. Fanny Brice hit
42. Louisiana political family
43. Loosen
44. Discharge
46. Boutique
47. Spanish painter
50. Made unfriendly sounds
52. Handy throwaways
55. Ensnare
56. Old Japanese coin
59. Stentorious person
60. *The Wayward* ___
61. Evict
65. Military inst.
67. Flowers of a W.W. I song
68. Laughing sounds
69. Annapolis student
70. Ulysses' temptress
72. Residents: Suffix
74. Probability
75. Fairylike
76. Maturing
77. One of two certainties
79. Poet Edmund Waller's flowery command
81. Erie landmark
85. Kind of hit or pay
86. Moslem deity
88. Comes to rest
90. Outfit
91. Dries, as mortar
93. Genus of Asian evergreens
95. Playing a small wind instrument
97. Greek serf
99. Andrea ___
100. Ruin
101. Kind of tide
102. Cheap hangout
103. Optimistic
104. Feature of some dogs
105. Rake
106. Athletic field
107. Dickens girl
110. French demonstrative
111. Lat. catchall

187 Lyrical Ladies By Manny Miller

A cast of characters immortalized in song.

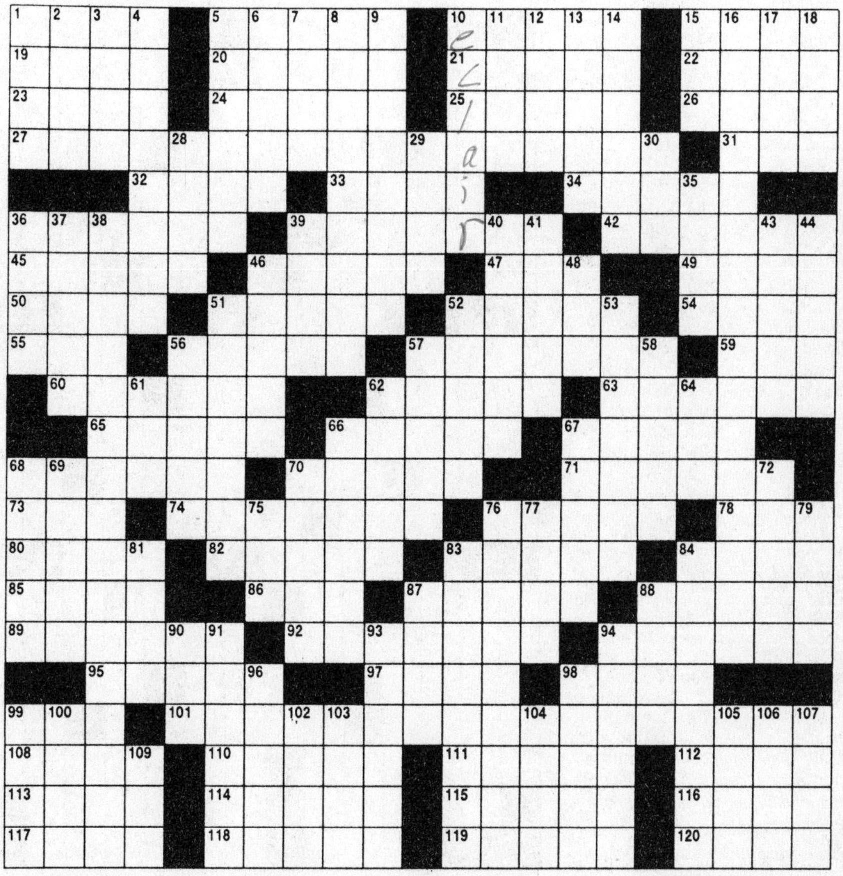

ACROSS

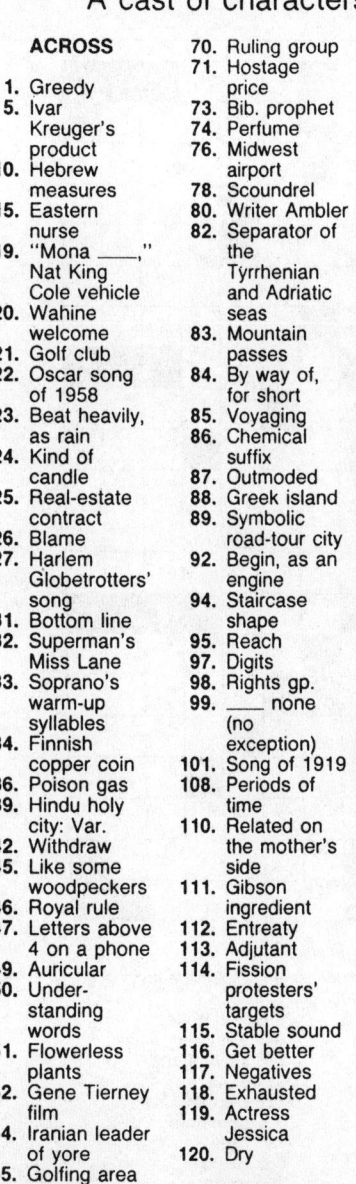

1. Greedy
5. Ivar Kreuger's product
10. Hebrew measures
15. Eastern nurse
19. "Mona ___," Nat King Cole vehicle
20. Wahine welcome
21. Golf club
22. Oscar song of 1958
23. Beat heavily, as rain
24. Kind of candle
25. Real-estate contract
26. Blame
27. Harlem Globetrotters' song
31. Bottom line
32. Superman's Miss Lane
33. Soprano's warm-up syllables
34. Finnish copper coin
36. Poison gas
39. Hindu holy city: Var.
42. Withdraw
45. Like some woodpeckers
46. Royal rule
47. Letters above 4 on a phone
49. Auricular
50. Understanding words
51. Flowerless plants
52. Gene Tierney film
54. Iranian leader of yore
55. Golfing area
56. Speak pompously
57. Kittens' loss
59. Ethyl or butyl ending
60. Plastered
62. Canonical hour
63. Henley Regatta river
65. Greek tourist attractions
66. Leather shoe strips
67. Seat for Helen Morgan
68. Of high quality
70. Ruling group
71. Hostage price
73. Bib. prophet
74. Perfume
76. Midwest airport
78. Scoundrel
80. Writer Ambler
82. Separator of the Tyrrhenian and Adriatic seas
83. Mountain passes
84. By way of, for short
85. Voyaging
86. Chemical suffix
87. Outmoded
88. Greek island
89. Symbolic road-tour city
92. Begin, as an engine
94. Staircase shape
95. Reach
97. Digits
98. Rights gp.
99. ___ none (no exception)
101. Song of 1919
108. Periods of time
110. Related on the mother's side
111. Gibson ingredient
112. Entreaty
113. Adjutant
114. Fission protesters' targets
115. Stable sound
116. Get better
117. Negatives
118. Exhausted
119. Actress Jessica
120. Dry

DOWN

1. Matterhorn's range
2. Picture-postcard showing
3. Man, for one
4. Part of a news dispatch
5. Popular sing-along song
6. Lily plants
7. Volume, in Barcelona
8. *What Price Glory?* theme song
9. Tapestries and curtains, e.g.
10. Elongated cream puff
11. Commoner
12. Listen
13. Fabled writer
14. Shish-kebab holder
15. Give it ___ (try)
16. Cab Calloway's best-known song
17. Fever
18. Grade-school study: Abbr.
28. Tom Mix's horse
29. "___ old cowhand . . ."
30. Dir.
35. Mil. stripers
36. Mine passage
37. Floral purchases
38. Waltz in a Betty Grable film
39. Lahr or Wheeler
40. Marbles
41. Closes
43. *Seventh Heaven* song
44. Enlarges, old style
46. Studies
48. Neighbor of Eng.
51. Song popularized by Artie Shaw
52. *The Story of G.I. Joe* tune
53. Upas tree poisons
56. Chilled
57. Carlo beginning
58. Alan Ladd film
61. Madame's affirmative
62. One of the Reagans
64. Response: Abbr.
66. Brook
67. Talk foolishly
68. Stingy
69. Colt or filly
70. Denim trousers
72. Girl of the radio Street Singer's song
75. Depot: Abbr.
76. Stephen Foster song
77. Door fastening
79. Conflict using seconds
81. Charitable foreign-aid gp.
83. Third party with you and me
84. Wins
87. Swift Malayan sailboat
88. Sgts.-to-be
90. Japanese statesman
91. Home of the Acropolis
93. Bear witness
94. Meager
96. Confess
98. In ___ (briefly)
99. Coffee source
100. Melody
102. Relative of the cod
103. Egyptian sun disk
104. Detroit footballer
105. Away from the wind
106. Kind of guard or admiral
107. Ivy League member
109. French possessive

188 Casting a Spell By Marjorie Pedersen

In which some liberties are taken.

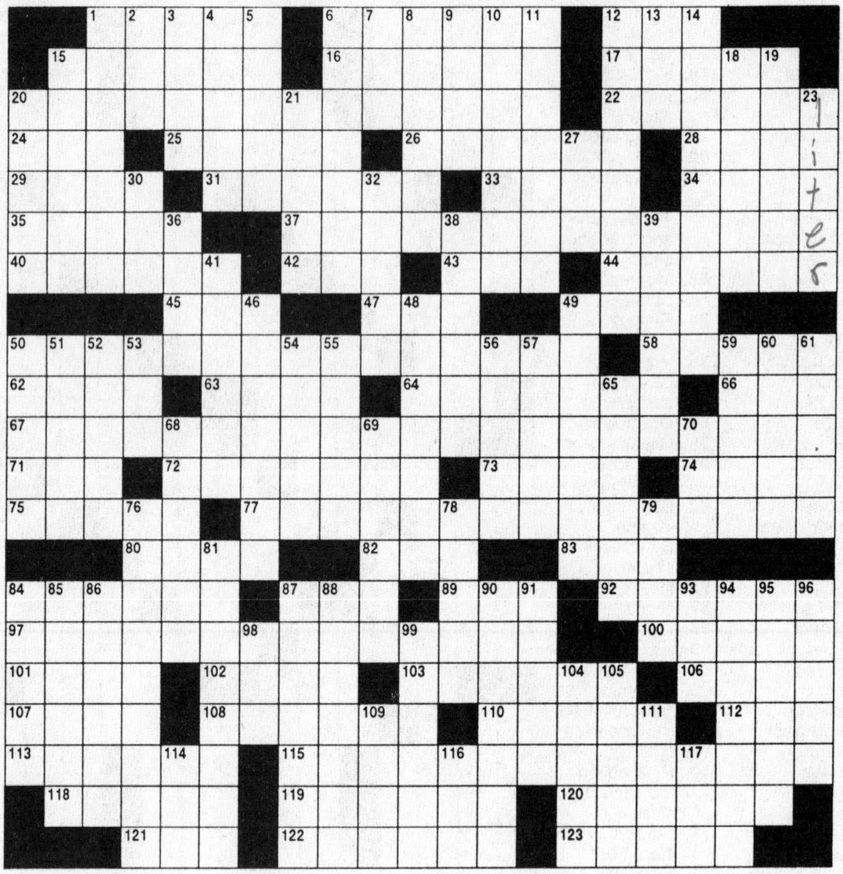

ACROSS

1. Defend
6. ". . . ridicule is the best ___ truth": Chesterfield
12. Quiche base
15. Stove-top unit
16. "___ Grecian Urn"
17. Boom type
20. Sailors' snapshots?
22. Like a tail
24. Finless fish
25. Pilfered
26. He made a last stand
28. Sonoran Indian
29. Enjoy shallow water
31. Bari is its capital
33. Prefix for dynamics
34. Superior of a lieut.
35. Workers on a cake
37. Pimlico photo finish?
40. Scold, in Scotland
42. Former campus org.
43. No longer active: Abbr.
44. Sword-shaped
45. Spanish Mrs.
47. Suitable
49. "I earn that ___ . . .": *As You Like It*
50. What the impetuous doctor did?
58. Spectral body
62. Ancient strongbox
63. Cask stave, in Scotland
64. Loggerhead turtle, in Brest
66. ___ *pro nobis*
67. Astronaut on a Christmas ride?
71. Waiter's due
72. Way in for a driver
73. Specialized educ. group
74. Coin of Iran
75. Hide away
77. Martial-tread maneuver?
80. Center of activity
82. Columbus campus
83. Word before cent
84. ___ limb (stranded)
87. Traffic sign
89. Roman 1501
92. ___ in the bud (aborted)
97. Booming business?
100. Wristbones
101. Prop for Aladdin
102. Merit
103. Muse of astronomy
106. Mediocre
107. Israeli airline
108. Veteran
110. Elder statesmen of Japan
112. ___ Hindenburg
113. Lutes' relatives
115. Like an autumn leaf in a book?
118. Winter beverage
119. Common Market locale
120. Corrects a manuscript
121. Ames and Begley
122. Straight drinks
123. Asian civet

DOWN

1. Netherlands coin
2. Samovar
3. Hill insects
4. "Birdie, ___ little longer": Tennyson
5. Sag
6. Dried, after a bath
7. Old English letter
8. Harbor seal
9. Balsam tree
10. "All the good ___ married!" (spinster's complaint)
11. Most rapid
12. One holding money in trust
13. Gazelle of Tibet
14. TV programs from a veld?
15. Violation
18. Philosophical concepts
19. It's red for V.I.P.s
20. Lapwing
21. Boners
23. Gas measure in England
27. Hesitant sounds
30. Before
32. Where ___ (scene of action)
36. Cummerbund
38. Go it alone
___ up (choice)
39. Tooth layer
41. Light refractor, in Spain
46. Goddess of fertility
48. Vagabonds
49. "Marriage ___ so grave . . .": Stevenson
50. Shoe parts
51. Fretful, in Scotland
52. ___ Flow
53. Between tic and toe
54. Town in Zaire
55. "But ___ man is Christ's stamp . . .": Herbert
56. Rub with oil, old style
57. Musical fanfare
59. ___ up (do an addition chore)
60. Noisy
61. In a coarse way
65. Relative of a Quonset hut
68. Sea urchins
69. "No morn, ___, no dawn . . .": Hood
70. Sea eagle
76. Imposing landmark, e.g.
78. Angry one
79. The Red
81. Miss Redgrave's namesakes
84. Makes eyes at
85. Finnish language group
86. Salad staple
87. Predicaments
88. In the ___ (over a period)
90. Cake decorations
91. Gave lodging to
93. Ballet step
94. Stipulate
95. Downs and salts
96. Double compound: Suffix
98. Hood's weapon
99. Computer arrow
104. Deduce
105. Bouquet
109. Architect Saarinen
111. Mining products
114. Steiger
116. N.Y.C. or S.F.
117. Weight units: Abbr.

189 Go-Togethers By Herman Surasky

Like Mom and Pop, or bread and butter.

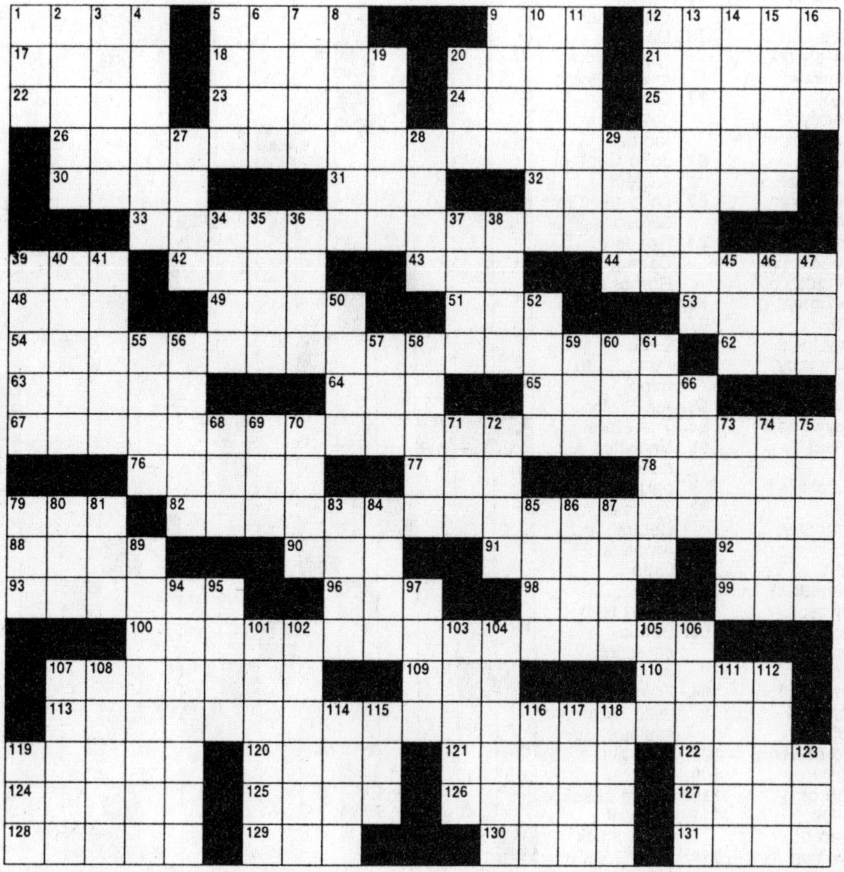

ACROSS

1. Incite
5. Bell town
9. Alps or Andes: Abbr.
12. Wrong
17. Cordon ___
18. Bounds' partners
20. Actress Witherspoon
21. Highway divisions
22. Aaron of duel note
23. Bay
24. Word of assent
25. Aligns
26. Diamond trio
30. ___ of clay
31. Greek nickname
32. Southern cookery pioneers
33. Masculine trio
39. Wind dir.
42. Like a Richard
43. ___ loco (in its own place)
44. Yearbook
48. Reverence
49. Govt. agent
51. Depression org.
53. Town in France
54. John Van Druten trio
62. Mountain
63. Go to court again
64. St. Anthony's cross
65. Upstate New York city
67. Dumas trio
76. One of 50
77. Damage
78. Allen of *Zelig*
79. Sellout initials
82. Crossing trio
88. Young salmon
90. Transgress
91. Fit out a sailboat again
92. The way, in China
93. Low form of life
96. Haul
98. Western cont.
99. Like some folks at home
100. Bearish trio
107. Issue
109. Baton Rouge campus
110. French month
113. Altruistic trio
119. Dress style
120. Part of Q.E.D.
121. Heron
122. Bunting bird
124. Cotton-field worker
125. Dainty
126. Renew a lube job
127. Swiss painter
128. African villages
129. Mat. day
130. Roman 651
131. Meeting: Abbr.

DOWN

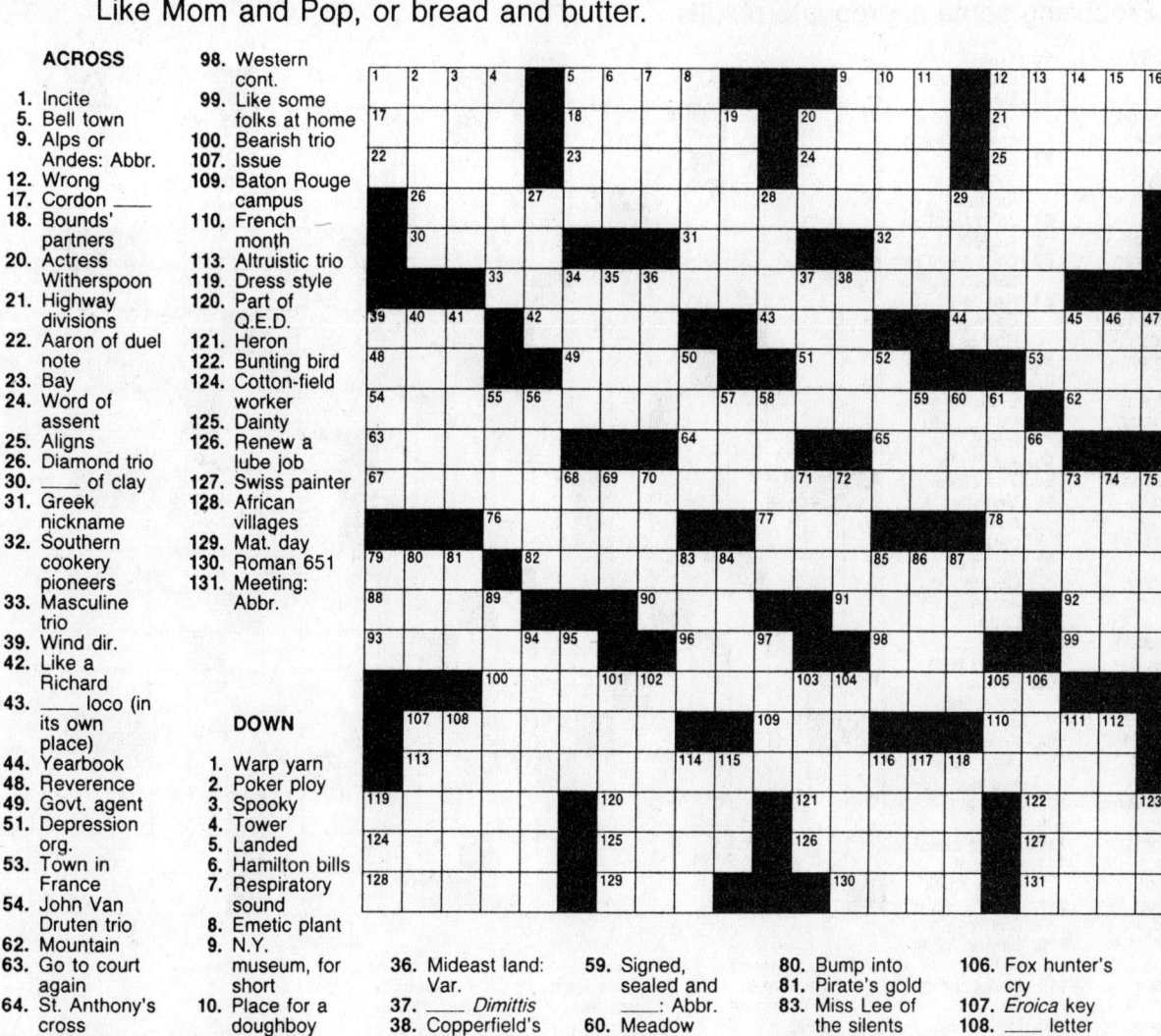

1. Warp yarn
2. Poker ploy
3. Spooky
4. Tower
5. Landed
6. Hamilton bills
7. Respiratory sound
8. Emetic plant
9. N.Y. museum, for short
10. Place for a doughboy
11. Miss Dee
12. Brass wind instrument
13. Miss Monroe's namesakes
14. Habituate
15. Bird fare
16. Draft initials
19. Baby bird
20. Heel
27. "___ the presses!"
28. Island off Sumatra
29. Buddhist monastery
34. Marquand's sleuth
35. Major-___
36. Mideast land: Var.
37. ___ *Dimittis*
38. Copperfield's first wife
39. Native Israeli
40. Like Sue or Adeline
41. Renege on a bet
45. Miss Hagen
46. Everything
47. Cut off
50. Norse night deity
52. Later
55. Nilotic people
56. Wins over
57. Negative of sorts
58. Italian cathedral
59. Signed, sealed and ___: Abbr.
60. Meadow
61. Small centipede
66. Ancient shrine
68. Mike's friend
69. Western Indian
70. House members, for short
71. Egyptian cotton
72. Sandarac tree
73. Homey saying
74. Perfectly suited
75. Church group
79. Resort
80. Bump into
81. Pirate's gold
83. Miss Lee of the silents
84. "Come ___" (inviting words)
85. Indigence
86. Thrash
87. Roman coin
89. Stayed
94. Engages in teasing
95. Oriental nurse
97. Festival
101. Sparta's old rival
102. Illinois city
103. TV's Lou Grant
104. Poked
105. Legal profession
106. Fox hunter's cry
107. *Eroica* key
108. ___ letter (use the postbox)
111. Functional
112. Radials, in England
114. NATO, for one
115. French season
116. Gator's cousin
117. Safe, in Germany
118. Gudrin's husband
119. Away: Abbr.
123. Bandleader Brown

190 Reverse Gear By Bernice Gordon

Producing some appropriate results.

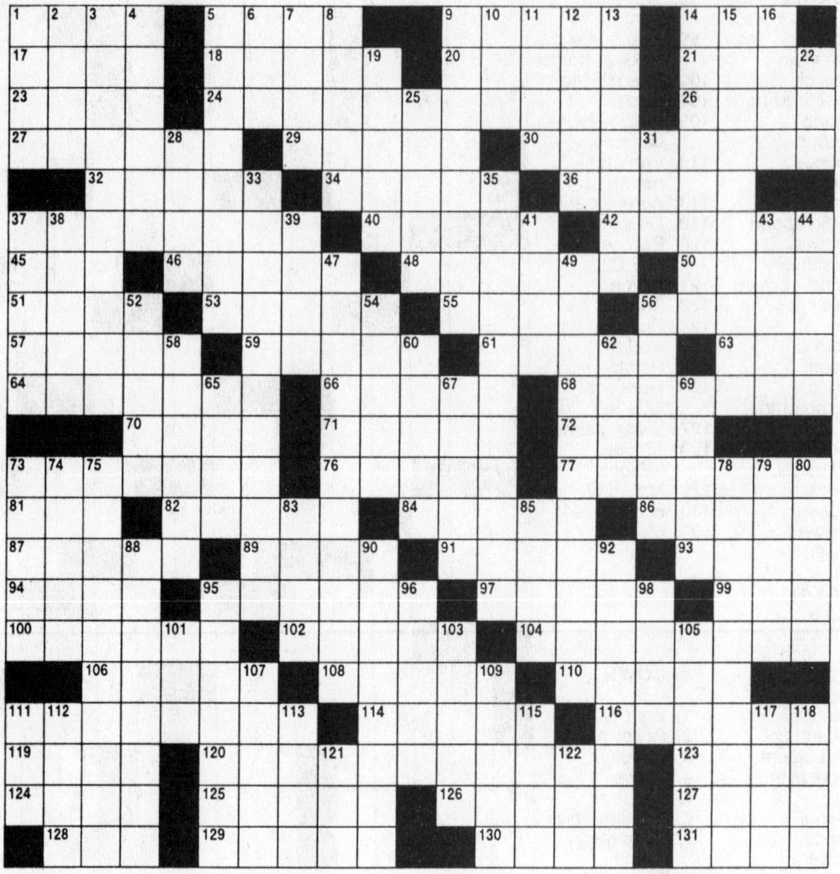

ACROSS

1. Does crewelwork
5. Sidewalk edge
9. Speedy
14. Shareholder's abbr.
17. Coagulate
18. Small oxen
20. Babylonian hero
21. Handled jug
23. Stringed instrument of yore
24. Posy for a funny lady?
26. Polish title
27. Bovary or X
29. Hollywood's Sunset
30. Shy
32. Churchill's *The Gathering* ___
34. Upper chamber in France
36. Film actor Thatcher
37. Heirs
40. Complication
42. Loch and Eliot
45. Kind of verb: Abbr.
46. Bean or Welles
48. Indian of New York
50. Kind of corner
51. Small container
53. Eye afflictions
55. Tangle, old style
56. Proclaim loudly
57. Clair and Coty of France
59. Site of a well-known dam
61. Irregular
63. Creek
64. Social standings
66. Like O'Neill's ape
68. Opened oysters
70. Coarse hominy
71. Dancing girls in Cairo
72. Half an Oriental disease
73. The candlenut
76. Do a supermarket checker's job
77. Ground covered in football
81. John Gunther subject
82. Loop used by surgeons
84. Roads to Caesar's Rome
86. Flynn
87. Tithe
89. Endure
91. Put ___ to (stop)
93. Air: Prefix
94. Therefore
95. Uninvited sleeping partner
97. Trees of Central America
99. Onto
100. Two-___ (short film)
102. Sound-detecting device
104. Framework used by a sculptor
106. Lazy girl
108. Nips
110. Of the cheek
111. State of being stuck
114. Wound, as a textile yarn
116. Singer Willie or Rick
119. Bert Lahr in Oz
120. Measuring stick for a rock 'n' roll star?
123. River in Spain
124. Hope springs eternal for him
125. Wading bird
126. Old hat
127. Actress Patricia
128. Thing, in law
129. Blackmore girl
130. Was indebted
131. Source of the Blue Nile

DOWN

1. Rip-off
2. Martinelli of the screen
3. Gift from an artist?
4. Layers
5. Food suppliers
6. Número ___
7. Gypsy men
8. Northern Europeans
9. Turns the soil over again
10. An ocean: Abbr.
11. Shoe combo
12. Coastal cove
13. Beach in Florida
14. Tit-for-tat action
15. Logo of an author?
16. Swiss herdsman
19. Temptress
22. Equipment
25. Young boys, in Barcelona
28. Detective Mr.
31. Wrath
33. Gem for a hostess?
35. Heredity factor of a fighter?
37. Book for an *élève*
38. Lake Indians
39. Sauce beans
41. Scorch
43. Hair-raising
44. Golf veteran Sam
47. Haircut for a TV star?
49. Average for a comic?
52. To say the ___
54. West German river
56. Paris bread spread
58. Stiffness
60. Rain clouds
62. Home to the Mets
65. Flightless bird
67. Gear for a vaquero
69. Spanish citron
73. Kind of space
74. Rhone feeder
75. Desire of an actress?
78. Insect of a comedienne?
79. TV's Pyle
80. Emulate Romeo and Juliet
83. Inventor of the diving bell
85. Midianite king
88. Antiknock solvents
90. Marine animal
92. Insisted upon
95. Browned in fat
96. Bowl in Florida
98. Store-ad word
101. Winding curve
103. Lets
105. Great gift
107. "Do ___ gentle into that good night": Thomas
109. Sixth, in Italy
111. High mountain
112. Boutique name
113. Peter of the keyboard
115. Tie
117. Port in Algeria
118. Vincent Lopez favorite
121. Cyst
122. Cheer for El Cordobés

191 Giving the Go-By By Robert Roop

Concentrating on entries with a certain affinity.

ACROSS

1. QE2, e.g.
6. Kind of pneumonia
11. Bed or fire follower
14. Stroll
15. One who cheapens
17. Lively, in mus.
19. Instrument often boxed
20. Chemical parallel
21. Garment-rack abbr.
23. Eastern Church title
24. Ending for major or farmer
26. Horne et al.
27. Savalas
28. Portly
30. Gorge
32. Freedom from emotion
34. American painter
36. Left
38. Oriental continent
39. Omar's offering
40. Huntress of Greek myth
42. Housetop
44. Bedouin
46. School-system off.
48. Scatter
50. Sweet potatoes
54. Egyptian snake
57. Charles Lamb
59. Woodwind
60. Petulance
62. Regions
64. Rodgers and Hammerstein musical
66. Peddler
67. Interloper
69. Incapable of emotion
71. Handel oratorio
72. Advance
74. Snicker___
75. September flowers
76. Drugstore: Abbr.
77. Old Portuguese coins
79. Stray
80. Fuss
81. Glued
83. She wrote *Gentlemen Prefer Blondes*
85. Tijuana ladies: Abbr.
87. Kind of vark or wolf
89. Solar phenomenon
94. Irish Rose's mate
98. ___ dixit
100. New or Fair
102. Macao money
103. Catwalk
106. Chemical suffixes
108. Nuisances
109. Las Vegas machines
110. Red dye
112. ___ ex machina
114. H.S. test
115. Burstyn or Terry
116. Dreidel
118. Submissive
120. Greek theaters
121. Instruct
122. He wrote *Phèdre*
123. Between els and ens
124. English explorer of the Nile
125. "With ___ at the end of his nose": Lear

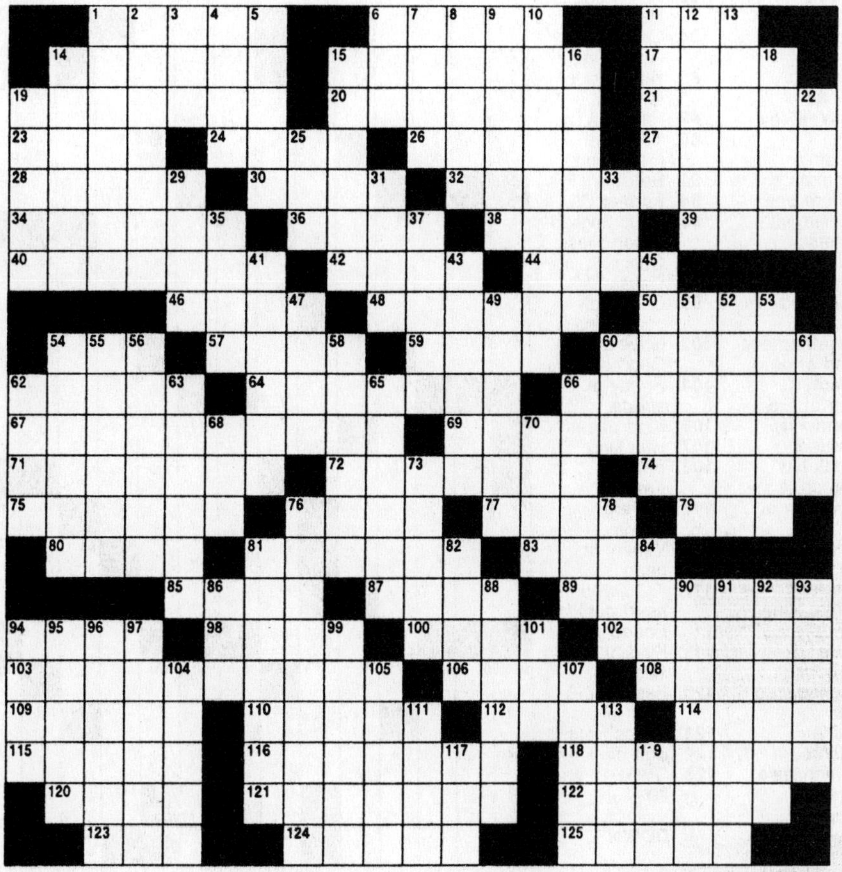

DOWN

1. Flickering
2. Deadlock
3. Knicks and Celtics org.
4. Otherwise
5. Takes five
6. ___ *Misérables*
7. Old Greek coin
8. Restrained
9. Tone deafness
10. Privilege of returning
11. Harasses
12. Turmoil
13. Kind of magazine
14. Kind of baron
15. Weight watcher
16. Breathe
18. Honeydew or casaba
19. West Indian mahogany
22. Peer ___
25. Playing marble
29. Billing times: Abbr.
31. Son of Seth
33. Motorists' org.
35. Savage Island
37. Mapmaking abbr.
41. Spatter
43. Wool or silk
45. Encircling road
47. Sesame plants
49. Lodger
51. Venetian book of high quality
52. Dues payer
53. Arctic hunting ship
54. Apprehend
55. Takes care of
56. Stayed out of the bidding
58. Hebrew letters
60. Mayday's relative
61. Nautical dirs.
62. Hindu life principle: Var.
63. Agnew namesakes
65. Printing mistakes
66. Transistors
68. Shoe widths
70. Rind
73. Mountain nymph
76. Countersigns
78. Nuts' predecessor
81. Capital of the Society Islands
82. Between zwei and vier
84. Kind of dragon or bean
86. Fit
88. Pamper
90. Enters
91. Fleeting
92. Musical interval
93. Savor
94. Part of a basilica
95. Verdi's *Un ___ in Maschera*
96. Wagner heroine
97. Respect
99. Relax
101. Shelter
104. Persian card game
105. Once, in Scotland
107. Above: Prefix
111. Bismarck is its capital
113. German basin
117. Pierre's summer
119. ___-fi

192 Solitaire By Sidney Robbins

Keeping things on an individual basis.

ACROSS

1. Ill-tempered person
6. Nigerian people
9. W.W. II spy org.
12. Room's roommate
17. Where one parliament meets
19. Dumb girl
21. Miss Farrow
22. Fast sled or yacht
23. Togetherness
27. Kind of devil
28. Hilarity
29. Part of E.S.T.
30. Cartoonist Gardner
31. Small bits
32. Anarchist Goldman et al.
33. Made good spiritually
35. Scatter
39. "What Kind of Fool ___?"
40. Choir response
41. Dog-induced fear
47. Edible mushroom
51. Brünnhilde's horse
52. Jungle attention-getter
53. Brutus' 13
54. Take exception
55. Harden
56. Wet-eyed
58. Part of a gross
59. Suggest
60. Bone: Prefix
61. Castro
62. Apes an owl
63. Diego or Salvador
65. Zero
69. Bread type
70. Twerp
72. Prides' prides
73. Heraldic band
75. Old World apples
76. Poe or Guest
77. Unlikely story
79. Ending for hill or bull
82. Shows devotion
83. Armstrong or Hamilton
84. One of a Great five
85. Recipient of largess
87. Part of A.D.
88. Tonsorial instruction
91. British V.I.P.s
94. Former G.I.
95. Early English assemblies
96. Chain, to Caesar
99. Chemical compound
102. Novelist George
104. Bobby of sports
105. Kind of set
107. Hun king
108. Bitter ___ to swallow
112. Revere words
116. Variety of bean
117. "___ your heart out!"
118. Ended
119. Kind of streak
120. Passover feast
121. Winos' woes
122. Soft drink
123. 'Twixt 12 and 20

DOWN

1. Survival requirement
2. Volcano of note
3. Roman road
4. Umpire's call
5. One doubled
6. Takes it easy
7. Tree trunk
8. Mouths
9. Cows' stomachs
10. Delta deposits
11. Garage event
12. Town near Mt. Etna
13. Paddle's relative
14. Undeveloped oak
15. Adorée of films
16. Apprehension
18. Wild Asian sheep
20. Puny
24. Cleric's robe
25. Hoover or Grand Coulee
26. Beat, in England
31. Credits' offsets
32. Eastern biggie
34. Again
35. Go to the ___
36. Concerning
37. Jazz style
38. Place for a con
39. Not at home
40. Hebrew letter
42. Get into shape
43. Rocky eminence
44. Mass departure
45. 8B, 9C, etc.
46. Ice, in Toledo
48. Gas-gauge reading
49. What a doctor feels
50. Suffix for green or tomfool
54. God, in Italy
57. Story-telling slave: Var.
58. Fast-food spot
60. Single file
61. Windup
62. Artificial fishing fly
63. Disdain
64. Isle off Scotland
66. West German port
67. Hocus-pocus
68. Prize name
71. Curve
74. Like a reef
75. Baden Baden, for one
76. Baseball's Slaughter
77. Worry
78. Breathing necessity
79. Upon
80. Gael
81. Florida's tip
84. Eternally
86. German physicist
89. Exaggerate
90. Set on fire
92. "Win ___ the Gipper"
93. Fishhook feature
96. Relatives of condos
97. Palmer of the links
98. Tendency
99. Showy display
100. Figures, for short
101. Heavy weight
102. Stow away
103. Ex-ring champ
106. Looked at
107. Overwhelmed
108. Ernie or Howard
109. Capri or Elba
110. Trotsky
111. Congres-sional achievements
113. Follower: Suffix
114. Tenn. project
115. Do some wagering

193 On Cue By Louis Baron

A matter of coming up with logical conclusions.

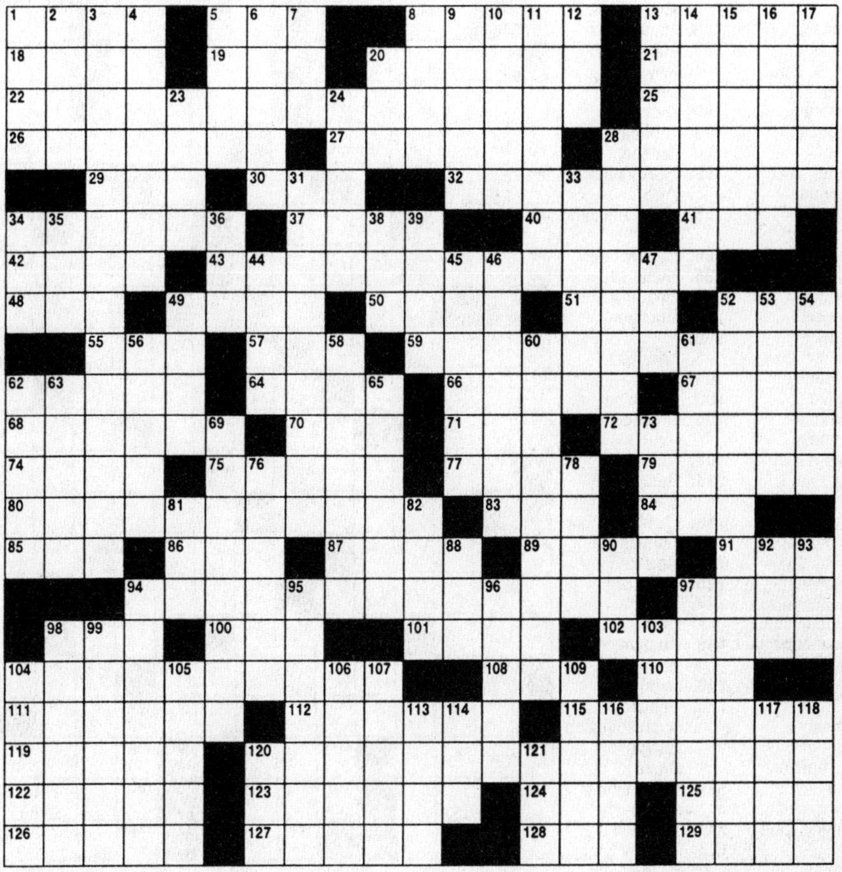

ACROSS

1. ". . . have mercy on such ___"
5. Parapsychology study
8. "___ Street Blues"
13. Business downer
18. Hiker's thing
19. Opposite of paleo
20. *Lost Horizon* star
21. Pavarotti, e.g.
22. READY, AIM
25. LuPone role
26. Takes up a case again
27. Yacht mooring
28. Resort near St. Moritz
29. Can. province
30. "___ sells seashells . . ."
32. AND BOARD
34. Borneo sultanate
37. Pre-J.H. school
40. Bowstring hemp
41. Printing spaces
42. Entertain
43. OF THE MOHICANS
48. Urgent call
49. Coffee
50. Melville opus
51. From ___ Z
52. Police-blotter abbr.
55. Tell's canton
57. It's coddled sometimes
59. ON THE BARREL
62. Paste-on
64. Function
66. Basket-maker's willow
67. Out of town
68. Rouse
70. Greek letters
71. Switched on
72. Penny-pinch
74. Port of Yemen
75. Top-level orders
77. Consider
79. Zodiacal animal
80. NOW I LAY ME DOWN TO
83. Geneticist's abbr.
84. Cow genus
85. Pre-grads
86. Cameo appearance
87. Two-toed sloth
89. Is way off
91. Life story
94. LET THERE BE
97. Exam
98. Songster's syllable
100. Samoan wattlebird
101. Ability prover
102. Rely on
104. C-CUT TH-THAT O-OUT!!
108. Weddell or Ross
110. Congo native
111. Taros
112. Irish patriot: 1879–1916
115. Order to a little star
119. Chaplain
120. AND NAIL
122. In a tough spot
123. Trial locales
124. Lend a hand
125. Speedway for the 500
126. Elephant groups
127. Dictation taker
128. Zetterling of films
129. Money-changer's fee

DOWN

1. Ripening agent
2. Name with Coburg or Gotha
3. SWEET SMELL OF
4. Saint-___, city near Lyons
5. RR driver
6. The Grinch's author
7. Luau serving
8. Peccary's relative
9. Puckish
10. ___ acid
11. Wyoming city
12. Helmsman's dir.
13. Cubic meter
14. Young hare
15. Concord
16. Maxims
17. Flat-bottomed boat
20. Oriental tea
23. Nickname for Hawthorne
24. Troutlike food fish
28. Inventors
31. Half dodecagonal
33. Recently
34. Marquand's ___ *Daughter*
35. Car-museum exhibit
36. ___ hurry
38. Ike's war turf
39. Apple-pie pros
44. "Did you ___?"
45. To have's partner
46. From Indiana
47. Bulg. capital
49. Cast off
52. AU R OR A
53. Type of orange
54. "___! I wrote the 'PurpleCow'": Burgess
56. Actor Claude
58. Sitter's muscle
60. Slow down, in music
61. Lorre role in *The Maltese Falcon*
62. Starts a call
63. Biblical witch's home
65. Early Jewish sectarian
69. Likenesses
73. Filing aids
76. "___ so?"
78. Playwright Connelly
81. Kimono prettifier
82. Breathe hard
88. Western Indian
90. Czar-buster
92. Writer Fleming
93. On in years
94. Not effortless
95. Carolyn Wells poem
96. Elizabeth I's favorite
97. Cactus group
98. "The will to do, the soul ___": Scott
99. Tiller's attachment
103. George Orwell's real first name
104. Bathymeter reading
105. Yorkshire city
106. Sierra ___
107. Ob River feeder
109. Entrance courts
113. Prefix for stat
114. French possessive
116. Desert gully
117. Napoleonic victory site
118. Greek war goddess
120. Boob tubes
121. Beret's kin

194 Cooling It By William Canine

Keeping the temperature under control.

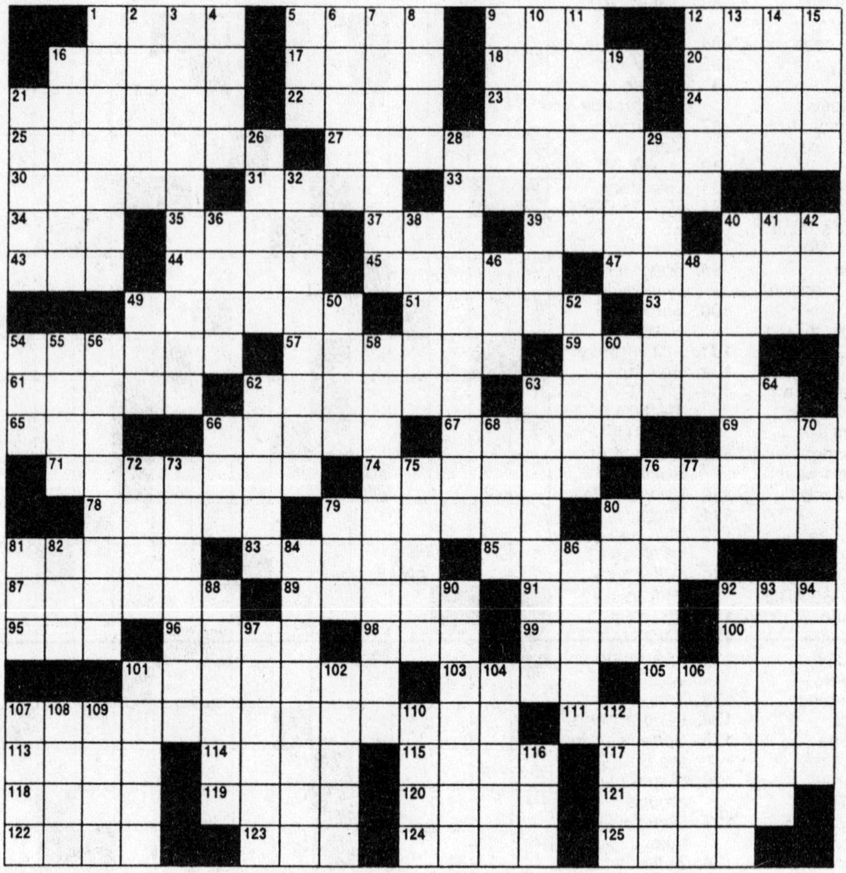

ACROSS

1. Cornfield sounds
5. This, in Spain
9. Rhine tributary
12. Refresher
16. Site of Miletus and Ephesus
17. Dollop
18. Framework
20. Severn tributary
21. Concoct
22. Rose or Cotton
23. More or less
24. Substance
25. Metallic sulfides
27. Summery twosome of a song
30. Topsoil, e.g.
31. Profound
33. Bootmakers
34. One of the formicidae
35. Of a Pindaric form
37. African tribe
39. Tennille of TV
40. Pay-TV channel
43. Docs
44. Dart feather
45. Use a divining rod
47. Lightning unit
49. Pick
51. Foxy
53. Lariat
54. Manhattan's skid row
57. Tank up
59. SST's forte
61. Memorable actor Maurice
62. Florida city
63. Window décor
65. Kind of picker or wit
66. Culvert
67. Surpluses
69. Offs and ___
71. Propriety
74. Skyscrapers
76. *As You Like It* girl
78. Incurred
79. Hut
80. Inferior
81. Measure for Noah's ark
83. ___ Park, Colorado
85. Pundits
87. Having no key, musically
89. Dispatch
91. Biblical brother
92. Hundredth: Abbr.
95. Old Tunisian ruler
96. Ceremony
98. Sicily or Crete: Abbr.
99. Stagger
100. ". . . ___ I saw Elba"
101. Trifling thing
103. Describe
105. Bremen's river
107. Jilt
111. Pub customer
113. Out of control
114. Cause: Prefix
115. Bowsprit
117. Forage clover
118. Festive occasion
119. Minute
120. "There ___ such thing as justice": Darrow
121. What Poirot seeks
122. So be it
123. Military V.I.P.s
124. Silent-star Wallace
125. River to the North Sea

DOWN

1. Hiding places
2. In regard to
3. Kestrels
4. Surfeit
5. Flood's opposite
6. Keyholes
7. Blondie
8. Efficient
9. Marketplace
10. Lightning-control device
11. ___ the occasion
12. Western lily plant
13. Furnace's relative
14. Encumber
15. Opposed
16. Not maritime
19. Quite a few
21. Type of girder
26. Poland Chinas
28. Popeye's exclamation
29. Site of Asmara
32. Baked Alaska base
36. Augustin ___ of theater note
38. Petty officer
40. Summer misery
41. Cave denizen
42. Volga tributary
46. ___ ammoniac
48. Nothing, in Paris
49. D.C. bigwig
50. Low-caste Hindu
52. The Romanovs
54. Crenshaw of golf
55. Roman poet
56. Gunga Din was one
58. Put up the K's, in baseball
60. Word of request: Abbr.
62. Cherry or plum
63. ___ *for May,* 1939 musical
64. Author Bagnold
66. Actress Joanne
68. Former G.I.s
70. Assert
72. His postman rang twice
73. Rochester's lake
75. Kilns
76. Former character actor
77. Aurora
79. RR stop
80. Kind of duck
81. Hackie's place
82. Shoshonean
84. Bed-linen material
86. Evening, in Berlin
88. Kind of finch
90. Oval
92. More of a nuisance
93. Brooks' relatives
94. ___ Haute
97. Dogmatic
101. Weasel's relative
102. Sailors' cries
104. Native of Isfahan
106. Follow
107. Batty
108. Shiite leader
109. Field mouse
110. Region of Saudi Arabia
112. Risqué
116. Curtain holder

195 Getting the Count By Jo Lundy

With any number of things to be considered.

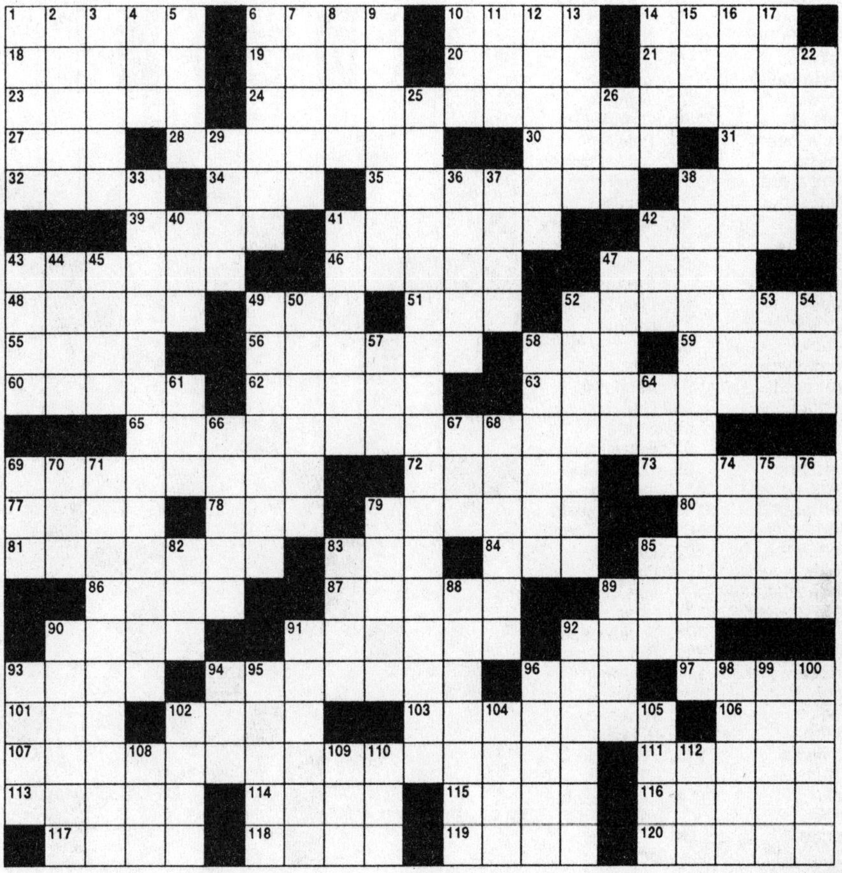

ACROSS

1. Kind of boat or engine
6. Irritable stinger
10. Wheelchair convenience
14. Facts
18. Blood distributor
19. Winglike parts
20. ___-Neisse Line
21. Cosmetics case: Var.
23. Employed
24. Eight hundred
27. U.N. workers' agency
28. Word on an unpaid bill
30. Turn to liquid
31. Large planet: Abbr.
32. Cowardly Lion Lahr
34. Tax org.
35. Kind of triangle
38. Remain
39. Linden and Holbrook
41. Start again
42. Former governors in Turkey
43. Mountain divider
46. As good ___
47. Left: Prefix
48. Turn away
49. Heating unit: Abbr.
51. Med. people
52. Lead ores
55. Mail
56. Wharton and Head
58. Prepare for battle
59. Nearest
60. Kind of minister or number
62. Indian shrine town
63. Brags about
65. Slogan for a July day
69. Incorrect term
72. Mrs. Copperfield and others
73. Zsa Zsa or Eva
77. Came down
78. "___ longa, vita . . ."
79. Convince
80. A climber
81. Tam, beret, cloche, Panama, fedora and tricorn
83. Aggregate: Abbr.
84. Parts of egos
85. Neutral place to sit
86. Prefix for graph or phone
87. Quick drink
89. Came ashore
90. Units of resistance
91. Some churches have them
92. Japanese ship name
93. Euterpe or Clio
94. High canvas on a ship
96. Eye part
97. ___ the Red
101. Habit
102. Truck rig
103. ___ Valera
106. Early Tokyo
107. L. Gordon Cooper
111. Diminish gradually
113. Dinsmore or Venner
114. Generous sandwich
115. Rocky eminence
116. Freshly washed
117. Appear
118. Solicits
119. Congers
120. Like Rome's topography

DOWN

1. Sir, in India
2. Sheer fabric
3. Lapse
4. Corroded
5. Australian fish
6. Crisp cookies
7. Then, in Dieppe
8. Ibn-___
9. Studies
10. Fabulous bird
11. Fuss
12. Human sea denizens
13. Dress for show
14. Skillful
15. Legal figure: Abbr.
16. Blackjacks
17. Trojan hero
22. Catch sight of
25. Twice-told tales
26. Spanish cheer
29. Despicable
33. Zither music in a 1949 film
36. Mimics
37. Ayres and Cody
38. Needle-and-pin area of N.Y.C.
40. Carpenter ___
41. Forearm bone
42. ___ canto
43. File
44. State
45. A first word for Caesar
47. Joseph ___ of the Supreme Court: 1910–16
49. Foul-weather jackets
50. Psychologist Alfred and family
52. Complains
53. Central line: Prefix
54. Personnel: Abbr.
57. ___-la-la
58. "All ___!"
61. That, to Juan
64. Fine silver: Abbr.
66. Tropical timber tree
67. Dawn goddess
68. Pears, peaches, etc.
69. College degrees
70. River of China
71. Intuitive power
74. Restrain
75. Fairy-tale start
76. Part of a clarinet
79. Embryo sacs
82. Pacino and Jolson
83. Nile menaces
85. Kind of cry
88. Backslide
89. Actress Cheryl
90. European blackbirds
91. Porcupine quills
92. Gold diggers
93. Voiceless
94. Pro ___
95. W.W. II invasion beach
96. Kind of anesthetic
98. Drive off
99. Perfectly suited
100. Like some jokes
102. Ark passenger
104. Nutmeg product
105. Do certain art works
108. Ascot or Windsor
109. Annoy
110. Refusals
112. Mohammed's son-in-law

196 On the Plus Side By Norma Steinberg

Whether unusual, pleasant or what.

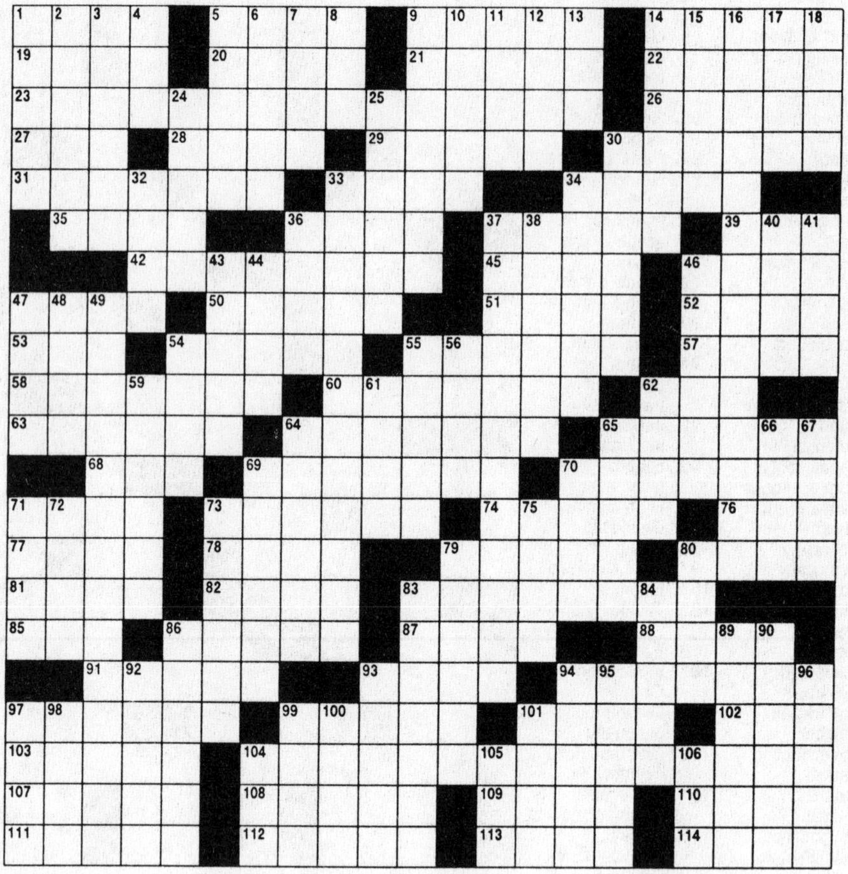

ACROSS

1. Does buffing
5. Latin declension word
9. Saying
14. Wide open
19. Sailing
20. Rani's dress
21. Metes out
22. Entrance hall
23. TV show about daredevil feats
26. April 1 people
27. Poetic word
28. Words at weddings
29. Miss Horne and others
30. Outcome
31. Vagabond
33. Gun sound
34. More pleasant
35. Fluids
36. Make one's way
37. Trick
39. Certain Alaskan: Abbr.
42. Sleeve addenda
45. Conflicts
46. A gender
47. Make out
50. Makes money
51. "Or ___!" (ultimatum)
52. "An apple ___ . . ."
53. Mal de ___
54. Late
55. Stone markers
57. Finishes a j
58. Houses, in Paris
60. Was a cocky winner
62. ___ diem
63. Hall and Oakley
64. Dye ingredient
65. Swamp
68. Certain bank savings: Abbr.
69. Advance
70. Like pure water
71. Miss Verdon
73. Pulled crab grass
74. Paradises
76. Fond du ___
77. Wedding throwaway
78. Input for a smasher
79. Armada
80. Before Oct.
81. Pale
82. ___, *Lucille:* Gershwin musical
83. Most slippery
85. "___ Clown"
86. Steve or Ethan
87. Like Sellers' panther
88. ___ for the hills
91. Infuriates
93. Gait
94. Stutter
97. Perpetrate
99. ___ of the evening
101. Recipe word
102. Golfer's grip
103. Of birds
104. Postal service
107. Char
108. Urban oases
109. Reveal
110. Mountain: Prefix
111. Trimmed
112. Rubbish
113. Timetable, for short
114. ". . . ___ but not heard"

DOWN

1. Marked R or PG
2. Wedding attendants
3. Kind of cap
4. Watched the kids
5. Stage whisper
6. Big house
7. Circle parts
8. Galahad, for one
9. Parts of sums
10. In action
11. Goya's duchess
12. Sets
13. Suffix for Japan
14. Influence
15. Main dish for the Cratchits
16. "The Alphabet Song" start
17. ___-mell
18. Formerly, of old
24. Shankar's instrument
25. Antelopes
30. Beauty-parlor procedures
32. Wear
33. King of Swing
34. Drank slowly
36. Hospital section
37. Barbershop quartet's gal
38. Loftier
40. Strip of wood
41. Padlock accessories
43. The ___ to an end
44. Confederate-flag units
46. City near Fresno
47. Mme. Bovary
48. Penn or O'Casey
49. Mr. Right?
54. *On Your___.* Rodgers-Hart musical
55. Did a cobbler's job
56. London gallery
59. Poitier or Lanier
61. Curtain material
62. Flower holders
64. New Orleans settler
65. Three-card ___
66. Before dash or stick
67. Religious group
69. Daisy sections
70. Catch a glimpse
71. Snatch
72. Sagacious
73. Billfold
75. Hit the ___
79. Friendly horse of fiction
80. Pipe part
83. Kind of omelet or onion
84. Puppeteer Lewis
86. Straightened
89. Electrical unit
90. B.A., for one
92. "Man is God's ___": Herbert
93. Fills a suitcase
94. Metric unit
95. Installed flooring
96. Synthetic fabric
97. A ___ in point
98. Roman poet
99. Go a few rounds
100. Zeus' spouse
101. Neighbor of Neb.
104. Harbor: Abbr.
105. Weights: Abbr.
106. Your, in Ypres

197 Lying in State By Wilson McBeath

Not necessarily in a dignified way.

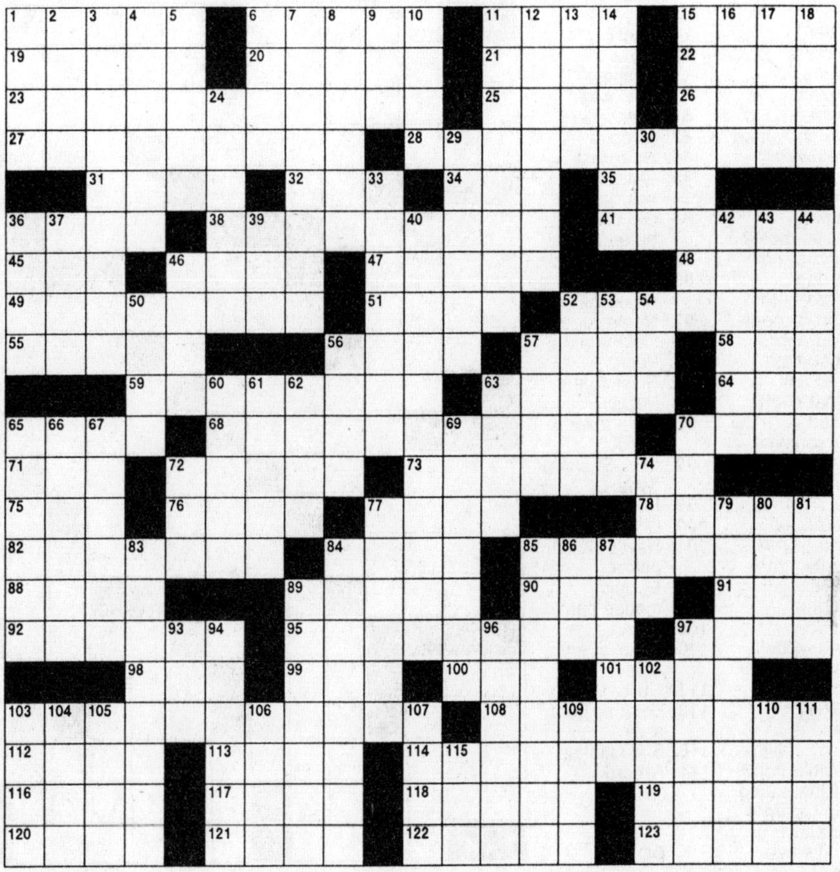
1 2 3 4 5 6 7 8 9 10 11 12 13 14 15 16 17 18
19 20 21 22
23 24 25 26
27 28 29 30
31 32 33 34 35
36 37 38 39 40 41 42 43 44
45 46 47 48
49 50 51 52 53 54
55 56 57 58
59 60 61 62 63 64
65 66 67 68 69 70
71 72 73 74
75 76 77 78 79 80 81
82 83 84 85 86 87
88 89 90 91
92 93 94 95 96 97
98 99 100 101 102
103 104 105 106 107 108 109 110 111
112 113 114 115
116 117 118 119
120 121 122 123

ACROSS

1. Appears
6. Fitzgerald and Raines
11. Wife of Hercules
15. Applaud
19. Photographer Adams
20. Old West Indies people
21. Part of a molecule
22. City on the Big Island
23. Seminole door openers
25. Locale of The Little Brown Church
26. Soviet sea
27. Reckoned
28. Beaver path of a sort
31. First garden
32. Rent
34. Before
35. Morse-code symbol
36. Kind of rubber
38. Oddball
41. Supports in a subway
45. Half of CIV
46. Part of a harness
47. Suffix for Anglo or biblio
48. Part of Q.E.D.
49. Inserted in an envelope
51. Pitcher parts
52. Bridge
55. Lulu
56. TV's Johnson
57. Nurtured
58. Diminutive suffix
59. Benny Goodman's instrument
63. Word before meal or work
64. Disencumber
65. Do in
68. A state-ly dessert
70. Replaces a lawn
71. French city in the Pyrenees
72. Permit
73. Highest card below an honor
75. Govt. agency
76. Has-____
77. Affectation
78. Gossips
82. Circuitous routes
84. Sounds from the dovecote
85. Short negligee
88. River in Hesse
89. Grass used for syrup
90. Author Kingsley
91. Condensed moisture
92. Presidential name
95. Pennsylvania town on the Delaware
97. Visits
98. Born
99. Wallach
100. Antiquity
101. Dutch painter
103. Southern radio operator
108. Elevator's alternative
112. Singer Adams
113. Spanish bull
114. Western digger's find
116. College military org.
117. Overwhelmed
118. Radon
119. He watched Salome dance
120. Name for Athena
121. Boys
122. Oceans, to Shelley
123. Donkeys

DOWN

1. Yegg's target
2. Photog. blowups
3. Recondite matters
4. Capital of Yucatán
5. Thin mud
6. French state
7. City near Tampa
8. German songs
9. Prefix for thing or place
10. Mediocre
11. Foolish talkers, in Scotland
12. Whatnot's relative
13. Machete
14. Corrects
15. French cathedral city
16. Coin on the Corso
17. Soviet range
18. Large-scale count of noses
24. Cha-cha and samba
29. Withdraw
30. Small child
33. Like some candles
36. Annapolis freshman
37. Eldest, in Paris
39. Hasten
40. Place for a choo-choo
42. Toscanini
43. Wan
44. Horses
46. Middle Eastern weight
50. ____ Stoner (certain libber)
52. Migrates
53. Summarize
54. Netherlands city
56. Once more
57. Cold Swiss wind
60. More skillful
61. Chest sounds
62. Image: Var.
63. Window part
65. Black widow
66. City on the Rio Grande
67. Novelist Jane
69. Supple
70. Depots: Abbr.
72. ____-Bakr, Mohammed's successor
74. Elevator name
77. She discussed the quality of mercy
79. Polaris and others
80. Swiss painter
81. Stitches
83. Address for Santa Ana's neighbor
84. Scuttles
85. Valentines' source
86. Doctors' org.
87. Accident
89. Daubed
93. Wreath
94. Kind of floss
96. Ester of an acid
97. Candidate lists
102. Hawaiian greeting
103. Actress Miles
104. Matinee ____
105. Ceremony
106. Amana's state
107. Obey
109. Swindles
110. American Indian
111. Lightning diverters
115. Engraved stamp

198 Queries By Emory Cain

In which some apt answers are called for.

ACROSS

1. Hoard
6. Draw a ___ (aim)
12. Luzon volcano
16. Flamboyance
18. Delaware Indian
19. Detective Lupin
22. Arctic mole?
25. Kind of cow or dog
26. Word before chat or nous
27. Map abbr.
28. Soak flax
29. Q–U link
30. What's left
31. Quad personality
32. Nationality suffix
33. ___ Na Na
34. Unrefined
38. One of the Cartwrights
39. Biblical prophet
40. SOS!
41. Kind of belt
43. River to the Roanoke
44. Pottery or china
48. Mine, in Nice
49. Robin's pop?
53. Off the sauce
54. Don't slam it
55. Theater grp.
56. Tidal wave
57. Small songbirds
58. Having limits
60. Tapered structure
61. Bolshoi offering
62. Tissue layer
63. European blackbird
64. All ___ (the works)
65. Soprano Maria
68. Bait for oglers
69. Viragoes
71. Shakespearean sprite
72. Concerto endings
73. Certain club
74. ___ out (fire tactfully)
77. Salon treatment
78. Warning label in small print?
80. Minute quantity
81. Grid wear
82. Deli order
83. Appoint
84. Hoarfrost
85. Colloidal solutions
86. Did the butterfly
88. Units of force
89. Poker winnings
92. Name for a caliph
93. Pack
94. River to the Fulda
97. Latin lover's word
98. ___ Shamra, Syria
99. Mac's cap
100. Coeur d'___
101. Haw's partner
104. Myopic mouse hero?
109. Suit ___
110. Ester of an acid
111. Guilty feeling
112. Back or front area
113. S.A.T. taker
114. A Ford

DOWN

1. Writer Seton
2. Crop
3. Ones needing liniment
4. Glistened
5. Groups
6. Kind of alert or blood
7. Slithery fish
8. One of the Bahamas
9. ___ *Divine Comedy*
10. Chose
11. Take-home pay
12. Hires
13. Rugged ridges
14. Residue
15. Sly looks
16. Ltr. addenda
17. Mimic
20. Vintage car
21. Miss Kett
23. Food scrap
24. "Poems ___ by fools . . ."
31. Pigeon pad
34. African lake
35. San ___, Italy
36. Distant
37. Not haunted?
38. Merry sound
39. Like a lot
41. Occasional sleigh driver
42. Leather or luncheon ending
44. Like Atlas?
45. Labor leader I. W. or actor Walter
46. Glassmaker Lalique
47. Formerly, of old
49. Flunks
50. Musical repetition
51. Greets
52. Cruel man
53. Marshy area
59. Grid Hall of Famer Greasy
60. French council
61. Ready to yawn
63. Mild ogle-bait
64. "___ you go again!": Reagan
65. Cavil
66. Elaborate melody
67. Swedish soprano
68. Sheds
69. Six or seven, at bridge
70. Gown fabric
72. Orchestra member
73. Agana's island
75. To ___ extent
76. Uncles, in Edinburgh
79. Cause erosion
82. Delayed
85. A Roosevelt Vice President
86. ___ rights
87. Australian animal
88. ". . . such stuff as ___ are made on . . .": Shak.
89. What a crew cut doesn't have
90. 1847 adventure novel
91. Now
93. Vapid
94. Plumbing joint
95. Steel-plow pioneer
96. Over
100. Nautical position
101. Friend or Guide
102. Dawn goddess
103. Chemical ending
105. Airline abbr.
106. Kind of rod or seat
107. French season
108. Scot's strong emotion

199 Kooky Clues By Alfio Micci

Making sense out of a little nonsense.

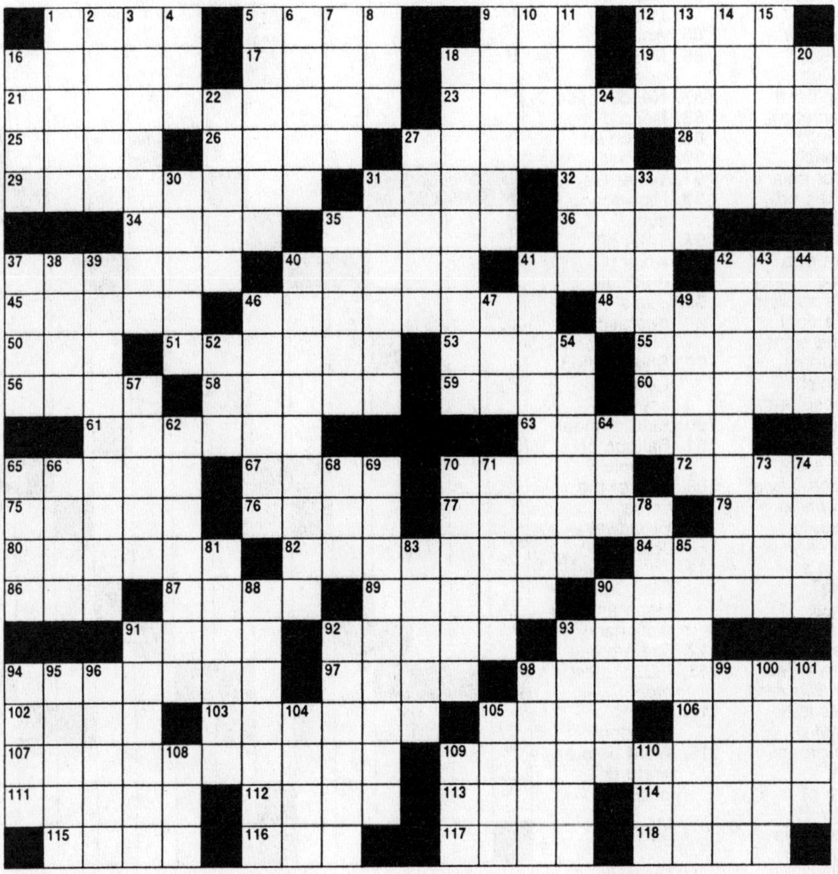

ACROSS

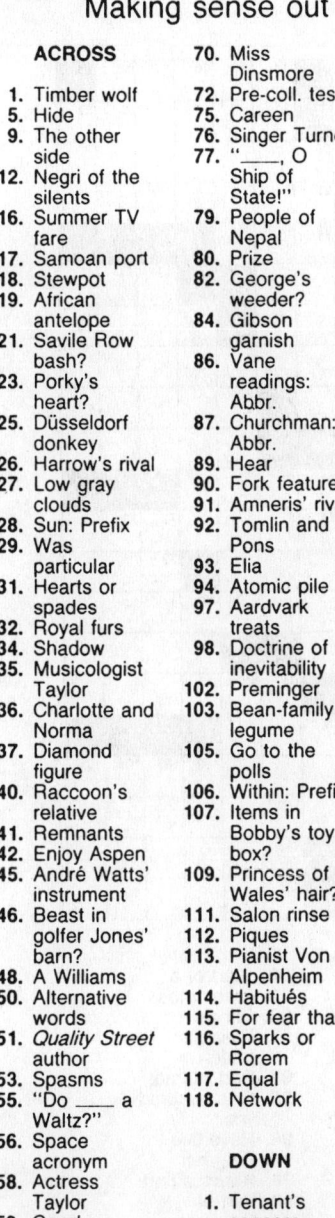

1. Timber wolf
5. Hide
9. The other side
12. Negri of the silents
16. Summer TV fare
17. Samoan port
18. Stewpot
19. African antelope
21. Savile Row bash?
23. Porky's heart?
25. Düsseldorf donkey
26. Harrow's rival
27. Low gray clouds
28. Sun: Prefix
29. Was particular
31. Hearts or spades
32. Royal furs
34. Shadow
35. Musicologist Taylor
36. Charlotte and Norma
37. Diamond figure
40. Raccoon's relative
41. Remnants
42. Enjoy Aspen
45. André Watts' instrument
46. Beast in golfer Jones' barn?
48. A Williams
50. Alternative words
51. *Quality Street* author
53. Spasms
55. "Do ___ a Waltz?"
56. Space acronym
58. Actress Taylor
59. Good fortune, in England
60. Omni or Brendan Byrne
61. Anatomical folds
63. Discharge, as cargo
65. Curve formed by vaults
67. Stern's opposite
70. Miss Dinsmore
72. Pre-coll. test
75. Careen
76. Singer Turner
77. "___, O Ship of State!"
79. People of Nepal
80. Prize
82. George's weeder?
84. Gibson garnish
86. Vane readings: Abbr.
87. Churchman: Abbr.
89. Hear
90. Fork features
91. Amneris' rival
92. Tomlin and Pons
93. Elia
94. Atomic pile
97. Aardvark treats
98. Doctrine of inevitability
102. Preminger
103. Bean-family legume
105. Go to the polls
106. Within: Prefix
107. Items in Bobby's toy box?
109. Princess of Wales' hair?
111. Salon rinse
112. Piques
113. Pianist Von Alpenheim
114. Habitués
115. For fear that
116. Sparks or Rorem
117. Equal
118. Network

DOWN

1. Tenant's concern
2. Bay window
3. Kind of board
4. Lennon's widow
5. Artist's medium
6. Ceremonial apron
7. Celebrity
8. Spigot
9. Coquettes
10. Kafka heroine
11. Part of E.D.T.
12. South Seas staple
13. Salep
14. Compare
15. White poplar
16. Map abbrs.
18. Their outlook is bright
20. Garden bloom
22. Lace anew
24. Harangue
27. Like tallow
30. Pod-yielding tree
31. Certain Navy man
33. Handel masterpiece
35. TV character Gillis
37. *Once ___ a Mattress*
38. Star in Cetus
39. Dad's favorite games?
40. Member of the band
41. Act of debarring
42. Ovine relatives?
43. N.J. governor
44. Soprano Petina
46. Chicken-part preference
47. Grenoble goose
49. Snap the fingers
52. Rainbow
54. Infirm
57. Flo's TV friend
62. ___ *the Wind*
64. ___ de Urgel, Spain
65. Campbell of song
66. Trick
68. Bambi's aunt
69. Virility
70. Products of 93 Across
71. Bert's folks
73. Eat like ___ (gluttonize)
74. Summer acquisitions
78. Bellini heroine
81. Bordeaux wines
83. Greek letter
85. Word with oblige
88. Vitamin A source
90. Etonian parent
91. Future oaks
92. ___ up (accepted eagerly)
93. Former's opposite
94. ___ ha-Shanah
95. Lionel's sister
96. In agreement
98. *Cabaret* director
99. Map detail
100. Cubic meter
101. Rolling stone's lack
104. Had on
105. Despicable
108. Make lace
109. Canapé enhancer
110. Grand-tour site: Abbr.

200 Decibel Limit By Frances Hansen

Roosters aren't alone in greeting the new day.

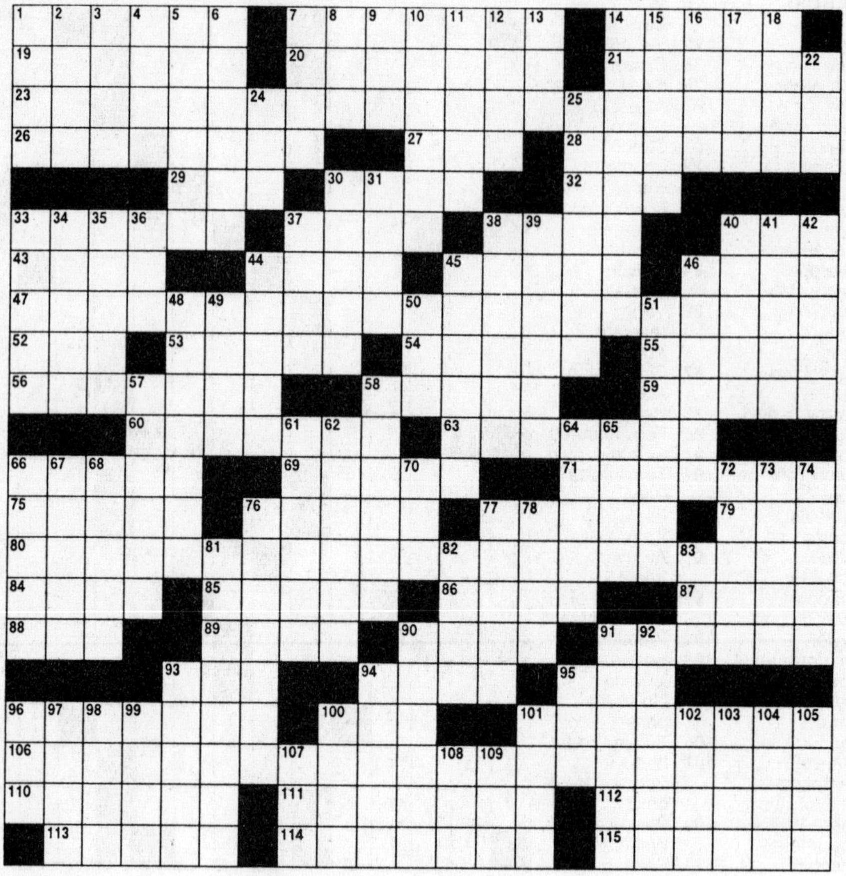

ACROSS

1. Danny or Marlo
7. Easily misplaced
14. Cosmetics, quaintly
19. Monaco glitter-palace
20. Makes do
21. Has a mind like ___ trap
23. Start of a verse
26. He's spoiling for a fight
27. Seine sight
28. Western, Spanish, cheese, etc.
29. Wriggly one
30. Days of ___
32. Fido's doc
33. Robert Taylor in *Camille*
37. Head, in Hyères
38. Aid in a crime
40. Ginger
43. Lot's city of refuge
44. Ibsen's Peer
45. *The Sun Also Rises* lady
46. Planet of little green men
47. More of verse
52. Kind of trip
53. Projecting window
54. Funeral oration of old
55. ___ air (outdoor painting style)
56. Telephone operator, once
58. Ms. Watling of *G.W.T.W.*
59. Squiffed
60. Dunk
63. Swirling about
66. Europe's largest river
69. Danish national-song lyricist
71. Tristesse
75. Kind of squash
76. "___ Kick Out of You"
77. *South Pacific* sine qua non
79. Slave girl of *Turandot*
80. More of verse
84. Luck, in Limerick
85. An Oop
86. Mystical poem
87. Needle case
88. Hosp. hubs
89. Observed
90. Defraud
91. Writer Gay
93. High-school subj.
94. Take off weight medically
95. *Pag*'s operatic companion
96. She's slated for a mad scene
100. Kind of meal
101. Balloon or dirigible
106. End of the verse
110. Broadway Joe
111. ___ bound (like Crosby, Hope and the dictionary)
112. Grain bread
113. "___, *c'est moi*"
114. More impudent
115. Word before world or lands

DOWN

1. Tongue-clucking sounds
2. Between hic and hoc
3. Glacial ridges
4. Cape Breton Island bay
5. Keep ___ mind (reserve judgment)
6. Increased the car power, with "up"
7. Glassmaking oven
8. Trappist cheese
9. Ninth mo.
10. Have high hopes
11. "Wedding Day" writer Kay
12. Velez, the Mexican Spitfire
13. D.D.E.'s command
14. South Carolina's tree
15. Up to now
16. Type of type: Abbr.
17. Hawaiian bird
18. Outdoor wedding precaution
22. Vegas preceder
24. Short kin
25. "___ Neighbor," Der Bingle's advice
30. Streisand film of 1983
31. Actor Kruger
33. Early Mexican
34. Blush substitute
35. Massenet opera
36. *Exodus* hero
37. Practice "The quick brown fox . . ."
38. Matthew or Benedict
39. Panhandled
40. Jury group
41. Pyle or Ford
42. Mind one's ___ Q's
44. Cunning
45. Sent a month-end notice
46. Calumniate
48. Winners in 1066
49. Metric weight
50. Bishopric
51. Two-syllable poetic foot
57. Nineveh stood on its banks
58. Clyde or Warren
61. Ply with goodies
62. Where the Riksdag meets
64. Memorable Belgian violinist
65. Relative of 51 Down
66. Explorer da Gama
67. Paint pigment
68. Loamy deposit
70. ___-di-dah
72. Top-drawer
73. Source of some snuffles
74. Cantor's girl of song
76. Under the counter
77. Old enough to know better
78. Like a root cellar
81. Edison ended this era
82. "___ go bragh!"
83. Congeal
90. Sticky sentimentality
91. Kiltie's plaid
92. Start of a French toast
93. Prince Valiant's bride
94. Port of Iraq
95. One hundred yrs.
96. Have title to
97. Ring out
98. Harness part
99. Part of Q.E.D.
100. Repute
101. Hebrew zither
102. Loretta of *M*A*S*H*
103. Mary Roberts Rinehart spinster
104. Bellum introducer
105. Russian ruler
107. Diplomatic rep.
108. Flying formation: Abbr.
109. Bar rocks

201 Samples By Gary Schmunk

Leading to somewhat fuller explanations.

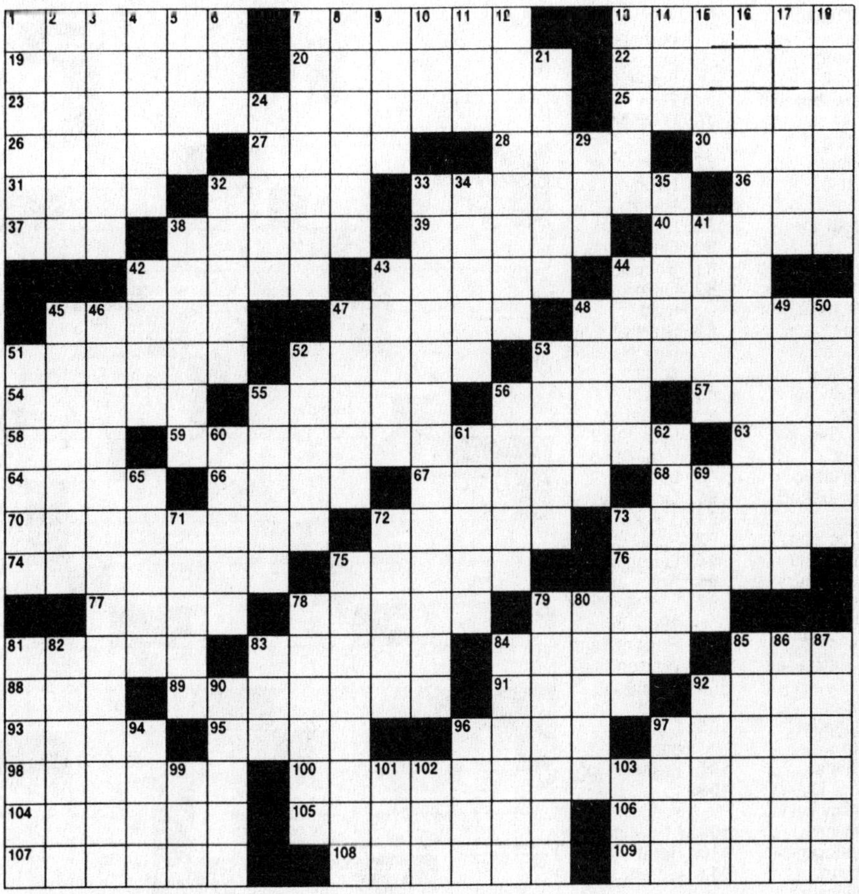

ACROSS

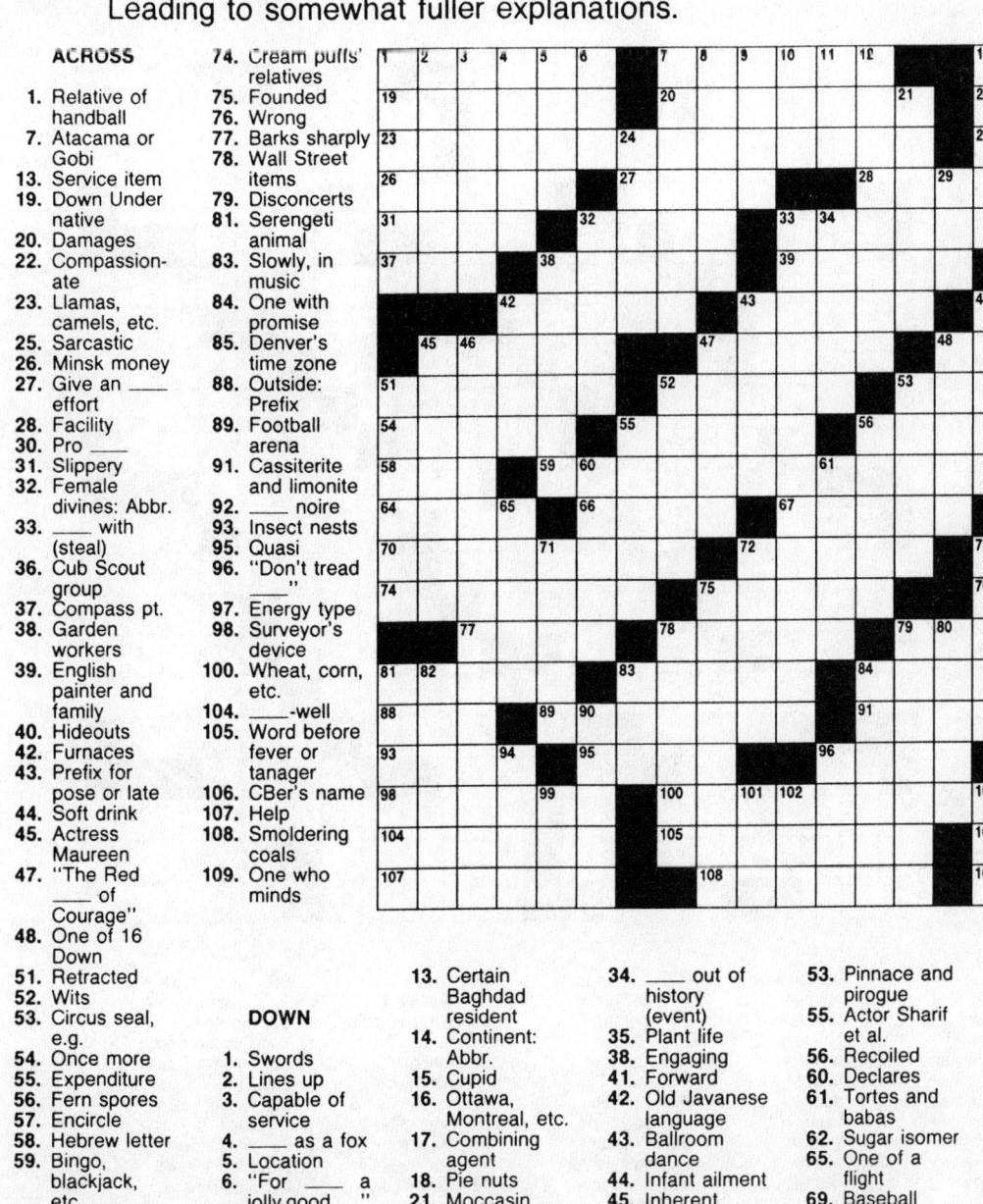

1. Relative of handball
7. Atacama or Gobi
13. Service item
19. Down Under native
20. Damages
22. Compassionate
23. Llamas, camels, etc.
25. Sarcastic
26. Minsk money
27. Give an ___ effort
28. Facility
30. Pro ___
31. Slippery
32. Female divines: Abbr.
33. ___ with (steal)
36. Cub Scout group
37. Compass pt.
38. Garden workers
39. English painter and family
40. Hideouts
42. Furnaces
43. Prefix for pose or late
44. Soft drink
45. Actress Maureen
47. "The Red ___ of Courage"
48. One of 16 Down
51. Retracted
52. Wits
53. Circus seal, e.g.
54. Once more
55. Expenditure
56. Fern spores
57. Encircle
58. Hebrew letter
59. Bingo, blackjack, etc.
63. Three, in Italy
64. Feminine endings
66. Fluctuate
67. Tarries
68. Preceding
70. Muscatel makers
72. Two-wheelers
73. Those who scoff
74. Cream puffs' relatives
75. Founded
76. Wrong
77. Barks sharply
78. Wall Street items
79. Disconcerts
81. Serengeti animal
83. Slowly, in music
84. One with promise
85. Denver's time zone
88. Outside: Prefix
89. Football arena
91. Cassiterite and limonite
92. ___ noire
93. Insect nests
95. Quasi
96. "Don't tread ___"
97. Energy type
98. Surveyor's device
100. Wheat, corn, etc.
104. ___-well
105. Word before fever or tanager
106. CBer's name
107. Help
108. Smoldering coals
109. One who minds

DOWN

1. Swords
2. Lines up
3. Capable of service
4. ___ as a fox
5. Location
6. "For ___ a jolly good . . ."
7. Disagrees
8. Adorn
9. Railroad siding
10. Give ___ to (heed)
11. Disencumber
12. Mountain demarcation area
13. Certain Baghdad resident
14. Continent: Abbr.
15. Cupid
16. Ottawa, Montreal, etc.
17. Combining agent
18. Pie nuts
21. Moccasin and boa
24. Of a certain grain
29. Desperate call
32. Sea goose
33. Jesus' parables, Plato's dialogues, etc.
34. ___ out of history (event)
35. Plant life
38. Engaging
41. Forward
42. Old Javanese language
43. Ballroom dance
44. Infant ailment
45. Inherent
46. Stars, comets, etc.
47. Ross of flag note
48. Mountain lakes
49. Hellions
50. Commands
51. Grammar case
52. Prosecutors
53. Pinnace and pirogue
55. Actor Sharif et al.
56. Recoiled
60. Declares
61. Tortes and babas
62. Sugar isomer
65. One of a flight
69. Baseball stats
71. Basketry palms
72. African tribesman
73. Stares
75. Innkeeper
78. Obscures
79. Makeups of books, magazines, etc.
80. Moslem ruler
81. Harem
82. Deportees
83. ___ Vegas
84. Give
85. Tune
86. Permanent paper clip
87. More concise
90. Fortunetelling card
92. Carried
94. Biblical initials
96. Shield border
97. Wound result
99. Ames and Wynn
101. Predicament
102. Sphere
103. Unit of conductance

202 All Out By Alfio Micci

But the solver should put it all in.

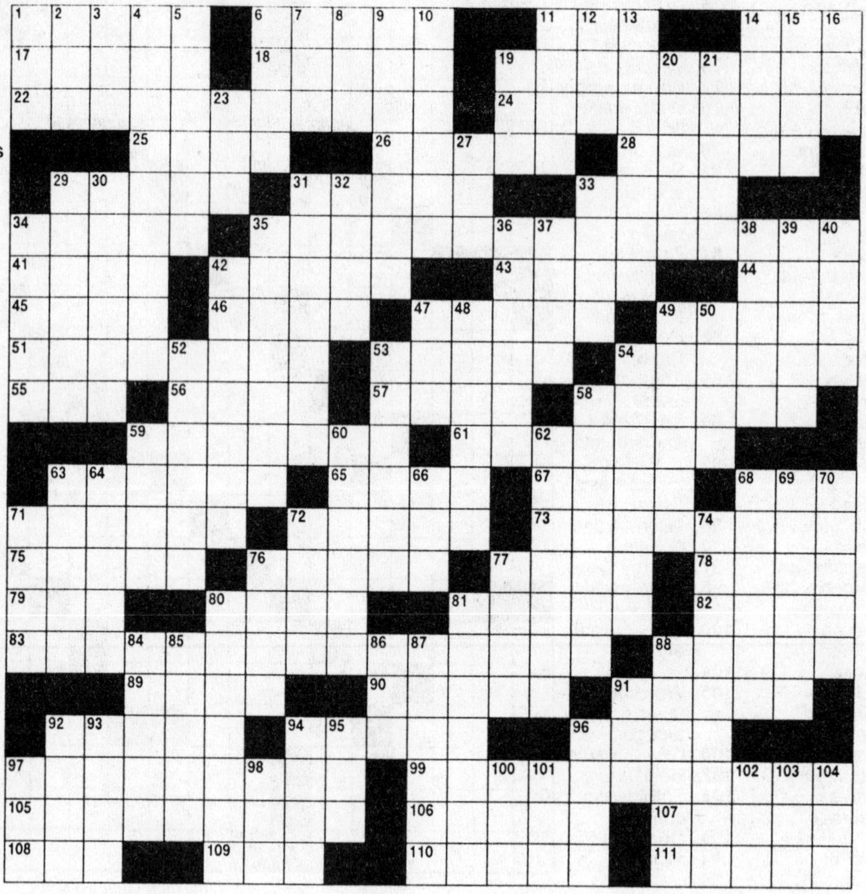

ACROSS

1. Moving
6. ___ Flow
11. Servicemen
14. Row
17. Poet's concern
18. Israeli dances
19. Worth the risk
22. Dance troupe
24. Practice gets one here, it's said
25. ___ avis
26. Emulate Rosie
28. Toot
29. Old Greek coins
31. Pirandello
33. ". . . baked in ___"
34. Garlic unit
35. Motto à la Musketeers
41. Leslie Caron role
42. Like an unsharpened knife
43. Proper
44. Dramatist Betti
45. Twain's "___ Diary"
46. Energy units
47. Kind of development
49. Sonata movement
51. Freshwater fish
53. Circa
54. Caught between
55. Depot: Abbr.
56. Protection
57. Island off Sumatra
58. Hotel-room Bible
59. Bestowed
61. Protect
63. Believing, in a saying
65. Mare's ___
67. Baseball team
68. Actress Balin
71. Tarkington lad
72. Certain types: Abbr.
73. Ethel Merman musical
75. ". . . a new beginning, ___ on the inarticulate": Eliot
76. U. of Maine site
77. Beaver works
78. Evening, in Variety
79. Snapshot
80. Con game
81. Snouts
82. Go on the road
83. Start of a Gay Nineties song
88. Petrol measure
89. Prominent Virginia family
90. Got along
91. Thicket
92. Pipe
94. Laughing
96. Arp's art
97. Sky visitor of 1985–86
99. Robert Penn Warren title
105. Welcome word
106. Conger catcher
107. French story
108. "___ the season . . ."
109. I finisher
110. Burst forth
111. Golem

DOWN

1. Rainbow
2. "___ 'nuff!"
3. Scandinavian god
4. Ad lib
5. Kind of value
6. Mets' home
7. Male swan
8. Common verb
9. New England athlete
10. Designate
11. Pesky insect
12. Neighbor of Leb.
13. Solar patch
14. Off Broadway award
15. Sheltered
16. Mixture of sodium salts
19. Stolen jewelry
20. Fasten anew
21. Concur
23. Bacheller's "___ and I"
27. Contend
29. Biblical mount
30. Henry VIII's second
31. Most clamorous
32. Samovars
33. Yemeni port
34. Balls of yarn
35. Peeling
36. Surprise attack
37. Undiluted
38. Baseball-practice bat
39. Nash of poesy
40. Cross
42. Outlaw
47. ___ supra (where mentioned above)
48. Uses the oven
49. Turn in coupons
50. Fragrant stream?
52. Sentence ender
53. Of the llamas' range
54. Harrison Ford film of '85
58. Shine
59. One of Odin's wolves
60. Bury
62. Ready for shipping
63. Printer's stroke
64. Portray
66. Road warning
68. Sherwood's "___ Delight"
69. Mother ___
70. ___ bagatelle
71. Haydn sobriquet
72. Dies ___
74. Trattoria offering
76. Baron ___ of "Der Rosenkavalier"
77. Peace symbol
80. Organic compound
81. Violent wind
84. Beethoven's "Für ___"
85. Do a double take
86. "___ body meet a . . ."
87. South Carolina river
88. Paying guest
91. Fire
92. Double this for a disease
93. Bar orders
94. Mil. unit
95. Possessive
96. Gossip
97. Alt.
98. L-P connection
100. Chosen, in Chartres
101. Catch, in old England
102. Fairy queen
103. Kind of trip
104. After taxes

203 Lit Course By Don Nardizzi

All the way from the classics to the juveniles.

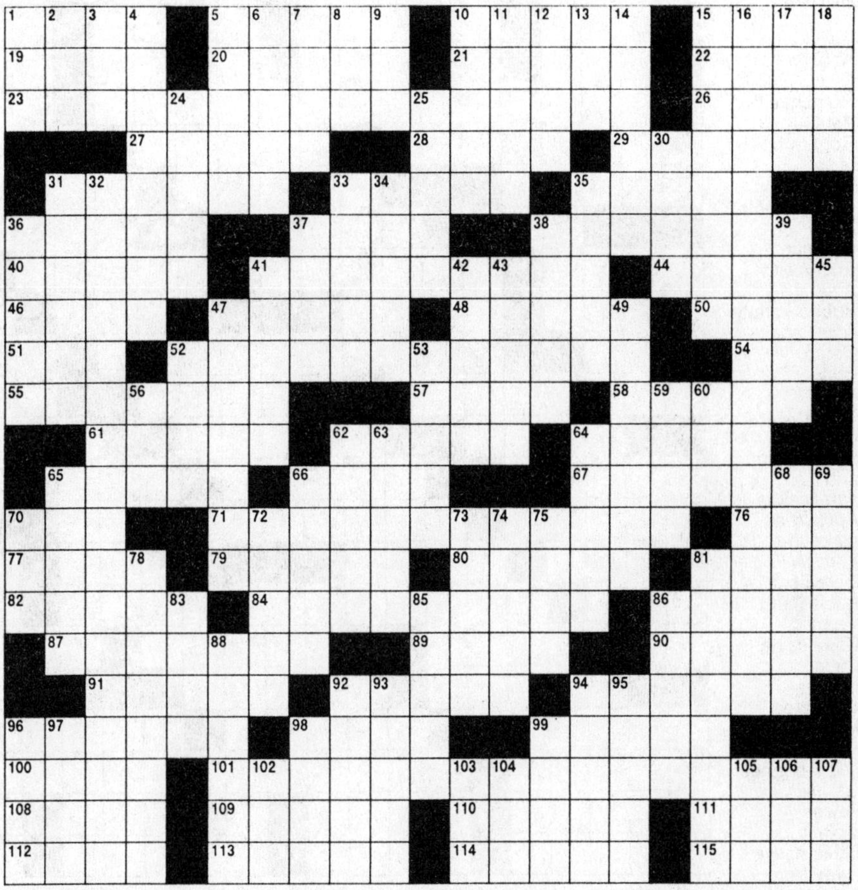

ACROSS

1. Basics
5. American code man
10. Evil one
15. Moby Dick's pursuer
19. Gather
20. Liquid part of a fat
21. Silly
22. "Once ____ unto the breach . . ."
23. Rostand's nosy hero
26. Breakfast food
27. Benefactor Rhodes
28. ____ even keel
29. Hooky player
31. Telephone inventor of film
33. Darth of "Star Wars"
35. ____ Ste. Marie
36. Dagger's spying partner
37. Heredity transmitter
38. Walter Raleigh's tavern
40. "And thereby ____ a tale"
41. Cartridge belt
44. Saw wood, in a way
46. Gaelic
47. Word before blind or bearer
48. Atelier adjunct
50. "____ she blows!"
51. Roman 52
52. Flaubert heroine
54. Orel's river
55. Film ingredient
57. Chemical endings
58. Word before coeur or bleu
61. Importunes
62. Curves
64. Pieman's noncustomer
65. Word before storm or trust
66. Wild ox
67. Like all planets
70. Name
71. Oliver's light-fingered friend
76. Angeles or Gatos preceder
77. Arrow poison
79. Join a card game
80. Arkin and Ladd
81. Kind of fountain
82. Insufficient
84. Lute's cousins
86. Indian lancer
87. More compassionate
89. Hindu deity
90. French writer and family
91. Chanel and others
92. Unevenly edged
94. ____ de Balzac
96. The Age of ____
98. Frigg's husband
99. "And the smile on the face of the ____"
100. Early bloomer
101. Pooh's friend
108. Give the ax
109. Small quantity
110. Made a pledge
111. Armbone
112. Nourish
113. Track events
114. Roots for making poi
115. Chinese dynasty

DOWN

1. Kind of light
2. Turkish title
3. Street or side
4. It began with Sputnik I
5. Cadge
6. Song of yesteryear
7. Film holder
8. Relative
9. Opposite of WSW
10. Actress Hasso
11. Close by, to a poet
12. Mountain pool
13. A California Santa
14. Bee's gathering
15. Moving about
16. Forester's naval hero
17. Island off Ireland
18. Propensity
24. Bottle parts
25. Famous Beverly Hills drive
30. Sugar-cane drinks
31. King of the Visigoths
32. Tarkington's nobleman-barber
33. Asp's injection
34. British spy hanged in 1780
35. More withered
36. Lobster claw
37. Festival
38. Western hills
39. English navigator and buccaneer
41. Augurs
42. Sierra ____
43. Building features
45. Paleozoic, for one
47. Chains of connected events
49. Basic amino acids
52. Wise trio
53. Fundamental
56. Singing syllable
59. Love, to Lepidus
60. Heart
62. Finally, to Pierre
63. Hobe or Puget
64. Uses the dotted line
65. Banana cluster
66. Rose perfume
68. Treat with an antiseptic
69. Peter and Nicholas
70. Romans' Pluto
72. Hoarfrosts
73. Evans and Robertson
74. Martini extra
75. "Two Years Before the Mast" author
78. Like an old oaken bucket
81. Resonant
83. Tortilla with filling
85. Having teeth: Suffix
86. More rational
88. Sarge, e.g.
92. Proclamation
93. Emulates a balloon
94. Sacred: Prefix
95. Fairy-tale villains
96. Predecessor of raff
97. Iroquoian
98. Caen's river
99. Norse god of thunder
102. Cry's companion
103. East, to Heine
104. Agcy. of the Depression
105. Color of the sky in Napoli
106. Du Maurier's "Jamaica ____"
107. Mediocre horse

204 Who's Who By Dorothy Smitonick

People who relate to better-known people.

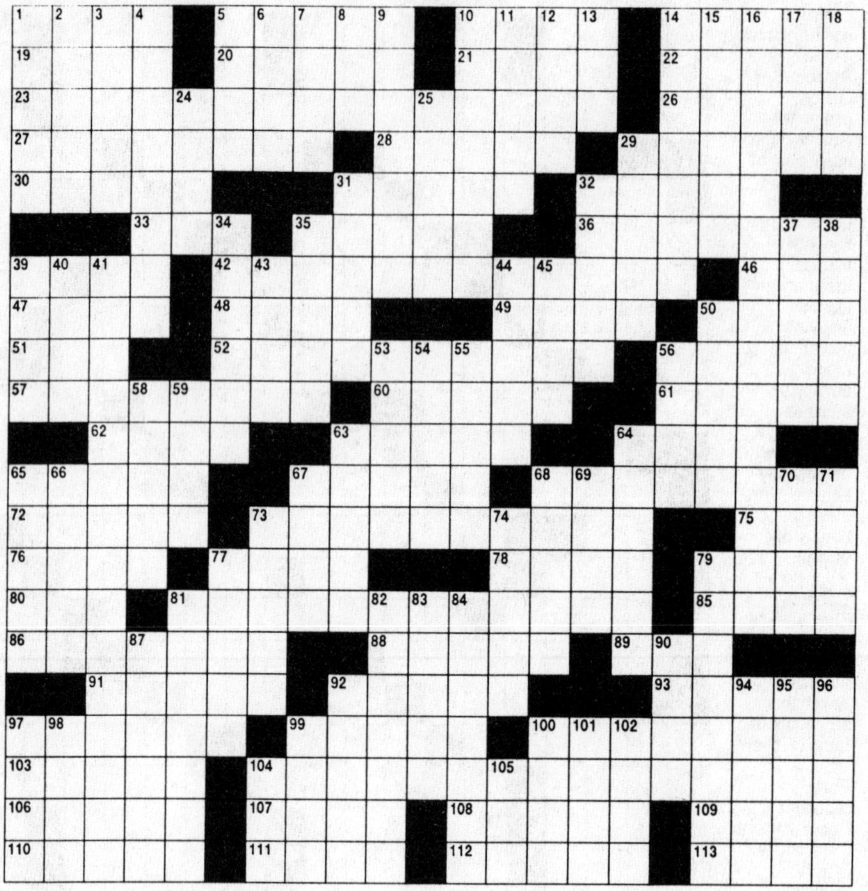

ACROSS

1. Gender: Abbr.
5. "___ Romance," Astaire-Rogers hit
10. Miss Hayworth
14. Garden tools
19. Seed covering
20. Angry with
21. Ages
22. Potato variety
23. Andri and Ostap
26. Bridge, in Italy
27. "God bless us ___"
28. Miss Verdon and namesakes
29. Applied a makeup
30. Varnish ingredient
31. Adolescent years
32. Body cavity
33. Curtain material
35. Ventilated
36. Modified
39. Have ___ in one's bonnet
42. Claudius
46. Power project
47. Baltic native
48. Away from the wind
49. Observes
50. "___ was no lady . . ."
51. Timber tree
52. Like many dungeons
56. Actress Adams
57. Hollywood hopefuls
60. Loved ones
61. ___-ski
62. Be in want
63. Coal deposits
64. Neckwear
65. Relatives of love seats
67. Balm
68. Street of neon fame
72. Swarm
73. Game with two stakes
75. Freshwater fish
76. Prefixes for shoulders
77. "I could ___ horse!"
78. Minerals
79. Have ___ (be upset)
80. Rate of speed: Abbr.
81. Penelope
85. Half: Prefix
86. Woo ___ (seek poetic inspiration)
88. Uses a towel
89. "___ Rheingold"
91. Gratifies
92. Kind of steak
93. Leaflike part
97. "Fire ___" (battle order)
99. Hair: Prefix
100. "___ to Garcia"
103. French exclamation
104. Number One
106. ___ words (briefly)
107. Like anthracite
108. Wolfe and others
109. Mediterranean volcano
110. Acts
111. Zoo animals
112. Irregular
113. "Simon ___"

DOWN

1. One of the almas
2. Get ___ review
3. Fathers
4. Woodwind
5. Eastern pulpit
6. Satyr's relative
7. Not working
8. Catch a felon
9. Display stand
10. Ships again
11. ___ out (smooths)
12. Light colors
13. Fool
14. Fencer's thrust
15. Stir
16. Guinevere
17. Villa d'___
18. Throw off
24. "For auld lang ___"
25. "How ___ it is!"
29. Costly car, for short
31. Like a bathroom wall
32. Confronts
34. Defrosted
35. Final words
37. Get away
38. Palm-tree yields
39. Word of regret
40. Get the ___ of (outdo)
41. Zeena
43. Landed
44. Consumers
45. Loch of note
50. Recorded
53. Medieval estates
54. Use a loom
55. Metallic materials
56. Mother of Hermes
58. ___ the riot act (scolds)
59. ___ majesty
63. Roosevelt and Teasdale
64. Kind of salad
65. Lacking
66. Pizzazz
67. Drunkards
68. Karloff or Godunov
69. Ridge of coral
70. Take ___ view of
71. Abominable Snowman
73. Gabby or Helen
74. Inventor Elias and family
77. One of the Fords
79. Sets a value on
81. Fugitives
82. Koch and Kennedy
83. Archangel
84. Vatican chapel
87. Posted
90. Org.
92. Portion
94. Ravioli, e.g.
95. Torment
96. Singer Horne and others
97. Eager
98. Pitch
99. Fellow
100. Height: Prefix
101. Units of conductance
102. Facility
104. Chinese tea
105. Ever, to a poet

205 Star Attraction By Reginald Johnson

Presenting one from Hollywood's early era.

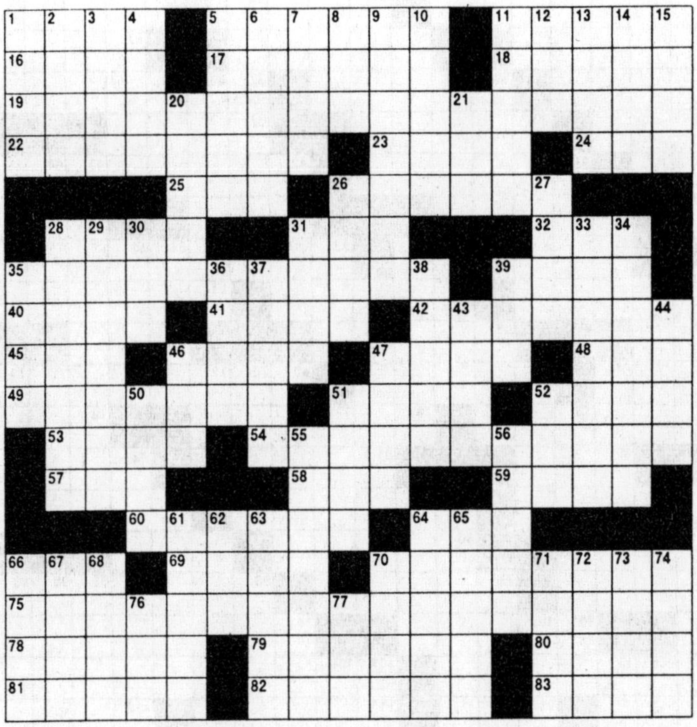

ACROSS

1. French cleric
5. Waldorf and fruit
11. 23d, e.g.
16. Fence part
17. Lacking vigor
18. Kind of active
19. Classic film for 35 Across
22. Truth, to fiction
23. London home
24. Explosive
25. Part of an Iowa city
26. More sagacious
28. "Now ____ this"
31. Rhine feeder
32. Ararat lander
35. Pioneer movie star
39. To ____ (perfect fit)
40. French concept
41. ____ de Boulogne
42. Manors
45. Violin-string tightener
46. Reverberate
47. Choir member
48. Bank-book entry: Abbr.
49. Unnamed bloke
51. Kind of roof
52. Dirk of yore
53. Military group
54. Film for 35 Across
57. Banner: Abbr.
58. French article
59. Where hops are dried
60. Whole
64. McGraw's Mel
66. ____ Palmas
69. German article
70. Nonbelievers
75. Film for 35 Across
78. ". . . for man or ____"
79. Excites
80. One of five
81. One of nine
82. Holding period
83. Craze

DOWN

1. Beaux-____
2. Thai money
3. German suds
4. Tuscan isle
5. NCO, familiarly
6. They make the pot
7. Annealing oven
8. Latin grammar word
9. Isn't the same
10. Climb
11. Chatter
12. Made a lap
13. Mine entry
14. King of a sort
15. ____ Blanc
20. Lemur of Madagascar
21. Forty winks
26. Emcee's place
27. Pro ____
28. Ugly
29. Posh
30. Pub order
31. Exchange premium
33. Eye parts
34. Sharpest
35. Things to smack
36. Fundamentals
37. Not at all
38. "Howdy!"
39. From ____ Z
43. Beef concoction
44. Editor's marking
46. N.Y. fast time
47. Post for a young officer
50. Brood of pheasants
51. English river
52. Kind of farer
55. Halo
56. Fas and sols, e.g.
61. Under, in poetry
62. Kind of horn
63. Map part
64. Different
65. Pronoun
66. Place for a ring
67. Neighborhood
68. Ship's pole
70. Alaskan island
71. Route for Caesar
72. Marsh bird
73. Advanced math
74. Pintail duck
76. Before D.D.E.
77. Enthusiast

206 This and That By Herman Surasky

With a few questions to be answered.

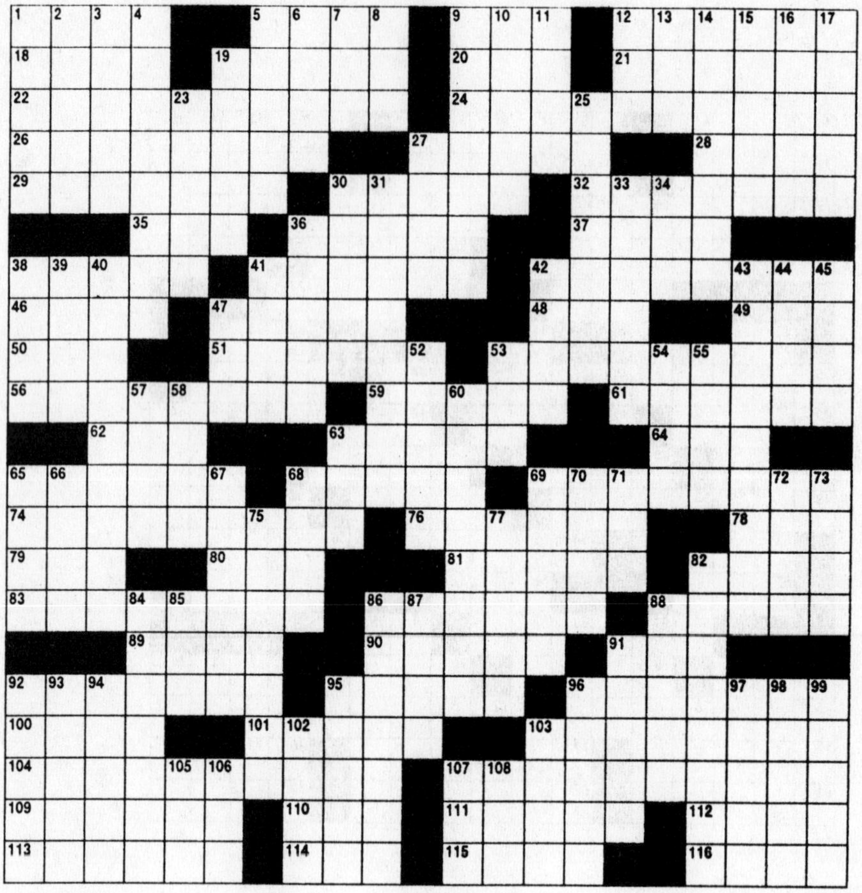

ACROSS

1. Sonny's TV partner
5. Aria
9. Tax savings acct.
12. Sycophant
18. Robust
19. Shankar's instrument
20. Today
21. Interstice
22. Fast
24. J.R.'s real mother
26. Bleach
27. Chekhov's Uncle
28. Rockfish
29. Cleans again
30. Cockneys' drug problems
32. Penzance people
35. Rel.
36. Soap plant
37. Longfellow or Frost
38. Frolic
41. Forest clearings
42. Holiday dessert
46. Ogled
47. Hoity's follower
48. Cuckoo
49. Plus
50. Greek nickname
51. Enrapture
53. Supermarket bonus for nondieters?
56. Drink for an Edsel?
59. Shanty
61. Carpenter, at times
62. Counterpart of 35 Across
63. Pyle of TV
64. Modernist
65. P.I. successor to Marcos
68. Prance
69. Alpine maid in Berlin?
74. Super Bowl treats?
76. Cesar of films
78. Davis or Walker ___
79. Wrong: Prefix
80. Pay dirt
81. Polite refusal
82. Roman patriot
83. Marsh-mallow's occasional destination?
86. Stupes
88. Hank of baseball
89. Met offering
90. Weddings, in France
91. Short nights
92. ___ in a teapot
95. Athletic team
96. Hawaiian vacation?
100. Mideast land: Var.
101. "Peace ___ time"
103. Apocalypse quartet
104. Part of T.L.C.
107. Rock magician?
109. Blissful
110. French possessive
111. Singing birds
112. Mining conveyance
113. More compact
114. Id ___
115. ___ bien
116. Counting-out word

DOWN

1. Render a siss-boom-bah
2. Waste maker
3. Spanish hero
4. Moved to new quarters
5. Filters
6. Western Indian
7. Thai native
8. Fort near Monterey
9. Pen pals?
10. Horse colors
11. Distorted
12. Sweet potato
13. Pitcher's stat.
14. Saw-toothed
15. Choral composition
16. Straighten
17. Nursemaids
19. Goes for flies
23. Miss Dinsmore
25. Jabbering
27. Wicked
30. Fine fiddle
31. Health spa?
33. Sea off Greece
34. Family room, for short
36. Vibrant
38. Make airtight
39. Combustible heap
40. Pay back
41. Spur
42. Heavy mallet
43. Train accom-modation
44. Arrow poison
45. Fulda feeder
47. Word before la
52. Four-bagger
53. Sun. talk
54. Sounded
55. Feudal estate
57. O'Neill character
58. Petty taboo
60. Hollywood Lake
63. Fuel
65. Air: Prefix
66. Sally
67. Egg-shaped bodies
68. Canadian Indian
69. Witticisms
70. Author Leon
71. Connective
72. Sedan or coupe
73. Hep
75. Eccentric
77. Lowed
82. Tape case
84. Prandial conveniences
85. "For shame!"
86. Judicial inquiry
87. Sullen
88. It equals a mile
91. Brews, as coffee
92. Like many bathrooms
93. Wear away
94. So-called expert
95. Tender spots
96. Canal features
97. Mood, in Italy
98. French author
99. Foe
102. Title
103. March animal
105. Never, in Germany
106. Detecting device: Abbr.
107. Deli sandwich
108. Household god

207 Salad Course By Connie Cowan

With an appropriate mixture provided.

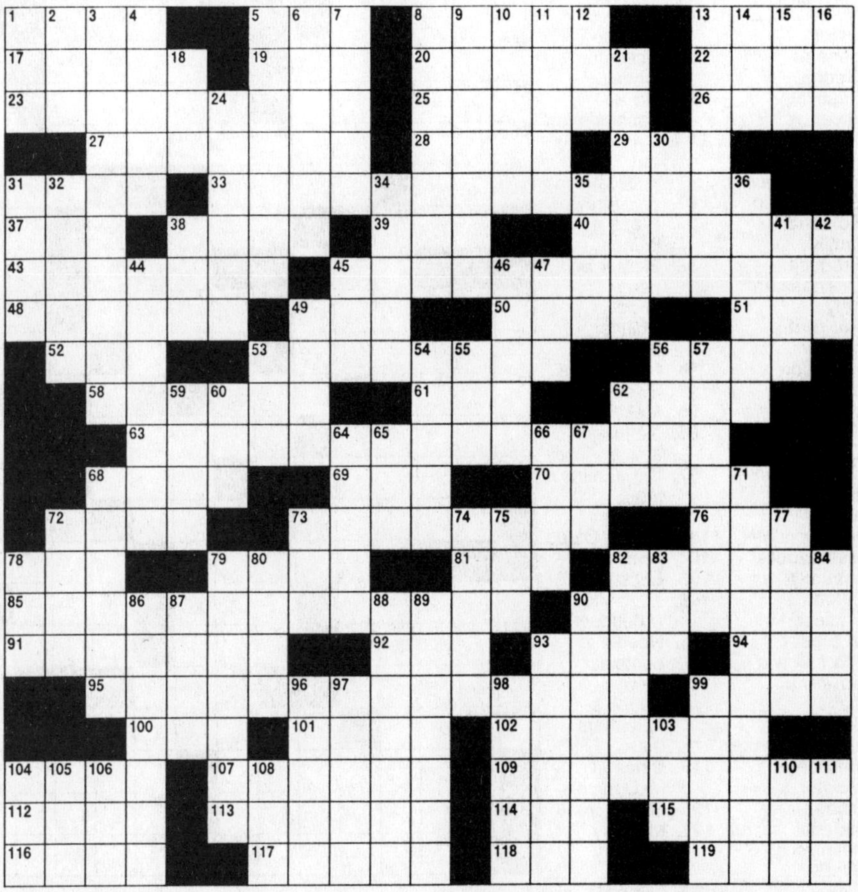

ACROSS

1. Pahlavi was one
5. Pouch
8. Of ___ (mediocre)
13. ___ Bator
17. Part of TV reception
19. Legal abbr.
20. Burmese viols
22. Zilch
23. Accumulated lore
25. Ladylove, in Paris
26. Pious talk
27. Character in "G.W.T.W."
28. Poisonous fish of Japan
29. Swiss river
31. Go by
33. Fruit of politics?
37. Southern constellation
38. Agreement
39. Words before king
40. Verse writings
43. Accused fruit?
45. Reptilian fruit?
48. Go by again
49. Pipe joint
50. "___ Rhythm"
51. B.&O. et al.
52. 100 cts.
53. Relating to thoughts
56. Birlers' footings
58. Parisian star
61. Half a bray
62. After ready, aim
63. Literary fruit?
68. Whale
69. Abner's radio friend
70. Only, in Bonn
72. "It's a ___ world"
73. Renounce
76. Summit
78. Three-toed sloths
79. Disquiet, of old
81. "___ was saying . . ."
82. Santa's vocal trademark
85. Okie fruit?
90. One who testifies
91. Did up a present again
92. Uncle, in Perth
93. Circle dance
94. Decline
95. Unfriendly fruit?
99. Lincoln and Vigoda
100. Cedar Rapids college
101. Sally of the fans
102. Huge
104. Peter of cartoons
107. Banns, in England
109. Beastly fruit?
112. Sirius or Deneb
113. If in time, it's a saver
114. Chaney
115. ___ in the bucket
116. Hammer part
117. Feed the fire
118. Letters
119. Words of agreement

DOWN

1. Held a session
2. Charioteer Ben
3. Fruit of antifeminism?
4. Keeps out of sight
5. Staple for Popeye
6. Make ___ of (stress)
7. Crete's capital
8. ". . . and laugh ___": Browning
9. Early Japanese V.I.P.
10. French storm
11. Accumulated, as bills
12. Word of reproach
13. Like stale crackers
14. Mauna ___
15. Actress Harding
16. Not gross
18. Kuwait export
21. Fisherman's wader
24. Smokers' purchases, in Lille
30. Tenor John ___
31. Shoe grouping
32. Prepared for hostilities
34. Gully, in India
35. Capable of
36. Candle, in Paris
38. Dance step
41. "I'm all ___"
42. Grads-to-be
44. Kind of ware
45. Drink
46. Generous one
47. ___ of discretion
49. Biographer Leon
53. Class
54. Subject
55. Comparative suffix
56. City in Austria
57. Bird: Prefix
59. Trio in an inning
60. Rink surface
62. Five-spot
64. Kind of grease
65. Hamburger holder
66. Tibetan creature
67. Cry of contempt
68. Winter melon
71. Downy fruit?
72. Bog down
73. Sandy's sound
74. Garden and pearly
75. Hardwood tree
77. Flycatcher: Var.
78. Soil cult.
79. Ineffectual
80. Knob
82. Tender of sheep
83. W.W. II agency
84. Heavenly bodies
86. Movie fare for some
87. Vancouver event of 1986
88. Hillbilly's relative
89. ". . . ___ alien corn": Keats
90. French town on the Marne
93. "___ the Range"
96. Once around, in space
97. "Thursday's child has ___ go"
98. Target, in France
99. Town in Sweden
103. Sports org.
104. Nile menace
105. Way to go: Abbr.
106. Scottish refusal
108. "___ no use!"
110. Anonymous Richard
111. Security guards: Abbr.

208 Music Lesson By Dorothea Shipp

Given an instrument at a time.

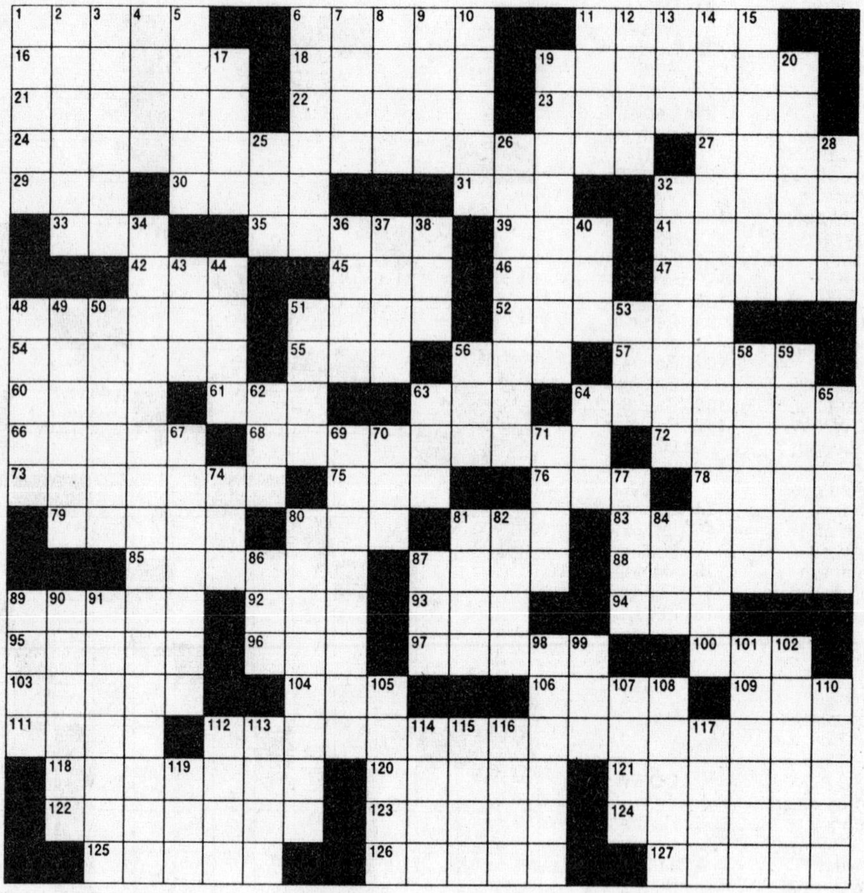

ACROSS

1. Union general George
6. Festivals
11. River of forgetfulness
16. Passionate
18. Praying figure
19. The Swamp Fox and family
21. Produce
22. Oneness, in Italy
23. Arc of the horizon
24. King Cole's callees
27. Yarn fiber
29. Neighbor of Que.
30. Continent in a French atlas
31. Small pouch
32. Minneapolis suburb
33. Fetch
35. Endless time, to a poet
39. Pi's follower
41. Dot on a map
42. Bumbling fellow
45. Kind of shooter
46. Ribbed material
47. Relative of a civet
48. Canny
51. What a bridesmaid carries
52. "Gay Robin ____ no more"
54. Secular
55. Baking chamber: Var.
56. Miss Lupino
57. Chaplain
60. Baltic S.S.R.
61. Composer Delibes
63. Literary scraps
64. Minute puncture
66. Change
68. There were 76 of them
72. Hebrew month
73. Hot-pot accessories
75. Mrs. Nixon
76. Roman 1002
78. Word form for Chinese
79. Actress Ada
80. Felipe or Alfonso
81. Eccentric wheel
83. Do a cobbler's job
85. One putting out publications
87. ____ breve
88. Stops a launch
89. Plaster of paris
92. Wing
93. Chinese leader
94. Neighbor of Swed.
95. Make true
96. No longer active: Abbr.
97. Did a steno's job
100. Rorem
103. Plotter Oates
104. Army men
106. Ericson
109. ____ Alte (Adenauer)
111. Needle container
112. Lewis Carroll's "Elephant that ____"
118. Dines at McDonald's
120. Like a crone
121. Mentally deficient person
122. Immobile sculpture
123. Effort toward a goal
124. Small cavity
125. Blot out
126. Clown's prop
127. Disseminate

DOWN

1. Manly
2. Going wrong
3. "____ Fideles"
4. Unheeding
5. Abstract beings
6. Singer Robert
7. English composer
8. Wild animal's pad
9. Hill dwellers
10. Box-score listings, for short
11. Idle
12. Lake or canal
13. Comedian Conway
14. John Peel's company when he was "far far away"
15. Draws in a trap
17. Knight and Mack
19. Italian noblewoman
20. Polishes
25. Sine ____
26. Xanthippe, for one
28. Tardy
32. Dail ____
34. What Thomas Haynes Bayly's troubadour did
36. Body of poetry
37. Musical hiatus
38. Negative word
40. Harvest goddess
43. ____ loss for words
44. Toppled
48. Moslem supreme being
49. Hornpipe dancer
50. Word before tattle
51. Like one Richard
53. Roof adornment
56. Daughter of Cadmus
58. Brighter
59. Kite
62. Diminutive suffixes
63. German composer Franz
64. Greek letter
65. Organic compounds
67. Argues logically
69. Like a Met production
70. Kind of day or fly
71. Lazarus or Goldman
74. Hospital assts.
77. Oil country
80. Assign to left field
81. Statesman Henry
82. Off balance
84. Central American tree
86. Former Mideast org.
87. Sum: Abbr.
89. San Francisco's is golden
90. Upper-crust people
91. Locate
98. Firstborn
99. ____ volente
101. Newspaper V.I.P.
102. Besmirch
105. Kenton and Musial
107. Andes native
108. TV's Jamie and family
110. Refurbish
112. Petits ____
113. Govern
114. Monogram part: Abbr.
115. Spanish agreement
116. Hebrew month
117. Measures
119. U.S. aid agency

209 Getting Offbeat By Robert Malinow

Wherein some doubtful logic is called for.

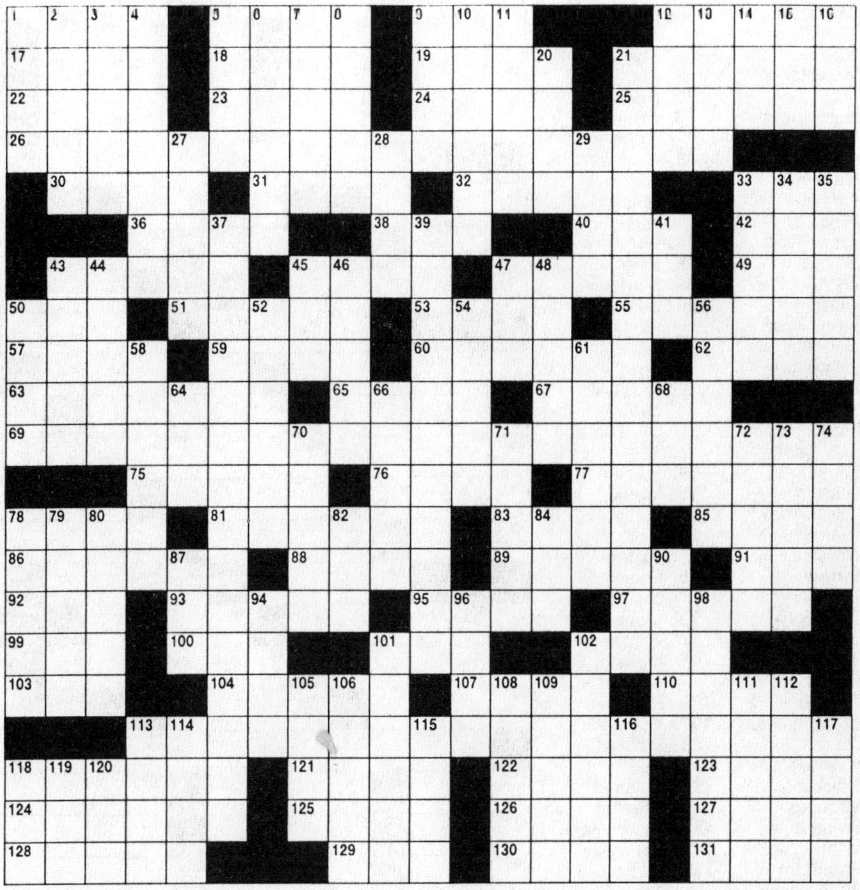

ACROSS

1. Pretense
5. Mine, to Pierre
9. Big Board listing
12. Gush
17. Arabian land
18. Fat
19. Took cards
21. Word with pen or oak
22. Sinbad or Popeye, e.g.
23. Prefix with trust or social
24. Facility
25. Whole
26. Prefight ritual
30. Idi
31. Togo's capital
32. Word after ant or lotus
33. ___ Tech
36. Memo
38. Reverence
40. Between Mao and tung
42. Org. for doctors
43. Kind of nut
45. Nick's dog
47. Dart
49. Free
50. Marsh
51. Shrubby tract
53. Brain tissue
55. Food for Elsie
57. War god
59. Yesterday, in Nice
60. Poet's early digs
62. Harrow's rival
63. Like some triangles
65. Noble, in Essen
67. Yellow pigment
69. Feats for Liz if she had played ball?
75. Prepare for knighthood
76. Take the sun
77. Khachaturian's homeland
78. 1958 Pulitzer author
81. Scoreboard info
83. He loved an Irish Rose
85. Active one
86. ___ plenty
88. "___ chance!"
89. Miss Bernhardt
91. Roman 551
92. Silkworm
93. Throat problem
95. Lusty look
97. Perked up the punch
99. "Peer Gynt" woman
100. Haggard novel
101. Slippery one
102. King of Israel
103. ___ Plaines
104. Organic compound
107. Comic strip's Etta
110. Portico
113. Grew a glutted spice crop?
118. Famed barber
121. Desertlike
122. Hammer or sickle, e.g.
123. "___ and her Aeneas . . ."
124. Baseball-game unit
125. Number of heads for Hydra
126. Besides
127. Prefix for derm or plasm
128. Bore measurement
129. Bard's word
130. Clarinet part
131. Trotsky or Blum

DOWN

1. Part of P.M.
2. City near Boys Town
3. Witch-trial city
4. Weave
5. Jai ___
6. Mutilate
7. Prefix for doxy or graphy
8. Argot
9. It's often linked to a bulb
10. Irish port
11. Contemporary of Edison
12. "___ and Lovers"
13. Gist
14. Mex. neighbor
15. "Arabian Nights" bird
16. Explosive
20. Cross threads
21. Liverpool features?
27. Long-missing Arden
28. Bit of derring-do
29. Mother of Apollo
33. Weight for Diamond Lil
34. José's pal
35. Full up
37. Hound's quest?
39. Gossiped?
41. W.W. II area
43. Stalin's hatchet man
44. Hector, to Achilles
45. Supped
46. Unit of evidence?
47. Title for Galahad
48. Mediterranean tree
50. Kind of food or lane
52. Fliers
54. Composer Edouard and family
56. Tottered
58. Smooth
61. Bakery product
64. Cambodia's ___ Nol
66. Society function
68. Initials for 33 or 45
70. Coeur d'___
71. Edict from Peter the Great
72. Battery terminal
73. Sign at a road junction
74. Indian dress
78. Leading
79. Prickly shrub
80. U.S. Indians
82. Caveman Alley
84. Type of stool
87. Wild Bill Donovan's gp.
90. Cruel
94. Word with parade or arm
96. Nevada city
98. The Kremlin is one
101. Coat fur
102. Indolent
105. Word of comparison
106. Eagle's abode
108. Word on a door
109. Oar adjunct
111. In reserve
112. Increase
113. Nixon chief of staff
114. Nurse of Poseidon
115. First home
116. Arctic conveyance
117. Shortly
118. Kind of leaf for Eve
119. Actress Balin
120. African antelope

210 Gridiron Echoes By Wilson McBeath

What the Bard and others have to say about the game.

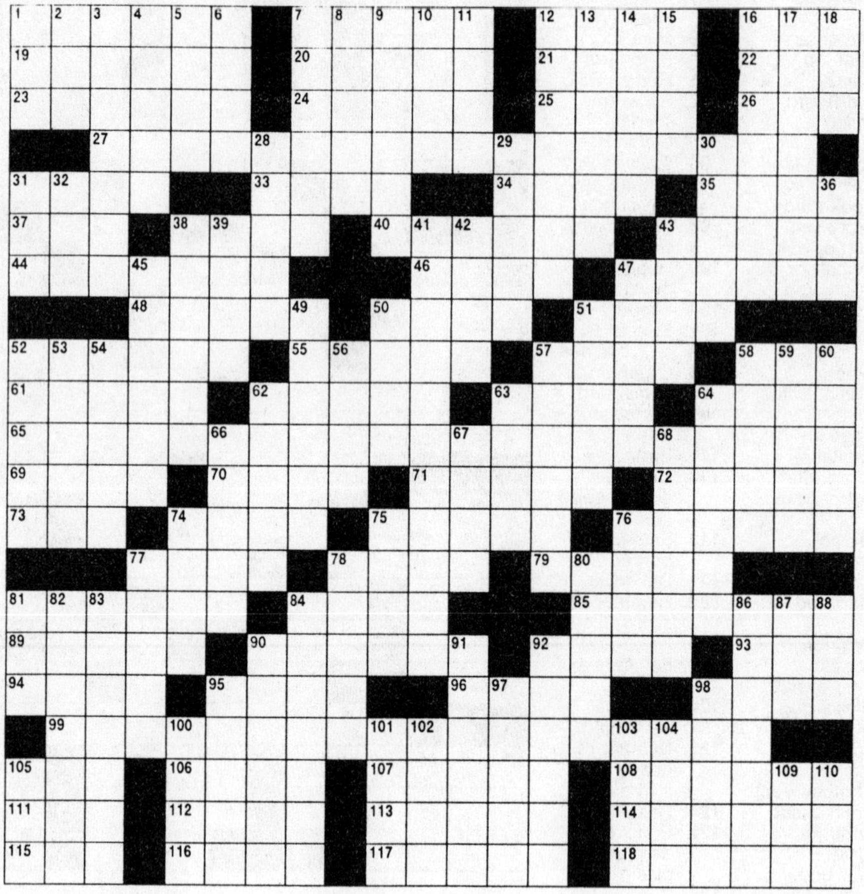

ACROSS

1. Resting
7. Music org.
12. Three, in Heidelberg
16. Navy noncom
19. Mackerel: Var.
20. Mine excavation
21. Restraint
22. Cry of triumph
23. Rides a bike
24. Goddess of agriculture
25. Spiritual being, in France
26. ___ capita
27. Shakespeare's advice to a quarterback
31. Word of sorrow
33. Anent
34. Common Latin verb
35. Reed instrument
37. Fall mo.
38. Farming area
40. Of sovereignty
43. Stock-market optimists
44. Everlasting
46. Weather for Maugham
47. Most plain
48. Exterior
50. ___ de Londres (dress fabric)
51. Preserve with salt
52. Debussy
55. Filmdom's Flynn
57. Exhausted
58. London V.I.P.'s
61. Singer Frankie
62. Hungarian composer
63. V.P. Morton under Harrison
64. House, in Mexico
65. Horace's comment to a quarterback
69. Despicable
70. Very, to Pierre
71. Subdued
72. Greek meeting places
73. Compass direction
74. Vientiane's land
75. Applaud
76. Concedes
77. Chums
78. Cote sounds
79. Carousal
81. In a mean way
84. Dynamic one
85. Fined
89. Monadic
90. 3.26 light years
92. Pitfall
93. Ovid's advice to a ball carrier, with 99, 105 and 114 Across
94. Roman 1551
95. Metric measures
96. Andy's partner
98. Snaky weapon
99. More of 93 Across
105. More of 93 Across
106. Moreover
107. Theme
108. Embryonic sac
111. Writer Fleming
112. No, in Bonn
113. Eat away
114. End of 93 Across
115. Baseball's Mel
116. Counsels: Abbr.
117. Inferior
118. Raises

DOWN

1. TV network
2. Doll or top, e.g.
3. Monaco is one
4. French wings
5. Manuscript mark
6. Far or Near
7. Rise
8. Beef animal
9. Monopolize
10. Imitated
11. Mosquito or gnat
12. Cart driver
13. Kind of income
14. Number of furlongs in a mile
15. Relative of curare
16. Accomplished
17. Carbolic acids
18. Sculler's need
28. Gate holder
29. Indian princesses
30. Grieve
31. Santa ___
32. Naval record
36. Superlative ending
38. Noisier
39. Prefix for chamber or date
41. "I stand a wreck on ___": A. I. Menken
42. Reading is one
43. Word with dance or storm
45. Posh waiting room
47. Kind of acid
49. Town officers
50. Novelist Shirley Ann ___
51. Under ___ (hidden)
52. British pioneer in India
53. ___ Quarter
54. Church area
56. Greek letters
57. Composer Karl Maria and family
58. Nearsighted Mr. of cartoons
59. Cry of impatience
60. Gorges
62. Dodecanese island
63. Part of the ear
64. Knife vendor
66. The Boot
67. Digits
68. Dormant
74. Speech disorder: Suffix
75. Miler Sebastian's family
76. What Virgil sang of
77. Jeopardy
78. Major street in Rome
80. Do a grammatical exercise
81. Loafer
82. "___ is so rare as a day . . . ?"
83. Jutting outward
84. Evil spirits: Var.
86. Whodunit poison
87. Geologic time
88. Unearthed
90. German toast
91. Star in Gemini
92. Chewy candy
95. End of a shoelace
97. Domestics
98. ___ siècle
100. Actress Turner
101. Merganser
102. Spanish bull
103. Gentle one
104. Scandinavian giant
105. Spanish uncle
109. Like Hemingway's fisherman
110. Cape

211 Luckless Year By Sidney Robbins

Period with three days to worry about.

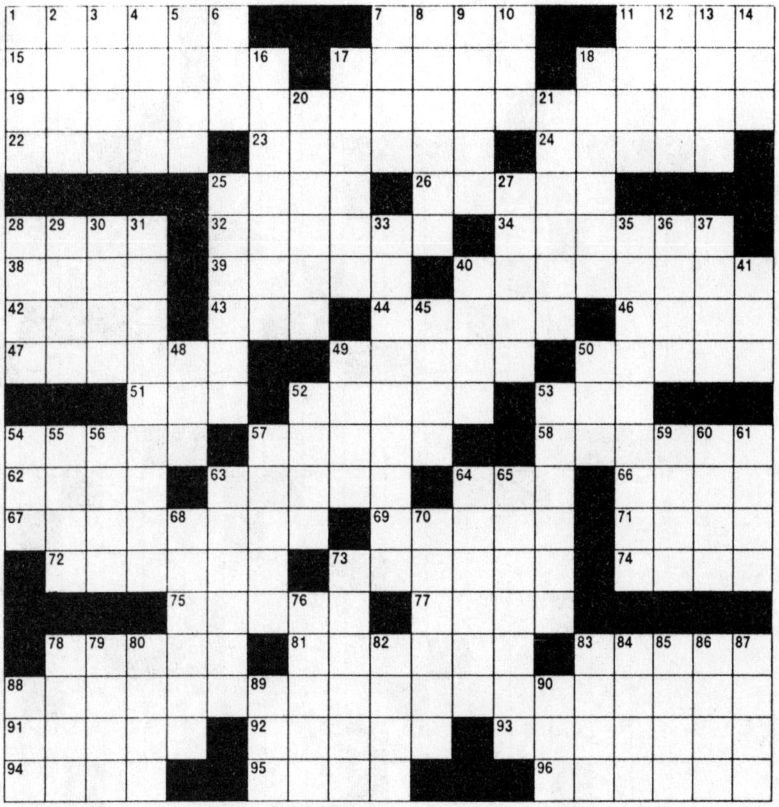

ACROSS

1. Trying periods
7. Movie dog
11. Tibetan monk
15. Sends an R.S.V.P.
17. Czech capital, to Czechs
18. Feasts
19. Black-cat day?
22. Mah-jongg pieces
23. Sisterly name
24. Sharpens
25. Savoir faire
26. Whiskers
28. Goes wrong
32. Carson and Rivers, e.g.
34. Prodded
38. Fracas
39. Having nerves: Suffix
40. Month for 88 Across
42. Genesis for a patent
43. Scout unit: Abbr.
44. Shows pleasure
46. Taste, in Scotland
47. Cuddle
49. ____ of burden
50. Spent
51. Comparative ending
52. Month for 88 Across
53. Greek letter
54. ____ the salt
57. Comedian Jack
58. Gangster's thing
62. Kind of will
63. Similar
64. Heat-measure initials
66. Subtle quality
67. Month for 88 Across
69. Reception room
71. Trolley
72. Passover feasts
73. Surmise
74. Squirmy fish
75. Files
77. Holds a session
78. He had a sling
81. St. Francis locale
83. Hives
88. Year with three black-cat months
91. Hot spots
92. Writer Ernest Thompson
93. Ship route
94. Eft
95. Org.
96. Meeting places

DOWN

1. Use a sieve
2. Religious initials
3. Sin
4. Novelist André
5. Greek letters
6. Beef cut, in Scotland
7. Comic Johnson
8. Indian titles of respect: Var.
9. Yours, poetically
10. Swiss river
11. Mortgage
12. Queen of lace note
13. Champs of 1986
14. Kind of tray or can
16. Fulton built one
17. Beat steadily
18. Asian cedar
20. Involuntary spasm
21. Heart actions for a teenager
25. Person in a camp
27. Representative
28. Miss Moran of TV
29. Use a taxi
30. Anonymous Richard and others
31. Posted
33. Avidity
35. Kind of bridge
36. Peer
37. After zwei
40. Scale bearer
41. Urge
45. Risqué
48. Wallace or Ayres
49. Willie Sutton's target
50. ____ rule
52. Golda
53. Trims
54. Container
55. Cupid
56. Amour
57. Hallow
59. Honshu port
60. Of a time period
61. Highland wear
63. Scrape
64. Somewhat down in the dumps
65. Small birds
68. Earns
70. Delegate a task
73. Plus things
76. Window parts
78. Swan, for one
79. Once more
80. Opening
82. Swiss town
83. Backup soldiers' org.
84. Depend
85. Stowe girl et al.
86. Depression
87. Change of a five
88. French denial
89. That, in Madrid
90. Still and all

212 On the Gridiron By Ernie Furtado

Dealing exclusively with the no-nos of the game.

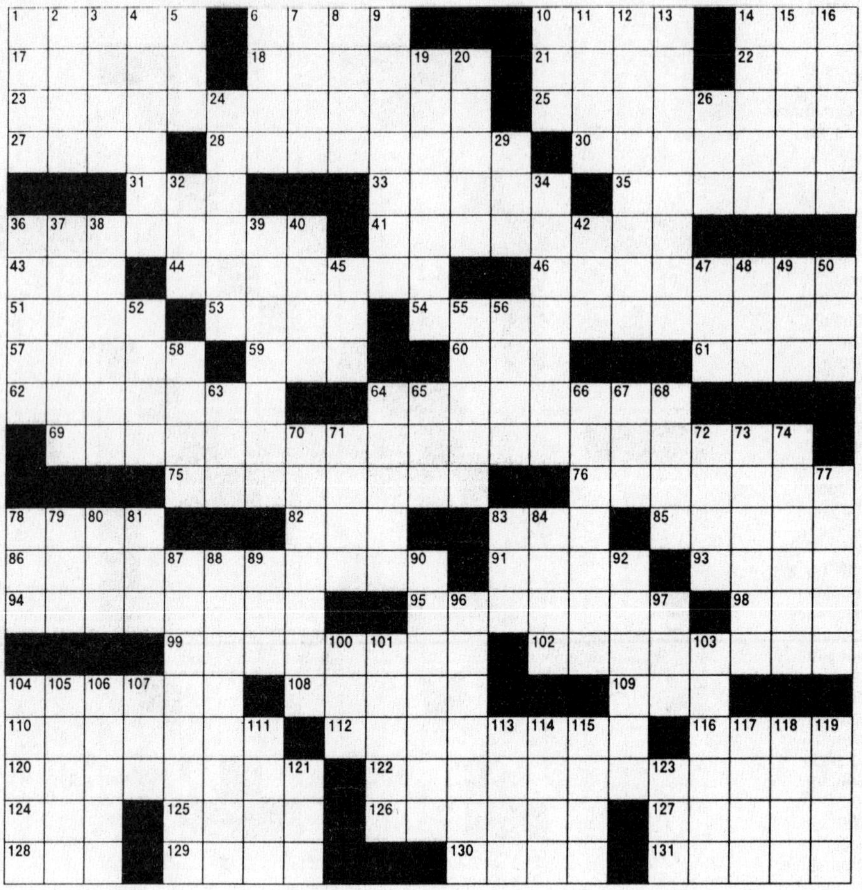

ACROSS

1. Elan
6. Rose or Fountain
10. Theatrical producer Joseph
14. Middling grade
17. Cosmetic
18. Ancestor: Lat.
21. Track
22. Neighbor of Fla.
23. ILLEGAL ENTRY
25. Lets go
27. Japanese beverage
28. Spa frequenter
30. UNSPORTS-MANLIKE ___
31. Capuchin monkey
33. Fish eaters
35. Underground events
36. BEYOND THE LINE OF SCRIMMAGE
41. Sororal
43. "___ of Me," 1931 song
44. High-level rapproche-ment
46. "Change the subject!"
51. Irritate
53. Dream, to Debussy
54. PROTRAC-TION
57. Comic Kovacs
59. Ump's counterpart
60. Resembling: Abbr.
61. It springs eternal
62. Twice a pentagon
64. Suitable for estimating
69. WHAT THE OFFICIAL DID
75. What aspirin does for some
76. ___ of (testimonial words)
78. Atmosphere
82. First lady
83. Viewed
85. Difficult, to Bardot
86. ILLEGAL TACKLE
91. Word before dash
93. New Jersey five
94. Snapped the ball
95. Idiotic
98. Non-Jew: Var.
99. Kind of well
102. GANGING UP
104. Sweater material
108. "No man is an island" penner
109. Dined
110. GRABBING ILLEGALLY
112. "___ as Apple Cider"
116. Third or mono
120. Familiarized
122. HINDRANCE OF A RECEIVER
124. Mil. officers
125. Stoneware, to a Frenchman
126. Town near Jerusalem
127. Vehicles
128. After dees
129. Method: Abbr.
130. LP's
131. Rhone feeder

DOWN

1. Mars's counterpart
2. Barrett of gossipdom
3. Sidestep
4. Monster
5. Old car
6. Speed of movement
7. Number endings
8. ___ Shanter
9. Earth's highest point
10. ___ favor (please, in Spain)
11. With, in France
12. Stanford's home
13. Have ___ (be well supplied)
14. ___ belli
15. Do a November job
16. Bridge seats
19. Like a rookie
20. British guns
24. Add ___ (tack on to a bill)
26. Lemon follower
29. Soak flax
32. Abet's partner
34. Town near Singapore
36. Rowed
37. Small flower
38. Recoil
39. Timeless
40. Ballesteros of golf
42. "The Bridge of San Luis ___"
45. Ship-shaped clock
47. E-I connection
48. U.N. farm unit
49. Mischief-maker
50. Peg for Peete
52. Fibber
55. These, in Spain
56. Claim
58. River to the Elbe
63. Chit word
64. "Nevermore" sayer
65. Mature
66. Town near Delhi
67. Novelist Deighton
68. Hebrew measure
70. Made a baseball play
71. Son of Jacob
72. Forsaken
73. Bacon ___ breakfast
74. Caesar's query to Brutus
77. Copal
78. Part of C.P.A.
79. Rubber tree
80. Jimmy's successor
81. A.B.A. member
83. Ukr., e.g.
84. Askew
87. Preliminary court events
88. Knight's activity
89. Tennis unit
90. Issuing from
92. Pontius ___
96. Kind of novice general
97. Townsman
100. Oneself, in Paris
101. Kind of ink
103. Sea god
104. Make ___ -in-one
105. Opposite of sur, in Toledo
106. Musical slide, for short
107. "___ to Billy Joe"
111. Turns right
113. "The Way We ___"
114. Cordage fiber
115. Newts
117. Frenchhandle
118. Worker on cakes
119. ___ majesty
121. Summer time: Abbr.
123. Baseball stat

213 Phraseworthy By Louis Baron

Putting some logic of sorts in word combos.

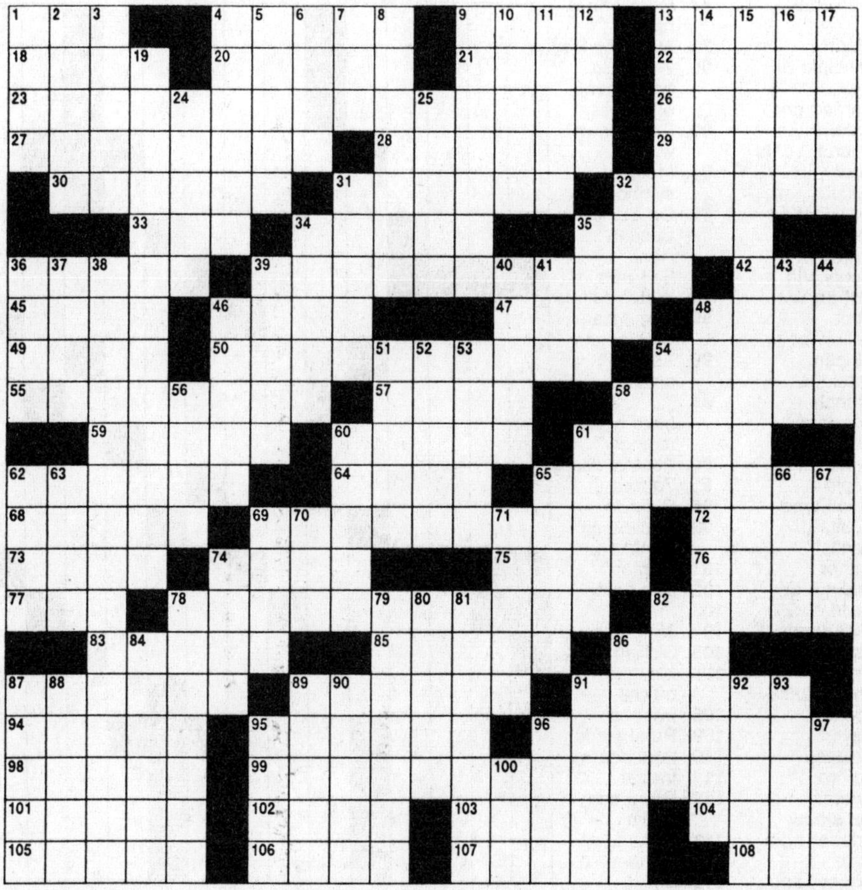

ACROSS

1. Kind of goblin or nob
4. Veered suddenly
9. Robin Hood's Marian
13. Texas Indians
18. Mighty piece of writing
20. Duck
21. Spore sacs
22. District of Portugal
23. See it another way
26. Dance of the 1930's
27. Most saline
28. Pathologists' specimens
29. Bookbinding worker
30. Arrival
31. Old Testament book
32. Adult
33. River to Lake Balkhash
34. "Nutcracker ___"
35. Sea-lane traveler
36. Becomes sparse
39. Align the cheesecake
42. Neighbor of Ill.
45. Lip ___
46. Bog yield
47. Desert builder
48. Quote
49. Basilica area
50. Include a joker
54. Unaccompanied chorale
55. Lays new flower beds
57. Pram pusher
58. Happy Jewish occasion
59. Jots
60. ___ the moon
61. Mea follower
62. Of the wrist
64. "___ She Sweet?"
65. Uzbek Republic native
68. Dueling props
69. Censure an ogler
72. Guaranteed
73. Ruth's husband
74. Prado great
75. "Wellaway!"
76. Colorado peak
77. Guidonian notes
78. Fix up a Connecticut retreat
82. Disastrous
83. Bentley sleuth
85. Dortmund parent
86. Whale group
87. Boot-camp order
89. Arctic geese
91. Mississippi Valley Siouan
94. Stay in place, at sea
95. Charpentier opera
96. Mocking
98. Force
99. Turn in a false alarm
101. Maison room
102. Plentiful
103. Franck's "___ Angelicus"
104. Russian river
105. Lock of hair
106. "___ is as good as a wink": Scott
107. Low-grade stuff
108. Lumberman's implement

DOWN

1. Food seasoner
2. Bouffe or comique
3. Forked
4. Resident of San'a
5. Popeye's advisory
6. Poverty
7. Old Tokyo
8. Down payment
9. One using an iron
10. "Paint me ___": Cromwell
11. Sacred figures
12. Repeats incessantly
13. Erie-Ontario canal
14. Fly
15. Let a stray follow you home
16. "Halt!" e.g.
17. Zelda ___ Fitzgerald
19. Persuade a bandleader
24. Cambodian coins
25. Steamed
31. ___ Arenas, Chile
32. Weather report
34. Standees' lacks
35. Dragged out
36. Autocrat
37. Adman's specialty
38. Install an epi
39. Word on a nickel
40. Nile dam
41. Air-control agcy.
43. Virginia willow
44. Adam's third son
46. Like some servitude
48. Relax an art-class nude
51. ". . . bombs bursting ___"
52. Singer Ross of radio
53. Ekberg or Louise
54. Coconut yield
56. Mindanao people
58. Rides the breakers
60. Brilliant bird
61. Town south of Bourges, France
62. Philippine island
63. ". . . all my fame for ___ of ale . . .": "Henry V"
65. A Charlie Chan portrayer
66. Water buffalo
67. Actress Patricia
69. Word of warning
70. Polyphemus had one
71. Ripples' big brothers
74. Actor Raymond
78. Gives shoes a new life
79. ___ oneself of (used)
80. Old German guild
81. Stab
82. Bed-of-nails ascetic
84. Badger look-alikes
86. Flashy
87. Tilting
88. Turkish fief
89. Islands south of Japan
90. Italian baritone Titta
91. Bold challenges
92. Common masthead name
93. Palindromic fruit
95. Turin tip
96. Wynter of films
97. Chew at
100. Tympanum site

214 Figuratively By Robert Roop

Some phrases that can't be taken literally.

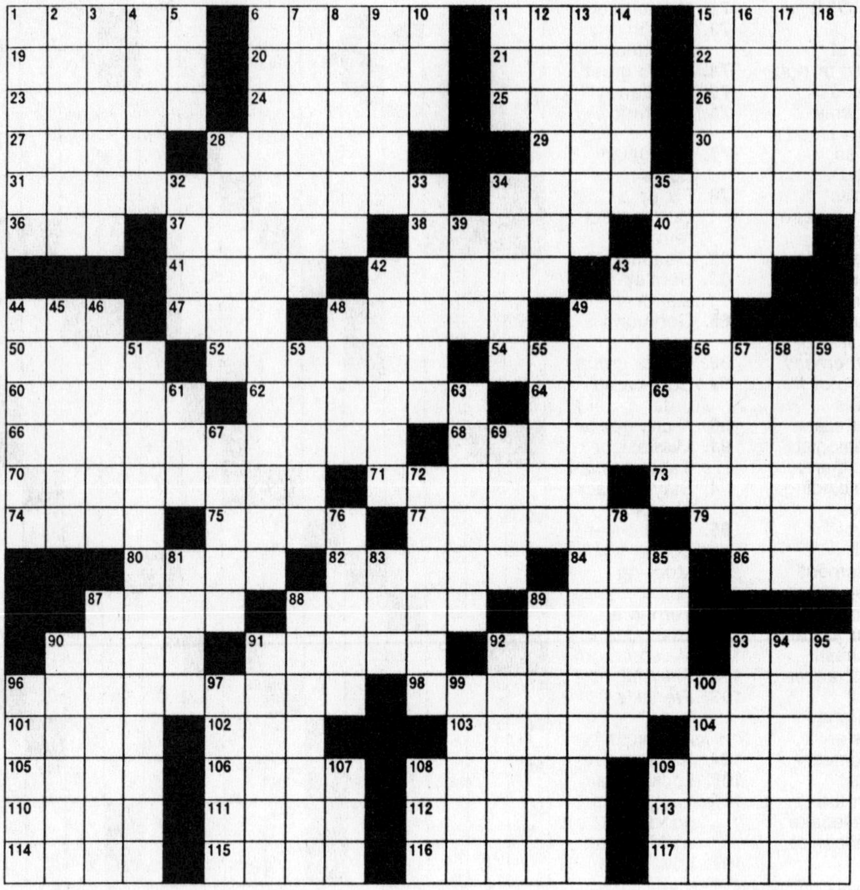

ACROSS

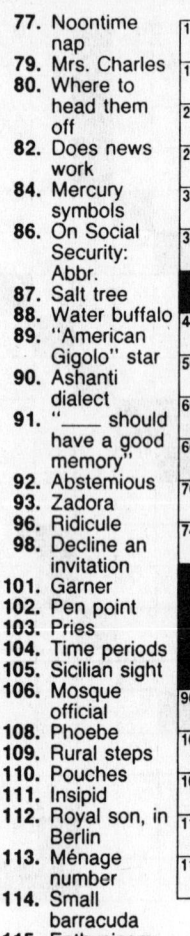

1. Hindu principle of life
6. Carried on
11. Ruler units
15. Church seats
19. Booty, in Padua
20. Architect's pattern
21. A wife of Henry VIII
22. Not genuine: Abbr.
23. Yellow color
24. African antelope
25. French weapon
26. Ship for Columbus
27. Cupid
28. Small type
29. "Delta of Venus" author
30. Ending for cyclo
31. Mint words
34. Assist
36. Sin
37. Philadelphia hockey player
38. Release
40. Before gamma
41. Cat's-paw
42. Gripper on a shoe
43. Singer Lane
44. Abbr. used in prefabrication
47. Dallas campus
48. Vigilant
49. Ratify
50. Man of the ___
52. Certain Frenchman
54. Exclamations
56. At a distance
60. Strong man
62. East African native
64. Dorm sharer
66. Chew the rag
68. Get out of hand
70. ___ to (concerning)
71. Petrarchan form
73. ___ Dame
74. Lower Burma people
75. Same, in a notation
77. Noontime nap
79. Mrs. Charles
80. Where to head them off
82. Does news work
84. Mercury symbols
86. On Social Security: Abbr.
87. Salt tree
88. Water buffalo
89. "American Gigolo" star
90. Ashanti dialect
91. "___ should have a good memory"
92. Abstemious
93. Zadora
96. Ridicule
98. Decline an invitation
101. Garner
102. Pen point
103. Pries
104. Time periods
105. Sicilian sight
106. Mosque official
108. Phoebe
109. Rural steps
110. Pouches
111. Insipid
112. Royal son, in Berlin
113. Ménage number
114. Small barracuda
115. Enthusiasm
116. Atmosphere probe
117. Methods

DOWN

1. "___ in the Sun"
2. Minor earthquake
3. Autobiography
4. Dress up
5. Code word for "N"
6. Advice to a careless talker
7. Clothes
8. Segovia's instrument
9. Costume designer and family
10. Agnus ___
11. Noted columnist's monogram
12. Sincere
13. Fur of royalty
14. Vogue
15. Accuse
16. Arabian chief's domain
17. Minnesota county
18. Abide
28. Poise
32. P.M.'s
33. Terry and Burstyn
34. Reluctant
35. Eban of Israel
39. "___ the ramparts . . ."
42. Heat-lightning locales
43. Fabulist
44. Summer uniforms
45. Showing fondness
46. Supports for levers
48. Business-letter abbr.
49. Converse airily
51. Recall times better forgotten
53. ___ vie
55. TV's Johnson et al.
57. Constituent
58. Pied-___
59. Usher elsewhere
61. Droop
63. Kindle
65. Andy Gump's wife
67. Hoist
69. Wallet contents
72. Willows
76. Kind of Scout badge
78. Concurs
81. Arabic letter
83. Genetic initials
85. Rank above Cpl.
87. With suspicion
88. Selma's state
89. Good fortune
90. Specialty dance
91. Farm or cracker
92. "Than wish a ___ May's new-fangled mirth"
93. Sentence ender
94. Genoa's land, to Bizet
95. Evaluate
96. One of the estates
97. Amalgamate
99. January, in Juárez
100. Prefix for grade or gress
107. Certain people
108. Second letter addn.
109. Religious degree

215 Also Known As By William A. Smith

Getting to know more about entertainment folk.

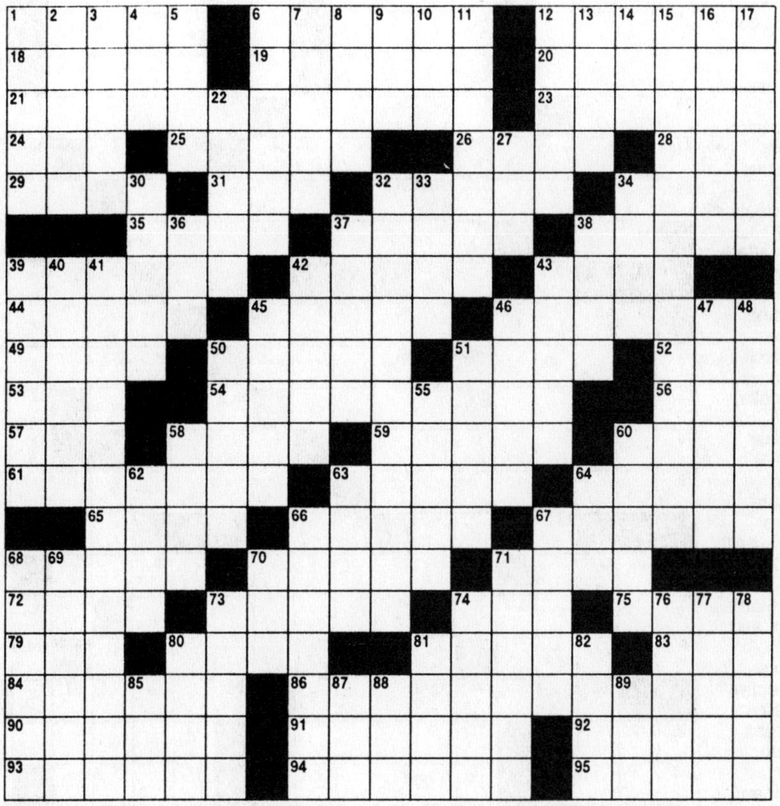

ACROSS

1. Brigitte Bardot, offstage
6. Greek assembly places
12. Humperdinck, offstage
18. Few: Prefix
19. Solar-eclipse sight
20. Dancer in "Peer Gynt"
21. Edna Gilhooley, onstage
23. Directs the attention of
24. Recline
25. Efface
26. Between good and poor
28. Duct
29. Spanish muralist
31. Goddess of discord
32. Helen Hayes, offstage
34. Bristle: Prefix
35. Elder, in France
37. Mound of stones
38. Bicuspid's neighbor
39. John Forsythe, offstage
42. Establish
43. Lugosi
44. Jeweler's glass
45. Lodging-house offerings
46. Vehicular passage
49. Margin
50. Wire: Abbr.
51. Gravy container
52. Mr. Olds's car
53. Opposite of SSW
54. Elizabeth Enke, onstage
56. Finish
57. Legislative fig.
58. Cruising
59. Capital of Morocco
60. Snicker follower
61. Grommets
63. Gray-flannel suit people
64. Old Thai money
65. What strokes use
66. Allyson and Havoc
67. Gentle touch
68. Cartoon pig
70. City near Stuttgart
71. Window part
72. African plant
73. Editor in a TV series
74. Govt. unit
75. Roy Rogers, offstage
79. Ayres or Cody
80. Old English letters
81. Court decree
83. Architects' org.
84. Away from home
86. Stevland Morris's stage name
90. Perfumery liquid
91. White fur
92. Warble
93. Pepsin is one
94. Lacking
95. Like some spinach

DOWN

1. Grey and McCrea
2. "Kate and ___," TV series
3. More nasty
4. Iron or teen
5. Isolated
6. Having a sharp point
7. Growth on a moor
8. Mount for a cockney
9. Go bad
10. One or another
11. Redd Foxx, offstage
12. Singer Bobby
13. Unique person
14. Moroccan range
15. Sidney Leibowitz, onstage
16. Printing boo-boos
17. P.L.O. chief Arafat
22. Mark of disgrace
27. Beard of wheat
30. Brownish gray
32. James Garner, offstage
33. Speeds, in Scotland
34. Realtor's favorite sign
36. Suffix for salt or Alp
37. Australian cry
38. Potatoes' partner
39. Strip a whale
40. Dangerfield
41. Michael Landon, offstage
42. Rock layers
43. Toot one's own horn
45. Counsels, old style
46. Kind of nose
47. Trojan hero
48. Sings at Chamonix
50. Examines
51. "___ in Arms"
55. Women, in Germany
58. Ethereal
60. Begets
62. Ann Sothern, offstage
63. Greek court
64. Light color
66. David Meyer, onstage
67. Baseball's Rod ___
68. Buckingham, for one
69. Ethylene is one
70. Residue
71. Strained food
73. Confuse
74. Sea water
76. Romansh
77. Relinquish
78. Worm-catching kind of bird
80. Ancient kingdom
81. Agog
82. Young ones
85. Ending for rook or bean
87. Italian three
88. Scottish uncle
89. Gun gp.

216 Filmy Scriptures By Cathy Millhauser

Wherein the Bible and Hollywood get together.

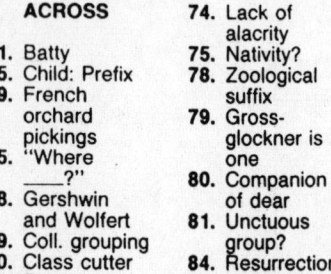

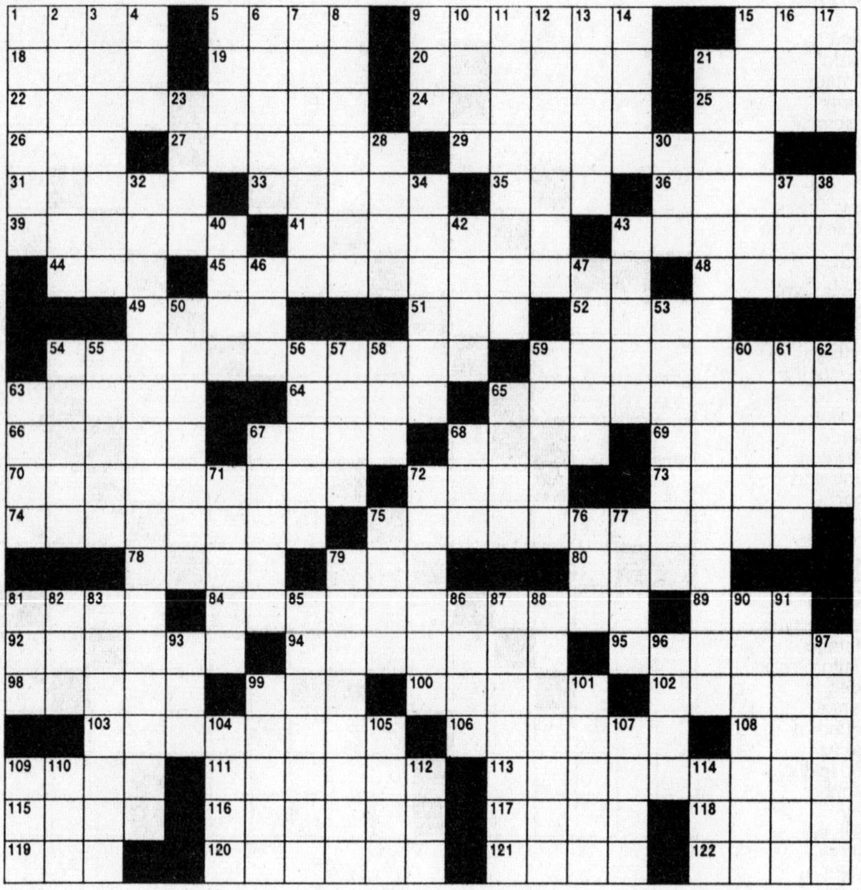

ACROSS

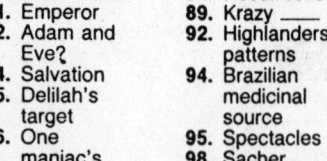

1. Batty
5. Child: Prefix
9. French orchard pickings
15. "Where ___?"
18. Gershwin and Wolfert
19. Coll. grouping
20. Class cutter
21. Emperor
22. Adam and Eve?
24. Salvation
25. Delilah's target
26. One maniac's problem
27. Mystery Queen
29. Magis' journey?
31. Wicker: Var.
33. Guthrie namesakes
35. Humorist George
36. Ammonia derivative
39. Punishes, biblically
41. Luigi's Mrs.
43. Miss Bryant and others
44. Crete's high point
45. Abel?
48. Plexus
49. Meadows
51. Word of request: Abbr.
52. Florida's ___ Raton
54. Exodus? (with "The")
59. Dictator
63. Manhattan and London districts
64. Partner
65. It's often romantic
66. "Don't look ___ horse . . ."
67. Turkish titles
68. Rosin recipients
69. Apollo's birthplace
70. Viewed with scorn
72. ___ Gracia, Argentina
73. Debtors
74. Lack of alacrity
75. Nativity?
78. Zoological suffix
79. Gross-glockner is one
80. Companion of dear
81. Unctuous group?
84. Resurrection?
89. Krazy ___
92. Highlanders' patterns
94. Brazilian medicinal source
95. Spectacles
98. Sacher ___ (rich cake)
99. Latin grammar case: Abbr.
100. Metric measure
102. Sphere
103. Noah's ark?
106. Wood louse
108. Greek letters
109. Blackthorn
111. Doone and Luft
113. Jonah's perspective?
115. Emulates Barabbas
116. Eastern rulers
117. Just open
118. First-floor apartment no.
119. Israel ender
120. Scottish lowlands
121. Snoopy
122. Promontory

DOWN

1. Cons with no future
2. Japanese paper-folding art
3. Major artery
4. C.I.A. predecessor
5. Clout
6. ___ Gay
7. Scattered
8. Too bright, as a room
9. Typesetter: Abbr.
10. There are lodes of these
11. Dijon et al.
12. Australian for whom a nut was named
13. Habituate
14. Manuscript marking
15. As high ___
16. Avril's follower
17. Kind of verb: Abbr.
21. Jesus of Nazareth?
23. Big shoe size
28. Middle English letter
30. Fled
32. Sodom and Gomorrah?
34. Curt
37. Turner or King Cole
38. Chin follower
40. Bit of data
42. Escutcheon border
43. Make ___ of (jot down)
46. Place for a rep.
47. Borders on
50. Side of town
53. Spain's former capital
54. "Taras Bulba" writer
55. Ionesco critter
56. Wise men
57. Outfitted
58. Than, in Thuringia
59. Gamal Abdel's successor
60. Herod was one
61. Embellish
62. Hardy heroine
63. Pouches
65. Greek letter
67. Anatomical loops
68. Sandwich order
71. Rewards of old
72. Former Turkish coins
75. Part of T.A.E.
76. Corporation abbr.
77. Bishops' posts
79. Fliers' paths
81. Choose
82. Mideast gp.
83. Piercing site
85. Horny-handed one
86. Degenerates
87. Of a math theorem
88. Orange tree, in Spain
90. Buttercup variety
91. Teachers' goals
93. Dict. entry
96. Author John Dickson
97. Gives lip
99. Large constrictor
101. Miss Kett and others
104. T.V.A. power type
105. Biblical weed
107. Weird
109. Hindu title
110. Realty unit
112. Snaky sound
114. It's charged

217 Friendly Consonants By John Hales

Some letter combinations that go together.

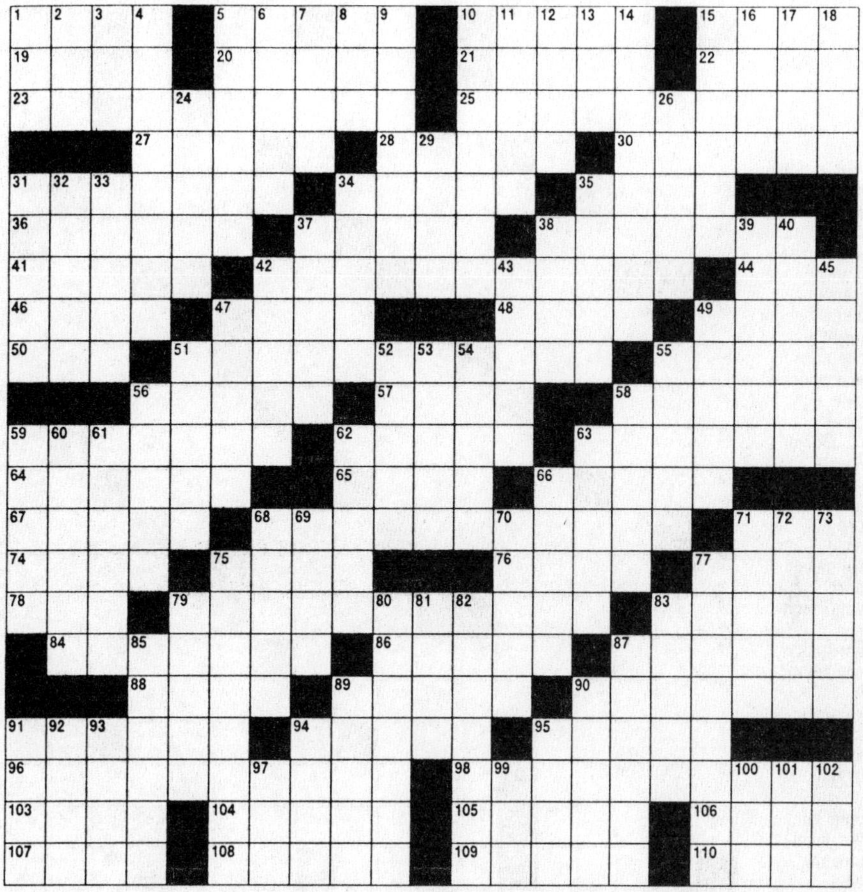

ACROSS

1. ___ kiri
5. Horselaughs
10. Ethiopian province
15. "When I was ___"
19. Assert
20. Ryan or Tatum
21. Way to serve oysters
22. Pro ___
23. Lake Erie port
25. Sleight-of-hand artist of a sort
27. "Please come home; ___ forgiven"
28. Discernment
30. Fuel gas
31. Kind of French cri
34. Roman halls
35. Being, in Spain
36. Item for the mistake-prone
37. Primp
38. Modified
41. Canada's highest mountain
42. Ibsen woman
44. Deface
46. Date for Caesar
47. Alliance initials
48. German song
49. Star in Cetus
50. Roman bronze
51. Zealous one
55. Specialty stores
56. Poe or Burroughs
57. Hardly done
58. Depends
59. One who corrupts
62. Pools
63. Medicinal plant
64. Slick surface
65. Like some rumors
66. Post-coup ruling group
67. Highway stopover
68. Scottish girl of old song
71. Ethiopian title
74. Old English moneys
75. Dormouse genus
76. ___ of Judah (Selassie title)
77. Mousebird
78. Insignificant, to a Glaswegian
79. Top-drawer
83. French novelist Lesage
84. Country within a country
86. Not a soul
87. Sistine Chapel feature
88. Hindu deity
89. Miss Kett et al.
90. Bound with a thread
91. Vanity
94. Derived from an acid
95. Duelist Burr
96. Hiker
98. Jersey city near N.Y.C.
103. Will-___-wisp
104. Roi's wife
105. Prefix for cept or fere
106. Sewing kit
107. Prying
108. Hall of Fame golfer
109. Golda's family
110. Word with drum or honor

DOWN

1. TV's Linden
2. Films' Gardner
3. Kind of hall, for short
4. Land of Opportunity state
5. Fleet Street headwear
6. Walking ___ (elated)
7. Low places
8. Bleacher occupant
9. Like a blind
10. "Bonanza" cook
11. TV's Gillette
12. Pilaf requirement
13. Half an antiaircraft gun
14. Showed remorse
15. William Tell, for one
16. "Mighty ___ Rose"
17. Solar deity
18. Palm-tree yield
24. Unfamiliar
26. Web-footed swimmer
29. Environs
31. Festival of Apollo
32. Disintegrate
33. Storms
34. Eagerness
35. Aunt in "Oklahoma!"
37. Associate of Paul and Mary
38. Rose's friend
39. Character in "The Winter's Tale"
40. Site of Keats's peak
42. Ishmael's mother
43. Rodrigues ___, former president of Brazil
45. Civet native to China
47. Film actor Conrad
49. Pêche ___
51. Ill-fated vehicle
52. Meat stew in Africa
53. Inventor Pliny ___
54. Unsteady
55. Al ___ (not overcooked)
56. Singer Emma
58. Kidney enzyme
59. Dealers' cars, for short
60. Huge, in France
61. Site of a historic W.W. II march
62. Capital of Belorussia
63. Impresario Sol
66. Orange yield
68. Basque province
69. French Riviera resort
70. King and Bates
71. Friars Club occasion
72. Albee's "Tiny ___"
73. Ecclesiastical council
75. Beginners' textbooks
77. Charwoman's need
79. Part of a brooch
80. Did a stage routine
81. French entree word
82. Early Italian mystic
83. Gaseous element
85. Inoffensive oath
87. Brickkiln workers
89. "Maria ___," 1933 song
90. One of an L.A. team
91. Black
92. Argentine music
93. Words of woe, in the Highlands
94. Migrant worker of the 1930's
95. Play beginning
97. Focal point: Abbr.
99. Pierre's donkey
100. From ___ Z
101. ___-de-sac
102. Distance meas. on the Continent

218 Goal-Line Stand By Louis Sabin

Doings of sorts on the football field.

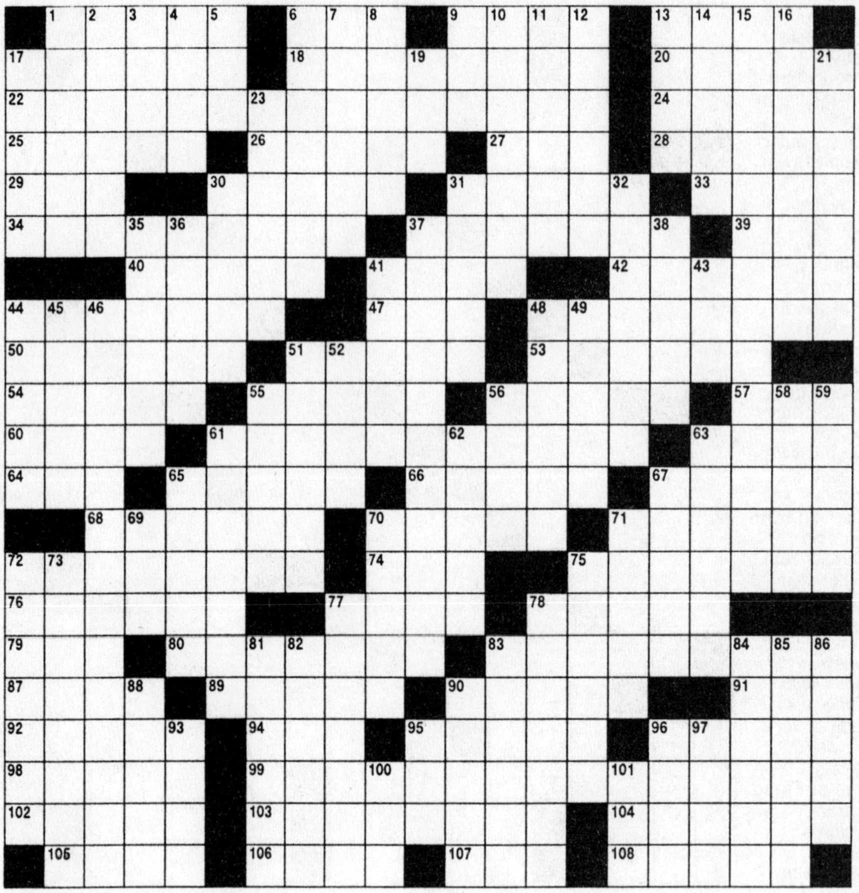

ACROSS

1. "Turandot," e.g.
6. Chafe
9. Vipers
13. .367 career hitter
17. Enter quietly
18. Joiner
20. Van Gogh setting
22. Get a huge signing bonus?
24. Reject haughtily
25. Collegiate wall covers
26. Tickle
27. Douse
28. ____-Coeur
29. Golfer's concern
30. Heiden and Blore
31. Worse
33. Hebrides island
34. Measure of grid greatness?
37. Many-rayed fish
39. Short mo.
40. Lahore lady
41. For men only
42. Bad guy
44. Nominal
47. Hippie joint
48. Fixed firmly
50. Mistreats
51. "Casablanca" actor
53. Food fish
54. Unmasks
55. Prepared for shipping
56. "____ moi le . . ."
57. Lackland or Keesler: Abbr.
60. Samovars
61. Position for driving fullbacks?
63. Roman 251
64. Weather vane rdg.
65. Prove false
66. Patio piece
67. Dervish's relative
68. Arrange
70. Comic George
71. Grew insipid
72. Overlord was one in 1944
74. Charlotte of films
75. Field hands
76. Northern jacket
77. Chalcedony
78. Pickler's supply
79. Gun an engine
80. Bequeathed
83. Stoppers of a Chicago team?
87. Definite articles
89. Cocktails
90. "Ladies and germs," said he
91. Precept
92. Blood carrier
94. Land measure
95. Harangue
96. Sherman or Reynolds
98. Untrained
99. How to run a halfback?
102. Serfs' cousins
103. Capable of being raised
104. Main course
105. Old Norse epic
106. Pedestal part
107. Took the van
108. Pried

DOWN

1. "Twelfth Night" countess
2. Having more evergreens
3. Olympic blade
4. Spanish rivers
5. Dancer Miller
6. Cut again
7. Do a returning tourist's chore
8. Penman's smudges
9. Petition
10. In a dither
11. Bernadette or Jean
12. Sonnet part
13. Singer Elliot
14. Killer whales
15. They help raise the victory flag?
16. Dessert choice
17. Shrewdly: Var.
19. Rocks
21. Played the villain
23. More hair-raising
30. Heating vessels
31. Pairs
32. Gadabout
35. Members of a Moslem sect
36. Willy Loman's goal
37. Buys a round for the defense?
38. Film units
41. Snoopy person
43. Bit of refreshment
44. Don'ts: Var.
45. Construction units
46. Upset the offense?
48. Drives
49. Rivera specialty
51. Gully
52. Order to the helm
55. Brazilian port
56. Not fer
58. Chuck Yeager or Wiley Post
59. Hitchcock subject
61. Shoots over
62. Muffed
63. Guest
65. Stale
67. Indistinct
69. Relative of eterne
70. Scottish slopes
71. French pear
72. Hauling fee
73. Kind of town
75. County Kerry port
77. Scattered
78. At anchor
81. Spurred
82. Dawn
83. John Lennon was one
84. Tempt
85. Troubled
86. Malmö native
88. Trusty mount
90. Prepare a steak
93. Handle, to Ovid
95. Former Giant star
96. Florence's river
97. Plenty
100. Sarge
101. Star wearer: Abbr.

219 Window Dressing By Isaac Miller

Featuring a multipurpose convenience.

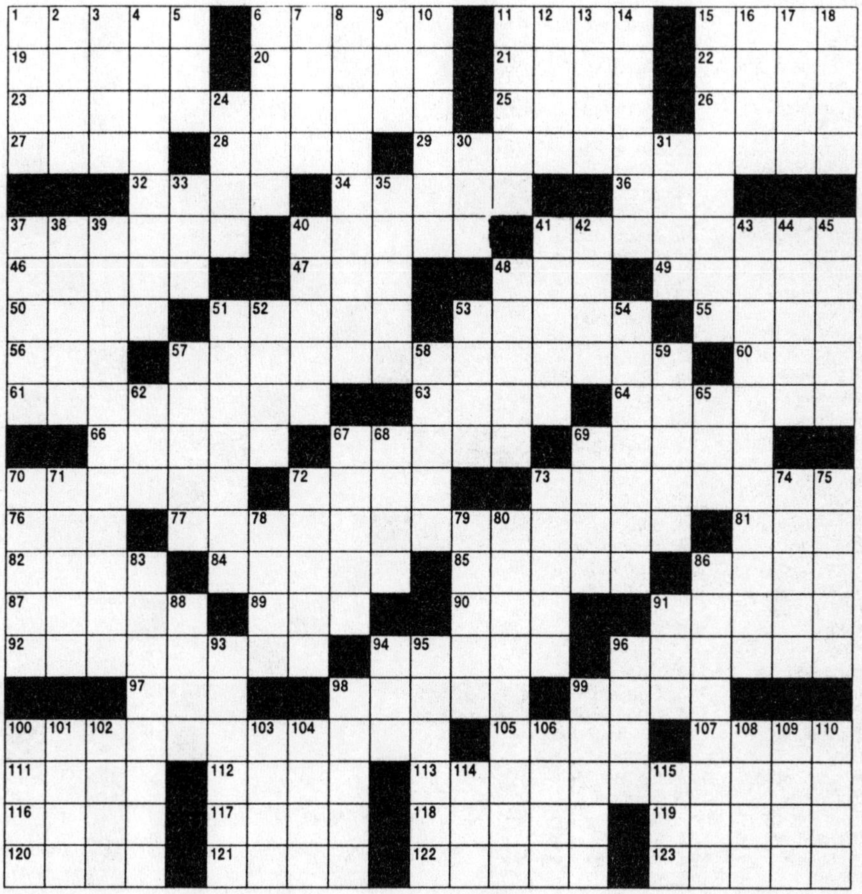

ACROSS

1. Proverb
6. Songwriters' org.
11. Biblical brother
15. ___ colada
19. Sedate
20. Ball queen
21. Eastern garment
22. Norse god
23. Big moment for an actor
25. Neat
26. Fix over
27. Writer Murdoch
28. Asian festivals
29. Hitchcock film
32. ___-Neisse Line
34. Off. worker
36. Floral wreath
37. Onions' relatives
40. Money or aleck
41. Cresting wave
46. Dorm for a sultan's wives
47. Chance
48. "___ Wore a Yellow Ribbon"
49. Burst forth
50. Stravinsky
51. "Not ___ loved Caesar less . . ."
53. Trinket
55. Pennsylvania port
56. Seek office
57. Bathroom item
60. Sailor
61. Of the chest
63. Vigoda and Lincoln
64. Spanish wind
66. ___ the weather (ill)
67. Unit
69. Play part
70. Quick raid
72. London district
73. Laundry whiteners
76. Urge, in Aberdeen
77. Preliminary event
81. Cambodia's Angkor ___
82. Sound from a crowd
84. Type of finish
85. County and city in Nevada
86. Casino game
87. Negative ion
89. Aurora
90. ___ du Diable
91. Former Italian coin
92. Shaped like a spire
94. Exhorted
96. Jaunted along a highway
97. Resort
98. Strike, in England
99. Not straight
100. What a valance conceals
105. Dare, in Marseilles
107. Counterpart of nuts
111. S-shaped curve
112. Part of Al Capone's nickname
113. High point in a stage play
116. Winglike
117. "___ Lynne"
118. Thai or Mongol
119. Red dye
120. Smack one's ___
121. Dopes
122. Milk: Prefix
123. Discharge

DOWN

1. Spore sacs
2. Gloomy
3. Shelter
4. Recovers
5. Time division
6. Li'l one
7. Religious denomination
8. Fellow student
9. Winner's take, sometimes
10. Animal raised for fur
11. Houston athlete
12. Farm building
13. Greenland explorer
14. Horseshoe crabs
15. Doorway drape
16. Thought
17. Spider nests
18. At another time
24. Inhabitants: Suffix
30. Toronto is its cap.
31. Network
33. Rep. rival
35. Snouty mammal
37. Bird sound
38. Netherlands' The ___
39. Cold-war divider
40. Shoulder covering
41. "___ in a name?"
42. Juno, in Greece
43. Ornamental building exterior
44. Of bees
45. Feather: Prefix
48. Fragment
51. Situation after a sixth World Series game
52. Frosty coating
53. Land of the libre
54. Errors
57. Containing a salt base
58. Criterion
59. One who perceives
62. Explosive
65. Weeks in a year, to Caesar
67. Items found around castles
68. Buckeyes' home
69. As well
70. Ice pinnacle
71. Maine town
72. ___ pigeon
73. Cycled
74. It's often avant
75. Endured
78. Ostrich
79. ___ of Terror
80. Symbolic
83. Farm alarm clocks
86. March through mud
88. Asian palm
91. Dombey's relative
93. Speakers' stands
94. Hairy bean
95. Scamp
96. Actress Garr
98. Havens
99. Form of bingo
100. Fuel
101. Tangelo, in England
102. Harvest
103. Campus sports org.
104. Scrape
106. R.B.I. or E.R.A.
108. Seine feeder
109. Les Etats-___
110. Confined
114. 109 Down in another form
115. Once named

220 Centerpieces By Wilson McBeath

Where all the romantic action is.

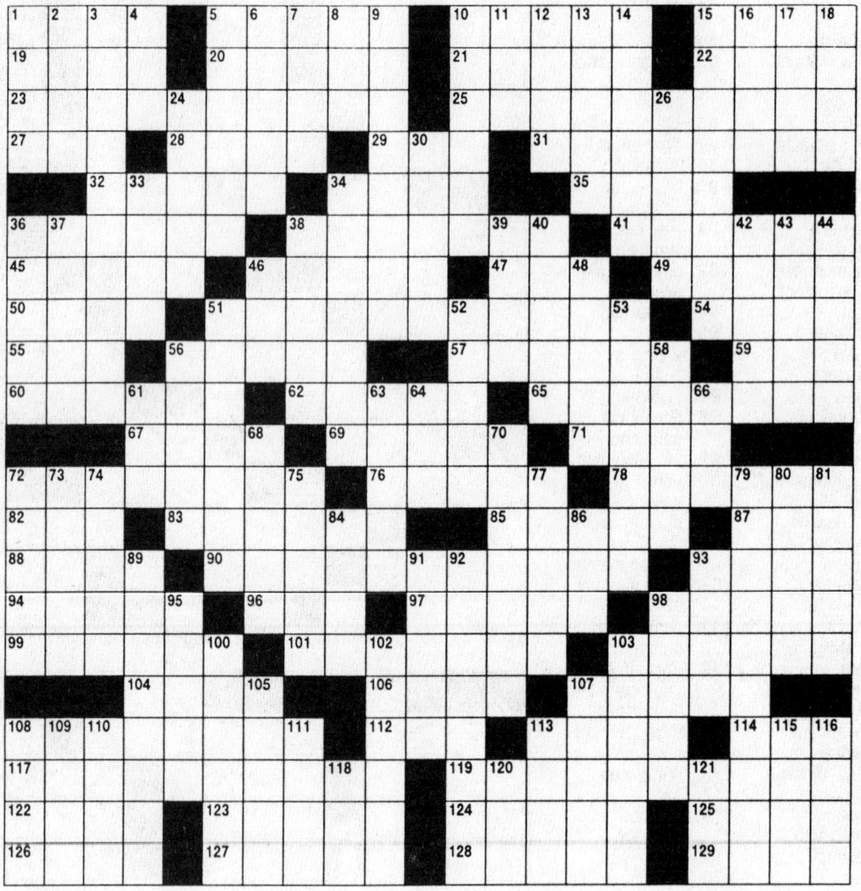

ACROSS

1. Thai monetary unit
5. Leaning
10. Journalist Joseph
15. Verge
19. 1934 Nobel chemist
20. Stalin's secret-police head
21. Painting on dry plaster
22. Organic element: Prefix
23. Valentine-shaped mollusk
25. The one and only
27. Household god
28. Pay attention
29. Lake, to Renée
31. What navigators take
32. "To ___ own self be true": "Hamlet"
34. Sandwich filler
35. A ___ Able
36. Forsake
38. Founder of the cult of quietism
41. Jovial
45. Manipulate
46. Pineapples, in Spain
47. Nanny's offspring
49. Main Street unit
50. Netherlands cheese
51. Sympathetic
54. Greek org. of W.W. II
55. Bandleader Brown
56. Fiction for U.F.O. believers
57. Crocodile's cousin
59. Trygve of the U.N.
60. Minor quake
62. Foul-up
65. Roman and Arabic items
67. One of a Kipling trio
69. Do theatrics
71. Craze
72. Disparage
76. Vernon's dancing partner
78. Garment insert
82. Focal line: Prefix
83. Crosses home plate
85. Records
87. Minuscule
88. Gorge
90. Like Hannah of a song
93. Withered
94. Blanch
96. Bushy mass
97. Gibe
98. Coil of yarn
99. "See oursels as ___ see us": Burns
101. Oven pan
103. Strikes
104. Extinct birds
106. Garlands
107. California's ___ Valley
108. Godless ones
112. Cobra
113. Sea eagles
114. Shoe width
117. It never won fair lady
119. Be merciful
122. Support a felon
123. Make happy
124. West, to Luigi
125. Solo
126. Singer Columbo
127. Challenged
128. Natives of Bergen
129. Western Indians

DOWN

1. Inlaid cabinetwork
2. Tract
3. Pansy
4. Odin's son
5. Missing
6. Snicker
7. Angered
8. Diamond ___
9. Actress Bankhead
10. Refuse receptacle
11. Golfer Elder
12. Incrustation
13. Plant sheath
14. Ingredient of soap or glass
15. Covered with bristles
16. Mend
17. Drink for seamen
18. Recedes
24. Hot-corner base
26. Attempts
30. Liqueur flavor
33. Tiller
34. Annuity scheme
36. ". . . that I ___ in marble halls"
37. Sea duck
38. Offends
39. Gumbo
40. Union job action
42. City in Missouri
43. Hikers' route
44. Assents
46. Luau dish
48. Take exception
51. Withdraw a race entry
52. Kind of angle
53. Hurt
56. Varieties
58. Ethiopian title
61. Spring month in Paris
63. Mennonite group
64. Pro
66. Legal matter
68. Brag
70. Main courses
72. Opera singer
73. Precise
74. Indian water vessel
75. Slip
77. Diner
79. Sigma Chi figure
80. Uncanny
81. High-school ages
84. Taro root
86. For each
89. Periodic-table contents
91. Double curves
92. Song to be chanted
93. Revue unit
95. Legal claim
98. Go to work on an atom
100. Having window frameworks
102. Winged
103. Legislative assembly
105. Inscribed pillar
107. Garb
108. ___ cry (distant)
109. Forbidden
110. Hastens
111. Mosel tributary
113. Anon's partner
115. Canal completed in 1825
116. Greek letters
118. Hwy.
120. Monetary unit of Macao
121. ___ Claire, Wis.

221 Globe-trotting By Bernice Gordon

Getting here and there around the map.

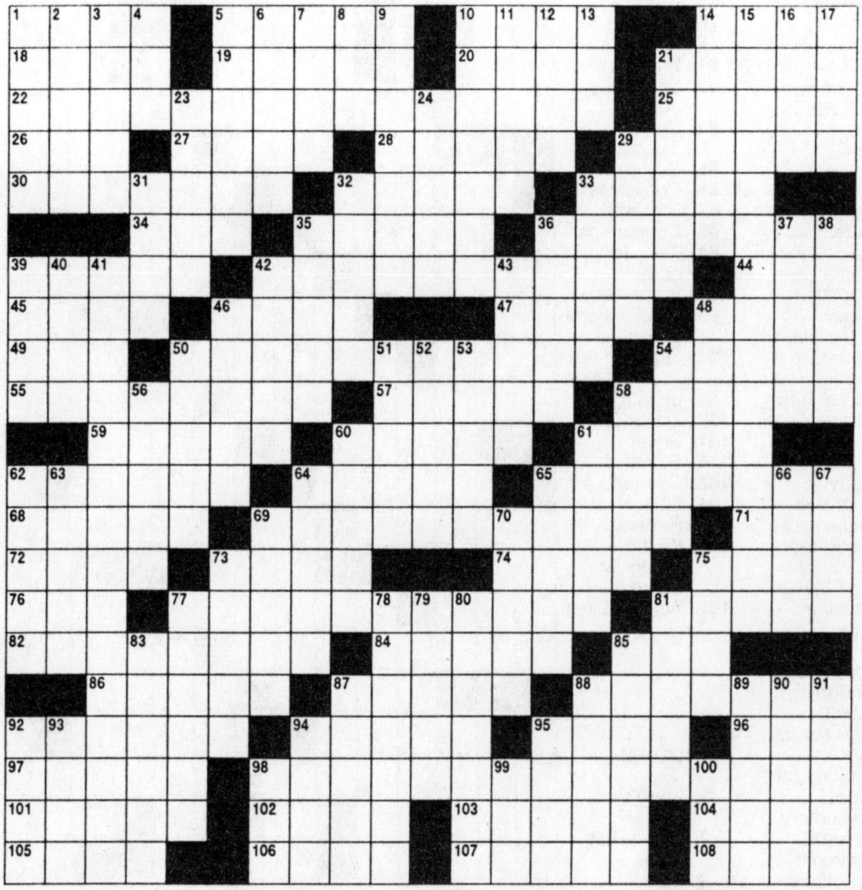

ACROSS

1. Desert in Mongolia
5. Scarf
10. Roman Censor
14. Scottish explorer and family
18. Once follower
19. Took an oath
20. Russian range
21. South American plain
22. Oriental von Sternberg movie, with "The"
25. Have an ___ the hole
26. Poetic contraction
27. Covering on a seed
28. Port opposite Copenhagen
29. Punish by fining
30. Old World bunting
32. Antler branches
33. Half, in France
34. Moon-landing vehicle
35. Gossipy woman
36. Literary excerpts
39. Singer John
42. Film starring Sabu
44. Altar in the sky
45. Comedian Lew
46. Author Victor
47. Something special
48. Hitch
49. City on Huon Gulf
50. Window decorations
54. Ingredient of a girl
55. Writer France et al.
57. Religious cup
58. Does art work
59. Saturday-night ailment
60. Eagle's weapon
61. Dried tubers
62. Like a prison window
64. Lawyer Melvin
65. Fixture for easing muscle pain
68. Eastern Indians
69. Well-known air
71. S.A. cruise port
72. Place for a boa
73. Like Hilton's horizon
74. Heights: Abbr.
75. Japanese native
76. Former Spanish queen
77. Flowers that bloom in the spring
81. Map part
82. Lines to go off on
84. Then, in Paris
85. Korean G.I.
86. Cite
87. Finery
88. Street opening
92. Leaps' partners
94. Braid
95. Coins of Rumania
96. Greek letters
97. Ireland, to Spenser
98. Du Maurier novel
101. One taking it on the lam
102. Moss of "Act One"
103. ". . . could ___ fat"
104. Egg on
105. Ward off
106. Hudson or Stanley Steamer
107. Romantic kind of boat
108. He defeated Carnera in 1934

DOWN

1. Enthusiasm
2. Biblical land of wealth
3. Crow
4. "Holiday ___," Crosby movie
5. Hindu religious retreat
6. Beau
7. Wind into rings
8. Assn.
9. Abounding
10. Like some maple growths
11. Flowering plants
12. Poi ingredient
13. Cheer
14. Flower cluster
15. Gershwin person
16. Grand tale
17. All there
21. Early English novel heroine
23. Greek physician
24. ___ Domingo
29. Robin of an early song
31. Swan genus
32. Mortise's partner
33. Where Aconcagua is
35. Hindu disciplines
36. Subjoin
37. Stretch of land
38. Profound people
39. ___ Mae Morse, jazz singer
40. Director David
41. Notable Bogart-Hepburn film
42. Division of ancient Babylonia
43. Antiseptic: Var.
46. ___ out (sank a putt)
48. Carny's lecture
50. Wanders
51. Heat, as milk
52. Hunting cry
53. Bitter cathartic
54. Piquant
56. River to the Caspian
58. TV's Jack and family
60. Slaughter avenue
61. Paintings by a Spanish muralist
62. William or Stephen
63. Atlanta's Omni, e.g.
64. Pears
65. Lends a hand
66. Place for Clementine's father
67. Be sullen
69. Singer Lehmann
70. Type of farm
73. Famous acting pair
75. Egyptian cross
77. East Indian cedar
78. Gulf on the Ionian Sea
79. Lenore, of stage note
80. Had an aversion to
81. Column order
83. Opened the throttle
85. Payment of a sort
87. On one's toes
88. Biblical food
89. Wagnerian forte
90. City in Belgium
91. Sand ridge
92. Sock
93. Heraldic border
94. Indonesian boat
95. Moderate
98. Federal mortgage gp.
99. Cause damage
100. ___ elbows (mingle)

222 Value Received By Dorothy Smitonick

Wherein nothing comes very cheaply.

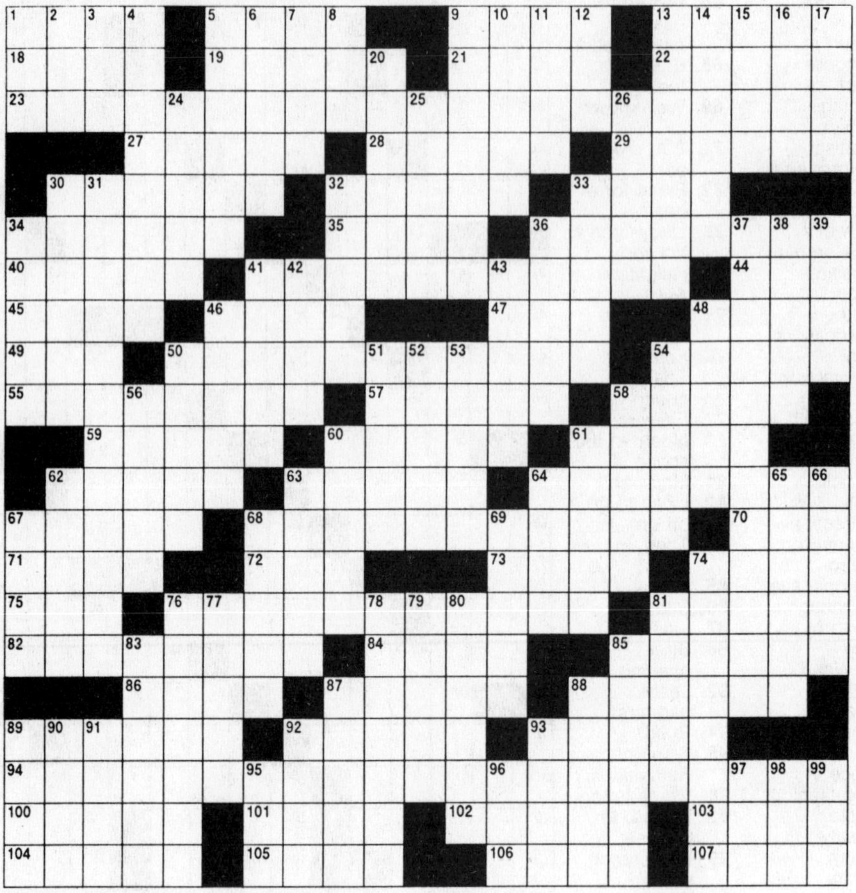

ACROSS

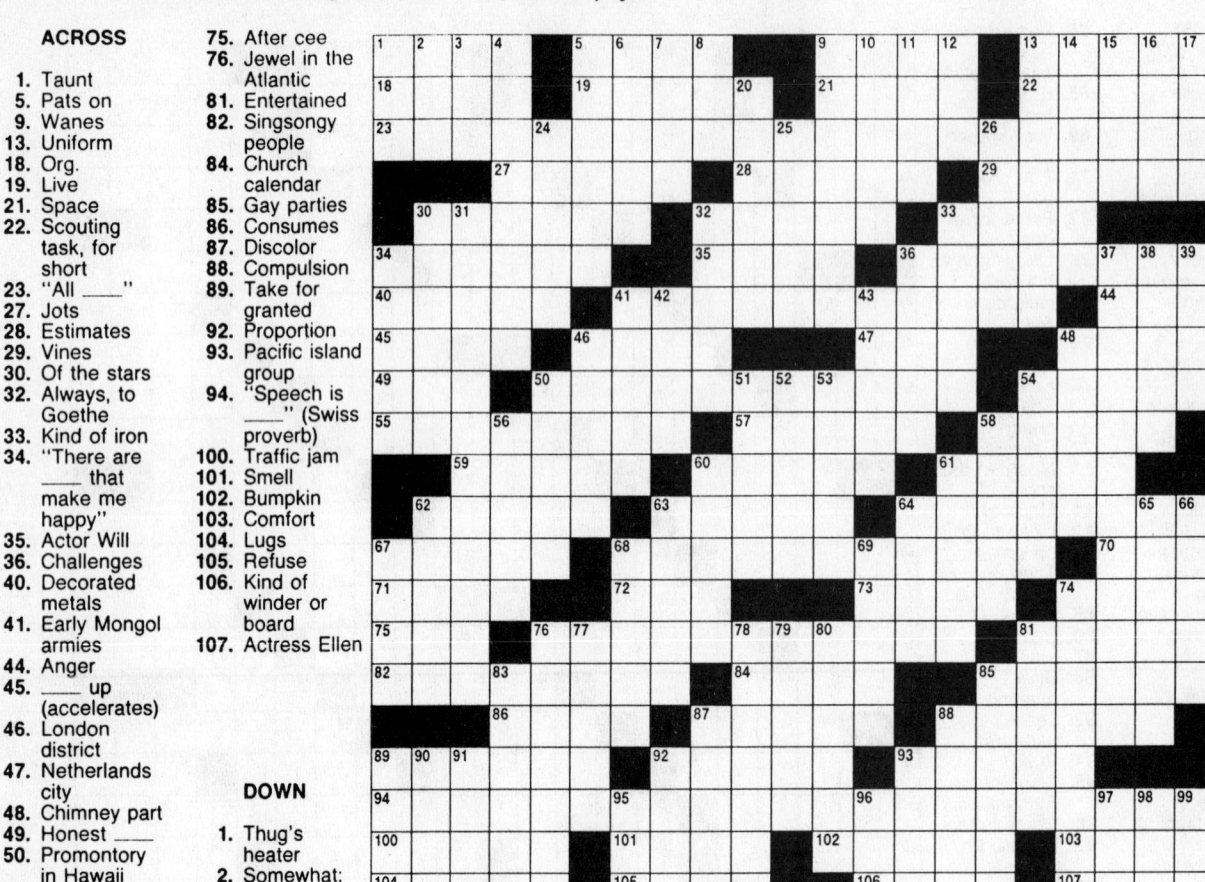

1. Taunt
5. Pats on
9. Wanes
13. Uniform
18. Org.
19. Live
21. Space
22. Scouting task, for short
23. "All ___"
27. Jots
28. Estimates
29. Vines
30. Of the stars
32. Always, to Goethe
33. Kind of iron
34. "There are ___ that make me happy"
35. Actor Will
36. Challenges
40. Decorated metals
41. Early Mongol armies
44. Anger
45. ___ up (accelerates)
46. London district
47. Netherlands city
48. Chimney part
49. Honest ___
50. Promontory in Hawaii
54. Mammoth and others
55. Chinese rulers of the early 1900's
57. Tests
58. Waits
59. Bundles
60. Boxes
61. ___ by verdict (court term)
62. Goes for treasure
63. Unbends
64. Intent on
67. Joins
68. Neighbor of 50 Across
70. French lady: Abbr.
71. "___ well that . . ."
72. "___ the greatest": Ali
73. Gives free ___ to
74. Playwright Elmer
75. After cee
76. Jewel in the Atlantic
81. Entertained
82. Singsongy people
84. Church calendar
85. Gay parties
86. Consumes
87. Discolor
88. Compulsion
89. Take for granted
92. Proportion
93. Pacific island group
94. "Speech is ___" (Swiss proverb)
100. Traffic jam
101. Smell
102. Bumpkin
103. Comfort
104. Lugs
105. Refuse
106. Kind of winder or board
107. Actress Ellen

DOWN

1. Thug's heater
2. Somewhat: Suffix
3. Daniel Beard's gp.
4. Gives a right to
5. River areas
6. Based around a central line
7. Partners of pieces
8. Fast plane
9. The Great ___ (early Atlantic queen)
10. Thorny bush
11. Good Queen ___
12. ___ Diego
13. Marcel Marceau, for one
14. Envoy
15. Sacred object
16. Russian peninsula
17. Objectives
20. Designated
24. Skirt parts
25. Lustrous fiber: Var.
26. A movie Charlie Chan
30. Micro-organism
31. Emperor Jones's downfall
32. Snowy domicile
33. Prepared apples
34. Ice-cream soda adjunct
36. Musical endings
37. Paul Revere and others
38. Sets right
39. Observes
41. Spurs
42. Electrical units
43. Cool one's ___
46. Fathers
48. Gets washed-out
50. Dimwits
51. Without face value
52. Southern accent
53. Severe
54. Beverage
56. England's ___ End
58. Indians' meat source
60. Indian thrush
61. John Adams's wife, familiarly
62. Actress Hayes
63. Rips
64. Russian city
65. Johnny Carson et al.
66. Acts
67. African ravine
68. Hudson River sights
69. Crime of Mrs. O'Leary's cow?
74. Closed again
76. Nail polishes
77. Measuring device
78. State-run numbers game
79. Exhaust
80. Foolishness
81. City in North Dakota
83. Hors d'___
85. Botch
87. Literary do
88. Treated
89. Staff person: Abbr.
90. ___-Japanese War
91. Venetian-blind part
92. ___ at anchor (lie)
93. Polynesian amulet
95. Earth
96. Goddess of dawn
97. Women's gp.
98. Suffix for Japan
99. Novel

223 Back to Nature By Jo Lundy

And the bounties provided therefrom.

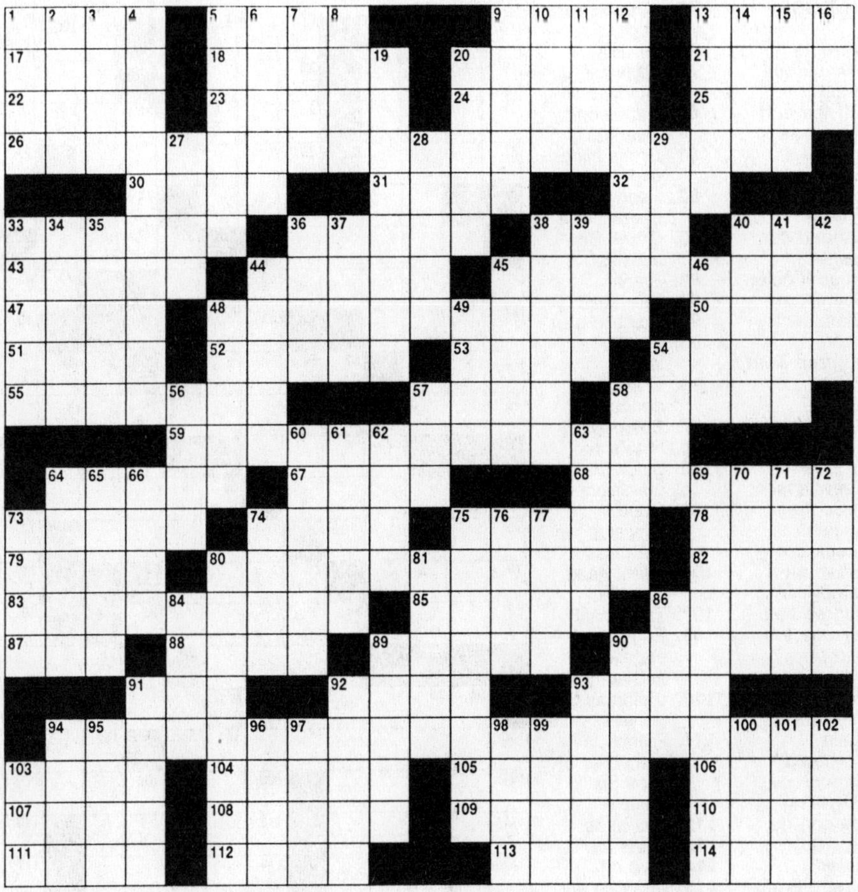

ACROSS

1. Arabic letter
5. Autocratic ruler
9. Orangs
13. Steamer
17. Petty taboo
18. Lubricated
20. Hunger for
21. Where drones hang out
22. Light shade
23. Of days past, poetically
24. It has locals
25. Give forth
26. "____ never pry": Browning
30. Scottish grandchildren
31. Cereal grasses
32. Ended, to poets
33. Small hackney coach
36. Cautions
38. Wander
40. Wind direction
43. Name on a W.W. II atomic plane
44. Prefix for grade or meter
45. Bittersweet plant
47. Soil: Prefix
48. It occasionally has four leaves
50. Change
51. College mil. group
52. Employed
53. College in N.C.
54. Fish features
55. Have a ____ (join the betting)
57. Ancient Mariner's sighting
58. Entire
59. Yielder of small fruit
64. Flying saucers
67. Canyon mouth
68. Hydrocarbons
73. Actress Davis
74. Ice mass
75. Insipid
78. Weaver's frame
79. Big bird
80. Things of beauty not planned
82. H.R.E. emperor
83. It looks too heavy to fly
85. Old coins of India
86. Follow
87. Forage vetch
88. Hops dryer
89. "This is only ____"
90. "Alice ____ live here anymore"
91. Make a mistake
92. Bowlike lines
93. Lancelot and Raleigh
94. "Sweeter also than ____": Psalm 19
103. Actress Cheryl
104. Caesar's veni
105. Book of the Apocrypha
106. Entertainer Adams
107. Sheltered
108. Katmandu's land
109. Room for free action
110. Nick Charles's wife
111. Dressed
112. Older relative, for short
113. Pay attention
114. Hard journey

DOWN

1. Turn over ____ leaf
2. Ness, for one
3. Concerning
4. Late afternoon bloomer
5. Fits ____
6. Mournful breaths
7. Plant of the lily family
8. California rockfish
9. English composer and family
10. Poker holding
11. Old reveler's cry
12. Deliver
13. Encourage
14. Sketch
15. It's often rara
16. Encountered
19. Exiled
20. Religious groups
27. South American wildcat
28. Lose control
29. Bambi, for one
33. Dreads
34. Steel-mill unit
35. Trunk artery
36. Milldam
37. Word before bellum
38. Insurrection
39. Microwave ____
40. Enlarge
41. Move like a crab
42. Inner selves
44. Confucius country
45. Madness, in France
46. Musical combo
48. Makes a buzzing sound
49. Faithful, in Scotland
54. Indian butter
56. Behold, to Ovid
57. Health spot
58. Writer H. G.
60. Agnes De Mille's field
61. Dwelling place
62. Book intro: Abbr.
63. Crowd sounds
64. Take exception
65. Articles
66. Much-used pencil
69. Abloom
70. Small bits
71. Away
72. Young salmon
73. Miss Daniels of the silents
74. Little lies
75. Herbs of the aster family
76. Barley beards
77. Tidy
80. Tiring
81. Gate fastening
84. Old knowledge
86. Backer of the redcoats
89. Russian co-op
90. Counted calories
91. Finished
92. Madison Avenue figure
93. Marsh bird
94. Corridor
95. Small theaters
96. Maple genus
97. California wine area
98. High, in Bonn
99. Woodwind
100. Reputation
101. Bog down
102. Pelican feature
103. Varnish ingredient

224 Antipodes By Kenneth Haxton

Going to extremes to designate certain people.

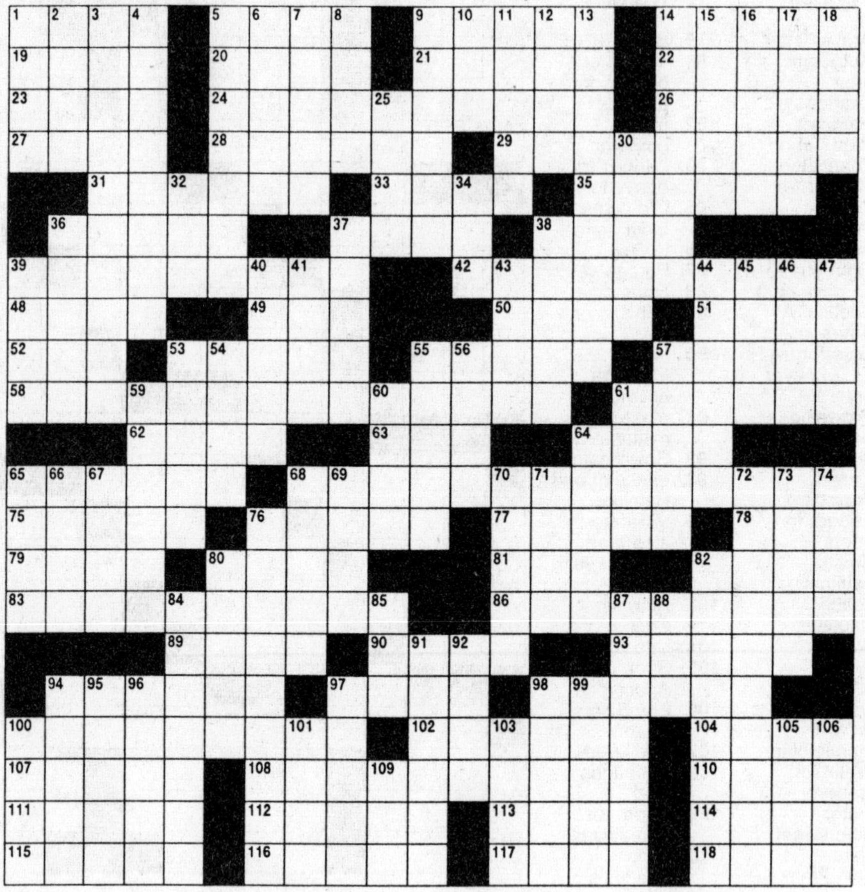

ACROSS

1. Verboten
5. Wimbledon great
9. Off the cuff
14. Foie-gras treats
19. Solar cult object
20. Three-handed card game
21. Neutral color
22. Dismal, in Glasgow
23. Pear
24. "Citizen Tom Paine" author?
26. Storm, in Lyon
27. ___ facto
28. Straw basket, in Scotland
29. Ancient Greek coin
31. Finish off a vampire
33. Degree field
35. Dosage form
36. Bad buy
37. Having wings
38. Roman 1106
39. Used davits again
42. "Patterns" author?
48. "Anything you can do, ___ do better"
49. Mouth: Prefix
50. Bauxite and others
51. Bacchanalian cry
52. Masterson
53. Indian transport
55. Celebes oxen
57. Loon's relative
58. "A Place in the Sun" actress?
61. Cavalry swords
62. Affectedness
63. Roll-call notation: Abbr.
64. Rail bird
65. De Medici great
68. "The Fire Next Time" author?
75. Stage device
76. Roof worker
77. "Deutschland uber ___"
78. Mr. Hill
79. Pedestal block
80. Napoleonic weapon
81. Gross minus expense
82. Teeny-bopper woe
83. Greek film actress?
86. Frantic
89. Like shad
90. Chinese port
93. Combo lead-in
94. Brazilian dances
97. Bus depot
98. Riga's sea
100. Black-magic practitioner
102. Quote "Invictus" for the class
104. Infant head covering
107. Tibetan city
108. English statesman and author?
110. Diplomas for lawyers
111. French composer of "Les Six" group
112. Sea birds
113. Mars: Prefix
114. Give off
115. Dislodge an ash
116. Pritikin and Scarsdale
117. "East of Eden" star
118. Cabinet V.I.P.'s

DOWN

1. Japanese sock
2. On
3. Silent-screen charmer?
4. Rare
5. Depth charges
6. Scandinavian toast
7. Part of a ship's bow
8. Airport abbrs.
9. Thracian city of simpletons
10. ___ Moines
11. Sings merrily
12. Stravinsky
13. Casts a spell on
14. TV mimic and impressionist?
15. Of the ear
16. Vestige
17. Pieces of ___
18. Appear
25. Money of Iran
30. Ossie or Skeeter
32. Taro product
34. Song syllable
36. Descendant of Judah
37. Good-bye, to Deneuve
38. Hess and Breckinridge
39. Barbecue offerings
40. Broadway awards
41. Love god
43. Othello was one
44. Like fennel or thyme
45. Eternally
46. Ear part
47. Dregs
53. Poetic region
54. Prefix for space
55. Bead material
56. Agent Eliot
57. Hart and Cooper
59. Attacked
60. Musical Auntie
61. Aching
64. Chokes with mud
65. Moslem judge
66. Glacial ridges
67. Kind of splitting
68. Carter
69. Title for Athena
70. Blues great
71. Not aweather
72. Witty English playwright?
73. ___ Domingo
74. Capt. Hook's ally
76. Passed across
80. "Or as ___ defensive to a house"
82. Magazine offerings
84. "Charlotte's Web" author?
85. Posed
87. Stacks
88. Suffix for differ
91. Quagmire
92. Begins, to Keats
94. Synagogue
95. Mites
96. Food of love, to Shakespeare
97. Diamond, for one
98. Mitterrand's lager
99. Confused
100. Swedish king
101. Indian title
103. Dressed
105. Caucasian language
106. W.W. II boats
109. N.Y. opera house

225 No Man's Land By Bert Kruse

Omissions that need to be allowed for.

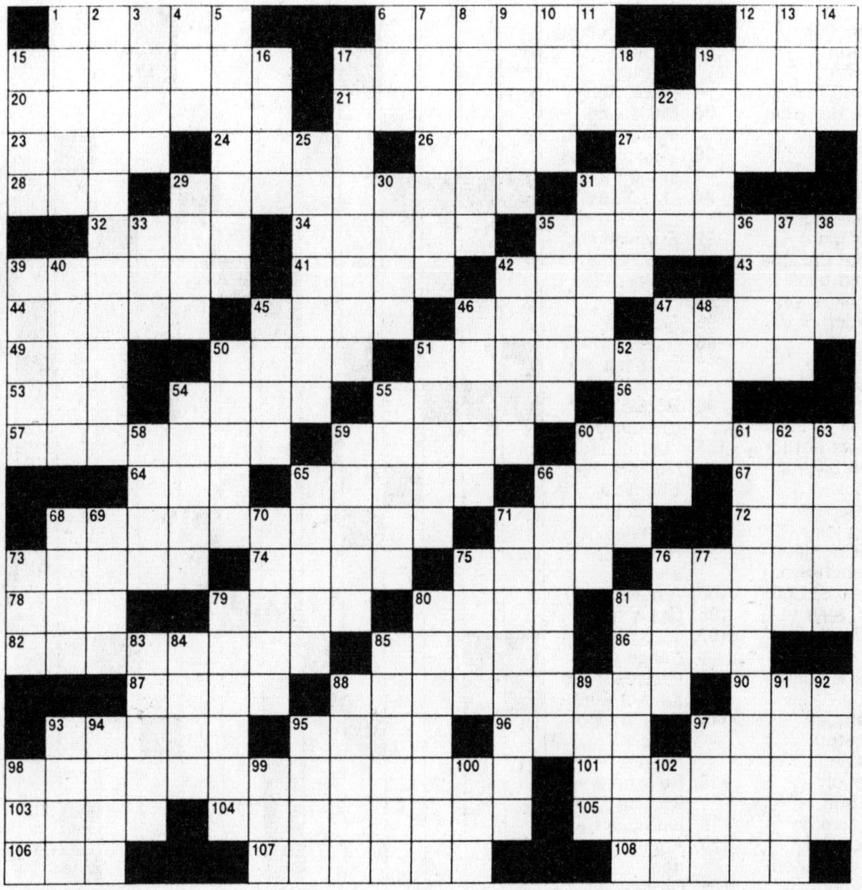

ACROSS

1. Shopping area for Xanthippe
6. Panoplies
12. Beat it
15. Pianos
17. Pilots
19. Ice unit
20. Flamboyance
21. Presidential title: Abbr.
23. Work units
24. Bridge hand
26. Cold European wind
27. Fragrant
28. Summer, to Sartre
29. Puccini opera
31. ___-dieu (religious bench)
32. Pro ___
34. Smear, in Scotland
35. Made a snappy comeback
39. Synagogue leaders
41. Karachi's province
42. Broadway musical
43. Possess, in Scotland
44. Farm measurements
45. Two-wheeler
46. Et ___
47. Egg-shaped
49. Fish dish
50. Wild plum
51. Factory bosses
53. Women's-lib goal
54. Intend
55. Partners of bounds
56. Hockey name
57. Makes beloved
59. Months, to an Indian
60. Sentimental guff
64. Beachwear
65. Deserves
66. Nutty
67. Three-toed sloths
68. Insect seemingly in church
71. Western elevation
72. Between Q and U
73. Service club
74. Aphrodite lover
75. Sidekicks
76. Was required
78. Doctors' org.
79. Low card
80. Dear, in Italy
81. More highly flavored
82. Mead or Mitchell
85. Board game
86. The old sod
87. The Greatest and Baba
88. Oscar-winning composer
90. Eminence
93. Lively dance
95. Hemingway
96. Memorizing method
97. Kind of bargain
98. Old Broadway comedy
101. Royal furs
103. Jockey's need
104. Asked without smiling
105. Office machines
106. Rah's companion
107. Judge
108. Family of movie-house note

DOWN

1. Separate
2. Bakery personage for a child
3. Fuegian Indians
4. Kind of room
5. Belonging to a Greek goddess
6. Coin of Macao
7. 19th-century French poet
8. Element discovered by the Curies
9. Major explosion
10. Past
11. ___ Lanka
12. Spoil
13. Lend a hand to
14. Ship-shaped clock
15. Graf ___
16. Circus barker
17. ___ a fool (gets silly)
18. Short drinks
19. Encourage
22. Media advertising award
25. Meeting
29. Elevator name
30. Sugar source
31. Kind of jury
33. Lincoln
35. Pours
36. "___ she blows!"
37. Beanery come-on
38. Sandra or Ruby
39. Street performance
40. Squirrel fare
42. Applauds
45. "Gil ___"
46. Alda and King
47. Fairy-tale frights
48. Actress Miles
50. Eastern overnight stop
51. Laborers
52. Main artery
54. Tyler Moore and Martin
55. Lemur
58. Israeli name
59. Chummy, in Britain
60. Russian agency
61. Famous English theologian
62. French shopper's need
63. El ___, Guatemalan town
65. Plume source
66. David ___ of theater note
68. Egyptian cotton
69. Lion's voice
70. Nostrils
71. Like heretics at the Inquisition
73. Getaway
75. Henry VIII's sixth
76. Spy name
77. "___ my brother's keeper?"
79. Photographer's aid
80. Absurd reports
81. Washington was one
83. Greek physician
84. Drug plant
85. Give testimony
88. Laughs
89. Newspaper bit
91. Suggestive looks
92. Become history
93. Indian butter
94. Song
95. Loo cards
97. Heap
98. Attempt
99. Teachers' org.
100. French possessive
102. "O sole ___"

226 Ship Ahoy! By Ruth Smith

Spotting some vessels that ply or plied the deep seas.

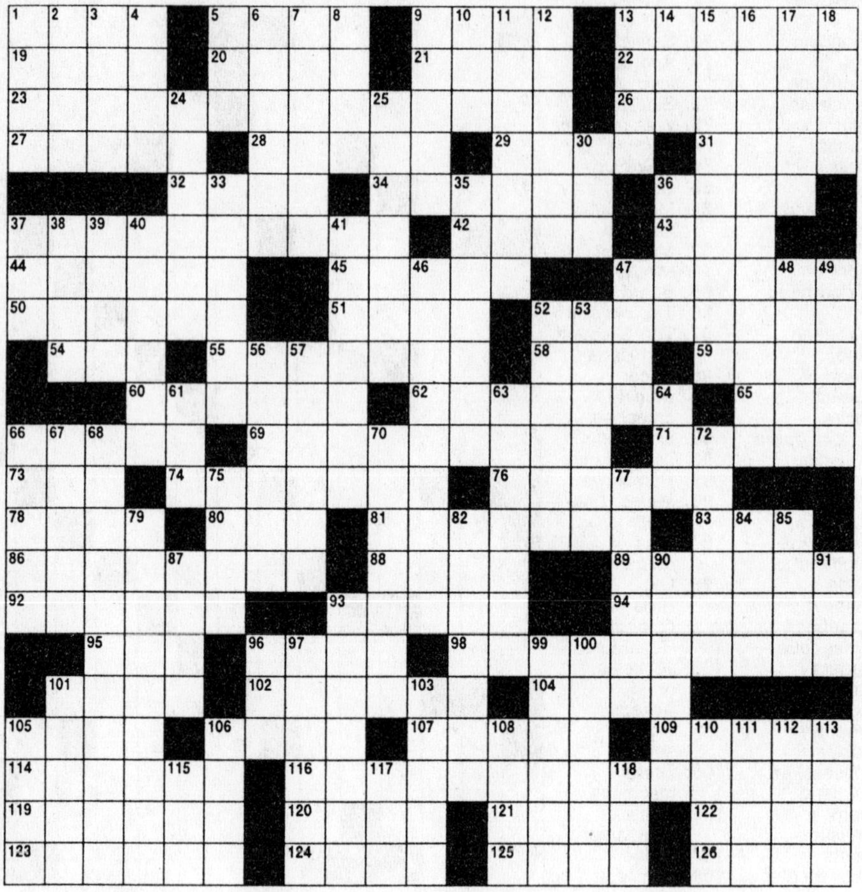

ACROSS

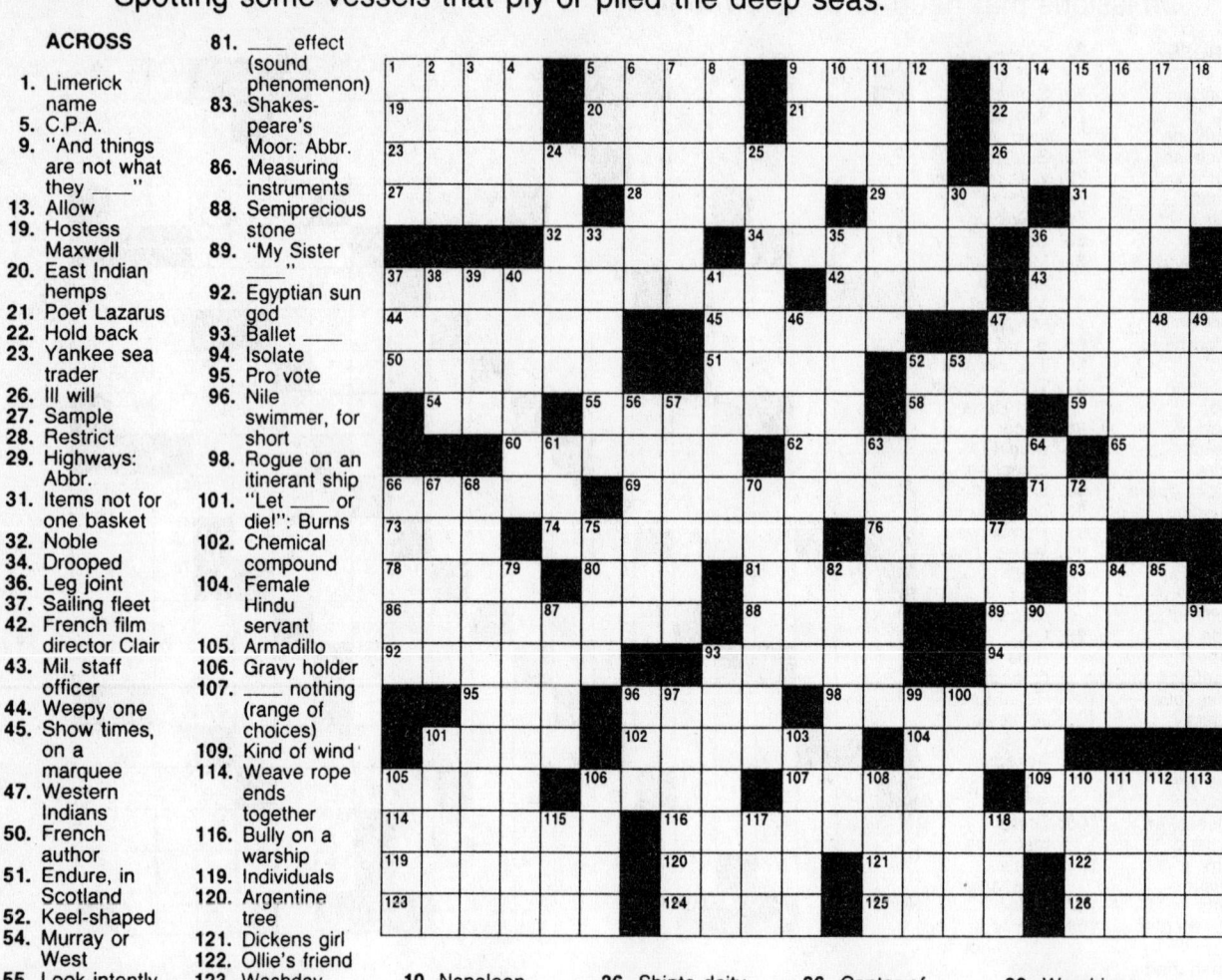

1. Limerick name
5. C.P.A.
9. "And things are not what they ___"
13. Allow
19. Hostess Maxwell
20. East Indian hemps
21. Poet Lazarus
22. Hold back
23. Yankee sea trader
26. Ill will
27. Sample
28. Restrict
29. Highways: Abbr.
31. Items not for one basket
32. Noble
34. Drooped
36. Leg joint
37. Sailing fleet
42. French film director Clair
43. Mil. staff officer
44. Weepy one
45. Show times, on a marquee
47. Western Indians
50. French author
51. Endure, in Scotland
52. Keel-shaped
54. Murray or West
55. Look intently
58. British mil. school
59. It's often rapid: Abbr.
60. Tropical food staple
62. Closes tightly again
65. Quarter pints: Abbr.
66. Noncoms
69. Talk on a Southern sailboat
71. George ___, English dramatist
73. Greek letter
74. Of a Peruvian culture
76. Asian parade ground
78. Storage-battery part
80. Sun god
81. ___ effect (sound phenomenon)
83. Shakespeare's Moor: Abbr.
86. Measuring instruments
88. Semiprecious stone
89. "My Sister ___"
92. Egyptian sun god
93. Ballet ___
94. Isolate
95. Pro vote
96. Nile swimmer, for short
98. Rogue on an itinerant ship
101. "Let ___ or die!": Burns
102. Chemical compound
104. Female Hindu servant
105. Armadillo
106. Gravy holder
107. ___ nothing (range of choices)
109. Kind of wind
114. Weave rope ends together
116. Bully on a warship
119. Individuals
120. Argentine tree
121. Dickens girl
122. Ollie's friend
123. Washday appliances
124. Toboggan
125. ___ bien
126. German article

DOWN

1. Discourse: Abbr.
2. Miss Raines
3. "No exchange or refunds"
4. Engrossed
5. "The Hairy ___"
6. One uttering oaths
7. Número uno in Havana
8. Dialect of Ghana
9. Dividing walls
10. Napoleon was one: Abbr.
11. Comes into view
12. Weasellike animal
13. Anglo-Saxon letters
14. School org.
15. Bride's helper
16. Certain harbor fee
17. Feudal vassal
18. At loose ___
24. Kind of corn or mint
25. Serve as a role model
30. Netherlands commune
33. Way out
35. Host, at times
36. Shinto deity
37. Draft agency
38. Soil
39. Work, in Spain
40. Glued on, as a pupa
41. Like closed drapes
46. Pendant shapes
47. Spoken
48. In any way
49. Be aware of
52. Kind of embroidery
53. Charlotte ___
56. Liz or Deems
57. Makes use of
61. Balaam's animal
63. Bit of needlework
64. Evian or Bath
66. Center of Islam
67. Medium for James Watt
68. Attack by a trireme
70. "Irma ___"
72. Of an organic compound
75. Sailing
77. Trickles, in England
79. Hard baseball hit
82. Pale colors
84. Brim, in Italy
85. Pilot's place
87. Indonesian boat
90. Latin words for 3 Down
91. Fiber knot
93. Of a platform
96. ___-Magnon
97. Does a double take
99. Worshiper
100. Carrara diggings
101. One of the crusts
103. Water nymph
105. Evaluated: Abbr.
106. Good queen
108. Easter ends it
110. Shine's partner
111. Italian wine city
112. College official
113. Ocean bird
115. Wax: Prefix
117. Rubber tree
118. Literary initials

227 Q. and A. By Emory Cain

Wherein the Q. part is provided.

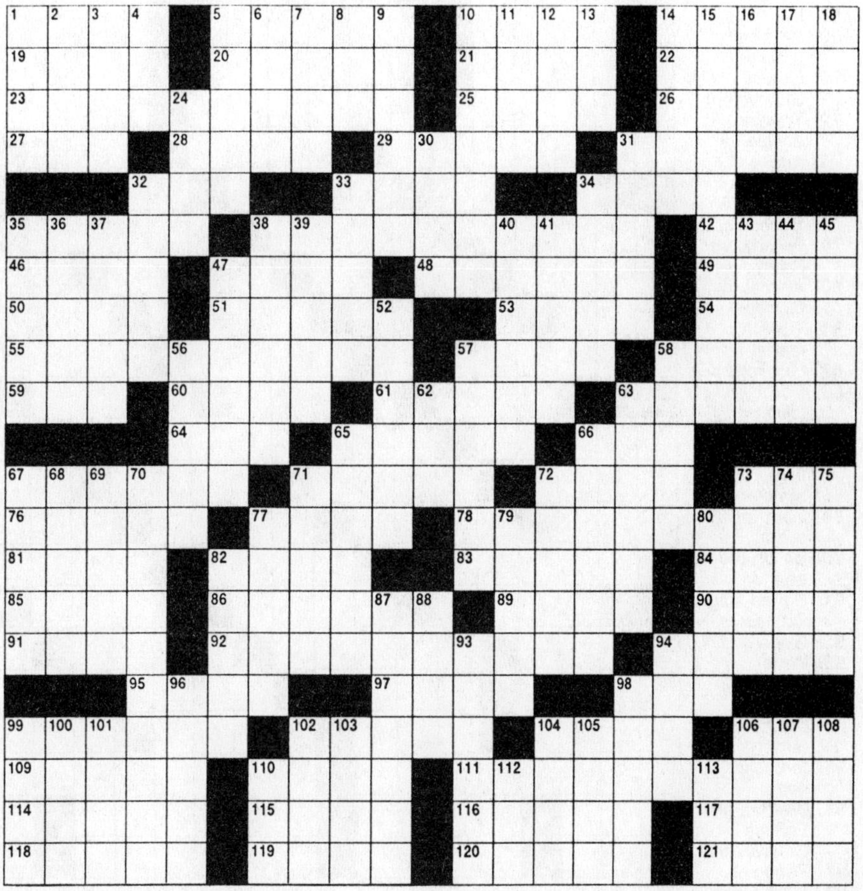

ACROSS

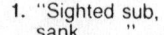

1. "Sighted sub, sank ___"
5. Daunted
10. Oft-seen sign
14. Moslem rulers
19. Gem
20. Pass over
21. Ligurian Sea feeder
22. Realtor's sign
23. Underachiever?
25. On one's ___ (recovered)
26. ___ Vista, Mexican War site
27. Coin of Norway
28. "To ___, a bone . . ."
29. Surmise
31. General played by George C. Scott
32. W.W. II org.
33. Repute
34. Kind of salts or towel
35. Quick-witted
38. Slum leveler?
42. Infatuation, to a teener
46. Prefix for pathy
47. Lovely lady
48. Drums
49. Went ___ (checked)
50. Olive genus
51. African antelope
53. Seldom seen
54. English school
55. Unbookish one?
57. Sea birds
58. View
59. Tool
60. English composer
61. Packing a rod
63. Essential
64. British letter
65. Kind of boat or limit
66. Big or Gentle
67. Went around
71. Luster
72. ___ good example
73. Jeff Davis' realm
76. Neglects
77. Kind of start or lettuce
78. Edam?
81. Miss Gam
82. Max or Buddy
83. Mamba or krait
84. Jason's craft
85. Winged pest
86. Dillon portrayer
89. Marina structure
90. Has-___
91. The old days
92. Football jersey?
94. Billiard shot
95. Manx and Persians
97. Like ___ of bricks
98. Toper
99. Meager
102. Body trunk
104. Connery
106. U.S. humorist
109. Mideast dances
110. Bottle
111. Well-fed?
114. "Have ___ journey!"
115. Anent
116. Remove
117. At ease
118. Lash marks
119. Nuisance
120. Up the ___ (in stir)
121. Hammer part

DOWN

1. London district
2. On ___ with
3. Tom or cob, e.g.
4. Sprite
5. Phobias
6. Inter ___
7. Vitality
8. Dutch commune
9. Scoff
10. Flavoring for rice
11. Family ___
12. Unique thing
13. Poker winning
14. In the box
15. Tongue?
16. "___ a Song Go . . ."
17. Adriatic feeder
18. Ollie's partner
24. Pant
30. Socialites, in England
31. Do a grammar job
32. Mountain nymph
33. Sheeplike
34. Sudsy quaffs
35. Plant pore
36. Geometric curve
37. Coeur d'___
38. Florida city
39. Turkish decree
40. Spoiled
41. It's often X, in TV ads
43. Swelled 13 Down
44. Actor Lewis
45. Sharpened
47. Squinted
52. Hung in folds
56. Levels
57. Corrects a text
58. French assembly
62. Female ruff
63. ___ regions (Hades)
65. Unselfish one
66. Nautical rope
67. Bess's man
68. Acid type
69. Shankar's instrument
70. Air Force One?
71. "___ evil"
72. Case or well
73. Largest asteroid
74. Herbs
75. Make amends
77. Nags
79. Loosen
80. Moroccan capital
82. Sew
87. Filmdom hopeful
88. Speedy jets
93. Vaudeville hack
94. Prefix with plane
96. Onagers
98. Sword
99. G. B. or Artie
100. Propound
101. Soviet sea
102. Antler part
103. Rows
104. Eastern European
105. Part of a two-word threat
106. Right-hand man
107. Proof notation
108. Where it all started
110. Big shot
112. Swiss canton
113. Quick swim

228 Out On a Limb By Tap Osborn

Or at least somewhere in the arboretum.

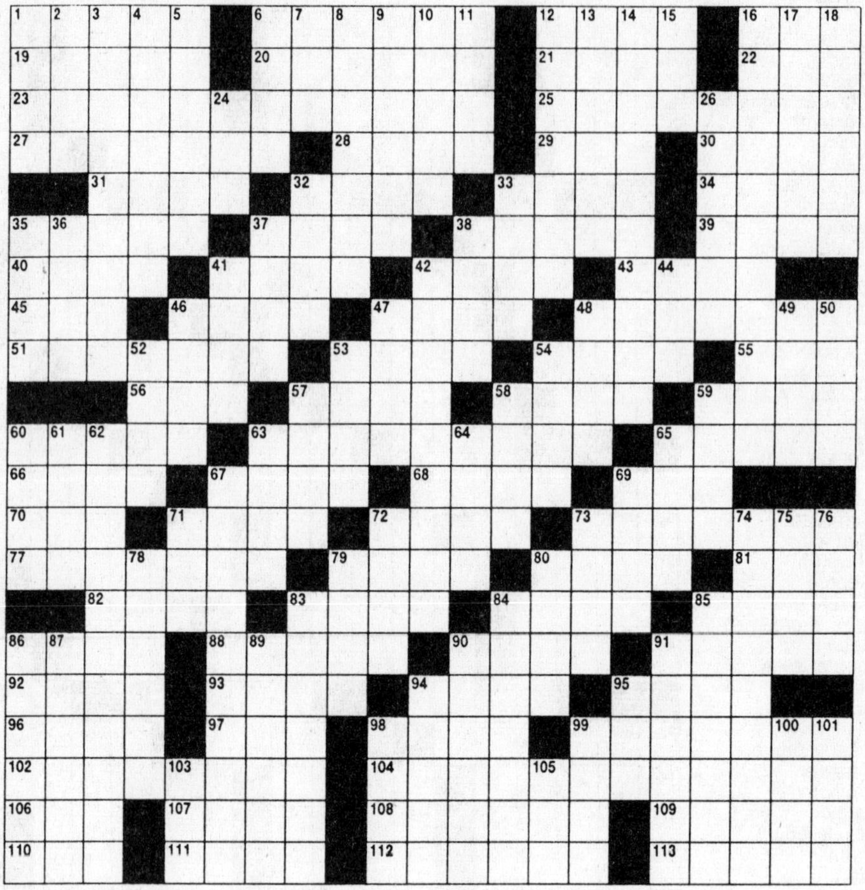

ACROSS

1. Salmon varieties
6. One with a big I.Q.
12. It has a thin waist
16. Bad ___, Germany
19. Command at sea
20. Chalk chaser
21. Ionian Sea gulf
22. Iacocca
23. Venetian school painter
25. Singer from Peru
27. From head to toe
28. Derby entry
29. Chaney
30. Monthly payout
31. It makes arrows lethal
32. Evergreens
33. Clayey soil
34. Con ___
35. Word in the 4-H motto
37. Auctioneer's word
38. Nairobi's locale
39. Antiquing compound
40. They're out on passes often
41. Make out
42. Cassowary or skua
43. Armbone
45. Ending for consul
46. Smelly
47. Place
48. Narcissistic one
51. Tackles, guards, etc.
53. Simon's follower
54. Spare-tire changer, in a way
55. Additionally
56. Provoke
57. Of the congregation
58. Money holder
59. Seafood-platter item
60. College protest
63. Salemite of fame
65. Actress Mansfield
66. Wolfish greeting
67. Tip off
68. Flu siege
69. Visibility blocker
70. Quaff
71. Benevolent
72. Training device for rats
73. Toronto athlete
77. Second ___
79. Entertainer Danny
80. Animal for Goldilocks
81. Turkish leader
82. Guy-rope
83. Dorothy or Lillian
84. Ladder unit
85. Atlantic food fish
86. Male ant
88. Spot for a glider
90. Be on the agenda
91. Sound-stage fixtures
92. Goes bad
93. Writer Dinesen
94. Certain stabber's target
95. In-basket item
96. Word in an Erskine Caldwell title
97. Penpoint
98. 1932 Greta portrayal
99. Show great joy
102. Henry Ward and family
104. Leslie Howard role
106. Rav or div ending
107. Melodic piece
108. Blanche DuBois's sister
109. "I ___ Say No"
110. Gem wts.
111. Grid coach Fielding
112. Starts
113. Bordoni or Castle

DOWN

1. Matador's cloak
2. Racetrack
3. Star of "Barney Miller"
4. Marie and Donny
5. Barrel pieces
6. Occult one
7. Circle part
8. Antidote
9. On land
10. Diamond and Hamilton
11. Gait
12. ___ Flowers of TV
13. Place for weekend drill
14. One of a comic duo
15. "N'est-ce ___?"
16. Lewis's preacher
17. Stinker
18. Part of a military front
24. Churchill letter
26. Suave
32. Competitor of G.M.
33. Signifying little
35. Grow scar tissue
36. Con
37. Achieve
38. Bird or toy
41. Show one's muscles
42. Former Indiana Senator
44. Ending for drop or book
46. Portentous thing
47. Fashion purchase
48. Stack
49. Of the dawn
50. Queen's garment
52. Kind of eye
53. Bishop's poor relative
54. Force
57. Chef's cooking need
58. Kind of blue
59. Bird holder
60. Pahlevi, for one
61. Hercules's captive
62. Actress Helen, or what this puzzle has
63. "___ it all!"
64. Soft mud
65. Bon follower
67. Actor-playwright Sir Arthur ___
69. Mark for attention
71. Relatives
72. Do a potato chore
73. South ___
74. Old-time comic actor
75. Fit of shivering
76. Chatters
78. Interstellar space measure
79. Squawk
80. Hokum
83. Goes for the brass ring
84. Detroit headaches
85. Corresponding
86. Arafat's tongue
87. Harmful
89. Egyptian god
90. ___ Lao
91. Noted Florentine
94. Do stitching
95. Gullet
98. Large-scale
99. Actor Robert
100. Neighbor of Ky.
101. Villa d'___
103. What money ain't
105. Yalie

229 Numero Uno By Robert Malinow

Concerning some people who made it all the way.

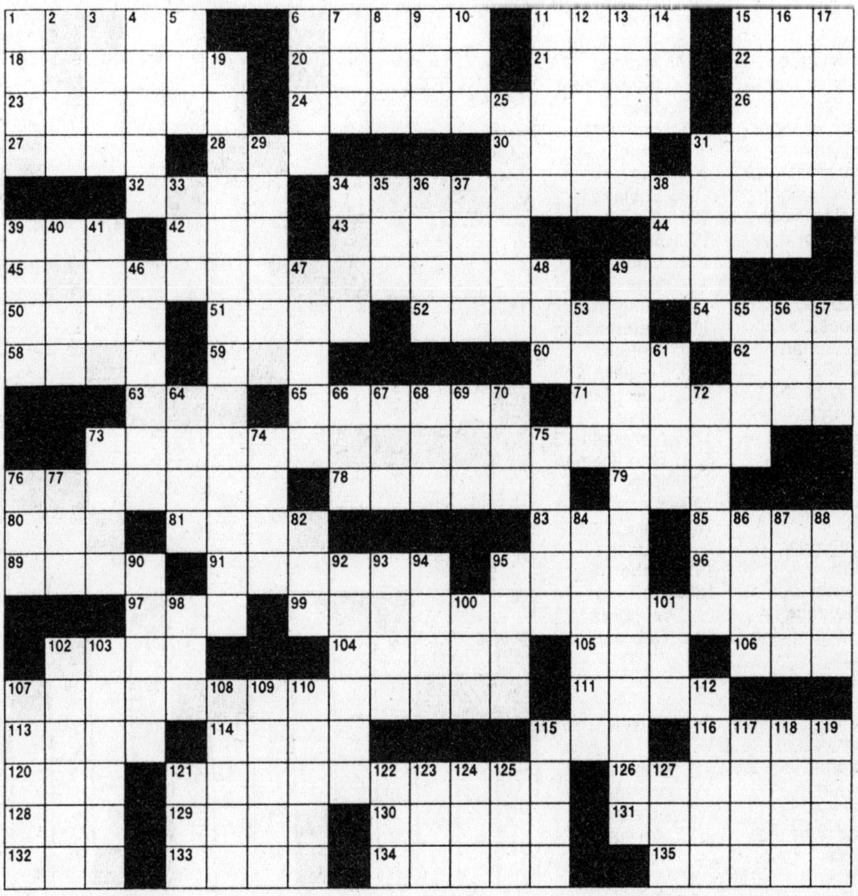

ACROSS

1. Nut native to the U.S.
6. Electron tube
11. Kind of beer
15. Possessive
18. Interference of a sort
20. Fatuous
21. Persian Gulf land
22. ____-jongg
23. Luanda's country
24. First nonelected President
26. Mideast initials
27. Asian weight
28. Rels. of 45's
30. One-armed bandit locale
31. "Iliad," e.g.
32. Have a bath
34. Old Rough and Ready President
39. Germ cells
42. Nose grower?
43. Admit
44. Deli order
45. Red Fox President
49. Former Fidel aide
50. Before dote or macassar
51. Part of a bird's bill
52. Financier who served three Presidents
54. Ostrich's kin
58. Great Barrier, for one
59. Big Ten campus
60. An ai has 12
62. Stripe
63. U.N. agency
65. Opera singers
71. Tallinn is its capital
73. President turned Chief Justice
76. "____ Durward," Scott novel
78. Nebraska Indian
79. It's found on the face, at times
80. Neighbor of Mex.
81. Duchin
83. Mason, for one
85. Buck character
89. Wine: Prefix
91. Sells for
95. Tiny bit
96. Julie Christie portrayal
97. All-purpose truck, for short
99. Back to Normalcy President
102. Mr. ____, Lorre role
104. Muralist Rivera
105. Time period
106. Bashful
107. The New Freedom President
111. Certain degrees
113. Actor Ray
114. An apple has one
115. Sort of: Suffix
116. Once, once
120. Former Dodger Hodges
121. First dark-horse President
126. Newscast feature
128. Nautical dir.
129. Word of regret
130. Sine, for one
131. President who once led a union
132. Thing, in law
133. Type of ad
134. Actor John
135. About

DOWN

1. H.S. junior's exam
2. Sicilian landmark
3. Home, to some birds
4. Bikini, e.g.
5. Nothing
6. Archaeologists' sites
7. Suffix for mar or can
8. Thole adjunct
9. Genetic initials
10. Lamprey
11. Certain con
12. Socratic ____
13. Sibyl's prop
14. Type of run
15. African antelope
16. Soap ingredient
17. Blacksmith, at times
19. Business-minded President
25. Top follower
29. Irritates
31. First V.P. to move up
33. Baba
34. Grey of the purple sage
35. Religious wear
36. Early weapon
37. Hour, in Spain
38. Word before tray or can
39. Bradley
40. Wind indicator
41. Comic Johnson
46. Lunch, to Clive
47. Island off Venezuela
48. Hardware item
49. The Gentleman Boss President
53. Campus figure
55. It is often helpful
56. Biblical judge
57. Initials on a police blotter
61. Frat social
64. Der ____
66. Elec. unit
67. ____ Na Na
68. Barnyard animal
69. Confess, with "up"
70. Thus, to Burns
72. "Shall flow with tears ____": Blake
73. Remove from
74. ____-China
75. Tickle the memory again
76. "____ Vadis?"
77. Purpose
82. Evergreen
84. Where to find an agora
86. Secular
87. River of Florence
88. Hungarian premier Imre ____
90. Best
92. Miss Thompson et al.
93. Seed cover
94. ____ bien
95. Party to
98. Crag
100. Kind of trip
101. Cheer
102. Illinois city
103. Scads
107. Concern at 30 Across
108. City near Silver Springs
109. Termagant, for one
110. Seize control
112. Napoleon III's Waterloo
115. Image
117. Storm
118. The Man of baseball
119. Sheik of Araby's digs
121. Part of a vise
122. Crab-eating monkey
123. ____ de deux
124. Hall of Fame name
125. Roman 52
127. Kind of soup

230 Point of Disorder By Sidney Robbins

As presented in a quatrain of misfortune.

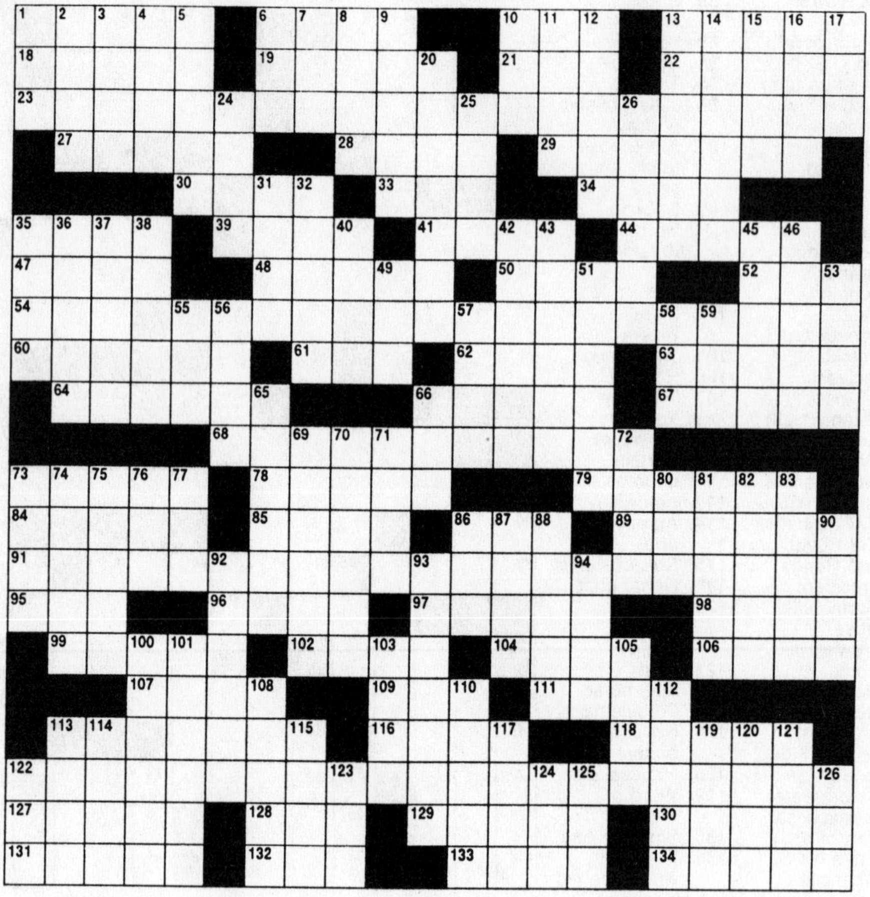

ACROSS

1. Nebs
6. Mortgage
10. Constrictor
13. Slopes
18. Lox wrapper
19. Egyptian measure
21. Swiss sight
22. Ratite birds
23. Start of a four-line verse
27. Voodoo land
28. Mozart's "___ fan tutti"
29. God of the earth's waters
30. Difficulty
33. British version of inc.
34. Arthurian lady
35. Barn's locale
39. Pub drinks
41. Scandinavian rugs
44. Not mounted
47. Beverly Sills forte
48. Marsh bird
50. Capone feature
52. Regret
54. Line 2 of the verse
60. Ancient celibate
61. Also
62. Ohio city
63. Remove fastenings
64. Montana's capital
66. Dozed
67. Take to a different jury
68. Member of a church sect
73. Disgrace
78. Tangle
79. Repeat an oath
84. Knoblike
85. Words of proportion
86. Lion or cougar
89. Sound system
91. Line 3 of the verse
95. Word before cent
96. Turn down
97. Mideast trouble spot
98. Clamp
99. Projecting shelf
102. Old dirk
104. Soviet city
106. Miss Kett
107. Merit
109. One ___ time
111. Stuffy person
113. Determined
116. Mature
118. Regions
122. End of the verse
127. National bird
128. Grid lineman
129. Pyle
130. Stone: Prefix
131. Take the rudder
132. Robert E.
133. Decimal numbers
134. Rub out

DOWN

1. Commercial degree
2. Apiece
3. Mexican water
4. Military cap
5. Slovens
6. Resin
7. N.Y.C. subway line
8. Instruction: Abbr.
9. Rose-scented liquid
10. Obstruction
11. Margarine
12. Swiftly
13. Stay
14. Alters
15. Bill of fare
16. Opposites of calls
17. Draft org.
20. Scatter
24. A Columbus ship
25. Well-ordered
26. Professor's goal
31. Too
32. Insect joints
35. ___ the music
36. Break out in ___ (be allergic)
37. Final wash
38. Actress Normand
40. Apply one's John Hancock
42. More pale
43. Shrimp dish
45. Ape Mount St. Helens
46. Piano adjuster
49. Advanced degree
51. Vishnu incarnation
53. Irritable
55. Opposite of WSW
56. Landlord's due
57. Fitzgerald
58. Sable or ermine
59. After 12:59
65. Poison gas
66. Archway city: Abbr.
69. Insertions
70. Ours is indivisible
71. Hard stuff
72. Snug home
73. Cut hair
74. Ritz or Waldorf
75. Worship
76. Chinese hero
77. Antlered animal
80. Noshed
81. Spirited energy
82. Sphere of activity
83. Tiniest
86. Billiard aid
87. Jason's vessel
88. Jerk
90. Music halls
92. Act excessively
93. Former
94. State
100. Untrimmed paper
101. Diving-board maneuver
103. Peer
105. Munchausen, for one
108. Stair post
110. Nautical direction
112. Search blindly
113. Become senile: Var.
114. "Bravo!"
115. Have a repast
117. Serf of old
119. Pitcher
120. Theatrical org.
121. Weights of India
122. Affirmative vote
123. Soft drink
124. Kind of pan or ear
125. ___ Moines
126. Fictitious John

231 Paging Bruce Catton By Reginald Johnson

Or any Civil War expert who might help a solver.

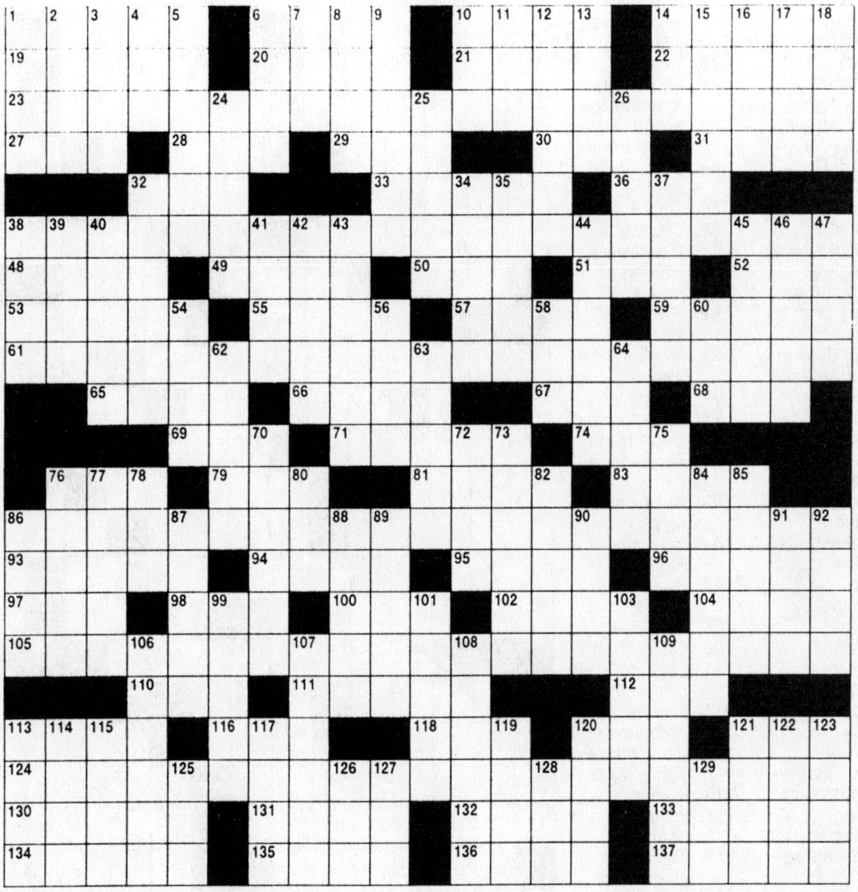

ACROSS

1. Couples
6. Soapy leavings
10. Historic island
14. Parisian school
19. Property of value
20. Court order
21. Like Cassius's look
22. Wherewithal
23. April 12, 1861
27. Shoe width
28. One of a trio
29. Port of Morocco
30. N.Y. time
31. Jab
32. Perform
33. Polishes, literarily
36. Scottish explorer
38. July 21, 1861
48. "It ___ necessarily so"
49. Alone, as an actress
50. Literary monogram
51. Before theta
52. Chemical ending
53. ___ fatuus (marsh light)
55. Edible root
57. French political unit
59. Fiber plant
61. Sept. 4, 1862
65. Close a letter
66. ___ up (prepared to drive)
67. Harry's successor
68. Part of Gt. Brit.
69. Southeast Asian
71. Worthless stuff
74. Opposite of WNW
76. TV initials in Toronto
79. White stuff in Scotland
81. Hor. lines on a map
83. "Woe is me"
86. July 1-3, 1863
93. Bank holdup
94. North Pacific island
95. Vicinity
96. Queer
97. Have
98. Muscular contraction
100. Winter home expense: Abbr.
102. Times after sunset, to poets
104. Mother of Apollo
105. March, 1864
110. Grampus
111. Drop ___ to (correspond)
112. ___ adjudicata
113. Cruising
116. Rhone feeder
118. Reply to a ques.
120. Oriental or shag
121. Mine production
124. April 9, 1865
130. Lé Carre characters
131. Mild oath
132. Install overhead covering
133. Ankle bones
134. Takes care of
135. Utah's flower
136. Advantage
137. British naval vessel

DOWN

1. Head
2. Tennis name
3. Words of under-standing
4. Whistle blower: Abbr.
5. It's often in time
6. Emulate a seal
7. Coffee vessel
8. Uses a shovel
9. Companion of lost and strayed
10. Mischievous one
11. The Lip of baseball
12. Most empty
13. Picnic guests
14. Large bird
15. Force
16. Aware of
17. Onion's cousin
18. Brontë's Jane
24. Rosters
25. Consumer advocate
26. Swagger
32. Clothing
34. Loafed
35. Sample
37. Wing-shaped
38. "Hurry up and ___"
39. Up in the air
40. Two wives of Henry VIII
41. Partners of pans
42. Braid
43. Merited
44. Move (oneself)
45. Kind of numeral
46. Manipulating
47. Want
54. County ___
56. "___ There"
58. Pierre's friend
60. Malt drink
62. Explosion
63. Hitler
64. Repeat aloud
70. Whole
72. Long narrative
73. Hi-fi component
75. Otherwise
76. Grinds, in a way
77. Existing
78. TV network
80. Hgt.
82. Like a precipice
84. White poplars
85. More certain
86. Quaker pronoun
87. Petal perfume
88. Green Mountain Allen
89. Exceed
90. Sharp taste
91. "Rio ___"
92. Earth study, for short
99. Of an Andes empire
101. Influence corruptly
103. Antitoxin
106. Made oneself heard
107. Riding academy
108. Card combination
109. Nullify
113. Right-hand man: Abbr.
114. Movie extra, for short
115. Leprechaun land
117. Roman date
119. Hurried
120. Part
121. Other, in Toledo
122. Bonheur
123. Way out
125. Letter
126. Musical kind of time
127. Fuss
128. Guinea
129. Restaurant bill

232 Field Trip By Dorothea Shipp

Some of the smaller bits of wildlife around.

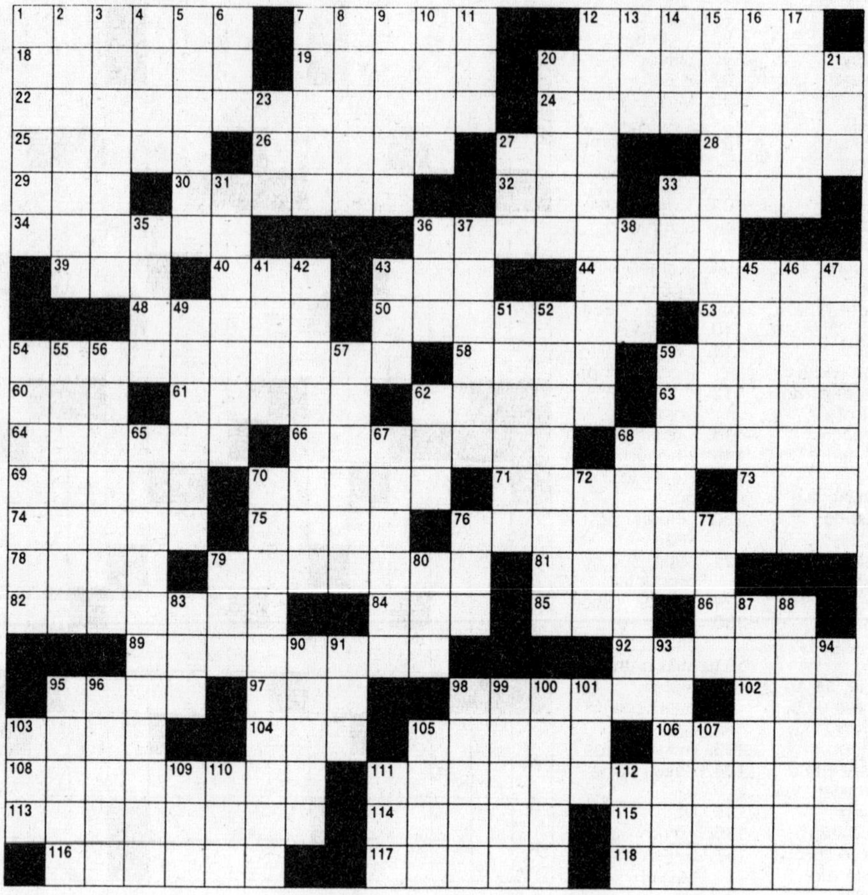

ACROSS

1. Houston team
7. Excoriates
12. In order to
18. Orange oil
19. Prefix for U.S.S.R.
20. Reflected
22. Web-spinning primate?
24. North African
25. Cruising
26. Resentment
27. Army unit: Abbr.
28. Roundworm
29. Vietnamese New Year
30. Spread hay
32. Coin of Sweden
33. Shocking fish
34. Floors of a maison
36. Bank offering
39. Winter fall, to Mac
40. Christie's Indians
43. Harem accommodation
44. As ___ a daisy
48. Havana's ___ Castle
50. Marsh plant
53. Taboo
54. Features of some figures
58. March and Linden
59. ___ great store by (distrust)
60. Corse or Martinique
61. Place to find an élève
62. Small yard of old
63. Quivery poplar
64. Andes and Rockies
66. Purify
68. Change
69. German president Friedrich
70. Christmas decoration
71. Author of "The Green Hat"
73. Parts of dols.
74. Forsyte account and others
75. "Step ___!"
76. Place for selling Fido's pests?
78. Desert lizards
79. Old Roman magistrates
81. Singer Della
82. Body tremors
84. Butterfly catcher
85. Depot: Abbr.
86. Cruces or Palmas
89. Having no future
92. Robert or Zachary
95. Manna from heaven
97. Dandy
98. Prop for Bugs Bunny
102. Royal-flush card
103. Al of comic strips
104. Law, to Pierre
105. Puzo or Lanza
106. Red dye
108. Clergyman
111. Clothing for a coward?
113. Strains' companions
114. Do a house agent's job
115. Manor
116. Emulates a peacock
117. Facing a glacial side
118. Conked

DOWN

1. Having a handle
2. Musical groups
3. Isolde's love
4. Cycled
5. Acid salt
6. ___ Roger de Coverley
7. Palm leaf
8. Fencing maneuver
9. Questioned
10. North Sea feeder
11. Sauce in Chinatown
12. Charm-bracelet addition?
13. Assn.
14. Prefix for foil or pan
15. Not-so-cozy home?
16. Shakespearean prankster
17. Harness groupings
20. French city official
21. Nucleic acid initials
23. Alice's Hatter
27. On the ___ (punctual)
31. Leaves the straight and narrow path
33. Suffix for Malt or Chin
35. Large umbrella
36. Actress Lupino
37. Patriot Hale
38. ___ king of folklore
41. Blore or Portman
42. Part of a missile
43. Mil. school
45. Pain easer
46. One of the Dionne quints
47. "Least said is ___ mended"
49. Little hooters
51. Of a part of the foot
52. Tailors, at times
54. Trusses firmly
55. Its capital is Montgomery
56. Its capital is Dakar
57. "___ like it is"
59. Health-spa features
62. Full of joie de vivre
65. Sweet cocktail
67. Singer John et al.
68. Souvenir
70. Words describing Pegasus?
72. Kentish freedman
76. Tightly shut: Abbr.
77. Depend on
79. Zip
80. Musical notes
83. Free electron
87. Native of Nome
88. Organization, in Paris
90. Diving birds
91. Prefix for tome
93. Military command
94. Leased
95. Thai money
96. MOMA offering
98. Beautiful: Prefix
99. Rhone city
100. Mass-violence acts
101. Compete at Henley
103. Stenos' duplicates: Abbr.
105. Athletic event
107. Eight: Prefix
109. Baton Rouge campus
110. Ending for bomb or ball
111. Groups of mos.
112. Confederate general Stuart

233 Togetherness By Herman Surasky

Presenting some inseparable combinations.

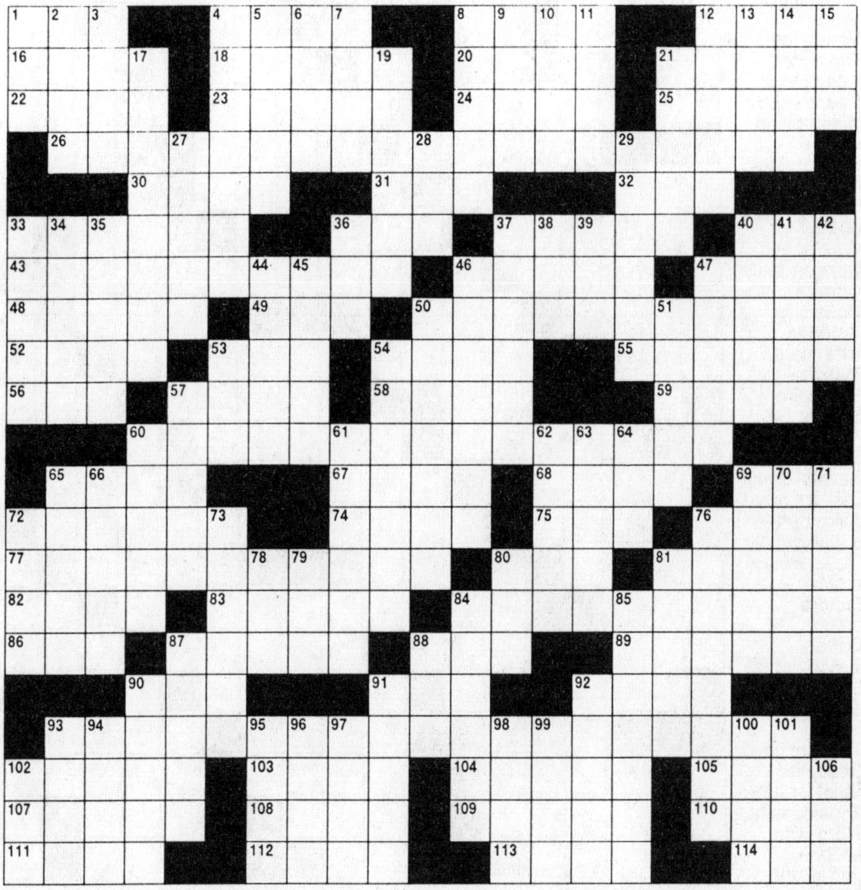

ACROSS

1. Male swan
4. Croat
8. "What's the ___?" (who cares?)
12. Quahog
16. Sharp point
18. Cookie
20. Broadway stage hero
21. Pirandello
22. Sky light
23. Related maternally
24. Uris's "___ 18"
25. Mail
26. TV spies
30. "Kiss Me ___"
31. Incumbents
32. Loving Latin word
33. Withdraw
36. Anger
37. Glowed
40. Daytimes, for short
43. First mates
46. Triad
47. Nigerian natives
48. Road sign
49. English isle
50. Famed twins
52. 2,000 pounds
53. Engine speed: Abbr.
54. Former South African assembly
55. Prince of beasts
56. Wind dir.
57. "I ___ man with . . ."
58. Great Lake
59. Medical picture
60. Ravel ballet
65. Always
67. Alaskan city
68. Maugham-inspired play
69. Doubles: Abbr.
72. Dancer Markova
74. Conked out
75. Roof ornament
76. Kind of code
77. Hill climbers
80. Bankbook entry
81. Joined, in Madrid
82. Actor Roscoe
83. Toots
84. The Gumps
86. Legal matter
87. Queen of
88. ___ mode
89. Glacial epoch
90. The Red Baron was one
91. Be plural
92. Winged
93. Royal romance figures
102. Tuck, for one
103. Israeli airline
104. Motif
105. Norse war god
107. Writer Cleveland ___
108. Kennedy matriarch
109. Lorelei
110. Lopez theme
111. Weight allowance
112. German valley
113. Saucy
114. Insurgent

DOWN

1. TV initials
2. Feed-bag treat
3. Bric-a-___
4. Add to the kitty
5. Fer-de-___
6. At a distance
7. Interdiction
8. Condemns
9. Abbr. in a footnote
10. Thin coating
11. N.C. cape
12. Objet d'art
13. Delineate
14. Avid
15. Russian village
17. Railroad workers
19. Fix an electrical system
21. Delibes opera
27. "M*A*S*H" character
28. Dijon donkey
29. Beach footwear
33. Heroine of 68 Across
34. Redacts
35. Dugout
36. One of the leagues
37. Added a nuance of color
38. Short word of endearment
39. Assn.
40. Sphere of action
41. Bank's supply
42. NCO
44. Intensity
45. Violinist Mischa
46. Linked
47. Worship
50. Chewy candy
51. Ford's predecessor
53. Agt.
54. Dirties again
57. "West Side Story" girl
60. Card collections
61. Nehru's daughter
62. Dogma
63. Mrs. Rockefeller
64. Roman 52
65. Thrill
66. Evils
69. ___ donna
70. Probe anew
71. River of France
72. Partly open
73. Flower part
76. Singer Marian
78. Cee's follower
79. Thrust
80. Geneticist's concern
81. Open a bottle
84. Tocsins
85. Mild disorder
87. Like a horror movie
88. Fortify
90. Cognizant
91. Polly or Larry
92. Gunsight user
93. Bombeck
94. Designer Christian
95. Earl ___ Biggers
96. Baseball brother
97. Poet Ogden
98. Liner
99. Withered
100. Bouquet
101. Asp's milieu
102. Obese
106. Seize

234 Happy Face By Betty Jorgensen

Not a frown to be found anywhere.

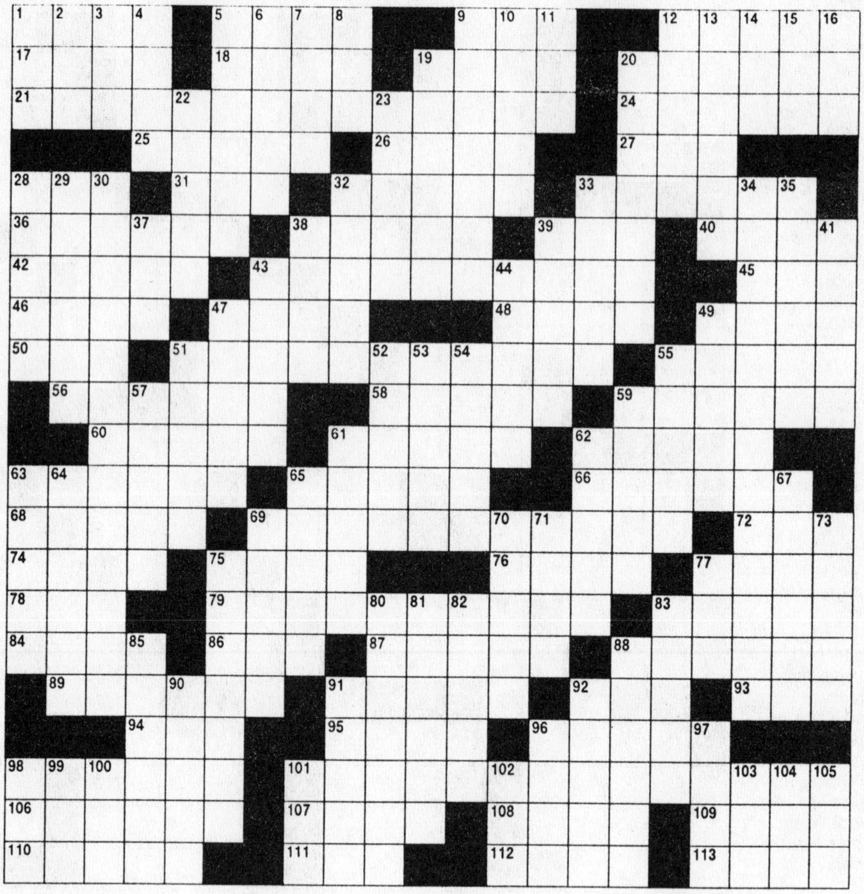

ACROSS

1. Grin
5. Deneb, for one
9. Behave
12. Forward
17. Caen's river
18. Matador's target
19. Muff, as a chance
20. Pet name
21. "Let a Smile ___ . . ."
24. Make fragrant
25. Legal documents
26. Eight: Prefix
27. Vessel for three men
28. Slip off course
31. Some M.D.'s
32. "If you've time to spare, travel ___"
33. Deserves
36. Resounds
38. Dominion
39. Old Japanese money
40. Quaker pronoun
42. Hitchcock's "The 39 ___"
43. "When you ___, smile," said the Virginian
45. Classifieds
46. Thrall
47. ___ Raton
48. Tops
49. School gps.
50. ___ generis (unique)
51. "There are smiles that ___"
55. Moisten
56. Laud
58. "Tanglewood ___"
59. Flitted
60. English historian
61. Army subdivision
62. Slaughter avenue
63. Respond
65. Cut sharply
66. Printing process
68. He wrote "The Merry Widow"
69. "___ Your Smile"
72. Variety of lion
74. Assert
75. Pedro's room
76. White-tailed eagle
77. Kind of line
78. Merry month
79. "___ Smiles at Me"
83. Wax poetic
84. Concert halls
86. Comics' Alley
87. Hollers
88. Antenna
89. At a slant
91. Make silly
92. Pourboire
93. Begley and Asner
94. Baby food
95. Sailors' saint
96. Dial sounds
98. Take part in a walkout
101. "___ wears a smile" (actors' credo)
106. Did a Tuesday task
107. Lebanon's Gemayel
108. Rotter
109. Thought
110. Occupied
111. Color of a portside light
112. Word with shoppe
113. End of the field

DOWN

1. Cut short
2. Before
3. "Indeed, I have not ___"
4. Tabby's talk
5. Emulates Gypsy Rose Lee
6. Tipsters
7. "___ and the Man"
8. One of the Roys
9. Unsurpassed to date
10. Hue
11. Rival of Pan Am
12. Thighbone
13. Welsh ___
14. Notable period
15. Word in R.S.V.P.
16. Haw's partner
19. Make motionless
20. Cold-war thaw
22. Impulses
23. Word with flush or welcome
28. Agreeable words
29. Misbehaves
30. "___ Are Smiling"
32. Pacific island country
33. Labor leader George
34. "Smile, boys, ___" (kit packer's advice)
35. Staid
37. Unlatch, poetically
38. Water channel
39. Hunts bargains
41. Ancient chariot
43. Fountain drinks
44. Nixon collection
47. More lowly
49. Segments
51. Clementine's dad
52. Greek porticoes
53. Rough
54. Omega's opposite
55. Canadian tourist park
57. Sadat
59. Crusoe's creator
61. Do housework
62. Village resident
63. Place to remember
64. Elko's state
65. Drag oneself: Var.
67. Yoked
69. Two-state resort lake
70. Parceled out the deck
71. Symbols of royal power
73. Golden-___
75. Exchanged: Var.
77. Haggard's ageless one
80. Of bone marrow
81. Sycophant
82. Life fluid
83. Turn away
85. Growing above the timberline
88. Conclusion
90. Like a certain bucket
91. Road shoulder
92. Played with
96. Asian weight
97. Gulp down
98. Make a lap
99. Musical syllable
100. Korean soldier
101. Block
102. "___ stole my heart away?"
103. ___ Annie of "Oklahoma!"
104. Affirmative vote
105. Frivolous gal

235 Making Connections By Louis Sabin

With the help of a preposition.

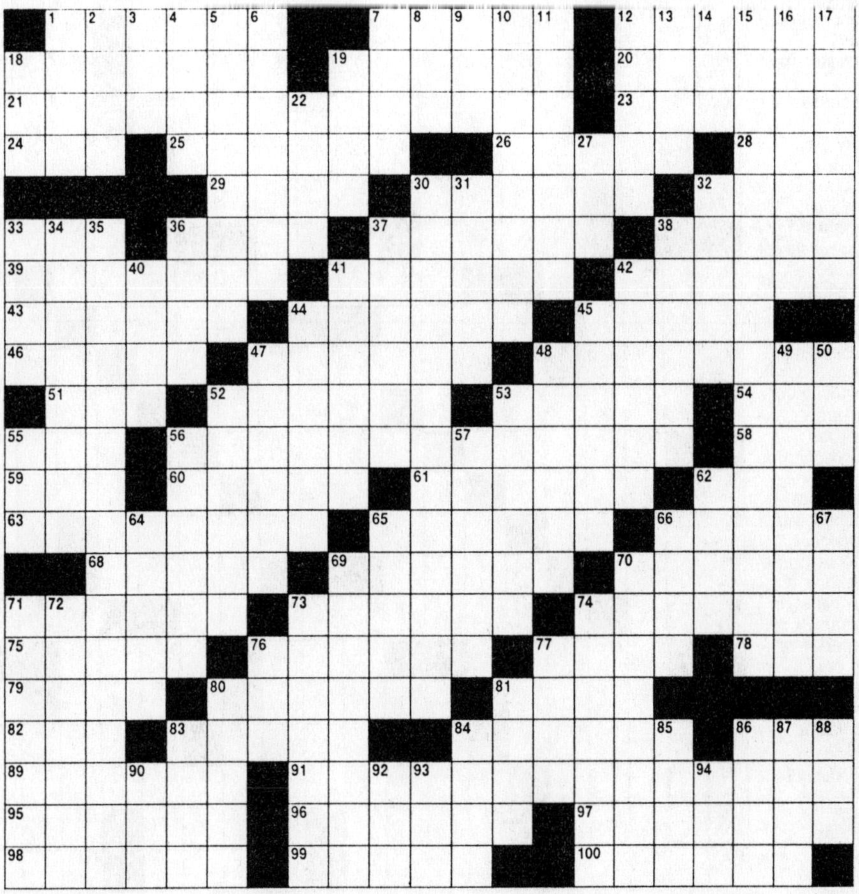

ACROSS

1. Royal digs
7. Sorcerer
12. Puts on
18. Loser
19. Author Gordimer
20. Most wan
21. Hit the N.Y.-Hollywood trail
23. "Swan Lake" role
24. Old English letter
25. Hash mark
26. Dumas swordsman
28. High place
29. Yorkshire river
30. American financier
32. Southern bread
33. Work unit
36. Kind of cap
37. Strong points
38. Barbecue site
39. Headwear at Ascot
41. Guinea pigs
42. Former Turkish brass
43. Least receptive
44. He's often one, indeed
45. Sample
46. Shore fliers
47. Sheds, in England
48. Like some vacant flats
51. Followers of ees
52. "Do I ___ eat a peach?"
53. Sari wearer
54. Nerd
55. Greatly
56. Speak pointlessly
58. Famous tomb name
59. Sioux
60. Van Gogh setting
61. Kane and Hayes
62. Orch. section
63. Made an observation
65. Like a non-women's libber
66. Medicinal tonic
68. Crane's kin
69. Guide
70. Chief
71. One with a fixed look
73. Promising people
74. Fruit dish
75. Miscued
76. Tree cobras
77. Platform
78. Word for Churchill's R.A.F.
79. Widow's asset
80. "___ and yet so far"
81. "___ Free"
82. Altar assent
83. Promenades for Plato
84. Composed
86. Resort
89. Rec-room staple
91. Lower oneself to advantage
95. Glaze
96. Headdresses
97. Annual periods
98. Long step
99. Comported
100. Prepares pekoe

DOWN

1. Drudge
2. "The Nazarene" author
3. "The ___ Sanction"
4. Parseghian and others
5. Flamenco dancer's prop
6. Contestants
7. Medieval weapon
8. Ruckus
9. Actress Scala
10. Like some nuts
11. Founds
12. Golf club
13. Young ones
14. Tap tap
15. Solve
16. Tallinn is its capital
17. Sound systems
18. Wear
19. "Unh-unh"
22. Flag
27. Exclamations
30. Bus driver's litany
31. Gray and Moran
32. Trattoria offering
33. She sang for Ernie
34. Put fresh life into
35. Show delight
36. Rodin subject
37. ___ see (not comprehend)
38. Soft color
40. Apiarist's charges
41. Vinegar holders
42. Civic groups
44. Like some tongues
45. Occupant
47. Lawn-game tool
48. Least refined
49. Tennyson or Masefield
50. Newt
52. More shaded
53. Dig findings
55. Pro
56. Did road surfacing
57. Witches
62. Goof
64. Jibe
65. Lion
66. Pentagon purchases
67. Scads
69. Butler or housemaid
70. Indicate
71. Some Middle Easterners
72. Neptune's scepter
73. Card game
74. Venezuelan hub
76. Pasture call
77. Fuddy-duddy
80. Stone slab
81. Pimlico handle
83. Rank, in tennis
84. Fokker's foe
85. Grafted, in heraldry
86. ___ pump
87. Swords' stoppers
88. ___ gratia artis
90. Cadets' acad.
92. Nose-bag unit
93. Tram contents
94. "___ Sera, Sera"

236 Close Ties By Isaac Miller

Presenting various degrees of familiarity.

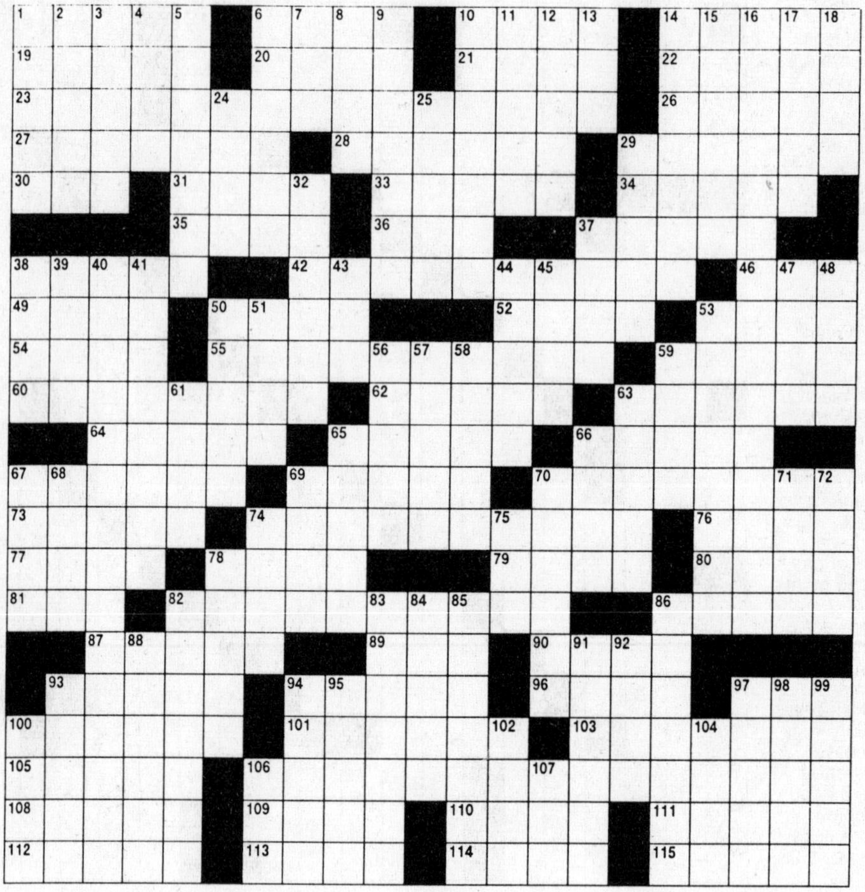

ACROSS

1. Tears down, in Soho
6. Spavined horses
10. Part of a deck
14. Cold
19. Swiftly
20. Brontë heroine
21. Not astir
22. Kind of bin
23. Robert Young TV series
26. Framework
27. Poem of eight lines
28. Take a risk
29. Give
30. Sault ___ Marie
31. Object of devotion
33. Prepare beef
34. Mountain nymph
35. Forbidden act
36. Hound
37. Don Adams TV role
38. Confuse
42. See 74 Across
46. Half a bray
49. Verve
50. French shouts
52. Charged particles
53. Take out
54. Town in France
55. Roz Russell role
59. All in
60. Talking aimlessly
62. Leopards' ID's
63. Figures of speech
64. Observing
65. Plants of a region
66. Writer Jong
67. Seat for the mighty
69. Cast out
70. Whatnots
73. Intervening, in law
74. Film about Francis of Assisi, with 42 Across
76. Portico
77. Assistant
78. Coconut-husk fiber
79. Elevator man
80. "It ___ Necessarily So"
81. New Deal agency
82. One's sister's son's daughter
86. Liqueur flavor
87. Eastern Christian
89. Sea eagle
90. Cheese
93. Thickening agents
94. On the level
96. Horace or Thomas
97. Native: Suffix
100. Stupid ones
101. Wipes out
103. Instilled with courage
105. Dine at home
106. Chekhov play
108. Current style
109. Human or rat
110. Preceder of bus or present
111. Occupied
112. Suit fabric
113. Fine or liberal
114. Pheasant group
115. Bactrian

DOWN

1. Large numbers
2. Separated
3. French composer
4. Resound
5. Doing a falconer's task
6. Free-swimming sea animals
7. Author Rand
8. Diluted rum
9. ___ Folly (Alaska)
10. Crop for Mrs. Wiggs
11. Third man and others
12. Electrical switch
13. Insecticide
14. Sacred Moslem book
15. Car for temporary use
16. Coppola sequel, with "The"
17. The lady ___ (Dillinger woman)
18. Fabric worker
24. Decorate anew
25. Hawley-___ Tariff Act
29. Singer Perry and family
32. About to be defeated
37. Unit of loudness
38. Carry
39. Kazan
40. Subject of traveling-salesman jokes
41. Ark procession, cut by half
43. Doer: Suffix
44. Lasso
45. Pops' mates
47. Sheltered
48. Ties the knot
50. Queeg's ship
51. Ladder part
53. Of a church district
56. Small land mass
57. Time period
58. "Le ___ d'Arthur"
59. Relative of alg.
61. Boundary
63. Prefix for lucent or port
65. Narrow inlet
66. Needle case
67. Treasury agent
68. ___ apparent
69. Shamrock land
70. Respect
71. Ages
72. Satisfy
74. Gravy dish
75. Fabulous bird
78. Insensitive
82. Department of France
83. Makes ineffective
84. Kind of coffee or whiskey
85. Begin
86. Having a memory loss
88. Christening
91. Small African fish
92. Against
93. Not ___ in the world
94. Hungarian composer
95. Upright
97. Intestinal part
98. Pithy
99. Henry Ford's son
100. Tennis units
102. Truck
104. Lab burner
106. Refrain syllable
107. Last part

237 One More Time By Ernie Furtado

A matter of going on and on with a thing.

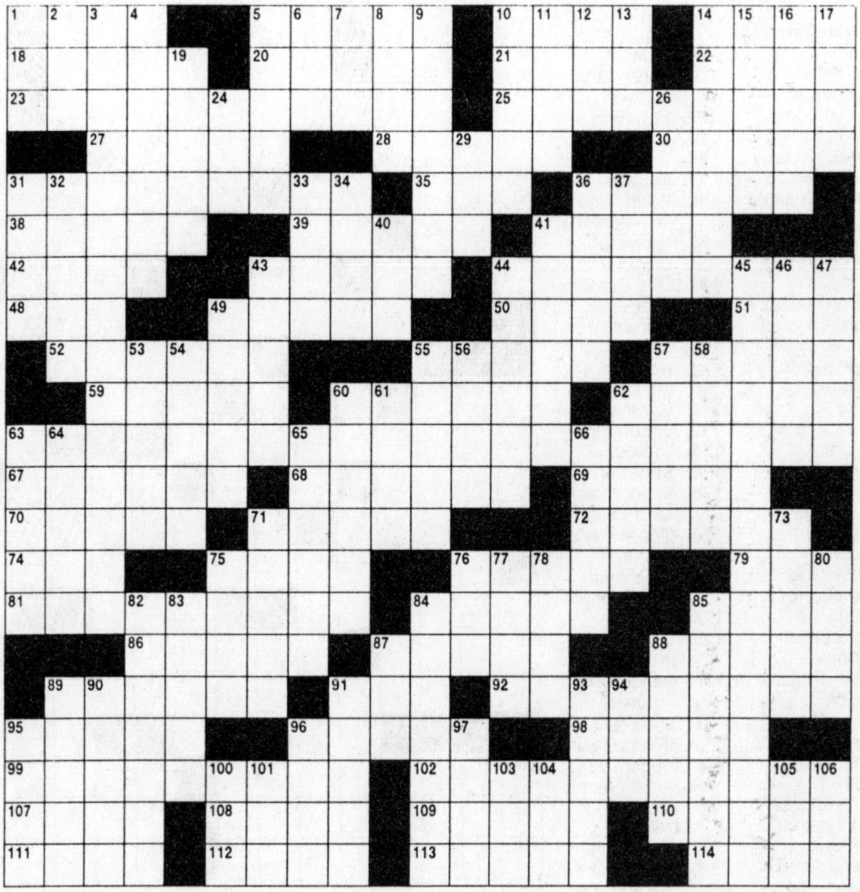

ACROSS

1. Squabbles
5. Motorized bike
10. Louise or Turner
14. Andy's partner
18. Orient
20. Cordial flavoring
21. Ended
22. Good, in Napoli
23. Dis-agreements
25. Genghis Khan follower, plus
27. Old Lithuanian coins
28. Ruhr city
30. Hindu garments
31. Latin dance, plus
35. Popular street name
36. Egyptian goddess of love
38. Flycatcher
39. Abrasive
41. Word with firma or cotta
42. "It's ___ world": Dickens
43. Something to put up
44. Antiaircraft gun, plus
48. ___ vous plaît
49. Solo
50. Sweetsop
51. "___ live and breathe!"
52. ___ la Real, city near Granada
55. Japanese painter of the 1400's
57. "Our ___ Havana," Guinness movie
59. Jones of song
60. Counterparts of hommes
62. Argentine poet Jorge Luis ___
63. Big Apple, plus
67. Garland
68. "___ Nightingale"
69. "___ of dust alone remains . . .": Pope
70. Certain spies
71. Future soph
72. "___ Knowledge," Nicholson film
74. Kind of gotten gains
75. Duo
76. Discover
79. Hindu caste member
81. Start of a nursery rhyme, plus
84. Billiard stroke
85. Combust-ibles: Abbr.
86. Sleds
87. Wooden shoe
88. Spondulix
89. Teacher, sometimes
91. Tavern
92. North American tree, plus
95. Suspect's need
96. Fusses
98. Mob-scene player
99. Goof, plus
102. Functioning
107. Bone: Prefix
108. Time of day
109. Pitcher Ryan
110. Poet Paul Hamilton ___
111. U.S.A. Olympics rival
112. Magazine in Paris
113. Data, for short
114. Kind of dancer

DOWN

1. Vallone of films
2. Harem room
3. Washington river, plus
4. Edited tape
5. Legerdemain
6. Yoko
7. More, in music
8. Italian family
9. Sweet-tooth gratifier
10. Emblem
11. Lendl of tennis
12. Saul's grandfather
13. Tatum of jazz
14. Hebrew patriarch
15. Paris subway
16. Walking ___
17. Indian weights
19. Tax
24. Aeronautics gp.
26. Houston baseballer
29. Stallone, to friends
31. April V.I.P.'s
32. Blood condition: Suffix
33. Man of the hour
34. Theban deity
36. John Wayne roles
37. Stringed instruments, to a cockney
40. Compass dir.
41. Take ___ (censure)
43. Side
44. Old Roman cup
45. Samoan harbor plus, phonetically
46. Willow
47. Russian city
49. Wake-up aid
53. Scottish firth
54. Bitter drug
55. English woman composer
56. Melville novel
57. Lawn machine
58. Nazi racial word
60. Sardou's hat drama
61. Rams' mates
62. "Borstal Boy" playwright
63. Desert of South-West Africa
64. ___ Gay
65. Water wheels
66. Mother-of-pearl
71. Pencil tycoon Eberhard ___
73. Moore's "___ Rookh"
75. Leaf
76. Testing place
77. Fabler: Var.
78. Nick and Nora's pet
80. "I came, ___ . . ."
82. Prattle
83. Video counterpart
84. Strands
85. "The king can do ___"
87. Kind of sack
88. Young herring
89. Shine
90. Outbreaks
91. Pat or Richard
93. Alienates
94. Early abbr. on a painter's signature
95. Ben Adhem
96. Cat's-paw
97. Espy
100. Quarter of four
101. S.A. country
103. Guido's high note
104. Squeal
105. Branch of math.
106. Between Virgo and Cancer

238 Ownership By Marjorie Pedersen

Possible possessions for well-known people.

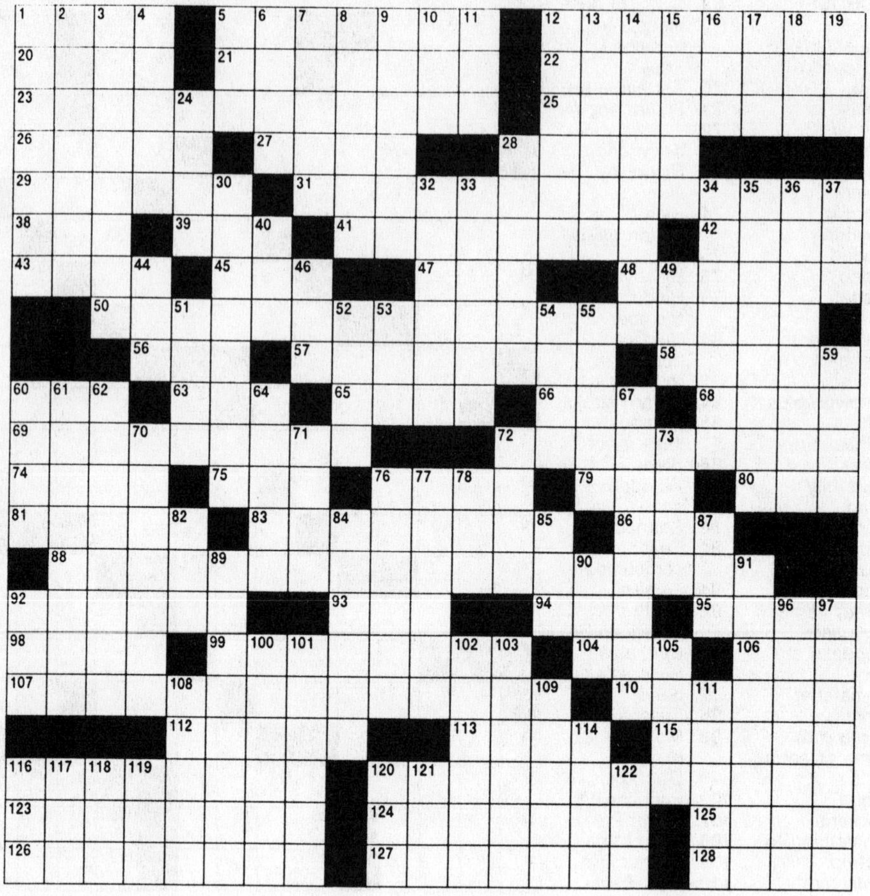

ACROSS

1. Swan genus
5. Pulpit canopies
12. Eagles and birdies, for one pro?
20. Peau de ___
21. Gasoline-rating units
22. Transvaal capital
23. Cheer for one astronaut?
25. Dispute
26. Testimonial-dinner host
27. Aware of
28. Hike
29. Biblical place of balm
31. Jazz pianist's keen ear?
38. Fiji island
39. Stiffen
41. Most unyielding
42. Small ones: Suffix
43. Noncoms
45. Carney
47. Kind of spoon
48. Ancient ascetic
50. One writer's digit?
56. "The Black Cat" author
57. Former movie short
58. Stupid ones
60. O'Shanter
63. Large container: Abbr.
65. Natives, for short
66. Inlet
68. Fish dishes
69. One economist's theory?
72. One actor's beast?
74. Lima land
75. Expert
76. German rocket of W.W. II
79. Corn spike
80. Jap. currency units
81. Large South American snake
83. Native of Gary or Kokomo
86. Part of Washington's sig.
88. Siblings' parent and in-laws?
92. Fanatic
93. Be sorry
94. ___ Paulo
95. Morays
98. What "line" or "man" has
99. Native of Erivan
104. Dos Passos trilogy
106. Favorite
107. One social worker's motivation?
110. Harangue
112. Secure firmly
113. Lifeless
115. Street show
116. Soup choice for a child
120. One writer's instrument?
123. Numismatist's treasure
124. Flier
125. To ___ (exactly)
126. Dance of a Dolphin?
127. Trims with shears again
128. Biggers's middle name

DOWN

1. Upstate N.Y. city and river
2. Covering with fertile soil
3. Shelf lining
4. Appomattox signature
5. Prepositions
6. Nymph who pined away
7. Overcharged
8. French pastries
9. Implant
10. Agcy. that supervised power lines
11. "Quiet!"
12. Meager
13. Irish exclamations
14. Measurer of elec. resistance
15. Buddhist shrine
16. ___ de plume
17. Before
18. An, in Bonn
19. Gram. case
24. Town-meeting votes
28. Bridge sequence
30. Letter opener to Miss Bombeck
32. Try out anew
33. Garson and namesakes
34. Italian tragedienne Adelaide
35. Visionary speculation
36. Twenty minus one
37. Proceed, in Scotland
40. Prefix for pod
44. Weaken
46. Super rating
49. Papal initials
51. Rifles
52. Part of M.I.T.
53. Bahamas island group: Abbr.
54. Hearty sandwich
55. Slur over
59. Russian pol. units
60. Pacific cloth
61. "We've a war, an' ___ flag . . .": Lowell
62. Pirate, sometimes
64. Of a beetle group
67. As pale ___
70. Joining in merrymaking
71. Do bar duty
72. Wander
73. Corner
76. Fine wool
77. Admit
78. Hoisting devices: Abbr.
82. Bond rating
84. Most terrible
85. Digits: Abbr.
87. Natural mineral
89. Lake in Ont.
90. Greek letter
91. Force apart
92. Pop's partner
96. Onetime film actor Francis
97. More costly
100. Disguise anew
101. High point in Sicily
102. Dried mushroom
103. Babylonian sun god
105. Brings into the open
108. Study of spiders: Abbr.
109. Central Italian town
111. Sudanese town
114. Tear or rain unit
116. Suffix for dull
117. Thai people
118. For the emergency: Abbr.
119. "For ___ a jolly good . . ."
120. Damage
121. Lex. or Mad.
122. Time periods: Abbr.

239 Sound System By Robert Wolfe

Some results of playing words by ear.

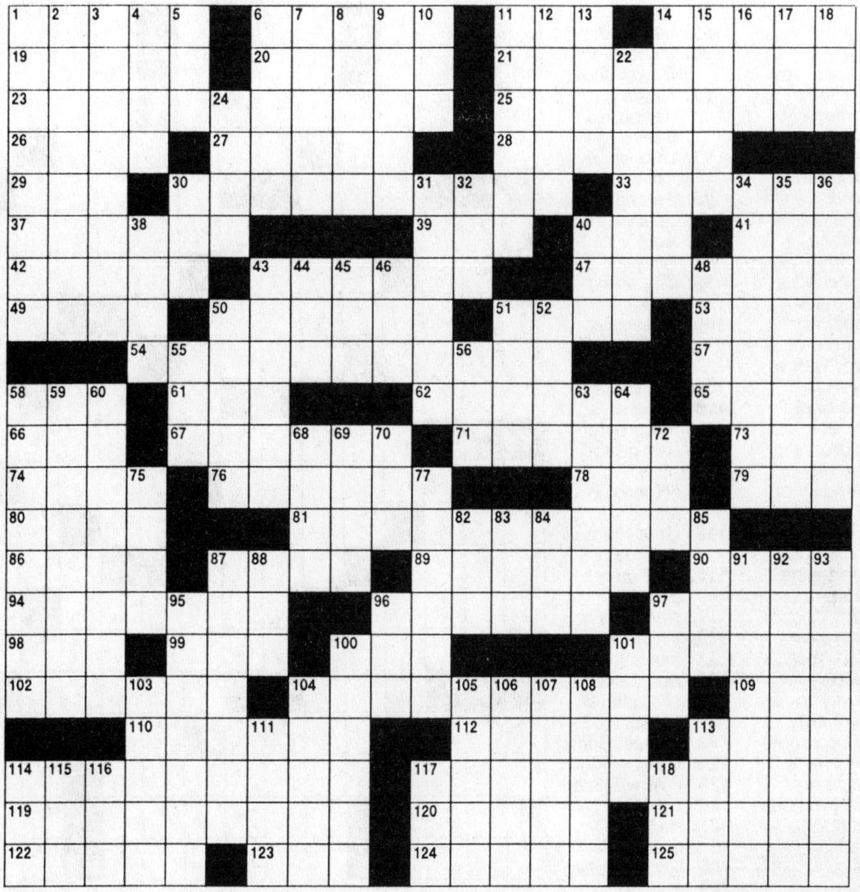

ACROSS

1. Greeting shout
6. South American monkeys
11. Hiatus
14. Wooden pin
19. ___ a million (rara avis)
20. First name on a W.W. II plane
21. Kind of park
23. Rich young heiress?
25. Place for a baseball-playing cleric?
26. Followers of zetas
27. Asphyxia
28. Bite repeatedly
29. ___ Alamos
30. Young cook?
33. Disarranged
37. Friendly
39. Eden hostess
40. Follower of wonder
41. Roof ornament
42. Insect nest
43. Thin and light
47. Thespian
49. Ruby and Sandra
50. Lighter fluid
51. Eur. country
53. Inter ___
54. Reckless in a zenana?
57. Wire measures
58. Periodical, for short
61. Women's ___
62. A quarter blown?
65. Santa's bane
66. Mr. Baba
67. Dinner course in France
71. Acid salt
73. Opposite of SSW
74. Possess
76. Stet emphatically?
78. Old card game
79. Georgia or Armenia: Abbr.
80. Belgian town
81. Strong and headed for bivalves?
86. Cowboy's need
87. Buss
89. Lamentation
90. Ivory Coast language
94. Firm
96. Boxer Carnero and others
97. Actress Irene
98. Wandering ___ (plant)
99. Deer
100. Roman 1002
101. "___ Hot Tin Roof"
102. Agree
104. Hidden weakness in a K.O. by Cassius?
109. Know, formerly
110. Leg bones
112. Noel ___ of "Superman"
113. Son of ___
114. Token for a punt receiver?
117. Pitiless deer sculpture?
119. Send to another jurisdiction
120. Eared seal
121. Political alliances
122. Imagines, long ago
123. Bit of turf
124. Frozen
125. Assistants

DOWN

1. Native soil
2. Université medical study
3. Put off an Oahu gift?
4. Eye parts
5. Mrs. Lennon
6. Musical beat
7. Turkish statesman
8. Colorer
9. Of the intestine
10. Utter
11. Use mouthwash
12. Have ___ to (feel inclined)
13. ___ damper on (deter)
14. Fail to pay
15. Overlooks
16. Small
17. Do a phot. job
18. Inc., in England
22. A bit of what Betsy Ross did?
24. Season for cider
30. Musical syllables
31. When this occurred
32. Certain league
34. What safari people do?
35. Greek letters
36. Shipwreck or earthquake
38. Ham's eldest son
40. It's often in the fire
43. Indian village
44. Air: Abbr.
45. Dance step
46. Ref. book
48. Batters
50. Actor Keith
51. Mount where Moses saw Canaan
52. Moslem prince
55. Kaline and Capp
56. Carl Reiner's son
58. Indian prince
59. Thin silks
60. Stop and think of dog tricks?
63. Claws
64. Ale's cousin
68. Nav. officers
69. It's often ex machina
70. Certain railways
72. Long time
75. Kind of sch.
77. ___ de corps
82. Actor Wallach
83. On the ___ (in flight)
84. Life story, for short
85. Caress, in Scotland
87. Like a pretty good granny?
88. Brooklyn follower
91. Unsatisfactory moral goal?
92. Proclaim
93. Orderly quality
95. Flowered plants
96. ___ mater
97. Dennis or Doris
100. Interlocked
101. Young animal
103. Endless, in poesy
104. Ipso ___
105. Spanish explorer
106. Wild
107. Lemony prefix
108. Harold of the silents
111. Inflammatory ending
113. King of the Huns
114. Not many
115. Miss Borden's weapon
116. Hwy.
117. Porcine beast
118. U.S. business group

240 Rarae Aves By Sara Helleny

Some possible additions to a bird-watcher's vocabulary.

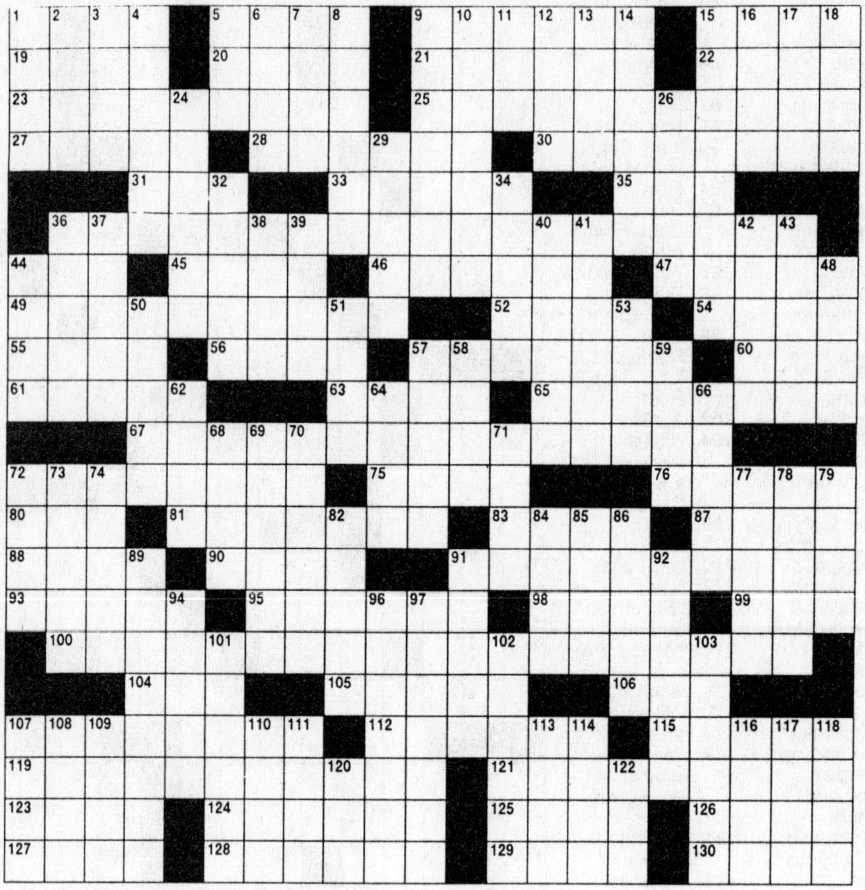

ACROSS

1. Ingrid's "Casablanca" role
5. She loved Radames
9. "Each ___ seven kits"
15. Adherents: Suffix
19. As silent as the ___
20. Lump in yarn
21. Flattened at the poles
22. Appoint
23. Lament of a lover with a cold?
25. Mad bank official?
27. Colonist's greeting to an Indian
28. ___ a dime
30. What to do to the vote
31. Varangians
33. Pivots
35. U.S. warplane type: Abbr.
36. Ongoing activity for a deadbeat?
44. Spring runner
45. River nymph
46. ___ even keel (remains stable)
47. Leather flasks
49. Movie bird-dog?
52. Some are martial
54. Bit of skulduggery
55. Prefix for dynamics
56. Fall faller
57. Bites for Bugs Bunny
60. Take advantage of
61. General drift
63. Dread
65. "You're ___ best things that . . ."
67. Cartoon singer?
72. Leopards' relatives
75. Kind of admiral
76. Obliterate
80. Minor pol. party
81. Indiana athlete
83. Place for Zeno
87. "The fat ___ the fire"
88. Mighty mote
90. Incite a dog, Down Under
91. Like a newborn baby?
93. Greek city-state
95. Setting, in Spain
98. Author Wiesel
99. City ways: Abbr.
100. Stravinsky opus for right now?
104. Consumed
105. Have an ___ the ground
106. City on the Miss.
107. "Honest Injun!"
112. Gets the golf ball ready
115. "Ulalume" poet's signature
119. James Bond movie?
121. Steinbeck characters' workplace?
123. Places: Suffix
124. Marshy inlet
125. Overwhelmed
126. Labyrinth
127. Hamelin quarry
128. Roman robes
129. Ibn-___
130. "Them There ___"

DOWN

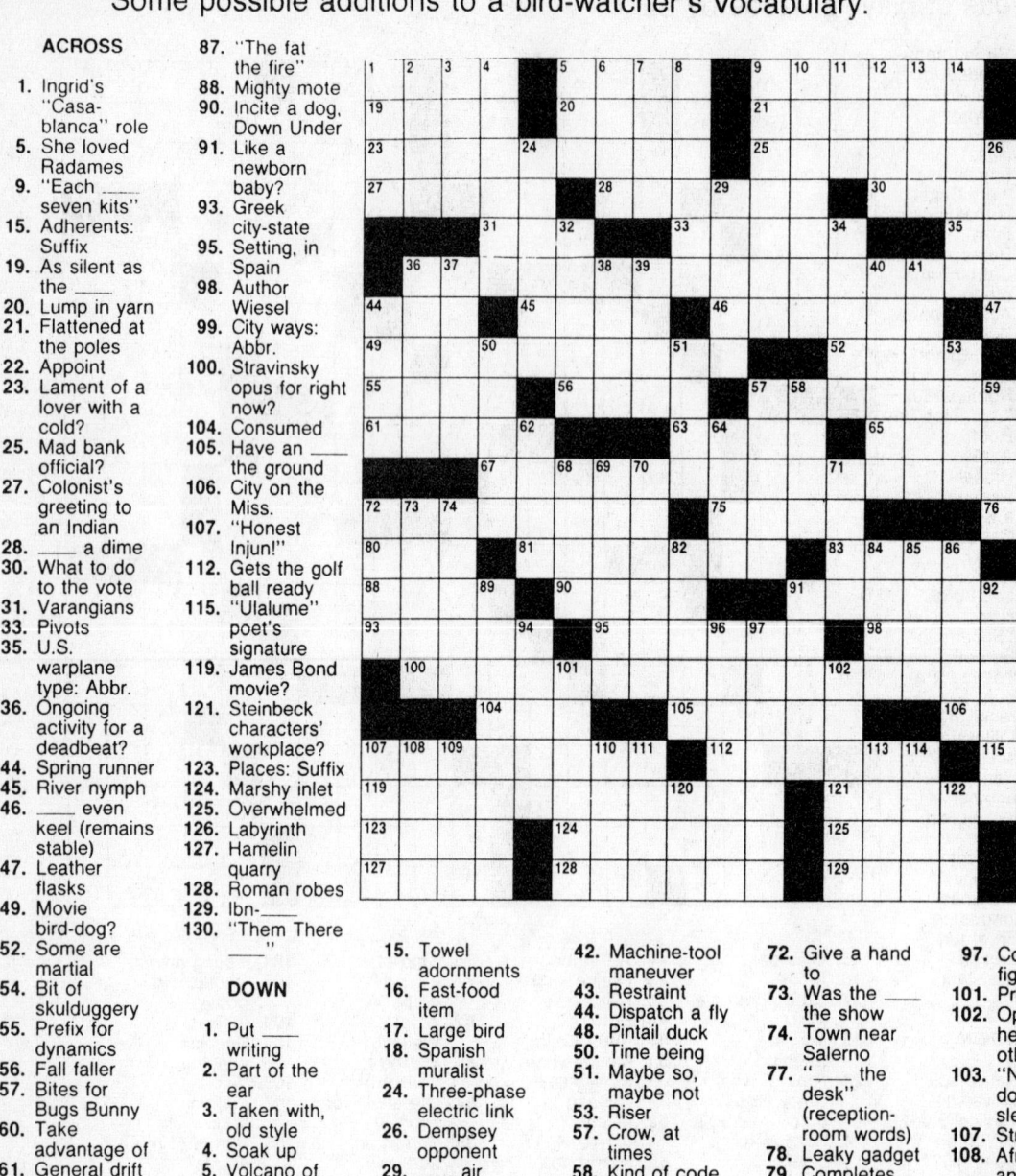

1. Put ___ writing
2. Part of the ear
3. Taken with, old style
4. Soak up
5. Volcano of Japan
6. Grandfather of Priam
7. Attic accumulation
8. Give ___ to (help)
9. Hues, in England
10. Have ___ pick
11. Insurance-policy letters
12. Do an art-gallery chore
13. Stub ___
14. With dexterity
15. Towel adornments
16. Fast-food item
17. Large bird
18. Spanish muralist
24. Three-phase electric link
26. Dempsey opponent
29. ___ air school of painting
32. Slow mover
34. Detecting device
36. Less common
37. ___ citato
38. Lonesome tree
39. "¿Cómo ___ usted?"
40. Christie's avian detective Hercule?
41. "___ and Cleopatra"
42. Machine-tool maneuver
43. Restraint
44. Dispatch a fly
48. Pintail duck
50. Time being
51. Maybe so, maybe not
53. Riser
57. Crow, at times
58. Kind of code
59. Silk, in France
62. "How ___ the little busy bee . . ."
64. To be, in Brest
66. Spanish market fete
68. Ancient temple
69. Actress Goldberg
70. ___ as a lemon
71. First, in Frankfurt
72. Give a hand to
73. Was the ___ the show
74. Town near Salerno
77. "___ the desk" (reception-room words)
78. Leaky gadget
79. Completes
82. ___ France
84. Nailed obliquely
85. Wreath on a helmet
86. "___ in the Dark"
89. Actress Carmen and family
91. Recipe direction
92. One of the genders
94. ___ threads (man's suit)
96. Balance, to Cicero
97. Corrida figures
101. Proves false
102. Operatic heroine and others
103. "Now ___ down to sleep"
107. Stravinsky
108. African antelope
109. Dress feature
110. V.M.I. or R.P.I.
111. Outside: Prefix
113. New Zealand county
114. French tire
116. "Let us ___"
117. Seep
118. Rams' mates
120. Loki's daughter
122. Do sums

241 Progress By Jo Lundy

Various ways of getting places.

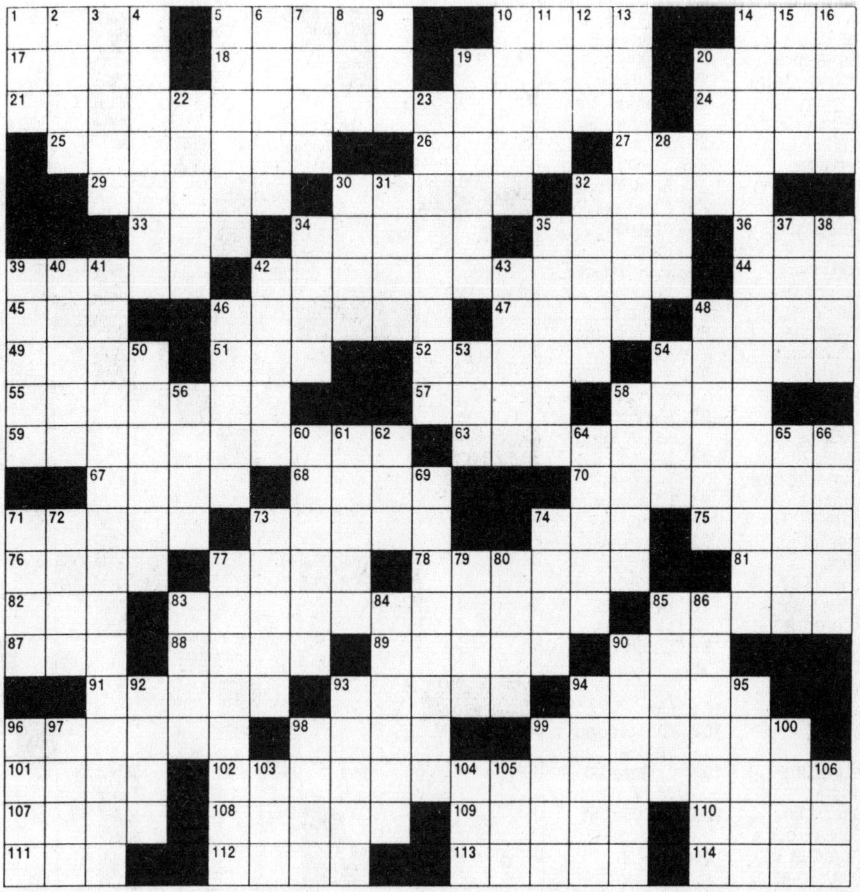

ACROSS

1. Spanish home
5. Grants
10. Brilliant stroke
14. Huck's friend on the river
17. "There ought to be ___."
18. Coral island
19. French W.W. I soldier
20. Boorish
21. Spidery suggestion
24. Latin love
25. Containing more info
26. Hard-to-beat combo
27. Elementary
29. City conduits
30. Spanish hero
32. Article of virtu
33. Map abbr.
34. Country gallant
35. Fairy of Irish folklore
36. Utensil, to Caesar
39. Israel's Meir
42. Suggestion to a volunteer
44. Old cloth measure
45. Honshu port
46. Staffs used in Bacchic rites
47. Matadors' prizes
48. Sky animal
49. Meadows
51. Scottish explorer
52. Tilt
54. Above
55. Common pain reliever
57. Clock-climbing trio
58. London's is Marble
59. Ill-wisher's suggestion
63. Aim wide of trouble
67. Track shape
68. "___ she blows!"
70. Lack of vigor: Var.
71. Comic actress Polly
73. Kind of angle
74. Concurred: Abbr.
75. Fern spores
76. Actor Richard
77. Bone up for an exam
78. Type of agent
81. Major ref. work
82. Pixie
83. Suggestion to a mountaineer
85. Territories
87. ___ Aviv
88. Wing, in Nice
89. Sidles
90. G-man
91. Raconteurs' spinnings
93. Port in Brittany
94. Neckwear
96. Japanese musical drama
98. Writer Uris
99. Raging flood
101. Having wings
102. Ex post facto suggestion
107. Legal wrongs
108. Film actor Lew
109. Fine-print type
110. Heraldic border
111. Have miseries
112. Period of fasting
113. Of bottom quality
114. Require

DOWN

1. Cornfield call
2. Cranston or Alda
3. Capital on the Willamette
4. Having two left feet
5. Pointed tooth
6. Feminine suffixes
7. It sometimes has a knocker
8. Endangered tree
9. Tricky
10. Prepared an apple for baking
11. Many paintings
12. Gums: Prefix
13. Posse people, at times
14. Suggestion to bossy
15. Baal, for one
16. Kind of bagatelle
19. Al of "The Godfather"
20. Branches
22. "___ plane?" (No, it's Superman)
23. Dove's thing
28. Made angry
30. Vessel
31. Times around the track
32. Plot a course
34. Eye infection
35. Stephen Foster's river
37. Besides
38. Prelude to a duel
39. Soviet prison camp
40. Overweight, in Spain
41. Suggestion to an outfielder
42. Dub a stroke in golf
43. Hit back
46. Courtroom drama
48. Relatives
50. Of forest trees
53. Fleur-de-___
54. Killer whale
56. "Paper Moon" O'Neal
58. German poet
60. "___ Upon the Midnight Clear"
61. Hitchhiker's digit
62. Devour
64. Expectant
65. Made public
66. Forays
69. Nontransient
71. Encounter
72. Amorous stare
73. Seed covers
74. He hates 23 Down
77. Impersonal
79. Poultry products
80. President Arthur's nickname, maybe
83. Burden with anxiety
84. Valorous ones
85. Hear
86. Appended
90. Weasel's relative
92. Subtle atmosphere
93. Hem in
94. Canoes, catamarans, etc.
95. Dorm sound
96. Hindu god of love
97. Russian range
98. Forsaken
99. Metal beam
100. Painted metalware
103. Caustic substance
104. Hee's partner
105. Kind of maniac
106. Grange or Barber

242 National Assets By Bernice Gordon

Holdings that might be appropriate to places therein.

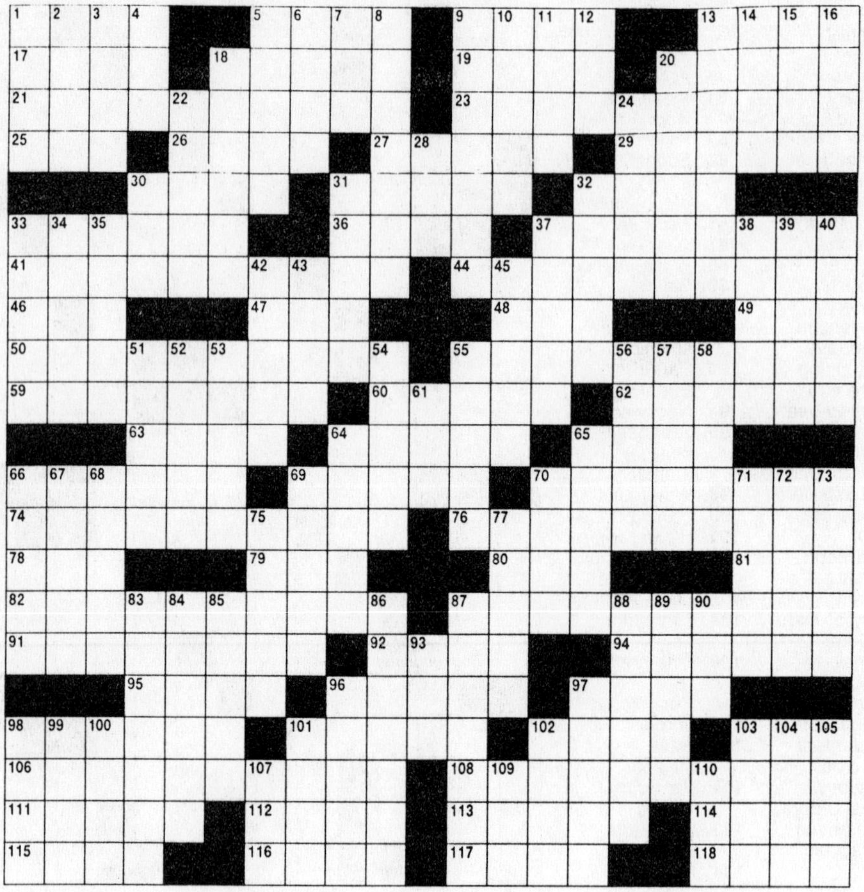

ACROSS

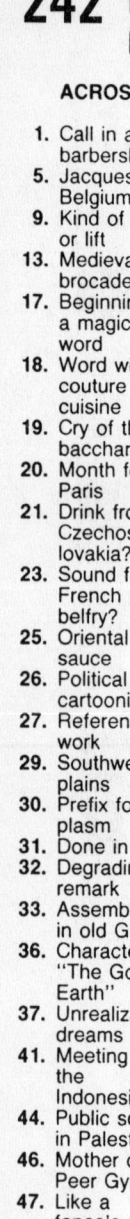

1. Call in a barbershop
5. Jacques from Belgium
9. Kind of card or lift
13. Medieval brocade
17. Beginning of a magician's word
18. Word with couture or cuisine
19. Cry of the bacchanals
20. Month for Paris
21. Drink from Czechoslovakia?
23. Sound from a French belfry?
25. Oriental sauce
26. Political cartoonist
27. Reference work
29. Southwestern plains
30. Prefix for plasm
31. Done in
32. Degrading remark
33. Assemblies in old Greece
36. Character in "The Good Earth"
37. Unrealizable dreams
41. Meeting of the Indonesians?
44. Public square in Palestine?
46. Mother of Peer Gynt
47. Like a fence's wares
48. Needlefish
49. Brynner
50. Location for the Armada?
55. Baby carrier in Ireland?
59. Delaware Bay cape
60. Actor Jeremy
62. Makes amends
63. Told a fib
64. Plunder
65. Actor ___ Julia
66. ". . . drinking ___ of milk a day": Henry Wallace
69. Homer temptress
70. Abstains
74. Spoils found in Montana?
76. Plum served at a ski lodge?
78. Wee bit of land
79. Inclined
80. Altar in the sky
81. Bronze Age trumpet
82. Export from the Aegean?
87. Big top in Belgium?
91. Changed into vapor
92. Nimbus
94. Beagles, e.g.
95. Salamanders
96. Brief bio sketches
97. Latch on to
98. ___ as a bird
101. Up
102. All-purpose vehicle
103. O'Hara's Joey
106. Building in Michigan?
108. Flier in Peking?
111. Indian noble
112. First homicide victim
113. Having overhangs
114. Goldwater's state: Abbr.
115. Comply with
116. Sum, ___, fui
117. Formal assembly
118. Bank on

DOWN

1. Takes a siesta
2. Mediterranean feeder
3. Roentgen's gift to mankind
4. Schoolyard game
5. Chaliapin or Pinza
6. Litter's also-ran
7. Ike's command
8. In a lawful way
9. Knocking down
10. Of birds
11. Mountain passes
12. Kingklip or moray
13. Attire
14. Spring: Prefix
15. "So long!" in Italy
16. "___ well"
18. Gangster's rod
20. Go into ___ (decline)
22. Well-known Mohican
24. Designer Perry ___
28. Chinese pagoda
30. Silkworm
31. Conductor Georg
32. Villain of "Jaws"
33. Disconcert
34. Quebec peninsula
35. New York city
37. Peter and Paul, e.g.
38. Dress material
39. Unclouded sky
40. Jonas of polio note, and kin
42. Sultan of Turkey
43. Banking deal
45. Torment
51. ___ ease (uncomfortable)
52. Black, in Brest
53. Small barracudas
54. City in France
55. Housing for pigeons
56. Estonian island
57. Moviegoer's receipts
58. Decorated tin plates
61. Sinbad's transport
64. Regional flora and fauna
65. Comedian Dan
66. Fiber of the Philippines
67. Paper quantity
68. Absolute
69. ___ with (handled)
70. Links word
71. Debbie or Steve
72. Kind of house or table
73. Some Spanish paintings
75. Fancy fabrics
77. Western lake
83. Gene of the screen
84. Exhausted
85. Locations
86. Prickly plant
87. Took a quick look
88. Item in a sewing kit
89. Afternoon TV offerings
90. Place for three men
93. Dined
96. Liana and ivy
97. Relative of the civet
98. Hairdo
99. Thick slice
100. Excellent
101. ___ of beef
102. Swing music
103. Fiery heap
104. Blue dye
105. Like Susan
107. Miss West
109. "Bali ___"
110. Damage

243 Assortment By Manny Miller

A weaving of words around no particular subject.

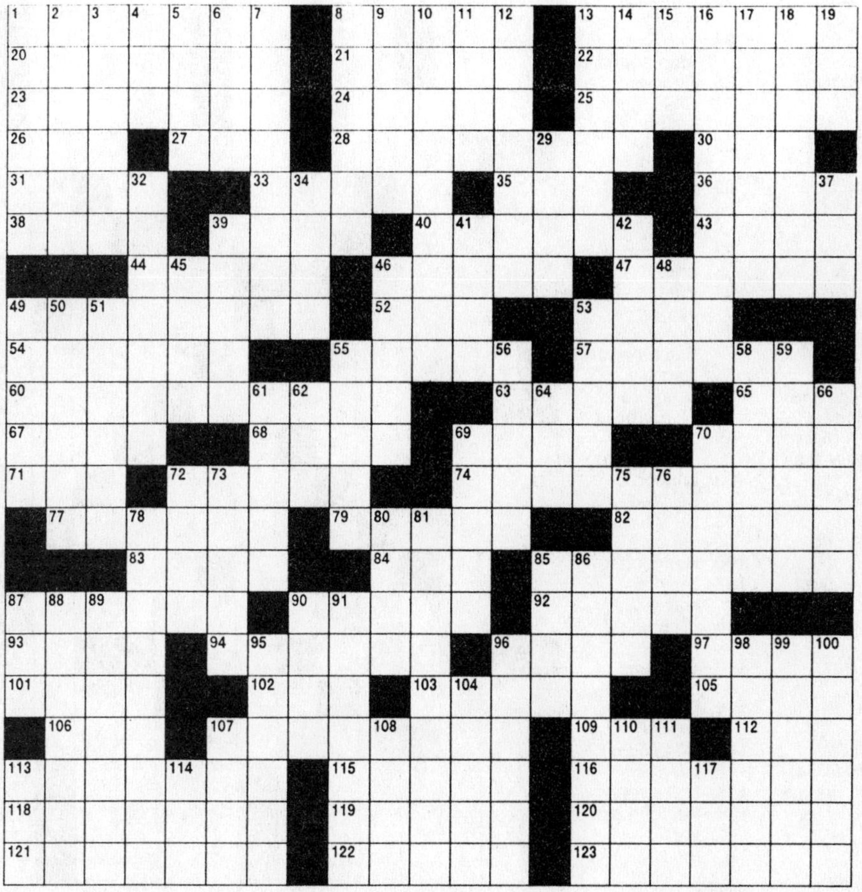

ACROSS

1. Quartz or feldspar
8. Truman's birthplace
13. Most daring
20. Harmonica's relative
21. Came up
22. Receiver of property
23. Feels indignant
24. Swings around
25. Say again
26. W.W. I weapon
27. One of the Carsons
28. Capitol people
30. Printing measures
31. Matured
33. Belt area
35. Chemical suffix
36. Place for poultry
38. Italian saint
39. "By ____!" (zounds)
40. Cancels
43. Caroline Islands group
44. Bowling mark
46. Life-history accts.
47. Perches
49. Wreaths
52. Lineman
53. Castor or Pollux
54. Stritch or May
55. Facilitates
57. Foster's "____ in de Cold Ground"
60. Tennis players, in a way
63. Common Latin phrase
65. Kind of service
67. To ____ (exactly)
68. Bits of thread
69. Greek promenade
70. Death-row distance
71. Type of stitching
72. Salad plant
74. Big blows
77. Town near Boston
79. Bangkok people
82. Beaver or mouse, e.g.
83. Indian queen
84. Traveler's stop
85. Cliburn and Borge
87. Mojave or Arabian
90. It's occasionally crashed
92. Chips in
93. Units
94. 21-gun event
96. Flute's relative
97. Musical gp.
101. Chicks
102. Bandleader Brown
103. Writer Hobson
105. Peter of the keyboard
106. Roman 106
107. Military units
109. Donald or Arthur beginning
112. Library section, for short
113. Unseated one
115. Coin for Gandhi
116. Former
118. Clothes
119. Dunne or Bordoni
120. Disentangle
121. Does ironing
122. Staff people: Abbr.
123. Sibyl

DOWN

1. Helen or Henry
2. Pleistocene epoch
3. A Mubarak predecessor
4. Poetic word
5. Skating floor
6. Opposed
7. Final say
8. Scottish miss
9. Rhone city
10. Adams and McKinley
11. Cruising
12. Taking ten
13. Container for monkeys
14. Chihuahua cheers
15. French lily
16. Sonar and radar, e.g.
17. Charms
18. Starts a trip
19. Golfing item
29. Burden
32. Feel an aversion to
34. Bird class
37. Rec. areas
39. Gaynor or Leigh
41. Swelling
42. Misses, in Mex.
45. Glass piece
46. Beauty's friend
48. Kiln
49. Ancient Hebrew weight
50. Having wings
51. Flower cluster
53. Kind of campaign
55. Director Lubitsch
56. Position
58. Straightens
59. Movie from way back
61. Tree resin
62. Ice, on the Elbe
64. Flying insect
66. Vermin and such
69. Like an unpowdered nose
70. President or avenue
72. Scorch
73. Carries on
75. Burned up
76. Pine yield
78. Russian and French
80. Trumpeter Al
81. Impalas and gazelles
85. Poker holding
86. Scandalous
87. Lhasa apso or keeshond
88. Lawmaker
89. Fabric's finished edge
90. Entreaty
91. Lippizaner's land
95. Lanes
96. Signal flares
98. Experience again
99. Offenses
100. Ritz, Waldorf, etc.
104. About
107. Mère's mate
108. Possessive
110. Baxter or Bancroft
111. Part of a bird's beak
113. Postal purchase: Abbr.
114. ____ Moines
117. Partner of feather

244 Phrasemaking By Cathy Millhauser

Leading to some apt responses.

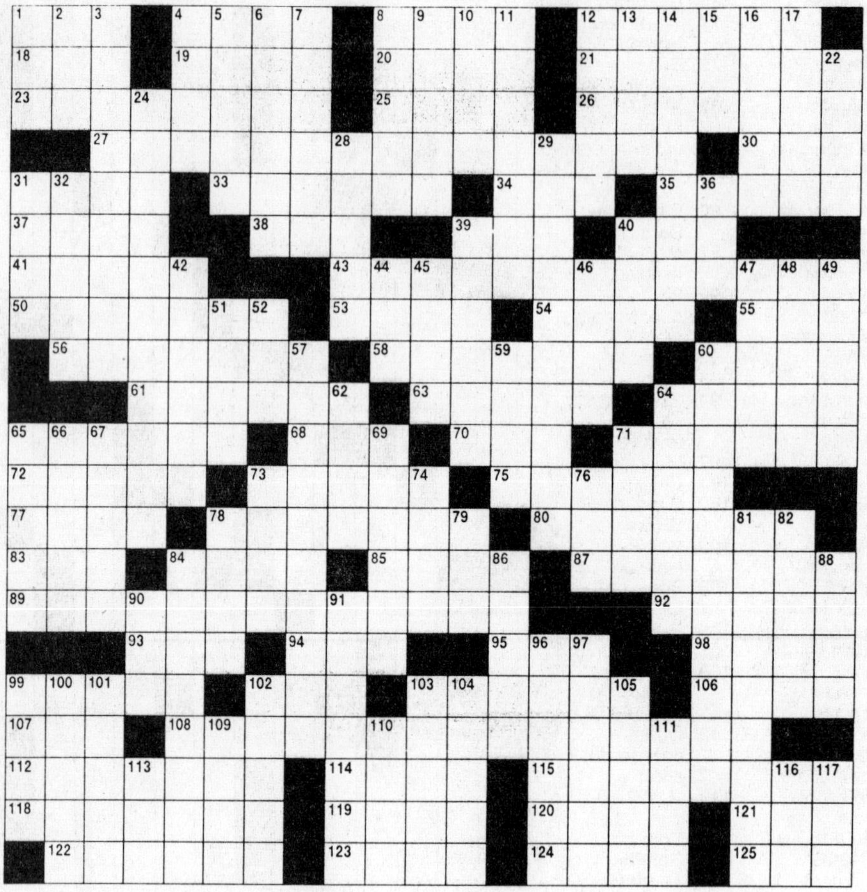

ACROSS

1. Rumanian coins
4. Hemingway handle
8. Indian-corn meal
12. Finn's friend
18. Shady tree
19. Pick and battle
20. Prompter
21. Medical priority-settings
23. Fever relievers
25. Soil: Prefix
26. Bothersome condition
27. Pole's place?
30. Salvator's six
31. Flit
33. Jesuit's cousin
34. Old World cont.
35. Be the host, for a fee
37. Straight: Prefix
38. Fast train: Abbr.
39. Summer time in L.A.
40. Baby syllables
41. Oil or vinegar holder
43. Tack's place?
50. Córdoba cooler
53. Fasten
54. Edible exclamation
55. German article
56. Silk gum
58. Dr. Dolittle's charges
60. Russian saint
61. Had a premiere
63. Climb
64. Says it's so
65. Noels
68. Nu followers
70. Samuel's teacher
71. Statements of belief
72. Drab color
73. Soak
75. Damage
77. Wings
78. In harmony
80. Some treasurers
83. Offensive festival?
84. Part of a train sound
85. Bedouin
87. Child's gun ammo: Var.
89. Desk's place?
92. Cawdor Castle's county
93. San Luis was one
94. What a drunk ties on?
95. Org. for Eagles and Rams
98. Maine-to-Florida hwy.
99. Noble robber?
102. Lennon's beloved
103. St. Vitus's dance
106. Remainder
107. Spanish wave
108. Umbrella's place?
112. Set free, conditionally
114. Cat or dove chaser
115. Reaping's keepings
118. Make ready
119. White-tailed eagle
120. British carbine
121. Hemp fibers
122. Shooting star
123. Person with a list
124. Stool sitter
125. Summer on the Riviera

DOWN

1. Herd's hangout
2. Subways' opposites
3. Entreat
4. Head line of a sort
5. Truth about math
6. Corre-spondent of a sort
7. Classify
8. Scrams
9. Zero
10. Only
11. Great ability
12. Beatles' beater
13. Seed covering
14. Serval and margay
15. Thanksgiving vegetable
16. Discharge
17. Actress Adorée
22. Commotion
24. Needle's place?
28. Rovers' cousins
29. Finger's place?
31. Severinsen and others
32. Tapestry
36. Silvery gray
39. Raid participants
40. New York nine
42. Baseball clout
44. Teachers' assn.
45. Does leather work
46. Scuff slipper
47. Stayed in neutral
48. Amazon tributary
49. Pot, for some
51. Frosts
52. Caledonian one
57. One's place?
59. Bamako's country
60. Hoop's place?
62. "Mon ____!"
64. Ascended
65. Snouted animal
66. Fred or Ethan
67. Laredo loop
69. House's relative
71. Custody
73. Pack
74. Lima locale
76. Tavern
78. Sailing call
79. Pop
81. Repeat
82. Ecological stages
84. Leaf scallops
86. "You ought to know ____"
88. Pique
90. Sis's sib
91. Used cocaine
96. Most like a bird
97. Type of shed
99. Philologist Franz
100. Frighten
101. Peep show
102. Less usual
103. Dresden specialty
104. Wife of Menelaus
105. Bewildered
109. Unholy Roman emperor
110. Common vetch
111. Red deer
113. Choose
116. Received
117. Fleecy female

245 Around the Country By H. Hastings Reddall

Getting familiar with how some places are known.

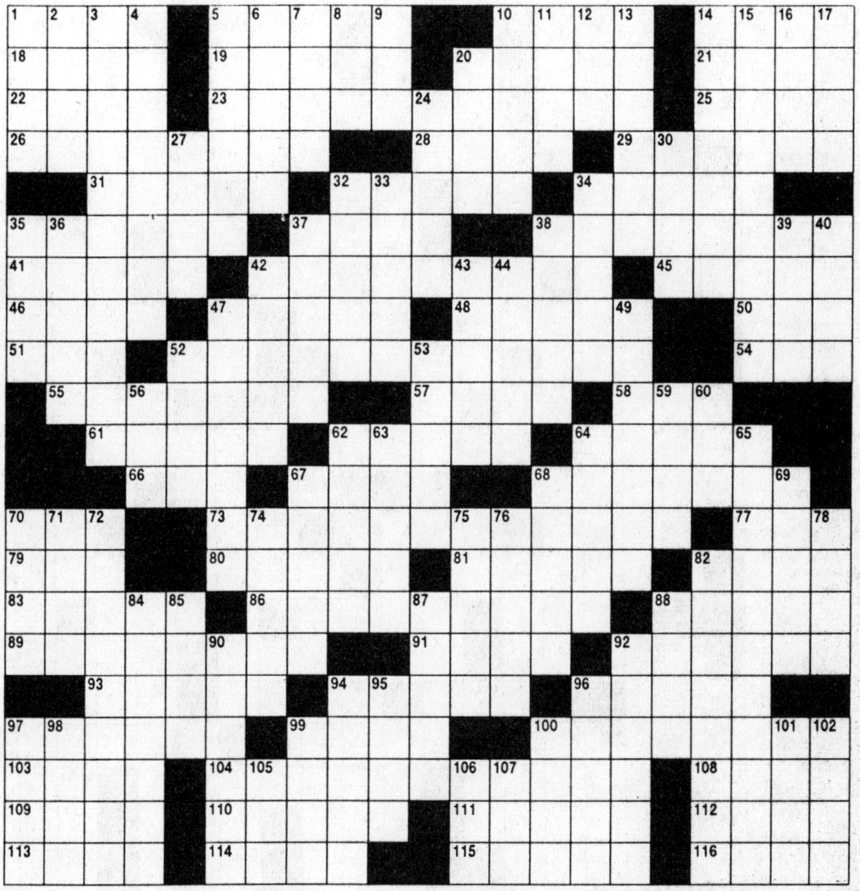

ACROSS

1. Get rid of
5. Handlelike parts
10. African fox
14. Roman 301
18. Bring into line
19. Requires
20. Go onstage
21. Desertlike
22. Yodelers' locale
23. New Jersey
25. Dole out
26. Novice rowers' woes
28. "I met ___ with . . ."
29. Trousers feature
31. Fish-pole parts
32. Chairman's need
34. Inclined
35. Metric measures
37. Musical rendering
38. Plunders
41. Nuisances
42. "But mice and rats, and such ___": "King Lear"
45. Bend over
46. Consumes
47. Speedily
48. Orphan girl
50. Neither's partner
51. Period of time
52. Certain group of 50
54. Do a mole job
55. Mussolini confederate
57. Cats and dogs, often
58. More than one: Abbr.
61. U.S. poet
62. Certain writing
64. Trident part
66. ___ volente
67. TV emcee Jack
68. Greek earthquake
70. Headed the parade
73. New Hampshire
77. Word before cent
79. Holiday time
80. Tall tales
81. Active ones
82. Queens stadium
83. Openings
86. Certain passes
88. Fetid
89. Murderer's plea, often
91. Common abbr. on a list
92. Crude
93. The Red and others
94. Sanctify
96. Public walks
97. Delaware tribe
99. "Too bad"
100. Condensed, as an article
103. Destination of a certain witch
104. South Dakota
108. Hindu god of love
109. Fog's relative
110. Mountain ridge
111. More wan
112. News piece
113. Too
114. Bridge term
115. Mimics
116. Loch of note

DOWN

1. Brief try
2. Annie or Monty
3. New York
4. Ice cream, cake, etc.
5. One's own children, always
6. Approaches
7. Indian weights
8. Accumulate
9. Compass direction
10. Conductor Dorati
11. Musial of baseball
12. Tennis unit
13. Constructs
14. Arthurian Eden
15. Inventions
16. Townsmen
17. French notion
20. Salinger girl
24. Part of U.S.N.R.
27. Cumberland river
30. Van Winkle and Torn
32. Kind of musical note
33. Bothered
34. High nest
35. Graf ___
36. Bored to ___
37. Tropical tree
38. Parking-lot souvenirs
39. Belt holder
40. Agile
42. Clove or nutmeg
43. Teenage activities
44. Growing out
47. Partial resemblance
49. Lively qualities
52. Exhort
53. Football or baseball, e.g.
56. Connective
59. Finish last
60. Like a spinster: Abbr.
62. Satin finish
63. Do a roof job
64. Anjou and Bosc
65. Minnesota
67. Fend off
68. Bessemer product
69. Searches for
70. Son of Jacob
71. Balanced
72. Stupidity
74. Floats
75. Prepares copy
76. Soft drinks
78. Comedienne Martha
82. Aquatic animal's pelt
84. Italian port
85. Clip
87. Pee Wee of baseball
88. Part
90. Polar cover
92. N.B.A. players
94. Ink smudges
95. Tardy
96. Clerical cap
97. Southwestern hill
98. Harmful
99. Certain votes
100. Small valley
101. Scottish uncles
102. Hoover and others
105. Mouths
106. Mineral spring
107. Valve or spout

246 Bar None By Jim Page

Everybody's welcome to some activities.

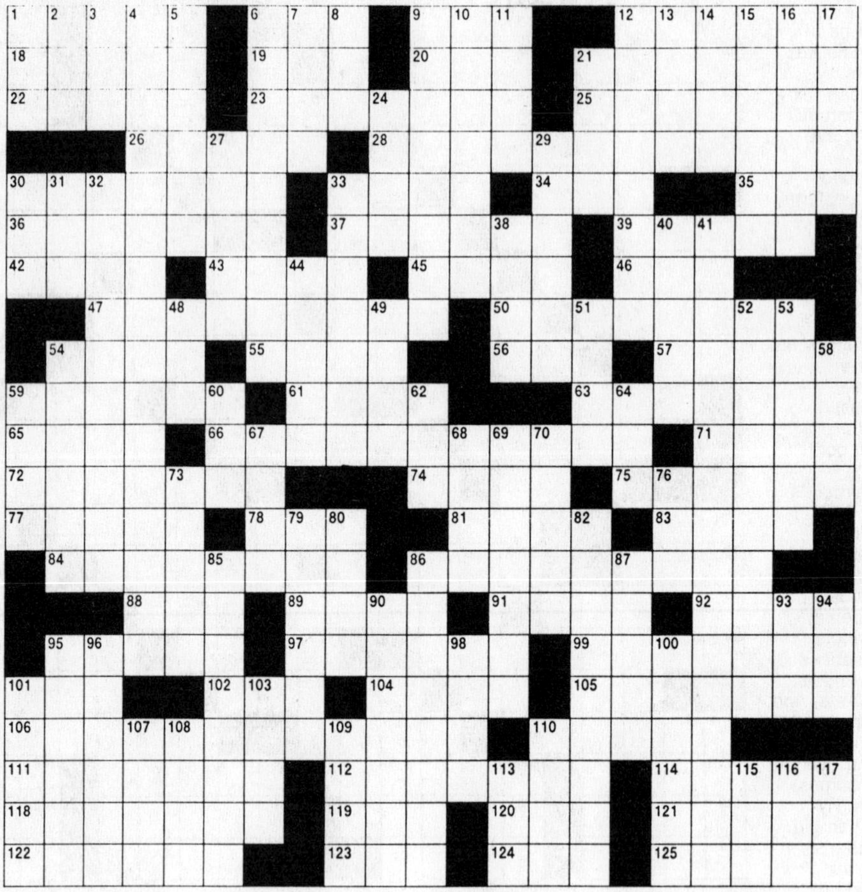

ACROSS

1. Nonprofessionals
6. Also
9. Spanish Mrs.
12. Gadgets
18. Moslem god
19. Aster finish
20. Rec. of brain activity
21. Far away
22. Phone-call opening
23. Methuselah was one
25. High-level agreement
26. Deficiencies
28. What Scrooge did at bedtime?
30. Kneecap
33. Author Pierre
34. Rubber tree
35. Piano's relative: Abbr.
36. Color-treated a fabric
37. Overdue debt
39. ___ aves (unusual ones)
42. ___ Spee
43. Textile screw pines
45. Weapons
46. "The ___ of Wonderful Nonsense"
47. Drainer's words?
50. Lets in again
54. Bird-beak part
55. Feeling no ___ (squiffed)
56. Jerusalem is its cap.
57. Ones easily flimflammed
59. Out-and-out
61. Linden tree
63. Come ___ (agree)
65. Belgrade native
66. What a dumbwaiter did?
71. Finger noise
72. More shaggy
74. Lucy's ex
75. Standards of conduct
77. Outfit for Mr. T
78. Blue Eagle org.
81. Cleveland cagers
83. "___ You Were Here"
84. Bloodhounds' targets, often
86. How a trout drinks?
88. ___ Koussi (Sahara's highest peak)
89. N.Y.C. museum
91. Indian or state
92. Bristle
95. Intrinsically
97. Turkish peak
99. Crimson color
101. Sea bird
102. Road material
104. Inside info
105. Florentine irises
106. What a down-to-earth quarterback did?
110. Retail store V.I.P.
111. Most diabolic
112. "Do not ___"
114. Weeper who was stoned
118. Trig lines
119. Org. for April
120. Bando or Mineo
121. Mink's kin
122. Drifts
123. Woe!, to Cicero
124. Juin, juillet, etc.
125. Oaters: Abbr.

DOWN

1. ___-di-dah:
2. "Cakes and ___"
3. ___-gotten (like some gains)
4. What the tent-raising camper did?
5. Like a sand bar
6. What the batter at the plate did?
7. Lubricates
8. Outré
9. Prepare an ambush
10. More slender
11. Taj Mahal site
12. Pepped up Miss Rogers?
13. Narrow strip of land: Abbr.
14. Dele's opposite
15. "Man of La ___"
16. Like most TV shows
17. Footprints
21. Satan, to a Scot
24. Restaurateur Toots
27. Athlete's gripper
29. Edith Cavell and others
30. Book production: Abbr.
31. What dreamers walk on
32. Wintergreen fruits
33. Scotch damsels
38. Of an ancient Indus culture
40. Medieval helmet
41. What a toaster does?
44. Violinmaker
48. Knockout number
49. Military group
51. Commedia dell'___
52. Agents that dull luster
53. Field shrub: Var.
54. Bring into being
58. Biological classes: Abbr.
59. East African people
60. Article
62. Headed
64. Be indebted
67. Normandy river
68. Prefix for liter or meter
69. High ___ (stewed)
70. "Hawaii ___" (TV show)
73. Mosque leaders
76. ___-nighter (double-header)
79. Comment
80. Zitherlike instrument
82. What a pair of glasses did?
85. Religious ones
86. French encyclopedist
87. Land of enchantment
90. White wine
93. ___-hee
94. Blurbs, e.g.
95. One who verifies
96. Tempt
98. Engagement: Abbr.
100. Heretofore
101. Discharge
103. Pretends
107. Ladd
108. Await decision
109. Roman 1504
110. Snippy child
113. ___ up (consume)
115. Giant Giant
116. Big ___
117. Speech pauses

247 Encore By Calista Luminati

The first time isn't always enough.

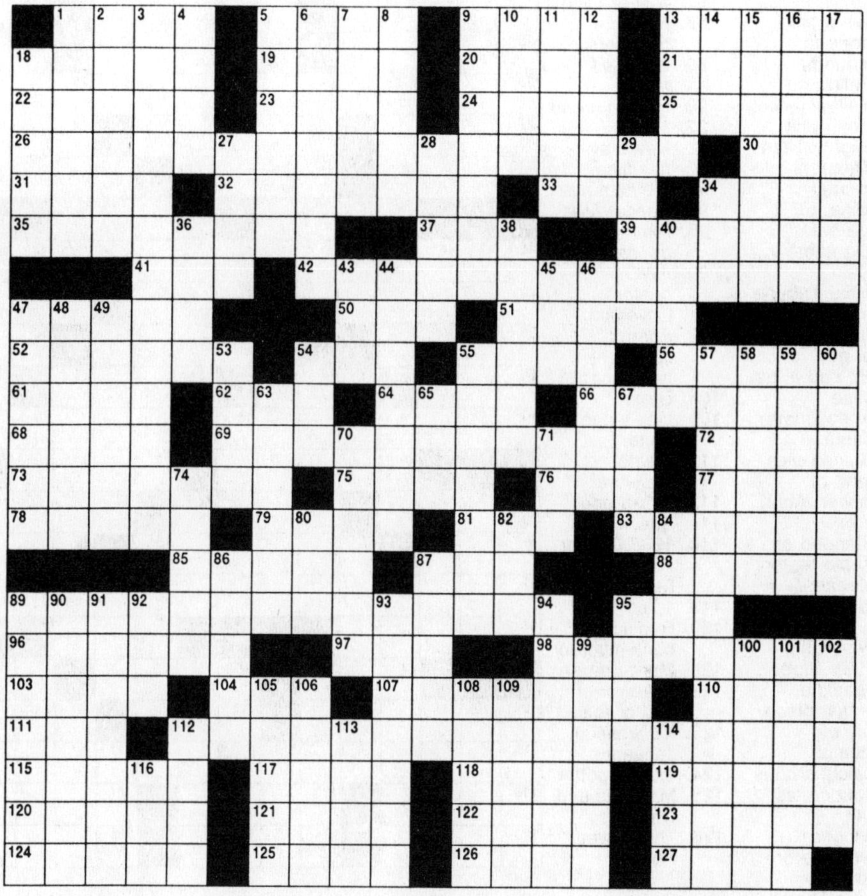

ACROSS

1. Renowned Surrealist
5. Rope fiber
9. Nanny's vehicle
13. Actress Irene
18. Raise your partner again
19. Vulcan's forge
20. Rank
21. Spinachlike plant
22. Having wings
23. Mouthful for an oaf
24. Riviera seasons
25. K.P. worker
26. Song popularized by Bing Crosby
30. Panay native
31. Concealed: Prefix
32. Surveyor's instrument
33. Ott or Allen
34. "When the frost ___ the punkin . . ."
35. Torments
37. Dog tags
39. Undergo absorption
41. Helios
42. Hawthorne story collection
47. I.R.S. action
50. Wee worker
51. Hefty
52. Metric measures
54. Former campus org.
55. Keel extension
56. ___ over (studies)
61. Dove domicile
62. "___ your age!"
64. Bone: Prefix
66. Cast a poor mold
68. Well-known cartel
69. Song that gave Doris her stage name
72. Renown, to Gina
73. Chinese nuts
75. Moist
76. Genetic initials
77. Moslem prince
78. Malayan headmen
79. Romantic archer
81. Crowbar
83. University official
85. Stately dance
87. Holy ___
88. Gets bogged down
89. Woody Allen movie
95. Antithesis of quiet
96. Kind of equation
97. Daughter of Cadmus
98. Forms of atomic elements
103. Freeman Gosden role
104. Sixth sense
107. "Rhinoceros" author
110. Pinocchio feature
111. Before Oct.
112. Rescheduled production
115. Billiard shot
117. Italian painter Guido
118. Handclasp
119. Moth
120. Loon
121. Can. province
122. Hamlet, for Burton
123. Legal claims
124. Discontinue
125. Shadow
126. Cheers for Manolete
127. Writer Claude

DOWN

1. Mislead
2. Humiliated
3. Popular Brownie song
4. Thought: Prefix
5. Happened
6. Democritus was one
7. Bun binder
8. Polish range
9. Antedate
10. Old Irish stronghold
11. Mr. T's vehicle
12. Middle, in law
13. He translated Homer
14. Macaw
15. Sunburn preventer
16. Vinegary
17. Lourdes and the Alamo
18. Moslem month
27. Seize
28. Nantes pronouncement
29. Bumpkins
34. "___ Yankee Doodle . . ."
36. Yea or nay, e.g.
38. Furnace feeder
40. Strides
43. Bankroll
44. ___ as (to what extent)
45. Brit. decoration
46. What Watson was for Holmes
47. ___ as ice
48. Thomas More's country
49. Discover
53. His name produced an ism
54. Dirty digs
55. Siberian features
57. Finnigin's words to Flannigan
58. Rover
59. Weasel
60. Stings
63. Tapioca source
65. Religious degree
67. Jewish month
70. Hebrew name for God
71. Carry Nation, for one
74. Secret agent, in Spain
80. Newsstand buy, for short
82. Former power org.
84. Gush
86. ". . . lovely as ___"
87. Be inquisitive
89. Of a blood component
90. Green cooler
91. Eye malformation
92. "___, my darling daughter"
93. Hanky ornament
94. Put in the wrong folder
95. It sometimes has a keeper
99. Clarence Darrow defended him
100. Silk cloth
101. Suffix for opal or phosphor
102. Sibyl and Pythia, e.g.
105. Certain fussy eater
106. ___ grape (feed Mae West)
108. River to the Amazon
109. Famous Flynn
112. Network
113. Against
114. Indian fair
116. Titanic's call

248 Headlines By William Canine

Sports achievements as reported locally.

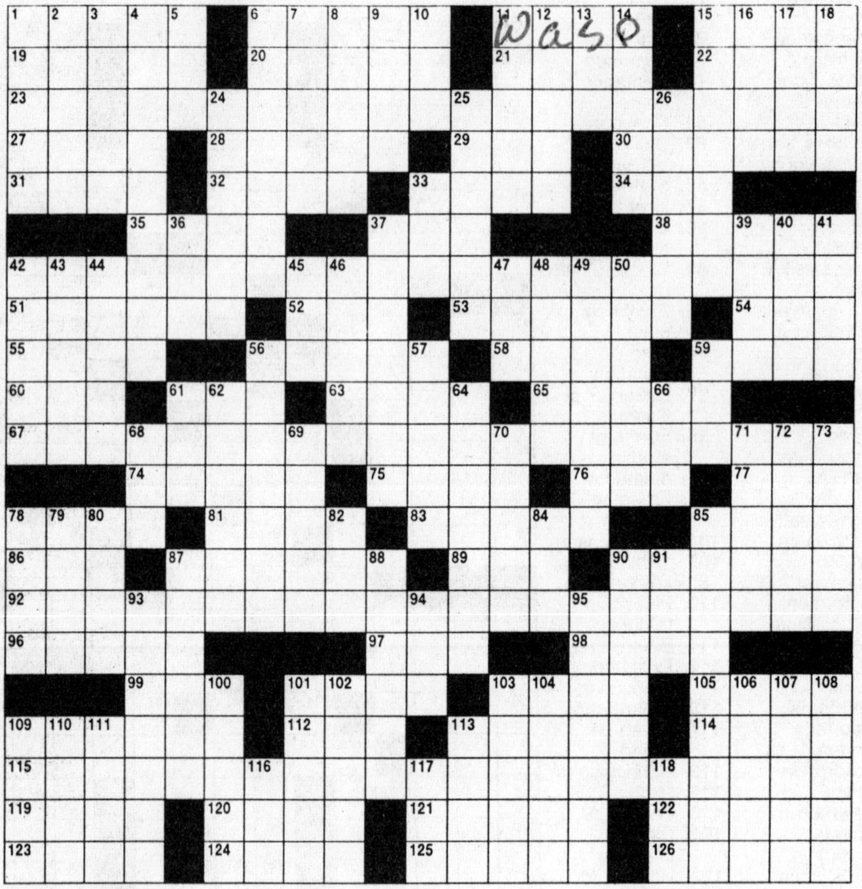

ACROSS

1. What time does to wounds
6. Following
11. Yellow jacket
15. Soap unit
19. Mighty Titan
20. Tempera-mental
21. Mine, to Marcel
22. Big name in Oslo
23. 1959 Tribune headline
27. Ballesteros of golf
28. He had a last case
29. Affectionate name
30. Guinea pigs
31. Kind of power: Abbr.
32. Frees
33. Stepped on
34. Apple tester
35. Mediter-ranean port
37. ___ generis
38. Wipe out
42. 1986 Globe headline
51. In last place
52. Cry of triumph
53. Calcutta lutes
54. Bounce, as bait
55. Winged
56. Word before ho
58. ___ Alto
59. Withhold
60. Latvia or Estonia: Abbr.
61. Brazilian timber tree
63. Swingy rhythm
65. Mountain crest
67. 1980 Press headline
74. Swedish tenor
75. Christie's "Death on the ___"
76. Leaders: Abbr.
77. Speed
78. Verdi's "___ Nome"
81. Flavoring herb
83. Nostrils
85. Caution
86. Word before way or thing
87. NATO members
89. Off one's rocker
90. Held in dread
92. 1983 Newsday headline
96. Vietnam hub
97. Dancer Miller
98. Himmel's opposite
99. AWOL hunters
101. Covenant
103. Former late-night TV presence
105. Dross
109. Lion's-den visitor
112. Metric measure
113. Italian poet
114. Speck
115. 1985 Courier-Journal headline
119. 1,760 yards
120. Reo's contemporary
121. More precise
122. Follower of bed or road
123. It's white in January
124. Three-spotter
125. Madeline and Otto
126. The Velvet Fog

DOWN

1. Part of a ship's bow
2. Waters or Barrymore
3. Animate
4. Inconsiderate theater patron
5. Compass pt.
6. Artist's cupid
7. Outwitted
8. Municipalities
9. Prepare for print
10. Rembrandt van ___: Var.
11. Ocean game fish
12. Change
13. Bribe
14. Chessboard item
15. Change
16. Russian range
17. Welles role
18. Newts
24. Bosporus, for one
25. Destructive insects
26. Certain oranges
33. Parson bird
36. Speed meas.
37. G.B.S. specialist
39. Assistant
40. Look over
41. Observe
42. Elegance
43. English composer
44. Cognizant
45. Dundee denial
46. Command-ment verb
47. Restaurant-table leaving
48. Hokkaido city
49. Moslem rulers
50. Wore down
56. In a bold manner
57. North Carolina town
59. Soc. page gal
61. Stout's relative
62. Hawk
64. Caryatid's relative
66. A's, B's, etc.: Abbr.
68. Self
69. Franks' ___ Law
70. Caravansary
71. Busy takeoff spot
72. Electrician, sometimes
73. Imparts
78. Available funds
79. Column
80. Pitcher Nolan
82. Coin of Rumania
84. Wynn and Begley
85. Attacks vigorously
87. Wing-footed
88. Actress Sissy
90. Actress Mia
91. Conclude
93. Campaign choice
94. Explosive
95. Temporary occupants
100. Virgule, for one
101. Hesitate
102. Literary cockroach
103. B'rer Rabbit's brier home
104. Pale
106. Hermit
107. Mr. T's "The ___"
108. "En ___!"
109. Mil. decorations
110. Samoan city
111. Mistress Quickly
113. Chinese tea
116. ___ Harbor, Maine
117. Sign
118. Violin or harp suffix

249 Urban Connections By Elaine Schorr

What some cities might aptly be called.

ACROSS

1. In a reverie
5. Victim of the Russian Revolution
9. Concubine of Abraham
14. Nonprofit TV
17. Mischa of the films
18. Without profit
21. "G.W.T.W." name
22. Marsupial, for short
23. City lynching
26. It's often bitter
27. Sandwich fish
28. Matisse, in Soho
29. Regarding
30. Major Hoople's word
31. City's fortune
36. Mom-and-pop place
39. Piqued
40. Pollster's quest
41. Wired messages: Abbr.
42. City lavatory
46. Prior to
47. Electrical pioneer Nikola
48. Part of Caesar's pronouncement
49. Plaintiff's opp.
52. Time period
53. Novelist Murdoch
54. So soon, in France
55. Arena sound
57. Blackout convenience
59. Attorney-___
60. Pregame event
61. Miss Teasdale concurs
66. Colonel killed at the Alamo
68. Pugilistic
69. Figaro's creator
72. Give in
73. "It's ___ country, isn't it?"
74. Musician Brubeck
75. Sci. of plants
76. Always, to a poet
77. Age category
78. Novelist Joyce Carol
79. Way: Abbr.
80. City political front
85. Evening, in Nice
86. Small crayfish
88. Fencing sword
89. Schemers' dupes
90. Island explosive traps
93. Bilker's art
95. ___ to (stopped, at sea)
96. Biblical brother
97. Made a billiard shot
101. "Exodus" character
102. City retreats
108. U.S.S.R. native
109. Upper crust
110. Rodin creation
111. Tennis score
112. Honshu bay
113. ___ man (Romeo)
114. Pans' partners
115. Lacoste of tennis

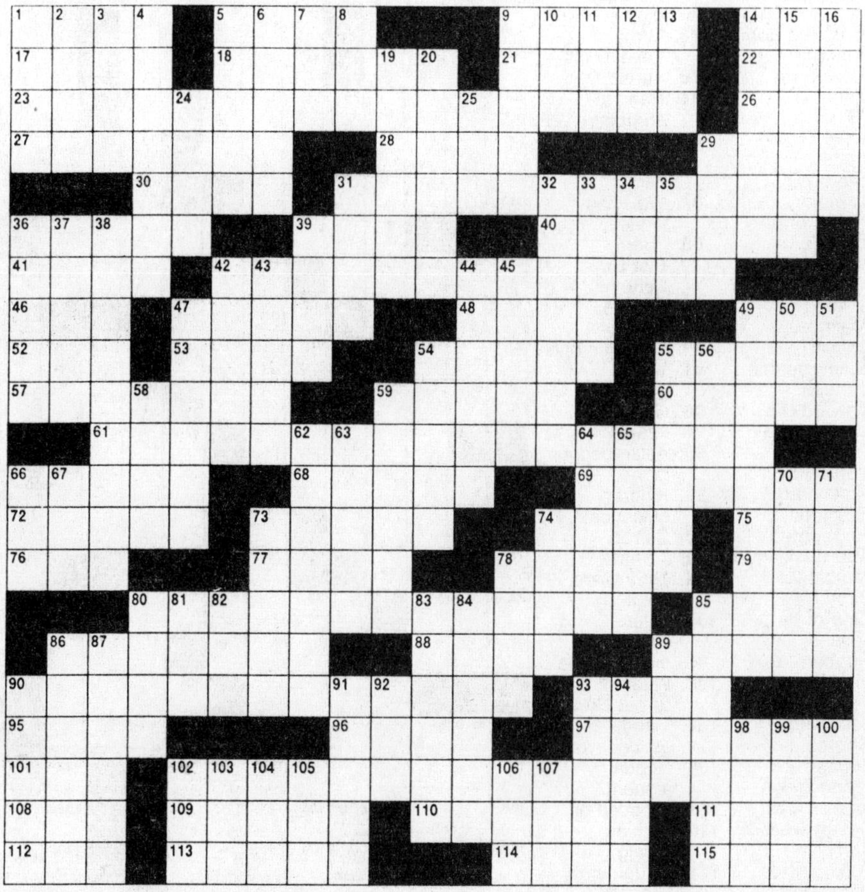

DOWN

1. Riches' counterpart
2. Emanation
3. M.P. member
4. Wall Street figures
5. Early rabbi
6. Pegasus was one
7. C.P.A.
8. Korean soldier
9. Words to a hitchhiker
10. Cry of surprise
11. Needlefish
12. Creative endeavor
13. Stinging fish
14. Near, in Italy
15. Stylish society
16. Sinful biblical city
19. ___ middle course (be uncommitted)
20. Partner of Evers and Chance
24. Rifle firing pin
25. Silkworm
29. Lively: Music abbr.
31. Hawaiian gooseberry
32. Alit
33. Sailing spar
34. Branco or Bravo
35. Upward: Prefix
36. Gary product
37. Kind of firma
38. City reply
39. Weighing implements: Abbr.
42. Baseball's Yogi
43. Exploiting
44. With sinister intent
45. Cowpea of the Philippines
47. Like a wedding cake
49. City intellectual
50. Slithery one
51. Playwright Christopher
54. Kind of prison or secret
55. Turning points
56. Bowlers and cloches
58. Kangaroo feature
59. Go along with
62. Gave a choice
63. Begets
64. Persona non ___
65. Like a web
66. Tennis seeding
67. French goose
70. Out
71. Passages
73. Dined en famille
74. Subject of a "South Pacific" song
78. Is insolvent
80. Hold in distaste
81. Piercing tool
82. Stringed instrument: Abbr.
83. Extends a membership
84. Baby simian
85. Urn
86. Refrain of a song
87. Blue-pencil
89. Prefix for mutuel
90. Lamb Chop's Lewis
91. Two of a kind
92. Nigerian native
93. Buffalo Bill was one
94. Places for croissants
98. See 103 Down
99. Yeats's home
100. Unit of force
102. ___ canto
103. In fashion, with 98 Down
104. Disencumber
105. Dirty place
106. Kind of session
107. Pou ___ (place to stand)

250 Vegetable Plate By Frances Hansen

Presenting a varied menu of indigestibles.

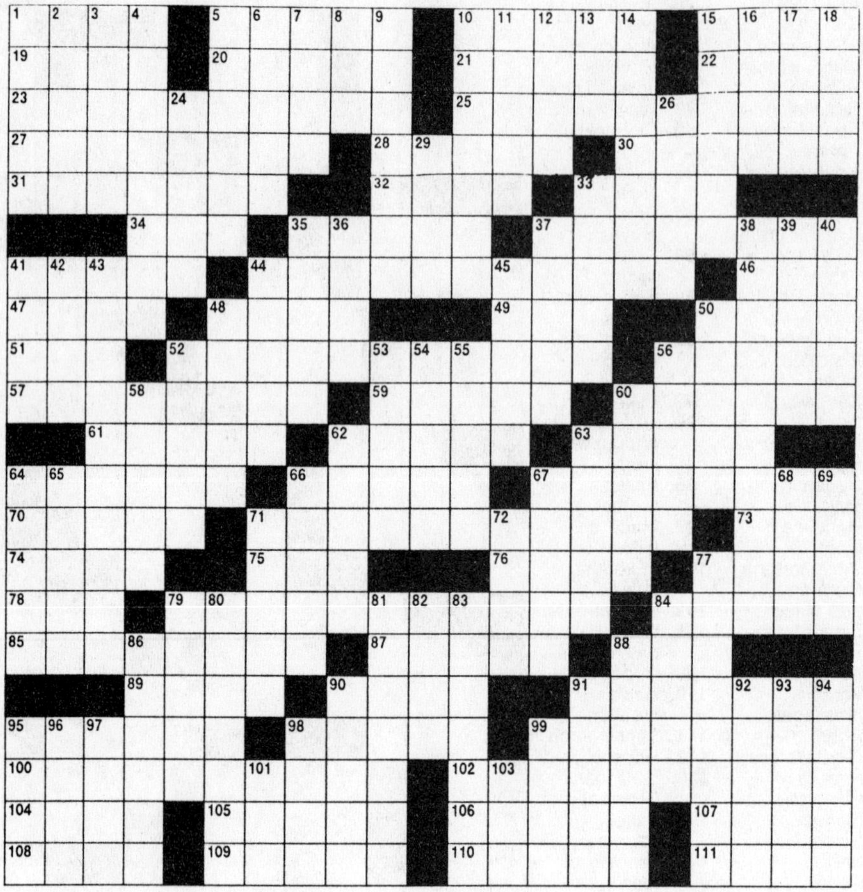

ACROSS

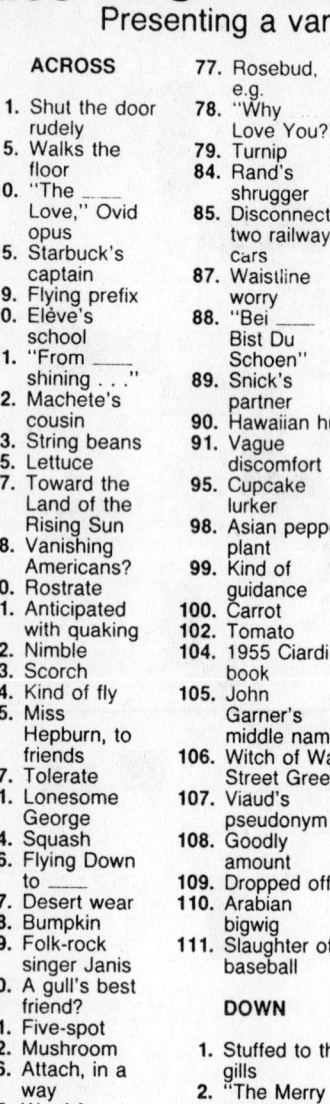

1. Shut the door rudely
5. Walks the floor
10. "The ___ Love," Ovid opus
15. Starbuck's captain
19. Flying prefix
20. Elève's school
21. "From ___ shining . . ."
22. Machete's cousin
23. String beans
25. Lettuce
27. Toward the Land of the Rising Sun
28. Vanishing Americans?
30. Rostrate
31. Anticipated with quaking
32. Nimble
33. Scorch
34. Kind of fly
35. Miss Hepburn, to friends
37. Tolerate
41. Lonesome George
44. Squash
46. Flying Down to ___
47. Desert wear
48. Bumpkin
49. Folk-rock singer Janis
50. A gull's best friend?
51. Five-spot
52. Mushroom
56. Attach, in a way
57. Word for Fosdick
59. Eero's father
60. Needing storm windows
61. Bounded over
62. Ecstasy
63. Prefix for glyphic
64. Greasy hair stuff
66. Psalm word
67. First name in art
70. Draw out
71. Spinach
73. Feel under par
74. Take ten
75. Turner or Cole
76. Dobbin's dish
77. Rosebud, e.g.
78. "Why ___ Love You?"
79. Turnip
84. Rand's shrugger
85. Disconnect two railway cars
87. Waistline worry
88. "Bei ___ Bist Du Schoen"
89. Snick's partner
90. Hawaiian hub
91. Vague discomfort
95. Cupcake lurker
98. Asian pepper plant
99. Kind of guidance
100. Carrot
102. Tomato
104. 1955 Ciardi book
105. John Garner's middle name
106. Witch of Wall Street Green
107. Viaud's pseudonym
108. Goodly amount
109. Dropped off
110. Arabian bigwig
111. Slaughter of baseball

DOWN

1. Stuffed to the gills
2. "The Merry Widow" man
3. Hit the deck
4. Composite pictures
5. Squinted
6. "Feed ___ and starve a fever"
7. Kind of cat
8. Cockney purgatory
9. "Ev'ry little breeze ___ whisper Louise"
10. One with high hopes
11. All set
12. G.I.'s lullaby?
13. Citizen: Suffix
14. Refrain from
15. Established in one's stateroom
16. Lean on the horn
17. On the sheltered side
18. Hopalong Cassidy portrayer
24. Ride with Daisy of song
26. Intended
29. Tropical herb
33. Adamant
35. "Heaven ___, Mr. Allison"
36. Tacks on
37. Stone chip
38. Rhubarb
39. Gorno-Altai of the U.S.S.R., formerly
40. Actor Cox of "Apple's Way"
41. Fish-landing spear
42. Off Broadway award
43. Corn
44. Start of a San Francisco song
45. Building lots
48. Light pancake
50. Queen's coiffure-disturber
52. Forest clearing
53. ". . . know ___ am not great": Tennyson
54. Homeric work
55. Like an angler's tall story
56. Tendency
58. Do a double take
60. Fashionable creations
62. Midler or Davis
63. Native ___ (homeland)
64. In hiding
65. Greek theater
66. Plumbing tool
67. Percolate
68. "When I said I would ___ bachelor . . .": Shak.
69. Auto pioneer
71. Say ___ (concede defeat)
72. Blast-furnace knob
77. Use a garrote
79. ___ Wars (Rome-Carthage hassle)
80. Having no fixed limits
81. Needled
82. Artifice
83. The dapper Menjou
84. Choreographer Alvin
86. Become inflexible
88. Long-suffering one
90. Ergo
91. Smooth finish
92. Suffix for exped or extrad
93. Painter Andrea del ___
94. ___ Bell (Emily Brontë)
95. Clean a pipe
96. Looped handle
97. Put ___ a nutshell (summarize)
98. Follower of Mercedes
99. We do a lot for his sake
101. Chinese leader
103. Dream stage, briefly

251 Americana By Sidney Robbins

Some things having to do with the union.

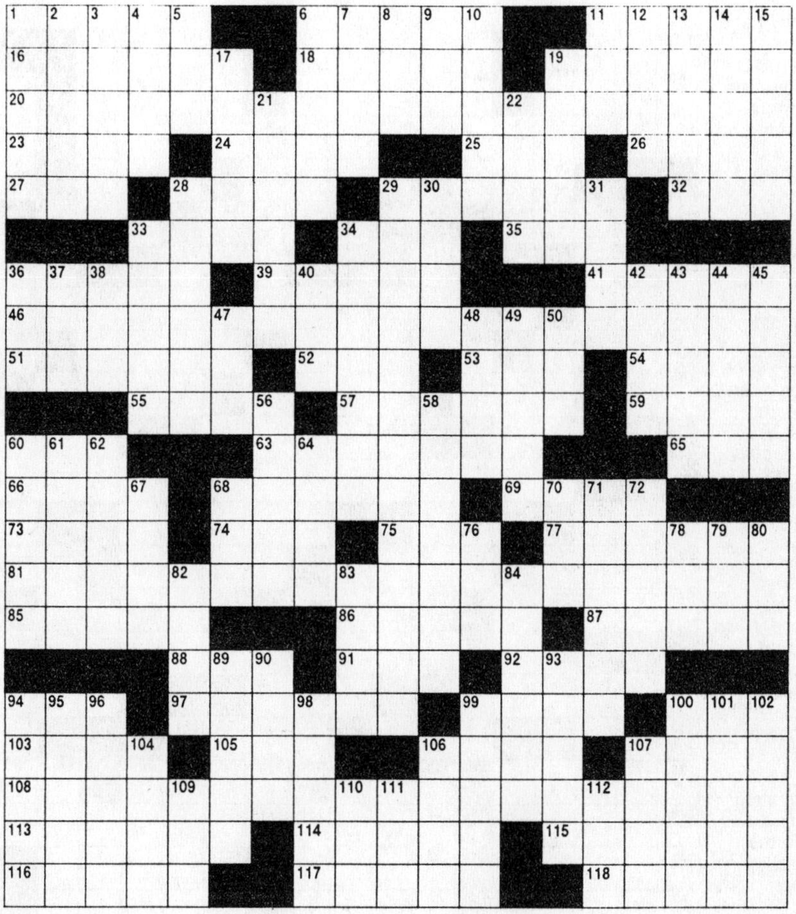

ACROSS

1. Stolen-goods receiver
6. Fancy banquet
11. Inventor Nikola
16. "All ___!"
18. Feature of a cow
19. Tool of war
20. "Most widely unread book in America"
23. Suffix for differ
24. Let stand
25. A.F.L. partner
26. Sharpen
27. Color
28. Part of a bird's beak
29. Originate
32. ___ Vegas
33. Wormwood product
34. Bluegrass
35. U.S.A. neighbor
36. Eastern V.I.P.
39. Be a scholarly flop
41. Furious
46. U.S. date to remember
51. Inferior racehorse
52. Tropical shrub
53. Christmas or New Year's ___
54. Neighbor of Tex.
55. What Simon does
57. Doted on
59. Archer William
60. Pep
63. Henbane of old
65. Summer time, for short
66. Length times width
68. It closes Saturday night
69. Kind of worm or measure
73. Forsaken
74. "___ Yankee Doodle . . ."
75. Collection
77. Goose variety
81. One of 100
85. Exist, in Spain
86. Partner of washy
87. Make amends
88. Critic Huxtable
91. We, to Cicero
92. Hilly city
94. Obtained
97. Broadway stage name
99. "___ Rose": Willson song
100. Delaware Water ___
103. Barbary ___
105. Sheepish bleat
106. Necklace part
107. Combo
108. Javits, Moynihan, etc.
113. Verified
114. Liberace's candelabra holder
115. Rank snuff
116. Word after dog or lop
117. Dutch painter
118. In want

DOWN

1. Went head-on
2. Dark, heavy wood
3. Time being
4. Bird container
5. Go off target
6. Red flare
7. Redact
8. Commotion
9. Old Japanese coin
10. Vestige
11. Golfer's place
12. Apiece
13. Thread holder
14. Blackmore girl
15. South American backbone
17. Spay
19. Scribbled
21. Bombard furiously
22. Writer O'Flaherty
28. Eye part
29. Value received
30. Go after leaves
31. Egress
33. Track events
34. Lahore native
36. Sixth sense
37. Tormé
38. A Gabor
40. Grassland
42. Peasant of India
43. Showed curiosity
44. Does farm work
45. Lift up
47. Attempt
48. Florida's ___ Beach
49. Occurrence
50. Sparks of the movies
56. Frauds
58. Unity
60. Worth
61. Does laundry work
62. Earn
64. It's moi, said Louis
67. Wall column
68. Caesar of TV
70. King toppler
71. Canal Zone area
72. Maternally related
76. Tray or tree
78. From ___ Z
79. Ameche
80. Exist
82. Periods of time
83. Bristly
84. Native of Damascus
89. Energetic person
90. Winglike
93. More peculiar
94. Quebec peninsula
95. "Carmen" or "Norma"
96. Quartet member
98. Stingers
99. Detroit flop
100. Grasp for
101. Broadcast
102. Slow
104. Make an S.&L. deposit
106. ___ up (study hard)
107. Italic or elite
109. Spread hay
110. Conniption
111. Charlotte of films
112. Pale

252 Meanings By Reginald Johnson

What some word combinations might indicate.

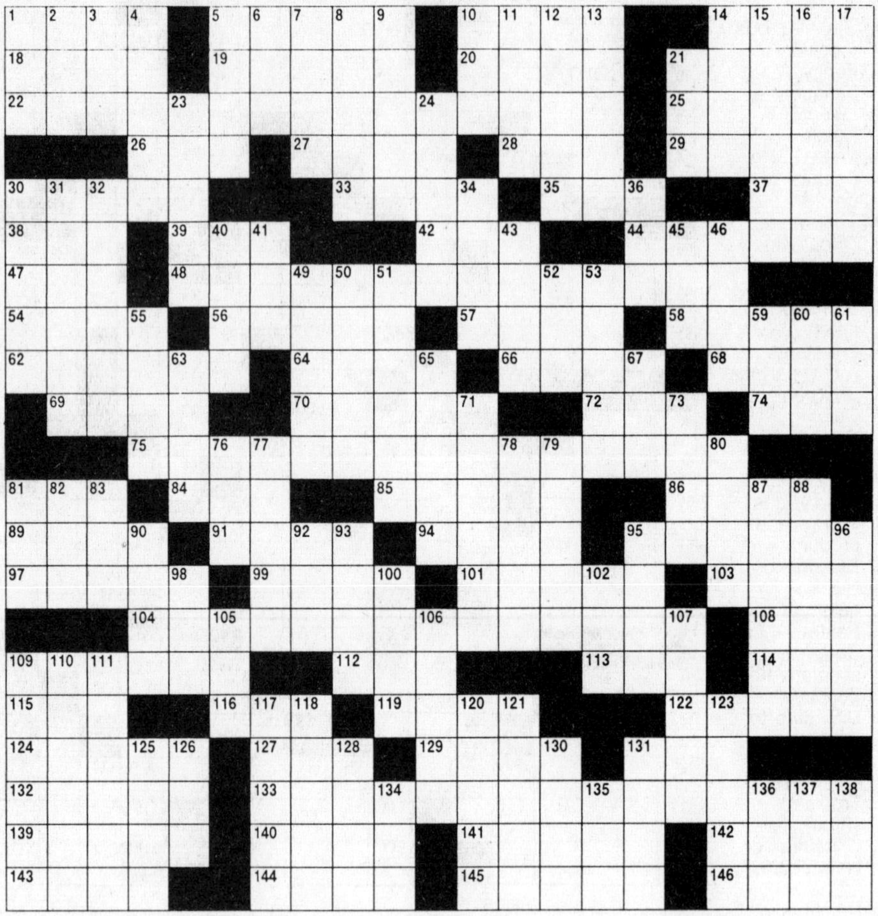

ACROSS

1. Partner of Phi and Kappa
5. It's light or grand
10. Camper's need
14. Smell ___
18. Plaza de Toros sounds
19. One of Dickens's "Tale"
20. In a line
21. Do mountaineering
22. Phrase suggesting golf
25. Stroll
26. Ocean bird
27. Put away
28. Look
29. Contradict
30. Mother: Prefix
33. Town near Caen
35. Barn's neighbor
37. Wrath
38. Lupino
39. Nation formed in Ala.
42. Attention
44. Kind of egg or bonnet
47. Kind of cat
48. Phrase suggesting racing
54. Part of Q.E.D.
56. Seed: Prefix
57. Eye part
58. Pieces of ___
62. Trusts
64. Frost
66. Noun ending
68. Crude
69. Exploit
70. ___-so (unnamed bloke)
72. Second person
74. N.J. clock setting
75. Name suggesting baseball
81. Upset, with "over"
84. Fed. power operation
85. Kind of heat
86. Paper or book
89. Port of Yemen
91. Handy Latin phrase
94. River to the Yellow Sea
95. Leatherneck
97. Ligurian port
99. Like a boat to China
101. Trace
103. Business-letter abbr.
104. Words suggesting Diana Ross
108. Ungentlemanly one
109. Do a job on Patty Hearst
112. Born, in France
113. "___ culpa"
114. Handle
115. Exist
116. Put on an ___
119. Marx
122. Brooder
124. Stair part
127. What Pizarro sought
129. Coward of the stage
131. Finial
132. Afghan or Thai
133. Phrase suggesting bowling
139. Midterms
140. To be, in France
141. Mails
142. De Valera's land
143. Superlative endings
144. Ooze
145. Cereal disease
146. College official

DOWN

1. Reptile with a hug
2. Dutch ___ disease
3. Kind of party
4. Late bloomer
5. Sign on a store door
6. Golfer's target
7. Cupid
8. Breaks in friendships
9. A "My Fair Lady" setting
10. Greek letter
11. Goofs
12. Things to count
13. Sound of spring
14. Peak
15. Kind of ears
16. Vamp's strong point
17. Seesaw
21. Men's org.
23. Halloween threat
24. Wise one's young
30. Bishop's hat
31. Was crazy about
32. Mexican dish
34. Where Diamond Head is
36. Affirmative vote
40. Meeting: Abbr.
41. Book addition, for short
43. French dream
45. One-shot court point
46. Variety of milk
49. Trunk
50. Hunter in space
51. Wanderers
52. Cicero's X
53. Barney Oldfield, e.g.
55. Bound
59. Turn right
60. Owns
61. Explosive
63. Polish a manuscript
65. Delight in
67. A Gabor
71. Expand
73. Ferber
76. 5th is one
77. Island off China
78. Kind of apple acid
79. Lindbergh case's Hauptmann
80. Good old days
81. Baseball putout
82. Chemical ending
83. Sword's superior
87. Beggar's prop
88. Put in a box
90. Common or proper
92. Mont Blanc, e.g.
93. Bereft
95. Small lake
96. Church official
98. ___ rule (generally)
100. One of 52
102. Chew for Junior
105. Health spot
106. Intended
107. Buccaneers' home
109. Kind of self-defense
110. Garden flowers
111. Discontinue
117. Apple throwaways
118. Commonplace
120. Excite
121. Outcast
123. Soused
125. Consumes
126. Hosp. workers
128. Demon
130. "It's a ___ way . . ."
131. Formerly, of old
134. Wise to
135. Japanese herb
136. Golfer's concern
137. Period
138. Itch

253 No Decision By Bert Kruse

A cynical observation on personal diversity.

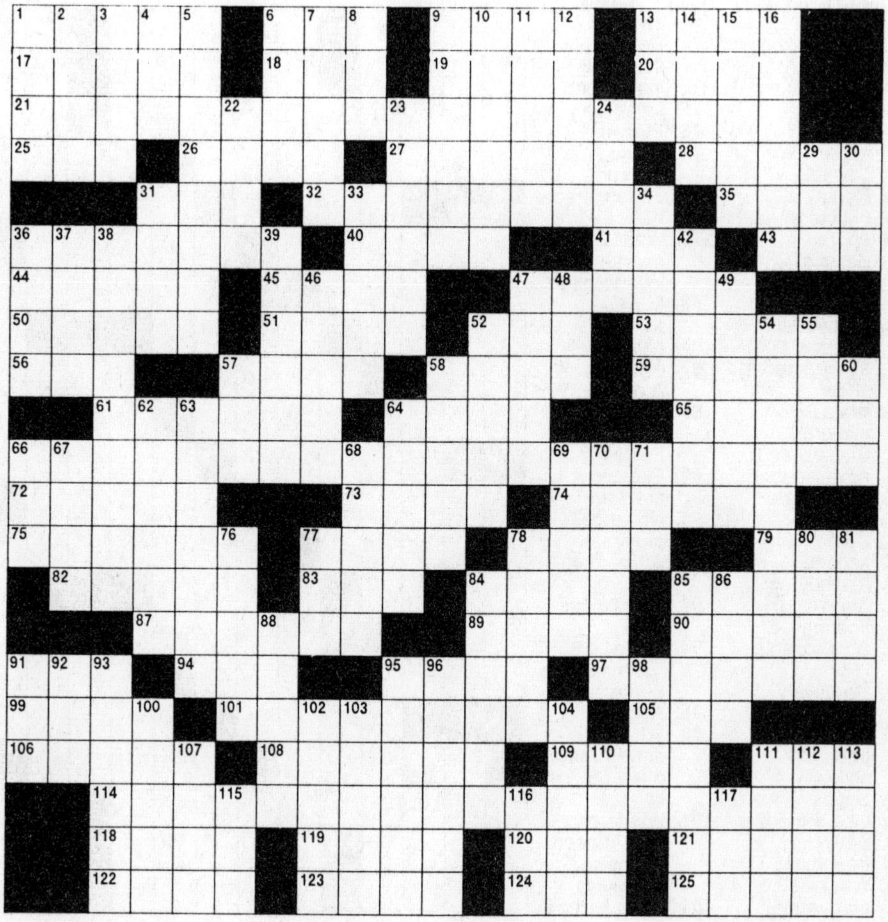

ACROSS

1. Cake's crown
6. Total up
9. Like some cheese
13. Leap
17. Count of music
18. ____-Magnon
19. Olive genus
20. Location
21. Start of an epigram
25. Old Japanese coin
26. Colors
27. Release a claim to
28. Places to build
31. Kind of code
32. ____ of one's wits
35. Little harbor
36. Tiara
40. English school
41. "____ 'nuff!"
43. Stout or Reed
44. Primate, for short
45. Unemployed
47. Author Graham
50. Carries on
51. No longer good
52. Chinese leader
53. "Divine Comedy" author
56. Finger count
57. Actress Negri
58. Fishhook part
59. Loves extravagantly
61. Pollute
64. Central European
65. Tennis players, at times
66. Epigram continued
72. City in Kansas
73. Wine residue
74. Most simple
75. Be ambitious
77. You love, to Caesar
78. Buzzers
79. Reign, in India
82. Medieval slaves
83. Guided
84. Clarinet, e.g.
85. Mozart's was magic
87. No place for a bowling ball
89. To be, in Paris
90. Indian queen
91. "H. M. Pulham, ____"
94. Word with cent or diem
95. Ear part
97. Writer Catherine ____ Bowen
99. Oaf
101. Gibberish
105. Dined
106. France's longest river
108. Horse in a claiming race
109. Endure
111. Wye's follower
114. Epigram concluded
118. Carry
119. Tool place
120. Belfry denizen
121. Modern factory hand
122. Tater
123. Repairs a lawn
124. Before, to Byron
125. Drench

DOWN

1. Nile heron
2. Kind of society
3. "No man ____ island . . ."
4. Nothing
5. Certain horses
6. Throb
7. Attire
8. Name with Jones
9. Bullfighter
10. ". . . ____ are created equal"
11. Decorated again
12. Italian poet
13. ____ alai
14. Coffee makers
15. Physician
16. Clergyman
22. Italic or Roman, e.g.
23. Held forth
24. W.W. I battle river
29. First lady
30. Spoof for Mae West
31. Temperate or Torrid
33. "As You Like It" daughter
34. Bara of the silents
36. Egyptian church member
37. Helmet wreath
38. Bits of precipitation
39. City near Rome
42. Out with a sweetie
46. Gave grudgingly
47. Ninotchka portrayer
48. Hold up
49. Arden and namesakes
52. Retail centers
54. Place for a yellow ribbon
55. Weird
57. ____ mater
58. Venerable and Adam
60. Papal title: Abbr.
62. Going after morays
63. Sudden outburst
64. Sam of the links
66. F.D.R. work program
67. Lighten
68. Lewis's Gantry
69. Arabian leader
70. Required
71. A.M.A. members
76. Glyceride, e.g.
77. Tavern order
78. Kind of nut
80. To ____ (precisely)
81. Scoff
84. Like some Christians today
85. Wastes, with "away"
86. Abbe or Priscilla
88. Balderdash
91. Building wing
92. American canals
93. Dionnes, e.g.
95. Shaped, as a board
96. Mountain nymphs
98. Tear down a Soho flat
100. Scout unit
102. Like some boxers' jaws
103. Virile
104. English composer
107. Caesar's inclusive words
110. Comedian Johnson
111. Humped bovine
112. Slaughter of baseball
113. Ending for room or kitchen
115. Sportswriter Smith
116. Lincoln
117. Pasture sound

254 Collaborations By Alfio Micci

People who get together to form bigger things.

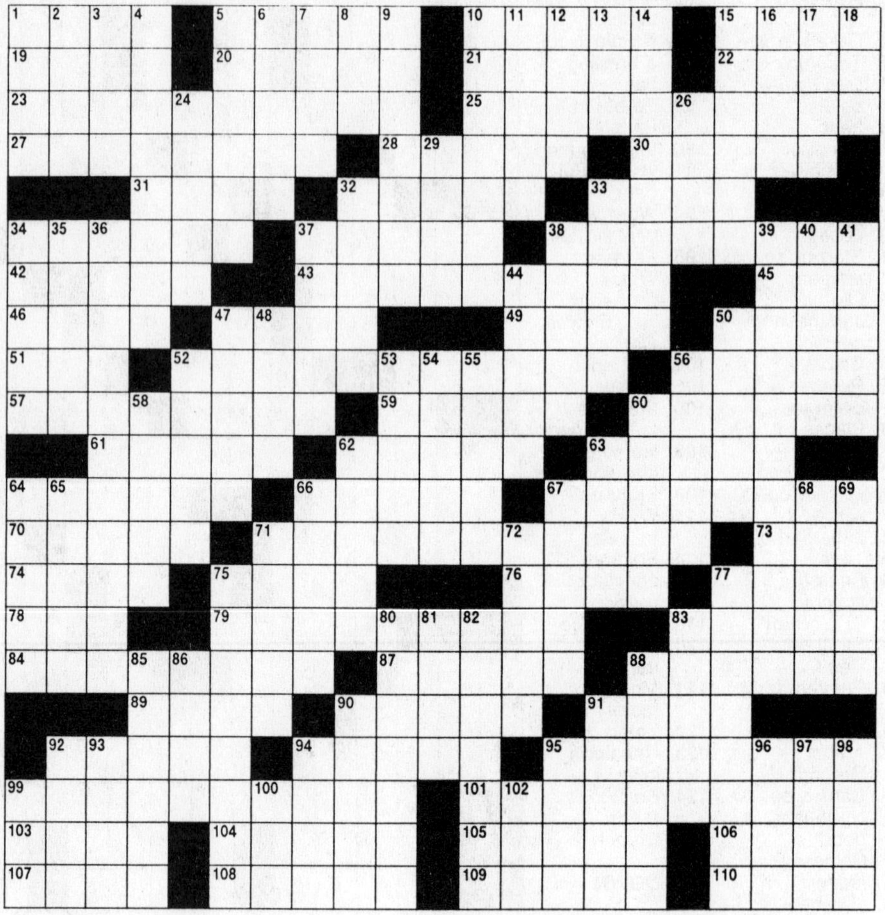

ACROSS

1. Tito was one
5. Do upholstering
10. Bombeck and namesakes
15. Capable
19. Deputy
20. Lucine of the opera
21. Ballet's Shearer
22. Security
23. Gladys and Al enjoy one at the late show
25. What explorer Richard and novelist John can't abide
27. Aardvark
28. Come in second
30. Playboy girl
31. Shower flooring
32. Beethoven's "Für ___"
33. Do gallery work
34. Circuitous path, old style
37. Unties
38. Like a trellis
42. Early freedmen
43. What Helen and Johnny could use
45. Medieval tale
46. Shield border
47. Footless
49. Loretta Swit's were hot
50. Tabula ___
51. Olive yield
52. What Glenn and Jim are
56. More demure
57. Aesop, for one
59. "___ flowing with milk . . ."
60. Obey
61. Kind of orange or Indian
62. Fred's sister
63. Veranda
64. Roman god of agriculture
66. Skyline sight
67. Public ___
70. Pilasters
71. What Bobby and dramatist David collaborate on
73. The, Italian style
74. Despicable sounding instrument
75. Incentive
76. Elec. units
77. Mexican laborer
78. Endangered tree
79. What Emily and Lena love to play
83. Moves through slush
84. Lab activity
87. Antelope of Africa
88. River for Stephen Foster
89. Plumbing problem
90. Nerve-cell process
91. At the drop of ___
92. N.Z. timber tree
94. Carroll's "The Hunting of the ___"
95. Abstruse
99. What Julie and Phileas often get lost in
101. What John and Al need on losing their keys
103. Anne Nichols hero
104. Oil: Prefix
105. Urban district in Surrey
106. Play start
107. Hollywood's Tuesday
108. Mark Van ___
109. One-masted vessels
110. "High" or "Purple"

DOWN

1. Iranian nomad
2. Waterfall, in Scotland
3. Mine entrance
4. Live monotonously
5. Word between shake and roll
6. Dais figure
7. Carson's predecessor
8. Dada pioneer
9. Mottled, as a horse
10. Home abroad for a V.I.P.
11. Rolls's partner
12. Swampy ground
13. Drunk or tank trailer
14. Holy days
15. African river
16. Misery
17. Like Albee's Alice
18. Miss or Bull
24. Former Secretary of State and kin
26. One of the litter
29. Was untruthful
32. Former Met conductor Alberto
33. Door fasteners
34. Cool
35. Bernstein song
36. What Ma and Timothy wear
37. Jack or David
38. Scottish landowner
39. What statesman Henry and actor Walter shoot at
40. Picasso prop
41. Anne Frank's recording
44. Genetic replica
47. Straighten
48. Sit
50. Actress Ruth
52. Ennis is its county seat
53. The pits
54. Warn
55. Cotton units
56. Brooklyn's Island
58. Customary
60. Bistros
62. Nautical position
63. Insect secretion
64. Thrifty one
65. Old-womanish
66. "Quiet!"
67. Like Congress's building
68. Marry in haste
69. Beauty salon offering
71. Pediatrician Benjamin
72. Sunburnt, in Lyons
75. Injured an ankle
77. Coal-mine worker
80. Pentagon's big brother
81. Swan genus
82. Irritated
83. Hits
85. Slipped by
86. Prefix for dynamics
88. Blacksmiths, at times
90. Miss Dickinson
91. Crookedly
92. Honshu port
93. Indigo
94. Fly
95. Repeat
96. Puerto ___
97. "Tell ___ the marines"
98. Boxer's target
99. Order's partner
100. Ziegfeld
102. USSR city

255 Body English By Ernie Furtado

What some notables might be noted for.

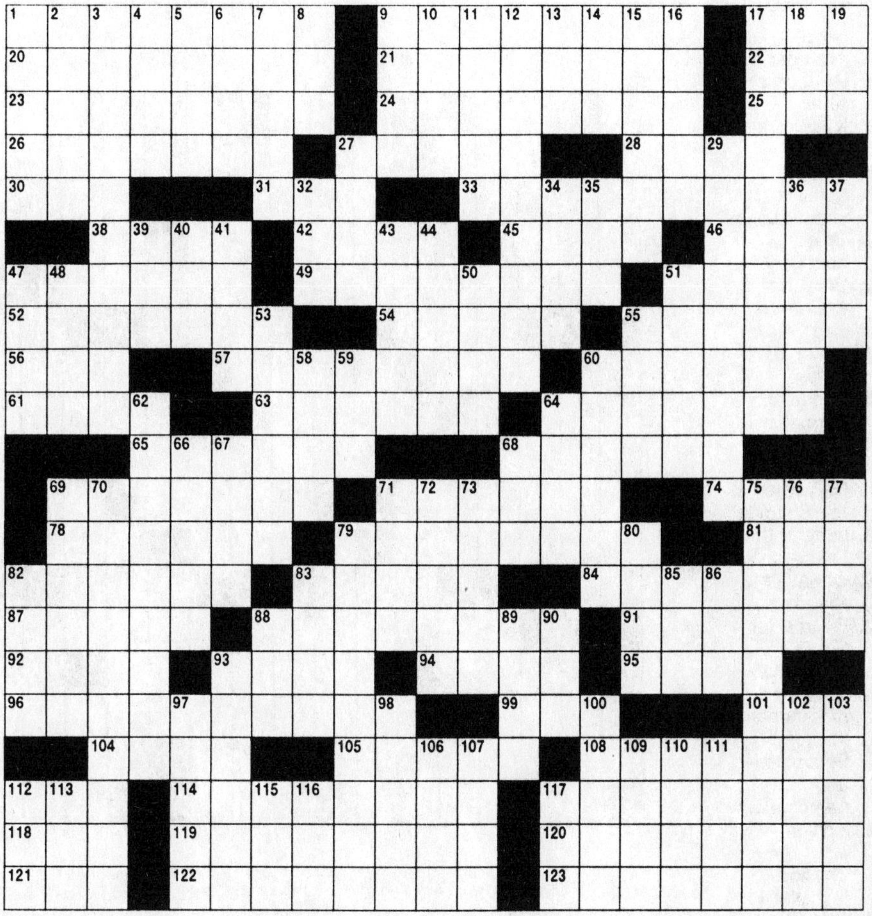

ACROSS

1. Baseballer Pete's features?
9. "What ___, what are plans?": Schiller
17. Angora or Persian
20. Insert
21. Asa Gray was one
22. Bullring sound
23. Ones who condescend
24. Cupids
25. Composer Rorem
26. "If we do not make common ___ save . . .": Lincoln
27. Tolerate
28. Right and acute: Abbr.
30. Choose
31. Four-in-hand
33. Actress Blanche's weakness?
38. ___ to (stopped, at sea)
42. Fruit pie
45. Clydesdale, to a cockney
46. Top rating
47. Fantasies
49. Certain transport to China
51. Dot one's ___ and cross one's t's
52. One ___ (singly)
54. Undeveloped lands
55. Skull points
56. Thrice: Prefix
57. Essences
60. Intend
61. Bible bk.
63. Backbones
64. ___ Wonders (1906 White Sox)
65. Detected
68. Common alga
69. Examine by touch
71. Jacob's son et al.
74. Swiss painter
78. "As good ___!" (almost finished)
79. Young doctors
81. Hilo music maker
82. Get ___ (shape up)
83. Word with ear or tube
84. Sherlock Holmes, at times
87. Of hearing
88. Letter holder
91. Farce
92. Lay ___ the line
93. "Picnic" penner
94. Hindu land grant
95. Clan
96. Comedian Foxx's feature?
99. River in north Portugal
101. "___ to Billy Joe"
104. Christiania, today
105. Ruffle, as hair
108. Forward-looking person
112. L.A. footballer
114. Piano soft pedal
117. Literary justification
118. Dutch commune
119. Punt ___ (grid specialist)
120. Some film-scene endings
121. ___ Passos
122. Cooking in a way
123. Actress Karen's feature?

DOWN

1. Missouri town
2. Ready
3. Mystery writer Rex's feature?
4. God of love
5. Bing's "Road" companion
6. "___ a man with . . ."
7. Serbian town
8. City ways: Abbr.
9. Blind as ___
10. Capital of Italia
11. Coats and collars
12. Cherry and oak, e.g.
13. Song from "A Chorus Line"
14. Coal mine
15. The press is the fourth
16. Restrict
17. Most of the alphabet
18. October brew
19. Turner or Williams
27. Stamp
29. Pitcher Gossage's feature?
32. "___ Magic"
34. Periods
35. Superlative ending
36. S.A. timber trees
37. "If I ___ Million"
39. Feed-bag unit
40. Where Stonewall Jackson taught
41. Salinger girl
43. Partner of Martin
44. Doubly
47. Tryst
48. 1 and 66, e.g.
50. Diner orders, for short
51. Author Calvino
53. Impassion
55. Tartan pattern
58. "Of ___ I Sing"
59. Free
60. Overlooked
62. Actress Anna's feature?
64. Instrument, often tin
66. Mar
67. Breathe heavily
68. Saul's uncle
69. Western Indian
70. Aircraft sections
71. Bancroft or Jackson
72. Stone pillar
73. Egret
75. Clare Boothe's feature?
76. Got by, with "out"
77. Spooky
79. Shareholders
80. Parts of mins.
82. Spend, in Scotland
83. Actress Swenson
85. Buck's mate
86. Ref's counterpart
88. Compass dir.
89. Jerry of golf
90. Ostrich's cousin
93. Laundry worker
97. Book-jacket plug
98. City near Rome
100. Dismay
102. Godhood
103. Obliterate
106. South Yemen port
107. Marionette maker Tony
109. Town south of Chicago
110. Templeton
111. Recess
112. Cincinnati player
113. Word in a Shakespeare title
115. ___ standstill
116. ___ bono (for whose benefit?)
117. Mil. installation

256 Cool Reception By Joy Wouk

Sometimes one finds a distinct lack of warmth.

1 2 3 4 5 6 7 8 9 10 11 12 13
14 15 16 17 18
19 20 21
22 23 24
25 26 27
28 29 30 31 32
33 34 35 36 37 38 39 40 41
42 43 44
45 46 47 48
49 50 51
52 53 54
55 56 57 58
59 60 61 62 63 64 65 66
67 68 69 70 71
72 73 74
75 76 77
78 79 80

ACROSS

1. Boys
5. Arab garment
8. Pidgeon or Abel
14. New York city
16. "The ___" (musical about Oz)
17. Of a continent
19. What one of le Carré's spies did
22. I love, to Cato
23. Canadian lawman
24. Dressed to the ___
25. He wrote "In the Clearing"
28. Inlet, in the Orkneys
29. Odense's island
30. Degree for a C.E.O.
33. Lost color
36. Girls' hair ornaments
39. Miss Dinsmore and namesakes
42. Appian Way, e.g.
43. Physics Nobelist
44. Stayed put longer
45. January sound
49. Russian coins
50. Actress Witherspoon
51. Saroyan hero
52. In the center of
53. Expensive
54. Grasp, in Naples
55. Stranger: Prefix
56. Bear, in Spain
58. After avril
59. January garment
67. Pacific Coast Indian
70. ". . . Lord sitting upon ___": Isa. 6:1
71. L-P connection
72. Showy flower
75. Rochester's river
76. Young sheep
77. Pierre's aunt
78. Dashboard extras
79. Coll. board members
80. Prejudice

DOWN

1. "From bar ___ to gates ajar" (Burma Shave ditty)
2. It is remembered
3. Leave the army, to a Tommy
4. So, in Scotland
5. Appalling
6. Pear, in Bonn
7. Nitrogen
8. Like eyes in January
9. Kind of tray
10. Property claims
11. Implied
12. Collar type
13. Irritate
15. Hunter
18. Bank offerings: Abbr.
20. Observe
21. Offends
26. Turned inside out
27. ___ kind (unique)
30. Distress, to a Parisian
31. Blessed women
32. Allergic disorder
33. Rock breakers' tool
34. Ready for visitors
35. A ___ the dark (risky action)
36. Restaurant section
37. Kimono accessory
38. Shrink back
40. Dasht-i-___ (Iranian desert)
41. Derived from fat
43. ___ one's laurels
46. Highway monsters: Abbr.
47. Tibetan antelope
48. Hockey great
53. Performs, biblically
54. Part of P.T.A.
57. Avers
58. Waiter's offering
59. Gave a thrill to
60. Twenty: Prefix
61. Margaret Mitchell's Butler
62. Abalone
63. Geodes
64. Muscat native
65. O'Day or Bryant
66. ___ down (softens)
67. Communication: Abbr.
68. Unique person
69. Madam, in Portugal
73. Recent: Prefix
74. Collar part

257 Starting the Car By Louis Sabin

Or, more accurately, starting with a car.

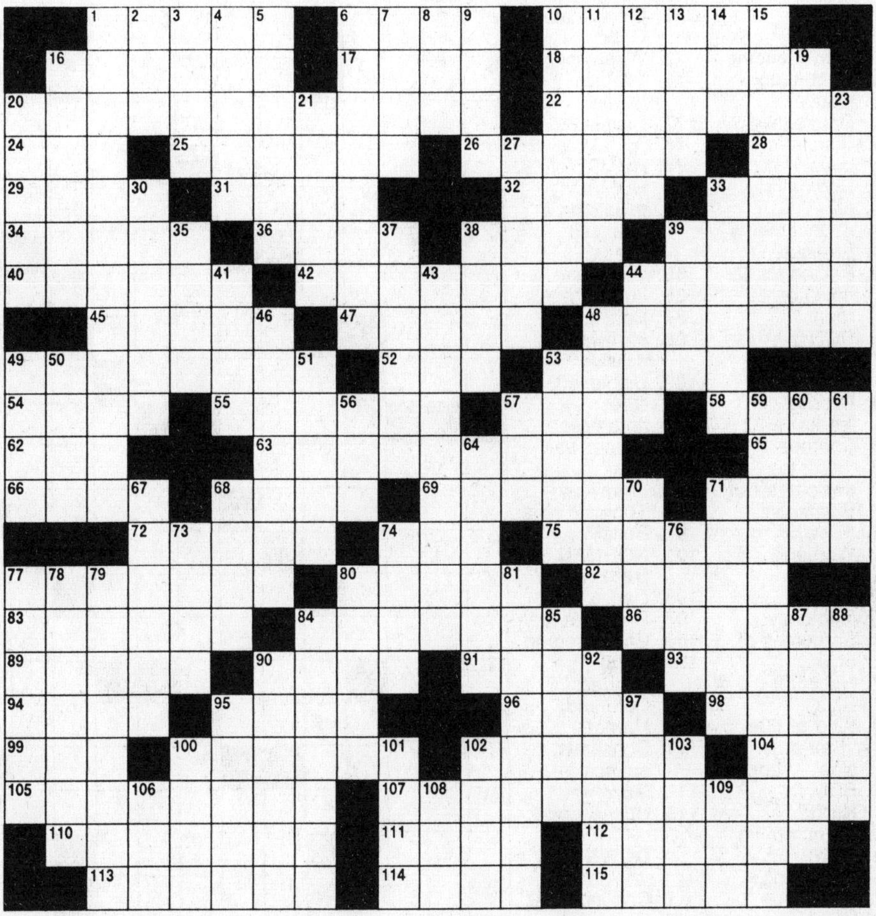

ACROSS

1. Supply food
6. Clean a pipe
10. Unseat
16. Gambler's mecca
17. Therefore
18. 55th-anniversary gift
20. Post-1865 opportunist
22. 1942 naval battle site
24. Calder's work
25. Flotsam
26. Joyous
28. Indisposed
29. Dylan Thomas, for one
31. Check
32. Pamplona sounds
33. Fit of pique
34. Jostle
36. Gather in
38. Urge
39. Spice
40. Prepare to fire again
42. Golf driver's problem
44. Loudmouthed one
45. Rose oil
47. Golden Hind's commander
48. What baseball pros are often on
49. Kitchen adjuncts
52. Land measure
53. Pooh's creator
54. Kindergarten refrain
55. Holdings
57. Geraldine or Patti
58. Unpleasant memory
62. Homer hitter's greeting
63. Making insert marks
65. Miss MacGraw
66. Corner
68. Like a hymn's foundation
69. Edward or Matthew
71. Rugged rock
72. Bond is one
74. Volga feeder
75. Making horsy sounds
77. Overdone, as steak
80. Sediment
82. Column type
83. Radio had a green one
84. Acid salt
86. Corso people
89. Lopsided
90. Studies
91. Coolidge et al.
93. Arrive
94. First-grade reward
95. Same, in Soissons
96. Soaks hemp
98. Hill for a camel
99. Mark for a gymnast
100. Brady's apparatus
102. Lower
104. Cartoonist Gardner
105. Fragrances
107. Colorful flier
110. Japanese warrior
111. A. k. a. Lamb
112. Embellish
113. Anya and Mother
114. Clan
115. Exhausted

DOWN

1. Total freedom
2. "Orphan Annie" character
3. In a 0–0 or 10–10 situation
4. Matriculate
5. Highwayman
6. Actor Gardiner
7. Work units
8. Epoch
9. Partner of less
10. The Commandments
11. Chewed the scenery
12. Deauville parents
13. Mouthward
14. Actor Mineo
15. "Hamlet" setting
16. Landis or Lombard
19. Rescue
20. Prance
21. Zodiac sign
23. Makes changes
27. Actor Greene
30. Beeped
33. Spartacus and Aesop, e.g.
35. Steam-engine pioneer
37. Lafitte was one
38. Medieval weapon
39. Mint
41. Go with
43. Absent owner's stand-in
44. Chest sound
46. Cancel
48. Made puppylike motions
49. Move fast
50. Building piece
51. Jump
53. Massenet opera
56. Extension
57. Mat victory
59. Thomas Nast was one
60. Ameche of football
61. Actress Diana
64. Like "Othello"
67. Salaried employee
68. Yardstick units
70. Fashion leader
71. Rang
73. Developed
74. Leftovers
76. Limey's potion
77. Pure
78. Mesta, e.g.
79. Sen. Bumpers's state
80. Metroliner car
81. Gave the once-over
84. Revenge deliverer
85. Varnish base
87. Forty-____ of S.F.
88. Golf great
90. Abase
92. Gems
95. Long: Prefix
97. Official mark
100. English king: 1017–35
101. Winners
102. Nerd
103. North Sea feeder
106. Angus's uncle
108. Flagon filler
109. Word before ton or soir

258 Moments of Truth By Nancy Ross

Pertinent observations by impertinent characters.

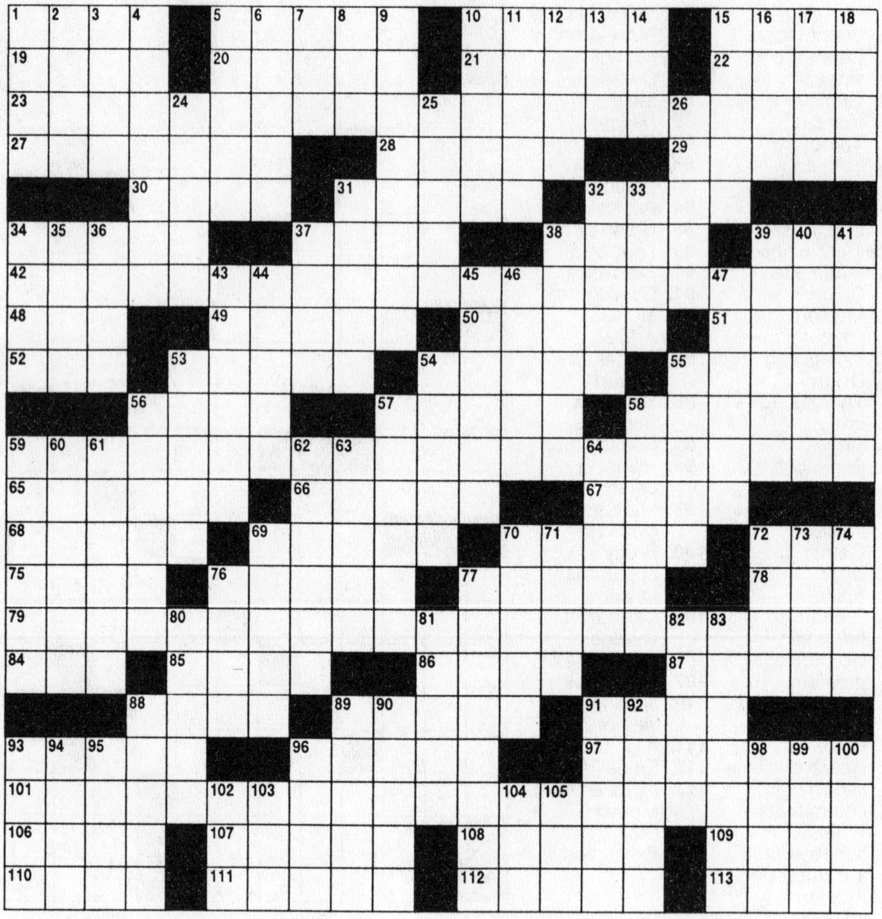

ACROSS

1. Joker
5. Planet ending
10. Contributor
15. Hoover Dam's lake
19. Clarinet's cousin
20. Dogmatic pro-nouncements
21. Straighten
22. Ending for novel or room
23. DON JUAN
27. Give a new name to
28. Exodus leader
29. Soothes
30. "___ the sweetheart of Sigma Chi"
31. "Two Women" actress
32. Droop indolently
34. Sorceress of myth
37. Native of Riga
38. Kind of tale
39. "See other side": Abbr.
42. BRÜNN-HILDE
48. Comprehend
49. What everything's coming up
50. Brooks
51. Pacific grass
52. Explosive initials
53. March animals
54. Twofold
55. Becomes tedious
56. Truck rig, for short
57. Verdi's "Un ___ in Maschera"
58. Small appendage
59. LADY CHAT-TERLEY
65. Cockney's fox chasers
66. Hoffmann products
67. Seasonal word
68. Pottery fragment
69. Dissolves
70. Needle cases
72. Disciplinary G.I.'s
75. Weedy plant
76. TV Vice locale
77. Disdain
78. ___ king
79. HUMBERT HUMBERT
84. Initials on a bounced check
85. Coop fliers
86. Luzon lake
87. Poet's feet
88. Highway division
89. Disbursed
91. Does arithmetic
93. Homer was one
96. Emmy or Tony
97. Boils
101. NORMAN BATES
106. Dry
107. Rhone feeder
108. Crude person
109. Earth goddess
110. Cole and Hentoff
111. Consumer advocate
112. Gaze
113. Chess piece

DOWN

1. Coconut fiber
2. Competent
3. Carrot or turnip
4. Contrived
5. Confuse
6. Ceremonies
7. German pronoun
8. Indian
9. Big beasts of the past
10. "___ Macabre"
11. Like times of yore
12. Asther of earlier films
13. "No ___ but you"
14. Source book: Abbr.
15. ___ detector
16. Biblical suffixes
17. To ___ (precisely)
18. Pol. people
24. Wharton's Frome
25. Way from a man's heart
26. The tube, in Britain
31. Delaware resort
32. Soup server
33. Auto magnate
34. Fog
35. First place
36. Something to go on
37. Come in second
38. Candle component
39. Spanish rice dish
40. Library listings
41. Horace and Keats
43. Hobos
44. Andrea ___
45. Strumpets
46. Double: Prefix
47. Combs' targets
53. What children shouldn't be
54. Appointments
55. S.A. rodents
56. Sound system
57. Sweden's sea
58. Regal wear
59. Auchincloss's "The Rector of ___"
60. Bares one's head
61. ___ Bethlehem
62. Bargains
63. Spiced game dish
64. Commuters' place
69. Pooh's creator
70. Brilliance
71. Hard work
72. Harm
73. Commoner
74. Be impertinent
76. Aspect
77. Hopefuls at the plane gate
80. Uniform color
81. Roman ways
82. Bill adjunct
83. More flavorful
88. Shows the way
89. Vowed
90. One writing a check
91. Famed old N.Y. hotel
92. Crusoe's creator
93. Fed
94. ___ avis
95. Send forth
96. Not yet up
98. Role for a star
99. Within: Prefix
100. Pierre's state: Abbr.
102. One of seven
103. "I wandered lonely ___ cloud"
104. Lunch
105. Asian sheep

259 One for the Books By Mary Murdoch

Getting inside the publisher's product.

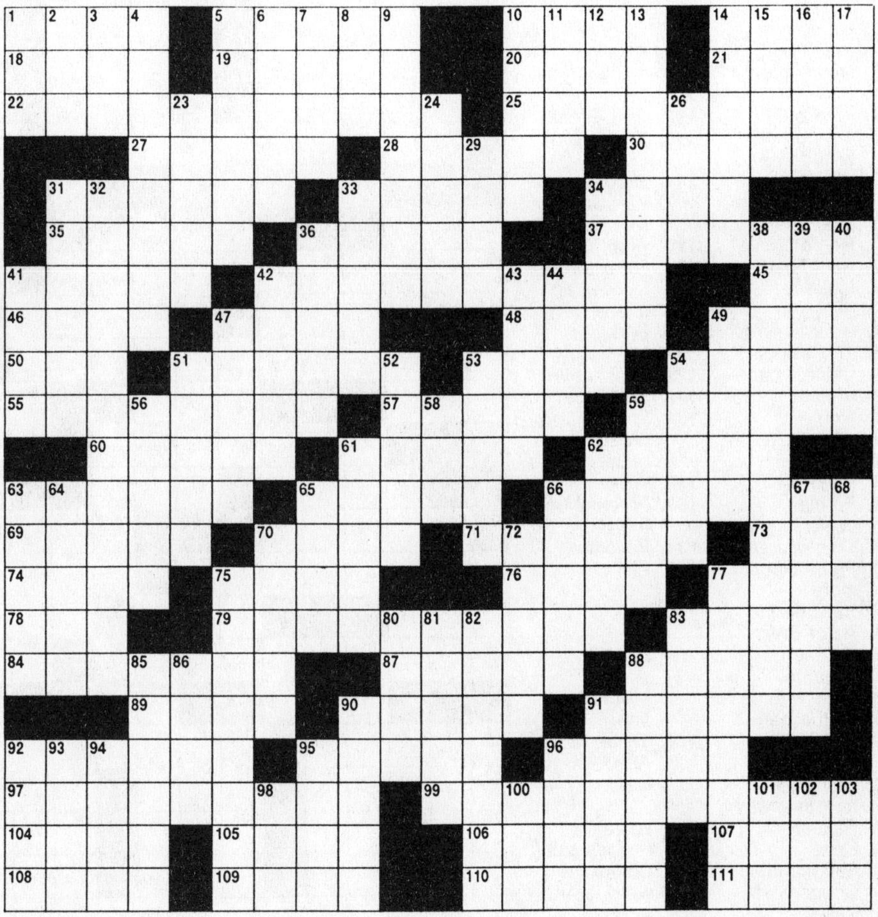

ACROSS

1. Modest poker holding
5. Alleviates
10. Andy of the old comics
14. Head or tooth follower
18. Villa d'___
19. Steep slope
20. Scope
21. Dash
22. Famous short story by O. Henry
25. Star's part, often
27. Double curves
28. Church parts
30. Icons
31. Rise
33. Refers to
34. ___ were
35. Car-trunk item
36. Old hat
37. "___ the South Pacific"
41. Revue parts
42. Kind of biography preferred by the subject
45. Con's partner
46. Byway
47. A Guthrie
48. Kyle of football
49. Bring up
50. ___ pro nobis
51. Like insensitive eyes
53. Place for an adit
54. Comedienne Anne
55. Type of security
57. Baffle
59. Luxurious
60. River craft
61. Second man and namesakes
62. Roman 1154
63. Strands
65. Joins the also-rans
66. Ruth Etting favorite
69. Links sites
70. Breath freshener
71. Poetically infinite
73. Abner's pal
74. Ratite birds
75. "Arrivederci ___"
76. Have ___ (scuffle)
77. Actor Robert
78. Dream letters
79. Wear for an English student
83. Cloth strainer
84. Composer Lecuona
87. Medicinal plants
88. Nonstop talkers
89. Side glance
90. Hidden spoilers
91. Overshoe
92. Eastern greeting
95. Forbidding
96. Man-made material
97. Ben Hecht–Charles MacArthur subject
99. Perennial gripers
104. Footless one
105. This, in Toledo
106. Work on a statue
107. Female ruffs
108. Totem poles
109. Venture
110. Diaphanous
111. Part of Babe Ruth's nickname

DOWN

1. Kind of project
2. Hardwood tree
3. Native: Suffix
4. Move
5. Ascetic of Palestine
6. Performed
7. My gal et al.
8. Poetic word
9. Kind of Armada or main
10. They're sometimes pearly
11. Author Leon
12. Lincoln Center unit
13. Fence for defense
14. Loosen the soil
15. Shoe type
16. Robust
17. Chemical endings
23. Ripening agents
24. Skinny's counterpart
26. Writer Ludwig
29. Go off course
31. African soldier
32. Backbone
33. The Censor and the Younger
34. Tête-___
36. Beat
38. Be full of meaning
39. "___ Ben Jonson"
40. "An eye ___ eye . . ."
41. Plod
42. O'Hara's "___ to Live"
43. Crocuses and gladioluses
44. Zip-code listing
47. Actor Ray et al.
49. Ignited anew
51. Hackman and Wilder
52. Baker's need
53. Parsonage
54. Alan Alexander ___
56. Vetches
58. Contend
59. Inadequate
61. Schwarzenegger role
62. Kind of badge
63. ___ Khan, Kipling's tiger
64. Jethro's sidekick
65. Luxury auto
66. Allots
67. Bullheaded
68. Certain rulers: Abbr.
70. Kind of bike or boat
72. Gate receipts
75. Treat steel anew
77. Christmas figures
80. Actress Curtin
81. Panic
82. Fine brandies
83. Rental-sign words
85. Antelopes
86. Enthrone
88. Big headline
90. Salisbury ___
91. Stand of trees
92. African port
93. Italian instrument
94. Swag
95. Certain noncoms
96. Plot of land
98. "___ was saying"
100. ___-di-dah
101. Unused
102. Cha or pekoe
103. Modern flier

260 Spray-Gun Fodder By Herman Surasky

Examining the smaller constituents of nature.

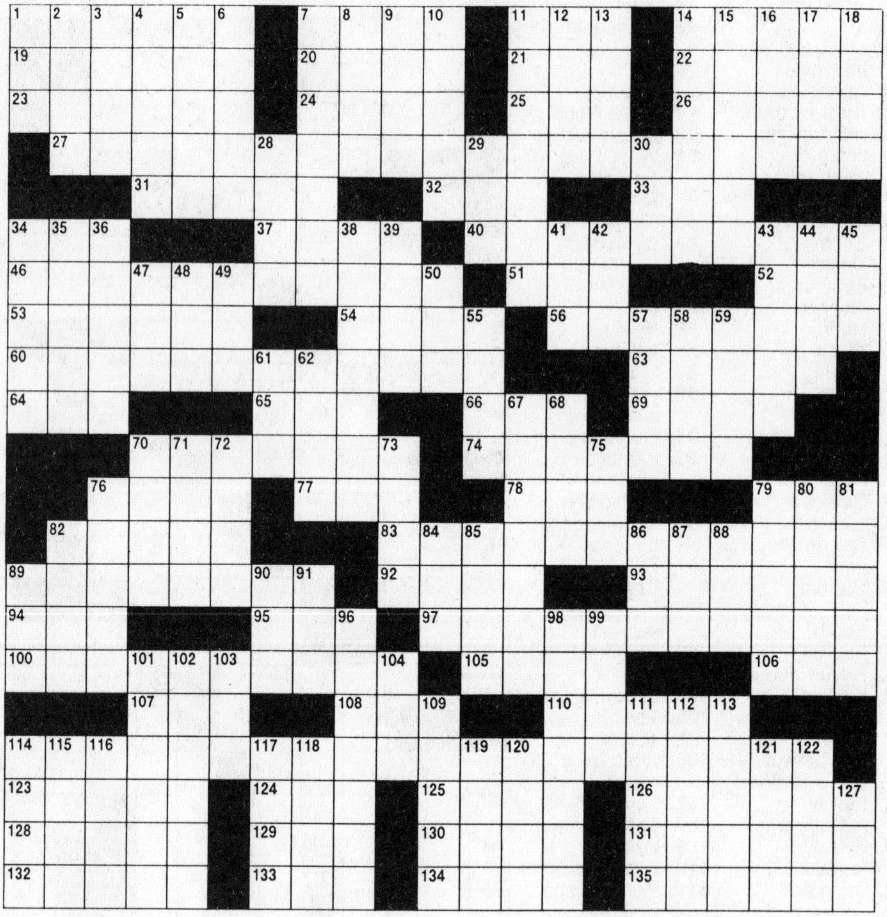

ACROSS

1. He cometh, to O'Neill
7. Heavy blow
11. Bankroll
14. Kind of skinned or witted
19. Whodunit inquiry focus
20. Green land
21. Regret
22. Bast fiber
23. Make a ___ (flirt)
24. Hebrew lyre
25. The works
26. Clerical cape
27. Popular 1985 film
31. Wall St. term
32. Corrode
33. Long fish
34. Former power agcy.
37. Coin of Iran
40. Poe's cipher story
46. Bar offering
51. Actor Erwin
52. Southern campus
53. Watercourse
54. Of the ear
56. Chippendale chairs, etc.
60. Camphor ball, in a way
63. Rakes
64. Exist
65. Salamander
66. Choose
69. Yalies
70. Lighthouse with wings
74. Sticky-wicket game
76. Cave, to a poet
77. Petty-officer class: Abbr.
78. W.W. II area
79. Future grads
82. Reproduce genetically
83. No coat for the Masters golf champ
89. Aristophanes satire
92. Great Barrier Island
93. Stimulate
94. Charged atom
95. U.N. agency
97. Type of tractor
100. Church council
105. Calif. rockfish
106. Alkaline solution
107. Incumbents
108. Gas: Prefix
110. First five of 26
114. Rimsky-Korsakov tour de force
123. Actor Greene
124. Excessively
125. Dunce-cap shape
126. Parka
128. Mr. Gantry
129. Possessive
130. Seed coat
131. ". . . all ___ created equal"
132. Winged
133. Forerunner of the C.I.A.
134. Favorites
135. Plant louse

DOWN

1. Mischievous one
2. Timber dowel
3. Although, to Cato
4. ___ solemnis
5. Sailor's call
6. Colonist's word to an Indian
7. Cruise
8. Kind of bone
9. Arafura Sea islands
10. Succinct
11. Apparitions
12. ___ lang syne
13. Printer's mark
14. Garden implement
15. Berlioz's Italian traveler
16. Mosque leader
17. That, in Paris
18. Avid
28. Card game
29. Mike's friend
30. Old car
34. Lizard
35. Faux pas
36. Menu
38. Matthew or John
39. Baltic native
41. Greek vowel
42. Rev the engine
43. Hill St. officers
44. Exploits
45. Gloomy guy
47. Old cry of surprise
48. Neighbor of Isr.
49. Relative of 14 Down
50. Meadow barley
55. Gator's cousin
57. Hegira
58. Hercules's captive
59. Give up
61. Behold
62. Maybe so, maybe not
67. Bishop or abbot
68. Yugoslav leader
70. Cleaving tool
71. New Rochelle college
72. Hwys.
73. String toy
75. Intimidate
76. Astronaut senator
79. Brain protection
80. Iterate
81. Cubic meter
82. Locomotive sound
84. Catchall abbr.
85. Limerick man
86. Tokyo's land: Abbr.
87. "Exodus" hero
88. Mountain pass
89. Partner of tac and toe
90. Pendulum's partner
91. Road sign
96. Spellbinders
98. Glazes
99. Of a synagogue leader: Abbr.
101. Seal
102. Belong
103. Speedy plane
104. Affirmative of a sort
109. News summary
111. Fasten
112. Sand hills, in England
113. Dark-colored wood
114. Kind of market
115. Take it easy
116. "___ La Douce"
117. Roman emperor
118. Enemies
119. Caliber
120. Entity
121. Epochal
122. British noble
127. New Zealand parrot

261 Advisories By Louis Baron

None of them having to do with the weather.

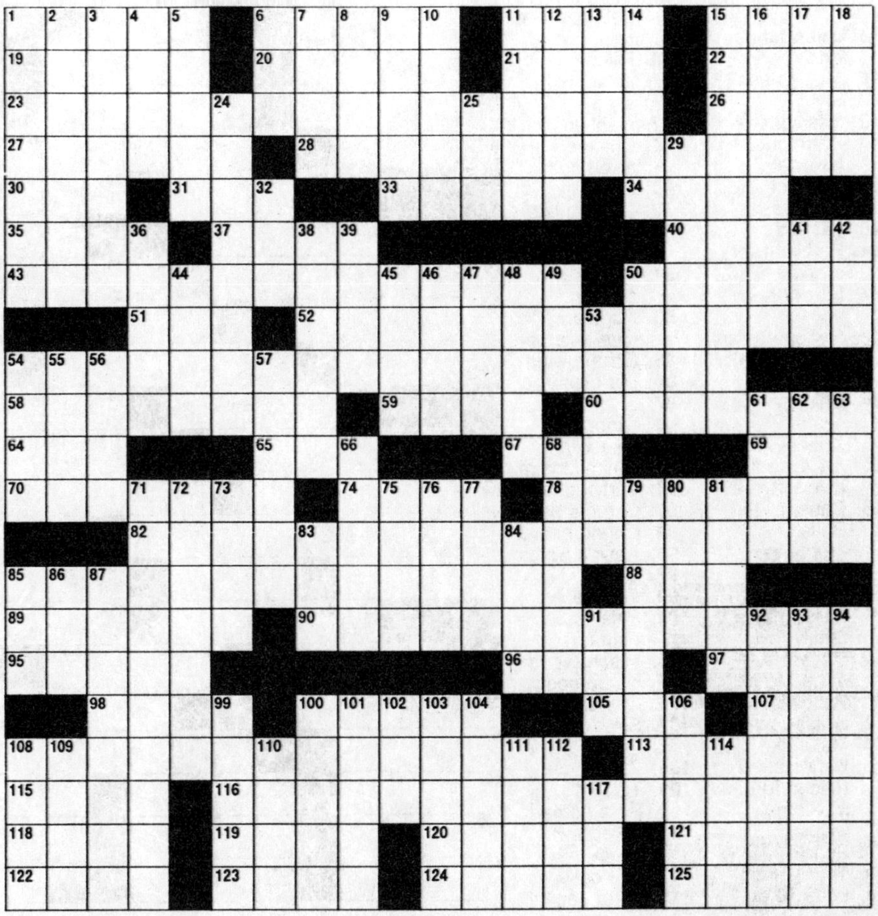

ACROSS

1. Of apples
6. Let up
11. Fateful date
15. Old English chattel law
19. Act with schmaltz
20. Demons
21. Bonkers
22. Norwegian capital
23. "How does one raise a baby vampire?"
26. Humorist Bill and family
27. Handel work, 1734
28. "What's an order for an honest poker deal?"
30. Region of Morocco
31. Hog's home
33. Alcohol heaters
34. Make turbid
35. Feverish chill
37. Entre ___
40. Of anatomical tissue
43. "Shall I use this one-armed blacksmith?"
50. Curtain raiser
51. An antiseptic: Prefix
52. "What can one do about a charging rhino?"
54. "What's best at a shark alert?"
58. Gloomy forecaster
59. Glacial ridges
60. Struggles with a b'ar
64. Opp. of small
65. Juliette Low's org.
67. Macho quality
69. Report-card jackpot
70. Mock orange
74. ___ B'rith
78. City near Munich
82. "Should I remarry my ex-wife?"
85. "How do I get to the auto races?"
88. N.Y.C. subway
89. Welcomes
90. "How do I grab a quick high?"
95. John Wayne film, 1953
96. Cad
97. Escutcheon border
98. Singer Petina
100. Pyongyang's land
105. N.Y.C. building
107. Moslem Easter
108. "Does this bank have branches?"
113. "A man in debt is so far ___": Emerson
115. West Indian rodent
116. "May I ask one more question?"
118. Micro or macro ender
119. Spelunker's turf
120. Mexicali cash
121. Crested ridge
122. Haws' mate
123. Actress Martha
124. Finnish lake, to Swedes
125. Waited

DOWN

1. Shul candelabrum
2. Vespucci
3. Opposite of hateful, formerly
4. Natives: Suffix
5. Documents: Abbr.
6. Application entry
7. Between Phi and Kappa
8. Indigo
9. Book-cover feature
10. Shell crew
11. Actress Massey
12. Frowzy ones
13. Old French coins
14. Lethargic sleep
15. They don't count calories
16. ___ as a dandelion
17. Guinness or Waugh
18. Islamic temple: Var.
24. "And, when I ope my lips, ___ bark!": Shak.
25. Fled
29. Gunslinger's scorings
32. "___ and who else!"
36. Prepares for a deadline
38. Ones who spur
39. Big Apple stadium
41. Mot compilation
42. Alfonso XIII, e.g.
44. Hindu discipline
45. Other, to Goya
46. Spoils
47. ___ Gora, Macedonian mountain
48. Ether, in Italy
49. Sty occupant
50. Leaf-cutting ant
53. Real gone
54. U.N. license-plate initials
55. Bacchanal
56. Kind of do-well
57. Deny
61. Foliage, to Fritz
62. James ___ Carter
63. Solomonic
66. Home
68. Protected, in St.-Lô
71. Reveries, in a Gershwin song
72. "___ without sticklers": Howell
73. Natl. outputs
75. ". . . kindness to say ___ once": Publilius Syrus
76. Asian hill people
77. African hemps
79. Train's snack section
80. Marsh bird
81. "___ not let us quarrel . . .": Browning
83. ___ it (go on foot)
84. Cussword
85. From E to I
86. Tail: Prefix
87. Companion of Marxism
91. Part of %
92. Feared
93. Uplift
94. Like 5 A.M. plane riders
99. It's omitted by 'arry
100. Rogue
101. Mink's kin
102. Headland
103. Troop bivouac
104. "Stormy Weather" composer
106. Make ___ at (try)
108. Lots
109. Western Indian
110. It had one hoss
111. Actress Martinelli
112. Get an ___ excellence
114. Small lemur
117. Full of: Suffix

262 Clock Watching By Betty Jorgensen

Especially when it goes ahead an hour.

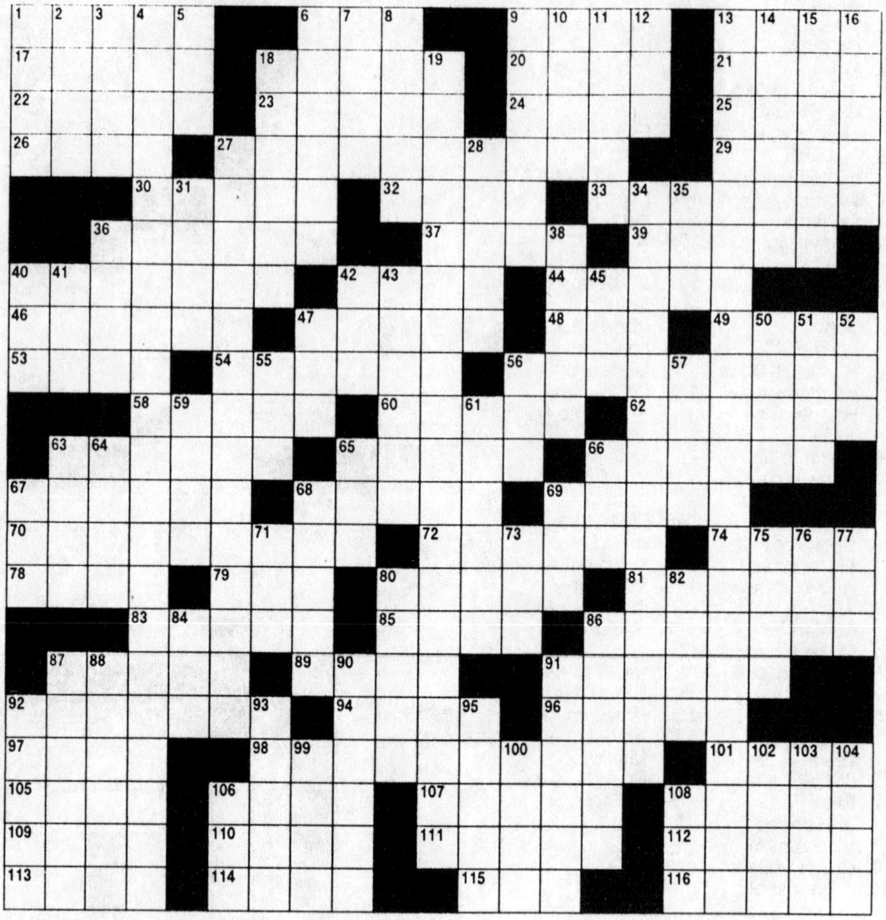

ACROSS

1. Set bounds on
6. Inc., British style
9. Fashioned
13. Farfetched, as a tale
17. Overact
18. Buenos ___
20. Excited
21. Highlight for a diva
22. Site of rainy plains
23. Congressmen usually don't need this
24. Chinese secret society
25. An X on a love letter
26. Cans, to the British
27. "Early in ___ our song . . ."
29. Italian noble family
30. He wrote "The Merry Widow"
32. Swiss town
33. Make like Katy's swain
36. Places for Moslem wives
37. Snack
39. Tear-jerker
40. Ester of an acid
42. Put one's John Hancock on
44. Deck with jewels
46. Province of Abruzzi, Italy
47. Mrs. Chaplin's namesakes
48. Old card game
49. Paradise
53. Munich mister
54. Fashionable
56. Songlike, in music
58. Greek letter
60. Sponsorship
62. Pain: Suffix
63. It goes with a bottle of rum
65. Springe
66. Lets up
67. Beach bungalow
68. ___ la Paix
69. Something politicos love to press
70. Filled up again, old style
72. Flunked
74. Cheese with a red coat
78. Ethereal
79. ___ a plea
80. ___ da Gama
81. Having two shapes
83. Hugs on a love letter
85. Off the wind
86. Let these be
87. ___ und Drang
89. Like Wilt Chamberlain
91. Partial ones
92. Camera part
94. Congo native
96. Having wings
97. Coy
98. Intolerably
101. Pelée's output
105. Mischievous Norse god
106. Ostrich's kin
107. Street, in Spain
108. Sturdy
109. Tied
110. Be a nomad
111. Hiked a check
112. Tea cake
113. Extra benefit, for short
114. The A in B.A.
115. ___ Angeles
116. Coil of yarn

DOWN

1. "___ we forget"
2. Body of African warriors
3. Don't do it at the bar
4. D.S.T. according to Robert Service
5. Two fives
6. Liquid measures
7. Trolley, in England
8. Populace
9. Morning prayers
10. Dramatic conflict
11. Big Ben sounds
12. Good ___ (nice guy)
13. D.S.T. according to Thales
14. Highborn one, for short
15. Attend
16. Powerful beam
18. "Ain't it ___ about Mame?"
19. Advice to clock setters
27. D.S.T. according to the Walrus
28. Times of day
31. He was, to Cicero
34. "I have ___" (D.S.T. complaint by R.L.S.)
35. One, in France
36. Scion
38. French cry of despair
40. German exclamation
41. Fidel's sidekick
42. ___-disant (self-styled)
43. Senseless
45. Pierre's denial
47. Fatima's room
50. Eat formally
51. First Olympic games site
52. Education org.
55. Indian tribe
56. Co., to Pierre
57. Miss Rehan and namesakes
59. "___ soit qui . . ."
61. Tend to the squeaks
63. Kind of lock
64. Upper, in Munich
65. Opposite of norte
66. The Brits like theirs warm
67. Accounts expert: Abbr.
68. Transfer a plant
69. Ziegfeld
71. Boo's partner
73. Hot diamonds
75. British tutors
76. "How ___ you?"
77. Metric lengths: Abbr.
80. Treasure
82. "___ a kick out of you"
84. Leftover
86. Sent an invoice
87. ___ Tuesday
88. Bib's partner
90. Record holders
91. Valuable furs
92. Dried orchid tubers
93. Hearsay
95. Thin as ___
99. ___ as a pin
100. Palo ___
102. African lily
103. Wine: Prefix
104. Capital of South Yemen
106. Women's lib goal
108. Draft initials

263 Odd Pairings By Kenneth Haxton

How some people of note might get together.

ACROSS

1. Cigar leavings
6. V.P. under Coolidge
11. End
14. Applied leeches
18. Thirty, in Italy
20. Earth color
21. Card game of yore
22. Tibetan priest
23. Actress Shelley weds singer Bobby
25. Like some highways
27. Cosmetician Lauder
28. Relating to Micronesia: Var.
30. Actress Mary Tyler weds producer Sol
36. Type of row
37. Freud contemporary
38. River in Spain
39. Kett of the comics
41. Actor Keenan weds writer Anita
45. W.W. II craft
47. Cole and Turner
51. Actor Wallach
52. Breakfast item for Deneuve
53. Crusader Sojourner weds U.N.'s Trygve
56. Virginia dance
58. Russian saint
59. Depend on
60. Repair a circuit
61. Without, to Mendelssohn
63. Kind of split or republic
65. Sis-boom-bah, for one
66. Round of firing
69. ". . . gold in them ___ hills"
72. Weight allowance
73. Sorts
74. Baobab and deodar
75. Abductee of Zeus
77. Dog, to a flea
79. Medium in "Blithe Spirit"
81. Predatory gull
82. Dawn affair
84. Catchall abbrs.
88. Comedian Madeline weds philosopher Immanuel
90. Lambs, to Caesar
91. Kanga's offspring
92. Stared at
93. Org.
94. Actress Irene weds painter Henry Varnum
98. Bidding, of old
100. Fish offal
102. "Bring ___ fire, snow to . . ."
103. Swimsuit parts
105. Actress Eva Marie weds novelist Joseph
109. Soggy weather condition
112. Chemical sugar
113. Underwear for milady
114. Singer Gladys weds singer Dennis
121. Egyptian cross
122. Cleo's worm
123. Boredom
124. Fitted with entries
125. Actress Edna
126. Sibling
127. "Mene, mene, ___, upharsin"
128. Angular bolt fittings

DOWN

1. Pac.'s counterpart
2. Broadway letters
3. Female lobster
4. Norwegian lake
5. Tonight, in Turin
6. Took medicine
7. German expletive
8. Word before dunit
9. Goof
10. Bristly
11. Change
12. Keokuk's state
13. Comics' Mullins
14. Actress Karen weds Justice Byron R.
15. Veranda
16. Rectify
17. June honoree
19. Drama org.
24. Rumpus room
26. Pianist Eugene
29. Like a honeycomb
30. Town in Saskatchewan
31. Hypothetical force
32. Argentine river
33. Tropical herb
34. Old name for Tokyo
35. Ancient Egyptian rattles
39. Old English letter
40. Boris or Ivan
42. "High ___"
43. Expunge
44. Wrench type
46. Composer Jule
48. Sigourney Weaver film
49. Effete
50. Magi, e.g.
54. Designer de la ___
55. Straits
57. Actress Bessie weds producer George
62. Asian flowering plant
63. Journalist Heywood
64. Wise goddess
66. Money risked
67. Adorn
68. Milk, to Cantinflas
70. Corn leavings
71. Colorado river
76. Arts supporter
78. Music critic Downes
80. Miss Claire and namesakes
82. Russian country house
83. Cry of disgust
85. Fish while moving
86. Actor Robert
87. Sister, to Nero
89. Summer-time initials
95. "Das ___ gut"
96. "Crime ___ pay"
97. Added to a load
99. Anglo-Saxon laborer
101. "A ___, a tasket"
103. Sauerkraut curer
104. Puts in order
105. Oozes
106. Nothing, to Cicero
107. Insecticide
108. Lew of tennis
110. Cleopatra's attendant
111. ___ prius (first court)
113. Scientist's area
115. Opp. of SSW
116. Writing fluid
117. Old Shetland viol
118. Joanne ___
119. Aged: Abbr.
120. Length units for a QB

264 Getting Around By Gary Schmunk

And reaching a few appropriate places.

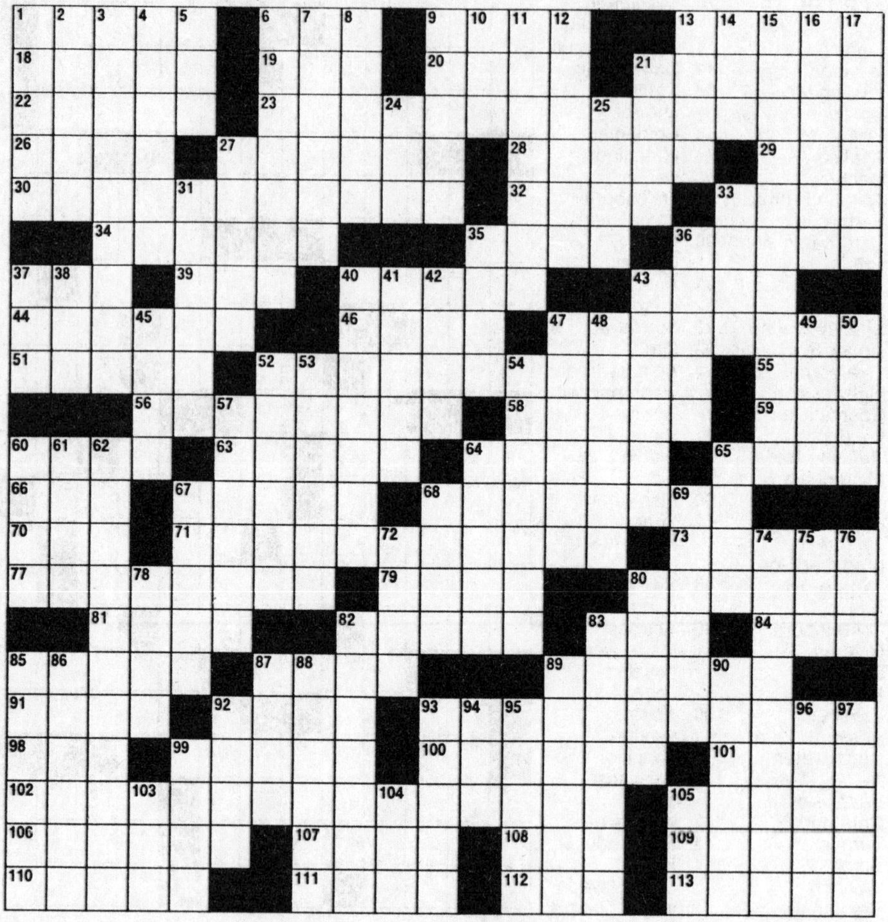

ACROSS

1. Zodiac sign
6. ___ Lanka
9. Rebuff
13. Turkish official
18. "The Woman ___"
19. Kind of lettuce
20. Soft drink
21. Something to sing for
22. King of Norway
23. Swimming stroke
26. Hitler or Hess, e.g.
27. Harmonize
28. Kovacs of comedy
29. Born, to Brigitte
30. Dairy product
32. Follower of tan or pun
33. Weaver's bobbin
34. Epistle
35. Church calendar
36. Armor plate
37. Vase
39. Serling or Steiger
40. Arctic abode
43. Suspire
44. One of the genders
46. Toothy smile
47. ___ out (hit a nadir)
51. Spare
52. Connector of oceans
55. Soviet river
56. What refiners remove
58. White poplar
59. Clique
60. Float lightly
63. Mountain crest
64. Insinuating
65. African fox
66. Ben ___
67. Position properly
68. Essential
70. Wrath
71. Waterfowl
73. Star in Orion
77. Formal orders
79. Soupe du ___
80. Impostors
81. Remedy
82. Pub game
83. For
84. Follower: Suffix
85. West Indian tree
87. John ___, U.S. naturalist
89. Child's art implement
91. Essen exclamations
92. Moat
93. Body of water
98. Sgt., for one
99. Lightning strokes
100. Of a blue color
101. City street sight
102. Dogs
105. Rabbit fur
106. ___ Vincent Millay
107. "___ each life . . ."
108. Grant's foe
109. Of sheep
110. Certain button
111. Magi's guide
112. Drunk or cow ending
113. Safecrackers

DOWN

1. Detroit team
2. Relative of a sort
3. Mixture partner of a pecan and a cashew
4. Amend
5. Part of speech: Abbr.
6. Denounced
7. Distance-running horse
8. Emanate
9. Rocky debris
10. Mauna ___
11. Briskly, in music
12. Like the ark animals
13. Dark red
14. Spring mo.
15. Southern tree adornment
16. Choppers
17. Dahl or Francis
21. Tizzy
24. Coal units: Abbr.
25. ___ Domini
27. Thespian
31. "Down by the Old Mill ___"
33. Half a Samoan city
35. Charlie's widow
36. Name
37. One, in Soissons
38. Oedipus ___
40. Lit
41. Barred frame
42. Like some rickeys
43. More hackneyed
45. Third: Prefix
47. Indulges
48. Tense
49. ___ out (supplements)
50. Social engagement
52. Acid derivative
53. Combat zones
54. Comedian Eddie and family
57. Sense of taste
60. Caprice
61. Subtle quality
62. Band instruments
64. Proboscis
65. Inter ___
67. "Not ___ in the world"
68. Stravinsky
69. Dry gully
72. Slightly open
74. Lab animal
75. Sullivan and McMahon
76. Landing vehicle: Abbr.
78. Batman and Robin et al.
80. Marseille money
82. Take issue with
83. Commended
85. Feed box
86. Consent
87. Small particles: Abbr.
88. "Give ___ day our . . ."
89. Fire leaving
90. Musical interval
92. Holy-water basin
93. Olympian's blood
94. Comedian Louis
95. One of the "Our Gang" rascals
96. Chopping
97. Baseball teams
99. Rope fiber
103. Miss West
104. School gp.
105. Actress Myrna

265 Underwear By Robert Malinow

At least in the sense that apparent items are concealed.

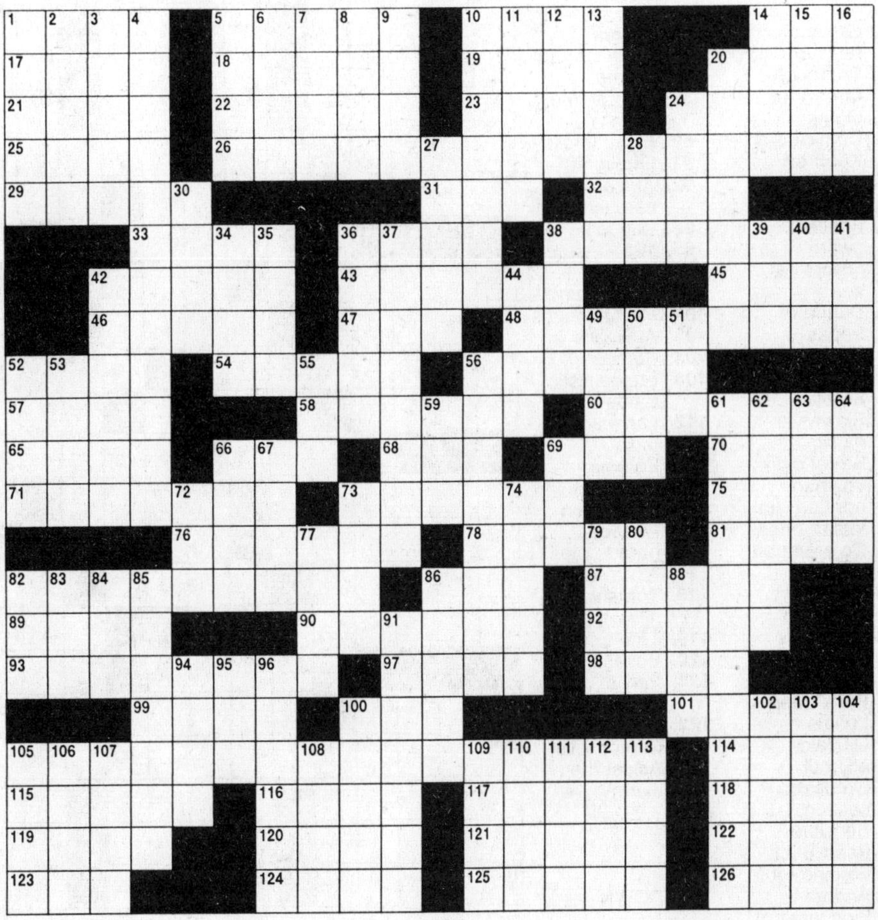

ACROSS

1. It calls a vespiary home
5. Bogart role
10. Caruso's dear
14. Word in a Shakespeare title
17. Before "Brute"
18. Fudd or Gantry
19. Dust-bowl adjective
20. Unbalanced
21. Kismet
22. Pope after John X
23. Subjunctive, for one
24. Bowling division
25. Gooey stuff
26. Garment found in a Govt. search?
29. Actress Burstyn
31. Cheer for Manolete
32. 1947 Nobelist family name
33. After-bath wear
36. Northern capital
38. ___ Stripes
42. Van Winkle sound, perhaps
43. "G.W.T.W." Oscar-winner McDaniel
45. Out of the wind
46. An Asia or Ursa
47. Lawyers' org.
48. Anklets found among the elite?
52. Guinness
54. "The Mark of ___"
56. Horse color
57. Hard wood
58. Wainwright surrendered it in '42
60. Lamp owner of note
65. Anent
66. Food at a luau
68. Be human
69. Before clear or star
70. Roof adjunct
71. Income-producing cargo
73. Do a mad scientist's job
75. Things sometimes stick in here
76. First coat of paint
78. Discernment
81. "___ Misbehavin'"
82. Neckwear found on a political elephant?
86. Jazz form
87. Emulate certain lovers
89. Acre's measurement
90. "Gil Blas" author
92. With force
93. Lustful
97. Munich's river
98. Like Hilton's horizon
99. Dial ___
100. Between Sault and Marie
101. Mount or drum
105. Moslem headwear lost in a demonstration
114. Entertainer Tennille
115. Act the penitent
116. Poet Teasdale
117. Papal cape
118. Rainbow: Prefix
119. Son of Rameses I
120. Slattern
121. Sign up
122. ___ in a lifetime
123. Prior to
124. Suffix for kitchen
125. Like coral
126. ___-do-well

DOWN

1. Pie serving
2. Bikini is one
3. Bar adjunct
4. Footwear dropped on the bread?
5. Before esteem
6. Commoner
7. Frenchman's possessive
8. Hindu goddess
9. Emerald Isle
10. Arthurian home
11. Heeded the alarm
12. Haymarket Square event
13. Person helped by Synanon
14. Jai ___
15. Major follower
16. Kind of shop
20. Fabergé was one
24. Jamie of "M*A*S*H"
27. River of Ghana
28. Gazelle of Tibet
30. Siesta hour
34. Josip ___ (Tito)
35. Saarinen
36. "Butterfield 8" author
37. Footwear destroyed by a vandal?
38. Very, in Stuttgart
39. Loser to Franklin in 1936
40. Once-named
41. Kind of drop or lap
42. Like finger painting
44. Religious object
49. Test
50. Market
51. Guido's high note
52. Leave ___ (reward the waiter)
53. Singer Horne
55. Homer hitter's stat
56. Robe seen at a racetrack?
59. Drama or dance, etc.
61. Headgear lost in a guillotine operation?
62. "Silent, upon a peak in ___"
63. Denisovich of a prison novel
64. "Eye of ___ . . .": "Macbeth"
66. Norms, at St. Andrews
67. Of a poem
69. Loser to D.D.E.
72. W.W. II org.
73. Allot
74. Candle
77. Shed
79. Duck
80. Patron saint for a sailor
82. Word with generation
83. Iceman Bobby
84. Little, in Nice
85. Bar order
86. More vile
88. Potter's need
91. Put in place
94. Captive of Hercules
95. Terminus
96. River to the Oder
100. Play the rooster
102. Carried
103. In safekeeping
104. Jockey
105. Bit of work for Hammer
106. Brain passage
107. Elizabeth Stanton goal
108. U.S.-Soviet negotiations
109. South African
110. "Rule, Britannia" composer
111. N.B.A.'s Archibald
112. Symbol on a staff
113. Spooky

266 Signs of the Times By Robert Roop

What people might expect to run into these days.

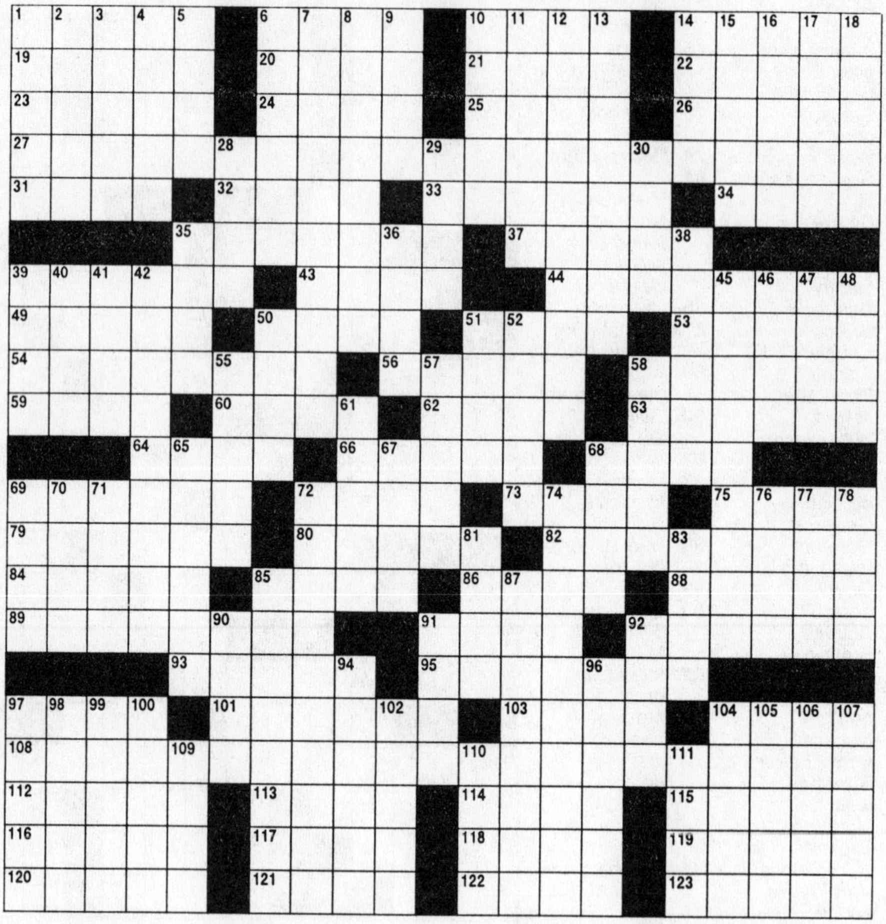

ACROSS

1. Onion's relative
6. Thoroughfare: Abbr.
10. Outfit
14. Domiciles
19. Keep on subscribing
20. Great Lake
21. Fencing sword
22. "Stop!" at sea
23. Dunne or Papas
24. Desire, in Spain
25. Serbian city
26. Slowly, in music
27. Street sign
31. Town in northern Italy
32. Indian beans
33. Do a Detroit auto job
34. Vetch
35. One who embraces
37. Early French king
39. Petty despot
43. Labels
44. Oil-field adjunct
49. Orchestra section
50. Sensible
51. Pearl Buck heroine
53. Andrea ____
54. Sign west of Omaha
56. Poe's bird
58. Do a suitcase job again
59. Org.
60. High naval off.
62. Rave's partner
63. Obliterates
64. Horse color
66. Ramp sign
68. Nigerians: Var.
69. Elephant driver
72. Ivy League school
73. Sheltered
75. Site of a Darius palace
79. Indian city
80. Kind of boy or cloth
82. Place for documents
84. Injures
85. Bairn's broth
86. Tramp
88. ____ a time (singly)
89. Expel forcibly
91. Of aircraft
92. African grain sorghum
93. Dugouts
95. 1957 Peace Nobelist
97. "____ homo"
101. Recital bonus
103. Afrikaans
104. Portico
108. Euphemistic taboo
112. Language of India
113. Potpourri
114. Love god
115. Decoration
116. "Ready ____, here I come"
117. "____ who?"
118. Yorkshire river
119. Tête-____
120. Boxes
121. Part of Q.E.D.
122. Rogers and Campanella
123. Adjust the alarm

DOWN

1. Shrink, in Scotland
2. Leander's love and others
3. Bumbling
4. Blood carriers
5. Pitcher
6. Journey for Mohammed
7. Race-track sign
8. Airplane's width
9. Affirmative of sorts
10. Painting style
11. Each
12. Eatery sign
13. Obligated
14. Saintly aura
15. Plain
16. Divine food
17. Chemical compound
18. Ensile
28. Turkish town
29. Deviates
30. Bass or treble
35. Dramatis personae
36. Bavarian river
38. Star: Prefix
39. Cries
40. "It's ____!"
41. Playthings
42. Sign in a public building
45. Two-lane road sign
46. Time periods
47. "Street Scene" author
48. Oxen of Tibet
50. Final song
51. White House office
52. ____ hand (help)
55. Speechify
57. Sports-complex sign
58. Early fiddle
61. Bone marrow: Prefix
65. What mare nostrum means
67. Division word
68. Saarinen
69. Roman 3100
70. Native maid in India
71. Chinese dynasty
72. Specific
74. Science-building sign
76. Part of the eye
77. Char
78. Italian wine city
81. One-time Korean leader
83. East Indian weight
85. Cloak for desert wear
87. Handel opus
90. Comply
91. Mime
92. Evergreen oak
94. Capital of Bulgaria, to a native
96. Talks back
97. Culture of a group
98. Bird sound
99. Showy flower
100. Biblical witch's home
102. Perch
104. Eastern monks' settlement
105. Flood and ebb
106. Explorer of New Mexico
107. End of a shoelace
109. Cases
110. Imminent
111. FitzGerald translated his poetry

267 Master of Suspense By A. J. Santora

Recalling one of the giants of the film world.

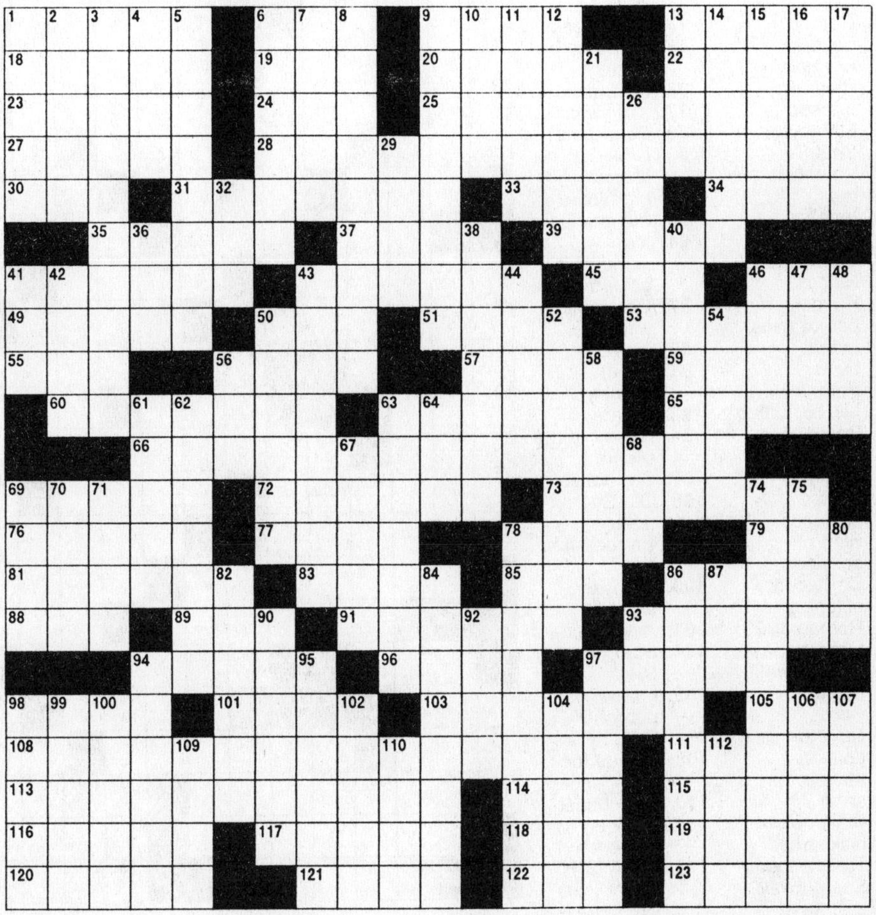

ACROSS

1. Start of a remark by 108 Across
6. Sugar amt.
9. Sharif bridge call
13. Capital of Guam
18. "___ You Now," Crane-Jacobs song
19. Kind of cry or lord
20. "Some Like ___"
22. Fashionable beach resorts
23. Arnold of the old Berle show
24. Nigerian native
25. Part 2 of the remark
27. Number for a skat game
28. Part 3 of the remark
30. Stitch
31. Most soppy
33. Actress Deborah
34. While starter
35. In a high-hat way
37. On foot?
39. Send a check
41. Theory of oneness
43. Treeless plain
45. Marino or Rather
46. Genetic initials
49. A Murphy
50. Hwy.
51. "My Three ___"
53. More frilly
55. Inner: Prefix
56. Kind of dorm
57. Writes
59. Velvety cloth
60. Couple
63. Spenser's Queene
65. The end
66. End of the remark
69. He entered the Promised Land
72. Kol ___ (Judaic prayers)
73. Bony fish
76. On ___ (carousing)
77. ___ about
78. Give up
79. Burst
81. Sniveling sound
83. Kind of plaid
85. "We ___ the World"
86. Look after
88. One of a deadly seven
89. Pepper or York: Abbr.
91. Diner seats
93. Prince Kong?
94. Concorde stop
96. Sp. miss
97. In any way
98. Fraternal initials
101. A Khan
103. Lamaist, for one
105. Swimsuit part
108. Speaker of 1 Across
111. Murkiness
113. ___ Magazine, source of the remark
114. Mouth: Prefix
115. ___ up (botch)
116. Have ___ (settle finally)
117. Lucy or Harlan Fiske
118. Energy source
119. Kovacs
120. Zip and area
121. This, in Avila
122. Letter
123. Passover meal

DOWN

1. Tools for Sugar Ray
2. ___ qui vive
3. Film by 108 Across
4. Word on the wall
5. How to get a word in
6. Out of the teens
7. Type of footwear
8. Went to a higher authority
9. Indy refuelings
10. Part of N.C.A.A.
11. Valentino role
12. Pele's game
13. Hebrew letter
14. Gin or vodka drink
15. Bay off Sonora
16. "___ ands or buts"
17. Plus item
21. Arranged row above row
26. Regular
29. Netman Arthur
32. Village-green shader
36. Roman 102
38. Heroic poems
40. A pig ___
41. Daisy ___ of Dogpatch
42. Force out
43. Brewing, as tea
44. January, in Juárez
46. Sup in style
47. Mass., Conn., etc.
48. Neighbor-hood
50. A cheese
52. Brandy glasses
54. Frequent role for 108 Across
56. Fort Ord bed
58. Withdraw
61. Fetish
62. Privately
63. Searches out
64. Proficient one
67. Worshiped ones
68. Bar drink
69. Rig compart-ments
70. Thine, in Quebec
71. Uris
74. Movie by 108 Across
75. Kind of board
78. Hoosegow
80. Poker winnings
82. See 106 Down
84. Arm of the Atlantic
86. Sequins
87. Swedish delicacy
90. Acrobats' wear
92. Of hearing
93. ___ standstill
94. In hiding
95. Type of Moslem
97. Music-maker Chet
98. Underlying
99. Planet
100. Land ___ (sleep)
102. Kind of pressure: Abbr.
104. Beiges
106. Sweet girl of song, with 82 Down
107. Arab ruler: Var.
109. Noshes
110. Copper
112. Learning

268 Couplings By Elaine Schorr

Some people just like to go together.

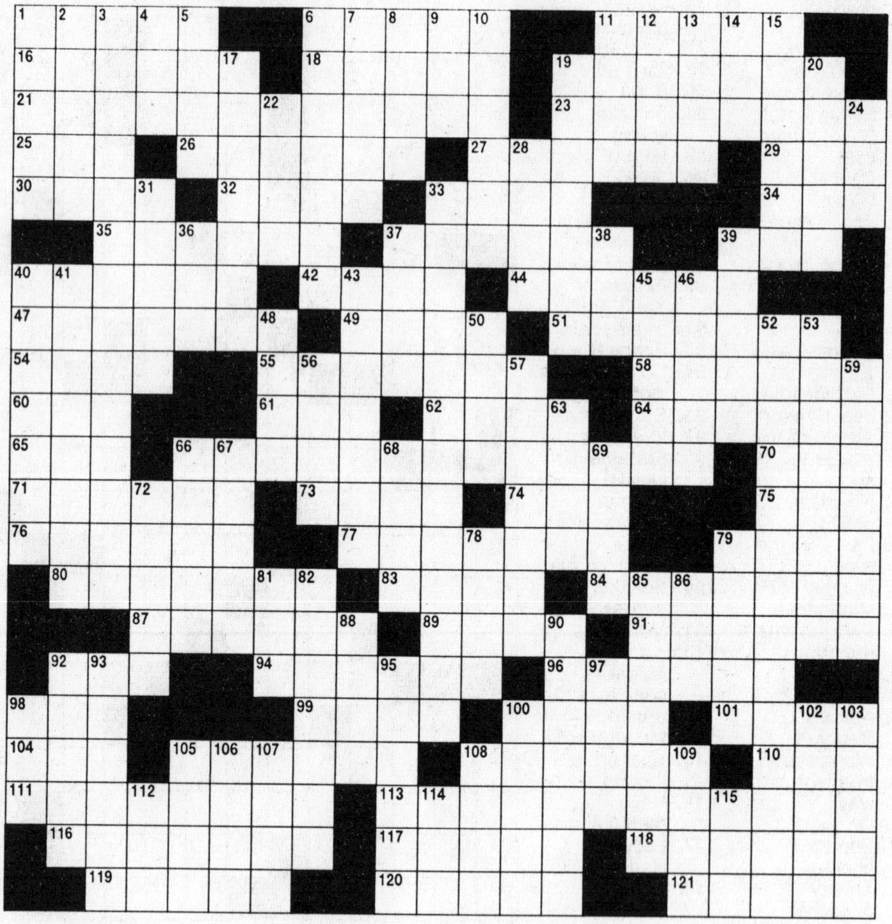

ACROSS

1. Good-conduct principle
6. River transports
11. Flame lovers
16. South American beer
18. Vinegar vessel
19. Scorecard listings
21. Revolutionary patriot joins Laurel's buddy
23. Potencies
25. Mil. recruiting
26. Baseball shutout listing
27. Secret societies
29. Kind of session
30. Do falconry stitching
32. Roman 1003
33. Delta deposit
34. Poet Lowell
35. Eat one's words
37. Up-and-coming athlete, for short
39. Stallone's nickname
40. Take a tour
42. Scare away
44. ___ race (become a candidate)
47. Apple variety
49. Airboard abbrs.
51. Scene of an Israeli plane rescue
54. French wave
55. Prospecting device
58. Capital of Albania
60. Attached one's John Hancock: Abbr.
61. Fraternal member
62. Templeton
64. Represents
65. Spanish wave
66. Novelist joins with singer
70. Hospital areas: Abbr.
71. Thousands, in France
73. Playing or calling ___
74. Decamped
75. Hindu barber caste
76. Just make it
77. ___-wear
79. Forefronts
80. Driver's-license procedure
83. Pull one's leg
84. It's sometimes golden
87. Directional wind
89. Newt: Var.
91. Tooth crusting
92. Imitate
94. Renée of the silents
96. Say it's so
98. Old English letter
99. Be foolish: Var.
100. Malayan sailboat
101. Actor Richard
104. Start of many titles
105. Former publisher Dorothy
108. Wands for cheerleaders
110. Wildebeest
111. Draw an inference
113. "M*A*S*H" player joins film actress
116. Oriental drudges
117. Of ancient Troy
118. Metric volume units
119. Clumsy fellow
120. At ___ for words
121. Like fizzy drinks

DOWN

1. Enlarges, of old
2. Macbeth was one
3. English actress joins Chicago ex-mayor
4. Cold stuff
5. Sleuth Charlie
6. Dutch canal boats
7. Skull: Prefix
8. Possessive pronoun
9. Tie the knot
10. Thwart
11. Kind of skirt
12. ___-cat (street game)
13. Land areas: Abbr.
14. Gesture of affection
15. Like some staircases
17. Genus of beetles
19. ___ cold (was unconvincing)
20. One side of life
22. Albanian river
24. C.I.A. target
28. River of England
31. Formal court reception
33. Singer-pianist joins silent-film actress
36. These, in Paris
37. Generic suffix
38. Alp: Abbr.
39. Native-born Israeli
40. Golf grouping
41. Resembling a circle
43. Metal-cutting tool
45. Ordnance site near Dumas, Tex.
46. Sign again
48. Canadian beaver skin
50. ___ out (betrayed)
52. English essayist joins family of English actress
53. Fascinate
56. Acid: Suffix
57. Pack again for moving
59. Foundations, in France
63. Social group
66. People, in Germany
67. ___ Park, Colo.
68. Smell ___
69. Connectives
72. "Camelot" composer
78. Busy place
79. Brink
81. RR stop
82. Chemises
85. Archipelago units
86. Scottish love
88. Something to raise
90. Highland wear
92. Kind of committee
93. Carbolic acid
95. Fiber for mats
97. Diving bird
98. Catchall abbr.
100. Old Turkish coins
102. Puts up
103. Loony
105. French W.W. II site
106. Place for corn
107. Long of Louisiana
108. Con ___ (with spirit)
109. Train-yard activity: Abbr.
112. ___ Canals
114. In toto
115. Affirmative

269 Gazetteer By Bernice Gordon

Featuring mainly places enjoyed by people.

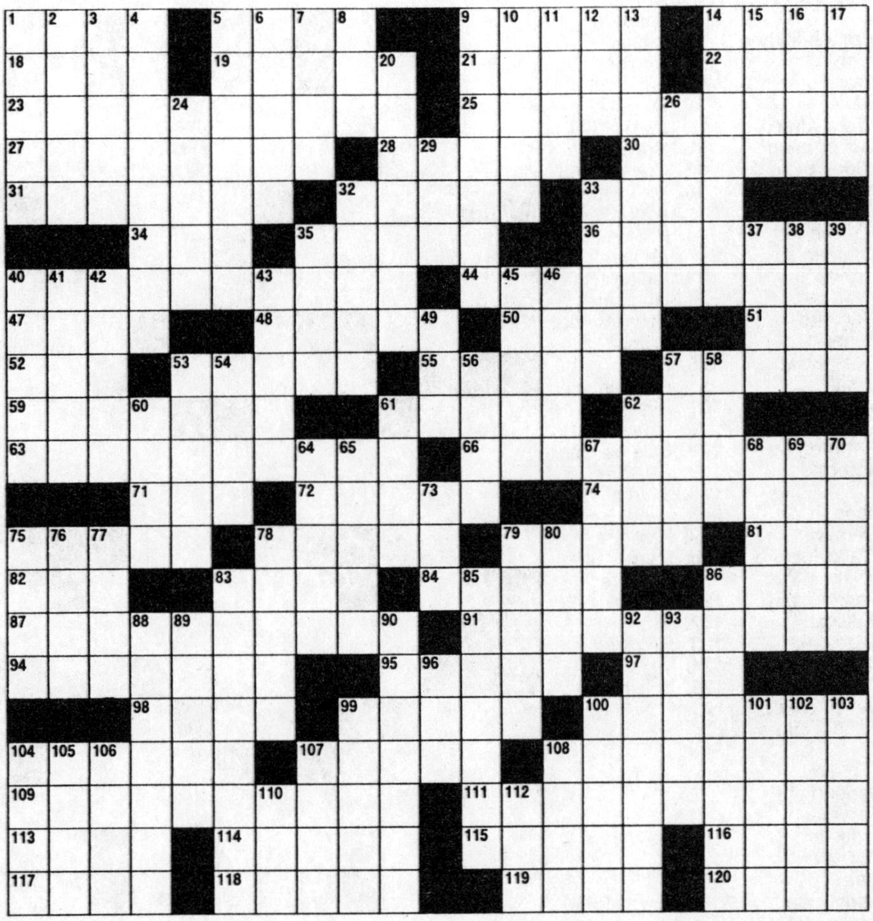

1 2 3 4 5 6 7 8 9 10 11 12 13 14 15 16 17
18 19 20 21 22
23 24 25 26
27 28 29 30
31 32 33
34 35 36 37 38 39
40 41 42 43 44 45 46
47 48 49 50 51
52 53 54 55 56 57 58
59 60 61 62
63 64 65 66 67 68 69 70
71 72 73 74
75 76 77 78 79 80 81
82 83 84 85 86
87 88 89 90 91 92 93
94 95 96 97
98 99 100 101 102 103
104 105 106 107 108
109 110 111 112
113 114 115 116
117 118 119 120

ACROSS

1. Peggy Wood role
5. "___ boy!"
9. Shifted, at sea
14. Rio beach, for short
18. Do a blue-pencil job
19. Sir, in Jaipur
21. Crowded airport
22. Templeton
23. Where Claus meets Miss Bow?
25. Where Veronica meets Eddie?
27. "___ Day," Carrie Jacobs Bond song
28. Lehmann of opera
30. American or National
31. Gibraltar and Bosporus
32. Fran's pal
33. Ananias
34. Dernier ___
35. Sound of distress
36. DDT targets
40. Where Markham met Ponti?
44. Home for a certain Boy?
47. Son of Aphrodite
48. Sierra ___
50. Places to take the cure
51. Undercover agcy.
52. Give assistance
53. Gone
55. "___ a Stranger"
57. In the course of
59. Gets set
61. Drone
62. Rita or Bravo
63. Prussian city for Woody and Gertrude?
66. Oil magnate's domain?
71. Cistern
72. Water wheel
74. Rehearsed one's lines
75. Shower time
78. Widow's share
79. Chief Justice: 1941–46
81. Little Stowe girl
82. Mauna ___
83. Highest note
84. Story for Hildy Johnson
86. Charlotte and Norma
87. Hideaway for Huey?
91. Where Heather trips?
94. Green onion
95. States of being
97. "___ Town"
98. Teeny bit
99. One of the flus
100. An S.S.R. republic
104. Village in Illinois
107. Upset for Killy
108. At the helm
109. Wine named for Bea?
111. Where writer Buck bathed?
113. Sea eagle
114. Rhone feeder
115. Song by Burt Bacharach
116. Le Moko of the Casbah
117. Carpenter's medium
118. Transferred
119. Cap with a visor
120. ___ en point

DOWN

1. Small plateaus
2. Adjust
3. Any of the Seven Dwarfs
4. Pulls to itself
5. Austere
6. Soft minerals
7. To such an extent
8. Bearing
9. Moving bumpily
10. "Oh, how ___ to get up . . ."
11. Use the oven
12. Before
13. Business activities
14. Musical about prewar Berlin
15. Designer Cassini
16. Home of Yma Sumac
17. Entr'___
20. Plaything for Malcolm Forbes
24. Burning
26. Tenant's paper
29. Palm leaf: Var.
32. Man-made fiber
33. Turkish pounds
35. Mushroomed
37. Actor James
38. Castor, e.g.
39. Hosiery mishap
40. Stiller's partner
41. Large bay window
42. Of a swelling
43. Willa Cather's "___ Lady"
45. First name in cosmetics
46. MOMA presentation
49. Omega
53. Newspaper edition
54. For fear that
56. Korbut
57. Oise feeder
58. Timber wolf
60. Hindu goddess
61. Concerning
62. Hillbilly Irene
64. ___ Gay
65. Keokuk resident
67. Figure of speech
68. Of an eye part
69. Join the evoe crowd
70. Hula-skirt material
73. Income-tax collector: Abbr.
75. Beginning of a Shakespeare title
76. Milne character
77. Frog genus
78. Mouth of a river
79. ___-law
80. Garb for Gaius
83. Confidential
85. Tree with showy flowers
86. Early maturing fruit
88. Shone
89. Massey of the films
90. Yearned for
92. Siren of the Rhine
93. Fretful one
96. Zilch
99. River to the Orinoco
100. Raised, as an anchor
101. Phileas Fogg enactor
102. Awkward
103. See eye to eye
104. Cast out
105. Matador's foe
106. Cartoonist Peter
107. Small building
108. Call by the ump
110. Mao ___-tung
112. Wapiti

270 Busy Year By Norman Wizer

It was 1936, when all sorts of things took place.

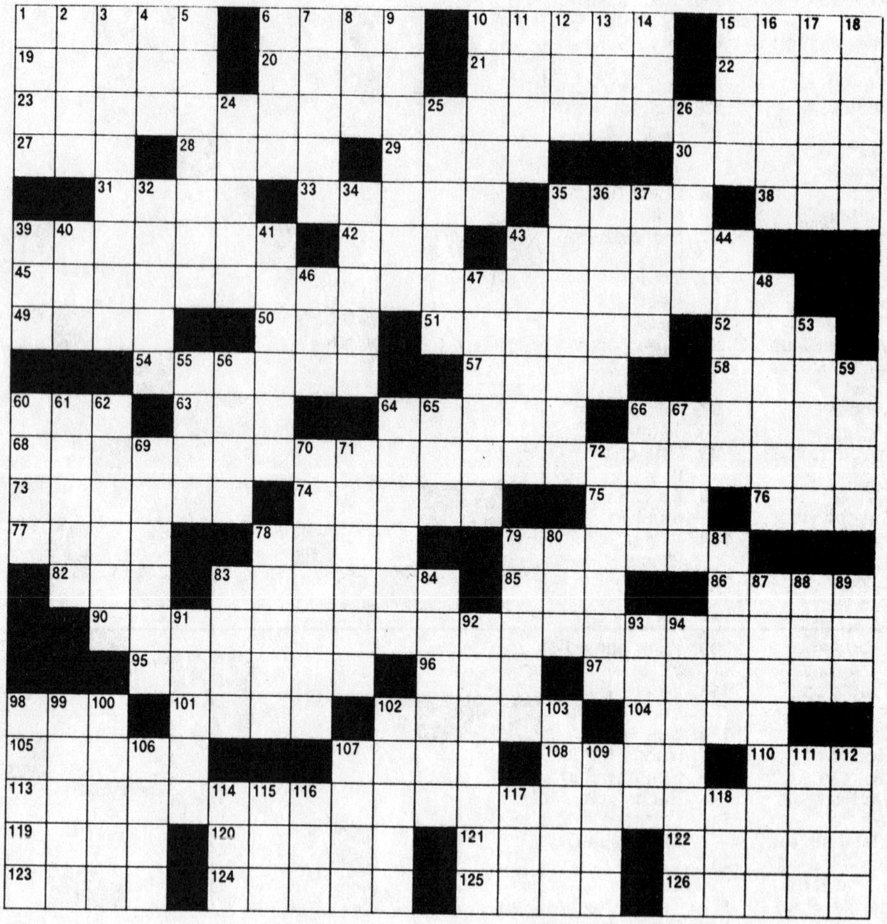

ACROSS

1. French library loan
6. War god
10. Lariat
15. Word after ear or snap
19. Close by, old style
20. Confident
21. Mosaic
22. Ol' Man ____
23. Sports headline
27. Haggard novel
28. Tone down
29. Shaft
30. Water bird
31. Golda
33. Between sei and otto
35. "To ____, a bone . . ."
38. Gershwin
39. Rialto feature
42. Flying prefix
43. Bring to view
45. Political headline
49. Bone: Prefix
50. Word with wet or clear
51. Fished with a net
52. "Eureka!"
54. Dangerfield
57. Enzyme suffixes
58. Morse or area
60. Insecticide
63. City in Israel
64. Purport
66. French Pointillist
68. Military headline
73. Rubber-stamp necessity
74. In ____ (angry)
75. Meadow
76. Controversial org.
77. One of Caesar's words
78. American reformer
79. Amass
82. June bug
83. "My Sister ____"
85. N.C.A.A.'s relative
86. Shake-spearean villain
90. Engineering headline
95. Derisive looks
96. Draw
97. Constructed
98. Harvest goddess
101. Pile, in England
102. Indian language
104. Great Barrier Island
105. Hindu untouchable
107. Bird of the rail family
108. Salamander
110. Guevera
113. Journalistic headline
119. Paradise
120. Painter of dancers
121. ____ avis
122. Lieu
123. Remainder
124. Vigilant
125. British gun
126. Rash

DOWN

1. Girl
2. Move slowly
3. Impassioned
4. Aries
5. Hermit
6. ____ were
7. Norse poems
8. Energy unit
9. Anesthetized
10. Ransack
11. Arrow poison
12. ____ mode
13. Do handwork
14. Affirmatives: Var.
15. Weather condition
16. Maid of paradise
17. Willow
18. Seed coat
24. Enticed
25. Spear carriers
26. On the up-and-up
32. Avid
34. Kind of bird
35. Straighteners
36. Does a kitchen job
37. Inst.
39. Ring result
40. Possessive pronoun
41. African republic
43. Menlo Park name
44. Item for the Mad Hatter
46. Quaff
47. Freshman's hat
48. Navigation aid
53. Scottish cartographer
55. Spanish jar
56. Slovenly woman
59. Lab burner
60. Roman 604
61. Companion of wined
62. Fine tuner or channel selector, e.g.
64. Provoked
65. Incite to action
66. Dagger of old
67. Brother of Jacob
69. Greek region on the Ionian Sea
70. Scolders
71. Plants used for pipe making
72. Light up, to a poet
78. Performs at a horse show
79. Measured, with "off"
80. Hawaiian bait fish
81. Speak one's ____
83. Robert ____
84. It's indivisible, in an oath
87. Diplomats' assistants
88. A thousand bucks
89. Strange
91. Free of an obstruction
92. Coinmakers
93. Move stealthily
94. Latvian
98. Houston player
99. It preceeds a fall
100. Vaults
102. Lift
103. Toughen
106. Air outlet
107. Peter or Nicholas
109. Israeli statesman
111. Passion
112. Whirlpool
114. Nabokov heroine
115. Set
116. Iron or Bronze
117. Butter measure
118. Depot: Abbr.

271 Common Cause By Dorothea Shipp

Things that are shared by persons of note.

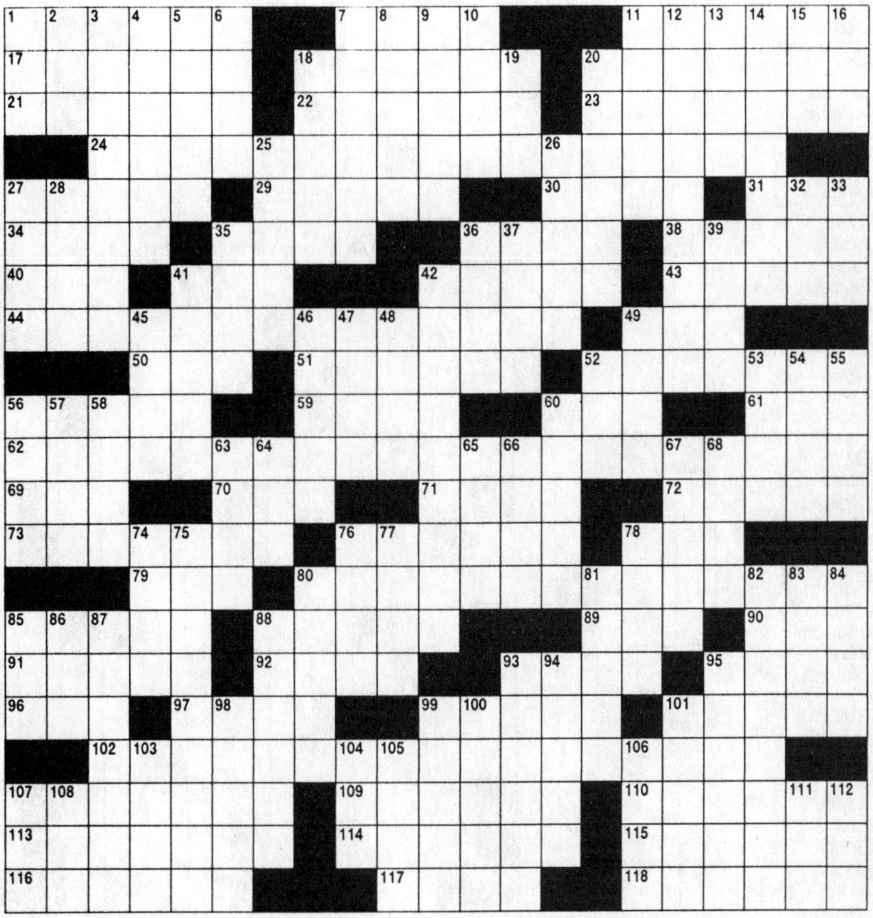

ACROSS

1. "From ___ with Love"
7. Indian mulberry trees
11. Forms
17. Bistro clientele
18. Monastery heads
20. Base runner, at times
21. Onmi and Cobo Hall
22. Novelist Charles and family
23. Pens
24. Actors
27. Gay ___
29. Board member: Abbr.
30. Olive genus
31. Kind of money
34. Eastern potentate
35. Triumphant cries
36. Reykjavik's land: Abbr.
38. Family girl
40. Tiriac of tennis
41. Martinique or Corse
42. Don Ho's welcome
43. Gift receiver
44. Actors
49. Grant or Costello
50. "Ode ___ Nightingale"
51. Mariner Abel
52. Muscle relaxer
56. Northwestern highway
59. Blue: Prefix
60. Hawaiian provender
61. Actress Mary
62. Actors
69. Friend, to Athos
70. Alfonso's queen
71. Copper center in Venezuela
72. Certain cash
73. Sea cow
76. Novelist Alice Tisdale ___
78. Evergreen
79. "A Shropshire ___"
80. Entertainer and a Mae West creation
85. Product of Toledo
88. Do a grammar job
89. Swedish coin
90. Peer Gynt's mother
91. Bactrian
92. Part of Civil War signature
93. Suffragist Carrie
95. Comb: Prefix
96. Levin or Eaker
97. Nail in a mine
99. Beauty's friend
101. Kind of lightning or music
102. Singer and composer
107. California seafood item
109. Trousers feature
110. "___ humanum est"
113. Took over for a dinner host
114. Laird's wear
115. Barnum's partner
116. Ladd or Tiegs
117. North Sea feeder
118. "___ Fideles"

DOWN

1. U.S. caricaturist
2. Org. for Nasser
3. At the helm
4. Letter mailer
5. Moslem decree
6. Southern holly
7. White poplars
8. Addis ___
9. Mine seams
10. Prank or game follower
11. One of the Ages
12. DeSoto and namesakes
13. Tributary of the Rhine
14. Baby's place
15. Squirmy fish
16. Certain citizens: Abbr.
18. Macaw
19. Fast plane
20. Spring flower
25. Far blue yonder
26. Warm Alpine wind
27. Anguish
28. Mine, to Pierre
32. Cream or berg
33. Word in a society notice
35. Italy's ___ Longa
36. Parts of the intestine
37. Kind of bread or ball
39. Markers
41. Actress Massey
42. Worthy of praise
45. Settlement in Greenland
46. City on the Mohawk
47. Site of the first miracle
48. Apocrypha book: Abbr.
49. Nonclerical
52. Dairy sound
53. Dorothy's Em
54. Cave, to a poet
55. Spooky
56. Man in a palindrome
57. Capital of Peru
58. Second man
60. Rio de la ___
63. Exigency
64. Compass letters
65. Toward the mouth
66. Lemur
67. Deem
68. Twerp's relative
74. Sheltered
75. Münchhausen specialty
76. ___ and now
77. Seine feeder
78. Ord or Knox
80. Early film star Nita
81. "God Bless Our Home," e.g.
82. Certain football passes
83. Words of understanding
84. Mardi Gras follower
85. ___-fi
86. Brea output
87. Arise
88. Rang
93. Sid or Julius
94. Ski resort
95. René's darling
98. Skirt feature
99. South Africans
100. Put on cloud nine
101. Valuable violin
103. Tenor John
104. Outside: Prefix
105. Australian lobster
106. McEntire of country music
107. Bank saver's abbr.
108. Word of disgust
111. No longer working: Abbr.
112. Storm center

272 Manege Time By Marjorie Pedersen

At least as far as the animal is concerned.

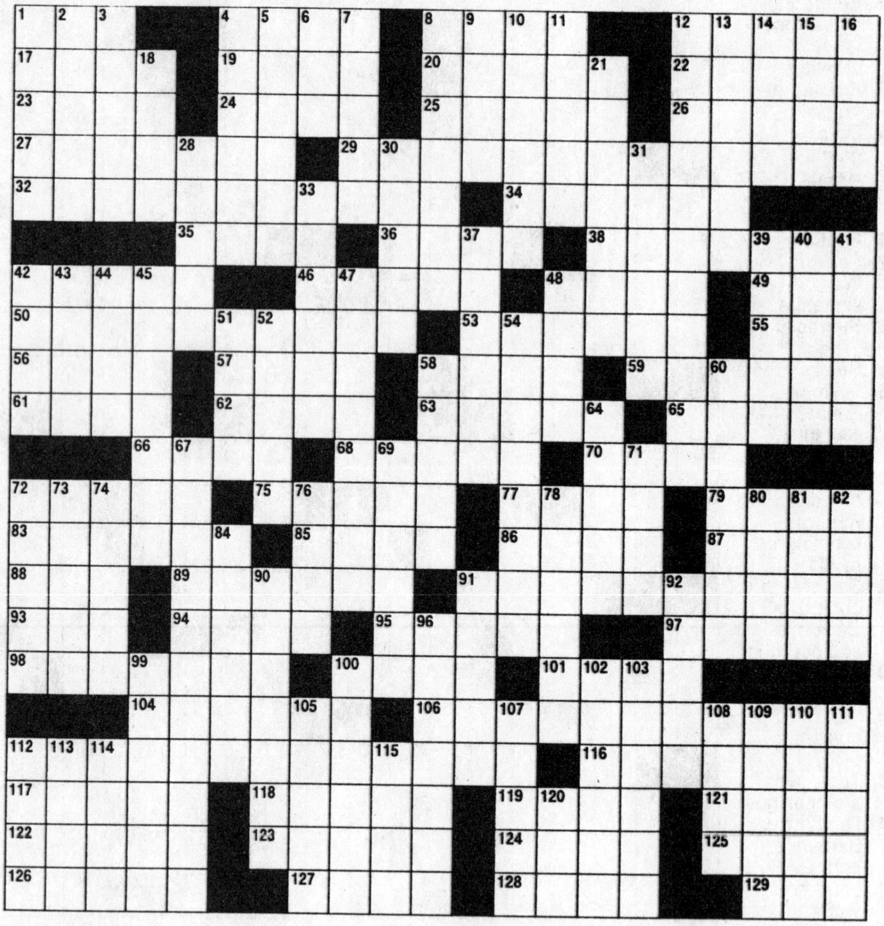

ACROSS

1. Suited
4. Observed
8. Rum cake
12. Waste producer
17. Part of D.A.R.
19. If not
20. Clock type
22. Triple Crown horse
23. Light shade
24. Speech flaw
25. Town in Missouri
26. Employees' Christmas extra
27. Mouthful for Demosthenes
29. Days of yore
32. Strategic offering
34. Mrs. O'____ cow
35. Approaching
36. Depots: Abbr.
38. Readies a latecomer's meal
42. Claiborne of culinary fame
46. Part of R.K.O.
48. Kind of chamber
49. A.E.C.'s successor
50. Good judgment
53. Actress Ralston
55. Early sailing ship
56. Employer
57. Weight allowance
58. Guitar part
59. Q-X span
61. High plateau
62. Writer Seton
63. Weariness
65. Gardner and namesakes
66. Honor, in Germany
68. Granular snows
70. Passport endorsement
72. Flier Balbo
75. "____ bleu!"
77. Have ____ for (hold a grudge)
79. Tiki, Siva and Thor
83. Williams's streetcar
85. Harbor fixture
86. ____ Rabbit
87. Rapier's relative
88. High note
89. Damascene
91. Draft animal
93. Capuchin monkey
94. Shoe width
95. Woodwinds
97. Tippecanoe's partner
98. Class of bony fishes
100. Mil. infraction
101. "So long!"
104. Soccer, basketball, etc.
106. Kid
112. Balderdash
116. More zany
117. Potentate
118. Facing a ship's keel
119. Contender
121. ____ cat
122. Rinse type
123. Back: Prefix
124. Malayan boat
125. Yardsticks: Abbr.
126. Joins a poker game
127. Fed. safety agency
128. Back talk
129. Beast of burden

DOWN

1. Expert
2. Trotter's cousin
3. Word before jet or fan
4. Moon goddess
5. Elevator man Otis
6. Feminine ending
7. Kidney: Prefix
8. Elizabeth ____ Browning
9. MacGraw and Baba
10. Swiss city and canton
11. Old money boxes
12. Trikes' predecessors
13. ". . . was stirring, not even ____"
14. Chanted
15. Gangster
16. This does it
18. Topic, for short
21. Sovereign
28. Actress Hope
30. Actor Davis
31. Austrian folk dance
33. Islands off Scotland
37. Actor Brian
39. Abrogate
40. Paddock installation
41. Ungainly craft
42. Sidekick
43. ". . . like a red, red ____"
44. War god
45. Sabra
47. Southwestern cattle range
48. Famous last words
51. Asterisk
52. Sea birds
54. Reasonable
58. Craze
60. "Othello," for one
64. Like hallowed halls
67. Oaters
69. Previously, poetically
71. Concerning
72. That is
73. Tissue layers
74. Ancient Mariner's sighting
76. ". . . blackbirds baked in ____"
78. Rendezvous
80. Milky stone
81. Printing mark
82. Soothsayer
84. "The ____ Texas are upon you"
90. Type of tire
91. "The ____ Purple"
92. Onset
96. Region of Czechoslovakia
99. Early ascetic
100. Daisylike flowers
102. Trojan hero
103. Zodiac sign
105. Prohibition
107. Invitation letters
108. Siouans
109. Rockies range
110. Requires
111. Rubbish
112. Merry sounds
113. Sign
114. Budget item
115. Muddle
120. Tax-shelter initials

273 Possessions By Sara Helleny

Things that some people might own.

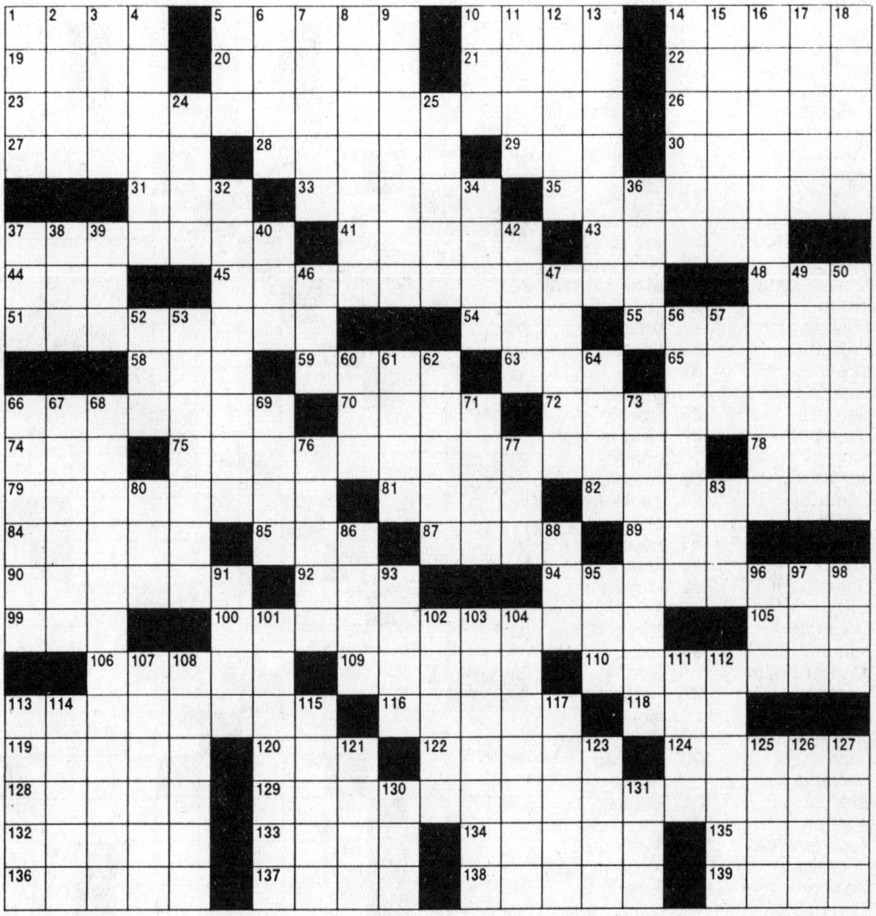

ACROSS

1. Kemo ___ (Lone Ranger)
5. S.A. constrictor
10. Smasher material
14. Of a large quantity
19. Ending for poet or tact
20. Glacial block
21. Pedro's assent
22. Hendricks of baseball
23. GRAHAM
26. Pro Football Hall of Famer Bobby
27. Brash
28. Utters, biblical style
29. Family member, for short
30. "___ my ten command-ments in your face": Shak.
31. Common Market initials
33. Squirrel away
35. Acid salts
37. "Iliad" loudmouth
41. Cathode's opposite
43. Large European lake
44. Former Mideast gp.
45. RAY
48. Helium-style craft: Abbr.
51. Most extensive
54. ___ loss for words
55. "___ ancient Mariner"
58. Mixture of sodium salts
59. Like still waters
63. Globe
65. Spanish hero
66. Do a foreman's job
70. ___ -and-potatoes man
72. ___ jig (English dance of yore)
74. Negative of sorts
75. VAN
78. "Born in the ___"
79. Genus of fungi
81. Medieval estate
82. ___ case of nerves (is edgy)
84. Pooped
85. Librarian's deg.
87. Seed appendage
89. "Lord, is ___?": Matt. 26:22
90. Jai alai
92. Take it on the ___
94. Never
99. French connectives
100. CHARLIE
105. Quixote
106. Piece of armor
109. "The Green Hat" author
110. Exact
113. Emulates Mel Tillis
116. Songbird
118. Pitcher Maglie
119. ___ Haute
120. Wood sorrel
122. Soprano Mitchell
124. Drunkard
128. "Chocolate Soldier" composer Straus
129. BILL
132. "Rose is a rose" writer
133. ___-high to a grasshopper
134. African lake and river
135. Composer Jerome
136. ". . . girl who cain't ___"
137. Hot or back follower
138. Alamogordo's county
139. Fast fliers

DOWN

1. Kind of language
2. Farm unit
3. Max or Buddy
4. Cricket-team number
5. Mrs. Gynt
6. She was a Good Queen
7. Killer whales
8. Kind of bliss
9. ". . . than ___ hot tin roof": Williams
10. Inquire
11. Father's Day purchases
12. "Hamlet" courtier
13. "___, since you went away, dear"
14. Of a yellow color
15. Turkish mountain chain
16. BILLY
17. Actress-singer Blakley
18. "Golden Boy" author
24. Moscow negative
25. Time: Prefix
32. "___ or high water"
34. Old Norse writing
36. Years, to Cicero
37. Bench warmer
38. Uncle Remus's Baby
39. Cockney idol
40. French laugh
42. "___ Perpetua": Idaho's motto
46. Relative of inc.
47. Loup-___ (werewolf)
49. "Whose hands are four, whose ___ limb": Huxley
50. ". . . the varied year, sullen ___": Thomson
52. Abbr. at J.F.K.
53. Plane's arrival
56. Has an inclination
57. U.N. labor group
60. Large bird
61. Saarinen
62. Zoo treasure
64. Nonsense
66. Not live
67. Knave
68. TOM
69. Barren, to Angus
71. Dictator
73. Places for wet dishes
76. Umpire's call
77. The, in Naples
80. "O Sole ___"
83. River island
86. Actress Thompson
88. Gibbon
91. Church part
93. Griffin of TV
95. Recipe meas.
96. Amin
97. Parts of yrs.
98. Chem. suffix
101. Puts the baby back to sleep
102. Craftily: Var.
103. Toast start
104. Street game
107. Ellington's transport
108. Breastbone: Prefix
111. Let up
112. Times
113. Facing a glacier
114. Seed covering
115. Tea cake
117. One-___ (direct competition)
121. Cruising
123. Winged
125. All-purpose trucks
126. Ilk
127. Sea eagles
130. Wager
131. Nav. worker

274 Put Another Way By Helen Bernhardt

Giving familiar phrases a new twist.

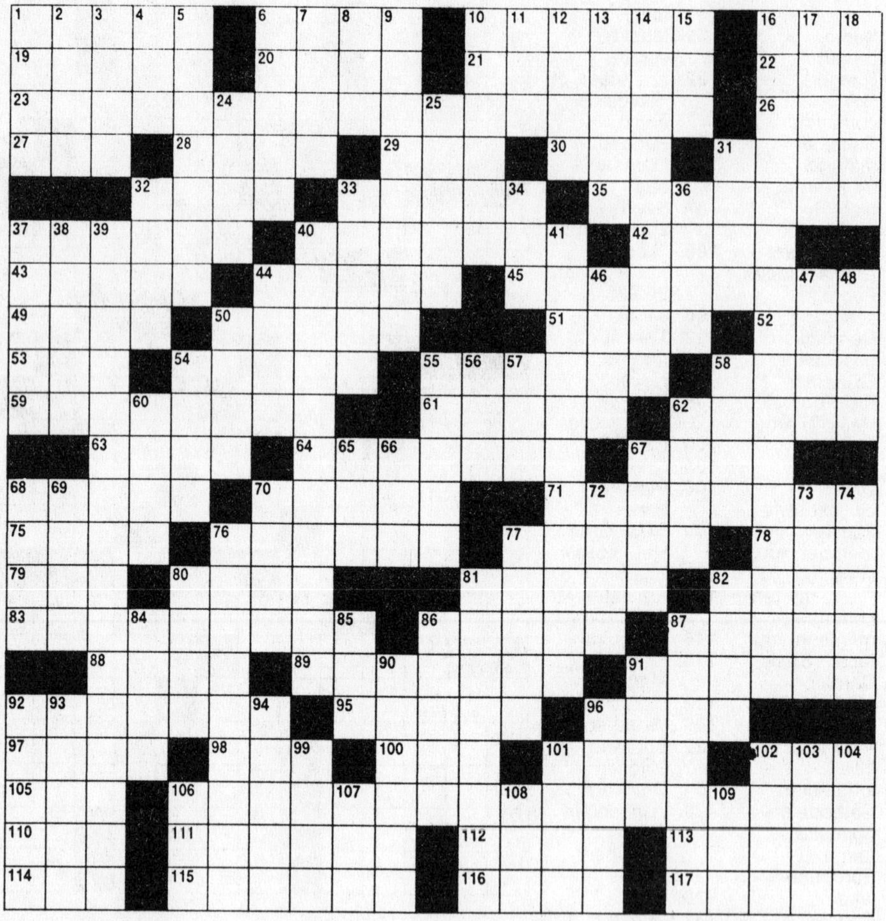

ACROSS

1. Chan portrayer Sidney
6. Swindle
10. John the Baptist's downfall
16. Snead or Palmer, e.g.
19. Musical study
20. Presently
21. Of a singing group
22. Male gypsy
23. Prepare a street for a parade?
26. Seraglio chamber
27. King of Judah
28. Pump or loafer
29. 144 items: Abbr.
30. Chemical suffix
31. Oriental nurse
32. Kind of beam or struck
33. Hebrew abode of the dead
35. Alexandra's title
37. Wait on
40. Popular pre-Christmas mailing
42. Baseball's Speaker
43. Nobel physicist and family
44. Man's man
45. Lowest ship platform
49. S-curve molding
50. Braved
51. German one
52. ___ Na Na
53. Crude
54. Fastens
55. British naturalist, 1660–1753
58. Invent
59. Rock formations
61. Dwelling
62. On the ___ (undecided)
63. First class
64. Eastern Cuban province
67. Swiss river
68. Like Huxley's hay
70. Blazing
71. Hemmed in
75. Comedian Mort
76. Sergeant of lonely-hearts note
77. Hawaiian love
78. Actress Francis of the 1930's
79. Niño's uncle
80. Malay vessel
81. Dublin theatre
82. Swiss city
83. Bare possibility
86. Bobbin
87. King Minos's home
88. Hoodlum
89. Technical skill
91. Hebrew letters
92. Make an aerobic move
95. Miró's home
96. "___ a Song Go Out . . ."
97. Toward the mouth
98. Break bread
100. German conjunction
101. Pilaster
102. ___ volente
105. Avocado or onion mixture
106. Talking to cager Larry Bird
110. Burrows or Beame
111. Occurring in pairs
112. Teen problem
113. Like many Poe works
114. His, in Lille
115. Faulkner family
116. Rouge et ___
117. Scare off

DOWN

1. Honduran port
2. Elevator man
3. Moon goddess
4. Dutch city
5. Motives
6. Mehta's handful
7. Concerning
8. Mauna ___
9. Dubbed by King Arthur
10. Marm's place
11. Vancouver native
12. Film actor Edmund
13. Praying figure
14. Significant point in life
15. Luther's opponent
16. Pledges bed and board?
17. Japanese movie monster
18. Siouan tribe
24. Sandaled
25. Prodigious
31. Dry
32. Only
33. Kind of slip or resistance
34. Card game
36. Cockney strings
37. Halt a rocket
38. Roman wear
39. Wino's hangover?
40. Jokers in a deck?
41. Lubricate a funny bone?
44. Weathercock
46. Occupation
47. Modish
48. Helen or Citizen
50. Wine and ___
54. Judge's seat
55. Diaphanous
56. Chaney of films
57. Elsewhere
58. Large mackerel
60. Irritate
62. White House pet
65. One of the tides
66. Dander
67. In pain
68. Anent
69. Innocent
70. Endless time
72. December song
73. Fifth largest planet
74. Units of force
76. Made a swaggering entrance
77. Overhead, in the sticks
80. Illumination unit
81. Of garden pests
82. Writer Harte
84. Campus figure
85. Abstract being
86. White trumpeters
87. Became sunny
90. Musical works
91. Choir voice
92. Fountain and water
93. Clan
94. "I ___ way of knowing" (wasn't told)
96. Deduce
99. Snare
101. God of fire
102. Scurry
103. Lake found by Jolliet in 1669
104. River of Poland
106. Not present: Abbr.
107. Follower of printemps
108. Sgt. or cpl.
109. Very small

275 On the Occult Front By Evelyn Benshoof

Plumbing some of the darker sides of life.

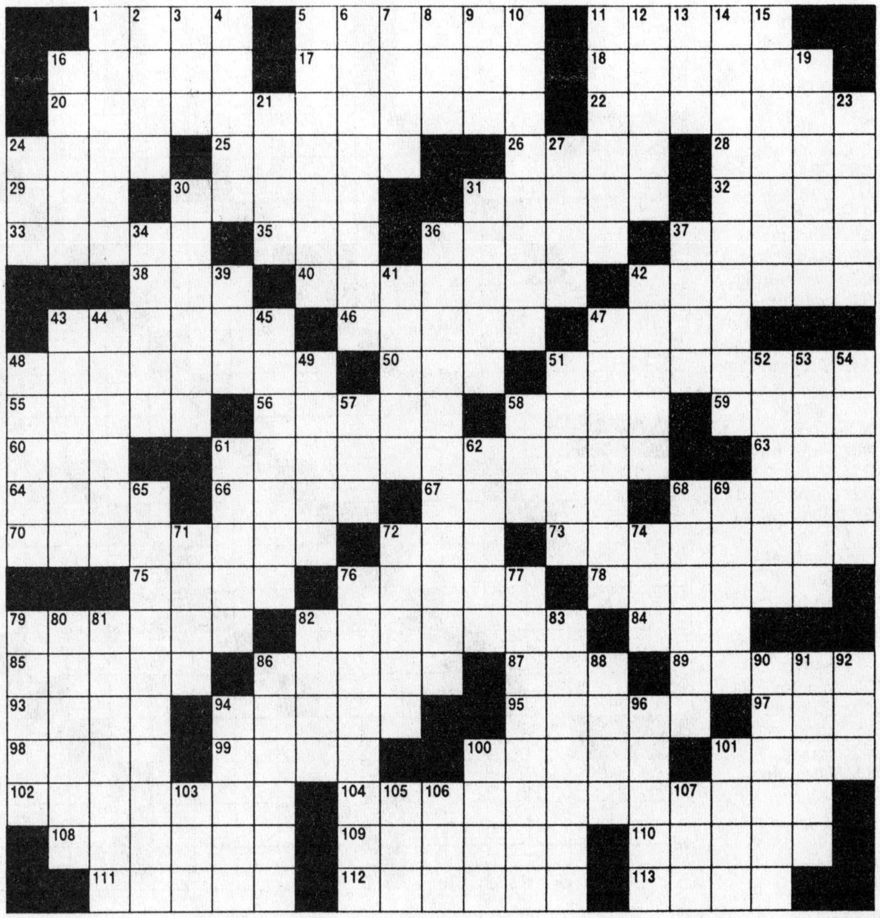

ACROSS

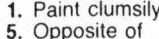

1. Paint clumsily
5. Opposite of proximal
11. Small lumps
16. Game of chance
17. Arthurian woman
18. Coaster or derby
20. State of fascination
22. Made current
24. Fish-eating bird
25. Best
26. London gallery
28. Contend
29. Emolument
30. Short: Prefix
31. Spring or scarlet
32. Joint
33. Late, in Seville
35. Theological inst.
36. Cables
37. Revise
38. Spanish king
40. Complains
42. Crows
43. Throw off balance
46. Showed affection
47. Mild epithet
48. Airport user
50. Math initials
51. One who hoodwinks
55. Scandinavian god
56. Jewish law
58. Prefix for naut or dynamic
59. Bullfighter's cloak
60. News service
61. Trickery
63. Camper's need
64. Type of TV antenna
66. War god
67. ___ off (intermittently)
68. Military camp
70. Big beer glass
72. Decree
73. Matured
75. African republic
76. Summoned
78. Delegate
79. Comes up again
82. Dye user
84. Balsam's relative
85. Originated
86. Swain
87. Painter ___ Borch
89. Buddhist king of India
93. Show surprise
94. Crossed out
95. In any way
97. Kind of money
98. This, in Spain
99. Addict
100. Horowitz's instrument
101. Power
102. Clerics
104. Entrancing
108. Siding for a house
109. Release from a bobbin
110. Roof parts
111. Poly follower
112. Flaunt
113. Scandinavian rugs

DOWN

1. "___ at Eight"
2. Stake
3. Cry of disgust
4. Auger, for one
5. Hand over
6. Inopportune
7. Corresponding
8. Fasten
9. Miss Landers
10. Cultured
11. Swift's Yahoos, e.g.
12. Horse, at times
13. Classic
14. Sorcery
15. ___ cap for (try to get)
16. City near Cleveland
19. Feel contrite
21. Pub drinks
23. Exploits
24. Newt
27. City rtes.
30. Warning device
31. Mulcted
34. Force
36. Mumbo-jumbo expert
37. Superior
39. Brynner
41. Kind of bear or front
42. Part of B.L.T.
43. Capricorn or Cancer
44. Relish-tray item
45. ___ out (faded gradually)
47. Ridiculed
48. Dull sounds
49. "All right!"
51. Martin and Stockwell
52. Like some stares
53. High-flown poetry
54. Appraised
57. Legal point
58. Doctors' org.
61. Turner and Wood
62. Make a beginning
65. Trickery
68. Observation
69. City on the Loire
71. Elbe feeder
72. Had troubles
74. Troops of W.W. I
76. Conceals
77. Intricate
79. Stormed
80. Rubs out
81. Having ribs
82. Composer Porter
83. Altar structure
86. Landlord
88. Raja's wife
90. Expresses a view
91. Chess pieces
92. Insect
94. Blockhead
96. Recluse
100. "Guilty," for one
101. Singer
103. Calendar abbr.
105. Acid initials
106. Be incorrect
107. Doris or Dennis

276 Bit of English By H. Hastings Reddall

Some references to the people across the ocean.

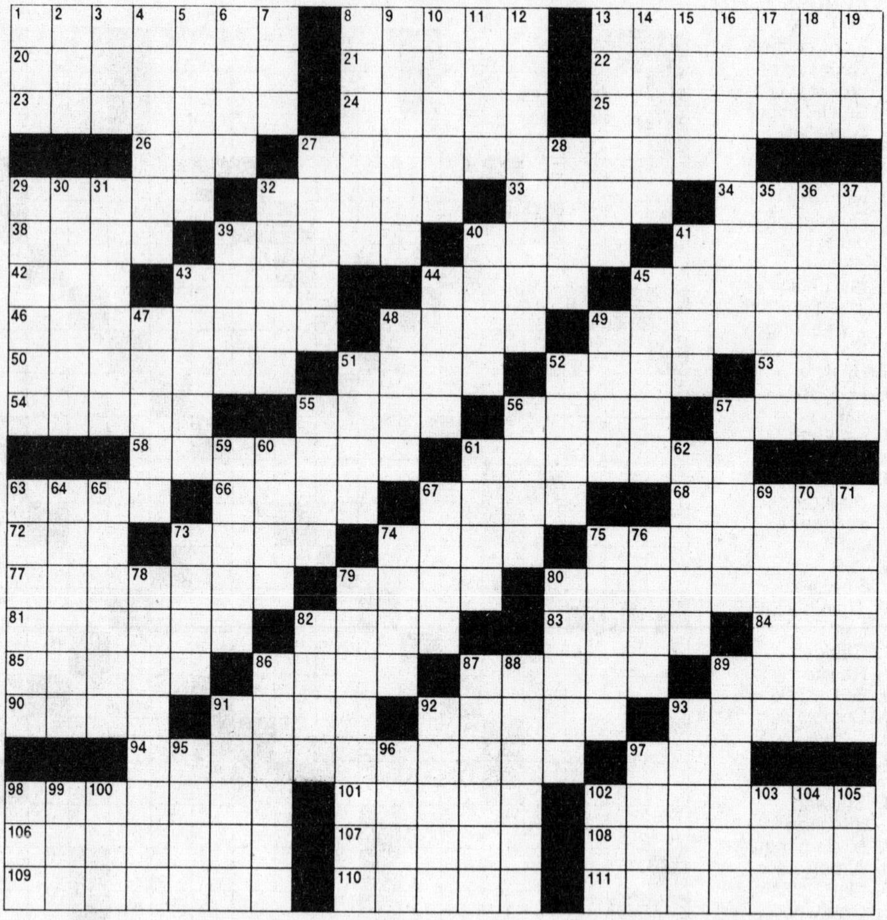

ACROSS

1. Scepter'd isle of note
8. "___ wha hae wi' Wallace bled"
13. Daydream
20. Failed to follow suit
21. Chicago gateway
22. Unyielding
23. Complains
24. Tree product
25. Ore-digging processes
26. "Le Coq ___"
27. Abbey with a Poet's Corner
29. German city
32. Bygone times
33. Writer Anita
34. Smith or Bede
38. Diving bird
39. Goes after a trout
40. Sauna user
41. Unit of volume
42. Sea eagle
43. Wrongful act
44. Moderate
45. Demons
46. Having a skull
48. Bloody queen
49. Spring flowers
50. Completely
51. Injure
52. Stuffy person
53. Compass dir.
54. Used a vacuum
55. Muffin ingredient
56. Lowly worker
57. Superlative suffixes
58. Give in marriage
61. Bread browner
63. Mischievous ones
66. Appraise
67. Duke of ___
68. Took a new mate
72. Spoil
73. Endings for cash and bombard
74. Golf warning
75. Appease
77. Charles and Andrew
79. Swing around
80. Rubber bands
81. Not visible
82. Gold item for a pupil
83. Despicable
84. Article
85. Abounds
86. The ___ of battle
87. Blemishes
89. Hart or elk
90. Gaelic
91. Unheeding
92. Solitary
93. ___ Lord of the Admiralty
94. Buckingham Palace people
97. Noise
98. Flute player
101. Avoid
102. Connected
106. Symbols of tone deafness
107. Stair component
108. Western Hemisphere native
109. Wash
110. Suffixes for song and young
111. Communication

DOWN

1. Boot one
2. Born
3. Govt. output statistic
4. Netherlands city
5. Shmuel Yosef ___, Israeli author
6. ___-do-well
7. Dentist's degree
8. Most painful
9. Cedar and hope items
10. Kilns
11. Balance a ship
12. Old-age syndrome
13. European garlic
14. Prepares a paper
15. Wind indicator
16. Some Mideast nations
17. Sought office
18. Gerundial ending
19. French connectives
27. Squander
28. "___ but the brave . . ."
29. Puts in office
30. Anne ___ Lindbergh
31. Give
32. Gala affair
35. Repudiates
36. Fervent
37. Military dining places
39. Hard or soft fuel
40. Old MacDonald's place
41. Warble
43. Does jousting
44. Home, to a cow
45. Very dim
47. Neck areas
48. Old gray animal
49. Those in favor
51. Firefighting gear
52. Top
55. Severs
56. Study carefully
57. Upright
59. Dress fussily
60. Boat movers
61. Ripped
62. Obliterate
63. Ascribe
64. Silas of Raveloe
65. Moves with a lever: Var.
67. Possessive
69. Futile call in a cafe
70. Does artwork
71. Wasteland
73. Orange and lemon desserts
74. Small apartment
75. Table-setting piece
76. Young girl
78. Class of marine worm
79. Office workers
80. Dark wood
82. Close tightly
86. Funeral vehicle
87. Baseball pitch
88. Raft movers
89. Iranian coins
91. Color workers
92. Entertain
93. Rasps
95. "The Good Earth" heroine
96. Came down
97. Township of Attica
98. Crystalline salt: Abbr.
99. Olive product
100. Singleton
102. Battering ___
103. Mexican aunt
104. Locomotive operator: Abbr.
105. Follower of H.S.T.

277 Companionship By Roger Courtney

Some people have a lot in common.

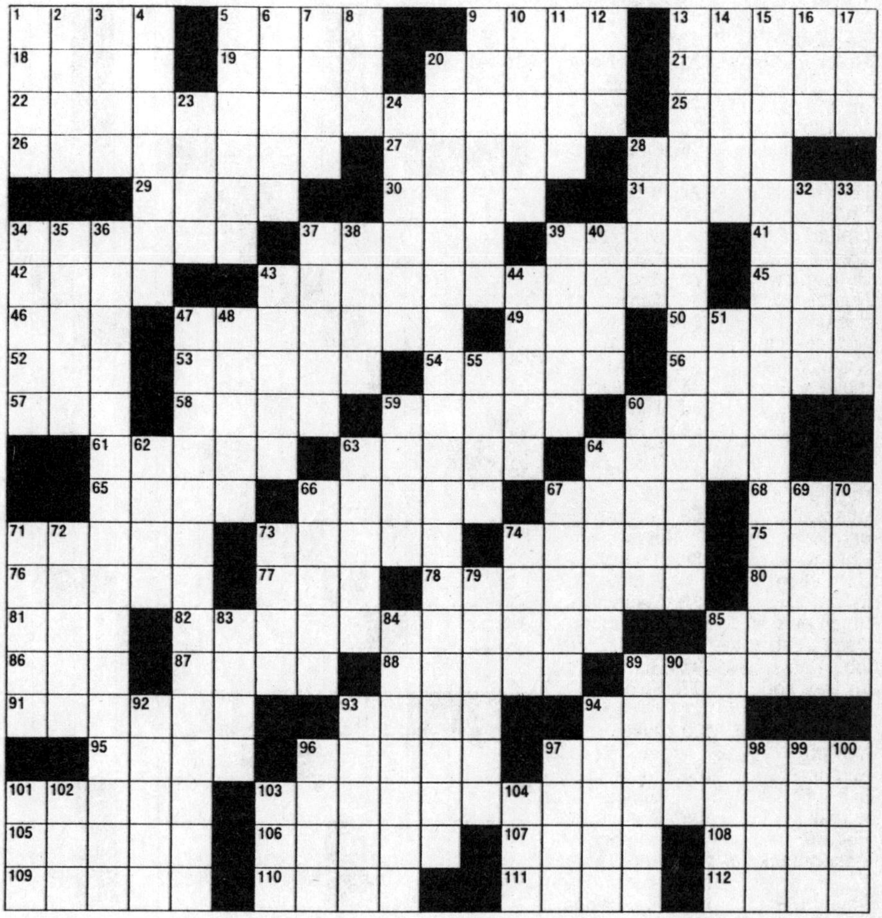

ACROSS

1. Tattle
5. Harris's Fox
9. Type of cut
13. Synagogue leader
18. Dynamics preceder
19. Tabula ___
20. Fixed percentage
21. Mountain nymph
22. Boxer turns actor
25. O'Casey and Penn
26. Stupid
27. Ignited again
28. Alpha follower
29. Olympic scores
30. Sinn ___
31. Come forth
34. Embraces once more
37. Construction-site object
39. Portuguese lady
41. Word after pro
42. Wood sorrels
43. Potent drink
45. Biblical lang.
46. Suit maker: Abbr.
47. "Doesn't that ___?" (really!)
49. Fury
50. Unavailable
52. Attention
53. Boleyn and Bancroft
54. Wight and Man
56. Like some cups or seals
57. Pig's pad
58. Peat places
59. Pound and Stone
60. Profession for the Lunts: Abbr.
61. McCrea and Harris
63. "Till We Meet ___"
64. Misuse, in Milan
65. Airport abbrs.
66. Arafat and Assad
67. Wide-flanged beam
68. Smidgen
71. Canelike plant, in Malaysia
73. Slur over
74. Town in India
75. Alice's TV friend
76. Alamogordo event
77. Train terminal: Abbr.
78. Foot lever
80. Charles or Milland
81. Spanish yeses
82. Go ___ (argue violently)
85. Apportion
86. Mother's offering: Abbr.
87. Gray coating
88. Australian aborigines' club
89. Gary the golfer
91. Clog
93. German title
94. Mortgage
95. Choir voice
96. Oscar the writer
97. Dog from England
101. Small cases
103. Bandleader turns author
105. Judy of "Laugh-In" fame
106. Color of envy
107. Keep ___ (persist)
108. Football positions
109. Term of endearment
110. Geog. area
111. Economical letter
112. ___ majesty

DOWN

1. ___ California
2. Ames of the movies
3. War god
4. Genus of fungi
5. Boston skaters
6. Bromfield's "The ___ Came"
7. Basic Latin word
8. Reign, in India
9. Having more ringlets
10. Thinking man's sculptor
11. French political unit
12. Sickly
13. Comedienne turns chemist
14. Mountain crest
15. Maude becomes a uke player
16. Outlaw
17. Psyche parts
20. Royal lady becomes a cosmetics giant
23. Neighbor of Wash.
24. "Summer, winter ___ . . ."
28. With diction, it's a blessing
32. Silly people
33. Fix firmly
34. Sea sounds
35. Brilliance
36. Trumpeter turns film actor
37. Pigeons' homes
38. Narrow inlets
39. Challenges
40. Turkish units of weight
43. July 4 sounds
44. Home of a noted opera house
47. Baseball superstar turns movie actress
48. Chemical compounds
51. Former D.C. baseballers
55. Indian titles
59. Oath for Hoople
60. Have ___ (whoop it up)
62. Planets
63. Doer: Suffix
64. "Gin ___ meet . . ."
66. Sacred place
67. Villain, e.g.
69. Winged
70. Charles of the Casbah
71. Matting fibers
72. Like a listing boat
73. This, in Spain
74. Kind of duck or head
79. Sketched again
83. Word before sorry
84. Home owner, for example
85. Machinist's tool
89. Bluebeard was one
90. Lascivious look
92. Author of "Common Sense"
93. One in concealment
94. Legitimate
96. "The Way We ___"
97. About
98. Top-notch
99. Law degrees
100. "Or ___!"
101. Plane formation: Abbr.
102. Confucian principle
103. Dart board, for one: Abbr.
104. Smith or Fleming

278 Echoes By Cathy Millhauser

A matter of waxing slightly poetical.

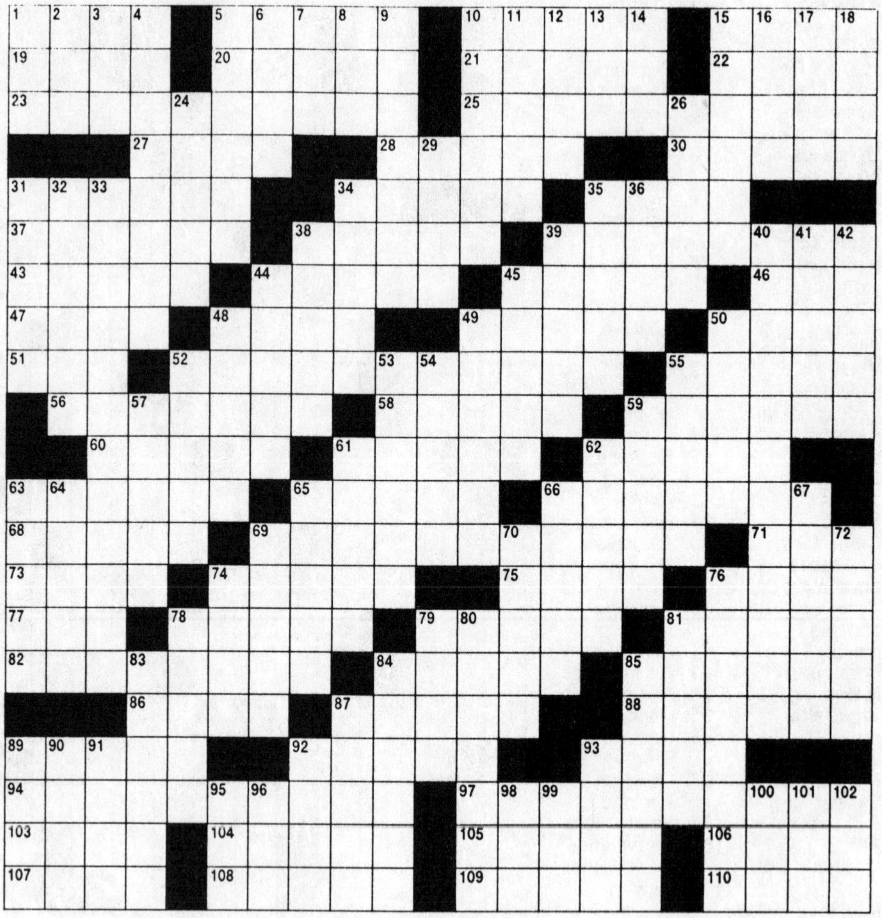

ACROSS

1. Seaweed
5. Holey roll
10. Defrock a flock
15. Spot for a tot
19. Love god
20. Port of Honshu
21. English prelate of the 1600's
22. Betting city
23. Neater cheater
25. Midget digit
27. One on the move
28. Imitators
30. Handy ___ (fixers)
31. Poodle noodle
34. Atlanta university
35. Knelled
37. Correction list
38. Small eels
39. Does a lab job
43. Trotsky and Uris
44. Wooer-cooer, with 45 Across
45. See 44 Across
46. His wife looked back
47. "___ Rhythm"
48. He abhors a matador
49. Prepared a baking apple
50. Part of a bird's bill
51. Part of USSR
52. Hare wear
55. Candidates' list
56. Gotham newspaper
58. They're hard and soft
59. Saved from the rod
60. Styles
61. Kingly titles
62. Moslem rulers: Var.
63. Played to the gallery
65. Types
66. Crypt writing
68. Fulcrum's partner
69. Enough stuff
71. Cross the road like a toad
73. New Haven people
74. Jalopies
75. Depend
76. Floor model, often
77. A Stooge
78. Bright sprite, with 79 Across
79. See 78 Across
81. Certain words
82. Impart heart
84. Dictatorial
85. Turn aside
86. Sum, ___, fui
87. Transit for a tyke
88. Some bridge bids
89. Kind of lightning
92. Secrecy protectors
93. Light colors
94. Glad dad
97. Soleful bowlful
103. Away from the gale
104. Fountain-coin number
105. Song from long ago
106. Odor encoder
107. Roe or doe
108. Word after sooth
109. Repair the turf
110. Place for a Campbell

DOWN

1. Neighbor of Neb.
2. Large bird
3. Chop off
4. Full of meaning
5. Wine cellar
6. Assyrian deity
7. Space
8. ___ out (scrounge)
9. Wyoming tourist city
10. Feasts
11. Like O'Neill's ape
12. Sea predators
13. Turpentine resin
14. He reigns in Spain
15. Cower
16. Split
17. Like a squid's defense
18. Lads
24. Yells for the team
26. Violet's relative
29. Menhaden
31. Places for salami
32. Where to find Eugene and Josephine
33. Slick flicks
34. Poetic finale
35. Hard hat's bolt
36. New no longer
38. Trees of the rose family
39. One Day
40. Double bubble
41. German pastry
42. Knight's mount
44. Parts of ears
45. Sun-dried bricks, for short
48. Made a wildcat a mildcat
49. Tender touch
50. Red Cross founder Barton
52. Addition to a bill
53. Manipulates a baton
54. Writer Bret
55. Ill will
57. Certain bags
59. Showing glee
61. Sentimental
62. Petition for a job
63. Tropical resin
64. Casaba or honeydew
65. Clever
66. Board for nails
67. Spanish chap
69. High nest
70. Get up
72. Puts up bail
74. Possessive
76. Making schemes
78. Like a spray
79. Kitchen wrap
80. Requests
81. Article of food
83. Young chick
84. Mule, often
85. Drove a certain cart
87. Redskin's place
89. Herring's relative
90. Force to court
91. Fencing sword
92. Agile
93. Containing sulfur
95. Parts of qts.
96. Cry of jubilation
98. ___ de France
99. Student org. of the 60's
100. José's sun
101. Part of Cong.
102. Yearning

279 Phrasing Out By Robert Wolfe

Alliterative descriptions of familiar combinations.

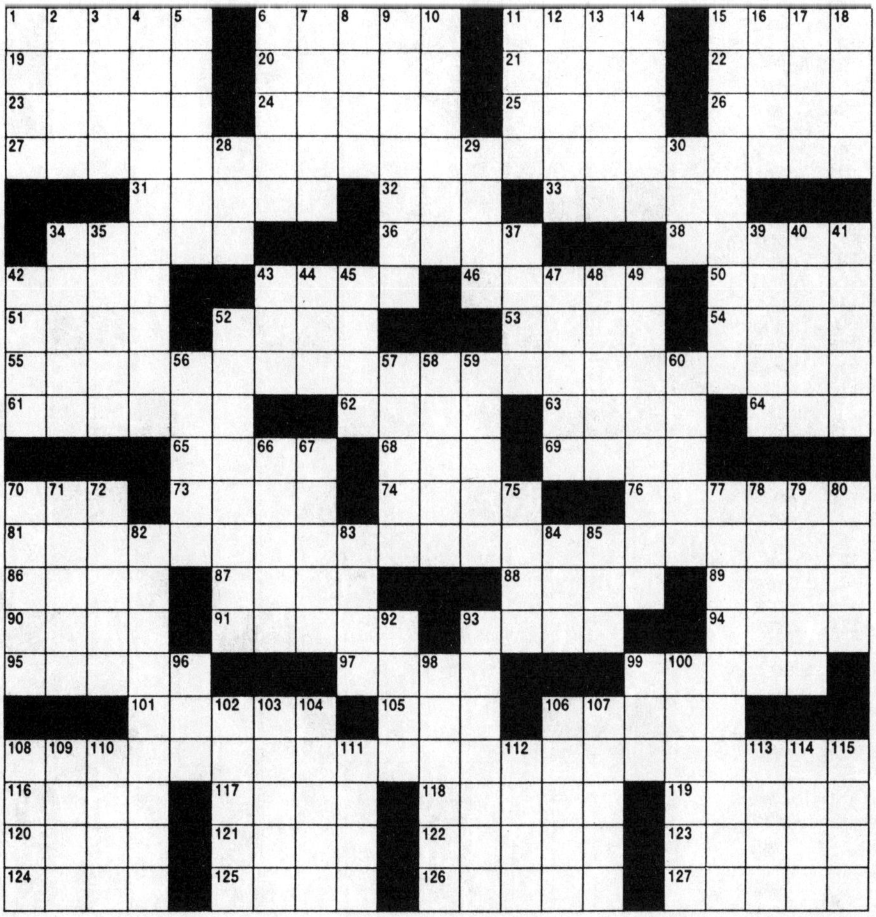

ACROSS

1. Insipid ones
6. Tibetan V.I.P.'s
11. Rehan and namesakes
15. Actress Tyne
19. Venerate
20. Few: Prefix
21. Sword handle
22. Assam silkworm
23. Dormouse
24. Kidney enzyme
25. Celebes ruminant
26. High pool
27. Fosters feline freedom
31. Helots' relatives
32. Part of E.T.A.
33. Range sight
34. Dog-pedigree listing
36. What tecs do at times
38. Crinkled cloth
42. Talkative Jack
43. Plexus
46. East Indian milkweeds
50. Word before lasting or more
51. Nuclear abbr.
52. Of aircraft
53. Insect feeler
54. Asian palm
55. Santa's salutations
61. Wits
62. Scarlett's HQ
63. Kind of bell or prize
64. Comic Louis
65. Clicking sounds
68. Legal thing
69. Area of Morocco
70. Nile killer
73. Rib order
74. "___ We Be Friends?"
76. George Ade writings
81. Shadow a spawning salmon
86. Louise or Turner
87. Ferber
88. Certain truant
89. "Tell ___ the Marines"
90. Rich Little, often
91. Exudes
93. Stride
94. Third of a 1970 film title
95. Elemi or copal
97. Kind of soap or sell
99. Threefold
101. Actor Lloyd
105. Whopper
106. Kilmer opus
108. Modular misfit
116. Injured
117. Golden Fleece ship
118. Jack-in-the-pulpit, for one
119. Closet wood
120. French river
121. Beget
122. Strong thread
123. Palm
124. School orgs.
125. Yalies
126. Ridicule
127. Attention getters

DOWN

1. Kind of flower
2. ___ fixe
3. Comic Sahl
4. Thriving
5. Sofa
6. Sophia
7. Smart ___ (cocky ones)
8. Starling's cousin: Var.
9. Stir up
10. State south of Arizona
11. At the drop of ___
12. De Laurentiis and Martin
13. Up
14. Aver
15. Hindrance
16. Stately horse
17. Corso money
18. Yin's counterpart
28. Shoulder trough
29. "Exodus" author
30. TV's ___ Ramsey
34. Enjoy Jones Beach
35. Continued
37. Easy gait
39. Par ___ (French airmail)
40. Spirited
41. Rub out
42. Brenner or Donner
43. Ump's cousin
44. Go wrong
45. Whistle blast
47. ___ Gras
48. Distant
49. Recipe amount
52. Slakes
56. Tropical fish
57. Chagall et al.
58. Be the host
59. Doesn't own
60. Tuck was one
66. Calling
67. Notre Dame's river
70. "___ Is Born"
71. Filch
72. Grieves
75. Part of "TW 3"
77. Elizabeth's subjects
78. Admit
79. ___ nous
80. Portico
82. Steeps in spices
83. Siestas
84. Ram's dam
85. ___ a plea
92. Arias
93. Soap ingredient
96. Neither's mate
98. Student hurdles in the spring
99. Bo Derek figure
100. Porter
102. Hire
103. Time for a fool
104. Pola of the silents
106. Linen fabric
107. More loutish
108. Mall unit
109. Resign
110. ___ Major
111. Decamps
112. Midler flower
113. Poetic works
114. Milk: Prefix
115. Paleozoic and Cenozoic

280 Spectrum By Wayne Williams

What some of the bands might stand for.

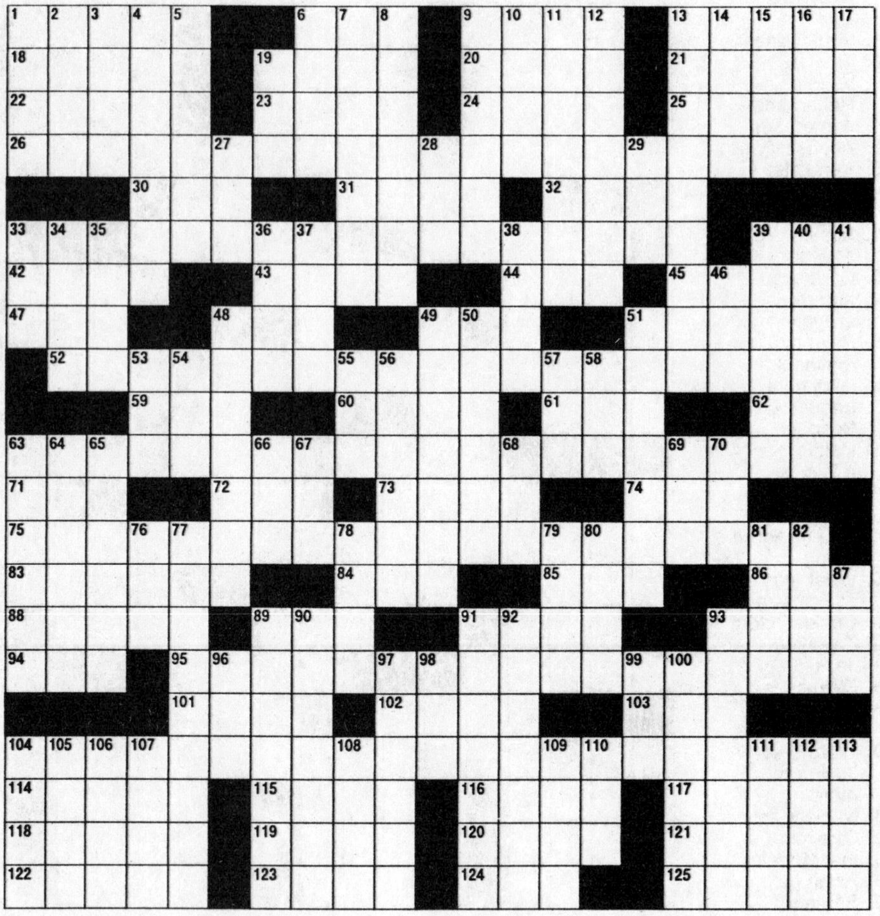

ACROSS

1. Stradivari's teacher
6. Preceder of amas
9. Clerical robes
13. Roman temple
18. Burdened
19. Slick-tongued
20. Weakly colored: Prefix
21. Pygmy antelope
22. Food item
23. Stirs in
24. Skirt length
25. Like some porridge
26. RED
30. Tic-tac-toe win
31. Angers
32. Hagen and namesakes
33. ORANGE
39. Dosage meas.
42. Prime-time segment
43. Liberate
44. Pres. advisory group
45. Sturdy as ___
47. Want ___
48. Secluded
49. You, to Helmut
51. Handsome god
52. YELLOW
59. Onassis
60. Charged meson
61. Paul Scott's "The ___ Quartet"
62. Roman 502
63. GREEN
71. Acapulco gold
72. Sine ___ (without a date)
73. Seep
74. Shoe width: Abbr.
75. BLUE
83. Also-rans
84. Nabokov book
85. Asian holiday
86. Van Gogh's loss
88. ___ France
89. Astronaut Grissom
91. Jot
93. Author Ferber
94. Crowded cont.
95. INDIGO
101. Actress Loretta
102. Demolish, British style
103. Summer mo.
104. VIOLET
114. Star belt's location
115. Egg on
116. The old sod
117. Cafeteria stack
118. "___ My Souvenirs"
119. Arikaras
120. Sweetsop
121. Heronlike bird
122. Prom guests
123. Formerly, formerly
124. Coloring matter
125. Sits out

DOWN

1. Thomas ___ Edison
2. Primary
3. One ___ (dosage)
4. O.K., to a CB-er
5. Like rainy-day activity
6. Ray of ***"We're No Angels"***
7. Birth specialist
8. Celebrate
9. Close but no cigar
10. Explorer Ericson
11. Nonsensical mouthings
12. Of the hip
13. Jesters' headwear
14. Composer Khachaturian
15. Actress Naldi
16. "Deutschland ___ Alles"
17. Coquette
19. Four qts.
27. Position: Abbr.
28. Defendants, in law
29. Operated
33. "Eureka!"
34. Covers a lawn
35. Give the heave-ho
36. Nigerian people
37. Church calendar
38. Freshly
39. Piña ___
40. Containing lime
41. Chicago suburb
46. S.F. hill
48. Coiffures
49. Blind spot in vision
50. Dissolve salt
51. Secondary addition
53. Vallone of "Bitter Rice"
54. Before, to poets
55. Seamen's org.
56. Went for a spin
57. S.A. country
58. ___ in Romeo
63. Hockey position
64. Imitation gold leaf
65. Freer
66. Thor's wife
67. Favorite
68. In the: It.
69. Bleacher sound
70. To's opposite
76. British ref. source
77. Russian and French
78. Botch up
79. Aleutian island
80. Films' Patricia
81. Hostess to a swan
82. Tug violently
87. "Norma ___"
89. Variety of lace
90. One who speaks
91. In its place
92. Fatŝo's problem
93. Feed ravenously
96. Possess
97. Pulitzer author Poole
98. Writer Santha Rama
99. Household god
101. His mill was rushed
104. Urge on
105. "___ la Douce"
106. Mob action
107. Solitary
108. Matures
109. Canadian tribe
110. Loser to D.D.E.
111. Thole fillers
112. Turgenev's turndown
113. Mach-plus fliers

281 Paging Robinson Crusoe By Kenneth Haxton

Some other places that he might have been stranded on.

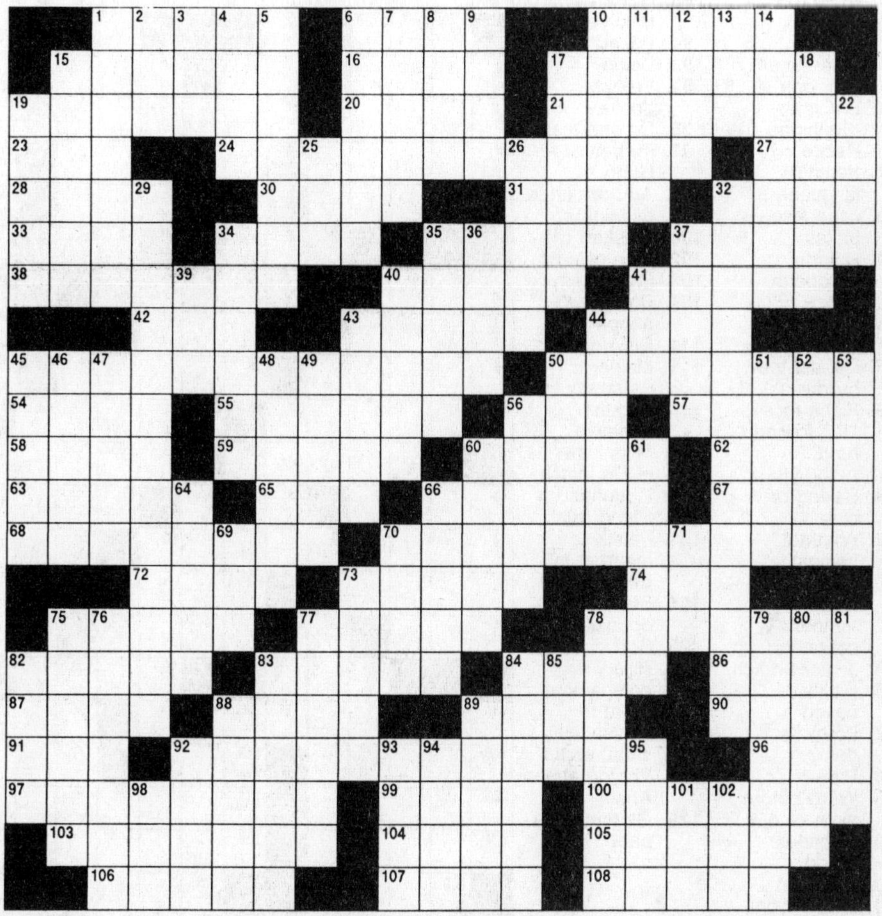

ACROSS

1. Belief in a personal God
6. Semitic deity
10. Spite
15. Having a foot: Prefix
16. Island for Napoleon
17. Russian urn
19. South Pacific island group
20. Fields, to Caesar
21. Tobago's island partner
23. Miss Hagen
24. Largest island in 19 Across
27. Spire ornament
28. Parade day in Russia
30. Lung sound
31. Arrow poison
32. Meerschaum, e.g.
33. Solar disk
34. Port in Israel
35. Brooklyn institute
37. Court judgment
38. Andalusian city
40. Fiber foods
41. Homeric epic
42. Goof
43. Fair person
44. N.C. college
45. Island with large dogs
50. Islands in Indonesia
54. Venezuelan town
55. Studying intently
56. Winter boot
57. Passed the cards
58. Dillon of "Gunsmoke"
59. Express gratitude
60. Wise men
62. Word before Shoppe
63. You were, to Deneuve
65. Black cuckoo
66. Smear with oil
67. Insect in a Mussorgsky song
68. Island due to be taken over by China
70. Island province of Canada
72. Em, to Dorothy
73. Electric measures
74. Anecdote collection
75. Town in Iraq
77. Aegean island
78. Mixture
82. Knievel namesakes
83. Gilroy drama subject
84. Certain witty offerings
86. Gaelic
87. Dull
88. Like Hilton's horizon
89. Formerly, of old
90. Bristle
91. Eisenhower bailiwick
92. Island east of Australia
96. Fabray, to friends
97. Island off Italy
99. Countenance
100. Wheat storehouse
103. Shriveled grapes
104. Nautilus captain
105. Cumbersome, old style
106. Wasp's offering
107. Island off Ireland
108. Heart trunk

DOWN

1. One who procrastinates
2. Tokyo, formerly
3. "___ Woman," Reddy song
4. Stump, to a yokel
5. Balearic island
6. Darwin's ship
7. Seaweeds
8. Dugout
9. Rested
10. Scoundrel
11. Nellie Forbush's love
12. "___ of the above"
13. Egg: Prefix
14. Portuguese wine island
15. Certain salad base
17. Restrains
18. Had a bull session
19. Common field plant
22. One was of Worms
25. Nasser's org.
26. Edible item
29. Galapágos island
32. Island of Queensland or Alaska
34. Sudden
35. Tine
36. "Atlas Shrugged" author
37. Hearable
39. Rio de ___
40. Application ___
41. Unwell
43. Russian pancakes
44. Tertiary subdivision
45. Borneo town
46. Poetry muse
47. Brünnhilde's father
48. ___ Vic, George Sand's home
49. Sturm und ___
50. Expertise of Merlin
51. Lily type
52. Birch's relative
53. Word after home or bed
56. French peacocks
60. Stews
61. Prepares clams
64. Predatory gulls
66. Guthrie and namesakes
69. Neighbor of Mich.
70. Corn bread
71. Genetic initials
73. Prospect
75. Incarnation
76. Sucking fishes
77. Roles for Price, Callas, etc.
78. Leewards island
79. Windwards island
80. Having a fixed look
81. Labor leader George
82. Summers in Lille
83. Competing in a regatta
84. Atomic particle
85. Salty initials
88. Soviet hero
89. Dropsy
92. Unless, to Caesar
93. Actress Turner
94. Eponymous Hebrew ancestor
95. Florence's river
98. Companion of dah
101. Bus-terminal abbr.
102. Something to pick

282 Dowsing By Dorothea Shipp

A search for water that gets somewhere.

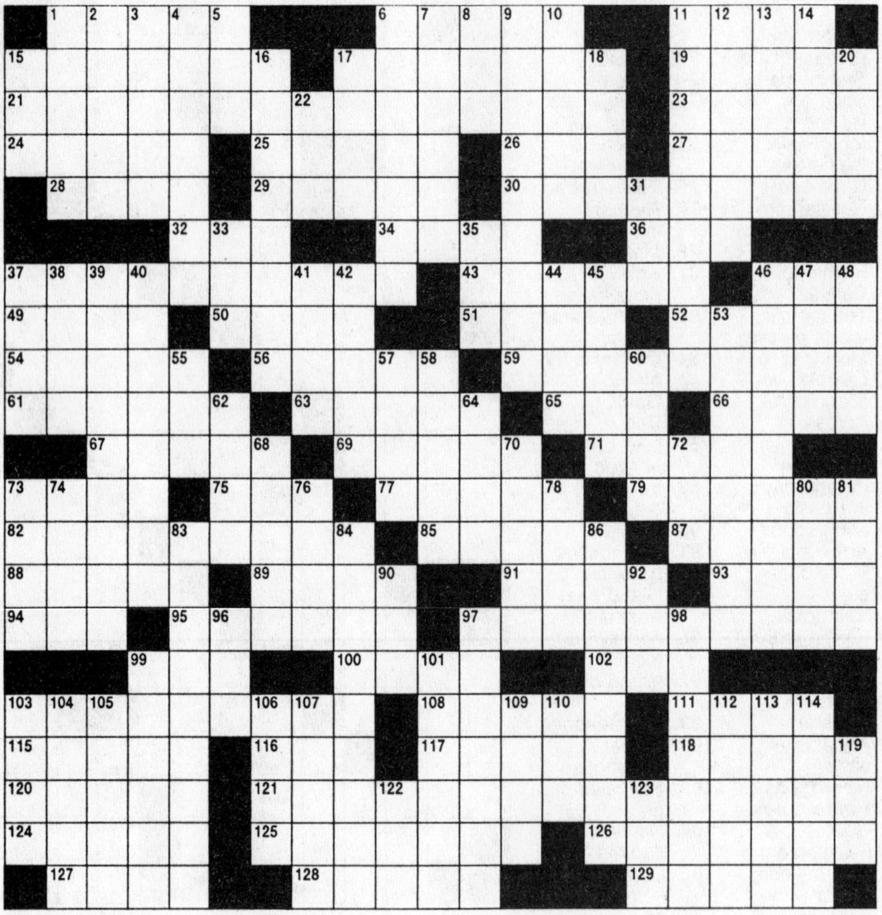

ACROSS

1. Country ___
6. Solar-lunar year gap
11. Emulates Xanthippe
15. Recite
17. Semitic language
19. Japanese boxes
21. Colorful European dance
23. Daft
24. Caravansary
25. Donald the builder
26. Place for "the lowing herd"
27. Actor Stu
28. Baking or club
29. Abstract beings
30. Overbearing manner
32. Vintner's container
34. Junior branch
36. Biblical haven
37. Lorelei's gem?
43. Pure
46. Word before night or day
49. Hebrides island
50. Saarinen
51. Living room in Seville
52. Gaboriau or Zola
54. Cartoonist Thomas and family
56. Antisub gear
59. In name only
61. Picturesque cave
63. Whey
65. Piper's son
66. Family ___
67. Time off
69. Trick's opposite
71. Ship pole
73. Asian border river
75. Supplement
77. Island in the Firth of Clyde
79. D.C. group
82. Shays' or Whiskey
85. Bred
87. Kind of servitude
88. Mark over a Spanish "n"
89. Gator's relative
91. Paced
93. Beige
94. French donkey
95. Do shorthand
97. Furbearer for Henry?
99. An hour after midnight
100. Alaskan city
102. Sign of a hit
103. Pied-à-terre
108. Boadicea's people
111. Disintegrates
115. Maine university site
116. Scottish negative
117. Miss Hawkins of Dogpatch
118. Liquefies
120. String freak
121. Family member in England?
124. Stem's opposite
125. Sort
126. Hillary's companions
127. Word in Massachusetts' motto
128. Photographer Ansel
129. Gloomy, to a poet

DOWN

1. Fire and garage events
2. Cape Cod resort
3. Mountain nymph
4. Diffuse
5. Airport info
6. Hermit
7. American fruit shrub
8. Doctors' org.
9. Canadian writer Morley ___
10. Strength of a solution
11. Egyptian color?
12. Eskimo's parka
13. Adult
14. Certain boom
15. Government dept.
16. Agreements between nations
17. Touch
18. Peter or Paul
20. New Year word
22. Place for a Keats ode
31. Kind of cake or meal
33. Avail oneself of
35. Ending for plast or hyster
37. Lardner
38. Icy covering
39. Unanswerable
40. Chattered, on Fleet Street
41. Brazilian town
42. Musical composition
44. "Thanks ___"
45. Island in the Aegean
46. Combativeness
47. Winnie ___ Pu
48. Ottoman officials
53. Certain performances
55. Depot: Abbr.
57. Irish exclamation
58. Sorry ones
60. Dennis or the Katzenjammers
62. Shape of some cameos
64. French spouse
68. Command
70. Estonian port
72. Ribbed material
73. Ionian Sea inlet
74. Chow ___
76. Dumb one
78. Wimp's relative
80. Irish kings' home
81. Hebrew month
83. Songstress from Russia?
84. Superfluous
86. Personnel files
90. Top person in a corp.
92. Flying insect
96. Shoulder: Prefix
97. Goddess of Hades and namesakes
98. Type of storm
99. Soccer positions
101. Go wide of the mark
103. Fling
104. Tub-thump
105. Plaited
106. Spanish numerals
107. Transparent sea creature
109. Old English letters
110. Boris Becker's never
112. Chicago airport
113. Port in Florida
114. Use bad language
119. Call-up org.
122. Agricultural org.
123. Religious deg.

283 Also Known As By Don Nardizzi

Presenting proper introductions for some celebrities.

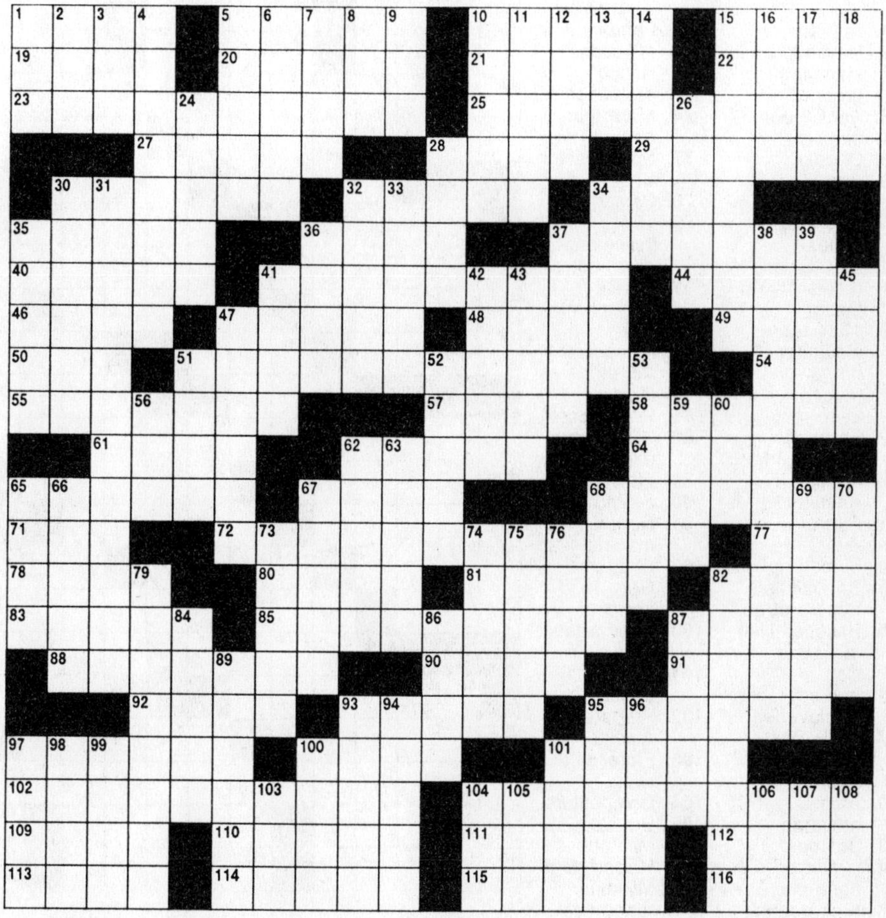

ACROSS

1. Sound of the Twenties?
5. Nut for a pie
10. Western
15. Bellow
19. English composer
20. Camel's kin
21. Palate projection
22. "God's Little ___"
23. Allen Stewart Konigsberg
25. Alfred Morris
27. California rockfish
28. Song for Pons
29. Sedative
30. Arctic marina sights
32. Alma or pia
34. Piano-violin piece, for one
35. Watches over
36. Smirch
37. Perform like an ecdysiast
40. "John Brown's Body" author
41. Lucille Collier
44. Dorm sound
46. Unique person
47. Rough
48. Hercules's captive
49. Latin I word
50. Tip
51. Virginia McMath
54. "Rose ___ rose . . ."
55. Of one of the Muses
57. Son of Seth
58. Comes up
61. Spider nests
62. Fine loam
64. Screwball
65. Chinese silver ingots
67. Medics
68. Low-rank servants
71. Flap or drum
72. Maureen Fitzsimmons
77. Studebaker's relative
78. Too much, to Pierre
80. Comic-strip light bulb
81. Scents
82. Scheme
83. Bits of intelligence, for short
85. Eugene Dennis McNulty
87. Dull talk
88. Uses seven-league boots
90. Future-tense person
91. Budding artists' homes
92. Ending for tonsil
93. Attendant of Bacchus
95. Provides employees
97. Kind of column
100. Broz
101. Former treaty group
102. Lazlo Loewenstein
104. Arthur Jefferson
109. Pub offerings
110. Iroquoians
111. Group for 10 Across
112. Cager Archibald
113. Thomas Hardy girl
114. Perch
115. Toady's words
116. Art ___

DOWN

1. Kind of recruit
2. Spanish Main loot
3. Year, in Yucatán
4. Comic-strip cowboy
5. Pirate's short walk
6. Fitzgerald and Logan
7. Coolidge and others
8. Soul, in France
9. A Bobbsey twin
10. Bizarre
11. Word before dupois
12. Sandwich fish
13. TV Tarzan
14. Branchlike
15. Choir member
16. Recorded proceedings
17. Legal document
18. Unaspirated
24. Something to get a rise out of
26. Imitators
28. Mythical king of the Huns
30. More perceptive
31. Anna Maria Italiano
32. Frenchman's world
33. To love, in France
34. More dreadful
35. Choice meat cut
36. Bug-in-a-rug feeling
37. Removes, in printing
38. William Henry Pratt
39. Remove, pencilwise
41. English composer
42. Social bigwigs
43. Trademarks
45. Greek letters
47. Good voter's quality
51. French novelist
52. Singer Della
53. Carpenters, at times
56. Old school or railroad
59. Indian prince
60. Here, in Le Havre
62. Sophia
63. Arctic or Indian
65. Bristle: Prefix
66. Tall tales
67. Easterns in westerns
68. Contrary girl
69. Smallest ones
70. Units of loudness
73. Assistants
74. Inquisitive
75. More quaint
76. Kind of frost
79. State of having small openings: Var.
82. Intensely felt
84. Indian string instrument
86. "To know her ___ love her"
87. Río de la ___
89. Phyllis of comedy
93. Begets
94. "This is ___" (loudspeaker warm-up)
95. Horse or common
96. "___ of the South Pacific"
97. Domestic quarrel
98. Soccer star
99. Followers: Suffix
100. Kingston, for one
101. Impudence
103. Coronado's quest
104. Catch sight of
105. Digit
106. Scottish explorer
107. Common abbr.
108. Zodiac animal

284 Spine Chillers By Frances Hansen

The eerier side of moviegoing life.

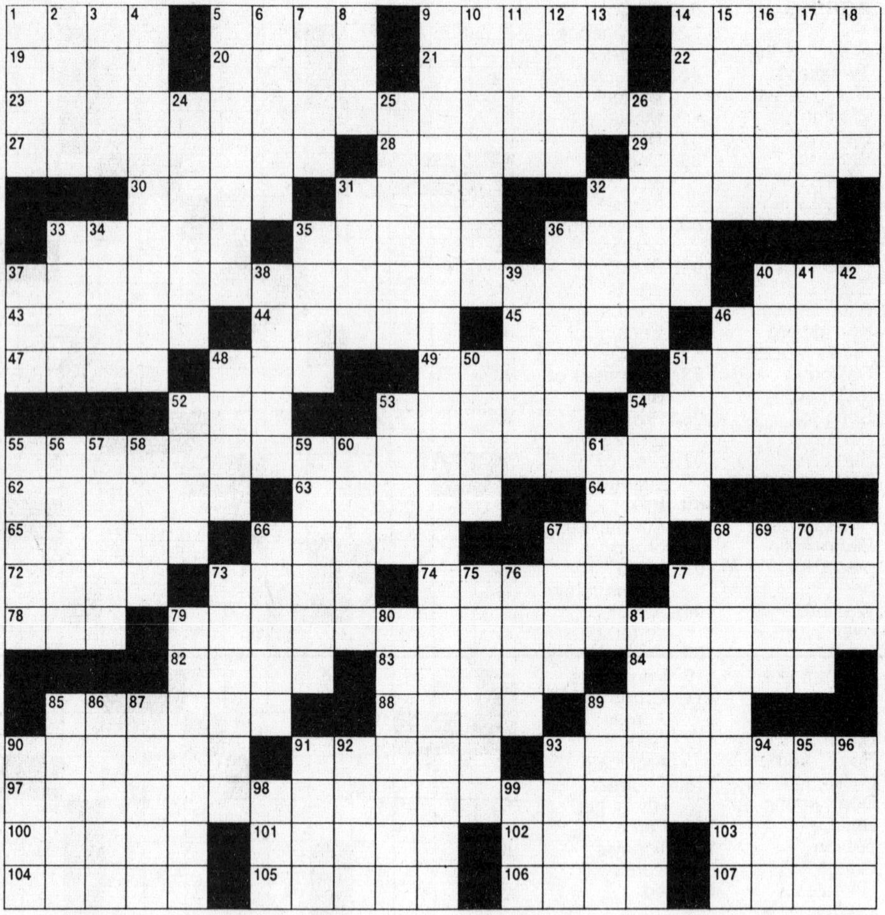

ACROSS

1. Cupid
5. Hayseed's stamping ground
9. Auctioneer's platform
14. Chores
19. Ade candidate
20. One of the codes
21. ___ Soleil (Louis XIV)
22. Deem
23. 1984 teen-slaughter horror
27. Placed
28. Lace mat
29. Forgoes one's rights
30. Emulated Ananias
31. Part of A.D.C.
32. Firmed up
33. Dr. Dolittle's Sophie et al.
35. Baseball Hall of Famer Cap
36. Parker House or cloverleaf
37. 1959 "like father, like son" horror
40. Animal offspring
43. Betimes
44. Grand or band place
45. King beaters
46. Except
47. Nautical hail
48. It's the limit, sometimes
49. Certain shadow-remover
51. Bridge expert Charles
52. Un ___ (a little, in Lille)
53. Debussy favorite
54. Shakespeare's "The Comedy of ___"
55. 1961 arch-criminal horror
62. ___-than-thou
63. John Milton masque
64. A March girl
65. Arabian bigwig
66. Flower part
67. Snoop
68. Eddie Fisher sang of him
72. Fender affliction
73. Castle protection
74. More than enough
77. Sportscaster Stan
78. Parseghian
79. 1981 "slice-and-dice" horror
82. Hera's belligerent boy
83. Pinnacles
84. Actress Rainer
85. Prado locale
88. ___ monde (high society)
89. Flesh: Prefix
90. Strand
91. Dotted material
93. Shattered
97. Gory 1973 horror
100. Shed a tear or two
101. European thrush
102. Prepare an Alaska
103. Florence's river
104. Competitors
105. Bel ___, mild cheese
106. Raised dogs
107. Minimum-range tide

DOWN

1. Before "poor Yorick"
2. Mary Quant's skirt
3. Skip over
4. At stated intervals
5. Most like Sydney Greenstreet
6. Prepared for battle
7. Interpret
8. Damage
9. Kinky 1967 horror
10. Permissive
11. City on the Oka
12. African bird
13. Miss Novak of "Satan's Triangle"
14. Completely
15. "___ Fool's Day," 1986 horror
16. Colander
17. Used a joint to attack
18. Movie-lot sights
24. "Airport" author Arthur
25. Wizard of Menlo Park
26. Toffs
31. Mrs. Roosevelt's first name
32. Errand boy
33. Pahlavi's title
34. Eliel's son
35. Bohemian
36. Tape
37. Sympathy's partner
38. Turkish name of Skoplje
39. One of the nuts
40. Loup-___ (werewolf)
41. Tinker's target
42. Up-tight
46. Old World apple tree
48. Scorch
50. Second of a Latin trio
51. Actress Coleen of "Kiss of Death"
52. Where to hear "Bon voyage!"
53. One of the beans
54. Oscar's cousin
55. First name in vamps
56. Four-bagger
57. Miss Verdugo
58. Fare
59. Vast amounts
60. Relative of bingo
61. Less common
66. Stuck a stick into
67. In addition
68. The Blue Knight, for one
69. Andy's friend
70. Aching window part?
71. Fall River weapon
73. Breed of sheep
75. "The world will pardon ___ . . ."
76. Chaucer or Ciardi
77. Annie of song
79. "Childe ___ Pilgrimage," Byron poem
80. Ladies of Hawaii
81. Slipped by, as time
85. New Zealand Polynesian
86. Golfer Palmer
87. Overly fond one
89. "___ People," 1968 Karloff horror
90. 1605, to Fabius
91. Predatory northern flier
92. Like Nestor
93. Structural beam
94. Part of a bird's beak
95. Sicilian city
96. "___ Me Before I Kill," 1961 import
98. Alley or Oola
99. Recede

285 Progress By Sidney Robbins

Largely a matter of getting somewhere.

ACROSS

1. Proverb
6. Beachside wear
10. Nursemaid of India
14. Agitate
18. Scientist Pauling
19. Solar deity
20. Ripped
21. "Skoal" or "prosit"
22. Often-welcome action at a meeting
25. Russian coin
26. Blue dye
27. Season in Paris
28. Wine goddess
29. Ballroom queens
30. Miss Williams
32. Secluded valley
33. Rent
34. Facing a central line
37. Kind of wave
38. Business degree
41. Problem
45. Young executive's goal
48. Tibetan creatures
50. Peaks
52. Indefinite amount
53. Hebrides isle
54. Steak's relative
55. Pleasant
56. Low islands
58. Units of inheritance
59. One of the estates
60. Possessing knowledge
62. Condition: Suffix
63. Morose
64. Old Japanese coin
65. "Soon to be a major ___" (book-ad words)
69. Frequently, to poets
72. Rusk of J.F.K.'s Cabinet
74. German spa
75. Reveler
77. Beelzebub
79. Kind of breath
80. Stain
82. River to the Seine
83. Comic Lew
84. Arrow poison
85. U.S.-Canada canals
86. ". . . upon ___ of gold"
88. Sports site
90. Performance
93. Paths
94. Peeping ___
95. City of Poland
97. Tasty tidbit
99. Leaves out
101. Famed office
103. Condemned
107. Senility
109. Quote
110. Couple
111. Misses the mark
113. Liver's friend
114. Words for an earbender's tongue
118. Scents
119. Sheltered
120. Bring under control
121. Liqueur
122. Italian artist
123. Münchhausen, for one
124. Metal containers
125. "We're off ___ the Wizard"

DOWN

1. ___ mater
2. Saturn satellite
3. Opponents
4. Wrongdoing
5. Inner: Prefix
6. Hopeless spot
7. U.S. Indian
8. Constrictor
9. Marriage within a social group
10. Make amends
11. "He's putting ___!"
12. Sked abbr.
13. Former egg
14. Spirits
15. Stalled at a meeting
16. Capri, for one
17. Road-map abbrs.
21. NATO or SEATO
23. Require
24. Dessert
29. Arthur or Lillie
31. Rabbit
33. Horne and namesakes
35. Hospital photo
36. Charged particles
37. ___ Abe
39. Life accounts, for short
40. Nile lurkers
41. Twinges
42. Reckon
43. Be helpful at a meeting
44. Former spouses
46. Coordinates
47. Type of column
49. Tan
51. Offshoot
57. Perform
58. Gawked
59. Entreaty
61. Fed
62. "Well, what do you know!"
63. Garbo
66. Blasco ___, Spanish novelist
67. Like a certain cereal
68. Certain alien visitor
70. Heraldic bar
71. Lock of hair
73. Make a salary
76. Short-billed crake
77. Wood strip
78. Word before plane
79. Feathered friends
80. ___ de Boulogne
81. Author Anita
85. Dagger
87. Marc's friend
89. Straightens
91. Furious
92. Lumps
96. Native: Suffix
98. Appear ahead
100. Pacific native
101. Plant sheath
102. Venomous snake
104. Washington subway
105. Lake and canal
106. Word after hippo
107. Entrance
108. Wave on la mer
110. ". . . nothin' like a ___"
112. Dagger of old
114. Joey was one
115. Whitney or Yale
116. Ill-fated republic
117. Sept. follower

286 Word Tampering By Ernie Furtado

With the idea of coming up with offbeat results.

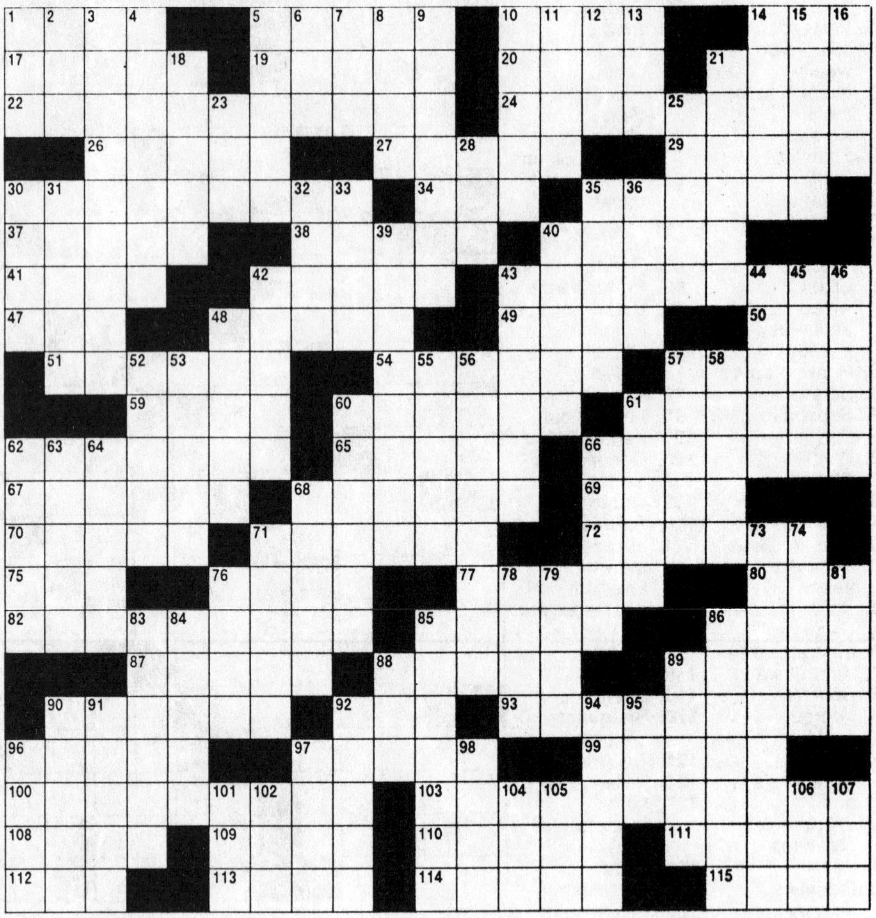

ACROSS

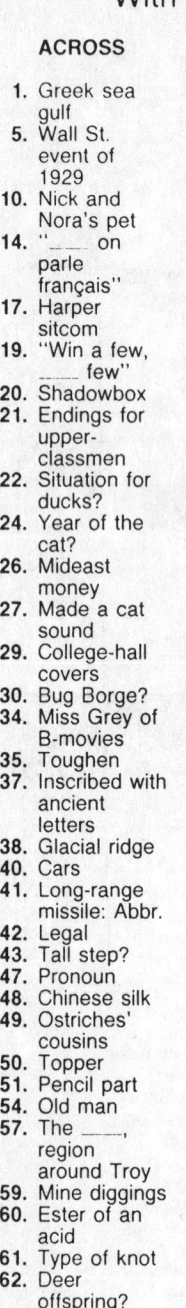

1. Greek sea gulf
5. Wall St. event of 1929
10. Nick and Nora's pet
14. "___ on parle français"
17. Harper sitcom
19. "Win a few, ___ few"
20. Shadowbox
21. Endings for upper-classmen
22. Situation for ducks?
24. Year of the cat?
26. Mideast money
27. Made a cat sound
29. College-hall covers
30. Bug Borge?
34. Miss Grey of B-movies
35. Toughen
37. Inscribed with ancient letters
38. Glacial ridge
40. Cars
41. Long-range missile: Abbr.
42. Legal
43. Tall step?
47. Pronoun
48. Chinese silk
49. Ostriches' cousins
50. Topper
51. Pencil part
54. Old man
57. The ___, region around Troy
59. Mine diggings
60. Ester of an acid
61. Type of knot
62. Deer offspring?
65. Saltpetre
66. Holders of Peete's pegs?
67. Words after bitter and tail
68. Hay ___ (cheap racehorse)
69. Austrian statesman
70. Waits
71. Close again
72. Capers
75. Uris hero
76. Entertain
77. Third man et al.
80. Give ___ go (attempt)
82. Old bird?
85. Town in Arkansas
86. Companion of means
87. Piano part
88. Test a new jacket
89. Dig oneself into ___ (get in deep)
90. Mother Carey's chicken
92. Parseghian
93. Sad contests?
96. Adage
97. Roman magistrate
99. Musical about the Peróns
100. Dolphin gridder grip?
103. Lazy cocktail?
108. Queen of scat
109. Cousin of P.D.Q.
110. Johnny Carson, for one
111. Angle: Prefix
112. Fast plane
113. Tense
114. German industrial city
115. ___ Park, New York

DOWN

1. Sandy's articulation
2. Greek letter
3. Drag Gene Kelly?
4. For the action, in law
5. Nurse Barton
6. Balderdash
7. Residue
8. Appear
9. Lagomorph snare?
10. Poplar
11. What a G.I. used to peel
12. Salt
13. Airport abbr.
14. Ancient Greek region
15. Pitiless
16. Doctrines
18. Bearded, as a plant
21. Buy an E-bond
23. The same, in prescriptions
25. Japanese aborigines
28. Strife
30. Gray, in Grenoble
31. Dress trimming
32. Teutonic denial
33. Bait, in Italy
35. Foretell
36. Certain degrees
39. Almighty dollar in Rome?
40. Evangelist McPherson
42. Bodies of knowledge
43. One who grades hides
44. Actress Massey
45. Old Chinese weight
46. Nelson et al.
48. Lamarr and namesakes
52. Two-time Pulitzer drama winner
53. Animal disorders
55. Famed volcano
56. Token person?
57. Halloween choice
58. Hebrew spiritual leader
60. Burdens
61. Heart cherries
62. Exclude
63. Dream: Prefix
64. Of Norse literature
66. Words before la
68. Asian palm
71. Stately
73. Luigi's parting words to vacationland?
74. Ton
76. Cover a dice bet
78. ___ tube
79. Sicilian resort
81. Peer's mother et al.
83. Best conditions
84. Nuclear physicist Enrico
85. Russian bishopric?
86. Give ___ (treat roughly)
88. Part of TNT
89. Maturing
90. Buckets
91. Glorify
92. Skilled
94. Because of, in Germany
95. Virgil's 56
96. French wives: Abbr.
97. Birthright seller
98. "Desire Under the ___"
101. Cask
102. O.T. book
104. Mil. school
105. Tiny
106. Zag's companion
107. Menagerie

287 Wishful Thinking By Judith Perry

A bit of meditation for lovers of lotteries.

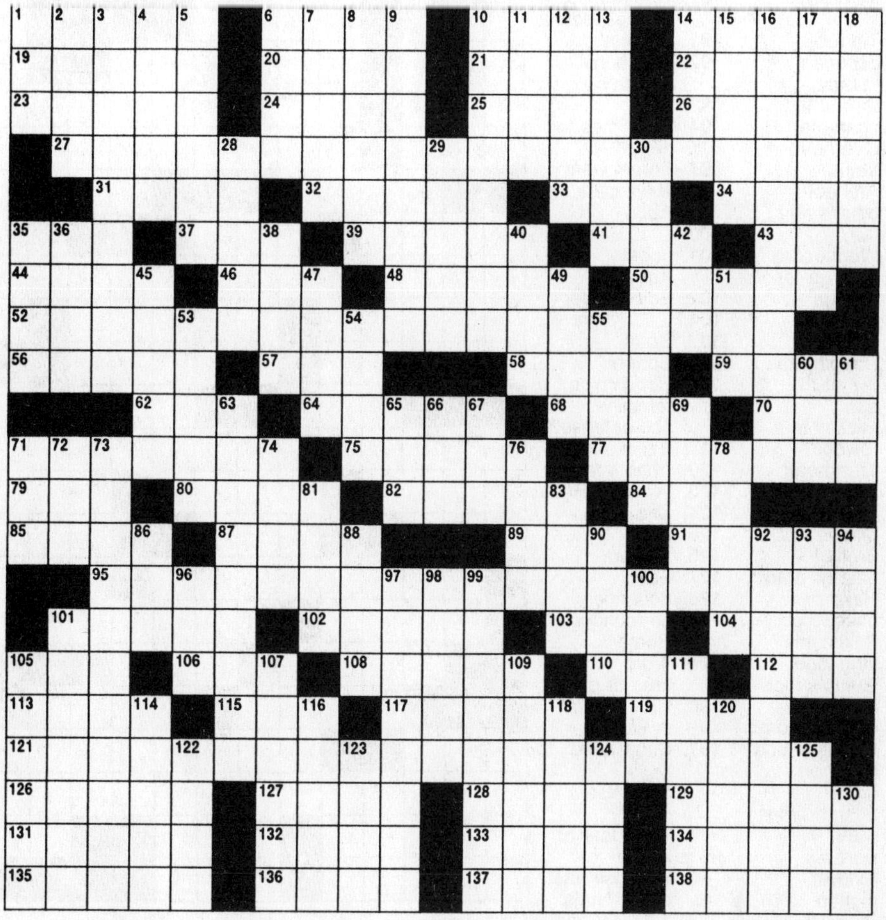

ACROSS

1. Shade
6. Man Fri.
10. Popular TV rerun
14. Rum cakes
19. Marsh birds
20. Bangkok resident
21. "___ La Douce"
22. Rocket type
23. Terminate
24. Fine-grained mineral
25. Fine thing to sew
26. Ferber novel
27. Start of a lottery-oriented verse
31. Ignoble Roman
32. Starchy ground meal
33. Papal name
34. Equipment
35. Plant sci.
37. Zilch
39. Bogs
41. Explosive
43. Writer's monogram
44. Son of Isaac
46. Bean for a sauce
48. Sheer fabric
50. Pyramids' contents
52. Second line of verse
56. "Roots" author
57. Josephine of mysteries
58. "G.W.T.W." setting
59. Kind of shirt
62. Associates of M.D.'s
64. Speedy
68. H.S. subject
70. Black gold
71. Sudanese province
75. Israeli dances
77. Supplied
79. Large bird
80. Do choir duty
82. Legendary friend
84. Hit-show sign
85. Help with the dishes
87. Spanish painter
89. Corpulent
91. Davit
95. Third line of verse
101. Apportion
102. Usurp
103. Adage
104. Cat's-paw
105. Co., in France
106. Scale syllables
108. Accumulate
110. Part of R&R
112. Word for Anthony Wayne
113. "Full Moon and Empty ___"
115. Sgt., for one
117. Eastern Indians
119. Lynda Bird ___
121. End of verse
126. Detection device
127. Miss Horne
128. New Mexico resort
129. Variety of chalcedony
131. Extreme
132. Duad
133. Bovary or Woodhouse
134. Birth-related
135. Nuisances
136. Slough off
137. Cherished
138. Fish-line leader

DOWN

1. Dos Passos trilogy
2. Hordes
3. Moth variety
4. Street show
5. To the rear
6. Legal people: Abbr.
7. Pine needles
8. Gesture of obeisance
9. Titillating
10. Wasted
11. Locale
12. Trivial
13. Memorable Dane
14. Asian evergreen
15. Ripening
16. British publisher and politician
17. Treats metal with heat
18. Butterflies
28. Assurance
29. Spooky
30. Antitheses
35. A Little Woman
36. Govt. safety unit
38. Confused
40. Chimney lining
42. Digit
45. Exploiters
47. French river
49. Biblical builder
51. Carto-grapher's output
53. Avian mimics
54. Indian nursemaid
55. "Mila 18" novelist
60. Golfing term
61. Superan-nuated
63. Disregarding
65. Pea's home
66. Savings acct.
67. Beaver or Hoover
69. Kind of unrequited-love song
71. London district
72. Parisian friend
73. Additions
74. Celebes animal
76. Cushioned item
78. Removed the center
81. Fleeces
83. Some votes
86. Conger
88. On the briny
90. Dictator
92. Foreshadow
93. California wine valley
94. Surveyed
96. Nonsense
97. Employee's work validation
98. Plateau across Arkansas
99. Ceased
100. Nerd's relative
101. Vent
105. Hamburger topping
107. Reaps a questionable profit
109. Ali Baba's word
111. Vaudevillian family
114. Modish
116. West Indian witchcraft
118. Anatomical opening
120. Started
122. Periods
123. Unicorn fish
124. Glacial ridges
125. Inclusive Latin abbr.
130. Wing

288 Phrasemaking By Robert Malinow

Involving a change or so here and there.

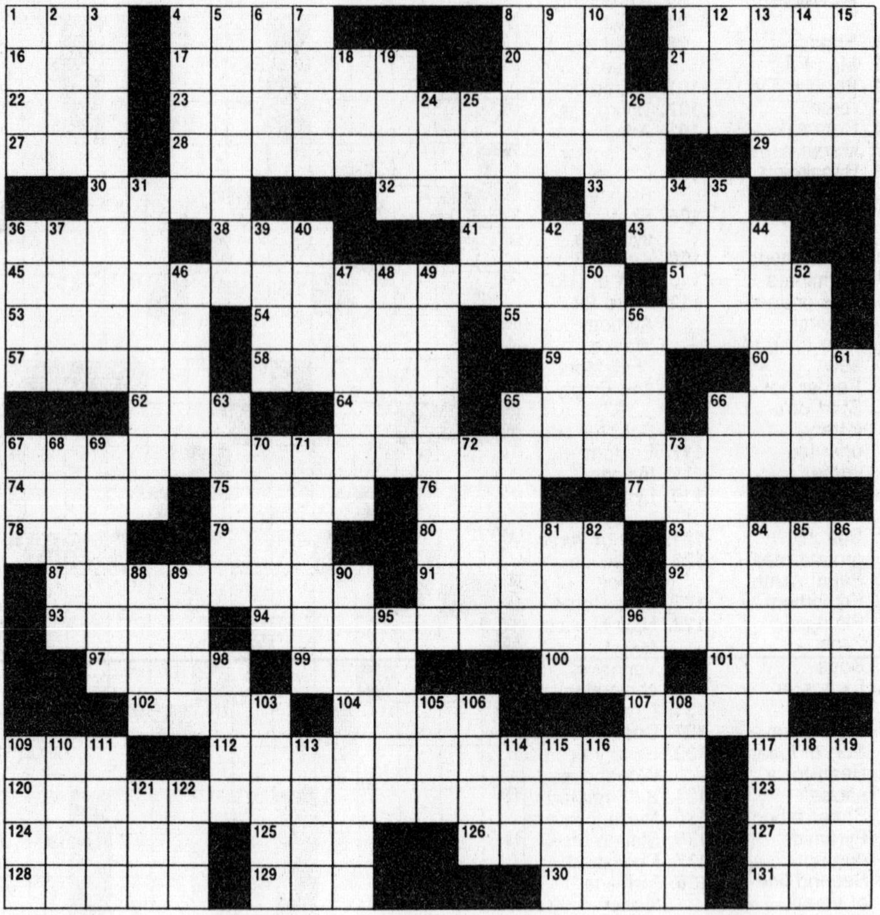

ACROSS

1. Tin-roof occupant
4. "Lorna Doone" character
8. Overhead trains
11. Archeologist's find
16. ___ Wednesday
17. Sign up for college
20. Burns's refusal
21. Hopping mad
22. 7-7 at the gun
23. Mickey in a rowboat
27. Thickhead
28. Hailstones?
29. Part of to be
30. Matinee ___
32. Prefix for cast or gram
33. Hake or dace, e.g.
36. Pakistani language
38. Guido's high note
41. Clean-air org.
43. Falling sound
45. Bette on high?
51. Length times width
53. Bores
54. Kind of pigeon
55. Sin
57. Winter fall
58. Earl, for one
59. Prefix for angle
60. "The Waste Land" initials
62. French preposition
64. Hawkshaw
65. Filly, in the future
66. Borscht base
67. Moriarty, to Sherlock?
74. He eclipsed Cobb in hits
75. Get an ___ effort
76. Disabuse
77. Shower mo.
78. Miami Dolphins' div.
79. In addition
80. Habituate
83. Actress Berger
87. "Indeed!" to Shakespeare
91. Criminal
92. Bassoons' relatives
93. Solo
94. Bad times for Jekyll?
97. Forum wear
99. Navy clerk: Abbr.
100. ___ Baba
101. Lobster of Australia
102. Edible tuber
104. ___ Kong
107. Roué
109. Sphere
112. Concerning feminine self-defense?
117. Bar order
120. Ahab's fate?
123. White or Red
124. Chou ___
125. Nautical dir.
126. Esteem
127. Sash
128. Legendary co-founder of Rome
129. Word before tape or coat
130. U.S. admiral in W.W. I
131. Court need

DOWN

1. The Elder of Rome
2. Expanse east of the Urals
3. ". . . cat and ___"
4. Certain rocket
5. Respirator
6. Eins plus zwei
7. Rumanian king's title
8. Warehouse
9. Lion portrayer
10. Hamlet's ___ troubles
11. Bravo or Grande
12. Stat for Koufax
13. Zhivago's love
14. Road for Diocletian
15. Relinquish
18. Old card game
19. Air, to Ludwig
24. Sault ___ Marie
25. Certain fisherman
26. Word after ego
31. What a blunt knife has
34. Kind of dash or shot
35. Hour, in Spain
36. Diamond callers
37. Currency of Iran
39. "___ Horizon"
40. Con
42. Arteries
44. Tease
46. Poly ending
47. Walk like a small child
48. Golf-course features
49. Do a TVA job
50. Iron: Prefix
52. Property, for one
56. Palio race site
61. Ordinal ending
63. Make sure of
65. Vehicle for Glenn
66. Sans saddle
67. ___-la-la
68. Former teamsters' leader
69. Kind of service
70. In progress
71. Like T.R.'s smile
72. Penalized in a way
73. Downs or salts
81. Painter Bonheur
82. Chemical compound
84. "I received nor rhyme ___"
85. Mexican Indian
86. Like an uncleaned fireplace
88. Haymarket Square had one
89. Long-running prose
90. Aped a jackass
95. Moonshine
96. Blunderbuss or musket
98. Ending for buck
103. The godfather's can't be refused
105. Teachers' org.
106. Fiesta
108. Henry VIII had two
109. ___-Neisse Line
110. Descartes
111. Salve
113. Lion's main attraction?
114. Actor Beatty
115. Mil. awards
116. Roman 2002
118. Ear piece
119. Stage direction
121. Before upsilon
122. ___ and hers

289 Liquid Diet By Bernice Gordon

Not necessarily for the infirm.

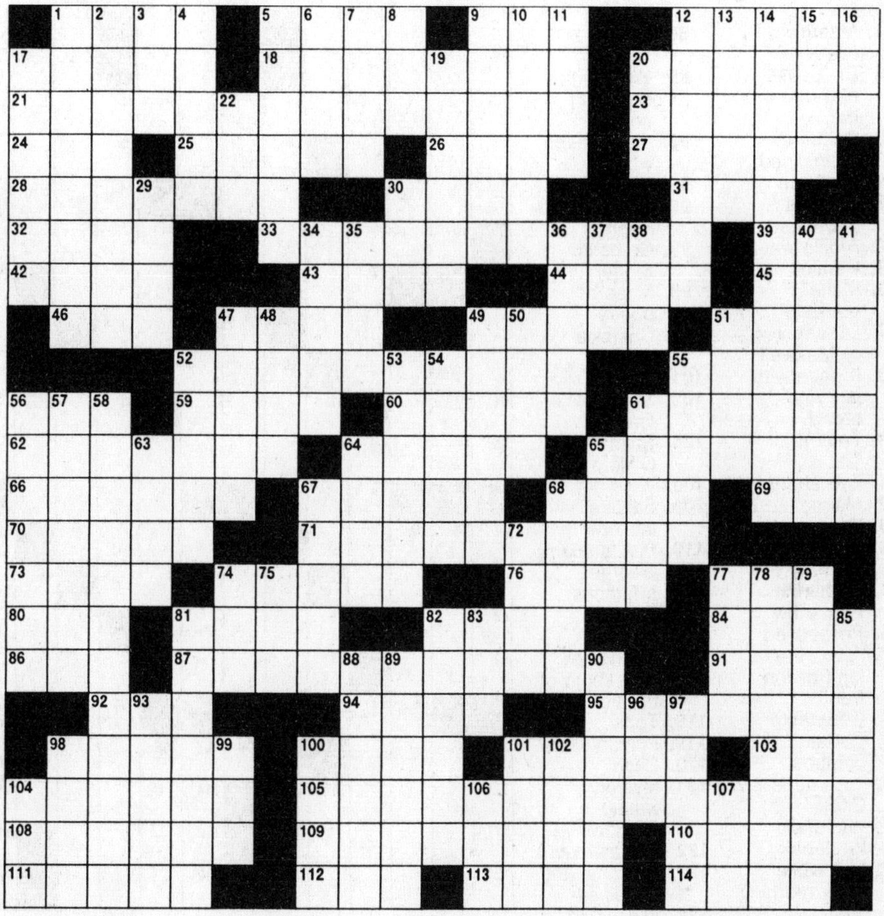

ACROSS

1. Dress-shirt fitting
5. Reliquary
9. Make a survey
12. Italian lawn game
17. Kind, in Paris
18. Weary from walking
20. Frontier-town oasis
21. Tops
23. Hydrocarbon
24. Wood sorrel
25. Of ancient Troy
26. Rake
27. Edwards or Robertson
28. Russian symbol
30. Hardy lass
31. Hole filler?
32. Perry's creator
33. Sticky field growth
39. Decline
42. Kind of river or six
43. Sounds of disapproval
44. Expresses
45. Bikini half
46. Q-U filler
47. Coward of the stage
49. Squeeze out water
51. Like Death Valley
52. Brotherhoods
55. Intermingle
56. Van area
59. Piece of news
60. Billy's mate
61. Pride of Spain's Philip II
62. Agamemnon's son
64. Simon's "Plaza ___"
65. With energy
66. Gave off a stench
67. Lint-prone fabric
68. One is golden
69. His, to Yves
70. Wimbledon winner Hart, 1951
71. Neighbor of Tampa
73. Where the Brenner Pass is
74. Places of worship
76. Colonizers
77. Songwriter Garfunkel
80. Needlefish
81. Port ___, Egypt
82. Patty the golfer
84. Bearberry
86. Native: Suffix
87. Base for cosmetics
91. Notion, in Nîmes
92. Three, to Luciano
94. Dumb ___
95. Where Kiev is
98. Pure air
100. Abbrs. on bargain clothing
101. Counting-out word
103. Peak: Prefix
104. Engaged in fencing
105. Film starring Deborah Kerr
108. Canadian physician and family
109. Erodes
110. Bacchanalian cries
111. Disordered
112. Soul, in France
113. Peacock blue
114. Cooking aid

DOWN

1. He had an apprentice
2. Foot levers
3. Actress Hagen
4. Withdraw from office
5. Uphold a judgment
6. List
7. Bacteriology pioneer of the 1800's
8. Had a snack
9. Gloomy
10. Stir
11. Le Moko of the Casbah
12. "Reading Gaol," etc.
13. Of an acid
14. Intervals at the office
15. Hoodlike cap
16. Wayside, for one
17. Made a touchdown
19. ___ up (botches)
20. Part of S.P.C.A.
22. Spanish wave
29. Branch of a family
30. Ref's decision
34. Construction piece
35. Lounge
36. Won't-tell flower
37. Safety or straight
38. Assn.
40. Horse with a streaky coat
41. ". . . that in ___, we can vividly recall . . .": Schopenhauer
47. Well-known
48. Pindaric works
49. Fall follower
50. Director Clair
51. Charity
52. Locales
53. Accrues
54. Coniferous northern forest
55. Prickly plant
56. Ropes in a ship's rigging
57. Small spaces
58. Popular nosh during TV
61. Where Van Gogh painted sunflowers
63. Equipment for the Mahres
64. Put on the market
65. Victim of a joke
67. Old Italian coin
68. Scope
72. Kind of hog
74. ___ Paulo
75. ___ jacet (epitaph)
77. Inter ___
78. Wintertime room hisser
79. Dug a protective ditch
81. Stage hangings
82. Sacs of the body
83. Greek letter
85. Noah and Wallace
88. Having reveries
89. Ester of an acid
90. Writer Damon
93. Actors' quests
96. Miss Hunter
97. Drive back
98. River in England
99. MS people
100. Virginia willow
101. ___ May Oliver of the screen
102. This, in Spain
104. DeLuise
106. Little swig
107. Miss Gardner

290 Hearths By Betty Jorgensen

Places that some people call home.

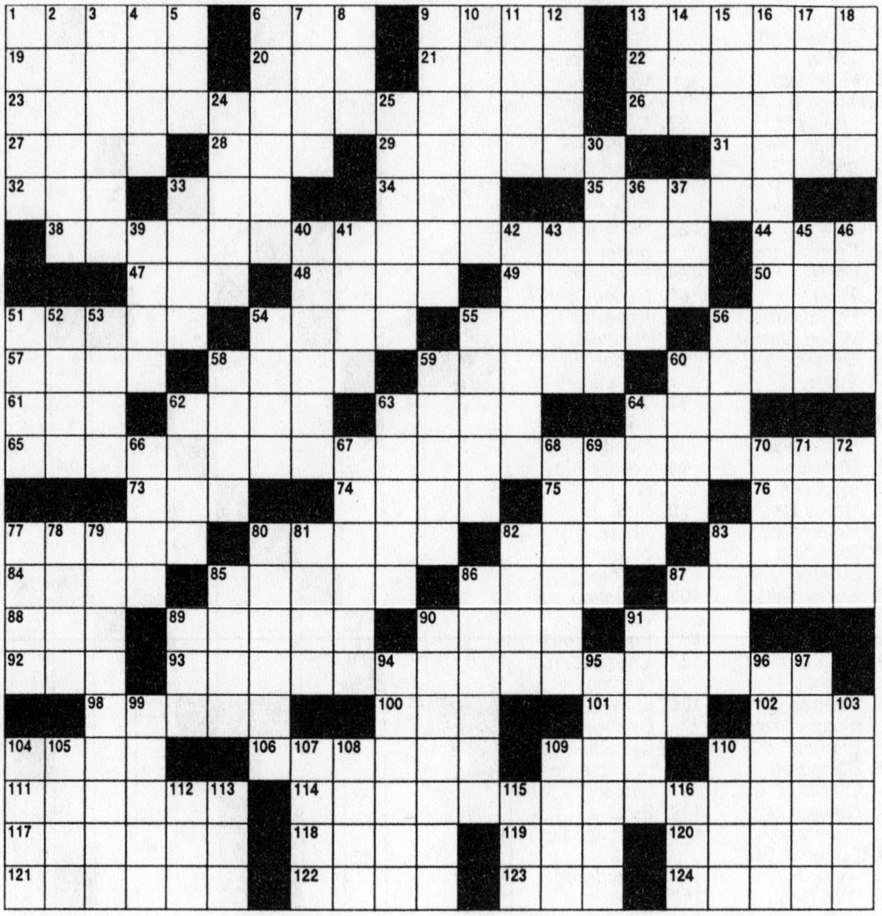

ACROSS

1. Mammy's li'l boy
6. Dr. Seuss had one in a hat
9. Doctrines
13. Disinclined
19. Kingdom
20. Onassis
21. Tube light
22. Atoll's waters
23. Hamlet
26. Make possible
27. Lanchester or Maxwell
28. It goes with jam and bread
29. Thelma or Tex
31. Eye shutters
32. Mauna ___
33. Pronoun
34. Turn gray
35. German city
38. Catherine Earnshaw
44. Possessed
47. "___ the land of the free . . ."
48. Debatable
49. Certain combos
50. ___ de la Cité
51. Wakefield Whiteoak
54. In a while
55. Early morning sound
56. Gin variety
57. Hautboy
58. Billboard
59. Straighten
60. Lamprey fisherman
61. Tennis shot
62. Dover treat
63. So be it
64. Native of: Suffix
65. Sherlock Holmes
73. Fedora or boater
74. Thaw
75. Editor's take-out word
76. Stadium sound
77. Pierre's mom
80. Sugar supplier
82. Officer's helper
83. Bog down
84. Isles in Galway Bay
85. Famous clinic brothers
86. As well
87. Poisonous weed
88. Wayside shelter
89. Word with colony or code
90. Comparison words
91. Dine
92. Land east of Eden
93. Catherine Sloper
98. Muse of poetry
100. Chemical suffix
101. Place
102. St. Agnes's time
104. Scarlett O'Hara
106. Wise old man
109. Sailor's jacket
110. M.P.'s quarry
111. George ___, a famous Disraeli
114. Edward Rochester
117. Nap south of the border
118. Tops
119. Primary color
120. Dash
121. Mystery writer Dorothy
122. Not as much
123. Personal and classified
124. Always, to Hans

DOWN

1. Dizzy
2. Holler
3. Bahamas' capital
4. Lamb's a.k.a.
5. President after L.B.J.
6. Vocation
7. Space
8. Muscle spasm
9. Understanding
10. Parlor piece
11. Shed feathers
12. Word with snicker
13. Porter's relative
14. In the ___ (leading)
15. Same, to Pierre
16. Soames Forsyte
17. Word on a realty sign
18. Helm positions
24. Different
25. Spanish region
30. Engage again
33. Mets' home
36. Arrest
37. Draft letters
39. Musical quality
40. Cymbeline's daughter
41. Between A.M. and P.M.
42. "___, therefore I am"
43. Show pleasure
45. African lily
46. Antelope's playmate
51. Shake up
52. "Baby, Take ___"
53. Gray wolf
54. Storage structure
55. Part of a sports shoe
56. Prognosticator
58. Flue flakes
59. Saunter
60. Feminine ending
62. Grown-up ugly duckling
63. Tasman et al.
64. Man or Capri
66. "It is later ___ you think"
67. Town near Florence
68. Menlo Park
69. Update the décor
70. Mavourneen's land
71. Little pitchers have them
72. "___ asked me how I knew . . ."
77. It is bounding
78. River of 67 Down
79. Rebecca de Winter
80. Charles ___ of murder fame
81. Indian nanny
82. Choir section
83. Spy's first name
85. "Some hae ___ and canna eat"
86. Behind, at sea
87. Tightly stretched
89. New Deal org.
90. Snubs
91. Peer
94. Radons
95. Exceeds a certain limit
96. Prepare leftovers
97. Unfold
99. Increase
103. "Oklahoma!" aunt
104. Soviet press agency
105. Leontyne Price forte
107. Kin of etc.
108. It was lost because of a nail
109. Like Hamelin's piper
110. Attention-getter
112. Liner: Abbr.
113. Chemical abbr.
115. Lippo Lippi's title
116. Roman 506

291 Word Assortment By William A. Smith

Presenting a collection of general entries.

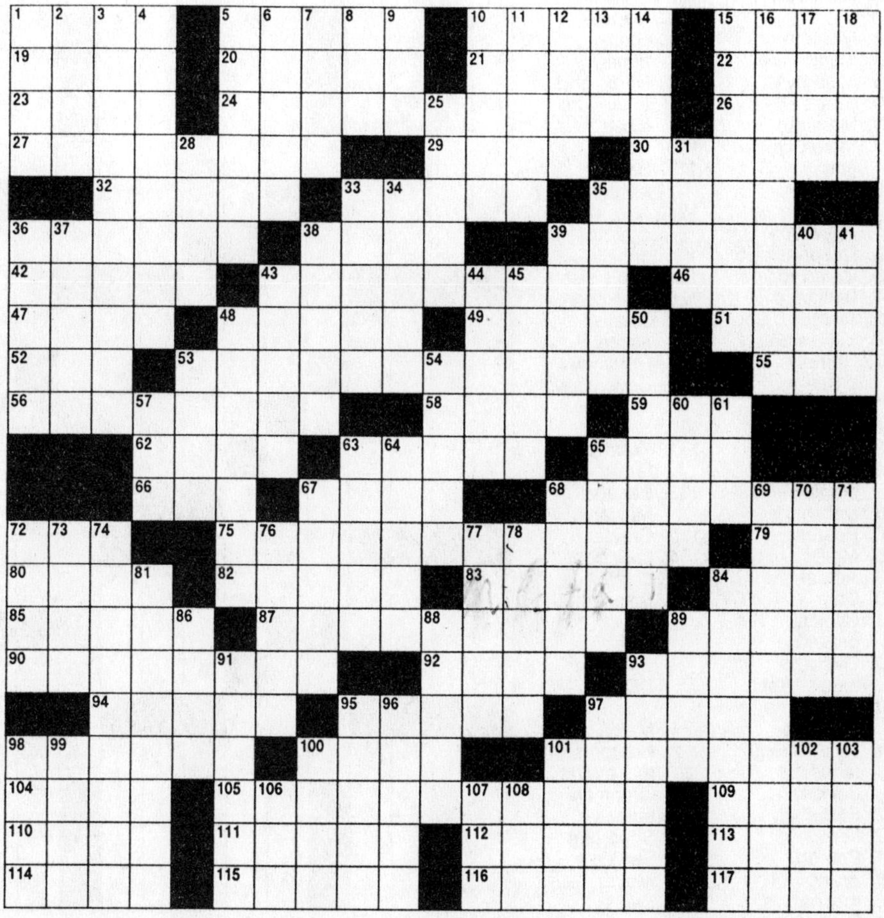

ACROSS

1. Poison tree
5. Black: Prefix
10. Praline maker's need
15. It's sometimes wrinkled
19. Capital of Togo
20. Run off
21. Make amends
22. Miss Moreno
23. Holiday song
24. Everlasting
26. Organic compound
27. Goldenrod or ragweed, to some
29. Roman road
30. Sugar-coated nut
32. More chilling
33. Disrupt
35. Overfills
36. Diving duck
38. Whale chaser
39. Mineral of iron
42. Miss Black
43. Place for an overnight guest
46. Passover feast
47. City of Rumania
48. Two on the ___
49. Indian buffalo
51. Place to get cold cuts, etc.
52. Small bit of liquor
53. Posture
55. Cape
56. Retired but holding a title
58. Hodgepodge
59. Shelter
62. Greek god
63. Game for Karpov
65. From a distance
66. Place for physical ed.
67. Blind part
68. Food thickener
72. Relative of Bub
75. Busy one-armed men
79. Freshwater fish
80. Roast to overexercise
82. Five Boy Scouts make one
83. Rock musician Eddy
84. Shelter
85. Plant pore
87. Draft
89. Johnson's vaudeville partner
90. Name with ceremony
92. What the ten o'clock scholar was
93. She got John's head
94. Facing trouble
95. Southwest winds
97. Wedge: Prefix
98. Most ignoble
100. Region
101. Contend
104. Abbr. on a business letter
105. Something a nurse takes
109. Money in Teheran
110. Guinness
111. Fix firmly
112. Aladdin's friend
113. Killer whales
114. Beget
115. Means of restraint
116. Heating vessels
117. Roy Rogers's real name

DOWN

1. Armbone
2. Game using 16 balls
3. Improve
4. Chosen
5. Scanty
6. Fudd or Gantry
7. Kind of shark
8. Follower of Mar.
9. Teachers' org.
10. Singer Page
11. Miss Merman
12. Coconut fiber
13. Actress Harding
14. Haystack hider
15. Showed life
16. Close-up fight fan
17. Siouan tribe
18. Cloth ridge
25. She turned to stone
28. Nothing, to Pierre
31. Boring routines
33. "Thou ___ not . . ."
34. Polynesian skirt
35. Yankee pitcher Lefty ___
36. Play ice hockey
37. Billiard shot
38. Orbital point
39. Angle: Prefix
40. Tissue layer
41. Discordant goddess
43. Position, to Cato
44. Tracks
45. Local birdlife
48. Try
50. Migration of wriggly fish
53. Vivacious
54. Biblical word of action
57. Kind of time
60. Up to one's ___ in trouble
61. Roaring 20's, e.g.
63. Athenian demagogue
64. Heavenly instruments
65. Ten per-center
67. Edgar Lee Masters river
68. Wide open
69. Certain 1890's beauty
70. Pertinent, in law
71. French queen
72. Not fem. or neut.
73. Hormone initials
74. Certain singer
76. Curved
77. Sahara desert region
78. Nights, in Paris
81. Position of distinction
84. Lively movements, in music
86. Fireproof materials: Abbr.
88. "On a ___ day . . ."
89. Honolulu is its main city
91. Shred
93. Binges
95. Old French land unit
96. Nurtures
97. Narrow groove
98. Sheepish sounds
99. Hun king
100. Dextrous preceder
101. Cordage fiber
102. Frilly
103. Other
106. Scottish uncle
107. Golden or ripe old
108. Asian holiday

292 Simple Truths By Wilson McBeath

Quotations presenting some basic premises.

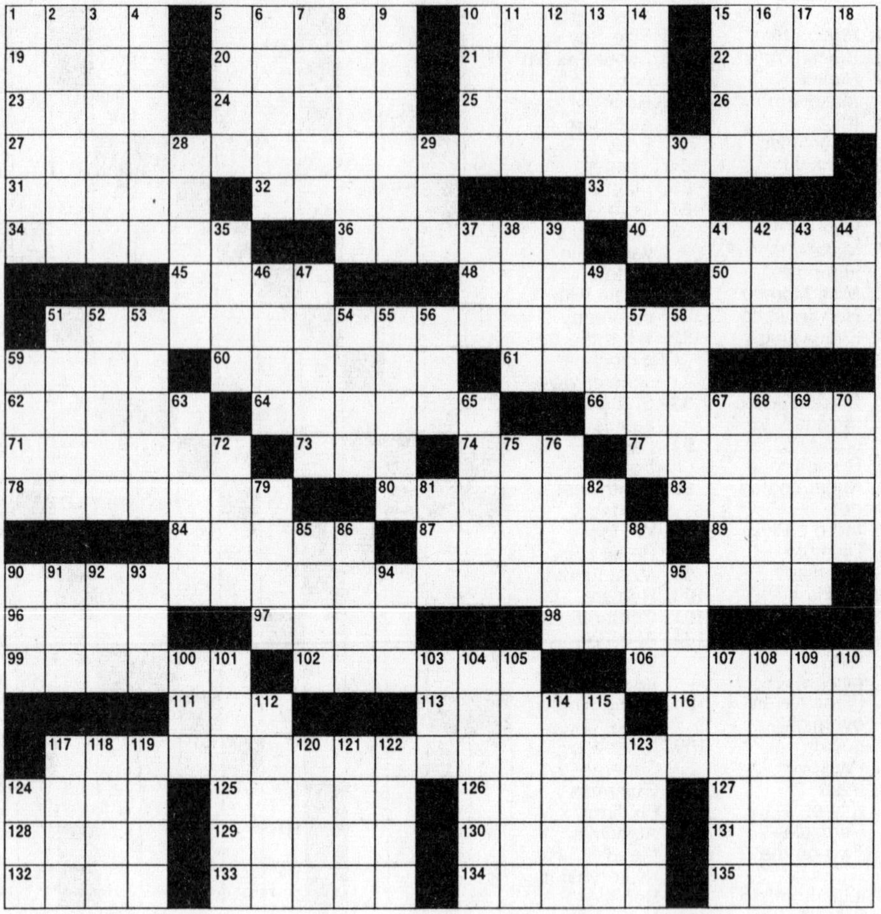

ACROSS

1. Moslem judge
5. Miss by ___
10. Spars
15. Meditate
19. Indian Ocean gulf
20. Basic principle
21. Apportion
22. Responsibility
23. Iowa Indians
24. Brilliance
25. Aviator Balbo
26. ___ majesty
27. Homely proverb
31. Uncle Miltie
32. Cubic meter
33. Spot
34. Property items
36. Delay
40. Posture
45. Mollify
48. Actual
50. Char
51. Cynical proverb
59. Lively, in music: Abbr.
60. Like some windows
61. ___ detector (airport device)
62. Stendhal hero
64. Poured
66. Branch of mechanics
71. Red wine
73. Caustic
74. Poetic contraction
77. Drums
78. Sail-hoisting tackle
80. Pinched
83. Move suddenly
84. Dean Martin affair
87. Phonograph's successor
89. Literary collections
90. Homely proverb, with 117 Across
96. Verdi opera
97. Rothenburg gentleman
98. They number seven
99. Ancient Greek hub
102. Spanish inn
106. Gaped
111. Stop ___ dime
113. Radio and television, e.g.
116. Dodge
117. See 90 Across
124. "Nor any ___ to drink"
125. Clio's sister
126. Like neon
127. Juan's assent
128. Ceremony
129. Covered with ravelings
130. Snake
131. Yoko and family
132. Baseball's Musial
133. Creates
134. Lauder of cosmetics
135. Dispatched

DOWN

1. Melon
2. Contents of this puzzle
3. Ornamentations
4. Shoe part
5. Served a winner
6. Clubs
7. Lagoon
8. Longshoreman
9. All
10. Principal
11. Der ___
12. Croat
13. Metalware pieces
14. Mall establishments
15. Water game
16. Change for a five
17. Oxidize
18. Compass pt.
28. Restrain
29. Place
30. Rent
35. "___ who!"
37. "___ longa . . ."
38. Enlarge a hole
39. Roy's spouse
41. Residue
42. Modern: Prefix
43. Presidential nickname
44. Sooner than
46. Blind part
47. Atelier appurtenance
49. Realtors' units
51. ___ Gay
52. Kind of pneumonia
53. Board material
54. Part of Miss Muffet's meal
55. Virile ones
56. Citric quencher
57. Percheron's repast
58. Designs
59. Author of "The Nazarene"
63. Ascertain
65. Beyond one's ___
67. Soviet republic
68. Native of Tabriz
69. Horn: Prefix
70. Fast planes
72. Walked
75. Foil's kin
76. Fiddler and pianist
79. Track event
81. Follower of novel or social
82. Editor's note
85. Bandleader Fields
86. Novice: Var.
88. Harem rooms
90. Scale notes
91. Tear
92. Crete peak
93. Corn unit
94. Shoes or gloves: Abbr.
95. Poly ending
100. Haul
101. British saint
103. Aggregate: Abbr.
104. Deduce
105. Handsome young man
107. Dispatch boats
108. Loosely woven fabric
109. Prolific inventor
110. Partner of cease
112. Roman courtyards
114. Foolish
115. Consent
117. Fortitude
118. Musical round
119. Golf tournament
120. Aaron or Bauer
121. Diminutive suffix
122. Beans
123. Raison d' ___
124. A.M.A. members

293 English Lesson By Helen Bernhardt

A matter of saying exactly what you mean.

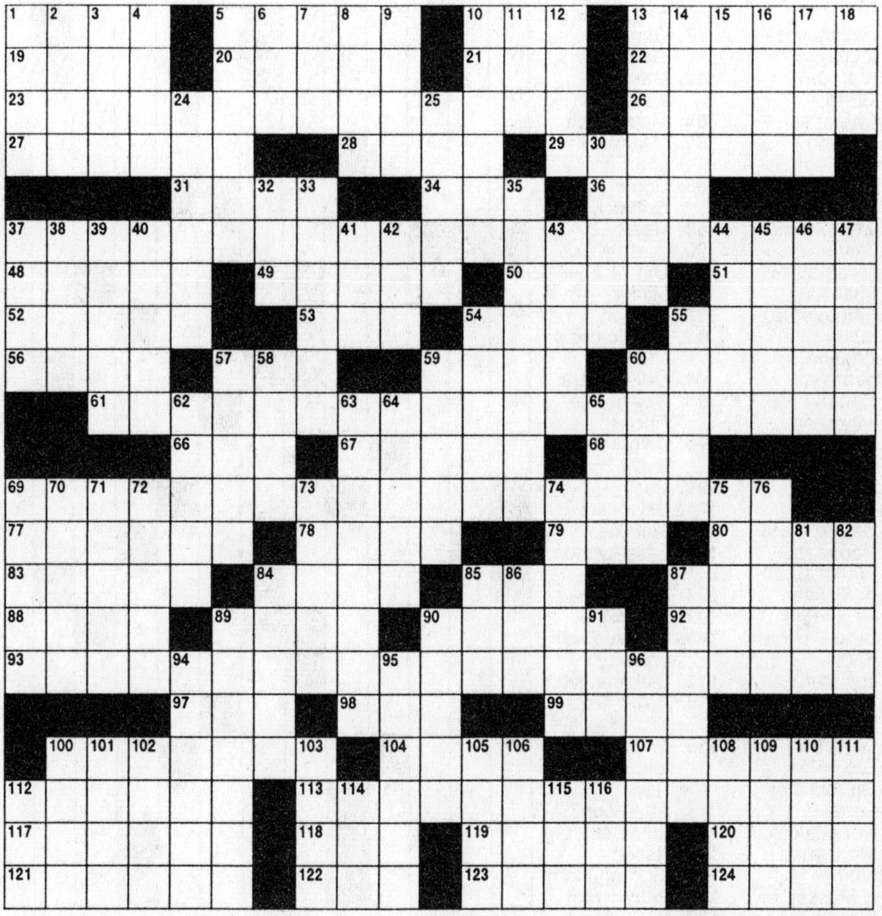

ACROSS

1. Island for terriers
5. New York's Mario ___
10. Pay-TV unit
13. Dance form
19. Spree
20. Producer Spelling
21. Durable wood
22. Even though
23. Start of a semantic quote
26. Rio Grande city
27. Balanchine's field
28. Socials
29. Golf handicap
31. Cuckoopint
34. "___ the king of Siam . . ."
36. ___ gratia
37. Quote continued
48. Bewail
49. "Golden Boy" dramatist
50. Shipshape
51. Rearranged wd.
52. TV awards
53. French article
54. Old Siamese coins
55. Blazing
56. Mount for Moses
57. Insecticide
59. Assert
60. Mary and John Jacob
61. More of quote
66. Junior hotel
67. Scottish cormorant
68. School org.
69. Quote continued
77. Razor clams
78. Code signals
79. Jenny or jack
80. Scottish isle
83. Sharif and Khayyám
84. Brave
85. Summer hrs.
87. Singer Paul and family
88. Singer Jenny
89. Fictional captain
90. "The Tempest" spirit
92. Noblemen
93. More of quote
97. Mindanao peak
98. Toby
99. First king of Israel
100. Stand on one's own ___
104. Sled
107. Feathery
112. Upholstery material
113. End of quote
117. ___ d'armes, fencing teacher
118. Mother of Seth
119. Flavor
120. Patricia of filmdom
121. Swimmer Williams
122. "___ the land of . . ."
123. Resource
124. Ferrara family name

DOWN

1. Wound
2. Tropical nut
3. Dog's greeting to the moon
4. Common Latin abbr.
5. Friend of Guevara
6. Mich.-based union
7. ___ pro nobis
8. Feminist Lucretia
9. Start of "The Raven"
10. Power tool
11. Cry of contempt
12. Endorse
13. Most unbelievable
14. Norway's patron saint
15. River in Spain
16. High-school age
17. ___ -de-camp
18. Request to a flier reader: Abbr.
24. Hankers
25. Split ___ (make trivial)
30. Egyptian skinks
32. E.T.'s craft
33. "To do ___ to God" (Scout motto)
35. California bay
37. Augury
38. Capital of Latium
39. Disney elephant
40. Fossil genus
41. Wine: Prefix
42. Sun-dancing Indian
43. Test anew
44. Handles
45. Cation's opposite
46. Roman author
47. Throw out
54. Have, to Pierre
55. Chinese or Indian
57. Units of force
58. Contradict
59. Hairdos
60. Motors
62. Property claims
63. Sharp-edged, as a leaf
64. Sentimental person
65. Musical work
69. Capri or Elba, to an Italian
70. Man: Prefix
71. "___ flowing with milk and honey"
72. "Requiem" composer
73. Swelling disease
74. Horse operas
75. Flaxen fabric
76. Country bumpkin
81. Not one
82. U.S. holly
84. "Roxana" author
85. Parched
86. Wife of Thor
87. Handsome one
89. Royal-linen custodian
90. Dispute
91. Mauna ___
94. William ___, author of the quote
95. Indiana resort town
96. Tuffet sitter
100. Polynesian warriors
101. Speck
102. Pledge
103. Kojak
105. Wooden clogs
106. Nestling
108. Sea eagle
109. Does coloring
110. Zodiac animal
111. Kind of log or candle
112. Mrs., in Nice
114. Hail, to Caesar
115. Curve
116. Fr. holy woman

294 Quiz Time By Calista Luminati

Some questions that need answers of sorts.

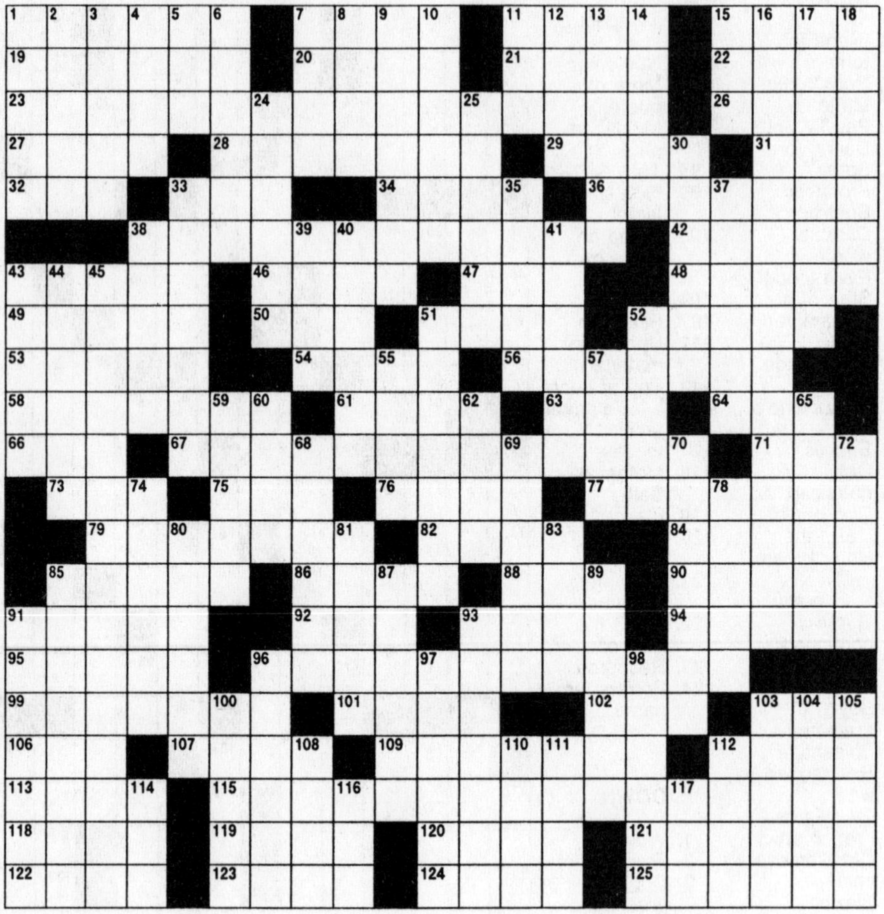

ACROSS

1. Evangeline's locale
7. Mat. days
11. Up to
15. Calendar offering
19. Ali's aide
20. It's usually cheaper when round
21. Jester
22. Mountain goat
23. "What's up, pussy?"
26. Engage, as gears
27. Hebrew zither
28. Helmet-shaped
29. Revue segment
31. Before theta
32. Hoosegow
33. Walter Scott or Raleigh
34. Ravine, in India
36. Short signature
38. "What price hot money?"
42. "A votre ____!"
43. On this side: Prefix
46. Not clerical
47. Word with bred or will
48. A Musketeer
49. Son of Jacob
50. Cambridge fellow
51. Marsh growth
52. Walking ____ (happy)
53. Undomesticated
54. Moslem mystic
56. Royal headgear
58. Gas-pump attendants
61. Apiece
63. Left port: Abbr.
64. Nigerian people
66. Stout, for one
67. "Where has my little dog gone?"
71. Wave, in Spain
73. Short for kindness
75. Hoover or Aswan
76. Kopf, to a Frenchman
77. Grim one
79. Germ killers
82. Make watertight
84. Maui porch
85. "Damned spot"
86. Cop's bailiwick
88. Heart
90. "____ Kick Out of You"
91. Midler
92. Landon
93. Missile-crisis site
94. Little letters
95. City on the Rhone
96. "Where's the fire?"
99. Chair
101. Skyrocket
102. Moccasin
103. Fifth Avenue carrier
106. Install a bug
107. Antitoxins
109. Croesus was one
112. Dickens girl
113. Tell it like ____
115. "What follows 'Dog Day Afternoon?'"
118. Turns sharply
119. Raced
120. Kind of guard
121. Petty tyrant
122. Naturalness
123. Marquee listing
124. Italian wine area
125. Radiator sounds

DOWN

1. Tin Pan Alley org.
2. Begin's opposite
3. Take steps
4. French or Dutch item
5. Imaret
6. Dance duet
7. Small-airport acronym
8. Spanish skill
9. Symbol of sea fallibility
10. Wayside shelter
11. Continent: Abbr.
12. Arena calls
13. Be a Peeping Tom
14. Mischievous
15. Kind of wit
16. "What makes Sammy run?"
17. He has a way with a will
18. Breathes out
24. Byron's Childe
25. Sunshine girl of song
30. Herbal tea
33. Like Hawthorne's letter
35. Bothered
37. Japanese floor mat
38. Of a region
39. Luang Prabang's land
40. Beethoven or Haydn piece
41. Sort of worn
43. Rich silk fabric of old
44. Arthurian woman
45. "Who's afraid of Virginia Woolf?"
51. Adjective for Midas
52. More unusual
55. Fait accompli
57. Arabic letter
59. Auguste of sculpture
60. Read the headlines
62. "I ____ definitions": Disraeli
65. Acid salt
68. Simple organisms
69. It needs a handle to handle
70. Type of vitamin acid
72. Sutherland solos
74. English composer Eric
78. Dray or wain
80. Double dagger, in printing
81. Hawks
83. Wolf
85. Genus of bacteria
87. Waterborne
89. Pungent snuff
91. Christen
93. Containers for claret
96. Feudal lord's due
97. Spanish president: 1931–36
98. Louisiana division
100. Depressions
103. Chicago athletes
104. Armbones
105. Cuffs
108. Taj Mahal site
110. Suffix for thermo
111. Indian title of respect
112. McAuliffe's word
114. Opposite of NNW
116. Feminine pronoun
117. Happy, in Paris

295 Who's Who By Dorothy Smitonick

Cluing in on some people of note.

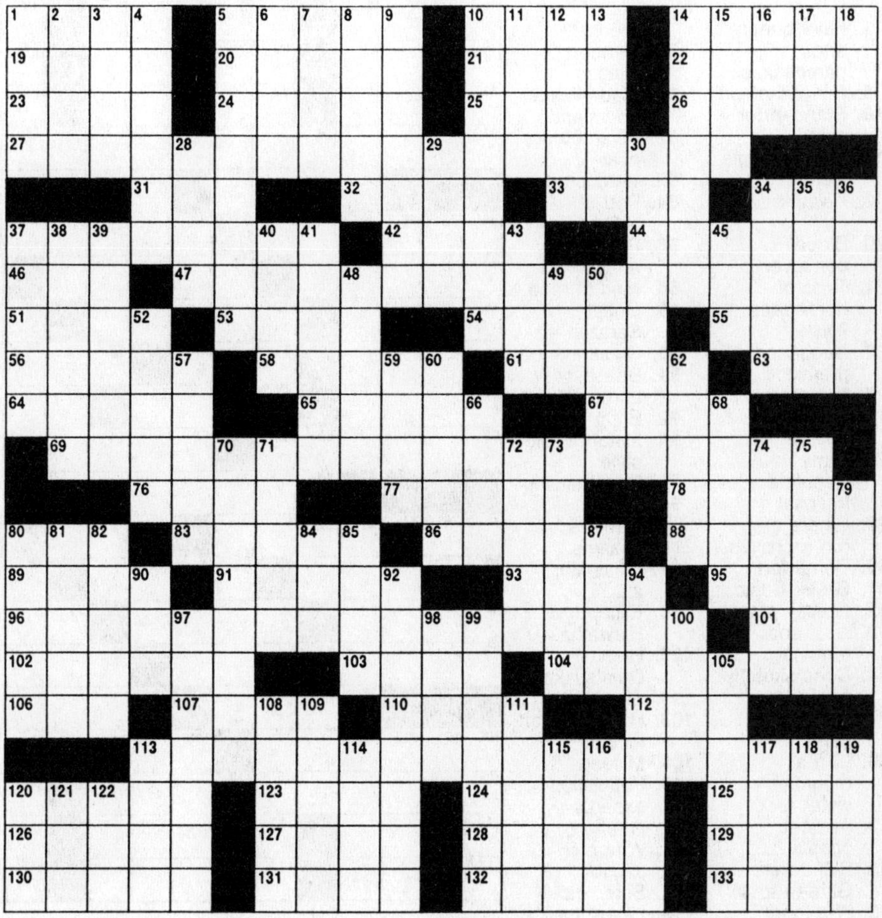

ACROSS

1. Reps.
5. Lions' features
10. ___ in (contribute)
14. Marner or Scrooge, i.e.
19. Writer Roald
20. Convex moldings
21. One of the Chaplins
22. Make amends
23. Exchange fee
24. Word before the raven's "more"
25. Lombardi city
26. Tierney and Lockhart
27. Sheridan Whiteside
31. Stay behind
32. Frosts
33. Unending time
34. Haggard heroine
37. Religious-festival times
42. Metal fastening
44. Tends the furnace
46. Spanish Main loot
47. Thomas More
51. Public disturbance
53. Norse mythical giant
54. Art of reason
55. Rational
56. Postpone
58. Barker's pitch
61. Dakota tribe
63. ___ Cruces
64. Growing out
65. Presley
67. Merkel and others
69. Sir Percy Blakeney
76. Get rid of, in a way
77. Writer Nevil
78. Candy items
80. Depot: Abbr.
83. Conditional sale
86. Minneapolis suburb
88. Herring
89. Comic Johnson
91. Things often blown
93. Elephant Boy of films
95. Persian poet
96. Uncas, almost
101. Counterpart of an adm.
102. Sinatra's "Eleven"
103. ___ Alto
104. Edible
106. Teachers' org.
107. Handful
110. Six, on a die
112. Cheer for Escamillo
113. Philip Nolan
120. Fall flower
123. Jai ___
124. Abalone's home
125. Navigator Bartholomeu
126. Prepared apples
127. Actor Rip
128. Weird
129. Entry fee of a sort
130. Leaves the scene
131. Bachelor's party
132. Dickens's Edwin
133. Close

DOWN

1. "Batman" actor West
2. In a dither
3. Slender
4. "Though the mills of God grind ___, yet . . ."
5. One kind of marriage
6. ___ plaisir
7. Variable star
8. Tropical resin
9. "Little ___"
10. Huge
11. Mount of Oregon
12. Setting for "Jewel in the Crown"
13. Revolutionary writer
14. Purplish red
15. Roman road
16. Dombey's partner
17. Compass reading
18. Thing, in law
28. "Mary ___ little lamb"
29. Rend
30. Missile part
34. Viking toast
35. Hair tint
36. Curves
37. Golden ___ (Mongol force)
38. Christie's Express
39. Sponge from a tropical gourd
40. Sweet potatoes
41. Sharpshooter
43. Chart
45. W.W. II spy outfit
48. Lace trimming, for one
49. Sweater size: Abbr.
50. Keep late hours
52. French heads
57. Turn the dial again
59. Preholiday times
60. Limber
62. Certain cops
66. Small spade for weeding
68. Ginger cookies
70. "Would that I were under the ___ the . . ."
71. Alaskan native
72. "Be of good cheer; ___"
73. Threat
74. Infuriate
75. Heavy
79. Restrict
80. Boutique
81. Vestige
82. Bewildered
84. Somewhat: Suffix
85. Turnip, in Scotland
87. Bedouin robes
90. Air-travel guess: Abbr.
92. Outstandingly good
94. Still warm
97. Moving ahead
98. Stew
99. Deceived
100. Sea off Borneo
105. ___ ear
108. Hits a fly
109. Lindbergh was one
111. Ozone
113. Sporting event
114. O'Hara's home
115. Flying prefix
116. Muse of history
117. Fork part
118. Pro ___
119. River in Belgium
120. Playing card
121. White or Red
122. Prefix for cycle or corn

296 Stretch Runs By Michael McWane

Taking a look at the sport of kings.

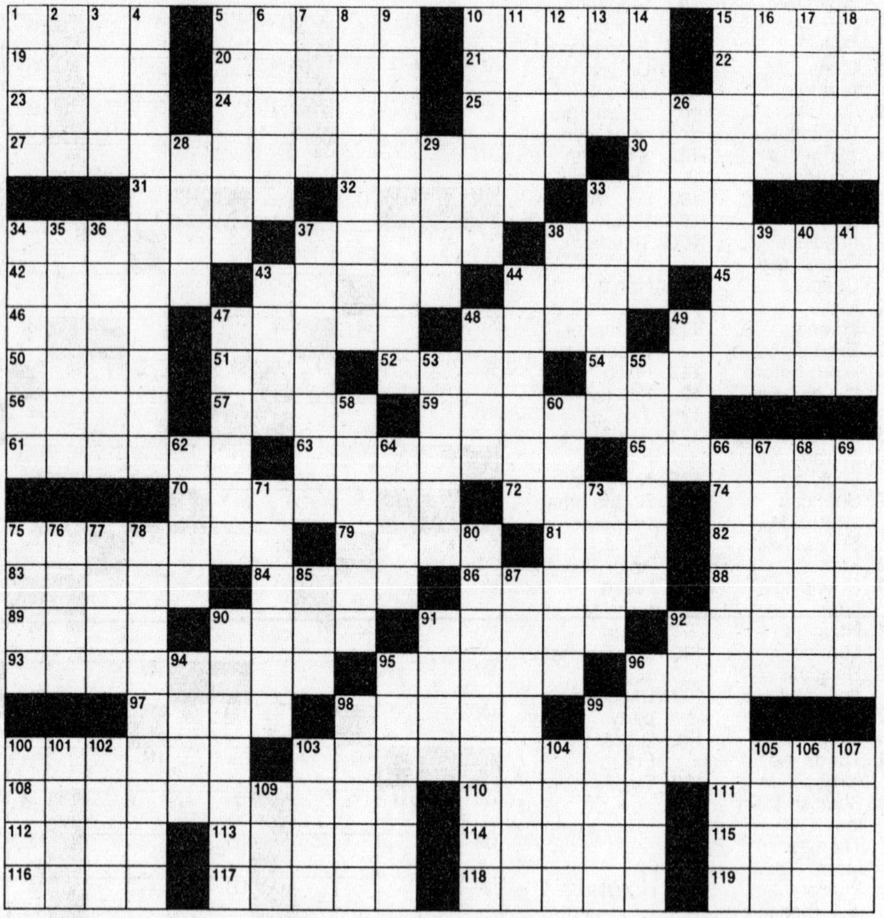

ACROSS

1. Fairy queen and namesakes
5. Bill of fashion
10. Stand-in for cash
15. Major Hoople word
19. "Winnie ___ Pu"
20. Blood conveyer
21. Type of horse-race finish
22. Hungarian premier
23. Not reg.
24. Dyad plus one
25. Army front-line hospital
27. Where they run for roses
30. Come forth
31. Greek Cupid
32. Grassy plain
33. ___ and terminer
34. Does sketchy sewing
37. Stadium parts
38. Like a mountain vista
42. Ancient chests
43. Blunderers
44. Garden tools
45. "So long!"
46. One on the move
47. Cassia plant
48. Minnesota Fats's game
49. Waits
50. 1936 Oscar actor
51. Medieval poem
52. Make a canine warning
54. Unfastens
56. Nick's dog
57. Work units
59. In succession
61. Curl up snugly
63. Chemical element
65. William Tell, for one
70. Enthusiastic tribute
72. Rabbit's tail
74. Meshed fabric
75. Austrian sound theorist
79. Vertebral or slipped
81. Made like a gourmand
82. Asian border river
83. Verdi product
84. Part of N.E.A.
86. Places of refuge
88. Kind of race
89. Golfer Sarazen
90. Countenance
91. Beach barriers
92. Bring
93. Instance, old style
95. Does hauling
96. Jesse James's chasers
97. "Kiss Me, ___"
98. Group for Hiawatha
99. Hoover Dam's lake
100. Slow up
103. Hambletonian locale
108. Miserly
110. Population expert's criterion
111. Wife of Jacob
112. Sgts., etc.
113. Like some milk
114. Act the femme fatale
115. Scat-singing great
116. Teut. people
117. Flatfish
118. Flub
119. Triple Crown winner Seattle ___

DOWN

1. Varied: Abbr.
2. Xanadu's river
3. Tangy cheese
4. Triple Crown winner
5. Mawkishness
6. Nocturnal lemur
7. Seed cover
8. 4 Down, for one
9. Gear for 4 Down
10. Engenders
11. Twilled cotton
12. Gats
13. Possessive pronoun
14. Ringlike textile devices
15. Intestinal disorder
16. Greedy, in Ayr
17. Excited
18. Unit of force
26. Word of agreement
28. Canadian tribe
29. Sculls
33. Peacock's spots
34. Bribe collector
35. Stir up
36. Gets on the trail of
37. "West Side Story" song
38. Great Lakes canals
39. Suffix for motor or aqua
40. Solar god
41. Girl
43. Endure
44. V.I.P.'s at 27 Across
47. Magician's hiding spot
48. Hunger signal
49. South African
53. Sign gases
55. Mexican basket grasses
58. Spake
60. Removes from a box
62. Miss Falana
64. Pork cut
66. Beer-commercial animals
67. ___ and flowers
68. Intertwine
69. Trouble areas on the links
71. Tillable
73. Shoshoneans
75. Venetian magistrate
76. Afford access
77. Indites
78. Pimlico happening
80. Manège maneuver
85. Understand
87. Animal with a special diet
90. Suitability
91. Fallow deer
92. 4 Down, at first
94. Paramount
95. Wave tops
96. Alloy for utensils
98. Greenland settlement
99. Animated, to Liszt
100. Ladder part
101. Suffix for differ
102. Stravinsky
103. Work hard
104. Expensive
105. Miss Gwyn
106. Hill's opposite
107. "Pygmalion" author
109. Mail-service initials

297 Winners By William Canine

All of whom showed their stuff in the same year.

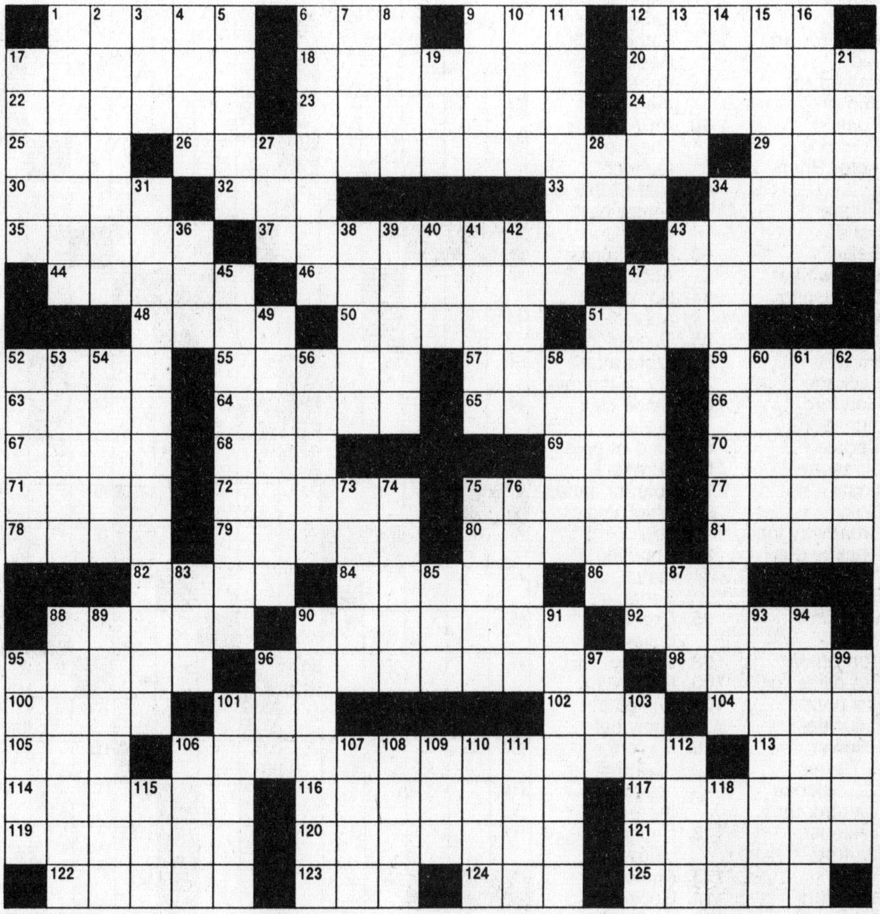

ACROSS

1. Twinges
6. Wonder
9. QB's encouragement
12. Cancel a launch
17. Debussy
18. Revel
20. Arranges
22. John Updike animal
23. Lindbergh or Post
24. Doodad
25. Attys.' group
26. 1978 Oscar film
29. Italian poet Betti
30. Minstrel
32. Six, to Verdi
33. Comparative suffix
34. Thimble Theater character
35. Vilify
37. 1978 Pulitzer author
43. Former Czech president
44. Asian salt tree
46. Soup ingredients
47. Show and gravy
48. Sprawl
50. Operatic voice
51. Symptom
52. Site of a famed campanile
55. Saar ___ (coal area)
57. Digger ___ of old radio
59. RR stops
63. Outback birds
64. Harbingers
65. Jeopardy
66. Marquee
67. "Beowulf," for one
68. Pugilists' org.
69. Writer Compton-Burnett
70. Samoan port
71. Mother of Apollo
72. Biblical juniper
75. Schmidt and Wallace
77. Rhode Island senator
78. Scads
79. Maine U. site
80. Mites
81. Emblem of Wales
82. Rorschach item
84. Organ stops
86. Pintail duck
88. Flourish
90. Valenzuela and Ballesteros
92. Located
95. Yacht-race markers
96. 1978 U.S. Open golf champ
98. Forbidden things
100. "Dear me!"
101. Sage of Concord's initials
102. Kind of tent
104. Nothing, to Ramón
105. Attorney's degree
106. Sharer of the 1978 Nobel Peace Prize
113. Mil. leaders
114. Tenant
116. Nonwelcoming sign
117. Samples
119. Doltish
120. Oval
121. Good-natured
122. Bowsprits
123. Knock
124. Neighbor of Leb.
125. Farm workers

DOWN

1. Southern football power
2. Joel Grey's film hangout
3. Activity center
4. Prepare copy
5. Clockmaker Thomas and others
6. Nova Scotian
7. Whitecap
8. Lake port
9. Wife of Boaz
10. Without ___ (penniless)
11. Ruptures
12. More sapient
13. Woodwind: Abbr.
14. Disencumber
15. Salve
16. 1978 Grammy winners
17. Grumbles
19. Paddle
21. Comes to a halt
27. Common Market initials
28. Finger count
31. 1978 Super Bowl winners
34. 1978 Emmy-winning comedienne
36. Defunct car
38. Spring bird
39. Items of interest
40. 1960's antiwar group
41. Columnist Stewart
42. Hollow stone
43. Quagmire
45. 1978 Pulitzer novel
47. 1978 Heisman winner
49. Unit of brightness
51. Shavings
52. Trims away
53. Urge
54. Retinue
56. Old Pacific alliance
58. Thomas Mann's writer-daughter
60. Home on the plains
61. Infirm
62. Celery unit
73. Done
74. Listless
75. Large: Prefix
76. More glacial
83. ___ Altos
85. Chaney
87. "___ Heldenleben"
88. 1978 N.B.A. champions
89. Stockpiles
90. Gym shoe
91. Pearly Gates keeper
93. Put through, as a bill
94. 1978 N.L. champions
95. Spheroids
96. Arista
97. Cuddle
99. Impudent
101. Cattails
103. Hurl
106. Golda of Israel
107. That, in France
108. Succor
109. Prefix for carp or cure
110. Swabs
111. Common phone signal
112. Okinawan capital
115. Health spot
118. Member of Cong.

298 Wood Craft By Bernard Meren

Concentrating on uses for a piece of lumber.

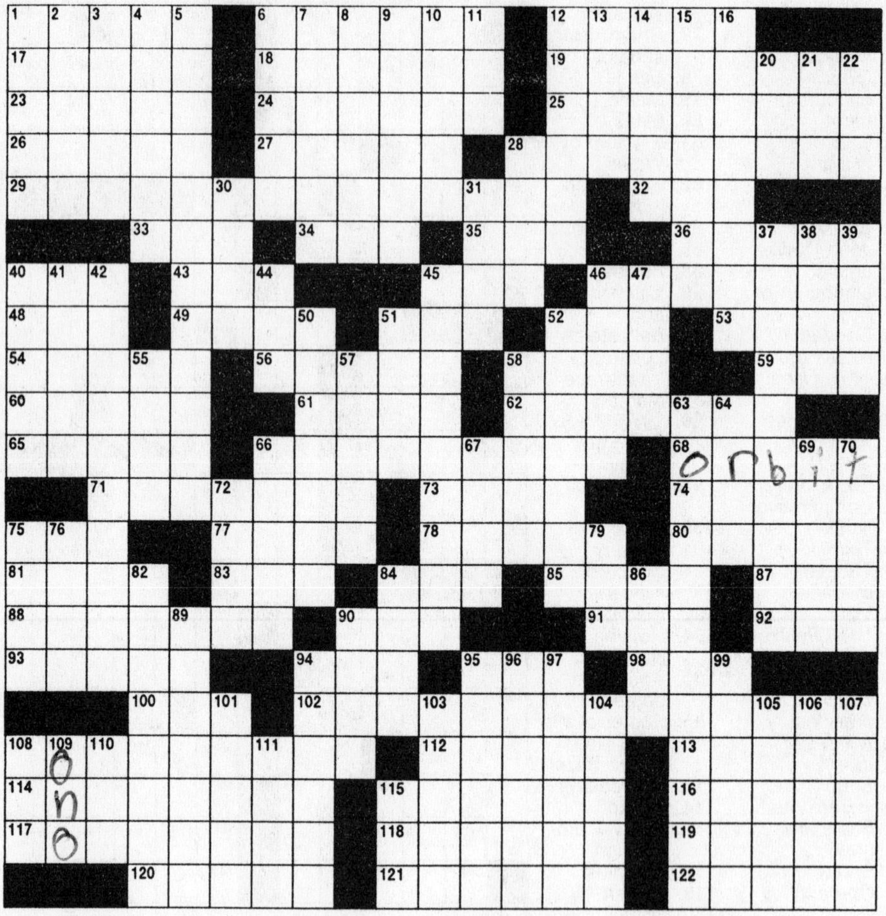

ACROSS

1. Conquer an Alp
6. Talked on and on
12. Fumes
17. Pi is one
18. Actor Brian ___
19. Rubber bands
23. Bellini's sleepwalker
24. Exhausting
25. Evict physically
26. Party package
27. Hundred simoleons
28. Certain pleasure boats
29. Do a Broadway job
32. Hockey star
33. Never, in Berlin
34. V.I.P. in Wash.
35. Iron holder
36. Put aside for the nonce
40. Fleur-de-follower
43. A Turner
45. ___ glance
46. Taverns for Toulouse-Lautrec
48. Squid's emission
49. Kind of stake out West
51. What R.N.'s dispense
52. Highway sign
53. Lampreys
54. "___ unto my feet"
56. Roll with a hole
58. Neat as ___
59. Stout's relative
60. Nerve networks
61. Broad-topped hill
62. Made do
65. Printers' marks
66. House-siding material
68. Satellite's path
71. Difficult, old style
73. City of Siberia
74. Flora and fauna
75. Explorer with LaSalle
77. Father of the Reo
78. Enhanced the pot
80. An Abbey Theatre founder
81. Half of this is somewhat better
83. Metric units: Abbr.
84. Not public: Abbr.
85. Obligation
87. Word after dry or tommy
88. Blood clot: Prefix
90. Kind of pole
91. "Bravo!"
92. John or Jane
93. Chief Vedic god
94. Shooting match, in Sedan
95. Org. for drivers
98. Johnny ___
100. Explosive
102. Win-place-show bet
108. Place for casino hopping in the East
112. Daphnis's beloved
113. Abalone
114. Gooselike
115. Ex-South African P.M. and family
116. Anoint, once
117. Tightness relaxant
118. Woodworkers' tools
119. Subscribe again
120. Oodles
121. "No Exit" Nobelist
122. Potions

DOWN

1. Talent
2. Truman's first home
3. Ending for add
4. Ancient Cretan
5. Plane-ticket adjunct
6. Mrs. Wiggs's property
7. Fine white wines
8. Air-breathing organism
9. Minor sea deity
10. Nine: Prefix
11. A.B. or B.A.
12. Trash
13. "Thanks ___"
14. "Ninotchka" star
15. Small warships, often
16. Salt of a fatty acid
20. Ending for super
21. Cow's second chew
22. Map abbrs.
28. Czech river
30. Drop of sorrow?
31. Campus gp.
37. Slicing surface for 81 Across
38. Lounge
39. Being, to Livy
40. Credibility stretchers
41. Cove
42. Wheels of a sort for the young
44. Beat-up boat
45. Last call for a commuter
46. Alley or date
47. Hebrides island
50. Sentimental songs
51. Occasional worker, for short
52. Gave impetus to
55. Dyna or ere chaser
57. Eggs on
58. "Lives like a drunken sailor on ___": Shak.
63. Be neglected
64. Pennsylvania port
66. Instrument for Casals
67. Atlanta Hawk's home
69. ". . . your cake and have ___"
70. Sample
72. Grant's ___
75. High: Prefix
76. Late attorney Roy
79. ___ Alte
82. Bastion
84. Henry VIII's last
86. Expose
89. Lathing spindle
90. Clock sound
94. Old German coins
95. Building stone
96. Oblique
97. Penitent one
99. Third largest island
101. Interlace
103. Florida city
104. Wiesbaden is its capital
105. Last words
106. Book by D. S. Freeman
107. U.S. actor John and family
108. Palais bash
109. Yoko ___
110. Kyushu volcano
111. Over again
115. AWOL retrievers

299 Placements By Alfio Micci

Finding the what from the where.

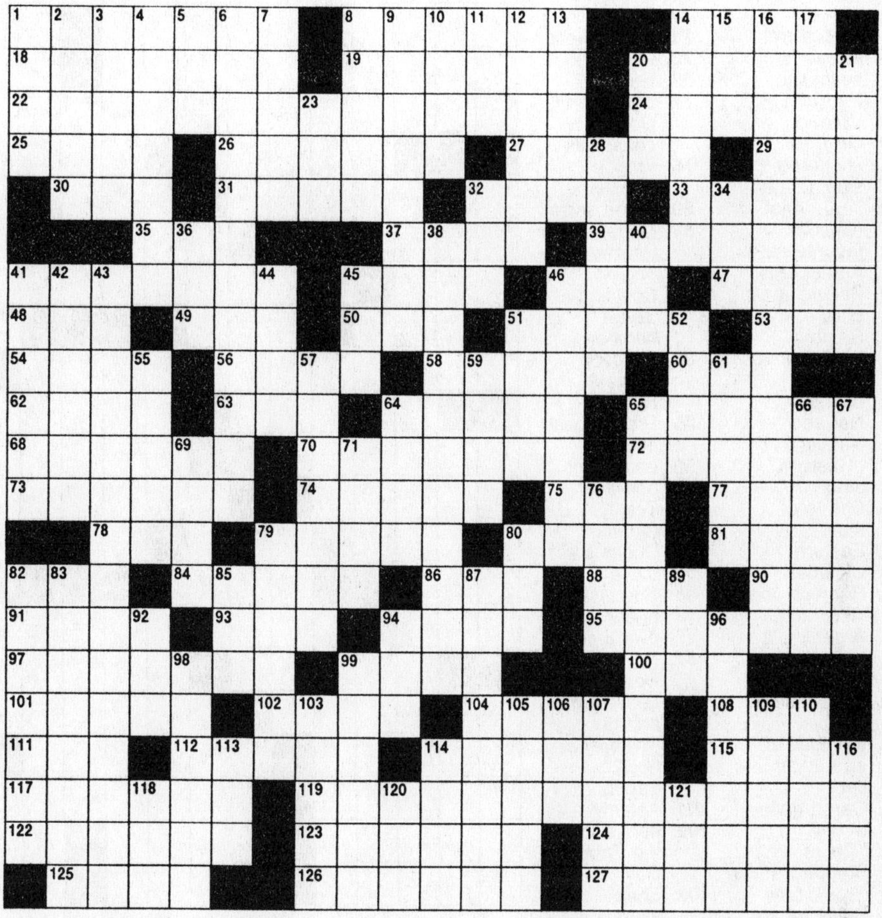

ACROSS

1. Type of triangle
8. Lofty
14. Carry on
18. Milk protein
19. Went on the road
20. Emigration
22. stoles hold
24. "Cymbeline" heroine
25. Single performances
26. Not as complicated
27. Bust on a pillar
29. Possessed
30. Chinese river
31. "___ Is Born"
32. Woody's son
33. Diva Adelina
35. Sphere
37. ___ facto
39. Feeling of futility
41. Luncheonette
45. Friedkin's "To Live and Die ___"
46. Morning moisture
47. Words of supposition
48. Sharp-cornered: Abbr.
49. Items for Caesar's omelet
50. Golfers' org.
51. "Western Star" poet
53. Number for Bo
54. Hatched
56. Is human
58. Baker's need
60. Own, in the highlands
62. Ali ___
63. Pod occupant
64. Special talent
65. Hot
68. Woman adviser
70. More trite
72. "___ bragh!"
73. Rebellious one
74. Diadem
75. Harry ___ Zell
77. ___ Fein (Irish society)
78. Actress Munson
79. African river
80. It's often conjugated
81. Pianist Petri
82. Spoil
84. Western resort
86. Dietary abbr.
88. Nourished
90. Charle-magne's dom.
91. Compass points
93. Actor Cariou
94. Norse god
95. Acted the coquette
97. Unstinting
99. Greet the villain
100. Canticle
101. Rhone feeder
102. Mil. truancy
104. Rod of baseball
108. Face the target
111. Red or Dead
112. Transparent
114. Fake
115. Durrell heroine
117. Atelier
119. elected 1 1 chief
122. Harmonize
123. Give chapter and verse
124. Strauss's "___ auf Naxos"
125. Potato features
126. Became tiresome
127. Mrs. Browning's output

DOWN

1. Director Gene
2. Athenian demagogue
3. White poplar
4. Actress Ida's folks
5. Cassowary's cousin
6. 9 average
7. Willingham's "___ a Man"
8. Courtyards
9. Threatening, as the sky
10. Contented sound
11. Author Levin
12. Kidney: Prefix
13. Detroit lemon
14. Charts anew
15. Past
16. DARKNESS; DARKNESS
17. Formal account
20. That fellow
21. Hearth item
23. N.Y. time
28. Paca or squirrel, e.g.
32. Botanist Gray
34. Bee: Prefix
36. Pi follower
38. cavort lyrics
40. Lamb's mother
41. Put a label on
42. Madden
43. RIPEN; PULCHRI-TUDE
44. Reduce
45. Bark-beetle genus
46. Merit
51. Lessen
52. U.S. missile
55. Singer Bobby
57. Bushy-tailed animal
59. Emerald Isle
61. Stand
64. Pond denizen
65. 0 X
66. Snub
67. Slipped on, as a garment
69. "I earn that ___": Shak.
71. Caen's river
76. German composer Carl
79. Claws
80. Heflin
82. Entertainer Manchester
83. Cordial
85. ___ mode
87. Separate
89. Performed
92. Sun. talk
94. Castor-bean product
96. ___ agreement (settle a dispute)
98. Lacs
99. Stinger
103. Dams
105. ___ as a beet
106. Indian novelist Raja ___
107. Lab burners
109. ___ France
110. Denoted
113. Work the garden
114. Satanic
116. Quaffs
118. Owed
120. Wood sorrel
121. Wrongdoing

300 In Style By Frances Hansen

Some ways of identifying creators of fashion.

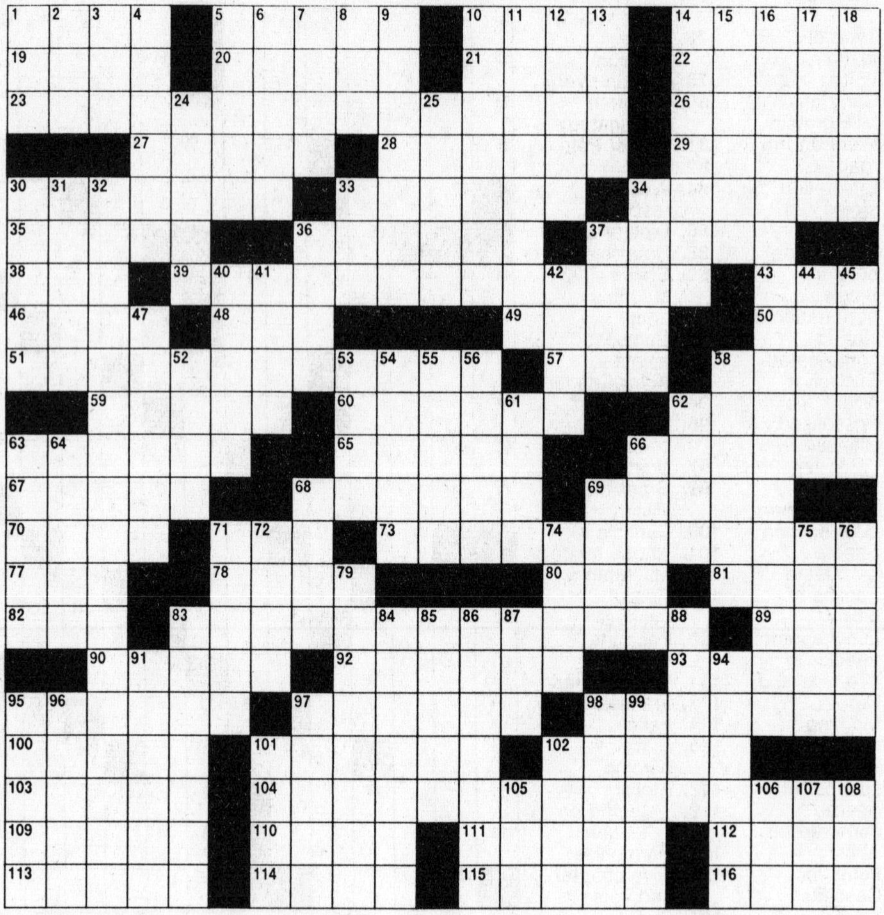

ACROSS

1. Mecca trek
5. Nasser's successor
10. Part of T.A.E.
14. Vote in
19. On the sheltered side, asea
20. "___ mio!" (Gucci's favorite air?)
21. Author Uris
22. Balenciaga's chair
23. Ralph's family moves to sheik country
26. Nat and Natalie
27. "Gaslight" actor
28. Shade of blue
29. Eastern Christian
30. Home of the "lily maid"
33. Argentina's capital: 1852–62
34. "___ fideles . . ."
35. Member of an Iranian sect
36. Oared galley of old
37. "Christ Stopped at ___": Levi
38. Suffix for ox or brom
39. Stocking time for Saint Laurent?
43. Bird's beak
46. Barbecue offering
48. Still
49. Carter's middle name
50. Alphabetic sequence
51. Oscar opens an agency?
57. Comedian Louis
58. Whisky trailer
59. Sans assistance
60. Cesar of filmdom
62. Round relief
63. Actress Andress
65. Popular Dixie jelly
66. Weigh down
67. Galling as all get-out
68. Desert growth
69. Bristles
70. Trucker's rig
71. Mil. address
73. Cheer for Halston?
77. She wasn't clothes-conscious
78. French Christian
80. Wood sorrel
81. Magazine for Pauline Trigère
82. Downing Street number
83. Simpson reads Hersey?
89. Draw a bead on
90. Lou Grant portrayer
92. Testify formally
93. Dueler's move
95. Coco was one in her own time
97. Not likely to wear a bikini
98. Leave high and dry
100. "Where ___ now?": Sandburg
101. Aplenty
102. Item aboard the Enola Gay
103. Soap ingredient
104. Geoffrey quotes Sid Caesar?
109. C'est-___ (that is to say)
110. Miss Best of the films
111. Patou's notions
112. Pin down
113. Food, shelter and such
114. Insect eggs
115. 7 Down, to Pierre Cardin
116. In proper fashion

DOWN

1. Linden or Holbrook
2. In the style of
3. Game, to Givenchy
4. Small jumping rodent
5. "War and Peace" girl
6. Elegance, for one
7. Entry
8. Landon, informally
9. P.M. refreshment wagon
10. Heart of Dixie
11. Native of Beirut
12. Marc Bohan's "Behold!"
13. Medical-school subj.
14. Cape Verde coins
15. A Barrymore
16. Perry rapt in wild surmise?
17. Golf-shoe projection
18. Certain bud
24. Of the wind
25. Composer Ned
30. "___ in the hand . . ."
31. Maugham's Miss Thompson
32. Bill turns zookeeper?
33. Greek letters
34. White poplar
36. Deck post
37. "I've Told ___ Little Star," 1932 song
40. Jungle laugher
41. Coty
42. Town on Hiroshima Bay
44. Ooze, as charm
45. Romantically-shirted poet
47. Greyhound-like dog
52. ___-poly
53. Pamplona's river
54. Shrink's need
55. Fine violin
56. Gun the motor
58. Jimmy Dorsey favorite
61. Foolhardy
62. Makarova's miniskirt
63. Fluster
64. "Superman" Christopher
66. "Borstal Boy" author
68. "Neato!"
69. Humane soc.
71. Included in
72. Kind of glass
74. Daché's iodine
75. Few: Prefix
76. San 'a is its capital
79. Like a waft from the kitchen
83. Appropriates
84. Homburgs' kin
85. Part of op. cit.
86. Fruit of a certain flower
87. Busy colonizer
88. "___ of God, who takest away . . ."
91. His icebox was a good buy
94. Relax
95. Father of Leah
96. Eat away
97. Moslem prophet
98. Red as ___
99. Idaho hub
101. Actress Verdon
102. Declare
105. Pother
106. Water, to Christian Lacroix
107. Zilch
108. Culbertson of bridge fame

1

ALEC TUTUS PANIC STAR
VOLE INURE ELIDE POGO
EVANESCENT LICENTIOUS
CENTRALS SLICK TORTES
AONE DOUCE RUNA
ACCUSE DOURA TOPOLOGY
THERE CENTENNIAL BLE
HANS ORLO ENSE PSAS
OST FLUORESCENT BLORE
SEEDLESS TOADY HEALED
NOONE SHAMS SORTE
CLARET BLAKE STRESSES
LORIS TRANSLUCENT CRO
ERIC ARAN DALE LEAF
ANA CENTIGRADE PINTA
RANSACKS MAULS RECTOR
AGES SPELL MERE
KEATON MERLE BASENESS
ACCENTUATE OPALESCENT
TAME EDITS UINTA ERIA
EDEN DODOS TREAT DOPY

2

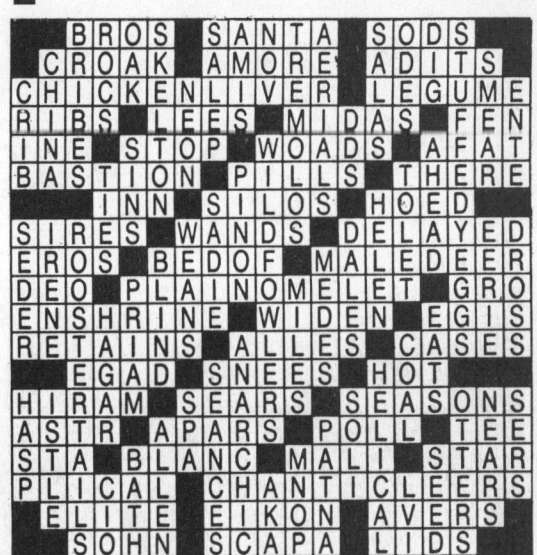

BROS SANTA SODS
CROAK AMORE ADITS
CHICKENLIVER LEGUME
RIBS LEES MIDAS FEN
INE STOP WOADS AFAT
BASTION PILLS THERE
INN SILOS HOED
SIRES WANDS DELAYED
EROS BEDOF MALEDEER
DEO PLAINOMELET GRO
ENSHRINE WIDEN EGIS
RETAINS ALLES CASES
EGAD SNEES HOT
HIRAM SEARS SEASONS
ASTR APARS POLL TEE
STA BLANC MALI STAR
PLICAL CHANTICLEERS
ELITE EIKON AVERS
SOHN SCAPA LIDS

3

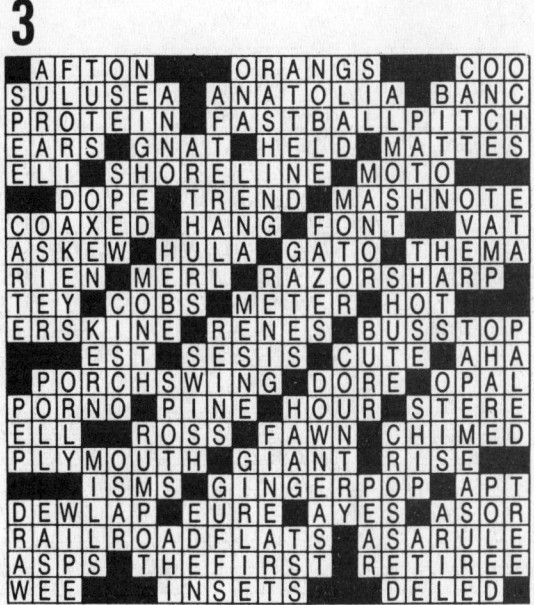

AFTON ORANGS COO
SULUSEA ANATOLIA BANC
PROTEIN FASTBALLPITCH
EARS GNAT HELD MATTES
ELI SHORELINE MOTO
DOPE TREND MASHNOTE
COAXED HANG FONT VAT
ASKEW HULA GATO THEMA
RIEN MERL RAZORSHARP
TEY COBS METER HOT
ERSKINE RENES BUSSTOP
EST SESIS CUTE AHA
PORCHSWING DORE OPAL
PORNO PINE HOUR STERE
ELL ROSS FAWN CHIMED
PLYMOUTH GIANT RISE
ISMS GINGERPOP APT
DEWLAP EURE AYES ASOR
RAILROADFLATS ASARULE
ASPS THEFIRST RETIREE
WEE INSETS DELED

4

ASTA SAGS SALAD MATCH
STUN PREP ALIBI ADELA
PONT ORLY GIVES NIXON
SWEETIE TAKETHESTAND
BOLSTER ERS GASSES
PETER TOTEM OAR
ANELES WHEELSANDDEALS
CARL TWIN REUSES AMOK
ECRU RETOP ACHS IRANI
STAMPED ASTRE BOSSES
FASTONTHEDRAW
PLANCK ENTRE ABASHES
LOBES MESH RECTI TEST
ODER RANEES NOSE RATA
WILDCATSTRIKES DEARER
AVA PARTS NITES
PERUSE MOA NOSHING
ICANTSTANDIT RASHERS
ELIDE ARDOR PRIM TAIL
RASER SNIPE LIMB ESTE
STERS KETTS OOPS NEED

5

SCAPE CID OFA SHIM
PASARS ATATURK ELAINE
ARTIST PANACEA PAULAS
TOONESDELIGHT GOULASH
TULE OLIO RES ITE
ESA VIOLA STOAT ACRES
RET ETNA MERRYANDREW
ANSE TACIT CADI
BORGE SPES AHHA LAG
ONEAT HANAU AGAU CASA
HAPPINESSISAWARMPUPPY
ELLE EASE SPANG ARIEL
ALY IMRE IRAE TINNY
PLAT ABIND OSTE
STRINGALONG FUME ACE
TAHOE OLLAS ALTAR BAR
EME HOB AGIO LAVA
BARMAID SEMPERFIDELIS
ERMINE GERAINT CAROLE
TIARAS CHARADE IRONER
SALE ARS NAD TIERS

6

DEBT SETA ATAN OIDS
ADAR IRON ROMA NDAK
METARZANYOUJANEEYRE
TIDES PRIOR VOLTAS
PARANGS SONNY DECLINE
ADENO ACRO GENA NSA
COSIFANTUTTEFRUTTI
ERE BOOT DOOM MMES
RELATIVE JOURS ABBESS
SEMELE ORCUS PORTER
CALLMEMADAMIMADAM
GETSIT LENIN ARECAS
UNESCO INNED ENTRENCH
MADE OSSA CLEO AHO
DASRHEINGOLDFINGER
SPR BETA IOTA SEEMS
CRETANS BOLUS THETREE
REMITS ALTON SEOUL
TOBEORNOTTOBEMYLOVE
ITER LAKE DEEP TSAR
LETS STER SERE SSTS

7

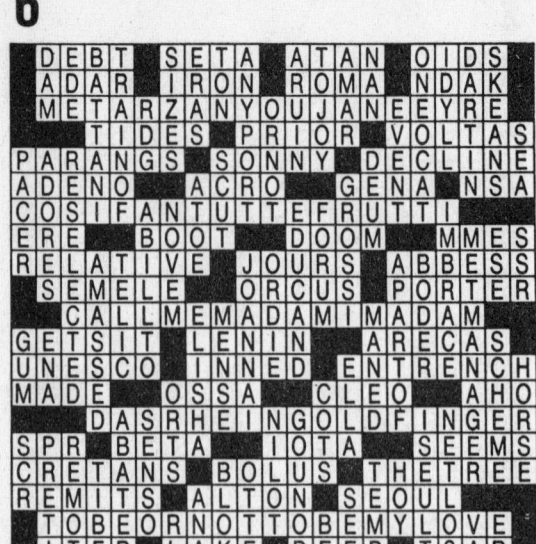

ACHIP GRIMY TEA
AMP ELUDE RENEE HAS
PAL RIGOR EVERS ERY
ERELONG IOWA CAMETO
ALAI CELLO TINAMOU
ROSE HRE HULA DAB
EFREMS PEKIN RAF
MED ASU ATIMEFORALL
ALOAN GISH OSS UCLA
DANCINGCHEEKTOCHEEK
RIOT DEA GLOW ORAGE
INTHEARMSOF OSU BED
DES SKIES STEROL
QAT NITA LOT SEEN
SPUMING SCOTT LENO
CREAMY HEAR ALLOWED
RUE ALLOT ANNIE ERA
ADZ TOILE SIGNS SOL
GEE ENIDS SLOGS

8

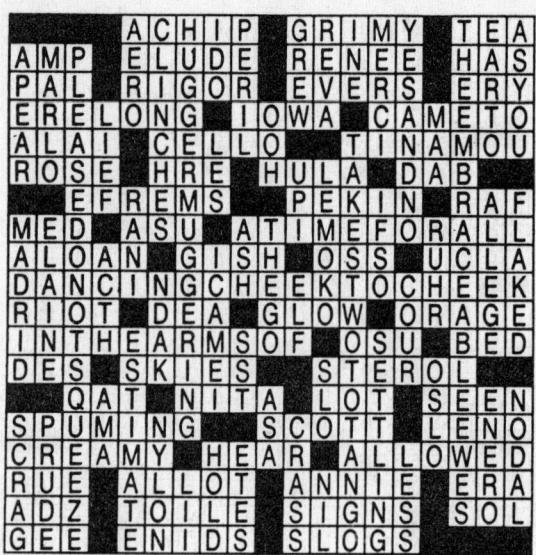

HEATER DEED IFS EMYDS
INCOME ATLI LEA LEVEE
SAHLINTHEFAMILY IDOLS
TRIO BEAU SINES
FORE ALMAOLDCOWHAND
ICECAP EARL CREATE
ETA MOSHEDIAHANN ITBE
FACTUAL WECRY DENHAM
HOR ICON TEA AGENE
AMID BEL RENDERS TAR
BON ROSAKILLARNEY ENG
ORG EXTERNS OES BRAE
MAFIA SAE IMPS OAR
BLONDE IRATE CAUTION
SERT RHETTBUTTONS BRO
DEADER ORAE STOLEN
BARBARASEVILLE SEME
TAMPA SATE REAP
ODORS MICHAELREDBRAVE
RENEE INC LYON OBERON
ANETS AGO LENA MAYANS

9

INCA GRAB MOODS MOP
MAAM AURAS AUDILE AVE
ARNO BRESTSTROKES NET
MANEGE SIEPI REASSURE
EBOLI SCENA SVENS
ASSAULTS HEEDS ENACTS
SIC TEAMS DEVIL ERROL
SEAR LUPO SADAT LINA
ANNES ITERS LETIT PAT
MASCARA WOOF INEPTLY
ATEN SNORT NEAL
DAMPISH ONEA LACEDUP
ORO NIECE GARBO HAUTE
BESS TROAD KIEV STIR
BACON OLDER FEEDA CLI
SLOPED DICED TRENCHES
WUWEI ELIOT SPIRO
COMPEERS ACRES OLIVES
ABU SPANISHSTEPS MEAT
LIL TENONS ORALE ENCY
FEE RIDGE AMOS ASHE

10

SPRIG LESS TOO INTER
PRONE ATTU ANTA DIONE
HEADOFTHESCHOOL ESNES
ESSE AINT HON CRAIG
RET ARNO PIE FUEL USA
ENESCO FOE CEIL SEEP
TROT EAROFCORN SPITE
AUSTRAL OCT AIN
INNATELY AVOID UNCLE
POODLE AREOLA LEHUA
INN NOSEFORNEWS ECT
PIETA THIRST RAGERS
SCORN BOGIE UPSTROKE
FIN THC STREAMY
PAYEE POTATOEYE FADS
EROS PLUS EOS FUSEES
ACU MEAT TNT BAAL LAP
ROOTS ROT AUST RIBE
HELLO MOUTHOFTHERIVER
ARIES AIDE SATE SPEAR
LAPSE LEM ARES TERRY

11

BETES LASH MGRS PASSE
ADELE ALTO ARUM ASPEN
INNERTUBES OUTERSPACE
TANAGER SPARE WATER
ELIS IPIL STRESA
INF SENECA STY EASED
BREAST ENERO RANN TAD
SMARTALEC ALBINOS
CARFARE HUDDLE MESHES
BLT ACARE USSS OARS
EMEUS FINN BETH AFRIT
RIEN SYST TABOO STD
GARGLE TERETE CLASSED
ACCEDES LAKEPOETS
ARM STIR PSALM SHALOM
GUEST DNA ENSUES PLN
ORLESS NARA SLIM
OATES OPALS ANABATA
OLDMASTERS YOUNGTURKS
ASIAN ALAE SAND ASCOT
STAND YAKS TROS STOSS

12

PATER NABOB ACTH THEM
OVULE ERASE DHOW EAVE
WILLSCARLET LADYINRED
ELIA ARA REAP SADDLE
RAP RUDYSPANIEL LES
NOSY KEYS RAD RHOD
TRIBE AIRE DOSED EGO
LEONE STUDYINSCARLET
ASTA BLTS ALSO IOLES
ILO TIER BAWL ASA
CARNATIONLILYLILYROSE
OKS EONS ENTS BET
CADRE ATMO MANO MEAN
CRIMSONRAMBLER BASRA
XIS ASNOT OUTS PONES
ISBA SUP SYNE EARN
ALA MOULINROUGE CPA
ERRATA LION AGE BARS
VERMILION REDREDROBIN
EREB VOGT EMDEN MALDE
RIDS ANYA DESDE STEER

13

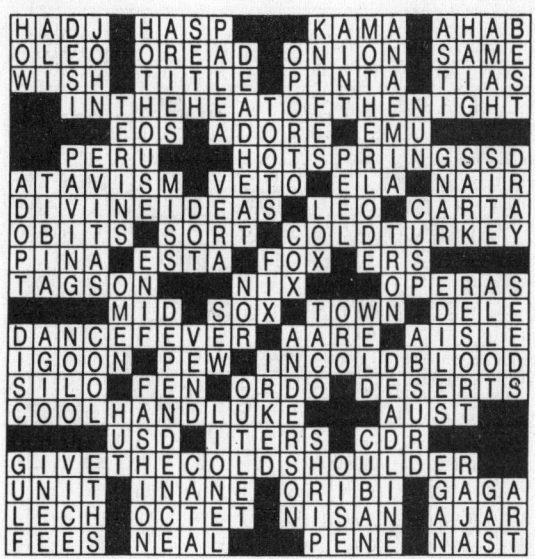

HADJ HASP KAMA AHAB
OLEO OREAD ONION SAME
WISH TITLE PINTA TIAS
INTHEHEATOFTHENIGHT
EOS ADORE EMU
PERU HOTSPRINGSSD
ATAVISM VETO ELA NAIR
DIVINEIDEAS LEO CARTA
OBITS SORT COLDTURKEY
PINA ESTA FOX ERS
TAGSON NIX OPERAS
MID SOX TOWN DELE
DANCEFEVER AARE AISLE
IGOON PEW INCOLDBLOOD
SILO FEN ORDO DESERTS
COOLHANDLUKE AUST
USD LITERS CDR
GIVETHECOLDSHOULDER
UNIT INANE ORIBI GAGA
LECH OCTET NISAN AJAR
FEES NEAL PENE NAST

14

BELL STOMP LADES ARMS
ALEE EATER ISONE RHEA
JUSTINTIME CHEVALIERS
ALL NATS ATHOS PESTLE
ERATO SCREW COMET
MAYAN ORPHAN HARASSED
AWAKES ELEM FORTY AGE
KANE ELLIS MOORS DIRE
ERN OCEAN WOODY AILED
REDDFOXXTROTTS AVASTS
ORAN ORT BENI
REWORD HOLMONTHERANGE
ERNST MAULS ORALS TOT
MOSS TONTO UTILE WHOA
IDA WILDS SPAT SHIEST
TENDERLY REDTOP ESSES
ORLES SOARE ELIHU
ATTICS OHARA MOOD NAE
DAHLHOUSES FLIPWILSON
AXEL UPSET TITLE OENO
MIRS TSARS STEER UTES

15

ABBEY CARAT PARC
SLATE CHROMA ARAPAHOS
PUTONTHECUFF PUTONICE
SEEN RAMAS TRASH GLEE
RETIRE OSS OLAS
PUTONESNOSEOUTOFJOINT
ELANDS LXX ION
CAKES TSHELA OSTS MAP
AMES PUTONANACT TRACE
NAN ORNATE ECCE LINER
BUYERS CLAWED
GETAT UTES POURED JAG
AMONG PUTAWORDIN SAGA
GUM RASP REDDEN BASIN
HOB ODA SARONG
PUTAWAYCHILDISHTHINGS
ITEM OUI UNTIES
PTNS EUROS SHORN GAGE
PEUTETRE PUTONEOVERON
ARRESTED APICES INCUR
ERSE SINKS ZESTY

16

RICK STAG SORDID SMOG
INRO PERU OTOOLE PASA
BAERBELLI SOMMERMUNTZ
SENDON OTT PET ANNEE
NANDA ALFA SIKH
CEASE MERRILLLIND ASP
ATL DOOR EMPERY ANTA
RAYE SOIT DESTE BIDES
PINK UNCURL ENCODERS
INNER STEELEMILL LEE
SERB TIRED CUTS
CAB CURTINCOWL SAHIB
INAFUROR RISING NORA
DIRER KIOWA LIO GRID
ETTE SEALABS AGAL NNE
RAH MENDELBLOCH OCEAN
RAIL LEAN THROB
SOARS ERE GEM BAREST
KNIGHTMAYER AIKENBACH
ATTU IMPEDE CREA AMOI
TOTE PATRON TEAM NETS

17

LAMB SETUP EDIT BOWS
OREL ASIDE NACHT AMIE
BEAUTYSPOT TREEOFLIFE
EATERIES SHRED ULSTER
FITS AHEAD RIA
EQUIP BROWN LONESOME
DUNS TRAMPSTEAMER FOX
DISH ROLE PRAY PROA
ACT ACADEMIES THERM
KOPECKS LICE CARAFES
PAYEE JONES ANOSE
DOPIEST UPON SNIPERS
ORALS AMERICANS ENL
GIBS TEMP OGEE PNOM
MEL TAKESTHEPASS ICON
ALESALES RIDES ONETO
THE LULUS LOVE
OPTION MEDOC MINERALS
SIGNETRING ADAMSRIVAL
SKIT SADIE TOGAE COZY
OAFS MIND EGEST HWYS

18

PAC GUARD ROAST FLOW
ISLE ELDER ENTER AULA
CHIMPANZEE BALDEAGLES
TEMPERA LABILE ENOUGH
SNEAKERS MARL STET
LED CLINT FOOTSORE
BRAES CHINCHILLAS REV
OILS OLIN DEAD LANA
SOL GRIZZLYBEAR MONAD
STILETTO EOAN TOGGLE
GENIE LUNT BAYOU
JUAREZ IAINT ARRESTED
ALTOS ASIATICLION AYE
SCOT LEAD ACTS INRE
PER REDKANGAROO ASSAM
ERSKINES INSET OWL
ENTS SLAP TORNARIA
UBANGI BASTED NIEMANN
RHINOCEROS CROCODILES
GAME LLANO TOALL CEPA
ERST ESSEN SPREE STE

19

SONIC PARIAH JUICED
EPICAL EVERSO ARCANE
MILITARYINTELLIGENCE
DIN TSETSE YULE NOD
STEER COO BOWLS WORE
CESSATION TOTAL WANED
SWOON PRIOR PAT
FRA DON DIAL DIVERSE
LAUREL SUNG STAKERACE
ATSEA SALTI TIME SVEN
ATHLETICSCHOLARSHIP
ATEE NENE OAKEN TENTH
PARAKEETS MIES REDEEM
ETERNAL HERR GOA SRS
SOS SEEDY SAULT
CLEAT STORY POSTTIMES
LOLL TERSE SUR HOERS
OCA SHEA STRATH SAT
SANITARYSEWERSYSTEMS
ELEVEN ETOILE RENTEE
RETYPE DANGER STARS

20

DUB SLOES KAPPA IKON
ITEM LARCH IDEAL NILE
SABU AMATO MALTA CELA
CHERRYBLOSSOMFESTIVAL
AYES HEN KIT
LASSER PROPOSE ADEEM
ASTAS DAUNT HEW ASSAI
ISAK BARGE BOREAL TNT
KAMIKAZE CAGIER TOGO
AMP ONES AGUE ROSSO
ATTS JAPAN BALK
SAMOA PAIR ARNE MSS
ALBA MASUDA NAGASAKI
ZEN ASPENS ARTIE TRIN
OPENS OUT GREEN BRINE
TRAIL DYNAMOS BRINKS
INE ISR ALAN
THELANDOFTHERISINGSUN
AIRS TIBER SATIN UPSA
LENO EMILE TREAD PEER
EDEN NESTS SEANS ERA

21

DADO TREES FARO RILL
EDER RANAT AMAN OBEAH
NOBODYGETSADIME METRO
ERR ISERE LIEUT ARSON
BEAIIIT ORSON SHA IISA
RISE PEGS !SPAHAN
ARNA USSR TORTONI
SHOWACREDITCARDOR NFC
TATLER ARGUERS CUKOR
APH SALT CDT RESPIRE
ISIT WHOSQUEALED STET
RONDELS IUM OSSA OSO
EDGES PLEASER ELEVEN
SYD THISISNTHALLOWEEN
ONEIRIC EENY ERNE
TRIESTE ALEE SILL
SENT ANS INLET NOLOAN
ANGLO ITALO PRIAM IDA
RAPID CRUISECANCELLED
STOKE AILE VODKA SOLE
APES LADS ATEAR UFER

22

SCALAS COBALT ABBA
TAMALE ORATOR SAULT
MONUMENTVALLEY HELPED
EGALE RENEE STERLING
SIDED CENT STEV ENOS
SEAT FRET BASSI TER
ARA RECAP LEI
ABC DITTYBAG BALANCE
CARELESS ENSLAVER AMS
CLOVEN EARN ITA ORIA
EDWARDS STORM LAPLAND
DINS OBI NANO CRIMEA
ENE OFFENDER ACCIDENT
GRADATE REAFFIRM LTS
NEI KAREL VUE
ASA RESIT OKIE ALAS
EDIT FILM ERIC DRIVE
CAROLINA PELEE ERGOT
AMALIE VERNONVIRGINIA
STIEL IRONIC REAVED
SAND CETANE ASSESS

23

SKIP LOPE PAPPI CHOP
AUTO EASEL ORION EURO
THEEDUCATEDSOUTHERNER
ENAMELER PRESS EDISON
SNED SHARE ORES
AFFAIR REAMS MINERAL
LAIRS HANNA KITS ELI
LUNE JOIST SKIT LAIT
ANE SOUSE CHIN BUDGE
HASNOUSE BLOND FORANR
TEASE TRUNK DRAIN
EXCEPT SEINE GOESDOWN
LEADS EASY ERGOT THE
INKS MARK TWAIN SHIN
TIE GAEL SIEVE GEESE
EASTEND SABRE CLERKS
ENDS ELVES ARES
FASCIA ADAIR ALABAMAN
ATTHEBEGINNINGOFAWORD
LOAN ERECT ABAFT ETTA
AMBO LASTS SALT DESK

24

RICE COMFY TOAD GOVT
ALAN OVERT SEULE ELEE
WELCOMEMAT LATECOMERS
LIENS REARS IDIOTS
COLTS DIRKS ASUN
ROSE RUSE INIMICAL
COMERS COMESINTO OLE
AWED UNTO MAIN EMIT
SES UPANDCOMING TRENT
TROUSER ATONE PARSES
USURY SCAPE CAROB
AETNAS NEHRU OSTLERS
TOWEL COMEUPPANCE TAI
ASIA ARTI ANYA TWIN
MIT NEWCOMERS LAREDO
INHOCKTO CUTE TIES
FAYE SETHS SATAN
IREFUL AMATI UNTIL
COMEDOWNON COMEACROSS
EMIR SINKS ANEEL UNIT
SALS ENSE LEASE NONE

25

SHARP CAPA BOUND
APACHE ROWAN ELASTIC
GARRETHOBART MARSHALL
ATREE AMAR SUMMER TIO
NEYS AMPLE HEED ARNE
ASS INLET JILTS FLITS
TINTED LOMAS BIMBOS
BARONET MAHAN JENSEN
ETUDES CONN SOIE
SAMAR LILAC SHINDIG
STAT WILLIAMKING MEIN
NEMESIS LAIRS ABODE
ALLA HINT ALURES
JANGLE LEONS ALLEGES
COLONS ROGUE APPOSE
OHARA HERON ARLEN DSC
ANBA COMA TRIOS NATO
SSA SHRINE ADAM AILED
TOMPKINS ALBENBARKLEY
NATIVES SAONE STEALS
NADER TROT HESSE

26

CALF DEBUT AAR SWAB
RIEL ABASH ARMOR HOWE
ODEA CORNERSTONE ANON
WARTORN FACES CASTLE
TROY PANEL RENT
FIJIAN ALIGN SUITABLE
ENURE FIRETRAPPS UAR
ACME AMIE IMET DRIN
SUP ABANDONHOPE HENRI
TRISTATE BAITS DIVIDE
NORSE IRT LIMON
LEGREE GRECO DERANGED
ALBEE CROSSRHODES BEA
CIEL PLOT YEAR CURT
KHA TRIPHAMMER BASIE
SUNSHINE RUINS BOTHER
CAME CITRA LOLA
ARCANE HOSEA ELOCUTE
POUR RAISEDCAINE OPEN
ELBA SIREN LINTY MDLI
SLAB TEC ELTON BOLD

27

ALEPH DUB SPA CHASE
DIXIE EROSION OATEN
ASPEN SIXTEENTHNOTE
MAL KENT RASPS
EGO PRIMA SANE
NATAL LOTS ALI LASS
EXILE ALE OXEN POE
VIVA BYE SKIDS MESA
ALEXIUS SARAS SAXON
INN TIDAL LAX
SEXES TEXAS FELINES
AXIS MANET DOG MERY
CII AXES HEX MIXIN
STIR NET KOBE AZTEC
OATS SEATS REO
ASANA FLEX FRA
EXPRESSIONIST PEKIN
SLEET EXPENSE EXIST
SEEDS WEE GET GENES

28

GOLF ASH SOI ESTA
EVIAN ITOR ERN ATOR
ROBROYRUSTYNAILSOUR
ARMED TEAS TIERRA
GITA ARAL MEDIA ESS
ADIGE OLEG EARTH
BLOODYMARYBULLSHOT
SEN MAES RISES RUED
CURS PORES POSER
ARMAND CASTS LINENS
LAIRD TORCH GALE
BIRD TRITO ARIL MOW
DAIQUIRIPINACOLADA
COUNT ENID WILES
SOL IGETA SLAT NASH
ADEPTS WRIT TUBER
GIMLETMARTINIRICKEY
ALAI EON OLEO DUETO
NENE NAG LON TYES

29

BAN TART FEIST GEAR
SYNE LUNAR ESTEE RARE
ALAW AROSE STERN ERIN
CAMBODIA NOT MINDANAO
SWEETEN STRAD FEET
RON SWOLLEN REVERS
SHINE MAINE FEZ PILOT
HOT CATT SLEEP CLUE
OREL ALI ARIADNE TEST
PARISIAN CANTS STONE
EASY DANKE BEAR
PECOS HEDGE PATRIOTS
RESH OLIVIER ETA ASEA
ERST NORIA EROS LAB
SLEET PAL MANOR ECOLE
TENNIS MEGATON ETH
STOA DULLS ASTASIA
SANTIAGO TEA GOTEBORG
ALOE RIVET THERE LAKE
YETI ELATE LILTS IVES
SEEN DELED SETA SED

30

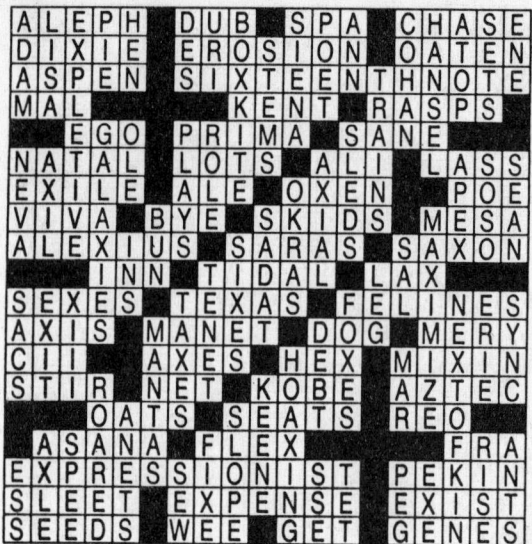

MECCAN ACTI TEAMSTER
AVERSE POUF ARMATURE
BERATE ALTO PIECESOF8
UTI ALLURES ERR DEB
TALENTS ISAR FRONTERA
HEED ESSE LIAR SOREL
ERA DRIES LEGIST ESEL
9INNINGS SETOUT
OPENARMS 4HORSEMEN
LAGOS EMCEES NEGATE
ELIS 7DEADLYSINS BIAS
ATREUS ELSECO PELTS
FIDDLERS3 STRINGER
MADAME CHAPTER1
TAPE SOREST SLUBS LAS
AYRES ANTE MEMO METO
KEENNESS EASE UNRIVEN
EAT OXA ASFATAS IRA
5YEARPLAN OLAN AGATHA
ESTEEMED RENO DOGEAR
STARLETS 2MAN DREDGE

31

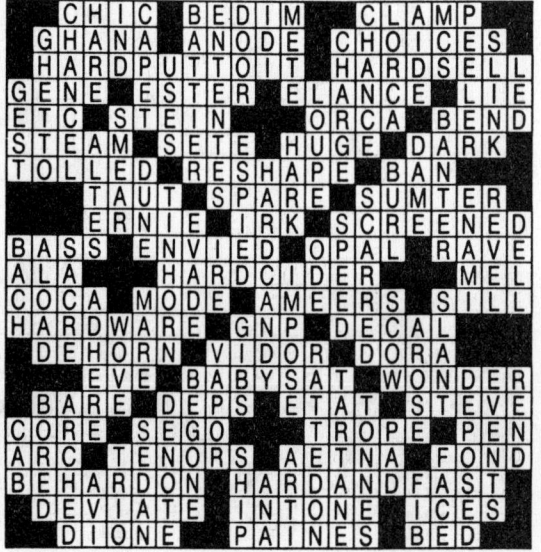

CHIC BEDIM CLAMP
GHANA ANODE CHOICES
HARDPUTTOIT HARDSELL
GENE ESTER ELANCE LIE
ETC STEIN ORCA BEND
STEAM SETE HUGE DARK
TOLLED RESHAPE BAN
TAUT SPARE SUMTER
ERNIE IRK SCREENED
BASS ENVIED OPAL RAVE
ALA HARDCIDER MEL
COCA MODE AMEERS SILL
HARDWARE GNP DECAL
DEHORN VIDOR DORA
EVE BABYSAT WONDER
BARE DEPS ETAT STEVE
CORE SEGO TROPE PEN
ARC TENORS AETNA FOND
BEHARDON HARDANDFAST
DEVIATE INTONE ICES
DIONE PAINES BED

32

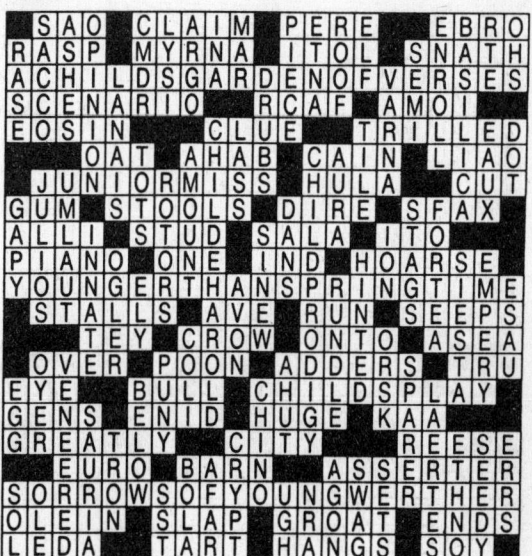

SAO CLAIM PERE EBRO
RASP MYRNA ITOL SNATH
ACHILDSGARDENOFVERSES
SCENARIO RCAF AMOI
EOSIN CLUE TRILLED
OAT AHAB CAIN LIAO
JUNIORMISS HULA CUT
GUM STOOLS DIRE SFAX
ALLI STUD SALA ITO
PIANO ONE IND HOARSE
YOUNGERTHANSPRINGTIME
STALLS AVE RUN SEEPS
TEY CROW ONTO ASEA
OVER POON ADDERS TRU
EYE BULL CHILDSPLAY
GENS ENID HUGE KAA
GREATLY CITY REESE
EURO BARN ASSERTER
SORROWSOFYOUNGWERTHER
OLEIN SLAP GROAT ENDS
LEDA TART HANGS SOY

33

SERAI BOTH ELSE SCRAP
ACORN ERIE METE ERICA
CHUCKWAGON PHILOSOPHY
KOT BESS CLEAR PASSES
FLAT WHIRR SAMS
MAROONS AMMO RULE DSC
ABORT CHEERLESS FOAL
LUGE AKRON ATA DONNA
ITES UNTO RAYON ROWDY
CORTEGE MANOR SIDE
ENA THENICKOFTIME NOB
NAUT ALCES CORRODE
RADII EPICS MEEK EWES
IRONS TEA HORSE PONT
SMUT TORCHSONG HOUSE
EST TONY OINK STARRED
SONS DUKES TOIT
SALAMI CUSHY PARR ALB
IRAACCOUNT BILLANDCOO
VIOLA ARNO ETAL EUROS
ASSET KEEN EATS TEENS

34

DEBAR ASIS AREA CHKS
STARE REPLETION HORA
CHRISTMASISLAND REINS
ENDEAR OCTAL REISSUE
ORO TRES EHS CESS SST
NEWS PSAND SHANT KIT
MALT STIB CHAR EMIR
ELSAS NEUROTIC ADINF
TAINT NOWISE SENOR
CFH NOON SCENTS SEGNO
ALA TOPIS SMITE LES
COPRA ECHOES AURA EST
TOPIC THANKS SMILE
IDYLL SORCERER SALMI
NEAT LOAD TORE ROAD
AME UHLAN EASEL LICE
NOW SOUS BEN ELIA TAM
ALYSSUM CURIE EASTER
TEETH ACHRISTMASCAROL
SAGO NOISELESS ARENA
TRET DONT ESTE PARIS

35

HEPTA ALPS CAMB DAME
ACRID GARE RTEI PERAK
DRONE EMENDATED ONINE
JUSTPRESSDOWNTOCLOSE
PETE IER ARIETTAS
PIER TRADE ARN TREATY
ARC PROBE ANO STEN
SATURATE ATNOTIME ERE
PULLTABTODETACH
EAST SIRE MAROONED
TRAILER MISSA LENTILS
APOLOGIA TAXI ELMO
TWISTTOOPENSEAL
ASP ELEANORS ENLISTED
PERS UPS DREAD RNA
EMOTER HTS PATEN SEEM
TIMENOTE NAN ETTE
TURNHERETOLIFTTHELID
COLLI RENOVATOR ERICA
ANGES MAIN CERE INNER
BEET STDS ESAS REESE

36

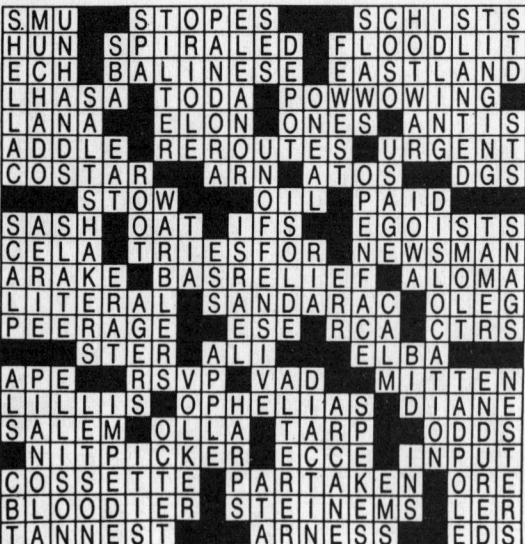

SMU STOPES SCHISTS
HUN SPIRALED FLOODLIT
ECH BALINESE EASTLAND
LHASA TODA POWWOWING
LANA ELON ONES ANTIS
ADDLE REROUTES URGENT
COSTAR ARN ATOS DGS
STOW OIL PAID
SASH OAT IFS EGOISTS
CELA TRIESFOR NEWSMAN
ARAKE BASRELIEF ALOMA
LITERAL SANDARAC OLEG
PEERAGE ESE RCA CTRS
STER ALI ELBA
APE RSVP VAD MITTEN
LILLIS OPHELIAS DIANE
SALEM OLLA TARP ODDS
NITPICKER ECCE INPUT
COSSETTE PARTAKEN ORE
BLOODIER STEINEMS LER
TANNEST ARNESS EDS

37

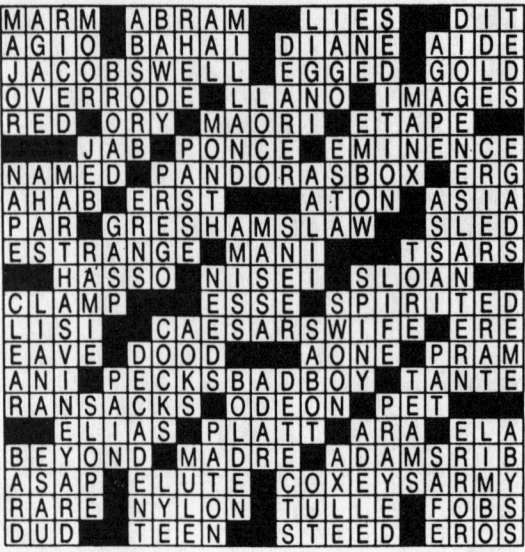

MARM ABRAM LIES DIT
AGIO BAHAI DIANE AIDE
JACOBSWELL EGGED GOLD
OVERRODE LLANO IMAGES
RED ORY MAORI ETAPE
JAB PONCE EMINENCE
NAMED PANDORASBOX ERG
AHAB ERST ATON ASIA
PAR GRESHAMSLAW SLED
ESTRANGE MANI TSARS
HASSO NISEI SLOAN
CLAMP ESSE SPIRITED
LISI CAESARSWIFE ERE
EAVE DOOD AONE PRAM
ANI PECKSBADBOY TANTE
RANSACKS ODEON PET
ELIAS PLATT ARA ELA
BEYOND MADRE ADAMSRIB
ASAP ELUTE COXEYSARMY
RARE NYLON TULLE FOBS
DUD TEEN STEED EROS

38

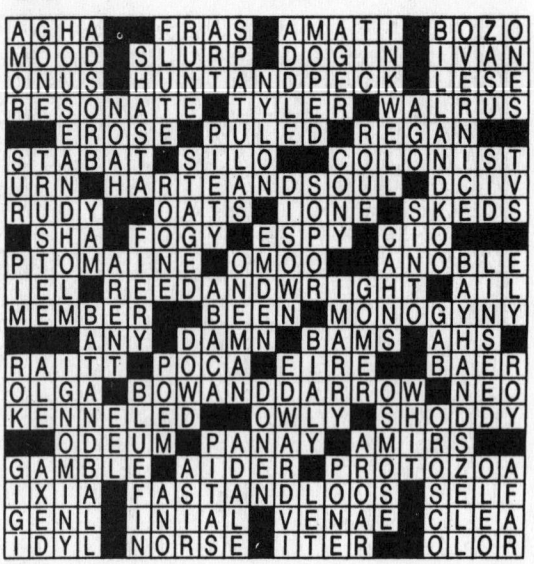

AGHA FRAS AMATI BOZO
MOOD SLURP DOGIN IVAN
ONUS HUNTANDPECK LESE
RESONATE TYLER WALRUS
EROSE PULED REGAN
STABAT SILO COLONIST
URN HARTEANDSOUL DCIV
RUDY OATS IONE SKEDS
SHA FOGY ESPY CIO
PTOMAINE OMOO ANOBLE
IEL REEDANDWRIGHT AIL
MEMBER BEEN MONOGYNY
ANY DAMN BAMS AHS
RAITT POCA EIRE BAER
OLGA BOWANDDARROW NEO
KENNELED OWLY SHODDY
ODEUM PANAY AMIRS
GAMBLE AIDER PROTOZOA
IXIA FASTANDLOOS SELF
GENL INIAL VENAE CLEA
IDYL NORSE ITER OLOR

39

SHAD MIST ADELA COPT
TOTE ANTE LOSES ANAIL
AURA OTIS IDEAS PERFS
IRID ACTING FORE&AFT
NIP&TUCK REEF CERAM
GENTLER SOB ASLOPE
SECOND EMIT ROAD LUTE
PRONTO ROTI TOLES RAN
UNSEEN TAM STARTS
MET DES ETE ISSUANCE
ESEL HIDE&SEEK GEOL
STRIPPED TEN AIR SAL
EARLES INA NETTLE
BED DIVAN DAME STOLEN
STEP META ETON TOWERS
CAMERA EKE ORATION
UNITS EGER BILL&COO
FAR&NEAR RESALE GANG
ARRIS LEPER RIRE OVER
DIENE AMATI ENCE WIRE
ARKS DOUSE AGES NESS

40

HEATER SASHAYS CARPAL
ALPINE EMPIRIC AVERSE
RAILAT PERSONA REMOTE
THEDRAFT AMST BRIBER
EERIE ANA LOTTERY
CHIS DEMANDSUPON
LAD ASS DAH NRA FEAST
ASTAR PATE COMEANDGO
STAGEDOOR RIOT NICETY
PAGANINI ASTIR DRESS
AMENDE GLASSY
MARCO CURIO CAUTIONS
MILIEU IMIN STOPANDGO
ALLBUTHAD SOPS LODAR
CLASS ANU AWE ABE EIR
ADAMSNEEDLE TROY
CHARADE ADD ATREE
REFOLD NEMO TOANDFRO
ENTAIL IMPULSE TEDIUM
SCONCE MEATIER EMERGE
SENSED BUNSENS SYRIAN

41

RADOM COOLER APHID
DINERO ARRIVED IRENE
LOVEMEORLEAVEME ROAST
EMOTIONAL DERANGE RTE
MELO OVUM MITE STAN
ASI LOVEPOTION LAMONT
VOWEL BOAR GIFTS
LAVER RIMMED CALM
ABELES CELEB ILOVEYOU
METS WOMENINLOVE HRS
ILSE SERI AUBE BEBE
SIF SWEETHEARTS LAIR
HEARTILY OLDIE SMARTS
LOAM STOVES ALIST
SOLON AKES ADORE
ELISSA HEARTACHES CAN
RENT BREN ETTE LOPE
VOL COOLIES LIRIPIPES
IOOTO DIDNTHAVEAHEART
CIVIL SOIREES TRIGLY
ELECT SAYSIT OESES

42

ANT ADEPT BELT NEIN
ROW ERROR UTAH ORLE
AVE ROARINGTWENTIES
BALLAST DALE FINEST
VATS LESE WACO
ISERE PANT GATEWAYS
GLAD FORTYNINER POE
NIP WALK IVES TRUE
IDOLIZE CAVES BAIRN
SATE COVER FURL
PATCH HUMAN JUMPFOR
ISLE MARE POMP IMA
ETE NINETOFIVE AFAR
DISTENDS VANE SUTRA
OPUS MERE CONE
SARLAT PART LOITERS
THEELEVENTHHOUR NIL
USED LIES EAGLE TVA
BOLO YARE RIODE HEM

43

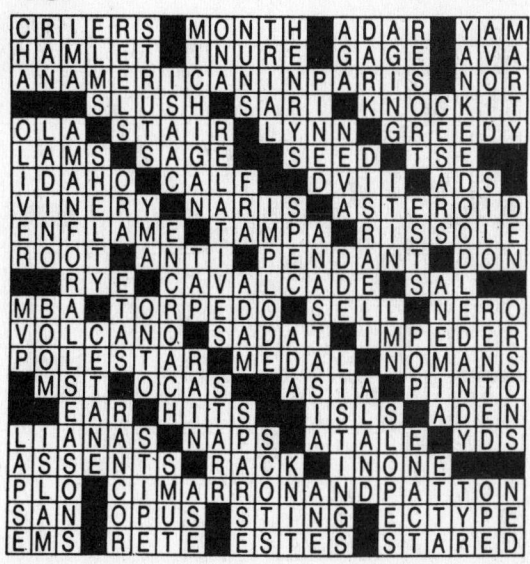

CRIERS MONTH ADAR YAM
HAMLET INURE GAGE AVA
ANAMERICANINPARIS NOR
SLUSH SARI KNOCKIT
OLA STAIR LYNN GREEDY
LAMS SAGE SEED TSE
IDAHO CALF DVII ADS
VINERY NARIS ASTEROID
ENFLAME TAMPA RISSOLE
ROOT ANTI PENDANT DON
RYE CAVALCADE SAL
MBA TORPEDO SELL NERO
VOLCANO SADAT IMPEDER
POLESTAR MEDAL NOMANS
MST OCAS ASIA PINTO
EAR HITS ISLS ADEN
LIANAS NAPS ATALE YDS
ASSENTS RACK INONE
PLO CIMARRONANDPATTON
SAN OPUS STING ECTYPE
EMS RETE ESTES STARED

44

ERRED RIATA ASS LAW
LIEGES BOSLEY PEPTONE
OFFONESROCKER REROUTE
NEE OLIO HATE DAWNED
RATED PILE BALING
GARDEN CHAIRWOMEN EDH
ALAI AMOI HUBS CLEO
YALTA ORAL SOLOS HILL
SADDLESHOES SIZED
ADS TRES SCUP SENATE
LITERAL SOT SPEARER
APODAL CORE DIET DDS
MOODY JOHNNYBENCH
OLLA RAZES ERIC EMBER
DAPS ONOS ESEL ALOE
ERI COUNTYSEAT ASCENT
GROSSE OINK TREES
EXEUNT NUNC HUGE SAW
PRONGED OTTOMANEMPIRE
HANGERS THEDAY REINED
AYS RST ASRED DEGAS

45

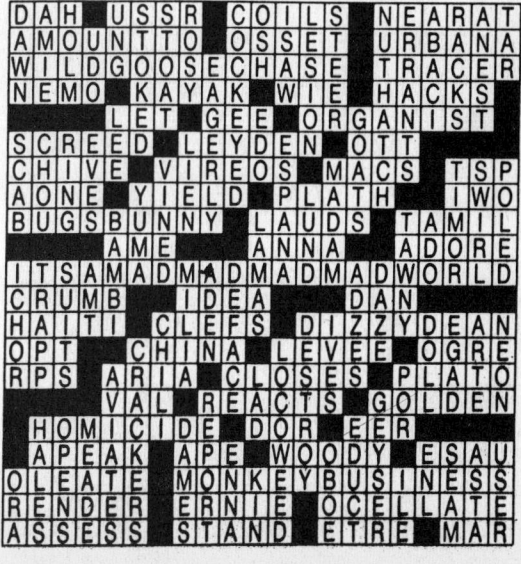

DAH USSR COILS NEARAT
AMOUNTTO OSSET URBANA
WILDGOOSECHASE TRACER
NEMO KAYAK WIE HACKS
LET GEE ORGANIST
SCREED LEYDEN OTT
CHIVE VIREOS MACS TSP
AONE YIELD PLATH IWO
BUGSBUNNY LAUDS TAMIL
AME ANNA ADORE
ITSAMADMADMADMADWORLD
CRUMB IDEA DAN
HAITI CLEFS DIZZYDEAN
OPT CHINA LEVEE OGRE
RPS ARIA CLOSES PLATO
VAL REACTS GOLDEN
HOMICIDE DOR EER
APEAK APE WOODY ESAU
OLEATE MONKEYBUSINESS
RENDER ERNIE OCELLATE
ASSESS STAND ETRE MAR

46

```
STAB SADIST CRAFT
ECOLE ENORME REPROS
RAISEARUCKUS ANTENOR
WILL CRICK TENT ETUI
OCA PHIAL CIRCE FIND
KARMA ALE PANNE SONDE
OTO SAVINGS CARESS
COVERT RITES LAMA
PARENTIS RCA REBELLED
ERNST SELAH GAGA LEDA
RBI BATTLEROYAL GIT
DOTH ENID SABOT ACUTE
UNHIDDEN LIN NEWCOMER
TRIS SONAR SOTTED
SYSTEM SPOTTED NIE
PECHE CHINO HEM OSCAR
IMRE CHINS ASIAN ABA
NEED RANG ASPEN FLAW
SNEEZER ANYTHINGGOES
INCEPT REDOES LEASE
SKEES NOSIDE OLLA
```

47

```
TRAP MOWED CARMEL SST
OONA IRANI ANITRA THE
WYNNBLAISEANDSHAW OEN
ECU AINT TARES SERED
RELATE CHOP URARE
HOUKLAINEANDSINGER
MILAN RUNNY REACT ESE
ODOR SALAD HEDDA ASTR
REDDYWILLIGANDABEL
RAG AITS OKAY SETAL
ITE HTS PATES SOT AMO
SERIO DONT MILA BAR
LOCKESTACKANDBERLE
COLE LANAI HINGE LIIN
ORA FETID CADET OOZES
WAYNEWYMANANDSOONG
STONE OPTO BIERCE
LOVED ASONE ASTO EEL
IRE BALLBOKANDKENDALL
PIR ATTAIN NAZIS IDLE
SOS GHETTO AGENT NEON
```

48

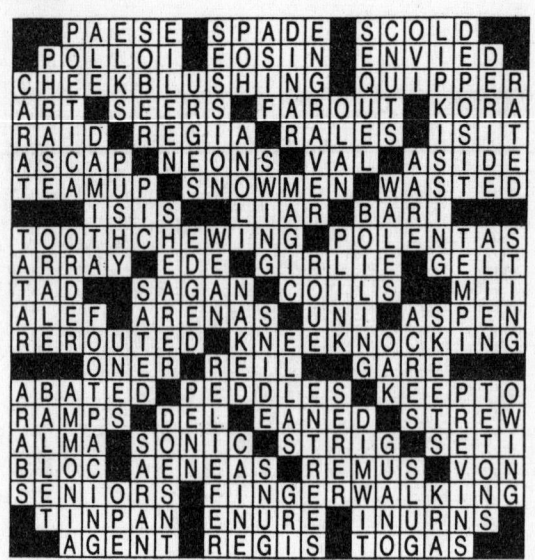

```
PAESE SPADE SCOLD
POLLOI EOSIN ENVIED
CHEEKBLUSHING QUIPPER
ART SEERS FAROUT KORA
RAID REGIA RALES ISIT
ASCAP NEONS VAL ASIDE
TEAMUP SNOWMEN WASTED
ISIS LIAR BARI
TOOTHCHEWING POLENTAS
ARRAY EDE GIRLIE GELT
TAD SAGAN COILS MII
ALEF ARENAS UNI ASPEN
REROUTED KNEEKNOCKING
ONER REIL GARE
ABATED PEDDLES KEEPTO
RAMPS DEL EANED STREW
ALMA SONIC STRIG SETI
BLOC AENEAS REMUS VON
SENIORS FINGERWALKING
TINPAN ENURE INURNS
AGENT REGIS TOGAS
```

49

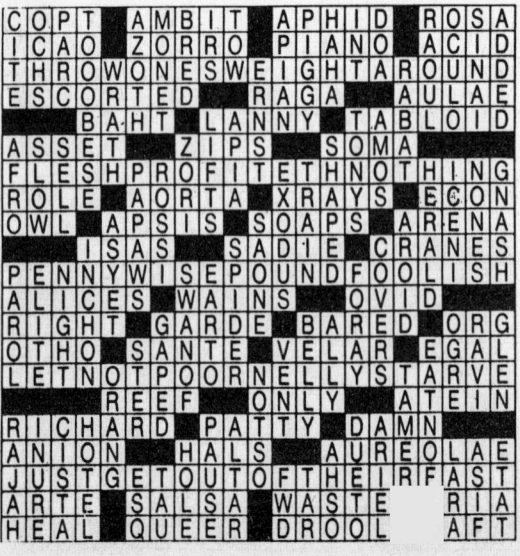

```
COPT AMBIT APHID ROSA
ICAO ZORRO PIANO ACID
THROWONESWEIGHTAROUND
ESCORTED RAGA AULAE
BAHT LANNY TABLOID
ASSET ZIPS SOMA
FLESHPROFITETHNOTHING
ROLE AORTA XRAYS ECON
OWL APSIS SOAPS ARENA
ISAS SADIE CRANES
PENNYWISEPOUNDFOOLISH
ALICES WAINS OVID
RIGHT GARDE BARED ORG
OTHO SANTE VELAR EGAL
LETNOTPOORNELLYSTARVE
REEF ONLY ATEIN
RICHARD PATTY DAMN
ANION HALS AUREOLAE
JUSTGETOUTOFTHEIRFAST
ARTE SALSA WASTE RIA
HEAL QUEER DROOL AFT
```

50

```
APORT LANKA PEAL
POWER DEMEAN BAILIFFS
THEQUEENANDI ELSINORE
EXCISED SSE CEREA
ETC SPAN ICHOR INTER
PRESTO PASHA EASY
SOLA SOURCHARITY FAT
ONLY EUBIE RELEE SIVA
MAINE TOM MADAM SCRIP
SORT APHID PELISSE
SGT EASTSIDESTORY TOD
WOODCUT GASPE NEDS
ERNST ESTHS ONS RETRO
ASTO ENDOW ANTHO IRON
REH NOTHINGGOES SEAT
ECOL ORATE CAMERA
BORON BOLET FAUN TSP
AGORA AND IDEALLY
ELONGATE GOODBYEDOLLY
REFUELED ANGELA ADOBE
ARID ISERE YEAST
```

51

GARE SLID RAVI ATTA
OMIT TATA EVEN SHOR
FIFTHAMENDMENT HERA
ONLEAD MIRO TALESOF
ROE LIP SIRE CINEMA
FOURTHESTATE VET
ACNE MAR REAM STE
PRIES MIA LAW ANSE
PENTAS BRIG TIMOTHY
EAT FIRSTFAMILY HIE
ATHLETE SILO ERASES
LESE UTE APO AMOST
YEA ASSN UNC INTO
ADM FIRSTINPEACE
REPAIR EAVE SPA ASP
INHIBIT TEES ELISHA
VIOL SECONDWORLDWAR
ERNE EDER LADE LARK
ROYS SSTS EKED ENDS

52

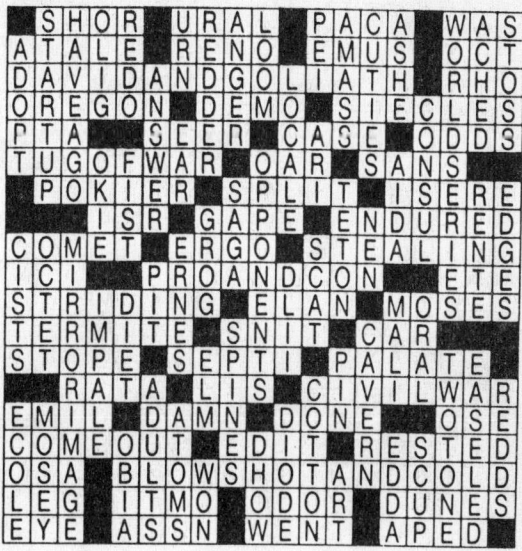

SHOR URAL PACA WAS
ATALE RENO EMUS OCT
DAVIDANDGOLIATH RHO
OREGON DEMO SIECLES
PTA SEER CASE ODDS
TUGOFWAR OAR SANS
POKIER SPLIT ISERE
ISR GAPE ENDURED
COMET ERGO STEALING
ICI PROANDCON ETE
STRIDING ELAN MOSES
TERMITE SNIT CAR
STOPE SEPTI PALATE
RATA LIS CIVILWAR
EMIL DAMN DONE OSE
COMEOUT EDIT RESTED
OSA BLOWSHOTANDCOLD
LEG ITMO ODOR DUNES
EYE ASSN WENT APED

53

BARGAIN SMELL SHORTS
AVARICE PEORIA COVERT
TOTALED ACTIAN ANEMIA
TWIN FATHERSUPERIOR
LAND COARSE ITE CLE
ELEPHANTS RHINE DOLED
AEDES STUNG VALET
FARMER ALIGN PILE
OTOOLE PRIME GLEE MAN
STOSS BRIDE DRAW TOPO
SITE SOUSE GOATS HALL
IRES CONE ANODE HENIE
LED CANE ADORE ROGETS
MARE DRUMS ERODES
TSARS UNITE KNEAD
FIKED ISAAC UNCLEMAME
AGE SMU HELIOS ORAL
THEMANFROMAUNT TRIM
ATTILA PLEURA MACHINE
LEERER ELINOR GRIEVER
ENRAGE RANTS SCORERS

54

ALAR EDDA RESHIP MAT
PELE ERRED ESPANA ORE
EVEL NOOSE STERES RES
RICEANDWILDEOATES EAT
GREEN LEPRE UGH
DAGAMAS VOIDS SPRANG
ELATED LILT ESP OLOR
EGRETS UNI BACCA WERE
RADS COOKEBURNSLAMB
SEN SPEE EEL INTENSE
EMAIL BLARE BEARD
DERANGE AEC PERT FRA
READESNOWWHITE PRON
ARNI KARLS MOE STROUD
CODS ISO TAMP PRESTO
OSBORN HBOMB COASTER
UNA SCORN CORGI
BAT STEELEGRAYBRIDGES
ALL PANAMA ACCRA ERNE
DIE ERASES MILAN NETS
EAR DETEST IDES TWOS

55

JOHN CAWED CHIC
HOUSE ALATE HULAS
HOUSTONTEXAS AMENTS
EAST LACE MINTS AOK
ART WITH WIRES CVII
DESPITE CANED ELECT
USH GALES AGAR
ERASE LOCKS INGRATE
RASH COATI ANNEALED
EDT LANDINGGEAR FAG
CARNAGES SEERS ALME
TROOPER SPENT BRASS
NEED BEAST FEE
SHALL FARCE BLASTED
IOUS BELIE HEAR AME
POT KOREA OAST AREA
SPITED FLIGHTCENTER
SCARE ULTRA ASTER
SUNS LYSES REAR

56

DRAT MORPH SOLAR CSA
EACH TORERO UTILE OHM
MYHEARTSTOODSTILL NIB
SETSHOT PTAH IDLE
PUTSAFOOTINTHEDOOR
TYPOS NESW EYEWASH
SOUTHPAWDELIVERIES
ADS AHAB NADER EDA
RES NARY ALLIS PAYER
LYCEES EROSE ROBERT
FALLHEADOVERHEELS
ADONIS ANGLE EMMETS
BIOTA ARTIE OGLE RUE
APT RUNON COOS AND
READINGISTOTHEMIND
STEUBEN HAEC LENYA
CLEARINGONESTHROAT
HEAP SEAS EXTINES
EAR SPEAKFROMTHEHEART
EVE PANDA DORIAN RILE
RED ALDER ANSON SLEW

57

ARAB SABIN CASAS
MEDAL PURSE OCULO
OPERA EBONS NEILS
READTHERIOTACTTO
ALLI EDEL BEAST
CAGEY CABAL
APO LID BABEL SSR
DEWIER ORNE ETTA
DANCEATTENDANCEON
ELEE ETNA GEORGE
DER ARMET REE NYE
SMEAR LENDS
AGLEE SAND ESSA
DRINKTHEHEALTHOF
MIAMI SEROW ATOLL
EMMET ALARE EERIE
MESSY RICED ENDA

58

USSR NOM RVS BEAST
TATI EMIL BEIT AVENUE
ABUNDANCE OTOE TENANT
HUNGARIANGOULASH ERIN
ILE ABRADE BALSA
SPANISHONIONS ROES
PUNG TERATOS RAPT COT
INN LASS MICE BLUR
NYET SENT SWISSCHEESE
EDEN BOONE ELATE
MEXICANJUMPINGBEANS
AURAS JONAS ALLY
FRENCHTOAST LILY SAMP
ARCS EARN SANE LIE
RAT BALD SATURNS BERN
DOLL CANADIANBACON
LATEX OKAPIS AAS
OWEN SWEDISHMEATBALLS
ONEIDA CREE PORCELAIN
TENSES KENS SUCH TINA
DYERS SST SHY STEP

59

GASP SALEP PURER PHAR
ETTA AMOLE OPERA OESE
ETAL TOPDRESSING SATE
SURPRISE TEED OUTDID
AINT BLAST AURUM
GAMBLE ARAN ALTERANT
ONALL ACUTABOVE ESAU
DINE PINIC EREA STIB
ETO MAKETHEFURFLY EVE
TARTARE AIR EAGRES
ONIN SARTO OSLO
EMBOGS TNT LAISSEZ
TOR THERAZORSEDGE ASE
HOUR MAIA EERIE BUTS
ESSE MARCHHARE TAROT
REHASHED OERS CANOPY
ACTOR GERMS MALI
CASHEW LAIS PARISIAN
ASIF LEARNEDHAND TOGA
LIDO EPODE DONNE ENID
ISER RISER SITAR RANA

60

CAGY BANAL CABOT ABED
AURA ELENA AGAPE SOLO
STOKERANDFURNESS HOBO
ERA AARE INNER TARTAR
DYNASTY STIES MARAH
TEE SITAR AUTOMATA
EPHOD SWEETANDLOW NIP
ZOOM TUAN ODER EDGE
REM FASTANDLOOS CALOR
AMERICAS ORES SATINY
ROBIN PRATE SOREN
CHALET ATMO SCIENCES
LINER CASHANDCARY OKA
OLDS COBH ERRS CLEF
SUP BLUEANDGREY RONDE
EMIGRANT AULAE HEL
DEIST UNCUT LANTERN
UGGAMS TREAT JUNE LIE
TIER WHISTLERANDWOLFE
ALOE AUDIT NUDGE HELD
HAND READE STEEL ONES

61

SAAR SPAT BED ROSES
ORME TORAH ALTO UNCLE
MEASURETREASURE NAHUM
MASHNOTE RELEE GOGOL
ASSAILS PESOS CRUEL
POL SETON PROTRACT
PACES SNOOPGROUP ROI
ERRS SEEN OISE RSVP
LIE LEASTBEAST MODES
FLATWORK ARISE MEMORY
TRIES SPURT FIDEL
CRUETS SCENE CONSOLED
HARES SHORTSNORT ARE
ONES MEAT APTS CRIB
PUT EARTHGIRTH LOSES
SPECTATE ERNES GIN
ALANS BLOCS MASCARA
SCENT SALSA AIRLINES
BOHAN STRESSESTRESSES
ELEVE POOR ESTEE EASE
GORED AWN PART REES

62

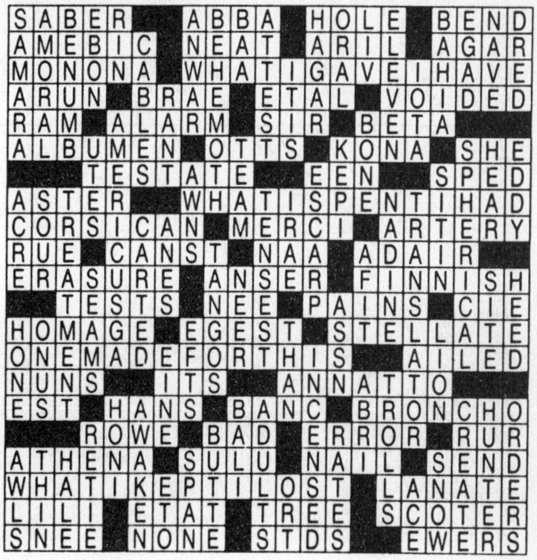
SABER ABBA HOLE BEND
AMEBIC NEAT ARIL AGAR
MONONA WHATIGAVEIHAVE
ARUN BRAE ETAL VOIDED
RAM ALARM SIR BETA
ALBUMEN OTTS KONA SHE
TESTATE EEN SPED
ASTER WHATISPENTIHAD
CORSICAN MERCI ARTERY
RUE CANST NAA ADAIR
ERASURE ANSER FINNISH
TESTS NEE PAINS CIE
HOMAGE EGEST STELLATE
ONEMADEFORTHIS AILED
NUNS ITS ANNATTO
EST HANS BANC BRONCHO
ROWE BAD ERROR RUR
ATHENA SULU NAIL SEND
WHATIKEPTILOST LANATE
LILI ETAT TREE SCOTER
SNEE NONE STDS EWERS

63

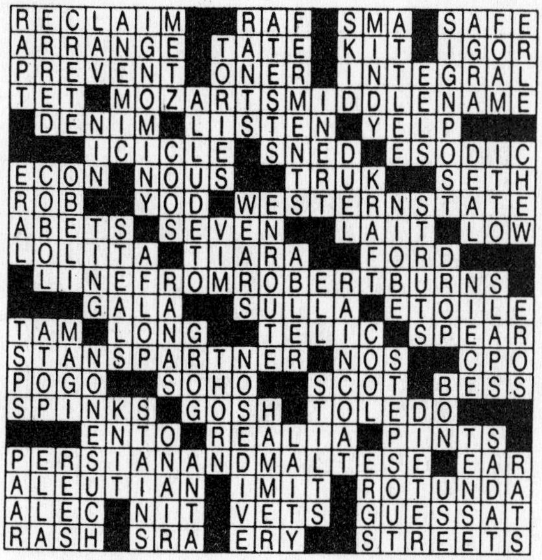
RECLAIM RAF SMA SAFE
ARRANGE TATE KIT IGOR
PREVENT ONER INTEGRAL
TET MOZARTSMIDDLENAME
DENIM LISTEN YELP
ICICLE SNED ESODIC
ECON NOUS TRUK SETH
ROB YOD WESTERNSTATE
ABETS SEVEN LAIT LOW
LOLITA TIARA FORD
LINEFROMROBERTBURNS
GALA SULLA ETOILE
TAM LONG TELIC SPEAR
STANSPARTNER NOS CPO
POGO SOHO SCOT BESS
SPINKS GOSH TOLEDO
ENTO REALIA PINTS
PERSIANANDMALTESE EAR
ALEUTIAN IMIT ROTUNDA
ALEC NIT VETS GUESSAT
RASH SRA ERY STREETS

64

ARCH BAREGE CAB TBAR
BEAR PARADOX LAO OLIO
ALLSTEAMEDUP IRRIGATE
SAC OWL ADE MAENAD
ETAGE IRR ALLBURNEDUP
SERE SMEAR SET ERA
TEA STEP SHAW FRAT
STRONG IFI SERA ISLE
POINTS LOINS WORST
INNER SONNET AMPUTATE
TASSE ESSE ELLA DOVES
ELEGANCE ROWELS EBERT
OTOES SHAGS ETERNE
BETA ODOR ORR LETTER
ALIT NENE STAR ANI
RUM ESS SNITS ELSE
BLEWONESTOP DOS ODEUM
ZODIAC ILL ERR ANO
AMORETTO READYTOBURST
RAND REO EASIEST SNEE
TREY ENL ESSENE SSTS

65

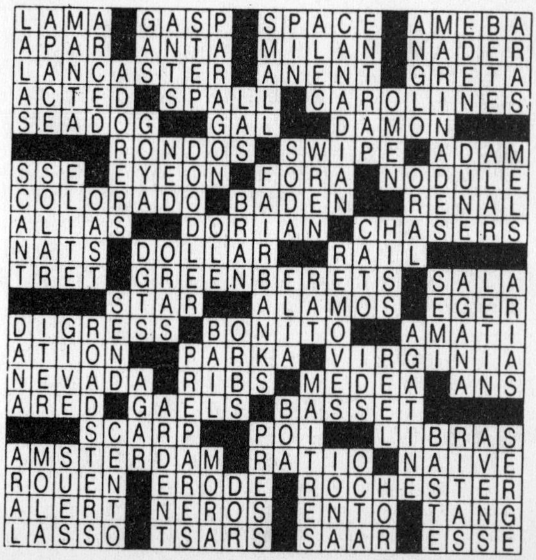
LAMA GASP SPACE AMEBA
APAR ANTA MILAN NADER
LANCASTER ANENT GRETA
ACTED SPALL CAROLINES
SEADOG GAL DAMON
RONDOS SWIPE ADAM
SSE EYEON FORA NODULE
COLORADO BADEN RENAL
ALIAS DORIAN CHASERS
NATS DOLLAR RAIL
TRET GREENBERETS SALA
STAR ALAMOS EGER
DIGRESS BONITO AMATI
ATION PARKA VIRGINIA
NEVADA RIBS MEDEA ANS
ARED GAELS BASSET
SCARP POI LIBRAS
AMSTERDAM RATIO NAIVE
ROUEN ERODE ROCHESTER
ALERT NEROS ENTO TANG
LASSO TSARS SAAR ESSE

66

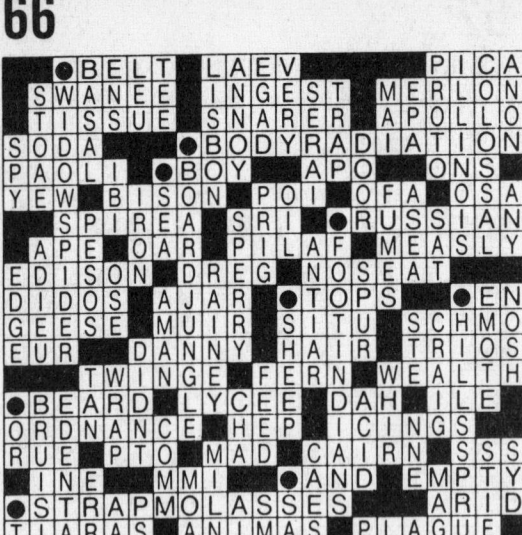

●BELT LAEV PICA
SWANEE INGEST MERLON
TISSUE SNARER APOLLO
SODA ●BODYRADIATION
PAOLI ●BOY APO ONS
YEW BISON POI OFA OSA
SPIREA SRI ●RUSSIAN
APE OAR PILAF MEASLY
EDISON DREG NOSEAT
DIDOS AJAR ●TOPS ●EN
GEESE MUIR SITU SCHMO
EUR DANNY HAIR TRIOS
TWINGE FERN WEALTH
●BEARD LYCEE DAH ILE
ORDNANCE HEP ICINGS
RUE PTO MAD CAIRN SSS
INE MMI ●AND EMPTY
●STRAPMOLASSES ARID
TIARAS ANIMAS PLAGUE
ENTERS BELUGA SONICS
AGED STER TWICE

67

BESSES DALLAS BRUNCH
AMULET ELOISE RESOLE
REGALED COOKIEMONSTER
GRAVYTRAIN ESSE DREAM
AIRE SAC GEN ROE ANI
ITA CTS TEALEAD SST
NANA SOUPANDFISH EYES
DURO ARCA ANTUNG
PISTOL LAC URN AGAPE
EXPOSED WEST EADS PON
LII SMALLPOTATOES PSI
LOC ENKI TYES KNELLED
SNEER MAS RYE DRIERS
ASSAIL SELS RSVP
SPAR TUTTIFRUTTI YIPS
ORT PASSANT MHO EAT
LET ART ASA ENC SORA
ILIAC EONS TURKEYTROT
PUMPKINPAPERS ANEEDLE
EDESSA EPOPEE CAREER
DESEAM CATHER ISERES

68

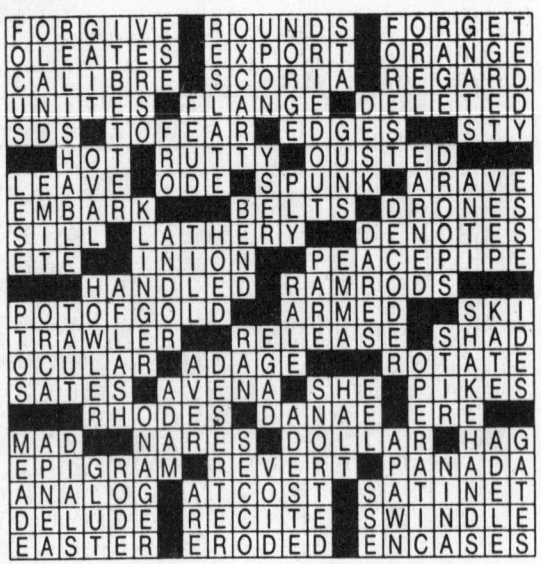

FORGIVE ROUNDS FORGET
OLEATES EXPORT ORANGE
CALIBRE SCORIA REGARD
UNITES FLANGE DELETED
SDS TOFEAR EDGES STY
HOT RUTTY OUSTED
LEAVE ODE SPUNK ARAVE
EMBARK BELTS DRONES
SILL LATHERY DENOTES
ETE INION PEACEPIPE
HANDLED RAMRODS
POTOFGOLD ARMED SKI
TRAWLER RELEASE SHAD
OCULAR ADAGE ROTATE
SATES AVENA SHE PIKES
RHODES DANAE ERE
MAD NARES DOLLAR HAG
EPIGRAM REVERT PANADA
ANALOG ATCOST SATINET
DELUDE RECITE SWINDLE
EASTER ERODED ENCASES

69

HEBE BASER SENSE FRIT
OMAN OPERA CLAIR LALO
PUCCINIANDLEONCAVALLO
ISH CIEL IONIA DETEST
LIED KORAN BITS
SPIES BAMA BRAC ELS
BERNSTEINANDBEETHOVEN
OLENT SKIN EERIE RENA
REPS AKIN SCANT STROP
ANA OMEN SPAT TOI
HAYDNBRITTENANDMOZART
OUI RANT IRAN REO
ARGUS BAIRD AZAN GASP
BANG ULNAE SCAM REGIO
BRAHMSANDRACHMANINOFF
YET AQUA MAES ANENT
COUE MOONS FIGS
SIERRA BEARD EILE ABE
TCHAIKOVSKYANDBERLIOZ
AHEM EDDIE LONER ODOR
NOUS RASON STARS BABA

70

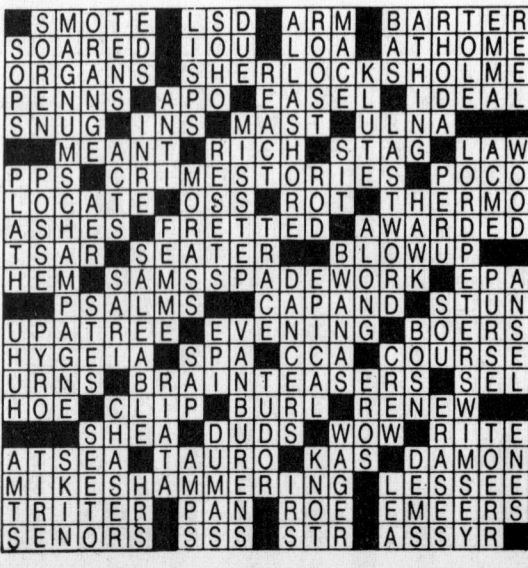

SMOTE LSD ARM BARTER
SOARED IOU LOA ATHOME
ORGANS SHERLOCKSHOLME
PENNS APO EASEL IDEAL
SNUG INS MAST ULNA
MEANT RICH STAG LAW
PPS CRIMESTORIES POCO
LOCATE OSS ROT THERMO
ASHES FRETTED AWARDED
TSAR SEATER BLOWUP
HEM SAMSSPADEWORK EPA
PSALMS CAPAND STUN
UPATREE EVENING BOERS
HYGEIA SPA CCA COURSE
URNS BRAINTEASERS SEL
HOE CLIP BURL RENEW
SHEA DUDS WOW RITE
ATSEA TAURO KAS DAMON
MIKESHAMMERING LESSEE
TRITER PAN ROE EMEERS
SENORS SSS STR ASSYR

71

TODD CLAMP RENO DAWN
OMOO AIDER ELATH EROO
LARGESTZOO MOSTOSCARS
ARRESTEE SHORT SHANDY
ATOR SAURO SPAY
SCORER SHINS SLIPSHOD
ARLES THICKESTICE INE
LADD KEAN EPEE AGES
ANE NEARESTSTAR SOHOT
DISTANCE PILOT HONERS
TENTH LINEN POSES
SCHWAS BORGE CLOISTER
ALOES DRIESTPLACE NRA
LARS PAIR HIGH BORI
EIS LONGESTBONE HITON
PRETEENS TRENT MISERY
ATTY CRONY DOVE
SEETHE ALATE SIDECARS
TALLESTMAN FATTESTCAT
ERIE SWING IMITS ERLE
YSER INGE TAROT DEEP

72

TOTEMS SETOUT AFL PRO
APELET TRIPLE ROOMIER
BANANA RATINE CROONED
ARTHURJASONANDHENRY
CTS KAY ISSUES
LIED EDO GRE CLUB
RUSSELLANDJOSEPHINE
TEAPOT ASP RAU LENDA
ONION ATE CAPT TURNON
GIS ABE ELMO MIMI
ADAMALEXISIANANDBETTY
ALOT CPOS ROY ROE
RESOLE LIAS PEP SPELL
OSTIA ALN ION ATONAL
OTISHARRYANDRAYMOND
FORT DUE OAT OOPS
REDEEM EGO MIO
JUNEDONJIMMYANDJACK
ABALONE DENIER FAIRER
GENERAL ACEDIA ORGANA
ODE ALA STEINS RESTIS

73

SLED RATES RAINS SAFE
PARR ELIDE ULNAE INON
ETRE VANED BASEL ETON
THEWHITERABBIT ENSILE
SED USES LOIN CET
AMI AILS STEAMER
LAWN THEMADHATTER OXA
AVON ORB ROAD CCCI
VIN THEDODO IND RAKES
ADD HORA ERASE BUSTLE
EMILS SLAVE BANTU
ERRAND DEANE AERO ROB
LOLLS TEL GRYPHON TRE
AMAT TERM MIA ILES
TAN THEMARCHHARE NEST
ENDOWED ELIA NNE
RIA SLAT AIDE ANS
RECENT CHARLESDODGSON
SLOG ECLAT ESTER ETNA
VETO READE STOAS NECK
PEEN SEWED SENSE TREE

74

TSAR MAST AMAZED
ROMAINE ALOU MADURO
ORANGES GLOB ADONIS
MADANTHONY ALTARIST
UTA ONEND MIMI
LOSS SWIT ERN INCAS
ORACLE COMTE ANGOLA
RUEDE ARISTA BOT
MADEIRA ADAGIO TINE
ARIES MADDING ERASE
NANS HEREON MADISON
ERE MINING SAGAN
TARMAC EOSIN EDAMES
STOOD ELI NOIR LANO
IRAN DAMON DCI
CREDIBLE MADAGASCAR
OOLOGY UNIT PORTAGE
MADRAS GENE ESCAPEE
EDSELS EYES THOR

75

NEGRI ABBE SPEND
ELIEL TRUE AQUEOUS
BULLFIGHTERS BULLSEYE
ARI AROIDS SLIP BMA
KOPT COWCATCHER TIBS
UNSHY PEA RODE CHLOE
SERAPES AVER SHELL
OLOR CID LEAF
PEWITS BROODCOW ACHE
TENSES NEIL ROAN THOR
ETATS FERDINAND STING
SETH ALLY NONE SCENES
TREE BULLRING PERDAY
BRIE ESE OTIC
SHUTE MATT ARAPAHO
SHALE ALEC ANS SLAVE
PILL COWHEARTED FRET
ILL ICES RETINA ORA
COWHIDES VATICANBULLS
HARNESS ODAS SARDI
YESES WEST ERASE

76

CRAT OCTET SPASM MUD
LARI POOLE GARGLE ARE
ABET ENOLA URANUS RAN
PATIENTTAKESATURN SLY
STELLAR ASHES ENE
LENA MARYS SEISM
NIPAND COTS IDA CLEO
YALTA ADO DECOR KLAN
SLUE INEPTUNEWRITERS
EST PUNT WED SERIFS
OWING EDITS ESKER
SCATHE SON ORTS ABE
EARTHENWAREPOTS GNAR
ARAT LUAUS OBI RACER
RETA MER MOOS RISERS
LEIGH CHAFE JEST
CEE SPLAY OVERUSE
ALA MICROWAVEOVENUSER
SOL PRAISE ASTIR LUNG
TIL EARNED STOAT ARNO
ANY NESTS TEENS SPAT

77

PROPS AGAIN RAVER
GRETEL TANGO OLAFII
ARETINO TUTORSSUITORS
POMES EMILE STALL TAT
SWIM VEERS CEARA COKE
ETE GAYLE NAMBY FRUIT
SHRILLED WIRES GUESS
STEED HELEN CEDE
USHANT TAILS LANDLORD
RIALS HURRYSCURRY CII
BEMY MITE ALOE BEAN
ANI HARUMSCARUM FRANK
NARRATES MOVES DAINTY
OPED RILEY COLDS
DIALS WELTS HOUSEMAN
GEMMY TOTES LANGE ORE
RAPS CURRY PARCH ETNA
ALA MORSE LAPEL PLIER
FENDERBENDERS ATALOSS
REDSEA CEASE VOLENS
LEARN HERES EDENS

78

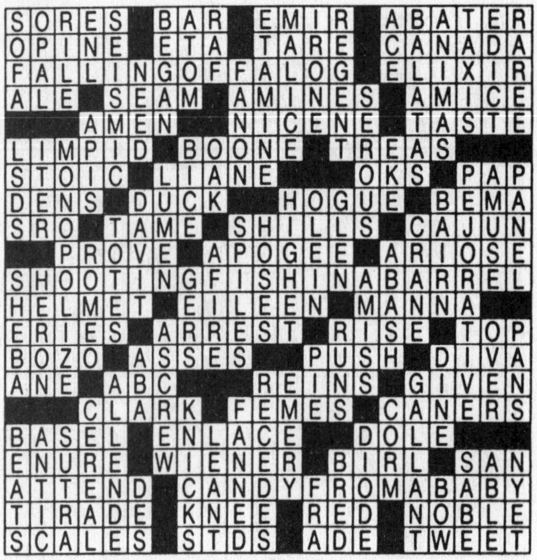
SORES BAR EMIR ABATER
OPINE ETA TARE CANADA
FALLINGOFFALOG ELIXIR
ALE SEAM AMINES AMICE
AMEN NICENE TASTE
LIMPID BOONE TREAS
STOIC LIANE OKS PAP
DENS DUCK HOGUE BEMA
SRO TAME SHILLS CAJUN
PROVE APOGEE ARIOSE
SHOOTINGFISHINABARREL
HELMET EILEEN MANNA
ERIES ARREST RISE TOP
BOZO ASSES PUSH DIVA
ANE ABC REINS GIVEN
CLARK FEMES CANERS
BASEL ENLACE DOLE
ENURE WIENER BIRL SAN
ATTEND CANDYFROMABABY
TIRADE KNEE RED NOBLE
SCALES STDS ADE TWEET

79

BALM CAAMA BRIMS CADI
ALEE ONTOP REMIT ONIT
NONEBUTAMERICANS PONE
GESTAPO EAST FINER
BON SEAN AGIN
FATHEN GUARDIANANGELS
ASHES CARR TRAIN ROE
DOUR SORGO SATIN BRAW
OFGRACEDEFENDUS ALADA
RIDE BIAS MATER
TASSELS MALTY DIEHARD
OMUTA PALI SOWN
BARAS LIKESOMEWATCHER
ETES FATAS ROANS IOLE
ACT ARBOL DIMS ALLOT
THEETOANUNNERY AMIENS
ATEN AERA AMO
CHEKA TOPI DONTYOU
HOPI YEOMENOFTHEGUARD
INON EELER CAROB FRAT
NESS TEENY ARECA ADDS

80

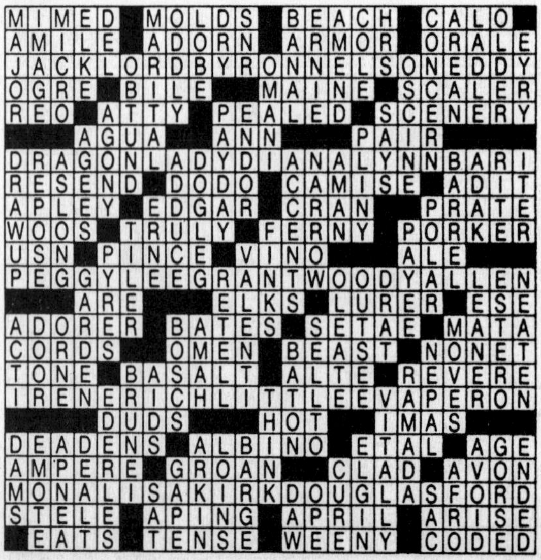
MIMED MOLDS BEACH CALO
AMILE ADORN ARMOR ORALE
JACKLORDBYRONNELSONEDDY
OGRE BILE MAINE SCALER
REO ATTY PEALED SCENERY
AGUA ANN PAIR
DRAGONLADYDIANALYNNBARI
RESEND DODO CAMISE ADIT
APLEY EDGAR CRAN PRATE
WOOS TRULY FERNY PORKER
USN PINCE VINO ALE
PEGGYLEEGRANTWOODYALLEN
ARE ELKS LURER ESE
ADORER BATES SETAE MATA
CORDS OMEN BEAST NONET
TONE BASALT ALTE REVERE
IRENERICHLITTLEEVAPERON
DUDS HOT IMAS
DEADENS ALBINO ETAL AGE
AMPERE GROAN CLAD AVON
MONALISAKIRKDOUGLASFORD
STELE APING APRIL ARISE
EATS TENSE WEENY CODED

81

SPAS PEER SHEA DASH
TELEO LATE TEAR DOGMA
ENOCH ACRE EAST EURUS
ACARE THEDRAPESOFBATH
DEFENSE AMS TROT
TROD WOVE MUTE THE
DELAYS WATERBEDS TEEN
OMAR BATON ARY AHEAD
SIDI BASES ITE WRESTS
ELLA ASTR ASH SHIP
REEL BREAKTHEICE APED
PLEA RAT VDAY CANA
SCHOOL GUY BAERS IVAN
ELIOT POM TODAY FETE
PULL PERSPIRES ARISES
TET DULY HEIR ALEC
PASI NOR DECODES
HEALTHCLUBSAUNA ECOLE
ELSIE AERI SNAP NEWAR
LITER NASA HINT TASTE
LEAD SPES ETAS NEER

82

USED ETRE TAB TAFT
NILE SHERE ITO OMAR
SEVENKEYSTOBALDPATE
EVE OESE ARISTA TET
RESPIRES DATING
URSA EVELYNKEYES
FRERE ALAR IAGO
BALE APRILS PRESTON
INO SERAI WROTH
ANOPENANDSHUTCASE
REEDS CIANO ELD
PETARDS WALTER BELA
ATON ASTA ROREM
THEGLASSKEY SLAM
SURETE STUMBLED
OCT BEARON TOTO ERI
THEKEYSOFTHEKINGDOM
TELA OOP HARES ROSE
ORLY UNS LEST INES

83

SAGA MIKES RETAG OGLE
PURR ALIKE EVITA ALIT
ITEM COWED CELLI FARO
NOWOMANISANISLAND SEN
IOWA TOP SWEEPS
SPURNS LOITER DRAWER
ARNES CANOE ITE SOMA
BOWS WOMENDICANT SMOG
OVO LANAI THROES ETE
TOMTIT SLOTS PLATANES
EAVES LURAY AROMA
CANTERED TITAN ONAGER
AGT REPAST RAISE ELI
BAIL DISWOMANTLE PRES
ATOE AHA ODETS WAIVE
LANCET NAPERY CAREER
AHORSE DUN LOVE
CUB NONCOMPOSWOMENTIS
ONLY MATRI INANE TARA
IDEE BRANT DICED ALMA
LOST ALLES STORY LEAR

84

AMOR GAGS DEER AWE
CRETE SAMOA ELSA NELL
HEARTSTRING MISHANDLE
ISSORARE GAME ESTADIO
ALIT ASAN AMISS
PRINCECHARMING FRAN
RACIEST FORMEANDMYGAL
EPICS NABS ARS DUE
SHAH LAIR EAVE ARA
SENORITA ASTRA MAGYAR
LOVECONQUERSALL
RAMSES IRAQI LARGESSE
ANY UNIT BELT ATAR
HOO IMP DRAT AMOUR
VALENTINESDAY PATERNO
DMUS SWEETHEARTDEAL
REFER OWEN ALIE
ILLNESS NAST GLANCING
GLADSTONE PHILANDERER
SEME ALEC AEDES ERATO
NED BEAK NEAT DANS

85

CANNAE USIA ANYAS PHI
AREOLA SENSATIONS ION
BEATAROUNDTHEBUSH EAR
ANTHILL AIES LAE AARE
LASI ESTER DIS ATL
NOTATES BECKYSHARP
SINGSING BANK ISOMER
ARAFAT DIANE ANEMONE
BELLYUPTOTHEBAR NEDDY
ESSA LAHRS GRAS ESS
TRAPERO TONEROW
DAP ARAT AVAST IBET
ARIAN WASOFLITTLENOTE
LEANTOS ALIAS ELGARS
ANNIES SCAT ASSESSES
IGOTRHYTHM TABASCO
TRS ARA TOTAL FRAT
AQUA AKA URFA SESSILE
GUN AFIFTHOFBEETHOVEN
TIE TIMEOFYEAR TENANT
STR AGASP SELA ANGLES

86

LOBES LIARS AGHA ARTY
AWAIT IBSEN DRUB SHOO
MEARA NAOMI MISE PINK
ADLERNERNSTEINSTEINGE
TOMS TRAY DREAD
OBSCENE TARTAN AWE
ARPERONEALDALDENIROME
FAUN NCOS MAN VAS
SENT DIVOT YESES DENS
ELITE HALER SERGE
OHARAVELGARKINGRESTON
POLES ROUGE SERAC
TOLD LAPSE TRUSS ALMS
ICE TAT GOYA NOEL
CHERODEANKABELMANTONY
ARS LEASES ERASMUS
ADAMS WASP ONER
GARBOGARTHURISTOWELTY
OREL RIME RADIO ALOHA
RENE AVER SNEER LINER
ADAR FEDS AGARS SAGAN

87

TATA MOLAR IDLER STOP
OMAR ATONE NOISE IONA
FOURINHAND FIVEFINGER
UNTANNED RHINE EDGARS
YSER DEAD TREE
REMAPS LISLE ARRESTER
EMILS FIRSTLADIES HIE
EELS SONG FRED BIDE
VEL THREEMASTER CARED
ERITREAN IDIOM SUNDRY
ORION SCORN PAREE
ANNEAL BARRE CARESSED
VIAND SECONDHANDS TAR
ACID MENE ERGS CAGE
SER HUNDREDDAYS PATES
TREMOLOS PIERS CANERS
AUER ISMS MONT
SLANGY GUCCI AESTHETE
SIXTHSENSE SIXSHOOTER
TOLL AGAIN ELITE OATS
SNEE WORSE SOLAR KLEE

88

HIES ZASU RITE PUCKA
ACLU ALOFT ELIS APLEY
TELLINGYOURMONEYWHERE
PRIES PEONY ONIONS
ACHIER CEARA FUEL
AROIDS ALLS MORELLOS
DENTS INCOMETAXES EGO
LOVE KNOT RYE EDEN
ILE TOGOINSTEAD GAGES
BARBITON EARNS POSES
TAROT PUTIT PLIER
VIBES AERIE GRANDDAD
LOBED OFWONDERING ORO
ILLS DOE NINE AMOY
ETE WHEREITWENT BLAME
FASCIATE RHEA FABIAN
ENNS BORIS LORANS
ASTROS VENOM SERIC
THEAVERAGEBANKACCOUNT
NORTE USER ROUSE RABI
OWNER BETS BATS EWES

89

WELTS HATS CIST DANCE
ALOOP IMET OSLO ERECT
FIRMA SALA CRUX CIRIO
THEBROTHERSKARAMAZOV
UNESCO GRIPES APO
ERROR GIL BRONCOS
CHARLEYSAUNT BIGDADDY
HONEY AMPS METE EEN
ASEA TAR EIRENE OFFRE
FEN PAL ANNULE SPA
FATHERLAND MOTHERSDAY
ERA STEFAN STY OLE
SIGNE BORDEN UTA ARIA
ENL SANE RIIS EDICT
CRYUNCLE GRANDMAMOSES
TONNEAU BAA TAINE
AWL PATRIE STRASS
YESMYDARLINGDAUGHTER
PARKA ROTI PERI ISERE
OLSEN ELON URIM NINUT
DEEDS WING TSPS GNOME

90

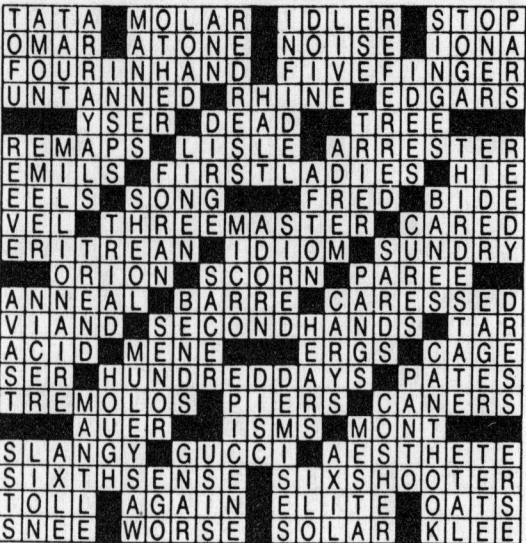

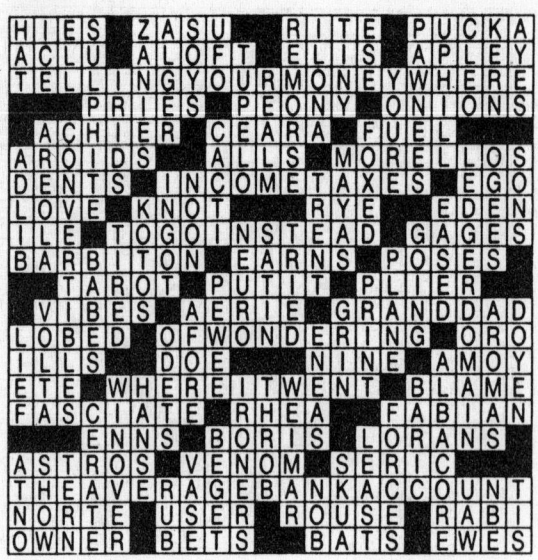

MATES TREPID SPAR
TANANA ROTATE COROT
ROCKCORNISHHEN APICES
ARHAT DOTES RILLE KAT
PEI COTES DAZED MYCO
TUNE ONOR RITES DEMUR
PERTAIN GOREN CANAPE
ROTC PECKS HONOR
FERAL SINKS ROMANCED
ANOTE ATTIC SORTS ILO
COCA KNUTEROCKNE MADE
ELK REINS YULES LONER
DAFFIEST ASTER ALORS
ORALE MUTER FROE
SARANS SODAR PRISSED
AUDIT PANEL CLAN TARE
ALFS RATON SHACK RAF
LAI PEWIT STINT SPLIT
EILEEN ROCKYMOUNTAINS
TERSE ENSILE ROUSES
SNOW SEATED ENDOR

91

BALD SENOR CAITS CLEF
AGAR ANILE AVERY HORA
ARNO DENIM TIROS AKIM
AGOODMANISHARDTOFINE
PREY THEN OWE
SIMIAN TATAR BOLL PIP
ANENT OMAR SEMI HERA
CUDGELUPALITTLECLOSER
KRI ISIS RAIN ORONO
SEALANE STERE TINSEL
ISURRENDERDEERE
CARESS AMISS ETERNAL
OMEGA STEP PALE ONE
LOVEISTHESWEETYSTHING
ORES EYER ISLE EERIE
REL ITER ENTER CAREER
ALF FACE SORE
HOURLOVEISHERETOSTAY
ANTE RELEE MODAL IRIS
SEAN TROLL ELITE CAPE
HAHA HANDS DETER SMEW

92

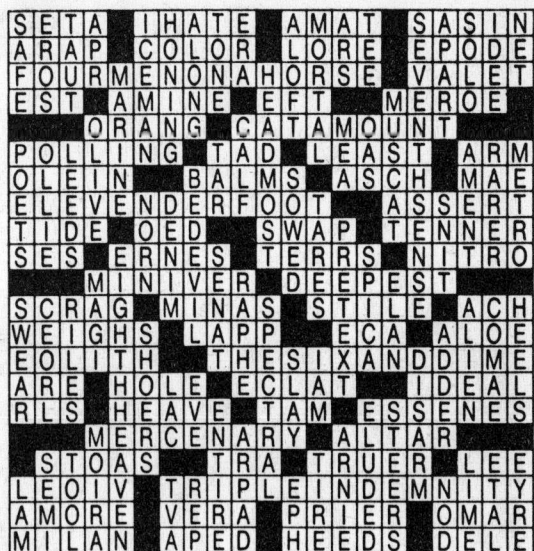

SETA IHATE AMAT SASIN
ARAP COLOR LORE EPODE
FOURMENONAHORSE VALET
EST AMINE EFT MEROE
ORANG CATAMOUNT
POLLING TAD LEAST ARM
OLEIN BALMS ASCH MAE
ELEVENDERFOOT ASSERT
TIDE OED SWAP TENNER
SES ERNES TERRS NITRO
MINIVER DEEPEST
SCRAG MINAS STILE ACH
WEIGHS LAPP ECA ALOE
EOLITH THESIXANDDIME
ARE HOLE ECLAT IDEAL
RLS HEAVE TAM ESSENES
MERCENARY ALTAR
STOAS TRA TRUER LEE
LEOIV TRIPLEINDEMNITY
AMORE VERA PRIER OMAR
MILAN APED HEEDS DELE

93

DEAF SPOOK BAA SAWS
EDNA CELLA LLB PLAT
WITH OLDER ABE YOGI
YEARSOFSOLITUDE HEN
EATS RAM YEAST
HINTS SATAN REV
LETHE COIR THEBEARS
BREED HONOR SPANIEL
SARI CEN MOSTEL STY
TRA EMBOW ALE
EAU AVERNO EEL ASTA
DEFAMER ONEAL USUAL
SCOMPANY ENRY SYRUP
OAT ASSES DUPES
SPURN AMO SORI
URN THEMOONANDPENCE
SOIR ERE BEFOG CALL
ANTE AIR ORARE EPOS
NEED PES LORES SETA

94

BALM ARTIE GIGOT RACE
ALEE RAZOR OCALA OLAN
LINDAEVANS ROGERMOORE
DESIGNER KOINE HOMER
COOL HILLS TETE
DEPART FINAL CHEERED
OVERA MIKEFARRELL DRS
RITE HARE OARS EDIT
ITE ROBERTBLAKE PRIED
CARPETED ARISE FRIED
GAVEL APINT ELENA
GRUEL TRIBE DRESSLER
TOALL LAURENTEWES BAA
ALVA MOLL ALIT FERN
DDE MARIEWILSON FORTE
ASTORIA HOOTS FORTHE
OTIS MANSE BLUE
SAUTE GOTAT FEARSOME
ANNSOTHERN SALLYFIELD
NEIL TONTO EDILE DIXI
DELE ANEST ACTED ELIE

95

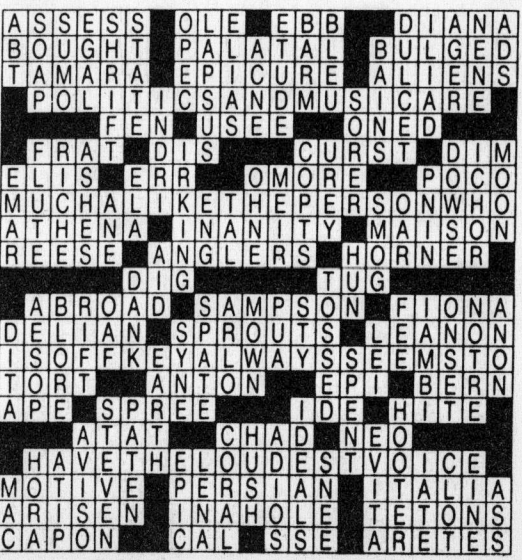

ASSESS OLE EBB DIANA
BOUGHT PALATAL BULGED
TAMARA EPICURE ALIENS
POLITICSANDMUSICARE
FEN USEE ONED
FRAT DIS CURST DIM
ELIS ERR OMORE POCO
MUCHALIKETHEPERSONWHO
ATHENA INANITY MAISON
REESE ANGLERS HORNER
DIG TUG
ABROAD SAMPSON FIONA
DELIAN SPROUTS LEANON
ISOFFKEYALWAYSSEEMSTO
TORT ANTON EPI BERN
APE SPREE IDE HITE
ATAT CHAD NEO
HAVETHELOUDESTVOICE
MOTIVE PERSIAN ITALIA
ARISEN INAHOLE TETONS
CAPON CAL SSE ARETES

96

STUMP SERB GRATA
MYOPIA SOFIA RETREE
MARLINS PUTONSIDEARMS
ARID TSARS JULEP OBI
LINO SALAAM OIL ESSEN
ANGLO DEI EAST MANORS
READFROMNASH FINALS
JAI SEW STEALUP
CHOLLA DAR ARRET NOW
BOOKLETS KEMPER STORE
EDGE DROVEHISCAR OBIT
BEAST ORISON TREMOLOS
ERN OLPES ENC SHAKEN
LOUISES OHO ADA
BUSKIN SAWANANALYST
MANTIS BEER MIL MOOLA
IDEST DOT KABOBS NUIT
FLA HEATH TENET GAME
FORGOTWHATFOR RAINIER
TEAMEN NEONS TITANS
DRESS ELBE ADOPT

97

SLIP EVOE ALAR ITISAN
TARA MART ZANY MEMORY
OMAR BLUEBONNETPLAGUE
MATA EOS AREA HEARSTS
PREMEDICATEDMURDER
OLDS GAS TOE YVES
PERUSE ANA AMON ILA
ORAN DEMENTIAPEACOCKS
LISTS LOW ENGI RUBIES
YEP ATE RETIA UPI
PSYCHOCERAMICSYMPTOMS
IAN ROGET ASE SOO
CASTRO EMIR KEW DEMON
LIKEAWOMANSCORNS VISA
ARI LING APE TRACER
YENS DDT RTE CAUL
THEHEMLOCKMANEUVER
JULIANA AYAH ORD AONE
ABANDAGEONMYKNEE TINE
MERGER ERNE ATEE ELIS
BRASSY LIED TENS DESE

98

REND YAWN IDS ARAGON
ARAR UVEA NEED REFUSE
FREETRIALOFFER MARIST
SITAR ALIPED TOLET
LASSO TOSTO AROA TIL
ARNE BENCHWARMER ACNE
STARVE ASSIS GISMO
HEP ANSON RTS SALMON
PLAINTIFF PROLAPSE
JEU CASTRO ION LAW
CRUDEOIL WAR RUSTLERS
HAD CLI ANCIEN AIX
EDGERTON SKEDADDLE
RAMADA EAN ASSAM SAG
ETONS STOSH RATTLE
PONS TENNISCOURT OLAN
ONT ASSE MESNE EROSE
MEDES SALTON AUSTR
AMALFI LAYSDOWNTHELAW
DAYLIT SORI VEER NERO
ENSATE SOS ODDS TAPE

99

CROWN ITERATE ORHATE
RICHES FIREMAN FEARED
IFHERLIFEISONEOFSHAME
SNOOTY ORG WRINGER
ELAS MALAY LAS
SPAVIN CAMEL MINT SRO
WADE MACO DISCO CON
EVERYBODYKNOWSHERNAME
EEL OASIS ALES ORAN
PRELUDE BELA OFFEND
ERASTUS ALLEGRO
ACROSS OSLO THERAPE
SHUN RUIN TATAR TAB
WOEISMEIAMSOBLAMELESS
ARD MONEL LOOS ANTE
NEE ENGS INANE ATNOON
ATI GNOME BLOC
SHEARER RSM SEALED
IAMVIRTUOUSLYNAMELESS
SIMONE KILDARE ODONTA
SLANGY INTENSE OTTER

100

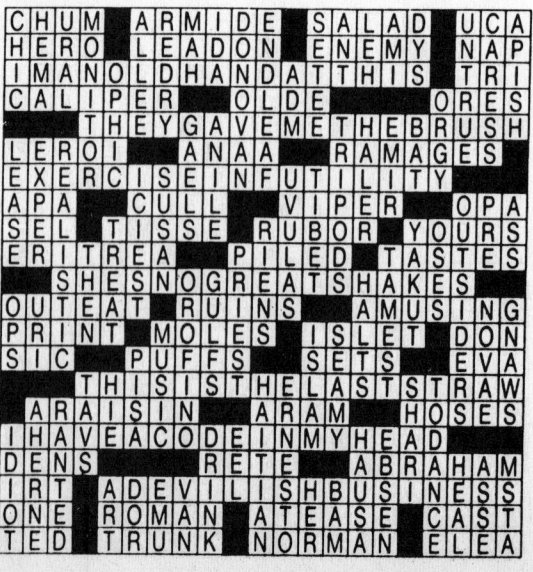

CHUM ARMIDE SALAD UCA
HERO LEADON ENEMY NAP
IMANOLDHANDATTHIS TRI
CALIPER OLDE ORES
THEYGAVEMETHEBRUSH
LEROI ANAA RAMAGES
EXERCISEINFUTILITY
APA CULL VIPER OPA
SEL TISSE RUBOR YOURS
ERITREA PILED TASTES
SHESNOGREATSHAKES
OUTEAT RUINS AMUSING
PRINT MOLES ISLET DON
SIC PUFFS SETS EVA
THISISTHELASTSTRAW
ARAISIN ARAM HOSES
IHAVEACODEINMYHEAD
DENS RETE ABRAHAM
IRT ADEVILISHBUSINESS
ONE ROMAN ATEASE CAST
TED TRUNK NORMAN ELEA

101

NOMADS RASP LASSO
IBERIA IDEAS PELOTA
CALAMITYJANE TAPPER
ENDS LEA STAKED
POLL OILER SAKE
SISTER ANNIEOAKLEY
TOTAL DBL GNP LEONE
INURE EELS RODEOS
FIDO ENROOT SUN
FASTESTGUNINTHEWEST
CTS TINIER OENO
CREOLE ACNE KOREA
AORTA IBM UAR EDIES
WYATTBSEARP DESERT
SSTS ABASE MIEN
SCARCE ASP SASS
GAUCHO DAVYCROCKETT
EILEEN AREEL SOIREE
OLAND ASHE EXPORT

102

PANT SALEP DOGMA PACS
OMOO TRALA OLEUM EBOE
DAMP ACTES RIATA ERLE
SARAHCHILDRESSPOLK
CAROLE TAME SIEGE
AVAIL SRO PARMA NYACK
NELLIEHERRONTAFT ETTA
IRES PAT ASSERTER EON
STS CID MME CONE DRE
LADYBIRDJOHNSON
ALE ARO ULO TIO
MARYTODDLINCOLN
UPS IMET IIO INS BAA
RAH SINEBADA AGE KEGS
FROM CAROLINEHARRISON
AARON NYXIS LAR ENTRE
BERET EEEE ENDEAR
DOLLEYPAYNEMADISON
ALIE PADUA ENOLS ELAN
TINY ERECT SOUSE SERE
ACES DANAE ARRAS SEAT

103

OSSA APSES BARA RIAL
ROIL TAURO ORMER ENNA
CAMINOREAL CATFISHROW
APPEALED DOTES SWAINS
NILE HIRES TIS
MOTIF GEEST WASHTUB
URIS PRIMROSEPATH ONA
RANT RAMA DOGE ABIT
ALP ESPLANADE PRATE
LEAFLESS DANA MINCES
NOONE TITIS COMIC
BEARDS HEAL CONAMORE
ADLAI BOULEVARD RES
RELY FEAR ENDA SOIT
EME ALCANHIGHWAY KANE
DAYBOOK ELLAE RYDER
ORR STEER FLEW
AGOUTI SETSA PEASANTS
PASSAGEWAY MAINSTREET
ROTE EXITS ELECT DINE
ALES NEMO DARES SLOW

104

DANCE STRAUSS SLAMS
ONION ARISTAE APERIES
TANGO DISCOVERYLAUNCH
STEN SITE PIRAEUS DUR
ASTRO KIOSK REVERE
ELECTIONYEAR ING IRED
ROW APNEAL ISDEAD
STEPPE LENGTHS NESTS
TIROL ONEPAIN COOTIE
LEONI PRO TANGENT
URAL SUPERPOWERS ASTA
RESULTS NEE REAIM
SETTEE TARPANS CEASE
ASIAN CLEMSON LISTEN
NASSER LISBON ORE
ACCT EOS OLYMPICGAMES
BALSAM SCRAP EROSE
AVA BIVOUAC ANDS ROTE
COMPUTERSCIENCE CANEA
AROUSED PLEDGER OTTER
TRIES SERVERS PEONS

105

PUSHOFF BARB CORNUS
ASTORIA GAPERS AMOUNT
THECATBIRDSEAT KETTLE
RERUN USAGE CAGER CEP
IRES ELIDE HEROD TRAP
KNOTS SOFIA PHASE
OMINOUS BISON LARCH
REPELS WATER HUROK
ABASES SANTA JACKWEBB
RIDES BENJI TORI ARLO
OTO PIGEONHOLED SAO
MAWR LOUD GAITS MOURN
ALLOCATE EDITS SERINE
AMANA TRULY DONATE
BREVE PRICE BRADLEY
PEKOE QUICK FLOPS
ALLS GURUS BEAUS ATMO
NIE CLAIM DOING ASHEN
DEMILO SPRINGCHICKENS
EVOKES THEMEN TRIESTE
RENEWS SPED SADDEST

106

107

108

109

110

111

ALASKAN TRES KIBOSH
REROUTE ESHARP AMERCE
CARLROWANHENRYSTANLEY
ADE INSIDES EASTEND
NE[illegible] [illegible] ATA
ARTBUCHWALDPAULHARVEY
ONEEAR APIA ORDERS
AMB TRAY AYES TOMS
SALTIER INST JOKY RNS
SNARES ODD EMIT LEET
ENDED PREY NONE METER
REEK LEAR COX DIVIDE
TDS AWES ODES FELINES
ILIA HOES TONI ADS
SLANTS RONA MONIES
TEDKOPPELEDWARDMURROW
RMA EDDYLINE SORE
IMPRESS ITERATE TIS
PATBUCHANANTHOMASNAST
ETOILE HONEYS TREETOP
SARSEN ADDS SOLVENT

112

THEBUD ODD BEA FED
HONORER FOR PEAR ACE
ELGRECO ADO RACY COX
ILL YOUKNOWYOUHAVENT
SOUP YEN SAC NIDOR
MATER ENCEPHAL COMO
PIGTAIL EYES WIS
STOPPEDTALKINGSINCE
APO POR MOEN AWN
CANAL CGS BYALL TROD
ICAMEHEREYOUMUSTHAVE
DELA ELOPE PIA HELEN
IER UTAH NOR PRY
BEENVACCINATEDWITHA
LAS ALPH RENAILS
ORTH DOODLING LOPAT
OTHER MAE LIB SANA
PHONOGRAPHNEEDLE CAL
EIN BEAR ION OUTSIDE
REI ONYX GLO LETONES
SRA TEE HAS SALOME

113

DICED ASTRA MASSA
AERATE ATTAIN PASTURE
FLASHINTHEPAN ASSORTS
RETE AUER LEGIS VEES
ODER OMANI ARRA ERLE
NAP ALKALI GAP
TRUSTEES EIN PREDICTS
HUR ORTHO TIDED SPOIL
ELI MASONIC IDS ENNA
WESKIT ESTHER REHEAT
EZE STEELER ENA
STATED ARNICA CATENA
COLT ARG WATCHER MIR
ADULT SEENA SEISM ICI
DOMESTIC ORE DESERTED
OER ESSENE EDE
SURF ENDO GRIND PEPE
OLAF PEERS ANTE UVEA
ATTILAS RANGEOFCOLORS
PRESENT EGRESS BASKET
ASHES LEAST CREES

114

LEGUP MUMPS SAMPS
TULANE ALERT QUEANS
MILKOFAMNESIA UNTRAIN
EEL LICIT GROAT TREE
TRAP TETRA SLURS YEGG
ARBOR STARE ERE YPRES
LAYMEN SPIRITS AMISS
PLIE ERNS DIAL
SCHOOLTABLET PURSLANE
TAINT ELA DEFILE SLED
ONT GRASP RILLS IVE
IDOL ANNEAL LEA SEVEN
COROLLAS NAMEDROPPERS
SEAL BERI DALI
AREAS SALVEOF TALONS
SCORN ATL ANVIL TOPOT
ARTS SCALE SEXES GAVE
MOAB TIROL RUNAT LIN
ASTAIRE OILOFPOLITICO
SELLER NOONE RELINE
SMEWS STOOD ESTEE

115

HARD PADS HASTO STAB
EWER LORRE ALLAN CHOO
LOLA ESTER ROAMS REND
PL8GLASSWINDOW TRALEE
SIRE CALF PRIM8
MITTEN DAIRY GRIP GAM
ACHED POUND SLAKE ELI
DOER LAWN CONE SOIL
ASS W8UNTILDARK CIRCE
MATTRESS REEDY BOLGER
RAISE HINTS ALGAE
ST8IST WASTE TRANSACT
THANT FISHORCUTB8 PLO
AINT FONT OLES CLAW
IND MERCY STILL SHERE
DEN ALTE WHILE STAYED
ABIDE POEM PAIR
SHREDS GOLDENG8BRIDGE
TORA PARIS LOIRE SEAT
AMOS AMINE ARDOR MEMO
NEWT RUNTY GMEN AMEN

116

SLAB MARAT TORRID WET
LAMA ORATE AREOLA ILE
ALIS TAMER PASSER TIN
MODELOFPERFECTION HAT
MORAS ARLEN EPA
TYPESET PARSE SLAGGY
WEANED SATE LIP IRAE
EMITS ECO AGAMA NABS
EENS KEEPALOWPROFILE
TNT ADEN LID ATTUNES
STRIA OLLAS CARLO
ESTREAT RIA ETNA FRO
GOHEADOVERHEELS TSAR
ADEM ENOLA DAB BRAND
DOTO MSU VITA TRALEE
SMOLTS ADITS POINTER
WOE SATIE SARAS
AWN SETTHEWORLDONFIRE
PER TRALAS CAIRN EDEN
INE EUGENE ARMET RENO
ADD ESSEDS SAYSO SATS

117

BEAR ASP BASH DEBIT
ORNE ROTOR ACTI ELITE
WATCHEDONESSTEP METED
RANON LATIN MOVER
SPIELER LAPIN LATE
ORNATE SETON LEGENDOF
MITTS COVERGROUND RUE
ACHE OHRE INCA TATS
SEE SNAILSPACE RAGIS
LAMESA NEWER CAPONE
PROTEAM APO LACINGS
RENTAL AWFUL SERENE
EGGAR GOUPSTAIRS SMA
CARR ECHO ACTE AFAR
ULU STEALAMARCH ALERT
TENSPOTS TORSO ARLENE
LANE STORE INCITES
SEERS TEASE STEEN
FIXER DANCEATTENDANCE
ALIVE DISH ROAST LEAN
NOTED ELEE SER LEND

118

TRAPP LAPP SAMAR
LOOTER UBER ALIENEE
REPLETE LANE PODIATRY
ASPEN SALT&PEPPER AMA
DIES MELEE ADLER SKIP
IOR PINED BREED OPENS
INSTANCE CLEMS BRINE
ARTE CLARA POET
ATARMS ALECS DOWN&OUT
RAG&A CREAK AERI PIRO
ENIF SUGAR&SPICE OLGA
CIRE AMOR WATCH BLEED
ATLANTIS CHILE BAIRDS
TEEN SHINY TOSS
ASHES BHATS SHOEHORN
ALTER FIORE MEETS SAO
REAR SALPA SOARS SMIT
AGR PICK&CHOOSE DIODE
LAKEERIE TOUR MOUSSES
RETREAD ESNE IMPAIR
RATEL REDS NOELS

119

AMBOS DASH WEDS STRIP
MARAT ALTO OTRA ERATO
ELATE ROAR RUED GAVEL
NIGHTCLUBS LIGHTOPERA
SAID ERD GEE
RIPTORN CRISPY LLAMAS
ONION GIRAFFE DESPISE
MANNS SHOC ATNO TIMID
ANTI SPACE IRATE AIDE
ESCAPADES ROPEDANCER
TUT SID
CENTERRING SHOOTOUTS
LEER SOPOR TERNS RAID
ARIAS LAMA AIR AISLE
SILVERS ANAGRAM PESKY
HELENE ADDLES EMPLOYS
DAV SSH FLOE
CARTOONIST ACROBATICS
OMAHA NAHA NEED LOCAL
LOSER ETON DREI EROSE
ASHES SEED SODA DINED

120

LADY SPAT ASEA APPS
UBOAT LALA TINT PLIES
COCKALORUM ONTHEEARTH
AUK JAPAN PAHIS YOUR
STIR MEDIC TREE SUPS
NAB SITO GRAF THE
BROKEN SEMINAL PROTON
AIREDALE ENOS RUETHE
LAB EVE ARAT HAEC EMB
SLIP ARCS HOISTED
ASTI RELIC INTHE NIPS
NIRVANA TEEN ANIL
PEP TEED NERO EST TEA
HEAVEN MIRA APERFECT
INNAME MANAGED SURREY
ALS COLE ENVY EEE
MATH BODE SLASH TSAR
ELEA ROUND ANEAR TRE
MILLVALLEY ACCUSATION
OCALA IASK REEL MANSE
ESAU ERSE ASST OGEE

121

MACO PASTA SCAPA MAR
ALOT ALOOP TIMER PINO
ABUT REMORSECODE ARNO
MONADS ALICE RECARTED
TWIN OLIPO AMAH
TREATISE SOLAR SESQUI
EER SPLAY NENE ROUND
ASST OSAR STABS LADE
REPEL PEWIT ADAPT KEA
STYRENE LARK ROOTERS
REAP STUNG BOOR
ONTARIO ASOR ENTICED
LOI SAKES STOOD HORNE
DICT DECAL SOLI SONE
ASKER CRUD MARAT WED
SEEDED EATER VERANDAS
RICE SHIED TRIB
ASTOUNDS ESTES ISEULT
BEAU VIGORMORTIS CRUS
LAPS ENTIA OMASA ESTA
ETE RESIN KORAN STER

122

FLED SAP ABCS SETS
RODE MOWER ABEET PTAH
OMAR ALARE PLANE AURA
MAMMYYOKUM PERTAINING
BONE ORE DEMO
LABORS STOAT RELATES
TENORS SEESRED REVOLT
ETAL MANLY TOA ERIA
SUGARDADDY BROTHERRAT
SSE ERNES LEA HAM ESS
AIDS EAT ILIE
APO DEA ARC ABELE SST
FATHERTIME SISTERKATE
ASHE ETO SPREE IBEX
CHEERS TOLKIEN MALLET
EARLIER NEALS PANNER
SEEA ATL AIRS
UNCLEREMUS AUNTIEMAME
PORE ELATE GROTE ENID
OTOE SINES EASEL ADZE
NEWS SNAS LED DYER

123

WEAR CHAD CARGO SUMS
ALDA LORE ARIEL EMIT
ALIT SERIF TABLE ABLY
CATCHAFALLINGSTAR REX
HINT ANI TYPE
ACCESS CATSPAW EARLS
CHATS PUREE TIS LILAC
ROTS CATASTROPHE MADO
IRE SALEM OPERAS CAP
DERMAL RIVAL SURCOAT
PYLON SITES GLOAT
CIGARET STOOP ANKARA
CUL DIMOUT DRAPE LOS
ORLO CATSANDDOGS SPAS
LEAPS NUN IRENE OHARA
DRAMA PRESIDE BRASSY
THUS SUN POOL
TOR THECATSKILLS SLIDE
OGEE CLARE STOIC ODER
ULAN ASTIR TAPE WEBS
REDD NEEDS OLES SATE

124

OPS EGAD PEP COPT
PRESSURE AEOLIS LUNAR
EIGHTMINUSSEVEN ARENA
RANEE SIT ITOLDTHEM
AMO SUEDE SAWED ASP
ISLANDERS SHILL
SNEAKS ODA REEF
SQUATS EMOTERS SATES
SOURCE ATON BETS FIXE
PIANO APOGEE OIL MUN
ORR WERENUMBERONE ELL
NEE SAM LOOPED PASTA
GERI ROTA RAID TACTIC
ESOPS REGRETS RENOWN
OSIS TEE AUSTRO
TOTAL SINGLETON
MAO TIOGA SAYER PPD
OFFCENTER TIR OLLIE
OFOUR ONEDIVIDEDBYONE
RINDS STANCE INSISTED
EXES ENA PETS SDS

125

SILICA ASP COPA EMEND
INADRY LOA ANOM AEAEA
MIKEINDIANOVEMBERXRAY
ATEAM RAP RESOIL ILLS
SERA ALLEN CAC
ETC ALPHADELTA IDOUBT
LEOS SEINES CDI NAH
DANTE RNA PTAH EAGLE
JULIETALPHAZULUZULU
ADV TYRONE ILUS
CHARLIEHOTELOSCARPAPA
AONE TROCAR HSE
WHISKEYECHOECHOKILO
COMTE SANA GRO NEVER
AHA YAO ARENAS TIME
WOLFER YANKEEECHO DUM
ODD EBOAT CONK
SWAG ORSELL ERR ENATE
TANGOROMEOINDIASIERRA
OKIES MAIS EDS PLEIAD
WELDS ANNS EYE ALLAYS

126

SCRAPES STRAP STRAFE
ELEMENT TRALEE ARISEN
TOFORGIVEISANDYDEVINE
TWERP PINTER GADS ACR
ENRY MUSS REHIT NEO
ESS POLS DOMO OSLO
ASTAIREWAYTOHEAVEN
THIRST ENLACES TIRE
RIALTO FAT MEN ABSENT
ALTE ARTOF DADA
LONGAGOANDFARRAHWAY
ANON ROBIN ULES
REWARD TAP ORL VIRAGO
ATOR MANILLA ENSIGN
THOUSHALTNOTCAVETT
THAN ISTO MARS RAP
CID RUINS SANS MESH
ALI INTO ACACIA ZEPPO
LORENTOLABORANDTOWAIT
ENTREE LIONEL IONESCO
BAYARD RUSSE SMARTEN

127

ASTER SHAPE DAR FWD
SCONE PEKING EVEL RIO
SANTODOMINGO SAMISENS
ALAR STINT TAP IMPEDE
MALABO DOMINO SAITH
NASTY ANDTHE NOOK
DEBTS HEAPS RIA WEE
EROS LITTLEROCK BANKY
BIG FEN PARAS IBIS
AVOCET LAYUP SMOOTHED
RATELS ORG PET STEELE
SNARLING OTARU TIPTOP
TONE LEARN CON MIT
UKASE CHARLESTON GASH
FIN RAH LETIT DANES
ANAT MORONI CELEB
SLOPE TRANCE AMORAL
SHOGUN FED AMMAN ROMA
PAGOPAGO INDIANAPOLIS
ASI AGAR RAGLAN ANENT
SAC END WEEMS YESES

128

ABET APPLE CARPS FLAT
MASH NADIA ABASE LEDA
ALAR INGER BASIE SAMS
NIUE MISUNDERSTD EDIT
EDUC ECT LIT RATE
ARISES GURU DENIER
CARTN WAR MIE SMEARED
AGAG MINE EMMA ERNEST
RENEGING INPUT DENE
IRISINS ASTARTE ASKED
DRTDRSALESMAN
BRISE NATURES BRASSIE
EINE WHEYS TERTIARY
DERMAT SURF THRW LTER
SLEIGHS RSI HIS BVINE
CARATS LSES SCENES
ADAM EPI AMT PIER
GILA SHARPSHTERS SAVE
GAIT HERAS SENAT PREY
INAS ENAMI ANISE NINE
EASE RASPS YNDER SAID

129

STATE REAM ISLET HEX
ARBOR EDNAS DOONE EAR
BORGE MAINE OARED ASA
UNA JIMMYWALKER TREY
HORAS MES VJE
EVADERS TORTS EASTERN
DIMES PARSON OTT OOO
TABLET HIE OISE SNOW
ELTORO PWS DOE
CHA PANT PECOS RAJAH
OHM ROBERTFWAGNER ORE
THEME ITEMS PRIN HAM
IDA IES ATTAIN
BAWL DICT MOM SERVAL
USO AHS OCHERS GALBA
THEOREM PLATO SPINIER
VIR ARR EOSIN
NOVA EDWARDIKOCH DON
AVE SNOOT ECOLE PESTO
SAN START RAKED ERATO
ALA ESSEN LOSE RAYON

130

CETTE CRI BAMA EVER
LARES RAT POORER TIRE
AGENT ANE ENGANDCHANG
WRATHOFGRAPES TIL
SET STE NOM RITE PAS
ODES SSD AGESOFROCK
FROE MINNOW ANTI
DOTERS AIRY LEET TEED
JERRYANDTOM ADORES
AMIS DOZEN CAT DIG
TEC ENTERS THRICE ONE
INK LEA RAITT LOVE
SYSTEM MARCHOFIDES
AMAH SEGO ADAH RETIRE
HOPE ADELES RENT
EVEANDADAM SSE TURK
MEX ARCS MLI STS AAA
PEA BEANSTHESPILL
DOGSANDCATS TOE TANGO
AREA CIVETS LPS AIKEN
GATO HAIR OSE BLARE

131

REID MUDPIE STRIP
FEARME ONEONTA ERODE
SANFRANCISCOCHRONICLE
PROTEGEE ARR SALT KEN
TOLEDOBLADE BEE
SEAR TELEVISIONNEWS
BRASSY IDE SCENIC
ODOROUS REACT ESTER
NEWYORKTIMES TIE TALE
ALLOT ADAM ENG DDE
THEBOSTONHERALD
RIM STA VIOL ARUBA
ELAM ALL BALTIMORESUN
NONES LOCAL ELEGANT
ENESCO ORR SISTER
WASHINGTONPOST LEPO
AIR ENTERTAINED
SOP TOED ADA ROOMMATE
THECINCINNATIENQUIRER
EROIC ORBITAL DUSTER
SENTA TALESE SEES

132

CAPH THUD ROAR PSALMS
OLLA ORNO ESTA OCREAE
PLUMBTHEDEPTHS PRIMPS
TOMMYS ADDLE PIPEDUP
SWEET ARENA ASTEW REP
REENTRANCE EDB IRA
BBL EDH TOTER AMASS
LOOTER ISM PAOLI
TORCHSONGS BRITTLEST
AWAKE ERA EAGER SIRE
DUC ARTA TEDA LIV
SPIT SETTA MIA ALICE
SCARIFIED GOLDBRICKS
LEARN MIR RETOOL
ALPEN AGAIN CER NNE
PEA DIM ATTHERANCH
TAV EDEMA HONOR LEASE
FLORIDA MERCI SOARED
FLORIO HADANAXTOGRIND
LEVANT DISC MDII TONY
STANGS IMET PEEL STAS

133

NEON SCOPE PTAS HILO
ALIE TAKEN RAFTS ODOR
SASE ELAND EXTRACTION
THEDAILYNOOSE ILLCOME
LANA ARLES POOR
RACERS ONSET STOPOVER
ERASE BITES BEEP SEGO
AIR IALS IRAS SARA
PENDANTS MASSES ABLER
SLEEVES SALOON FROSTS
YEP RATLINE IAN
ASLANT ESTERS ALBERTS
BLOTS PLIERS PRESSURE
BORT DUAN BOAR CUE
OPAH EFTS STANS ASHER
TENERIFE BEARS USHERS
RACA MEANT ANTI
CREATED YANKEECLIPPER
DISCARDING ARNIE PARI
VASE SERAL REDDS ENID
ILES RISE DROSS DEES

134

PASHA SLOE SPAR LUST
ASHEN TURN TARA ANTIC
SPARE ENERGETIC CLEAR
TIRE IRA ORR DEN AERO
ACETOSE BLUNT RATTRAP
INTO ULNAE SIC
PARCEL ASST PARACHUTE
OSE EDIT IDOL PRO
LOVES ELECT DEA SASIN
ENISLES ROWS DEPRESS
STATE SWEET SCENT
AVIATOR LEER IGNITES
VOTRE TAB TRIED TEILS
ETE SEGO MEET NET
REDOUNDED GAMS ADAGES
NRA EERIE LIAR
PASTORS STAND INVESTS
ACTA LES ENT ANT OTRA
SMART THIRDRATE CLOUT
SERIO TOR ETON SAUCE
STOP EPE ELMS TETES

135

BRER ASPER TIBER ADIT
UELE BARRE AMOLE RATA
SAMCLEMENS WILLPORTER
SPORULES TINTS ADEEMS
ESE IVORY TRIES
RAJAH ADORE BEERSTEIN
OMIT ANELE CORDES DNA
CAMEMBERT COB DRAWBAR
KIM ALAS HOMBRES RUNE
SNICKER LUMPIER MERES
CHER RABBONI SAAR
OPHIR MEMBERS BECKONS
REEL HISPART FUEL UIT
BENISON RRS BALDEAGLE
IVE PRIDED SLILY WHEN
TERRITORY SPURS BASSO
ADANA ACERB PAR
AVOCET PANIC ABERDEEN
MIKEROGERS KENROBERTS
OSA RAREE LIKEN RANT
RAY YOYOS ESSAY STAD

136

MEAT SPCA MAW PASOS
ANNO STEAM COSH ARULE
JUGORHULLABALOO ROVER
ORE AUNT TORT ASSUAGE
RELENT SCENEOF ILS
ITEA HUGE ASLEEPAT
SIGNS BEARORBETTY ELI
USES NOTI ARAS TAIL
RAN TOMORHOBNOB LOCKE
FRESHMAN ASIDE LASHES
RHEAS GRINS MERCY
ACARID TOPEE TEACAKES
CATER SEWORTHRASH ERA
ENID FERN EUGE BEEF
REO MINESORLAKE ERNIE
BANQUETS COIR RORY
URN ACCOSTS BONBON
WIZARDS RUST HUES UTE
EVORA SWELTERORSEETHE
SALTY TOOT NURSE FEED
TRASS SON SETA TORY

137

CLUB LAPPS OPAL MCCC
HALE ADLAI OPINE ARLO
AMTS TOURNAMENTS NOEL
PARTNERS MINE SPASMS
ARISE POETS BEATS
LAMENT RACE CORLEONE
INAWE LOSER PAYS SEVER
SIRS SOUSA AGROS ERA
PSI THREENOTRUMP ROT
ENTREES LEES RAY
ERIES MEESE RILES
APR SOLI CANASTA
OTB EMPLACEMENTS RID
AHA RERAN TORUS PALE
TORSO CARDSHARP RATEL
SUBTRACT KENO CARESS
ARENA LAIRS BRING
CAROLI BIDE TOENAILS
PAIL MARKEDCARDS ICAL
ORAL AGEES ABEET BARA
SENS LEND DEEDS ALKY

138

PITH CURSE AWNS VAMP
ASHE ONEAL TREAT EXAM
CREAMPUFFS HOTDOGGERS
SROS TEAPOT EPEE
INASTEW ELEF LETSA
MELTS ALPHA UFO ATMO
BITS FROLIC IRRA BRAN
EGO OLDFASHIONED LATE
DEFORESTS ERNES EWER
TWAS MESA SNEE BUS
THECHOCOLATESOLDIER
CHE HYLA INES ADOR
LIEB DROOD CONTOURED
UNAU SMARTCOOKIES YER
MORT EAVE RERIGS ABLE
PUTT NNE ESTEE ISLES
THEGO LAVA RECTORS
RIRE REMORA CERN
BEEFEATERS SUGARDADDY
OVAL SADAT ALIBI EERO
GARY TONS RESET ASSN

139

BABE FACTOR AMAZONIAN
ANYA ASHINE RELOCATES
RTES THEREGOESMYHEART
TIBETS WAS GATOS LSD
PYLE MEDICI OSIER
ARE YOUREDEVASTATING
ROBESON EYER ADEEM
ATAN TIDED NBA PEASE
COBRA SEL SWEETHEARTS
ANYONE FACIE ALE SEA
LOVEANDMARRIAGE
SMA ORR VOLES LOGJAM
KISSMEAGAIN VIA DRURY
ANANA SEV PENNI ESME
TOPED INMY GLOTTAL
WHEREHAVEYOUBEEN IDO
RELET NORMAL TONI
KLM OLTEN RBS COSTLY
YOURCHEATINHEART MILE
ABYSSINIA BERLIN AMON
TESTAMENT CASTES NESS

140

MAST MARO SHOPS JAG
NORIA ALECS TERRE IDO
EVENTHOUGHANUMBER NAN
SENATE MARLO ESTRANGE
TRAILED LETTS ZANIER
ELIA OUTS ETC
CARESSES OFPEOPLEHAVE
ALIA TSAR PLO OLEG
SACRO SURGE SEAFARING
SIENNA RIALS CORSETS
TRIEDNOONEHAS
ATTRACT APRIL MOHAVE
TRAIPSING EELED NOSEY
TURF OUR LEVI RISE
YETFOUNDAWAY ENGRAFTS
LON ENOL SERE
STEELS OMAHA RASCALS
CREDITED ASIDE ITALIA
AIR TODRINKFORALIVING
LEI ERGOT AISLE VIBES
ADE SEEPS SEES ELIS

141

142

143

144

145

146

B	I	B	B		M	S	B	A				P	A	V	E		S	P	A	R
A	R	E	A		A	C	E	R	B		A	R	R	A	N		H	E	M	O
J	O	L	L	Y	R	O	G	E	R		D	E	A	N	S	L	I	S	T	S
A	N	A	L	E	C	T	S		A	N	V	I	L		L	A	N	O	S	E
			P	A	H	S			Z	E	E	S		C	A	K	E			
C	A	M	A	S			A	Y	E	A	R			O	V	E	R	L	A	P
A	M	E	R		S	I	L	E	N	T	B	U	T	L	E	R		I	D	A
P	O	R	K		O	R	E	G				L	I	D	S		T	B	A	R
E	R	R			L	O	N	G	J	O	H	N	S			B	U	E	N	O
K	E	Y	S	T	O	N	E		A	P	I	A			R	E	T	R	O	S
		A	T	O	N	E		I	S	T	L	E		M	A	L	T	A		
C	A	N	I	N	G			C	O	I	L		M	A	N	T	I	L	L	A
O	D	D	L	Y			F	A	N	C	Y	D	A	N	S			A	I	X
M	O	R	E		S	K	I	N				O	R	N	O		B	R	E	L
I	R	E		S	W	E	E	T	W	I	L	L	I	A	M		E	T	T	E
C	O	W	S	L	I	P			A	T	A	L	E			P	A	S	O	S
			K	A	N	T		B	R	E	T			S	E	R	T			
S	T	R	O	N	G		F	E	M	M	E		B	E	G	O	N	I	A	S
G	R	E	A	T	S	C	O	T	T		S	I	L	L	Y	B	I	L	L	Y
T	I	L	L		B	R	O	T	H		T	R	U	M	P		K	L	A	N
S	O	Y	S		Y	U	L	E				S	E	A	T		S	E	R	E

147

		S	T	R	A	D		M	A	N	E	T				P	A	N	G	S
	B	L	O	U	S	E		A	L	A	M	E	D	A		A	B	E	L	E
D	E	A	T	H	O	F	A	D	R	U	M	M	E	R		S	A	T	A	N
I	N	T	E	R	F	E	R	E		T	A	P	P	E	T	S		T	D	S
G	E	E	R			R	O	U	T			E	O	A	N		C	E	D	E
S	T	S		S	E	R	A	P	H	D	U	S	T		T	A	R	R	E	D
			S	O	L	A	R		W	E	S	T				G	O	I	N	
		S	P	A	L	L		C	A	L	E	S	A		I	R	A	N		
S	A	T	I	R	E		L	A	R	E	S		U	P	S	E	T	T	H	E
A	V	E	R			T	A	R	T	S	A	N	D	A	L	E		H	E	N
L	O	R	E		A	I	R	E				E	I	R	E		N	E	S	T
E	I	N		F	R	E	E	D	O	M	H	A	L	L			E	R	S	E
P	R	O	F	O	U	N	D		V	O	I	L	E		S	A	W	Y	E	R
		N	O	R	M		O	L	E	I	N	E		C	O	N	T	E		
	S	T	A	T				E	R	S	T		P	O	U	T	S			
M	A	H	L	E	R		E	A	S	T	E	R	H	A	R	E		T	R	E
A	D	E	S		A	R	A	P			D	A	I	S			B	R	A	G
D	I	R		S	T	A	T	I	O	N		G	A	T	H	E	R	I	N	G
A	R	O	S	E		T	E	N	L	I	T	T	L	E	O	S	A	G	E	S
M	O	O	R	E		A	N	T	O	N	I	A		R	O	S	C	O	E	
E	N	F	I	N				O	R	A	N	G		S	T	E	E	N		

148

A	B	B	E		A	M	B	O				S	L	E	W		A	L	B	A
L	O	R	D		P	I	L	A	R		P	H	O	T	O		T	A	A	L
P	L	A	I	T	P	L	A	T	E		H	I	G	H	E	R	H	I	R	E
S	E	N	T	I	E	N	T		C	H	A	R	Y		F	I	O	R	D	S
			I	L	L	E		M	O	O	S	E			U	L	M			
C	A	B	O	T			P	A	I	N	E			F	L	E	E	R	E	D
O	L	A	N		W	H	O	R	L	E	D	W	O	R	L	D		A	T	E
V	E	R	S		E	A	R	S				A	W	A	Y		V	I	A	L
E	R	R			S	I	G	H	T	S	I	T	E			L	A	N	G	E
S	T	E	A	D	I	L	Y		R	E	S	T			T	E	N	S	E	D
		N	E	O	N	S		M	Y	T	H	S		S	A	V	E	R		
V	I	B	O	R	G			A	S	T	A		O	C	C	I	D	E	N	T
A	M	A	N	A			M	I	T	E	M	I	G	H	T			I	E	R
T	A	R	S		T	M	A	N				T	R	I	O		A	G	R	A
I	G	O		F	R	I	E	Z	E	F	R	E	E	Z	E		E	N	V	Y
C	E	N	T	R	A	L			L	E	E	R	S			A	S	S	E	S
			H	E	N			W	O	R	M	S		P	A	C	T			
A	B	O	R	T	S		R	H	I	N	O		P	U	R	C	H	A	S	E
F	L	E	E	S	F	L	E	A	S		T	U	R	N	S	T	E	R	N	S
T	A	N	A		E	A	G	R	E		E	R	A	T	O		T	A	U	T
S	H	O	D		R	O	O	F				D	Y	A	N		E	R	G	S

149

P	I	L	L		D	O	R	A			A	B	O	U	T		S	P	A	D
E	R	I	E		A	M	O	N	G		N	O	D	T	O		A	R	N	A
P	I	T	C	H	K	E	T	T	L	E	D	A	D	A	M		L	I	N	K
O	N	E	T	O	O	N	E		A	M	A	S	S		A	L	I	C	I	A
	G	R	U	N	T	S		S	M	E	L	T			H	O	N	K	E	R
			R	E	A		M	O	O	R	E			H	A	R	E	M		
A	B	B	E	Y		M	E	R	R	Y	G	O	D	O	W	N		E	M	S
D	E	E	D		S	E	R	E				C	O	R	K		S	D	A	K
I	L	L		S	M	E	L	L	S	M	O	C	K	S		T	H	A	N	E
P	A	L	A	T	I	N	E		L	A	R	U	E		C	U	E	I	N	G
		I	T	A	L	Y		D	I	N	A	R		S	O	L	A	N		
D	E	B	A	T	E		P	A	T	E	R		S	P	L	I	N	T	E	R
A	M	O	L	E		W	H	I	S	T	E	R	P	O	O	P		I	L	E
T	I	N	E		B	A	I	L				O	R	O	N		L	E	O	N
A	T	E		B	E	L	L	Y	T	I	M	B	E	R		R	O	S	I	E
		S	T	O	A	T			S	T	A	L	E		C	A	L			
L	U	T	H	E	R			M	A	C	L	E		S	A	I	L	E	D	
O	T	H	E	R	S		S	A	R	A	I		P	E	N	N	I	N	E	S
M	I	E	S		K	E	A	K	I	N	G	H	O	D	D	Y	P	E	A	K
A	L	O	E		I	D	L	E	S		N	A	S	A	L		O	R	N	A
N	E	W	S		N	O	T	A	T			D	Y	N	E		P	O	E	T

150

O	K	A	Y		F	U	L	D	A		L	O	W	E	R		A	T	T	A
N	I	T	E		I	S	A	A	C		E	N	A	T	E		S	H	O	D
T	O	H	A	V	E	A	N	D	H	A	V	E	N	O	T		T	E	N	D
O	W	E		E	R	G	O		I	M	E	A	N		R	A	R	O	I	A
P	A	L	A	N	C	E		B	L	U	R	T		S	A	L	A	L		
			G	A	E		S	A	L	S	E		S	H	I	E	L	D	E	D
G	O	G	O	L		S	T	R	E	E	T	S	C	E	N	E		W	A	R
U	P	O	N		B	A	R	I				L	I	D	S		M	I	T	E
S	A	N		T	O	B	A	C	C	O	R	O	A	D		W	A	V	E	S
T	H	E	M	O	N	E	Y		U	N	I	T			C	O	R	E	R	S
		W	A	T	E	R		C	R	A	G	S		B	I	R	D	S		
A	L	I	N	E	D			H	I	L	I		P	A	R	T	I	T	A	S
R	E	T	E	M		T	H	E	O	L	D	B	U	N	C	H		A	B	E
R	A	H	S		S	U	E	R				I	R	A	E		G	L	U	T
A	R	T		W	I	L	L	I	A	M	T	E	L	L		T	E	E	T	H
U	N	H	A	R	M	E	D		S	O	I	R	S		S	I	R			
		E	L	A	P	S		S	T	U	N	S		S	T	O	M	A	C	H
A	S	W	I	P	E		S	C	A	R	Y		S	H	A	G		N	A	Y
C	H	I	C		R	E	T	U	R	N	T	O	P	A	R	A	D	I	S	E
R	A	N	I		E	X	U	L	T		I	N	A	N	E		A	M	E	N
E	D	D	A		D	O	B	L	E		M	A	R	K	S		M	A	Y	A

151

```
CASH■CARAT■RACK■■FRAU
ARPA■AVERS■INRE■FLUBS
BARD■MANTA■SIER■LATEN
■BYJUPITER■STARLIGHT■
■■■■POLES■LOAM■ENG■■■
MINED■■■■AIL■POST■MOO
ONETOUCHOFVENUS■YEARN
OTRA■NOOSE■■AFT■■NINA
REOS■LURER■FIFES■RAES
ENL■MACS■■LEA■■COO■■■
■TILLTHECLOUDSROLLBY■
■■■LIC■■EAU■■HOTE■LUM
ABBA■HOUND■FLOAT■COPE
BRAM■■USS■■ABACI■HOPS
RABAT■THESKYSTHELIMIT
IDE■ROSE■URE■■■■ATSEA
■■■BAR■RANA■ABEAD■■■■
■THECOMETS■MOONBEAMS■
BEIGE■ATOP■ARRAY■ROAD
SALAD■ATNO■ITEMS■MATA
ARON■■MEET■MARIS■STEM
```

152

```
■FLORA■CHAIRS■WINDBAG
ERASER■HARDEN■HARRIER
NESTLE■ARMADA■INCENSE
TETEATETE■■ARCS■■AGOG
■■■■YEST■■STEEPS■DEPS
ADITS■SERAPE■DEE■SSS■
IRRA■PAROLE■PARTI■■■■
REALLY■■DIAPER■■CLEFT
SINKOR■BEAKER■■SCORIA
■■■AERIE■■OPORTO■QASR
■PUTWORDSINONESMOUTH■
MESH■LASTRE■■OPERA■■■
RAMOSE■■AISLES■DECADE
SLANT■■KISMET■■ASIDES
■■■■POSER■INADAY■TALC
■ETO■APR■UNITES■SYRIA
ASOF■RIBAND■■LIST■■■■
THAT■■ESPS■■GIFTOFGAB
LATERAL■PAVLOV■OPIATE
ARENTWE■AFFINE■LONGED
SPEARER■LEWDER■ENDAS■
```

153

```
SPAN■TEACH■FLOUR■BONG
ORDO■ENSUE■LITRE■ALOE
BEARDSTHELIONINHISDEN
SYMMETRY■PRODS■ENISLE
■■■ALAE■EMERY■SAUL■■■
APPLE■■CAAN■■PQRS■ADA
BUILDABETTERMOUSETRAP
ORGY■BURSE■EERIE■IBIS
WIG■TRIO■■ADLIB■SPORE
■MYSOUL■VISION■ENTRY■
■■■CAPTAINKANGAROO■■■
■BLEST■LEVELS■CRUETS■
POINT■ISNEW■■ATAT■RUB
AXLE■SCANS■DIJON■RIDE
LETSTHECATOUTOFTHEBAG
MRS■AIRE■■SNIB■■OVENS
■■■ALPS■SHAGS■CITE■■■
BIGTOP■GOUGE■ROBERTAS
INAONEHORSEOPENSLEIGH
DRUM■ROBES■NUDGE■NERO
EELS■SPINY■SPOON■DRAW
```

154

```
PAST■EMBER■STOIC■OPAL
ATOY■DIANE■LOTTO■LANE
YOUKNIGHTS■ONTOP■ESTA
SPLEEN■■RELET■■ERASER
■■■■OARDANE■ORT■UNE■■
■SCAN■IRITIS■ERAS■NEE
LULUS■SEN■■TENANT■GIN
AMAN■SEA■HUEMAIN■AERO
TWIT■INDIAN■IMP■ACRES
HORSED■■MHO■RESORT■■■
ENE■CLASP■■■ADEPT■BAA
■■■DUETEA■SET■■ESTERS
MACES■RAS■MEEKER■HERO
ETON■MOWSHUN■ALA■EDEN
TOM■RUPEES■■RPI■ROUTE
AMP■ASHE■TABOOS■ELEE■
■■ORG■YDS■BEAKERS■■■■
TRUESO■■AZTEC■■OODLES
AONE■WEAVE■THREWWEIGH
LIDS■LADES■LEASE■EDGE
ELSE■START■ESTES■ROSA
```

155

```
SWABS■AMASS■IBIS■HUME
LANAI■NEMAT■DUNE■ENOW
IRONE■NAOMI■ELAN■AIDE
DYANSCANNONBALLSERVES
■■■ITALY■AGE■SLEET■■■
■BASAL■■■NYET■■■SWAYS
BELT■■ERGS■NABOB■OGEE
ALIE■ICON■■■HALO■RANT
CLARABOWANDARROWSMITH
HASSLE■■TOOL■ANET■NAS
■■■■ARES■ONI■SADA■■■■
LAG■RIRE■SNEE■■OUSTER
ASUBMARINEANDCLUBTOGO
NINE■NONE■■■ALIT■RUGS
CANA■SLEEP■SMUT■■ETAS
ENSUE■■■ROSA■■■SPEAR■
■■■FLEAS■PAR■SWEAT■■■
BROOKESHIELDSTHESWORD
LAIR■RIAL■VITAE■SINAI
ERST■IDLE■ONAIR■USERS
TEES■EELS■SABRE■PERAK
```

156

MALABAR TACIT FETTLE
APARADE ENOCH CURIOUS
DRUMSALONGTHE ANONYMS
FIRS RESOLE FENDS SBE
ODE ATNO ALLEY DIAN
RENT ASIS ALOSS TINGE
HAVEA ADOSE MOTTOS
LABORED AEONS TENTH
ITALIC STILE HONEYED
NOBEL STOOL EGIS AER
ONES THEMUSICMAN ATTU
SES LEAN HARPS ESTES
RICARDO MOTES EXCISE
NORSE TOURS EXPECTS
BETRUE PROSY AXION
ANODE MEESE MUTT TAPS
RAYS GORSE BADE CAP
BBL BANAT SUPINE SURA
ALABAMA LITTLEDRUMMER
RENEGED ELATE EILEENS
ADDERS SATES DETENTE

157

BERM SCALA COAL ERST
ACEA ALLER FAUNA TOUR
SONGSMYMOTHERTAUGHTME
ALTITUDE WANDS GLOSSY
LEE ARE PIRNS HAS
SRA SETTE ICES RAE
WAITTILLTHECLOUDSROLL
OSSA AYR ILL ESEL
OHMYDARLINGCLEMENTINE
LES INKY ARRAS RUINER
NAGS CEE MAMA
ARCANE TORTE LATE OCT
SILVERTHREADSAMONGTHE
SLOE IRA CRI ITAL
NEVERBEENINLOVEBEFORE
SSE OLDE MOIRA ART
BUA SPILE ANI IST
SHARES TOAST ANACUSIA
MANONTHEFLYINGTRAPEZE
OLIO EERIE NORIA OREL
GOLD DYNA GRASS NESS

158

ALAN CWT EDP ♥FELT
SOLE UAR LEI TINGE
INAT PROTECTS ORIEL
RICHARDTHELION♥ED
REP SSE ALLI
PAIRED ♥BREAKHOUSE
ALT EIS LES EARNED
SAY SALTIERS STALED
EARLOBE TIDY
KIND♥SANDCORONETS
LOST IODINES
ALLITS WONDERED AMB
PLACEA ING SER NAY
SOMEWHERE♥S SWEET♥
IDEM SIE ARC
MY♥BELONGSTODADDY
AMINE RENITENT SORE
TAKEN STP RAT ETAT
♥LESS SHA ESO DEMI

159

CASK SNAP OPEC WUN
ULNAS SNAP TOGA SCENE
POINTOFNORETURN ELSIE
INFORM ALIX RETREATED
DEF INCLOSE STOPSUP
PIA ORB DADOES
LADDS POINTSOUT WEIGH
ALIE AURA SCRIP SNEE
BOSC MALTA CANNOT TSP
SPARGE ORLE DIRECT
PEAN POINTER NINA
SPEEDY GIDE TODDLE
WHO AEOLIA SWAGE REIN
HAIR DYERS ICED UTES
ERNES OUTPOINTS ENSUE
TETRAD SUD SRS
MAVISES GETSOUT ABI
ONETONINE HAHA HEAVEN
LONER POINTLESSREMARK
PATSY ELSE SMIT MAINE
EHS SAME ANY SLED

160

GLAIR COLADA SOUSA
RUBLE AVALON OCTAVES
HALLOA BENITO FRENEAU
ONLY CHINESEDATE ASTI
RDA SHANS IDEAL TET
EMBROILS TARZAN OSANE
BAYONNE BONIER CUP
MAG CURSED ALPACAS
ATTAR FATTEN ALIENATE
LOAN BANTER PLUM ISTS
PARC ENNIS CRIME SPIT
ETTA GOON SAUDIS HALO
REANOINT MANNAN AMRAS
TENDERS DONNED PTA
LST MELTED PATIENT
SPREE BUTTES BALINGER
HEE SOUSE ILIAC AMY
OTTO GRECIANBEND OLES
TEACHES TOROSE INSIST
ERITREA ORATED NOLTE
LOESS RAMONS SLOES

161

ASTI MALI CAPER BIALI
REAM APED ARENA ECLAT
ARMISTICE TROIS ABOVE
THEGHOSTANDMRSMUIR
ROSARY AIS SUET DES
ACUTE DENS STLO
THEOWLANDTHEPUSSYCAT
HERR OMEGA MORE TREE
ERS OVATE RESINS GAT
ANET MANIA ANGORA
THEWINDANDTHELION
ODESSA AURAS RAPT
BOA SHORTS LANDS GAP
INCH AMAH AIMEE FORE
THEDEVILANDMISSJONES
NIKE EDER ANETO
ASH PEAR EWE ANTRES
THEOLDMANANDTHESEA
LINGO IRATE REVISITED
ALIEN NENES ARID NOVA
SLEET DEANS POLE EDAM

162

LALO PGNS ANITRA IDS
ANIFORANI BEGONE LAMP
SYCAMORES AWLESS ITOI
NEVA TEA ADAGE
ALI SIGHTFORSOREIS
GEL NEARER SMART ELM
ENATIC MAY BEIGE SOI
DESIRE GESTE ASAN
SHORTHAIRED UPEND
OUTRAN PAIDONES
YELLOWTOTHEJAUNDICEDI
AWOMANSI SELLTO
LINNS LITTLENECKS
INDO HOWES TIANTS
EGO GENIE UMP KOREAN
SSS DEALT ENDMAN ETO
IONLYHAVEISFOR LEW
BIRDS HRE TWAS
ALER SAVIOR SHOWROOMS
REDO PROSIT PANHANDLE
TIP SOLIDS ASSY GAVE

163

ATSEA DOME ACER
ANITAS UPON FORUM
SPANISHSTEPS EDISON
AIL RELICS TIRE SRA
SNOB LATH MANS SIAM
EGGED REHEATS STALE
TEA ALEE DARNED
DEFERS TRI CIGAR
EARL SINBAD REAPING
AVE SEPTO UNITS VII
RENDERS RETUNE FELL
CENTO ACT REARED
ATHENS RICH SAT
KAPPA PUSHUPS TERSE
RIAS BUNT NELL SECT
OPS BONN SCREAM BAN
NETTED ITALIANOPERA
IRATE NORE VENICE
YEAS GRAS ESTES

164

ASP TITLES BRER TATAR
BOA ENRAGE ROVE ANAME
JOYCECAROLOATES ROYAL
UNION DIS XIS TOTAL
RENT TEA HIS ALBA OLD
ERG GERTRUDESTEIN ROY
SON HIE TESS SCAN
BRAND POUT LESS SHANE
LAGO LAM DART COIL
UNAWARES TIME SLANDER
RET BEATRIXPOTTER WAE
BEHOLDS IBIS GOOSEEGG
APED SMEE VIN ELLE
OSCAR STIR WIFE ALLES
KOHL STAN THE AES
RUR VIRGINIAWOOLF DUD
ALI ALOE ONT CBS RENE
STILL STE ETE EOSIN
MATIN LOUISAMAYALCOTT
ARIEL ERIC DIVERS TEE
EMERY ROTE SLEDGE ODD

165

PROSER ARTIST MACHO
PRORATE BORNEO ALAIN
CLOSEBUTNOCIGAR ROUGE
HATE UNIO KNAR SOUGHT
ONE NTHS TOSIR HEW
SECONDRATE SHAPE ATRO
ESTREAT ELKE DENOVO
RAREE PELT CARAFES
ABLATE NOSEDOUT ALFIN
BEE STATS LORNA NOBLE
LEFT OBITS MALTS NAEL
ONTAP ARIES HEEPS SEL
OTATE NEARMISS LINENS
MOTTOED LION STONE
TENSOR AGIO ESCAPES
SEHR SNARL OFFTHEPACE
TSE MESTA BNAI ROD
APPLES HIER RSTU PALE
PIOUS FOLLOWTHELEADER
LASSO ALASKA ENEMIES
ELTON RETEES DOSERS

166

CHEWS TOGAS MILORD
RUSHED REGALED OLIVER
ASPIRE EMPLACE RACEME
WHATSNEWPUSSYCAT EROS
LUNT STR ALAI ERS
SPAIN CATBURGLARS ASE
NAP PARSERS OPTED
ADAGIO MISDO ANU
RATTLE WEARESIAMESE
ETHOS PARR NNE SNAP
TEEN TRUSS NISAN ISLE
ERNS RUG IMET SNIDE
ACHESHIRECAT CUTLER
AEF SERER OTHERS
COSTA TAINTED PRE
ONT PUSSYFOOTED ACTED
NEE SNEE LOT ORME
FOES CATONAHOTTINROOF
UNREEL STAMINA CANUTE
STEPPE EUGENES SIEVER
EARTHS SYSTS FREDS

167

WAIST STILT SISI AND
ESCARP RILLE ARUT TOO
THEVIRGINIAN VERACRUZ
SERENER AMAT DELAINE
REGAG CANEA LISPS
AMBS OPUS STANWYCK
LAR ELAM STYE SEBUM
IDIOM SABOT RHEA TARE
DAGMAR GARYCOOPER LET
ATHENA DARE WERE LYE
TRIMS OVALS RINGO
GEL AROE INEE EARFUL
ABE SOULSATSEA STIFLE
BRAC DRIP STRUT AMINO
SOFAS EXIT AERA RAN
SHERIDAN DAME GEES
CABAL REBEL SAVOR
SONANTS RARA RECEDES
HIGHNOON SERGEANTYORK
ALL ORLY CIGAR SEEMLY
DSO NODE ODETS TREES

168

BSA CAB SLAG REB
LADD DEVON PARR ARAM
OTHO ALONE ANTE VIRUS
WEEWILLIEWINKIE ANKLE
SERENE DREW STAG ILE
NELL SLIGHT TEASED
SAVE SEA ODDITY
KEW WILLOTHEWISP USS
ARIA ADONAI NCO NEW
FALLIN SURD ECHO IRE
ISLAND TSP HAS AMULET
REO OSSO FISH MERLIN
FAN HUT ARIOSI NINA
STY BETHEREAWILL NES
SCHEME EAR CLAR
CHERIE TOTALS YUMA
ROY STAR GOAL HUBERT
ELUDE WILLOWWAREPLATE
WAKER AVIS ESTER EDEN
ROLL SILT REELS SORT
NEY HAYS TRY WYO

169

CARGO APB ALP CRAMP
SALIAN MORAVIA REMORA
ELAPSE BRAVEST ADORES
GOB PULITZERPRIZE ASS
ARAM POE OLE RISE
LIMIT ANNIEHALL GENET
SEASON TINEARS AUGERS
SNOW SALVO SUNG
BRIM TOLAN OMENS IFFY
LONI REINE CADET ERIE
ODIN EVA GAR JENA
NEON DINAR RIEKA AYES
DONE ANGLE EDSEL CAST
SEME ANAME RICK
SALOME PREMIER ASSERT
TROTS TOMWATSON TONIO
RARA PIE DOE NAVY
ABE KENTUCKYDERBY BIE
PITMEN ELLISON BUTLER
SATURN SNIDEST ELVERS
NANNY SAP RES DEARE

170

ABETS OPEC BARB RANG
NOVAE FATA OBOE ALOUD
THEMANFROMUNCLE MERLE
HER EST ELIDE GLUMLY
EMENDS SPRAT ANITA
MISERS SONOFAGUN NEB
ATTA SWANS ERASE CAR
UPTON ALOT SPORE
MAJ GRANDMAMOSES HUNT
BLOWHOT ASONE ISIS
LAYETTE TITUS ATELIER
CASE SALON ROMANCE
AVER MOTHERTONGUE SUB
LIBYA RAID POUTS
DER SHIRT ARETE TOSS
ADO SOBSISTER PEWTER
TREVI IOTAS ARLENE
ETHANE MAGNA AER ASE
GHENT FATHERCHRISTMAS
GORGE ALAE DOIN CRETE
USED TEND SOBE TIRES

171

OBEY SCALPS FIRTHS
APALE IHEARA ALSORAN
GERMANSERMON BESTOWED
ORES OST PSS RSO IALU
RAT SOY TOA DAH KILN
ATTACK CHOICE ASSAI
SEALE FRENCHBENCH ADA
INDIANS ROADRUNNER
RAJ TALC BIND ATESTS
ABAT WOOD ESA AMERCE
SAMOA SWISSMISS SAINT
LASSIE MOE ROTH LOTA
HOICKS RIOT DRAM NEG
ENCASEMENT SODAPOP
PEA IRAQIHOCKEY PHASE
NONES SEVERN ASIDES
BABA SCH ENA ANY ETS
ALAR RAU FRA LLD ALTA
MUCILAGE ISRAELIDAILY
LONGIES GEISHA ERNES
ANGELS STOPIN WEAR

172

AHABS FANON TAB FARO
IBERIA ITERO ERE IVAN
FLAMETHROWER CONCRETE
WET RERENTS ADHERES
ERIC SECCO ISA SAP
NUI RENEWALS FLEET
ANGELICA TORCHBEARER
SOP KNOCK ENTAIL CORA
SIAM TOKAY TONNE ESOP
ASDIC LEMON ENIF
MESCAL RANAMOK DRIVER
RYAL PERLE ERODE
ROTO NOTED LAIRD ELIE
ALOW COOLIE LENIN CCS
CIGARETTIPS GENERATE
KNAVE SEASONAL TAN
EAR MNO EPISC MODE
STOODUP LAIGLON LAW
CONVENED HOTCHOCOLATE
ARCE UTE CLEAT OLIVER
TEEN PEW HARLS ALTAR

173

HARD CUBA PLAT CADI
AROE ISAR RANI AXIS
HALFANEYE EYEAPPEAL
ABLAZE ATOM TREADLE
CURE EPIC ABB
STEERAGE TERM ALEPH
TAY EMAIL ROOD EYRE
APED ADDUP POUF EER
BABEL IONIC RELAPSE
ALOP SALIC LOGO
FILLOUT REGAL PEPYS
ILL SCAT SARAS SPAT
LIED EXIT REBID ELI
MODEL ICON DEMURRER
SOP SWAB LORE
TEMPURA EYED LOCALE
EYEOPENER LAYEYESON
ARAN SKYE OREO SEND
LAND SHED WEAN SAGO

174

ANTA ABACA JABS RASH
BAHN SALON EOLIC OSTE
EVEN HILLSOFHABERSHAM
LEGERITY EVANS PETERS
RATES BRATS PTER
EELER BOITE PRIVATE
TREES REUNE JUICE HMS
HAND PONTE ARMS NEBO
ASP ARNAS CULPA SALEM
WEARIED TIDAL ANSARA
SONGOFTHEOPENROAD
POTATO ROILS ACOLYTE
ELULS FAUNS AUGHT OAR
BIRD HUNG ALLEY EFTS
AVE TENCH TRIAL MATTE
ESTRADA MAKER PITHY
REDS GOLAN DANSE
ATSINA OUTON MIRACLES
GRANDCANYONSUITE RARE
AUBE HOMER ALLAN OKRA
LEES EKED SMELT WEST

175

JADE ADEPTS STOPUP EPIS
EVIL REGAIN ERRATA RARE
RATS CARNEYSMIDWAY EGAN
KITED LETS TITIS RECENT
SLY EMITS ARTIE SORT
FENS ADIEU ILLS CAS
ECHOING FORDSMODELT ARM
PLOWED RANEE ZEES ILA
SUPER HAREM SCANT ABNER
OMEN LEIS APART FLUENT
MPS MEADOWSLARK ARIOSE
DRYADS INERT ANONYM
VIANDS STACKEDDECK URI
RIATAS PECKS OMSK ATOR
ALMAS BATHE MERIT FRISK
ILO TOLA WORST MINNIE
SON WELLESFARGO MONEYED
END RAES CERES FETE
AIMS GRAMS DODOS BAN
CRYPTS SHORT AERI TERSE
RASP TALEOFHOFFMAN GETA
ABEL ERINGO FREETO OVER
MIRE RITTER TORRES SERS

176

```
ALEC■SAIC■OLAV■PLAN
LANO■OSSA■LAGO■ROVE
ACCOUNTABILITY■AVOW
STELLAR■ONIT■ADVENT
■■■AER■LONE■AGED■■■
SIGNS■CASE■AMENABLE
HOLT■SAUERKRAUT■UAR
ANA■STUD■■AMIR■GRIN
RADICAL■RATED■DOLCE
■■SCAT■CITED■AONE■■
MOTOR■EASES■AMNESTY
IRON■AARE■■ALOE■QUE
FEN■APPENDICES■CUBA
FLESHPOT■INRE■SHEER
■■■TARE■LACE■ETA■■■
GAZEBO■DELI■SPINALS
AMOR■AMBASSADORSHIP
OBOE■COLD■ORAD■OONA
LIMO■HESS■RAKE■NYET
```

177

```
BANJO■DAVID■PPS■SCOFF
ALOUD■EROSE■ROT■MARLO
SIRLANCELOT■ALEXANDER
SEMI■EARTH■■IDLE■DEEM
INSURE■ISE■AREAR■LACE
■■■SERIF■LAHIRE■PILED
ABACA■REI■GEES■DAN■■■
EMBARGO■NANA■■■ARGINE
ROBE■ONEEYEDJACKS■COT
ACES■AWARNS■OLA■EDEMA
■■■ASSISTS■CHALICE■■■
METRE■LEI■WINTER■AFAR
AMA■PALLASATHENA■DONE
JUDITH■■■ALEA■DESMOND
■■■NEA■BALD■YEA■TALES
BARIT■HECTOR■PREEN■■■
ADAM■BOGEY■ARI■INSETS
OMNI■IGOT■■CIGAR■HAIL
BIGCASINO■CHARLEMAGNE
AREAS■EIN■PETAL■INRED
BERLE■RAE■ALAMO■IDEAS
```

178

```
VALA■SARSA■■FIN■■APOD
ANAT■STAEL■IODO■ASORE
MYHARTEBELONGSTODADDY
POOLE■NEATAS■■TPI■■■■
ENROL■■■LISI■SHIR■LIS
DEES■■HOLMESSWEETHOME
■■■SACER■ESTEES■YOUNG
MIT■PARCH■■ENDED■UPON
ONELAP■HAVARTI■ROSETO
MALAISE■SOI■■SPINE■■■
■TOBRINGHOMETHEBACON■
■■■OOZER■■ERI■ABRASED
WHARFE■ADDENDS■LOTSOF
HADA■DATER■■YOKEL■ENC
ALORS■PINITE■TESLA■■■
MOVEALONGFELLOW■■LACE
SSE■BITE■TABA■■■LAMAS
■■■■RAH■■SOONAS■AMOST
WHATAREYOURWORDSWORTH
ARMES■GASP■ESTAR■SERE
YEAR■■MME■■DESKS■ASOR
```

179

```
SMEAR■PAMPER■APICAL
TAXCO■AREOLA■COLONY
OLAND■CONDESCENSION
RAGE■GEMS■PHASE■NIX
ERG■TARA■THEN■■RENE
■■EMITS■CHAR■FLIRTS
MARINE■WARN■■LIN■■■
OVATE■TIBET■MANGOES
PETE■IONIA■SAGE■BRA
PSI■OSTENTATION■SAM
ETO■REED■ERIAN■HOSP
TANTRUM■ONENO■GALEA
■■■AIL■■PINT■TAVERN
MOLEST■SENT■TALES■■
ARIL■■FANG■PERE■CHA
GIS■ADAMS■AONE■HEAD
METAMORPHOSIS■CONGO
ANEMIC■LOBULE■OSCAR
STREAK■EPIRUS■STERE
```

180

```
MANORS■■BOHR■■■BEATTY
AZALEA■BESOOT■BANSHEE
IOIDALMATIANS■RIVIERA
TRAS■VORTEX■HAILY■3RS
RED■SANDER■LILAS■IMET
ESS■AGTS■■4IRON■BTU■■
■■■GLEE■MALATE■GRIST■
■ABRAS■POSERS■ALASKAN
PSEUD■MAMBAS■OBEY■EXE
ASHE■■ONEIF■AXON■■TIP
JAIL■3RINGCIRCUS■DECA
AYN■■PACT■LORAN■■REAL
MID■BAYS■HOWARD■BARBI
ANTLERS■SAVANT■SWISS■
■GHOST■CADENT■CHAN■■■
■■EGO■RULER■■ARAN■IRR
IN8O■CETUS■CINEMA■TAO
REB■FLASK■POWDER■RITA
AVAILED■17YEARLOCUSTS
NULLIFY■STLUKE■COBALT
ISLETS■■■HERE■■KEYNES
```

181

LUSTED SHERE STEELY
ATTIRE AURORA STELLAS
THEPAWNBROKER TARTINE
EELS OBOES AMAIN ZER
XRAYS TANS ONAIR LAS
HEATS FERN NOB
BEQUEATH AFFIX BATES
EMULATE STRAD BRUITED
GUESTS RATAL HAIR HAI
ETH EATIN ARGUABLE
WANE CHECKMATE SIST
EXORABLE KITED PIS
ALF BRAD MINER GRAHAM
RETREAT DINTS LEONORE
SHOTS HANGS BICUSPID
EOS SUMO SINKS
ANT BEGAT MIRE TATAR
CRI AUTOS WAGER RATI
REGATTA KNIGHTSGAMBIT
ATHLETE SONNET AREOLE
BETTES MEARA LEROTS

182

SHARE ABUMP REBS CHAT
TALON SEPIA EXIT HOPI
ONEMEATBALL SONATINAS
MORE TOO ISER TAMER
PIT TWOPERSPECTIVES
LEAP BEAT IOO STAR
SPIER SEND ASSN MIO
PEONS THREETIMESALADY
ORIN NEAT ELSA GENA
OIL SEER PANE PEN
FOURWINDSANDSEVENSEAS
HAN PROS NITA DRU
BOER ELIS LUCE MILE
FIVEMINUTESMORE BALED
ONE NANS AARE HAZES
BERG CCC ENTE KOBE
EIGHTHOFJANUARY IMP
OXBOW ERGO NRA EROO
THELOOKOF SIXTEENTONS
AIRE RUNE EMAIL ANNES
MOTT MISS SATES TASTE

183

SLEEPS AMATI ELATE
SEATRIP REPINE SIRENS
TWOTIMESTWENTY SEANCE
RACE ALLEES EELED PAD
IBO LARD ARLEN ELSA
PLOW LEVY CRIED CRUET
SENATORS COOT PRESSE
FADS BOXER ELECT
MUFFLE COALS ROASTHEN
ANILE PLASM FISTS IRA
LIFE FOURTIMESIO ARND
IOT TRINS NIVEN ARTIE
ANYTHING CURES PREYER
MARAT POSER SATO
SHINER TALC RAVELERS
TINGE DORIC BALE ABET
OPUS MUSIC CUBA OVA
OPS GUESS CASBAH ANIL
PITIED EIGHTTIMESFIVE
SEEDED DANIEL EXERTED
SNAKY NURSE DADOES

184

MAYS SPAS NDAK APR
ANOA TANANA SOELA TAU
LAUGHINGBOY COMEDIANS
ARTERIA ENE INLET
JOYFOREVER CPDS ALLY
URAL URIS CATANIA
RALE PAN MERRYENGLAND
OTTERS BALLES TAIPEI
REATA KERMESS DERANGE
COULOMB JAG NERO
HAPPYDAYSAREHEREAGAIN
EDIE ELS ATONERS
LASAGNA CATHEAD OCALA
PLANET TORIES PROPEL
SENSEOFHUMOR ATA RIPE
KNEEPAN CLOS FATA
LAPP ELLS MAKESFUNOF
EDAMS LIE CORONAL
AMUSEMENT OPERABOUFFE
RAS CARES DERAIL SOLD
NNE TASS ONLY KEYS

185

MAEWEST AWASH MANMADE
EMERSED CARTA UNIATES
TYRANTS CIDER LINTELS
TEA HELENKELLER
BATHS BADEN EPEE INCH
ANAS SOLED KNOT SCALE
INS ICIER FEES DIETER
LATERALS DEED TENSIVE
ELEVENS SEEN PALS VET
ESSEN HEAD TILT SERO
NEWTOWN PRELATE
DIRS AIRS BOAR ARSES
ODE GINS DENY MANIPLE
LEADING PINE PICKFORD
LASERS HAND TUNES KEA
ATOLL HERS FASTS GENT
RENI SORA TUBAS CANOE
CLARABARTON TON
ATTAINS ODOUR BRONTES
RESTATE LOIRE REPEALS
SNEERED ASSET SYSTEMS

186

187

188

189

190

191

192

193

194

195

196

RUBS AMAS ADAGE AGAPE
ASEA SARI DOLES FOYER
THATSINCREDIBLE FOOLS
EEN IDOS LENAS RESULT
DRIFTER BANG NICER
SERA WEND STUNT ESK
ARMBANDS WARS MALE
ESPY EARNS ELSE ADAY
MER TARDY STELES DOTS
MAISONS GLOATED PER
ANNIES COALTAR MORASS
CDS PROCEED POTABLE
GWEN WEEDED EDENS LAC
RICE ATOM FLEET SEPT
ASHY LALA SLICKEST
BEA ALLEN PINK HEAD
RILES PACE STAMMER
COMMIT SHANK STIR PGA
AVIAN SPECIALDELIVERY
SINGE PARKS BARE OREO
EDGED TRASH SKED SEEN

197

SEEMS ELLAS HEBE CLAP
ANSEL TAINO ATOM HILO
FLORIDAKEYS VALE ARAL
ESTIMATED OREGONTRAIL
EDEN LET ERE DOT
PARA CHARACTER STRAPS
LII REIN PHILE ERAT
ENCLOSED EARS TRESTLE
BEAUT ARTE BRED ULE
CLARINET PIECE RID
SLAY BAKEDALASKA SODS
PAU ALLOW NINESPOT
IRS BEEN POSE TALKS
DETOURS COOS CAMISOLE
EDER SORGO AMIS DEW
RONALD MATAMORAS SEES
NEE ELI ELD HALS
VIRGINIAHAM ESCALATOR
EDIE TORO IDAHOPOTATO
ROTC AWED NITON HEROD
ALEA LADS DEEPS ASSES

198

AMASS BEADON TAAL
PANACHE LENAPE ARSENE
SPYWHOCOULDNTTAKEHEAT
SEA ENTRE RTE RET RST
REST COED ESE SHA
CRASS HOSS AMOS
HELP SEAT DAN WARE
AMOI FATHERHOOD SOBER
DOOR ANTA EAGRE WRENS
FINITE SPIRE BALLET
TELA MERLE TOLD
CALLAS MINIS SHREWS
ARIEL CODAS GLEE EASE
RINSE ELITEGUARD ATOM
PADS BLT NAME RIME
GELS SWAM DYNES
POT ALI STOW EDER
AMO RAS TAM ALENE GEE
RODENTTHATBELLEDALION
TOATEE OLEATE REMORSE
YARD TESTEE EDSEL

199

LOBO PELT FOE POLA
RERUN APIA OLLA ORIBI
TAILORSHOP PIGSTICKER
ESEL ETON STRATI HELI
SELECTED SUIT ERMINES
TAIL DEEMS RAES
UMPIRE COATI ENDS SKI
PIANO BOBBYSOX ESTHER
ORS BARRIE TICS IHEAR
NASA RENEE SELE ARENA
PLICAE UNSHIP
GROIN STEM ELSIE PSAT
LURCH TINA SAILON KHA
ESTEEM SANDSHOE ONION
NES RECT LEARN PRONGS
AIDA LILYS LAMB
REACTOR ANTS FATALISM
OTTO COWPEA VOTE ENTO
SHORTSTOPS DISTRESSES
HENNA TRES ILS USERS
LEST NED PEE RETE

200

THOMAS LOSABLE PAINT
CASINO EKESOUT ASTEEL
HEAROURHAPPYPOLLYANNA
SCRAPPER ILE OMELETS
EEL YORE VET
ARMAND TETE ABET PEP
ZOAR GYNT BRETT MARS
TUNINGUPTOSINGHOSANNA
EGO ORIEL ELOGY PLEIN
CENTRAL BELLE OILED
IMMERSE EDDYING
VOLGA EWALD SADNESS
ACORN IGETA ADAME LIU
SHEISGLADTHEDAYBEGINS
CESS ALLEY RUNE ETUI
ORS SEEN BILK TALESE
ALG BANT CAV
OPHELIA OAT AEROSTAT
WEAREGLADSHEISNTTWINS
NAMAT MOROCCO ARISTA
LETA BRASHER NETHER

201

SQUASH DESERT TEACUP
AUSSIE IMPAIRS HUMANE
BEASTSOFBURDEN IRONIC
RUBLE AFOR EASE RATA
ELLY SIES WALKOFF DEN
SSE HOERS OPIES LAIRS
KILNS TRANS COLA
OHARA BADGE TORONTO
DREWIN SENSE BALANCER
AGAIN OUTGO SORI GIRD
TAV GAMESOFCHANCE TRE
INES VARY WAITS PRIOR
VINTNERS BIKES GIBERS
ECLAIRS BASED AMISS
YIPS BONDS FAZES
ZEBRA LENTO COMER MST
EXO STADIUM ORES BETE
NIDI ASIF ONME SOLAR
ALINER MAJORFARMCROPS
NEERDO SCARLET HANDLE
ASSIST EMBERS OBEYER

202

ASTIR SCAPA GIS OAR
RHYME HORAS INSURABLE
CORPSDEBETS CARNEGIEH
RARA RIVET SPREE
OBOLI LUIGI APIE
CLOVE FORONEANDONEFOR
LILI BLUNT MEET UGO
EVES RADS URBAN RONDO
WEYEPIKE ABOUT WEDGED
STN EGIS NIAS GIDEON
GRANTED SHELTER
SEEING NEST NINE INA
PENROD ITALS CMEMADAM
ARAID ORONO DAMS NITE
PIC SCAM NOSES TOUR
AFTERTHEBISOVER LITRE
LEES FARED COPSE
BRIAR RIANT DADA
HEYSCOMET THEKINGSMEN
GREETINGS EELER ETAGE
TIS DOT ERUPT ROBOT

203

ABCS MORSE SATAN AHAB
REAP OLEIN INANE MORE
CYRANODEBERGERAC BRAN
CECIL ONAN TRUANT
AMECHE VADER SAULT
CLOAK GENE MERMAID
HANGS BANDOLEER SNORE
ERSE COLOR EASEL THAR
LII MADAMEBOVARY OKA
ACETATE ANES SACRE
URGES ESSES SIMON
BRAIN ANOA INORBIT
DUB ARTFULDODGER LOS
INEE SITIN ALANS SODA
SCANT MANDOLINS SOWAR
HUMANER DEVA ANETS
COCOS EROSE HONORE
REASON ODIN TIGER
IRIS CHRISTOPHERROBIN
FIRE OUNCE SWORE ULNA
FEED MEETS TAROS SUNG

204

MASC AFINE RITA RAKES
ARIL MADAT ERAS IRISH
TARASBULBASSONS PONTE
EVERYONE GWENS ROUGED
RESIN TEENS FOSSA
NET AIRED ALTERED
ABEE HAMLETSUNCLE TVA
LETT ALEE SEES THAT
ASH WINDOWLESS MAUDE
STARLETS DEARS APRES
NEED SEAMS TIES
SOFAS SALVE BROADWAY
HORDE HORSESHOES IDE
OMOS EATA ORES AFIT
RPM ODYSSEUSWIFE SEMI
THEMUSE DRIES DAS
SATES SWISS SEPAL
ATWILL CHAET AMESSAGE
VOILA CHARLIECHANSSON
INFEW HARD NEROS ETNA
DEEDS APES EROSE SAYS

205

ABBE SALADS PSALM
RAIL ANEMIC RADIO
THEBIRTHOFANATION
STRANGER FLAT TNT
DES DEEPER
HEAR AAR ARK
LILLIANGISH ATEE
IDEE BOIS ESTATES
PEG ECHO ALTO INT
SOANDSO TILE SNEE
UNIT WAYDOWNEAST
STD UNE OAST
ENTIRE OTT
LAS EINE ATHEISTS
ORPHANSOFTHESTORM
BEAST ELATES ERIE
EARTH TENURE RAGE

206

207

208

209

210

211

SIEGES ASTA LAMA
INVITES PRAHA DINES
FRIDAYTHETHIRTEENTH
TILES EILEEN HONES
TACT BEARD
ERRS EMCEES GOADED
RIOT NEURA FEBRUARY
IDEA TRP GRINS PREE
NESTLE BEAST ALLIN
IER MARCH PSI
BELOW BENNY RACKET
IRON ALIKE BTU AURA
NOVEMBER SALON TRAM
SEDERS ASSUME EELS
RASPS SITS
DAVID ASSISI UREDO
NINETEENEIGHTYSEVEN
OVENS SETON SEALANE
NEWT ASSN TRYSTS

212

ARDOR PETE PAPP CEE
ROUGE ATAVUS OVAL ALA
ENCROACHMENT RELEASES
SAKE RESORTER CONDUCT
CAI ERNES ATESTS
OFFSIDES SISTERLY
ALL DETENTE GETOFFIT
ROIL REVE DELAYOFGAME
ERNIE REF SIM HOPE
DECAGON RATEABLE
THREWAFLAGONTHEPLAY
RELIEVES INHONOR
AURA EVE SAW ARDUE
CLOTHESLINE SLAP NETS
CENTERED MORONIC GOI
ARTESIAN PILINGON
ANGORA DONNE ATE
HOLDING IDASWEET RAIL
ORIENTED INTERFERENCE
LTS GRES ATARUT BUSES
EES SYST RECS ISERE

213

HOB YAWED MAID WACOS
EPIC EVADE ASCI EVORA
REFORMANOPINION LINDY
BRINIEST ORGANS LACER
ADVENT PSALMS MATURE
ILI SUITE LINER
THINS CENTERAFOLD WIS
SYNC PEAT SAND CITE
APSE ENTAILAWAG MOTET
REPLANTS NANA SIMHAH
IOTAS MANIN CULPA
CARPAL AINT TURKOMAN
EPEES DECRYAWOLF SURE
BOAZ GOYA ALAS ETNA
UTS RENEWAHAVEN FATAL
TRENT VATER GAM
ATEASE BRANTS DAKOTA
LIETO LOUISE DERIDING
IMPEL INFLAMEAFIREMAN
SALLE RIFE PANIS LENA
TRESS ANOD TRASH SAW

214

ATMAN WAGED FEET PEWS
PREDA EPURE PARR IMIT
LEMON IPITI ARME NINA
AMOR AGATE NIN TRON
COINAPHRASE LENDAHAND
ERR FLYER LOOSE BETA
TOOL CLEAT ABBE
KDF SMU ALERT SEAL
HOUR BRETON HAHS AFAR
ATLAS WATUSI ROOMMATE
KICKAROUND GOTOPIECES
INREGARD SONNET NOTRE
SGAU IDEM SIESTA NORA
PASS EDITS HGS RET
ATLE ARNEE GERE
TSHI ALIAR SOBER PIA
POKEFUNAT SENDREGRETS
REAP NIB NOSES ERAS
ETNA IMAM PEWEE STILE
SACS TAME PRINZ TROIS
SPET ELAN SONDE MODES

215

JAVAL AGORAS DORSEY
OLIGO CORONA ANITRA
ELLENBURSTYN REFERS
LIE ERASE FAIR VAS
SERT ATE BROWN SETI
AINE CAIRN MOLAR
FREUND FOUND BELA
LOUPE ROOMS ROADWAY
EDGE TELEG BOAT REO
NNE EDIEADAMS END
SEN ASEA RABAT SNEE
EYELETS ADMEN TICAL
OARS JUNES CARESS
PORKY AALEN PANE
ALOE ASNER BUR SLYE
LEW EDHS ARRET AIA
AFIELD STEVIEWONDER
CITRAL ERMINE TRILL
ENZYME NEEDED SANDY

216

LOCO PEDO POMMES AMI
IRAS UNIV TRUANT TSAR
FIRSTLOVE RESCUE HAIR
EGO ELLERY STARTREK
RATAN ARLOS ADE AMINE
SMITES SIGNORA ANITAS
IDA THETHIRDMAN RETE
LEAS PLS BOCA
GREATESCAPE AUTOCRAT
SOHOS ALLY INTERLUDE
AGIFT AGAS BOWS DELOS
CONTEMNED ALTA OWERS
SLOWNESS ASTARISBORN
ODEA ALP NEAR
OPEC DELIVERANCE KAT
PLAIDS ARAROBA SCENES
TORTE ABL STERE ARENA
LIFEBOAT SLATER MUS
SLOE LORNAS INTERIORS
ROBS EMEERS AJAR ONEE
ITE CARSES NOSY NESS

217

HARA BOFFS HARAR ALAD
AVER ONEAL ONICE RATA
LACKAWANNA PICKPOCKET
ALLIS TASTE ETHANE
DERNIER ATRIA ENTE
ERASER PREEN ALTERED
LOGAN HEDDAGABLER MAR
IDES NATO LIED MIRA
AES EAGERBEAVER DELIS
EDGAR RARE RELIES
DEBASER MERES HENBANE
ENAMEL IDLE JUNTA
MOTEL ANNIELAURIE RAS
ORAS GLIS LION COLY
SMA CRACKERJACK ALAIN
ENCLAVE NOONE FRESCO
RAMA ETTAS LIGATED
EGOISM OLEIC AARON
BACKPACKER HACKENSACK
OTHE REINE INTER ETUI
NOSY SNEAD MEIRS ROLL

218

OPERA RUB ASPS COBB
SLIPIN ENLISTEE ARLES
LINEONESPOCKETS SCORN
IVIES ELATE WET SACRE
LIE ERICS DIRER SKYE
YARDSTICK SUNSTAR APR
RANEE STAG MEANIE
TITULAR PAD IMBEDDED
ABUSES RAINS MULLET
BARES BALED APRES AFB
URNS REVERSEGEAR CCLI
SSE BELIE GRILL FAKIR
NEATEN BURNS PALLED
CODENAME RAE TOILERS
ANORAK SARD BRINE
REV LEGATED BEARTRAPS
THES SOURS BERLE LAW
AORTA ARE ORATE ALLIE
GREEN DOWNTOTHEGROUND
ESNES ERECTILE ENTREE
EDDA DADO LED NOSED

219

ADAGE ASCAP ABEL PINA
SOBER BELLE SARI ODIN
CURTAINCALL TRIM REDO
IRIS TETS TORNCURTAIN
ODER STENO LEI
CHIVES SMART WHITECAP
HAREM HAP SHE ERUPT
IGOR THATI CHARM ERIE
RUN SHOWERCURTAIN TAR
PECTORAL ABES SOLANO
UNDER MONAD ACTII
SORTIE SOHO BLUEINGS
ERT CURTAINRAISER WAT
ROAR PHOTO ELKOS FARO
ANION EOS ILE SOLDO
CONOIDAL URGED TOOLED
SPA PRANG BENT
CURTAINRODS OSER SOUP
OGEE SCAR CURTAINLINE
ALAR EAST ASIAN EOSIN
LIPS SAPS LACTO EGEST

220

BAHT ATILT ALSOP EDGE
UREY BERIA SECCO CARB
HEARTSHELL HEARTTHROB
LAR HEED LAC BEARINGS
THINE TUNA ASIN
DESERT MOLINOS HEARTY
WIELD PINAS KID STORE
EDAM SOFTHEARTED ELAS
LES SCIFI CAIMAN LIE
TREMOR SNAFU NUMERALS
ARAG EMOTE RAGE
BELITTLE IRENE GUSSET
AXO SCORES TAPES WEE
SATE HARDHEARTED SERE
SCALD TOD SNEER SKEIN
OTHERS ROASTER SMITES
MOAS LEIS DEATH
ATHEISTS ASP ERNS EEE
FAINTHEART HAVEAHEART
ABET ELATE OVEST ARIA
RUSS DARED NORSE UTES

221

GOBI■ASCOT■CATO■■RAES
UPON■SWORE■URAL■PAMPA
SHANGHAIGESTURE■ACEIN
TIS■ARIL■MALMO■AMERCE
ORTOLAN■TINES■ADEMI■■
■■■LEM■YENTA■ANALECTS
ELTON■SONGOFINDIA■ARA
LEHR■HUGO■■■ONER■SNAG
LAE■ROMANSHADES■SPICE
ANATOLES■CALIX■PAINTS
■■FEVER■TALON■SALEP■■
BARRED■BELLI■HEATLAMP
ERIES■LONDONDERRY■RIO
NECK■LOST■■■ALTS■AINU
ENA■DUTCHTULIPS■INSET
TANGENTS■ALORS■ROK■■■
■■QUOTE■ARRAY■MANHOLE
BOUNDS■PLAIT■BANI■PIS
IRENA■FRENCHMANSCREEK
FLEER■HART■EATNO■URGE
FEND■■AUTO■DREAM■BAER

222

GIBE■DABS■■EBBS■ALIKE
ASSN■EXIST■AREA■RECON
THATGLITTERSISNOTGOLD
■■■IOTAS■RATES■LIANAS
■ASTRAL■IMMER■CAST■■■
SMILES■■GEER■CONTESTS
TOLES■GOLDENHORDE■IRE
REVS■SOHO■■■EDE■■FLUE
ABE■DIAMONDHEAD■CAVES
WARLORDS■ORALS■BIDES■
■■BALES■SPARS■AIDER■■
■HUNTS■THAWS■OBSESSED
WELDS■PEARLHARBOR■MME
ALLS■■IAM■■■REIN■RICE
DEE■EMERALDISLE■FETED
INTONERS■ORDO■■BASHES
■■■EATS■STAIN■DURESS■
ASSUME■RATIO■TONGA■■■
SILVERSILENCEISGOLDEN
SNARL■ODOR■YOKEL■EASE
TOTES■DENY■■SIDE■DREW

223

ALIF■TSAR■■■APES■CLAM
NONO■OILED■CRAVE■HIVE
ECRU■AGONE■UNION■EMIT
WHERETHEAPPLEREDDENS■
■■■OYES■■OATS■■OER■■■
FIACRE■WARNS■ROVE■SSE
ENOLA■CENTI■FEVERTWIG
AGRO■WHITECLOVER■REDO
ROTC■HIRED■ELON■GILLS
STAKEIN■■■SAIL■WHOLE■
■■■■CRABAPPLETREE■■■■
■DISCS■ABRA■■■OLEFINS
BETTE■FLOE■BANAL■LOOM
EMEU■WILDFLOWERS■OTTO
BUMBLEBEE■ANNAS■TRAIL
ERS■OAST■ATEST■DOESNT
■■■ERR■■ARCS■■SIRS■■■
■HONEYANDTHEHONEYCOMB
LADD■ICAME■TOBIT■EDIE
ALEE■NEPAL■SCOPE■NORA
CLAD■GRAN■■■HEED■TREK

224

TABU■ASHE■ADLIB■PATES
ATEN■SKAT■BEIGE■OURIE
BOSC■HOWARDSLOW■ORAGE
IPSO■CASSIE■TRIDRACHM
■■IMPALE■ARTS■TABLET■
■LEMON■■ALAR■MCVI■■■■
REHOISTED■■AMYHIGHELL
ICAN■■ORI■■■ORES■EVOE
BAT■CANOE■ANOAS■GREBE
SHELLEYSUMMERS■SABRES
■■■AIRS■■ABS■■SORA■■■
COSIMO■JAMESHAIRYLOSS
ASIDE■TILER■ALLES■SAM
DADO■ARME■■■NET■■ACNE
IRENEMAMAS■■DESPERATE
■■■■BONY■AMOY■■INTRO■
■SAMBAS■STOP■BALTIC■■
OCCULTIST■RECITE■CAUL
LHASA■THOMASLESS■LLDS
AURIC■ERNES■AREO■EMIT
FLICK■DIETS■DEAN■SECS

225

■AGORA■■■ARRAYS■■■RAN
SPINETS■AVIATORS■CUBE
PANACHE■COMDERINCHIEF
ERGS■EAST■BISE■OLENT■
ETE■ONLESCAUT■PRIE■■■
■■RATA■SLAUM■RETORTED
RABBIS■SIND■CATS■■HAE
ACRES■BIKE■ALII■OVATE
ROE■■SLOE■PLANTAGERS■
ERA■MEAN■LEAPS■ORR■■■
ENDEARS■MOONS■TREACLE
■■■BRA■EARNS■BATS■AIS
■PRAYINGTIS■MESA■■RST
LIONS■ARES■PALS■HADTO
AMA■■TREY■CARA■GAMIER
MARGARET■DARTS■ERIN■■
■■■ALIS■HENRYCINI■ALP
■GALOP■PAPA■ROTE■PLEA
THREEONAHORSE■ERMINES
REIN■DEMANDED■MAILERS
YEA■■■ASSESS■■■LOEWS■

226

LEAR ACCT SEEM ENABLE
ELSA PUAS EMMA DETAIN
CLIPPERSHIPPER HATRED
TASTE STINT RTES EGGS
PEER SAGGED KNEE
SLOOPGROUP RENE ADC
SOBBER NITES OMAHAS
SARTRE DREE CARINATE
MAE STAREAT RMA TRAN
CASAVA RESEALS GLS
MSGTS YAWLDRAWL PEELE
ETA SALINAR MEIDAN
CELL SOL DOPPLER OTH
CALIPERS OPAL EILEEN
AMENRA RUSSE ENISLE
YEA CROC TRAMPSCAMP
USDO RESENE DASI
APAR BOAT ALLOR TRADE
SPLICE CRUISERBRUISER
SELVES TALA NELL STAN
DRYERS SLED TRES EINE

227

SAME FAZED STOP AMIRS
OPAL ELIDE ARNO TOLET
HALFGAINER FEET BUENA
ORE ARAG INFER PATTON
OSS ODOR BATH
SHARP DIVEBOMBER PASH
TELE PERI SNARES INTO
OLEA ELAND RARE ETON
MINDREADER ERNS SCENE
AXE ARNE ARMED NEEDED
ZED SPEED BEN
PASSED SHEEN SETA CSA
OMITS HEAD DUTCHTREAT
RITA BAER SNAKE ARGO
GNAT ARNESS PIER BEEN
YORE SPORTSHIRT MASSE
CATS ATON SOT
SPARSE TORSO SEAN ADE
HORAS VIAL FULLBODIED
ASAFE INRE ERASE IDLE
WELTS PEST RIVER PEEN

228

COHOS SAVANT WASP EMS
AVAST ERASER ARTA LEE
PALMAVECCHIO YMASUMAC
ALLOVER COLT LON RENT
INEE FIRS MARL BRIO
HANDS GONE KENYA AGER
ENDS FARE BIRD ULNA
ATE OLID SITE PREENER
LINEMEN PURE DIET TOO
VEX LAIC TILL CRAB
SITIN HAWTHORNE JAYNE
HOWL WARN BOUT FOG
ALE KIND MAZE BLUEJAY
HELPING KAYE BEAR AGA
VANG GISH RUNG SCUP
ANER PORCH PEND MIKES
ROTS ISAK BACK MEMO
ACRE NIB MATA RADIATE
BEECHERS ASHLEYWILKES
INE ARIA STELLA CAINT
CTS YOST SETSIN IRENE

229

PECAN DIODE LITE ITS
STATIC INANE IRAN MAH
ANGOLA GERALDFORD PLO
TAEL LPS RENO TALE
LAVE ZACHARYTAYLOR
OVA LIE ALLOW SLAW
MARTINVANBUREN CHE
ANTI CERE BARUCH RHEA
REEF OSU TOES ILK
FAO BASSOS ESTONIA
WILLIAMHOWARDTAFT
QUENTIN PAWNEE EGG
USA EDDY JAR OLAN
OENO GOESAT IOTA LARA
UTE WARRENGHARDING
MOTO DIEGO ERA COY
WOODROWWILSON NTHS
ALDO CORE ISH ERST
GIL JAMESKPOLK UPDATE
ENE ALAS RATIO REAGAN
RES WANT ASTIN ANENT

230

BEAKS LIEN BOA RAMPS
BAGEL ARDEB ALP EMEUS
ACUPUNCTURETREATMENTS
HAITI COSI OCEANUS
SNAG LTD ENID
FARM ALES RYAS UNSET
ARIA SNIPE SCAR RUE
CANBEROUGHWEHAVEFOUND
ESSENE AND LIMA UNPEG
HELENA SLEPT RETRY
TRINITARIAN
SHAME SNARL REAVOW
NODAL ISTO CAT STEREO
ITOOKONEINOURWATERBED
PER VETO NEGEV VISE
LEDGE SNEE OREL ETTA
EARN ATA PRIG
DECIDED RIPE AREAS
YOUKNOWIALMOSTDROWNED
EAGLE END ERNIE PETRO
STEER LEE TENS ERASE

231

PAIRS SUDS ELBA ECOLE
ASSET WRIT LEAN MONEY
THEFIRINGONFORTSUMTER
EEE TOM SLA EST POKE
ACT EDITS RAF
WHATHAPPENEDATBULLRUN
AINT SOLA RLS ETA OSE
IGNIS TARO ETAT RAMIE
THEREBSINVADEMARYLAND
SEAL TEED IKE ENG
TAI DROSS ESE
CBC SNA LATS ALAS
THEBATTLEOFGETTYSBURG
HEIST ATTU AREA EERIE
OWN TIC HTG EENS LETO
USGRANTMADETOPGENERAL
ORC ANOTE RES
ASEA AIN ANS RUG ORE
SURRENDERATAPPOMATTOX
SPIES EGAD CEIL TARSI
TENDS SEGO EDGE EBOAT

232

ASTROS FLAYS SOTHAT
NEROLI RUSSO MIRRORED
SPIDERMONKEY ALGERIAN
ATSEA ANGER DIV NEMA
TET TEDDED ORE EELS
ETAGES INTEREST
SNA TEN ODA FRESHAS
MORRO CATTAIL NONO
WASPWAISTS HALS SETNO
ILE LYCEE GARTH ASPEN
RANGES CLEANSE MUTATE
EBERT HOLLY ARLEN CTS
SAGAS ONIT FLEAMARKET
UMAS PRETORS REESE
PALSIES NET STN LAS
HOPELESS TAYLOR
BOON FOP CARROT ACE
CAPP LOI MARIO EOSIN
CHAPLAIN YELLOWJACKET
STRESSES RELET ESTATE
STRUTS STOSS BEANED

233

COB SLAV DIFF CLAM
BARB WAFER ABIE LUIGI
STAR ENATE MILA ARMOR
SCARECROWANDMRSKING
KATE INS AMO
SECEDE IRE SHONE AMS
ADAMANDEVE CHORD AROS
DINER ELY CHANGANDENG
ITON RPM RAAD LIONET
ESE META ERIE XRAY
DAPHNISANDCHLOE
EVER NOME RAIN PRS
ALICIA DIED EPI AREA
JACKANDJILL DEP UNIDO
ATES TEARS ANDYANDMIN
RES SHEBA ALA ICEAGE
ACE ARE ALAR
EDWARDANDMRSSIMPSON
FRIAR ELAL THEME ODIN
AMORY ROSE SIREN NOLA
TARE RUHR PERT REB

234

BEAM STAR ACT FRESH
ORNE TORO BLOW DEARIE
BEYOURUMBRELLA EMBALM
WRITS OCTO TUB
YAW GPS BYAIR MERITS
ECHOES REALM SEN THEE
STEPS CALLMETHAT ADS
ESNE BOCA AONE PTAS
SUI MAKEUSHAPPY BASTE
PRAISE TALES DARTED
INNES CORPS TENTH
ANSWER SLASH OFFSET
LEHAR THESHADOWOF SEA
AVER SALA ERNE STAG
MAY WHENMYBABY RHYME
ODEA OOP YELLS FEELER
ASLOPE BESOT TIP EDS
PAP ELMO TONES
STRIKE BROADWAYALWAYS
IRONED AMIN HEEL IDEA
TAKEN RED OLDE GOAL

235

PALACE MAGUS STAGES
ALSORAN NADINE PALEST
GOCOASTTOCOAST ODETTE
EDH STRIPE ATHOS TOR
AIRE MELLON PONE
ERG KNEE FORTES PATIO
DERBIES CAVIES PASHAS
ICIEST FRIEND TASTE
ERNES MOULTS RENTABLE
EFS DARETO RANEE OAF
FAR TALKTOTHEWALL TUT
OTO ARLES HELENS STR
REMARKED SEXIST ALOES
EGRET DIRECT PRIMAL
STARER COMERS COMPOTE
ERRED MAMBAS DAIS FEW
MITE SONEAR BORN
IDO STOAS SEDATE SPA
TEEVEE STOOPTOCONQUER
ENAMEL TIARAS AUTUMNS
STRIDE ACTED STEEPS

236

237

238

239

240

241

CASA CEDES COUP JIM
ALAW ATOLL POILU RUDE
WALKINTOMYPARLOR AMOR
NEWSIER ACES SIMPLE
MAINS ELCID CURIO
RTE SWAIN SHEE VAS
GOLDA STEPFORWARD ELL
UBE THYRSI EARS URSA
LEAS RAE SLANT ONTOP
ASPIRIN MICE ARCH
GOFLYAKITE STEERCLEAR
OVAL THAR ANAEMIA
MORAN ACUTE AGD SORI
EGAN CRAM SECRET OED
ELF CLIMBHIGHER LANDS
TEL AILE EDGES FED
YARNS BREST BEADS
KABUKI LEON TORRENT
ALAR CLOSETHEBARNDOOR
MALA AYRES AGATE ORLE
AIL LENT WORST NEED

242

NEXT BREL FACE ACCA
ABRA HAUTE EVOE APRIL
PRAGUESNOG LILLESPEAL
SOY NAST ATLAS LLANOS
ECTO SLAIN SLUR
AGORAE OLAN CHIMERAS
BALIS RALLY GAZASPLAZA
ASE HOT GAR YUL
SPAINSMAIN CORKSSTORK
HENLOPEN IRONS ATONES
LIED BOOTY RAUL
AQUART CIRCE FORBEARS
BUTTESLOOT STOWESSLOE
AIT APT ARA LUR
CRETESMEAT GHENTSTENT
AERIFIED HALO HOUNDS
EFTS VITAE GRAB
ASFREE RISEN JEEP PAL
FLINTSMINT CHINASMYNA
RANEE ABEL EAVED ARIZ
OBEY ESSE DIET RELY

243

MINERAL LAMAR BOLDEST
OCARINA AROSE ALIENEE
RESENTS SLUES RESTATE
GAS KIT SENATORS EMS
AGED WAIST INE COOP
NERI JOVE ANNULS TRUK
SPARE BIOGS ROOSTS
GARLANDS END STAR
ELAINE EASES MASSAS
RACKETEERS IDEST LIP
ATEE LINT STOA MILE
HEM CRESS HURRICANES
DEDHAM THAIS RODENT
RANI INN PIANISTS
DESERT PARTY ANTES
ONES SALUTE FIFE ORCH
GALS LES LAURA NERO
CVI PLATOONS MAC LIT
STANDEE RUPEE ONETIME
TOGGERY IRENE UNRAVEL
PRESSES ASSTS SEERESS

244

LEI PAPA SAMP SAWYER
ELM AXES CUER TRIAGES
ASPIRINS AGRO AILMENT
ONTOPOFTHEWORLD SEI
DART MARIST EUR CATER
ORTH LTD PST MAS
CRUET ONTOSOMETHING
SANGRIA SEAL NUTS DER
SERICIN ANIMALS OLGA
OPENED SCALE AVERS
CAROLS XIS ELI CREDOS
OLIVE STEEP IMPAIR
ALAE ATTUNED BURSARS
TET CHOO ARAB BEEBEES
INABROWNSTUDY NAIRN
REY ONE NFL RTEI
BARON ONO CHOREA REST
OLA UNDERTHEWEATHER
PAROLED TAIL ENSILAGE
PREPARE ERNE STEN TOW
METEOR DEAN TOAD ETE

245

SHED ANSAE ASSE CCCI
TAME NEEDS ENTER ARID
ALPS GARDENSTATE METE
BLISTERS AMAN CREASE
REELS GAVEL ATILT
STERES ARIA DESPOILS
PESTS SMALLDEER STOOP
EATS APACE ANNIE NOR
ERA UNITEDSTATES SPY
STARACE PETS PLU
ENGLE PROSE PRONG
DEO PAAR SEISMOS
LED GRANITESTATE PER
EVE YARNS DOERS SHEA
VENTS FREERIDES REEKY
INSANITY ETAL COARSE
ERICS BLESS MALLS
LENAPE ALAS DIGESTED
OVEN COYOTESTATE KAMA
MIST ARETE PALER ITEM
ALSO PASS APERS NESS

246

LAICS TOO SRA GISMOS
ALLAH OID EEG DISTANT
HELLO OLDSTER ENTENTE
LACKS HADANIGHTCAP
PATELLA LOTI ULE HPS
TIEDYED ARREAR RARAE
GRAF ARAS ARMS ERA
BOTTOMSUP READMITS
CERE PAIN ISR ESAUS
ARRANT TEIL TOTERMS
SERB HOISTEDAFEW SNAP
HAIRIER DESI ETHICS
ATEAM NRA CAVS WISH
ESCAPEES LIKEAFISH
EMI MOMA IOWA SETA
PERSE ARARAT DEEPRED
ERN TAR DOPE ORRISES
GOTAPICKMEUP BUYER
EVILEST DISTURB NIOBE
SECANTS IRS SAL OTTER
TRENDS VAE ETE WSTNS

247

DALI BAST PRAM PAPAS
REBID ETNA RATE ORACH
ALATE FOOT ETES PARER
JUSTONEMORECHANCE ATI
ADEL ALIDADE MEL ISON
BEDEVILS IDS OSMOSE
SOL TWICETOLDTALES
AUDIT ANT OBESE
STERES SDS SKEG PORES
COTE ACT OSTE MISFORM
OPEC DAYAFTERDAY FAMA
LICHEES DAMP RNA AMIR
DATOS AMOR PRY REGENT
PAVAN SEE MIRES
PLAYITAGAINSAM DIN
LINEAR INO ISOTOPES
AMOS ESP IONESCO NOSE
SEP REPEATPERFORMANCE
MASSE RENI GRIP EGGER
IDIOT ALTA ROLE LIENS
CEASE TAIL OLES ANET

248

HEALS AFTER WASP CAKE
ATLAS MOODY AMOI OLAF
WHITESOXWINTHEPENNANT
SEVE TRENT HON CAVIES
ELEC RIDS TROD EVE
ORAN SUI ERASE
CHAMPIONSHIPTOCELTICS
LOWEST AHA SITARS DAP
ALAR HEAVE PALO DENY
SSR APA LILT RIDGE
STEELERSTAKESUPERBOWL
GEDDA NILE HDS HIE
CARO DILL NARES WARN
ANY ALLIES MAD FEARED
STANLEYCUPTOISLANDERS
HANOI ANN ERDE
MPS PACT PAAR SLAG
DANIEL ARE TASSO IOTA
SPENDABUCKISTHEWINNER
MILE NASH NICER STEAD
SALE TREY KAHNS TORME

249

RAPT TSAR HAGAR PBS
AUER ATCOST OHARA ROO
GREATNECKTIEPARTY END
SARDINE ENRI ASTO
EGAD PEKINGSRANSOM
STORE SORE OPINION
TELS BUCHARESTROOM
ERE TESLA VIDI DEF
ERA IRIS SITOT CHEER
LANTERN ATLAW RALLY
SARAGOSSALONGWITH
BOWIE FISTY ROSSINI
YIELD AFREE DAVE BOT
EER TEEN OATES RTE
HAVERSTRAWMAN SOIR
CRAWLIE EPEE PAWNS
SHETLANDMINES SCAM
HOVE ABEL CAROMED
ARI BARSTOWEROFIVORY
RUS ELITE STATUE ADIN
ISE LADYS POTS RENE

250

SLAM PACES ARTOF AHAB
AERO ECOLE SEATO BOLO
THINPEOPLE PAPERMONEY
EASTERLY MAIDS BEAKED
DREADED SPRY SEAR
GAD KATIE STANDFOR
GOBEL INDOORSPORT RIO
ABAS CLOD IAN TERN
FIN GROWSWIFTLY TIEON
FEARLESS ELIEL DRAFTY
LEAPT BLISS HIERO
POMADE SELAH LEONARDO
EDUCE UNTIDYBEARD AIL
REST NAT OATS SLED
DOI POCKETWATCH ATLAS
UNCOUPLE WIDTH MIR
SNEE HILO MALAISE
RAISIN BETEL PARENTAL
ENTICEMENT PRETTYGIRL
ASIF NANCE HETTY LOTI
MANY DOZED EMEER ENOS

251

FENCE FEAST TESLA
ABOARD UDDER WEAPON
CONGRESSIONALRECORD
ENCE STET CIO HONE
DYE CERF CREATE LAS
MOXA POA MEX
EMEER FLUNK IRATE
SEVENTEENSEVENTYSIX
PLATER AJI EVE OKLA
SAYS ADORED TELL
VIM HEBENON DST
AREA SATIRE TAPE
LORN IMA ANA CANADA
UNITEDSTATESSENATOR
ESTAR WISHY ATONE
ADA NOS ROME
GOT SELWYN LIDA GAP
APES MAA BEAD TRIO
SENATORSFROMNEWYORK
PROVEN PIANO RAPPEE
EARED STEEN NEEDY

252

BETA OPERA TENT ARAT
OLES PARIS AROW SCALE
AMATTEROFCOURSE AMBLE
ERN STOW SEE REBUT
MATRI STLO STY IRE
IDA CSA EAR EASTER
TOM KEPTONTHETRACK
ERAT SPORO UVEA EIGHT
RELIES RIME ENCE MEAN
DEED SOAND EVE EST
DIAMONDJIMBRADY
TIP TVA SOLAR NOTE
ADEN ETAL YALU MARINE
GENOA SLOW TINGE ENCL
USSUPREMECOURT CAD
KIDNAP NEE MEA USE
ARE ACT KARL MOPER
RISER ORO NOEL EPI
ASIAN RIGHTUPOURALLEY
TESTS ETRE SENDS EIRE
ESTS SEEP ERGOT DEAN

253

ICING ADD TART JUMP
BASIE CRO OLEA AREA
IFALLTHEWORLD'SMINDS
SEN DYES REMISE SITES
ZIP SCAREDOUT COVE
CORONET ETON SHO REX
ORANG IDLE GREENE
PLIES VOID MAO DANTE
TEN POLA BARB ADORES
DEFILE SERB ACERS
WERELAIDENDTOENDTHEYD
PAOLA LEES MEREST
ASPIRE AMAS BEES RAJ
ESNES LED REED FLUTE
GUTTER ETRE RANEE
ESQ PER LOBE DRINKER
LOUT RIGMAROLE ATE
LOIRE PLATER LAST ZEE
NOTREACHANAGREEMENT
TOTE SHED BAT ROBOT
SPUD SODS ERE SOUSE

254

SLAV REPAD ERMAS UPTO
AIDE AMARA MOIRA BAIL
KNIGHTCAPP BYRDBRAINE
ANTEATER PLACE BUNNY
TILE ELISE HANG
AMBAGE FREES LATTICED
LAETS REDDYCASH LAI
ORLE APOD LIPS RASA
OIL CLOSENABORS COYER
FABULIST ALAND COMPLY
OSAGE ADELE LANAI
SATURN SPIRE DEFENDER
ANTAE SHORTSTOREY GLI
VIOL SPUR AMPS PEON
ELM POSTHORNE SLOPS
RESEARCH ELAND SWANEE
LEAK AXONE AHAT
KAURI SNARK ESOTERIC
LONDONFOGG LOCKESMITH
ABIE ELAIO ESHER ACTI
WELD DOREN DHOWS NOON

255

ROSEHIPS AREHOPES CAT
INTROMIT BOTANIST OLE
STOOPERS AMORETTI NED
CAUSETO STAND ANGS
OPT TIE SWEETTOOTH
HOVE TART ORSE ONEA
DREAMS SLOWBOAT ISAND
ATATIME WILDS STENIA
TER EXTRACTS MEANTO
ESTH CHINES HITLESS
ESPIED NOSTOC
PALPATE ASHERS KLEE
ASDONE INTERNES UKE
WITHIT INNER DEDUCER
AURAL ENVELOPE COMEDY
ITON INGE ENAM SEPT
REDDBREAST TUA ODE
OSLO TEASE PLANNER
RAM UNACORDA APOLOGIA
EDE RETURNER FADEOUTS
DOS BRAISING BLACKEYE

256

TADS ABA WALTER
OLEAN WIZ ASIATIC
CAMEINFROMTHECOLD
AMO MOUNTIE NINES
ROBERTLEEFROST
VOE FYN MBA
PALED BOWS ELSIES
ITER RABI OUTSAT
CHATTERINGOFTEETH
KOPEKS CORA ARAM
AMIDST DEAR PRESA
XEN OSO MAI
WINTEROVERCOAT
MODOC ATHRONE MNO
SNOWONTHEMOUNTAIN
GENESEE TEG TANTE
RADIOS TRS BIAS

257

CATER REAM DEPOSE
CASINO ERGO EMERALD
CARPETBAGGER CORALSEA
ART DEBRIS ELATED ILL
POET REIN OLES SNIT
ELBOW REAP PROD CLOVE
RELOAD SLICING ROARER
ATTAR DRAKE WAIVERS
DINETTES ARE MILNE
ABCD ESTATE PAGE SCAR
RAH CARETTING ALI
TREE FIRM ARNOLD CRAG
AGENT OKA NEIGHING
CHARRED DREGS DORIC
HORNET NITRITE ROMANS
ASKEW DENS CALS GETIN
STAR MEME RETS DUNE
TEN CAMERA DEMOTE REA
ESSENCES CARDINALBIRD
SAMURAI ELIA EMBOSS
SETONS SEPT SPENT

258

CARD ARIUM DONOR MEAD
OBOE DICTA ALINE ETTE
ILOVEDTHEMANDLEFTTHEM
RETITLE MOSES EASES
SHES LOREN LOLL
MEDEA LETT TALL PTO
IDIDNTDOWHATDADDYSAID
SEE ROSES RILLS NETI
TNT HARES DUPLE PALLS
SEMI BALLO EARLET
JUSTAPASSATLOWERCLASS
UNTERS TALES XMAS
SHARD MELTS ETUIS MPS
TARE MIAMI SCORN ALA
ITOOKILLICITLIBERTIES
NSF HENS TAAL IAMBS
LANE SPENT ADDS
GREEK AWARD SEETHES
MAMAISABOYSBESTFRIEND
ARID ISERE YAHOO ERDA
NATS NADER STARE ROOK

259

PAIR EASES GUMP ACHE
ESTE SCARP AREA ELAN
THELASTLEAF TITLEROLE
OGEES NAVES IMAGES
ASCEND CITES ASIT
SPARE PASSE TALESOF
SKITS AUTHORIZED PRO
LANE ARLO ROTE REAR
ORA GLASSY MINE MEARA
GILTEDGE EVADE SILKEN
CANOE CAINS MCLIV
SHORES LOSES MEANTOME
HOLES MINT ETERNE LUM
EMUS ROMA ATIT CULP
REM ETONJACKET TAMIS
ERNESTO ALOES BORES
LEER SNAGS GALOSH
SALAAM STERN ARNEL
FRONTPAGE MALCONTENTS
APOD ESTA CARVE REES
XATS RISK SHEER SWAT

260

ICEMAN SWAT WAD THICK
MOTIVE EIRE RUE RAMEE
PASSAT ASOR ALL ORALE
KISSOFTHESPIDERWOMAN
ATPAR EAT EEL
AEC RIAL THEGOLDBUG
GRASSHOPPER STU LSU
ARROYO OTIC ANTIQUES
MOTHRESISTER ROUES
ARE EFT OPT ELIS
FIREFLY CRICKET
GROT YEO ETO SRS
CLONE YELLOWJACKET
THEWASPS OTEA AROUSE
ION ILO CATERPILLAR
CONSISTORY RENA LYE
INS AER ABCDE
LIGHTOFTHEBUMBLEBEE
LORNE TOO CONE ANORAK
ELMER HER ARIL MENARE
ALATE OSS PETS PSYLLA

261

MALIC ABATE IDES NAAM
EMOTE GENII LOCO OSLO
NEVERLETITGROWUP NYES
ORESTE ALLHANDSONDECK
RIF STY ETNAS ROIL
AGUE NOUS TELAR
HOLDYOURHORSES ACTONE
IOD GETOUTOFTHEWAY
DONTGONEARTHEWATER
PRESAGER OSAR RASSLES
LGE GSA EGO AAA
SYRINGA BNAI AUGSBURG
DONTLOOKFORTROUBLE
FULLSPEEDAHEAD IRT
GREETS GETASTEPLADDER
HONDO HEEL ORLE
IRRA KOREA RCA EED
MONEYISNTATREE ASLAVE
UTIA THATSALLFORTODAY
COSM CAVE PESOS ARETE
HEMS HYER ENARE BIDED

262

LIMIT LTD MADE TALL
EMOTE AIRES AGOG ARIA
SPAIN STAMP TONG KISS
TINS THEMORNING ESTE
LEHAR SION STUTTER
HAREMS NOSH ONION
ACETATE SIGN ENGEM
CHIETI OONAS LOO EDEN
HERR MODISH CANTABILE
THETA AEGIS ODYNIA
YOHOHO SNARE ABATES
CABANA RUEDE FLESH
PLENISHED FAILED EDAM
AERY COP VASCO BIFORM
OOOOO ALEE BYGONES
STURM IALL SIDERS
SHUTTER LUBA ALATE
ARCH UNBEARABLY LAVA
LOKI EMEU CALLE SOLID
EVEN ROAM KITED SCONE
PERK ARTS LOS SKEIN

263

ASHES DAWES AIM BLED
TRENTA OCHRE LOO LAMA
LONGANDSHORT TWOLANED
ESTEE OCEANICAN
MOOREANDLESSER SKID
ADLER ODIEL ETTA
WYNNANDLOOS LSTS NATS
ELI OEUF TRUTHANDLIE
REEL OLGA RELY REWIRE
OHNE BANANA CHEER
SALVO THAR TRET KINDS
TREES EUROPA HOST
ARCATI SKUA DUEL ETCS
KAHNANDKANT AGNI ROO
EYED ASSN RICHANDPOOR
HEST STOSH OILTO
BRAS SAINTANDHELLER
RAININESS IDOSE
LINGERIE KNIGHTANDDAY
ANKH ASP ENNUI DOORED
BEST SIS TEKEL TNUTS

264

LIBRA SRI SLAP PASHA
INRED COS COLA SUPPER
OLAVV AUSTRALIANCRAWL
NAZI ATTUNE ERNIE NEE
SWISSCHEESE GENT PIRN
LETTER ORDO TASSE
URN ROD IGLOO SIGH
NEUTER GRIN BOTTOMED
EXTRA PANAMACANAL OKA
IMPURITY ABELE SET
WAFT ARETE SNIDE ASSE
HUR ALINE INTEGRAL
IRE CANADAGOOSE RIGEL
MANDATES JOUR FRAUDS
CURE DARTS PRO IST
MAHOE MUIR CRAYON
ACHS FOSS INDIANOCEAN
NCO BOLTS CYANIC TAXI
GERMANSHEPHERDS LAPIN
EDNAST INTO LEE OVINE
RESET STAR ARD YEGGS

265

WASP SPADE CARA ADO
ETTU ELMER ARID ALOP
DOOM LEOVI MOOD FRAME
GLOP FBIINVESTIGATION
ELLEN OLE CORI
ROBE OSLO STARSAND
SNORE HATTIE ALEE
MINOR ABA CHOSENFEW
ALEC ZORRO SORREL
TEAK BATAAN ALADDIN
INRE POI ERR ALL EAVE
PAYLOAD MUTATE CRAW
PRIMER TASTE AINT
GOPMASCOT BOP ELOPE
AREA LESAGE AMAIN
PRURIENT ISAR LOST
TONE STE TABOR
CIVILDISTURBANCE TONI
ATONE SARA ORALE IRID
SETI SLUT ENTER ONCE
ERE ETTE REEFY NEER

266

CHIVE HGWY GARB HOMES
RENEW ERIE EPEE AVAST
IRENE GANA NISH LENTO
NOPARKINGHERETOCORNER
ESTE URDS RECALL TARE
CLASPER EUDES
SATRAP TAGS REFINERY
OBOES SANE OLAN DORIA
BOYSTOWN RAVEN REPACK
SYST RADM RANT ERASES
ROAN YIELD EBOS
MAHOUT PENN ALEE SUSA
MYSORE ALTAR ARCHIVES
MAIMS BROO HOBO ONEAT
CHASEOUT AERO HEGARI
ABRIS PEARSON
ECCE ENCORE TAAL STOA
THANKYOUFORNOTSMOKING
HINDI OLIO EROS MEDAL
ORNOT SAYS AIRE ATETE
SPARS ERAT ROYS RESET

267

FORME TSP PASS AGANA
INEED WAR ITHOT LIDOS
STANG EBO THECINEMAIS
THREE NOTASLICEOFLIFE
SEW WETTEST KERR ERST
ICILY SHOE REMIT
MONISM STEPPE DAN DNA
AUDIE RTE SONS LACIER
ESO COED PENS PANNE
TWOSOME FAERIE OMEGA
BUTAPIECEOFCAKE
CALEB NIDRES TELEOST
ATEAR ONOR CEDE POP
BOOHOO GLEN ARE SEETO
SIN SGT STOOLS APELET
PARIS SRTA ATALL
BPOE AGHA TIBETAN BRA
ALFREDHITCHCOCK GLOOM
SUNDAYTIMES ORI LOUSE
ITOUT STONE SUN ERNIE
CODES ESTA ESS SEDER

268

ETHIC SCOWS MOTHS
CHICHA CRUET LINEUPS
HALEANDHARDY ENERGIES
ENL NORUNS MAFIAS RAP
SEEL MIII SILT AMY
RECANT PHENOM SLY
TRAVEL SHOO ENTERA
WINESAP ARRS ENTEBBE
ONDE LOCATOR TIRANA
SGD ELK ALEC ENACTS
OLA LEWISANDCLARK ORS
MILLES CARD RAN NAI
EKEOUT WASHAND VANS
EYETEST TWIT SILENCE
WESTER EVET SORDES
APE ADOREE ALLEGE
EDH DOAT PROA EGAN
THE SCHIFF BATONS GNU
CONSTRUE FARRANDWYATT
COOLIES ILIAN STERES
LOOBY ALOSS GASSY

269

MAMA ATTA JIBED COPA
EDIT SAHIB OHARE ALEC
SANTACLARA LAKEALBERT
APERFECT LOTTE LEAGUE
STRAITS OLLIE LIAR
CRI GROAN INSECTS
MONTECARLO GEORGETOWN
EROS LEONE SPAS CIA
AID FLOWN NOTAS ALONG
READIES IDLER RIO
ALLENSTEIN GETTYSBURG
VAT NORIA RANOVER
APRIL DOWER STONE EVA
LOA EELA SCOOP RAES
LONGISLAND ANGELFALLS
SHALLOT ENTIA OUR
IOTA ASIAN ARMENIA
STANNE SPILL STEERING
PORTARTHUR PEARLRIVER
ERNE ISERE ALFIE PEPE
WOOD CEDED KEPI ENTE

270

LIVRE ARES RIATA SHOT
ANEAR SURE INLAY MOSE
SCHMELINGDEFEATSLOUIS
SHE MUTE AXLE EGRET
MEIR SETTE ARAG IRA
THEATER AER ELICIT
KINGEDWARDABDICATES
OSTE ALL SEINED AHA
RODNEY ASES CODE
DDT LOD TENOR SEURAT
CIVILWARBEGINSINSPAIN
INKPAD ARAGE LEA NRA
VENI RIIS PILEUP
DOR EILEEN AAU IAGO
BOULDERDAMCOMPLETED
SNEERS TIE ERECTED
OPS DESS HINDI OTEA
IRAVA COOT NEWT CHE
LIFEMAGAZINEPUBLISHED
EDEN DEGAS RARA STEAD
REST ALERT STEN HASTY

271

```
RUSSIA##AALS###SHAPES
EATERS#ABBOTS#STEALER
ARENAS#READES#CORRALS
##EDDIEALBERTFINNEY##
[illegible]#[illegible]##[illegible]#PIN
AMIR#AHAS##ICEL#NIECE
ION#ILE###ALOHA#DONEE
NIGELBRUCEDERN#LOU###
###TOA#TASMAN#MASSAGE
ALCAN##INDI##POI##URE
DIAHANNCARROLLOCONNOR
AMI##ENA##AROA##PETTY
MANATEE#HOBART#FIR###
###LAD#NEILDIAMONDLIL
STEEL#PARSE###ORE#ASE
CAMEL#ELEE##CATT#CTEN
IRA#SPAD##BEAST#SHEET
##NATALIECOLEPORTER##
ABALONE#CREASE#ERRARE
CATERED#TARTAN#BAILEY
CHERYL###YSER##ADESTE
```

272

```
APT##SEEN#BABA##HASTE
DAUS#ELSE#ALARM#OMAHA
ECRU#LISP#RISCO#BONUS
PEBBLES#HORSEANDBUGGY
TROJAN[illegible]#[illegible]###
####NEAR#STAS#REHEATS
CRAIG##KEITH#ECHO#NRC
HORSESENSE#ESTHER#NAO
USER#TRET#FRET#RSTUVW
MESA#ANYA#ENNUI#ERLES
###EHRE#NEVES#VISA###
ITALO#SACRE#ITIN#GODS
DESIRE#PIER#BRER#EPEE
ELA#SYRIAN#CLYDESDALE
SAI#EEEE#OBOES##TYLER
TELEOST#AWOL#TATA####
###SPORTS#HORSEAROUND
HORSEFEATHERS#NUTTIER
AMEER#ABEAM#VIER#ONEO
HENNA#DORSI#PRAU#STDS
ANTES##OSHA#SASS##ASS
```

273

```
SABE#ABOMA#ATOM#MACRO
ICAL#SERAC#SISI#ELROD
GREENESCRACKERS#LAYNE
NERVY#SAITH#SIS#IDSET
###EEC#STORE#CYANATES
STENTOR#ANODE#ONEGA##
UAR##MILLANDSGUN##LTA
BROADEST###ATA#ITISAN
###REH#DEEP#ORB#ELCID
OVERSEE#MEAT#OLDNOLLS
NAW#CLIBURNSGUARD#USA
TREMELLA#ODAL#HASABAD
ALLIN#DLS#ARIL#ITI###
PELOTA#LAM###ATNOTIME
ETS##PRIDESHORSE##DON
##TASSE#ARLEN#PRECISE
STUTTERS#VIREO#SAL###
TERRE#OCA#LEONA#SOUSE
OSKAR#COSBYSCOLLECTOR
STEIN#KNEE#TANAS#KERN
SAYNO#SEAT#OTERO#SSTS
```

274

```
TOLER#BILK#SALOME#PRO
ETUDE#ANON#CHORIC#ROM
LINEASTRAIGHTWALK#ODA
ASA#SHOE#GRO#ENE#AMAH
###MOON#SHEOL#TSARINA
ATTEND#CATALOG#TRIS##
BOHRS#VALET#ORLOPDECK
OGEE#DARED###EINS#SHA
RAW#BINDS#SLOANE#COIN
TERRANES##HOUSE#FENCE
##AONE#ORIENTE#AARE##
ANTIC#AFIRE##ENCLOSED
SAHL#PEPPER#ALOHA#KAY
TIO#PROA###ABBEY#BERN
OFFCHANCE#SPOOL#CRETE
##GOON#KNOWHOW#ALEPHS
STRETCH#SPAIN#ILET###
ORAD#EAT#UND#ANTA#DEO
DIP#ADDRESSINGFORWARD
ABE#BINATE#ACNE#EERIE
SES#SNOPES#NOIR#DETER
```

275

```
##DAUB#DISTAL#BLOBS##
#BINGO#ELAINE#ROLLER#
#ENTHRALLMENT#UPDATED
ERNE#ELITE##TATE#COPE
FEE#BREVI##FEVER#KNEE
TARDE#SEM#WIRES#AMEND
###REY#REPINES#BOASTS
#TRIPUP#DOTED#DANG###
TRAVELER#LCD#DECEIVER
HODER#TORAH#AERO#CAPA
UPI##LEGERDEMAIN##COT
DISH#ARES#ONAND#ETAPE
SCHOONER#ACT#SEASONED
###CHAD#CITED#DEPUTE#
RECURS#COLORER#FIR###
AROSE#LOVER#TER#ASOKA
GASP#DELED##ATALL#PIN
ESTO#USER##PIANO#DINT
DEACONS#SPELLBINDING#
#STUCCO#UNREEL#EAVES#
##ESTER#PARADE#RYAS##
```

276

ENGLAND SCOTS REVERIE
RENEGED OHARE ADAMANT
REPINES RESIN MININGS
DOR WESTMINSTER
EMDEN PASTS LOOS ADAM
LOON CASTS FINN STERE
ERN TORT BATE FIENDS
CRANIATE MARY PANSIES
TOTALLY HARM PRIG ENE
SWEPT CORN PEON ESTS
ESPOUSE TOASTER
IMPS RATE YORK REWED
MAR IERS FORE PLACATE
PRINCES SLUE ELASTICS
UNSEEN STAR BASE THE
TEEMS HEAT SPOTS DEER
ERSE DEAF ALONE FIRST
ROYALFAMILY DIN
TOOTLER ELUDE RELATED
TINEARS RISER AMERIND
CLEANSE STERS MESSAGE

277

BLAB BRER CREW RABBI
AERO RASA QUOTA OREAD
JOELOUISJOURDAN SEANS
ANSERINE RELIT BETA
TENS FEIN EMERGE
REHUGS CRANE DONA TEM
OCAS BOILERMAKER HEB
TLR BEATALL IRE INUSE
EAR ANNES ISLES EARED
STY BOGS EZRAS ACTG
JOELS AGAIN ABUSO
ARRS ARABS HBAR DAB
BAMBU ELIDE DEOLI FLO
ATEST STA TREADLE RAY
SIS HOTANDHEAVY METE
TLC HOAR WADDY PLAYER
STOPUP HERR LIEN
BASS WILDE AIREDALE
ETUIS TEDLEWISCARROLL
CARNE GREEN ATIT ENDS
HONEY TERR NOTE LESE

278

KELP BAGEL SHEAR CRIB
AMOR OSAKA EARLE RENO
SUPERDUPER DINKYPINKY
GOER APERS ANDYS
DOGNOG EMORY RUNG
ERRATA SNIGS DISSECTS
LEONS LOVEY DOVEY LOT
IGOT TORO CORED CERE
SOV RABBITHABIT SLATE
NYTIMES WARES SPARED
MODES SIRES AMIRS
EMOTED SORTS EPITAPH
LEVER AMPLESAMPLE HOP
ELIS HEAPS RELY DEMO
MOE MERRY FAIRY VERBS
INSPIRIT BOSSY DIVERT
ESSE TRIKE RAISES
SHEET SEALS TANS
HAPPYPAPPY FISHYDISHY
ALEE THREE OLDIE NOSE
DEER SAYER RESOD GLEN

279

WIMPS LAMAS ADAS DALY
ADORE OLIGO HILT ERIA
LEROT RENIN ANOA TARN
LETSTHECATOUTOFTHEBAG
PEONS ARR STEER
BREED TAIL CRAPE
PAAR RETE SOMAS EVER
ATNO AERO PALP NIPA
SHOUTSFROMTHEROOFTOPS
SENSES TARA DOOR NYE
TUTS RES IFNI
ASP RARE CANT FABLES
SWIMAGAINSTTHECURRENT
TINA EDNA AWOL ITTO
APER SEEPS STEP TORA
RESIN SOFT TRINE
NOLAN LIE TREES
SQUAREPEGINAROUNDHOLE
HURT ARGO AROID CEDAR
OISE SIRE ISLE ARECA
PTAS ELIS SNEER PSSTS

280

AMATI AMO ALBS FANUM
LADEN GLIB LEUC ORIBI
VIAND ADDS MINI OATEN
ANYFOLLOWEROFKARLMARX
OOO IRES UTAS
ASOURCEOFVITAMINC CCS
HOUR FREE NSC ANOAK
ADS HID SIE APOLLO
STREAKONACOWARDSBACK
ARI MUON RAJ DII
GOLFERSPUTTINGSURFACE
ORO DIE OOZE NAR
AMOODOFTHEMELANCHOLY
LOSERS ADA TET EAR
ILEDE GUS IOTA EDNA
EUR SOUTHERNBULLSNAKE
SWIT RASE AUG
GIRLINPEANUTSCARTOONS
ORION URGE EIRE TRAYS
AMONG REES ATES EGRET
DATES ERST DYE RESTS

281

DEISM BAAL VENOM
PEDATI ELBA SAMOVAR
SOLOMON AGRI TRINIDAD
UTA BOUGAINVILLE EPI
MAYI RALE INEE PIPE
ATEN ACRE PRATT ARRET
CORDOBA BRANS ILIAD
ERR BLOND ELON
NEWFOUNDLAND MOLUCCAS
AROA PORING PAC DEALT
MATT THANK SAGES OLDE
ETAIS ANI ANOINT FLEA
HONGKONG PRINCEEDWARD
AUNT VOLTS ANA
ARBAT TINOS AMALGAM
EVELS ROSES PUNS ERSE
TAME LOST ERST SETA
ETO NEWCALEDONIA NAN
SARDINIA ABET GRANARY
RAISINS NEMO UNRIDE
STING ARAN AORTA

282

STORE EPACT NAGS
NARRATE ARAMAIC INROS
BLUEDANUBEWALTZ LOONY
SERAI TRUMP LEA ERWIN
SODA ENTIA ARROGANCE
TUN TWIG ARK
RHINESTONE CHASTE MID
IONA EERO SALA EMILE
NASTS SONAR NOMINALLY
GROTTO SERUM TOM TIES
LEAVE TREAT SPRIT
AMUR ADD ARRAN SENATE
REBELLION SIRED PENAL
TILDE CROC TROD ECRU
ANE NOTATE HUDSONSEAL
IAM NOME SRO
TOWNHOUSE ICENI ROTS
ORONO NAE SADIE THAWS
SAVER OLDFATHERTHAMES
STERN SPECIES SHERPAS
ENSE ADAMS DREAR

283

ROAR PECAN OATER BAWL
ARNE LLAMA UVULA ACRE
WOODYALLEN TONYMARTIN
RENAS ARIA OPIATE
KAYAKS MATER DUET
TENDS SOIL DISROBE
BENET ANNMILLER SNORE
ONER CRUDE IOLE ERAT
NEB GINGERROGERS ISA
ERATIVE ENOS ARISES
NIDI LOESS WACK
SYCEES DOCS MENIALS
EAR MAUREENOHARA REO
TROP IDEA ODORS PLAN
INFOS DENNISDAY PROSE
STRIDES SEER LOFTS
ITIS SATYR STAFFS
SPINAL TITO SEATO
PETERLORRE STANLAUREL
ALES ERIES POSSE NATE
TESS ROOST YESES DECO

284

AMOR FARM BLOCK TASKS
LIME AREA LEROI OPINE
ANIGHTMAREONELMSTREET
SITUATED DOILY WAIVES
LIED AIDE GELLED
SEALS ANSON ROLL
THERETURNOFTHEFLY GET
EARLY STAND ACES SAVE
AHOY SKY RAZOR GOREN
PEU LAMER ERRORS
THEDIABOLICALDRMABUSE
HOLIER COMUS AMY
EMEER PETAL PRY PAPA
DENT MOAT AMPLE LOMAX
ARA HEKNOWSYOUREALONE
ARES ACMES LUISE
MADRID HAUT SARC
MAROON SWISS INPIECES
DONTLOOKINTHEBASEMENT
CRIED OUSE BAKE ARNO
VIERS PAES BRED NEAP

285

ADAGE ROBE AYAH STIR
LINUS ATON TORE TOAST
MOTIONTOADJOURN RUBLE
ANIL ETE OENO BELLES
ESTHER GLEN LEASE
ADAXIAL HEAT DBA
POSER PROMOTION YETIS
APEXES ANY IONA CHOP
NICE CAYS GENES PRESS
GNOSTIC IASIS GLUM
SEN MOTIONPICTURE OFT
DEAN BADEN FEASTER
SATAN BATED BLOT OISE
LEHR INEE SOO ACROSS
ARENA RENDITION LANES
TOM LODZ RISSOLE
OMITS OVAL DOOMED
DOTAGE CITE DUO ERRS
ONION PERPETUALMOTION
ODORS ALEE TAME CREME
RENI LIAR ORES TOSEE

286

ARTA CRASH ASTA ICI
RHODA LOSEA SPAR IORS
FOWLWEATHER PURRANNUM
DINAR MEWED IVIES
GRATEDANE NAN ANNEAL
RUNED ESKER AUTOS
ICCM LICIT HIGHSTILE
SHE HONAN EMUS LID
ERASER GAFFER TROAD
LODE OLEATE GRANNY
DOEBOYS NITRE TEEBAGS
ENDERS BURNER RAAB
BIDES RESEAL ANTICS
ARI FETE ABELS ITA
ROCOFAGES ADONA WAYS
PEDAL TRYON AHOLE
PETREL ARA BAWLGAMES
MAXIM EDILE EVITA
MIAMIVISE SLOWGINFIZZ
ELLA ASAP EMCEE GONIO
SST TAUT ESSEN REGO

287

UMBRA ASST MASH BABAS
SORAS THAI IRMA AGENA
ABORT TALC SEAM GIANT
SWEEPSTAKESALLCONVEY
NERO SALEP LEO GEAR
BOT NIL MIRES TNT RLS
ESAU SOY NINON TOMBS
THISMESSAGETOOUREAR
HALEY TEY TARA POLO
RNS RAPID HIST OIL
KASSALA HORAS STOCKED
EMU SING DAMON SRO
WIPE GOYA FAT CRANE
PERHAPSTODAYSTHEDAY
ALLOT SEIZE SAW DUPE
CIE TIS AMASS REC MAD
ARMS NCO ERIES ROBB
THEMEGABUCKSSTOPHERE
SONAR LENA TAOS AGATE
ULTRA PAIR EMMA NATAL
PESTS SHED DEAR SNELL

288

CAT RIDD ELS RELIC
ASH ENROLL NAE IRATE
TIE THEMOUSETHATOARED
OAF RAINOFTERROR ARE
IDOL TELE FISH
URDU ELA EPA PLOP
MIDLERONTHEROOF AREA
PALLS STOOL TRESPASS
SLEET TITLE TRI TSE
DES TEC MARE BEET
THEGREATESTFOEONEARTH
ROSE EFOR RID APR
AFC TOO INURE SENTA
FORSOOTH FELON OBOES
ARIA THEHYDESOFMARCH
TOGA YEO ALI CRAY
TARO HONG RAKE
ORB OFMACEANDMEN ALE
DEATHOFAWHALESMAN SOX
ENLAI ENE ADMIRE OBI
REMUS RED SIMS NET

289

STUD ARCA MAP BOCCI
SORTE FOOTSORE SALOON
CREAMOFTHECROP OLEFIN
OCA ILIAN ROUE CLIFF
REDSTAR TESS ACE
ERLE MILKWEEDPOD EBB
DEEP BOOS AIRS BRA
RST NOEL WRING ARID
SODALITIES BLEND
CAB ITEM NANNY ARMADA
ORESTES SUITE BRISKLY
REEKED SERGE RULE SES
DORIS CLEARWATER
ALPS SHULS ANTS ART
GAR SAID BERG LARB
ESE COCOABUTTER IDEE
TRE DORA UKRAINE
OZONE IRRS EENIE ACR
DUELED TEAANDSYMPATHY
OSLERS EATSINTO EVOES
MESSY AME PAON LARD

290

ABNER CAT ISMS AVERSE
REALM ARI NEON LAGOON
ELSINORECASTLE ENABLE
ELSA TEA RITTER LIDS
LOA SHE AGE ESSEN
WUTHERINGHEIGHTS HAD
OER MOOT TRIOS ILE
JALNA SOON CHIRP SLOE
OBOE SIGN ALINE EELER
LOB SOLE AMEN ITE
TWOTWOONEBBAKERSTREET
HAT MELT DELE RAH
MAMAN MAPLE AIDE MIRE
ARAN MAYOS ALSO TANSY
INN PENAL ISTO EAT
NOD WASHINGTONSQUARE
ERATO INE PUT EVE
TARA NESTOR PEA AWOL
ARLISS THORNFIELDHALL
SIESTA AONE RED VERVE
SAYERS LESS ADS IMMER

291

UPAS MELAN PECAN BROW
LOME ELOPE ATONE RITA
NOEL AMARANTHINE ENOL
ALLERGEN ITER DRAGEE
ICIER SPOIL GLUTS
SCOTER AHAB GOETHITE
KAREN SPAREROOM SEDER
ARAD AISLE ARNEE DELI
TOT ATTITUDINIZE RAS
EMERITUS OLIO LEE
ARES CHESS AFAR
GYM SLAT AGARAGAR
MAC PAPERHANGERS IDE
ACHE TROOP DUANE ABRI
STOMA CONSCRIPT OLSEN
CHRISTEN LATE SALOME
INBAD AFERS SPHEN
BASEST AREA STRUGGLE
ATTN TEMPERATURE RIAL
ALEC EMBED GENIE ORCS
SIRE REINS ETNAS SLYE

292

CADI AMILE MASTS PORE
ADEN CANON ALLOT ONUS
SACS ECLAT ITALO LESE
AGOODDEEDISNEVERLOST
BERLE STERE SEE
ASSETS RETARD STANCE
EASE REAL SEAR
EVERYLAWHASALOOPHOLE
ANIM SASHED METAL
SOREL TEEMED STATICS
CLARET LYE EEN SNARES
HALYARD NIPPED START
ROAST STEREO ANAS
FRIENDSHIPTHEOLDERIT
AIDA HERR SEAS
SPARTA POSADA STARED
ONA MEDIA EVADE
GROWSTHESTRONGERITIS
DROP ERATO INERT SISI
RITE LINTY VIPER ONOS
STAN MAKES ESTEE SENT

293

SKYE CUOMO HBO TOETAP
TOOT AARON OAK ALBEIT
ALWAYSWATCHTHE LAREDO
BALLET TEAS HALFONE
ARUM IAM DEI
ORDEROFYOURWORDSIHAVE
MOURN ODETS NEAT ANAG
EMMYS UNE ATTS AFIRE
NEBO DDT AVER ASTORS
ONLYEYESFORYOUISNOT
INN NORIE PTA
IHAVEEYESFORYOUONLY
SOLENS DITS ASS IONA
OMARS DEFY DST ANKAS
LIND NEMO ARIEL PEERS
ANDISAFARCRYFROMONLYI
APO MUG SAUL
TWOFEET LUGE FLEDGY
MOHAIR HAVEEYESFORYOU
MAITRE EVE TASTE NEAL
ESTHER OER ASSET ESTE

294

ACADIA SATS ABLE DATE
SECOND TRIP FOOL IBEX
CATONAHOTTINROOF MESH
ASOR GALEATE SKIT ETA
PEN SIR NALA INITIAL
ACOOLMILLION SANTE
CITRA LAIC ILL ATHOS
ASHER DON REED ONAIR
FERAL SUFI DIADEMS
FUELERS EACH SLD IBO
ALE TOCATCHATHIEF OLA
TLC DAM TETE FROWNER
IODINES SEAL LANAI
STAIN BEAT COR IGETA
BETTE ALF CUBA NOTES
ARLES HELLZAPOPPIN
PRESIDE SOAR PAC BUS
TAP SERA AMASSER NELL
ITIS NIGHTOFTHEIGUANA
ZIGS TORE REAR SATRAP
EASE STAR ASTI HISSES

295

AGTS MANES CHIP MISER
DAHL OVOLI OONA ATONE
AGIO NEVER LODI GENES
MANWHOCAMETODINNER
LAG ICES AEON SHE
HOLYDAYS HASP STOKES
ORO AMANFORALLSEASONS
RIOT YMIR LOGIC SANE
DEFER SPIEL TETON LAS
ENATE ELVIS UNAS
THESCARLETPIMPERNEL
SELL SHUTE CANES
STA TIEIN EDINA SPRAT
ARTE FUSES SABU SADI
LASTOFTHEMOHICANS GEN
OCEANS PALO ESCULENT
NEA WISP SICE OLE
MANWITHOUTACOUNTRY
ASTER ALAI SHELL DIAS
CORED TORN EERIE ANTE
EXITS STAG DROOD NEAR

296

MABS BLASS SCRIP EGAD
ILLE AORTA PHOTO NAGY
SPEC TRIAD AIDSTATION
CHURCHILLDOWNS EMERGE
EROS LLANO OYER
BASTES TIERS SCENICAL
ARCAE BOOBS HOES TATA
GOER SENNA POOL BIDES
MUNI LAI GNAR LOOSENS
ASTA ERGS ENSUITE
NESTLE HALOGEN ARCHER
OVATION SCUT LENO
DOPPLER DISC ATE YALU
OPERA ASSN OASES DRAG
GENE ABET DUNES FETCH
ENSAMPLE CARTS POSSES
KATE TRIBE MEAD
REININ THEMEADOWLANDS
UNGENEROUS TTEST LEAH
NCOS SPILT TEASE ELLA
GERS SOLES ERROR SLEW

297

ACHES AWE RAH SCRUB
CLAUDE CAROUSE ALINES
RABBIT AVIATOR GADGET
ABA THEDEERHUNTER UGO
BARD SEI IER JEEP
SMEAR CARLSAGAN BENES
ATLEE NOODLES BOATS
LOLL BASSO SIGN
PISA BASIN ODELL STAS
EMUS OMENS PERIL TENT
EPIC WBA IVY APIA
LETO RETEM MIKES PELL
SLEW ORONO ACARI LEEK
BLOT DOLCI SMEE
BLOOM SENORES SITED
BUOYS ANDYNORTH NONOS
ALAS RWE PUP NADA
LLD MENACHEMBEGIN CGS
LESSEE KEEPOUT TASTES
STUPID ELLIPSE CHEERY
SPARS RAP SYR HANDS

298

CLIMB PRATED RAGES
RATIO AHERNE ELASTICS
AMINA TIRING FORCEOUT
FAVOR CNOTE OUTBOARDS
TREADTHEBOARDS ORR
NIE SEN ORE TABLE
LIS NAT ATA BISTROS
INK GRUB TLC SLO EELS
ALAMP BAGEL APIN ALE
RETIA LOMA MANAGED
STETS CLAPBOARD ORBIT
BESTEAD OMSK BIOTA
ACO OLDS ANTED YEATS
LOAF MLS PRI DEBT ROT
THROMBO TAD RAH DOE
INDRA TIR AAA REB
TNT ACROSSTHEBOARD
BOARDWALK CHLOE ORMER
ANSERINE MALANS ANELE
LOOSENER PLANES RENEW
SLEWS SARTRE DOSES

299

SCALENE ALPINE RANT
ALBUMIN TOURED HEGIRA
KEEPUNDERWRAPS IMOGEN
SOLI EASIER HERMA HAD
NEN ASTAR ARLO PATTI
ORB IPSO DESPAIR
TEASHOP INLA DEW IFSO
ANG OVA PGA BENET TEN
BRED ERRS YEAST HAE
BABA PEA FORTE TORRID
EGERIA CORNIER ERINGO
DEFIER CROWN VON SINN
ONA CONGO VERB EGON
MAR TAHOE RDA FED HRE
ENES LEN ODIN FLIRTED
LIBERAL HISS ODE
ISERE AWOL CAREW AIM
SEA SHEER ERSATZ CLEA
STUDIO INOVERONESHEAD
ATTUNE RECITE ARIADNE
EYES STALED SONNETS

300

HAJJ SADAT ALVA ELECT
ALEE OSOLE LEON SILLA
LAURENSOFARABIA COLES
BOYER COBALT UNIAT
ASTOLAT PARANA ADESTE
BAHAI BIREME EBOLI
IDE CHRISTMASYVES NEB
RIBS YET EARL WXY
DELARENTACAR NYE SOUR
ALONE ROMERO TONDO
URSULA GUAVA BURDEN
PESKY CACTUS SETAE
SEMI APO HIPHIPHURROY
EVE DIOR OCA ELLE
TEN ADELEFORADANO AIM
ASNER DEPONE LUNGE
LEGEND MODEST ABANDON
AREWE GALORE ABOMB
BORAX WHEREHAVEIBEENE
ADIRE EDNA IDEES NAIL
NEEDS NITS PORTE DULY